INTRODUCTION TO

Psychology

NINTH EDITION

INTRODUCTION TO

Psychology

NINTH EDITION

Rita L.
ATKINSON

Richard C.
ATKINSON
University of California, San Diego

Edward E.
SMITH
University of Michigan

Ernest R.
HILGARD
Stanford University

HARCOURT BRACE JOVANOVICH, PUBLISHERS
San Diego   New York   Chicago   Austin
London   Sydney   Tokyo   Toronto

ISBN: 0-15-543682-1

Library of Congress Catalog Card Number: 85-82651

Printed in the United States of America

Preface

An old English proverb states that a cat has nine lives. The allusion is probably to the cat's ability to land on all four feet when dropped from a height that would mean death for most animals. This is the ninth edition of this textbook; we are pleased that it has had nine lives, and we hope that it will have many more. *Introduction to Psychology* was first published in 1953. In the intervening years it has become one of the most widely used textbooks in the history of college publishing and has been translated into many languages, including Russian, Chinese, French, and Spanish. Many of the young students studying the text today will have parents who used an earlier edition. In fact, since the 1950s more introductory students have used this text than any other.

Students take introductory psychology for a variety of reasons, but few of them are motivated by the desire to know the field in detail. Most students are concerned with what is relevant to their lives and to the problems confronting society. As in previous editions, we have attempted to write for the student, but in a manner that will satisfy the critical psychologist as well. Our goal has been to be responsive to student interests without sacrificing scientific rigor or scholarship.

To accomplish this goal, we have relied on feedback from three sources: students, instructors, and specialists. To make certain our subject matter was comprehensible to students and pertinent to the issues with which they are concerned, we asked a number of students to comment on each section of the manuscript in terms of interest and clarity. Their responses were extremely helpful.

Several college instructors who specialize in teaching the introductory course read the manuscript as it evolved, commenting on its suitability for their students and on problems they foresaw in teaching the material. We also benefited from the comments and suggestions we received from instructors who used the previous edition.

To keep abreast of research developments, we asked experts to review the material. Typically several specialists commented on each chapter both in the early stages of revision and in its final form. By such consultation, we sought to ensure that the coverage was attuned to current research. The reviewers are listed following the preface.

This edition represents a major revision. As a simple measure of the amount of change, over one-third of the references have been published since the last edition went to press. Those familiar with the text will realize that the three chapters of Part Three ("Consciousness and Perception") have been reordered: "States of Consciousness" now comes first, followed by "Sensing" and then "Perceiving." This reordering reflects the renewed interest of psychologists in the study of consciousness and the central role that it plays in the cognitive approach to psychology. This chapter also introduces some extremely interesting material early in the book, thereby helping to motivate the reader for the more difficult topics that follow.

New to this edition is an appendix called "How to Read a Textbook: The PQRST Method." It describes a method for reading a textbook designed to improve the reader's understanding and recall of key ideas and information. Considerable research and experience demonstrate the effectiveness of this method, and we thought it warranted the attention of our readers. Two appendices retained from the last edition, "Brief History of Psychology" and "Statistical Methods and Measurement," provide additional material for readers who want a more thorough coverage of these topics than is presented in the text proper.

We have tried to cover contemporary psychology in a textbook of reasonable length. But each instructor must design his or her course according to course objectives and available time. Even if all chapters are not assigned, students will have them for reference. For a short course, we believe that it is better to treat fewer chapters fully than to cover the entire text. Two possible 14-chapter courses are proposed below, one for a course with an experimental-biological emphasis, the other for a course with a personal-social emphasis. For the instructor with very limited time, a briefer 10-chapter course is also proposed. These proposals only illustrate possible combinations, however. The order of chapters can be changed. For example, some instructors feel that student interest can be

CHAPTER	EXPERIMENTAL-BIOLOGICAL EMPHASIS	PERSONAL-SOCIAL EMPHASIS	SHORT GENERAL COURSE
Nature of Psychology	1	1	1
Biological Basis of Psychology	2	—	—
Psychological Development	3	3	3
States of Consciousness	4	4	4
Sensing	5	—	—
Perceiving	6	6	—
Learning and Conditioning	7	7	7
Memory	8	8	8
Thought and Language	9	—	—
Basic Motives	10	—	—
Emotion	—	11	11
Mental Abilities and Their Measurement	12	12	—
Personality and Its Assessment	13	13	13
Stress and Coping	14	14	14
Abnormal Psychology	—	15	—
Methods of Therapy	—	16	—
Social Information Processing	17	17	17
Social Influence	—	18	18

aroused better by beginning the course with material on personality, abnormal psychology, and social psychology, while leaving more experimental topics, such as memory, perception, and physiological psychology, until later. The authors have tried this approach but have not found it satisfactory. Beginning with the more personally relevant and intriguing topics may get the course off to a fast start, but it often gives the students a distorted idea of what psychology is about. In addition, many students are ill prepared for, and disgruntled by, the experimental material when it is sprung on them later. Our preferred approach is to cover the chapters on developmental psychology and states of consciousness early in the course, thereby exposing students to a range of provocative topics in psychology. Then we turn to the more technical areas, such as perception, memory, and motivation, and end the course with personality, abnormal psychology, and social psychology. But each instructor must choose the order of topics he or she finds congenial; the book has been written so that a variety of arrangements is possible.

The many decisions that must be made in teaching the introductory psychology course are discussed in the Instructor's Handbook. Instructors are urged to obtain a copy of this handbook, which is useful for both beginning and experienced instructors, as well as for teaching assistants. As a further instructional aid, we have again provided a Study Guide for students.

Edward E. Smith, who has contributed to previous editions, is now a full-fledged coauthor. Daryl J. Bem, of Cornell University, has reorganized and rewritten his two chapters on social psychology, which, as usual, are engaging and provocative. John M. Foley, of the University of California, Santa Barbara, has provided an up-to-date and well-integrated treatment of perception in his authorship of Chapters 5 and 6. These contributions from two outstanding scientists and teachers add immeasurably to the quality of this book.

RITA L. ATKINSON
RICHARD C. ATKINSON
EDWARD E. SMITH
ERNEST R. HILGARD

ACKNOWLEDGMENTS

Lyn Abramson, *University of Wisconsin, Madison*

Barbara L. Andersen, *University of Iowa*

Richard Aslin, *University of Rochester*

Lynn L. Atkinson, *Medical College of Virginia*

Cyrus Azimi, *University of Central Florida*

Jack Badaracco, *American River College*

Barbara H. Basden, *California State University, Fresno*

Andrew Baum, *Uniformed Services University of the Health Sciences*

Gordon Bear, *Ramapo College*

J. Morris Beene, Jr., *East Texas State University*

Robert Boynton, *University of California, San Diego*

Ross Buck, *University of Connecticut*

John Cacioppo, *University of Iowa*

Anthony Caggiula, *University of Pittsburgh*

Gerald L. Clore, *University of Illinois*

Patricia W. Crigler, *U.S. Naval Academy*

Sheldon M. Ebenholtz, *State University of New York*

Nancy Etcoff, *Massachusetts Institute of Technology* and *Harvard Medical School*

Aaron Ettenberg, *University of California, Santa Barbara*

Rand B. Evans, *Texas A & M University*

Larry Fenson, *San Diego State University*

Alfred Finck, *Temple University*

David Funder, *University of Illinois*

Michael Gabriel, *University of Illinois*

Russell Geen, *University of Missouri*

Richard W. Giroux, *Tacoma Community College*

Robert Glaser, *University of Pittsburgh*

Arnold L. Glass, *Rutgers University*

Kenneth Graham, *Muhlenberg College*

Philip Groves, *University of California, San Diego*

Judith Harackiewicz, *Columbia University*

Sandra L. Harris, *Rutgers University*

Lynn Hasher, *Duke University*

Dan Hays, *University of Alabama, Huntsville*

William Hoover, *Suffolk County Community College*

Judith A. Hunt, *California State University, Hayward*

John Ieni, *Albert Einstein College of Medicine*

Rick Ingram, *San Diego State University*

Robert M. Kaplan, *San Diego State University*

Stephen Kiefer, *Kansas State University*

John Kihlstrom, *University of Wisconsin*

Michael J. Lambert, *Brigham Young University*

Marcy Lansman, *University of North Carolina, Chapel Hill*

Stephen Lehmkuhle, *University of Missouri, St. Louis*

Herschel W. Leibowitz, *Pennsylvania State University*

Charles F. Levinthal, *Hofstra University*

Carlton Lints, *Northern Illinois University*

Kenneth R. Livingston, *Vassar College*

Alexandra W. Logue, *State University of New York, Stony Brook*

Jack Loomis, *University of California, Santa Barbara*

Sandra Davis Markwald, *Central Virginia Community College*

Donald McBurney, *University of Pittsburgh*

Gail McKoon, *Northwestern University*

Robert B. McLaren, *California State University, Fullerton*

Spencer A. McWilliams, *Winthrop College*

Douglas Medin, *University of Illinois*

Robert Miles, *Long Beach City College*

Alan Monat, *California State University, Hayward*

Maribel Montgomery, *Linn-Benton Community College*

Richard Moreland, *University of Pittsburgh*

Jay Neitz, *University of California, Santa Barbara*

Thomas F. Oltmanns, *University of Virginia*

Valerie R. Padgett, *Mississippi State University*

Allen Parducci, *University of California, Los Angeles*

Ronald H. Peters, *Iowa State University*

Roger Ratcliff, *Northwestern University*

John Robertson, *North Hennepin Community College*

Judith Rodin, *Yale University*

Herbert Roitblat, *Columbia University*

S. A. Rollin, *Florida State University*

Jerome M. Sattler, *San Diego State University*

Hans A. Schieser, *DePaul University*

Fred Schwartz, *East Los Angeles Community College*

Stephanie Shields, *University of California, Davis*

Paul G. Shinkman, *University of North Carolina, Chapel Hill*

Robert F. Smith, *George Mason University*

Mark Snyder, *University of Minnesota*

Charles D. Spielberger, *University of South Florida*

James R. Stellar, *Northeastern University*

Hans H. Strupp, *Vanderbilt University*

Michael Swanston, *Dundee College of Technology*

David Swinney, *City University of New York*

Philip Tetlock, *University of California, Berkeley*

Charles P. Thompson, *Kansas State University*

William Timberlake, *Indiana University*

Susan Warner, *University of Arizona*

W. B. Webb, *University of Florida*

Shelly Williams, *University of Montana*

Timothy D. Wilson, *University of Virginia*

Robert Woodson, *University of Texas, Austin*

John W. Wright, *Washington State University*

James L. Zacks, *Michigan State University*

Contents

Part One

PSYCHOLOGY AS A SCIENTIFIC AND HUMAN ENDEAVOR

1

Nature of Psychology   4

Part Three

CONSCIOUSNESS AND PERCEPTION

4

States of Consciousness 108

5

Sensing 146

6

Perceiving 180

Part Four

LEARNING, REMEMBERING, AND THINKING

7

Learning and Conditioning   214

8

Memory   244

9

Thought and Language 280

Part Five

MOTIVATION AND EMOTION

10

Basic Motives 314

11

Emotion 350

Part Six

PERSONALITY AND INDIVIDUALITY

12

Mental Abilities and Their Measurement   382

13

Personality and Its Assessment   416

Part Seven

STRESS, PSYCHOPATHOLOGY, AND THERAPY

14

Stress and Coping   458

15

Abnormal Psychology   488

16

Methods of Therapy   526

Part Eight

SOCIAL BEHAVIOR

17

Social Information Processing   564

18

Social Influence   596

Appendices

Glossary   655

References and Index
to Authors of Works Cited

Index

INTRODUCTION TO

Psychology

NINTH EDITION

Part One

JERRY N. UELSMANN   Untitled, 1981.

PSYCHOLOGY AS A SCIENTIFIC AND HUMAN ENDEAVOR

1 / Nature of Psychology

Nature of Psychology

A method for effectively reading a textbook is described in Appendix I; the reader may wish to read the appendix before starting this chapter.

PSYCHOLOGY TOUCHES ALL ASPECTS OF our lives. As society has become more complex, psychology has assumed an increasingly important role in solving human problems. Psychologists are concerned with an astonishing variety of problems. Some are of broad concern. What child-rearing practices produce happy and effective adults? How can mental illness be prevented? What family and social conditions contribute to alienation and aggression? What can be done to make people sensitive to the needs and problems of others?

Other problems are more specific. What is the best way to break a drug habit? Can men care for infants as ably as women can? To what extent are political surveys self-fulfilling prophecies? Can one recall childhood experiences in more detail under hypnosis? How should the instruments in an air traffic control tower be designed to minimize human errors? What effects does prolonged stress have on the immune system and the likelihood of illness? How effective is psychotherapy in the treatment of depression? Can learning be improved by the use of drugs that facilitate neural transmission? Psychologists are working on these and many other questions.

Psychology also affects our lives through its influence on laws and public policy. Laws concerning discrimination, capital punishment, pornography, sexual behavior, and the conditions under which individuals may be held legally responsible for their actions are influenced by psychological theories and research. For example, laws pertaining to sexual deviancy have changed markedly in the past 30 years as research has shown that many sexual acts previously classed as perversions are "normal" in the sense that most people engage in them.

The effect of television violence on children is of concern to parents and psychologists. Only since studies provided evidence of the harmful effects of such programs has it been possible to modify TV programming policies. More brutal TV fare is gradually being replaced with shows of other kinds. Some follow the model of *Sesame Street* and related programs, which represent concerted efforts by psychologists and educators to make learning interesting, fun, and effective.

Because psychology affects so many aspects of our lives, it is important, even for those who do not intend to specialize in the field, to know something about its basic facts and research methods. An introductory course in psychology should give you a better understanding of why people behave as they do and should provide insights into your own attitudes and reactions. It should also help you to evaluate the many claims made in the name of psychology. Everyone has seen newspaper headlines like these:

- New drug discovered to improve memory
- Anxiety controlled by self-regulation of brain waves
- Proof of mental telepathy found

- Hypnosis effective in the control of pain
- Emotional stability and family size closely related
- Homosexuality linked to parental attitudes
- Transcendental meditation facilitates problem solving
- Multiple personality linked to childhood abuse

How can you judge the validity of such claims? In part by knowing what psychological facts have been firmly established and by being familiar with the kind of evidence necessary to give credence to a new "discovery." This book reviews the current state of knowledge in psychology and examines the nature of research — how a psychologist formulates a hypothesis and designs a research study to prove or disprove it.

Psychology is a young science compared to other scientific disciplines, and recent years have seen a virtual explosion in psychological research. As a result, psychological theories and concepts continue to change and evolve. For this reason, it is difficult to give a precise definition of psychology. Basically, psychologists are interested in finding out why people think and act as they do. But there are different ways of explaining human actions. Before we provide a formal definition of psychology, it will be useful to consider some alternative approaches to psychological phenomena.

PERSPECTIVES ON PSYCHOLOGY

Any action a person takes can be explained from several different perspectives. Suppose, for example, you walk across the street. This act can be described as the firing of the nerves that activate the muscles that move the legs that transport you across the street. It can also be described without reference to anything within the body: the green light is a stimulus to which you respond by crossing the street. Or your action might be explained in terms of its purpose or goal: you plan to visit a friend, and crossing the street is one of many acts involved in carrying out the plan.

Just as there are different ways of describing the simple act of crossing the street, there are also different approaches to psychology. Many perspectives are possible, but the five presented here represent the major approaches to the modern study of psychology. Because these different approaches are discussed throughout the book, we will provide only a brief description of some main points.

One should bear in mind that these approaches are not mutually exclusive; rather, they tend to focus on different aspects of a complex phenomenon. There is no "right" or "wrong" approach to the study of psychology. Most psychologists take an eclectic viewpoint, using a synthesis of several approaches to explain psychological phenomena.

Neurobiological Approach

The human brain, with its 12 billion nerve cells and almost infinite number of interconnections, may well be the most complex structure in the universe. In principle, all psychological events are represented in some manner by the activity of the brain and nervous system. One approach to the study of human beings attempts to relate behavior to events taking place inside the body, particularly within the brain and nervous system. This approach seeks to specify the neurobiological processes that underlie behavior and mental events. For example, a psychologist studying learning from the neurobiological approach is interested in changes that take place in the nervous system as the result of learning a new task. Perception can be studied by recording the activity of nerve cells in the brain as the eye is exposed to various visual displays.

Recent discoveries have made it dramatically clear that there is an intimate relationship between the brain's activity and behavior and experience. Emotional reactions, such as fear and rage, can be produced in animals by mild electrical stimulation of specific areas deep in the brain. Electrical stimulation of certain areas in the human brain will produce sensations of pleasure and pain and even vivid memories of past events (see Figure 1-1).

Because of the complexity of the brain and the fact that live human brains are seldom available for study, tremendous gaps exist in our knowledge of neural functioning. A psychological conception of ourselves based solely on neurobiology would be inadequate indeed. For this reason, other methods are used to investigate psychological phenomena. In many instances, it is more practical to study antecedent conditions and their consequences without worrying about what goes on inside the organism.

Behavioral Approach

A person eats breakfast, rides a bicycle, talks, blushes, laughs, and cries. These are forms of *behavior:* the activities of an organism that can be observed. With the behavioral approach, a psychologist studies individuals by looking at their behavior rather than at their internal workings. The view that behavior should be the sole subject matter of psychology was first advanced by the American psychologist John B. Watson in the early 1900s. Before that, psychology had been defined as the study of mental experiences, and its data were largely self-observations in the form of *introspection.*

Introspection refers to an individual's careful observation and recording of his or her own perceptions and feelings; that is, self-reflection about the nature and course of his or her thoughts and feelings. Introspection ranges from reporting immediate sensory impressions to the onset of a stimulus (for example, the flash of a light) to the long-term probing of emotional experiences (for example, during psychotherapy). As unlike as these "introspections" may seem, they have in common a *private* quality that distinguishes them from observations in other fields of science. Any qualified scientist can replicate an observation in the natural sciences, whereas the introspective observation can be reported by only one observer.

Watson felt that introspection was a futile approach. He argued that if psychology were to be a science, its data must be observable and measurable. Only you can introspect about your perceptions and feelings, but others can observe your behavior. Watson maintained that only by studying what people do — their behavior — is an objective science of psychology possible.

Behaviorism, as Watson's position came to be called, helped shape the course of psychology during the first half of this century, and its outgrowth, stimulus-response psychology, is still influential. *Stimulus-response psychology* (or S-R psychology for short) studies the stimuli that elicit behavioral responses, the rewards and punishments that maintain these responses, and the modifications of behavior obtained by changing the patterns of rewards and punishments.

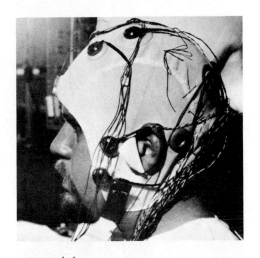

FIGURE 1-1

A Brain Wired for Pleasure *Micro-electrodes implanted in specific areas deep in the brain of this young man produce a sensation of pleasure when stimulated by a mild current. He had previously been driven to the brink of suicide by spells of deep depression. When the wired cap is attached to the microelectrodes, the man can produce pleasurable sensations by pressing a button on a control box. Brain stimulation studies with microelectrodes in animals are helping psychologists understand emotion-producing centers of the brain. Diagnostic procedures with humans, such as the one depicted here, are employed only in extreme cases, when other methods have failed to relieve suffering.*

John B. Watson

Stimulus-response psychology is *not* concerned with what goes on inside the organism, and for this reason it has sometimes been called the "black box" approach. The activities of the nervous system inside the box, so to speak, are ignored or blocked from view. S-R psychologists maintain that a science of psychology can be based strictly on what goes into the box and what comes out, without worrying about what takes place inside. Thus, a theory of learning can be developed by observing how learned behavior varies with environmental conditions — for example, what patterns of reward and punishment lead to the fastest learning with the fewest errors. The theory need not specify the changes that learning produces in the nervous system in order to be useful. In engineering, such an approach to the study of mechanical systems is referred to as an *input-output analysis*.

A strict S-R approach does not consider the individual's *conscious experiences*. Conscious experiences are simply the events that a person is aware of. You may be aware of the various thoughts that go through your mind as you solve a difficult problem. You know what it feels like to be angry or frightened or excited. An observer may judge from your actions which emotion you are experiencing, but the conscious process — the actual awareness of the emotion — is yours alone. A psychologist can record what a person *says* about his or her conscious experiences (the verbal report) and from this objective data draw *inferences* about the person's mental activity. But, by and large, S-R psychologists have not chosen to conjecture about the mental processes that intervene between the stimulus and the response (Skinner, 1981).*

Today, few psychologists would regard themselves as strict behaviorists. Nevertheless, many modern developments in psychology have evolved from the work of behaviorists.

Cognitive Approach

Cognitive psychologists argue that we are not passive receptors of stimuli; the mind actively processes the information it receives and transforms it into new forms and categories (see Figure 1-2). What you are looking at on this page is an arrangement of ink particles. At least, that is the physical stimulus. But the sensory input to the visual system is a pattern of light rays reflected from the page to the eye. These inputs initiate neural processes that transmit information to the brain and eventually result in seeing, reading, and (perhaps) remembering. Numerous transformations occur between the stimulus and your experience of reading. These include not only transformations of the light rays into some kind of visual image, but also processes that compare the image with others stored in memory.

Cognition refers to the mental processes of perception, memory, and information processing by which the individual acquires knowledge, solves problems, and plans for the future. *Cognitive psychology* is the scientific study of cognition. Its goal is to conduct experiments and develop theories that explain how mental processes are organized and function. But explanation requires that the theories make predictions about observable events, namely behavior. As we shall see, one can theorize about cognitive processes and how they work without resorting to neurobiological explanations.

The cognitive approach to the study of psychology developed partly in

---

* Throughout this book the reader will find references, cited by author and date, that document or expand the statements made here. Detailed publishing information on these studies appears in the reference list at the end of the book. The reference list also serves as an index to the pages on which the citations appear.

reaction to the narrowness of the S-R view. To conceive of human actions solely in terms of stimulus input and response output may be adequate for the study of simple forms of behavior, but this approach neglects too many interesting areas of human functioning. People can think, plan, make decisions on the basis of remembered information, and selectively choose among stimuli that require attention.

In its origin, behaviorism rejected the subjective study of "mental life" in order to make psychology a science. It provided a valuable service by making psychologists aware of the need for objectivity and measurement. Cognitive psychology represents an attempt to investigate mental processes once again, but—as later chapters will show—in an objective and scientific manner.

An analogy has been made between the S-R approach and an old-fashioned telephone switchboard: the stimulus goes in, and after a series of cross connections and circuits through the brain, the response comes out. The analogy for cognitive psychology is the modern high-speed computer—or what in its most general sense is called an *information-processing system*. Incoming information is processed in various ways: it is selected, compared and combined with other information already in memory, transformed, rearranged, and so on. The response output depends on these internal processes and their state at that moment.

Kenneth Craik, a British psychologist and one of the early advocates of cognitive psychology, proposed that the brain is like a computer capable of modeling or paralleling external events. He remarked,

> If the organism carries a "small-scale model" of external reality and of its own possible actions within its head, it is able to try out various alternatives, conclude which is the best of them, react to future situations before they arise, utilize the knowledge of past events in dealing with the future, and in every way to react in a much fuller, safer and more competent manner to the emergencies which face it. (Craik, 1943)

The notion of a mental model of reality is central to a cognitive approach to psychology.

Cognitive psychology is not restricted to the study of thought and knowledge. Its early concerns with the representation of knowledge and human thought processes led to the label of cognitive psychology, but in recent years the approach has been applied to virtually all areas of psychology (Mandler, 1985).

Psychoanalytic Approach

The psychoanalytic conception of human behavior was developed by Sigmund Freud in Europe at about the same time behaviorism was evolving in the United States. Unlike the ideas discussed thus far, psychoanalytic concepts are based on extensive case studies of individual patients rather than on experimental studies. Psychoanalytic ideas have had a profound influence on psychological thinking.

The basic assumption of Freud's theory is that much of our behavior stems from processes that are unconscious. By *unconscious processes* Freud meant thoughts, fears, and wishes a person is unaware of but which nevertheless influence behavior. He believed that many of the impulses that are forbidden or punished by parents and society during childhood are derived from *innate instincts*. Because each of us is born with these impulses, they exert a pervasive influence that must be dealt with in some manner. Forbidding them merely drives them out of awareness into the unconscious, where they remain to affect dreams, slips of speech, or mannerisms, and to manifest themselves through symptoms of mental illness or such socially approved behavior as artistic or literary activity.

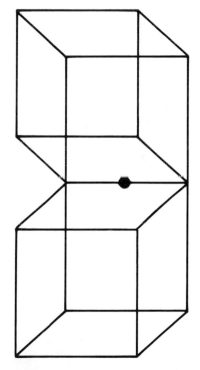

FIGURE 1-2

Perception as an Active Process *We continually extract patterns from objects we see, trying to match them with something meaningful. Stare at the dot in the center between the cubes to establish for yourself the fluctuating nature of perception. Your brain performs all sorts of transformations, seeking the different patterns inherent in the cubes.*

Sigmund Freud

Most psychologists do not completely accept Freud's view of the unconscious. They would probably agree that individuals are not fully aware of some aspects of their personality. But they prefer to speak of degrees of awareness rather than to assume that a sharp distinction exists between conscious and unconscious thoughts.

Freud believed that all of our actions have a cause but that the cause is often some unconscious motive rather than the rational reason we may give for our behavior. Freud's view of human nature was essentially negative: we are driven by the same basic instincts as animals (primarily sex and aggression) and are continually struggling against a society that stresses the control of these impulses. Freud's theories of personality and the psychoanalytic method for treating mental disorders will be discussed in later chapters.

Phenomenological Approach

The phenomenological approach focuses on *subjective experience*. It is concerned with the individual's personal view of the world and interpretation of events — the individual's *phenomenology*. This approach seeks to understand events, or phenomena, as they are experienced by the individual and to do so without imposing any preconceptions or theoretical ideas. Phenomenological psychologists believe that we can learn more about human nature by studying how people view themselves and their world than we can by observing their actions. Two people might behave quite differently in response to the same situation; only by asking how each interprets the situation can we fully understand their behavior.

In its emphasis on internal mental processes rather than behavior, the phenomenological approach is similar to the cognitive approach. There is a major difference, however, in the kinds of problems studied and in the scientific rigor of the methods used to study them. Cognitive psychologists are concerned primarily with how individuals perceive events and code, categorize, and represent information in memory. They seek to identify variables that influence perception and memory and to develop a theory of how the mind works so as to predict behavior. Phenomenological psychologists, in contrast, are concerned more with describing the inner life and experiences of individuals than with developing theories or predicting behavior. They are interested, for example, in a person's self-concept, feelings of self-esteem and self-awareness.

Phenomenological psychologists tend to reject the notion that behavior is controlled by unconscious impulses (psychoanalytic theories) or by external stimuli (behaviorism). They prefer to believe that we are not "acted on" by forces beyond our control but instead are "actors" capable of controlling our own destiny. We are the builders of our own lives because each of us is a *free agent* — free to make choices and set goals and, thus, accountable for our life choices. This is the issue of *free will* versus *determinism*. The ideas of phenomenological psychologists are similar to those expressed by existential philosophers such as Kierkegaard, Sartre, and Camus.

Some phenomenological theories are also called *humanistic* because they emphasize those qualities that distinguish people from animals: in addition to free will, primarily the drive toward *self-actualization*. According to humanistic theories, an individual's principal motivational force is a tendency toward growth and self-actualization. All of us have a basic need to develop our potential to the fullest, to progress beyond where we are now. Although we may be blocked by environmental and social obstacles, our natural tendency is toward actualization, or realization, of our potential.

With its emphasis on developing one's potential, humanistic psychology has been closely associated with encounter groups and various types of "consciousness-expanding" and mystical experiences. It is more aligned with literature and the humanities than with science. In fact, some humanists reject scientific psychology, claiming that its methods can contribute nothing worthwhile to an understanding of human nature.

As a warning that psychology needs to focus its attention on solving problems relevant to human welfare rather than studying isolated bits of behavior in the laboratory, the humanistic view makes a valuable point. But to assume that the difficult problems in today's highly complicated society can be solved by discarding all that we have learned about scientific methods of investigation is fallacious. To quote one psychologist concerned with this issue, "We can no more afford a psychology that is humanistic at the expense of being scientific than we can afford one that is 'scientific' at the expense of human relevance" (Smith, 1973).

Application of Different Approaches

The details of these different approaches to psychology will become clearer as we encounter them in subsequent chapters (see Figure 1-3). As noted earlier, any aspect of psychology may be viewed from several perspectives. For example, in studying aggression, the physiological psychologist would be interested in investigating the brain mechanisms responsible for such behavior. As we shall see in Chapter 11, aggressive behavior in animals can be controlled by electrical and

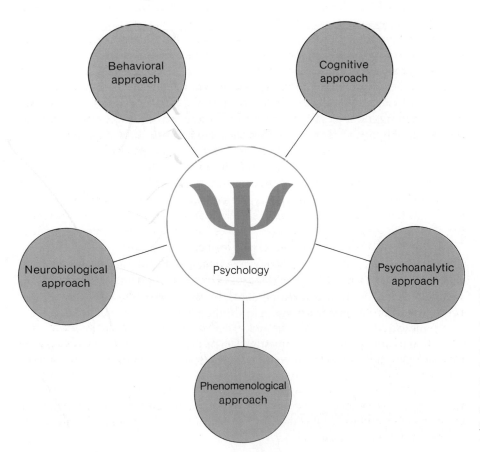

FIGURE 1-3
Viewpoints in Psychology *The analysis of psychological phenomena can be approached from several viewpoints. Each offers a somewhat different explanation of why individuals act as they do, and each makes a contribution to our conception of the total person. The Greek letter psi, ψ, is sometimes used as an abbreviation for psychology.*

chemical stimulation of specific areas in the brain. A behavioral psychologist might be interested in determining the kinds of learning experiences that make one person more aggressive than another. He or she might also study the specific stimuli that provoke hostile acts in a particular situation. A cognitive psychologist might focus on how individuals represent certain events in their minds (in terms of anger-arousing characteristics) and how these mental representations can be modified by providing people with different types of information. A psychoanalyst might want to find out what childhood experiences foster the control of aggression or its channeling into socially acceptable forms of behavior. The phenomenological psychologist might focus on those aspects of an individual's life situation that promote aggression by blocking progress toward self-actualization.

Each approach suggests a somewhat different way to modify or change an individual's behavior. For example, the physiological psychologist would look for a drug or some other biological means, such as surgery, for controlling aggression. The behaviorist would try to modify the environmental conditions to provide new learning experiences that reward nonaggressive behavior. Cognitive psychologists would use an approach similar to that of the behaviorists, although they might focus more on the individual's mental processes and strategies for decision making in anger-arousing situations. The psychoanalyst might probe the individual's unconscious to discover why the hostility is directed toward certain people or situations and then try to redirect it into more acceptable channels. A phenomenological psychologist might be concerned with helping the individual explore his or her feelings and express them openly in an attempt to improve interpersonal relationships. A broader goal for some phenomenological psychologists is to change the aspects of society that foster competition and aggression rather than cooperation.

In making these distinctions, we have overstated the case. Although some psychologists might consider themselves strict behaviorists and others might hold a firm psychoanalytic view, most are fairly eclectic. They feel free to select from several approaches the concepts that seem most appropriate for the problem with which they are working. Put another way, all of these approaches have something important to say about human nature, and few psychologists would insist that only one of them contained the "whole truth."

SCOPE OF CONTEMPORARY PSYCHOLOGY

Definition of Psychology

During the course of its brief history, psychology has been defined in many different ways.* The early psychologists defined their field as "the study of mental activity." With the development of behaviorism at the beginning of this century and its concern for studying only the phenomena that could be objectively measured, psychology was redefined as "the study of behavior." This definition usually included the investigation of animal as well as human behavior on the assumptions that (1) information from experiments with animals could be generalized to the human organism and (2) animal behavior was of interest in its

---

* A brief history of psychology is presented in Appendix II. One can gain a better understanding of contemporary psychology by viewing it in its historical context.

TABLE 1-1
Changing Definitions of Psychology

Psychology is the Science of Mental Life, both of its phenomena and of their conditions. . . . The phenomena are such things as we call feelings, desires, cognitions, reasonings, decisions, and the like.

William James, 1890

Psychology has to investigate that which we call internal experience — our own sensations and feelings, our thoughts and volition — in contradistinction to the objects of external experience, which form the subject matter of natural science.

Wilhelm Wundt, 1892

All consciousness everywhere, normal or abnormal, human or animal, is the subject matter which the psychologist attempts to describe or explain; and no definition of his science is wholly acceptable which designates more or less than just this.

James Angell, 1910

For the behaviorist, psychology is that division of natural science which takes human behavior — the doings and sayings, both learned and unlearned — as its subject matter.

John B. Watson, 1919

As a provisional definition of psychology, we may say that its problem is the scientific study of the behavior of living creatures in their contact with the outer world.

Kurt Koffka, 1925

Conceived broadly, psychology seeks to discover the general laws which explain the behavior of living organisms. It attempts to identify, describe, and classify the several types of activity of which the animal, human or other, is capable.

Arthur Gates, 1931

Today, psychology is most commonly defined as "the science of behavior." Interestingly enough, however, the meaning of "behavior" has itself expanded so that it now takes in a good bit of what was formerly dealt with as experience . . . such private (subjective) processes as thinking are now dealt with as "internal behavior."

Norman Munn, 1951

Psychology is usually defined as the scientific study of behavior. Its subject matter includes behavioral processes that are observable, such as gestures, speech, and physiological changes, and processes that can only be inferred as thoughts and dreams.

Kenneth Clark and George Miller, 1970

Psychology is the scientific analysis of human mental processes and memory structures in order to understand human behavior.

Richard Mayer, 1981

own right. From the 1930s through the 1960s, most psychology textbooks used this definition. The cycle has come around again with the development of cognitive and phenomenological psychology; most current definitions of psychology include references to both behavior and mental processes (see Table 1-1).

For our purposes, we will define psychology as *the scientific study of behavior and mental processes.* This definition reflects psychology's concern with the objective study of observable behavior. It also recognizes the importance of understanding mental processes that cannot be directly observed and so must be inferred from behavioral and neurobiological data. But we need not dwell on a definition. From a practical viewpoint, we can get a better idea of what psychology *is* from looking at what psychologists *do.*

TABLE 1-2A

Field of Specialization   *The percentage of individuals holding a doctorate degree in psychology and their primary fields of specialization. (After Stapp & Fulcher, 1981)*

FIELD	PERCENTAGE
Experimental and physiological	6.9
Developmental, personality, and social	10.4
Clinical, counseling, and school	60.5
Engineering, industrial, and organizational	6.3
Educational	5.4
Other	10.5
	100.0

TABLE 1-2B

Employment Setting   *The percentage of individuals holding a doctorate degree in psychology and their principal employment settings. (After Stapp & Fulcher, 1981)*

SETTING	PERCENTAGE
Academic setting (university, medical school, college, other)	43.1
Schools and school systems	4.6
Clinics, hospitals, community mental health centers, and counseling centers	23.9
Private practice	14.7
Business, government, research organizations, industry	13.0
Other	.7
	100.0

Fields of Psychology

About half the people who have advanced degrees in psychology work in colleges and universities, although teaching is not always their primary activity. They may devote much of their time to research or counseling. Others work in the public schools, in hospitals or clinics, in research institutes, in government agencies, or in business and industry. Still others are in private practice and offer their services to the public for a fee; they represent a relatively small but growing fraction of the field. Table 1-2A gives an estimate of the proportion of psychologists engaged in different specialized fields; Table 1-2B gives proportions in terms of employment settings — that is, where psychologists work.

We now turn to a description of some of the fields of specialization in psychology.

EXPERIMENTAL AND PHYSIOLOGICAL PSYCHOLOGY   The term "experimental" is really a misnomer because psychologists in other areas of specialization carry out experiments too. But this category usually consists of those psychologists who use experimental methods to study how people react to sensory stimuli, perceive the world, learn and remember, respond emotionally, and are motivated to action, whether by hunger or the desire to succeed in life. *Experimental psychologists* also work with animals. Sometimes they attempt to relate animal and human behavior; sometimes they study animals in order to compare the behavior of different species (*comparative psychology*). Whatever their interest, experimental psychologists are concerned with developing precise methods for measuring and controlling psychological phenomena.

An area of research closely related to both experimental psychology and biology is physiological psychology. *Physiological psychologists* (also called *neuropsychologists*) seek to discover the relationship between biological processes and behavior. How do sex hormones influence behavior? What area of the brain controls speech? How do drugs like marijuana and LSD affect personality and memory? Two areas of interdisciplinary research are the *neurosciences* (concerned with the relationship between brain function and behavior) and *psychopharmacology* (the study of drugs and behavior).

DEVELOPMENTAL, SOCIAL, AND PERSONALITY PSYCHOLOGY   The categories of developmental psychology, social psychology, and personality psychology overlap. *Developmental psychologists* are concerned with human development and the factors that shape behavior from birth to old age. They might study a specific ability, such as how language develops and changes in the growing child, or a particular period of life, such as infancy, the preschool years, or adolescence.

Because human development takes place in the context of other persons — parents, siblings, playmates, and school companions — a large part of development is social. *Social psychologists* are interested in the ways interactions with other people influence attitudes and behavior. They are concerned also with the behavior of groups. Social psychologists are perhaps best known to the general public for their work in public opinion surveys and in market research. Surveys are now widely used by newspapers, magazines, TV networks, and government agencies such as the Bureau of the Census.

Social psychologists investigate topics such as propaganda and persuasion, conformity, and intergroup conflict. A significant part of their research effort is directed toward identifying the factors that contribute to prejudice and aggression.

To the extent that personality is a product of developmental and social factors, the province of personality psychology overlaps both of these categories. *Personality psychologists* focus on differences between individuals. They are interested in ways of classifying individuals for practical purposes, as well as in studying each individual's unique qualities.

CLINICAL AND COUNSELING PSYCHOLOGY   The greatest number of psychologists is engaged in clinical psychology, which is the application of psychological principles to the diagnosis and treatment of emotional and behavioral problems — mental illness, juvenile delinquency, criminal behavior, drug addiction, mental retardation, marital and family conflict, and other less serious adjustment problems. *Clinical psychologists* may work in mental hospitals, juvenile courts or probation offices, mental health clinics, institutions for the mentally retarded, prisons, or university medical schools. They may also practice privately, often in association with other professionals; their affiliations with the medical profession, especially psychiatry, are close.

Counseling psychologists serve many of the same functions as clinical psychologists, although they usually deal with less serious problems. They often work with high school or university students, providing help with problems of social adjustment and vocational and educational goals. Together, clinical and counseling psychologists account for about 55 percent of all psychologists in the United States.

SCHOOL AND EDUCATIONAL PSYCHOLOGY   The elementary and secondary schools provide a wide range of opportunities for psychologists. Because the beginnings of serious emotional problems often appear in the early grades, many elementary schools employ psychologists whose training combines courses in child development, education, and clinical psychology. These school psychologists work with individual children to evaluate learning and emotional problems; administering and interpreting intelligence, achievement, and personality tests is part of their job. In consultation with parents and teachers, they plan ways of helping the child both in the classroom and in the home. They also provide a valuable resource for teachers, offering suggestions for coping with classroom problems.

A youngster interacts with a clinical psychologist.

A psychologist counseling teenaged boys.

Educational psychologists are specialists in learning and teaching. They may work in the schools but more often are employed by a university's school of education, where they do research on teaching methods and help train teachers and school psychologists.

INDUSTRIAL AND ENGINEERING PSYCHOLOGY   *Industrial psychologists* (sometimes called *organizational psychologists*) may work for a particular company or as consultants for a number of business organizations. They are concerned with such problems as selecting people most suitable for a particular job, developing job training programs, and participating in management decisions that involve the morale and motivation of employees. They also conduct research on consumer behavior, including how advertising and consumer preferences influence the purchase of a particular product.

Engineering psychologists (sometimes called *human factors engineers*) seek to make the relationship between people and machines as satisfactory as possible; they design machines to minimize human errors. For example, engineering psychologists were involved in developing space capsules in which astronauts could live and function efficiently. Designing air traffic control systems and underwater habitats for oceanographic research are other examples of their work. In computer systems and complex machines, the design of the *person-machine interface*, the point at which the person interacts with the machine, is especially important. Misreading or ignoring human factors at this juncture can lead to costly and tragic design flaws.

Along with social psychologists and engineering psychologists, there is a group of psychologists concerned with environmental issues: problems of noise, air, and water pollution; overcrowding; and the psychologically optimal design of working and living areas. The term for this area of research is *environmental psychology.*

OTHER SPECIALTIES   In addition to the areas mentioned, there are other career possibilities in psychology. *Forensic psychologists* work within the legal, judicial, and correctional systems in a variety of ways. For example, they may consult with police departments and probation officers to increase their understanding of the human problems with which they must deal, work with prison

Forensic psychologist working with an inmate of a federal prison.

inmates and their families, participate in decisions about whether an accused person is mentally competent to stand trial, or prepare psychological reports to help judges decide on the most appropriate course of action for a convicted criminal.

Psychologists who have a subspecialty in *computer science* may plan the design and data analysis of large-scale experiments and surveys that require the complex calculations that can only be done with a computer. Or they may work in the field of *artificial intelligence,* developing computers and robots that can perform intellectual tasks considered characteristic of human thought. Or they may work in *computer-assisted instruction*, developing programs that play the role of a tutor in an instructional situation.

Because of their expertise in experimental design — the procedures for gathering and analyzing data — psychologists also work in the area of *evaluation* research. Many of the public and private programs designed to solve social problems involve large expenditures of money and personnel. Consequently, it is essential to determine whether such programs — aimed, for example, at establishing early education for underprivileged children, preventing drug abuse among high school students, or providing job training for unemployed youths — are effective. Psychologists are involved in the evaluation of such programs.

Behavioral and Social Sciences

The study of human behavior must go beyond what happens to an individual and must consider the institutional arrangements in which individuals live: the family, the community, and the larger society. Because these arrangements are much too varied to be understood from any single standpoint, a number of fields of inquiry have developed: anthropology, economics, linguistics, political science, sociology, and other specialties. Taken together, these are known as the *behavioral* and *social sciences.* The term "social science" used to be the more inclusive one, with behavioral science restricted to the fields that focused on individual behavior (psychology, linguistics, and aspects of anthropology). As all fields have grown to appreciate that individual and social behavior cannot be understood one without the other, the terms "behavioral science" and "social science" have come to be used somewhat interchangeably.

Social psychology would be viewed as part of the social sciences because it focuses on social phenomena. Physiological psychology, on the other hand, would be thought of as a behavioral science because it studies the biological basis of the behavior of individual organisms. Educational psychology, when it studies how an individual child learns to read or do arithmetic, would be labeled a behavioral science; but in its study of group interactions in the classroom, it would be a social science. Thus, psychology may be referred to as a behavioral science when the discussion emphasizes the individual and as a social science when the emphasis is on groups of individuals in interaction.

Cognitive Sciences

Cognitive science is another term used to describe certain areas of psychological research. The term was introduced in the 1970s to focus attention on how humans acquire and organize knowledge. By using this term, a number of scientists from diverse disciplines believed that sufficient progress had been made on various fronts to form a "new" science dedicated to understanding human cognition. The research agenda for cognitive science was presented in a widely discussed report issued in 1978: the new field's objective was to discover how information was represented in the mind (mental representations), what types of

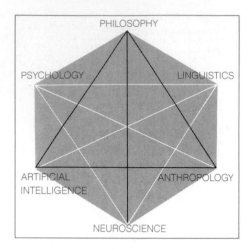

FIGURE 1-4

Cognitive Sciences *The figure shows the fields involved in cognitive science and their interrelationships. The solid lines indicate strong interdisciplinary connections and the broken lines indicate weak ties. Artificial intelligence refers to a branch of computer science concerned with (1) using computers to simulate human thought processes and (2) devising computer programs that act "intelligently" and can adapt to changing circumstances. This figure was included in an unpublished report commissioned by the Sloan Foundation (New York City) in 1978; the report was prepared by leading researchers in the cognitive sciences.*

computations could be carried out on these representations, and how they were realized biologically in the brain.

In addition to psychology, the disciplines that are particularly relevant to cognitive science are neuroscience, anthropology, linguistics, philosophy, and artificial intelligence. These disciplines will be familiar to most readers, except possibly the field of artificial intelligence. It is a branch of computer science concerned with developing computers that act intelligently and computer programs that can simulate human thought processes. The diagram in Figure 1-4 lists the contributing disciplines and their interrelationships.

Gardner, in discussing the emergence of cognitive science, argues that it is based on at least two beliefs:

> First of all, there is the belief that, in talking about human cognitive activities, it is necessary to speak about mental representations and to posit a level of analysis wholly separate from the biological or neurological, on the one hand, and the sociological or cultural, on the other. Second, there is the faith that central to any understanding of the human mind is the electronic computer. Not only are computers indispensable for carrying out studies of various sorts, but, more crucially, the computer also serves as the most viable model of how the human mind functions. (1985, p. 6)

Cognitive science, whether viewed as a new discipline or as a label for a group of disciplines working on a common problem, represents an important milestone in the history of science. Recent developments in neuroscience, computers, linguistics, and psychology suggest that the necessary ingredients are in place to solve a problem that has intrigued the human species throughout history: the nature of knowledge and how it is represented in the brain.

RESEARCH METHODS

The aim of science is to provide new and useful information in the form of verifiable data — data obtained under conditions such that other qualified people can repeat the observations and obtain the same results. This task calls for orderliness and precision in investigating relationships and in communicating them to others. The scientific ideal is not always achieved, but as a science becomes better established, it rests on an increasing number of relationships that are taken for granted because they have been validated so often.

Experimental Method

The experimental method can be used outside the laboratory as well as inside. Thus, it is possible in an experiment to investigate the effects of different psychotherapeutic methods by trying these methods out on separate but similar groups of emotionally disturbed individuals. The experimental method is a matter of logic, not of location. Even so, most experiments take place in special laboratories, chiefly because the control of conditions usually requires special facilities, computers, and other instruments.

The distinguishing characteristic of a laboratory is that it is a place where the experimenter can carefully control conditions and take measurements in order to discover *relationships among variables*. A *variable* is something that can occur with different values. For example, in an experiment seeking to discover the relationship between learning ability and age, both learning ability and age can have different values. To the extent that learning ability changes systematically with increasing age, we can find an orderly relationship between these two variables.

The ability to exercise precise control over variables distinguishes the experimental method from other methods of observation. If the experimenter seeks to discover whether learning ability depends on the amount of sleep a person has had, the amount of sleep can be controlled by arranging to have several groups of subjects spend the night in the laboratory. Two groups might be allowed to go to sleep at 11:00 P.M. and 1:00 A.M., respectively, and a third group might be kept awake until 4:00 A.M. By waking all the subjects at the same time and giving each the same learning task, the experimenter can determine whether the subjects with more sleep master the task more quickly than those with less sleep.

In this study, the different amounts of sleep are the antecedent conditions; the learning performances are the results of these conditions. We call the antecedent condition the *independent variable* because it is independent of what the subject does. The variable affected by changes in the antecedent conditions is called the *dependent variable;* in psychological research, the dependent variable is usually some measure of the subject's behavior. The phrase *is a function of* is used to express the dependency of one variable on another. Thus, for the experiment above, we could say that the subjects' ability to learn a new task is a function of the amount of sleep they had.

An experiment concerned with the effect of marijuana on memory may make the distinction clearer between independent and dependent variables. Subjects were randomly assigned to four groups. When subjects arrived at the laboratory, they were given an oral dose of marijuana in a "brownie cookie." All subjects were given the same type of cookie and the same instructions. But the dosage level of the marijuana was different for each group: 5, 10, 15, or 20 milligrams of THC, the active ingredient in marijuana.

After consuming the marijuana, the subjects were required to memorize several lists of unrelated words. One week later, the subjects were brought back to the laboratory and asked to recall as many words as possible. Figure 1-5 shows the percentage of words recalled for each of the four groups. Note that recall decreases as a function of the amount of marijuana taken at the time the subject studied the lists.

The experimenters had worked out a careful plan before bringing the subjects to the laboratory. Except for the dosage of marijuana, they held all conditions constant: the general setting for the experiment, the instructions to the subjects, the material to be memorized, the time allowed for memorization, and the conditions under which recall was tested. The only factor permitted to vary across the four groups was the dosage of marijuana — the *independent variable*. The *dependent variable* was the amount of material recalled one week later. The marijuana dosage was measured in milligrams of THC; memory was measured by the percentage of words recalled. The experimenters could plot the relationship between the independent and dependent variables as shown in Figure 1-5. Finally, the experimenters used enough subjects (a sample of 20 per group) to justify expecting similar results if the experiment were repeated with a different sample of subjects. The letter N is generally used to denote the number of subjects in each group; in this study, $N = 20$.

The degree of control possible in the laboratory makes a laboratory experiment the preferred method when it is appropriate. Precision instruments are usually necessary to control the presentations of stimuli and to obtain exact measures of behavior. For example, the experimenter may need to produce colors of known wavelengths in vision studies or sounds of known frequency in audition studies. It may be necessary to expose a visual display for a precisely timed

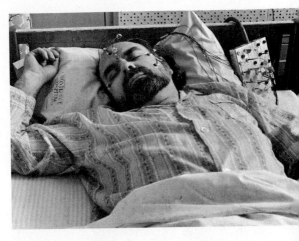

Recording a subject's brain activity while he sleeps.

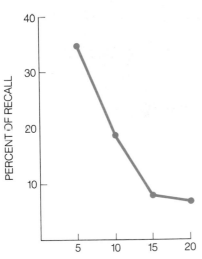

FIGURE 1-5

Marijuana and Memory *Subjects memorized word lists after taking varying dosages of THC (the active ingredient in marijuana). Recall tests administered a week later measured how much of the memorized material was retained. The figure shows the relationship between dosage level (independent variable) and recall score (dependent variable). (After Darley et al., 1973)*

FIGURE 1-6
Baboons Observed in Their Natural Habitat   *Such naturalistic studies tell more about social behavior than strictly experimental studies can. For example, grooming behavior, as shown in the picture, is a common form of social contact among baboons in the wild.*

fraction of a second in a memory experiment. With precision instruments, time can be measured in thousandths of a second, and physiological activity can be studied by means of very slight electrical currents amplified from the brain. Thus, the psychological laboratory has audiometers, photometers, oscilloscopes, electronic timers, electroencephalographs, and computers.

It is not essential that all psychological problems be brought into the laboratory for study. Some sciences, such as geology and astronomy, are experimental only to a very limited extent. Now that we have seen the value of the laboratory approach, we turn to other methods used in psychological investigations.

Observational Method

In the early stages of research on a given topic, laboratory experiments may be premature and progress can be best made by simply observing the phenomenon of interest as it occurs naturally. Careful observation of animal and human behavior is the starting point for a great deal of research in psychology. Observation of primates in their native environment may tell us things about their social organization that will help us later to conduct laboratory investigations (see Figure 1-6). Study of preliterate tribes reveals the range of variation in human institutions, which would go unrecognized if we confined our study to men and women of our own culture. Motion pictures of newborn babies reveal the details of movement patterns shortly after birth and the types of stimuli to which babies are responsive.

In making observations of naturally occurring behavior, however, there is a risk that interpretive anecdotes may be substituted for objective descriptions. We may be tempted, for example, to say that an animal known to have been without food for a long time is "looking for food" when all we observe is heightened activity. Investigators must be trained to observe and record accurately to avoid projecting their own wishes or biases into what they report.

Observational methods have also been brought into the laboratory. In their extensive study of the physiological aspects of human sexuality, Masters and Johnson (1966) developed techniques that permitted direct observation of sexual responses in the laboratory. The intimate nature of the research required careful planning to devise procedures for making the subjects feel at ease in the laboratory and to develop appropriate methods for observing and recording their responses. The data included (1) observations of behavior, (2) recordings of physiological changes, and (3) responses to questions asked about the subject's sensations before, during, and after sexual stimulation.

Masters and Johnson would be the first to agree that human sexuality has many dimensions in addition to the biological one. But, as they point out, we need to know the basic anatomical and physiological facts of sexual response before we can understand the psychological aspects. Their research has shown that some of the psychological hypotheses regarding sex (for example, the nature of the female orgasm or factors that contribute to sexual adequacy) are based on false biological assumptions.

Survey Method

Some problems that are difficult to study by direct observation may be studied through the use of questionnaires or interviews. For example, prior to the Masters and Johnson research on sexual response, most of the information on how people behave sexually (as opposed to how laws, religion, or society said they should behave) came from extensive surveys conducted by Alfred Kinsey and his associates 20 years earlier. Information from thousands of individual interviews was analyzed to form the basis of *Sexual Behavior in the Human Male* (Kinsey, Pomeroy, & Martin, 1948) and *Sexual Behavior in the Human Female* (Kinsey, Pomeroy, Martin, & Gebhard, 1953).

Surveys have also been used to obtain information on political opinions, consumer preferences, health care needs, and many other topics. The Gallup poll and the United States census are probably the most familiar surveys. An adequate survey requires a carefully pretested questionnaire, interviewers trained in its use, a sample of people selected to ensure they are representative of the population to be studied, and appropriate methods of data analysis, so that the results can be properly interpreted.

Test Method

The test is an important research instrument in contemporary psychology. It is used to measure all kinds of abilities, interests, attitudes, and accomplishments. Tests enable the psychologist to obtain large quantities of data from people with minimal disturbance of their daily routines and without elaborate laboratory equipment. A test essentially presents a uniform situation to a group of people who vary in aspects relevant to the situation (such as intelligence, manual dexterity, anxiety, and perceptual skills). An analysis of the results then relates variations in test scores to variations among people.

The construction of tests and their use are not simple matters. They require many steps in item preparation, scaling, and establishing norms. Later chapters will explore in some detail the problems of testing.

"How would you like me to answer that question? As a member of my ethnic group, income group, or religious category?"

Drawing by D. Fradon, © 1969 *The New Yorker Magazine* Inc.

Case Histories

Scientific biographies, known as case histories, are important sources of data for psychologists studying individuals. There can, of course, be case histories of institutions or groups of people as well.

Most case histories are prepared by *reconstructing the biography* of a person on the basis of remembered events and records. Reconstruction is necessary because the individual's history often does not become a matter of interest until that person develops some sort of problem; at such time, knowledge of the past is important in understanding present behavior. The retrospective method may result in distortions of events or oversights, but it is often the only approach available.

Case histories may also be based on a *longitudinal study*. This type of study follows an individual or group of individuals over an extended period of time, with observations made at periodic intervals. The advantage of a longitudinal study is that it does not depend on the memories of those interviewed at a later date.

MEASUREMENT IN PSYCHOLOGY

Whatever methods psychologists use, sooner or later they find it necessary to make statements about *amounts*, or *quantities*. Variables have to be assessed in an objective manner so that investigations can be repeated and verified by others. Occasionally a variable can be sorted into *classes*, or *categories*, as when boys and girls are separated for the study of sex differences. Sometimes the variables are subject to ordinary *physical measurement*—for example, hours of sleep deprivation, dosage level of a drug, or time required to press a brake pedal when a light flashes. Sometimes variables have to be *scaled* in a manner that places them in

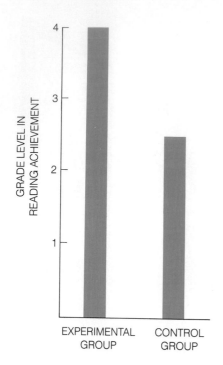

FIGURE 1-7

Experimental and Control Groups
Each day, grade school children in the experimental group participated in a computer-assisted learning (CAL) program in reading. The computer was programmed to present different types of materials and instructions to each student, depending on the difficulty a student was having at any point in the reading curriculum. CAL has the advantage of working with each student in a highly individualized way, concentrating on those areas in which the student is having the most difficulty. The control group had no supplementary CAL in reading. At the end of the third grade, all students in both groups were given a standardized reading test. It was administered by testers who had no knowledge of which students had received CAL and which had not. As the figure indicates, students in the experimental group scored higher on the test than students in the control group, suggesting that CAL had been beneficial. In this experiment, the independent variable is the presence or absence of CAL; the dependent variable is the student's score on the reading test. (After Atkinson, 1976)

some sort of order; in rating a patient's feelings of insecurity, a psychotherapist might use a five-point scale ranging from never through rarely, sometimes, often, and always. Usually, for purposes of precise communication, *numbers* are assigned to variables. The term *measurement* is used when a procedure is specified for assigning numbers to different levels, amounts, or sizes of a variable.*

Experimental Design

An investigator must plan all the details of an experiment. This includes specifying equipment and measuring instruments, the procedure to be used in collecting data, and how the data will be analyzed. The expression *experimental design* is used to describe the steps that must be planned before an experiment is conducted. Part of the experimental design is to specify how measurements are to be made.

The simplest experimental designs, as noted earlier, are those in which the investigator manipulates one variable (the independent variable) and studies its effects on another variable (the dependent variable). The ideal is to hold everything constant except the independent variable so that at the end of the experiment a statement like this can be made: "With everything else constant, when X is increased, Y also increases." Or, in other cases, "When X is increased, Y decreases." Almost any content can fit into this kind of statement, as is indicated by the following examples: (1) "When the dosage of THC is increased, the recall of memorized material decreases"; (2) "The more early stimulation children receive, the better their ability to learn as adults"; (3) "When the physical frequency of a tone is increased, the perceived pitch increases"; or (4) "The more prolonged stress one is under, the greater the likelihood of ulcers."

Sometimes an experiment focuses only on the influence of a single condition, which can be either present or absent. (Such a condition is an independent variable with two values, one representing its presence, the other its absence.) In this case, the experimental design calls for an *experimental group* with the condition present and a *control group* with the condition absent. The results of such an experiment are presented in Figure 1-7. Inspecting the figure, we see that the experimental group, which received computer-assisted learning, scored higher on reading achievement tests than the control group, which did not receive such instruction.

Limiting an investigation to the effects of only one independent variable is too restrictive for some problems. It may be necessary to study how several independent variables interact to produce an effect on one or even several dependent variables. Studies involving the simultaneous manipulation of several variables are called *multivariate experiments* and are frequently used in psychological research. The experimental design of such studies can be quite complicated, but sometimes the questions being asked can be answered only through a multivariate experiment.

Interpreting Statistical Statements

Psychological research usually involves making measurements on not just one subject, but a sample of many subjects. Thus, the outcome of the research is data in the form of a set of numbers that must be summarized and interpreted. Basic to this task is *statistics*, the discipline that deals with sampling data from a population of individuals and then drawing inferences about the population from that

---

* This discussion is designed to give the reader a brief introduction to the problems of measurement and statistics. A more thorough discussion is provided in Appendix III.

sample. Because statistics plays an important role in psychological research, it is helpful to be familiar with a few of its basic concepts.

The most common statistic is the *mean*. The mean is simply the technical term for an arithmetic average; it is the sum of a set of scores divided by the number of scores. In studies involving an experimental and control group, there are two means to be compared: a mean for the scores of the subjects in the experimental group and a mean for the scores of the subjects in the control group. The difference between these two means is, of course, what interests us. If the difference is large, we may accept it at face value. But what if the difference is small? What if our measures are subject to random error? What if a few extreme cases are producing the difference?

Statisticians have solved these problems by developing tests of the *significance of a difference*. A psychologist who says that the difference between the experimental group and the control group is "statistically significant" means that a statistical test has been applied to the data and that the observed difference is "trustworthy." The psychologist is not commenting on the practical significance of the results but is telling us that the statistical test indicates that the difference observed is extremely likely to occur again if the experiment is repeated. Many chance factors can influence the results of an experiment. By using statistical tests, psychologists can judge the likelihood that the observed difference is, in fact, due to the effect of the independent variable rather than an unlucky accident of chance factors.

Correlation as an Alternative to Experimentation

Sometimes an experimental approach to a problem is not possible. For example, the researcher interested in the human brain is not free to remove portions surgically. But when brain damage occurs through disease or injury, we can study how parts of the human brain are related to behavior. For instance, by keeping records on patients who have accidental damage to a particular area of the brain, a relationship may be found between the extent of the damage and the amount of loss in language ability. A controlled study that experimentally manipulates brain damage has *not* been conducted, but important information has been obtained. This method of investigating relationships between variables is known as *correlation*. Results of correlational studies can be summarized using the *coefficient of correlation*, usually symbolized by the lowercase letter r. The correlation coefficient is an estimate of the degree to which two variables are related and is expressed as a number between 0 and 1. No relationship is indicated by 0; a perfect relationship, by 1. As r goes from 0 to 1, the strength of the relationship increases.

COEFFICIENT OF CORRELATION The nature of a correlation coefficient can be made clearer by examining a graphic presentation of data from an actual study. In this study, subjects were tested for their susceptibility to hypnosis and were given a score: a low score indicated minimal susceptibility, whereas a high score indicated that they were easily hypnotized. Several weeks later, they were tested again to obtain a second measure of their susceptibility to hypnosis. The study was concerned with how effectively one can predict hypnotizability on one occasion from performance on a prior occasion. Each tally in Figure 1-8 represents the results for one subject on the two tests. For example, note that two subjects made scores of 1 on both test days (the two tallies in the box to the lower left), and two subjects made scores of 13 on both days (box to upper right). One subject (see lower right portion of diagram) made a score of 11 on the first test but only 5 on the second test, and so on.

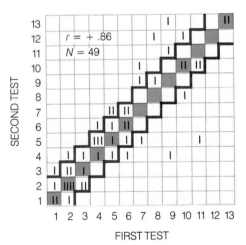

FIGURE 1-8
A Scatter Diagram Illustrating Correlation *Each tally indicates the scores of one subject on two separate tests of hypnotic susceptibility. Tallies in the colored area indicate identical scores on both tests; those between the solid lines indicate a difference of no more than one point between the two scores. The correlation of $r = +.86$ means that the performances were fairly consistent on the two days. There were 49 subjects in this study; thus, $N = 49$. (After Hilgard, 1961)*

If all subjects had exactly the same score on both tests, all of the tallies would have fallen in the diagonal squares (in color), and the coefficient of correlation would have been $r = 1$. Enough tallies fall to either side, however, so that in this study the correlation was $r = .86$. A correlation of .86 indicates that the first test of hypnotizability is a very good, but not perfect, predictor of hypnotizability on a later occasion. The numerical method for calculating a correlation coefficient is described in Appendix III. At this point, however, we will set forth some rules of thumb that will help you interpret correlation coefficients when you encounter them in later chapters.

A correlation can be either $+$ or $-$. The sign of the correlation indicates whether the two variables are positively or negatively correlated. For example, if the number of times a student is absent from class correlates $-.40$ with the final course grade, then the correlation between the number of classes attended and the course grade would be $+.40$. The strength of the relationship is the same, but the sign indicates whether we are looking at classes missed or classes attended.

The strength of the relationship between two variables is specified by the absolute value of r. As r goes from 0 to 1, the degree of the relationship increases. Let us consider a few examples of correlation coefficients:

- A correlation coefficient of about .75 between grades in the first year of college and the grades in the second year.
- A correlation of about .70 between scores on an intelligence test given at age 7 and a retest of intelligence at age 18.
- A correlation of about .50 between the height of a parent and the adult height of the child.
- A correlation of about .40 between scores on scholastic aptitude tests given in high school and grades in college.
- A correlation of about .25 between scores on paper-and-pencil personality inventories and judgments by psychological experts of individuals in a social setting.

In psychological research, a correlation coefficient of .60 or more is judged to be quite high. Correlations in the range from .20 to .60 are of practical and theoretical value and useful in making predictions. Correlations between 0 and .20 must be judged with caution and are only minimally useful in making predictions. One should be suspicious of investigators who make strong claims that are based on correlation coefficients in this lower range.

CAUSE-AND-EFFECT RELATIONSHIPS   Before concluding this section, we should emphasize an important distinction between experimental and correlational studies. In an experimental study, one variable (the independent variable) is systematically manipulated to determine its effect on some other variable (the dependent variable). Such *cause-and-effect relationships* cannot be inferred from correlational studies. The fallacy of interpreting correlations as implying cause and effect can be illustrated with a few examples. The softness of the asphalt in the streets of a city may correlate with the number of sunstroke cases reported that day, but this does not mean that soft asphalt gives off some kind of poison that sends people to hospitals. We understand the cause in this example: a hot sun both softens the asphalt and produces sunstroke. Another common example is the high positive correlation obtained for the number of storks seen nesting in French villages and the number of childbirths recorded in the same villages. We shall leave it to the reader's ingenuity to figure out possible reasons for such a correlation without postulating a cause-and-effect relationship between storks and babies. These examples provide sufficient warning against giving a cause-

and-effect interpretation to a correlation. When two variables are correlated, variation in one may *possibly* be the cause of variation in the other, but in the absence of experimental evidence, no such conclusion is justified.

OVERVIEW OF THE BOOK

Psychologists today are in the process of investigating thousands of different phenomena ranging from microelectrode studies of how individual brain cells change during learning to studies of the effects of population density and over-crowding on social behavior. Deciding how to classify these investigations topi-cally and how to present the topics in the most meaningful order is difficult. In older sciences, such as physics and chemistry, where facts and theories are well established, most introductory textbooks arrange their topics in approximately the same order—starting with basic concepts and proceeding to the more com-plex. In a science as young as psychology, however, where theories are often very speculative and so much remains unknown, there is no natural order of topics.

If you examine a number of introductory psychology texts, you will find considerable variation in the grouping and ordering of topics. Should we know how people perceive the world around them in order to understand how they learn new things? Or does learning determine how we perceive our environment? Should we discuss what motivates a person to action so that we can understand his or her personality? Or can motivation be better understood if we look first at the way personality develops over the course of a lifetime? Despite such unre-solved questions, we have tried to arrange the topics in this book so that the understanding of the issues in each chapter will provide a background for the study of problems in the next.

To understand how people interact with their environment, we need to know something about their biological equipment. In Part Two ("Biological and Developmental Processes"), the first chapter describes how the nervous and endocrine systems function to integrate and control behavior. Since behavior also depends on the interaction between inherited characteristics and environmental conditions, this chapter includes a discussion of genetic influences on behavior. The second chapter in Part Two provides an overview of the individual's psycho-logical development from infancy through adolescence and adulthood. By noting how abilities, attitudes, and personality develop and the problems that must be faced at different stages of life, we can appreciate more fully the kinds of ques-tions to which psychology seeks answers.

When we talk about the "mind," we are talking about consciousness—the perceptions, thoughts, feelings, and memories that we are aware of and that guide our actions at a given moment. Information about the world must be registered by our sense organs in order to reach consciousness; the sense organs mediate the sensations of light, sound, touch, and taste. Through the process of perception, this sensory information is organized into meaningful patterns. Part Three ("Consciousness and Perception") examines the characteristics of human con-sciousness under both normal and altered states and discusses how the sense organs register incoming information and how the organism interprets and reacts to patterns of stimuli.

Part Four ("Learning, Remembering, and Thinking") is concerned with the processes by which we acquire skills and knowledge, remember them, and use them for purposes of communication, problem solving, and thinking.

Part Five ("Motivation and Emotion") deals with the forces that energize and direct behavior; these include biological needs, as well as psychological motives and emotions.

The ways in which individuals differ from one another, both in personal characteristics and abilities, is the substance of Part Six ("Personality and Individuality"). Coping with stress and the development and treatment of abnormal behavior provide the topics for Part Seven ("Stress, Psychopathology, and Therapy").

Part Eight ("Social Behavior") is concerned with social interactions: how we think, feel, and act in social situations and how social situations, in turn, influence our thoughts, feelings, and actions; how we perceive and interpret the behaviors of other people; how beliefs and attitudes are shaped; and how groups influence their members and vice versa.

SUMMARY

1. The study of psychology can be approached from several viewpoints. The *neurobiological approach* attempts to relate our actions to events taking place inside the body, particularly in the brain and nervous system. The *behavioral approach* focuses on those external activities of the organism that can be observed and measured. *Cognitive psychology* is concerned with the way the mind processes incoming information by transforming it internally in various ways. The *psychoanalytic approach* emphasizes unconscious motives stemming from sexual and aggressive impulses repressed in childhood. The *phenomenological approach* focuses on the person's subjective experiences, freedom of choice, and motivation toward self-actualization. A particular area of psychological investigation can be analyzed from several of these viewpoints.

2. *Psychology* is defined as the *scientific study of behavior and mental processes*. Its numerous areas of specialization include experimental and physiological psychology; developmental, social, and personality psychology; clinical and counseling psychology; school and educational psychology; and industrial and engineering psychology.

3. Psychology, along with anthropology, economics, political science, sociology, and several other fields, is classified as one of the *behavioral* and *social sciences*. Another term used to describe certain aspects of psychological research is *cognitive science;* the term focuses attention on how humans acquire and organize knowledge.

4. When applicable, the *experimental method* is preferred for studying problems because it seeks to control all variables except the ones being studied. The *independent variable* is the one manipulated by the experimenter; the *dependent variable* (usually some measure of the subject's behavior) is the one being studied to determine if it is affected by changes in the independent variable.

5. Other methods for investigating psychological problems include the *observational method*, the *survey method*, the *test method*, and *case histories*.

6. *Measurement* involves specifying a procedure for assigning *numbers* to different levels or amounts of some variable. The expression *experimental design* is used to describe the array of procedures to be followed in conducting an experiment. In the simplest experimental designs, the experimenter manipulates one variable (the independent variable) and observes its effect on another variable (the dependent variable).

7. In many experiments, the independent variable is something that is either present or absent. In this case, the experimental design includes an *experimental group* (with the condition present for one group of subjects) and a *control group* (with the condition absent for another group of subjects). If the difference in *means* between the experimental and control groups is *statistically significant*, we

know that the experimental condition had a reliable effect; that is, if the study was repeated, a similar difference in means would be observed.

8. Another approach to research is by way of *correlation*. If an independent variable cannot be experimentally manipulated, it is still possible to observe how two variables are related. One can make many observations of the same two variables as they happen to occur in nature and then use the data to determine how one variable changes as the other changes. *Cause-and-effect relationships* cannot be inferred from a correlational study, but such studies are extremely important, particularly when experiments are not possible.

9. The *correlation coefficient, r,* is a useful way of describing the degree of relationship between two variables. It is a number between 0 and 1. No relationship is indicated by 0; a perfect relation, by 1. As r goes from 0 to 1, the strength of the relationship increases. The correlation coefficient can be positive or negative depending on whether one variable increases with another (+) or one variable decreases as the other increases (−). The sign of the correlation does not affect the strength of the relationship.

FURTHER READING

The topical interests and theories of any contemporary science can often be understood best according to their history. Several useful books are Hilgard, *Psychology in America: A Historical Survey* (1987); Murphy and Kovach, *Historical Introduction to Modern Psychology* (3rd ed., 1972); Wertheimer, *A Brief History of Psychology* (rev. ed., 1979); and Schultz, *A History of Modern Psychology* (4th ed., 1987). A brief history of psychology is presented in Appendix II to this book.

The various conceptual approaches to psychology are discussed in Hall and Lindzey, *Theories of Personality* (3rd ed., 1978); Anderson, *Cognitive Psychology and Its Implications* (2nd ed., 1985); Royce and Mos (eds.), *Humanistic Psychology: Concepts and Criticisms* (1981); Bower and Hilgard, *Theories of Learning* (5th ed., 1981); Lundin, *Theories and Systems of Psychology* (3rd ed., 1985); Mandler, *Cognitive Psychology: An Essay in Cognitive Science* (1985); and Gardner, *The Mind's New Science: A History of the Cognitive Revolution* (1985).

The methods of psychological research are presented in Wood, *Fundamentals of Psychological Research* (3rd ed., 1986); Johnson and Solso, *An Introduction to Experimental Design in Psychology: A Case Approach* (2nd ed., 1978); and Ray and Ravizza, *Methods Toward a Science of Behavior and Experience* (2nd ed., 1984).

A simple but elegant introduction to basic concepts in statistics is Phillips, *Statistical Thinking: A Structural Approach* (2nd ed., 1982).

Appendix IV to this book lists some of the major psychology journals and gives a description of the types of articles they publish. These journals are available in most college and university libraries. Current issues of the journals generally can be found on racks in an open section of the library. An excellent overview of psychology can be gained by spending some time perusing recent issues of these journals.

To find out more about career opportunities in psychology and the training required to become a psychologist, write to the American Psychological Association (1200 Seventeenth Street N.W., Washington, D.C. 20036) for a copy of their booklet, *A Career in Psychology.*

Part Two

JERRY N. UELSMANN

Untitled, 1978

BIOLOGICAL AND DEVELOPMENTAL PROCESSES

Biological Basis of Psychology

2

BEHAVIOR, FROM BLINKING AN EYE TO playing tennis or writing a computer program, depends on the integration of numerous processes within the body. This integration is provided by the nervous system with help from the endocrine system.

Consider, for example, all the processes that must coordinate effectively for you to stop your car at a red light. First you must see the light; this means that the light must register on one of your sense organs, your eye. Neural impulses from your eye are relayed to your brain, where the stimulus is analyzed and compared with information about past events stored in your memory: you recognize that a red light in a certain context means "stop." The process of moving your foot to the brake pedal and pressing it is initiated by the motor areas of the brain that control the muscles of your leg and foot. In order to send the proper signals to these muscles, the brain must know where your foot is as well as where you want it to go. The brain maintains a register of the position of body parts relative to one another, which it uses to plan directed movements. You do not stop the car with one sudden movement of your leg, however. A specialized part of your brain receives continual *feedback* from leg and foot muscles so that you are aware of how much pressure is being exerted and can alter your movements accordingly. At the same time, your eyes and some of your other body senses tell you how quickly the car is stopping. If the light turned red as you were speeding toward the intersection, some of your endocrine glands would also be activated, leading to increased heart rate, more rapid respiration, and other metabolic changes associated with fear; these processes would speed your reactions in an emergency. Your stopping at a red light may seem quick and automatic, but it involves numerous complex messages and adjustments. The information for these activities is transmitted by large networks of nerve cells.

Many aspects of behavior and mental functioning cannot be fully understood without some knowledge of the underlying biological processes. Our nervous system, sense organs, muscles, and glands enable us to be aware of and to adjust to our environment. Our perception of events depends on how our sense organs detect stimuli and how our brain interprets information coming from the senses. Much of our behavior is motivated by such needs as hunger, thirst, and the avoidance of fatigue or pain. Our ability to use language, to think, and to solve problems depends on a brain structure that is incredibly complex. Indeed, many physiological psychologists believe that specific patterns of electrical and chemical events in the brain are the very basis of our most intricate thought processes.

Some of the research relating psychological events to biological processes will be discussed when we talk, for example, about perception or motivation and emotion. This chapter provides an overview of the nervous system. Students with a background in biology will find most of the material familiar.

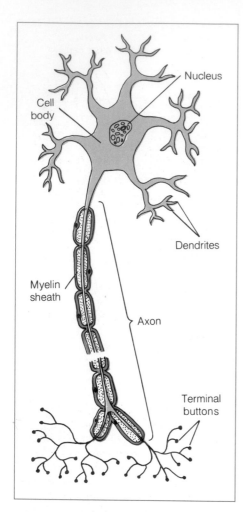

FIGURE 2-1
Neuron *An idealized diagram of a neuron. Stimulation of the dendrites or the cell body activates an electrochemical nerve impulse that travels along the axon to the axon terminals. The myelin sheath covers the axons of some, but not all, neurons; it helps to increase the speed of nerve impulse conduction.*

BASIC UNITS OF THE NERVOUS SYSTEM

The human brain is composed of 12 billion or more specialized cells called *neurons,* the basic units of the nervous system. It is important to understand neurons, for they undoubtedly hold the secrets of learning and mental functioning. We know their role in the transmission of nerve impulses, and we know how some types of neural circuits work; but we are just beginning to unravel their more complex functioning in learning, memory, emotion, and thought.

Neurons and Nerves

Although neurons differ markedly in size and appearance, depending on the specialized job each performs, they have certain common characteristics (see Figure 2-1). Projecting from the *cell body* are a number of short branches called *dendrites* (from the Greek word *dendron,* meaning "tree"). The dendrites and cell body receive neural impulses from adjacent neurons. These messages are in turn transmitted to other neurons (or to muscles and glands) by a long, slender tube-like extension of the cell called an *axon.* At the end of the axon is an array of small terminals, called *axon terminals.*

The axon terminal does not actually touch the neuron that it will stimulate. Rather, there is a slight gap between the axon terminal and the cell body or dendrites of the receiving neuron. This junction is called a *synapse* and the gap itself is called the *synaptic gap.* When a neural impulse travels down the axon and arrives at the axon terminals, it triggers the secretion of a chemical called a *neurotransmitter.* The neurotransmitter substance travels across the synaptic gap and stimulates the next neuron, thereby carrying the impulse from one neuron to the next. The axons from a great many neurons (perhaps 1,000) may synapse upon the dendrites and cell body of a single neuron (see Figure 2-2).

Although all neurons have these general features, they vary greatly in size and shape. A neuron in the spinal cord may have an axon two to three feet long, running from the tip of the spine to the big toe; a neuron in the brain may cover only a few thousandths of an inch with all its parts (see Figure 2-3).

There are three types of neurons. *Sensory neurons* transmit impulses received by *receptors* to the central nervous system. The receptors are specialized cells in the sense organs, muscles, skin, and joints that detect physical or chemical changes and translate these events into impulses that travel along the sensory neurons. *Motor neurons* carry outgoing signals from the brain or spinal cord to the effector organs, namely the muscles and glands. *Interneurons* receive the signals from the sensory neurons and send impulses to other interneurons or to motor neurons. Interneurons are found only in the brain and spinal cord.

A *nerve* is a bundle of elongated axons belonging to hundreds or thousands of neurons. A single nerve may contain axons from both sensory and motor neurons. Closely interwoven among the neurons are a large number of *glial cells* (from the Greek word *glia,* meaning "glue"). The glial cells help to hold the neurons in place and provide them with nutrients.

Axonal Conduction

The movement of a nerve impulse along an axon is quite different from the flow of electric current through a wire. Electricity travels at the speed of light (186,300 miles per second), whereas a nerve impulse in the human body may travel from 2 to 200 miles per hour, depending on the diameter of the axon and other factors. The analogy of a firework fuse has sometimes been used: when a fuse is lighted, one part of the fuse lights the next part, the impulse being regenerated along the way. However, the details of neural transmission are more complex. The process is *electrochemical*. The thin membrane that holds together the protoplasm of the cell is not equally permeable to the many different types of *ions* (electrically charged atoms and molecules) that float in the protoplasm of the cell and in the liquid surrounding the cell. In its resting state, the cell membrane tends to keep out positively charged sodium ions (Na^+) and tends to keep within the cell various negatively charged ions. As a result, there is a small electrical potential, or voltage difference, across the membrane; the inside of a nerve cell is more negative than the outside.

When the axon is stimulated, the electrical potential across the membrane is reduced at the point of stimulation. If the reduction in potential is large enough, the permeability of the cell membrane suddenly changes, allowing Na^+ ions to enter the cell. This process is called *depolarization;* now the inside of the cell membrane becomes less negative than it was before. This change affects the adjacent portion of the axon, causing its membrane to depolarize. The process, repeating itself down the length of the axon, is the nerve impulse. Because the nerve impulse is generated anew at each stage along the axon, it does not diminish in size during transmission.

Depolarization occurs because the cell membrane acts as a highly selective filter, ensuring different concentrations of ions inside and outside the cell. Ions can pass into and out of the cell only by way of *ion channels* and *ion pumps* embedded in the cell membrane. Ion channels are protein structures that form a pore across the cell membrane. The protein structure regulates the flow of ions by opening and closing the pore. When the gates of the channels are open, ions rush through the pores and tend to equalize the differences in ion concentrations that exist between the interior and exterior of the cell. The ion channels may open or close in response to neurotransmitters binding to them or in response to a change in the voltage across the membrane. In contrast to ion channels, ion pumps use metabolic energy to pump Na^+ ions (and other ions) back out of the cell to restore the resting potential of the membrane.

The axons of most neurons are covered by a thin fatty sheath, the *myelin sheath*, which serves to insulate them. The sheath consists of a series of short segments separated by small gaps (see Figure 2-1). The insulating function of the myelin sheath allows the nerve impulse to jump along from gap to gap, thus greatly improving the speed of conduction. The myelin sheath was a late development in evolution and is characteristic of the nervous systems of higher animals. *Multiple sclerosis*, a disease characterized by severe sensory and motor nerve dysfunction, is due to degeneration of areas of the myelin sheath.

Synaptic Transmission

The synaptic junction between neurons is of tremendous importance because it is there that nerve cells transfer signals. A single neuron discharges, or "fires," when the stimulation reaching it via multiple synapses exceeds a certain threshold level. The neuron fires in a single, brief burst and is then inactive for a few thousandths of a second. The size of the neural impulse is constant and cannot be triggered by a stimulus unless it reaches threshold level; this is referred to as the *all-or-none principle* of action. The impulse, once started, travels down the axon to its many axon terminals.

As we have said, neurons do not connect directly at a synapse; there is a slight gap across which the signal must be transmitted (see Figure 2-4). Although in a few areas of the nervous system the electrical activity in one neuron can stimulate another neuron directly, in the vast majority of cases, neurotransmitters are

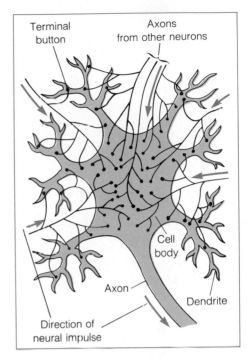

FIGURE 2-2
Synapses at the Cell Body of a Neuron
Many different axons, each of which branches repeatedly, synapse on the dendrites and cell body of a single neuron. Each branch of an axon ends in a swelling called an axon terminal, which contains chemicals that are released and transmit the nerve impulse across the synapse to the dendrites or cell body of the next cell. The neurons may undergo growth and rearrangement, establishing connections with new cells and severing old ties. It has been theorized that such changes are part of the physiological basis of learning and memory.

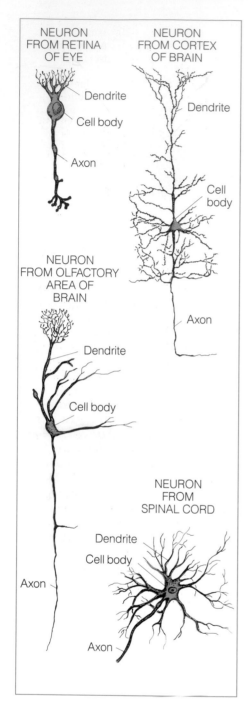

NEURON FROM RETINA OF EYE

Dendrite

Cell body

Axon

NEURON FROM CORTEX OF BRAIN

Dendrite

Cell body

Axon

NEURON FROM OLFACTORY AREA OF BRAIN

Dendrite

Cell body

Axon

NEURON FROM SPINAL CORD

Dendrite

Cell body

Axon

Axon

FIGURE 2-3
Shapes and Relative Sizes of Neurons
The axon of a spinal cord neuron (not shown is its entirety in the figure) may be several feet long.

responsible for transmitting the signal. When a nerve impulse moves down the axon of a neuron and arrives at an axon terminal, it stimulates *synaptic vesicles* in the terminal to discharge neurotransmitters. The neurotransmitter molecules diffuse across the synaptic gap and combine with molecules in the cell membrane of the receiving neuron. The two types of molecules lock together and cause a change in the permeability of the receiving neuron. Some neurotransmitters tend to have an excitatory effect and increase permeability in the direction of depolarization; others tend to be inhibitory and have the opposite effect.

A given neuron receives synapses from many other neurons, and some of these synapses release neurotransmitters that are excitatory, while others release neurotransmitters that are inhibitory. Depending on their pattern of firing, different axons will release their neurotransmitter substances at different times. If, at any moment, the excitatory effects become large relative to the inhibitory effects, then depolarization occurs and the neuron fires an all-or-none impulse.

Once a neurotransmitter substance is released and diffuses across the synaptic gap, its action must be very brief. Otherwise, it will exert its effects for too long, and precise control will be lost. The brevity of the action is achieved in one of two ways. For some neurotransmitters, the synapse is almost immediately cleared of the chemical by *reuptake;* the process in which the neurotransmitter is reabsorbed by the axon terminals from which it was released. Reuptake cuts off the action of the neurotransmitter and spares the axon terminals from having to manufacture more of the substance. The effect of other neurotransmitters is terminated by *degradation;* the process in which enzymes in the membrane of the receiving neuron react with the neurotransmitter to break it up chemically and make it inactive.

Neurotransmitters

Over 40 different neurotransmitters have been identified, and more will be discovered in the future. *Acetylcholine* (ACh) is the most common. In general, it is an excitatory transmitter, but it can be inhibitory depending on the type of receptor molecules in the membrane of the receiving neuron. ACh is found in many synapses in the brain and spinal cord. It is particularly prevalent in an area of the brain called the hippocampus, which plays a key role in the formation of new memories. Alzheimer's disease, a devastating disorder that affects many older people, involves impairment of memory and other cognitive functions. It has been demonstrated that brain cells producing ACh tend to degenerate in Alzheimer patients, and consequently the brain's production of ACh is reduced; the less ACh the brain produces, the more serious the Alzheimer symptoms.

ACh also is released at every synapse where a nerve terminates at a skeletal muscle fiber and hence is responsible for muscle contraction. Certain drugs that affect ACh can produce muscle paralysis. *Botulinum toxin,* which forms from bacteria in improperly canned foods, blocks receptors for ACh at nerve-muscle synapses and can cause death when the muscles for breathing become paralyzed. Some nerve gases developed for warfare and many pesticides cause paralysis by destroying the enzyme that degrades ACh once the neuron has been fired; when the degradation process fails there is an uncontrolled buildup of ACh in the nervous system so that normal synaptic transmission becomes impossible.

Norepinephrine (NE) is an important neurotransmitter that is produced mainly by neurons in the brain stem, although their axons project to a wide area of the brain. Two well-known drugs, *cocaine* and *amphetamines,* prolong the action of NE by slowing down its reuptake process. Because of this delay of the reuptake, the receiving neurons are activated for a longer period of time, thus giving rise to the stimulating psychological effects of these drugs. In contrast, *lithium* is a drug that speeds up the reuptake of NE, causing a person's mood level to be depressed. Any drug that causes NE to increase or decrease in the brain is correlated with an increase or decrease in the individual's mood level.

Another prominent neurotransmitter is *gamma-aminobutyric acid* (GABA). This substance acts as an inhibitory transmitter. For example, the drug *picrotoxin* blocks GABA receptors and produces convulsions, because without GABA's inhibiting influence there is a lack of control for muscle movement. The tranquilizing properties of certain drugs used to treat patients suffering from depression are related to a facilitation of GABA activity.

Some mood-altering drugs, such as *chlorpromazine* and *LSD,* create their effects by causing an excess or deficiency of specific neurotransmitters. Chlorpromazine, a drug used to treat schizophrenia, blocks the receptors for the neurotransmitter *dopamine* and allows fewer messages to get through. Too much dopamine at the synapse may cause schizophrenia, but Parkinson's disease results when too little is present. LSD is similar in chemical structure to the neurotransmitter *serotonin,* which affects emotion. Evidence shows that LSD accumulates in certain brain cells, where it mimics the action of serotonin and overstimulates the cells. (See the Critical Discussion, pp. 36–37.)

ORGANIZATION OF THE NERVOUS SYSTEM

All parts of the nervous system are interrelated. But for purposes of discussion, the nervous system can be separated into the following divisions and subdivisions:

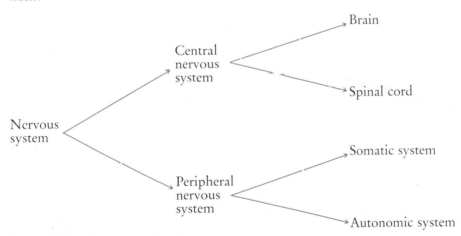

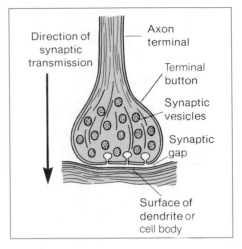

FIGURE 2-4

Synaptic Junction *When a nerve impulse reaches the end of an axon, it triggers the discharge of a chemical neurotransmitter into the synaptic gap. The neurotransmitter molecules combine with receptor molecules in the membrane of the receiving neuron in a lock-and-key type of action. The combination of molecules changes the membrane permeability of the receiving cell, making the cell either more likely to fire (excitatory synapse) or less likely to fire (inhibitory synapse). For many years, it was believed that a given neuron had only one type of neurotransmitter in all of its axon terminals. But recent evidence suggests that a neuron can secrete many different neurotransmitters and that even a single axon terminal may contain two or three types of neurotransmitters.*

The *central nervous system* includes all the neurons in the brain and spinal cord. The *peripheral nervous system* consists of the nerves connecting the brain and spinal cord to the other parts of the body. The peripheral nervous system is further divided into the *somatic system* and the *autonomic system.*

The sensory nerves of the somatic system transmit information about external stimulation from the skin, muscles, and joints to the central nervous system; they make us aware of pain, pressure, and temperature variations. The motor nerves of the somatic system carry impulses from the central nervous system to the muscles of the body, where they initiate action. All the muscles we use in making voluntary movements, as well as involuntary adjustments in posture and balance, are controlled by these nerves.

CRITICAL DISCUSSION*

Neurotransmitters and Psychoactive Drugs

When the electrical impulse reaches the end of an axon, *neurotransmitter molecules* are released that cross the synaptic gap and combine with *receptor molecules* in the membrane of the target neuron. The neurotransmitter and receptor molecules fit together in the same way that one piece of a jigsaw puzzle fits another or a key fits a lock. The *lock-and-key* action of the two molecules changes the electrical properties of the target cell, either causing it to fire or preventing it from firing.

To serve its function, every key requires a lock and every neurotransmitter requires a receptor. Many commonly used drugs—from tranquilizers such as Valium to street drugs like heroin and cocaine—interact with receptor molecules in very much the same way as neurotransmitters. Molecules of these drugs are shaped enough like those of the neurotransmitters to work as if they were keys to the lock of receptor molecules.

A good example is the *opiates*, a class of drugs that includes heroin and mor-

* Critical discussions are introduced from time to time to point out controversial issues or to treat a topic in more detail. They may be omitted at the discretion of the instructor.

phine. In molecular shape, the opiates resemble a group of neurotransmitters in the brain called *endorphins*, which have the effect of blocking pain. The discovery that opiates mimic naturally occurring substances in the brain has prompted considerable research on the chemical control system in the body that copes with stress and pain. Individuals who appear indifferent to pain may have an unusual ability to increase the production of these natural painkillers when they are needed. Research with one of the endorphins, called *enkephalin*, has helped explain why a painkiller like morphine can be addictive. Under normal conditions, enkephalin occupies a certain number of opiate receptors. Morphine relieves pain by binding to receptors that are left unfilled. Too much morphine can cause a drop in enkephalin production, leaving opiate receptors unfilled. The body then requires more morphine to fill the unoccupied receptors and to reduce pain. When morphine is discontinued, the opiate receptors are left unfilled, causing painful withdrawal symptoms. The fact that the brain synthesizes substances which resemble opiates has been invoked to explain all sorts of effects. Joggers tout the theory that physical exertion increases enkephalin production to induce a "runner's high." Acu-

The nerves of the autonomic system run to and from the internal organs, regulating such processes as respiration, heart rate, and digestion. The autonomic system, which plays a major role in emotion, is discussed later in the chapter.

Most of the nerve fibers connecting various parts of the body to the brain are gathered together in the *spinal cord,* where they are protected by the bony spinal vertebrae. The spinal cord is remarkably compact—barely the diameter of your little finger. Some of the simplest stimulus-response reflexes are carried out at the level of the spinal cord. One example is the knee jerk, the extension of the leg in response to a tap on the tendon that runs in front of the kneecap. Frequently a doctor uses this test to determine the efficiency of the spinal reflexes. The natural function of this reflex is to ensure that the leg will extend when the knee is bent by the force of gravity, so the organism remains standing. When the knee tendon is tapped, the attached muscle stretches, and a message from sensory cells embedded in the muscle is transmitted through sensory neurons to the spinal cord. There the sensory neurons synapse directly with motor neurons, which transmit impulses back to the same muscle, causing it to contract and the leg to extend. Although this response can occur solely in the spinal cord without any assistance from the brain, it can be modulated by messages from higher nervous centers. If you grip your hands just before the knee is tapped, the extension movement is exaggerated. Or if you consciously want to inhibit the reflex just before the

puncturists say their needles actuate enkephalins that act as natural anesthetics. There is, however, little scientific evidence to support these claims.

Drugs that influence mental functioning and mood, such as opiates, are called *psychoactive drugs.* They produce their effects by altering one of the various neurotransmitter systems. Most drug actions on the nervous system occur at synapses. Different drugs can have different actions at the same synapse. One drug might mimic the effect of a specific neurotransmitter, another might occupy the receptor site so that the normal neurotransmitter is blocked out, and still others might affect the reuptake or degradation processes. The drug action will either increase or decrease the effectiveness of neural transmission.

Two drugs, *chlorpromazine* and *reserpine,* have proved effective in treating schizophrenia (a mental illness to be discussed in Chapter 15). Both drugs act on norepinephrine and dopamine systems, but their antipsychotic action is primarily due to their effect on the neurotransmitter dopamine. It appears that chlorpromazine blocks dopamine receptors, whereas reserpine reduces dopamine levels by destroying storage vesicles in the axon terminals. The effectiveness of these drugs in treating schizophrenia has led to the *dopamine hypothesis,* which postulates that schizophrenia is due to an excess of dopamine activity in critical cell groups within the brain. The key evidence for the hypothesis is that antipsychotic drugs seem to be clinically effective to the extent that they block the transmission of impulses by dopamine molecules. Also, *amphetamines,* which can cause a schizophrenic-like state in normal individuals, appear to enhance dopamine activity. The dopamine hypothesis has wide support, but as yet, efforts to demonstrate an actual increase in dopamine concentrations in schizophrenics, as compared with normals, have not been successful.

Research on the relationship between psychoactive drugs and neurotransmitters has increased our understanding of how these drugs work. Other avenues of research have demonstrated that human memory can be temporarily enhanced by drugs that affect cholinergic activity (the activity of neurons that use ACh as a neurotransmitter). But due to the complexity of the cholinergic system, drugs that permanently enhance memory are still a long way off (Mohs et al., 1985). Many psychological problems will become clearer as we discover more about the intricacies of neural communication.

doctor taps the tendon, you can do so. The basic mechanism is built into the spinal cord, but it can be modified by higher brain centers.

The simplest reflex may involve only sensory and motor neurons, but most reflexes also involve one or more *interneurons* in the spinal cord, which mediate between incoming and outgoing neurons. Figure 2-5 shows a basic three-neuron reflex arc.

STRUCTURE OF THE BRAIN

Some brain structures are clearly demarcated; others gradually merge into each other, and this leads to debate about their exact boundaries and the functions they control. For our purposes, it will be helpful to think of the human brain as composed of three concentric layers that developed at different stages in evolution: (1) a primitive *central core;* (2) the *limbic system,* which evolved upon this core at a later stage of evolution; and (3) the *cerebral hemispheres* (together known as the *cerebrum*) responsible for higher mental processes. Figure 2-6 shows how these layers fit together. The three concentric layers may be compared with the more detailed cross section of the human brain in Figure 2-7.

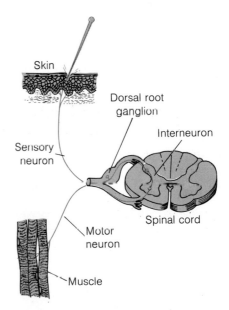

FIGURE 2-5
Three-neuron Reflex Arc *This diagram illustrates how nerve impulses from a sense organ in the skin reach a skeletal muscle by a three-neuron arc within the spinal cord. Awareness of this automatic reflex occurs because impulses also reach the cerebral hemisphere by way of an ascending tract. The H-shaped portion at the center of the spinal cord is gray matter, consisting largely of cell bodies and their interconnections.*

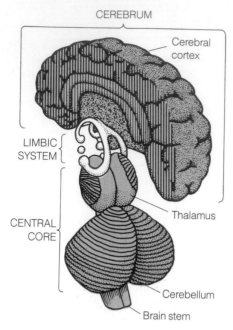

CEREBRUM

Cerebral cortex

LIMBIC SYSTEM

CENTRAL CORE

Thalamus

Cerebellum

Brain stem

FIGURE 2-6

Three Concentric Layers of the Human Brain *The central core and the limbic system are shown in their entirety, but the left cerebral hemisphere has been removed. The cerebellum of the central core controls balance and muscular coordination; the thalamus serves as a switchboard for messages coming from the sense organs; the hypothalamus (not shown but located below the thalamus) regulates endocrine activity and such life-maintaining processes as metabolism and temperature control. The limbic system is concerned with actions that satisfy basic needs and with emotion. The cerebral cortex, an outer layer of cells covering the cerebrum, is the center of higher mental processes, where sensations are registered, voluntary actions initiated, decisions made, and plans formulated.*

Central Core

The central core includes most of the brain stem. The first slight enlargement of the spinal cord as it enters the skull is the *medulla,* a narrow structure (about 1½ inches long) that controls breathing and some reflexes that help the organism maintain an upright posture. At this point, also, the major nerve tracts coming up from the spinal cord and descending from the brain cross over so that the right side of the brain is connected to the left side of the body, and the left side of the brain to the right side of the body. We will have more to say about the significance of this crossover later.

CEREBELLUM Attached to the rear of the brain stem, slightly above the medulla, is a convoluted structure, the *cerebellum.* The cerebellum is concerned primarily with the coordination of movement, and its structure is much the same in lower vertebrates (such as snakes and fish) as in humans. Specific movements may be initiated at higher levels, but their smooth coordination depends on the cerebellum. This structure regulates muscle tone and orchestrates the intricate movements of a fish swimming, a bird flying, or a human being playing a musical instrument. Damage to the cerebellum results in jerky, uncoordinated movements; often the person can no longer perform simple movements (such as walking) automatically but must concentrate on each component of the total action.

THALAMUS AND HYPOTHALAMUS Located just above the brain stem inside the cerebral hemispheres are two egg-shaped groups of nerve cell nuclei that make up the *thalamus.* One region of the thalamus acts as a relay station and directs incoming information to the cerebrum from the sense receptors for vision, hearing, touch, and taste. Another region of the thalamus plays an important role in the control of sleep and wakefulness and is considered part of the reticular system.

The *hypothalamus* is a much smaller structure, located just below the thalamus. Despite its size, the hypothalamus plays an extremely important role in many aspects of emotion and motivation. Centers in the hypothalamus govern eating, drinking, and sexual behavior. The hypothalamus regulates endocrine activity and maintains *homeostasis.* Homeostasis refers to the general level of functioning characteristic of the healthy organism, such as normal body temperature, heart rate, and blood pressure. Under stress, the usual equilibrium is disturbed, and processes are set into motion to correct the disequilibrium and return the body to its normal level of functioning. For example, if we are too warm, we perspire; and if we are too cool, we shiver. Both of these processes tend to restore normal temperature and are controlled by the hypothalamus. The hypothalamus contains control mechanisms that detect changes in body systems and correct the imbalance.

The hypothalamus also plays an important role in emotion and in response to stress-producing situations. We noted in Chapter 1 that mild electrical stimulation of certain areas in the hypothalamus produces feelings of pleasure, while stimulation of adjacent regions produces sensations that appear to be unpleasant or painful. By its influence on the pituitary gland, which lies just below it (see Figure 2-7), the hypothalamus controls the endocrine system and in turn the production of hormones. This control is particularly important when the body must mobilize a complex set of physiological processes (the "fight-or-flight" response) to deal with emergencies and other stress-producing events. The hypothalamus has been called the "stress center" in recognition of its special role in mobilizing the body for action.

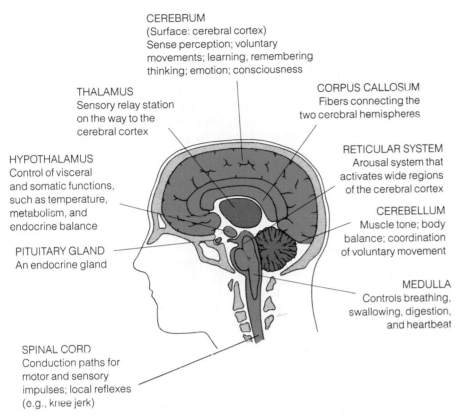

CEREBRUM
(Surface: cerebral cortex)
Sense perception; voluntary
movements; learning, remembering
thinking; emotion; consciousness

THALAMUS
Sensory relay station
on the way to the
cerebral cortex

HYPOTHALAMUS
Control of visceral
and somatic functions,
such as temperature,
metabolism, and
endocrine balance

PITUITARY GLAND
An endocrine gland

CORPUS CALLOSUM
Fibers connecting the
two cerebral hemispheres

RETICULAR SYSTEM
Arousal system that
activates wide regions
of the cerebral cortex

CEREBELLUM
Muscle tone; body
balance; coordination
of voluntary movement

MEDULLA
Controls breathing,
swallowing, digestion,
and heartbeat

SPINAL CORD
Conduction paths for
motor and sensory
impulses; local reflexes
(e.g., knee jerk)

FIGURE 2-7
The Human Brain *This schematic drawing shows the main subdivisions of the human central nervous system and their functions. (Only the upper portion of the spinal cord, which is also part of the central nervous system, is shown.)*

RETICULAR SYSTEM   A network of neural circuits that extends from the lower brain stem up to the thalamus, traversing through some of the other central core structures, is the *reticular* ("network") *system*. The reticular system plays an important role in controlling our state of arousal or awareness. When an electric current of a certain voltage is sent through electrodes implanted in the reticular system of a cat or dog, the animal goes to sleep; stimulation by a current with a more rapidly changing waveform awakens the sleeping animal. If lesions are made in the reticular system, the animal often becomes permanently stuporous (that is, goes into a coma).

The reticular system may also play a role in our ability to focus our attention. All of the sense receptors have nerve fibers that feed into the reticular system; and the system appears to act as a filter, allowing some of the sensory messages to pass to the cerebral cortex (to conscious awareness) while blocking others. Thus, in a moment of intense concentration, you may be unaware of the noises around you or a pain that was previously quite noticeable.

Limbic System

Around the central core of the brain, lying along the innermost edge of the cerebral hemispheres, are a number of structures that together are called the *limbic system*. From an evolutionary view, the limbic system is more recent than the central core; it is fully developed only in mammals. This system is closely interconnected with the hypothalamus and appears to impose additional controls over some of the "instinctive" behaviors regulated by the hypothalamus and brain stem. Animals that have only rudimentary limbic systems (for example, fish and reptiles) carry out activities such as feeding, attacking, fleeing from danger,

CRITICAL DISCUSSION

Computer-generated Pictures of the Brain

A number of new techniques have been developed to obtain detailed pictures of the living human brain without causing the patient distress or damage. Before these techniques were perfected, the precise location and identification of most types of brain injury could be determined only by exploratory neurosurgery or by autopsy after the patient's death. The new techniques depend upon sophisticated computer methods that have become feasible only recently.

One such technique is *computerized axial tomography* (abbreviated CAT or simply CT). This procedure involves sending a narrow X-ray beam through the patient's head and measuring the amount of radiation that gets through. The revolutionary aspect of the technique is that measurements are made at hundreds of thousands of different orientations (or axes) through the head. These measurements are then fed into a computer and, by making appropriate calculations, a cross-sectional picture of the brain is reconstructed that can be photographed or displayed on a television monitor. The cross-sectional slice can be at any level and angle desired. The term CT refers to the critical role of the computer, the many axes at which measurements are made, and the resulting image which is a cross-sectional slice through the brain (*tomo* is from the Greek word meaning "slice" or "cut").

A newer and even more powerful technique involves *magnetic resonance imaging* (abbreviated MRI). Scanners of this sort use strong magnetic fields, radio-frequency pulses, and computers to compose the image. In this procedure the patient lies in a donut-shaped tunnel surrounded by a large magnet that generates a powerful magnetic field. When the anatomic part to be studied is placed in a strong magnetic field and exposed to a certain radio-frequency pulse, the tissues emit a

signal that can be measured. As with the CT scanner, thousands of such measurements are made and then manipulated by a computer into a two-dimensional image of the anatomic part. Among scientists, the technique is usually called nuclear magnetic resonance because what is being measured are variations in the energy level of hydrogen atom nuclei in the body caused by the radio-frequency pulses. However, many physicians prefer to drop the term "nuclear" and simply call it magnetic resonance imaging, since they fear the public may confuse the reference to the nucleus of an atom with nuclear radiation.

While the indications for use of MRI are still evolving, it clearly offers greater precision than even the CT scanner in the diagnosis of diseases of the brain and spinal cord. For example, an MRI cross section of the brain shows features characteristic of multiple sclerosis that are not detected by a CT scanner; previously, diagnosis of this disease required hospitalization and a test in which dye is injected into the canal around the spinal cord. MRI is also useful in the detection of abnormalities in the spinal cord and at the base of the brain, such as herniated disks, tumors, and birth malformations.

While CT and MRI provide a picture of the anatomical detail of the brain, it is often desirable to assess the level of neural activity at different spots in the brain. A computer-based scanning procedure called *positron emission tomography* (abbreviated PET) provides this additional information. The technique depends upon the fact that every cell in the body requires energy to conduct its various metabolic processes. In the brain, neurons utilize glucose (obtained from the bloodstream) as their principal source of energy. A small amount of a radioactive "tracer" compound can be mixed with glucose so that each molecule of glu-

and mating by means of stereotyped behaviors. In mammals, the limbic system seems to inhibit some of the instinctive patterns, allowing the organism to be more flexible and adaptive to changes in the environment.

One part of the limbic system, the *hippocampus,* plays a special role in memory. Surgical removal of the hippocampus or accidental damage to the structure indicates that it is critical for the storage of new events as lasting memories, but it is not necessary for the retrieval of older memories. Upon recovery from such an operation, the patient will have no difficulty recognizing

cose has a tiny speck of radioactivity (that is, a label) attached to it. If this harmless mixture is injected into the bloodstream, after a few minutes the brain cells begin to use the radio-labeled glucose in the same way they use regular glucose. The PET scan is essentially a highly sensitive detector of radioactivity (it is not like an X-ray machine, which emits X rays, but rather like a Geiger counter, which measures radioactivity). Neurons of the brain that are most active require the most glucose and, therefore, will be the most radioactive. The PET scan measures the amount of radioactivity and sends the information to a computer which draws a color cross-sectional picture of the brain with different colors representing different levels of neural activity. The measurement of radioactivity is based on the emission of positively charged particles (called positrons), and hence the term positron emission tomography.

Comparing PET scans of normal individuals with those of persons who have neurological disorders indicates that a variety of brain problems (epilepsy, blood clots, brain tumors, and so on) can be identified using this technique. For psychological research, the PET scan has been used to compare the brains of schizophrenics with those of normals and has revealed differences in the metabolic levels of certain cortical areas. It has also been used to investigate the brain areas activated during such higher mental functions as listening to music, doing mathematics, or speaking—the goal being to identify the brain structures involved.

The CT, MRI, and PET scanners are proving to be invaluable tools for studying the relationship between brain and behavior. These devices are yet another example of how progress in one field of science forges ahead because of technical developments in another.

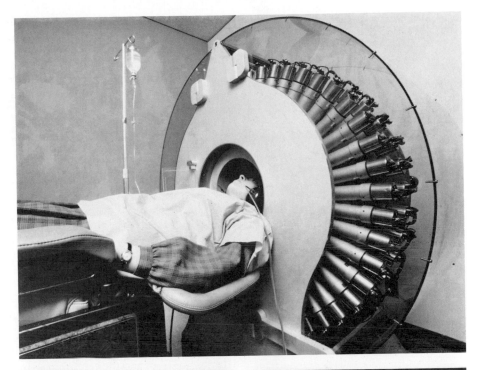

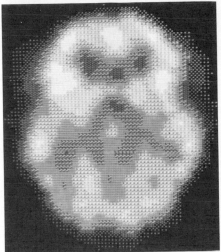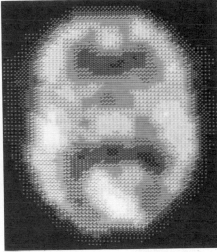

To monitor brain activity, a patient is injected with glucose plus a radioactive tracer. The PET scanner measures glucose metabolism (above). On the left is a scan of a normal person; on the right is a schizophrenic patient.

old friends or recalling earlier experiences; he will be able to read and perform skills learned earlier in life. However, he will have little, if any, recall of events that occurred in the year or so just prior to the operation. And events and people he met after the operation will not be remembered at all. For example, the patient will fail to recognize a new person with whom he may have spent many hours earlier in the day. He will do the same jigsaw puzzle week after week, never remembering having done it before, and will read the same newspaper over and over without remembering the contents (Squire, 1986).

Both playing (left) and fighting (right) appear to be controlled by the limbic system.

The limbic system is also involved in emotional behavior. Monkeys with lesions in some regions of the limbic system react with rage at the slightest provocation, suggesting that the destroyed area was exerting an inhibiting influence. Monkeys with lesions in other areas of the limbic system no longer express aggressive behavior and show no hostility, even when attacked. They simply ignore the attacker and act as if nothing had happened.

Treating the brain as three concentric structures—the central core, the limbic system, and the cerebrum—must not lead us to think of these interrelated structures as independent. We might use the analogy of a bank of interrelated computers. Each has specialized functions, but they still work together to produce the most effective result. Similarly, the analysis of information coming from the senses requires one kind of computation and decision process (for which the cerebrum is well adapted), differing from that which controls a reflexive sequence of activities (the limbic system). The finer adjustments of the muscles (as in writing or playing a musical instrument) require another kind of control system, in this case mediated by the cerebellum. All these activities are ordered into complex systems that maintain the integrity of the organism.

CEREBRAL CORTEX

Structure of the Cerebral Cortex

The cerebrum is more highly developed in human beings than in any other organism. The *cerebral cortex* is the layer of neurons about 3 millimeters thick covering the cerebrum; in Latin, *cortex* means "bark." The cortical layer of a preserved brain appears gray because it consists largely of nerve cell bodies and unmyelinated fibers—hence the term *gray matter*. The inside of the cerebrum, beneath the cortex, is composed mostly of myelinated axons and appears white. It is in the cerebral cortex that our more complex mental activities take place.

The cerebral cortex of a lower mammal, such as the rat, is small and relatively smooth. As we ascend the phylogenetic scale to the higher mammals, the amount of cortex relative to the amount of total brain tissue increases accordingly, and the cortex becomes progressively more wrinkled and convoluted, so that its actual surface area is far greater than it would be if it were a smooth covering over the surface of the cerebrum. There is a general correlation between the cortical development of a species, its position on the phylogenetic scale, and the complexity of its behavior.

All of the sensory systems (for example, vision, audition, and touch) project information to specific areas of the cortex. The movements of body parts (motor responses) are controlled by another area of the cortex. The rest of the cortex, which is neither sensory nor motor, consists of association areas. These areas are concerned with more complex aspects of behavior—memory, thought, and language—and occupy the largest area of the human cortex.

Before discussing some of these locations, we need to use a few landmarks in describing areas of the *cerebral hemispheres*. The two hemispheres are basically symmetrical with a deep division between them, running from front to rear. So, our first classification is the division into *right* and *left hemispheres*. Each hemisphere is divided into four *lobes:* the *frontal, parietal, occipital,* and *temporal*. The divisions between these lobes are shown in Figure 2-8. The frontal lobe is separated from the parietal lobe by the *central fissure*, running from near the top of the head sideways to the ears. The division between the parietal lobe and the occipital lobe is less clear-cut; for our purpose, it is sufficient to know that the parietal lobe is at the top of the brain behind the central fissure and that the occipital lobe is at the rear of the brain. The temporal lobe is demarcated by a deep fissure at the side of the brain, the *lateral fissure*.

Cortical Areas and Their Functions

MOTOR AREA The *motor area* (or *motor cortex*) controls the voluntary movements of the body; it lies just in front of the central fissure (see Figure 2-9). Electrical stimulation at certain spots on the motor cortex produces movement of specific body parts; when these same spots are injured, movement is impaired. The body is represented on the motor cortex in approximately upside-down form. For example, movements of the toes are mediated near the top of the head, whereas tongue and mouth movements are mediated near the bottom of the motor area. Movements on the right side of the body are governed by the motor cortex of the left hemisphere; movements on the left side, by the right hemisphere.

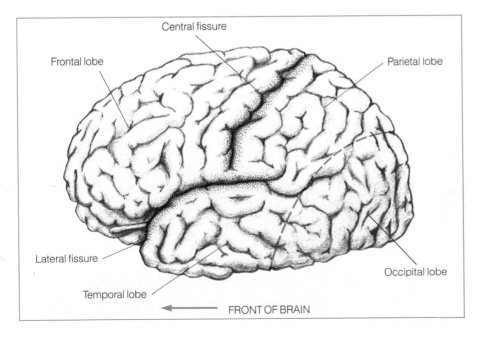

Central fissure

Frontal lobe

Parietal lobe

Lateral fissure

Temporal lobe

Occipital lobe

← FRONT OF BRAIN

FIGURE 2-8
The Four Lobes of the Left Cortex *The central fissure and lateral fissure are landmarks separating the lobes of the cortex.*

FIGURE 2-9

Localization of Function in the Left Cortex *Much of the cortex is involved in generating movements and in analyzing sensory inputs. These areas (which include motor, somatosensory, visual, auditory, and olfactory areas) are present on both sides of the brain in all species that have a well-developed cortex. Other areas are more narrowly specialized, often found on only one side of the brain, and present only in human beings. For example, Broca's area and Wernicke's area are involved in the production and understanding of language, and the angular gyrus is involved in matching the visual form of a word with its auditory form; these functions exist only on the left side of the human brain. The right side of the human brain, not shown in this figure, has its own specialized functions, including the analysis of complex visual scenes and some aspects of music perception.*

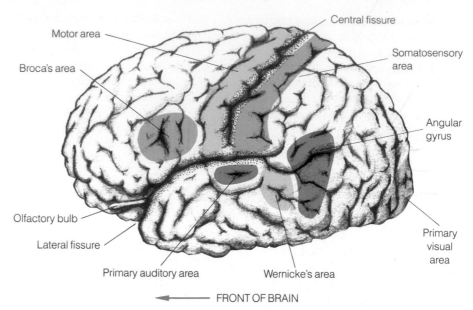

SOMATOSENSORY AREA In the parietal lobe, separated from the motor area by the central fissure, lies an area that if stimulated electrically produces a sensory experience somewhere on the opposite side of the body. It is as though a part of the body were being touched or moved. This is called the *somatosensory* (body-sense) *area* (or *somatosensory cortex*). Heat, cold, touch, pain, and the sense of body movement are all represented here. The lower extremities of the body are represented high on the area of the opposite hemisphere; the face, low on the area of the opposite hemisphere.

Most of the nerve fibers in the pathways that radiate to and from the somatosensory and motor areas cross to the opposite side of the body. Thus, the sensory impulses from the right side of the body go to the left somatosensory cortex, and the muscles of the right foot and hand are controlled by the left motor cortex.

It seems to be a general rule that the amount of somatosensory or motor cortex associated with a particular part of the body is directly related to its sensitivity and use. Among four-footed mammals, the dog has only a small amount of cortical tissue representing the forepaws, whereas the raccoon — which makes extensive use of its forepaws in exploring and manipulating its environment — has a much larger representative cortical area, including regions for the separate fingers of the forepaw. The rat, which learns a great deal about its environment by means of its sensitive whiskers, has a separate cortical area for each whisker.

VISUAL AREA At the back of each occipital lobe is an area of the cortex important in vision, known as the *visual area*. Figure 2-10 shows the optic nerve fibers and neural pathways leading from each eye to the visual cortex. Notice that some of the fibers go from the right eye to the right cerebral hemisphere and from the left eye to the left hemisphere, whereas others cross over a junction called the *optic chiasma* and go to the opposite hemisphere. Fibers from the right sides of *both* eyes go to the right hemisphere of the brain, and fibers from the left sides of both eyes go to the left hemisphere. Consequently, damage to the visual area of one hemisphere (say, the left) will result in blind fields in the left sides of both eyes, causing a loss of vision to the right side of the environment. This fact is sometimes helpful in pinpointing the location of a brain tumor or injury.

AUDITORY AREA The *auditory area,* found on the surface of the temporal lobe at the side of each hemisphere, is involved in the analysis of the more complex aspects of auditory signals. It is particularly concerned with the patterning of sound in time, as in human speech. There is some spatial mapping in the auditory area, one part being sensitive to high tones and a different part sensitive to low tones. Both ears are represented in the auditory areas on both sides of the cortex; however, the connections to the contralateral side are stronger.

ASSOCIATION AREAS The many large areas of the cerebral cortex that are not directly concerned with sensory or motor processes are called *association areas.* The *frontal association areas* (the parts of the frontal lobes anterior to — or in front of — the motor area) appear to play an important role in the thought processes required for problem solving. In monkeys, for example, lesions in the frontal lobes destroy the ability to solve a delayed-response problem. In this kind of problem, food is placed in one of two cups while the monkey watches, and the cups are covered with identical objects. An opaque screen is then placed between the monkey and the cups; after a specified time the screen is removed, and the monkey is allowed to choose one of the cups. Normal monkeys can remember the correct cup after delays of several minutes, but monkeys with frontal lobe lesions cannot solve the problem if the delay is more than a second or so. This delayed-response deficit following brain lesions is unique to the frontal cortex; it does not occur if lesions are made in other cortical regions (French & Harlow, 1962).

Human beings who have suffered damage to the frontal association areas can perform many intellectual tasks normally, including delayed-response problems. Their ability to use language probably enables them to remember the correct response. They do have difficulty, however, when it is necessary to shift frequently from one strategy to another while working on a problem (Milner, 1964).

The *posterior association areas* are located among the various primary sensory areas and appear to consist of subareas, each serving a particular sense. For example, the lower portion of the temporal lobe is related to visual perception. Lesions in this area produce deficits in the ability to recognize and discriminate different forms. A lesion here does not cause loss of visual acuity, as would a lesion in the primary visual area of the occipital lobe; the individual "sees" the forms (and can trace the outline) but cannot identify the shape or distinguish it from a different form. In contrast, the association areas of the parietal lobe are important for locating objects in sensory space and for maintaining internal "maps" of the environment.

ASYMMETRIES IN THE BRAIN

To the naked eye, the two halves of the human brain look like mirror images of each other. But closer examination reveals asymmetries. When brains are carefully measured during autopsies, the left hemisphere is almost always larger than the right hemisphere. Also, the right hemisphere contains many long neural fibers that connect widely separate areas of the brain, whereas the left hemisphere contains shorter fibers that provide rich interconnections within a limited area.

As early as 1861, the French physician Paul Broca examined the brain of a patient who had suffered speech loss and found damage in an area of the left hemisphere just above the lateral fissure in the frontal lobe. This region, known as *Broca's area* and shown in Figure 2-9, is involved in the production of speech sounds. Destruction of the equivalent region in the right hemisphere usually does

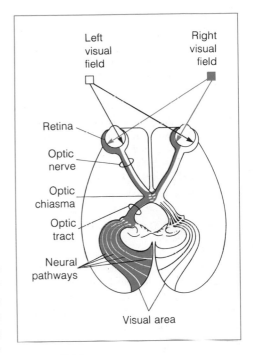

FIGURE 2-10
Visual Pathways *Light waves from objects in the right visual field fall on the left half of each retina; light waves from the left visual field fall on the right half of each retina. The optic nerve bundles from each eye meet at the optic chiasma, where the fibers from the inner, or nasal, half of the retina cross over and go to opposite sides of the brain. Thus, stimuli falling on the right side of each retina are transmitted to the occipital cortex of the right cerebral hemisphere, and stimuli impinging on the left side of each retina are transmitted to the left cerebral hemisphere. In terms of the visual field, this means that objects in the right visual field are projected to the left cerebral hemisphere, whereas objects in the left visual field are projected to the right hemisphere.*

not result in speech impairment. The areas involved in understanding speech and in the ability to write and understand written words are also usually located in the left hemisphere. Thus, a person who suffers a stroke that damages the left hemisphere is more likely to show language impairment than one whose damage is confined to the right hemisphere. This is usually true for right-handed individuals because their left hemisphere is almost always dominant. (Remember that the left hemisphere controls the motor functions of the right side of the body.) Some left-handed people have speech centers located in the right hemisphere or divided between the left and the right, but the majority have language functions in the left hemisphere (the same as right-handed individuals).

Although the left hemisphere's role in language has been known for some time, only recently has it been possible to investigate what each hemisphere can do on its own. In the normal individual, the brain functions as an integrated whole; information in one hemisphere is immediately transferred to the other by way of a broad band of connecting nerve fibers called the *corpus callosum*. This connecting bridge can cause a problem in some forms of epilepsy, because a seizure starting in one hemisphere may cross over and trigger a massive discharge of neurons in the other. In an effort to prevent such generalized seizures in some severe epileptics, neurosurgeons have surgically severed the corpus callosum. The operation has generally proved successful, resulting in a decrease in seizures. In addition, there appear to be no undesirable aftereffects; the patients seem to function in everyday life as well as individuals whose hemispheres are still connected. It took some very special tests to demonstrate how mental functions are affected by separating the two hemispheres. A little more background information is needed to understand the experiments we are about to describe.

We have seen that the motor nerves cross over as they leave the brain, so that the left cerebral hemisphere controls the right side of the body and the right hemisphere controls the left. We noted also that the area for the production of speech (Broca's area) is located in the left hemisphere. When the eyes are fixated directly ahead, images to the left of the fixation point go through both eyes to the right side of the brain and images to the right of the fixation point go to the left side of the brain (see Figure 2-11). Thus, each hemisphere has a view of that half of the visual field in which "its" hand normally functions; that is, the left hemisphere sees the right hand in the right visual field. In the normal brain, stimuli entering one hemisphere are rapidly communicated, by way of the corpus callosum, to the other, so that the brain functions as a unit. We will see what happens when the corpus callosum is severed — called a *split brain* — so that the two hemispheres cannot communicate.

Split-brain Subjects

Roger Sperry pioneered work in this field and was awarded the Nobel prize in 1981 for his research. In one of Sperry's test situations, a male subject who has undergone a split-brain operation is seated in front of a screen that hides his hands from view (see Figure 2-12A). His gaze is fixed at a spot on the center of the screen and the word *nut* is flashed very briefly (for one-tenth of a second) on the left side of the screen. Remember that this visual image goes to the right side of the brain, which controls the left side of the body. With his left hand, the subject can easily pick up the nut from a pile of objects hidden from view. But he cannot tell the experimenter what word flashed on the screen because speech is controlled by the left hemisphere and the visual image of *nut* was not transmitted to that hemisphere. When questioned, the split-brain subject seems unaware of what his left hand is doing. Since the sensory input from the left hand goes to the right hemisphere, the left hemisphere receives no information about what the left hand

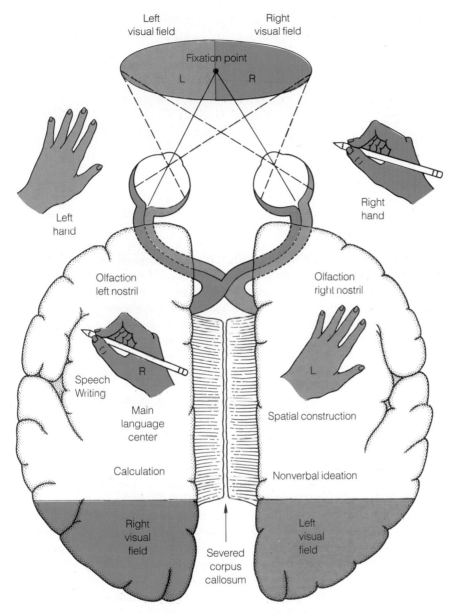

Left
visual field

Right
visual field

Fixation point

L   R

Left
hand

Right
hand

Olfaction
left nostril

Olfaction
right nostril

Speech
Writing

R

Main
language
center

Spatial construction

L

Calculation

Nonverbal ideation

Right
visual
field

Severed
corpus
callosum

Left
visual
field

FIGURE 2-11

Sensory Inputs to the Two Hemispheres *With the eyes fixated straight ahead, stimuli to the left of the fixation point go to the right cerebral hemisphere, and stimuli to the right go to the left hemisphere. The left hemisphere controls movements of the right hand, and the right hemisphere controls the left hand. Hearing is largely crossed in its input, but some sound representation goes to the hemisphere on the same side as the ear. Olfaction is received on the same side as the nostril. The left hemisphere is dominant for most people; it controls written and spoken language and mathematical calculations. The right hemisphere can understand only simple language. Its main ability seems to involve spatial construction and pattern sense.*

is feeling or doing. All information is fed back to the right hemisphere, which received the original visual input of the word *nut*.

It is important that the word be flashed on the screen for no more than one-tenth of a second. If it remains longer, the subject can move his eyes so that the word is also projected to the left hemisphere. If the split-brain subject can move his eyes freely, information goes to both cerebral hemispheres; this is one reason why the deficiencies caused by severing the corpus callosum are not readily apparent in a person's daily activities.

Further experiments demonstrate that the split-brain subject can communicate through speech only what is going on in the left hemisphere. Figure 2-12B shows another test situation. The word *hatband* is flashed on the screen so that *hat* goes to the right hemisphere and *band* to the left. When asked what word he saw, the subject replies, "band." When asked what kind of band, he makes all sorts of guesses — "rubber band," "rock band," "band of robbers," and so forth — and only hits on "hatband" by chance. Tests with other word combinations (such as

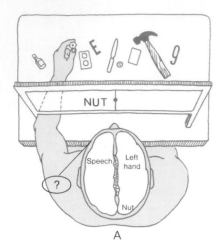 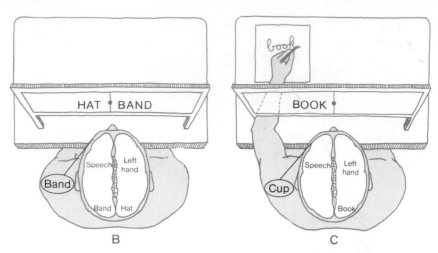

A   B   C

FIGURE 2-12
Testing the Abilities of the Two
Hemispheres   A. The split-brain subject
correctly retrieves an object by touch with
the left hand when its name is flashed to
the right hemisphere, but he cannot name
the object or describe what he has done.
B. The word **hatband** is flashed so that **hat**
goes to the right cerebral hemisphere and
band goes to the left hemisphere. The
subject reports that he sees the word **band**
but has no idea what kind of band. C. A
list of common objects (including book and
cup) is initially shown to both
hemispheres. One word from the list
(**book**) is then projected to the right
hemisphere. When given the command to
do so, the left hand begins writing the
word **book**, but when questioned the
subject does not know what his left hand
has written and guesses "cup." (After
Sperry, 1970; Nebes & Sperry, 1971)

keycase and *suitcase*), split so that half is projected to each hemisphere, show similar results. What is perceived by the right hemisphere does not transfer to the conscious awareness of the left hemisphere. With the corpus callosum severed, each hemisphere seems oblivious of the experiences of the other.

If the split-brain subject is blindfolded and a familiar object (such as a comb, toothbrush, or keycase) is placed in his left hand, he appears to know what it is; for example, he can demonstrate its use by appropriate gestures. But he cannot express his knowledge in speech. If asked what is going on while he is manipulating the object, he has no idea. This is true as long as any sensory input from the object to the left (talking) hemisphere is blocked. But if the subject's right hand inadvertently touches the object or if it makes a characteristic sound (like the jingling of a keycase), the speaking hemisphere immediately gives the right answer.

Although the right hemisphere cannot speak, it does have some linguistic capabilities. It recognized the meaning of the word *nut,* as we saw in our first example, and it can write a little. In the experiment illustrated in Figure 2-12C, a split-brain subject is first shown a list of common objects such as cup, knife, book, and glass. This list is displayed long enough for the words to be projected to both hemispheres. Next, the list is removed, and one of the words (for example, *book*) is flashed briefly on the left side of the screen so that it goes to the right hemisphere. If the subject is asked to write what he saw, his left hand will begin writing the word *book*. If asked what his left hand has written, he has no idea and will guess at any of the words on the original list. The subject knows he has written something because he feels the writing movements through his body. But because there is no communication between the right hemisphere that saw and wrote the word and the left hemisphere that controls speech, the subject cannot tell you what he wrote.

Hemispheric Specialization

Studies with split-brain subjects have made clear the striking differences between the functions of the two hemispheres. The left hemisphere governs our ability to express ourselves in language. It can perform many complicated logical and analytic activities and is skilled in mathematical computations. The right hemisphere can comprehend very simple language. It can respond to simple nouns by selecting objects such as a nut or comb, and it can even respond to associations of these objects. For example, if the right hemisphere is asked to retrieve from a group of objects the one used "for lighting fires," it will instruct the left hand to select a match. But it cannot comprehend more abstract linguistic forms. If the right hemisphere is presented with such simple commands as "wink," "nod," "shake head," or "smile," it seldom responds.

The right hemisphere can add simple two-digit numbers but can do little beyond this in the way of calculation. However, the right hemisphere appears to have a highly developed spatial and pattern sense. It is superior to the left hemisphere in constructing geometric and perspective drawings. It can assemble colored blocks to match a complex design much more effectively than the left hemisphere. When split-brain subjects are asked to use their right hand to assemble the blocks according to a picture design, they make numerous mistakes. Sometimes they have trouble keeping their left hand from automatically correcting the mistakes being made by the right hand.

Studies with normal individuals tend to confirm the different specializations of the two hemispheres. For example, verbal information (such as words or nonsense syllables) can be identified faster and more accurately when flashed briefly to the left hemisphere (that is, in the right visual field) than to the right hemisphere. In contrast, the identification of faces, facial expressions of emotion, line slopes or dot locations occurs more quickly when flashed to the right hemisphere. And *electroencephalogram* (EEG) studies indicate that electrical activity from the left hemisphere increases during a verbal task, whereas during a spatial task, EEG activity increases in the right hemisphere (Springer & Deutsch, 1985).

Thus, a range of evidence indicates that the two hemispheres operate in different ways. The left hemisphere controls speech, reading, writing, and arithmetic. It operates in a logical, analytical mode, focuses on details, and perceives in terms of individual features rather than holistic patterns. The right hemisphere, on the other hand, plays a special role in musical and artistic abilities, in imagery and dreaming, and in the perception of complex geometric patterns. Its perceptions are holistic, and it is particularly effective on tasks that require the visualization of relationships. The right hemisphere also shows more emotion and impulsiveness than its companion.

Some researchers have speculated that individual differences in *cognitive style* are related to individual differences in the relative efficiency of the two hemispheres. Thus, individuals who are very logical, analytical, and verbal would have highly efficient left-hemisphere functions, whereas those who are unusually holistic, musical, intuitive, and impulsive would have a balance in favor of the right hemisphere. The notion of a differential balance in hemispheric functioning to explain individual differences in cognitive style is an attractive idea, though it is based more on speculation than on direct experimental evidence.

One should not infer from this discussion that the two hemispheres work independently of each other. Just the opposite is true. The hemispheres differ in their specializations, but they integrate their activities at all times. It is this integration that gives rise to mental processes greater than and different from each hemisphere's special contribution. As noted by Levy,

> These differences are seen in the contrasting contributions each hemisphere makes to all cognitive activities. When a person reads a story, the right hemisphere may play a special role in decoding visual information, maintaining an integrated story structure, appreciating humor and emotional content, deriving meaning from past associations and understanding metaphor. At the same time, the left hemisphere plays a special role in understanding syntax, translating written words into their phonetic representations and deriving meaning from complex relations among word concepts and syntax. But there is no activity in which only one hemisphere is involved or to which only one hemisphere makes a contribution. (1985, p. 44)

CRITICAL DISCUSSION

Language and the Brain

A great deal of our information about brain mechanisms for language comes from observations of patients suffering from brain damage. The damage may be due to tumors, penetrating head wounds, or the rupture of blood vessels. The term *aphasia* is used to describe language deficits caused by brain damage.

As already noted, Broca observed in the 1860s that damage to a specific area on the side of the left frontal lobe was linked to a speech disorder called *expressive aphasia*. Individuals with damage in Broca's area have difficulty enunciating words correctly and speak in a slow, labored way. Their speech often makes sense, but it includes only key words. Nouns are generally expressed in the singular, and adjectives, adverbs, articles, and conjunctions are apt to be omitted. However, these individuals have no difficulty understanding either spoken or written language.

In 1874, Carl Wernicke, a German investigator, reported that damage to another site in the cortex (also in the left hemisphere but in the temporal lobe) was linked to a language disorder called *receptive aphasia*. People with damage in this location, *Wernicke's area,* are not able to comprehend words; they can hear words, but they do not know their meaning. They can produce strings of words without difficulty and with proper articulation, but there are errors in word usage and their speech tends to be meaningless.

Based on an analysis of these defects, Wernicke developed a model for language production and understanding. Although the model is 100 years old, its general features still appear to be correct. In recent years, Norman Geschwind has built on them and developed the theory known as the *Wernicke-Geschwind model.* According to the model, Broca's area is assumed to store "articulatory codes" that specify the sequence of muscle actions required to pronounce a word. When these codes are transferred to the motor cortex, they activate the muscles of the lips, tongue, and larynx in the proper sequence and produce a spoken word.

Wernicke's area, on the other hand, is where "auditory codes" and the meanings of words are stored. If a word is to be spoken, its auditory code must be activated in Wernicke's area and transmitted by a bundle of nerves to Broca's area, where it activates the corresponding articulatory code. The articulatory code in turn is transmitted to the motor cortex for the production of the spoken word.

If a word spoken by someone else is to be understood, it must be transmitted from the auditory cortex to Wernicke's area, where the spoken form of the word is matched to its auditory code, which in turn activates the word's meaning. When a written word is presented, it is first registered in the visual cortex and then relayed to the *angular gyrus,* which associates the visual form of the word with its auditory code in Wernicke's area; once the word's auditory code has been found, so has its meaning. Thus, the meanings of words are stored along with their acoustical codes in Wernicke's area. Broca's area stores articulatory codes, and the angular gyrus matches the written form of a word to its auditory code; neither of these two areas, however, stores information about word meaning. The

AUTONOMIC NERVOUS SYSTEM

We noted earlier that the peripheral nervous system consists of two divisions. The somatic system controls the skeletal muscles and receives information from the skin, muscles, and various sensory receptors. The autonomic system controls the glands and the smooth muscles, which include the heart, the blood vessels, and the lining of the stomach and intestines. These muscles are called "smooth" because that is how they look when examined under a microscope. (Skeletal muscles, in contrast, have a striated appearance.) The autonomic nervous system derives its name from the fact that many of the activities it controls are autonomous, or self-regulating — such as digestion and circulation — and continue even when a person is asleep or unconscious.

meaning of a word is retrieved only when its acoustical code is activated in Wernicke's area.

The model explains many of the language deficits shown by aphasics. Damage restricted to Broca's area disrupts speech production but has less effect on the comprehension of spoken or written language. Damage to Wernicke's area disrupts all aspects of language comprehension, but the individual can still articulate words properly (since Broca's area is intact) even though the output is meaningless. The model also predicts that individuals with damage in the angular gyrus will not be able to read but will have no problem in comprehending speech or in speaking. Finally, if damage is restricted to the auditory cortex, a person will be able to read and to speak normally; but he or she will not be able to comprehend spoken speech.

There are some research findings that the Wernicke-Geschwind model does not adequately explain. For example, when the language areas of the brain are electrically stimulated in the course of a neurosurgical operation, both receptive and expressive functions may be disrupted at a single site. This suggests that some brain areas may share common mechanisms for producing and understanding speech. We are still a long way from a comprehensive model of language function, but there can be no doubt that some aspects of language function are highly localized in the brain (Geschwind, 1979).

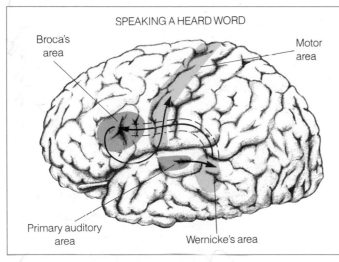
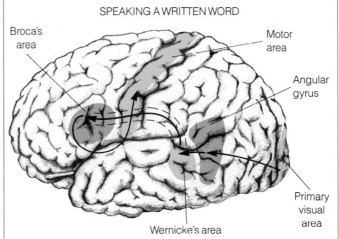

Wernicke-Geschwind Model *The left panel illustrates the sequence of events when a spoken word is presented and the individual repeats the word in spoken form. Neural impulses from the ear are sent to the primary auditory area, but the word cannot be understood until the signal is next transmitted to Wernicke's area. In Wernicke's area, the word's acoustical code is retrieved and transmitted via a bundle of nerve fibers to Broca's area. In Broca's area, an articulatory code for the word is activated, which in turn directs the motor cortex. The motor cortex drives the lips, tongue, and larynx to produce the spoken word.*

In the right panel, a written word is presented and the individual is to speak the word. The visual input to the eye is first transmitted to the primary visual cortex and then relayed to the angular gyrus. The angular gyrus associates the visual form of the word with the related acoustical code in Wernicke's area. Once the acoustical code is retrieved and the meaning of the word is established, speaking the word is accomplished through the same sequence of events as before.

The autonomic nervous system has two divisions, the *sympathetic* and the *parasympathetic*, which are often antagonistic in their actions. Figure 2-13 shows the contrasting effects of the two systems on various organs. For example, the parasympathetic system constricts the pupil of the eye, stimulates the flow of saliva, and slows the heart rate; the sympathetic system has the opposite effect in each case. The normal state of the body, somewhere between extreme excitement and vegetative placidity, is maintained by the balance between these two systems.

The sympathetic division tends to act as a unit. During emotional excitement, it simultaneously speeds up the heart, dilates the arteries of the skeletal muscles and heart, constricts the arteries of the skin and digestive organs, and causes perspiration. It also activates certain endocrine glands to secrete hormones that further increase arousal.

FIGURE 2-13
Autonomic Nervous System *Neurons of the sympathetic division originate in the thoracic and lumbar regions of the spinal cord; they form synaptic junctions with ganglia lying just outside the cord. Neurons of the parasympathetic division exit from the medulla region of the brain stem and from the lower (sacral) end of the spinal cord; they connect with ganglia near the organs stimulated. Most, but not all, internal organs are innervated by both divisions, which function in opposition to each other.*

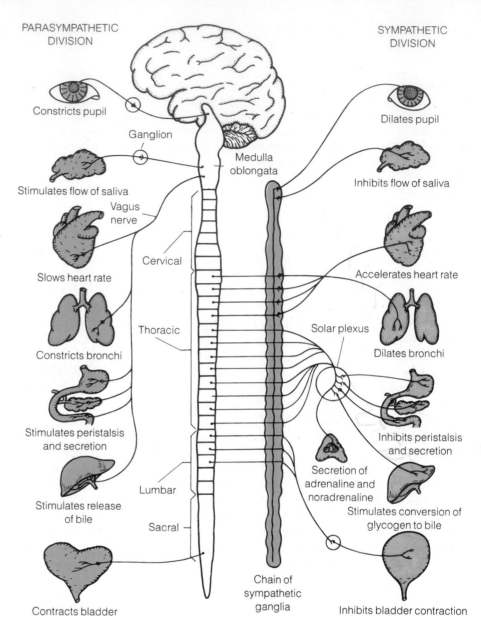

PARASYMPATHETIC DIVISION

SYMPATHETIC DIVISION

Constricts pupil

Ganglion

Stimulates flow of saliva

Vagus nerve

Slows heart rate

Cervical

Constricts bronchi

Thoracic

Stimulates peristalsis and secretion

Stimulates release of bile

Lumbar

Sacral

Contracts bladder

Medulla oblongata

Solar plexus

Chain of sympathetic ganglia

Dilates pupil

Inhibits flow of saliva

Accelerates heart rate

Dilates bronchi

Inhibits peristalsis and secretion

Secretion of adrenaline and noradrenaline

Stimulates conversion of glycogen to bile

Inhibits bladder contraction

Unlike the sympathetic system, the parasympathetic division tends to affect one organ at a time. If the sympathetic system is thought of as dominant during violent and excited activity, the parasympathetic system may be thought of as dominant during quiescence. It participates in digestion and, in general, maintains the functions that conserve and protect bodily resources.

While the sympathetic and parasympathetic systems are usually antagonistic to one another, there are some exceptions to this principle. For example, the sympathetic system is dominant during fear and excitement; however, a not-uncommon parasympathetic symptom during extreme fear is the involuntary discharge of the bladder or bowels. Another example is the complete sex act in the male, which requires erection (parasympathetic) followed by ejaculation (sympathetic). Thus, although the two systems are often antagonistic, they interact in complex ways.

ENDOCRINE SYSTEM

We can think of the nervous system as controlling the fast-changing activities of the body by its ability directly to activate muscles and glands. The *endocrine system* is slower acting and indirectly controls the activities of cell groups throughout the body by means of chemicals called *hormones*. These hormones are secreted by the various endocrine glands (see Figure 2-14) directly into the bloodstream. The hormones then travel through the body, acting in various ways on cells of different types. Each target cell is equipped with receptors that recognize only the hormone molecules meant to act on that cell; the receptors pull the hormone molecules out of the bloodstream and into the cell. Some endocrine glands are activated by the nervous system, while others are activated by changes in the internal chemical state of the body.

One of the major endocrine glands, the *pituitary*, is partly an outgrowth of the brain and lies just below the hypothalamus (refer back to Figure 2-7). The pituitary gland has been called the "master gland" because it produces the largest number of different hormones and controls the secretion of other endocrine glands. One of the pituitary hormones has the crucial job of controlling body growth. Too little of this hormone can create a dwarf, while oversecretion can produce a giant. Other hormones released by the pituitary trigger the action of other endocrine glands such as the thyroid, the sex glands, and the outer layer of the adrenal gland. Courtship, mating, and reproductive behavior in many animals are based on a complex interaction between the activity of the nervous system and the influence of the pituitary on the sex glands.

The relationship between the pituitary gland and the hypothalamus illustrates the complex interactions that take place between the endocrine system and the nervous system. In response to stress (fear, anxiety, pain, emotional events, and so forth) certain neurons in the hypothalamus secrete a substance called *corticotropin-release factor* (CRF). The pituitary is just below the hypothalamus and CRF is carried to it through a channel-like structure. The CRF stimulates the pituitary to release *adrenocorticotrophic hormone* (ACTH), which is the body's major "stress" hormone. ACTH, in turn, is carried by the bloodstream to the adrenal glands and to various other organs of the body, causing the release of some 30 hormones, each of which plays a role in the body's adjustment to emergency situations. This sequence of events indicates that the endocrine system is under the control of the hypothalamus and thereby under the control of other brain centers via the hypothalamus.

The *adrenal glands* play an important role in determining an individual's mood, level of energy, and ability to cope with stress. The inner core of the adrenal gland secretes *epinephrine* and *norepinephrine* (also known as *adrenaline* and *noradrenaline*). Epinephrine acts in a number of ways to prepare the organism for an emergency, often in conjunction with the sympathetic division of the autonomic nervous system. Epinephrine, for example, affects the smooth muscles and the sweat glands in a way similar to that of the sympathetic system. It causes constriction of the blood vessels in the stomach and intestines and makes the heart beat faster (as anyone who has ever had a shot of adrenaline knows). It also acts on the reticular system, which excites the sympathetic system and in turn stimulates the adrenals to secrete more epinephrine. Hence, a closed circuit is formed to maintain emotional arousal. Such a closed system is one reason why it takes a while for strong emotional excitement to subside even after the disturbing cause has been removed.

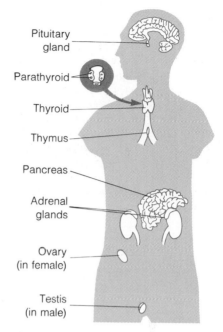

Pituitary gland
Parathyroid
Thyroid
Thymus
Pancreas
Adrenal glands
Ovary (in female)
Testis (in male)

FIGURE 2-14
Some of the Endocrine Glands
Hormones secreted by the endocrine glands are as essential as the nervous system to the integration of the organism's activity. The endocrine system and the nervous system, however, differ in the speed with which they can act. A nerve impulse can travel through the organism in a few hundredths of a second. Seconds, or even minutes, may be required for an endocrine gland to produce an effect; the hormone, once released, must travel to its target site via the bloodstream — a much slower process.

Norepinephrine also prepares the organism for emergency action. When it reaches the pituitary in its travels through the bloodstream, it stimulates the gland to release a hormone that acts on the outer layer of the adrenal glands; this second hormone, in turn, stimulates the liver to increase the blood-sugar level so the body has energy for quick action.

The hormones of the endocrine system and the neurotransmitters of neurons have similar functions; they both carry *messages* between cells of the body. A neurotransmitter carries messages between adjacent neurons, and its effect is highly localized. In contrast, a hormone may travel a long distance through the body and act in various ways on many different types of cells. The basic similarity between these chemical messengers (despite their differences) is shown by the fact that some serve both functions. Epinephrine and norepinephrine, for example, act as neurotransmitters when released by neurons and as hormones when released by the adrenal gland.

GENETIC INFLUENCES ON BEHAVIOR

To understand the biological foundations of psychology, we need to know something about hereditary influences. The field of *behavior genetics* (also called *psychogenetics*) combines the methods of genetics and psychology to study the inheritance of behavioral characteristics. We know that many physical characteristics — such as height, bone structure, and hair and eye color — are inherited. Behavioral geneticists are interested in the degree to which psychological characteristics — such as ability, temperament, and emotional stability — are transmitted from parent to offspring.

All psychological characteristics depend on the *interaction* between heredity and environment. The old heredity-versus-environment question is no longer meaningful. Instead, researchers ask how heredity limits the individual's potential and to what degree favorable or unfavorable environmental conditions can modify the inherited potential.

Chromosomes and Genes

The hereditary units we receive from our parents and transmit to our offspring are carried by structures known as *chromosomes*, which are found in the nucleus of each cell in the body. Most body cells contain 46 chromosomes. At conception, the human being receives 23 chromosomes from the father's sperm and 23 chromosomes from the mother's ovum. These 46 chromosomes form 23 pairs, which are duplicated each time the cells divide (see Figure 2-15).

Each chromosome is composed of many individual hereditary units called *genes*. A gene is a segment of *deoxyribonucleic acid* (DNA), which is the actual carrier of genetic information. The DNA molecule looks like a twisted ladder or a double-stranded helix (spiral), as shown in Figure 2-16. All DNA has the same chemical composition, consisting of a simple sugar (deoxyribose), phosphate, and four bases — adenine, guanine, thymine, and cytosine (A, G, T, C). The two strands of the DNA molecule are composed of phosphate and sugar, and the strands are held apart by pairs of bases. Due to the structural properties of these bases, A always pairs with T and G always pairs with C. The bases can occur in any sequence along a strand, and these sequences constitute the genetic code. The fact that many different arrangements of bases are possible is what gives DNA the ability to express many different genetic messages. The same four bases specify the characteristics of every living organism and, depending on their arrangement,

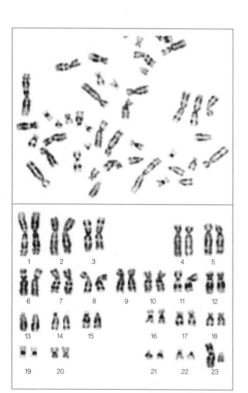

FIGURE 2-15

Chromosomes *The upper panel is a photo (enlarged about 1,500 times) of the 46 chromosomes of a normal human male. In the lower panel, the chromosomes are arranged in the appropriate pairs. A human female would have the same pairs 1 through 22, but pair 23 would be XX rather than XY. Each chromosome appears double here because the preparation was made while the cell was preparing to divide; each chromosome has duplicated itself and is about to split apart.*

determine whether a given creature turns out to be a bird, a lion, a fish, or Michelangelo.

A segment of the DNA molecule, the gene, will give coded instructions to the cell, directing it to perform a specific function (usually to manufacture a particular protein). Although all cells in the body carry the same genes, the specialized nature of each cell is due to the fact that only 5 to 10 percent of the genes are active in any cell. In the process of developing from a fertilized egg, each cell switches on some genes and switches off all others. When "nerve genes" are active, for example, a cell develops as a neuron because the genes are directing the cell to make the products that allow it to perform neural functions—which would not be possible if the genes irrelevant to a neuron, such as "muscle genes," were not dormant.

Genes, like chromosomes, exist in pairs. One gene of each pair comes from the sperm chromosomes and one gene comes from the ovum chromosomes. Thus, a child receives only half of each parent's total genes. The total number of genes in each human chromosome is around 1,000—perhaps higher. Because the number of genes is so high, it is extremely unlikely that two human beings would have the same heredity, even if they were siblings. The only exception is *identical twins*, who, because they developed from the same fertilized egg, have exactly the same genes.

An important attribute of some genes is *dominance* or *recessiveness*. The genes determining eye color, for example, act in a pattern of dominance and recessiveness. When both members of a gene pair are dominant, the individual manifests the form of the trait specified by these dominant genes. When one gene is dominant and the other recessive, the dominant gene again determines the form of the trait. Only if the genes contributed by both parents are recessive is the recessive form of the trait expressed. Blue eyes are recessive. Thus, a blue-eyed child may have two blue-eyed parents, or one blue-eyed parent and one brown-eyed parent who carries a recessive gene for blue eyes, or two brown-eyed parents, each of whom carries a recessive gene for blue eyes. A brown-eyed child, in contrast, never has two blue-eyed parents.

Some of the characteristics that are carried by recessive genes are baldness, albinism, hemophilia, and a susceptibility to poison ivy. Not all gene pairs follow the dominant-recessive pattern, and as we shall see, most human characteristics are determined by many genes acting together rather than by a single gene pair.

Even though most human characteristics are not determined by the actions of a single gene pair, there are some striking exceptions. Of special interest from a psychological viewpoint are neurological diseases like *phenylketonuria* (PKU), *Huntington's chorea*, and *multiple sclerosis*, which all involve deterioration of the nervous system and correlated behavioral problems. In recent years, scientists have identified the gene responsible for PKU, and they have been able to establish the approximate locations of the genes responsible for Huntington's chorea and multiple sclerosis. PKU, for example, results from the action of a recessive gene that is inherited from each parent. The infant cannot digest an essential amino acid (phenylalanine), which then builds up in the body, poisoning the nervous system and causing irreversible brain damage. PKU children are severely retarded and usually die before the age of 30.

If the PKU disorder is discovered at birth and the infants are placed on a diet that controls the level of phenylalanine, their chances of surviving with good health and intelligence are fairly high. Until the PKU gene was located, the disorder could not be diagnosed until an infant was at least 3 weeks old. Now it is possible to determine prenatally whether the fetus has the PKU gene so that the proper diet can begin at birth.

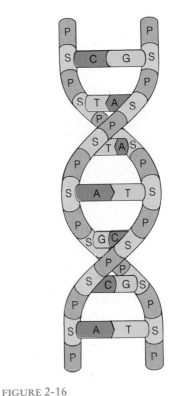

FIGURE 2-16
Structure of the DNA Molecule *Each strand of the molecule is made up of an alternating sequence of sugar (S) and phosphate (P); the rungs of the twisted ladder are made up of four bases (A, G, T, C). The double nature of the helix and the restriction on base pairings make possible the self-replication of DNA. In the process of cell division, the two strands of the DNA molecule come apart with the base pairs separating; one member of each base pair remains attached to each strand. Each strand then forms a new complementary strand using excess bases available in the cell; an A attached to a strand will attract a T, and so forth. By this process, two identical molecules of DNA come to exist where previously there was one.*

SEX-LINKED GENES   Male and female chromosomes appear the same under a microscope, except for pair 23, which determines the sex of the individual and carries genes for certain traits that are sex linked. A normal female has two similar-looking chromosomes in pair 23, called X chromosomes. A normal male has one X chromosome in pair 23 and one that looks slightly different, called a Y chromosome (see Figure 2-15). Thus, the normal female chromosome pair 23 is represented by the symbol XX, and the normal male pair by XY.

When most body cells reproduce, the resulting cells have the same number of chromosomes (46) as the parent cell. However, when sperm and egg cells reproduce, the chromosome pairs separate, and half go to each new cell. Thus, egg and sperm cells have only 23 chromosomes. Each egg cell has an X chromosome, and each sperm cell has either an X or a Y chromosome. If an X-type sperm is the first to enter an egg cell, the fertilized ovum will have an XX chromosome pair, and the child will be a female. If a Y-type sperm fertilizes the egg, the 23rd chromosome pair will be XY, and the child will be a male. The female inherits one X chromosome from the mother and one from the father; the male inherits his X chromosome from the mother and his Y chromosome from the father. Thus, it is the father's chromosome contribution that determines a child's sex.

The X chromosome may carry either dominant or recessive genes; the Y chromosome carries a few genes dominant for male sexual characteristics but otherwise seems to carry only recessive genes. Thus, most recessive characteristics carried by a man's X chromosome (received from his mother) are expressed since they are not blocked by dominant genes. For example, color blindness is a recessive sex-linked characteristic. A man will be color-blind if he inherits a color-blind gene on the X chromosome he receives from his mother. Females are less often color-blind, because a color-blind female has to have both a color-blind father and a mother who is either color-blind or carries a recessive gene for color blindness. A number of genetically determined disorders are linked to abnormalities of, or recessive genes carried by, the 23rd chromosome pair. These are called sex-linked disorders.

CHROMOSOMAL ABNORMALITIES   On rare occasions, a female may be born with only one X chromosome instead of the usual XX. Females with this condition, which is known as *Turner's syndrome*, fail to develop sexually at puberty. Although usually of normal intelligence, they show some specific cognitive defects: they do poorly in arithmetic and on tests of visual form perception and spatial organization.

Sometimes when the 23rd chromosome fails to divide properly, the developing organism ends up with an extra X or Y chromosome. An individual with an XXY chromosome is physically a male, with penis and testicles, but with marked feminine characteristics. His breasts are enlarged and his testes are small and do not produce sperm. This condition, known as *Klinefelter's syndrome*, is surprisingly common—about 1 in every 400 births.

Another sex chromosome abnormality in males has received considerable publicity. Men with an extra Y chromosome (type XYY) are taller than average and are reported to be unusually aggressive. Early studies suggested that the incidence of XYY males among prison inmates — particularly those convicted of violent crimes — was much higher than in the population at large. Newspaper accounts exaggerated these findings, portraying the XYY male as an individual genetically predisposed toward aggression and violence. Several XYY men were even acquitted of criminal charges on the grounds that they were helpless victims of their inheritance and, thus, could not be held responsible for their acts.

More recent studies, however, question whether there is a link between the presence of an extra Y chromosome and aggression. They find that XYY males in

"You can't talk to that crowd—they've all got extra Y chromosomes."

the general population are no more aggressive than normal males (Owen, 1972; Hook, 1973). Nevertheless, survey data indicate that males with this genetic makeup are more likely than normal males to be convicts. We do not know why this is so; however, XYY males do test lower on intelligence tests. Their higher incarceration rate may be related to low intelligence, which would increase the likelihood of being apprehended when committing a crime (Witkin et al., 1976).

Genetic Studies of Behavior

A few disorders result from chromosomal abnormalities, and some traits are determined by single genes. But most human characteristics are determined by many genes; they are *polygenic*. Traits such as intelligence, height, and emotionality do not fall into distinct categories but show continuous variation. Most people are neither dull nor bright; intelligence is distributed over a broad range, with most individuals located near the middle. Sometimes a specific genetic defect can result in mental retardation, but in most instances, a person's intellectual potential is determined by a large number of genes that influence the factors underlying different abilities. And, of course, what happens to this genetic potential depends on environmental conditions.

SELECTIVE BREEDING One method of studying the heritability of traits in animals is by selective breeding. Animals that are high or low in a certain trait are mated with each other. For example, to study the inheritance of learning ability in rats, the females that do poorly in learning to run a maze are mated with males that do poorly; the females that do well are mated with the males that do well. The offspring of these matings are tested on the same maze. On the basis of performance, the brightest are mated with the brightest and the dullest with the dullest. (To ensure that environmental conditions are kept constant, the offspring of "dull" mothers are sometimes given to "bright" mothers to raise so that genetic endowment rather than adequacy of maternal care is being tested.) After a few rodent generations, a "bright" and a "dull" strain of rats can be produced (see Figure 2-17).

Selective breeding has been used to show the inheritance of a number of behavioral characteristics. For example, dogs have been bred to be excitable or lethargic; chickens, to be aggressive and sexually active; fruit flies, to be more drawn or less drawn to light; and mice, to be more attracted or less attracted to alcohol. If a trait is influenced by heredity, it should be possible to change it by selective breeding. If selective breeding does not alter a trait, we assume that the trait is primarily dependent on environmental factors.

TWIN STUDIES Since breeding experiments cannot be carried out with human beings, we must look instead at similarities in behavior among individuals who are related. Certain traits often run in families. But families not only are linked genetically, they also share the same environment. Thus, if musical talent runs in the family, we do not know whether inherited ability or parental emphasis on music and music training is more important. Sons of alcoholic fathers are more likely than sons of nonalcoholic fathers to develop alcoholism. Do genetic tendencies or environmental conditions play the major role? In an effort to answer questions of this sort, psychologists have turned to twin studies.

Identical twins develop from a single fertilized egg and thus share the same heredity. They are called *monozygotic* since they come from a single zygote, or fertilized ovum. Fraternal twins develop from different egg cells and are no more alike genetically than are ordinary siblings; they are called *dizygotic*, or two-egged. Studies comparing identical and fraternal twins help to sort out the influence of environment and heredity. Identical twins are found to be more similar in

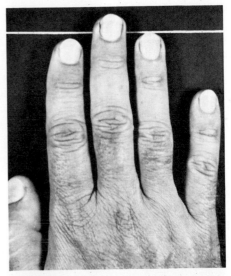

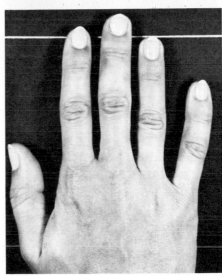

A sex-influenced gene seems to be responsible for the relative length of the index finger as compared to the other fingers. A gene that causes the index finger to be shorter than the fourth finger appears to be dominant in males and recessive in females. The male index finger (top) is shorter than the fourth finger, but the female index finger (bottom) is longer than the fourth finger. (Courtesy A. M. Winchester)

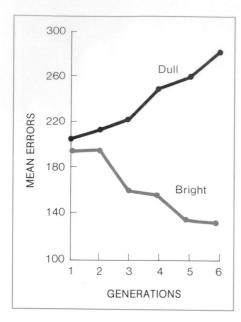

FIGURE 2-17
Inheritance of Maze Learning in Rats
Mean error scores of "bright" and "dull" rats selectively bred for maze-running ability. (After Thompson, 1954)

intelligence than fraternal twins, even when they are separated at birth and reared in different homes (see Chapter 12). Identical twins are also more similar than fraternal twins in some personality characteristics and in susceptibility to the mental disorder of *schizophrenia* (see Chapter 15). Twin studies have proved to be a useful method of investigating genetic influences on human behavior.

Environmental Influences on Gene Action

The inherited potential with which an individual enters the world is very much influenced by the environment that he or she encounters. This interaction will be made clear in the following chapters, but two examples will suffice to illustrate the point here. The tendency to develop diabetes is hereditary, although the exact method of transmission is unknown. Diabetes is a disease in which the pancreas does not produce enough insulin to burn carbohydrates (sugars and starches) as energy and store them for future use. Scientists assume that genes determine the production of insulin. But people who carry the genetic potential for diabetes do not always develop the disease; for example, if one identical twin has diabetes, the other twin will develop the disorder in only about half the cases. Not all of the environmental factors that contribute to diabetes are known, but one variable that seems fairly certain is obesity. A fat person requires more insulin to metabolize carbohydrates than a thin person. Consequently, an individual who carries the genes for diabetes is more likely to develop the disorder if he or she gains weight.

A similar situation is found in the mental illness called *schizophrenia*. As we shall see in Chapter 15, substantial evidence indicates a heredity component to the disorder. If one identical twin is schizophrenic, chances are high that the other twin will exhibit some signs of mental disturbance. But whether or not the other twin develops the full-blown disorder will depend on a number of environmental factors. The genes may predispose, but the environment shapes the outcome.

SUMMARY

1. The nervous system is composed of cells called *neurons*, which receive stimulation by way of their *dendrites* and *cell bodies* and transmit impulses via their *axons. Sensory neurons* carry messages from the sense *receptors* to the brain and spinal cord; *motor neurons* transmit signals from the brain and spinal cord to the muscles and glands. Axon fibers group together to form *nerves.*

2. Two aspects of the transmission of the nerve impulse are important: conduction along axon fibers and transmission across the synaptic junction between neurons. Axonal conduction involves an electrochemical process called *depolarization;* the nerve impulse, once started, travels down the axon to its many axon terminals. Chemical intermediaries called *neurotransmitters* pass the impulse from one neuron to the next across a *synapse.* Neurotransmitters are released from the *axon terminals* and act on the dendrites and cell body of the receiving neuron to change its membrane permeability; some neurotransmitters are excitatory and others are inhibitory.

3. The nervous system is divided into the *central nervous system* (the brain and spinal cord) and the *peripheral nervous system* (the nerves leading from the brain and spinal cord to other parts of the body). Subdivisions of the peripheral nervous system are the *somatic system* (which carries messages to and from the sense receptors, muscles, and the body surface) and the *autonomic system* (which connects with the internal organs and glands).

4. The human brain is composed of three concentric layers: a *central core*, the *limbic system*, and the *cerebrum.*
   a.   The central core includes the *medulla*, responsible for respiration and postural reflexes; the *cerebellum*, concerned with motor coordination; the *thal-*

amus, a relay station for incoming sensory information; and the *hypothalamus*, important in emotion and in maintaining homeostasis. The *reticular system*, which crosses through several of the above structures, controls the organism's state of wakefulness and arousal.

b. The *limbic system* controls some of the "instinctive" activities (feeding, attacking, fleeing from danger, mating) regulated by the hypothalamus; it also plays an important role in emotion and memory.

c. The *cerebrum* is divided into two *cerebral hemispheres*. The convoluted surface of these hemispheres, the *cerebral cortex*, controls discrimination, decision making, learning, and thinking—the "higher mental processes." Certain areas of the cortex represent centers for specific sensory inputs or for control of specific movements. The remainder of the cortex consists of *association areas*.

5. When the *corpus callosum* (the band of nerve fibers connecting the two cerebral hemispheres) is severed, significant differences in the functioning of the two cerebral hemispheres can be observed. The left hemisphere is skilled in language and mathematical abilities. The right hemisphere can understand some language but cannot communicate through speech; it has a highly developed spatial and pattern sense.

6. The *autonomic nervous system* is made up of the *sympathetic* and the *parasympathetic* divisions. Because its fibers mediate the action of the smooth muscles and of the glands, the autonomic system is particularly important in emotional reactions. The sympathetic division is usually active during excitement and the parasympathetic during quiescent states.

7. The *endocrine glands* secrete hormones into the bloodstream that are important for emotional and motivational behavior. They are essential to the nervous system in integrating behavior, and their action is closely tied to the activity of the hypothalamus and the autonomic nervous system.

8. An individual's hereditary potential, transmitted by the *chromosomes* and *genes*, influences psychological and physical characteristics. Genes are segments of *DNA molecules*, which store genetic information. Some genes are *dominant*, some *recessive*, and some *sex linked*. Most human characteristics are *polygenic*—that is, determined by many genes acting together, rather than by a single gene pair.

9. *Selective breeding* (mating animals that are high or low in a certain trait) is one method of studying the influence of heredity. Another method for sorting out the effects of environment and heredity is *twin studies*, in which the characteristics of identical, or *monozygotic*, twins (who share the same heredity) are compared with those of fraternal, or *dizygotic*, twins (who are no more alike genetically than ordinary siblings).

10. All behavior depends on the *interaction* between heredity and environment; the genes set the limits of the individual's potential, but what happens to this potential depends on the environment.

FURTHER READING

Good introductions to physiological psychology are Kolb and Whishaw, *Fundamentals of Human Neuropsychology* (2nd ed., 1985); Schneider and Tarshis, *An Introduction to Physiological Psychology* (3rd ed., 1986); Brown and Wallace, *Physiological Psychology* (1980); Cotman and McGaugh, *Behavioral Neuroscience: An Introduction* (1980); Carlson, *Physiology of Behavior* (3rd ed., 1985); Groves and Schlesinger, *Introduction to Biological Psychology* (2nd ed., 1982); Rosenzweig and Leiman, *Physiological Psychology* (1982); and Levinthal, *Introduction to Physiological Psychology* (2nd ed., 1983).

A survey of genetic influences on behavior is provided by Plomin, DeFries, and McClearn, *Behavioral Genetics: A Primer* (1980). For a review of psychoactive drugs and their effects on the body, brain, and behavior, see Julien, *A Primer of Drug Action* (4th ed., 1985).

For a survey of research on the function of the two cerebral hemispheres, see Springer and Deutsch, *Left Brain, Right Brain* (rev. ed., 1985).

Psychological Development

3

OF ALL MAMMALS, HUMAN BEINGS ARE the most immature at birth and require the longest period of development before they are capable of performing the activities and skills characteristic of their species. In general, the higher on the phylogenetic scale an organism is, the more complex its nervous system is and the longer the time it requires to reach maturity. For example, the lemur, a primitive primate, can move about on its own shortly after birth and is soon able to fend for itself; the newborn monkey is dependent for several months; and the infant baboon remains with its mother for several years. The human offspring, in contrast, is dependent for many years and requires a long period of learning and interaction with others before becoming self-sufficient.

We tend to think that development is complete once a person reaches physical maturity. But the circumstances of our lives and the way we deal with them continually shape us, so that development is actually a lifelong process. Developmental psychologists are concerned with describing and analyzing the regularities of human development throughout the life span. They study *physical development,* such as changes in height and weight, brain development, and the acquisition of motor skills; *cognitive development,* such as changes in thought processes, language abilities, and memory; and *personality and social development,* such as changes in gender role or moral behavior.

Developmental psychologists often study the average or "typical" rate of development. At what age, for instance, does the average child begin to speak? How rapidly does a typical child's vocabulary increase with age? Such normative data, in addition to being intrinsically interesting, are important for planning educational programs and for evaluating an individual child's development. Psychologists are concerned also with how certain behaviors develop and why they appear when they do. Why do most children not walk or utter their first word until they are about a year old? What physiological developments and behaviors must precede these accomplishments?

Environmental influences on behavior are another concern. Psychologists may study the effect of a child's viewing TV violence on his or her aggressive behavior or of different approaches to instruction on learning. More recently, they have been looking at the effects of day care, divorce, and parental unemployment on the emotional development of children.

In this chapter, we discuss several general principles of development, as well as some behavior and attitude changes that occur as the individual matures from infancy through adulthood. Our purpose is to provide an overview of psychological development. The development of certain specific abilities, such as language and perception, will be considered in later chapters devoted to these topics.

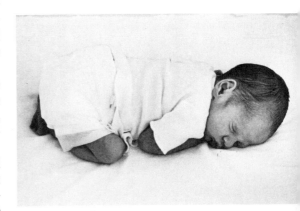

The human infant is helpless at birth.

BASIC QUESTIONS ABOUT DEVELOPMENT

Two basic questions underlie theories about the course of human development: (1) Is development a continuous process of change, or is it best understood as a series of distinct stages? and (2) Is development guided primarily by heredity (by genetic programs locked into the body's cells), or is it subject to fundamental changes determined by events in the environment? The assumptions that theorists make about these two questions—about continuity and the sources of change—shape their interpretations of what they observe and their proposals for guiding development.

Nature Versus Nurture

The question of whether heredity ("nature") or environment ("nurture") is more important in determining the course of human development has been debated through the centuries. The seventeenth-century British philosopher John Locke, for example, rejected the prevailing notion of his day that babies were miniature adults who arrived in the world fully equipped with abilities and knowledge and who simply had to grow in order for these inherited characteristics to appear. On the contrary, said Locke, the mind of a newborn infant is a "blank slate" *(tabula rasa)* with nothing written on it. What gets written on this slate is what the baby experiences—what he or she sees, hears, tastes, smells, and feels. According to Locke, all knowledge comes to us through our senses. It is provided by experience; no knowledge or ideas are built in.

The advent of Charles Darwin's theory of evolution (1859), which emphasizes the biological basis of human development, led a return to the hereditarian viewpoint. With the rise of behaviorism in the twentieth century, however, the environmentalist position gained dominance. Behaviorists such as John B. Watson and B. F. Skinner argued that human nature is completely malleable: early training can turn a child into any kind of adult. Watson believed that the environment has tremendous power to shape a child's development. "Give me a dozen healthy infants, well-formed, and my own specified world to bring them up in," he wrote, "and I'll guarantee to take any one at random and train him to be any type of specialist I might—doctor, lawyer, artist, merchant, chief, and, yes, even beggar man and thief!" (Watson, 1950, p. 104).

Today most psychologists agree that both nature and nurture are essential to development. Human development is determined by continuous interaction between heredity and environment. At the moment of conception, a remarkable number of personal characteristics are already determined by the genetic structure of the fertilized ovum. Our genes program our growing cells so that we develop into a person rather than a fish, a bird, or a monkey. They decide the color of our skin and hair, general body size, sex, and (to some extent) our intellectual abilities and emotional temperament. The genetically specified characteristics present at birth interact with the experiences encountered in the course of growing up to determine individual development. Our experiences depend on the specific culture, social group, and family in which we are raised.

The development of speech provides an example of the interaction between genetically determined characteristics and the experiences provided by the environment. Almost all human infants are born with the ability to learn a spoken language; other species are not. In the normal course of development, human beings learn to speak. But they are not able to talk before they have attained a certain level of neurological development—no infant less than a year old speaks in sentences. Children raised in an environment where people talk to them and reward them for making speechlike sounds will talk earlier than children who do not receive such attention. For example, children raised in middle-class American homes begin to speak at about 1 year of age. Children raised in San Marcos, a remote village in Guatemala, who have little verbal interaction with adults, do not utter their first words until they are over 2 years old (Kagan, 1979). The language children speak, of course, will be that of their own culture. Thus, the development of speech has both genetic and environmental components. Most other aspects of human development likewise depend on the interaction between inherited characteristics and environmental experiences.

MATURATION Genetic determinants are expressed through the process of *maturation*. Maturation refers to innately determined sequences of growth or bodily changes that are *relatively* independent of environmental events. We say relatively because such changes occur over a wide range of environmental conditions; however, an environment decidedly atypical or inadequate in some way will affect maturational processes. Although maturation is most apparent during childhood, it continues well into adult life. Some of the changes that occur at adolescence, as well as some of the changes that occur with aging (the appearance of gray hair, for instance), are regulated by a genetically determined time schedule.

Maturation is demonstrated clearly by fetal development. The human fetus develops within the mother's body according to a fairly fixed time schedule, and fetal behavior (such as turning and kicking) also follows an orderly sequence that depends on the stage of growth. Premature infants who are kept alive in an incubator develop at much the same rate as infants who remain in the uterus to the full term. The regularity of development before birth illustrates what we mean by maturation. However, if the uterine environment is seriously abnormal in some way, maturational processes can be disrupted. For example, if the mother contracts German measles during the first three months of pregnancy (when the fetus's basic organ systems are developing according to the genetically programmed schedule), the infant may be born deaf, blind, or brain damaged (the type of defect depends on which organ system was in a critical stage of development at the time of infection). Maternal malnutrition, smoking, and consumption of alcohol and drugs are among the other environmental factors that can affect the normal maturation of the fetus.

Motor development after birth — using the hands and fingers, standing, and walking — also follows a regular sequence. For example, such activities as rolling over, crawling, and pulling up to a standing position occur in the same order in most children. Unless we believe that all parents subject their offspring to the same training regimen (an unlikely possibility), we must assume that growth processes determine the order of behavior. As Figure 3-1 shows, not all children go through the sequence at the same rate; some infants are four or five months ahead of others in standing alone or walking. But the *order* in which they go from one stage to the next is generally the same in all infants.

Because the child's mastery of the movements necessary for sitting, standing, walking, and using hands and fingers follows such an orderly sequence, and because children in all cultures accomplish these skills at *roughly* the same age, motor development appears to be primarily a maturational process little influenced by the environment in which the child is reared.

Stages and Critical Periods

Many behaviors follow a natural sequence of development. Infants reach for an object before they are able to pick it up. Toddlers walk before they can run; they

FIGURE 3-1
Babies Develop at Different Rates
Although development is orderly, some infants reach each stage ahead of other infants. The left end of the bar indicates the age by which 25 percent of infants have achieved the stated performance, whereas the right end gives the age by which 90 percent have accomplished the behavior. The vertical mark on each bar gives the age by which 50 percent have achieved it. (After Frankenburg & Dodds, 1967; revised to include crawling)

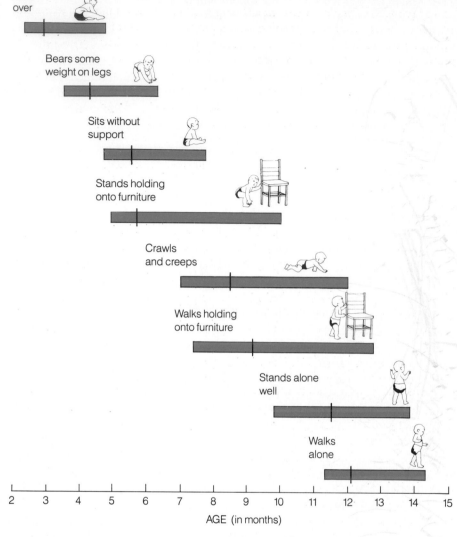

Rolls over

Bears some weight on legs

Sits without support

Stands holding onto furniture

Crawls and creeps

Walks holding onto furniture

Stands alone well

Walks alone

2   3   4   5   6   7   8   9   10   11   12   13   14   15
AGE (in months)

speak words before they can combine them into sentences. Children learn to count by rote before they understand the concept of numbers. Sequences in development usually proceed from simple behaviors to those that are more differentiated and complex. For example, newborn infants can clasp and unclasp their fingers and wave their arms about, occasionally managing to connect the thumb with the mouth. As infants mature, these simple actions become differentiated into more complex behaviors: patting an object, grasping it, picking it up, moving it toward the mouth, or throwing it.

Psychologists generally agree that there are orderly sequences in development that depend on the maturation of the organism as it interacts with its environment. In explaining developmental sequences, some psychologists prefer to interpret them as a *continuous process,* in which biological factors interplay with learning to produce a smooth and continuous change in behavior. Other psychologists agree on the sequential character of development but are less impressed by the continuity of the process; they see development more as a series of steps. For this reason, they have introduced the concept of *stages.*

We identify broad stages when we divide the life span into successive periods of infancy, childhood, adolescence, and adulthood. Parents use the term "stage" when they refer to their 2-year-old as going through a "negative stage" (saying no to every request) or their adolescent as being in a "rebellious stage" (challenging parental authority). When psychologists refer to developmental stages, they have a more precise concept in mind: the concept of stages implies that (1) behaviors at a given stage are organized around a *dominant theme*, (2) behaviors at one stage are *qualitatively different* from behaviors that appear at earlier or later stages, and (3) all children go through the same stages *in the same order*. Environmental factors may speed up or slow down development, but the order of stages is invariant; a child cannot achieve a later stage without going through an earlier one.

Later in this chapter, we will look at several stage theories: one focuses on stages of cognitive development; another, on stages of moral development; and the third, on stages of social development. Although some psychologists believe that stage theories are a useful way of describing development, others believe that development is better interpreted as a continuous process of acquiring new behaviors through experience. They do not accept the qualitative shifts in behavior that stage theories imply. We will examine the evidence for both the continuous process and the stage theory viewpoints as we go along.

Closely related to the concept of stages is the idea that there may be *critical periods* in human development—that is, crucial time periods in a person's life during which specific events must occur for development to proceed normally. Critical periods have been firmly established for some aspects of the physical development of the human fetus. For example, if the newly formed sex organ (the gonads) fails to produce the male hormone androgen at about seven weeks following conception, female genitalia will develop. During postnatal development, there is a critical period for the development of vision. If children who are born with cataracts have them removed before the age of 7, their vision will develop fairly normally. But if a child goes through the first seven years without vision, extensive permanent disability will result (Kuman, Fedrov, & Novikova, 1983).

The existence of critical periods in the psychological development of the child has not been established. However, there is evidence for periods that are *sensitive* in the child's development—if not critical. For example, the period from 6 to 9 months may be sensitive for the formation of close attachment to the parents. Other periods may be especially significant for intellectual development or the acquisition of language. Children who for some reason have not had sufficient exposure to language prior to the age of 6 or 7 years may fail to ever acquire it (Goldin-Meadow, 1982). The experiences of the child during such sensitive periods may shape his or her future course of development in a manner that will be difficult to change later.

EARLY YEARS

Newborn infants seem to be helpless creatures who spend most of their time sleeping, feeding, and crying; they appear to understand little of what is going on around them. However, research findings tell us that they are much more aware of their environment than had been previously supposed.

The Infant

CAPACITIES OF THE INFANT How do psychologists study the abilities of young infants? Since infants cannot talk, control their movements, or follow directions, they are hardly ideal subjects. The solution is to focus on responses

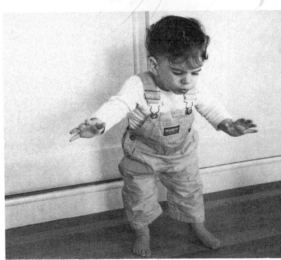

Motor Development in Infants
Sitting alone, crawling, and standing alone are major developments in an infant's mobility.

they do have, such as sucking, looking, and head turning or changes in respiration and heart rate.

For example, changes in heart rate can be used to determine whether newborns can detect the difference between two sounds. The investigator presents one sound for a series of trials while monitoring the infant's heart rate. When a baby — or anyone, for that matter — is presented with a new event, the heart rate slows down. Deceleration in heart rate is part of the *orienting reflex,* a response pattern that prepares the organism to process information (see p. 197). It is a sign that the infant is attending to the stimulus. After the sound is presented a number of times, the heart rate will no longer decelerate at the onset of the sound. Presumably, the sound has become familiar and the infant ceases to attend to it. This is called *habituation,* which is the reduction in the strength of a response to a repeated stimulus. The experimenter then presents a new sound. If the infant's heart rate decreases, the experimenter infers that the infant is attending to the new sound and hence is able to detect a difference between the two sounds. Studies using this method have shown that newborn infants can detect the difference between very similar sounds, such as two tones that are only one note apart on the musical scale (Bridger, 1961).

A surprising discovery is the ability of infants to discriminate nearly all of the phonetic contrasts of human speech. For example, 1-month-old infants can tell the difference between the sounds of *p* and *b.* The investigators used sucking as a response and a decrease in sucking rate as a measure of habituation. They discovered that the infants would suck strongly on a pacifier connected to a recording mechanism in order to hear the sound "bah." Gradually, they became habituated to that sound and sucked less. When the sound changed to "pah," they sucked harder again, indicating that they were hearing something new. Using this method, researchers have found that infants are able to discriminate most of the contrasts used by the world's languages, even though they may lose that capacity as adults. For example, babies can tell the difference between the sounds of *r* and *l,* although Japanese adults cannot (Eimas, 1975).

These findings and related research indicate that infants come into the world prepared to learn any language they hear spoken. In addition to being able to tell the difference between speech sounds, young infants can recognize the voices of different speakers. Infants as young as 3 days have shown that they prefer listening to their own mother's voice over that of an unfamiliar woman (DeCasper & Fifer, 1980).

Procedures that test preferential looking (see p. 203) have been used to study the visual ability of newborn infants (Fantz, 1961). The investigator presents infants with pairs of stimuli that differ in a particular way — such as a yellow circle and a red circle, or a gray square and a square with narrow black stripes. If the infants consistently look longer at one stimulus than the other (regardless of whether it is the right or the left element of the pair), the investigator draws two conclusions: the infants can tell the difference between the patterns, and they prefer one over the other. Using this method, investigators have discovered that newborns can discriminate fine print from gray surfaces, prefer complex patterns to plain ones, prefer patterns with curved lines to patterns with straight lines, and are especially interested in faces (see Figure 3-2). Newborns prefer to look at the outside contour of a face, but by 2 months they focus their attention on the inside of the face — the eyes, nose, and mouth (Haith, Bergman, & Moore, 1977). At this point a parent may notice, with delight, that the baby has begun to "look into my eyes"— that is, to make eye contact.

Newborns can follow a moving object with their eyes, but they cannot adjust the focus of their eyes to near or far stimuli until they are at least 2 months old.

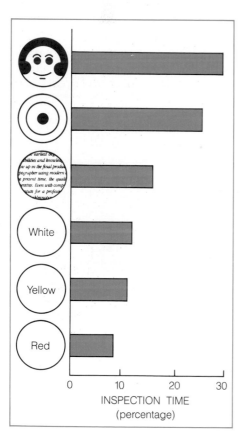

FIGURE 3-2

Visual Preferences *Newborns as young as 10 hours to 5 days old were shown disks that differed in particular ways — a facelike circle, a bull's-eye, an array of fine print, and disks colored white, yellow, or red. Infants could tell the difference between them and preferred one pattern over another. (After Fantz, 1961)*

They see things best at a distance of approximately one foot—which is about the distance of the parent's face when the parent is holding the baby.

Infants can discriminate differences in taste shortly after birth. They much prefer sweet-tasting liquids to those that are salty, bitter, sour, or bland. The characteristic response of the newborn to a sweet liquid is a relaxed expression resembling a slight smile, sometimes accompanied by lip licking. A sour solution produces pursed lips and a wrinkled nose. In response to a bitter-tasting solution, the baby will open its mouth with the corners turned down and stick out its tongue in what appears to be an expression of disgust.

Newborns can also discriminate among odors. They will turn their heads toward a sweet smell, and their heart rates and respiration will slow down, indicating attention (see Figure 3-3). Noxious odors, such as ammonia or rotten eggs, cause them to turn their heads away; heart rate and respiration accelerate, indicating distress. Infants are even able to discriminate subtle differences in smells. After nursing for only a few days, an infant will consistently turn its head toward a pad saturated with its mother's milk in preference to one saturated with another mother's milk (Russell, 1976). The innate ability to distinguish among smells has a clear adaptive value: it helps infants avoid noxious substances, thereby increasing their likelihood of survival.

In addition to certain innate perceptual abilities, newborns are also capable of simple forms of learning. In one study, infants only a few hours old learned to turn their heads right or left depending on whether they heard a buzzer or a tone. In order to taste a sweet liquid, the baby had to turn to the right when a tone sounded; when a buzzer sounded, the baby had to turn to the left to get the sweet drink. In only a few trials, the babies were performing without error—turning to the right when the tone sounded and to the left when they heard the buzzer. The experimenter then reversed the situation so that the infant had to turn the opposite way when either the buzzer or tone sounded. The babies mastered this new task in approximately ten trials (Siqueland & Lipsitt, 1966).

All in all, the research we have described challenges the view of the newborn as a "blank slate." It suggests that the infant enters the world prepared to perceive and recognize reality and to learn quickly the relations between events that are important for human development. Newborns appear to have innate knowledge of some elementary principles that help them sort and categorize the flood of stimuli they experience and that enable them to form abstract concepts long before they have any usable language. In a series of studies, 6- to 8-month-old infants were shown pairs of slides, one slide displaying three objects and the other, two objects (see Figure 3-4); the objects pictured in the slides changed from trial to trial. In addition, on each trial the babies heard either two or three drumbeats emanating from a hidden, centrally placed speaker. Results of the experiment show that infants tended to look longer at the slide that matched the number of drumbeats—that is, when two drumbeats sounded, the infants tended to look at the slide picturing two objects, whereas with three drumbeats they looked toward the slide with three objects (Starkey, Spelke, & Gelman, 1986). These results demonstrate that infants are able to abstract numerical information presented in two different modalities (visual and auditory).

Findings such as these have led some psychologists to propose that infants come into the world knowing certain implicit principles that guide and facilitate subsequent learning. Infants are not born with specific knowledge about numbers and other kinds of logical relations, but they appear to have a head start on other species.

INDIVIDUAL DIFFERENCES IN TEMPERAMENT In discussing the capacities of the infant, we have emphasized ways in which infants are alike. Barring some

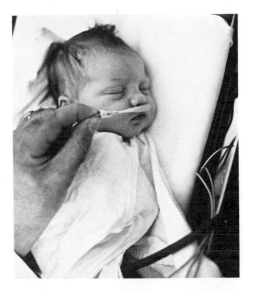

FIGURE 3-3
Testing the Newborn's Sense of Smell *Head turning and measures of heart rate and respiration are used to determine a 2-day-old infant's reaction to various odors.*

FIGURE 3-4
Forming Abstract Concepts *Infants preferred to look at the display in which the number of items matched the number of drumbeats that sounded from a speaker hidden behind the screen, thus demonstrating an ability to abstract numbers across sensory modalities. (After Starkey, Spelke, & Gelman, 1986)*

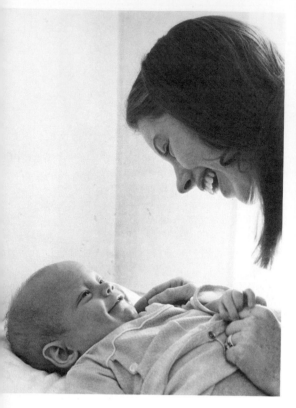

sort of physical damage, all babies have similar sensory abilities at birth and can experience the same kinds of events around them. But babies differ markedly in their general style of responding, or what is called *temperament*.

As early as the first weeks of life, infants show individual differences in activity level, responsiveness to changes in their environment, and irritability (see Chapter 13). One infant cries a lot; another cries very little. One endures diapering or bathing without much fuss; another kicks and thrashes. One is responsive to every sound; another is oblivious to all but the loudest noises. Infants even differ in "cuddliness." Some seem to enjoy being cuddled and mold their bodies to the person holding them; others stiffen and squirm and do less body adjusting (Korner, 1973).

The traditional view has been that parents shape their children's behavior. Parents of a fussy baby, for example, tend to blame themselves for their infant's difficulties. But research with newborns makes it increasingly clear that some temperamental differences are innate, and that the relationship between parent and infant is reciprocal — the infant's behavior also shapes the parent's response. An infant who is easily soothed, who snuggles and stops crying when picked up, increases the mother's feelings of competency and attachment. The infant who stiffens and continues to cry, despite all efforts to comfort it, makes the mother feel inadequate and rejected. The more responsive a baby is to the stimulation provided by the parent (snuggling and quieting when held, attending alertly when talked to or played with), the easier it is for the parent and child to establish a loving bond.

Researchers do not assume that a child's temperament is unchangeable or immune to environmental influences. Temperamental differences observed in infants often persist to some degree throughout childhood; thus, babies with "difficult" temperaments are more likely than "easy" babies to have school problems later on (Thomas & Chess, 1977). But temperamental traits can also change with development: an easygoing infant may become a tantrum-throwing toddler. Inborn temperament predisposes an infant to react in certain ways, but temperament and life experiences interact to mold personality. Nevertheless, regardless of how much an infant's temperament persists into childhood and beyond, it affects how parents and infant interact with one another.

Early Experience and Infant Development

A child's development from an alert but fairly helpless newborn to a walking and talking 2-year-old progresses at an astonishing rate. Indeed, changes occur more rapidly during the first two years of life than at any other period, except for the nine months before birth. As we noted earlier, the achievement of such physical skills as sitting, reaching for objects, crawling, and walking depends on the maturation of the muscles and nervous system. All babies achieve these skills without being taught. But psychologists have long been interested in whether environmental conditions can accelerate or retard maturational processes.

Although no training is required for a child to walk at the appropriate time, a certain amount of environmental stimulation appears to be necessary. Children raised in institutions who are handled infrequently and are given little opportunity to move about will sit, stand, and walk much later than normal. One study of an orphanage in Iran found that only 42 percent of the children were able to sit without support at 2 years, and only 15 percent could walk unaided at age 4 (Dennis, 1960). Contrast these percentages with the norms given for home-reared children in Figure 3-1 (p. 64). It should be emphasized that this particular orphanage provided a more impoverished environment than most. The caregivers had little education; they provided for the physical needs of the children but made no effort to play with or talk to them. Infants remained in their cribs all day except when being fed or changed. Older children were placed in a playpen for part of the day, but there were few toys to play with.

To determine whether increased stimulation and the opportunity to move about improve the development of motor skills, two psychologists tested 30 of the Iranian orphans on a scale measuring various aspects of infant development and then divided them into two groups. One group remained in their cribs as before. The other babies were taken to a playroom for an hour each day, propped into a sitting position, and allowed to play with a variety of toys. When the two groups were tested again a month later, the infants in the experimental group showed a marked gain in development compared with those who had remained in their cribs. Although motor development is largely dependent on maturation, the experiences of being able to move about freely and to reach for interesting objects are also necessary.

These studies demonstrate that when opportunities for exercise and movement are greatly restricted, there is some retardation in motor development, but the retardation can be remedied by appropriate stimulation. A related question, one that has long intrigued psychologists, is whether extra stimulation or special training can accelerate the development of basic motor skills. Some classic studies with identical twins in the 1920s and 1930s focused on this question (Gesell & Thompson, 1929; McGraw, 1935). Typically, one twin of a pair was given a lot of early practice on a particular skill (such as stair climbing). Later, the second twin was given a brief period of practice, and then the two twins were tested. In general, if the "untrained twin" had received even the briefest period of practice, the two performed almost equally well on the task. For the early motor skills, a small amount of practice later (when the muscles and nervous system are more mature) is as good as a lot of practice earlier.

More recent studies indicate that practice or extra stimulation can accelerate the appearance of motor behaviors to some extent. For example, newborn infants have a "stepping reflex"—if they are held in an upright position with their feet touching a solid surface, their legs will make stepping movements that are very similar to walking. (This reflex disappears within a few weeks, and real walking does not appear until many months later.) A group of infants who were given stepping practice for a few minutes several times a day during the first two months of life later began walking five to seven weeks earlier than babies who had not had this practice (Zelazo, Zelazo, & Kolb, 1972).

Long-term Effects of Early Experience

How permanent are the effects of early stimulation or deprivation? As far as motor skills are concerned, early experiences probably do not have a lasting effect. Children from the Iranian orphanage who were adopted before the age of 2 quickly attained, and thereafter maintained, normal development (Dennis, 1973). Infants in an isolated Indian village in Guatemala are kept inside the family's windowless hut for the first year of life in the belief that sunshine and air will cause sickness. They have little opportunity to crawl about, and their parents seldom play with them. When these children are allowed to leave the hut, they are behind American children in physical skills. But they catch up, and by the age of 3 they are as well coordinated as other children (Kagan & Klein, 1973).

In other areas of development—language ability, intellectual skills, and emotional development—the effects of early deprivation appear to be more lasting. Children whose learning opportunities are restricted during the first two or three years of life—who are not talked to, read to, or encouraged to explore their environment—will be seriously behind in language and intellectual skills by the time they enter school and may never catch up.

The importance of a stimulating environment in the early years for intellectual development is illustrated by a classic study by Skeels and Dye (1939). A group of orphaned children whose development at about 2 years of age was so retarded that they were not considered adoptable was transferred to an institution for the mentally retarded. In this institution, in contrast to the overcrowded orphanage, each child was placed in the care of an older, mildly retarded girl who served as a surrogate mother and spent great amounts of time playing with and talking to the child. In addition, the living quarters were spacious and well equipped with toys. As soon as the children could walk, they began to attend a nursery school where additional play materials and stimulation were provided. After a period of four years, this experimental group showed an average gain in intelligence of 32 IQ points; a group matched in age and intelligence that remained in the orphanage showed a loss of 21 points. A follow-up study over 20 years later found the experimental group still superior to the control group (Skeels, 1966). Most of the experimental group had completed high school (one-third had gone to college), were self-supporting, and had married and produced children of normal intelligence. Most of the control group, on the other hand, had not progressed beyond third grade and either remained institutionalized or did not earn enough to be self-supporting.

Although the number of subjects in this study was small and the possibility of some innate intellectual differences between the experimental group and control group cannot be completely ruled out, the results are sufficiently impressive to indicate the importance of a stimulating early environment for later intellectual development.

As we shall see later in this chapter, the lack of a close and caring relationship

An infant's intellectual development is dependent in part on environmental stimulation.

with an adult during the early years can have a profound effect on subsequent emotional and social development.

COGNITIVE DEVELOPMENT

Although most parents are aware of the intellectual changes that accompany their children's physical growth, they would have difficulty describing the nature of these changes. The Swiss psychologist Jean Piaget intensively studied children's cognitive development. After many years of careful observation, he developed a theory of how children's abilities to think and reason progress through a series of distinct stages as they mature (see Table 3-1).

Sensorimotor Stage

Noting the close interplay between motor activity and perception in infants, Piaget designated the first two years of life as the *sensorimotor stage.* During this period, infants are busy discovering the relationships between their actions and the consequences of these actions. They discover, for example, how far they have to reach to grasp an object, what happens when they push their food dish over the edge of the table, and that their hand is part of their body and the crib rail is not. Through countless "experiments," infants begin to develop a concept of themselves as separate from the external world.

TABLE 3-1
Piaget's Stages of Cognitive Development   *The ages given are averages. They may vary considerably depending on intelligence, cultural background, and socioeconomic factors, but the order of progression is assumed to be the same for all children. Piaget has described more detailed phases within each stage; only a very general characterization of each stage is given here.*

STAGE	CHARACTERIZATION
1. Sensorimotor (birth–2 years)	Differentiates self from objects Recognizes self as agent of action and begins to act intentionally: for example, pulls a string to set a mobile in motion or shakes a rattle to make a noise Achieves object permanence: realizes that things continue to exist even when no longer present to the senses
2. Preoperational (2–7 years)	Learns to use language and to represent objects by images and words Thinking is still egocentric: has difficulty taking the viewpoint of others Classifies objects by a single feature: for example, groups together all the red blocks regardless of shape or all the square blocks regardless of color
3. Concrete operational (7–12 years)	Can think logically about objects and events Achieves conservation of number (age 6), mass (age 7), and weight (age 9) Classifies objects according to several features and can order them in series along a single dimension, such as size
4. Formal operational (12 years and up)	Can think logically about abstract propositions and test hypotheses systematically Becomes concerned with the hypothetical, the future, and ideological problems

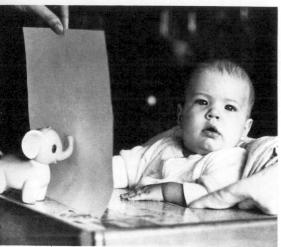

FIGURE 3-5

Object Permanence *When the toy is hidden by a screen, the infant acts as if it no longer exists. The infant does not yet have the concept of object permanence.*

An important discovery during this stage is the concept of *object permanence:* an awareness that an object continues to exist even when it is not present to the senses. If a cloth is placed over a toy that an 8-month-old is reaching for, the infant immediately stops and appears to lose interest. The baby seems neither surprised nor upset, makes no attempt to search for the toy, and acts as if it has ceased to exist (see Figure 3-5). In contrast, a 10-month-old will actively search for an object that has been hidden under a cloth or behind a screen. The older baby seems to realize that the object exists even though it is out of sight. He or she has attained the concept of object permanence. But even at this age, search is limited. If the infant has had repeated success in retrieving a toy hidden in one place, he or she will continue to look for it in that spot even after watching an adult conceal it in a new location. The baby repeats the action that produced the toy earlier, rather than looking for it where it was last seen. Not until about 1 year of age will a child consistently look for an object where it was last seen to disappear, regardless of what happened on previous trials.

Preoperational Stage

By about 1½ to 2 years of age, children have begun to use language. Words, as symbols, can represent things or groups of things, and one object can represent (symbolize) another. Thus, in play a 3-year-old may treat a stick as if it were a horse and ride it around the room; a block of wood can become a car; one doll can become a mother and another, a baby.

Although 3- and 4-year-olds can think in symbolic terms, their words and images are not yet organized in a logical manner. Piaget calls the 2- to 7-years stage of cognitive development *preoperational,* because the child does not yet comprehend certain rules or *operations.* An operation is a mental routine for transposing information, and it is reversible; every operation has its logical opposite. Cutting a circle into four equal pie-shaped wedges is an operation because we can reverse the procedure and put the pieces back to form a whole. The rule that we square the number 3 to get 9 is an operation because we can reverse the operation and take the square root of 9 to get 3. In the preoperational stage of cognitive development, a child's understanding of such rules is absent or weak. Piaget illustrates this deficit by some experiments on the development of what he calls *conservation.*

As adults, we take conservation principles for granted: the amount (mass) of a substance remains the same when its shape is changed or when it is divided into parts; the total weight of a set of objects will remain the same no matter how they are packaged together; and liquids do not change in amount when they are poured from a container of one shape to a container of another shape. For children, however, attainment of these concepts is an aspect of intellectual growth that requires several years.

In a study of the conservation of mass, a child is given some clay to make into a ball that is equal to another ball of the same material; after doing this, the child declares them to be "the same." Then, leaving one ball for reference, the experimenter rolls the other into a long sausage shape while the child watches. The child can plainly see that no clay has been added or subtracted. In this situation, children about 4 years old believe that the two objects no longer contain the same amount of clay: the longer one contains more, they say (see Figure 3-6). Not until the age of 7 do the majority of children perceive that the clay in the longer object is equal in amount to that in the reference ball.

The same kind of experiment can be used to study the conservation of weight. For example, children who know that equal things will balance on a scale

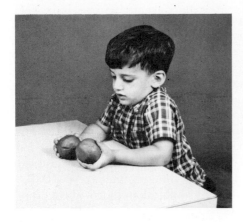
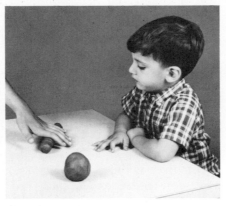

(they can test this with the two balls) are asked whether the sausage-shaped form will keep the scale arm balanced, as did the original ball. Conservation of weight is a more difficult concept than conservation of mass, and it comes a year or so later in development.

One reason why children younger than 7 have difficulty with conservation concepts is because their thinking is still dominated by visual impressions. A change in the appearance of the clay mass means more to them than less obvious qualities, such as weight. The young child's reliance on visual impressions is made clear by an experiment on the conservation of number. If a row of black checkers is matched one for one against an equal row of red checkers, the 5- or 6-year-old will say the rows have the same number of checkers. If the black checkers are brought closer together to form a cluster, the 5-year-old says there are now more red ones — even though no checkers have been removed (see Figure 3-7). The visual impression of a long row of red checkers overrides the numerical equality that was obvious when the black checkers appeared in a matching row. In contrast, 7-year-olds assume that if the number of objects was equal before, it must remain equal. At this age, numerical equality has become more significant than visual impression.

FIGURE 3-6
Concept of Conservation *A 4-year-old acknowledges that the two balls of clay are the same size. But when one ball is rolled into a long thin shape, he says that it has more clay. Not until he is several years older will he state that the two different shapes contain the same amount of clay.*

Operational Stages

Between the ages of 7 and 12, children master the various conservation concepts and begin to perform still other logical manipulations. They can order objects on the basis of a dimension, such as height or weight. They can also form a mental representation of a series of actions. Five-year-olds can find their way to a friend's house but cannot direct you there or trace the route with paper and pencil. They can find the way because they know they have to turn at certain places, but they have no overall picture of the route. In contrast, 8-year-olds can readily draw a map of the route.

Piaget calls this period the *concrete operational stage:* although children are using abstract terms, they are doing so only in relation to concrete objects — that is, objects to which they have direct sensory access. Not until the final stage of cognitive development, the *formal operational stage,* which begins around age 11 or 12, are youngsters able to reason in purely symbolic terms.

In one test for formal operational thinking, the subject tries to discover what determines the amount of time that a pendulum will swing back and forth (its period of oscillation). The subject is presented with a length of string suspended from a hook and several weights than can be attached to the lower end. He or she can vary the length of the string, change the attached weight, and alter the height from which the bob is released.

FIGURE 3-7
Conservation of Number *When the two rows of seven checkers are evenly spaced, most children report that they contain the same amount. When one row is then clustered into a smaller space, children under 6 or 7 will say the original row contains more.*

Children still in the concrete operational stage will experiment by changing some of the variables, but not in a systematic way. Adolescents of even average ability will set up a series of hypotheses and proceed to test them systematically. They reason that if a particular variable (weight) affects the period of oscillation, the effect will appear only if they change one variable and hold all others constant. If this variable seems to have no effect on the time of swing, they rule it out and try another. Considering all the possibilities—working out the consequences for each hypothesis and confirming or denying these consequences—is the essence of what Piaget called formal operational thought. This ability to conceive of possibilities beyond what is present in reality—to think of alternatives to the way things are—permeates adolescent thinking and is related to the adolescent tendency to be concerned with philosophical and ideological problems and to question the way in which adults run the world.

Nonstage Approaches

Piaget's theory provides a broad overview of cognitive development. It is the most comprehensive theory to date and has influenced much of the research on the way children think and solve problems. Most studies support Piaget's observations on the sequences in cognitive development, although the ages at which children reach the different levels vary considerably, depending on such factors as intelligence and experiences.

Newer, more sophisticated methods of testing the intellectual functioning of infants and preschool children indicate that Piaget, whose theories were based on naturalistic observations, underestimated their abilities. As we saw earlier, very young infants possess some intellectual abilities that they are unable to demonstrate under normal circumstances. And, as we will see shortly, preschoolers are capable of handling concepts more complex than those of Piaget's preoperational stage, given appropriate conditions of testing.

Recent research also raises questions about some of Piaget's ideas. For example, Piaget believed that early cognitive development depends on sensorimotor activities. He did not conceive of the possibility that infants' minds may be ahead of their motor abilities. He believed that infants do not recognize contingencies—that their own actions are making something happen—until at least 4 or 5 months when they begin to have some control of arm movements. At this age, for example, they discover that hitting a rattle suspended above the crib makes an interesting noise, and they delight in repeating the movement. Recent studies show that infants as young as 2 or 3 months, who cannot manipulate objects with their hands, can still recognize when something they have done has had an effect on the environment. If a mobile that can be operated by a pressure-sensitive pillow is attached to the crib, 2-month-old infants quickly learn to move their heads in a way that makes the mobile rotate. Moreover, after a few days of playing with the mobile, they begin to smile and coo at it (in advance of the normal time for this kind of emotional expression), suggesting that they are delighted by their ability to make something happen (Watson, 1983; Bahrick & Watson, 1985). This study indicates that sensorimotor activities (moving about and handling objects) may not be essential for early cognitive development, although they undoubtedly play a major role.

Studies show that Piaget also underestimated the abilities of preschool children. For example, if test conditions are carefully arranged in conservation experiments so that the children's responses do not depend on their language ability (their understanding of what the experimenter means by "more" or "longer"), then even 3- and 4-year-olds show some awareness of number conservation; they can distinguish between the number of items in a set and the way in which the items are spatially arranged (Gelman & Gallistel, 1978).

This and similar studies suggest that the quality of a child's thinking does not change dramatically from one stage to the next. Transition between stages of intellectual growth is gradual, involving a consolidation of earlier skills so they become automatic. Consider conservation of liquid. If the task is simplified in various ways (for example, by drawing the child's attention to both the height and the width of the containers), preschoolers are able to conserve. A 7- or 8-year-old, in contrast, hardly needs to glance at the containers. He or she *knows* that the quantity of liquid remains the same regardless of the shape of the container into which it is poured.

Instead of focusing on stages, some psychologists view cognitive development as a gradual increase in knowledge and in the ability to process information. One important cognitive skill is remembering. Many of the differences in performance between an older and younger child may be due to differences in their ability to remember (Case, 1985). The younger child may be unable to acquire certain concepts (such as conservation) because to do so would require holding more items of information in mind simultaneously than the child's current memory capacity permits.

Preschool children perform poorly on tests of memory compared with school-age children. With increasing age, their performance improves. For example, if children hear a list of 15 simple words and are then asked to recall them, a 6-year-old will recall about 4 words; a 9-year-old, 5 words; and an 11-year-old, 7 words (Yussen & Berman, 1981). The poorer performance of the younger children may be due to a limited memory capacity, which increases as they mature physically. But it seems more likely that what changes with age is the ability to use various strategies to improve memory. For example, as they grow older, children learn to rehearse information (to repeat it to themselves several times), to organize lists of words into meaningful categories and memorize them accordingly, and to use a variety of cues to aid memory (see Chapter 8).

PERSONALITY AND SOCIAL DEVELOPMENT

Our first social contacts are with the person who cares for us in early infancy, usually the mother. The manner in which the caregiver responds to the infant's needs — patiently, with warmth and concern, or brusquely, with little sensitivity — will influence the child's attitudes toward other people. Some psychologists believe that a person's basic feelings of trust in others are determined by experiences during the first years of life (Erikson, 1963, 1976; Bowlby, 1973). In the discussions that follow, we will use the word "mother" to refer to the primary caregiver, recognizing, nevertheless, that fathers and other family members sometimes assume this role.

Early Social Behavior

By 2 months of age, the average child will smile at the sight of its mother's face. Delighted with this response, mothers will go to great lengths to encourage repetition. Indeed, the infant's ability to smile at such an early age may play an important role in strengthening the mother-child bond. The first smiles tell the caregiver that the infant "recognizes (loves) me" — which is not true in any personal sense as yet — and encourages the caregiver to be even more affectionate

and stimulating in response. The infant smiles and coos at the mother; she pats, smiles, and vocalizes in return, thereby stimulating an even more enthusiastic response from her infant. Each reinforces social responses in the other.

Infants all over the world begin to smile at about the same age, whether raised in a remote African village or a middle-class American home. This suggests that maturation is more important in determining the onset of smiling than are the conditions of rearing. The fact that blind babies smile at about the same age as sighted infants (in response to their parents' voices rather than faces) adds support to this conclusion (Eibl-Eibesfeldt, 1970).

By their third or fourth month, infants show that they recognize and prefer familiar members of the household — by smiling or cooing more when seeing their faces or hearing their voices — but they are still fairly receptive to strangers. At about 8 months, however, this indiscriminate acceptance changes. The infant begins to show wariness or actual distress at the approach of a stranger (even while being held by the mother) and, at the same time, to protest strongly when left by the parent in an unfamiliar setting or with an unfamiliar person. Parents are often disconcerted to find that their formerly gregarious infant, who had always welcomed happily the attentions of a baby-sitter, now cries inconsolably when they prepare to leave — and continues to cry for some time after they have left.

"Stranger shyness" increases dramatically from about 8 months of age until the end of the first year (Bronson, 1972). Distress over separation from the parent — a distinct but related phenomenon — reaches a peak between 14 to 18 months and then gradually declines. By the time they are 3 years old, most children are secure enough in their parents' absence to be able to interact comfortably with other children and adults.

The waxing and waning of separation fears appears to be only slightly influenced by conditions of child rearing. The same general pattern has been found among American children raised entirely at home and those attending a day-care center, as well as in Israeli infants raised in a kibbutz, Indian children living in a Guatemalan village, and Bushmen children living in the Kalahari Desert (Kagan, 1979).

How do we explain these fears? Two factors seem to be important in both their onset and their decline. First is the growth of memory capacity. Beginning at about 8 months, an infant is able to form a mental image of people or situations. This image can be stored in memory and then retrieved for comparison with the present situation. Thus, a 1-year-old can wake up from a nap, confront an unfamiliar face, and realize that the mother's more familiar one is not present; this realization may generate feelings of uncertainty. In the months ahead, increased memory competence will be accompanied by an ability to anticipate the future. As the child's memory improves for past instances of separation and return, the child becomes better able to anticipate the return of the absent parent, and both uncertainty and distress decline.

The second factor is the growth of autonomy. One-year-olds are still highly dependent on care from adults, but children of 2 or 3 can head for the snack plate or toy shelf on their own. Also, they can use language to communicate their wants and feelings. Thus, dependency on caregivers in general, and on familiar caregivers in particular, decreases, and the issue of the parent's presence becomes less central for the child.

Attachment

The infant's tendency to seek closeness to particular people and to feel more secure in their presence is called *attachment*. The young of other species show attachment to their mothers in different ways. An infant monkey clings to its mother's chest as she moves about; puppies climb over each other in their attempts to reach the warm belly of their mother; ducklings and baby chicks follow their mother about, making sounds to which she responds and going to her when they are frightened. These early, unlearned responses to the mother have a clear adaptive value: they prevent the organism from wandering away from the source of care and getting lost.

Psychologists at first theorized that attachment to the mother developed because she, as a source of food, satisfied one of the infant's most basic needs. But some facts did not fit. For example, ducklings and baby chicks feed themselves from birth, yet they still follow their mothers about and spend a great deal of time with them. The comfort they derive from the mother's presence cannot come from her role in feeding. A series of well-known experiments with monkeys showed that there is more to mother-infant attachment than nutritional needs (Harlow & Suomi, 1970).

ATTACHMENT IN MONKEYS Infant monkeys were separated from their mothers shortly after birth and placed with two artificial "mothers" constructed of wire mesh with wooden heads: the torso of one mother was bare wire; the other was covered with foam rubber and terry cloth, making it more cuddly and easy to cling to (see Figure 3-8). Either mother could be equipped to provide milk by means of a bottle attached to its chest.

The experiment sought to determine whether the mother that was always the source of food would be the one to which the young monkey would cling. The results were clear-cut; no matter which mother provided food, the infant monkey spent its time clinging to the terry-cloth, cuddly mother. This purely passive but soft-contact mother was a source of security. For example, the obvious fear of the infant monkey placed in a strange environment was allayed if the infant could make contact with the cloth mother. While holding on to the cloth mother with one hand or foot, the monkey was willing to explore objects that were otherwise too terrifying to approach. Similar responses can be observed in 1- to 2-year-old children who are willing to explore strange territory as long as their mothers are close by.

FIGURE 3-8
A Monkey's Response to an Artificial Mother *Although fed via the wire mother, the infant spends more time with the terry-cloth mother. The terry-cloth mother provides security and a safe base from which to explore strange objects.*

Further studies revealed additional features that infant monkeys seek in their mothers. They prefer an artificial mother that rocks to an immobile one, and they prefer a warm mother to a cold one. Given the choice of a cloth mother or a wire mother of the same temperature, the infant monkeys always preferred the cloth mother. But if the wire mother was heated, the newborns chose it over a cool cloth mother for the first two weeks of life. After that, the infant monkeys spent more and more time with the cloth mother.

The infant monkey's attachment to its mother is thus an innate response to certain stimuli provided by her. Warmth, rocking, and food are important, but *contact comfort*—the opportunity to cling to and rub against something soft— seems to be the most important attribute for monkeys.

Although contact with a cuddly, artificial mother provides an important aspect of "mothering," it is not enough for satisfactory development. Infant monkeys raised with artificial mothers and isolated from other monkeys during the first six months of life showed various types of bizarre behavior in adulthood. They rarely engaged in normal interaction with other monkeys later on (either cowering in fear or showing abnormally aggressive behavior), and their sexual responses were inappropriate. When female monkeys that had been deprived of early social contact were successfully mated (after considerable effort), they made very poor mothers, tending to neglect or abuse their infants. For monkeys, interaction with other members of their species during the first six months of life appears to be crucial for normal social development.

ATTACHMENT IN HUMAN INFANTS   Although we should be careful in generalizing from experimental work on monkeys to human development, there is evidence that the human infant's attachment to the mother serves the same functions: it provides the security necessary for the child to explore his or her environment, and it forms the basis for interpersonal relationships in later years. Young children are much more willing to investigate strange surroundings when their mothers are nearby. The failure to form an attachment to one or a few primary persons in the early years can be related to an inability to develop close personal relationships in adulthood (Bowlby, 1973).

A series of studies designed to investigate attachment in young children has revealed some interesting differences in the quality of the mother-child relationship (Ainsworth, Blehar, Walters, & Wall, 1978). The laboratory setup, called the *Strange Situation,* involves the following episodes:

1. The mother brings the child into the experimental room, places the child on a small chair surrounded by toys, and then goes to sit at the opposite end of the room.
2. After a few minutes, a female stranger enters the room, sits quietly for a while, and then attempts to engage the child in play with a toy.
3. The mother leaves the room, leaving her handbag on her chair as a sign that she will return.
4. The mother returns and engages the child in play while the stranger slips out.
5. The mother leaves again, and the child is left alone for three minutes.
6. The stranger returns.
7. The mother returns.

The child is observed through a one-way mirror during the entire sequence, and any number of different measures can be recorded: child's activity level and play involvement, crying and other distress signs, proximity to and attempts to gain attention of the mother, proximity to and willingness to interact with the stranger, and so on. From studying the reactions of 1- to 1½-year-olds in the

Strange Situation, especially their behavior when reunited with their mothers, the investigators categorized children into three groups.

- *Securely Attached*   As long as the mother is present, these babies play comfortably with toys and are friendly to the stranger. They are clearly upset when the mother leaves; signs of distress range from fussing and visually searching for her to loud crying. When she returns, they go to her immediately, calm down after being held or hugged, and resume playing with the toys. About 65 percent of the children studied were classified in this category.
- *Insecurely Attached: Avoidant*   These babies pay little attention to the mother when she is in the room and do not seem distressed when she leaves. If distressed, they are as easily comforted by the stranger as the mother. They ignore the mother when she returns, or they may approach her tentatively, turning or looking away. About 25 percent of the sample fit into this pattern.
- *Insecurely Attached: Ambivalent*   These babies have trouble with the Strange Situation from the start. They stay close to their mothers and appear anxious when she is not at hand. They become very upset during the mother's absence and seem ambivalent toward her when she returns. They simultaneously seek and resist physical contact. For example, they may cry to be picked up and then squirm angrily to get down. They do not resume playing; instead they keep a wary eye on the mother. About 10 percent of the sample fit this category.

The first group of children, those who sought contact with their mothers on reunion, were labeled securely attached on the basis of observations in the home. They seemed generally more secure (cried less often, were more responsive to their mothers' verbal commands, and were less upset by their mothers' coming and going) than children who were either avoidant or ambivalent on reunion in the Strange Situation. The latter two groups showed signs of conflict in their relationship with their mothers. The avoidant babies seemed to dislike physical contact with her, while the ambivalent babies were clingy and seemed to demand more from their mothers than the mothers were willing to give (Ainsworth, 1979).

The investigators concluded, on the basis of these and other data, that all babies become attached to their mothers by the time they are 1 year old, but the quality of the attachment differs depending on each mother's responsiveness to her baby. Most babies show *secure attachment*, but some show *insecure attachment*. Insecure attachment is associated with insensitive or unresponsive mothering during the first year of life. The mothers of babies who show insecure attachment tend to respond more on the basis of their own wishes or moods than to signals from the baby. For example, they will respond to the baby's cries for attention when they feel like cuddling the baby but will ignore such cries at other times (Stayton, 1973). Mothers of infants who are securely attached are more responsive to their infants' needs, provide more social stimulation (talking to and playing with the infant), and express more affection (Clarke-Stewart, 1973).

ATTACHMENT AND LATER DEVELOPMENT   The pattern of early attachment appears to influence the way that an infant copes with new experiences during the next few years. For example, in one study, 2-year-olds were given a series of problems requiring the use of tools. Some of the problems were within the child's capacity; others were quite difficult. The toddlers who had been rated as securely attached (at 12 months of age) approached the problems with enthusiasm and persistence. When they encountered difficulties, they seldom cried or became angry; rather, they sought help from the adults who were present. Those who had been rated earlier as insecurely attached behaved quite differently. They became easily frustrated and angry, seldom asked for help, tended to ignore or

CRITICAL DISCUSSION

Working Mothers: Effects on Children's Development

More and more women today are working outside of the home. Over half of the mothers in the United States with children under 3 years of age are employed, and the number is increasing. In view of the research on infant attachment and on the benefits of a stimulating environment during the early years, it is important to consider how this trend will affect future generations.

Working mothers provide a variety of arrangements for their children's care. The majority leave their preschoolers at home to be cared for by a sitter or a relative while they work. The rest leave their young ones at someone else's home (to be cared for alone or with other children) or at day-care centers. Clearly, the effects of maternal employment on the child's development depend, to a large extent, on the quality of the substitute care. Research has focused on two broad areas: the general effects on children of having a working, versus a full-time, mother; and the effects of group child care versus those of individual child care.

Having a working mother appears to benefit girls more than it does boys. Daughters of working mothers tend to be more independent, better adjusted socially, and more likely to do well academically and aspire to a career than are daughters of mothers who are not employed (see Birnbaum, 1975; Gold, Andres, & Glorieux, 1979; Hoffman, 1980). Sons of working mothers are also more independent and better adjusted socially than are sons of nonworking mothers, but they do not do as well in school or on tests of cognitive ability (Banducci, 1967; Brown, 1970). How

do we explain these findings? There are a number of possibilities. It may be that the loss of intellectual stimulation when the mother works has an adverse effect on both boys and girls. But the daughter's loss may be offset by other benefits, such as increased independence and the model of a mother who has a career outside of the home. Little boys whose mothers stay home during the preschool years tend to be more intellectually able as adolescents, but they are also more conforming, inhibited, and fearful. The nonworking mother may be so immersed in her role that she encourages dependency and has difficulty letting her son develop mature behavior.

Any attempt to weigh the effects of group child care against those of individual care at home obviously depends on the quality of the child-care facility and the nature of the home. Most of the research has been conducted at university-affiliated day-care centers of high quality. Such centers are run by trained personnel in charge of small groups of children. They have good equipment, educationally stimulating activities, and they attempt to provide each child with emotional support. The experience of children in these centers is probably not representative of the experiences of day-care children in the United States as a whole. This limitation must be kept in mind when considering the reported findings.

In terms of intellectual development, children from middle-class families appear to do as well at a good day-care center as they do with parental care at home (Kagan, Kearsley, & Zelazo, 1978; Clarke-Stewart,

reject directions from the adults, and quickly gave up trying to solve the problems (Matas, Arend, & Sroufe, 1978).

Another study looked at the social behavior of nursery school children (age 3½ years) whose attachment relationships had been assessed at 15 months of age. The children rated earlier as securely attached tended to be the social leaders: they were active in initiating and participating in activities and were sought out by the other children. Their teachers rated them as forceful, self-directed, and eager to learn. The insecurely attached children tended to be socially withdrawn and hesitant about participating in activities. Their teachers rated them as less curious about new things and less forceful in pursuing their goals. These differences were not related to intelligence (Waters, Wippman, & Sroufe, 1979).

These studies suggest that children who are securely attached by the time they enter their second year of life are better equipped to cope with new experiences and relationships. However, we cannot be certain that the quality of chil-

1982). Children from homes with poorly educated parents who have low incomes benefit intellectually from their day-care experience. The enrichment programs provided seem to prevent the decline in intellectual performance that often occurs after the age of 2 if such children remain at home (Ramey, 1981). Middle-class mothers are better educated than lower-class mothers; they are more effective teachers and a greater source of intellectual stimulation for their children (Goldberg, 1978). The statement made earlier that sons of working mothers do not do as well academically as sons of nonworking mothers is true for boys from middle-class homes. Boys from very low income families, in contrast, score higher on tests of cognitive ability when their mothers work.

How does day care affect the emotional ties between parents and their children? Critics of day care have voiced concern that the repeated separations of mother and child that are a part of day care could seriously interfere with young children's attachment to their mothers. Most of the studies on this issue have compared the responses of home-reared children and day-care-reared children under the age of 2 in the Strange Situation. The findings indicate that day-care infants and toddlers are as securely attached to their mothers as children raised at home. Although they may form an affectionate relationship with a day-care teacher, they still clearly prefer their mothers, especially when tired or upset (Kagan, Kearsley, & Zelazo, 1978). The day-care toddlers did not stay as close to their mothers or seek as much physical contact when playing in the Strange Situation as did the home-raised children. However, this difference has been interpreted to indicate that day-care children become more independent as part of their adaptation to daily separation (Clarke-Stewart, 1982).

The most clear-cut influence of day care appears to be in the area of social development. Compared to home-raised children, those who attend day-care centers have been described as more self-sufficient, more cooperative with peers, and more comfortable in new situations. They are also less polite, less compliant with adults, and more aggressive (Clarke-Stewart & Fein, 1983). Some of these results may depend on the child-rearing attitudes of the parents and the teachers. Children attending day-care centers in the Soviet Union, Israel, and Sweden also show greater self-sufficiency and ease in social situations, but they do not act as aggressively or rudely as day-care children in the United States. Such behavior is strongly disapproved of by parents and teachers in those countries (Cole & Cole, 1987).

It should be emphasized again that all of these generally positive findings pertain to quality day-care centers. They undoubtedly do not hold for the many day-care facilities that provide for the child's physical needs but little more. Since experiences during the preschool years form the basis for later development, children who spend most of their waking hours under conditions that are not very stimulating lose a great deal. In view of the fact that the number of mothers of young children who are employed is steadily increasing, the provision of quality, affordable child care is a vital social issue.

The age of the child is important when deciding between individual care and group care for children of working mothers. Most experts recommend individual care in a home for the youngest children (up to age 2 or 3) and group care for older preschool children (Scarr, 1984). Infants and toddlers need the consistent care of one person (turnover of personnel is frequent in most day-care centers). Older children can benefit from the intellectual stimulation and peer interaction provided by a good day-care center. In fact, 3- and 4-year-olds attending day-care centers show better social and intellectual development than do their age-mates cared for at home by sitters (Clarke-Stewart, 1982).

Day-care centers provide children of working parents with social interaction and intellectual stimulation.

dren's early attachments is directly responsible for their later competence in problem solving and social skills. Mothers who are responsive to their children's needs in infancy probably continue to provide effective mothering during early childhood — encouraging autonomy and efforts to cope with new experiences, yet ready with help when needed. Thus, the child's competency and social skills at age 3½ may reflect the current state of the parent-child relationship rather than the relationship that existed two years earlier.

Moreover, some critics believe that the child's behavior in the Strange Situation and his or her competency as a preschooler reflect characteristics of the child more than the quality of the mother-child relationship (Chess & Thomas, 1982; Lamb et al., 1984). As we noted earlier, some children appear to be more cautious and easily upset than others almost from birth. Such children may find it hard to cope with new tasks and to form relationships, despite receiving quite adequate parenting.

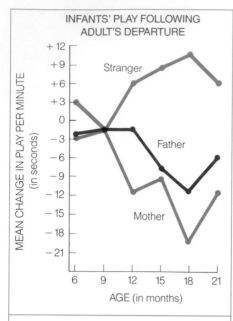

INFANTS' PLAY FOLLOWING
ADULT'S DEPARTURE

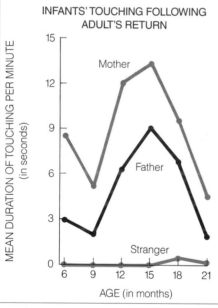

INFANTS' TOUCHING FOLLOWING
ADULT'S RETURN

FIGURE 3-9

Age Changes in Infants' Responses
Children (6 to 21 months) were observed in the Strange Situation with either their mothers, fathers, or a stranger. When the mother or father left briefly, the child's play was disrupted, although such responses to father's departure appeared at a later age. When the stranger left, the child played more actively, apparently feeling more comfortable alone than with a stranger. The return of either parent was followed by a period of touching or clinging.

Child-rearing practices may also affect the child's behavior in the Strange Situation. For example, Japanese child-rearing customs encourage a great deal of physical closeness between mother and child, little exposure to strange adults, and little experience in the sort of free play environment characteristic of the Strange Situation. As a result, Japanese babies tend to be anxious and wary throughout all episodes of the Strange Situation and are particularly upset when left alone — so distressed, in fact, that the experimenter usually curtails the alone episode (Takahashi, 1986).

Thus, at least some of the observed differences in infant attachment behavior that have been attributed to the mother's responsiveness may arise from temperamental predispositions of the child and cultural expectations that influence both mother and child. Nevertheless, it seems likely that early patterns of mother-child attachment have an important influence on later development.

ATTACHMENT TO FATHERS   Although an infant's primary attachment is to the person who provides most of the early care, other familiar persons are a source of security, too. Studies of the Strange Situation using the father indicate that infants react to his presence or absence in ways similar to those described for the mother, although attachment to the father seems to develop more slowly (Kotelchuck, 1976). For example, a 1-year-old usually cries and stops playing when mother leaves him or her alone; such responses to the father's departure do not appear (on the average) until the child is 15 months old. In addition, the 1-year-old infant usually protests the mother's departure more vigorously than the father's and clings to her somewhat longer on reunion. These differences lessen with age (see Figure 3-9).

Fathers differ greatly in the amount of time they devote to child care. Children whose fathers are actively involved in their day-to-day care tend to be less disturbed when left alone with a stranger than children from families in which mother provides most of the care (Kotelchuck, 1976). Yet babies also become attached to fathers who spend little time with them. Most of the brief interactions between fathers and their babies are play episodes. Fathers provide fun and excitement; they tend to engage in more physical, rough-and-tumble play than mothers. If given a choice of whom to play with, 18-month-old babies will choose their fathers more often than they will their mothers. But in times of stress, mothers are generally preferred (Clarke-Stewart, 1978).

Interaction With Peers

Although a close relationship with a warm and responsive adult is essential for a child's emotional development, interaction with other children plays an important role, too. As we have seen, infant monkeys that are raised only with their mothers and have no opportunity to play with other young monkeys do not develop normal patterns of behavior. When introduced to other monkeys later on, they may be abnormally fearful of contact — screaming in fright at the approach of another monkey — or overly aggressive. They also show inappropriate sexual responses (Suomi, 1977).

In the normal course of development, an infant monkey spends the first eight weeks of life exclusively with its mother. From then on, the young monkey spends more and more time swinging, chasing, and wrestling with its age-mates. From these early play activities, the young monkey learns to enjoy physical contact, to control aggression, and to develop the grasping and mounting responses that will lead to adult sexual behavior. Human children also learn many of their social skills by interacting with each other. They learn to give and take, to share in cooperative ventures, to enjoy each other's actions, and to understand

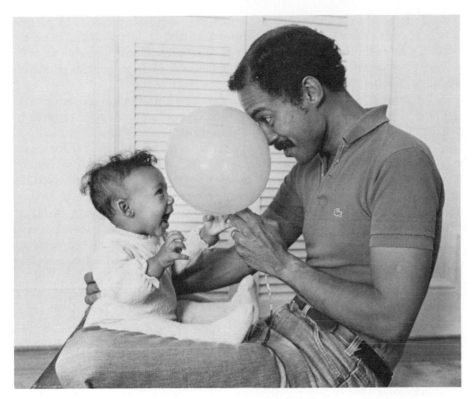

how another person feels. Peers become models to imitate as well as important dispensers of rewards and punishments. By watching the actions of peers, children may learn a new skill (how to build a bridge with blocks) or the consequences of certain behaviors (aggressive children get into trouble).

A number of experiments have shown the influence of peer models on children's behavior. For example, 4- and 5-year-olds who watched one of their classmates being very generous in sharing some prizes were much more generous when their turn came to share than were children who had not watched the generous model (Hartup & Coates, 1967). As we will see in Chapter 11, if a child watches a model being rewarded for certain behaviors, the child is more likely to imitate those behaviors than if he or she sees the model being punished.

The way in which other children respond to a child's behavior is also an important modifying influence. For example, selfishness that is accepted by doting parents may not be tolerated by the child's peers. Children reinforce certain actions in their playmates — by approval and attention — and punish others.

Moral Thought and Behavior

Understanding the values of society and regulating behavior accordingly are important parts of development. Children's concepts of right and wrong change in interesting ways as they grow older. Most 5-year-olds say that it is wrong to lie, to steal, or to injure another person. But their comprehension of these statements changes with age. Only gradually do they begin to understand what kinds of statements are lies, how borrowing differs from stealing, and that injuring someone intentionally evokes greater blame than accidental injury.

Children's ability to make judgments about moral issues is related to their cognitive development. Older children are more capable of handling abstract concepts and making inferences about social relationships than are younger children. Although maturing cognitive abilities play a role in the development of a child's sense of right and wrong, other factors (the models provided by parents and peers, for example) are equally important. And children's moral behavior (their ability to inhibit their actions that are disapproved of by society and to be concerned about the welfare of others) depends on much more than an understanding of moral problems.

Piaget was the first to investigate the development of moral reasoning (Piaget, 1932). He told stories to children of various ages and asked the children to make moral judgments about the fictional characters in the stories. For example, one story was about a boy who broke a teacup while trying to steal some jam when his mother was not home. Another boy broke a whole trayful of teacups, but it was just an accident; he was not doing anything wrong. Piaget asked his subjects, "Which boy is naughtier?" He presented a number of such stories, varying the amount of damage done, as well as the character's intentions. Piaget found that preschool children tend to attribute blame according to the amount of damage done, regardless of intention. Older children take motives or intentions into account. A person with good intentions is not considered morally blameworthy even if he or she does a great deal of damage.

The American psychologist Laurence Kohlberg has extended Piaget's work on moral reasoning to include adolescence and adulthood (Kohlberg, 1969, 1973, 1984). By presenting moral dilemmas, such as the following, in story form, he has sought to determine if there are universal stages in the development of moral judgments.

> In Europe, a lady was dying because she was very sick. There was one drug that the doctors said might save her. This medicine was discovered by a man living in the same town. It cost him $200 to make it, but he charged $2,000 for just a little of it. The sick lady's husband, Heinz, tried to borrow enough money to buy the drug. He went to everyone he knew to borrow the money. But he could borrow only half of what he needed. He told the man who made the drug that his wife was dying, and asked him to sell the medicine cheaper or let him pay later. But the man said, "No, I made the drug and I'm to make money from it." So Heinz broke into the store and stole the drug. (After Kohlberg, 1969, pp. 18–19)

The subject is asked, "Should Heinz have done that? Was it actually wrong or right? Why?" By analyzing the answers to a series of stories of this type, each portraying a moral dilemma, Kohlberg arrived at six developmental stages of moral judgment grouped into three broad levels (see Table 3-2). The answers are scored as appropriate to a certain stage, not on the basis of whether the action is judged right or wrong, but on the reasons given for the decision. For example, agreeing that Heinz should have stolen the drug because "If you let your wife die, you'll get in trouble" or condemning him for his actions because "If you steal the drug, you'll be caught and sent to jail" are both scored at Stage 1 of Level I. In both instances, the man's actions are evaluated as right or wrong on the basis of anticipated punishment.

Kohlberg believes that all children start at Level I, preconventional morality: they evaluate actions in terms of whether or not the actions avoid punishment or lead to rewards. His studies indicate that between age 7 (the youngest group tested) and age 10, preconventional responses are still dominant. Some people, criminals for example, never progress beyond this level. From age 10 on, responses at Level II, conventional morality, increase: youngsters begin to evaluate actions in terms of maintaining a good image in the eyes of other people. By age 13, a majority of moral dilemmas are resolved at Level II. In the first stage of this level (Stage 3), one seeks approval by being "nice." This orientation expands in

LEVELS AND STAGES		ILLUSTRATIVE BEHAVIOR
Level I	Preconventional morality	
Stage 1	Punishment orientation	Obeys rules to avoid punishment
Stage 2	Reward orientation	Conforms to obtain rewards, to have favors returned
Level II	Conventional morality	
Stage 3	Good-boy/good-girl orientation	Conforms to avoid disapproval of others
Stage 4	Authority orientation	Upholds laws and social rules to avoid censure of authorities and feelings of guilt about not "doing one's duty"
Level III	Postconventional morality	
Stage 5	Social-contract orientation	Actions guided by principles commonly agreed on as essential to the public welfare; principles upheld to retain respect of peers and, thus, self-respect
Stage 6	Ethical principle orientation	Actions guided by self-chosen ethical principles (that usually value justice, dignity, and equality); principles upheld to avoid self-condemnation

TABLE 3-2

Stages of Moral Reasoning   *Kohlberg believes that moral judgment develops with age according to the following stages. (After Kohlberg, 1969)*

the next stage (Stage 4) to include "doing one's duty," showing respect for authority, and conforming to the social order in which one is raised.

According to Kohlberg, many individuals never progress beyond Level II. He sees the stages of moral development as closely tied to Piaget's stages of cognitive development, and only those people who have achieved the later stages of formal operational thought are capable of the kind of abstract thinking necessary for postconventional morality at Level III. The highest stage of moral development (Level III, Stage 6) requires formulating abstract ethical principles and upholding them to avoid self-condemnation. Kohlberg reports that fewer than 10 percent of his subjects over age 16 show the kind of "clear-principled" Stage-6 thinking exemplified by the following response of a 16-year-old to Heinz's dilemma: "By the law of society he was wrong but by the law of nature or of God the druggist was wrong and the husband was justified. Human life is above financial gain. Regardless of who was dying, if it was a total stranger, man has a duty to save him from dying" (Kohlberg, 1969, p. 244). Because Stage-6 thinking occurs so rarely, Kohlberg no longer considers it to be an expected outcome of ordinary human development (Kohlberg, 1984).

Kohlberg views children as "moral philosophers" who develop moral standards of their own. These standards do not necessarily come from parents or peers; rather, they emerge from the cognitive interaction of children with their social environment. Movement from one stage to the next involves an internal cognitive reorganization rather than a simple acquisition of the moral concepts prevalent in their culture (Kohlberg, 1973).

Other psychologists disagree, pointing out that the development of a conscience, a sense of right and wrong, is not simply a function of maturing cognitive abilities. Children's identification with their parents and the way in which they are rewarded or punished for behavior in specific situations will influence their moral views, as will the moral standards espoused by the children's peers and by characters on television and in books. Studies have shown that moral judgments can be modified by exposure to models: when children see adults reinforced for expressing a moral viewpoint based on principles different from their own, they may change their judgments up or down a level (Bandura & McDonald, 1963).

Thus, although there are obviously *age trends* in the way children think about moral issues, these may be explained more simply by looking at what parents teach and reinforce in children at different ages than by proposing a set sequence of stages. Very young children may need the threat of punishment to keep them from doing something wrong ("If you hit your little sister, I will put you to bed *right now*"). As children mature, social sanctions become more effective ("If you hit your little sister, I will be very angry; good children don't hurt other people").

Researchers using stories much simpler than Kohlberg's and posing moral dilemmas more relevant to a child's daily experiences have found that children as young as 4 or 5 years (whom Kohlberg would place in the preconventional stage) have some awareness of important moral principles. For example, they begin to consider intentions as well as consequences (damage) in evaluating the "badness" of an act (Surber, 1977). They also show an ability to integrate the concepts of need and achievement in allocating rewards. In one study, children 4 to 8 years old were asked to play Santa Claus and to divide in a fair manner a fixed number of toys between two boys. Each of the boys was described by two pieces of information: how hard he worked (indicated by a picture showing how many dishes he had washed for his mother) and his need (indicated by a picture showing how many toys he already had). According to Piaget (1932), the younger children should have given greater weight to the objective information about achievement and less weight to the more subjective factor of need. However, the data showed essentially the same pattern for all age groups: the children considered need as important as achievement in deciding on a fair distribution of the toys (Anderson & Butzin, 1978).

These studies indicate that even preschoolers recognize some important moral principles when presented with situations they can understand. This is not to deny, of course, that ways of thinking about moral issues change with age.

MORAL BEHAVIOR   How well does *moral reasoning* — as measured by responses to moral dilemmas — correlate with *moral behavior*? Are youngsters who show advanced moral judgment more likely to resist temptation or behave unselfishly than those less advanced? There is clearly some relationship between moral thought and moral action. For example, juvenile delinquents show lower levels of moral judgment than law-abiding youngsters of the same age and intelligence (Kohlberg, 1969). And people who attain higher moral levels on Kohlberg's dilemmas are more likely than low scorers to offer help to a person in distress (Huston & Korte, 1976). But, in general, research relating Kohlberg's levels to behavior in specific situations — for example, whether a child will cheat on a test or behave unselfishly — has found low correlations (Mischel & Mischel, 1976; Rest, 1983).

Often we know how we *should* act, but we may not do so when our own self-interest is involved. For example, children's judgment of "fairness" tended to be more mature in a hypothetical situation (how should candy bars be distributed among workers in a group) than their reasoning was when the situation became real. Those who had suggested giving the most candy to the person who produced the most when the situation was hypothetical were apt to say that everyone should share equally when it came to dividing the candy among their own work group — particularly if they had been among the less productive workers. Some who had earlier advocated an equal division demanded the largest share in the real situation (Damon, 1977).

Moral conduct depends on a number of factors in addition to the ability to reason about moral dilemmas. Two important factors are the ability to consider the long-range consequences of one's actions (rather than the immediate gain) and to control one's behavior. Equally important is the ability to empathize with other people — that is, to be able to put oneself in someone else's place. Understanding what another person is feeling motivates us to help.

Child-rearing Practices and Later Behavior

Methods of child rearing vary considerably from country to country and from one social group to another. Even in middle-class homes in the United States, parents' attitudes have tended to fluctuate on such matters as toilet training, feeding schedules, bottle feeding versus breast feeding, and permissiveness versus firm control.

During the first third of this century, child-rearing practices were fairly strict. Parents were advised not to spoil their babies by picking them up every time they cried, to feed them only according to a fixed schedule (whether or not the children were hungry), and to toilet train them within the first year. Thumb sucking and handling the genitals were to be vigorously discouraged. This quite rigid approach was partly the result of the influence of behaviorism; the goal was to build "good" habits and extinguish "bad" ones — and the earlier the parents started, the better. The following quotation from John B. Watson, the father of behaviorism, carries to a ridiculous extreme the notion of a controlled, objective, unemotional way of handling children.

> There is a sensible way of treating children. Treat them as though they were young adults. Dress them, bathe them with care and circumspection. Let your behavior always be objective and kindly firm. Never hug and kiss them, never let them sit in your lap. If you must, kiss them once on the forehead when they say goodnight. Shake hands with them in the morning. Give them a pat on the head if they have made an extraordinarily good job of a difficult task. Try it out. In a week's time you will find how easy it is to be perfectly objective with your child and at the same time kindly. You will be utterly ashamed of the mawkish, sentimental way you have been handling it. (Watson, 1928, pp. 73–74)

It is doubtful that many parents followed such a rigid program, but this was the advice of the "experts" at the time.

During the 1940s, the trend shifted toward more permissive and flexible child-care methods. Views on child development were being influenced by psychoanalytic theory, which stressed the importance of the child's emotional security and the damage that might result from harsh control of natural impulses. Under the guidance of Dr. Benjamin Spock, parents were advised to follow their own inclinations and to adopt flexible schedules that fit both the child's and their own needs. Toilet training should be delayed until the child was old enough to understand its purpose (not before the middle of the second year), and neither thumb sucking nor genital touching was to be considered a matter of great concern.

Now the pendulum appears to be swinging back. Parents today seem to feel that permissiveness is not the answer. Their approach to child rearing includes a moderate degree of control, firm discipline, and even punishment when necessary. That children flourish under a variety of rearing methods is a tribute to their adaptability and probably an indication that specific methods are less important than the basic attitude of the parents.

Specific child-rearing methods are probably less important to the development of a child than is the basic attitude of the parents.

Attempts to relate specific child-rearing techniques — type of feeding schedule, age of weaning or of toilet training — to later personality characteristics have not been very successful. The inconsistent results obtained probably are due to several factors. For one thing, parents' reports of how they have handled their children may be fairly inaccurate, particularly when they are trying to recall the children's early days. Parents tend to report what they *think they should do* in handling their offspring rather than what they actually do. There are also numerous ways of applying any specific child-rearing method. For example, two children may be toilet trained at the same early age: one mother is firm but patient; whereas the other is firm and impatient, expressing disappointment when the child fails. Both mothers toilet train their children "early," but they communicate quite different attitudes to the child.

Although specific techniques may not be predictive of later personality traits, we do have some evidence of the kind of parent-child relationships that produce competent and self-confident youngsters. In a series of studies, 3- and 4-year-old children were observed at home and in nursery school and were rated on five measures of competency: self-control, the tendency to approach new or unexpected situations with curiosity and enthusiasm, vitality, self-reliance, and the ability to express warmth toward playmates. On the basis of ratings on these characteristics, three groups of children were selected for further study. Children in Group I were the most mature and competent, scoring high on all five characteristics. Group II children were moderately self-reliant and self-controlled but rather apprehensive in new situations and not much interested in interacting with other children. Group III children were the most immature; they were much less self-reliant and self-controlled than the children in the other two groups, were highly dependent on adults for help, and were apt to retreat from new situations.

The investigator next looked at the child-rearing practices of all the parents by interviewing them and by observing how they interacted with their children at home. The investigator focused on four dimensions of the parent-child relationship:

1. *Control* — how much the parents tried to influence the child's activities and modify the expression of dependent or aggressive behavior in line with their own standards
2. *Maturity demands* — the amount of pressure on the child to perform at his or her level of ability
3. *Clarity of parent-child communication* — how well the parents explained their reasons when they wanted the child to obey and the extent to which they took the child's opinions and feelings into consideration
4. *Parental nurturance* — the warmth and compassion the parents showed toward the child and their pleasure in his or her accomplishments

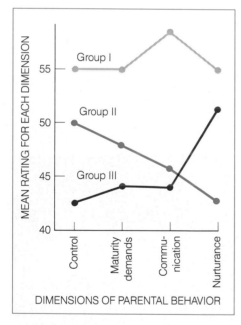

FIGURE 3-10

Parental Behavior as Related to Child Behavior *Nursery school children were evaluated in terms of competency and maturity. Members of Group I are the most competent children; members of Group III are the most immature and dependent. The figure shows how the parents of each group were rated on four dimensions: control of the child's activities, pressure demands for mature behavior, clarity of parent-child communication, and nurturance or warmth. (After Baumrind, 1967)*

As Figure 3-10 shows, the parents of the mature and competent children (Group I) are high on all four dimensions. They are warm and loving, and they communicate well with their children. Although they respect their children's opinions, they are generally firm and clear about the behavior they consider appropriate. The parents of the children who are moderately self-controlled and self-reliant but somewhat withdrawn and distrustful (Group II) tend to be fairly controlling but not very warm and affectionate toward their children or concerned with their opinions. The parents of the most immature children (Group III) are affectionate toward their children but not very controlling, demanding, or communicative. These parents tend to be ineffective and disorganized in running their households and lax in setting guidelines for behavior and in disciplining or rewarding their children.

In subsequent studies, the investigator proceeded in the reverse direction, selecting parents who fit these categories and then looking at the behaviors of their preschool children. Although the results are too detailed to describe here, we can draw some general conclusions. Parents who are fairly firm and consistent in their expectations of how their children should behave, but who are also warm and affectionate and respect their children's opinions, tend to produce competent and self-reliant preschoolers. When the parents are very controlling and more concerned with their own needs than with those of their children, their offspring may be fairly self-controlled but not very secure or confident in their approach to new situations or other people. Very permissive parents, who neither reward responsible behavior nor discourage immature behavior, produce youngsters with the least self-reliance and self-control. In summary, competence and self-confidence in young children seem best fostered by a warm and nurturant home where parents reward responsible behavior but also encourage independent actions and decision making (Baumrind, 1972).

IDENTIFICATION

As children develop, they acquire many attitudes and behavior patterns that are similar to those of their parents. Sometimes the resemblance between a youngster and a parent in such characteristics as manner of walking, gestures, and voice inflection is striking. The child is said to *identify* with the parent.

The concept of identification comes from psychoanalysis and played an important role in Freud's theorizing. In psychoanalytic theory, identification refers to the unconscious process by which one individual takes on the characteristics (attitudes, patterns of behavior, emotions) of another. Young children, by duplicating the attitudes and attributes of their parents, come to feel that they have absorbed some of the parent's strength and competency.

Identification, according to the psychoanalytic view, is more than the imitation of parental behavior; the child responds as if he or she *were* the parent. Thus, a young girl who identifies with her mother feels proud when her mother receives an award or honor—as if she herself had been the recipient. She feels sad when her mother suffers a disappointment. Through the process of identification, the child acquires the diverse behaviors involved in developing self-control, a conscience, and the appropriate sex role. For example, Freud believed that the child's conscience is formed by incorporating parental standards of conduct; the child acts in accordance with these standards even when the parent is absent and experiences guilt when he or she violates them.

Some psychologists question the psychoanalytic view of identification as an unconscious, unitary process. They point out that not all children identify with their parents in all respects. A girl, for example, may emulate her mother's social skills and sense of humor but not her moral values. These psychologists view identification as a form of learning: children imitate certain parental behaviors because they are rewarded for doing so. Siblings, peers, teachers, and TV heroes are other models who serve as sources of imitation or identification. According to this view, identification is a continuous process in which new responses are acquired as a result of both direct and vicarious experiences with parents and other models.

Most psychologists — regardless of how they define it — view identification as the basic process in the socialization of children. By modeling themselves after the important people in their environment, children acquire the attitudes and behaviors expected of adults in their society. Parents, because they are children's

A child identifies with the parent.

earliest and most frequent associates, serve as the primary source of identification. The parent of the same sex usually serves as the model for sex-typed behavior.

Sex Roles

All cultures define ways in which men and women are expected to behave. Certain personality characteristics, work tasks, and activities are considered appropriate for males, and others are appropriate for females. The definitions of sex-appropriate behavior vary from culture to culture and may change over time within a culture. Certainly, our view of appropriate masculine and feminine behavior today is radically different from what it was 50 years ago. Women are no longer expected to be dependent, submissive, and noncompetitive; men are not criticized for enjoying such domestic activities as cooking and child care or for expressing artistic and tender feelings. Standards of dress and appearance have also become much more unisex—indeed, from a distance it is often difficult to determine whether the individual in jeans and with medium-length hair is male or female. In the areas of education, work, and athletics, earlier sex-role differentiations have been breaking down. Nevertheless, within any culture the roles of men and women and the behavior expected of them still differ.

SEX TYPING *Sex typing* refers to the acquisition of characteristics and behaviors that a culture considers appropriate for females and males. Sex typing must be distinguished from *gender identity,* which is the degree to which one regards oneself as female or male. A girl may have a firm acceptance of herself as female and still not adopt all of the behaviors that her culture considers feminine or avoid all behaviors labeled masculine. A boy may identify with an artistic and sensitive father whose behavior does not fit the cultural masculine stereotype; the boy may be secure in his masculine identity, yet his behavior will not be strongly sex-typed.

Despite the current trend toward equality of the sexes, sex-role stereotypes are still prevalent in our culture. By *sex-role stereotypes,* we mean the belief that an individual should behave in certain ways or show certain characteristics because that person is male or female. For example, it is difficult to distinguish newborn boys from girls when their diapers are on. Yet adults, viewing newborn infants through the window of a hospital nursery, believe that they can detect differences. Infants thought to be boys are described as robust, strong, and large-featured; girls are seen as delicate, fine-featured, and "soft" (Luria & Rubin, 1974). To cite another example, college students viewed a videotape of a 9-month-old infant's responses to a variety of situations. Some students were led to believe that the infant was a boy, and others that the infant was a girl. When the infant showed a strong reaction to a jack-in-the-box, the reaction was more often labeled "anger" if the child was thought to be a boy and "fear" when the infant was thought to be a girl (Condry & Condry, 1976).

Children themselves evidence some knowledge of sex-role stereotypes as early as 2 years of age (see Table 3-3). They also begin to show sex-typed behavior in their choice of toys and play activities. In a day-care setting with a wide selection of toys available, male toddlers will spend more time playing with "masculine" toys (trucks, trains, tools) than "feminine" toys (dolls, tea sets) or "neutral" ones (chimes, stacking blocks). Likewise, female toddlers will spend more time with "feminine" toys (O'Brien & Huston, 1985). As they grow older, both boys and girls make increasingly more sex-typed choices. But boys show a

---

Both boys and girls believe that girls
    like to play with dolls
    like to help mother
    talk a lot
    never hit
    say "I need some help"
    will grow up to be a nurse or a
        teacher

Both boys and girls believe that boys
    like to play with cars
    like to help father
    like to build things
    say "I can hit you"
    will grow up to be boss

TABLE 3-3
Sex-Role Stereotypes in Young Children   *Two- and 3-year-olds were introduced to male and female paper dolls, Michael and Lisa, and then played a game in which they were asked to identify the doll that said or did certain things. For example, when the experimenter said "I like to play with dolls" and showed a sketch portraying dolls and a doll house, the child placed one of the two paper dolls in the picture. The children's choices for a number of such statements were tabulated. Many items were not sex typed. For example, neither boys nor girls believe that one sex more than the other is smart, runs fast, likes to play outside, says "I can't do it." On other items, boys and girls disagreed. For example, girls (but not boys) believe that boys like to fight, are mean, and say "I did it wrong." Boys (but not girls) believe that girls cry sometimes, and say "you hurt my feelings," or "you're not letting me have a turn." The items listed in the table are the sex-role stereotypes on which both boys and girls agreed. (After Kuhn, Nash, & Brucken, 1978)*

preference for same-sex toys earlier than girls, and they do so more consistently at every age. Boys appear to be more strongly sex-typed than girls.

How do we account for this difference? For one thing, there is an unfortunate tendency for both sexes to view "masculine" activities as superior to "feminine" ones. In addition, the taboos in our culture against feminine behavior for boys are stronger than those against masculine behavior for girls. Conforming to the masculine stereotype seems to be largely a matter of avoiding any behavior regarded as "sissyish." Four- and 5-year-old boys are more likely to experiment with feminine toys and activities (such as dolls, a lipstick and mirror, hair ribbons) when no one is watching than when an adult or another boy is present. For girls, the presence of an observer makes little difference in their choice of play activities (Hartup & Moore, 1963; Kobasigawa, Arakaki, & Awiguni, 1966). These findings suggest that young boys are interested in feminine activities but have learned to expect negative reactions for showing interest in them.

CAUSES OF SEX-TYPED BEHAVIOR   Parents clearly play a major role in sex typing. They serve as the child's first models of feminine and masculine behavior. Their attitudes toward their own sex roles and the way they interact with each other will influence the child's views. In addition, parents shape sex-typed behavior directly in numerous ways: by the toys they provide, the activities they encourage, and their responses to behaviors considered appropriate or inappropriate for the child's sex. From infancy on, most parents dress boys and girls differently and provide them with different toys. When they are old enough to be given household chores, girls are usually assigned such tasks as caring for younger children and helping with cleaning and food preparation. Boys are usually asked to do things outside the house, such as raking leaves or shoveling snow. Parents tend to emphasize independence, competition, and achievement in raising boys; girls are expected to be trustworthy, sensitive, and concerned with the welfare of others (Block, 1980).

Fathers appear to be more concerned with sex-typed behavior than mothers, particularly with their sons. They tend to react negatively (interfering with the child's play or expressing disapproval) when their sons play with "feminine" toys, whereas mothers do not. Fathers are less concerned when their daughters engage in "masculine" play, but they still show more disapproval than mothers do (Langlois & Downs, 1980).

Once children enter nursery school or kindergarten, their peers serve as models for imitation and also exert pressure toward sex-typed behavior. Parents who consciously seek to raise their children without the traditional sex-role stereotypes (by encouraging the child to engage in a wide range of activities without labeling any activity as masculine or feminine) are often dismayed to find their efforts undermined by peer pressure. Again, boys tend to experience more pressure than girls. Girls seem not to object to other girls playing with "boys'" toys or engaging in masculine activities. Boys, on the other hand, criticize other boys when they see them engaged in "girls'" activities. They are quick to call another boy a sissy if he plays with dolls, cries when he is hurt, or shows tender concern toward another child in distress (Langlois & Downs, 1980).

In addition to parental and peer influences, children's books and television programs play an important part in promoting sex-role stereotypes. Until recently, most children's books portrayed boys in active, problem-solving roles. They were the characters who displayed courage and heroism, persevered in the face of difficulty, constructed things, and achieved goals. Girls were usually much more passive. Female storybook characters were apt to display fear and avoidance of dangerous situations; they would give up easily, ask for help, and watch while

CRITICAL DISCUSSION

Sex Differences in Behavior

"Girls are more fluent verbally; boys are better at math." "Girls can memorize well, but boys are superior in abstract thinking." "Girls tend to be passive and to seek approval; boys are aggressive and independent." You have probably heard these and other claims about psychological differences between the sexes. What is the evidence? Do males and females differ consistently in abilities and personality traits? If so, are these differences the result of biology or of social learning? Two major reviews of the numerous books and research articles on the topic conclude that many common assumptions about sex differences are myths with no foundation in fact. But there do appear to be some real and interesting psychological differences between males and females (Maccoby & Jacklin, 1974; Deaux, 1985).

Tests of overall intelligence show no consistent sex differences — in part because the tests are designed not to. In constructing intelligence tests, care is taken either to eliminate items on which the sexes are found to differ or to balance items on which females have an advantage with those that give males an advantage. Tests of specific cognitive abilities, however, do show some sex differences. These differences, which are absent or negligible during childhood, begin to appear in early adolescence. For example, beginning at about 10 or 11 years of age, girls *on the average* outscore boys on many measures of *verbal ability* — vocabulary size, comprehension of difficult written material, and verbal fluency.

Although boys may lag behind in verbal skills, they tend *on the average* to be superior to girls on some tests of *visual-spatial ability* (Sanders, Soares, & D'Aquila, 1982). Visual-spatial skills are used in such tasks as conceptualizing how an object in space would look from a different perspective, aiming at a target, reading a map, or finding a simple geometric form embedded in a more complex figure (see Figure 3-11). The mathematical skills of boys also appear to increase faster than those of girls after age 13, but the differences are not as consistent as are those for spatial ability. Girls are about equal to boys on geometric and arithmetical problems, while boys excel in dealing with algebraic problems (Becker, 1983).

In talking about sex differences in cognitive abilities, two points should be stressed. First, the differences, although fairly consistent over studies, are *small* (Hyde, 1981). Second, it is important to remember that we are referring to *average* differences over large groups of youngsters; some girls are better at spatial and algebraic tasks than most boys, and some boys are more verbally fluent than most girls.

Because sex differences in these abilities do not emerge until adolescence, it seems reasonable to conclude that they reflect differences in training and social ex-

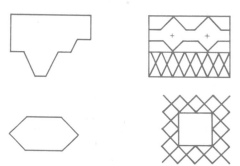

FIGURE 3-11
Embedded Figures Test *The subject must identify the simple figure on the left within the more complex one on the right.*

someone else achieved a goal. Similar differences have been noted in the sex roles portrayed in children's TV programs (Sternglanz & Serbin, 1974).

Attempts to modify children's sex-role stereotypes by exposing them to TV programs in which the stereotypes are reversed (for example, the girls win in athletic events or construct a clubhouse, or a girl is elected president) have shown some success (Davidson, Yasuna, & Tower, 1979). But exposure to television

pectations. After all, girls are usually encouraged to develop interests in poetry, literature, and drama; boys are expected to be more concerned with science, engineering, and mechanics. This is undoubtedly part of the cause, but it is also possible that some sex differences in ability may be based on biological differences that do not appear until the nervous system reaches a certain level of maturation—namely, puberty.

The timing of sexual maturity is related to specific abilities. A number of studies have found that late maturers outperform early maturers on visual-spatial tasks, independent of sex (Waber, 1977; Petersen, 1981; Sanders & Soares, 1986). There is also a maturation-related difference in the relative proficiency of verbal and visual-spatial skills within individuals: late maturers, like males, have higher spatial scores than verbal scores; whereas early maturers, like females, have higher verbal scores than spatial scores (Waber, 1977; Newcombe & Bandura, 1983). Mathematical ability may also be related to maturation rate. One study of 6,000 adolescents (ages 12 to 18) found that girls who matured late matched or outscored their male age-mates on tests of mathematical ability, and early-maturing boys had better verbal skills than late maturers (Carlsmith, Dornbusch, & Gross, 1983). Thus, early maturation appears to favor verbal skills, and late maturation favors spatial and mathematical abilities. Since females, on the average, mature earlier than males, rate of physical maturation may be one determiner of sex differences in ability.

The connection between maturity and cognitive skills is not known. It may be related to the rate at which the two hemispheres of the brain develop and become specialized for different abilities (see p. 48). Whatever the biological mechanism, the resulting differences in cognitive abilities are small, are not found in every sample studied, and are modifiable by experience (Waber, Mann, Merola, & Moylan, 1985).

In terms of personality traits, most studies have found surprisingly few differences between the sexes, particularly during the early years. Little girls are *not* more dependent than little boys, as is commonly believed, nor are they more sociable. Toddlers of both sexes seek to be close to their parents, especially when they are under stress, and they seem equally willing to leave their parents to explore a new environment (Maccoby & Jacklin, 1974). Differences in sociability show up only to the extent that boys during the elementary grades tend to play in "gangs," whereas girls are more apt to get together in groups of two or three.

The one area in which observed sex differences are consistent with popular beliefs is aggression. Boys are more aggressive than girls, starting at about age 2 or 3. Although there appear to be no differences in activity level, boys are much more prone than girls to engage in rough-and-tumble play—pushing, pulling, hitting, chasing, and wrestling with each other (Dipietro, 1981). This is true in a wide range of settings and for almost every culture that has been studied. Boys are not only more physically aggressive than girls but also more verbally aggressive; they are more likely than girls to exchange verbal taunts and insults.

Clearly, social learning has much to do with the expression of aggression. Many parents believe that a boy should be able to fight for his rights, and a boy has all kinds of aggressive models (in books, television, and movies) to show him how. Girls, on the other hand, are expected to get their way by more subtle means. In view of such social conditioning, it seems reasonable to assume that girls have the same potential for aggression as boys but inhibit its expression for fear of punishment. Some psychologists believe that this is the case (Feshbach & Feshbach, 1973). Others believe that, although social expectations and role models influence the expression of aggression, females are by their biological nature less aggressive (Maccoby & Jacklin, 1974). They point to the fact that girls show less aggression in their fantasies than boys. If girls are suppressing hostile impulses because of fear of punishment, such impulses might be expected to occur in fantasy or in "safe" situations. But even in an experimental situation where aggression is expected and encouraged—the subject is instructed to administer electric shocks to a "learner" whenever the learner makes a mistake—males tend to administer longer and stronger shocks to their victims than do females (Titley & Viney, 1969). These findings do not suggest that females have "bottled-up" aggression waiting for a safe outlet.

Studies of sex differences show that males and females are alike in more respects than is commonly supposed. Some of the differences found may be the result of social learning, and others may reflect biological predispositions. But even the differences that have a biological base can be modified by learning. For example, girls who initially score lower than boys on tests of visual-spatial ability can equal the boys' scores with a little practice. And certainly girls can be taught to be more aggressive (if necessary), and boys can learn to modify their aggressive responses.

In rearing their young, societies can accentuate what they believe to be innate differences, or they can choose to encourage in both sexes the characteristics most useful for their particular society.

cannot counteract real-life experiences. When 5- and 6-year-olds were shown films in which the usual sex-typed occupations were reversed (the doctors were women and the nurses were men), the children tended to relabel the occupations of the characters; when questioned about the films afterward and shown pictures of the actors, they were apt to identify the female actor as the nurse and the male as the doctor. Having a mother who worked outside the home or being exposed to female physicians and male nurses in real life increased the likelihood that the child would accept the less conventional roles (Cordua, McGraw, & Drabman, 1979).

Factors Influencing Identification

Many personal qualities are not strongly sex typed. Enthusiasm, sense of humor, friendliness, and integrity are characteristics shared by males and females. A child may learn such traits from *either* parent without violating the cultural sex roles. When college students were interviewed about their behavioral similarities to their parents in personality characteristics and interests, one-fourth of the men believed that they resembled their mothers in these respects, and a similar proportion of women thought they resembled their fathers; many reported resemblances to both parents (J. Hilgard, 1979).

Experiments give us clues as to the kinds of variables that influence identification. Several studies have shown that adults who are warm and nurturant are more likely to be imitated than those who are not. Boys who receive high scores on masculinity tests tend to have warmer, more affectionate relationships with their fathers than boys who receive low scores. Girls who are rated as quite feminine also have warmer, closer relationships with their mothers than do girls evaluated as less feminine (Mussen & Rutherford, 1963).

The adult's power in controlling the child's environment also affects the tendency to identify. When the mother is dominant, girls tend to identify much more with her than with the father, and in such cases, boys may have difficulty developing the masculine sex role. In father-dominant homes, girls are more similar to their fathers than in mother-dominant homes, but they still identify to a large degree with their mothers. For girls, a mother's warmth and self-confidence seem to be more important than her powerfulness (Hetherington & Frankie, 1967).

Another factor that influences identification is the perception of similarities between the child and the model. To the extent that a child has an objective basis for perceiving himself or herself as similar to the parent, the child will tend to identify with that parent. A girl who is tall and large-boned, with facial features similar to those of her father, may have more difficulty identifying with her petite mother than a younger sister who is similar to the mother in build.

To the extent that both parents are seen as nurturant, powerful, and competent, the child will identify with both, although the stronger identification generally will be with the parent of the same sex.

Identification With Siblings

Although parents are the primary identification figures, siblings play an important role, too. The sex of the other siblings influences the child's interests and behavior; girls with older brothers are likely to be more masculine (tomboyish) and competitive than girls with older sisters. Similarly, boys with older sisters tend to be less aggressive than boys with older brothers.

First-born or only children occupy a unique position in the family for several reasons. Parents have more time and attention to devote to their first child and are apt to be more cautious, indulgent, and protective. The first-born does not have to compete with older siblings; for a while, he or she has only adult models to copy and adult standards of conduct to emulate, whereas later-borns have siblings with whom to identify.

Research indicates that these factors do have an effect. First-born or only children are more likely to score at the upper extremes on intelligence tests, to do well in college, to earn graduate degrees, and to make it into the pages of *Who's Who* (Sutton-Smith, 1982). Among finalists for the National Merit Scholarship from two-children families, there are twice as many first-borns as second-borns. Among finalists from three-child families, there are as many first-borns as second- and third-borns combined (Nichols, 1968). First-born or only children have also been found to be more conscientious, cooperative, and cautious than later-born children (Altus, 1966). We should stress the fact that these are only *trends;* many famous achievers were later-born children (Benjamin Franklin, for example, was the 15th of 17 children), and many first-born children do not possess any of the characteristics just noted.

The more conscientious and cooperative nature of first-borns probably reflects an attempt to maintain their "privileged" status with the parents in the face of possible displacement by the newly arrived sibling. The later-born may feel less competent than the older sibling (not realizing that his or her inadequacies are a function of age) and may try to excel in other ways.

Although competition with younger siblings may partially account for the higher achievement of first-borns, it does not explain the equally high achievement of only children. The most likely explanation is that parents have more time and energy to devote to an only child (or to the first child), and thus may provide a richer, more stimulating environment. As the family becomes larger, the parents may pay increasingly less attention to each child.

ADOLESCENCE

Adolescence refers to the period of transition from childhood to adulthood. Its age limits are not clearly specified, but it extends roughly from age 12 to the late teens, when physical growth is nearly complete. During this period, the young person develops to sexual maturity, establishes an identity as an individual apart from the family, and faces the task of deciding how to earn a living.

A few generations ago, adolescence as we know it today was nonexistent. Many teenagers worked 14 hours a day and moved from childhood into the responsibilities of adulthood with little time for transition. With a decrease in the need for unskilled workers and an increase in the length of apprenticeship required to enter a profession, the interval between physical maturity and adult status has lengthened. Symbols of maturity such as financial independence from parents and completion of school are accomplished at later ages. Young people are not given many adult privileges until late in their teens; in most states, adolescents cannot work full-time, sign legal documents, drink alcoholic beverages, marry without parental consent, or vote.

A gradual transition to adult status has some advantages. It gives the young person a longer period in which to develop skills and to prepare for the future, but it tends to produce a period of conflict and vacillation between dependence and independence. It is difficult to feel completely self-sufficient while living at home or receiving financial support from one's parents.

Sexual Development

At the onset of adolescence, most youngsters experience a period of very rapid physical growth (the *adolescent growth spurt*) accompanied by the gradual

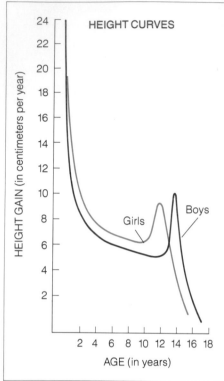

HEIGHT CURVES

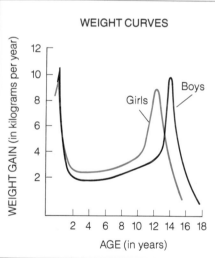

WEIGHT CURVES

FIGURE 3-12
Annual Gains in Height and Weight
The period of most rapid growth comes earlier for girls than for boys. (After Tanner, 1970)

development of reproductive organs and *secondary sex characteristics* (breast development in girls, beard growth in boys, and the appearance of pubic hair in both sexes). These changes take place over a period of about two or three years; *puberty,* the age at which the adolescent is theoretically capable of producing offspring, occurs toward the end. Puberty is marked by menstruation in girls and by the appearance of live sperm cells in the semen of boys.

There is wide variation in the age at which a youngster reaches puberty. Some girls menstruate as early as 11, others as late as 17; the average age is 12 years 9 months. Boys, on the average, experience their growth spurt and mature two years later than girls (see Figure 3-12). They begin to discharge semen with live sperm sometime between age 12 and 16; the average age is 14½ years. Boys and girls average the same height and weight until about 11, when the girls suddenly spurt ahead. Girls maintain this difference for about two years, at which point the boys forge ahead and remain there for the rest of their lives. This difference in rate of physical development is striking in seventh- and eighth-grade classrooms, where quite mature young women can be observed seated alongside immature boys.

Although girls on the average mature earlier than boys, there are large individual differences. Some girls will mature *later* than some boys. Numerous studies have investigated whether there are personality differences between early- and late-maturing children. How does a late-maturing boy feel when he is shorter than most of his classmates? How does an early-maturing girl feel when she towers over most of the boys in her class?

Late-maturing boys face a particularly difficult adjustment because of the importance of strength and physical prowess in their peer activities. During the period when they are shorter and less sturdy than their classmates, they may lose out on practice of game skills and may never catch up with the early maturers, who take the lead in physical activities. Studies indicate that boys who mature late tend to be less popular than their classmates, have poorer self-concepts, and engage in more immature attention-seeking behavior. They feel rejected and dominated by their peers. The early maturers, on the other hand, tend to be more self-confident and independent. Some of these personality differences between early and late maturers persist into adulthood, long after the physical differences have disappeared (M. C. Jones, 1965).

The effects of rate of maturation on personality are less clear-cut for girls. Some early-maturing girls are embarrassed by the fact that their bodies are more womanly in shape than those of their female age-mates—particularly since current standards for female attractiveness as promoted by the media emphasize the "lean, lithe look." They may also be troubled by being taller than most of their age-mates of either sex. Others take their greater physical maturity to be an asset, just as early-maturing boys do. One study found that whether an adolescent girl matured early or late did not influence her prestige among her peers (Harper & Collins, 1972). Another found that early-maturing girls were at a disadvantage in the late elementary grades because they were more grown up than their peers; but by junior high school the early maturers tended to be more popular among their classmates and to be leaders in school activities (Weatherly, 1964).

Sexual Standards and Behavior

The last 25 years have witnessed an almost revolutionary change in attitudes toward sexual activity in most Western societies. Views regarding premarital sex, homosexuality, extramarital sex, and specific sexual acts are probably more open and permissive today than they have been at any time in recent history. Young

Sexual maturity varies among young adolescents.

people are exposed to sexual stimuli in magazines, on television, and by the movies to a greater extent than ever before. Satisfactory birth control methods and the availability of abortions have lessened fear of pregnancy. All of these changes give the newly matured individual more freedom today. These changes may produce more conflict, too, since guidelines for "appropriate" behavior are less clear-cut than they were in the past. In some families, the divergence between adolescent and parental standards of sexual morality may be great.

Have more permissive attitudes toward sex been accompanied by changes in actual behavior? At first, some experts maintained that young people were simply being more open about activities that their predecessors carried on in secret. But the data indicate definite changes in adolescent sexual behavior. A nationwide survey of 13- to 19-year-olds in 1973 found that 59 percent of the boys and 45 percent of the girls had engaged in sexual intercourse, most of them before age 16 (Sorensen, 1973). A 1976 survey found that 55 percent of the 19-year-old females interviewed had experienced sex (Zelnik & Kanter, 1977). More recent estimates remain about the same as those for 1976: about half of all young men and women have experienced sexual intercourse by the age of 18 (Brozan, 1985).

Although strictly comparable data from earlier periods are not available, the studies conducted by Alfred Kinsey in the late 1930s and the 1940s found that fewer than 20 percent of the females and about 40 percent of the males reported experiencing sexual intercourse by the time they were 20 years old. Today's adolescents are engaging in sexual activity at an earlier age than their parents did. The change is most dramatic for girls, who are now as likely as boys to have intercourse while still in their teens (see Table 3-4).

The change in sex standards does not seem to be in the direction of greater promiscuity. Although some of the boys said they had experienced intercourse with several partners, most of the girls reported they had limited their sexual relations to one boy with whom they were "in love" at the time. These young people feel that sex is a part of love and of intimate relationships and that it need not necessarily be restricted to the context of marriage.

STUDY AND YEAR	PERCENTAGE REPORTING SEXUAL INTERCOURSE
Kinsey et al. (1938–1949)	18
Sorensen (1973)	45
Zelnik & Kantner (1976)	55

TABLE 3-4
Premarital Intercourse Among Teenage Females   *The table gives the percentage of 19-year-old, unmarried females who reported having experienced sexual intercourse. The period of data collection is given below each study. This and other evidence indicate a marked increase in premarital sexual experience over the past 50 years.*

CRITICAL DISCUSSION

Teenage Pregnancy

The most troubling aspect of the increase in adolescent sexual activity is teenage pregnancy. The pregnancy rate for unmarried mothers under age 18 has been increasing rapidly in the United States since 1960. Studies estimate that about 31 to 39 percent of teenage girls will become pregnant if current rates persist (Senderowitz & Paxman, 1985)—and many of them will be under age 15.

An adolescent girl who became pregnant 25 years ago usually married or gave up her baby for adoption. Abortion was not a legal option until 1973, when the Supreme Court ruled that the procedure could not be outlawed. Today, if a girl chooses not to abort her pregnancy (and some 45 percent of teenagers decide to follow this course), chances are she will keep the baby and raise it as a single parent. A decade ago, more than 90 percent of babies born out of wedlock were given up for adoption; today, almost 90 percent are kept by the mother.

Children raising children has enormous social consequences. Teenage mothers often do not complete high school, and many live below the poverty level, dependent on welfare. Their infants have high rates of illness and mortality and later in life often experience emotional and educational problems. Many are victims of child abuse at the hands of parents too immature to understand why their baby is crying or how their doll-like plaything has suddenly developed a will of its own.

With effective methods of contraception more widely available than ever before, why do so many girls have unplanned pregnancies? Part of the explanation is ignorance about the process of reproduction. Surveys find that fewer than half of the teenagers questioned know when in the menstrual cycle a woman is most likely to become pregnant (Morrison, 1985). Since low pregnancy risk due to "time of month" is a common reason adolescents give for not using contraception, this lack of information has important consequences. Other frequently reported bits of misinformation

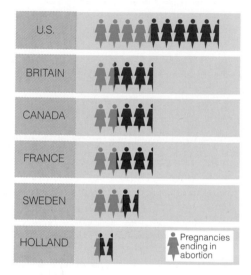

FIGURE 3-13

Teenage Pregnancy Rates *Shown are pregnancy rates per 1,000 teenage females; each figure represents 10 pregnancies. The teenage pregnancy rate in the United States (95 per 1,000) is more than double that of any of the other countries.*

Search for Identity

A major task confronting the adolescent is to develop a sense of individual *identity,* to find answers to the questions "Who am I?" and "Where am I going?" The search for personal identity involves deciding what is important or worth doing and formulating standards of conduct for evaluating one's own behavior as well as the behavior of others. It also involves feelings about self-worth and competence, as well as defining oneself with regard to sexuality and sex roles. While development of a self-image and sexual identity starts in early childhood and continues throughout the life span, adolescence is a particularly critical period. Compared to younger children, early adolescents, beginning about the age of 12, are highly self-conscious and have uncertain images of themselves.

include the belief that you cannot become pregnant from your first intercourse, or if you have sex infrequently, or if you do it standing up.

Fewer than one-third of sexually active adolescents regularly use a method of contraception. About 25 percent never use contraception; the rest do sometimes (Morrison, 1985). Among the reasons given for not using contraceptive methods (in addition to erroneous beliefs about the likelihood of getting pregnant) is the unplanned nature of intercourse and a generally negative attitude toward contraception. Many adolescents say that contraceptives are "embarrassing," "messy," or "unnatural" and interfere with the enjoyment of sex. A theme underlying these complaints is the feeling that being prepared robs sex of its spontaneity and is also somewhat immoral. Adolescent girls who are uncomfortable admitting their sexuality to themselves prefer to be swept away romantically rather than to prepare for sex: if you are swept away by passion, then you did not do anything wrong; but if you go on a date with a diaphragm or after taking the pill, then you are looking for sex and can be labeled "bad" or "promiscuous."

Teenage pregnancy rates in the United States are more than double that of any other industrialized country (see Figure 3-13). American adolescents are not more sexually active than their foreign peers. Nor is the difference due to higher abortion rates abroad; indeed, they are much higher here (Brozan, 1985). Most experts attribute the high rates of teenage pregnancy in this country to a cultural ambivalence about teenage sex. The popular

media—television, rock music, movies—encourage early experimentation with sex. They convey the message that to be sophisticated one must be sexually hip. Yet at the same time we are reluctant to acknowledge adolescent sexuality and to help teenagers prevent pregnancy. The TV networks are not willing to show programs dealing with contraception; many teenagers report that their parents are reluctant to discuss birth control; sex education in the schools is still a controversial topic; and high school clinics that give birth control counseling

and dispense contraceptives are even more controversial.

In contrast are countries like Sweden where schoolchildren, starting at age 7, receive instruction in reproductive biology and by age 10 or 12 have been introduced to the various types of contraceptives. The aim is to demystify sex so that familiarity will make the child less likely to fall prey to unwanted pregnancy and venereal disease. These efforts appear to be successful; Sweden has one of the lowest rates of teenage pregnancy.

Two posters prepared by the Children's Defense Fund for its campaign aimed at reducing teenage pregnancies. The theme of the campaign is "Having a baby when you're a teenager can do more than just take away your freedom, it can take away your dreams." (Courtesy Children's Defense Fund)

An adolescent's sense of identity develops gradually out of the various identifications of childhood. Young children's values and moral standards are largely those of their parents; their feelings of self-esteem stem primarily from their parents' view of them. As youngsters move into the wider world of junior high school, the values of the peer group become increasingly important, as do the appraisals of teachers and other adults. Adolescents try to synthesize these values and appraisals into a consistent picture. To the extent that parents, teachers, and peers project consistent values, the search for identity becomes easier.

When parental views and values differ markedly from those of peers and other important figures, the possibility for conflict is great and the adolescent may experience what has been called *role confusion:* the adolescent tries one role

Adolescence is a particularly critical period for the development of a self-image. Dressing according to a particular style enables a teenager to identify with a group.

after another and has difficulty synthesizing the different roles into a single identity. As one teenage girl put it,

> I'm fairly prim and proper at home because my parents have firm views about how a young girl should behave. At school, I toe the line too, although I don't hesitate to express my opinions. When I'm with my girl friends, I relax and act fairly silly; I'm usually the first to suggest smoking pot or doing something crazy. On a date, I tend to act helpless and docile. Who am I really?

In a simple society where identification models are few and social roles are limited, the task of forming an identity is relatively easy. In a society as complex and rapidly changing as ours, it is a difficult and lengthy task for many adolescents. They are faced with an almost infinite array of possibilities in terms of how to behave and what to do in life.

One way of approaching the identity problem is to try various roles and ways of behaving. Many experts believe that adolescence should be a period of role experimentation, in which the youngster can explore different ideologies and interests. They are concerned that today's academic competition and career pressures are depriving many adolescents of the opportunity to explore. As a result, some are "dropping out" temporarily to have time to think about what they want to do in life and to experiment with various identities. Youth movements, both political and religious, often provide temporary commitments to an alternative life-style; they give the young person a group to identify with and time to formulate a more permanent set of beliefs.

The search for identity can be resolved in a number of ways. Some young people, after a period of experimentation and soul searching, commit themselves to a life goal and proceed toward it. For some, the *identity crisis* may not occur at all; these are adolescents who accept their parents' values without question and who proceed toward adult roles that are consistent with their parents' views. In a sense, their identity "crystallized" early in life.

Still other young people adopt a *deviant* identity, one that is at odds with the values of their family or of society. For example, a young man who has been pressured all his life to go to law school and join the family firm may rebel and decide to become a bum. Some ghetto adolescents, rather than risk failure in attempting to rise above their social conditions, may adopt a deviant identity and take pride in being "nothing."

Other adolescents may go through a prolonged period of *identity confusion* and have great difficulty "finding themselves." In some cases, an identity definition may ultimately be worked out after much trial and error. In others, the person may never have a strong sense of personal identity even as an adult. This is the individual who never develops any commitments or loyalties.

An individual's personal identity, once formed, is not necessarily static. People can acquire new interests, ideas, and skills during their adult years that may change their sense of who they are. Married women, for example, often find a new sense of identity as their child-rearing duties diminish and they have time to develop new interests or pursue a career.

DEVELOPMENT AS A LIFELONG PROCESS

Development does not end with the attainment of physical maturity. It is a continuous process extending from birth through adulthood to old age. Bodily changes occur throughout life, affecting the individual's attitudes, cognitive processes, and behavior. The kinds of problems people must cope with change throughout the life span, too.

Erik Erikson has proposed a series of eight stages to characterize development from the cradle to the grave. He calls them *psychosocial stages* because he believes that the psychological development of individuals depends on the social relations established at various points in life. At each stage, there are special problems or "crises" to be confronted. Although these stages, shown in Table 3-5, are not based on scientific evidence, they call attention to the kinds of problems people encounter during life.

We touched on some of these problems earlier in the chapter, noting that an infant's feelings of trust in other people depend to a large extent on the way early needs are handled by the mother. During the second year of life (when children begin to move about on their own), they want to explore, to investigate, and to do things for themselves. To the extent that parents encourage such activities, children begin to develop a sense of independence or autonomy. They learn to control some of their impulses and to feel pride in their accomplishments. Overprotection—restricting what the child is permitted to do—or ridiculing unsuccessful attempts may cause the child to doubt his or her abilities.

During the preschool years (ages 3 through 5), children progress from simple self-control to an ability to initiate activities and carry them out. Again, parental attitudes—encouraging or discouraging—can make children feel inadequate (or guilty, if the child initiates an activity that the adult views as shameful).

During the elementary school years, children learn the skills valued by society. These include not only reading and writing but also physical skills and

TABLE 3-5
Stages of Psychosocial Development *Problems in relating to other people change with age. Erikson defines eight major life stages in terms of the psychosocial problems, or crises, that must be resolved. (After Erikson, 1963)*

STAGES	PSYCHOSOCIAL CRISES	SIGNIFICANT SOCIAL RELATIONSHIPS	FAVORABLE OUTCOME
1. First year of life	Trust versus mistrust	Mother or mother substitute	Trust and optimism
2. Second year	Autonomy versus doubt	Parents	Sense of self-control and adequacy
3. Third through fifth years	Initiative versus guilt	Basic family	Purpose and direction; ability to initiate one's own activities
4. Sixth year to puberty	Industry versus inferiority	Neighborhood; school	Competence in intellectual, social, and physical skills
5. Adolescence	Identity versus confusion	Peer groups and outgroups; models of leadership	An integrated image of oneself as a unique person
6. Early adulthood	Intimacy versus isolation	Partners in friendship and sex; competition, cooperation	Ability to form close and lasting relationships; to make career commitments
7. Middle adulthood	Generativity versus self-absorption	Divided labor and shared household	Concern for family, society, and future generations
8. The aging years	Integrity versus despair	"Mankind"; "My Kind"	A sense of fulfillment and satisfaction with one's life; willingness to face death

the ability to share responsibility and to get along with other people. To the extent that efforts in these areas are successful, children develop feelings of competence; unsuccessful efforts result in feelings of inferiority.

Finding one's personal identity, as we noted in the last section, is the major psychosocial crisis of adolescence.

Early Adulthood

During the early adult years, people commit themselves to an occupation, and many will marry or form other types of intimate relationships. Intimacy means an ability to care about others and to share experiences with them. People who cannot commit themselves to a loving relationship — because they fear being hurt or are unable to share — risk being isolated. Studies indicate that an intimate relationship with a supportive partner contributes significantly to a person's emotional and physical health. People who have someone to share their ideas, feelings, and problems with are happier and healthier than those who do not (see Traupmann & Hatfield, 1981).

The percentage of individuals who marry has declined since the late 1960s. More people are living alone or cohabitating without legal ties. Nevertheless, most people do marry, and most of them do so during the early adult years. Individuals tend to look for marriage partners whose ethnic, social, and religious backgrounds match their own. Contrary to popular opinion, women appear to be less romantic in their approach to mate selection than men. Men tend to fall in love more quickly than women and to be satisfied with the qualities of their prospective mate. Women, on the other hand, are more practical and cautious in deciding whom to marry (Rubin, 1973).

This finding is not surprising when we consider that marriage traditionally requires a greater change in life-style for women than for men. A married man usually continues in his career, whereas a woman may be required to give up the relative independence of single life for the demands and responsibilities of wife and mother. Egalitarian marriages in which family and financial responsibilities are shared and the careers of both partners are given equal consideration are increasing in number. Nevertheless, for most women, the person she marries determines where and how well she lives, as well as what her role in life will be.

Once married, both partners must learn to adapt to new demands and responsibilities. The arrival of children requires even greater adjustment. That such adjustments are not easy in a society as complex as ours is indicated by the high divorce rate. More than 38 percent of all *first* marriages in the United States end in divorce. Taking into account remarriages and divorces, about 40 percent of *all* marriages end in divorce.

A survey of 300 couples who had been happily married for 15 years or more provides some clues for a successful marriage. The most frequently named reason for an enduring and happy marriage was having a generally positive attitude toward one's spouse: viewing one's partner as one's best friend and liking him or her as a person. Among the characteristics that the partners liked in each other were qualities of caring, giving, integrity, and a sense of humor. In essence, they said, "I am married to someone who cares about me, who is concerned for my well-being, who gives as much or more than he or she gets, who is open and trustworthy and who is not mired down in a somber, bleak outlook on life" (Lauer & Lauer, 1985, p. 24). They also liked the fact that their spouses had changed and grown more interesting over the years.

Other elements important to a lasting marriage were a belief in marriage as a long-term commitment, agreement on common goals, and the ability to commu-

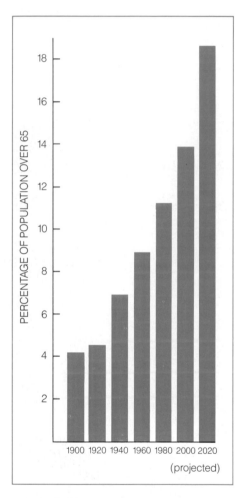

FIGURE 3-14
Aging America *The percentage of the population in the United States over age 65 is increasing at a steady rate and is projected to continue to increase. For babies born in the United States today, life expectancy is an unprecedented 71.1 years for a boy and 78.3 years for a girl. For those who survive through middle age, the expected length of life is dramatically longer. A man who reaches 65 today can expect to live until 79.5 and a woman, to 83.7. (U.S. Bureau of the Census, 1986)*

nicate with each other and to resolve problems calmly without venting anger. Surprisingly, agreement about sex was far down the list of reasons for a happy marriage. While most were generally satisfied with their sex lives, few listed it as a major reason for their happiness; those who were dissatisfied felt that sex was less important than understanding, friendship, and respect (Lauer & Lauer, 1985).

Middle Adulthood

For many people, the middle years of adulthood (roughly ages 40 to 65) are the most productive period. Men in their forties are usually at the peak of their careers. Women have less responsibility at home, because the children are growing up, and can devote more time to career or civic activities. This is the age group that essentially runs society, in terms of both power and responsibility.

Erikson uses the term *generativity* to refer to a concern in middle adulthood with guiding and providing for the next generation. Feelings of satisfaction at this stage in life come from helping teenage children become adults, providing for others who need help, and seeing your contributions to society as valuable. Feelings of despair may come from the realization that you have not achieved the goals set as a young adult or that what you are doing is not important.

As people approach their fifties, their view of the life span tends to change. Instead of looking at life in terms of time since birth, as younger people do, they begin to think in terms of years left to live. Having faced the aging or death of their parents, they begin to realize the inevitability of their own death. At this point, many people restructure their lives in terms of priorities, deciding what is important to do in the years remaining. A man who has spent his years building a successful company may leave it to return to school. A woman who has raised her family may develop a new career or become active in politics. A couple may leave their jobs in the city to purchase a small farm.

The Later Years

The years after 65 bring new problems. Declining physical strength limits the older person's activities; a debilitating illness can make the individual feel demoralizingly helpless. Retirement, which brings idle hours to be filled, may lessen feelings of worth and self-esteem. The death of a spouse, siblings, and friends can make life unbearably lonely, particularly for those whose children live far away. Since the proportion of older people in the population is progressively increasing (see Figure 3-14), such problems require renewed attention and research. Retirement villages and programs that actively involve older people in community life — as teacher aids, library assistants, guards at school crossings — have proved to be a step in the right direction.

Despite the obvious problems of aging, a study of 70- to 79-year-olds suggests that growing old is not as bad as is commonly thought: 75 percent reported that they were satisfied with their lives after retirement. Most were fairly active and not lonely, and few showed signs of senility or mental illness (Neugarten, 1971).

Erikson's last psychosocial crisis, of integrity versus despair, is concerned with the way a person faces the end of life. Old age is a time of reflection, of looking back on the events of a lifetime. To the extent that an individual has successfully coped with the problems posed at each of the earlier stages of life, he or she has a sense of wholeness and integrity, of a life well lived. If the elderly person looks back on life with regret, seeing it as a series of missed opportunities and failures, the final years will be ones of despair.

Volunteering at a day-care center and participating in athletic events are two of the many ways that seniors can stay active.

SUMMARY

1. Human development is determined by a continuous interaction between *heredity* or *nature* (characteristics specified by the individual's genes) and *environment* or *nurture* (the experiences encountered while growing up in a particular family and culture). Genetic determinants express themselves through the process of *maturation:* innately determined sequences of growth or bodily changes that are relatively independent of the environment. Motor development, for example, is largely a maturational process because all children master skills such as crawling, standing, and walking in the same sequence and at roughly the same age.

2. Development proceeds in *orderly sequences* from simple behaviors to those that are more differentiated and complex. Two unresolved questions concern (a) whether development should be viewed as a *continuous process* or a series of successive *stages* that are qualitatively different from each other, and (b) the existence of *critical periods* during which specific experiences must occur for psychological development to proceed normally.

3. Infants are born with well-functioning sensory systems, they are preprogrammed to learn about the world, and they show individual differences in *temperament*. Although the development of physical skills depends largely on maturation, restricted environments can delay motor development, and increased stimulation can accelerate it. Early deprivation or stimulation do not appear to have a lasting effect on motor skills, but development in other areas — language, intelligence, personality — may be permanently affected by early experiences.

4. Piaget's theory describes stages in *cognitive development,* proceeding from the *sensorimotor stage* (where an important discovery is *object permanence*), through the *preoperational stage* (symbols begin to be used), and the *concrete operational stage* (*conservation* concepts develop), to the *formal operational stage* (hypotheses are tested systematically in problem solving). Nonstage theories view cognitive development as a gradual increase in knowledge and information-processing skills, such as memory.

5. Early social attachments form the basis for close interpersonal relations in adulthood. Insensitive mothering may undermine the child's trust and produce *insecure attachment*. Children who are *securely attached* are better able to cope with new experiences and to relate to others. Interactions with siblings and peers are also important for normal development.

6. Children's concepts of right and wrong change as they mature. Younger children tend to evaluate moral actions in terms of anticipated *rewards* and *punishments;* with increasing age, *avoiding disapproval* and *conforming to social norms* become important. In the highest stage of moral reasoning, actions are evaluated in terms of one's own ethical principles. *Moral behavior* depends on a number of factors in addition to the ability to reason about moral issues.

7. Although no consistent relationships have been found between specific child-rearing techniques and later personality traits, a child's competency and self-confidence are best fostered by a warm and nurturant home where parents reward responsible behavior but also encourage independent actions and decision making.

8. Children acquire the attitudes and behaviors expected by society — self-control, a conscience, and the appropriate sex role — largely through the process of *identification. Sex typing,* the acquisition of those characteristics and behaviors society considers appropriate for a particular sex, develops through parental, peer, and cultural influences. It is distinct from *gender identity,* which is the degree to which one regards oneself as female or male. Children are most apt to identify with adults who are warm, nurturant, and powerful, and whom they view as similar to themselves in some way.

9. The age at which adolescents reach *puberty,* or sexual maturity, varies greatly, although girls, on the average, mature two years earlier than boys. Late-maturing boys tend to be less popular with their peers and to have poorer self-concepts

than boys who mature early; the effects of maturation rate on personality are less clear-cut for girls. Survey data indicate that adolescents today are engaging in sexual intercourse at an earlier age than did their parents.

10. In their search for personal *identity*, adolescents try to synthesize the values and views of people important to them (parents, teachers, and peers) into a cohesive self-picture. When these values are not consistent, adolescents may experience *role confusion*, trying out one social role after another before finding a sense of individual identity.

11. Development is a life-long process: individuals change both physically and psychologically, and they encounter new adjustment problems throughout life. Erikson's *psychosocial stages* describe problems, or crises, in social relations that must be confronted at various points in life. These range from "trust versus mistrust" during the first year of life, through "intimacy versus isolation" in early adulthood, to "integrity versus despair" as individuals face death.

FURTHER READING

Comprehensive textbooks on development include Skolnick, *The Psychology of Human Development* (1986); Fischer and Lazerson, *Human Development: From Conception Through Adolescence* (1984); Mussen, Conger, Kagan, and Huston, *Child Development and Personality* (6th ed., 1984); Bee, *The Developing Child* (4th ed., 1985).

Books focusing on infancy include Osofsky (ed.), *Handbook of Infant Development* (1979); Lamb and Campos, *Development in Infancy: An Introduction* (1982); and Rosenblith and Sims-Knight, *In the Beginning: Development in the First Two Years* (1985). A four-volume overview of the major theories and research in child development may be found in Mussen (ed.), *Handbook of Child Psychology* (4th ed., 1983).

Cognitive Development (2nd ed., 1985) by Flavell presents a thorough introduction to this topic. *The Development of Memory in Children* (2nd ed., 1984) by Kail provides a very readable summary of research on children's memory. For a brief introduction to Piaget, see Phillips, *Piaget's Theory: A Primer* (1981).

The problems of adolescence are dealt with in Conger and Peterson, *Adolescence and Youth: Psychological Development in a Changing World* (3rd ed., 1983); Kimmel and Wiener, *Adolescence: A Developmental Transition* (1985); and Rice, *The Adolescent: Development, Relationships, and Culture* (4th ed., 1984).

For the later years, see Kennedy, *Human Development: The Adult Years and Aging* (1978); and Poon (ed.), *Aging in the 1980s: Psychological Issues* (1980).

Part Three

ELLIOTT ERWITT
Venice, 1965

Gelatin-silver print, 9¼ × 13⅞″.
Collection, The Museum of Modern Art,
New York. Purchase.

CONSCIOUSNESS AND PERCEPTION

States of Consciousness

As you read these words, are you awake or dreaming? Hardly anyone is confused by this question. We all know the difference between an ordinary state of wakefulness and the experience of dreaming. We also recognize other states of *consciousness,* including those induced by drugs such as alcohol and marijuana.

A person's state of consciousness is changing all the time. At this moment, your attention may be focused on this book; in a few minutes, you may be sunk in reverie. To most psychologists, an *altered state of consciousness* exists whenever there is a change from an ordinary pattern of mental functioning to a state that *seems* different to the person experiencing the change. Although this is not a very precise definition, it reflects the fact that states of consciousness are personal and therefore subjective. Altered states of consciousness can vary from the distraction of a vivid daydream to the confusion and perceptual distortion of drug intoxication. In this chapter, we will look at some states of consciousness that are experienced by everyone (sleep and dreams, for instance), as well as some that result from special circumstances (meditation, hypnosis, and the use of drugs).

ASPECTS OF CONSCIOUSNESS

Many topics discussed in other chapters have a direct bearing on the study of consciousness. When psychologists ask how we interpret sensory information (Chapters 5 and 6), how we store and retrieve memories (Chapters 7 and 8), and how we think and solve problems (Chapter 9), they are essentially raising questions about consciousness.

But what is consciousness? We use the word most often as a collective term for an individual's perceptions, thoughts, feelings, and memories that are active at a given moment. In this sense, consciousness is synonymous with awareness. However, as we will see, consciousness also includes perceptions and thoughts of which the individual may be only dimly aware until his or her attention is drawn to them. Hence, there are degrees of awareness within consciousness.

The early psychologists equated "consciousness" with "mind." In fact, they defined psychology as "the study of mind and consciousness" (see Table 1-1, p. 13) and used the introspective method to study consciousness. As noted in Chapter 1, both introspection as a method and consciousness as a topic for investigation fell from favor with the rise of behaviorism in the early 1900s. John Watson, the founder of behaviorism, and his followers believed that if psychology were to become a science, its data must be objective and measurable. Behavior could be publicly observed and various responses could be objectively measured. In contrast, an individual's private experiences, as revealed through introspection, could not be observed by others or objectively measured.

Since the 1960s, the increasingly cognitive orientation of many psychologists, together with other developments, has revived interest in consciousness. A strict behaviorist insistence on observable actions now seems too confining, and most psychologists would hesitate to say that subjectivity and science are incompatible.

Consciousness

Despite the reemergence of the study of consciousness in psychology, there is still no common agreement on a definition of the term. For our purposes, we will adopt the following definition: we are conscious when we are aware of external and internal events, reflect on our past experiences, engage in problem solving, are selective in attending to some stimuli rather than others, and deliberately choose and execute an action in response to environmental conditions and personal goals. In short, consciousness has to do with (1) *monitoring* ourselves and our environment so that percepts, memories, and thoughts are accurately represented in awareness; and (2) *controlling* ourselves and our environment so that we are able to initiate and terminate behavioral and cognitive activities (modified from Kihlstrom, 1984).

MONITORING   Receiving information from the environment is the main function of the body's sensory systems, leading to awareness of what is going on in our surroundings as well as within our own bodies. But we could not possibly attend to all of the stimuli that impinge on our senses; there would be an information overload. Our consciousness focuses on some stimuli and ignores others. Often the information selected has to do with changes in our external or internal world. While concentrating on this paragraph, you are probably unaware of numerous background stimuli. But should there be a change in stimulation — should the lights dim, the air begin to smell smoky, or the noise of the air conditioning system cease — your attention would be drawn to it.

Our attention is selective; some events take precedence over others in gaining access to consciousness and in initiating action. Events that are important to survival usually have top priority. If we are hungry, it is difficult for us to concentrate on studying; a sudden pain crowds other thoughts out of consciousness until action is taken to alleviate it.

CONTROLLING   Another function of consciousness is to plan, initiate, and guide our actions. Whether the plan is simple and readily completed (such as meeting a friend for lunch) or complex and long-range (such as preparing for a career in medicine), our actions must be guided and arranged to coordinate with events around us.

In planning, events that have not yet occurred can be represented in consciousness as future possibilities; we may envision alternative "scenarios," make choices, and initiate appropriate activities.

Subconscious Processes and Preconscious Memories

From all that is going on around us now and from our store of knowledge and memories of past events, we can focus attention on only a few stimuli at a given moment. We ignore, select, and reject all the time, so that consciousness is continually changing. But objects or events that are not the focus of attention

Reflection is one aspect of consciousness.

can still have some influence on consciousness. For example, you may not be aware of hearing a clock strike the hour. After a few strokes, you become alert; then you can go back and count the strokes that you did not know you heard. Another example of peripheral attention is the *cocktail party phenomenon*: you are talking to someone in a crowded room, ignoring the other voices and general noise, when the sound of your own name in another conversation catches your attention. Clearly, you would not have detected your name in the other conversation if you had not, in some sense, been monitoring that conversation; you were not consciously aware of the other conversation until a special signal drew your attention to it. A considerable body of research indicates that we register and evaluate stimuli that we do not consciously perceive. These stimuli are said to influence us *subconsciously* or to operate at a subconscious level of awareness.

Many memories and thoughts that are not part of your consciousness at this moment can be brought to consciousness when needed. You may not be conscious right now of your vacation last summer, but the memories are accessible if you wish to retrieve them; then they become a vivid part of your consciousness. Memories that are available to consciousness are called *preconscious memories*. They include specific memories of personal events, as well as the information accumulated over a lifetime, such as one's knowledge of language, music, and the location of Alaska.

We can think of preconscious memories and subconsciously perceived events as being on the fringe of consciousness. They are not in the spotlight, but they influence consciousness nevertheless.

The Unconscious

According to the psychoanalytic theories of Sigmund Freud and his followers, some memories, impulses, and desires are not available to consciousness. Psychoanalytic theory assigns these to the *unconscious*. Freud believed that emotionally painful memories and wishes are sometimes *repressed* — that is, diverted to the unconscious, where they continue to influence our actions even though we are not aware of them. Thoughts and impulses repressed to the unconscious are assumed to reach consciousness only in indirect or disguised ways — through dreams, irrational behavior, mannerisms, and slips of the tongue. In fact, the term "Freudian slip" is commonly used to refer to unintentional remarks that are assumed to reveal hidden impulses. Saying "I'm sad you're better," while intending to say "I'm glad you're better," would be an example.

Freud believed that unconscious desires and impulses are the cause of most mental illnesses. He developed the method of psychoanalysis, the goal of which is to draw the repressed material to consciousness and, in so doing, cure the individual (see Chapter 16).

The concept of the unconscious remains controversial in modern psychology. A more contemporary approach talks about *levels* of awareness rather than a sharp dichotomy between conscious and unconscious determinants of behavior. We are more sensitive to stimuli around us than we are consciously aware of or are able to report. Thus, we are unaware of some things that influence us, not because they are repressed to the unconscious, but because they entered consciousness at a level below our ability to report them (Bowers, 1984; Kihlstrom, 1984).

In this section we have introduced four concepts — consciousness, subconscious processes, preconscious memories, and the unconscious — and assigned them definitions. Not all psychologists believe that these concepts are necessary or agree with the definitions given here. Nevertheless, versions of these concepts

"Good morning, beheaded — uh, I mean beloved."

Drawing by Dana Fradon; © 1979 *The New Yorker Magazine*, Inc.

Divided consciousness: extreme familiarity with a skill makes actions automatic, so that we can perform two tasks simultaneously.

are so pervasive in psychology that one needs to be familiar with the ideas, even though different theorists define them somewhat differently.

Divided Consciousness

An important function of consciousness is the control of our actions. But some activities are practiced so often that they become habitual, or automatic. Learning to drive a car requires intense concentration at first. We have to concentrate on coordinating the different actions (shifting gears, releasing the clutch, accelerating, steering, and so forth) and can scarcely think about anything else. However, once the movements become automatic, we can carry on a conversation or admire the scenery without being conscious of driving — unless a potential danger appears that quickly draws our attention to the operation of the car.

The more automatic an action becomes, the less it requires conscious control. Another example is the skilled pianist who carries on a conversation with a bystander while performing a familiar piece. The pianist is exercising control over two activities — playing and talking — but does not think about the music unless a wrong key is hit, alerting his or her attention to it and temporarily disrupting the conversation. You can undoubtedly think of other examples of well-learned, automatic activities that require little conscious control. One way of interpreting this situation is to say that the control is still there (we can focus on automatic activities if we want to) but has been *dissociated* from consciousness.

The French psychiatrist Pierre Janet (1889) originated the concept of *dissociation*. He proposed that under certain conditions some thoughts and actions become split off, or dissociated, from the rest of consciousness and function outside of awareness or voluntary control, or both. Dissociation differs from Freud's concept of repression because the dissociated memories and thoughts can become available to consciousness. Repressed memories, in contrast, can be brought to consciousness only with great difficulty, if at all; they have to be inferred from signs or symptoms (such as slips of the tongue). Dissociated memories, therefore, are more like memories in the preconscious or subconscious.

When faced with a stressful situation, we may temporarily "put it out of our minds" in order to be able to function effectively; when bored, we may lapse into reverie or daydreams. These are mild examples of dissociation; they involve dissociating one part of consciousness from another. More extreme examples of dissociation are demonstrated by cases of multiple personality.

Multiple Personality

Multiple personality is the existence of two or more integrated and well-developed personalities within the same individual. Each personality has its own set of memories and characteristic behavior. Typically, the attitudes and behavior of the alternating personalities are markedly different. For example, if personality A is shy, inhibited, and rigidly moral, personality B may be extraverted, unrestrained, and prone to excessive drinking and sexual promiscuity. Frequently, some of the personalities have no awareness of the experiences of the others. In fact, periods of unexplained amnesia — the loss of memory for hours or days each week — are a clue to the presence of multiple personality.

One of the most famous cases of multiple personality is that of Chris Sizemore, whose alternative personalities — Eve White, Eve Black, and Jane — were portrayed in the movie *The Three Faces of Eve* (Thigpen & Cleckley, 1957) and later elaborated more fully in her autobiography *I'm Eve* (Sizemore & Pittillo, 1977). Another well-studied case of multiple personality is that of Jonah, a 27-year-old man who was admitted to a hospital complaining of severe headaches that were often followed by memory loss. Hospital attendants noticed striking changes in his personality on different days, and the psychiatrist in charge detected three distinct secondary personalities. The relatively stable personality structures that emerged are diagrammed in Figure 4-1 and can be characterized as follows:

- *Jonah.*   The primary personality. Shy, retiring, polite, and highly conventional, he is designated "the square." Sometimes frightened and confused during interviews, Jonah is unaware of the other personalities.
- *Sammy.*   He has the most intact memories. Sammy can coexist with Jonah or set Jonah aside and take over. He claims to be ready when Jonah needs legal advice or is in trouble; he is designated "the mediator." Sammy remembers emerging at age 6, when Jonah's mother stabbed his stepfather and Sammy persuaded the parents never to fight again in front of the children.
- *King Young.*   He emerged when Jonah was 6 or 7 years old to straighten out Jonah's sexual identity after his mother occasionally dressed him in girl's clothing at home and Jonah became confused about boys' and girls' names at school. King Young has looked after Jonah's sexual interests ever since; hence he is designated "the lover." He is only dimly aware of the other personalities.
- *Usoffa Abdulla.*   A cold, belligerent, and angry person. Usoffa is capable of ignoring pain. It is his sworn duty to watch over and protect Jonah; thus he is designated "the warrior." He emerged at age 9 or 10, when a gang of white boys beat up Jonah, who is black, without provocation. Jonah was helpless; but Usoffa emerged and fought viciously against the attackers. He too is only dimly aware of the other personalities.

The four personalities tested very differently on all measures having to do with emotionally laden topics but scored essentially alike on tests relatively free of emotion or personal conflict, such as intelligence or vocabulary tests.

In cases of multiple personality, consciousness is divided so sharply that several different personalities seem to be living in the same body. Observers note that the switch from one personality to another is often accompanied by subtle changes in body posture and tone of voice. The new personality talks, walks, and gestures differently. There may even be changes in such physiological processes as blood pressure and brain activity. Studies of *evoked potentials* (the brain's electrical response to a series of repeated sounds or light flashes) have found distinct patterns for as many as three different personalities in the same multiple-personality patient. Actors who pretend to have multiple personalities do not exhibit these kinds of differences (Putnam, 1984).

Although individuals with multiple personalities are relatively rare, enough cases have been studied to uncover some common features that provide us with clues as to how multiple personalities develop in an individual. The initial dissociation seems to occur in response to a traumatic event in childhood (usually between ages 4 and 6). The child copes with a painful problem by creating another personality to bear the brunt of the difficulty (Frischholz, 1985). In Jonah's case, Sammy—"the mediator"—emerged when Jonah had to deal with his mother's attack on his stepfather. This hypothesis is supported by the fact that most cases of multiple personality were physically or sexually abused as young children.

The second factor in the development of multiple personality appears to be an enhanced susceptibility to self-hypnosis, a process by which one is able to put oneself at will into the kind of trance state characteristic of hypnosis (see p. 137). There is evidence that multiple-personality patients make excellent hypnotic subjects, and some report, when hypnotized for the first time, that the trance experience is identical to experiences they have had dating back to their

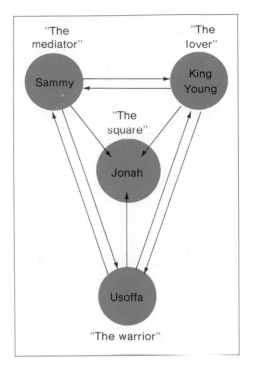

FIGURE 4-1
Jonah's Four Component Personalities
The three personalities on the periphery have superficial knowledge of each other but are intimately familiar with Jonah, who is totally unaware of them. (After Ludwig et al., 1972)

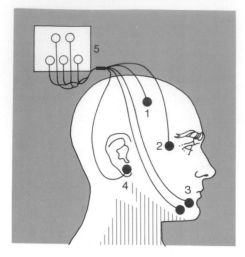

FIGURE 4-2

Arrangement of Electrodes for Recording the Electrophysiology of Sleep *The diagram shows the way in which electrodes are attached to the subject's head and face in a typical sleep experiment. Electrodes on the scalp (1) record the patterns of brain waves. Electrodes near the subject's eyes (2) record eye movements. Electrodes on the chin (3) record tension and electrical activity in the muscles. A neutral electrode on the ear (4) completes the circuit through amplifiers (5) that produce graphical records of the various patterns (see Figure 4-3).*

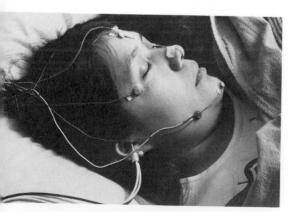

childhood. One of the personalities of a patient said, "She creates personalities by blocking everything from her head, mentally relaxes, concentrates very hard and wishes" (Bliss, 1980, p. 1392). This description sounds very much like self-hypnosis.

Once individuals discover that creating another personality by self-hypnosis relieves them of the emotional pain, they are apt to create other personalities in the future when confronted by emotional problems. Thus, when Jonah was beaten by a gang of white boys at age 9 or 10, he created a third personality, Usoffa Abdulla, to handle the problem. Some multiple-personality patients become so accustomed to defending against problems by means of alternate personalities that they continue the process throughout adulthood, creating new personalities in response to new problems; thus they may end up with a dozen or more different personalities (Spanos, Weekes, & Bertrand, 1985).

SLEEP AND DREAMS

Sleep seems the opposite of wakefulness, yet the two states have much in common. We think when we sleep, as dreams show, although the type of thinking in dreams departs in various ways from the type we do while awake. We form memories while sleeping, as we know from the fact that we remember dreams. Sleep is not entirely quiescent: some people walk in their sleep. People who are asleep are not entirely insensitive to the environment: parents are awakened immediately by their baby's cry. Nor is sleep entirely planless: some people can decide to wake at a given time and do so. We know a good deal about this most familiar altered state of consciousness.

Sleep

Many aspects of sleep have interested investigators. Researchers have looked at normal rhythms of waking and sleeping, the depth of sleep at different periods of the night, and individual and environmental factors that affect sleep.

SLEEP SCHEDULES Newborn babies tend to alternate frequently between sleeping and waking. Much to the relief of parents, a rhythm of two naps a day and longer sleep at night is eventually established. An infant's total sleeping time drops from 16 hours per day to 13 hours per day within the first six months of life. Most adults average about 7½ hours of sleep per night, but this time varies greatly. Some people manage on as little as 3 hours of sleep per night, and there are occasional reports of people who get by on less. Sleep patterns also vary from person to person. We all know "larks" who go to bed early and rise early and "owls" who go to bed late and rise late (Webb, 1975).

Many of our body functions (such as temperature, metabolism, blood and urine composition) have their own inherent tidelike ebb and flow, peaking sometime during the day and slowing down at night in approximate 24-hour cycles. These cyclical patterns form a kind of biological clock known as the *circadian rhythm*. Interestingly, in conditions in which a person has no way to mark the passing of day and night, the cycle tends to have a natural period of 25 hours. The cause of this departure from a 24-hour cycle is a matter of speculation. In any case, exposure to the normal environment of light and dark modifies the natural rhythm in favor of a 24-hour period (Aschoff, 1965).

A blind person may have a natural rhythm that departs from the 24-hour cycle, and this rhythm may prove very resistant to change. In one carefully studied case, a young professional man, blind since birth, had a circadian rhythm of 24.9 hours. As a consequence, he was completely out of phase with the night-day cycle about every two weeks. The only way he could stay in phase and meet the requirements of his professional life was to take heavy doses of stimulants and sedatives to counteract the rhythmical changes during the different phases of his cycle. Careful efforts to modify his sleep cycle by monitoring and controlling his sleep in a sleep laboratory did not prove successful (Miles, Raynal, & Wilson, 1977).

The jet lag that bothers many people when they travel to a different time zone is caused by disruption of the normal circadian rhythm. Their internal timekeepers that regulate sleep and metabolism are "out of sync" with the new light-dark cycle, and it may take several days before they adjust to the new schedule. The fatigue and lack of alertness characteristic of jet lag are not simply the result of the rigors of travel: travel in a north-south direction with no changes in time zones does not produce the same symptoms.

Most people find that traveling east is worse than traveling west. For one thing, if you fly from New York to California, your day simply becomes three hours longer. Westbound travelers also tend to arrive at their destinations in time to go to sleep when the natives do. Traveling east, the sun rises earlier (rather than later, as in westward journeys), so your body is required to start a new day hours earlier than its timekeepers are accustomed to (Kowet, 1983).

DEPTH OF SLEEP   Some people are readily aroused from sleep; others are hard to awaken. Research begun in the 1930s (Loomis, Harvey, & Hobart, 1937) has produced sensitive techniques for measuring the depth of sleep, as well as for determining when dreams are occurring (Dement & Kleitman, 1957). This research uses devices that measure electrical changes on the scalp associated with spontaneous brain activity during sleep, as well as eye movements that occur during dreaming. The graphic recording of the electrical changes, or brain waves, is called an *electroencephalogram,* or EEG (see Figures 4-2 and 4-3).

Analysis of the patterns of brain waves suggests that sleep involves five stages: four depths of sleep and a fifth stage, known as *rapid eye movement* (or *REM*) sleep, in which dreams commonly occur. When a person closes his or her eyes and relaxes, the brain waves characteristically show a regular pattern of 8 to 12 vibrations (hertz, or Hz) per second; these are known as *alpha waves.* As the individual drifts into *Stage 1* sleep, the brain waves become less regular and are reduced in amplitude with little or no alpha. *Stage 2* is characterized by the appearance of *spindles* — short runs of rhythmical responses of 12 to 16 Hz, slightly more rapid than alpha — and occasional rises and falls in the amplitude of the whole EEG. The still deeper *Stages 3 and 4* are characterized by slow waves (1 to 2 Hz), which are known as *delta waves.* The sleeper generally is hard to awaken during Stages 3 and 4, although he or she can be aroused by something personal, such as a familiar name or a child crying. A more impersonal disturbance, such as a loud sound, may be ignored.

After an adult has been asleep for an hour or so, another change occurs. The EEG pattern of Stage 1 reappears, but the subject does not wake. Instead, rapid eye movements appear on the record. This stage is known as *REM sleep;* other stages are known as *non-REM sleep* (or NREM). The stages alternate throughout the night. The exact pattern varies from person to person and with age. Newborn infants, for instance, spend about half their sleeping time in REM sleep. This proportion drops to 20 or 25 percent of sleeping time by the age of 5 and then remains fairly constant until old age, when it drops to 18 percent or less. For people of all ages, the deeper stages (3 and 4) tend to disappear in the second half of the night as REM becomes more prominent (see Figure 4-4).

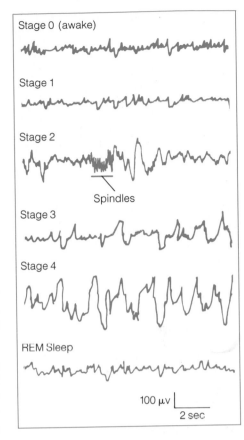

FIGURE 4-3
Electrophysiological Activity During Sleep   *The figure presents EEG recordings during wakefulness and during the five stages of sleep. Note the similarity of the EEG records for Stage 1 and REM sleep; these two stages do not differ in EEG activity, but REM sleep is accompanied by rapid eye movements whereas Stage 1 is not. Note the spindles that occur during Stage 2 and the irregularity that characterizes Stages 3 and 4 (the deeper stages of sleep). The calibration for the EEG record is given at the bottom; its amplitude is in microvolts, and time is in seconds.*

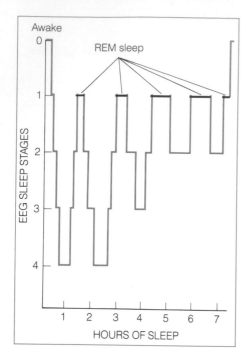

FIGURE 4-4

Succession of Sleep Stages *The graph provides an example of the sequence and duration of sleep stages during a typical night. The subject started in Stage 0 (awake) and then went successively through Stages 1 to 4 during the first hour. He then moved back through Stages 3 and 2 to REM sleep. REM sleep is like Stage 1 in terms of its EEG pattern, but it is accompanied by rapid eye movements. The width of each horizontal line segment indicates the duration of the corresponding stage of sleep. There are considerable differences from one subject to the next. However, the general pattern is to proceed through the first four stages during the initial hour of sleep before REM occurs. The deeper Stage 3 and Stage 4 tend to disappear in the second half of the night as REM becomes more prominent. (After Cartwright, 1978)*

REM AND NREM SLEEP During NREM sleep, eye movements are virtually absent and the heart rate and respiration are slowed, but there is still considerable tonus in the muscles. In contrast, during REM sleep, rapid eye movements occur approximately 40 to 60 times per minute, respiration and heart rate are more rapid and irregular, and the muscles become very relaxed, particularly around the head and neck. Physiological evidence indicates that in REM sleep the brain is isolated to a large extent from its sensory and motor channels; stimuli from other parts of the body are blocked from entering the brain, and there are no motor outputs. Nevertheless, the brain is still very active in REM sleep, being spontaneously driven by the discharge of giant neurons that originate in the brain stem. These neurons extend into parts of the brain that control eye movements and motor activities. Thus, during REM sleep, the brain registers the fact that the neurons normally involved in walking and seeing are activated, even though the body itself is doing neither (Hobson & McCarley, 1977).

Sleepers awakened during REM sleep almost always report having a dream, but when awakened during NREM sleep they will report a dream only about 30 percent of the time. The dreams reported when aroused from REM sleep tend to be visually vivid and have a bizarre, illogical character — they represent the type of experience we typically associate with the word "dream." In contrast, NREM dreams are more like normal thinking, neither as visual nor as emotionally charged as REM dreams, and more related to what is happening in waking life. Thus, mental activity is different in REM and NREM periods, as indicated by the type of dream we report (bizarre and illogical versus thoughtlike) and the frequency of reporting a dream (almost always versus occasionally).

It is important to realize that we become conscious of a dream only if we awaken while dreaming. If we then pay attention and make an effort to remember the dream, some of it will be recalled at a later time. Otherwise, our dream is transient and fades quickly; we may know that we have had a dream but will be unable to remember its contents.

If you are interested in remembering your dreams, keep a notebook and pencil beside your bed. Tell yourself you want to wake up when you have a dream. When you do, immediately write down the dream. As your dream recall improves, look for patterns. Underline anything that strikes you as odd and tell yourself that the next time something similar happens, you are going to recognize it as a sign you are dreaming. The problem, of course, is that you will lose some sleep if you follow this regime.

Theorists have proposed that sleep fulfills two separate functions: one being physical restoration and the other, psychological restoration. The physical restoration presumably takes place during the slow-wave, deep-sleep stages, whereas the psychological restoration occurs during REM sleep. There is some evidence to support this view. For example, strenuous physical exercise increases the time spent in slow-wave sleep (particularly Stage 4 sleep) without affecting REM time. In contrast, a higher percentage of REM sleep has been found to occur in hospital patients who have serious psychological problems. Further, women tend to have longer REM periods during their premenstrual phase, a time characterized by irritability, depression, and anxiety (Hartmann, 1984).

Sleep Disorders

Most people have good control over their ability to sleep or stay awake, though some have greater control than others. A study of college students found that 20 percent of the sample could nap at will; another 40 percent could nap if they had lost sleep recently; and the final 40 percent never napped (Orr, 1982).

INSOMNIA   The inability to sleep at night, *insomnia,* is very troubling to some people. In a large survey of adults, 6 percent of the males and 14 percent of the females complained that they often had great difficulty falling asleep or staying asleep throughout the night (Kripke & Gillin, 1985). A perplexing feature of insomnia is that people seem to overestimate their sleep loss. One study that monitored the sleep of people who identified themselves as insomniacs found that only about half of them were actually awake as much as 30 minutes during the night (Carskadon, Mitler, & Dement, 1974). The problem may be that light or restless sleep sometimes feels like wakefulness or that some people remember only time spent awake and think they have not slept because they have no memory of doing so. Table 4-1 provides some helpful information on how to ensure that you have a restful sleep.

NARCOLEPSY AND APNEA   Two relatively rare but severe disorders of sleep, narcolepsy and apnea, are characterized by a lack of control over the onset of sleep. A person with *narcolepsy* may fall asleep while writing a letter, driving a car, or carrying on a conversation. If the student falls asleep while a professor is lecturing, that is perfectly normal; but if the professor falls asleep while lecturing, that may indicate narcolepsy. In a study of 190 patients who complained that they could not stay awake in the daytime, 65 percent were diagnosed as having narcolepsy (Dement, 1976). Usually, the sudden, brief periods of sleep in narcolepsy are accompanied by muscular relaxation; the person may simply nod or may collapse. However, some narcoleptics are able to continue automatic behavior that they are not aware of, such as driving a car satisfactorily for some miles.

In *sleep apnea,* the individual stops breathing while asleep (either because the windpipe closes or because the brain centers that control respiration are not functioning properly). People with apnea must awaken repeatedly throughout the night in order to breathe, although they are unaware of doing so. For these people, daytime sleepiness is a function of nighttime sleep deprivation. Sleep apnea is common among older men. Sleeping pills, which make arousal more difficult, lengthen periods of apnea (during which the brain is deprived of oxygen) and in some cases may prove fatal. Apnea and narcolepsy show that complex voluntary and involuntary control systems are involved in sleep.

SLEEP DEPRIVATION   The need for sleep seems so important that we might expect being deprived of sleep for several nights to have serious consequences. Numerous studies have shown, however, that the only consistent effects of sleep deprivation are drowsiness, a desire to sleep, and a tendency to fall asleep easily. Subjects kept awake for 50 hours or more show nothing more noticeable than "transient inattentions, confusions, or misperceptions" (Webb, 1975). Even sleepless periods exceeding four days produce little in the way of severely disturbed behavior. In one study in which a subject was kept awake for 11 days and nights, there were no unusually deviant responses (Gulevich, Dement, & Johnson, 1966). Intellectual activities such as answering short test questions seem unaffected by several nights of sleep deprivation.

If sleep deprivation has no serious consequences, what about dream deprivation? This question has been investigated by depriving subjects of REM sleep. Dement (1960) woke his subjects at the onset of every REM period. He found that after five nights there was a *rebound effect,* with an abnormal amount of time spent in REM sleep during the recovery night. Control tests were run by awakening subjects an equal number of times during NREM sleep; no rebound of REM was found. Dement's findings have been confirmed by many others. Researchers had hoped that REM deprivation would provide clues to the function of REM sleep, but answers have not been forthcoming even though the search has continued. Some minor effects of REM deprivation on memory have been reported, but

TABLE 4-1
Advice for a Good Night's Sleep   *There is considerable agreement among researchers and clinicians on how to avoid sleep problems. These recommendations are summarized in the table; some are based on actual research, and others are simply the best judgments of experts in the field.*

REGULAR SLEEP SCHEDULE

Establish a regular schedule of going to bed and getting up. Set your alarm for a specific time every morning, and get up at that time no matter how little you may have slept. Be consistent about naps. Take a nap every afternoon or not at all; when you take a nap only occasionally, you probably will not sleep well that night. Waking up late on weekends can also disrupt your sleep cycle.

ALCOHOL AND CAFFEINE

Having a stiff drink of alcohol before going to bed may help put you to sleep, but it disturbs the sleep cycle and can cause you to wake up early the next day. In addition, stay away from caffeinated drinks like coffee or cola for several hours before bedtime. If you must drink something, try milk; there is evidence to support the folklore that a glass of warm milk at bedtime induces sleep.

EATING BEFORE BEDTIME

Don't eat heavily before going to bed, since your digestive system will have to do several hours of work. If you must eat something before bedtime, have a light snack.

EXERCISE

Regular exercise will help you sleep better, but don't engage in a strenuous workout just before going to bed.

SLEEPING PILLS

Be careful about using sleeping pills. All of the various kinds disrupt the sleep cycle, and long-term use inevitably leads to insomnia. Even on nights before exams, avoid using a sleeping pill. One bad night of sleep tends not to affect performance the next day, whereas a hangover from a sleeping pill may.

RELAX

Avoid stressful thoughts before bedtime and engage in soothing activities that help you relax. Try to follow the same routine every night before going to bed; it might involve taking a warm bath or listening to soft music for a few minutes. Find a room temperature at which you are comfortable and maintain it throughout the night.

WHEN ALL FAILS

If you are in bed and have trouble falling asleep, don't get up. Stay in bed and try to relax. But if that fails and you become tense, then get up for a brief time and do something restful that reduces anxiety. Doing push-ups or some other form of exercise to wear yourself out is not a good idea.

memory disturbances have also been found to occur after deprivation of NREM sleep (McGaugh, Jensen, & Martinez, 1979).

Dreams

Dreaming is an alteration in consciousness in which remembered images and fantasies are temporarily confused with external reality. Investigators do not yet understand why people dream at all, much less why they dream what they do. However, modern methods of study have answered a great many questions about dreaming.

DOES EVERYONE DREAM?   Although many people do not recall their dreams in the morning, REM-sleep evidence suggests that nonrecallers do as much dreaming as recallers. Researchers have proposed several hypotheses to account for differences in dream recall. One possibility is that nonrecallers simply have more difficulty than recallers in remembering their dreams. Another hypothesis suggests that some people awaken relatively easily in the midst of REM sleep and thus recall more dreams than those who sleep more soundly. The most generally accepted model for dream recall supports the idea that what happens on awakening is the crucial factor. According to this hypothesis, unless a distraction-free waking period occurs shortly after dreaming, the memory of the dream is not consolidated (Koulack & Goodenough, 1976).

HOW LONG DO DREAMS LAST?   Some dreams seem almost instantaneous. The alarm clock rings, and we awaken to complex memories of a fire breaking out and fire engines arriving with their sirens blasting. Because the alarm is still ringing, we assume that the sound must have produced the dream. Research suggests, however, that a ringing alarm clock or other sound merely reinstates a complete scene from earlier memories or dreams. This experience has its parallel during wakefulness when a single cue may tap a rich memory that takes some time to tell. The length of a typical dream can be inferred from a REM study in which subjects were awakened and asked to act out what they had been dreaming (Dement & Wolpert, 1958). The time it took them to pantomime the dream was almost the same as the length of the REM sleep period, suggesting that the incidents in dreams commonly last about as long as they would in real life.

DO PEOPLE KNOW WHEN THEY ARE DREAMING?   The answer to this question is "sometimes yes." People can be taught to recognize that they are dreaming, and their awareness does not interfere with the dream's spontaneous flow. For example, subjects have been trained to close an open switch when they notice that they are dreaming (Salamy, 1970).

Some people have *lucid dreams* in which events seem so normal (lacking the bizarre and illogical character of most dreams) that they feel they are awake and conscious. Only on awakening do they realize it was a dream. Lucid dreamers report doing various "experiments" within their dreams to determine whether they are awake or dreaming. A Dutch physician, van Eeden (1913), was one of the first to give an accurate account of initiating actions within a lucid dream to prove that events were not occurring normally. In a later report, Brown (1936) described a standard experiment in which he jumped and suspended himself in the air. If he did this successfully, he knew he was dreaming. Both Brown and van Eeden report an occasional "false awakening" within a dream. For example, in one of Brown's dreams, he discovered that he was dreaming and decided to call a taxicab as an indication of his control over events. When he reached into his pocket to see if he had some change to pay the driver, he thought that he woke up. He then found the coins scattered about the bed. At this point, he really awoke and found himself lying in a different position and, of course, without any coins.

CAN PEOPLE CONTROL THE CONTENT OF THEIR DREAMS?   Psychologists have demonstrated that some control of dream content is possible by making suggestions to subjects in the presleep period and then analyzing the content of the dreams that followed. In a carefully designed study of an *implicit predream suggestion*, researchers tested the effect of wearing red goggles prior to sleep. Although the researchers made no actual suggestion, and the subjects did not understand the purpose of the experiment, many subjects reported that their visual dream worlds were tinted red (Roffwarg, Herman, Bowe-Anders, & Tauber, 1978). In a study of the effect of an *overt predream suggestion*, subjects

"Greetings. You are now entering the Rapid Eye Movement phase of your sleep cycle."

Drawing by Ed Fisher. Reprinted by permission of Tribune Media Services.

CRITICAL DISCUSSION

Theories of Dream Sleep

A great deal of research on sleep and dreams has been conducted in recent years, and a number of new theories have been proposed. Here we summarize two theories of dream sleep, one proposed by Evans (1984) that takes a cognitive approach to the phenomenon and the other by Crick and Mitchison (1983) that takes a neurobiological perspective.

Evans' theory views sleep as a period when the brain disengages from the external world and uses this "off-line" time to sort through and reorganize the vast array of information that was input during the day. According to the theory, the brain is like a computer with large data banks and an assortment of control programs. Some of these programs are inherited and relate to what we call instincts; others are acquired, adapted, and continually modified by experience. Sleep, particularly REM sleep, is when the brain comes off-line, isolating itself from the sensory and motor neural pathways. In this off-line period the various data banks and program files are opened and become available for modification and reorganization based on the experiences of the day. According to Evans, the reorganization of memory that occurs dur-

ing REM sleep involves updating the memory files and programs rather than erasing or deleting information. In the language of computer science, the reorganization process is an "interlocking" procedure in which computer instructions are never erased; rather, new ones are added.

In Evans' theory, dreams are of two types. Type A dreams are the full array of off-line processing that occurs during REM sleep; we are not consciously aware of this processing. Type B dreams are nothing more than a small segment of Type A that we remember if we are awakened during REM sleep; they represent a momentary glimpse by the conscious mind of the vast amount of material being scanned and sorted during Type A dreams. During Type B dreams the brain comes back on-line and the conscious mind observes a small sample of the programs being run. When this occurs, the brain attempts to interpret the information in the same way it would interpret stimuli in the outside world, giving rise to a kind of pseudo-event that characterizes dreams. Evans believes that Type B dreams can be useful in inferring the full array of processing that occurs during Type A dreams, but they represent a very small

were asked to try to dream about a personality characteristic that they wished they had. Most of the subjects had at least one dream in which the intended trait could be recognized (Cartwright, 1974).

A *posthypnotic predream suggestion* is another way of influencing dream content. In one extensive study using this method, detailed dream narratives were suggested to highly responsive hypnotic subjects. After the suggestion, the subject slept until roused from REM sleep. Some of the resulting dreams reflected the thematic aspects of the suggestion without including many of the specific elements, whereas other dreams reflected specific elements of the suggestion (Tart & Dick, 1970).

SLEEPTALKING AND SLEEPWALKING?   Laboratory studies of sleeptalkers and sleepwalkers have shown that most of these behaviors take place during NREM sleep. In one study, researchers found that about 80 percent of sleeptalking occurred during NREM sleep, and 20 percent during REM (Arkin, Toth, Baker, & Hastey, 1970). Virtually all research on sleepwalking, however, indicates that it occurs *only* in NREM periods. Typically, people will sleepwalk during the first third of the night; sometimes they just sit up in bed, but at other times they may leave the room or even the house. Though the sleepwalker's eyes may be open, they are glassy and unseeing, so the person could have a serious accident. Sleepwalkers usually forget about what they have done, and the dreams they report bear no resemblance to what they do while walking about (Jacobson & Kales, 1967). About 15 percent of children have one or more episodes of sleepwalking, but these usually stop before age 15 and have no aftereffects.

sample on which to base inferences.

Crick and Mitchison base their theory on the fact that the cortex—unlike other parts of the brain—is made up of richly interconnected *neuronal networks,* where each cell has the capacity to excite its neighbors. They believe that memories are encoded in these networks, with neurons and their many synapses representing different features of a memory. These networks are like spiderwebs, and when one point in the web is excited, perhaps by hearing a few notes of a song, a pulse travels throughout the net prompting recall of the rest of the song. The problem with such network systems is that they malfunction when there is an overload of incoming information. Too many memories in one network may produce either bizarre associations to a stimulus (fantasies) or the same response whatever the stimulus (obsessions), or associations may be triggered without any stimulus (hallucinations).

To deal with information overload, the brain needs a mechanism to debug and tune the network. Such a debugging mechanism would work best when the system was isolated from external inputs and would have to have a way of randomly zapping the network in order to eliminate spurious connections. The mechanism Crick and Mitchison propose is REM sleep: the hallucinatory quality of dreams is nothing more than the random neural firing needed for the daily cleanup of the network. As noted earlier, the brain is very active during REM sleep, barraged with neural signals traveling from the brain stem to the cortex. According to the theory, these signals somehow erase the spurious memory associations formed during the previous day; we awake with the network cleaned up, and the brain ready for new input. Crick and Mitchison also suggest that trying to remember one's dreams—a key aspect of psychoanalysis—may not be a good idea. Such remembering could help to retain patterns of thought that are better forgotten, the very patterns the system is attempting to tune out.

The two theories have some common features but there are clear differences. Evans views REM sleep as a time when the brain reorganizes memory by a process of updating, rather than deleting, information. Crick and Mitchison, on the other hand, see REM sleep as a time when spurious or useless information is purged from memory. Evans regards conscious dreams as a surface indicator of the rich reorganizational process taking place during REM sleep, whereas Crick and Mitchison suggest that dreams are little more than random noise with no real content. But both theories assume that REM sleep is a critical factor in the memory storage process and in preparing the brain from day to day to deal with new information inputs. Neither theory assigns to dreams the rich symbolism and concealed meaning that typifies a psychoanalytic approach. Indeed, Crick and Mitchison question the scientific value of analyzing dream content using psychoanalytic methods.

We still have no direct test to prove one theory clearly superior to the other. The same comment, of course, applies to psychoanalytic theories of dreams. Thus these theories must be regarded as speculative, awaiting the outcome of further research. In the meantime, however, each provides intriguing possibilities about the nature of dreams.

Dream Content

Freud's theory that dreams are mental products that can be understood and interpreted was one of the earliest and most comprehensive attempts to explain the content of dreams without reference to the supernatural. In his book, *Interpretation of Dreams* (1900), Freud presented his controversial notion that dreams are a disguised attempt at *wish fulfillment.* By this he meant that the dream touches on wishes or needs that the individual finds unacceptable and *represses* (or banishes) from consciousness. These wishes then appear in symbolic form as the *latent content* of the dream. Freud used the metaphor of a censor to explain the conversion of latent dream content to *manifest content* (the characters and events that make up the actual narrative of the dream). In effect, Freud said, the censor protects the sleeper, enabling him or her to express warded-off impulses while avoiding the frightening intensity of the unconscious wish that is being expressed. However, sometimes the "dream work," as Freud called it, fails, and anxiety awakens the dreamer (Freud, 1965).

The cognitive side of dreaming—its role in problem solving and thinking—has been increasingly recognized (see the Critical Discussion, "Theories of Dream Sleep"). Although cognitive psychologists reject many of Freud's ideas, they also note that his theory has cognitive aspects. In fact, Freud's emphasis on thought transformations through free association goes far beyond the oversimplified popular notion that all the transformations in dreams can be explained as wish fulfillment.

PSYCHOACTIVE DRUGS

Since ancient times, people have used drugs to alter their state of consciousness —to stimulate or relax, to bring on sleep or prevent it, to enhance ordinary perceptions, or to produce hallucinations. Drugs that affect behavior, consciousness, and mood are called *psychoactive*. They include not only "street drugs" such as heroin and marijuana but also tranquilizers, stimulants, and such familiar drugs as alcohol, tobacco, and coffee. Table 4-2 lists and classifies the psychoactive drugs that are commonly used and abused.

It may be difficult for students today to appreciate the major changes in patterns of drug-taking behavior that have occurred over the past 30 years. In the 1950s, very few young people used drugs—other than cigarettes and alcohol. Since the 1950s, however, we have moved from a relatively drug-free society to a drug-using society. A number of factors have contributed to this change. For instance, the widespread use of tranquilizers for the treatment of mental illness and emotional problems, which began in the 1950s, and the appearance of oral contraceptives in 1960 did much to change people's attitudes toward drugs. Drugs became an option available to solve problems—problems other than physical illness. In the 1960s and 1970s, Americans also explored new life-styles, following the opportunities provided by easier transportation and expanding job markets. With increased leisure time people looked for new outlets, and the recreational use of drugs became one.

For these and other reasons, drug use, particularly among students, increased steadily through the 1970s. Figure 4-5 shows the increasing percentage through 1979 of high school seniors who experimented with drugs such as marijuana, stimulants, sedatives, and hallucinogens. In 1980, however, drug use began a downward trend that hopefully will continue. The social changes contributing to the decline in high school drug use are many, but an important factor appears to be an increased concern for health and physical fitness.

All of the drugs listed in Table 4-2 are assumed to affect behavior and consciousness because they act in specific biochemical ways on the brain. With repeated use, an individual can become physically or psychologically dependent on any of these drugs. *Physical dependence*, also called addiction, is characterized by *tolerance* (that is, with continued use, the individual must take more and more of the drug to achieve the same effect) and *withdrawal* (if use is discontinued, the person experiences unpleasant physical symptoms). *Psychological dependence* refers to a need that develops through learning. People who habitually use a drug to relieve anxiety may become dependent on it, even though no physical need develops. For example, marijuana smokers do not appear to build up tolerance for the drug, and they experience minimal withdrawal symptoms. Nevertheless, a person who learns to use marijuana when faced with stressful situations will find the habit difficult to break. With some drugs, such as alcohol, psychological dependence progresses to physical dependence as more and more of the substance is consumed.

Depressants

Drugs that depress the central nervous system include the minor tranquilizers, barbiturates (sleeping pills), and ethyl alcohol. Of these, the one most frequently used and abused is alcohol. Almost every society, primitive or industrialized, consumes alcohol. It can be produced by fermenting a wide variety of materials: grains, such as rye, wheat, and corn; fruits, such as grapes, apples, and plums; and vegetables, such as potatoes. Even flowers, milk, and honey can be fermented to

TABLE 4-2
Psychoactive Drugs That Are Commonly Abused   *Only a few examples of each class of drug are given. The generic name (for example, psilocybin) or the brand name (Miltown for meprobamate; Seconal for secobarbital) is used, depending on which is more familiar.*

DEPRESSANTS (SEDATIVES)

Alcohol (ethanol)
Barbiturates
   Nembutal
   Seconal
Minor tranquilizers
   Miltown
   Valium

OPIATES (NARCOTICS)

Opium and its derivatives
   Codeine
   Heroin
   Morphine
Methadone

STIMULANTS

Amphetamines
   Benzedrine
   Dexedrine
   Methedrine
Cocaine
Nicotine
Caffeine

HALLUCINOGENS (PSYCHEDELICS)

LSD
Mescaline
Psilocybin
PCP (Phencyclidine)

CANNABIS

Marijuana
Hashish

become alcoholic beverages. Through the process of distillation, the alcoholic content of a fermented beverage can be increased to obtain "hard liquors" such as whiskey or rum.

EFFECTS OF ALCOHOL   In small quantities, alcohol appears to increase people's energy and make them feel lively and sociable. In reality, it is a central nervous system depressant, not a stimulant. The initial stimulating effect of alcohol is believed to occur because the inhibitory synapses in the brain are depressed slightly earlier than the excitatory synapses. Since the brain's neurons maintain a close balance between excitation and inhibition, the depression of inhibitory synapses results in behavioral excitation, or stimulation. However, the excitatory synapses soon become depressed, too; the stimulating effects are over-ridden, causing drowsiness and slowed sensory and motor functions.

Measuring the amount of alcohol in the air we exhale (as in a breath analyzer) gives a reliable measure of alcohol in the blood. Consequently, it is easy to determine the relationship between blood alcohol concentration (BAC) and behavior. At concentrations of .03 to .05 percent in the blood (that is, 30 to 50 milligrams of alcohol per 100 milliliters of blood), alcohol produces light-head-edness, relaxation, and release of inhibitions. People say things they might not ordinarily say; they tend to become more sociable and expansive. Self-confidence may increase, whereas motor reactions begin to slow (a pair of effects that makes it dangerous to drive after drinking).

At a BAC of .10 percent, sensory and motor functions become noticeably impaired. Speech becomes slurred, and people have difficulty coordinating arm and leg movements. Some people tend to become angry and aggressive; others grow silent and morose. The drinker is seriously incapacitated at a level of .20 percent, and a level above .40 percent may cause death. The legal definition of intoxication in most states is a BAC of .10 percent (that is, one-tenth of 1 percent).

How much can a person drink without becoming legally intoxicated? The relationship between BAC and alcohol intake is not simple. It depends on a person's sex, body weight, and speed of consumption. Alcohol is distributed throughout the body fluids, including the blood. The heavier the person, the more body fluid and the lower the concentration of blood alcohol. Women have less fluid than men of the same weight because women have more fat; thus, their concentration of alcohol will be higher. For example, after drinking two 4-ounce glasses of wine (or two 12-ounce beers, or two 1-ounce cocktails of 100-proof liquor) over the period of an hour, a 150-pound man will have a BAC of .05, whereas a 150-pound woman's BAC will be .06; a 100-pound woman will have a BAC of .09. Drinking four glasses of wine within an hour will bring the 100-pound woman well above the point of legal intoxication, with a BAC of .18; her 150-pound boyfriend will just be approaching a BAC of .10 after consuming the same amount.

Drinking is viewed as an integral part of social life for many college students. It promotes conviviality, eases tensions, releases inhibitions, and generally adds to the fun. Nevertheless, social drinking can create problems in terms of lost study time, poor performance on an exam because of feeling hung over, and arguments or accidents while intoxicated. People must weigh these potential problems against the social benefits when deciding how much and how often to use alcohol. The most serious problem clearly is accidents: alcohol-related auto-mobile accidents are the leading cause of death among 15- to 24-year-olds. When the legal drinking age was lowered from 21 to 18 years of age in a number of states, traffic fatalities of 18- and 19-year-olds increased 20 to 50 percent. Most states have since raised their minimum drinking age, and a significant decrease in traffic accidents has followed.

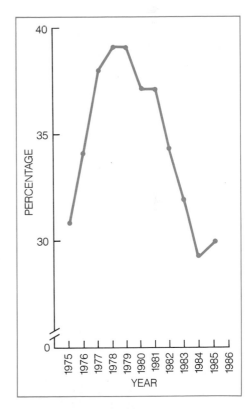

FIGURE 4-5

Illicit Drug Use   *Percentage of American high school seniors who reported using an illicit drug in the 30 days prior to the study. Drugs include marijuana, hallucinogens, cocaine, and heroin and any nonprescribed use of opiates, stimulants, sedatives, or tranquilizers. (After Johnston, O'Malley, & Bachman, 1986)*

About two-thirds of American adults report that they drink alcohol. At least 10 percent of them have social, psychological, or medical problems resulting from alcohol use. Probably half of that 10 percent are physically dependent on alcohol. Heavy or prolonged drinking can lead to serious health problems. High blood pressure; stroke; ulcers; cancer of the mouth, throat, and stomach; cirrhosis of the liver; and depression are some of the conditions associated with the regular use of substantial amounts of alcohol.

Alcohol can also produce risks for a developing fetus. Mothers who drink heavily are twice as likely to suffer repeated miscarriages and to produce low birth-weight babies. A condition called *fetal alcohol syndrome*, characterized by mental retardation and multiple deformities of the face and mouth, is caused by maternal drinking. The amount of alcohol needed to produce this syndrome is unclear, but it is thought that as little as a few ounces of alcohol a week can be detrimental. Women drinking one ounce per day in early pregnancy show fetal alcohol syndrome rates between 1 and 10 percent (Streissguth, Clarren, & Jones, 1985).

ALCOHOLISM   The stereotype of an alcoholic—the skid-row drunk—constitutes only a small proportion of the individuals who have drinking problems. The depressed housewife who takes a few drinks to get through the day and a few more to gear up for a social evening, the businessman who needs a three-martini lunch to make it through the afternoon, the overworked physician who keeps a bottle in her desk drawer, and the high school student who drinks more and more to gain acceptance from peers—all are on their way to becoming alcoholics. There are various definitions of alcoholism, but almost all of them include the *inability to abstain* (the feeling that you cannot get through the day without a drink) or a *lack of control* (an inability to stop after one or two drinks). Table 4-3 lists some questions to help people determine whether they have a drinking problem.

The peak drinking years for most people are between ages 16 and 25. In the late 20s to early 30s, the average drinker decreases his or her alcohol consumption. The alcoholic, in contrast, maintains or increases his or her drinking pattern and has the first major alcohol-related life problem (for example, job or marital difficulties, series of drunk-driving arrests) during this period. The average alco-

The sooner you recognize a drinking problem in yourself, the easier it is to get out from under it. Below are some questions that will help you learn how dependent you are on drinking. This is a time to be absolutely honest with yourself — only *you* can know how seriously you are being hurt by the role alcohol plays in your life.

1. Has someone close to you sometimes expressed concern about your drinking?
2. When faced with a problem, do you often turn to alcohol for relief?
3. Are you sometimes unable to meet home or work responsibilities because of drinking?
4. Have you ever required medical attention as a result of drinking?
5. Have you ever experienced a blackout — a total loss of memory while still awake — when drinking?
6. Have you ever come in conflict with the law in connection with your drinking?
7. Have you often failed to keep the promises you have made to yourself about controlling or cutting out your drinking?

If you have answered yes to any of the above questions, your drinking is probably affecting your life in some major ways and you should do something about it — before it gets worse.

TABLE 4-3
Signs of Alcoholism   *Questions developed by the National Institute on Alcohol Abuse and Alcoholism to help people determine whether they have a drinking problem.*

holic seeks help in the early 40s after a decade of difficulties. If the alcohol problems continue, the person is likely to die 15 years earlier than the life expectancy for the general population (Schuckit, 1984).

While this scenario describes the *average* alcoholic, it should be emphasized that heavy drinking can progress to alcoholism at any age. People who become psychologically dependent on alcohol — who habitually use alcohol to handle stress and anxiety — stand a good chance of becoming alcoholics. They are apt to become trapped in a vicious cycle. By resorting to alcohol when confronted with problems, they handle these problems ineffectively. As a consequence, they feel even more anxious and inadequate and consume more alcohol in an attempt to bolster their self-esteem. Prolonged heavy drinking leads to physical dependency: a person's tolerance rises so that more and more alcohol must be consumed to achieve the same effect, and the individual begins to experience withdrawal symptoms when he or she abstains from drinking. Withdrawal symptoms may range from feelings of irritability and general malaise to tremors and intense anxiety. In some instances, they include confusion, hallucinations, and convulsions. This syndrome, called *delirium tremens* (DTs), usually occurs only in chronic alcoholics who stop drinking after a sustained period of heavy alcohol consumption.

Although our definition of alcoholism includes the inability to abstain from drinking or the lack of control after starting to drink, very few alcoholics stay drunk until they die. They usually alternate periods of abstinence (or light drinking) with periods of serious abuse. Thus, the ability to go for weeks, or even months, without drinking does not mean that an individual is not an alcoholic. Perhaps the most useful criterion for diagnosing alcoholism is whether alcohol is causing problems with health, job performance, or family relationships.

Opiates

Opium and its derivatives, collectively known as *opiates*, are drugs that diminish physical sensation and the capacity to respond to stimuli by depressing the central nervous system. (These drugs are commonly called "narcotics," but "opiates" is the more accurate term; the term "narcotics" is not well defined and covers a variety of illegal drugs.) Opiates are medically useful for their painkilling properties, but their ability to alter mood and reduce anxiety has led to widespread illegal consumption. Opium, which is the air-dried juice of the opium poppy, contains a number of chemical substances, including morphine and codeine. Codeine, a common ingredient in prescription painkillers and cough suppressants, is relatively mild in its effects (at least at low doses). Morphine and its derivative, heroin, are much more potent. Most illegal drug use involves heroin because, being more concentrated, it can be concealed and smuggled more easily than morphine.

Heroin can be injected, smoked, or inhaled. At first, the drug produces a sense of well-being. Experienced adult users report a special thrill, or "rush," within a minute or two after an intravenous injection. Some describe this sensation as intensely pleasurable, similar to an orgasm. Young people who sniff heroin report that they forget everything that troubles them. Following this, the user feels "fixed," or gratified, with no awareness of hunger, pain, or sexual urges. The person may "go on the nod," alternately waking and drowsing while comfortably watching television or reading a book. Unlike the alcoholic, the heroin user can readily produce skilled responses to agility and intellectual tests and seldom becomes aggressive or assaultive. The changes in consciousness produced by heroin are not very striking; there are no exciting visual experiences or feelings of being transported elsewhere. Apparently, it is the change in mood — the feeling of euphoria and reduced anxiety — that prompts people to *start* using this dangerous drug. However, heroin is very addictive; even a brief period of usage can create physical dependency. After a person has been smoking or "sniffing" (inhaling) heroin for a while, tolerance builds up, and this method no longer produces the desired effect. In an attempt to recreate the original "high," the individual may progress to "skin popping" (injecting under the skin) and then to "mainlining" (injecting into a vein). Once the user starts mainlining, stronger and stronger doses are required to produce the high, and the physical discomforts of withdrawal from the drug become intense (chills, sweating, stomach cramps, vomiting, headaches). Thus, the motivation to *continue* using the drug stems from the need to avoid pain and discomfort.

Most heroin users who restrict themselves to smoking or "sniffing" are able to give up the habit. Only about 7 percent of American soldiers who sniffed heroin regularly in Vietnam (where the drug was easily available) continued to use the drug after they returned to the United States (Robins, 1974). However, once larger amounts are absorbed into the body through injection, the majority of users become physically dependent, or addicted.

The hazards of heroin use are many. Death from an overdose is always a possibility because the concentration of street heroin fluctuates widely. Thus, the user can never be sure of the potency of the powder in a newly purchased packet. Death is caused by suffocation resulting from depression of the brain's respiratory center. Less fatal dangers of heroin usage include hepatitis and other infections associated with unsterile injections. Acquired Immune Deficiency Syndrome (AIDS) has also been found among individuals who inject drugs. Heroin use is generally associated with a serious deterioration of personal and social life. Because maintaining the habit is costly, the user often becomes involved in illegal activities.

In the 1970s, researchers made a major breakthrough in understanding opiate addiction with the discovery that opiates act on very specific receptor sites in the brain (see Chapter 2, p. 36). In molecular shape, the opiates resemble a group of neurotransmitters called *endorphins*. One of these endorphins, *enkephalin*, occupies a certain number of opiate receptors. Morphine or heroin relieve pain by binding to receptors that are unfilled. Repeated heroin use causes a drop in enkephalin production; the body then requires more heroin to fill the unoccupied receptors and to reduce pain. The person experiences painful withdrawal symptoms when heroin is discontinued because many opiate receptors are left unfilled (since the normal enkephalin production has decreased). In essence, the heroin has replaced the body's own natural opiates.

The research findings on opiate receptors have led to two important treatment methods. First, there are drugs called opiate antagonists that can block the action of an opiate — such as heroin or morphine — because they have a greater affinity for the receptor site than do the opiates themselves. Thus, an opiate antagonist, such as *naloxone*, is often used in hospital emergency rooms to reverse the effects of a drug overdose. Interestingly, this drug is very specific: it will reverse the potentially fatal depression of the respiratory center caused by an opiate overdose but will not reverse depression resulting from other classes of drugs such as alcohol or barbiturates.

Second, a synthetic opiate called *methadone*, which prevents withdrawal symptoms by occupying the opiate receptor sites, is sometimes used to treat heroin-dependent individuals. Methadone is addictive, but it produces less psychological impairment than heroin and its effects last much longer. When taken orally in low doses, it suppresses the craving for heroin without producing feelings of euphoria.

Stimulants

AMPHETAMINES In contrast to depressants and opiates, stimulants are drugs that increase arousal. Amphetamines are powerful stimulants, sold under such trade names as Methedrine, Dexedrine, and Benzedrine and known colloquially as "speed," "uppers," or "Bennies." The immediate effects of consuming such drugs are an increase in alertness and a decrease in feelings of fatigue and boredom. Strenuous activities that require endurance seem easier when amphetamines are taken. As with other drugs, the ability of amphetamines to alter mood and increase self-confidence is the principal reason for their use. People also use them to stay awake, to increase endurance and strength during athletic competition, and to lose weight. Most prescription weight-control medications contain amphetamines.

Low doses that are taken for limited periods to overcome fatigue (as during nighttime driving) seem to be relatively safe. However, as the stimulating effects of amphetamines wear off, there is often a period of compensatory letdown during which the user feels depressed, irritable, and fatigued. He or she may be tempted to take more of the drug. Tolerance develops quickly, and the user needs increasingly larger doses to produce the desired effect. Since high doses can have dangerous side effects—agitation, confusion, heart palpitations, and elevated blood pressure—medications containing amphetamines should be used with caution. Amphetamines do decrease the appetite, but only temporarily (for three or four weeks at most). And controlled studies show that weight lost while taking diet pills containing amphetamines is regained once the patient discontinues medication.

When tolerance develops to the point at which oral doses are no longer effective, many users inject amphetamines into a vein. Large intravenous doses produce an immediate pleasant experience (a "flash" or rush); this sensation is followed by irritability and discomfort, which can be overcome only by an additional injection. If this sequence is repeated every few hours over a period of days, it will end in a "crash," a deep sleep followed by a period of lethargy and depression. The amphetamine abuser may seek relief from this discomfort by turning to alcohol or heroin.

Long-term amphetamine use is accompanied by drastic deterioration of physical and mental health. The user, or "speed freak," may become inappropriately suspicious or hostile and may develop psychotic symptoms that are indistinguishable from those of acute schizophrenia (see p. 511). These symptoms include paranoid delusions (the false belief that people are persecuting you or "out to get you") and visual or auditory hallucinations. The paranoid delusions may lead to unprovoked violence. For example, in the midst of an amphetamine epidemic in Japan (during the early 1950s when amphetamines were sold without prescription and advertised for "elimination of drowsiness and repletion of the spirit"), 50 percent of the murder cases in a two-month period were related to amphetamine abuse (Hemmi, 1969).

COCAINE   Like other stimulants, cocaine, or "coke," a substance obtained from dried leaves of the coca plant, increases energy and self-confidence; it makes the user feel witty and hyperalert. In the early part of this century, cocaine was widely used and easy to obtain; in fact, it was an ingredient in the early days of Coca-Cola. Its use then declined, but recently its popularity has been increasing, even though it is now illegal. Indeed, cocaine is the drug of choice for many conventional and upwardly mobile young adults who consider it safer than heroin or amphetamines. Further, its use by teenagers has nearly doubled in the past ten years; while the use of other drugs by high school seniors has leveled off or declined since 1980, cocaine usage has increased (Johnston, O'Malley, & Bachman, 1986).

One of the earliest studies of the effects of cocaine is reported by Freud (1885; reproduced in Freud, 1974). In an account of his own use of cocaine, he was at first highly favorable to the drug and encouraged its use. He noted

the exhilaration and lasting euphoria, which in no way differs from the normal euphoria of the healthy person. . . . You perceive an increase of self-control and possess more vitality and capacity for work. . . . In other words, you are simply normal, and it is so hard to believe that you are under the influence of any drug. . . . Long intensive mental or physical work is performed without any fatigue. . . . This result is enjoyed without any of the unpleasant after-effects that follow exhilaration brought about by alcohol. (1974, p. 9)

Freud soon withdrew this unreserved support, however, after he treated a friend with cocaine and the results were disastrous. The friend developed a severe addiction, demanded larger dosages of the drug, and was debilitated until his death.

Cocaine can be inhaled (snorted) by placing the powder high into the nasal passages where it is rapidly absorbed. Or it can be made into a solution and injected directly into a vein. It can also be converted into a flammable compound known as "crack" and smoked, usually in a water pipe.

Despite earlier reports to the contrary, and as Freud saw, cocaine *is* addictive. Tolerance develops with repeated use, and withdrawal effects, while not as dramatic as with the opiates, do occur. The restless irritability that follows the euphoric high becomes a feeling of "depressed anguish" for heavy users. The down is as bad as the up was good and can be alleviated only by more cocaine.

Heavy cocaine users can experience the same abnormal symptoms as high-level amphetamine users, including hallucinations and paranoid delusions. A common visual hallucination is flashes of light ("snow lights") or moving lights. Less common but more disturbing is the feeling that bugs are crawling under the skin — "cocaine bugs." The hallucination may be so strong that the individual will use a knife to cut out the bugs. These experiences (sensory stimulation in the absence of sensory input) occur because cocaine is causing the sensory neurons to fire spontaneously.

Hallucinogens

Drugs whose main effect is to change perceptual experience are called *hallucinogens*, or *psychedelics*. Hallucinogens typically change the user's perception of both his or her internal and external worlds. Usual environmental stimuli are experienced as novel events — for example, sounds and colors seem dramatically different. Time perception is so altered that minutes may seem like hours. The user may experience auditory, visual, and tactile hallucinations and will have a decreased ability to differentiate between himself and his surroundings.

Some hallucinogenic drugs are derived from plants — such as mescaline from cactus and psilocybin from mushrooms. Others are synthesized in the laboratory, such as LSD (lysergic acid diethylamide) and PCP (phencyclidine).

LSD   The drug LSD, or "acid," is a colorless, odorless, tasteless substance (solution or powder) that is often sold dissolved on sugar cubes or pieces of blotter. It is a very potent drug that produces hallucinations at low doses. Some users have vivid hallucinations of colors and sounds, whereas others have mystical or semireligious experiences. Anyone can have an unpleasant, frightening reaction (or "bad trip"), even those who have had many pleasant LSD experiences. Another adverse LSD reaction is the "flashback," which may occur days, weeks, or months after the last use of the drug. The individual experiences illusions or hallucinations similar to those experienced when using the drug. Since LSD is almost completely eliminated from the body within 24 hours after it is taken, the flashback is probably a restoration of memories of the prior experience.

More threatening to the LSD user is the loss of reality orientation that can occur during mystical states associated with the drug. This alteration in consciousness can lead to highly irrational and disoriented behavior and, occasionally, to a panic state in which the victim feels that he or she cannot control what the body is doing or thinking. People have jumped from high places to their death when in this state. LSD was popular during the 1960s, but its use has declined, probably due to widespread reports of severe drug reactions, as well as reports of genetic damage to users and their offspring.

PCP   Next to alcohol, PCP is now the most widely misused drug in Western cultures. Although it is sold as a hallucinogen (under such street names as "Angel Dust," "Shermans," and "Superacid"), PCP is technically classified as a "dissociative anesthetic." It may cause hallucinations, but it also makes the user feel dissociated or apart from the environment.

PCP was first synthesized in 1956 for use as a general anesthetic. It had the advantage of eliminating pain without producing a deep coma. However, its legal manufacture was discontinued when doctors found that the drug produced agitation, hallucinations, and a psychotic-like state resembling schizophrenia among many patients. Because the ingredients are cheap and the drug is relatively easy to manufacture in a "kitchen laboratory," PCP is widely used as an adulterant of other, more expensive street drugs. Much of what is sold as THC (the active ingredient in marijuana) is really PCP.

PCP can be taken in liquid or pill form, but more often it is smoked (by dusting it on marijuana or parsley cigarettes) or snorted. In low doses it produces an insensitivity to pain and an experience similar to a moderately drunken state —one of confusion, loss of inhibition, and poor psychomotor coordination. Higher doses produce a disoriented, comalike condition. Unlike the person who experiences LSD, the PCP user is unable to observe his or her drug-induced state and frequently has no memory of it.

The effects of PCP are not clearly understood. While the drug reduces a person's sensitivity to pain, the user also seems to experience heightened sensory input; the person feels bombarded by an overload of stimuli. This may explain why trying to talk down or physically handle a person on PCP usually makes things worse.

Contrary to the popular image, PCP users are seldom violent. When the police or someone else try to help the person because he or she looks drunk or sick, the increased stimulation of being picked up or grabbed increases the PCP user's arousal. In flailing around to get away, the user may injure others and himself, especially since the user is insensitive to pain.

Cannabis

The *cannabis* plant has been harvested since ancient times for its psychoactive effects. The dried leaves and flowers, or *marijuana*, is the form in which it is most often used in this country, while the solidified resin of the plant, called *hashish* ("hash"), is commonly used in the Middle East. The active ingredient in both substances is THC (tetrahydrocannibol). Taken orally in small doses (5 to 10 milligrams), THC produces a mild "high"; larger doses (30 to 70 milligrams) produce severe and longer-lasting reactions that resemble those of hallucinogenic drugs. As with that of alcohol, the reaction often has two stages: a period of stimulation and euphoria followed by a period of tranquility and, with higher doses, sleep.

Regular users of marijuana report a number of sensory and perceptual changes: a general euphoria and sense of well-being, some distortions of space and time, changes in social perception, and a number of out-of-body experiences (Tart, 1975). Not all marijuana experiences are pleasant. Sixteen percent of regular users report anxiety, fearfulness, and confusion as a "usual occurrence," and about one-third report that they occasionally experience such symptoms as acute panic, hallucinations, and unpleasant distortions in body image (Halikas, Goodwin, & Guze, 1971; Negrete & Kwan, 1972).

Marijuana interferes with performance on complex tasks. Motor coordination and signal detection (the ability to detect a brief flash of light) are significantly impaired by low to moderate doses; and tracking (the ability to follow a moving stimulus) is especially sensitive to the effects of marijuana (Institute of Medicine, 1982). These findings make it clear that driving while under the drug's influence is dangerous. The number of automobile accidents related to marijuana use is difficult to determine because, unlike alcohol, THC declines rapidly in the blood, quickly going to the fatty tissues and organs of the body. A blood analysis two hours after a heavy dose of marijuana may show no signs of THC, even though an observer would judge the person to be clearly impaired. Nevertheless, it is estimated that one-fourth of all drivers involved in accidents were under the influence of marijuana alone or marijuana in combination with alcohol (Jones & Lovinger, 1985).

The effects of marijuana may persist long after the subjective feelings of euphoria or sleepiness have passed. A study of aircraft pilots using a simulated flight-landing task found that performance was significantly impaired as much as 24 hours after smoking one marijuana cigarette containing 19 milligrams of THC—despite the fact that the pilots reported no awareness of any aftereffects on their alertness or performance (Yesavage, Leier, Denari, & Hollister, 1985). These findings have led to concern about marijuana use by those whose jobs involve the public safety.

Most studies of the effects of long-term marijuana usage have been confounded by the subjects' use of other drugs. One study in which this factor was carefully controlled found few measurable effects of prolonged use (Schaeffer, Andrysiak, & Ungerleider, 1981). The subjects, all Caucasians born and raised in the United States, were members of a religious sect that uses marijuana, in the form of ganja, as part of its religious sacrament. Members of the sect abstain from alcohol and other psychoactive drugs. The subjects had used between 2 and 4 ounces of ganja-tobacco mixture each day for over seven years, and their urine specimens indicated the presence of large amounts of THC. Nevertheless, their intelligence levels were unimpaired, they performed adequately on other cognitive measures, and they showed no signs of poor health. However, the long-range effect that smoking may have on these subjects' lungs remains to be determined. Indications are that marijuana smoke is at least as harmful to the lungs as tobacco smoke (Tashkin et al., 1985).

Drug Dependence

All of the drugs we have discussed—with the possible exception of marijuana—have profound effects on the central nervous system, and an individual can become psychologically or physically dependent on any of them.

While surveys show a slight downward trend in drug usage since 1980, drug abuse is still a major problem, particularly among high school and college students. The fact that students as young as 11 and 12 years are experimenting with drugs is of concern not only because of possible damage to the still-developing nervous system but also because early involvement with drugs predicts a more extensive use of drugs later on.

A longitudinal study of high school students in New York State indicates the following stages in the sequence of drug usage:

beer and wine → hard liquor → marijuana → other illegal drugs

This does not mean that the use of a particular drug invariably leads to the use of others in the sequence. Only about one-fourth of the students who drank hard liquor progressed to marijuana, and only one-fourth of the marijuana users went

CRITICAL DISCUSSION

Prevention and Treatment of Drug Abuse

Drug abuse is a major problem in the United States. Because the problem is so large, a great deal of money and effort is being directed toward prevention and treatment.

One approach to prevention is to make drugs difficult to obtain. This, of course, is what our laws restricting the importing and sale of drugs attempt to do. A review of drug use over the past hundred years shows that when psychoactive drugs are cheap and easily available, a relatively high percentage of individuals use them (Ray, 1983). Legal restrictions, however, will never completely prevent traffic in illegal drugs. For one thing, new information about the molecular structure of opiates and stimulants is making it possible for someone even with a modest knowledge of chemistry to synthesize new drugs which act like their counterparts and differ only by an atom or two in their molecular structure. Thus, an "underground chemist" can produce a cheap and *legal* drug that mimics the action of heroin, amphetamines, or cocaine and sell it as the real thing. A new drug such as this remains legal until the government has time to identify and classify it as a controlled substance. Numerous deaths and cases of permanent brain im-

pairment have been traced to such "designer drugs" (Shafer, 1985).

Another approach to prevention is to educate people about the effects of drugs. Most public schools and colleges have drug awareness programs. While many people believe in the value of such programs, there is little solid evidence so far of their effectiveness.

There are numerous programs for the treatment of drug dependence. Some take a biological approach. For example, methadone (see p. 127) is widely used in the outpatient treatment of opiate dependence. The individual is given decreasing doses of methadone, usually over a three-week period, until he or she is "clean." "Hard-core addicts" are maintained on methadone for longer periods, sometimes indefinitely. Methadone maintenance programs have been criticized because they do not cure the user; they transfer his or her dependence from one drug to another. Nevertheless, such programs enable many opiate-dependent individuals to lead productive lives.

Another biological approach is the use of *antabuse* (disulfiram) in the treatment of alcoholism. This drug alters the body's ability to metabolize alcohol and causes extreme discomfort (nausea, vomiting, and

on to try such drugs as LSD, amphetamines, or heroin. The students stopped at different stages of usage, but none of them progressed directly from beer or wine to illegal drugs without drinking liquor first, and very few students progressed from liquor to hard drugs without trying marijuana first (Kandel, 1975; Kandel & Logan, 1984). Positive experiences with one drug may encourage experimentation with another.

This stepping-stone theory of drug usage has been criticized because the majority of young people who smoke marijuana do not go on to use other drugs. Nevertheless, heavy use of marijuana does appear to increase the likelihood of using other illegal drugs. A nationwide survey of men 20 to 30 years of age showed that, of those who had smoked marijuana 1,000 times or more (roughly equivalent to daily usage for three years), 73 percent later tried cocaine and 35 percent tried heroin. In contrast, less than 1 percent of the nonsmokers surveyed used these harder drugs. Of those who had used marijuana fewer than 100 times, only 7 percent later tried cocaine and 4 percent tried heroin (O'Donnell & Clayton, 1982). Heavy marijuana smoking does increase the risk of becoming involved with more dangerous drugs.

WHY PEOPLE USE DRUGS Researchers have conducted many studies to determine what personality characteristics and social factors prompt people to use psychoactive drugs. Because some of these studies involved individuals who were already taking drugs, the results must be viewed with caution. For example,

breathing difficulties) if one drinks while taking it. Since antabuse must be self-administered daily, its success depends on the individual's motivation to stop drinking. For the alcoholic who wants to stay sober, the drug prevents impulse drinking because he or she must stop taking antabuse 12 hours before consuming alcohol.

Psychologically based treatment programs use a variety of methods. They teach problem-solving skills and more effective ways of handling stress, focus on the adverse life consequences that drug use has had, help the individual relate more warmly and openly to others, and, in general, try to provide some satisfaction in the person's life to replace the "highs" obtained with drugs.

No single approach has proved better than any other. The success of a drug treatment program seems to depend less on the particular methods used than on the attributes of the drug user. This is not too surprising. One would scarcely expect long-standing social and personal problems that led to drug dependence to be overcome by a brief interlude of treatment. In general, the more gratifying the person's life before the period of drug abuse — including satisfaction with his job and personal relationships

— the more likely he is to benefit from a treatment program. The individual who had some good things in his life and then lost them as a result of drug abuse is more likely to succeed in giving up drugs than the individual who had little or nothing going for him before he started to abuse drugs.

However, there are some general characteristics of drug treatment programs that are associated with success: (1) residential treatment programs (where drug abusers live together in a hospital or other facility) are more successful than nonresidential, or outpatient, programs; (2) structured, active programs are better than unstructured, nondirective ones; and (3) programs with extended follow-up care (such as weekly therapy or rap groups) are more successful than those without aftercare (Rosenhan & Seligman, 1984).

Many treatment programs for alcoholism insist on regular attendance at meetings of Alcoholics Anonymous (AA), which is a worldwide organization of recovering alcoholics dedicated to helping others overcome drinking problems. It offers group support in the struggle to control drinking, and it offers hope; the alcoholic realizes that many of the members, some of whom have been sober for years,

were once desperate drunks. Although AA protects the anonymity of its membership and does not encourage research, the available evidence is promising (Alford, 1980). AA now includes among its membership people with drug problems other than alcohol.

Patient receiving counseling at a methadone treatment center.

heroin addicts have been described as antisocial personalities who have difficulty relating to other people and who seek to escape responsibility through drugs. But we cannot be certain that these characteristics did not *result from* addiction rather than precede it. Nevertheless, the following factors seem important in determining whether a person will try illegal drugs.

1. *Parental influences.* One finding is that young people who come from unhappy homes, those where parents show little interest in their children or inflict harsh physical punishment, are more apt to use drugs than young people who come from happier home environments (Baer & Corrado, 1974). Parental values also play an important role in drug usage. Youths from conservative homes, where traditional social and religious values are emphasized, are less apt to become involved with drugs than youths from more permissive and liberal homes, where "doing your own thing" is encouraged (Blum et al., 1972). Perhaps the most powerful influence is the degree to which parents model drug use. The children of parents who freely use alcohol, tranquilizers, and other legal drugs are likely to sample drugs themselves (Smart & Fejer, 1972).

2. *Peer influences.* Numerous studies have revealed a correlation between the variety of drugs a young person tries, and the likelihood that his or her friends are users. This finding is subject to several interpretations: drug-using friends may encourage the youth to experiment with drugs, or the youth may start using drugs and then select friends who are drug users. Both explanations may be true.

3. *Personality factors.*   No single personality "type" is associated with drug use. People try drugs for a variety of reasons, such as curiosity or the desire to experience a new state of consciousness, escape from physical or mental pain, or relief from boredom. However, one personality trait that is predictive of drug usage is social conformity. People who score high on various tests of social conformity (who see themselves as conforming to the traditional values of American society) are less apt to use drugs than those who score low on such tests. The nonconformist may be either a "loner" who feels no involvement with other people or a member of a subculture that encourages drug use. A study of teenagers identified several additional personality traits, related to social conformity, that are predictive of drug use. Eighth- and ninth-graders who were rated by their classmates as impulsive, inconsiderate, not trustworthy, lacking in ambition, and having poor work habits were more likely to smoke, drink alcohol, and take other drugs. They were also more likely to start using these drugs early and to be heavy users 12 years later as young adults (Smith, 1986).

These factors may influence initial drug use, but once an individual becomes physically dependent, the motivation changes radically. The person has acquired a new need that may be so powerful he or she ignores all other concerns and lives only for the next "fix."

MEDITATION

In *meditation,* a person achieves an altered state of consciousness by performing certain rituals and exercises. These exercises include controlling and regulating breathing, sharply restricting one's field of attention, eliminating external stimuli, assuming yogic body positions, and forming mental images of an event or symbol. The result is a somewhat "mystical" state in which the individual is extremely relaxed and feels divorced from the outside world; the person loses self-awareness and gains a sense of being involved in a wider consciousness, however defined. That such meditative techniques may cause a change in consciousness goes back to ancient times and is represented in every major world religion. Buddhists, Hindus, Sufis, Jews, and Christians all have literature describing rituals that induce meditative states.

Traditional Forms of Meditation

Traditional forms of meditation follow the practices of *yoga,* a system of thought based on the Hindu religion, or *Zen,* which is derived from Chinese and Japanese Buddhism. Two common techniques of meditation are an *opening-up meditation,* in which the subject clears his or her mind for receiving new experiences, and a *concentrative meditation,* in which the benefits are obtained through actively attending to some object, word, or idea. The following is a representative statement of opening-up meditation:

> This approach begins with the resolve to do nothing, to think nothing, to make no effort of one's own, to relax completely and let go of one's mind and body . . . stepping out of the stream of ever-changing ideas and feelings which your mind is in, watch the onrush of the stream. Refuse to be submerged in the current. Changing the metaphor, . . . watch your ideas, feelings, and wishes fly across the firmament like a flock of birds. Let them fly freely. Just keep a watch. Don't let the birds carry you off into the clouds. (Chauduri, 1965, pp. 30–31)

Here is a corresponding statement used in an experimental study of concentrative meditation:

> The purpose of these sessions is to learn about concentration. Your aim is to concentrate on the blue vase. By concentration I do not mean analyzing the different parts of the vase, but rather, trying to see the vase as it exists in itself, without any connections to other things. Exclude all other thoughts or feelings or sounds or body sensations. (Deikman, 1963, p. 330)

After a few sessions of concentrative meditation, subjects typically report a number of effects: an altered, more intense perception of the vase; some time shortening, particularly in retrospect; conflicting perceptions, as if the vase fills the visual field and does not fill it; decreasing effectiveness of external stimuli (less distraction and eventually less conscious registration); and an impression of the meditative state as pleasant and rewarding.

Experimental studies of meditation, which necessarily are of short duration, provide only limited insight into the alterations of consciousness that a person can achieve when meditative practice and training extend over many years. In his study of the *Matramudra,* a centuries-old Tibetan Buddhist text, Brown (1977) has described the complex training required to master the technique. He has also shown that cognitive changes can be expected at different meditative levels. (In this type of meditation, people proceed through five levels until they reach a thoughtless, perceptionless, selfless state known as concentrative samdhi.)

Meditation for Relaxation

A somewhat commercialized and secularized form of meditation has been widely promoted in the United States and elsewhere under the name of *Transcendental Meditation* or TM (Forem, 1973). The technique is easily learned from a qualified teacher who gives the novice meditator a *mantra* (a special sound) and instructions on how to repeat it over and over to produce the deep rest and awareness characteristic of TM.

A similar state of relaxation can be produced without the mystical associations of TM. Developed by Benson and his colleagues, the technique includes the following steps:

1. Sit quietly in a comfortable position and close your eyes.
2. Deeply relax all your muscles, beginning at your feet and progressing to your face. Keep them deeply relaxed.
3. Breathe through your nose. Become aware of your breathing. As you breathe out, say the word "one" silently to yourself. For example, breathe in . . . out, "one"; in . . . out, "one"; and so on. Continue for 20 minutes. You may open your eyes to check the time, but do not use an alarm. When you finish, sit quietly for several minutes at first with closed eyes and later with opened eyes.
4. Do not worry about whether you are successful in achieving a deep level of relaxation. Maintain a passive attitude and permit relaxation to occur at its own pace. Expect other thoughts. When these distracting thoughts occur, ignore them by thinking "oh well" and continue repeating "one." With practice, the response should come with little effort.
5. Practice the technique once or twice daily but not within two hours after a meal, since the digestive processes seem to interfere with the subjective changes. (Benson, Kotch, Crassweller, & Greenwood, 1977, p. 442)

During this kind of meditation, a person develops a reduced state of physiological arousal. Subjects report feelings quite similar to those generated by other meditative practices: peace of mind, a feeling of being at peace with the world, and a sense of well-being.

Meditation is an effective technique for inducing relaxation and reducing physiological arousal. Almost all studies of the phenomenon report a significant lowering of the respiratory rate, a decrease in oxygen consumption, and less elimination of carbon dioxide. The heart rate is lowered, blood flow stabilizes, and the concentration of lactate in the blood is decreased (Benson & Friedman, 1985; Shapiro, 1985). Early research findings suggested that meditation could be discriminated as a unique physiological state, but more recent experiments indicate that the physiological state is no different from that induced by other relaxation techniques such as hypnosis, biofeedback, or deep muscle relaxation. Holmes (1984, 1985), based on a review of the research literature, goes even further and argues that there is no reliable evidence to indicate that meditating is more effective in reducing physiological arousal than simply resting.

A number of people involved in *sports psychology* believe that meditation can be useful in getting maximum performance from an athlete (Syer & Connolly, 1984). Engaging in meditation helps reduce stress before an event, and with experience the athlete can learn to relax different muscle groups and appreciate subtle differences in muscle tension. The meditation may also involve forming mental images of the details of an upcoming event, such as a downhill ski race, until the athlete is in total synchrony with the flow of actions. The skier visualizes the release from the starting platform, speeding down the hill, and moving between the gates and goes through every action in his or her mind. By creating visual sensations of a successful performance, the athlete is attempting to program the muscles and body for peak efficiency. Golfing great Jack Nicklaus developed this technique on his own years ago. In describing how he images his performance, Nicklaus wrote:

> I never hit a shot, even in practice, without having a sharp, in-focus picture of it in my head. It's like a color movie. First, I "see" the ball where I want it to finish, nice and white and sitting up high on the bright green grass. Then the scene quickly changes, and I "see" the ball going there: its path, trajectory, and shape, even its behavior on landing. Then there's a sort of fade-out, and the next scene shows me making the kind of swing that will turn the previous images into reality. Only at the end of this short, private, Hollywood spectacular do I select a club and step up to the ball. (1974, p. 79)

The research literature on meditation is of mixed quality and some claims, particularly by those who have a commercial interest in the outcome, are suspect. But independent evaluations suggest that meditation reduces arousal, especially in easily stressed individuals, and may be valuable for those suffering from anxiety and tension. To summarize, we quote from Harré and Lamb:

> The value of meditating for an individual depends on attitude and context. In the spiritual market place many contemporary cults of meditation, with their emphasis on gurus and membership of self-defining elitist institutions, may perhaps be seen as an expression of the disintegration of the family system in the modern West and attendant uncertainty regarding parental and sexual roles and mores. Young people, often desperate for guidance, find parental substitutes in strange places and are liable to become brainwashed practitioners of powerful psychosomatic exercises, access to which is made dependent on cult membership and financial contribution. Only where meditation is used as a means to personal development, insight and above all autonomy can its true potential be realized. (1983, p. 377)

HYPNOSIS

Of all states of altered consciousness, none raises more questions than the *hypnotic condition*. Once associated with the bizarre and the occult, hypnosis has now become the subject of rigorous scientific investigation. As in all fields of psychological investigation, uncertainties remain, but by now many facts have been established. A definition of hypnosis proposed by Kihlstrom serves as an introduction to the topic:

> Hypnosis may be defined as a social interaction in which one person (designated the subject) responds to suggestions offered by another person (designated the hypnotist) for experiences involving alterations in perception, memory, and voluntary action. In the classic case, these experiences and their accompanying behaviors are associated with subjective conviction bordering on delusion, and involuntariness bordering on compulsion. (1985, pp. 385–86)

Hypnotic Experience

In hypnosis, a willing and cooperative subject (the only kind that can be hypnotized under most circumstances) relinquishes some control over his or her behavior to the hypnotist and accepts some reality distortion. The hypnotist uses a variety of methods to induce this condition. For example, the subject may be asked to concentrate all thoughts on a small target (such as a thumbtack on the wall) while gradually becoming relaxed. A suggestion of sleepiness may be made because, like sleep, hypnosis is a relaxed state in which a person is out of touch with ordinary environmental demands. But sleep is only a metaphor. The subject is told that he or she will not really go to sleep but will continue to listen to the hypnotist.

The same state can be induced by methods other than relaxation. A hyper-alert hypnotic trance is characterized by increased tension and alertness, and the trance-induction procedure is an active one. For example, in one study, subjects riding a stationary laboratory bicycle while receiving suggestions of strength and alertness were as responsive to hypnotic suggestions as were conventionally relaxed subjects (Banyai & Hilgard, 1976). This result denies the common equation of hypnosis with relaxation but is consistent with the trance-induction methods of sects like the whirling dervishes.

Modern hypnotists do not use authoritarian commands. Indeed, with a little training, subjects can hypnotize themselves (Ruch, 1975). The subject enters the hypnotic state when the conditions are right; the hypnotist merely helps set the conditions. The following changes are characteristic of the hypnotized state.

1. *Planfulness ceases.* A deeply hypnotized subject does not like to initiate activity and would rather wait for the hypnotist to suggest something to do.
2. *Attention becomes more selective than usual.* A subject who is told to listen only to the hypnotist's voice will ignore any other voices in the room.
3. *Enriched fantasy is readily evoked.* A subject may find herself or himself enjoying experiences at a place distant in time and space.
4. *Reality testing is reduced and reality distortion is accepted.* A subject may uncritically accept hallucinated experiences (for example, conversing with an imagined person believed to be sitting in a nearby chair) and will not check to determine whether that person is real.
5. *Suggestibility is increased.* A subject must accept suggestions in order to be hypnotized at all, but whether suggestibility is increased under hypnosis is a matter of some dispute. Careful studies have found some increase in suggestibility following hypnotic induction, although less than is commonly supposed (Ruch, Morgan, & Hilgard, 1973).

Involuntary movement of the arms or paralysis of movement may be produced by hypnotic suggestion.

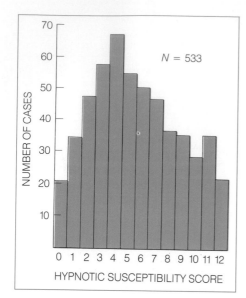

N = 533

FIGURE 4-6

Individual Differences in Hypnotizability *After using a standard procedure designed to induce hypnosis, researchers administered 12 test suggestions from the Stanford Hypnotic Susceptibility Scale to 533 subjects. The object of the experiment was to test the appearance of hypnotic responses such as those described in the text (for example, being unable to bend one's arm or separate interlocked fingers when the hypnotist suggests these possibilities). The response was scored as present or absent, and the present responses were totaled for each subject to yield a score ranging from 0 (totally unresponsive) to 12 (most responsive). As with other psychological measurements, most subjects fell in the middle ranges with a few very high and a few very low. (After Hilgard, 1965)*

6. *Posthypnotic amnesia is often present.*   When instructed to do so, a highly responsive hypnotic subject will forget all or most of what transpired during the hypnotic session. When a prearranged release signal is given, the memories are restored.

Responsiveness to suggestions is typical of relatively superficial levels of hypnosis. When highly responsive subjects are encouraged to go deeper into hypnosis, they eventually reach a state in which they are unresponsive to the hypnotist's suggestions (except when a prearranged signal returns them to a level at which they can communicate). People who have been deeply hypnotized describe a sense of mind-body separation, a feeling of oneness with the universe, an impression of gaining knowledge of a kind that cannot be communicated (Tart, 1979). This state seems similar to the kind of mystical experience reported by those who have had extensive training in meditation, suggesting that meditation may be a kind of self-hypnosis.

Not all subjects are equally responsive to hypnotic procedures (Figure 4-6). Responsiveness seems to have both learned and genetic components. The capacity to set ordinary reality aside and become deeply absorbed in reading a book, watching a play, listening to music, or enjoying nature is an important predictor of hypnotizability (Kihlstrom, 1985). This is probably a learned capacity, developed in early childhood through experiences with parents rich in imagination. Support for a hereditary component comes from studies of twins. For example, when identical (monozygotic) twins were compared with fraternal (dizygotic) twins, there was a significant difference between the groups. The identical twins achieved more similar hypnotizability scores than did the fraternal twins (Morgan, 1973).

Suggestions given to a hypnotized subject can result in a variety of behaviors and experiences. The person's motor control may be affected, new memories may be lost or old ones re-experienced, and current perceptions may be radically altered.

CONTROL OF MOVEMENT   Many hypnotic subjects respond to direct suggestion with involuntary movement. For example, if a person stands with arms outstretched and hands facing each other and the hypnotist suggests that the subject's hands are attracted to one another, the hands will soon begin to move, and the subject will feel that they are propelled by some force that she or he is not generating. Direct suggestion can also inhibit movement. If a suggestible subject is told that an arm is stiff (like a bar of iron or an arm in a splint) and then is asked to bend the arm, it will not bend, or more effort than usual will be needed to make it bend. This response is less common than suggested movement.

Subjects who have been roused from hypnosis may respond with movement to a prearranged signal from the hypnotist. This is called a *posthypnotic response.* Even if the suggestion has been forgotten, subjects will feel a compulsion to carry out the behavior. They may try to justify such behavior as rational, even though the urge to perform it is impulsive. For example, a young man searching for a rational explanation of why he opened a window when the hypnotist took off his glasses (the prearranged signal) remarked that the room felt a little stuffy.

POSTHYPNOTIC AMNESIA   At the suggestion of the hypnotist, events occurring during hypnosis may be "forgotten" until a signal from the hypnotist enables the subject to recall them. This is called *posthypnotic amnesia.* Subjects differ widely in their susceptibility to posthypnotic amnesia, as Figure 4-7 shows. The items to be recalled in this study were ten actions the subjects performed while hypnotized. A few subjects forgot none or only one or two items; most subjects forgot four or five items. However, a sizable number of subjects forgot all ten items. This type of bimodal distribution, showing two distinct groups of subjects, has been found in many studies of posthypnotic amnesia. The group of subjects with the higher recall is larger and presumably represents the average hypnotic responders; the smaller group, the subjects who forgot all ten items, has been described as hypnotic virtuosos. Differences in recall between the two groups following posthypnotic suggestion do not appear to be related to differences in memory capacity: once the amnesia is canceled at a prearranged signal from the hypnotist, highly amnesic subjects remember as many items as those who are less amnesic. Some researchers have suggested that hypnosis temporarily interferes with the person's ability to search for a particular item in memory but does not affect actual memory storage (Kihlstrom, 1985).

AGE REGRESSION   In response to hypnotic suggestion, some individuals are able to relive episodes from earlier periods of life, such as a birthday at age 10. To some subjects, the episode seems to be pictured as if it were on a TV screen; the subjects are conscious of being present and viewing the event but do not feel as if they are producing it. In another type of regression, subjects feel as if they are re-experiencing the events. They may describe the clothing they are wearing, run a hand through their hair and describe its length, or recognize their elementary school classmates. Occasionally, a childhood language, long forgotten, emerges during regression. For example, an American-born boy whose parents were Japanese and who had spoken Japanese at an early age but had forgotten it began speaking the language fluently again while under hypnosis (Fromm, 1970).

POSITIVE AND NEGATIVE HALLUCINATIONS   Some hypnotic experiences require a higher level of hypnotic talent than others. The vivid and convincing perceptual distortions of hallucinations, for instance, are relatively rare. Two types of suggested hallucinations have been documented: *positive hallucinations,* in which the subject sees an object or hears a voice that is not actually present; and *negative hallucinations,* in which the subject does not perceive something that normally would be perceived. Many hallucinations have both positive and negative components. In order not to see a person sitting in a chair (a negative hallucination), a subject must see the parts of the chair that would ordinarily be blocked from view (a positive hallucination).

Hallucinations can also occur as the result of posthypnotic suggestion. For example, subjects may be told that on arousal from the hypnotic state they will find themselves holding a rabbit that wants to be petted and that the rabbit will ask, "What time is it?" Seeing and petting the rabbit will seem natural to most of the subjects. But when they find themselves giving the correct time of day, they are surprised and try to provide an explanation for the behavior: "Did I hear someone ask the time? It's funny, it seemed to be the rabbit asking, but rabbits can't talk!" is a typical response.

Negative hallucinations can be used effectively to control pain. In many cases, hypnosis completely eliminates pain, even though the source of the pain — a severe burn or a bone fracture — continues. The failure to perceive something (pain) that would normally be perceived qualifies this response as a negative hallucination. The pain reduction need not be complete in order for hypnosis to be useful in giving relief. Reducing the pain by as little as 20 percent can make the patient's life more tolerable. Experimental studies have shown that the amount of pain reduction is closely related to the degree of measured hypnotizability (Hilgard & Hilgard, 1975). Pain reduction through hypnosis is useful in dentistry, obstetrics, and surgery, especially when chemical anesthetics are ill-advised because of the patient's condition (Wadden & Anderton, 1982) (see Figure 4-8).

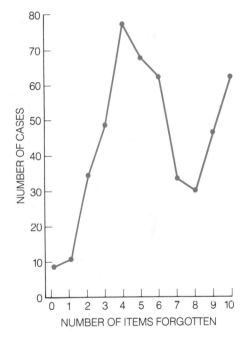

FIGURE 4-7

Distribution of Posthypnotic Amnesia
Subjects performed 10 actions while hypnotized and were then given posthypnotic amnesia instructions. When asked what occurred during hypnosis, subjects varied in the number of actions they failed to recall: the level of forgetting for a given subject ranged from 0 to 10 items. The experiment involved 491 subjects, and the graph plots the number of subjects at each level of forgetting. The plot shows a bimodal distribution for posthypnotic amnesia with peaks at 4 and 10 items forgotten. (After Cooper, 1979)

CRITICAL DISCUSSION

The "Hidden Observer" in Hypnosis

The neodissociation theory of hypnosis originated with Hilgard's (1977) observation that in many hypnotized subjects, a part of the mind that is not within awareness seems to be watching the subject's experience as a whole. His finding has been described as follows:

The circumstances of Hilgard's discovery of a doubled train of thought in hypnosis were suitably dramatic. He was giving a classroom demonstration of hypnosis using an experienced subject who, as it happened, was blind. Hilgard induced deafness, telling him that he would be able to hear when a hand was put on his shoulder. Cut off from what was going on around him, he became bored and began to think of other things. Hilgard showed the class how unresponsive he was to noise or speech, but then the question arose as to whether he was as unresponsive as he seemed. In a quiet voice, Hilgard asked the subject whether, though he was hypnotically deaf, there might be "some part of him" that could hear; if so,

would he raise a forefinger? To the surprise of everyone — including the hypnotized subject — the finger rose.

At this, the subject wanted to know what was going on. Hilgard put a hand on his shoulder so he could hear, promised to explain later, but in the meantime asked the subject what he remembered. What he remembered was that everything had become still, that he was bored and had begun thinking about a problem in statistics. Then he felt his forefinger rise, and he wanted to know why.

Hilgard then asked for a report from "that part of you that listened to me before and made your finger rise," while instructing the hypnotized subject that he would not be able to hear what he himself said. It turned out that this second part of the subject's awareness had heard all that went on and was able to report it. Hilgard found a suitable metaphor to describe this detached witness — the hidden observer. (Hebb, 1982, p. 53)

Thus, the hidden-observer metaphor refers

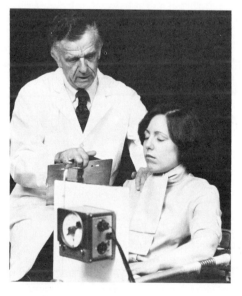

FIGURE 4-8
Pain Under Hypnosis   *Previously, when her hand was in the ice water, the subject felt no pain following suggestions of hypnotic anesthesia. By placing a hand on her shoulder, however, Dr. Hilgard can tap a "hidden observer" that reports the pain that the subject had felt at some level.*

Theories of Hypnosis

Experts have been arguing about what hypnosis is and how it works since the late 1700s, when Franz Mesmer claimed that it was caused by "animal magnetism." A hundred years later, the French neurologist Charcot suggested that hypnosis is a sign of hysteria and classified it as a neurological disturbance. His views were opposed by Bernheim, a physician who argued that hypnosis is the result of suggestion and insisted that normal people can be hypnotized. Although Bernheim won the argument, hypnosis remained a source of controversy.

Pavlov, famed for his work on conditioned reflexes (see Chapter 7, p. 216), believed that hypnosis is a form of sleep, from which, in fact, its name derives. His theory has been largely discredited by physiological studies that show a difference between sleep and hypnosis in the EEG and by demonstrations of alert hypnosis. Nevertheless, the tie between hypnosis and relaxation is still prominent (Edmonston, 1981).

A psychoanalytic theory suggests that hypnosis is a state of *partial regression* in which the subject lacks the controls present in normal waking consciousness and therefore acts impulsively and engages in fantasy production. The idea is that hypnosis causes a regression in the thought processes to a more infantile stage; fantasies and hallucinations during hypnosis are indicators of a primitive mode of thought uncensored by higher levels of control (Gill, 1972).

A theory based on the dramatic nature of many hypnotic behaviors emphasizes a kind of involuntary *role enactment* as a response to social demands. This theory does *not* imply that the subject is playacting in a deliberate attempt to fool the hypnotist; it assumes that the subject becomes so deeply involved in a role that actions take place without conscious intent (Coe & Sarbin, 1977).

to a mental structure that monitors everything that happens, including events that the hypnotized subject is not consciously aware of perceiving.

The presence of the hidden observer has been demonstrated in many experiments (Kihlstrom, 1985; Zamansky & Bartis, 1985). In studies on pain relief, subjects are able to describe how the pain feels, using automatic writing or speaking, at the same time that their conscious system accepts and responds to the hypnotist's suggestion of pain relief. In other studies using automatic writing, hypnotized subjects have written messages of which they were unaware while their attention was directed to another task, such as reading aloud or naming the colors on a display chart (Knox, Crutchfield, & Hilgard, 1975). Hilgard and his colleagues have compared these phenomena to everyday experiences in which an individual divides attention between two tasks, such as driving a car and conversing at the same time or making a speech and simultaneously evaluating his or her performance as an orator.

Hidden-observer experiments, although replicated in many laboratories and clinics, have been criticized on methodological grounds. Skeptics argue that implied demands for compliance may have produced the results (see, for example, Spanos & Hewitt, 1980). In a careful experiment designed to determine the role of compliance, researchers have shown that it is possible to distinguish the responses of the truly hypnotized from those of the merely compliant. They asked subjects of proven low hypnotizability to simulate hypnosis while highly responsive subjects behaved naturally. The experimenter did not know to which group each subject belonged. The simulators did conform to the implied demands in the way they were expected to, but their reports of the subjective experiences differed significantly from those individuals who were actually hypnotized (Hilgard et al., 1978; Zamansky & Bartis, 1985).

An unresolved problem is why some highly responsive hypnotized subjects do not have access to a hidden observer. One difference between the two groups has been reported. Subjects *without* a hidden observer are more "compliant" to suggestions of age regression — that is, they report feeling like children again — whereas those *with* a hidden observer invariably report a persistent duality of awareness. During age regression, they see themselves simultaneously as adult observers and as children. This division between an active participant and an observer is spontaneous and not suggested by the hypnotist (Laurence, 1980).

These are complex matters, not to be simply explained or lightly dismissed. They have implications not only for theories of hypnosis but for our view of consciousness in general. For a further discussion of this topic, see Hilgard (1977).

Yet another approach emphasizes the dissociative aspects of hypnosis. *Dissociation* involves a split of consciousness into several streams of thought, each somewhat independent of the others (see p. 112). Hypnosis theoretically induces a dissociative state in the subject so that he or she is not aware of all that is occurring in consciousness. The hypnotist, however, can tap into the various streams of thought. A special version of this theory, called *neodissociation theory*, has proved to be useful in analyzing hypnotic phenomena (see the Critical Discussion, "The 'Hidden Observer' in Hypnosis").

Competing theories of hypnosis were argued more vehemently in the 1960s and 1970s than they are today. With the facts and relationships now better understood, differences between explanations fade in importance. Each theory calls attention to some significant features of hypnosis, and as new data become available, differences are being resolved (Kihlstrom, 1985).

UNFOUNDED CLAIMS FOR THE MIND

No discussion of consciousness is complete without considering some esoteric and mystical claims about the mind that have attracted widespread interest. Whether they are associated with respected ancient religious and philosophical traditions or with more theatrical excursions into the occult, these beliefs ordinarily lie outside the province of a naturalistic psychology. When the claims are tangible, however, psychologists may examine them using ordinary scientific criteria (see the discussion of extrasensory perception in Chapter 6, p. 207).

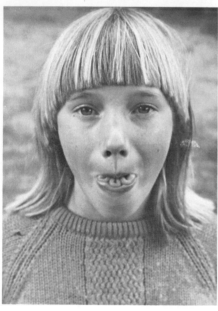

Voluntary Muscular Control
Not all people are able to groove their tongues, but this young woman is able to form up to three grooves when she wishes. (Courtesy of A. J. Hilgard)

Mind Over Body

A person's attitudes and expectations can control bodily processes. For centuries, experienced yogis have demonstrated remarkable control over processes that are ordinarily involuntary (Wenger & Bagchi, 1961). Until recently, it was assumed that such control resulted only from long and disciplined exercise. It now appears that similar, although less striking, effects can be achieved through biofeedback training, which is described in Chapters 7 and 14.

Simple practice, too, can lead to remarkable voluntary control over the body, as any skilled acrobatic performance shows. Even a trick like wiggling one's ears, which is beyond the capacity of most people, can be learned with patient practice. There need be no appeal to religion or other worldly powers for evidence of the mind's power over the body.

Another illustration of mind over body is firewalking, a religious ceremony carried out in many parts of the world. Even children in some cultures can walk barefoot over hot coals without injuring their feet. (Occasionally, a participant is seriously burned, but believers explain the injury as a consequence of the victim's having annoyed a responsible "spirit.") Surprisingly, firewalking can be explained by the physics of heat and materials, without resorting to otherworldly powers. Even though the coal bed is extremely hot, what is important is not the temperature but the conductivity of the material and the heat content. In a firewalk, we are dealing with the transfer of heat by wood, which is an extremely poor heat conductor; aluminum and copper, for example, are thousands of times more conductive than wood. Even more important is the heat content of the coals; in the final stages of a wood fire, when only the coals remain, the heat content is greatly reduced. Thus a person can walk on wood coals for very brief periods of time, and not enough heat will be transferred to cause burns (Leikind & McCarthy, 1985). To show confidence in this explanation, one of the investigators walked across a bed of coals several times and a friend joined him without mishap. On another occasion, he caught some embers between his toes and ended up with a few blisters. To observe a firewalk is a dramatic experience, but one does not need to invoke mystical powers to explain it.

Evidence of mental control over bodily functions should not be used to support such hoaxes as "psychic surgery," which is practiced in some parts of the Philippines. Without the use of a knife, the healer appears to open the skin, remove organic matter, and close the wound without a scar. Investigators have exposed the trick involved; but the belief dies hard (Randi, 1982).

Mind Over Matter

A young magician, Uri Geller, became famous in the United States and Great Britain by claiming paranormal (even supernatural) power. Geller managed to convince a number of scientists and even a few magicians (who are often better at detecting tricks than scientists) that his paranormal abilities were genuine (see Panati, 1976). Among his claims was the ability to bend keys and repair broken watches without touching them.

To make broken watches operate, Geller instructed participants to hold them in their hands and to think, "Work! Work! Work!" The watches often started, but not because of his power. Skeptics point out that most watches taken to a jeweler for repair are not actually broken; holding the watch for a few minutes and handling it to free the working parts will often start it running. In a test of the "Geller effect," six jewelers were asked to try to start broken watches by using the holding-and-handling method before opening the watch to inspect it. Of more than 100 watches brought in during one week, 57 percent started working. In one of Geller's stage performances, he was given 12 watches on stage; 4 started. Out of 17 watches that members of the audience held, 3 started. This yields 7 of 29 (24 percent), which is less success than that achieved by the jewelers (Marks & Kammann, 1977).

Reincarnation

Psychic researchers have long searched for tangible evidence of survival after death (Gould, 1977). Related to these efforts is an interest in *reincarnation,* the belief that life continues after death as the spirit of the dead person is reborn in the body of another person (Stevenson, 1977).

Instances in which individuals report experiences of prior lives while hypnotized have been cited as evidence of reincarnation. One case was a young American housewife, who under hypnosis described vividly her previous life in Ireland under the name of Bridey Murphy (Bernstein, 1956). A widely publicized account described the matter as a hoax (Gardner, 1975), but the refutation was questionable on the basis of later evidence (Wilson, 1982), and unresolved questions remain. Nevertheless, the case is not convincing evidence for reincarnation.

It is easy under hypnosis to produce fantasies of the birth experience or of an earlier life, and such evidence need not be taken seriously. One of the authors has been able to assign prior lives to hypnotizable subjects. These subjects produce quite satisfactory evidence of having lived at the time and place they were assigned. They have even given believable accounts when (on separate occasions) they were assigned prior lives in two different places at the same previous time. Clearly, under hypnosis, fantasy is interpreted as reality.

The desire to experience mysterious happenings is very great. The role of psychology is not necessarily to contradict occult beliefs but to understand why they have originated and why they persist.

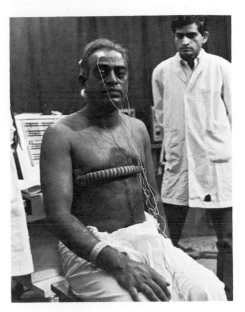

Control of Vital Functions
Ramanand Yogi has transducers attached for the study of EEGs, heart rate, and breathing as he prepares to reduce his oxygen needs while sealed in an airtight box. (After Calder, 1971)

SUMMARY

1. A person's perceptions, thoughts, and feelings at any moment in time constitute that person's *consciousness.* An altered *state of consciousness* is said to exist when mental functioning seems changed or out of the ordinary to the person experiencing the state. Some altered states of consciousness, such as sleep and dreams, are experienced by everyone; others result from special circumstances, such as meditation, hypnosis, or the use of drugs.

2. The main functions of consciousness are (a) *monitoring* ourselves and our environment so that we are aware of what is happening within our bodies and in our surroundings and (b) *controlling* our actions so that they coordinate with events in the outside world. Not all events that influence consciousness are at the center of our awareness at a given moment. Memories of personal events and of the knowledge accumulated during a lifetime that are accessible but are not currently part of one's consciousness are called *preconscious memories.* Events that affect behavior even though we are not aware of perceiving them influence us *subconsciously.*

3. According to psychoanalytic theory, some emotionally painful memories and impulses are *not* available to consciousness because they have been repressed — that is, diverted — to the *unconscious.* Unconscious thoughts and impulses influence our behavior even though they reach consciousness only in indirect ways — through dreams, irrational behavior, and slips of the tongue.

4. The notion of a divided consciousness assumes that thoughts and memories may sometimes be *dissociated,* or split off, from consciousness, rather than repressed to the unconscious. Extreme examples are cases of *multiple personality* where two or more well-developed personalities alternate within the same individual.

5. *Sleep*, an altered state of consciousness that everyone experiences, is of interest because of the rhythms evident in sleep schedules and in the depth of sleep. These rhythms are studied with the aid of the *electroencephalogram* (EEG). Patterns of brain waves show four stages (depths) of sleep, plus a fifth stage characterized by *rapid eye movements* (REMs). These stages alternate throughout the night. Dreams occur more often during REM sleep than during non-REM (NREM) sleep.

6. In 1900, Sigmund Freud proposed the most influential theory of dreams. It attributes psychological causes to dreams, distinguishing between the *manifest* and *latent content* of dreams and stating that dreams are wishes in disguise.

7. *Psychoactive drugs* have long been used to alter consciousness and mood. They include *depressants*, such as alcohol and tranquilizers; *opiates*, such as heroin and morphine; *stimulants*, such as amphetamines and cocaine; *hallucinogens*, such as LSD and PCP; and *cannabis*, such as marijuana and hashish. All of these drugs can produce *psychological dependence* (compulsive use to reduce anxiety), and most result in *physical dependence* (increased tolerance and withdrawal symptoms) if used habitually.

8. Alcohol is an integral part of social life for many college students, but it can create serious social, psychological, and medical problems. Prolonged heavy drinking can lead to *alcoholism*, which is marked by an *inability to abstain* from or a *lack of control* over drinking.

9. A number of factors may predispose people to drug usage, including an *unhappy home life*, parents who are *permissive* or who *model drug use*, *peer influences*, and a *lack of social conformity*.

10. *Meditation* represents an effort to alter consciousness by following planned rituals or exercises such as those of yoga or Zen. The result is a somewhat "mystical" state in which the individual is extremely relaxed and feels divorced from the outside world. Simple exercises combining concentration and relaxation can help novices experience meditative states.

11. *Hypnosis* is a responsive state in which subjects focus their attention on the hypnotist and the hypnotist's suggestions. Some people are more readily hypnotized than others, though most people show some susceptibility. Self-hypnosis can be learned by those who are responsive to hypnosis induced by others.

12. Characteristic hypnotic responses include enhanced or diminished *control over movements*, the distortion of memory through *posthypnotic amnesia*, *age regression*, and positive and negative *hallucinations*. The reduction of pain, as a variety of negative hallucination, is one of the beneficial uses of hypnosis in the treatment of burns and in obstetrics, dentistry, and surgery.

13. Theories of hypnosis have long been a source of controversy, with each explaining some aspect of hypnotic behavior but none explaining all. With better agreement on the empirical facts, the theories are gradually becoming complementary rather than antagonistic.

14. A great deal of control can be exercised over bodily processes without resorting to belief in occult agencies or paranormal processes. Some "miraculous" processes, such as firewalking, can be explained according to ordinary physical principles. Psychology as a science is committed to an open-minded testing of claims that are unusual or surprising, but it has an obligation to remain critical.

FURTHER READING

Several books deal in general with the problems of consciousness and its alterations, such as Tart (ed.), *States of Consciousness* (1975); Pope and Singer (eds.), *The Stream of Consciousness* (1978); and Bowers and Meichenbaum (eds.), *The Unconscious Reconsidered* (1984). Problems of divided consciousness are treated in Hilgard, *Divided Consciousness* (1977); and Kluft (ed.), *Childhood Antecedents of Multiple Personality* (1985).

Useful books on sleep and dreams include Arkin, Antrobus, and Ellman (eds.), *The Mind in Sleep* (1978); Cartwright, *A Primer on Sleep and Dreaming* (1978); Drucker-Colin, Shkurovich, and Sterman (eds.), *The Functions of Sleep* (1979); and Hauri (ed.), *Sleep Disorders* (1982).

General textbooks on drugs include Julien, *A Primer of Drug Action* (4th ed., 1985); and Ray, *Drugs, Society, and Human Behavior* (3rd ed., 1983). *Drug and Alcohol Abuse* (2nd ed., 1984) by Schuckit provides a guide to diagnosis and treatment. The Institute of Medicine summarizes research findings on the effects of marijuana in *Marijuana and Health* (1982). For a thoughtful discussion of the legal and social problems of heroin, as well as an evaluation of possible solutions, see Kaplan, *The Hardest Drug: Heroin and Public Policy* (1983).

On meditative practices, see Goleman, *The Varieties of Meditative Experience* (1977); or Naranjo and Ornstein, *On the Psychology of Meditation* (1977). On meditation for relaxing, see Benson, *The Relaxation Response* (1975). For a discussion of relaxation and mental images in athletics see Syer and Connolly, *Sporting Body Sporting Mind: An Athlete's Guide to Mental Training* (1984).

There are a number of books on hypnosis. Presentations that include methods, theories, and experimental results are E. R. Hilgard, *The Experience of Hypnosis* (1968); Fromm and Shor (eds.), *Hypnosis: Developments in Research and New Perspectives* (2nd ed., 1979); and J. R. Hilgard, *Personality and Hypnosis* (2nd ed., 1979).

There are many books on miraculous and paranormal experiences, but few of them have scientific merit. A serious effort to collect a variety of viewpoints, primarily of those who are committed to their beliefs, has been made by Wolman, Dale, Schmeidler, and Ullman (eds.), *Handbook of Parapsychology* (1985). This includes, in addition to the more usual problems of parapsychology, two chapters on life after death. Critiques of pseudo-scientific claims are Gardner, *Science: Good, Bad, and Bogus* (1981); Frazier (ed.), *Science Confronts the Paranormal* (1986); and Kurtz (ed.), *A Skeptic's Handbook of Parapsychology* (1985).

Sensing

5

TO SENSE OR PERCEIVE SOMETHING IS to become aware of it through our senses. How do we do this? Democritus (ca. 420 B.C.), a Greek philosopher, proposed that we perceive by means of small, faint "copies" (eidola) of objects that are transmitted from the objects to us (Jung, 1984). This idea became the basis of what may be called *copy theory.* According to this theory, copies enter the body through the sense organs and are carried by sensory spirits along hollow tubes to the sensory part of the brain, where they somehow evoke perceptual experiences. The idea that we perceive by means of copies of some kind dominated the field of perception through the first half of this century, although the specifics of the theory underwent changes as researchers learned more about the physics of sensory stimuli and the biology of the senses. In particular, after scientists discovered the electrical nature of the nerve response, the copies came to be thought of as electrical copies — that is, when an object is presented to the senses, an area of the brain becomes electrically activated in the shape of the object. Copy theory still has considerable appeal as a commonsense view of perception (Held, 1965a).

In 1825 Johannes Müller proposed a different idea. He theorized that the stimuli reaching our sense organs produce responses in sensory nerves and that each nerve evokes a specific type of sensation. His brilliant student, Hermann von Helmholtz, carried this idea further, proposing that each *individual nerve fiber* evokes a specific sensation. The magnitude of the neural response (rate of nerve impulses) determines the perceived intensity of the sensation. Such a system enables us to know what is going on around us because the activated neurons and the sensations they evoke are directly related to external stimuli.

In Helmholtz's view, each cell contains or is preceded by a filter that allows only a select set of stimuli to activate the cell. In a general sense, a *filter* is any device that allows some things to pass through it, but not others. A kitchen strainer is a good example: water passes through it, spaghetti does not. The filters in sensory systems pass some signals and not others. For example, a sensory filter might pass only blue light and filter out all other color lights. A cell in the sensory system that is preceded by a filter responds only to signals that pass through the filter; such a cell is said to be *tuned* to those signals. Different cells contain or are preceded by different filters and therefore respond to different sets of stimuli. Helmholtz thought that cells in the sense organs had one-to-one connections with cells in the sensory regions of the brain and that when one of these sensory brain cells responded, a specific sensation was evoked. Thus, according to this hypothesis, a scene is represented in our head not by a picture, but by a coded message in which specific neurons are activated by specific classes of stimuli and evoke specific sensations. This idea has been termed the *specific neuron code hypothesis.*

When Wilhelm Wundt, who had worked as Helmholtz's assistant, founded the science of psychology in the late 1800s, his goal was to model the new field after the science of chemistry. He wanted to break down human experience into its basic elements and analyze how they relate. His method, termed *analytic introspection,* was a highly controlled form of phenomenological observation in which trained observers describe their own experience of some object or event that they are currently experiencing. Wundt concluded that the basic elements of experience are sensations, and he proceeded to identify sensations and their attributes. He proposed that sensations are indivisible units of experience characterized by a quality and an intensity. Thus, "bright red" might describe a visual sensation and "loud, high-pitched," an auditory sensation (Boring, 1942).

Since Wundt's time, the principal goal of sensory research has shifted from the description of experience to the broader question of how stimuli are processed by the perceiver so as to guide behavior. Methods have changed as well. Although the preferred methods have always been experimental, today most experiments measure performance on a task for which the subject can be scored as right or wrong, rather than simply recording his or her introspections. The search for the biological basis of sensory processes has proceeded in close association with the study of sensory performance. Thus the dominant approaches to the study of sensory processes are cognitive and neurobiological, with phenomenological observation playing a secondary role (see Chapter 1).

Wundt and Helmholtz made a sharp distinction between sensation and object perception. Today the distinction no longer seems as sharp. *Perception* is now a general term to describe the whole process of how we come to know what is going on around us. It is viewed as a set of subprocesses that occur in a multilevel, interactive system. *Sensory processes* refer to the processes associated with the lower levels of this system, the parts closely associated with the sense organs. Sensory processes provide a selectively filtered *representation* of the stimuli that reach us. Higher level processes use this to form a representation of the scene.

PSYCHOPHYSICAL AND BIOLOGICAL METHODS

In sensory psychology, the *stimulus* refers to one of the forms of physical energy that we are sensitive to. To *discriminate* between two stimuli is to tell them apart. We show that we can discriminate among stimuli by responding differently to them. Discriminatory capacity is a fundamental psychological trait that all animals have to some extent. It can be assessed by objective experiments; most *discrimination experiments* measure absolute or difference thresholds.

Absolute Threshold

The *absolute threshold* is the minimum magnitude of a stimulus that can be discriminated from no stimulus at all (for example, the weakest light that can be discriminated from darkness), and the procedures used to study thresholds are called *psychophysical methods*. In the commonly used *method of constant stimuli*, the experimenter first selects a set of stimuli with magnitudes varying around the threshold. The stimuli are presented to a subject one at a time in random order with instructions to say yes if the stimulus is detected and no if it is not. Each stimulus is presented many times, and the percentage of yes responses is deter-

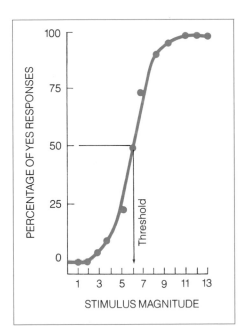

FIGURE 5-1

Psychometric Function   *Plotted on the ordinate is the percentage of times the subject responds, "Yes, I detect the stimulus"; on the abscissa is the measure of the magnitude of the physical stimulus. Psychometric functions may be obtained for any stimulus dimension.*

SENSE	THRESHOLD
Vision	A candle flame seen at 30 miles on a dark, clear night
Hearing	The tick of a watch at 20 feet under quiet conditions
Taste	One teaspoon of sugar in 2 gallons of water
Smell	One drop of perfume diffused into the entire volume of six rooms
Touch	The wing of a fly falling on your cheek from a distance of 1 centimeter

TABLE 5-1
Absolute Thresholds *Approximate values of absolute thresholds for various sense modalities. (After Galanter, 1962)*

mined for each stimulus magnitude. Figure 5-1 is a graph of the percentage of yes responses as a function of stimulus magnitude. This function is called a *psychometric function*. The data are typical of those obtained in this kind of experiment; the percentage of yes responses rises gradually over a range of stimulus magnitudes. In the graph of the figure, the subject detects some stimuli with magnitudes as low as three units and fails to detect some with magnitudes of eight units.

When performance is characterized by a psychometric function, the definition of a threshold must be somewhat arbitrary. Psychologists have agreed to define the absolute threshold as the value of the stimulus at which it is detected 50 percent of the time. Thus, for the data displayed in Figure 5-1, the absolute threshold is six units.

Table 5-1 lists some estimates of absolute thresholds for human senses in terms that are familiar. Of course, the absolute threshold may vary considerably from one individual to the next; the threshold for a particular individual will also vary from time to time, depending on the person's physical condition and motivational state.

Difference Threshold

Just as there must be a certain minimum stimulus before we can perceive anything, so there must be a certain magnitude of difference between two stimuli before we can distinguish one from the other. The minimum difference in stimulus magnitude necessary to tell two stimuli apart is the *difference threshold*. For instance, two tones must differ in intensity by a certain amount before one is heard as louder than the other; they must differ in frequency by a certain amount before one is heard as different in pitch than the other.

Like the absolute threshold, the difference threshold is defined statistically. In the method of constant stimuli, it is the amount of change necessary for a subject to detect a difference between two stimuli on 50 percent of the trials. Psychologists frequently use the term *just noticeable difference (jnd)* to refer to this amount of change.

An experiment to determine the difference threshold for lifted weights might proceed as follows. A stimulus that weighs 100 grams is presented on every trial along with a second weight that varies from trial to trial. The subject responds yes or no to indicate whether the second weight feels heavier than the first. If the subject can just barely discriminate a weight of 102 grams from a weight of 100 grams, then the difference threshold under these conditions is 2 grams. There are other methods for measuring thresholds, some of which do not use yes and no responses. However, different methods generally yield comparable values for thresholds. Sometimes, rather than referring to the threshold of a sensory system, we refer to its *sensitivity*. Sensitivity is the reciprocal of the threshold, that is,

$$\text{Sensitivity} = \frac{1}{\text{Threshold}}$$

When the threshold is low, sensitivity is high, and vice versa. These terms are used interchangeably; it seems more natural in some cases to refer to the sensitivity of a sensory system rather than to its threshold. (For further consideration of threshold determinations, see the Critical Discussion, "Signal Detection and Thresholds," pp. 152–53.)

Matching and Estimating

There are times when the sensory psychologist finds it useful to ask a subject for a description of his or her experience that goes beyond indicating whether a stimulus has been detected or not. Often a subject is given control of one stimulus and is instructed to adjust it until it matches another stimulus in appearance, either completely or in some dimension. For example, the researcher might say: "Vary the intensity of one light until it matches the brightness of another light, ignoring their colors." This is called *perceptual matching.*

Sometimes subjects are asked to indicate the magnitude of a perceptual dimension of a stimulus, such as the loudness of a sound. In the *method of magnitude estimation* (Stevens, 1975), the experimenter presents a standard stimulus and assigns to it a perceived magnitude, say, loudness = 10. Other stimuli are then presented in a random sequence and the subject is instructed to assign numbers to them, indicating their perceived magnitudes relative to the standard. Thus, if the standard has a loudness of 10, the subject should call a stimulus that sounds twice as loud "20," and one that appears half as loud should be called "5." Note that the subject indicates *perceived* magnitude, not physical magnitude. Usually, a stimulus that is perceived to be twice as intense as another will be physically much more than that. This is a property of all sensory systems.

Single-cell Recording

When a stimulus impinges on a sense organ, certain neural events are initiated in the organ and its neural pathways. These neural events can be thought of as messages sent from the sense organ to the brain, and the psychophysical methods described above are indirect ways of studying the events. It is also possible to record the electrical activity of individual receptor cells and neurons directly.

A typical *single-cell recording* experiment is illustrated in Figure 5-2. This is a vision experiment, but the procedure is similar for experiments that test the other senses. An animal (in this case a monkey) is placed in a restraining device that holds its head in a fixed position. The animal is anesthetized so it does not feel pain and also to prevent its eyes from moving. Facing the animal is a screen on which various stimuli can be projected. A thin wire (microelectrode), insulated except at its tip, is inserted into a selected area of the visual cortex through a small hole drilled in the animal's skull. The electrode is positioned so it will pick up the electrical response of a single neuron while the animal's eyes are being stimulated. These tiny electrical signals are amplified and displayed on an oscilloscope, which converts the electrical signals into a graph of the changing electrical voltage. Most neurons emit a series of nerve impulses that appear on the screen as vertical spikes. Even in the absence of a stimulus, many cells will respond at a slow rate (*spontaneous activity*). If a stimulus is presented to which the neuron is sensitive, a fast train of spikes will be seen. The electrode can be moved to test different cells.

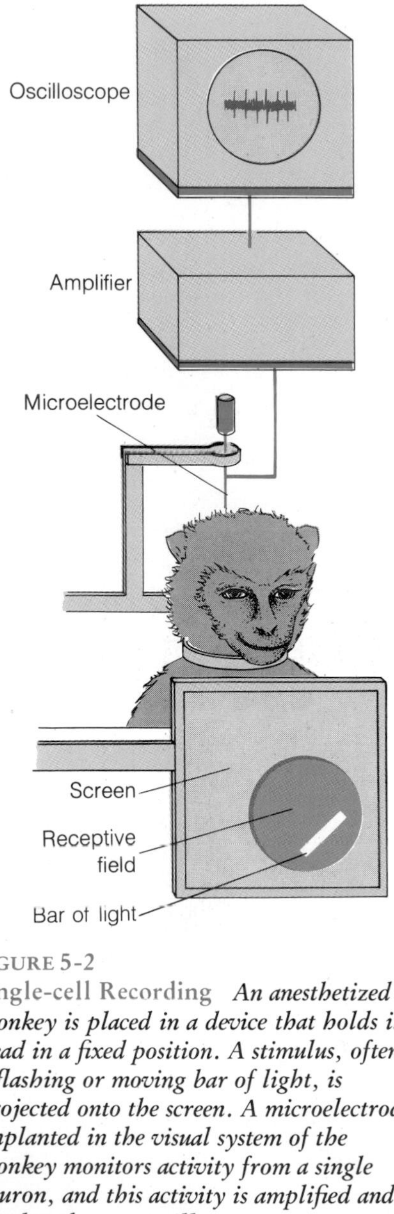

FIGURE 5-2
Single-cell Recording *An anesthetized monkey is placed in a device that holds its head in a fixed position. A stimulus, often a flashing or moving bar of light, is projected onto the screen. A microelectrode implanted in the visual system of the monkey monitors activity from a single neuron, and this activity is amplified and displayed on an oscilloscope.*

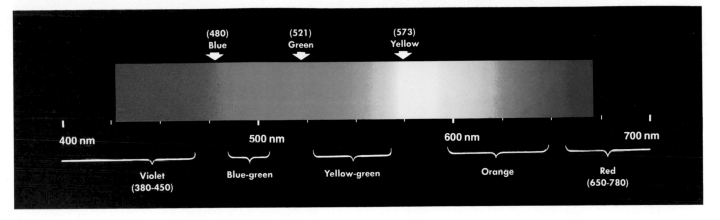

FIGURE 5-14
Solar Spectrum *The colors in sunlight as they are seen when a beam of sunlight passes through a prism or appears as a rainbow. Sunlight contains all of the visible wavelengths. The numbers given are the wavelengths of the various colors in nanometers (nm); a nanometer is one-billionth of a meter.*

FIGURE 5-15
Additive and Subtractive Color Mixtures *Additive color mixture (illustrated by the figure at the left) combines lights. Red and green lights are mixed to appear yellow; green and purple appear blue; and so on. In the center, where the three colors overlap, the mixture appears white.*

Subtractive color mixture (illustrated in the figure at the right) takes place when pigments are mixed or when light is transmitted through colored filters placed one over another. Usually blue-green and yellow will mix to give green, and complementary colors will combine to appear black. Unlike additive mixture, one cannot always tell from the color of the components what color will result. For example, blue and green commonly yield blue-green by subtractive mixture, but with some filters they may appear red. This depends on the exact nature of the filters.

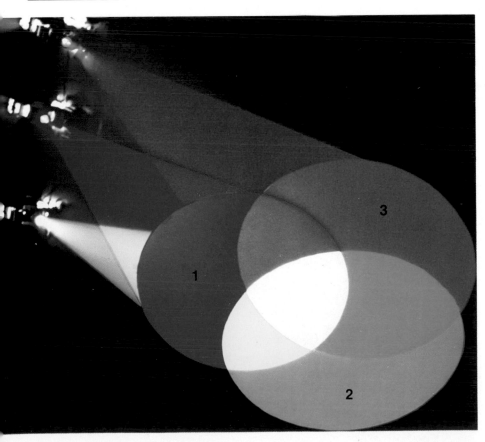

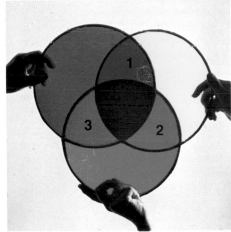

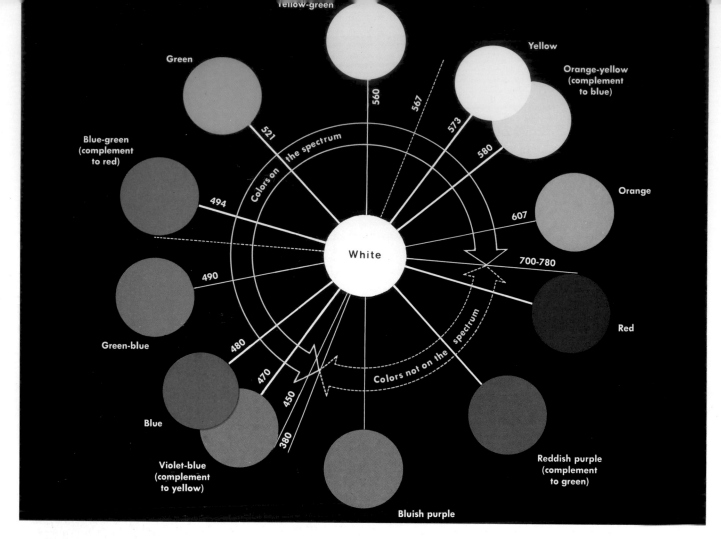

FIGURE 5-16
Color Circle *Wavelengths are indicated around the circle in nanometers. The spectral colors lie in their natural order on the circle, but their spacing is not uniform. Spectral lights do not go all around the circle. The nonspectral reds and purples are between the ends of the spectrum. Colors become less saturated toward the center, which is white. The colors opposite each other, called complementary colors, will appear white if mixed in the proper proportions.*

FIGURE 5-18
Color Solid *The three dimensions of color can be represented on a double cone. Hue is represented by points around the circumference, saturation by points along the radius, and lightness by points on the vertical axis. A vertical slice taken from the color solid will show differences in saturation and lightness of a single hue.*

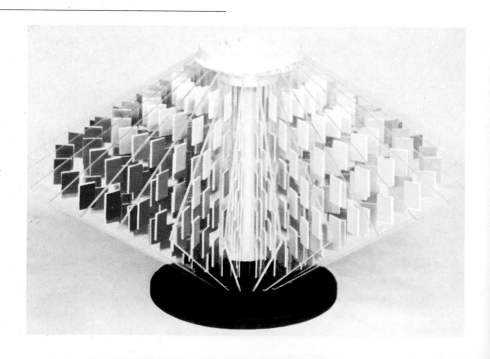

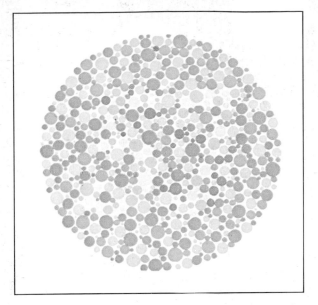 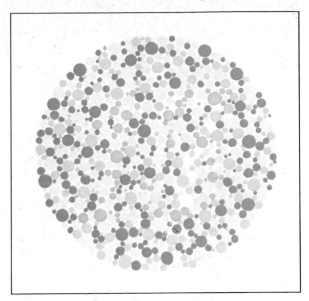

FIGURE 5-17
Tests for Color Blindness *Two plates used in color blindness tests. In the left plate, individuals with certain kinds of red-green blindness will see only the number 5; others see only the 7; still others, no number at all. Those with normal vision see 57. Similarly, in the right plate, people with normal vision see the number 15, whereas those with red-green blindness see no number at all.*

A Color-blind Comparison *A person who has red-green color blindness, the most common form of visual system deficiency, sees the vivid reds and greens of the roses (right) as shades of brown (below right).*

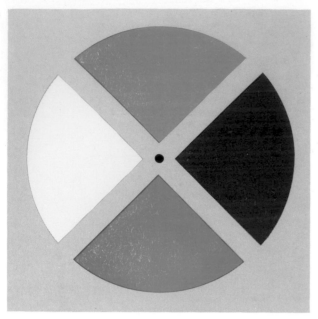 

FIGURE 5-19
Complementary Afterimages *Look
steadily for about a minute at the dot in the
center of the colors, then transfer your gaze
to the dot in the gray field at the right.
You should see a blurry image with colors
that are complementary to the original: the
blue, red, green, and yellow are replaced
by yellow, green, red, and blue.*

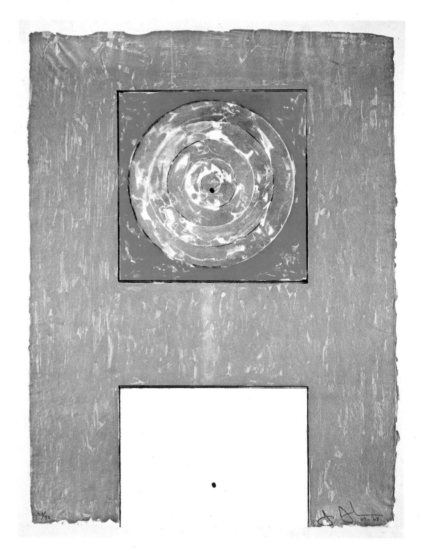

*Complementary afterimages are illustrated
in this contemporary work of art by Jasper
Johns. Stare at the dot in the middle of the
upper square for about a minute and then
shift your eyes to the dot in the middle of
the lower square. (*Targets, *litho from
nine stones and two aluminum plates,
1967–1968)*

VISUAL SENSE

Visual Stimulus

Each sense responds to a particular form of physical energy. The stimulus for vision is *light*. Light is *electromagnetic radiation* (energy produced by the oscillation of electrically charged matter) and belongs to the same continuum as cosmic rays, X rays, ultraviolet and infrared rays, and radio and TV waves. Think of electromagnetic energy as traveling in waves, with wavelengths (the distance from one crest of a wave to the next) varying tremendously from the shortest cosmic rays (4 trillionths of a centimeter) to the longest radio waves (several miles). Our eyes are sensitive to only a small range of this continuum — namely, wavelengths of approximately 400 to 700 nanometers (nm). Since a nanometer is one-billionth of a meter, visible energy makes up only a very small part of electromagnetic energy. Radiation within the visible range is called *light;* we are blind to all other wavelengths.

A light may be specified by the wavelengths it contains and the physical intensity (energy per unit time per unit area) at each wavelength; this is called the *energy spectrum* of the light. A prism and a radiometer may be used to determine the energy spectrum of a light. The prism refracts (bends) light of different wavelengths differently; the amount of refraction indicates the wavelength of a sample of light. The radiometer measures the light's intensity.

Visual System

The human visual system consists of the eyes, several parts of the brain, and the pathways connecting them. Figure 2-10 (p. 45) is a simplified illustration of the visual system. In the visual sense organ, the eye (see Figure 5-3), the most critical structure is the retina, which is a thin layer that covers the inside of the back of the eyeball and contains receptors and neurons. Also critical are the cornea and lens, which form an image on the retina of whatever is in front of the eye. Without them, we could see light, but not pattern.

The principal parts of the eye are illustrated in Figure 5-3. The cornea, the pupil, and the lens constitute the image-forming system of the eye. The *cornea* is the transparent front surface of the eye: light enters through the cornea, and rays are bent inward by it to begin image formation. The *lens* completes the process of focusing the light on the retina (see Figure 5-5, p. 154). To focus objects at different distances, the lens changes shape, becoming more spherical for near objects and flatter for far ones. In some eyes, the lens does not become flat enough to bring far objects in focus, although it focuses near objects well; people with such eyes are said to be *myopic* (nearsighted). In other eyes, the lens does not become spherical enough to focus on near objects, although it focuses well on far objects; people with such eyes are said to be *hyperopic* (farsighted). Such optical defects are common and can easily be corrected with eyeglasses or contact lenses.

The *pupil* is a circular opening in the iris (the colored part of the eye), which varies in diameter in response to the light level, being largest in dim light and smallest in bright light. This change helps to maintain image quality at different light levels. Pupil size is also sensitive to emotions and mental effort and is sometimes used as an indicator of these responses.

The *retina* is a thin layer that covers the inside of the eye except at the front. It contains the receptor cells for vision and a network of neurons (see Figure 5-6, p. 154), plus support cells and blood vessels. There are two types of receptor cells, *rods* and *cones,* and four principal types of neurons in the retina: bipolar

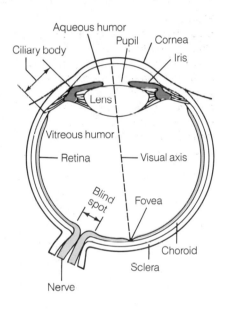

FIGURE 5-3

Top View of Right Eye   *Light entering the eye on its way to the retina passes through the following:* **cornea** — *a tough transparent membrane;* **aqueous humor** — *a watery fluid;* **lens** — *a transparent body whose shape can be changed by the ciliary muscles, thereby focusing near or distant objects on the retina; and* **vitreous humor** — *a transparent jellylike substance filling the interior of the eye. The amount of light entering the eye is regulated by the size of the* **pupil,** *a small hole toward the front of the eye formed by the* **iris.** *The iris consists of a ring of muscles that can contract or expand, thereby controlling pupil size. The iris gives the eyes their characteristic color (blue, brown, and so forth). (After Boynton, 1979)*

CRITICAL DISCUSSION

Signal Detection and Thresholds

The problems that confront researchers trying to establish thresholds can be illustrated by the following experiment. Suppose we want to determine the likelihood that a subject will detect a weak auditory signal. An experiment could be set up involving a series of trials, each initiated with a warning light followed by the auditory signal. On each trial the subject would be asked to indicate whether he or she heard the signal. Suppose that on 100 such trials the subject reported hearing the signal 62 times. How should this result be interpreted? On each trial, precisely the same signal is presented, and the responses presumably tell us something about the subject's ability to detect it. But if the subject knows that the same tone will be presented on each trial, what prevents him or her from always saying yes? Obviously nothing, but we assume that the subject is honest and is trying to do as good a job as possible. The task of detecting very weak signals is difficult, however, and even a conscientious subject will often be uncertain whether to respond yes or no on a given trial. Further, motives and expectations can influence judgment; even the most reliable subject may unconsciously tend toward yes answers to impress the experimenter with his or her ability.

To deal with this problem, we can introduce *catch trials* — on which there are no signals — to see how the subject will respond. The following results are typical of a subject's performance in an experiment involving several hundred trials, 10 percent of which are randomly selected as catch trials.

RESPONSE

	Yes	No	
Signal trials	.89	.11	*Hits*
Catch trials	.52	.48	*False alarms*

The entries in the table represent the proportion of times the subject answered yes or no when the signal was or was not presented. For example, in 89 percent of the trials on which a signal was presented, the subject said, "Yes, there was a signal." We refer to these correct responses as *hits*. When the subject says, "Yes, there was a signal" on a trial when the signal was not presented, the response is called a *false alarm*. In the example, the probability of a hit was .89 and the probability of a false alarm was .52.

How can we interpret the fact that the subject falsely reported the signal on 52 percent of the catch trials? We might think that the subject was careless or inattentive except for the fact that these results are typical of data obtained from dedicated, highly trained subjects. Even under the best conditions, subjects make false alarms.

Expectations also influence performance on this task. Suppose that the subject is tested for several days with the same signal but with the percentage of catch trials varied from day to day. Results of such an experiment in which the percentage of catch trials ranged from 10 to 90 are given in the table in Figure 5-4. These data show that hits and false alarms both change as the proportion of catch trials is manipulated. As this proportion increases, the subject becomes aware of this fact and biases his or her judgments by responding more often with no. Put another way, the subject's expectation of a large number of catch trials inhibits yes responses, which leads to a decrease in both hits and false alarms.

Originally, thresholds were thought to be determined by a fixed barrier in the sensory system. If a stimulus exceeded this barrier, it was sensed; otherwise, it had no effect. Not consistent with this idea is the occurrence of false alarms and changes in the subjects' hit rates as their expectations change. These phenomena led to a new theory of sensory signal detection. This theory, which is based on the mathematical

cells, ganglion cells, horizontal cells, and amacrine cells (Dowling & Boycott, 1966). The rods and cones absorb light and respond electrically. These responses are transmitted via synapses to *bipolar cells* and from the bipolar cells to *ganglion cells*. The long axons of the ganglion cells extend out of the eye to form the optic nerve to the brain. *Horizontal cells* make lateral (sideways) connections at a level

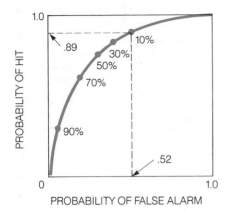

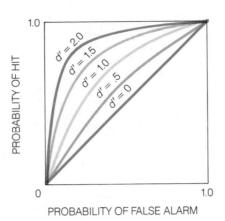

PERCENTAGE OF CATCH TRIALS	PROBABILITY OF A HIT	PROBABILITY OF A FALSE ALARM
10	.89	.52
30	.83	.41
50	.76	.32
70	.62	.19
90	.28	.04

FIGURE 5-4

Plotting ROC Curves From Data

The table presents data on the relationship between hits and false alarms as the percentage of catch trials is increased. The left-hand figure plots these same data in the form of an ROC curve. The right-hand figure presents ROC curves for several different values of d'. The more intense the signal, the higher the value of d'; the d' value for the data in the table is 1.18.

theory of signal detection (Green & Swets, 1966), explains the effect of expectation by saying that, instead of a fixed barrier, sensory systems have a *variable criterion* that changes with expectations. When a stimulus is expected, the criterion is low; when it is unexpected, the criterion is high. False alarms are explained by the existence of random activity (called *noise*) in sensory systems. Sometimes, in the absence of a stimulus, noise will exceed the criterion and the subject will say yes. This is particularly likely when the criterion is low.

Obviously, there is no fixed probability that the subject will detect a given signal; the probability varies as the proportion of catch trials is manipulated. At first glance, this is a discouraging picture, and one may question whether a simple measure can be devised to describe the subject's sensitivity level for a particular signal. Fortunately, the theory of sensory signal detection provides such a measure. It requires plotting the hit and false alarm probabilities, as is done in the left-hand graph of Figure 5-4. Note, for example, that the point farthest to the right is for data obtained when 10 percent of the trials were catch trials; referring to the table, we see the hit rate plotted on the ordinate is .89 and the false alarm rate on the abscissa is

.52. When all five points are plotted, an orderly picture emerges. The points fall on a symmetric, bow-shaped curve. If we ran still other experiments with the same signal but different percentages of catch trials, the hit and false alarm probabilities would differ from those in the table, but would fall somewhere on the curve. This curve is called the *receiver-operating-characteristic curve* — or more simply, the *ROC curve*. The term "ROC" describes the fact that the curve measures the operating, or sensitivity, characteristics of a person receiving signals.

The points that are plotted in the left-hand figure are for a fixed signal intensity. When the signal is more intense, it is more detectable and the ROC curve arches higher; when the signal is weaker, the ROC curve is closer to the diagonal line. Thus, the curvature of the ROC curve is determined by the intensity of the signal. The measure used for the bowedness of the ROC curve is called *d'*. The right-hand graph in Figure 5-4 gives ROC curves for values of *d'* ranging from 0 to 2.

Thus, hit and false alarm rates can be converted into a *d'* value that is a psychological measure of the subject's sensitivity to a particular signal. Manipulating the percentage of catch trials (or other variables)

may affect hits and false alarms for a fixed signal, but the proportions will fall on an ROC curve corresponding to a particular *d'* value.

Even in a simple task like signal detection, performance is not just a function of the signal intensity; it depends on the experience, motives, and expectations of the perceiver. Signal detectability theory permits us to isolate these factors and obtain a relatively pure measure of the effect of the signal on the sensory system. These developments have led to an alternative definition of the threshold; from this perspective the threshold is defined as the stimulus value at which *d'* has a particular value, such as 1.

near the receptors. *Amacrine cells* make lateral connections at a level near the ganglion cells. A consequence of these lateral connections is that many receptors provide inputs to a single bipolar cell, and many bipolar cells provide inputs to a single ganglion cell. This is reflected by the fact that there are about 130 million receptor cells in the human eye and 1 million ganglion cells.

FIGURE 5-5
Image Formation in the Eye *Each point on an object sends out light rays in all directions, but only some of these rays actually enter the eye. Light rays from the same point on an object pass through different places on the lens. If a sharp image is to be formed, these different rays have to come back together (converge) at a single point on the retina. For each point on the object, there will be a matching point in the retinal image. Note that the retinal image is inverted and is generally much smaller than the actual object. Note also that most of the bending of light rays is at the cornea. (After Boynton, 1979)*

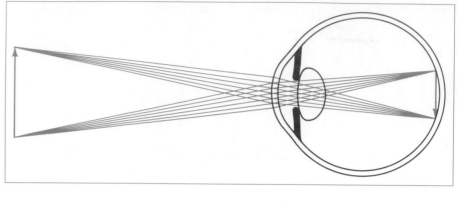

As its anatomy suggests, the retina has a more complex function than simply transmitting receptor activity to the brain. Curiously, the receptors are located in the layer of the retina farthest from the cornea, behind the other neurons and blood vessels. Note the direction-of-light arrow in Figure 5-6. In the center of the retina is a region called the *fovea* which appears as an indentation in a cross section of the eye (see Figure 5-3). In the fovea, the receptors are relatively unobstructed, thinner, and more closely packed together. Not surprisingly, this is the region of best detail vision. At the place where the optic nerve leaves the eye, there are no receptors. We are blind to a stimulus in this region (see Figure 5-7).

Except for the cornea, the eye is covered by a strong protective tissue called the *sclera* (the white of the eye). The spaces between the cornea and the lens and between the lens and the retina are filled with transparent fluids. Attached to the outside of the eyeball are six muscles which move the eyes with great speed and precision. This movement is essential because only the fovea is capable of fine detail vision. (Try reading this book while looking off to the side of the page.)

FIGURE 5-6
Schematic Picture of the Retina *This is a schematic drawing of the retina based on an examination with an electron microscope. The bipolar cells receive signals from one or more receptors and transmit those signals to the ganglion cells, whose axons form the optic nerve. Interaction across the retina is produced by the horizontal and amacrine cells. Note that there are several types of bipolar and ganglion cells. (After Dowling & Boycott, 1966)*

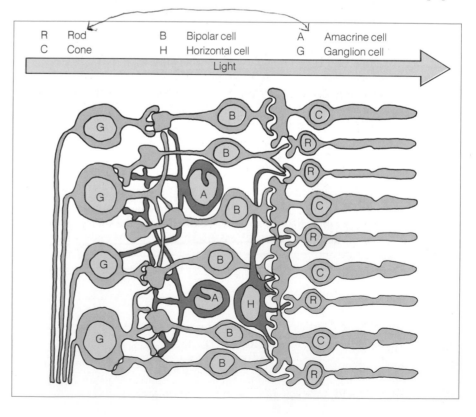

FIGURE 5-7
Locating Your Blind Spot *A. With your right eye closed, stare at the cross in the upper right-hand corner. Put the book about a foot from your eye and move it forward and back. When the black circle on the left disappears, it is projected onto the blind spot. B. Without moving the book and with your right eye still closed, stare at the cross in the lower right-hand corner. When the white space falls in the blind spot, the black line appears to be continuous. This phenomenon helps us to understand why we are not ordinarily aware of the blind spot. In effect, the visual system fills in the parts of the visual field that we are not sensitive to; thus, they appear like the surrounding field.*

Seeing Light

ABSOLUTE THRESHOLD FOR INTENSITY Although we see electromagnetic radiation within the 400- to 700-nanometer range, we are not equally sensitive to these wavelengths. This may be shown by measuring the absolute threshold for light flashes of different wavelengths presented to a subject sitting in a dark room. The results differ depending on whether the subject looks directly at the flash, so the light falls on the center of the fovea, or off to the side, so that it falls on the periphery of the retina. Threshold intensities from both experiments are shown in Figure 5-8.

Not only are thresholds lower in the periphery than in the fovea, but the minimum thresholds for the areas also occur at different wavelengths; about 500 nanometers in the periphery, as opposed to 550 nanometers in the fovea. The curve for the periphery is attributed to the rods because its shape is closely related to the absorption of light by the rods; thresholds are lowest at wavelengths that rods absorb best. The curve for the central fovea is mediated by the cones, since there are no rods and many cones in this part of the retina.

DIFFERENCE THRESHOLD FOR INTENSITY Consider next an experiment in which a circular spot of light is flashed in front of a subject and on top of it another, smaller spot (increment) is flashed for a shorter duration. This threshold measurement is repeated with increasingly intense flashes to find out how the difference threshold depends on intensity. Results of such an experiment are shown in Figure 5-9. As intensity increases, the difference threshold for intensity increases. In this case, it increases quite rapidly, and at high intensities the increment cannot be seen no matter how intense it is.

Ernst Weber (1834) measured difference thresholds for intensity for vision, audition, and several other senses. He noted that difference thresholds increase with intensity, and he proposed that the difference threshold is a constant fraction of stimulus intensity (*Weber's law*). This means that if the difference threshold is 2 at an intensity of 100, it will be 4 at 200, 8 at 400, and so forth. This relation may be written as

$$\frac{\Delta I}{I} = k$$

where I is intensity, ΔI is the difference threshold, and k is *Weber's constant* (0.02 in our example). Weber's law describes the data of Figure 5-9 only roughly. It applies to data from some types of experiment, but in general it is only an approximation of the relation between difference threshold and intensity. Some approximate values of Weber's constant are given in Table 5-2.

TABLE 5-2
Weber's Constant *Approximate values of Weber's constant for various stimulus dimensions. The smaller the number, the smaller the ratio of the difference-threshold to the stimulus magnitude. (Data are approximate, from various determinations.)*

STIMULUS DIMENSION	WEBER'S CONSTANT
Sound frequency	.003
Sound intensity	.15
Light intensity	.01
Odor concentration	.07
Taste concentration	.20
Pressure intensity	.14

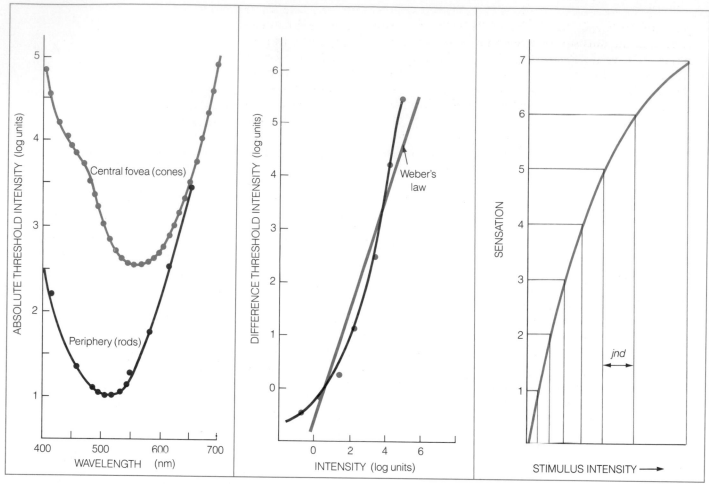

FIGURE 5-8
Absolute Threshold for Light Intensity at Different Wavelengths   *The graph plots the absolute threshold as a function of wavelength. The curve is different depending on whether the subject looks directly at the flash, so the image falls on the central fovea, or off to the side, so that it falls away from the fovea (on the periphery). The upper curve is attributed to the cones and the lower curve to the rods. Thus, the rods are more sensitive than the cones. The precise form of the curves and the value of the thresholds will depend on the duration of exposure, the area of the stimulus, and its exact retinal position. The thresholds are in log units; such units are often used for intensity. One log unit corresponds to a factor of 10; thus, when log intensity increases from 1 to 5, intensity increases 10 to the 4th power, or 10,000 times. (After Hecht & Hsia, 1945)*

FIGURE 5-9
Intensity Difference Threshold   *Here the subject's task was to detect the difference between a flash of intensity I and this same flash plus light of intensity ΔI. In this experiment the additional light was smaller in area and shorter in duration than the original flash. The difference threshold was measured at several different intensities. The graph shows that the difference threshold increases with intensity, but in a way that corresponds only roughly with Weber's law. (After Geisler, 1978)*

FIGURE 5-10
Intensity-Response Function   *If Weber's law is correct, and each* jnd *corresponds to a constant increase in sensation (the response of the sensory system), then sensation increases as a logarithmic function of stimulus intensity (Fechner's law). Research indicates that, in general, both laws are only approximately correct.*

Why does the difference threshold increase with intensity? Soon after Weber proposed his law, Gustav Fechner (1860) offered an explanation. Fechner theorized that the intensity of a sensation does not increase in proportion to the physical intensity of the stimulus. Instead, the sensation increases more and more slowly as physical intensity increases, as shown in Figure 5-10. Fechner assumed that the difference threshold corresponds to a constant change in sensation, so that sensation can be measured by counting successive *jnd*s. If this is the case and Weber's law holds, then sensation is proportional to the logarithm of physical intensity; that is, whenever intensity increases 10 times, sensation increases by a constant amount. This logarithmic relationship is known as *Fechner's law.* Like Weber's law, Fechner's law is only an approximation; modern researchers have proposed many variations on it to fit a wide variety of experimental results. Nevertheless, the logarithmic relation has been useful in practical applications of sensory psychology. Functions inferred from *jnd* data that relate sensation to physical intensity are usually called intensity-response functions, where "response" means the internal response of the sensory system.

BRIGHTNESS *Brightness* refers to the perceived intensity of light; it should not be confused with physical intensity, which is measured by a radiometer. If Fechner's hypothesis is correct, then we would expect that, as physical intensity of light increases, brightness will increase rapidly at first and then more and more slowly. When the relation between brightness and intensity is measured, this is what is found. You can demonstrate this to yourself by turning the switch on a three-way lamp. First, turn on 50 watts. It looks much brighter than the darkness that preceded it. Then turn to 100 watts; the lamp looks brighter, but not twice as bright. Then go to 150 watts; it looks only slightly brighter than 100. To double brightness, physical intensity must increase about nine times (Stevens, 1957). This is one of many phenomena that we will encounter where the subjective experience of an event does not agree with the physical measurement of that event.

LIGHT ADAPTATION So far we have been considering thresholds for flashes of light presented to a subject in a dark room. Suppose a subject looks at an illuminated surface for a few minutes. The person's visual system will change, adjusting to the prevailing level of illumination. This adjustment is called *light adaptation.*

Adaptation allows us to see well over a wide range of intensities, but our effective range at any moment depends on the prevailing level of illumination. Adaptation to a higher intensity is very rapid (Adelson, 1982), while adaptation to darkness or to a very low intensity may take half an hour or more. When you enter a dark movie theater from a bright street, you get a good demonstration of adaptation to a low light level. At first you can see hardly anything in the dim light reflected from the screen. If you try to proceed, you may kick someone or trip over something. However, in a few minutes you will be able to see well enough to guide yourself to a seat. Eventually you will be able to recognize faces in the dim light. When you re-enter the bright street, at first almost everything will seem painfully bright and it will be impossible to discriminate among these bright lights. Since adaptation to this higher light level is rapid, everything will look normal in about a minute. Figure 5-11 shows how the absolute threshold decreases with time in the dark after adaptation to a high intensity. The curve has two limbs. The upper limb is thought to be mediated by the cones and the lower limb by the rods. The rod system takes much longer to adapt, but it is sensitive to much dimmer lights.

As we adapt to a light, it appears to become dimmer. A dramatic illustration of this occurs when the retinal image is stabilized so there is no movement across

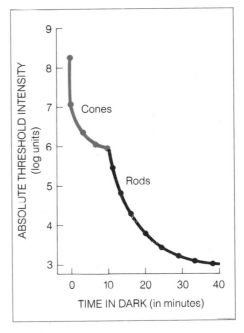

FIGURE 5-11
The Course of Light Adaptation
Subjects look at a bright light until the retina has become light adapted. When the subjects are then placed in darkness, they become increasingly sensitive to light, and their absolute thresholds decrease. This is called light adaptation. The graph shows the threshold at different times after the adapting light has been turned off. The color data points correspond to threshold flashes whose color could be seen; the black data points correspond to flashes that appeared white regardless of their wavelength. Note the sharp break in the curve at about ten minutes; this is called the rod-cone break. A variety of tests show that the first part of the curve is due to cone vision and the second part to rod vision. (Data are approximate, from various determinations.)

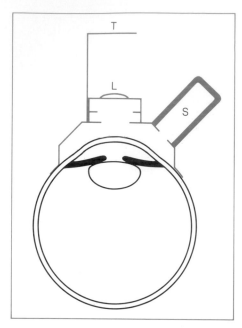

FIGURE 5-12

Retinal Image Stabilization   *This figure illustrates stabilization of the retinal image with a contact lens assembly. The target (T) is viewed through the powerful lens (L) mounted on a special type of contact lens. Unlike normal contact lenses, this lens does not slide around on the cornea; it is attached firmly with the aid of the sucker (S). With each movement of the eyeball, the lens and target also move so that the projected image always falls on the same area of the retina. After a few seconds, the image of the target will fade and then disappear. There are a number of other methods of stabilization, but the procedure illustrated here is one of the most reliable. (After Carpenter, 1977)*

the receptors. Even when we are trying to look steadily at a single point, our eyes are moving slightly. This means that the image is always moving over the retina. When this movement is eliminated, the visual world disappears within a few seconds. It takes delicate equipment to stabilize a retinal image completely (see Figure 5-12), but approximate stabilization will cause the image to fade and almost disappear. These phenomena appear to be a consequence of adaptation. The fact that the visual system ceases to respond to an unchanging stimulus indicates that it is designed to detect change. This is a general characteristic of sensory systems.

Adaptation to light appears to be due largely to processes in the retina rather than in the brain, because adaptation of one eye has little effect on thresholds in the other (Battersby & Wagman, 1962). Adaptation may take place in the rods and cones (that is, they may change the magnitude of their response after being exposed to light), or it may take place in the neurons that follow the receptors (Shapley & Enroth-Cugell, 1984).

Seeing Color

Sunlight, when passed through a prism, is spread into a band of light that appears multicolored. This multicolored light can be recombined into white light by means of a second prism. Isaac Newton described this phenomenon more than 300 years ago. Sunlight contains all the visible wavelengths, and the prism separates them by bending different wavelengths by different amounts so that one can experience the color evoked by each wavelength. Figure 5-14 (in the color section following p. 150) illustrates the appearance of the *solar spectrum*. All light is alike except for wavelength. The colors are created by our visual system.

WAVELENGTH DISCRIMINATION   If two wavelengths of light are presented side by side on a screen, the difference threshold for wavelength is found to be remarkably small. As shown in Figure 5-13, it is about 5 nm at the extremes of the range and only 1 nm at the most discriminable wavelengths. Between these extremes the threshold varies as an irregular function of wavelength. Usually we can discriminate wavelengths that are about 2 nm apart. Thus, between 400 and 700 nm there are about 150 wavelengths that we can discriminate.

COLOR MIXTURE   Light mixtures whose physical components are grossly different can appear identical and thus be indiscriminable. For example, a mixture of 650 nm light (red) and 500 nm light (green) in the proper proportions will look yellow; in appearance the mixture will perfectly match a light of 580 nm. Here and throughout this section we are referring to mixing light on a projection screen *(additive mixture)*. Since paint absorbs light, the rules of paint mixture *(subtractive mixture)* are different (see Figure 5-15 in the color section).

In general, *three widely spaced wavelengths can be combined to match almost any color of light*. A simple way to represent color mixture is by means of the *color circle* (Figure 5-16). The spectral colors are represented by points around the circumference of the circle. The two ends of the spectrum do not meet; the space between them corresponds to the nonspectral reds and purples, which can be produced by mixtures of long and short wavelengths. The inside of the circle represents mixtures of lights. Lights toward the center of the circle are less saturated (or whiter); white is at the very center. Mixtures of any two lights lie along the straight line joining the two points. When this line goes through the center of the circle, the lights, when mixed in proper proportions, will look white; such pairs of colors are called *complementary colors*. Since some lights that are grossly different physically always look identical to humans, we have to conclude that we are blind to the differences. Without this blindness, however, color reproduction would be impossible. Realistic color reproduction in television, photography, or painting relies on the fact that by mixing a few colors a wide range of colors can be produced. For example, examination of a television screen with a magnifying glass will reveal that it is composed of tiny dots of only three colors (red, green, and blue). Additive color mixture occurs because the dots are so close together that their retinal images overlap.

COLOR DEFICIENCY   Most people match a wide range of colors with a mixture of three appropriately selected lights—for example, red, green, and blue—and different people make similar matches. Such people are called *color normal*. Some people match colors with three lights but make matches different from those considered normal; they also generally have poor wavelength discrimination over part of the spectrum. They are called *color anomalous*. Still other people can match a wide range of colors by using mixtures of only two lights (*dichromats*) or, in rare cases, simply by adjusting the intensity of a single light (*monochromats*). Dichromats have a major weakness in wavelength discrimination; monochromats are unable to discriminate wavelength at all. Both groups are called *color-blind*. Screening for color deficiency is done with tests like that shown in Figure 5-17 (in the color section), a simpler procedure than conducting color mixture experiments.

Most color deficiencies are genetic in origin. They occur much more frequently in males than in females because the critical genes are recessive genes on the X chromosome (p. 55); these genes have been isolated and analyzed (Nathans, Thomas, & Hogness, 1986). About 6 percent of males are color anomalous and 2 percent are color-blind. For females, the percentages are both less than 1 percent, namely 0.4 percent and 0.03 percent, respectively. Some color-deficient persons make such skillful use of their remaining color vision, combining it with learned associations of the relative intensities and color names of familiar objects, that they are unaware of their deficiency.

COLOR APPEARANCE   Consider a spot of light seen against a dark background. Physically, it can be described by its energy spectrum, whereas its appearance is described by three dimensions: brightness, hue, and saturation. *Brightness* refers to the perceived intensity of the light. As we have already seen, this depends on the physical intensity but is not proportional to it. *Hue* refers to the quality described by the color name, such as red or greenish-yellow. *Saturation* means the colorfulness or purity of the light: unsaturated colors appear pale or whitish (for example, pink); saturated colors appear to contain no white. Both hue and saturation depend in a complex way on the energy spectrum. Albert Munsell, an artist, specified colored surfaces by assigning them one of ten hue names and two numbers, one indicating saturation and the other, lightness. The colors in the Munsell system are represented by the *color solid* (see Figure 5-18 in the color section). The term "lightness," rather than "brightness," is used when referring to a surface. *Lightness* refers to the shade (light to dark) of a surface, which depends on the percentage of light reflected by the surface.

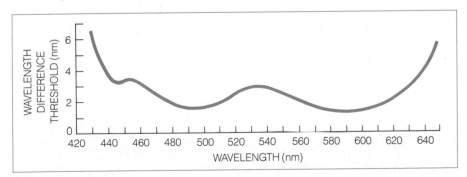

FIGURE 5-13
Wavelength Discrimination *This graph shows the difference threshold for wavelength at various wavelengths. In this experiment, lights of the two wavelengths were presented side by side, and the subjects had to judge whether they were the same or different. Over most of the range we can discriminate a change of 1 to 3 nm. (After Wright, 1946)*

A person who has red-green color blindness can still distinguish a traffic signal by the brightness and position of the light.

Although we can *match* colored lights by a mixture of *three wavelengths,* Ewald Hering (1878) noticed that all colors may be described phenomenologically as consisting of one or two of the following four sensations: red, green, yellow, and blue. Further, since nothing is perceived to be reddish-green or yellowish-blue, Hering described the *four basic color sensations* as belonging to two *opponent pairs:* red-green and yellow-blue.

When we adapt to (stare at) a colored light and then look at a neutral surface, we see markedly different colors than those to which we adapted (see Figure 5-19). The colors seen are usually the complement of those in the adapting light. These are called *complementary afterimages.*

COLOR THEORY   Thomas Young (1807) proposed that there are three types of receptors (now called cones) for color. These receptors act as three different light filters by absorbing some wavelengths better than others. The response of each receptor evokes a single color sensation: red, green, or violet. The ranges of wavelengths to which the different receptors respond overlap considerably, so that a single wavelength will evoke a mixture of sensations, and this mixture will vary from wavelength to wavelength. Fifty years later, Hermann von Helmholtz developed Young's theory and put it on a quantitative basis (Helmholtz, 1857). Since then it has been called the *Young-Helmholtz* (or trichromatic) *theory.* The theory explains wavelength discrimination in terms of the changes in the responses of the three receptors as wavelength changes; it explains color mixture by showing that a system of this kind will be blind to the differences between certain wavelength mixtures; and it explains color blindness by the absence of one or more receptor types.

The Young-Helmholtz theory has explained many phenomena, and it has become a prototype for theories of sensory processes. The theory, however, has not resolved two major problems. The first is finding out how the response of the three receptor types depends on wavelength. Researchers have pursued numerous approaches; the most successful approach has sought to isolate individual cone types and measure their thresholds. According to the theory, color-blind people have only one or two cone types. By measuring thresholds of color-blind subjects, researchers have determined the sensitivity curves of the three cone types (Smith & Pokorny, 1972). The curves are broad and overlapping, with peaks at 431, 534, and 560 nm. These three sensitivity curves are now known to be due to differential absorption of light by the three types of cones, and it has become possible to measure the absorption of light at different wavelengths in individual cones. This method produces absorption curves (shown in Figure 5–20) that are very similar to the sensitivity curves found in threshold experiments.

The second problem with the Young-Helmholtz theory is that it does not adequately account for our experience of colors. Since it assumes only three color sensations, each evoked by activating one of three color receptors, it does not explain, for example, why a mixture of red and green may look yellow and a mixture of yellow and blue may look white. Although Helmholtz and others invoked the idea that new sensations emerge from mixtures of the three fundamental sensations, many researchers did not accept this idea.

In the late nineteenth century, Hering proposed an *opponent-color theory.* He believed that the visual system contains two types of color-sensitive units that respond in opposite ways to the two colors of an opponent pair: one type of unit responds to red or green, the other to blue or yellow. For example, a unit might increase its response to one color and decrease it to another. Since a unit cannot respond in two ways at once, reddish-greens and yellowish-blues cannot occur. White is perceived when both types of opponent units are in balance. We perceive a single hue (red, green, yellow, or blue) whenever only one opponent unit is out of balance and combinations of hues when both units are out of balance.

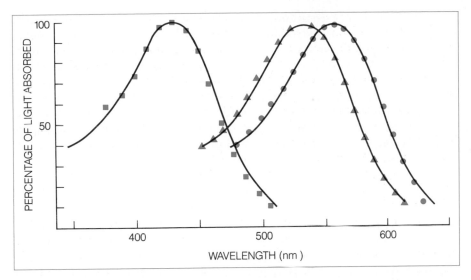

FIGURE 5-20
Absorption Spectra of Human Cones
These curves are average measurements of the absorption of light by individual human cones using a method called microspectrophotometry. In this method, a section of the retina is cut out of an eye that has been donated for research. Guided by a microscope, a very narrow light beam of one wavelength is shone on a single cone, and the proportion of light that is absorbed by the cone is measured. This is repeated using many wavelengths. The curves show the percentage of light absorbed at each wavelength relative to the amount absorbed at the peak of the curve. Each curve is the mean of several cones. These absorption curves change slightly with the density of the light-absorbing pigment in the cones. (After Dartnall, Bowmaker, & Mollon, 1983)

The opponent-color theory and trichromatic theory competed for more than half a century; each could explain some facts but not others. Some researchers proposed that the theories might be reconciled in a two-stage theory in which three types of receptors like those in the Young-Helmholtz theory feed into color-opponent units at a higher level in the visual system. The most completely developed theory of this kind is that by Jameson and Hurvich (Hurvich, 1981). This two-stage type of theory received a great impetus from the discovery of *color-opponent cells* in the retina (Svaetichin, 1956) and in the lateral geniculate nucleus of the thalamus (DeValois & Jacobs, 1984). The latter cells are spontaneously active, and they increase their activity rate in response to one range of wavelengths and decrease it in response to another. Four types of color-opponent cells have been identified: $+R-G$, $+Y-B$, $+G-R$, and $+B-Y$, where R, G, Y, and B refer to red, green, yellow, and blue, respectively; and $+$ refers to an increase in rate, $-$ to a decrease. So a $+R-G$ cell is excited by wavelengths in the red region of the spectrum and inhibited by wavelengths in the green region. There are also cells that are nonopponent (or achromatic) — that is, they respond in the same way to all wavelengths to which they are sensitive: the $+W-Bk$ cells are excited by light, and the $+Bk-W$ cells are inhibited by light.

Figure 5-21 is a schematic diagram of a *two-stage color theory*. The theory assumes that (1) excitation of each one of the four color-opponent cells gives rise

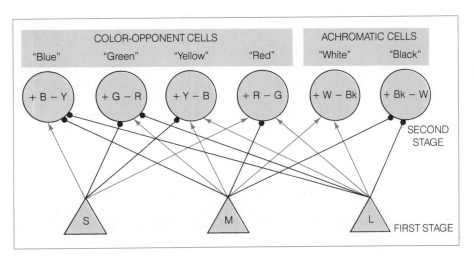

FIGURE 5-21
Two-stage Color Theory   *This is a schematic illustration of two-stage color theory. The triangles correspond to the three classes of cones with peak sensitivity at short (S), medium (M), and long (L) wavelengths. The circles correspond to the color-opponent cells and achromatic cells of the second stage. The lines represent excitatory and inhibitory synapses among the cells: ↑ corresponds to excitation and ↑ to inhibition.*

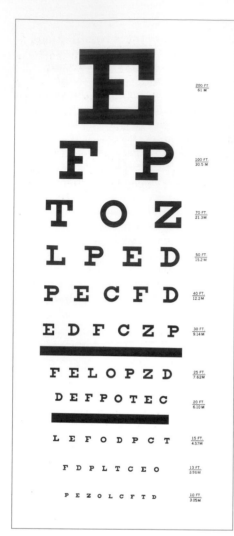

	200 FT. 61 M
	100 FT. 30.5 M
	70 FT. 21.3 M
	50 FT. 15.2 M
	40 FT. 12.2 M
	30 FT. 9.14 M
	25 FT. 7.62 M
	20 FT. 6.10 M
	15 FT. 4.57M
	13 FT. 3.96M
	10 FT. 3.05 M

FIGURE 5-22

A Visual Acuity Test *This is the Snellen letter chart, which is commonly used to measure visual acuity. An acuity of 20/20 means that a person can read a standard row of letters at a distance of 20 feet. A person who requires letters twice as large as this is said to have an acuity of 20/40. One that can read letters half the size of the 20/20 line has an acuity of 20/10, and so forth. Although 20/20 acuity is considered normal, many people can read the 20/10 line under optimal conditions. Note that this illustration is much smaller than the actual chart.*

to one of the four color sensations, (2) excitation of an achromatic cell gives rise to a sensation of whiteness or darkness, and (3) the ratio of opponent cell response to achromatic response determines saturation. The perceived color of any light is a combination of the sensations evoked by all the cells (color-opponent and achromatic) that it excites. This theory accounts for much of what is known about color vision. However, theories of this kind do not account for color constancy (Chapter 6), nor do they account for all known facts about the detection and appearance of isolated spots of light (Hood & Finkelstein, 1983). Nevertheless, the analysis of color vision is one of the major theoretical accomplishments of psychology to date, and it serves as a prototype for the analysis of other sensory systems.

Seeing Patterns

VISUAL RESOLUTION The problem that most often sends people to an eye specialist is difficulty in seeing patterns such as road signs or printed words. The capacity to see spatial patterns is called *spatial resolution*. Normally, resolution is measured by having a person look at a chart on which the patterns become progressively smaller, such as that shown in Figure 5-22. This kind of test allows the eye specialist to determine a threshold for the minimum size of detail that the tested person can detect. The result is expressed as a measure called *visual acuity*.

Recently, researchers have introduced a new approach to pattern detection. The stimuli are patterns of light and dark stripes called *sine-wave gratings* (see Figure 5-23). One reason for measuring sensitivity with sine-wave gratings is that any pattern can be analyzed into a sum of sine-wave gratings by a mathematical method called *Fourier analysis*. Instead of decreasing the width of the stripes until they can no longer be resolved, the experimenter keeps the stripe width fixed and varies the difference in intensity *(contrast)* between the bright and dark stripes to find the lowest contrast at which the stripes are detected *(contrast threshold)*. In a typical experiment, several gratings of different stripe width are selected. The gratings are presented one at a time, and the contrast of each is varied to find the contrast threshold. For very narrow stripes (high spatial frequency), the contrast threshold is high. As the stripes broaden, the contrast threshold decreases. For very broad stripes (low spatial frequency), the threshold increases again. This variation of threshold with spatial frequency is illustrated in Figure 5-24.

A similar phenomenon occurs when we try to discriminate whether a light is steady or flickering *(temporal resolution)*. If the flicker rate becomes very high, we cease to see any flicker. This is fortunate because most lights, such as fluorescent lamps, flicker at a fast rate. When a flicker becomes very slow, it again becomes difficult to detect.

What is responsible for the relation between stripe width and contrast threshold? The fact that we see some spatial frequencies better than others suggests that the visual system passes patterns through a filter that transmits some patterns better than others. A *pattern filter* can be envisioned as a device which, when presented with one image (input), computes another image (output). This output image is a part of the input image; it is the input image with some spatial frequencies removed, just as the water that goes through a kitchen strainer is the water-spaghetti mix with the spaghetti removed. In some cases, the filtered image will look like a blurry version of the input image. As we will see, many neurons in the visual system act like pattern filters. A pattern filter that passes intermediate frequencies best and passes both higher and lower frequencies less well would account for the way in which contrast sensitivity varies with spatial frequency (Figure 5-24). This same kind of filter can account for what we see in Figure 5-25. This is a pattern of black squares with white lines between them; the spots seen at

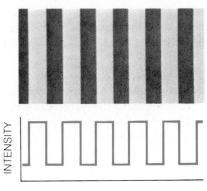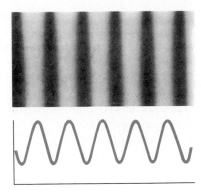

INTENSITY

POSITION

FIGURE 5-23
Gratings *The stripe pattern on the left is a square-wave grating; plotted below it is a curve giving intensity as a function of location. The pattern on the right is called a sine-wave grating because its intensity is a sinusoidal function of location. Different gratings can be constructed by varying* frequency *(number of cycles/cm),* contrast *(maximum difference between dark and light regions), and* orientation *(vertical, horizontal, 45 deg., and so on).*

the intersections of the white lines are produced by our visual system. Similar spots can be produced by filtering the pattern.

Again pursuing the approach used in color vision, we can ask if there may be *more than one* filter underlying the contrast sensitivity curve (Figure 5-24). In the 1960s, researchers proposed that there are several overlapping, broadly tuned spatial frequency filters in the human visual system (Campbell & Robson, 1968). Since then, a large number of experiments have provided evidence for the existence of such filters in the visual system (Olzak & Thomas, 1986).

NEURAL PROCESSING OF PATTERNS Rods and cones respond whenever light impinges on them. Cells higher in the system, particularly those in the visual cortex, are sensitive to the spatial pattern of the light that strikes the receptors in a

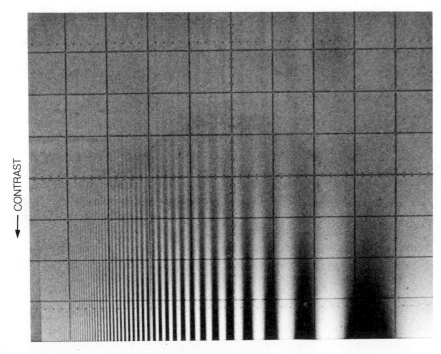

CONTRAST

STRIPE WIDTH →

FIGURE 5-24
Contrast Threshold and Stripe Width *In this photograph, stripe width increases from left to right; contrast increases from top to bottom. The middle-width stripes are seen at lower contrasts than the stripes at either end — that is, they are visible farther up the contrast axis. As stripe width increases, spatial frequency decreases. The picture illustrates how contrast sensitivity varies with spatial frequency. Sensitivity is high for spatial frequencies in the middle of the range and decreases for both low and high frequencies.*

FIGURE 5-25

Hermann Grid *Most observers will see dark spots at the intersections of the white lines. These are not in the physical stimulus; they are created by our visual system. If this intensity pattern is filtered using a pattern filter that passes middle frequencies best, similar spots will appear in the output image. This suggests that there are filters like this in the human visual system.*

given retinal area. The region of the retina associated with a neuron higher in the visual system is called the *receptive field* of that neuron. The sensitivity of neurons to visual stimuli can be studied by recording the response of the neuron while presenting different stimuli to the eye (see Figure 5-2).

Hubel and Wiesel (1968) were pioneers in *single-cell recording* from the visual cortex and shared a Nobel prize in 1981 for their research. They identified three types of cells in the *visual cortex* that can be distinguished by the features to which they respond.

Simple cells respond when the eye is exposed to a line stimulus (such as a thin bar or straight edge between a dark and a light region) at a particular orientation and position within their receptive field. Figure 5-26 illustrates how a simple cell will respond to a vertical bar and to bars tilted away from the vertical. The response decreases as the orientation varies from the optimal one. Other simple cells are tuned to other orientations and positions.

A *complex cell* also responds to a bar or edge in a particular orientation, but it does not require that the stimulus be at a particular place within its receptive field. A complex cell responds to the stimulus anywhere within its receptive field, and it responds continuously as the stimulus is moved across its receptive field.

Hypercomplex cells require not only that the stimulus be in a particular orientation, but also that it be of a particular length. If a stimulus is extended beyond the optimal length, the response will decrease and may cease entirely.

All three types of cells have been called *feature detectors* because they respond to simple stimuli that can be thought of as basic features or elements of more complex stimuli. The specific features that these cells detect is still debated. Hubel and Wiesel recorded the largest response to light and dark bars and characterized the cells as bar detectors. But other researchers have shown that many of these cells are more sensitive to a grating consisting of several bars than to a single bar—that is, the cells may be more like spatial frequency detectors than bar detectors (DeValois & DeValois, 1980; Shapley & Lennie, 1985).

Since anything we see can be approximated by a series of line segments at angles to each other, these feature detectors may be the building blocks for recognizing more complex forms. Theories of how we recognize complex patterns will be discussed in Chapter 6; as we will see, feature detectors play an important role in these theories.

FIGURE 5-26

Response of a Simple Cell *This figure illustrates the response of a simple cortical cell to a bar of light. The stimulus is on the top, the response on the bottom; each vertical spike on the bottom corresponds to one nerve impulse. When there is no stimulus, only an occasional impulse is recorded. When the stimulus is turned on, the cell may or may not respond depending on the position and orientation of the light bar. For this cell a horizontal bar produces no change in response, a bar at 45 degrees produces a small change, and a vertical bar produces a very large change.*

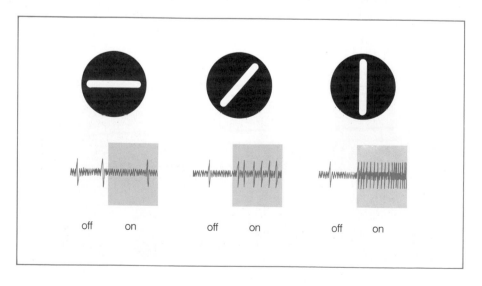

AUDITORY SENSE

Auditory Stimulus

Sound is less mysterious than light. It originates from the motion or vibration of an object, which is then transmitted to the surrounding medium (usually air) as a pattern of pressure changes. When something moves, the molecules of air in front of it are pushed together. These collide with other molecules and push them together. In this way the pressure wave is transmitted through the medium, even though the individual air molecules do not travel far.

A sound wave may be described by a graph of air pressure as a function of time. A pressure-versus-time graph of one type of sound is shown in Figure 5-27. The pressure variation corresponds to a sine wave. This type of sound is called a *pure tone*. Just as spatial patterns can be analyzed into a sum of sine waves, so can sounds. Pure tones differ in their frequency (number of cycles per second, called *hertz* and abbreviated Hz), their intensity (pressure difference between peak and trough), and the time at which they start (phase). Young adult humans can hear frequencies between 20 and 20,000 Hz; dogs, bats, and porpoises can hear much higher frequencies. Sound intensity is usually specified in *decibels*, abbreviated db, where a change of 10 db corresponds to a change in sound power of 10 times; 20 db, a change of 100 times; 30 db, a change of 1,000 times; and so forth. Table 5-3 shows the intensities of some familiar sounds.

Most sounds are not pure tones. The typical musical note, for example, will contain frequencies that are multiples (harmonics) of the frequency being played (fundamental). Different instruments produce different patterns of harmonics and thus different waveforms of the same note (see Figure 5-28).

Auditory System

The auditory system consists of the two ears, several centers in the brain stem, the medial geniculate nucleus of the thalamus, parts of the temporal lobe of the cortex, and the various connecting neural pathways. The scientific meaning of the word "ear" includes not just the appendages on the sides of the head, but the entire hearing organ, most of which lies within the skull. This is illustrated in Figures 5-29 and 5-30.

The ear consists of three main parts. The outer ear comprises the external ear and the auditory canal. The middle ear consists of the eardrum and a chain of

FIGURE 5-27

Pure Tone *As the tuning fork vibrates, it produces successive waves of compression and expansion of the air, which correspond to a sine wave. Such a sound is called a pure tone. It can be described by giving its frequency and intensity. If the tuning fork makes 100 vibrations per second, it produces a sound wave with 100 compressions per second and a frequency of 100 Hz. The intensity (or amplitude) of a pure tone is the pressure difference between the peaks and the troughs. The waveform of any sound can be decomposed into a series of sine waves of different frequencies with various amplitudes and phases. When these sine waves are added together, the result is the original waveform.*

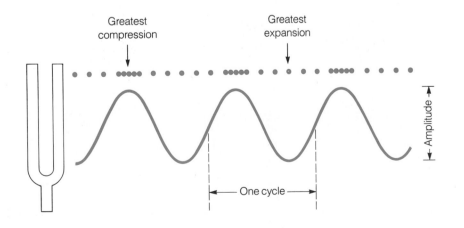

Greatest compression   Greatest expansion

Amplitude

One cycle

TABLE 5-3

Decibel Ratings and Hazardous Time Exposures of Common Sounds *This table gives the intensities of common sounds in decibels. An increase of 3 db corresponds to a doubling of sound power. The sound levels given correspond approximately to the intensities that occur at typical working distances. The right-hand column gives the exposure times at which one risks permanent hearing loss. Exposure to 150 db for a prolonged period causes death in laboratory rats.*

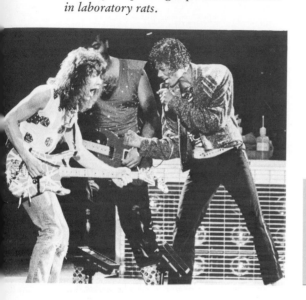

DECIBEL LEVEL	EXAMPLE	DANGEROUS TIME EXPOSURE
0	Lowest sound audible to human ear	
30	Quiet library, soft whisper	
40	Quiet office, living room, bedroom away from traffic	
50	Light traffic at a distance, refrigerator, gentle breeze	
60	Air conditioner at 20 feet, conversation, sewing machine	
70	Busy traffic, office tabulator, noisy restaurant (constant exposure)	Critical level begins
80	Subway, heavy city traffic, alarm clock at 2 feet, factory noise	More than 8 hours
90	Truck traffic, noisy home appliances, shop tools, lawnmower	Less than 8 hours
100	Chain saw, boiler shop, pneumatic drill	2 hours
120	Rock concert in front of speakers, sandblasting, thunderclap	Immediate danger
140	Gunshot blast, jet plane	Any exposure is dangerous
180	Rocket launching pad	Hearing loss inevitable

three bones (hammer, anvil, and stirrup). These middle-ear structures amplify the air pressure so that it can move the dense fluids of the inner ear. The inner ear, or *cochlea,* is a coiled tube of bone. It is divided longitudinally into three fluid-filled sections by two membranes, one of which, the *basilar membrane,* supports the auditory receptors *(hair cells).* These cells have hairlike structures (cilia) that extend into the fluid. The stirrup in the middle ear presses on the fluid of the cochlea at an opening called the *oval window.* Another window, the *round window,* is covered with a flexible membrane that pushes out when the oval window pushes in. Motion of the hairs on the hair cells causes them to bend, which produces an electrical response in the hair cells. In a cross section of the cochlea, four hair cells are visible (see Figure 5-30). Three of these, the outer hair cells, are

FIGURE 5-28

Musical Notes *Oscilloscope pictures of the same note played on two different instruments.*

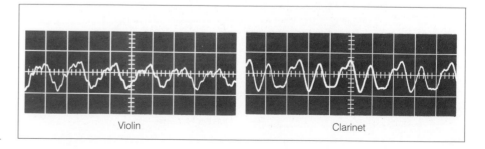

Violin   Clarinet

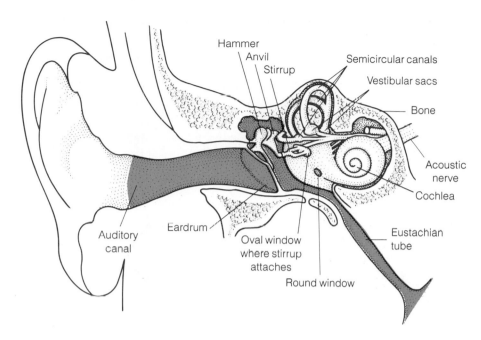

FIGURE 5-29
A Cross Section of the Ear *This drawing shows the overall structure of the ear. The inner ear includes the cochlea, which contains the auditory receptors, and the vestibular apparatus (semicircular canals and vestibular sacs), which is the sense organ for our sense of balance and body motion.*

on one side of the tunnel of Corti, and the fourth, the inner hair cell, is on the other side. The neurons that synapse with the hair cells have long axons that form part of the acoustic nerve. There are about 31,000 auditory neurons in the acoustic nerve, many fewer than the 1 million neurons in the optic nerve. Most of these neurons innervate a single inner hair cell; a few of them run along the basilar membrane and innervate about ten outer hair cells (Yost & Nielson, 1985). The central auditory pathways are relatively complex. The pathway from each ear

FIGURE 5-30
Schematic Diagram of the Middle and Inner Ear *The cochlea is shown on the left as if it were partially uncoiled. Vibration of the eardrum causes the stirrup to move the oval window, producing a pressure in the fluids of the cochlea and causing the basilar membrane to move and the cilia on the hair cells to bend. The bending produces an electrical response in the hair cells which is transmitted via synapses to the neurons of the acoustic nerve. On the lower right is a cross-section of the cochlea.*

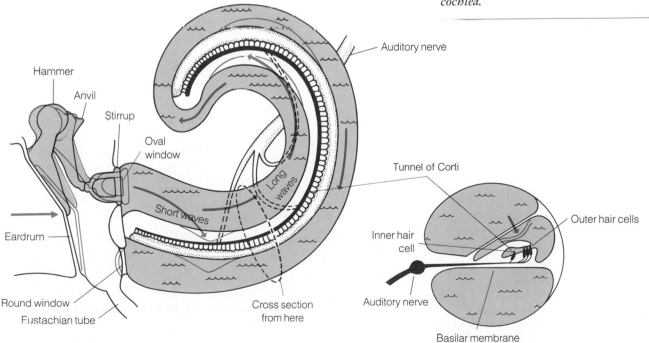

Viewing a Sound Wave   *Using an oscilloscope, we can produce pictures of sound waves. The vibration of the air molecules in a sound wave will cause the diaphragm of a microphone to vibrate. The vibrations are then transformed into an electrical signal, and the oscilloscope displays the signal as a graph on a screen.*

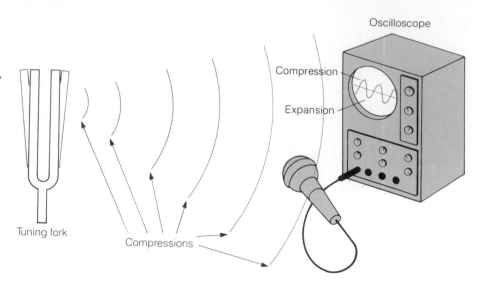

goes to both sides of the brain and has synapses in several nuclei before reaching the auditory cortex. Additional pathways descend from the cortex to the cochlea and modulate the activity in ascending pathways.

Hearing Sound

As with light wavelength, we are more sensitive to sounds of intermediate frequency than we are to sounds near either end of our frequency range. This is illustrated in Figure 5-31, which shows the absolute threshold for sound intensity as a function of frequency for young adults. The shape of this curve is largely a consequence of the transmission of sound by the outer and middle ear. The complex acoustics of these structures amplify the intermediate frequencies more than those at the extremes of the frequency range.

It is common for people to have thresholds substantially higher than those shown in Figure 5-31. There are two basic patterns to these hearing deficits. In one, thresholds are elevated roughly equally at all frequencies as the result of poor conduction in the middle ear *(conduction loss)*. In the other pattern of hearing loss, the threshold elevation is quite unequal, with large elevations occurring at higher frequencies. This pattern is usually a consequence of inner-ear damage, often the destruction of hair cells *(sensory-neural loss)*. Hair cells, once destroyed, do not regenerate. This type of loss occurs in many older people and in young people who are exposed to too much loud sound. It is curious that many people tolerate and even enjoy certain sounds at intensities that cause permanent hearing loss. Extensive exposure to sounds of 90 decibels or more risks permanent loss. Rock musicians, airport runway crews, and pneumatic drill operators commonly suffer major permanent hearing loss.

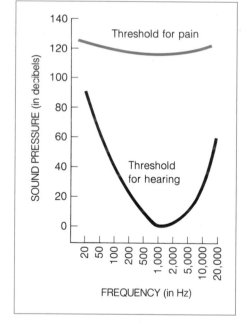

FIGURE 5-31
Absolute Threshold for Hearing   *The lower curve shows the absolute intensity threshold at different frequencies. The values given are typical of young adults. Sensitivity is greatest in the vicinity of 1,000 Hz. The upper curve describes the threshold for pain. (Data are approximate, from various determinations.)*

Hearing Pitch

Our experience of pure tones is characterized by *pitch* as well as by loudness. Pitch is a perceived quality of sound ordered on a scale from low to high. Different frequencies have different pitches, and pitch increases continuously as frequency increases. When frequency doubles (increases by one octave), pitch increases by an approximately constant amount. This psychological phenomenon is the basis of musical scales. As with the wavelength of light, we are very good at discriminating sound frequency. The difference threshold is less than 1 Hz at 100 Hz and increases to 100 Hz at 10,000 Hz.

There is nothing analogous to color mixture in audition. When two or more frequencies are sounded simultaneously, we can hear the pitch associated with each frequency, provided that the frequencies are sufficiently separated and we listen carefully. When the frequencies are close together, the percept is more complex but does not sound like a single, pure tone. In color vision, our ability to match most colors by a mixture of three lights led to the idea of three types of cones. The absence of a comparable phenomenon in audition suggests that, if there are receptors that are tuned to different auditory frequencies, then many different types must exist.

The possibility that there are filters in the auditory system that respond to different frequencies has been explored using the phenomenon of *masking*. If the threshold for a tone (signal) is increased by the simultaneous presentation of a second tone, the second tone (masker) is said to mask the first. This happens only when the tones are close in frequency. Assuming that masking occurs when the two tones are passed by the same filter, the lack of masking between widely separated frequencies implies that there are different filters for frequency, and it provides a way to determine what frequencies the filters pass and how well. The filters for frequency are found to be asymmetric and broadly tuned (see Figure 5-32).

How is the filtering of auditory frequency accomplished? In 1683, Joseph-Guichard Duverney, a French anatomist, proposed that auditory frequency filtering was done mechanically by resonance (Green & Wier, 1984). He theorized that the ear contained a structure like a stringed instrument. Different parts of this structure are tuned to different frequencies, so that when a frequency is presented to the ear, the corresponding part of the structure vibrates — just as when a tuning fork is struck near a piano, the piano string that is tuned to the frequency of the fork will begin to vibrate. This idea turned out to be essentially correct, except that the structure, the basilar membrane, is continuous, unlike a set of strings.

Helmholtz developed the resonance hypothesis into the *place theory* of pitch perception, which held that each place along the basilar membrane (and the neurons at that place) will, when it responds, lead to a particular pitch sensation. This does not mean that we hear with our basilar membrane, but the places on the membrane that vibrate do determine the pitches we hear.

How the basilar membrane actually moves was not established until the 1940s when Georg von Békésy (1960) measured its movement through small holes drilled in the cochlea. Working with the cochleas of guinea pigs and human cadavers, he showed that high frequencies cause vibration at the far end of the basilar membrane; as frequency increases, the vibration pattern moves toward the oval window. For this and other research on audition, von Békésy received a Nobel prize in 1961.

The place theory explains many phenomena of pitch perception, but not all. For example, the theory does not explain the *pitch of the missing fundamental*. As we noted earlier, a note produced by a musical instrument consists of one frequency (the fundamental) plus other frequencies that are multiples of the fundamental frequency — two times the fundamental, three times, four times, and so forth. When a note is played, the dominant pitch that is heard is that of the fundamental frequency. If the fundamental frequency is removed from the sound, we hear the same pitch. Such phenomena, which have been known since the nineteenth century, led to *temporal theories* of pitch perception. These theories propose that pitch depends on how the sound wave varies with time. Temporal theorists point out that the complex sound wave that produces the missing

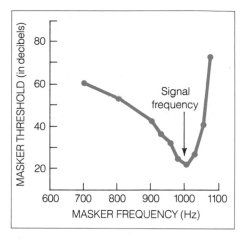

FIGURE 5-32

An Auditory Frequency Filter *The subject's task was to detect a 1,000-Hz tone of constant intensity (signal). The graph shows the intensity of a second tone (masker) that just masks the signal. As the masker frequency moves away from the signal frequency, the masker becomes less and less effective; its threshold increases. This curve closely resembles a threshold curve for a single neuron in the auditory nerve. It is thought to correspond to one of the frequency filters in the human auditory system. (After Moore, 1978)*

CRITICAL DISCUSSION

Artificial Ears and Eyes

The science fiction dream of replacing defective sense organs with artificial ones is becoming a reality. Researchers have been working for several years on artificial replacements *(prostheses)* for damaged eyes and ears. In November 1984, the U.S. Food and Drug Administration approved a device that directly stimulates the auditory nerve. This work has important implications both for the reduction of sensory handicaps and for the understanding of sensory processes.

Research on auditory prostheses has concentrated on devices that apply electrical stimulation to the auditory nerve. They are designed to aid people whose hair cells have been destroyed, and consequently suffer a total sensory-neural hearing loss, but whose auditory nerve is intact and functional. Most of these devices use an electrode, which is inserted through the round window into the cochlea, to stimulate the neurons along the basilar membrane (a *cochlear implant*). Although the electrode goes into the cochlea, the functional part of the ear is bypassed; the cochlea is simply a convenient place to stimulate auditory neurons, where they are accessible and laid out in an orderly array. In addition to the stimulating electrode, these devices have three other components: a microphone located near the external ear which picks up sound, a small battery-operated electronic processor worn on the outside of the body which converts sound waves into electrical signals, and a transmission system that transmits the electrical signal through the skull and to the electrode implanted in the cochlea. The signal from the microphone and electronic processor may be transmitted through the skull to the cochlear electrode by radio transmission to avoid a wire through the skull.

A relatively simple device of this kind was developed in the early 1970s by William House (Figure 5-33). The House implant extends only 6 millimeters into the cochlea and has only one electrode. The signal applied to this electrode is an electrical wave having essentially the same form as the sound wave, although extraneous frequencies are filtered out. When sound is presented to a patient using this device, he or she hears a complex noise that varies in loudness. These devices have been implanted in more than 600 profoundly deaf people, including young children who, it is hoped, will be aided in acquiring language. Most of the recipients believe that the device provides a marked improvement over their previously deaf state. With it, they do at least hear sounds and have some ability to discriminate intensity.

Still in the experimental stage are a number of other devices with multiple electrodes. These extend farther into the cochlea and are designed to stimulate independently several sets of neurons along the basilar membrane. Since the cochlea is only the size of a pea, with a solid bony shell and very delicate interior structures, the technical problems involved in designing and implanting the electrodes are challenging. Accompanying most of these multichannel implants is a more elaborate electronic processor that filters the sound into separate frequency bands, one for each electrode. The sound wave in each band is converted into an electrical signal and applied to one of the electrodes. Although preliminary results vary greatly, some patients show remarkably good performance, including word recognition scores of more than 70 percent correct (Loeb, 1985).

The multichannel devices are based on the place theory of auditory perception. The idea is to replace the mechanical filtering (which causes different frequencies to vibrate specific parts of the basilar membrane) with electronic filtering and then to apply the filtered signal to the same place that it would be applied in the normal ear. To some extent the success of the device vindicates the theory. When electrical stim-

fundamental pitch repeats itself at the frequency of the fundamental, even though the sound does not contain that frequency as one of its components. If the neural response follows the overall waveform of the sound, the auditory system could pick out and respond to this overall frequency. Temporal theories received support from the discovery that the pattern of nerve impulses in the auditory nerve follows the stimulus waveform, even though individual cells do not respond on every cycle of the wave (Rose, Brugge, Anderson, & Hind, 1967). This following

ulation is applied to a single small region on the basilar membrane, according to place theory, a sound with a pitch is heard and this pitch varies with place. However, contrary to place theory, the sound that is heard is not at all like a pure tone; it is more like the "quacking of ducks" or the "banging of garbage cans," even though it does have a crude pitch. Temporal theorists might expect that the sensation would change when the frequency of electrical stimulation changes. In fact, this produces only slight changes. The results suggest that another factor, apart from place and temporal pattern, is involved in pitch perception. This may be the complex spatiotemporal pattern of stimulation along the basilar membrane that cannot be mimicked by a few electrodes (Loeb, 1985).

The development of artificial eyes for the blind has not progressed as far as the development of artificial ears. The problem is not one of picking up the optical image; a video camera will do this very well. Rather, the problem is putting the image's information into the visual system in a form that the brain can use. Research has focused on the direct electrical stimulation of the visual cortex in volunteer subjects who are either blind or undergoing brain surgery. If we know what a person sees when different places in the cortex are stimulated, then by controlling the stimulation it would be possible to evoke different experiences at will. The next step would be to use a video camera to form an image of the scene in front of a blind person and then evoke an experience of that scene.

When a small region of the visual cortex in an awake subject is stimulated with a weak electrical signal, the person experiences visual sensations, called *phosphenes*. These have been described as small spots of light that are seen out in front of the person in different directions. They range in size from that of a "grain of rice" to a "coin." Most are white, but some are colored. If

several places in the visual cortex are stimulated simultaneously, the corresponding spots will usually be experienced together. Although this provides the basis for a crude pattern vision (Dobelle, Meadejovsky, & Girvin, 1974), it is questionable whether this approach will lead to a successful prosthesis for damaged eyes. The neural input to the cortex is so complicated that it is unlikely to be adequately duplicated. From

the point of view of visual theory, it is interesting that subjects in these experiments experience small spots rather than lines, edges, or more complex percepts. If the specific neuron code hypothesis is correct, then the cells responding to the electrical stimulation must evoke these spotlike sensations. Unfortunately, we do not know which cells in the cortex are being stimulated in these experiments.

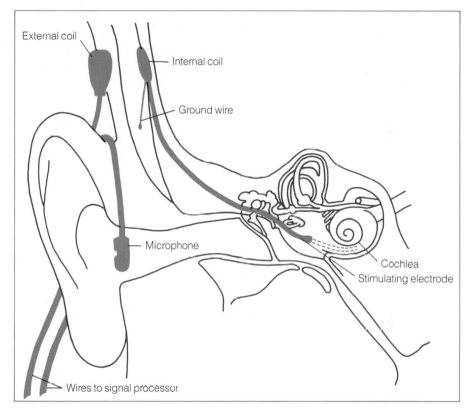

FIGURE 5-33

Cochlear Implant   *This diagram illustrates the auditory prosthesis developed by William House and his associates. Sound is picked up by a microphone and filtered by a signal processor (not shown) worn outside the body. The electrical waveform produced by the processor is then transmitted by radio waves through the skull to the electrode inside the cochlea.*

of the waveform, however, breaks down above 4,000 Hz, even though we hear pitch at much higher frequencies. There are other phenomena that temporal theory does not explain. This state of affairs led to the idea that pitch depends on both place and temporal pattern *(duplicity theory)*.

Unlike the two-stage color theory, duplicity theory has never been developed into a complete theory. The most recent trend is a return to place theories, but place theories that invoke a more complex relation between place (on the basilar membrane) and pitch than the one place – one pitch assumption of previous place theories (Goldstein, 1973; Wrightman, 1973). Although these theories say that the auditory system uses a complex code for frequency in the cochlea and auditory nerve, they do not rule out the possibility that in the brain one neuron evokes one pitch (a specific neuron code).

Localizing Sounds

The accuracy with which we can sense the direction of a sound source depends on a number of factors. Usually we can detect a change in direction of a few degrees, but confusions between sounds coming from in front of us and those coming from behind us are relatively common. If the frequency of the sound source is varied, accuracy of localization is worst for frequencies around 3,000 Hz (Stevens & Newman, 1936). This observation led to the idea that there are two stimulus cues to location: intensity differences in the sound arriving at the two ears due to the sound shadow cast by the head, and differences in arrival time of sound at the two ears. The physics of these two cues suggest that we localize by intensity differences at high frequencies and by arrival times at low frequencies. Intensity differences are greatest at high frequencies, because the head blocks high frequencies more; time differences are easiest to detect at low frequencies when the peaks of the waves are not close together (see Figure 5-34). A number of experiments support the two-cue theory. Front-back confusions are explained by the fact that both cues are almost the same for sound sources directly in front of and behind the observer. We can locate sound sources from differences in arrival time at the two ears as short as 10 microseconds (Durlach & Coburn, 1978).

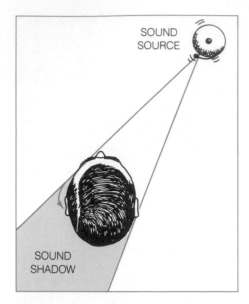

FIGURE 5-34

Cues to Sound Source Location *If a sound source is to the right of the head, the distance from the source to the right ear is shorter than the distance to the left ear. Consequently, the sound will arrive at the right ear first. This cue is effective at low sound frequencies. Because of the partial sound shadow cast by the head, intensity will be less at the left ear. This cue is effective at high frequencies.*

OTHER SENSES

Senses other than vision and audition are important; some would be very difficult to live without. But they lack the richness of patterning and organization that have led sight and hearing to be called the "higher senses." Our symbolic experiences are expressed largely in visual and auditory terms. Our spoken language is to be *heard;* our written language is to be *seen.* Musical notation permits music to be read or played on an instrument. Except for braille (printing in raised dots that permits the blind to read by touch), we do not have any comparable symbolic coding in the other senses.

Smell

Although smell plays a tremendously important role in the lives of animals, it is rarely essential for humans. Apart from occasionally warning us of danger (smoke, gas, spoiled food), it has little role other than to make life more pleasant or unpleasant.

From an evolutionary viewpoint, smell is one of the most primitive and most important of the senses. The sense organ for smell has a position of prominence in the head appropriate to a sense intended to guide behavior. Smell has a more direct route to the brain than any other sense. The receptors in the *olfactory epithelium*, high in the nasal cavity, are connected without synapse to the olfactory bulbs of the brain, which lie just below the frontal lobes. The olfactory bulbs in turn are connected to the olfactory cortex on the inside of the temporal lobes. In fish, the olfactory cortex makes up almost all of the cerebral hemispheres; in dogs, about one-third; in humans, about one-twentieth. These differences are

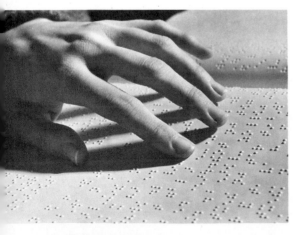

Braille, patterns of raised dots representing letters, allows blind people to read with their fingertips.

related to differences in sensitivity among these species. Taking advantage of the superior smell capability of dogs, both the U.S. Postal Service and the Bureau of Customs have trained them to check unopened packages for heroin or marijuana, and specially trained police dogs can sniff out hidden explosives.

A volatile substance, a substance that gives off molecules, is the stimulus for smell. The molecules must also be soluble in fat, since the receptors for smell are covered with a fatlike substance. Researchers have been hampered in their study of smell because the stimuli are difficult to control and cannot be described by a few dimensions as sounds and lights can. Absolute thresholds are as low as 1 part per 50 billion parts of air, but vary greatly from one substance to the next. Adaptation to odors is pronounced but not complete; when we are exposed to an odor, its perceived intensity is reduced by about 70 percent over a period of one minute. One odor can be masked by another; this is the principle on which air fresheners work. True odor mixture (in the sense of odors being mixed to match another odor) does not seem to occur.

Some researchers have proposed that there are only six basic odor sensations, and that all odors can be analyzed phenomenologically into one or more of these six sensations. Other researchers have proposed seven or more basic odors (Cain, 1978). The discovery that some odors are produced by classes of molecules of similar shape led to the hypothesis that a particular receptor is activated when the shape of a molecule fits the shape of a site on the receptor (Amoore, 1970). The theory remains speculative, however, and some researchers question even the basic relation between shape and odor (Schiffman, 1974). There seem to be a large number of different receptors, each responsive to at least two odorous substances, often more. Some people are insensitive to particular classes of odors, such as hydrogen cyanide; they may lack a receptor type.

In addition to odor receptors, the olfactory epithelium contains free nerve endings. These are receptors for a *common chemical sense* that responds to any odorant in high concentration. This sense resembles the sensitivity of the skin to noxious stimuli, which explains why some odors evoke unpleasant feelings in the nose, even pain.

Insects and some higher animals use their sense of smell as a means of communication. They secrete chemicals, known as *pheromones,* that float through the air to attract other members of the species. For example, a female moth can release a pheromone so powerful that males are drawn to her from a distance of several miles. It is clear that the male moth responds only to the pheromone and not to the sight of the female; the male will be attracted to a female in a wire container, even though she is blocked from view, but not to a female who is clearly visible in a glass container from which the scent cannot escape. Similar processes may be at work in humans in greatly attenuated form; males and females do have different odors that can be discriminated (Wallace, 1977). The perfumes and scents that people use are undoubtedly an attempt to enhance our vestigial olfactory communication.

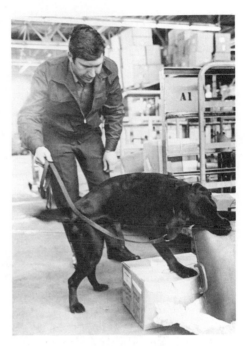

A dog at work for the postal service.

Taste

Taste gets credit for a lot of experiences that it does not provide. We say that a meal "tastes" good, but in fact, when smell is eliminated by a bad cold, dinner becomes quite an impoverished sensory experience. The stimulus for taste is a substance that is soluble in saliva, which is a fluid much like salt water. The taste receptors occur in clusters (*taste buds)* on the bumps on the tongue and around the mouth. At the ends of the taste receptors are short, hairlike structures which extend out and make contact with the solutions in the mouth. Sensitivity to different taste stimuli varies from place to place, with sensitivity to salty and

Taste discrimination by experts.

sweet substances best near the front of the tongue, salty along the sides of the tongue, and bitter on the soft palate. In the center of the tongue is a region insensitive to taste; that is the place to put an unpleasant pill.

Absolute thresholds for taste are very low, but difference thresholds for intensity are relatively high (Weber's constant is about 0.2). This means that if you are adding spices to a dish you must add more than 20 percent or you will not taste the difference. Adaptation to taste stimuli occurs, but recovery is relatively rapid, and exposure to one substance will temporarily change the taste of other substances. One taste can also mask another; sugar, for example, masks the bitterness of coffee. Toothpaste reduces the sweetness of sugar and makes citrus juice extra sour; it is best to brush your teeth after breakfast. There is a berry called miracle fruit *(Synsepalum dulcificum)* that can make anything eaten after it taste sweet. Although new tastes sometimes appear in mixtures (Schiffman & Erickson, 1980), we do not know if substances can be mixed to match the tastes of other substances in any general way. Researchers generally agree that any taste can be described as one or a combination of the four basic taste sensations: sweet, sour, salty, and bitter (McBurney, 1978). Single-cell recording from taste fibers reveals that a single fiber will respond to substances with quite different tastes. Different fibers will respond to many of the same substances, but each has its own pattern of sensitivities. Thus, as in other sensory systems, the fibers are broadly tuned and overlap in their tuning.

Skin Senses

Traditionally, humans have been thought to have five senses: sight, hearing, smell, taste, and touch. Today, touch is considered to include three skin senses (one of which responds to pressure, another to temperature, and the third to noxious stimulation) and a sense called *kinesthesis,* whose receptors are in the muscles and joints and which is sensitive to the position and movement of body parts. This recognition of the additional senses raises the question of what criteria should be used for distinguishing senses. Four criteria often used are that each sense should (1) respond to a distinct class of stimuli, (2) have the ability to discriminate among these stimuli, (3) possess a distinct set of receptors, and (4) lead to conscious experiences that differ qualitatively when the sense is stimulated. With respect to the skin senses, the critical issue has been the existence of distinct receptors for pressure, temperature, and noxious stimulation. Although the description of the different receptors has grown considerably more complex over the years, with at least 13 receptor types now being distinguished (Brown & Deffenbacher, 1979), the idea that there are distinct receptors for pressure, temperature, and noxious stimulation is supported by considerable evidence.

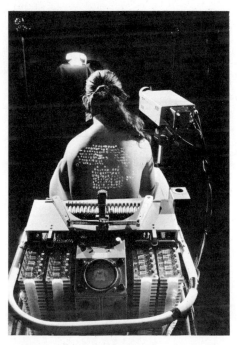

This electronic system enables a blind woman to "see" by skin sensation. The TV camera on her right converts the image of the telephone into the pattern of dots shown on the TV monitor behind her. Then hundreds of tiny cones vibrate against her back, allowing her to feel the dot pattern (shown here by fluorescent paint) and to perceive the image of the phone.

PRESSURE   Although we are not aware of steady pressures on the entire body (such as air pressure), we are sensitive to variations in pressure over the body surface. We can detect a force as small as 5 milligrams applied to a small area of the skin. The lips, nose, and cheek are most sensitive to pressure; the big toe is least sensitive. These differences are closely related to the number of receptors that respond to the stimulus at each of these body loci. If the stimulus vibrates up and down on the skin, we are most sensitive to vibration frequencies of about 250 hertz and less sensitive to higher and lower frequencies. The pressure sense shows profound adaptation effects. If you hold your boyfriend or girlfriend's hand for several minutes without moving, you will cease to feel the hand.

We are also sensitive to patterns of pressure applied to the skin. Most studies of pattern resolution have measured the *two-point threshold,* the minimum distance by which two very thin rods touching the skin must be separated before they are felt as two points rather than one. Like the pressure threshold, the

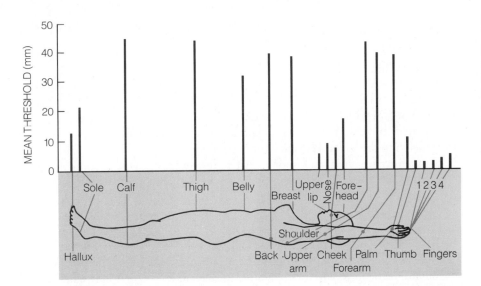

FIGURE 5-35
Two-point Threshold *This graph shows the two-point threshold in millimeters at different places on the body surface. The threshold is determined by touching the skin with two thin rods separated by a small distance. The subject indicates whether one or two rods are sensed. The rod separation is adjusted to find the minimum separation at which two rods are sensed. The data given are for females, but male thresholds are very similar. (After Weinstein, 1968)*

two-point threshold varies greatly over the body surface, but the correlation between the two is not perfect. The two-point threshold is lowest on the fingers and highest on the calves (see Figure 5-35).

Theory of the pressure sense is not highly developed. Threshold measurements and single-cell recording both provide evidence for the existence of filters in the system underlying the pressure sense that are tuned to different spatial and temporal frequencies of pressure stimulation (Loomis & Lederman, 1986).

TEMPERATURE Since maintaining body temperature is crucial to our survival, it is important that we can sense changes of temperature on the skin. The receptors for temperature are neurons with free nerve endings just under the skin. Cold receptors respond to a decrease in skin temperature, and warm receptors respond to an increase in skin temperature (Hensel, 1973). When the skin is at its normal temperature, we can detect a warming of 0.4 degrees centigrade and a cooling of 0.15 degrees centigrade (Nafe, Kenshalo, & Brooks, 1961). The temperature sense adapts completely to moderate changes in temperature, so that after a few minutes the stimulus feels neither cool nor warm. This adaptation explains the strong differences of opinion about the temperature of a swimming pool between those who have been in it for a while and those first sticking a foot in. A sensation of "hot" may be produced by stimulating adjacent regions of the skin with cool and warm temperatures (see Figure 5-36). This can be explained by the fact that cold receptors respond not only to low temperatures but also to very high temperatures (above 45 degrees centigrade). Consequently, a very hot stimulus will activate both warm and cold receptors, which in turn evoke a hot sensation.

NOXIOUS STIMULATION Any stimulus that is intense enough to cause tissue damage is a stimulus for pain. It may be pressure, temperature, electric shock, or irritant chemicals. The effect of such a stimulus is to cause the release of chemical substances in the skin, which in turn stimulate distinct high threshold receptors. These receptors are neurons with specialized free nerve endings, and researchers have distinguished at least four different types (Brown & Deffenbacher, 1979).

Experimental research on noxious stimulation of the skin is limited, because subjects for this type of research are difficult to find. Most of the research has been done with radiant heat. The threshold for pain is about 45 degrees centigrade; the upper tolerable limit is 61 degrees centigrade (Hardy, Wolff, & Goodell, 1947).

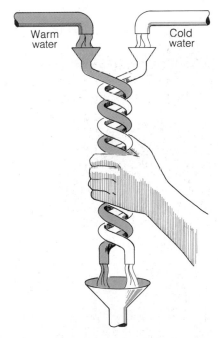

FIGURE 5-36
Warm Near Cold Feels "Hot" *When cold water (0–5 deg C) is circulated through one coil and warm water (40–44 deg C) through another intertwining coil, a person grasping the coils feels a hot, burning sensation. The experiment demonstrates that the sensation of "hot" is produced by stimulating warm and cold receptors together.*

Riding a roller coaster produces strong sensations of acceleration, deceleration, and side-to-side movement.

Experimental pain differs from clinical pain in that it is less affected by placebos or pain-killing drugs.

More than any other sensation, pain is influenced by factors other than the noxious stimulus. These factors include pressure stimuli, attitudes, motives, and suggestions, as well as hypnosis, drugs, and acupuncture. The existence of these influences led to the *gate control theory of pain* (Melzak & Wall, 1965; Melzak & Casey, 1968), in which the sensation of pain requires not only that pain receptors be activated, but also that a neural gate in the spinal cord allow these signals to continue on to the brain. Pressure stimulation tends to close the gate. This is why rubbing a hurt area may relieve pain. Attitudes, suggestions, and some drugs are thought to act through descending pathways from the brain, which also act to close the gate.

Kinesthesis

Kinesthesis, which literally means motion sense, is a sense of the position and movement of the head and limbs relative to the trunk. If you doubt whether you have such a sense, next time you wake in the middle of the night ask yourself where your arms are. Kinesthesis will enable you to answer correctly without looking. When we actively control our limbs, kinesthesis is aided by signals from the motor centers of the brain to the perceptual system, which represent commands to the muscles. Aspects of kinesthesis also include reflex activity and are not conscious. Kinesthesis is mediated by receptors in muscles, tendons, joints, and skin. When we perceive the shape of something by using the hand, the hand must generally be moved over the object *(active touch)*. This kind of perception involves the coordinated activity of the motor system, kinesthesis, and the skin senses. The word "touch" in our everyday language refers to this complex process (Loomis & Lederman, 1986). It is not a single sense. We can identify familiar objects very well by active touch, even though most of us are rarely required to identify by touch alone (Klatzky, Lederman, & Metzger, 1985).

Balance and Body Movement

We sense our orientation with respect to gravity and our acceleration through space. These two capacities are often grouped together because the sense organs for both are in the *vestibular apparatus* adjoining the inner ear (see Figure 5-29). Each of the senses utilizes hollow, fluid-filled chambers with hair cells whose cilia are bent by body tilt or acceleration. They do give rise to conscious sensations, but their main function is the largely unconscious regulation of motor activity.

The vestibular sacs, located between the base of the semicircular canals and the cochlea, contain the organs for our sense of balance and linear acceleration. They respond to the tilt or position of the head and to acceleration of the head in a straight line. The hair cells protrude into a gelatinous mass containing small crystals called *otoliths* (literally, "ear stones"). The normal pressure of the otoliths on the hair cells gives us the sense of upright position, and any distortion tells us that the head is tilted.

Our sense of angular (rotational) acceleration depends on the three semicircular canals (see Figure 5-29), each of which is roughly perpendicular to the others so that they lie in three planes. Movement of the fluid in these canals bends the cilia of the hair cells embedded in the canals and causes them to respond, producing a sensation of acceleration. The hair cells do not respond to motion at constant velocity. Extreme stimulation of this sense produces dizziness and nausea. Powerful illusions of the body movement sense are sometimes experienced in flying. For example, when a plane is increasing its speed gradually, a blindfolded subject may sense that the plane is climbing; if its speed is decreasing, the subject may sense that it is descending. Thus, under conditions of poor visibility, pilots must trust their instruments rather than their body motion sense.

SENSORY CODE

We now return to the question raised at the beginning of this chapter: How do we sense stimuli? Our discussion of the various senses makes it clear that in attempting to answer this question, we must consider two things: (1) How is the stimulus related to events in the sensory systems? (2) How are these events related to what we experience?

In answer to the first question, we have presented evidence indicating that neurons in sensory systems are tuned to respond to different classes of stimuli. There are neurons that respond to light whose wavelength is within a certain range, to sounds of certain temporal frequencies, to sets of visual gratings with particular spatial frequencies and orientations, to sets of molecules, and so forth. The tuning is brought about by filters of many different kinds in the sensory systems. These filters selectively pass sensory signals produced by one class of stimuli and in turn activate sensory neurons at a higher level in the system. The sets of stimuli to which different sensory neurons respond overlap considerably, so that one stimulus may activate several differently tuned neurons. Some stimulus dimensions have only a few classes of neurons (for example, wavelength of light); other dimensions have many classes (such as sound frequency). The picture is complicated by the fact that sensory systems have several levels, and the neural representation of a stimulus varies from one level to another. The wavelength of light is a good example. At the receptor level, three classes of cone receptors respond to it; at the opponent-cell level, four classes of opponent cells respond. In spite of such complications, it is clear that the representation of stimuli in sensory systems is not by means of copies, as Democritus thought. Helmholtz's idea that stimuli are represented by the neurons they activate is more consistent with the evidence.

How are the responses of cells in sensory systems related to what we experience? Helmholtz hypothesized that, when each sensory neuron in the brain is activated, it evokes a specific sensation. If more than one neuron type is active, then more than one sensation will be experienced. Helmholtz did not envision different levels in sensory systems at which the representation of the stimulus changes. He thought there were three types of color receptors, each with its own connecting fibers to the brain. Thus, he thought that the stimulus was represented in the same way at all levels of the system, and he was able to associate one sensation with each receptor and each neuron all through the system. This does not mean that he thought receptors alone could evoke sensations; rather, he believed that they could do so only by activating corresponding neurons in the brain.

Since sensory systems have several levels and the stimulus representation changes from one to the next, individual neurons may be associated with specific sensations at some levels but not others. At the lowest levels, unitary sensations such as "yellow" or "hot" depend on the relative activity of two or more neurons. This finding, however, does not rule out the possibility that in the brain the one neuron – one sensation rule does apply. Indeed, the opponent-color level of the visual system has four types of opponent neurons, each of which may be associated with one of four color sensations. It seems plausible that the same rule may apply to taste and smell, where sensory experiences are composed of a few basic sensations. A specific neuron code seems less likely for dimensions such as auditory frequency, in which the associated pitch sensations are unitary and unique, and also very numerous. For this dimension, a specific neuron code would require that, at the level where the pitch sensation is evoked, hundreds of pitch-specific neurons could be activated one at a time. The one neuron–one sensation rule is not the only possible one; unitary sensations could be evoked by an activity pattern across neurons. Nevertheless, the specific neuron code is our best current hypothesis (see Barlow, 1972).

SUMMARY

1. *Psychophysical methods* use overt responses to stimuli to study the senses. They include *threshold methods, matching,* and *magnitude estimation.* The *absolute threshold* is the minimum magnitude of a stimulus that can be detected. The *difference threshold* or *jnd* is the minimum difference between two stimuli that can be detected. In the *method of constant stimuli,* the percent detection is determined for a range of stimuli near threshold. The threshold is defined as the stimulus magnitude that can be detected on 50 percent of its presentations.

2. In *single-cell recording,* a microelectrode is used to record the electrical activity of receptors and neurons. This method has made it possible to study thresholds and sensitivity of single cells at different levels of sensory systems.

3. The stimulus for vision is electromagnetic radiation of 400–700 nanometers, and the sense organs are the two eyes. The *cornea* and *lens* of each eye form an image on the *retina,* which contains the visual receptors, the *rods* and *cones.* The central *fovea* in the center of the retina contains only cones, and the rest of the retina, called the periphery, contains mostly rods. The main visual pathway goes from *receptors* to *bipolar cells* to *ganglion cells* in the retina, and then to the thalamus and the *visual cortex.*

4. The *absolute threshold* for light is lowest for a light of about 500 nanometers presented to the periphery (rod vision). In the fovea, the threshold is generally higher and has a minimum at about 550 nanometers (cone vision). The *difference threshold* for light intensity increases with intensity and is approximately proportional to intensity *(Weber's law).* This increase may be explained by a curved *intensity-response function* that is approximately logarithmic *(Fechner's law). Magnitude estimates* of perceived *brightness* show a similar relation to intensity. *Adaptation,* the adjustment of the visual system to prevailing illumination, is associated with a change in the intensity-response function.

5. Light wavelength can be discriminated very well by most people, but a mixture of three lights (widely separated in wavelength) can be made to match perceptually almost any color of light. *Color anomalous* people make different matches than color-normal people, and *color-blind* people match any light with only one or two lights. There are four *basic color sensations:* red, yellow, green, and blue. Mixtures of these make up our perceptions, or experiences, of color, except that we do not see reddish-greens and yellowish-blues. These facts can be explained by a *two-stage color theory,* which postulates three types of cones (in agreement with Young and Helmholtz's trichromatic theory) followed by red-green and yellow-blue opponent processes (in agreement with Hering's opponent-color theory).

6. *Spatial resolution* refers to our ability to see fine detail; *visual acuity* is a measure of this ability. The *contrast threshold* is another measure of our ability to see spatial patterns; contrast thresholds are lowest for gratings of intermediate spatial frequency, increasing when the bars narrow or widen. Psychophysical and biological evidence indicates that the visual system contains spatial frequency filters (receptor and neuron units that pass some spatial frequencies and not others).

7. The stimulus for audition is vibration; all sounds can be analyzed into sine waves of different frequencies. The sense organ for hearing is the ear, and its principal

parts are the *ear canal*, *eardrum* and *middle-ear bones*, and *cochlea*. The receptors are the *hair cells* located on the *basilar membrane* in the cochlea.

8. *Absolute intensity thresholds* for hearing are lowest around 1,000 hertz and increase at higher and lower frequencies. Different types of hearing loss produce characteristic threshold increases; a *conduction loss* usually results in higher thresholds at all frequencies, and a *sensory-neural loss* tends to be concentrated at high frequencies. Auditory difference thresholds increase with intensity, and the intensity-response function is similar to that for vision.

9. *Pitch* increases with the frequency of sound. *Masking* and single-cell recording indicate that there are many overlapping *frequency filters* in the auditory system. According to *place theory*, each frequency stimulates one place along the basilar membrane, and each place, when stimulated, results in one pitch heard. *Temporal theories* state that the pitch heard depends on the temporal pattern of the sound wave and the corresponding temporal pattern of neural response in the auditory system. There is evidence for and against both theories. *Sound localization* is cued by intensity differences when the frequency is high and by arrival-time differences at the two ears when the frequency is low.

10. Smell and taste are much more important to nonhuman species than to humans. Many species use specialized odors *(pheromones)* for communication. In both smell and taste there seem to be relatively few sensations into which experiences can be analyzed. Both senses are characterized by broad, overlapping chemical filters at the lowest levels.

11. Three *skin senses* are distinguished: *pressure*, *temperature*, and *noxious stimulation*. Each has distinct receptors that respond to particular classes of stimuli. The unusual dependence of pain sensations on factors other than the intensity of the noxious stimulus led to the *gate control theory* of pain.

12. *Kinesthesis*, which is a sense of the position and movement of the limbs and head relative to the trunk, and the senses of *balance* and *body motion* are important in the control of movement.

13. According to the *specific neuron code hypothesis*, the brain contains different classes of neurons, each of which responds to a specific class of stimuli and evokes a specific sensation. There is much evidence to support the theory that different neurons respond to different classes of stimuli. This tuning is brought about by optical, mechanical, chemical, and neural filters in the sensory systems. The one neuron–one sensation rule does not always hold at the lower levels of sensory systems, for some sensations seem to depend on responses in two or more classes of neurons. The rule may hold, however, at the level of the brain.

FURTHER READING

Among the general texts on sensory processes and perception are Barlow and Mollon, *The Senses* (1982); Brown and Deffenbacher, *Perception and the Senses* (1979); Coren, Porac, and Ward, *Sensation and Perception* (2nd ed., 1984); Goldstein, *Sensation and Perception* (2nd ed., 1984); Levine and Shefner, *Fundamentals of Sensation and Perception* (1981); Schiffman, *Sensation and Perception* (1982); and Sekuler and Blake, *Perception* (1985).

For color vision see Boynton, *Human Color Vision* (1979); and Hurvich, *Color Vision* (1981). Introductory books on audition include Moore, *An Introduction to the Psychology of Hearing* (2nd ed., 1982); and Yost and Nielson, *Fundamentals of Hearing* (2nd ed., 1985). For smell see Engen, *The Perception of Odors* (1982); for touch, *Tactual Perception*, edited by Schiff and Foulke (1982); and for pain, *The Psychology of Pain*, edited by Sternbach (1978).

For reference there are four multivolume handbooks, each of which has several chapters on sensory systems. They are the *Handbook of Perception* (1974–1978), edited by Carterette and Friedman; the *Handbook of Sensory Physiology* (1971–1973), edited by Autrum et al.; the *Handbook of Physiology: The Nervous System:* Section 1, Volume 3, *Sensory Processes* (1984), edited by Darian-Smith; and the *Handbook of Perception and Human Performance:* Volume 1, *Sensory Processes and Perception* (1986), edited by Boff, Kaufman, and Thomas.

Perceiving

6 WE LIVE IN A WORLD OF OBJECTS AND people — a world that bombards our senses with stimuli. Only under unusual circumstances do we notice the individual features and parts of stimuli, such as their colors, brightness, exact shapes, lines, and contours. Instead, we see a three-dimensional world of objects and hear words and music. We react to elaborate patterns of stimuli, usually with little awareness of their individual parts. *Perception* is the process by which we organize, integrate, and recognize these patterns of stimuli. In the last chapter we were concerned with simple tasks performed with simple stimuli — such as detecting a flash of light or discriminating two tones — and simple experiences — such as "bright red." In this chapter we will be concerned with more complex tasks, such as judging distance, size, and shape and identifying objects and events. These tasks involve more complex stimuli which evoke more complex experiences that we call *percepts*. In considering these phenomena, we will address two principal questions: First, is the percept associated with a complex stimulus simply the simultaneous occurrence of the sensations evoked by each of its elements and features when presented alone? By *elements* we mean the parts that a stimulus can be divided into, and by *features* we mean the aspects that cannot be physically separated, such as color, size, and shape. Second, if the answer to the first question is no, then what else is involved in perception?

A century ago, a group of psychologists, called *structuralists,* believed that any percept was simply a bundle of sensations, each of which had a constant relation to an element or feature of the stimulus (Titchener, 1896). In Chapter 5 we described some exceptions to this idea, such as the white that is seen when complementary colors are mixed (p. 158) or the missing fundamental pitch (p. 169). Because of such phenomena, many researchers did not share the structuralists' simplistic view. The two main opposing theories were those of Helmholtz and the *Gestalt psychologists.*

Helmholtz (1857) hypothesized that perception depends on learned associations and inferences. This idea is credited to Bishop Berkeley (1709), but Helmholtz developed and promoted it. He believed that when a stimulus is presented the perceiver experiences a set of sensations and learns to associate sensations that occur together. Later, when a stimulus evokes one of the sensations, the person experiences the related sensations. Thus, when we look at a piece of sculpture in the distance, we experience a set of visual sensations. If we then walk up to the sculpture and touch it, we experience a set of kinesthetic sensations that correspond to its distance (amount of effort required to get there), shape (path of hand in scanning over sculpture), and size (separation of hands required to reach from one side to the other). After much experience of this kind, we learn the relations among these different sets of sensations. Thereafter, as soon as we look at an object, we use these learned associations to infer the object's properties. As

Helmholtz concluded, we perceive those objects that would, under normal conditions, be most likely to produce the sets of sensory stimulation that we are receiving. Helmholtz called the process by which the perceiver progresses from experiencing sensations evoked by an object to recognizing the properties of the object *unconscious inference*. We make this inference automatically and unconsciously, and eventually we do not even notice the sensations on which it is based. Helmholtz thought that unconscious inference is the basis of all distance and object perception.

Gestalt psychology is a movement that began in Germany early in this century. The Gestalt psychologists emphatically rejected the idea that perception is just the sum of the sensations evoked by each stimulus element or feature; they proposed a radically different view. According to Gestalt theory, the whole percept is different than the sensations evoked by each of its parts. Sensations are not the basic units of perception, and perception does not depend on learning. Instead, *whole forms* are the basic units of perception, and they are produced by a process of *perceptual organization* that takes place in the perceptual system, depending neither on learning nor on experience. The Gestalt psychologists formulated a number of laws describing the phenomena of perceptual organization, and they proposed that objects are represented in the brain by regions of electrical activity whose form corresponds to the shape of the object. It is now clear that this electrical copy idea was wrong, but the other Gestalt ideas are very much alive.

The Helmholtz and Gestalt theories raise several important questions about perception. First, what is the basic unit of perception? Is it the sensation or something more complex, like a whole form? Second, what kind of processes are involved in perception? Do they resemble logical inferences, or are they more like the formation of an electrical copy? Third, are perceptual processes learned or innate? There is a fourth question that did not become a major issue until recently, but it has its roots in these early controversies: What role do variables other than the stimulus have in perception? Of particular interest is whether context, expectations, and motives influence perception, and if so, to what extent and by what processes. Each of these questions is difficult, and psychologists do not yet have a definitive answer to any of them. The answers must rest on a detailed understanding of the relations between the percept and the variables that affect it.

ORGANIZING AND INTEGRATING

What the Gestalt psychologists called perceptual organization is quite a diverse set of phenomena and processes. We will distinquish between *perceptual organization*, which depends on the relations among the *elements* of a stimulus, and *perceptual integration*, which depends on the relations among the *features* of a stimulus. We will first consider the perceptual organization of stimulus elements and then perceptual integration as it manifests itself in distance perception, motion perception, constancies, and illusions.

Organizing the Elements of a Stimulus

The Gestalt psychologists devoted a lot of research to the study of how the percept depends on the *relations* among the *elements,* or parts, of a stimulus. Two examples of this are the figure-ground relationship and perceptual grouping.

FIGURE 6-1
Reversible Figure and Ground   *The reversible goblet illustrates figure-ground reversal. Note that you can perceive either the light portion (the goblet) or the dark portion (two profiles) as a figure against a background, but only one at a time.*

FIGURE AND GROUND If a stimulus contains two or more distinct regions, we usually see part of it as a *figure* and the rest as a *ground*. The regions seen as figure appear more solid than the ground and appear in front of the ground. But as Figure 6-1 illustrates, figure-ground organization can be reversible. The fact that either region can be recognized as a figure contributes to this reversibility. Figure 6-2 illustrates a more interesting reversible figure-ground effect. A stimulus need not contain indentifiable objects in order for a person to organize it into figure and ground.

We can perceive figure-ground relationships in senses other than vision. For example, we may hear the song of a bird against a background of outdoor noises or the melody played by the violin against the harmonies of the rest of the orchestra. Some of the factors that determine what is perceived as figure and what as ground will be considered in the discussion of selective attention (p. 197).

PERCEPTUAL GROUPING Even simple patterns of lines and dots fall into ordered relationships when we look at them. In the top part of Figure 6-3, we tend to see three *pairs* of lines, with an *extra* line at the right. But notice that the stimulus can equally well be described as three pairs beginning at the right with an extra line at the left. The slight modification of the lines shown in the lower part of the figure causes us to see the second pattern. This tendency to *organize* what we see is very compelling; our percepts often seem forced on us by the patterns of stimulation. The properties of the stimulus as a whole affect how the parts are perceived.

LAWS OF PERCEPTUAL ORGANIZATION The Gestalt psychologists proposed many laws for perceptual organization; most of which are concerned with specific phenomena like figure-ground organization or grouping. The *law of proximity*, for example, says that elements that are near one another will be grouped perceptually. Since many of these stimuli can be perceived in more than one way, the laws describe the most probable percept, not the only one. The Gestalt psychologists also proposed a general law of perceptual organization, which goes by several names but can be most meaningfully called the *law of*

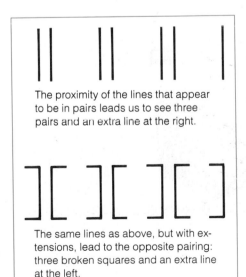

The proximity of the lines that appear to be in pairs leads us to see three pairs and an extra line at the right.

The same lines as above, but with extensions, lead to the opposite pairing: three broken squares and an extra line at the left.

FIGURE 6-3
Perceptual Grouping

simplicity: the percept corresponds to the simplest possible interpretation of the stimulus. This law captures an important idea, but theorists have not been able to give "simplicity" a precise definition that would enable the law to predict how new stimuli would be perceived (Hochberg, 1978).

Perceiving Distance

Distance perception puzzled early perception theorists because they thought of perception as a bundle of depthless sensations evoked by the flat visual image. Gradually, over many centuries, theorists realized that the dimensions of these flat images were related to the distances of the objects in the scene. Scientifically oriented artists such as Leonardo da Vinci, faced with the practical problem of depicting distance in a painting, played a large role in these discoveries. A stimulus dimension that is related to distance in a scene and evokes a percept of distance is called a *distance cue.* There are a number of distance cues that combine in complex ways to determine perceived distance. These can be classified as *monocular* or *binocular* depending on whether they involve one or both eyes. They may also be classified as cues to *egocentric distance* or *relative distance,* depending on whether they indicate how far something is from the perceiver or simply a relation between two distances—for example, that one object is farther than another or that one is two times the distance of the other.

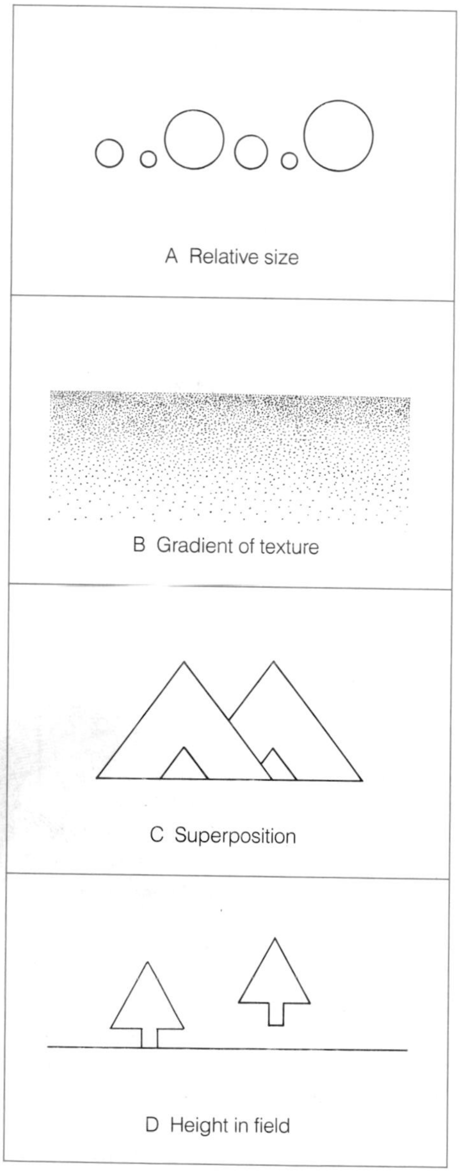

MONOCULAR CUES Although seeing with two eyes adds considerably to the precision of distance perception, people using only one eye can do remarkably well by picking up monocular distance cues. Figure 6-4 illustrates four of these cues. If an image contains an array of similar but different-sized objects, a person will interpret the objects as being at different distances from him or her, with the smaller images seen as being farther away (see Figure 6-4A). A related cue is a texture gradient of the kind that would occur in the image of an irregular surface, such as a rocky desert or the waving surface of the ocean (see Figure 6-4B). If one object has contours that cut through those of another, so that it obstructs the view of the other, a person will perceive the overlapping object as being nearer (see Figure 6-4C). Finally, objects that are higher in an image tend to be seen as farther away (see Figure 6-4D).

BINOCULAR CUES Seeing with both eyes has advantages over seeing with only one eye. The main advantage is that each eye views a scene from a slightly different angle and thus has a slightly different image of the scene. This *stereoscopic vision* provides a compelling impression of depth, which can be demonstrated by a device called a *stereoscope* (see Figure 6-5). The stereoscope displays a different photograph or drawing to each eye. If the two pictures are taken from slightly separated camera positions or drawn from slightly different perspectives, the viewer will perceive vivid depth.

Two binocular distance cues are available in stereoscopic viewing, *binocular parallax* and *binocular disparity* (see Figure 6-5). Binocular parallax requires only one visible point. It is the difference in directions of the point from the two eyes, which equals the angle between the two lines of sight. (This is the angle labeled binocular parallax in the figure.) Binocular disparity refers to the differences between the retinal images on each eye when we look at objects at different distances from us (Foley, 1978). Both cues are consequences of the fact that our eyes are separated. You can easily demonstrate these cues to yourself. Hold a pencil about a foot in front of you and, with only one eye open, line it up with a vertical edge on the wall opposite you. Then close that eye and open the other. The pencil will now appear in a different direction; the difference between these directions is binocular parallax. The two edges that were lined up in the first eye

FIGURE 6-4
Monocular Distance Cues   *The figure illustrates four monocular distance cues. These are used by artists to portray depth on a two-dimensional surface and are also present in photographs.*

Stereoscope *The Holmes-Bates stereoscope, invented by Oliver Wendell Holmes in 1861 and manufactured by Joseph Bates, was sold from the mid-1860s until 1939.*

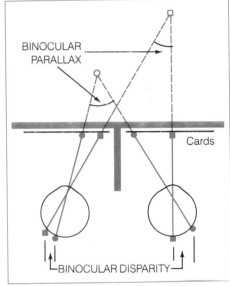

FIGURE 6-5

A Stereoscope and Binocular Distance Cues *A stereoscope is a device that presents different images to the two eyes. This very simple model holds a different card in front of each eye; a barrier between the eyes allows each eye to see only one card. If each card contains the same two symbols (here a circle and a square) separated by a different amount of space, the stimulus is the same as that produced by a circle and a square at different distances behind the cards. The dashed lines show how the images on the cards simulate two objects at different distances in space. When presented with stereo images such as these, people will experience vivid depth.* **Binocular parallax** *refers to the angle between the two lines of sight;* **binocular disparity** *refers to the difference between the separations of the retinal images of the two symbols in the two eyes.*

will appear separated when you open the second eye, and indeed the images in the eye are separated; the difference between the retinal images in the two eyes is binocular disparity. Binocular parallax is a cue to egocentric distance; binocular disparity is a cue to relative distance.

Just as artists can use distance cues to indicate depth in a picture, they can also use them to produce depth percepts that do not correspond to anything in the real world. In M. C. Escher's *Waterfall* (Figure 6-6), the water at the top is supplied from the bottom through a series of "level" channels.

Distance perception has been very important for perceptual theory. Phenomenologically, the impression of depth is usually immediate and compelling, particularly when binocular disparity is present. We are not conscious of inferring depth from flat sensations; yet even when each eye's image is only an array of random dots, we can experience vivid impressions of depth (Julesz, 1971). Researchers have found single neurons in the visual cortex of animals that are tuned to a limited range of binocular disparities (Barlow, Blakemore, & Pettigrew, 1967). This suggests that stereoscopic distance perception may be based on filters like those for light wavelength and sound frequency (see Chapter 5).

Perceiving Motion

Is perceiving motion just sensing an object at one position, then sensing it at another—a set of static sensations? The phenomenon of *stroboscopic motion* (see Figure 6-7), which was studied by the Gestalt psychologists, indicates that the answer to this question is no (Wertheimer, 1912). Stroboscopic motion is produced most simply by flashing a light in darkness and then, a few milliseconds later, flashing another light near the location of the first one. The light will seem to move from one place to the other in a way that is indiscriminable from real (that is, continuous) motion. When the time between the flashes is too short, they appear to be simultaneous; when it is too long, they appear as two isolated flashes without motion. The phenomenon is a convincing demonstration that motion is a distinct percept, and it illustrates nicely that the motion percept is not simply

FIGURE 6-6
An Artistic Experiment   *In this engraving by the Dutch artist M. C. Escher (*Waterfall, *1961), the artist uses depth cues which make the water appear to move uphill through a series of level channels.*

the joint occurrence of its parts (two static flashes); it depends critically on the space-time relation between its parts.

The motion that we see in movies is stroboscopic. The film is simply a series of still photographs (frames), each slightly different than the preceding. The frames are projected on the screen in rapid sequence, with dark intervals in between. The rate at which the frames are presented is critical. In the early days of motion pictures, the frame rate was 16 per second. This was too slow, and, as a consequence, movement in these early films appeared jerky and disjointed. Today, the rate is usually 24 frames per second. Even at this rate the picture would appear to flicker because of the fine temporal resolution of our visual system (p. 162); this perceived flicker is avoided by flashing each frame on and off three times while it is being presented.

Our visual system is very sensitive, of course, to *real motion*. Under optimal conditions, our threshold for seeing motion is very low: an object needs to move only about one-fifth the diameter of a single cone in the retina (Nakayama & Tyler, 1981). We are much better at detecting motion when we can see an object against a structured background *(relative motion)* than when the background is dark or neutral and only the moving object can be seen *(absolute motion)*. However, we do see motion in this latter case, and we see it even when we follow (track) the moving object with our eyes so that the image hardly moves on the retina. Our greater sensitivity to relative motion than to absolute motion causes us sometimes to see a static object in motion when another object actually moves *(induced motion)*. When a large object surrounding a smaller object moves, the smaller object usually appears to be the one that is moving. Thus, the moon appears to move through the clouds on a windy night.

Evidence from both psychophysical and single-cell experiments (p. 148) has shown that our sensory system has *motion filters*. These filters respond to some motions and not others, and each responds best to one direction and speed. The psychophysical evidence comes largely from experiments on *selective adaptation*. Selective adaptation is a loss in sensitivity to motion that occurs when we view motion; the adaptation is selective in the sense that we lose sensitivity to the motion viewed and to similar motions but not to motion that differs greatly in direction or speed. If we look at upward moving stripes, we lose sensitivity to upward motion, but our ability to see downward motion is not affected (Sekuler & Ganz, 1963). Scientists interpret this as indicating that some cells in the human visual system are tuned to different directions of movement. Numerous single-cell recording studies have found cortical cells tuned to direction of movement. Most of these cells are tuned to other features as well, but some are highly specialized for motion (Nakayama, 1985); there are even cells specifically tuned to detect an object moving toward the head (Regan, Beverley, & Cynader, 1979).

As with other types of adaptation, we do not usually notice the sensitivity loss, but we do notice the aftereffect produced by adaptation. If we view a waterfall for a few minutes and then look at the cliff beside it, the cliff will appear

FIGURE 6-7
Stroboscopic Motion   *The four circles in the top row correspond to four lights. If these are flashed one after the other with a short dark interval in between, they will appear to be a single light in continuous motion, such as that suggested in the second row. This is stroboscopic motion; all motion seen in movies and on television is of this kind.*

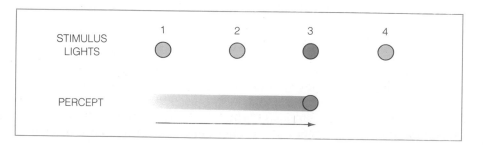

to move upward. Most motions will produce such a *motion aftereffect* in the opposite direction.

The motion that we see when we track a luminous object that is moving in darkness (such as an airplane at night) has important implications for understanding motion perception. Since our eyes follow the object, the image makes only a small, irregular motion on the retina (due to imperfect tracking), yet we perceive a smooth, continuous motion. This phenomenon suggests that information about how the eyes are moving must be sent to the visual system and must influence the motion that we see. In more normal viewing situations, there are both eye movements and large retinal image movements. The visual system must combine these two sources of information to determine the perceived motion.

Sensitivity to image motion has a number of functions in addition to just seeing motion. Among them are seeing depth, separating objects from backgrounds, controlling eye movements, and sensing body movement (Nakayama, 1985). When we move in a normal, illuminated environment, we produce complex patterns of retinal image motion. These are rich sources of information about both the scene and our own motion, and they are just beginning to be understood (Gibson, 1979; Ullman, 1979).

Perceptual Constancies

If you look around the room and ask yourself what you see, the answer is likely to be "a room full of objects" or "a room full of people and objects." Or you may pick out specific people or objects, but you are not likely to report that you see a mosaic of light and shadow. We tend to perceive *things* rather than their *features*. With effort, we are able to perceive features ("blueness," "squareness," or "softness"), but this is not our normal mode of perception. We perceive things such as blue flowers, square boxes, or soft pillows.

Our perceptual experiences are not isolated; they build a world of identifiable things. We usually perceive objects as remaining relatively constant regardless of a change in light conditions, the position from which we view them, or their distance from us. Your car does not appear to get larger as you walk toward it, distort in shape as you walk around it, or change in color when viewed in artificial light, even though the image on the retina of your eye does undergo these changes. This tendency is referred to as *perceptual constancy*. The constancy is not perfect, and some features are more stable than others.

LIGHTNESS AND COLOR CONSTANCY   Black velvet looks nearly as black to us in sunlight as it does in shadow, even though it reflects thousands of times more light toward our eyes when it is directly illuminated by the sun. We refer to this phenomenon as *lightness constancy*. Although the effect holds under normal circumstances, a change in the surroundings can destroy it. Attach the black velvet to a white board and throw a bright light on both, and the velvet still looks black. But now place an opaque black screen with a small opening in it between you and the velvet so you can see only a small patch of the velvet (see Figure 6-8). This screen reduces what you see through the opening to the actual light reflected from the velvet, independent of its surroundings. Now the velvet looks white because the light that reaches your eye through the hole is more intense than that from the screen itself. When we perceive objects in natural settings, several other objects are usually visible. Lightness constancy depends on the relations among the intensities of light reflected from the different objects.

Color constancy shows a similar dependence on the presence of a heterogeneous field. For example, if you look at a ripe tomato through a tube that obscures the surroundings and the nature of the object, the tomato may appear any color

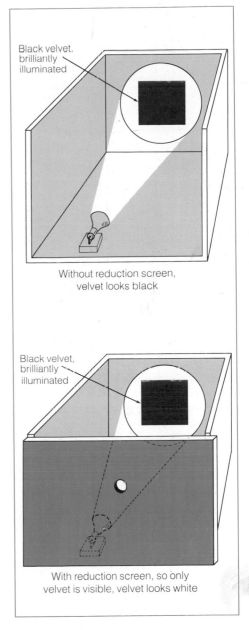

Without reduction screen, velvet looks black

Black velvet, brilliantly illuminated

Black velvet, brilliantly illuminated

With reduction screen, so only velvet is visible, velvet looks white

FIGURE 6-8
Effect of Surroundings on Lightness Constancy   *Even though the square of velvet is brilliantly illuminated, it still looks black if the illuminated white background is also visible. However, when one looks through the small opening in the reduction screen, so that only the black velvet is visible, the velvet looks white, even though the illumination on it is the same.*

—blue, green, or pink—depending on the wavelengths reflecting from it. On the other hand, when we view an object in a normal scene, the illumination can change quite a bit while affecting very little the colors we perceive. However, color constancy is far from perfect: shoppers sometimes learn this the hard way by picking clothing in store lighting, only to discover that the colors look different at home. Psychologists do not completely understand color constancy. Memory for colors may play a role, but the major influence is the relation between the light reflected from an object and the light reflected from surrounding surfaces (Land, 1977).

SHAPE AND SIZE CONSTANCY   When a door swings toward us, the shape of its retinal image goes through a series of changes (see Figure 6-9). The door's rectangular shape produces a trapezoidal image, with the edge toward us wider than the hinged edge; then the trapezoid grows thinner, until finally all that is projected on the retina is a vertical line the thickness of the door. Nevertheless, we perceive an unchanging door swinging open. The fact that the perceived shape is constant while the retinal image changes is an example of *shape constancy.*

As an object moves farther away from us, we tend to see it as remaining relatively constant in size. This is referred to as *size constancy.* Hold a quarter a foot in front of you and then move it out to arm's length. Does it appear to get smaller? Not noticeably so. Yet the retinal image of the quarter when it is 12 inches away is twice the size of its retinal image when it is 24 inches away (see Figure 6-10). We certainly do not perceive it as becoming half its size as we move it to arm's length.

Like other constancies, size constancy is not perfect. Very distant objects appear to be smaller than the same objects close up, as anyone who has looked down from a tall building or an airplane in flight knows. For near objects, constancy becomes imperfect as distance cues are eliminated. For example, the moving quarter just described appears to change more in size if it is viewed with one eye rather than two. In general, the less adequate the distance cues are, the more the size of an object will appear to change with distance.

LOCATION CONSTANCY   Despite the fact that a myriad of changing images strike the retina as we move, the positions of fixed objects appear to remain constant. We tend to take this *location constancy* for granted, but it requires that the perceptual system take account of both our movements and the changing retinal images. Consider the simple case where we move our eyes over a static scene. The image moves across the receptors in the same way it would if the

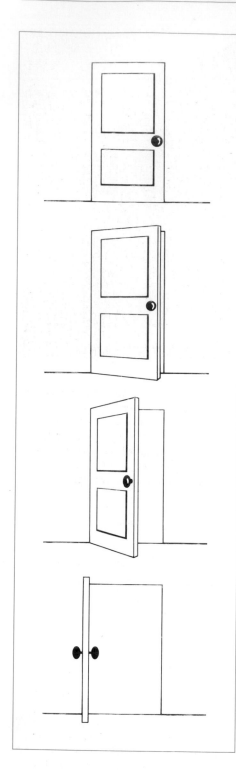

FIGURE 6-9
Shape Constancy   *The various retinal images produced by an opening door are quite different, and yet we perceive a door of constant rectangular shape.*

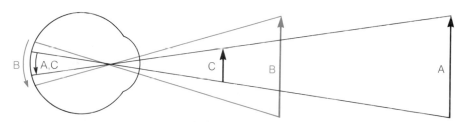

FIGURE 6-10
Retinal Image Size   *This figure illustrates the geometric relationship between the physical size of an object and the size of its image on the retina. Arrows A and B represent objects of the same size, but one is twice as far from the eye as the other. As a result, the retinal image of A is about half the size of the retinal image of B. The object represented by arrow C is smaller than that of A, but its location closer to the eye causes it to produce a retinal image of the same size as A.*

objects in the scene moved, yet we do not perceive movement in the scene. The visual system must receive information that the eyes are moving, and it must take this information into account in interpreting image motion. Using the single-cell recording method, researchers have found cells in the brain that respond only when an external stimulus moves, not when the eye moves over a static stimulus (Robinson & Wurtz, 1976).

Although all of the examples of constancy so far described are visual, and visual constancies are the most studied, constancies do occur in the other senses. For example, a person will hear the same tune if the frequencies of all of its notes double. All constancies depend on relations among features of the stimulus: the intensity of two adjacent regions, image size and distance, image movement and eye movement, and so forth. Somehow the perceptual system integrates these features to respond in a constant way, even though the individual features are changing.

Perceptual Illusions

An *illusion* is a percept that is false or distorted; it differs from the state of affairs described by physical science with the aid of measuring instruments. Some illusions are *physical*, such as the break we see in a stick where it enters water, the distorted images we see in fun-house mirrors, or the pitch change in a siren as a fire engine passes us; they are due to a distortion in the stimulus reaching our receptors. Other illusions are *perceptual*, arising as a consequence of processes in our perceptual system. These are the illusions that are of interest to psychologists.

Geometrical illusions constitute one large class of perceptual illusions that has received considerable attention. These are line drawings in which some aspect appears distorted — often the length, direction, or curvature of lines. Figure 6-11

A Perspective Illusion in a Real-life Scene *The two rectangles superimposed on the photograph are precisely the same size. Without the photograph, they would appear about the same size; yet when they are superimposed on the photograph, the upper one appears much larger. Cues in the photograph influence our perception of the rectangles.*

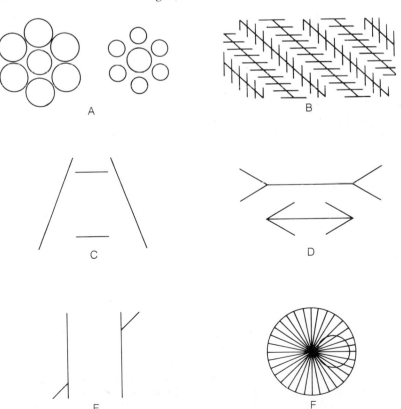

FIGURE 6-11
Some Geometrical Illusions *In A, the two center circles are physically equal in size; in B, the long lines are physically parallel; in C, the two horizontal lines are equal in length; the same is true in D; in E, the slanted lines are lined up with each other; in F, the smaller curved figure is a circle. Illusions A and B can be explained by pattern filtering of the kind described in Chapter 5. Illusions C, D, E, and F are a consequence of these patterns being processed as images of three-dimensional scenes.*

CRITICAL DISCUSSION

Understanding Constancy and Illusion

Early writers on perception, such as Bishop Berkeley who published an essay on the subject in 1709, held that perception consists of experiencing many sensations simultaneously while remembering other sensations that had previously been associated with them. Constancies and illusions, however, show that the percept is very different than the set of sensations evoked by each of its parts. Unlike some of the simpler phenomena discussed in Chapter 5, the perception of size, shape, and location (whether accurate or illusory) depends on at least two stimulus variables, often more. Understanding these more complex phenomena requires us to specify (1) how the percept is related to the stimulus variables that influence it and (2) what goes on in the perceptual system to bring about the percept. The relation between stimulus variables and percept can be illustrated by considering size perception.

Two variables that have long been recognized as important in size perception are the size of the retinal image and perceived distance. Emmert (1881) was able to separate the effects of these two variables by studying the perceived size of afterimages. He had people fixate on (stare at) the center of a high-contrast image for a minute or two. They then looked at a white screen and saw an afterimage. When the screen was far away, the afterimage looked large; when the screen was near, the afterimage looked small. Emmert's experiment is easy to do (see Figure 6-12). Perform the experiment before reading on.

In this experiment, the size of the adapted region of the retina remains constant, so something else must explain the

FIGURE 6-12

Emmert's Experiment *Hold the book at normal reading distance under good light. Fixate on the cross in the center of the figure for about one minute, then look at a distant wall. You will see an afterimage of the two circles that appears larger than the stimulus. Then look at a piece of paper held close to your eyes; the afterimage will appear smaller than the stimulus. If the afterimage fades, blinking can sometimes restore it.*

change in perceived size. Emmert proposed that the perceived size of an afterimage is proportional to its distance from the viewer (Emmert's law). Later, this was generalized into the *size-distance invariance principle*, which states that the ratio of perceived size, S', to perceived distance, D', is equal to the visual angle, θ (see Figure 6-13). The principle may be described in equation form as follows:

$$\frac{S'}{D'} = \theta \quad \text{or} \quad S' = \theta \times D'$$

shows six examples. Two of these, A and B, can be explained by the existence of *pattern filters* in the visual system (Chapter 5, p. 162). When these stimuli pass through filters like those at the lower levels of the visual system, the filter output is an image that is distorted in the same way that our experience is distorted when we look at these illusions. This suggests that these illusions are a product of pattern filtering. The other illusions shown in Figure 6-11 are based on the fact that they resemble images of *three-dimensional scenes* with cues to size and distance and so are processed by the visual system as three-dimensional scenes (Gillam, 1980). Figure 6-11C is a good example. The two horizontal lines are equal in length, but the slanted lines provide a cue that indicates that the upper part of the figure is farther away than the lower part. This cue is integrated with the image size of the upper line to make it appear larger. The process is explained in the Critical Discussion, "Understanding Constancy and Illusion." Illusions D,

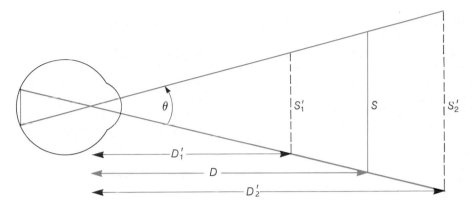

FIGURE 6-13
Size-Distance Invariance Principle
The angle θ, called the visual angle, is proportional to retinal image size. Suppose the object's true size is S and its distance is D. If the object is perceived at D_1', its perceived size will be S_1'. If it is perceived at D_2', its perceived size will be S_2'. The perceived size always fills the visual angle at the perceived distance.

The principle explains size constancy in the following way. When the distance to an object increases, its visual angle decreases. But if distance cues are present, perceived distance will increase. Thus the product of $θ \times D'$ will remain approximately constant. According to the principle, perceived size must therefore remain approximately constant.

The size-distance invariance principle seems to be fundamental to understanding a number of size illusions. A good example is the moon illusion: when the moon is near the horizon, it looks as much as 50 percent larger than when it is at its zenith, even though in both locations the moon produces the same size retinal image. The perceived distance of the horizon is judged to

be farther than the zenith by approximately the same amount.

As these examples illustrate, the size-distance invariance principle explains a wide range of diverse phenomena. There are, however, some reports of perceived size and distance that do not fit this principle. For example, a person judging the distance to the horizon when the moon is on the horizon often describes it as very close, just the opposite of how it is seen without the moon. It remains to be seen whether the principle needs to be modified or if these inconsistent reports have some other explanation. Theorists have proposed other invariance principles to explain constancies and illusions of shape, lightness, color, and location. The search for invariance princi-

ples shows a great deal of promise, but it is likely that invariances in relations among more than two variables will be needed to account for some of these percepts.

Let us now consider the second part of the problem of understanding constancies and illusions: What goes on in the perceptual system so that a particular relation among variables gives rise to a particular percept? Helmholtz proposed that a person arrives at the percept by inferring it from the sensations evoked by the stimulus. In the case of size perception, this means that the perceiver senses the retinal image size and the distance cues and infers the object's size from them. It is as if the perceiver inserts the values of D' and $θ$ in the size-distance equation and solves for S'. This is an example of *unconscious inference*. It happens very fast, and perceivers are not aware of either the sensations or the process of inference.

Without taking issue with Helmholtz's analysis, we can imagine biological bases for this process of inference. Given the discovery of many kinds of filters in perceptual systems, it is natural to ask if there might be higher-level filters tuned not to individual features but to the relations among features, such as the product of visual angle and distance. Although the idea has much appeal, psychologists have made little progress in discovering these invariance-sensitive filters. The closest we have come to this are the cells described in our discussion of location constancy, which seem to respond to the difference between the amount the eye turns and the amount the image moves on the retina.

E, and F can also be explained as a consequence of the figures being processed as three-dimensional scenes. Note the very close correspondence between these *perspective illusions* and size constancy. In each case, cues that indicate that something is farther away cause it to be perceived larger than it would otherwise be.

Scope of Perceptual Integration

We have considered a large variety of phenomena in which the percept depends on the relations among the features of a stimulus. The interpretation that we have given is that these features are processed together, or as the Gestalt psychologists would say, the stimulus is processed as a whole. But how large a stimulus can be processed as a whole? Perceptual properties of some very interesting stimuli called *impossible figures* suggest that the stimulus region that is processed as a

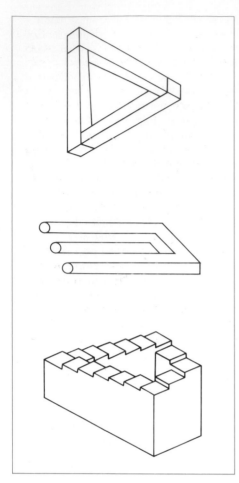

FIGURE 6-14
Impossible Figures *If one looks at any one part of these figures, it makes perceptual sense, but the whole does not. This suggests that the process of perceptual integration takes place over only a limited region at a time.*

whole does not extend beyond what the perceiver is able to take in with a single glance. Examples of impossible figures are shown in Figure 6-14. These figures appear to be tridimensional, but in no sense do they appear simple or even possible, an observation that is inconsistent with both Gestalt and Helmholtzian ideas about what we should see. On the other hand, each small region of the figures appears both possible and relatively simple. This suggests that the process of perceptual integration does not extend very far. Consistent with this is the fact that, if these figures are made small, so that their images fit in the fovea, they tend to lose both their depth and their impossible quality and will appear simply as lines on a flat surface (Hochberg, 1978).

Let us now reconsider one of the theoretical questions raised in the introduction to this chapter: What is the basic unit of perception? It is now clear that perception is not just the joint sensing of a bundle of stimulus features; the percept depends on the relations among the features. This suggests the existence of higher-level units that correspond to two or more features in a specific relation. Like sensations, these units may correspond to specific neurons in the brain. There may be a hierarchy of units in which lower-level units combine to form higher-level units. In that case, perception relies on several levels of units. The level that determines a particular percept will depend on the perceiver's task: sorting for color relies on one level; recognizing faces, on another.

RECOGNIZING

To recognize something is to associate it correctly with a category, such as "chair," or with a specific name, such as "John Jones." Recognition usually occurs when we see our car in the parking lot, hear a familiar tune, or look in the mirror in the morning. It is a high-level perceptual process, which requires learning and remembering.

There are many degrees of recognition, depending on the size of the category with which we associate something. Suppose that ten years from now you see someone at a party and sense that you know that person. If you are correct, you have already recognized the person — in the sense that you associated that person with the category of all people that you have ever known. You may be able to experience more complete recognition. For example, you might be able to say, "Podunk U., Class of '89," or even, "I'll be darned if you're not Gertrude Hasenpfeffer; you haven't changed a bit!"

Pandemonium Theory

What goes on in the perceptual system when we recognize something? Many of the ideas that we have about this come from scientists' efforts to make machines that can simulate the process of pattern recognition. One of the early theories that has some important resemblances to human recognition is called *pandemonium theory* (Selfridge & Neisser, 1960). It was designed to be implemented in a computer-based machine for the recognition of handwritten letters. According to this theory, when a test letter is presented, the machine senses its features, all more or less at the same time; processing several signals at the same time is called *parallel processing*. Pandemonium uses 28 features, such as the presence of vertical or horizontal lines, curves facing in different directions, and open spaces.

The theory assumes that letters can be represented in terms of a *feature list*. For example, the letter *H* consists of two lines that are roughly vertical, one line

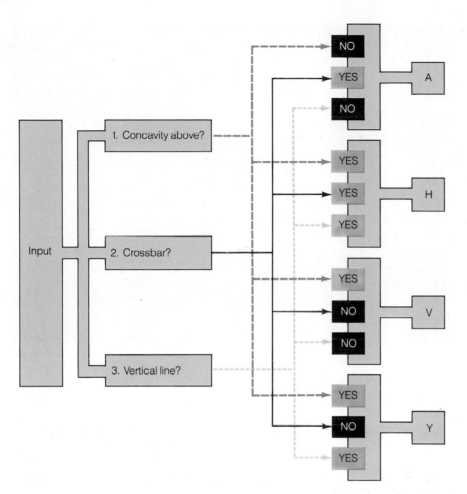

that is roughly horizontal, and an open space (concavity) at the top. These features taken together specify the letter *H*, but any of the features alone would not be enough to specify *H*. A feature list is stored in the computer's memory for each letter in the alphabet. When a test letter is presented, its features are sensed and compared with each of the feature lists in memory to determine which provides the best match.

The designers of pandemonium use the following analogy to describe their idea: "One might think of the various features as being inspected by little demons, all of whom then shout the answers in concert to a decision-making demon." The name "pandemonium" comes from this analogy to shouting demons. Figure 6-15 illustrates how the system might recognize one of the four letters, *A*, *H*, *V*, or *Y*.

From our point of view, there are two aspects to pandemonium theory that are particularly salient. One is that pandemonium processes features in *parallel*, not one after the other. The other is that pandemonium is completely *passive*: it has no preconceptions and makes no assumptions about the material that it senses. In other words, the sensors are activated automatically by the stimulus, and only the active sensors determine what is perceived. The perceiver's expectations, motives, and goals play no role. The percept depends on the immediate stimulus; all the perceiver has to do is open his or her eyes. As we will see, human perceptual systems are more complicated.

Pandemonium theory is extremely simple. Far more complex ones have been embodied in machines that are accurate in discriminating both hand-printed and

On the right is the painting La Parade *(1887–88) by Georges Seurat. An enlargement of one part of the picture illustrates how it is composed of separate daubs of paint. The total impression is greater than the sum of its parts.*

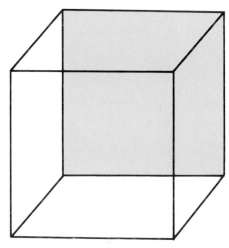

FIGURE 6-16
Necker Cube *An ambiguous stimulus devised in 1832 by the Swiss naturalist L. A. Necker. The tinted surface can appear as either the front or the rear of the transparent cube. The two percepts tend to alternate every few seconds.*

hand-written letters. Instead of parallel processing, some of these machines employ *serial processing,* which processes the features of the stimulus one after another. The technology is part of a larger field called *artificial intelligence,* whose goal is to develop machines capable of a wide variety of intelligent behavior.

Some of the greatest advances in artificial intelligence have been in the field of machine vision (Marr, 1982). Although most of these machines are still in an experimental stage, several have reached technological maturity. The postal service, for example, has installed Zip Code readers that can discriminate handprinted or typed digits, allowing the service to sort hundreds of letters in just minutes. Researchers are developing more sophisticated seeing machines that can infer three-dimensional scenes from two-dimensional images and hearing machines that can translate speech into written messages. Computer scientists, who are developing perception machines, and psychologists, who are trying to understand human perception, have formed a fruitful working relationship.

These various theories and machines have a common principle: a list of features is extracted from the stimulus and compared with a set of feature lists stored in memory. When a match occurs between the extracted feature list and one in memory, the stimulus has been identified. The human perceptual system may operate in a similar manner. Stored in your memory might be a feature list for "Aunt Sara"; it would include the width of her mouth, the slant of her nose, the color of her eyes, and so forth. When you encounter someone, the feature detectors are activated, and if the extracted features match the list in your memory for Aunt Sara, you know who it is. Another term for a feature list is *schema* (plural *schemata*). A subject has a schema of a stimulus stored in memory and recognizes the stimulus when the features extracted from it match the schema for that stimulus.

The process of extracting features from a stimulus and trying to match them with a feature list (schema) in memory is called *encoding;* that is, we are trying to form a code from the stimulus input that will allow us to locate information previously stored in our memory about the stimulus. The notion of encoding is an important concept in cognitive psychology and is discussed in greater detail in Chapter 8.

Ambiguous Stimuli

An *ambiguous stimulus* is one that can be perceived in more than one way. We have already seen one example in Figure 6-1, a picture with figure-ground ambiguity. Figure 6-16 is another; the Necker cube may be seen with the tinted surface either at the front or at the back; each of the two percepts is equally likely to be seen first, and if you continue to look at the figure, they will alternate. Figure 6-17 is an ambiguous stimulus that can be seen either as an old woman or as a young woman. This stimulus is not equally balanced; the old woman is more likely to be seen initially than the young one. The fact that a stimulus can be perceived in more than one way suggests that it must activate neurons in the perceptual system that correspond to more than one percept. The fact that only one of these percepts can be experienced at a time suggests that there must be a selective process that allows only one of these percepts to occur at a time.

Effects of Context, Expectations, and Motives

A *context effect* refers to the perception of a stimulus as it is influenced by the "meaning" of other stimuli near it in time and space. You can think of context as everything that might help you to guess what a stimulus is, apart from the stimulus itself. But context effects do not depend on conscious guessing or even on awareness of the context. When the context is one in which the stimulus usually occurs, the effect of context is facilitatory; familiar context increases both the speed and accuracy of perception. It is particularly beneficial in cases where the stimulus is ambiguous, blurred, or otherwise difficult to perceive; in the absence of context, recognition might fail to occur or might be in error. On the other hand, when a stimulus occurs rarely or for the first time in a particular context and so is unexpected, context has the opposite effect: recognition is slowed or erroneous, or simply does not occur.

When the stimulus is ambiguous, the percept that occurs depends on the context. If you have been looking at *unambiguous* pictures that resemble the young woman in Figure 6-17, you will tend to see the young woman first in the ambiguous picture. This effect of *temporal context* is illustrated with another set of pictures in Figure 6-18. Look at them in the sequence that you would look at a comic strip, from left to right and top to bottom. The pictures in the middle of the series are ambiguous. If you view the figures in the sequence just suggested, you will tend to see these ambiguous pictures as a man's face. If you look at them in the

FIGURE 6-17
Ambiguous Stimulus   *An ambiguous drawing that can be seen either as a young woman or as an old woman. Most people see the old woman first. Some hints may facilitate reversal. The young woman is turning away, and we see the left side of her face. Her chin is the old woman's nose, and her necklace is the old woman's mouth. (After Boring, 1930)*

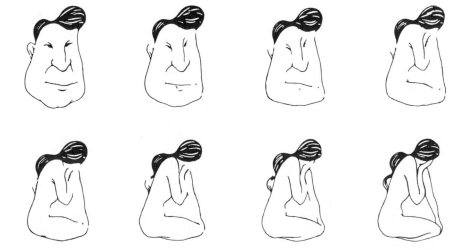

FIGURE 6-18
Effect of Temporal Context   *What you see here depends on the order in which you look at the pictures. The pictures in the middle of the series are ambiguous. If you have been looking at pictures of a man's face, they will appear to be distorted faces. If you have been looking at pictures of a young woman, they will look like a young woman. (After Fisher, 1967)*

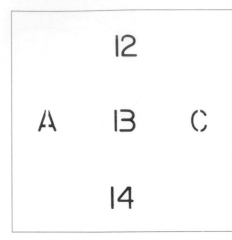

FIGURE 6-19
Effect of Spatial Context   *The figure in the center is ambiguous, and the way we see it depends on whether we are attending to the row or the column.*

opposite order, you will tend to see them as a young woman. Figure 6-19 illustrates how the spatial context provided by surrounding symbols influences our perception of an ambiguous symbol.

But the stimulus does not need to be ambiguous. Even in the simplest detection tasks, accuracy and speed of response depend on whether the subject knows what particular stimulus will be presented (Yager, Kramer, Shaw, & Graham, 1984). If a person is first shown a picture of a scene and then a picture of a single object is flashed briefly, identification of the object will be more accurate if the object is appropriate to the scene. For example, after looking at a kitchen scene, a subject will identify a loaf of bread correctly more often than he or she will a mailbox (Palmer, 1975). Likewise, when a scene is flashed very rapidly before a subject, who must then identify an object at some position in the scene, the subject will identify the object more accurately when it is in a normal location in the scene than if it is in an unusual location. For example, we have difficulty seeing fire hydrants on top of mailboxes (Biederman, 1981). We identify words, too, more rapidly in the context of meaningful sentences. Consider the sentence "Pete Rose swung his bat and hit the ⸻ ." The last word is recognized almost before the eye fixates it.

When a stimulus appears in an unusual context, we experience a negative effect of context. Recognizing the stimulus is often difficult and may be impossible. Students who see their professor at the lectern in coat and tie on weekdays will have difficulty recognizing him skinny-dipping at an isolated lake on Sunday afternoon. At the very least, recognition will take longer.

Context sometimes produces conscious expectations. Certainly when you are at an airport waiting for a friend to get off a plane, you have a conscious expectation. If that friend comes along, you are not likely to miss him or her, and recognition will be very rapid. Context, however, produces its effects even in the absence of conscious expectations: you do not even have to be aware of the context for the context effect to occur. If researchers flash a word on a screen for a few milliseconds and immediately follow it by a pattern of random lines, the viewer cannot report the word (backward masking). The unseen word, nevertheless, has an effect on the perception of a stimulus that follows. For example, if the word BREAD is flashed and masked, then the word BUTTER is flashed, subjects will recognize that "butter" is a word faster than they would if "bread" had not been presented (Schvaneveldt & Meyer, 1973; Marcel, 1983).

Although they are less studied than the effects of context and expectation, some evidence indicates that *motives* also influence perception. If we want to perceive something or fear perceiving it, our desires may affect perception. One study found, for example, that thresholds for undesirable words are higher than those for normal words (McGinnies, 1949), although this and similar results have been highly controversial. Some clinicians use the Rorschach Test to assess personality (see Chapter 13, p. 444). In this test, highly ambiguous inkblots (Figure 6-20) are presented to clients, who are asked to report everything that the inkblot looks like. The expectation is that the client's report will bring out motives and emotions that might otherwise remain hidden. Some psychologists have argued that motives and emotions influence only what people report and not what they perceive. This issue has not been settled, but evidence suggests that context acts directly on perception (see the Critical Discussion, "Context Effects in Letter Recognition," p. 202), and it would not be surprising if motives and emotions also influence perception (Erdelyi, 1974).

Just as recognition itself relies on our knowledge of concepts, objects, and events, context effects rely on a more general knowledge of the world. In particular, they depend on our knowledge of what is likely to happen in particular

FIGURE 6-20
Rorschach Inkblot   *This stimulus, created by spilling ink on a paper and folding it along a vertical line, is ambiguous. It can be perceived in many ways. Such stimuli are used in assessing personality.*

situations and what the specific cues are that indicate what is going to happen next.

Attention

Attention is a complex process that is just beginning to be understood. It has both overt behavioral components and internal components. When first-time campers hear a sound in the woods at night, they tend to jump and turn toward the sound; at the same time, physiological changes occur which produce alertness and readiness for action. This set of overt and internal responses is the *orienting reflex*. It is what the elementary school teacher is trying to elicit when he says, "Now pay attention!" Unfortunately for the teacher, although this reaction occurs automatically to unexpected stimuli, it ceases to occur to repeated stimuli.

Most of the time we are bombarded with many stimuli at once. We are unable to perceive all of them. Some of them intrude on our consciousness no matter what we do, but, within limits, we are able to select what we perceive. As you sit reading, stop for a moment, close your eyes, and attend to the various stimuli that are reaching you. Notice, for example, the tightness of your left shoe. What sounds do you hear? Is there any odor in the air? You probably were not aware of these stimuli until you attended to them. Without the ability to select, we would be overwhelmed by all these stimuli. Usually what we select depends on what is important to us at the moment, but certain salient stimuli are always perceived; we say that they "capture our attention." Factors that increase the likelihood that we will perceive a stimulus are intensity, size, contrast, movement, and novelty. The process by which we select is called *selective attention*.

SELECTIVE SEEING How much can you see in a flash? This has been studied in the laboratory by flashing before subjects random arrays of letters on a screen (see Figure 6-21). The array is flashed for just a few milliseconds, not long enough for the eyes to move. Immediately afterward, subjects try to write down as many of the letters as they can. College students score an average of 4.5 correct letters, and there is very little improvement with practice. Thus, we are sharply limited in how much we can see in a flash. However, if just as the letters are flashed subjects hear one of three tones that indicates which row to read, they can read any one row almost perfectly (Sperling, 1960). Thus, although we are *limited* in what we can see in a flash, we can *select* what part of the display it will be.

Another aspect of selective seeing becomes apparent when a person is given time to look at a picture or scene. If we watch the eyes of someone doing this, it is evident that the eyes are not stationary; they are scanning. Scanning is not a smooth continuous motion, however: the eyes are still for a brief period, then jump to another position, are still for another brief period, then jump again, and so on. The periods during which the eyes are still are called *fixations*, and the quick, almost instantaneous, movements between fixations are called *saccades* (*saccade* is French for "jump"). There are a number of techniques for tracking eye movements. The simplest method is to monitor the eyes with a TV camera in such a way that what the eye is gazing at is reflected on the cornea of the eye so it appears on television superimposed on the image of the eye. From this superimposed image, the experimenter can determine the point in the scene where the eye is fixated. The procedure provides an unobtrusive method for monitoring eye movements, and researchers can replay the TV tape to measure the duration of each fixation.

As noted in the previous chapter, the fovea has the best resolution; visual acuity diminishes rapidly toward the periphery of the retina. The eye movements used in scanning a picture ensure that different parts of the picture will fall on the

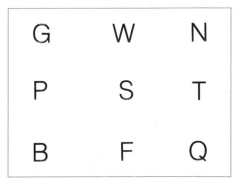

FIGURE 6-21
Random Letter Array *An array of the kind used by Sperling (1960) in his studies of selective seeing. If the array is flashed briefly, a subject can report only four or five letters. However, if the subject is asked to report a designated row just as the flash occurs, he or she can do so with almost perfect accuracy.*

fovea so that all of its details can be seen. The points on which the eyes fixate are not evenly distributed, nor are they random. They tend to be the places that are most informative about the picture, places where important features are located. Perceiving the picture requires the perceptual system to combine these various glimpses into a single representation of the scene, a process akin to assembling a picture from a series of snapshots of its parts (see Figure 6-22).

SELECTIVE HEARING   Hearing is also selective. Consider what happens at a crowded cocktail party. The sounds of many voices bombard our ears. We do not hear them all, and although we may think we can hear two or three, research shows that we can only perceive one message at a time. A common procedure in this research is to put earphones on a subject and play one speech message through one ear and another speech message through the other ear. The subject is asked to repeat (or *shadow*) one of the messages as it is heard. After proceeding in this way for a few minutes, the messages are turned off and the listener is asked about the unshadowed message. The person can report very little about this message. The listener's remarks are usually limited to the physical characteristics of the sound in the unshadowed ear — whether the voice was high or low, male or female, and so forth; he or she can say almost nothing about the content of the message (Moray, 1969).

At a real cocktail party, our task is even more difficult, because many messages come to both ears. However, we usually can select the message we want to follow; some of the cues that help us to do this are the direction of the sound, the lip movements of the speaker, and the particular voice characteristics of the speaker (pitch, speed, and intonation). Even in the absence of any of these cues, we can, with difficulty, select one of two messages on the basis of its meaning.

THE LOCUS OF SELECTION   At what level of the perceptual system do we select the stimuli to which we attend, and what happens to nonattended stimuli? An early idea was that nonattended stimuli are filtered out completely at a low level in the perceptual system (Broadbent, 1958). However, there is now considerable evidence that our perceptual system retains nonattended stimuli for a brief period and processes them to some extent, even though they never reach consciousness. The fact that a message can be selected or rejected on the basis of its meaning implies that quite a bit of processing must precede selection. Your own name, even when spoken softly in a nonattended conversation, often captures your attention. This could not happen if the entire nonattended message (such as another person's conversation across the room) were lost at lower levels of the perceptual system.

FIGURE 6-22
Eye Movements in Viewing a Picture
Below the picture of the young girl is a record of the eye movements made by a subject inspecting the picture for three minutes. (After Yarbus, 1967)

We selectively attend to the stimuli that impinge on our senses while retaining an awareness of the nonattended stimuli.

Contemporary Theory

A number of contemporary theories of recognition try to take account of context effects and selective attention, but none has been formulated in a precise fashion (Norman, 1976; Posner, 1982; Kahneman & Treisman, 1984). We have chosen to present a simplified theory that captures the main ideas of several theories, although it is most closely related to ideas proposed by Wickelgren (1979).

The theory proposes that conscious perception and recognition occur when the response of a specific neuron in the brain reaches a certain level of activation (recognition threshold). The neuron receives three kinds of input: stimulus input, attentional set, and selective attention (see Figure 6-23). *Stimulus input* depends on stimulus intensity and the sensitivity of the neuron to the stimulus. The neuron will be activated if it is sensitive to (tuned to) that stimulus and if the stimulus intensity surpasses the neuron's recognition threshold. *Attentional set* is an internal input to the neuron which depends on the momentary context, our expectations, and our motives. It results in a partial activation or inhibition of the neuron. Finally, *selective attention* is a decision process by which active neurons suppress the activity of other neurons. We do not know how this process works, but a plausible hypothesis is that it is based on mutual inhibition among competing neurons. This is indicated by the vertical lines in Figure 6-23. The reciprocal inhibition suppresses the less active neurons and makes the most active neurons still more active until some reach the threshold of recognition (Walley & Weiden, 1973).

It is likely that at every waking moment we have attentional sets for some percepts. These sets depend on what we are thinking about and what has been happening recently. They partially activate neurons, but generally not enough to produce conscious perception. When a stimulus arrives, it adds to the activation levels of the cells tuned to it, but even the attentional set and stimulus activation together may not produce enough activation for conscious perception. Selective attention then selects among these active neurons, and at that point we experience the stimulus and are able to respond to it. Note that in this theory, unlike pandemonium, there is no decision-making demon. The competitive attentional process produces the decision. It is like deciding who is the toughest kid on the playground by having a free-for-all that leaves only one kid standing; there is no need for a referee. According to this theory, the processing of stimuli is parallel up to a point, but if attention is required, the process becomes serial, because attention is limited to at most a few things at a time.

Reading

Reading is a remarkable cognitive skill and a critical process by which people become educated about the world around them. Adults read 100 to 400 words per minute, with college students averaging 300 words per minute for nontechnical material. This is much faster than we can read random letters or even random words, so clearly the context provided by the rest of the text has a large facilitatory role in reading.

EYE MOVEMENTS IN READING When we read, our eyes do not move continuously across the page; rather, they move in a series of saccades interspersed with fixations. Contrary to many people's impression, when reading our eyes move only a short distance in each saccade, about .5 to 1.5 words. The duration of fixations averages about 250 milliseconds, but varies greatly from one fixation to the next. As the readability of the text increases, saccades go farther and fixations become shorter (Rayner, 1978). Occasionally, a reader will move

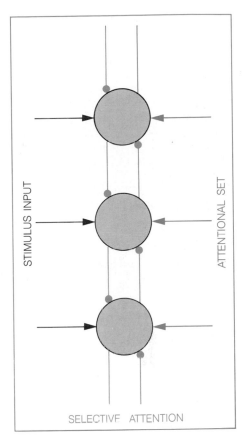

FIGURE 6-23
A Contemporary Theory of Recognition *The three circles symbolize three of the millions of neurons in the perceptual system. Each neuron, when sufficiently active, evokes a particular percept. Three types of input to each neuron determine its level of activation at any moment. These inputs are indicated by lines terminating in either arrows (excitatory inputs) or dots (inhibitory inputs). The three types of input are the* **stimulus input,** *which depends on the sensitivity of the neuron and the intensity of the stimulus;* **attentional set,** *which depends on momentary context, expectations, and goals; and* **selective attention,** *an inhibitory input from other active neurons (shown by the vertical lines in the figure). Stimulus input and attentional set may be either inhibitory or excitatory, although to avoid cluttering this illustration, only excitatory inputs are shown. When a neuron reaches a threshold level of activation, the associated percept is experienced.*

Eye Fixations in Reading *Eye fixations of a college student reading a scientific passage. A gaze is the total time a person fixates on a word or group of words. Gazes within each sentence are numbered sequentially above the fixated words, with the durations in milliseconds indicated below the sequence number. Note that there is only one regress — from fixation 4 to 5 in the second sentence. (After Just & Carpenter, 1980)*

1	2	3	4	5	6	7	8	9	1	2
1566	267	400	83	267	617	767	450	450	400	616
Flywheels	are	one	of the	oldest	mechanical	devices	known	to man.	Every	internal-

3	5	4	6	7	8	9	10	11	12	13
517	684	250	317	617	1116	367	467	483	450	383
combustion	engine	contains	a	small	flywheel	that converts	the	jerky	motion of the pistons	into the

14	15	16	17	18	19	20	21
284	383	317	283	533	50	366	566
smooth	flow	of	energy that	powers	the	drive	shaft.

his or her eyes backward to a word already passed, but skilled readers do this less often than beginners.

Figure 6-24 presents some eye movement data from an experiment by Just and Carpenter (1980). Their subjects read a series of passages that contained fairly difficult scientific material; the figure presents the fixation times of one subject reading two sentences from such a passage. The researchers combined consecutive fixations on the same word into units called *gazes* and numbered the gazes in sequence for each sentence. The duration of each gaze, recorded in milliseconds, is also indicated.

Note, first of all, that almost every word is fixated. The words that are not fixated tend to be short function words like "of," "a," and "the." This is the typical pattern when a reader encounters new text materials that are fairly difficult to comprehend. Note the word-to-word variation in the duration of gaze. For example, the word "flywheel" is fixated for over a second on each of its two occurrences; no other word was inspected for so long. Longer gazes occur for words that are unfamiliar to the reader or that have special thematic importance. Fixations at the end of a sentence also tend to be long, suggesting that the reader is taking time to integrate information from the whole sentence.

CONTEXT EFFECTS IN READING Three kinds of context effects facilitate normal reading. Our knowledge of words and how they are spelled speeds the identification of letters within the context of words. For example, when we fixate on "c_t," we attend for a vowel in the second position. Likewise, our knowledge of grammatical rules helps us to identify words in sentences, and our general knowledge of the world and the topic further augments the word identification. The possible words that can occur at any position in a text are limited both by grammar and by meaning.

How much information can we extract from the text in one fixation? One way to test this is to allow a reader to see only a small region around the fixation point and then determine how the size of this region affects reading performance. Using a computer-driven display controlled by the reader's eye movements, researchers masked all of the text except a small region around the fixation point. When the readers saw only one or two letters around the fixation point, their reading performance slowed and they made errors. As the amount of text seen by the readers increased, their performance improved, but they did not achieve normal reading speed until the window exposed about four words at a time (Rayner et al., 1981). This does not mean that we read four words in one fixation. The words in the periphery are too blurry to read, but apparently these blurs help somewhat, if only to guide the next fixation.

SPEED-READING Many speed-reading courses claim to increase both reading speed and comprehension. The idea behind these courses is to train readers to make fewer eye fixations and take in several words or a whole phrase in each fixation. Some groups even argue that one can register a whole line of printed text

in a single fixation and thus read straight from the top to the bottom of a page rather than from left to right on each line. Student readers are told to imagine a line down the center of the page and to move their eyes along that imaginary line, registering a whole line of print with each fixation. The instructor may suggest that they move the tip of a finger slowly down the center of the page at the same time, as a guide.

A common training exercise in speed-reading courses involves projecting short sentences on a screen for a very brief time (one-fourth of a second or less). The student attempts to register the sentence and read it aloud. If the exposures of sentences are well spaced, the student can learn to perceive a sentence of four or more words with practice; however, if the exposures occur rapidly, each new sentence will mask the last one. This exercise bears little resemblance to actual reading, in which the eyes move rapidly from one fixation point to the next.

Many claims have been made about the benefits of speed-reading courses — such as improved reading speed and comprehension — but the claims tend not to hold up when evaluated under carefully controlled conditions (Carver, 1981). Nevertheless, people who have taken speed-reading courses often are convinced that they have substantially improved their reading skills, and in a sense they are right. What they have learned is the skill of *skimming*. This enables them to pick out key words and main ideas and thereby obtain a great deal of information about the passage. Some reading material contains so little new information that skimming is all that is required. However, if the text presents new and challenging material, it cannot be comprehended by speed-reading. Under these conditions the reader must fixate on almost every word to comprehend the material.

These findings do not mean that there is no way to improve reading skills. On the contrary, we do know that the more reading a person does, the more his or her reading skills improve. This is particularly true for younger children. Attempts to force yourself to read at a faster rate, however, do not lead to improved reading skills.

Skimming is a valuable skill, and courses might be more effective if they were specifically designed to teach skimming rather than speed-reading. Even with difficult material, skimming can be helpful. For example, before reading a chapter in a textbook it is helpful to skim the material to identify key topics and gain a general impression of the chapter. The information gained by skimming helps to frame a context within which a person can read the material more carefully. Skimming can also help readers decide what materials are worth reading in detail (see Appendix I). For a consideration of how we recognize letters and words, see the Critical Discussion, "Context Effects in Letter Recognition" (p. 202).

"You have a choice of three courses. You could increase speed somewhat and retain your comprehension, you could increase speed considerably and reduce comprehension, or you could increase speed tremendously and eliminate comprehension completely."

PERCEPTUAL DEVELOPMENT

An age-old question about perception is whether our abilities to perceive are learned or innate — the familiar nature-nurture problem. Its investigation goes back to the philosophers of the seventeenth and eighteenth centuries. One group, the *nativists* (including Descartes and Kant), argued that we are born with the ability to perceive the way we do. In contrast, the *empiricists* (including Berkeley and Locke) maintained that we learn our ways of perceiving through experience with objects in the world about us. Contemporary psychologists believe that a fruitful integration of these two viewpoints is possible. No one today really doubts that practice and experience influence perception. The question is to what extent is perceptual capacity inborn and to what extent is it acquired as a function of experience.

CRITICAL DISCUSSION

Context Effects in Letter Recognition

If an array of random letters is flashed in front of us for a few milliseconds, we can report only four or five of them. Yet under the same conditions we can correctly report a word containing many more letters. How can this be explained? We will consider three hypotheses. Some psychologists believe that we still perceive only four or five letters of a word, but our knowledge of words and spelling rules allows us to *guess* the other letters. This means that the context provided by the word influences our decision of what to report but does not influence what we see. Another hypothesis is that the limit of four or five letters has to do with memory, not perception. We can perceive many more than four letters, but if they are random we can *remember* only four or five. If the letters form a word, though, we can readily remember them, because one word is easier to remember than several letters. Finally, other psychologists hypothesize that the context of the word actually helps us to *perceive* individual letters better. By this they mean that, if the experiment is done in a way that excludes memory and guessing, letters in words will still be recognized faster and more accurately than letters without this context.

Reicher (1969) performed an experiment designed to determine which of these three hypotheses is correct. He briefly flashed either a four-letter word or a random array of four letters on a screen. Then the subject saw a masking field where the array had been; above the masking field two test letters appeared, indicating the target position in the array (see Figure 6-25). One of the two test letters was the same as the letter in that position in the four-letter array previously viewed. The subject's task was to say which of the two

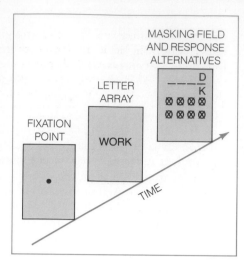

FIGURE 6-25
Reicher's Experiment   *This figure illustrates the sequence of stimuli in one trial of Reicher's experiment. First, subjects saw a fixation point, followed by a word or a random string of four letters, which was present for only a few milliseconds. Then Reicher presented a stimulus that contained a visual mask in the positions where the letters had been and two response alternatives, which were either directly above or directly below the position of the critical letter in the word or letter string. (After Reicher, 1969)*

letters was in that position in the array.

This sounds easy, but it was made hard by presenting the array for a very short time and following it with the masking field, which eliminated the afterimage. When the array formed a word, *both* of the test letters formed a word when combined with the other three letters. For example, when the array was WORK, the two test letters for the fourth position might be "K" and "D"; thus, knowledge of how words

For the modern researcher, the question "Must we learn to perceive?" has given way to more specific issues: (1) What discriminatory capacity do infants have, and how does this change with age under normal rearing conditions? (2) If animals are reared under conditions of controlled stimulation, what effects does this have on their discriminatory capacity? (3) What effects does rearing under controlled conditions have on perceptual-motor coordination?

Discrimination by Infants

It is hard for us to know what an infant perceives because it cannot talk or follow instructions and has a fairly limited set of behaviors. To study infant perception, a

are spelled would not aid guessing. Likewise, memory should not favor words over nonwords here, because the display contained only four letters and was followed by the two letters that the subject had to choose between. On half the trials, the subject was even told the target position and the two test letters in advance. Thus, by either the guessing hypothesis or the memory hypothesis, letters in this experiment should be seen no better in words than in nonwords. In fact, the results showed that letters were seen much better in words; the number of errors made for letters in words was only about half that for letters in random arrays. Reicher also showed that a letter in a word is detected better than a single letter with no context. These results have been replicated by several other investigators. Of the three hypotheses given here, only the hypothesis that the context of a word facilitates the perception of individual letters is consistent with these results.

McClelland and Rumelhart (1981) proposed a model of context effects in perception that was specifically designed to account for the effect of word context on letter recognition. According to the model, there is a hierarchy of detectors in the perceptual system. In particular, feature detectors activate letter detectors which in turn activate word detectors (see Figure 6-26). The critical property of the model is its interactive nature: as word detectors become active, they produce feedback that activates letter detectors for letters in the word and inhibits letter detectors for letters not in the word. When a word is presented, some of the letter detectors activate word detectors, which in turn feed back to activate letter detectors for *all* letters in that word. This is the basis of the word context effect. The authors call their theory an *interactive acti-*

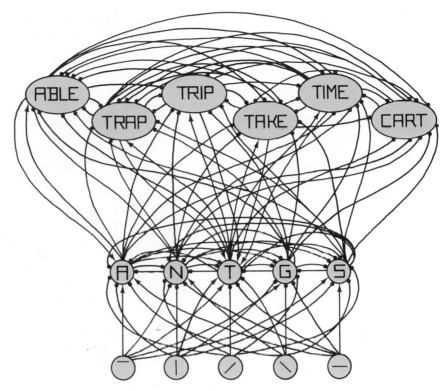

FIGURE 6-26
Interactive Activation Model *A model for the identification of letters in the context of words. The two sets of circles are detectors for features and letters; the ellipses, for words. Arrows correspond to excitatory inputs; dots to inhibitory inputs. Detectors excite other detectors with which they are compatible and inhibit detectors with which they are incompatible. The figure shows only a small part of the hierarchical perceptual network. (After McClelland & Rumelhart, 1981)*

vation model. They have simulated the model on a computer and have shown that it can account for many phenomena of letter detection. Figure 6-26 looks very complex even though it is only a small part of the model, which corresponds to only a

small part of the perceptual system. The whole system is certain to be even more complex. The building blocks of the model, however, are very simple. They consist of detectors joined by only two kinds of links, excitatory and inhibitory.

researcher needs to find a form of behavior through which an infant indicates what it can discriminate. The behavior most used for this purpose is an infant's tendency to look at some objects more than others, and psychologists study this by using the *preferential looking method* (see Figure 6-27). The method is very simple. Two stimuli are presented to the infant side by side. The experimenter, who is hidden from the infant's view, looks through a partition behind the stimuli and, by watching the infant's eyes, measures the amount of time that the infant looks at each stimulus. From time to time, the stimulus positions are switched randomly. If an infant consistently looks at one stimulus more than the other, we conclude that it can tell them apart (discriminate between them). The method would not work unless infants looked at some things more than others; thus,

FIGURE 6-27
Preferential Looking Apparatus
This "looking chamber" is used to study preferential looking in infants. A human infant lies in a crib and looks up at pictures and objects on the ceiling. The experimenter, watching through a peephole, records the infant's looking behavior. (After Fantz, 1961)

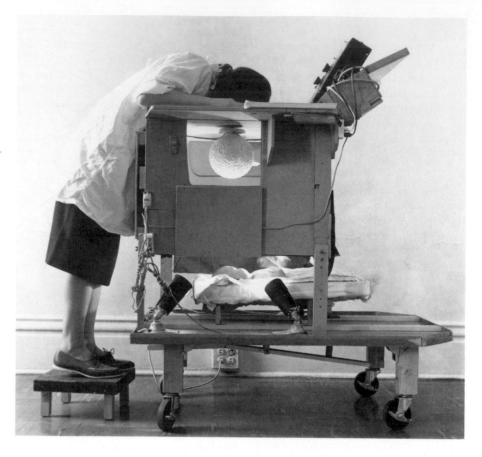

it shows that infants have definite looking preferences. For example, given a choice, infants will look at a pattern rather than a blank field (Fantz, Ordy, & Udelf, 1962).

Psychologists have also used *visual evoked potentials* to study infant perception. To record evoked potentials, an experimenter places electrodes on the back of the baby's head over the visual cortex; the electrodes are not annoying, and the infant quickly adapts to them. If a stimulus pattern consisting of broad stripes is presented to the infant, the electrodes will pick up an electrical response (the evoked potential); when the stripes are made very narrow, the response disappears. Psychologists believe the response is closely related to how well the stripes are seen.

A large number of studies have focused on acuity and contrast sensitivity in infants, the usual method being preferential looking, with a pattern of stripes as one stimulus and a uniform gray field as the other stimulus. The researcher decreases stripe width until the infant no longer shows a preference. When first studied at about 1 month of age, infants can see patterns, but their acuity is very low. Acuity increases rapidly over the first six months of life; then it increases more slowly, reaching adult levels between 1 and 5 years of age (Teller, Morse, Borton, & Regal, 1974; Pirchio, Spinelli, Fiorentini, & Maffei, 1978). Researchers have used the same method to study contrast sensitivity, with sine-wave gratings as stimuli (see Chapter 5, p. 162). Infant contrast sensitivity is better at low spatial frequencies than high but is less than adult sensitivity at all frequencies. Like acuity, contrast sensitivity increases rapidly over the first six months of life (Banks, 1982). Visual evoked potential studies give comparable results. The basis of this development in pattern vision is not completely understood, but researchers do know that the optics of the eye, the retina, and the cortex continue to develop over this period.

Infants as young as 2 months can discriminate colored lights from white ones (Teller, Peeples, & Sekel, 1978), but they may not have fully developed trichromatic color vision. By 3½ to 6 months of age, infants are able to discriminate depth using the binocular disparity cue (Fox, Aslin, Shea, & Dumais, 1980). At 5½ months, but not before, infants will reach for the nearer of two objects as indicated by the monocular relative size cue (Yonas, Pettersen, & Granrud, 1982). Perhaps the record for early testing goes to the psychologist who showed that one minute after birth infants will look toward the source of a sound (Wertheimer, 1961).

In summary, the youngest infants tested all showed considerable discriminatory ability, but this ability was well below adult levels. Discriminatory ability develops rapidly and, for acuity at least, is near adult levels by 1 year of age.

Perceptual abilities that require integration of stimulus features appear to take much longer to develop. For example, although there is some degree of size constancy in infancy, 8-year-old children still show considerably less constancy than adults (Zeigler & Leibowitz, 1957). There is no way for us to be sure what an infant is experiencing, but a number of investigators have been impressed by the fact that infants' natural responses to stimuli often resemble those of adults. They turn toward sounds, defend themselves when an object flies toward them, and do not fall off raised platforms (see Figure 6-28). Such behaviors are highly adaptive; in other words, they may have evolved because they help to keep people alive. The similarity of infant and adult responses to the same stimuli suggests that infants and adults may experience these stimuli in a similar way (Bower, 1982).

Rearing Without Stimulation

The earliest experiments using controlled stimulation kept animals in the dark for several months after birth until they were mature enough for visual testing. The theory behind these experiments was that if animals have to *learn* to perceive, they would be unable to do so when first exposed to the light. The results turned out as expected: chimpanzees reared in darkness for their first 16 months could detect light but could not discriminate patterns (Riesen, 1947). However, subsequent studies showed that dark rearing does more than prevent learning; it causes neuronal deterioration in various parts of the visual system. Apparently a certain amount of light stimulation is necessary to maintain the visual system. Without any light stimulation, nerve cells in the retina and visual cortex begin to atrophy. This fact is interesting in itself but does not tell us much about the role of learning in perceptual development.

Single-cell recording from the visual cortex in newborn cats and monkeys shows that they have simple, complex, and hypercomplex cells very similar to those in adult animals (p. 150) (Hubel & Wiesel, 1963; Wiesel & Hubel, 1974). Most cells in the visual cortex of the infant respond to stimulation in either eye, as do those of adults. Cells in newborn animals, however, respond more slowly and are less sharply tuned than adult cells. In kittens, for instance, the cells become adultlike in four to six weeks.

When they are introduced to an illuminated room, animals that have been raised in darkness act as though they are almost blind, and many of their cortical cells do not respond. Animals that are raised with one eye patched have few or no cells in the visual cortex that respond at all to stimulation of that eye, and they are essentially blind in that eye. When an animal is deprived of visual stimulation from birth, the longer the time of deprivation, the greater the deficit. Adult cats,

FIGURE 6-28
Visual Cliff *The "visual cliff" is an apparatus used to show that infants are able to see depth by the time they are able to move about. The visual cliff consists of two surfaces, both displaying the same checkerboard pattern and covered by a sheet of thick glass. One surface is directly under the glass; the other is several feet below it. When placed on the center board between the deep and the shallow sides, the infant refuses to cross to the deep side but will readily move off the board onto the shallow side. (After Gibson & Walk, 1960)*

FIGURE 6-29

Controlled Visual Environment   *In one experiment, kittens were kept in the dark from birth to 2 weeks of age. They were then placed in this tube for five hours a day and spent the rest of the time in the dark. The kitten is on a clear plexiglass platform, and the striped tube extends above and below it. It is wearing a neck ruff, which blocks its view of its own body and prevents head turning. The kittens did not appear to be distressed in this situation. After five months of this exposure, the kittens could see vertical stripes very well but were essentially blind to horizontal stripes. Further, single-cell recording found few cells in their cortices that responded to horizontal stripes. (After Blakemore & Cooper, 1970)*

on the other hand, can have one eye patched for a long period without losing vision in that eye. These observations led to the idea that a *critical period* exists for visual development early in life; lack of stimulation during this critical period impairs the visual system.

Rearing With Controlled Stimulation

Another line of research has studied the effects of rearing animals with stimulation in both eyes, but only of a certain kind. Kittens raised in an environment where they see only vertical stripes or only horizontal stripes (see Figure 6-29) become blind to stripes in the orientation that they do not experience and have few cells tuned to this orientation (Blakemore & Cooper, 1970; Hirsch & Spinelli, 1970). What happens to the cells that are not stimulated? Do they degenerate or do they become "rewired" to respond to the available stimuli? If degeneration occurs, there should be areas of the visual cortex that are unresponsive. The evidence on this issue is mixed, but it seems to favor the degeneration hypothesis (Movshon & Van Sluyters, 1981).

Although researchers do not deprive humans of normal visual stimulation, this sometimes happens naturally or as a consequence of medical treatment. After eye surgery, the operated eye is usually patched. If this happens to a child in the first year of life, the acuity of the patched eye is reduced (Awaya et al., 1973). If a person's eyes do not point in the same direction early in life (a condition called *strabismus*), he or she will not have binocular depth perception in later life, even if the strabismus is corrected by surgery. Likewise, if *astigmatism* (an optical defect that prevents horizontal and vertical contours to be in focus at the same moment) is not corrected early in life, the individual will later have low acuity for one orientation (Mitchell & Wilkinson, 1974). These facts suggest that there is a critical period early in the development of the human visual system similar to that in animals; if stimulation is restricted during this period, the system will not develop normally. The critical period is much longer in humans than in animals; it may last as long as eight years, but the greatest vulnerability occurs during the first two years of life (Aslin & Banks, 1978).

None of these facts indicate that we have to learn to perceive; but they do show that stimulation is essential for the *maintenance* and *development* of the perceptual capacity present at birth. Learning appears to play a role in the development of capacities that require perceptual integration; it is essential to our ability to recognize things and to explain the effects of context and expectation.

Perceptual-Motor Coordination

Although we may not need to learn to perceive, there is evidence that we must learn to coordinate motor responses with perception. The evidence comes from studies in which subjects receive normal stimulation but are prevented from making normal responses to that stimulation. Under such conditions, perceptual-motor coordination does not develop.

For example, kittens were reared in the dark until they were 4 weeks old. After that, they were placed in a lighted and patterned environment for six hours a day, where they were allowed to move about freely. While they were in this situation, they wore lightweight collars that prevented them from seeing their bodies or paws (see Figure 6-30). Except for this six-hour exposure period each day, they stayed in a dark room. After 12 days of this regimen, they were tested for visual-motor coordination. The test consisted of lowering the kitten (with one front paw held and the other free to move) toward a table that had horizontal prongs. The researcher was interested in determining if the kitten would extend a paw and guide it to a prong. This is a response that a normally reared kitten will make very reliably. All the experimental kittens extended their free paw as they approached the table, indicating that they could see that the table was within reach. But on 50 percent of the trials, the kittens missed the prongs, indicating that they had not learned to guide their limbs to a visual target. Fortunately, after a few hours without the collar in a normally illuminated room, the kittens learned the paw-placing response (Hein & Held, 1967).

Humans are not subjected to this kind of restricted rearing, but adults have volunteered for experiments in which they wear prism goggles that distort the directions of objects. Immediately after putting on these goggles, a person has trouble reaching for objects and often bumps into things. If a person moves about and attempts to perform motor tasks while wearing the goggles, he or she learns to behave adaptively. On the other hand, a person pushed in a wheelchair does not adapt. Apparently, self-produced movement is essential to prism adaptation (Held, 1965b). This result suggests that, not only is learning required for perceptual-motor coordination, but the learning also must involve self-produced movement in response to stimulation.

Is perception innate or learned? The answer to this question is clearly some of each. The evidence indicates that we are born with considerable perceptual capacity which is shaped and developed by learning. One way to conceptualize this joint role of heredity and environment is that the lowest levels in the perceptual system are intact at birth and higher levels develop as a result of learning.

EXTRASENSORY PERCEPTION

Is it possible for us to acquire information about the world in ways that do not involve sense-organ stimulation? The answer to this question is the source of a controversy within psychology over the status of *extrasensory perception* (ESP). Although some psychologists believe the evidence for ESP is incontrovertible, most remain unconvinced.

Three kinds of ESP are said to exist, and ESP itself belongs to a larger class of *parapsychological phenomena*. These phenomena may be described as follows:

1. Extrasensory perception (ESP)
   a. Telepathy, or thought transference from one person to another
   b. Clairvoyance, or the perception of objects or events that do not provide a stimulus to the known senses (for example, stating the number and suit of a playing card that is in a sealed envelope)
   c. Precognition, or the perception of a future event
2. Psychokinesis (PK), or the manipulation of objects by mental will, without the intervention of any known physical force (for example, willing that a particular number comes up in the throw of dice)

ESP Experiments

Although parapsychological phenomena are associated with many religions, most investigators of them describe themselves as scientists applying the usual rules of science. Yet the phenomena with which they deal are so extraordinary and so similar to what are widely believed to be superstitions that many scientists reject even the legitimacy of their inquiries. Such a priori judgments are out of

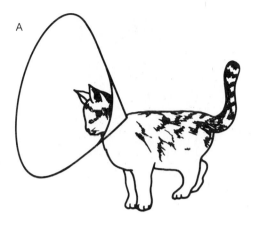

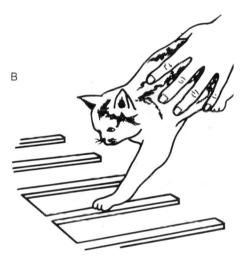

FIGURE 6-30
Learning Perceptual-Motor Coordination *A. Kitten wearing a collar that prevented it from seeing its limbs and torso. The collar was lightweight and had little effect on locomotion. Kittens were permitted to move freely six hours daily in a lighted and patterned environment while wearing the collar. The rest of the time, they were kept without collars in a dark room. B. Apparatus for testing visually guided paw placement. The prongs were 2.5 cm. wide and 7.5 cm. apart. During the test trials, the torso, hindlimbs, and one forelimb were supported as shown. The kitten was carried downward toward the pronged edge. The kitten was scored on the basis of whether or not its paw landed on a prong. (After Hein & Held, 1967)*

place in science; the real question is whether the empirical evidence is acceptable by scientific standards. Many psychologists who are not convinced are nevertheless ready to accept evidence that they find satisfactory. For example, the possibility of some sort of influence from one brain to another, other than by way of the sense organs, would not be inconceivable within the current framework of science. Some of the other phenomena, such as precognition, are more difficult to find believable; but if the experiments were convincing, beliefs would have to yield to facts.

Much of the early research on ESP was done by Rhine (1942) using a card "guessing" procedure. The typical ESP pack consists of 25 cards with five different symbols — so that by guessing alone, the person being tested should average five "hits," or correct answers, per pack (see Figure 6-31). Even very successful subjects seldom score as many as seven hits on a regular basis, but they may score above five often enough to meet accepted standards for statistical significance. In the typical experiment, the cards are shuffled and placed out of the subject's view; the subject then identifies the cards one at a time. If the experimenter, or "sender," looks at each card before the subject responds, the study tests telepathy. If the experimenter does not look at the card (it is face down), the study tests clairvoyance.

The card-guessing procedure may seem artificial and not conducive to good psychic performance, but it has several advantages: (1) the experiment can be carefully controlled to prevent the possibility of cheating; (2) the experiment can be repeated with the same subject at different times, or with different subjects; and (3) the significance of an experimental outcome (number of hits) can be evaluated using standard statistical techniques.

The kind of evidence used in support of the nonchance nature of the findings is illustrated by the successive runs of one "sensitive" subject, Mrs. Gloria Stewart, who was studied in England over a long period (see Table 6-1). If the evidence is viewed in the same way as evidence from any other experiment, it is clear that Mrs. Stewart responded above chance on the telepathy trials but not on the clairvoyance trials. These results meet certain objections regarding the possibility of nonrandom card order that are sometimes voiced against such experiments; her chance performance on the clairvoyance trials shows that above-chance scores are not an inevitable result related to the method of shuffling the cards.

Skepticism About ESP

Since a number of apparently sound experiments report statistically significant ESP or PK effects, why do these results not become part of established psychological science? Why do most psychologists not believe in these phenomena? Some of the resistance is due to the history of this field. In the past, many claims of parapsychological phenomena have been shown to be fraudulent. Likewise, many apparently decisive experiments have, on careful examination, been found

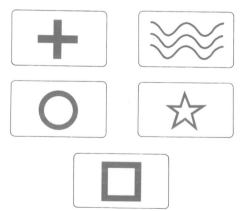

FIGURE 6-31
ESP Cards *Each card in the ESP pack bears one of five symbols (cross, wave, circle, star, rectangle). There are five of each symbol in a pack of 25 cards.*

YEAR OF SUCCESSIVE BLOCKS OF 200 TRIALS	HITS PER 200 TRIALS (EXPECTED = 40)	
	Telepathy Trials	Clairvoyance Trials
1945	65 58 62 58 60	51 42 29 47 38
1947	54 55 65	35 36 31
1948	39 56	38 43
1949	49 51 33	40 37 42
Total hits Expected hits (20% of 2,600) Difference Hits per 25 trials	707 520 +187 6.8	509 520 −11 4.9

TABLE 6-1
Results of an ESP Experiment *Results of telepathy and clairvoyance tests with one subject studied over a long period. (After Soal & Bateman, 1954)*

to be methodologically flawed. More important than these historical considerations, however, is the fact that *no parapsychological phenomenon can be reliably demonstrated*. Better methods, instead of yielding greater and more reliable effects, have tended to yield smaller and less reliable results. Procedures that produce significant results for one investigator do not do so for another. Even the same investigator testing the same individuals over a period of time may obtain significant results on one occasion and yet be unable to repeat the results later. Lack of reproducibility is a serious problem. In other scientific fields, an experimental finding is not considered established until the experiment has been repeated by several researchers with comparable results. Until ESP experiments can be shown to be reproducible, the authenticity of the phenomena remains open to question.

A second complaint about ESP research is that the results do not vary systematically with experimental variables. If we take the evidence at face value, however, this objection is not entirely fair. There is now a body of evidence that relates ESP and PK to other variables. Subjects tend to be more successful on early trials than on later ones; and subjects with a favorable attitude toward ESP produce positive results, whereas an unfavorable attitude leads to below-chance scores, which are equally puzzling. Researchers also have found that the emotional states of the sender and receiver are important; ESP is maximal when the sender is emotionally aroused and the receiver is reclining in a relaxed state. Other studies find ESP to be better when the receiver is dreaming or in a hypnotic state rather than in a normal, waking state. Effects in these studies are small but often statistically significant. Unfortunately, these studies have had the same problems of reproducibility that the more basic demonstrations of the phenomena do. For a review of these studies, see Kurtz (1985) and Frazier (1986).

The criticisms of parapsychological findings are not decisive. It is desirable to keep an open mind about issues that permit empirical demonstration. At the same time, the reservations of the majority of psychologists clearly are based on more than stubborn prejudice. For critiques of work in this field, see Hansel (1980) and Marks and Kammann (1980).

SUMMARY

1. *Perceiving* refers to tasks such as judging distance, size, and shape and identifying objects and events. *Structuralists* believed that a percept is simply the joint occurrence of sensations, while *Helmholtz* proposed that we learn to infer percepts from sensations. The *Gestalt psychologists* held that whole forms are the basic units of perception and are produced by a process of organization that does not depend on learning or experience.

2. When a stimulus consists of more than one part *(element)*, it is perceived in a way that depends on the relations among the elements *(perceptual organization)*. *Figure-ground* organization and *perceptual grouping* are examples of perceptual organization.

3. Distance perception is based on *distance cues*. There are a large number of such cues, some of which are *monocular* and some *binocular*. Most cues indicate only *relative distance*, but a few indicate *egocentric distance*. Motion perception can be produced by *real motion* or *stroboscopic motion* (a series of still images). There is evidence that some neurons in the brain are tuned to the direction and speed of motion. Motion seen while tracking an object moving in the dark indicates that the visual system receives and uses information about eye movements.

4. *Perceptual constancy* is a tendency for objects to appear the same in spite of large changes in the stimuli received by our sense organs. Examples of features for which constancy occurs are *lightness, color, shape, size,* and *location*. Constancy depends on relations among the features of a stimulus. It is rarely perfect. An *illusion* is a percept that is false or distorted. Some illusions are *physical;* others, *perceptual. Geometrical illusions* are perceptual illusions produced by line drawings. Some of them are explained by *pattern filtering;* others are a consequence of the drawing being processed as an image of a *three-dimensional scene*.

5. To *recognize* something is to associate it with a category or a specific name. An early theory of letter recognition, called *pandemonium,* proposed that features are detected *in parallel*. The detected features are then compared with feature lists for each letter that are stored in memory, and the letter whose feature list best matches the detected features is perceived.

6. An *ambiguous stimulus* is one that is perceived in more than one way. Examples are the Necker cube and the young woman–old woman figure. The fact that such stimuli can be seen only one way at a time suggests the existence of a selective process *(selective attention)*. The *context* in which a stimulus is presented will either facilitate perception (if it is a familiar context) or interfere with perception (if it is an unfamiliar context). Conscious expectations and motives also influence perception. These effects are particularly strong when the stimulus is ambiguous.

7. *Attention* refers to several processes including the *orienting reflex,* a general state of alertness, the control of looking behavior, and the process that underlies selective perceiving (selective attention). Looking behavior is an overt response; alertness and selective attention are internal responses; and the orienting reflex involves both overt and internal components.

8. According to a contemporary theory of *recognition,* neurons that evoke percepts receive three inputs: a stimulus input, an input due to context and expectation *(attentional set),* and an input due to a competitive process among percepts *(selective attention)*. When a neuron reaches a threshold level of activation, the associated percept is evoked.

9. In *reading,* the eyes jump *(saccade)* along a line of text in steps whose size depends on the skill of the reader and the difficulty of the text. Context effects

make it possible for us to read text much faster than we can read random words. It is not possible to read at speeds substantially higher than 400 words per minute without loss of comprehension. *Skimming,* however, is a valuable skill.

10. Infants have considerable perceptual capacity very early in life and probably at birth. This capacity improves rapidly during the first six months of life, and some perceptual abilities continue to improve over many years.

11. Animals have neurons in their brains that are tuned to stimulus features at birth. Animals raised in darkness suffer permanent visual impairment, and animals raised with a patch over one eye become blind in that eye. Adult animals do not lose vision even when deprived of stimulation for long periods. If stimulation is controlled early in life, so that certain kinds of stimuli are absent, both animals and people become insensitive to the stimuli of which they have been deprived. These results suggest a *critical period* early in life during which lack of normal stimulation produces an abnormal perceptual system. *Perceptual-motor coordination* must be learned. The development of visual-motor coordination requires visual stimulation, sight of limbs, and self-produced movement in response to stimulation.

12. *Parapsychological phenomena* include *extrasensory perception* in its various forms (telepathy, clairvoyance, precognition) and *psychokinesis*. In a number of apparently sound experiments, subjects have performed better than chance at these tasks. Nevertheless, none of these phenomena can be reliably demonstrated from one occasion to another, and most psychologists are not convinced that they exist.

FURTHER READING

Most of the textbooks listed under Further Reading in Chapter 5 also pertain to the topics considered in this chapter. Hochberg, *Perception* (2nd ed., 1978), and Rock, *The Logic of Perception* (1983), deal with various aspects of perceptual integration.

Problems of recognition and attention are discussed in Wickelgren, *Cognitive Psychology* (1979); Anderson, *Cognitive Psychology and Its Implications* (2nd ed., 1985); Spoehr and Lehmkuhle, *Visual Information Processing* (1982); and Posner and Marin, *Mechanisms of Attention* (1985). Marr, *Vision* (1982); and Boden, *Artificial Intelligence and Natural Man* (1981), treat perception from the viewpoint of artificial intelligence.

Bower, *Development in Infancy* (2nd ed., 1982), is concerned with early perceptual development. For a review of extrasensory perception, see Wolman, Dale, Schmeidler, and Ullman, (eds.), *Handbook of Parapsychology* (1985); Marks and Kammann, *The Psychology of the Psychic* (1980); Frazier (ed.), *Science Confronts the Paranormal* (1986); and Kurtz (ed.), *A Skeptic's Handbook of Parapsychology* (1985).

Part Four

AARON SISKIND   The End of The Civic Repertory Theater
1937–1938

LEARNING, REMEMBERING, AND THINKING

Learning and Conditioning

7

LEARNING PERVADES OUR LIVES. IT IS involved not only in mastering a new skill or academic subject but also in emotional development, social interaction, and even personality development. We learn what to fear, what to love, how to be polite, how to be intimate, and so on. Given the pervasiveness of learning in our lives, it is not surprising that we have already discussed many instances of it—how, for example, children learn to perceive the world around them, to identify with the appropriate sex, and to control their behavior according to adult standards. Now, however, we turn to a more systematic analysis of learning.

In this chapter, we focus on *associative* learning, or learning that certain events go together. This is among the most basic forms of learning. Traditionally, two kinds of associative learning have been of particular interest: *classical conditioning* and *operant conditioning*. In classical conditioning, an organism learns that one event follows another—for example, a baby learns that the sight of a breast will be followed by the taste of milk. In operant conditioning, an organism learns that a response it makes will be followed by a particular consequence; for example, a young child learns that striking a sibling will be followed by disapproval from his or her parents.

BEHAVIORIST APPROACH

Psychologists who have studied conditioning have usually taken a behavioristic approach (see Chapter 1, p. 7). This means they have operated according to the following general assumptions:

1. Simple associations of the classical or operant kind are the building blocks of all learning, no matter how complex. Thus, even something as complex as learning a language presumably is a matter of learning many simple associations (Staats, 1968).
2. The laws of learning are roughly the same for all species and can be revealed in experiments even with lower organisms in relatively barren environments. Thus, the laws that govern how a rat learns to run a maze presumably govern how a child learns long division (Skinner, 1938).
3. Learning can be better understood in terms of external or environmental causes than internal or intentional ones. That is, the ultimate causes of behavior presumably lie not inside the organism—not, for example, in a person's beliefs and desires—but rather in environmental events, particularly those that are rewarding or punishing. Thus, we may *not* be able to advance our understanding of how a child learns language by inquiring about his or her mental activities (Skinner, 1971).

Ivan Pavlov (center) with assistants in his laboratory.

These three assumptions have led behaviorists to focus on how the behaviors of lower organisms, particularly rats and pigeons, are influenced by rewards and punishments in simple laboratory situations.

The behaviorist approach has uncovered a wealth of findings about simple associative learning, and many of them will be presented in the first three sections of this chapter. In recent years, however, behaviorist assumptions have faced two serious challenges. The *ethological* approach disputes the behaviorists' claim that the laws of learning are the same for all organisms and all situations, while *cognitive* theory disputes the behaviorists assumptions that associations are the only building blocks of learning and that learning can be understood by considering only environmental factors. We will discuss these challenges in the final section of this chapter.

CLASSICAL CONDITIONING

The study of classical conditioning began in the early years of this century when Ivan Pavlov, a Russian physiologist who had already won the Nobel prize for research on digestion, turned his attention to learning. While studying digestion, Pavlov noticed that a dog began to salivate at the mere sight of a food dish. While any dog will salivate when food is placed in its mouth, this dog had learned to associate the sight of the dish with the taste of food. Pavlov decided to see whether a dog could be taught to associate food with other things, such as a light or a tone.

Pavlov's Experiments

BASIC EXPERIMENT   To prepare a dog for Pavlov's experiment, researchers attach a capsule to the dog's salivary gland in its cheek to measure salivary flow. The dog is then taken several times to a soundproof laboratory and is placed in a harness on a table. This preliminary training accustoms the dog to the harness so it will stand quietly in the apparatus once the actual experiment begins. The laboratory is arranged so that meat powder can be delivered to a pan in front of the dog by remote control and salivation can be recorded automatically. The

FIGURE 7-1
Classical-conditioning Apparatus
Arrangements used by Pavlov in classical salivary conditioning. During a typical experiment, a light (the conditioned stimulus) appears in the window and meat powder (the unconditioned stimulus) is delivered automatically to the food bowl. (After Yerkes & Margulis, 1909)

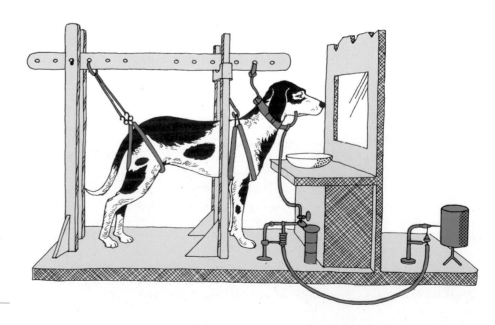

experimenter can view the animal through a one-way glass panel, but the dog is alone in the laboratory, isolated from extraneous sights and noises (see Figure 7-1).

In the experiment, a researcher turns a light on in a window in front of the dog. The dog may move a bit, but it does not salivate. After a few seconds, the apparatus delivers some meat powder and turns off the light. The dog is hungry, and the recording device registers copious salivation. This salivation is an *unconditioned response,* or UCR, for no learning is involved; by the same token, the meat powder is an *unconditioned stimulus,* or UCS. The procedure is repeated a number of times. Then, to test if the dog has learned to associate the light with food, the experimenter turns on the light but does not deliver any meat powder. If the dog salivates, it has learned the association. This salivation is a *conditioned response,* or CR, while the light is a *conditioned stimulus,* or CS. The dog has been taught, or conditioned, to associate the light with food and to respond to it by salivating. Pavlov's experiment is diagramed in Figure 7-2.

EXPERIMENTAL VARIATIONS Psychologists over the years have devised many variations of Pavlov's experiments. To appreciate these variations, we need to note some critical aspects of the conditioning experiment. Each paired presentation of the conditioned stimulus (CS) and the unconditioned stimulus (UCS) is called a *trial.* The trials during which the subject is learning the association between the two stimuli is the *acquisition* stage of conditioning. During this stage, repeated pairings of the CS (light) and UCS (meat) strengthen, or *reinforce,* the association between the two, as illustrated in the left-hand curve of Figure 7-3. If the CR is not reinforced (the UCS is omitted repeatedly), the response will gradually diminish; this is called *extinction* and is illustrated by the right-hand curve in Figure 7-3.

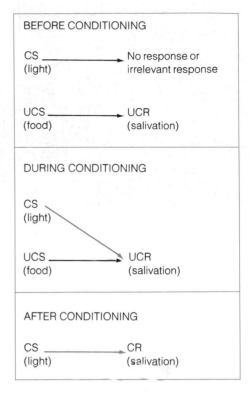

FIGURE 7-2

Diagram of Classical Conditioning *The association between the unconditioned stimulus and the unconditioned response exists at the start of the experiment and does not have to be learned. The association between the conditioned stimulus and the conditioned response is learned. It arises through the pairing of the conditioned and unconditioned responses. The conditioned response resembles the unconditioned one but generally differs in some details.*

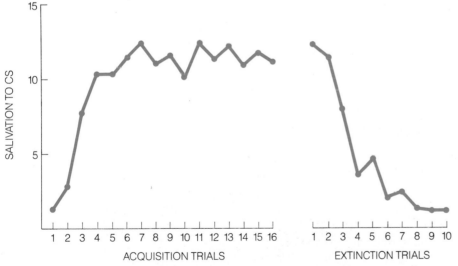

FIGURE 7-3

Acquisition and Extinction of a Conditioned Response *The curve in the panel on the left depicts the acquisition phase of an experiment using the trace-conditioning procedure. Drops of salivation in response to the conditioned stimulus (prior to the onset of the UCS) are plotted on the vertical axis; the number of trials, on the horizontal axis. The CR gradually increases over trials and approaches an asymptotic level of about 11 to 12 drops of saliva. After 16 acquisition trials, the experimenter switched to extinction; the results are presented in the panel at the right. Note that the CR gradually decreases when reinforcement is omitted. (After Pavlov, 1927)*

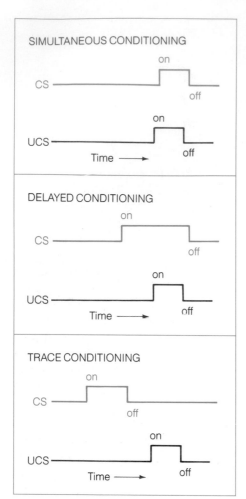

SIMULTANEOUS CONDITIONING

CS

UCS

Time ⟶

DELAYED CONDITIONING

CS

UCS

Time ⟶

TRACE CONDITIONING

CS

UCS

Time ⟶

FIGURE 7-4

Temporal Relations in Conditioning
Delayed conditioning is most effective when the CS precedes the UCS by approximately one-half second. Simultaneous conditioning is less effective, and both delayed and trace conditioning become progressively poorer as the time between CS and UCS increases.

Numerous experiments have varied the time interval between the presentation of the CS and UCS. Suppose that the CS is a light and the UCS is meat. In *simultaneous conditioning*, the light is turned on as the meat is presented and is left on until the dog salivates (the response). In *delayed conditioning*, the light is turned on several seconds before the meat is given and again is left on until the response occurs. In *trace conditioning*, the light is turned on first and then turned off before the meat appears, so that only a "memory trace" of the light remains to be conditioned. These three situations are illustrated in Figure 7-4. In delayed and trace conditioning, the experimenter knows that the subject has made the new association if the conditioned response (salivating) occurs before the UCS (meat) has been presented. With simultaneous conditioning, the experimenter has to use test trials withholding the UCS to determine if the subject has made the new association; if the dog salivates when the CS (light) is presented alone, we know that it has become conditioned.

What the subject seems to be learning in these situations is that the CS signals the occurrence of the UCS. Think of the CS as a road sign that signals a sharp curve in the road and of the UCS as the curve itself. In delayed and trace conditioning, the sign appears substantially before the curve, and hence the driver — or subject — can use it to predict and prepare for the curve. In contrast, in simultaneous conditioning the sign does not appear until the curve, and consequently it is of little use. This analogy suggests that the simultaneous procedure should result in the least conditioning, which is exactly what researchers have found. The analogy also highlights the adaptive value of classical conditioning: predictions about what follows what are learned (acquisition), and if things change so that these predictions are outdated, they are unlearned (extinction).

Scope of Classical Conditioning

Classical conditioning is pervasive in the animal kingdom and can occur with organisms as primitive as the flatworm. Flatworms contract their bodies when subjected to mild electric shock, and if they experience sufficient pairings of shock (the UCS) and light (the CS), eventually they will contract to the light alone (Jacobson, Fried, & Horowitz, 1967). At the other end of the spectrum, numerous human responses can be classically conditioned. Many of these are involuntary responses, such as *vasoconstriction*, which is a constriction of small blood vessels near the body surface that occurs automatically when our body is exposed to cold. If a buzzer (the CS) routinely sounds just before a person's left hand is immersed in ice water (the UCS), eventually vasoconstriction will occur in response to the buzzer alone (Menzies, 1937).

Classical conditioning also plays a role in emotional reactions such as fear. Suppose a dog is placed in an enclosed compartment where it is periodically subjected to electric shock (by electrifying the floor). Just before the shock occurs a tone sounds. After repeated pairings of the tone (the CS) and shock (the UCS), the tone alone will produce reactions that are indicators of fear, including crouching, trembling, and whining. The dog has been conditioned to be fearful when exposed to what was once a neutral stimulus.

Many human fears may be acquired in this way, particularly in early childhood. Perhaps the best evidence that they can be classically conditioned is that some of these fears, especially irrational ones, can be eliminated by therapeutic techniques based on classical-conditioning principles. A person with an intense fear of cats, for example, may overcome the fear by gradually and repeatedly being exposed to cats. Presumably, a cat was a CS for some noxious UCS a long time ago, and when the person now repeatedly experiences the CS without the

UCS the conditioned fear extinguishes. (See Chapter 15 for a discussion of conditioning and phobias and Chapter 16 for conditioning therapies.)

Some Basic Phenomena

SECOND-ORDER CONDITIONING Thus far in our discussion of conditioning, the UCS has always been biologically significant, such as food, cold, or shock. However, any stimulus can acquire the power of a UCS by being consistently paired with a biologically significant UCS. Recall the example of a dog exposed to a tone (CS) followed by electric shock (UCS), where the tone comes to elicit a conditioned fear response. Once the dog is conditioned, the tone acquires the power of a UCS. Thus, if the dog is now put in a situation where on each trial it is exposed to a light followed by the tone (but no shock), the light alone will eventually elicit a conditioned fear response even though it has never been paired with shock. (There must also be other trials where the tone is again paired with shock; otherwise, the originally conditioned relation between tone and shock will extinguish.) The existence of such *second-order* conditioning greatly increases the scope of classical conditioning, especially for humans where biologically significant UCSs occur relatively rarely.

GENERALIZATION AND DISCRIMINATION When a conditioned response has been associated with a particular stimulus, other similar stimuli will evoke the same response. Suppose that a person is conditioned to have a mild emotional reaction to the sound of a tuning fork producing a tone of middle C. (The emotional reaction is measured by the *galvanic skin response*, or GSR, which is a change in the electrical activity of the skin that occurs during emotional stress.) The person will also show a GSR to higher or lower tones without further conditioning (see Figure 7-5). The more similar the new stimuli are to the original CS, the more likely they are to evoke the conditioned response. This principle, called *generalization*, accounts in part for an individual's ability to react to novel stimuli that are similar to familiar ones.

A process complementary to generalization is *discrimination*. Whereas generalization is a reaction to similarities, discrimination is a reaction to differences. Conditioned discrimination is brought about through selective reinforcement and extinction, as shown in Figure 7-8 (p. 222). Instead of just one tone, for instance, now there are two. The low-pitched tone, CS_1, is always followed by a shock, and the high-pitched tone, CS_2, is not. Initially, subjects will show a GSR to both tones. During the course of conditioning, however, the amplitude of the conditioned response to CS_1 gradually increases while the amplitude of the response to CS_2 decreases. Thus, by the process of *differential reinforcement*, the subjects are conditioned to discriminate between the two tones.

Generalization and discrimination occur in everyday life. The young child who has been frightened by a snapping dog may initially respond with fear to all dogs (generalization). Eventually, through differential reinforcement, the child's range of fearful stimuli narrows to include only dogs that behave in a threatening way (discrimination).

Contiguity Versus Predictability

Since Pavlov, researchers have tried to determine the critical factor needed for classical conditioning to occur. Pavlov thought the critical factor was *temporal contiguity* of the CS and UCS — that is, the two stimuli must be close in time for an association to develop. Our earlier analogy in which the CS serves as a road sign suggests an alternative: perhaps the critical factor is that the CS be a *reliable*

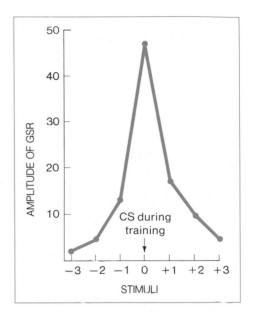

FIGURE 7-5

Gradient of Generalization *Stimulus 0 denotes the tone to which the galvanic skin response (GSR) was originally conditioned. Stimuli +1, +2, and +3 represent test tones of increasingly higher pitch; stimuli −1, −2, and −3 represent tones of lower pitch. Note that the amount of generalization decreases as the difference between the test tone and the training tone increases. (After Hovland, 1937)*

CRITICAL DISCUSSION

Cellular Basis of Elementary Learning

Classical and operant conditioning may be the simplest forms of *associative* learning, but there are more elementary forms of learning, namely those that are considered *nonassociative*. One example is *habituation*, by which an organism learns to ignore a weak stimulus that has no serious consequences—such as tuning out the sound of a loud clock. Another kind of nonassociative learning is *sensitization*, whereby an organism learns to strengthen its reaction to a weak stimulus if a threatening or painful stimulus follows. For instance, we learn to respond more intensely to the sound of a piece of equipment if it is frequently followed by a crash. Researchers have made remarkable progress in determining the biological bases of these two forms of learning.

Consider some of the research of Eric Kandel and his associates, who use snails in their work. The neurons of a snail are similar in structure and function to those of a human, yet its nervous system is simple enough to allow researchers to study individual cells. Indeed, the total number of cells in a snail is only in the thousands (compared to billions in a human). Moreover, the cells of a snail are collected into discrete groups (or *ganglia*) of 500 to 1,500 neurons, and a single ganglion can control an instance of habituation or sensitization. This makes it possible to give a "cell-by-cell" account of elementary learning.

The *Aplysia,* a large marine animal, is the snail of choice for researchers, and the behavior of particular interest is a withdrawal response. As shown in Figure 7-6, the *Aplysia's* gill is housed in a cavity that is covered by a protective sheet called the mantle shelf; the sheet ends in a fleshy spout called a siphon. When the siphon is stimulated by touch, both the siphon and gill

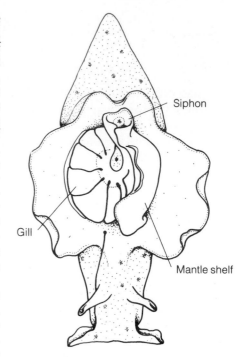

FIGURE 7-6
Gill Withdrawal in the *Aplysia* **When the siphon is stimulated, the animal retracts its gill into the protective sheet of the mantle cavity; this sheet is called the mantle shelf. (After Kandel, 1979)**

contract into the cavity. The withdrawal is controlled by a single ganglion and is subject to habituation and sensitization.

In studies of habituation, the researchers lightly touch the snail's siphon on each trial of the experiment. In the initial trials, the gill-withdrawal reflex is strong, but it gradually weakens after 10 or 15 trials. What cellular events mediate this habituation behavior? The stimulus to the siphon activates 24 sensory neurons, each of

predictor of the UCS. In other words, for conditioning to occur, perhaps there must be a higher probability that the UCS will occur when the CS has been presented than when it has not.

Rescorla (1967), in an important experiment, contrasted contiguity and predictability. On certain trials of the experiment, Rescorla exposed dogs to shock (the UCS), and on some of these trials he preceded the shock by a tone (the

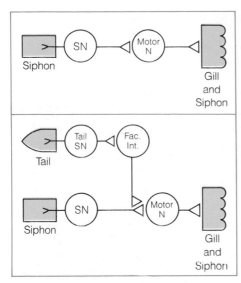

FIGURE 7-7
Partial Neural Circuits for Habituation and Sensitization *The top half of the figure illustrates the connection between a single sensory neuron (SN) and a single motor neuron (Motor N) for the gill-withdrawal reflex. Stimulation of the siphon excites the sensory neuron, which in turn excites the motor neuron. Stimulation of the motor neuron, in turn, innervates the gill. Habituation of gill withdrawal is mediated by a change at the synaptic connection between the sensory and motor neurons. The bottom half of the figure illustrates the connections involved in sensitization of gill withdrawal. Now, stimulation of the tail excites a facilitator interneuron (Fac. int.), which in turn facilitates the impulse being sent from the siphon's sensory neuron. (After Hawkins & Kandel, 1984)*

which activates the 6 motor neurons in the gill that innervate the contracting muscle. The structure of the system can be understood by looking at the neural connections for a single sensory neuron and a single motor neuron (see the top of Figure 7-7). The small triangles in the figure depict *synaptic* connections between neurons, where a synapse involves a space that must be bridged by a chemical *neurotransmitter*. In the *Aplysia*, a neurotransmitter released by the sensory neuron onto the motor neuron causes initial gill withdrawal, and a decrease in the amount of the neurotransmitter mediates the habituation of gill withdrawal. Thus, this form of elementary learning is due to chemically induced changes in synaptic connections between cells (Kandel, 1979).

Sensitization functions in a similar, though more complex, manner. To sensitize gill withdrawal, again the researchers apply a weak tactile stimulus to the siphon, but this time they also apply simultaneously a strong stimulus to the tail (see Figure 7-6). After a number of such trials, gill withdrawal becomes more pronounced. Some of the mediating neural connections are illustrated in the bottom half of Figure 7-7. Some neural connections from the tail are now added to the circuit from the siphon. The new connections include a synapse between a tail sensory neuron and a *facilitator interneuron* (a neuron that connects other neurons) and a synapse that connects the facilitator interneuron with the circuit that supports gill withdrawal. In essence, the neural activity from the strong stimulus to the tail modifies the neural connection that underlies gill withdrawal. Once more, learning is mediated by changes in the neurotransmitter that bridges the synapse between the

siphon's sensory neuron and the gill's motor neuron. But in this case, the change consists of an increase in the amount of the neurotransmitter released by the sensory neuron (Castelluci & Kandel, 1976).

Our discussion of sensitization suggests that a cell-by-cell analysis may be possible for classical conditioning. Gill withdrawal in the *Aplysia* can be classically conditioned; and such conditioning, like sensitization, involves modifying the gill withdrawal by a second stimulus. Indeed, researchers have proposed a cellular account of classical conditioning that is remarkably similar to that for sensitization (Hawkins & Kandel, 1984). This proposal has generated some controversy (Gluck & Thompson, 1986), but should the basic ideas of the proposal prove defensible, it would indicate that some forms of associative learning are built upon more primitive forms of nonassociative learning. It would also indicate that the biological basis of simple learning is not distributed diffusely through the brain; rather, it can be localized to the activity of specific neurons.

Aplysia, *a large marine snail*

CS). The procedures for two of the groups from the experiment are illustrated in Figure 7-9. The number of temporally contiguous pairings of tone and shock was the same in both groups; the variable was that tones preceded all shocks in Group A, whereas in Group B shocks were as likely to be preceded by no tones as tones, so the tone had no real predictive power for Group B. This predictive power of the tone proved critical: Group A became rapidly conditioned, whereas Group B

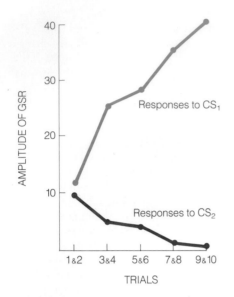

FIGURE 7-8

Conditioned Discrimination *The discriminative stimuli were two tones of clearly different pitch (CS$_1$ = 700 Hz and CS$_2$ = 3,500 Hz). The unconditioned stimulus, an electric shock applied to the left forefinger, occurred only on trials when CS$_1$ was presented. The strength of the conditioned response, in this case the GSR, gradually increased following CS$_1$ and extinguished following CS$_2$. (After Baer & Fuhrer, 1968)*

did not (determined by whether or not the dog responded to the tone in such a way as to avoid the shock).

In other groups in the experiment (not shown in Figure 7-9), the strength of the conditioning was directly related to the predictive value of the CS in signaling the occurrence of the UCS. Subsequent experiments support the conclusion that the predictive relation between the CS and UCS is more important than either temporal contiguity or the frequency with which the CS and UCS are paired (Rescorla, 1972; Fantino & Logan, 1979). Moreover, other studies show that once a subject learns that a particular CS (say, a tone) perfectly predicts a UCS (say, a shock), the subject is blocked from learning to associate another CS (for instance, a light coupled with the tone) with that UCS. Once predictability is established for one stimulus, there seems to be no need for further learning with other stimuli (Kamin, 1969).

Predictability is equally important for emotional reactions: if a particular CS reliably predicts that pain is coming, then the absence of that CS predicts that pain is not coming and the organism can relax. The CS is therefore a "danger" signal, and its absence represents a "safety" signal. When such signals are erratic, the emotional toll on the organism can be devastating. When rats have a reliable predictor that shock is coming, they respond with fear only when the danger signal is present; if they have no reliable predictor, they appear to be continually anxious and may even develop ulcers (Seligman, 1975).

There are clear parallels to human emotionality. If a doctor gives a child a danger signal by telling her that a procedure will hurt, the child will be fearful until the procedure is over. In contrast, if the doctor always tells a child "it won't hurt" when in fact it sometimes does, the child has no danger or safety signals and may become terribly anxious whenever in the doctor's office. As adults, many of us have experienced the anxiety of being in a situation where something disagreeable is likely to happen but no warnings exist for us to predict it. Unpleasant events are, by definition, unpleasant, but unpredictable unpleasant events are downright intolerable.

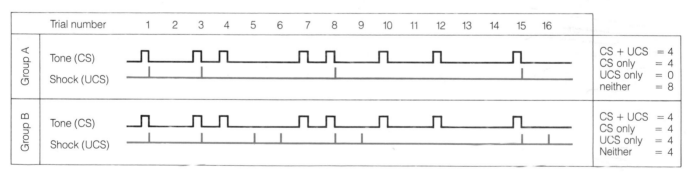

FIGURE 7-9

Rescorla's Experiment *The figure presents a schematic representation of two groups from Rescorla's study. For each group, the events for 16 trials are presented. Note that on some trials CS occurs and is followed by UCS (CS + UCS); on other trials CS or UCS occurs alone; and on still other trials, neither CS nor UCS occurs.*

The boxes to the far right give a count of these trial outcomes for the two groups. The number of CS + UCS trials is identical for both groups, as is the number of trials on which only the CS occurs. But the two groups differ in the number of trials on which UCS occurred alone (never in Group A and as frequently as any other type of trial in Group B). Thus, for Group

A, the experimenter established a situation where the tone was a useful (but not perfect) predictor that shock would follow shortly, whereas for Group B the tone was of no value in predicting subsequent shock. A conditioned response to CS developed readily for Group A but did not develop at all for Group B.

OPERANT CONDITIONING

In classical conditioning, the conditioned response typically resembles the normal response to the unconditioned stimulus: salivation, for example, is a dog's normal response to food. But when you want to teach an organism something novel — such as teaching a dog a new trick — you cannot use classical conditioning. What unconditioned stimulus would make a dog sit up or roll over? To train the dog, you must first persuade it to do the trick and *afterward* reward it with either approval or food. If you keep doing this, eventually the dog will learn the trick.

Much of real-life behavior is like this: responses are learned because they *operate* on, or affect, the environment. Referred to as *operant conditioning*, this kind of learning occurs in lower species, as well as in our own. Alone in a crib, a baby may kick and twist and coo spontaneously. When left by itself in a room, a dog may pad back and forth; sniff; or perhaps pick up a ball, drop it, and play with it. Neither organism is responding to the onset or offset of a specific external stimulus. Rather, they are operating on their environment. Once the organism performs a certain behavior, however, the likelihood that the action will be repeated depends on the nature of its consequences. The baby will coo more often if each such occurrence is followed by parental attention, and the dog will pick up the ball more often if this action is followed by petting or a food reward.

Law of Effect

The study of operant conditioning began at the turn of the century with a series of experiments by E. L. Thorndyke (1898). A typical experiment proceeded as follows. A hungry cat is placed in a cage whose door is held fast by a simple latch, and a piece of fish is placed just outside the cage. Initially, the cat tries to reach the food by extending its paws through the bars. When this fails, the cat moves about the cage, engaging in a variety of different behaviors. At some point it inadvertently hits the latch, frees itself, and eats the fish. The researchers then place the cat back in its cage and put a new piece of fish outside. The cat goes through roughly the same set of behaviors until once more it happens to hit the latch. The procedure is repeated again and again. Over trials, the cat eliminates many of its irrelevant behaviors, eventually efficiently opening the latch and freeing itself as soon as it is placed in the cage. The cat has learned to open the latch in order to obtain food.

It may sound as if the cat is acting intelligently, but Thorndyke argued that there is little "intelligence" operative here. There is no moment in time at which the cat seems to have an insight about the solution to its problem. Instead, the cat's performance improves gradually over trials. Even if at one point the experimenter places the cat's paw on the latch and pushes it down, thereby demonstrating the solution, the cat's progress continues to be slow. Rather than insight, the cat appears to be engaging in *trial-and-error* behavior, and when a reward immediately follows one of these behaviors, the learning of the action is strengthened. Thorndyke referred to this strengthening as the *law of effect*. He argued that in operant learning, the law of effect selects from a set of random responses just the responses that are followed by positive consequences. The process is similar to evolution, where the law of *survival of the fittest* selects from a set of random species variations just the changes that promote survival. The law of effect, then, promotes the survival of the *fittest responses* (Schwartz, 1984).

B. F. Skinner

Skinner's Experiments

B. F. Skinner has been responsible for a number of changes in how researchers conceptualize and study operant conditioning. His method of studying operant conditioning is simpler than Thorndyke's and has been widely accepted.

In a Skinnerian experiment, a hungry animal — usually a rat or a pigeon — is placed in a box like the one shown in Figure 7-10, which is popularly called a "Skinner box." The inside of the box is bare except for a protruding bar with a food dish beneath it. A small light above the bar can be turned on at the experimenter's discretion. Left alone in the box, the rat moves about, exploring. Occasionally it inspects the bar and presses it. The rate at which the rat first presses the bar is the baseline level of bar pressing. After establishing the baseline level, the experimenter activates a food magazine located outside the box. Now, every time the rat presses the bar, a small food pellet is released into the dish. The rat eats the food pellet and soon presses the bar again; the food *reinforces* bar pressing, and the rate of pressing increases dramatically. If the food magazine is disconnected so that pressing the bar no longer delivers food, the rate of bar pressing will diminish. Hence, an operantly conditioned response (or, simply, an *operant*) undergoes *extinction* with nonreinforcement just as a classically conditioned response does. The experimenter can set up a *discrimination* test by presenting food only if the rat presses the bar while the light is on, hence conditioning the rat through selective reinforcement. In this example, the light serves as a *discriminative stimulus* that controls the response.

Thus, operant conditioning increases the likelihood of a response by following the behavior with a reinforcement (often something that can satisfy a basic drive). Experimenters can measure the strength of an operantly conditioned response (or, simply, *operant strength*) in several ways. Because the bar is always present in the Skinner box, the rat can respond to it as frequently or infrequently as it chooses; the organism's *rate of response* is therefore a useful measure of operant strength (that is, the more frequently the response occurs during a given time, the greater its operant strength). Another useful measure of operant strength is the *total number of responses during extinction:* the more times the rat presses the bar, even though the experimenter is withholding reward, the greater the operant strength of the response (Skinner, 1938).

FIGURE 7-10

Apparatus for Operant Conditioning
The photograph shows the interior arrangement of the box used in the operant conditioning of a rat. This box has been named a "Skinner box" after its developer.

As is the case in classical conditioning, the temporal relations between the events in a trial are critical. In particular, immediate reinforcement is more effective than delayed; the more time between an operant and a reinforcer, the less the operant strength. Many developmental psychologists have noted that the delay of reinforcement is an important factor in dealing with young children. If a child acts kindly to a pet, the act can best be strengthened by praising (rewarding) the child immediately, rather than waiting until later. Similarly, if a child hits someone without provocation, this aggressive behavior will more likely be eliminated if the child is reprimanded or punished immediately, rather than waiting until both parents are home at night.

Scope of Operant Conditioning

Although rats and pigeons have been the favored experimental subjects, operant conditioning applies to many species, including our own. A particularly illuminating instance of operant conditioning in human behavior is illustrated by the following case. A young boy had temper tantrums if he did not get enough attention from his parents, especially at bedtime. Since the parents eventually responded, their attention probably reinforced the tantrums. To eliminate the tantrums, the parents were advised to go through the normal bedtime rituals and then to ignore the child's protests, painful though that might be. By withholding reinforcement (the attention), the tantrums should extinguish—which is just what happened. The time the child spent crying at bedtime decreased from 45 minutes to not at all over a period of only seven days (Williams, 1959).

Operant conditioning applies to many responses. For years, psychologists believed that operant conditioning occurred only with voluntary behavior (responses of skeletal muscles mediated by the somatic nervous system) and not with involuntary responses (responses of glands and viscera mediated by the autonomic nervous system). Responses mediated by the autonomic nervous system thus were thought to be susceptible to classical conditioning but not operant conditioning. Researchers have challenged this belief by ingeniously demonstrating that heart rate and other visceral responses can be operantly conditioned.

It might seem that life already provides such demonstrations, as some people — yogis in India and other Eastern countries, for example — are reputed to be able to control their heart rates. Yogis can indeed control their heart rate, but they do it *indirectly* by manipulating their skeletal muscles, specifically those in their chest and abdomen (see Kimble & Perlmuter, 1970). We are interested in the possibility of *directly* controlling heart rate. Think of the difficulties in demonstrating such direct control. The organism's skeletal muscles must be paralyzed (to prevent indirect control); but then how is the organism to breath since skeletal muscles are needed in breathing? And if the organism is paralyzed, what kind of reinforcer can it enjoy? Some remarkable experiments by Miller and his colleagues overcame these difficulties (for example, Miller, 1969) (see Figure 7-11). They injected rats with *curare*, a drug that paralyzes skeletal muscle but does not affect visceral reactions. An artificial respirator maintained the animals' breathing, and electrical stimulation of regions of the brain known to be associated with a feeling of reward served as reinforcement. Some animals were reinforced when their heart rate decreased; others were reinforced when their heart rate increased. The procedure worked: heart rate changed in accordance with reinforcement (see Figure 7-11). Experimenters have conditioned other autonomic responses using similar procedures. For example, curarized rats have learned to relax or contract their lower intestines.

These results have great practical implications. Human subjects have been trained by operant methods to control such autonomic responses as heart rate,

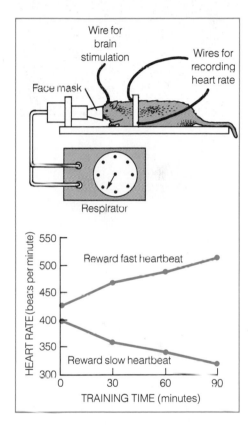

FIGURE 7-11
Operant Conditioning of Heart Rate
The top panel gives a schematic view of an apparatus used to study operant conditioning of heart rate. The rat, paralyzed by curare, is kept alive by a respirator. Reinforcement is administered through wires for brain stimulation; other wires record the rat's heart rate. The bottom panel shows the results of the experiment: heart rate increases when rats are reinforced for an increase and decreases when they are reinforced for a decrease. (After DiCara, 1970; © 1970 by Scientific American, Inc. All rights reserved.)

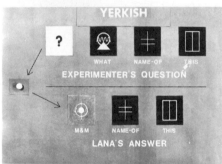

Animals have been taught very complex responses by means of shaping techniques. At the Yerkes Primate Research Center in Atlanta, a chimpanzee named Lana has learned to answer questions and to make requests by pressing symbols on a computer console. At bottom is an example of how the experiment works. A researcher outside the room asked Lana a question by pressing the symbols on the console for the words "What name of this" and also holding up a candy. The chimpanzee answered by pressing symbols for "M&M name of this."

blood pressure, and the secretion of stomach acids that may produce ulcers. To control blood pressure, for example, the individual watches a machine that provides continuous visual feedback about blood pressure. Whenever the blood pressure falls below a specified level, a light flashes. The subject then analyzes whatever he or she was thinking or doing when the blood pressure dropped and tries to repeat that thought or emotion to keep the blood pressure low. This procedure is called *biofeedback* training: the subject is given information (feedback) about some aspect of his or her biological state and is reinforced for altering that state.

The medical applications of such research are obvious. People with high blood pressure are better off learning to control it themselves rather than depending on medications that are only partially successful and that may have undesirable side effects. In addition to their use with high blood pressure, biofeedback techniques have been successfully used with a host of other disorders, such as cardiovascular disorders, migraine headaches, and visceral problems that range from the treatment of stomach ulcers in adults to toilet training children who have difficulty controlling their bowels (Miller, 1985). What is particularly noteworthy about these applications is that they were spawned by intricate experiments that used rats as subjects and were designed to demonstrate a scholarly point. The practical benefits of pure research are often difficult to foresee.*

Some Basic Phenomena

GENERALIZATION AND DISCRIMINATION What was true for classical conditioning holds for operant conditioning, as well: organisms generalize what they have learned, although generalization can be curbed by discrimination training. If a young child is reinforced by her parents for petting the family dog, she will soon generalize this petting response to other dogs. Since this can be dangerous (say, the neighbors have a vicious watchdog), the child's parents may provide some discrimination training, so that she is reinforced when she pets the family dog but not the neighbor's.

SHAPING Suppose you want to use operant conditioning to teach your dog a trick—for instance, to press a buzzer with its nose. You cannot wait until the dog does this naturally (and then reinforce it), because you may wait forever. When the desired behavior is truly novel, you have to condition it by taking advantage of natural variations in the animal's actions. To train a dog to press a buzzer with its nose, you can give the animal a food reinforcement each time it approaches the area of the buzzer, requiring it to move closer and closer to the desired spot for each reinforcer until finally the dog's nose is touching the buzzer. This technique of reinforcing only the responses that meet the experimenter's specifications and extinguishing all others is called *shaping* the animal's behavior.

Animals can be taught elaborate tricks and routines by means of shaping. Two psychologists and their staff have trained thousands of animals of many species for television shows, commercials, and county fairs (Breland & Breland, 1966). One popular show featured "Priscilla, the Fastidious Pig." Priscilla turned on the TV set, ate breakfast at a table, picked up dirty clothes and put them in a hamper, vacuumed the floor, picked out her favorite food (from among foods competing with that of her sponsor!), and took part in a quiz program, answering

---

* In these practical applications, however, the control of autonomic responses may be accomplished indirectly via the control of skeletal muscles, as was the case with yogis (see Chapter 4, p. 142).

questions from the audience by flashing lights that indicated yes or no. She was not an unusually bright pig; in fact, because pigs grow so fast, a new "Priscilla" was trained every three to five months. The ingenuity was not the pig's but the experimenters', who used operant conditioning and shaped the behavior to produce the desired result. Pigeons have been trained by the shaping of operant responses to locate persons lost at sea (see Figure 7-12), and porpoises have been trained to retrieve underwater equipment.

AUTOSHAPING Thus far, the phenomena of operant conditioning have been distinct from those of classical conditioning. But there are cases of behavior that appear to be determined by principles of both operant and classical conditioning. One is *autoshaping*. A hungry pigeon, never before an experimental subject, is placed in a chamber. A key in the chamber is lit once every minute for 6 seconds. When the light is turned off (by the automated apparatus), a bit of food is provided. The key then remains unlit for 54 seconds, turns on again, and so on. Note that food is delivered independent of the pigeon's behavior toward the key; that is, food appears whenever the light goes off whether or not the pigeon pecks the key. Nonetheless, after a few trials the pigeon begins to peck the key as soon as it is lit. The procedure is called *autoshaping* because it does not require an experimenter as shaping does (Brown & Jenkins, 1968).

FIGURE 7-12
Search and Rescue by Pigeons *The Coast Guard has used pigeons to search for people lost at sea. The pigeons are trained, using shaping methods, to spot the color orange — the international color of life jackets. Three pigeons are strapped into a plexiglass chamber attached to the underside of a helicopter. The chamber is divided into thirds so that each bird faces a different direction. When a pigeon spots an orange object, or any other object, it pecks a key that buzzes the pilot. The pilot then heads in the direction indicated by the bird that responded. Pigeons are better suited than people for the task of spotting distant objects at sea. They can stare over the water for a long time without suffering eye fatigue, have excellent color vision, and can focus on a 60- to 80-degree area, whereas a person can only focus on a 2- to 3-degree area. In tests by the Coast Guard, under conditions in which helicopter crews detect approximately 50 percent of targets, pigeons detect 85 percent. (After Simmons, 1981)*

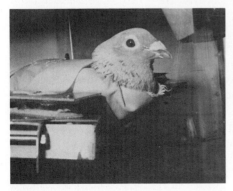

Pigeon sitting

Pigeon signaling

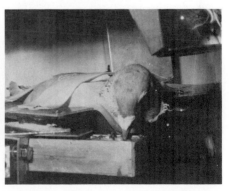

Pigeon rewarded

FIGURE 7-13
Water and Food Autoshaped Responses
The two photographs show the autoshaped responses of a pigeon at the moment of contact with the key. The top response is to a key paired with food, whereas the bottom response is to a key paired with water. The pigeon's beak movements are clearly different in the two situations. The top photo resembles a pigeon eating, whereas the bottom photo resembles a pigeon drinking. The pigeon appears to "eat" the key when working for food and "drink" the key when working for water. (After Jenkins & Moore, 1973)

Classical conditioning is involved in autoshaping: by virtue of repeated pairings of light and food, the light becomes a conditioned stimulus (CS) for the response to food (pecking, the UCR). Once the pigeon pecks the lit key, it is given food almost immediately, as in an operant-conditioning experiment. Hence, it is likely that operant conditioning serves to maintain an autoshaped response.

It seems that by pairing the lit key with food, the light comes to substitute for food and the pigeon responds to the light in a manner similar to the way it responds to food. Photographs of a pigeon's autoshaped pecks support this notion (see Figure 7-13). When the beak hits the key, it is positioned as if seizing food when food is the reinforcer but *not* when water is the reinforcer. Thus, stimuli paired with food come to elicit the same response as the food itself, as in classical conditioning (Schwartz & Gamzu, 1977).

PARTIAL REINFORCEMENT   In real life, rarely is every single instance of a behavior reinforced — sometimes hard work is followed by praise, but often it goes unacknowledged. If operant conditioning occurred only with continuous reinforcement, it might play little role in our lives. It turns out, however, that a behavior can be conditioned and maintained when it is reinforced only a fraction of the time. This phenomenon is known as *partial reinforcement,* and it can be illustrated in the laboratory by a pigeon who learns to peck at a key for food. Once this operant is established, the pigeon continues to peck at a high rate, even if it receives only occasional reinforcement. In some cases, pigeons who were rewarded with food on the average of once every five minutes (12 times an hour) pecked at the key as often as 6,000 times per hour!

Extinction following the acquisition of a response on partial reinforcement is much slower than extinction following the acquisition of a response on continuous reinforcement. This phenomenon, known as the *partial-reinforcement effect,* occurs because there is less difference between extinction and acquisition when reinforcement during acquisition is only partial. Human examples are plentiful. If a slot machine is broken, gamblers may still insert hundreds of coins into it, for they are accustomed to infrequent payoffs. When a food machine fails to operate, however, rarely will people insert more than one extra coin since vending machines operate on a continuous-reinforcement basis.

Other examples of partial reinforcement can be seen in child rearing. A parent who *occasionally* reinforces a child's temper tantrums by giving in to the child is ensuring more potent and more persistent tantrums than the parent who *always* gives in. The child with a history of partial reinforcement of tantrums will "throw" them with remarkable persistence even when the parent attempts to extinguish the tantrums by ignoring them.

Contiguity Versus Control

As was the case in classical conditioning, we want to know what factor is critical for operant conditioning to occur. Again, one of the options is temporal contiguity: an operant is conditioned whenever reinforcement immediately follows the behavior (Skinner, 1948). Another option, closely related to predictability, is that of *control:* an operant is conditioned only when the organism interprets the reinforcement as being dependent on its response. Some important experiments by Maier and Seligman (1976) provide more support for the control view than for the temporal contiguity view.

Their basic experiment includes two stages. In the first stage, some dogs learn that whether they receive a shock or not depends on (is controlled by) their behavior, while other dogs learn that they have no control over the shock. Think of the dogs as being tested in pairs. Both members of a pair are in a harness that restricts their movements, and occasionally they receive an electric shock. One member of the pair, the "control" dog, can turn off the shock by pushing a nearby panel with its nose; the other member of the pair, the "yoked" dog, cannot exercise any control over the shock. Whenever the control dog is shocked, so is the yoked dog; and whenever the control dog turns off the shock, the yoked dog's shock is also terminated. The control and yoked dogs therefore receive exactly the same number of shocks.

In the second stage of the experiment, experimenters place both dogs in a new apparatus — a box divided into two compartments by a barrier. On each trial a tone is first sounded, indicating that the compartment that the dog currently occupies is about to be subject to electric shock. To avoid shock, the dogs must learn to jump the barrier into the other compartment when they hear the warning tone. Control dogs learn this response rapidly, but the yoked dogs are another story: initially they make no movement across the barrier, and as trials progress their behavior becomes increasingly passive, lapsing finally into utter helplessness. Why? Because during the first stage the yoked dogs learned that shocks were not under their control, and this "belief" in noncontrol made conditioning in the second stage impossible. If a belief in noncontrol makes operant conditioning impossible, then a belief in control must be what makes it possible. Many other experiments support the notion that operant conditioning occurs only when the organism perceives reinforcement as being under its control (Seligman, 1975).

NATURE OF REINFORCEMENT

We have talked about reinforcement as if it has to be a biologically significant event and is always positive (food is a good example). We have also talked as if reinforcement is an all-or-none property of an event — food has it but a light does not. This description of reinforcement is somewhat misleading:

1. Many events that are not biologically significant can become *conditioned reinforcers*.
2. Whether or not an event is reinforcing can be determined only *relative* to the activity it reinforces.
3. Negative or *aversive* events, such as shock or painful noise, also have dramatic effects on behavior.

These three aspects of reinforcement are considered in the following discussion.

Conditioned Reinforcers

Most of the reinforcers we have discussed are called *primary* because, like food, they satisfy basic drives. If operant conditioning occurred only with primary reinforcers, it would not be as common in our lives, because primary reinforcers are not very common. However, virtually any stimulus can become a *secondary* or *conditioned* reinforcer by being consistently paired with a primary reinforcer; conditioned reinforcers greatly increase the range of operant conditioning.

A minor variation in the typical operant-conditioning experiment illustrates how conditioned reinforcement works. When a rat in a Skinner box presses a lever, a tone sounds momentarily, followed shortly by delivery of food (the food is a primary reinforcer; the tone will become a conditioned reinforcer). After the

CRITICAL DISCUSSION

Brain Stimulation and Reinforcement

In the 1950s, James Olds and Peter Milner made the startling discovery that electrical stimulation of certain regions of the brain can be reinforcing. Olds and Milner were investigating the rat's brain with microelectrodes. These tiny electrodes can be implanted permanently in specific brain areas without interfering with the rat's health or normal activity. When connected with an electrical source, they can supply stimulation of varying intensities to a very localized site in the brain. The researchers accidentally implanted an electrode in an area near the hypothalamus and delivered a very mild current through the electrodes. The animal repeatedly returned to the place in the cage where it had been when stimulated. Further stimulations at the same cage location caused the animal to spend most of its time there. Later, Olds and Milner found that other animals with electrodes implanted in the same region of the brain learned to press a bar in a Skinner box to produce their own electrical stimulation (see Figure 7-14). These animals pressed the bar at a phenomenal rate: a not unusual record would show an average of over 2,000 responses an hour for 15 or 20 hours, until the animal finally collapsed from exhaustion.

Since the initial discovery, experiments with microelectrodes implanted in many different areas of the brain and brain stem have been carried out using rats, cats, and monkeys in a wide variety of tasks. The reinforcing effects of stimulation in certain areas (primarily the hypothalamus) are powerful. If given a choice between food

and electric brain stimulation in a *T-maze* (a maze that has a straight runway ending in two armlike corridors that the animal must choose between — see Figure 7-15), even hungry rats may choose the arm that offers brain stimulation. On the other hand, stimulation of certain areas of the brain stem serves as a *punisher*. When the electrodes were moved to these different brain areas, rats that had previously pressed the bar at a rapid rate to receive stimulation suddenly

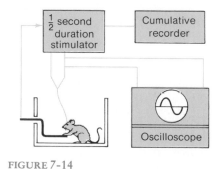

FIGURE 7-14
Brain Stimulation   *The animal's bar-press delivers a 60-cycle current for half a second, after which the animal must release the bar and press again for more current. The animal's response rate is recorded on the cumulative recorder, and the delivery of the current is monitored by means of the oscilloscope. Rats respond with rates up to 100 bar presses per minute when they have electrodes in the medial-forebrain region of the hypothalamus.*

animal has been conditioned in this way, the experimenter begins extinction, so that when the rat presses the lever neither the tone nor the food appears. In time, the animal virtually ceases to press the lever. Then the tone is reconnected but not the food. When the animal discovers that pressing the lever turns on the tone, its rate of pressing markedly increases, overcoming the extinction, even though no food follows. The tone has acquired a reinforcing quality of its own through classical conditioning: since the tone (the CS) was consistently paired with food (the UCS), it came to signal food.

Our lives abound with conditioned reinforcers. Two of the most prevalent are money and praise. Presumably, money is a powerful reinforcer because it has been paired so frequently with so many primary reinforcers — we can buy food, drink, and comfort, to mention just a few of the obvious things. And mere praise, without even the promise of a primary reinforcer, can sustain many an activity.

stopped responding and avoided the bar entirely. Apparently the new stimulation was unpleasant. And other animals have learned various responses to terminate stimulation in these areas—for example, pressing a lever to turn *off* the current. Considerable progress has been made in mapping the neutral, punishing, and reinforcing areas of the brain (Carr & Coons, 1982).

Part of the significance of brain stimulation studies lies in their potential to reveal the anatomical and neurological bases of reinforcement in general. It would be convenient for us to think that these studies map the anatomical location of reinforcement; that when we stimulate one brain area in a rat, the sensations are similar to those experienced when the animal is reinforced with food, and that the sensations in another area are similar to reinforcement with water. Unfortunately, the rat cannot describe its sensations. What data we have on human subjects are sparse and come from patients with abnormal conditions (such as epilepsy or the intractable pain of terminal cancer), so the results cannot be readily generalized to normal individuals. These patients report feeling relief from pain and anxiety and feeling "wonderful," "happy," and "drunk" following stimulation of certain areas of the limbic system (Campbell, 1973).

There are, however, some difficulties in interpreting studies of brain stimulation. In some experiments, brain stimulation may affect the nearby motor system, as well as the reward system. Consequently, in these studies the high rates of responding

obtained with stimulation may reflect heightened motor activity (Stellar & Stellar, 1985). Evidence for this comes from experiments where two different levels of stimulation were used. The stimulation level that

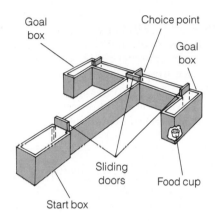

FIGURE 7-15

T-Maze *A maze used in the study of simple choice learning. Plexiglass covers on the start box and goal boxes are hinged so a rat can be easily placed in or removed from the apparatus. The sliding doors (which usually are operated by a system of strings and pulleys from above) prevent the animal from retracing its path once it has made a choice. Note that the goal boxes are arranged so that the rat cannot see what is in them from the choice point.*

rats responded to more was not always the one they preferred, if offered a choice. The level that led to the higher response rate may have done so because it activated the motor system, while the other level may have actually been the more rewarding. Brain stimulation has also been shown to produce an aftereffect consisting of a general motor arousal, which makes subsequent responding to receive electrical stimulation more likely and more vigorous (Gallistel, 1973).

The evidence that brain stimulation affects both the reward and motor system fits nicely with the hypothesis that the effects of brain stimulation are mediated by the neurotransmitter *dopamine* (Wise, 1984). Dopamine is known to be involved in motor functioning. Dopamine loss is a major cause of *Parkinson's disease*, which is a syndrome that includes such motoric dysfunctions as muscular rigidity and resting tremors. Dopamine production is also likely to be involved in the reward system, since drugs that stimulate dopamine production (such as cocaine and amphetamines) can be pleasurable and addictive—and dangerous. Perhaps the strongest evidence for the dopamine hypothesis comes from studies in which animals receiving brain stimulation are administered *neuroleptics,* drugs that disrupt the production of dopamine. Such drugs substantially reduce the rate of responding for brain stimulation. Moreover, this reduction in response is due to changes in the reward system, not the motor system (Stellar & Stellar, 1985).

Relativity of Reinforcement

It is natural to think of reinforcement as an all-or-none property of stimuli or events. But it is more useful to think of reinforcers as *activities;* it is not the food pellet that reinforces lever pressing, but the eating of the pellet. What must be the relation between the two activities such that one reinforces the other?

PREMACK'S PRINCIPLE   According to David Premack (1959), any activity that an organism performs can reinforce any other activity that the organism engages in less frequently. For example, Premack offered children the choice of operating a pinball machine or eating candy. Children who preferred eating candy would increase their rate of playing the pinball machine if playing the machine led to eating candy; thus, eating candy reinforced playing pinball. For children who preferred playing pinball, however, the reverse was true: they

Praise as a positive reinforcer: a student receives praise from a teacher on a task well done.

increased their intake of candy only if this increased their chance to play pinball.

From this experiment, Premack developed a two-tiered conception of reinforcement: (1) for any organism, a reinforcement hierarchy exists in which reinforcers at the top of the hierarchy are those activities engaged in with greatest likelihood, given the opportunity; and (2) any activity in the hierarchy may be reinforced (made more likely) by any activity above it—and may itself reinforce any activity below it. This second statement is *Premack's principle*. It expresses a technique that has long been applied by parents who require a child to do homework before going out to play rather than letting the child play first provided he or she agrees to do the homework later.

Teachers have also used Premack's principle in classrooms to give them control over children's activities. Allowing students to play after successfully completing a writing assignment, for example, has enhanced their writing abilities. Even 3-year-old nursery school children have responded well to use of the principle. For these "students," activities high on their reinforcement hierarchies included screaming and running around the room. These reinforcing activities were permitted if the children first displayed the desired behavior. For example, the behavior of sitting quietly while attending to the blackboard was followed occasionally by the sounding of a bell and the instruction "run and scream" (which was duly followed). After a few days, the teachers achieved virtually perfect control of classroom behavior (Homme et al., 1963).

IMPORTANCE OF DEPRIVATION Is the reinforcement hierarchy stable or does it change according to the organism's motivational state? Although eating candy did not reinforce pinball playing in the children who preferred pinball over candy, Premack found that when the children became sufficiently hungry, the reinforcement relation reversed: eating candy came to reinforce pinball playing. Premack (1962) also found similar results in more extensive studies with rats: a thirsty rat will run in order to drink, whereas a long-idle rat will drink for the chance to run in a running wheel. Other studies give an even greater role to deprivation in determining the reinforcement potency of an activity. Whenever an organism is deprived of its usual amount of a naturally occurring activity, such as running for rats, that activity becomes a more potent reinforcer (Timberlake & Allison, 1974).

Punishment and Avoidance

We have focused primarily on cases in which a behavior leads to a positive event or *reward* and have only briefly mentioned cases in which a behavior leads to an aversive event or *punishment*. But punishments have dramatic effects on behavior and therefore deserve a more systematic treatment.

PUNISHMENT AND LEARNING Suppose a young child is learning to draw with crayons; if he is slapped on the hand whenever he draws on the walls, he will learn not to do so. Similarly, if a rat learning to run a maze is shocked whenever it chooses a wrong path, it will soon learn to avoid past mistakes. In both cases, punishment is used to decrease the likelihood of an undesirable behavior.*

---

* It is worth noting the relation between the terms *reward* and *punishment* on the one hand, and *positive* and *negative reinforcers* on the other. *Reward* is sometimes used synonymously with *positive reinforcement*—an event whose occurrence following a response increases the probability of that response. But *punishment* is not the same as *negative reinforcement*. Negative reinforcement means termination of an aversive event following a response; this increases the probability of that response. Punishment has the opposite effect: it decreases the probability of a response.

Although punishment can suppress an unwanted response, it has several significant disadvantages. First, its effects are not as predictable as the results of reward. Reward essentially says, "Repeat what you have done"; punishment says, "Stop it!" but fails to give an alternative. As a result, the organism may substitute an even less desirable response for the punished one. Second, the by-products of punishment may be unfortunate. Punishment often leads to dislike or fear of the punishing person (parent, teacher, or employer) and of the situation (home, school, or office) in which the punishment occurred. Finally, an extreme or painful punishment may elicit aggressive behavior that is more serious than the original undesirable behavior.

These cautions do not mean that punishment should never be employed. It can effectively eliminate an undesirable response if the available alternative responses are rewarded. Rats that have learned to take the shorter of two paths in a maze to reach food will quickly switch to the longer one if they are shocked when in the shorter path. The temporary suppression produced by punishment provides the opportunity for the rat to learn to take the longer path. In this case, punishment is an effective means of redirecting behavior because it is informative, and this seems to be the key to the humane and effective use of punishment. A child who gets a shock from an electrical appliance may learn which connections are safe and which are hazardous; a teacher's corrections of a student's paper can be regarded as punishing, but they are also informative and can provide an occasion for learning.

Parents often wonder how and how much they should punish their children. In practice, most resort to some kinds of deprivation at times, if not to actually inflicting pain. Children often "test the limits" to see what degree of unpermitted behavior they can get away with. In such cases, it seems advisable to use discipline that is firm but not harsh and to administer it promptly and consistently. Nagging a child to conform may be less humane in the end than an immediate punishment. A child who is threatened with a vague and postponed punishment ("What kind of person do you think you will grow up to be?") may learn less and suffer more than one who pays a consistent penalty for infringement but afterward is welcomed back into the family circle.

Threat of punishment as a controller of behavior.

AVOIDANCE People often learn to avoid punishing events by being sensitive to signals that indicate the event is about to occur. We learn to avoid thunderstorms, for example, by going inside when we hear thunder. In a typical laboratory study of avoidance learning, a rat is placed in a box consisting of two compartments divided by a barrier. On each trial the animal is placed in one of the compartments. At some point, a warning tone is sounded, and five seconds later the floor of that compartment is electrified; to get away from the shock, the animal must jump the barrier into the other compartment. Initially, the animal jumps the barrier only when the shock starts; but with practice, the animal learns to jump upon hearing the warning tone, thereby avoiding the shock entirely.

Avoidance learning has generated a great deal of interest, in part because there is something very puzzling about it. What exactly is reinforcing the avoidance response? In the above study, what reinforces the animal for jumping the barrier? Intuitively, it seems to be the absence of shock, but this is a *nonevent*. How can a nonevent serve as a reinforcer? The best-known solution to this puzzle holds that there are two stages to the learning. The first stage involves classical conditioning: through repeated pairings of the warning (the CS) and the punishing event or shock (the UCS), the animal learns a fear response to the warning. The second stage involves operant conditioning: the animal learns that a particular response (jumping the hurdle) removes an aversive event, namely fear. In

CRITICAL DISCUSSION

Economics of Reward

The simple operant experiments that we have discussed fail to capture an important aspect of human behavior: most responses that we make represent a *choice* among alternatives. To study choice, operant researchers use experiments in which the animal has at least two responses. The choices that the animal has may differ in their reinforcer or in their schedule of reinforcement, or both. To illustrate, a pigeon may have a choice between two keys, where pecks on one key produce food and pecks on the other, water; alternatively, both keys may lead to food but may have different *schedules,* so that one key may require five pecks for a reinforcement while the other may require ten.

To analyze behavior in choice experiments, researchers have begun to rely on the concepts and principles of economics (Rachlin, 1980). To see the relation between economic principles and pigeons pecking keys, note that a pigeon in a choice experiment can be thought of as having to choose how to distribute its limited responses — its resources — whereas economic theory deals with questions about how to allocate one's limited resources.

We will illustrate the economic approach to operant conditioning by discussing three examples. In each case, we first provide the relevant economic principles and then consider their application to operant experiments.

DEMAND CURVES An important concept in economics is that of *demand* for a commodity; this is the amount of the commodity — say, bread or chocolate — that will be purchased at a given price. If we change the price, we generate a *demand curve* like those presented in Figure 7-16. Note that the curve for chocolate decreases sharply as price is increased; the more it costs, the less chocolate we will buy. The demand for chocolate is therefore said to be *elastic.* In contrast, the curve for bread is barely affected by price; we will purchase roughly the same amount of bread regardless of its cost. Thus, the demand for bread is *inelastic.* All of this conforms to the belief that bread is a necessity and chocolate is a luxury.

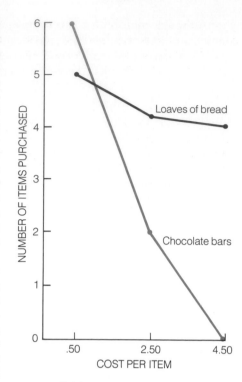

FIGURE 7-16

Hypothetical Demand Curves for Bread and Chocolate *As the price of a loaf of bread increases from $.50 to $4.50, the amount of bread purchased decreases hardly at all; the demand for bread is inelastic. In contrast, as the price of a chocolate bar increases form $.50 to $4.50, the amount purchased decreases sharply; the demand for chocolate is elastic.*

Consider now the relevance of this to operant conditioning. For rats and pigeons, the equivalent of price is the number of responses that must be made to "obtain" a reinforcer (which is the *schedule of reinforcement*). This equivalence is illustrated in Figure 7-17, which includes a rat's demand curve for food. The curve tells us how much food (reinforcement) a rat will "purchase" (work to obtain) at different "prices" (schedules of reinforcement). Rats purchase the same amount of food reinforcements regardless of whether they are rewarded after every two or every eight responses: the demand curve for food is inelastic. The other demand curve in Figure 7-17 is for brain stimulation. The demand for brain stimulation is clearly elastic, because the amount purchased decreases sharply with price (the number of responses required for a reinforcement).

The curves in Figure 7-17 have implications for questions about the nature of reinforcement. It is natural to ask whether one kind of reinforcement is more or less potent than another, say, food versus brain stimulation. In the past, researchers interested in this question had devised an experiment in which one response leads to food reinforcement, another leads to brain stimulation, and both are on the same schedule of reinforcement. As Figure 7-17 makes clear, the results from such an experiment will depend entirely on the choice of the schedule. Specifically when a reinforcement requires two responses, brain stimulation is the overwhelming choice, but at higher prices (eight responses) food is slightly preferred. The question of which reinforcer is more potent only has a straightforward answer when the demand for both reinforcers is inelastic, or when the demand for both are elastic and their demand curves are the same (Hirsh & Natelson, 1981).

SUBSTITUTABILITY OF COMMODITIES An economic analysis of choice considers the interactions between the choices. Suppose we are interested in a choice between gasoline and public transportation. Since the demand curves for both commodities are elastic, we expect that when gas prices increase, people more often choose public transportation. This of course is what happens, but it does so because gas and public transportation can *substitute* for one another. In contrast, consider the choice between gas and inexpensive downtown parking, where the two commodities *complement* one another (the more you have of one, the more you want of the other). Now, increases in gas prices will no longer lead to increases in the preference for the other commodity.

Similarly, operant studies of choice must consider whether the two reinforcers

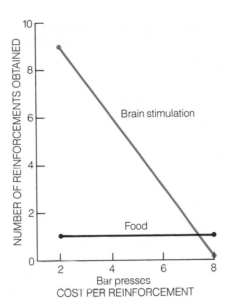

FIGURE 7-17

Demand Curves for Food and Brain-stimulation Reinforcers *As the "price" of a food pellet increased from two to eight bar presses, the amount of food reinforcement the rats obtained was essentially unchanged; the demand for food is inelastic. In contrast, as the price of brain stimulation increased from two to eight presses, the amount of reinforcement obtained decreased substantially; the demand for brain stimulation is elastic. (After Hirsh & Natelson, 1981)*

substitute for or complement one another. Suppose a pigeon can peck at either of two keys, and both are associated with food reinforcement. The reinforcers, therefore, are substitutes. Consequently, if we give one key a lower price (it requires only five responses per reinforcement, for instance, while the other key requires ten), the pigeon will increase its pecks to the lower price key and decrease its pecks to the more expensive one. In contrast, if the reinforcers are food and water, which are complements, and we lower the price on the key leading to food, the pigeon will peck at both keys more often (the more it eats, the

more it wants to drink). The influence of price differences on choice, therefore, depends on the relation between the commodities (Schwartz, 1982).

OPEN VERSUS CLOSED SYSTEM The economic principles that we have discussed so far hold only in a *closed system*—that is, in a situation where there are no alternative sources of the commodities. We can illustrate this concept with a commodity like soda, which has an elastic demand. A decrease in the price of soda should lead you to purchase more, but this is true only if you have no way of obtaining soda other than buying it at market prices. Should you have a benefactor who will supply you for free, there is no reason why your purchases should follow price changes; in this case we are in an *open system,* and the concept of demand does not apply.

There is a striking parallel to this in operant research. An operant experiment that uses, say, food reinforcement can be performed in two different ways, which correspond to open and closed systems. In the open-system version, if an animal does not obtain enough food reinforcement during an experimental session, it is given a supplement before the next session; the animal has an alternative way of obtaining the desired commodity. In the closed-system version of the experiment, there are no between-session supplements. If the reinforcement schedule is made increasingly demanding (100 rather than 50 responses are required for reinforcement), the resulting behavior differs for the two versions of the study. In the open-system version, the amount of reinforcement purchased decreases with very demanding schedules; this does not fit with the idea that the demand for food is inelastic. In the closed-system version, the amount of reinforcement purchased is the same regardless of the schedule, which is exactly what should happen if the demand for food is inelastic (Schwartz, 1982).

short, what first seemed to be a nonevent is actually fear, and we can think of avoidance as escape from fear (Mowrer, 1947; Rescorla & Solomon, 1967).

TWO CHALLENGES TO BEHAVIORISM

We mentioned at the outset that there have been two recent challenges to the behaviorist view of conditioning. One challenge is from *ethologists* (biologists and psychologists who study animal behavior in the natural environment), and the other is from cognitive psychologists. Ethologists claim that the laws of learning are not the same for all species; indeed, they differ even within a species for different situations. The cognitive psychologists believe that behavior, even for animals, can be understood only by considering internal factors, like goals and mental representations, as well as external factors. We will consider these challenges in turn.

Ethological Challenge

Though both ethologists and behaviorists are concerned with the behavior of animals, the two approaches differ in a number of respects. For one, ethologists usually study behavior by observing it in the natural environment, rather than by analyzing it in the laboratory, as is generally the case for behaviorists. Another difference is that ethologists place greater emphasis on genetics than on learning, while behaviorists do the reverse. In some cases, this difference in emphasis leads to a difference in what is studied — ethologists focusing on unlearned, innate behaviors, and behaviorists on learned ones. In other cases, this difference in emphasis leads to a clash of views: when ethologists turn their attention to learning, they argue that it is rigidly constrained by an animal's genetic endowment; behaviorists, on the other hand, assume that the laws of learning are the same for different species. As ethologists put it, when an animal learns, it must conform to a genetically determined "behavioral blueprint"; just as an architectural blueprint imposes constraints on the kinds of functions that a building may serve, so a behavioral blueprint imposes genetic constraints on the kinds of associations that an organism may learn.

Some early support for the ethological view came from psychologists who were using operant techniques to teach animals tricks. These trainers reported that instead of learning the desired trick, occasionally the animal learned something else that was closer to one of its instinctive behaviors. In one case, the trainers tried to get a chicken to stand still on a platform, but the chicken insisted on scratching the ground instead. Scratching the ground is related to the chicken's instinctual food-gathering behavior, which successfully competed with the behavior that the trainers were trying to instill. Thus, an instinct sets limits on what could be acquired. In other cases, an animal would succeed initially in learning the desired response only to drift later to a response that was an instinctual food-gathering behavior of its particular species (Breland & Breland, 1961).

CONSTRAINTS IN CLASSICAL CONDITIONING   Some of the best evidence for constraints in conditioning comes from studies of *taste aversion*. In a typical study, a rat is permitted to drink a flavored solution — say, vanilla. After drinking it, the rat is mildly poisoned and made ill. When the rat recovers, it is again presented the vanilla solution. Now the rat scrupulously avoids the solution because it has learned to associate the vanilla taste with poison. There is good evidence that such avoidance is an instance of classical conditioning: the initial taste of the solution is the CS, the feeling of being sick is the UCS, and after conditioning, the taste signals that sickness is on its way.

According to the behaviorist perspective, a light or a sound should play the same signaling role as taste. An association between a light and feeling sick should be no more difficult to establish than one between a taste and feeling sick. But the facts turn out to be otherwise, as revealed by the following experiment. Rats are allowed to lick at a tube that contains a flavored solution; each time the rat licks the tube, a click and a light are presented. Thus the rat experiences three stimuli simultaneously—the taste of the solution, as well as the light and the click. Subsequently, the rat is mildly poisoned. The question is, What stimuli—the taste or the light-plus-click—will become associated with feeling sick? To answer this, in the final phase of the study, the rat is again presented the same tube; sometimes the solution in the tube has the same flavor as before but there is no light or click, while other times the solution has no flavor but the light and click are presented. The animal avoids the solution when it experiences the taste, but not when the light-plus-click is presented; hence, the rat has associated only taste with feeling sick. These results cannot be attributed to taste being a more potent CS than light-plus-click, because in another condition of the experiment, instead of being mildly poisoned the rat is shocked. Now, in the final phase of the study, the animal avoids the solution only when the light-plus-click is presented, not when it experiences the taste alone (Garcia & Koelling, 1966).

Thus, taste can signal sickness but not shock, while light-plus-sound can signal shock but not sickness. Why does this selectivity of association exist? It does not fit with the behaviorist perspective: since taste and light-plus-click can both be effective CSs, and since being sick and being shocked are both effective UCSs, then either CS should have been associatable with either UCS. In contrast, this *selectivity of association* fits perfectly with the ethological perspective. In their natural habitat, rats (like other mammals) rely on taste to select their food. Consequently, there may be a genetically determined, or "built-in," relation between taste and intestinal reactions, which constrains what associations the rat may learn. In particular, the built-in relation fosters an association between taste and sickness but not between light and sickness. Furthermore, in a rat's natural environment, pain resulting from external factors like cold or injury is invariably due to external stimuli. Consequently, there may be a built-in relation between external stimuli and "external pain," which fosters an association between light and shock, but not one between taste and shock.

If rats learn to associate taste with sickness because it fits with their natural means of selecting food, then another species with a different means of selecting food might have trouble learning to associate taste with sickness. This is exactly what happens. Birds naturally select their food on the basis of looks rather than taste, and they readily learn to associate a light with sickness, but not a taste with sickness. In short, if we want to know what may be conditioned to what, we cannot consider the CS and UCS in isolation; rather, we must focus on the two in combination and consider how well that combination reflects built-in relations. This conclusion differs considerably from the behaviorist assumption that the laws of learning are the same for all species and situations.

CONSTRAINTS IN OPERANT CONDITIONING   Constraints on learning also occur in operant conditioning, though now the constraints involve response-reinforcer relations. We can illustrate this point with pigeons in two different situations; *reward learning,* where the animal acquires a response that is reinforced by food; and *escape learning,* where the animal acquires a response that is reinforced by the termination of shock. In the case of reward, pigeons learn much faster if the response is pecking a key rather than flapping their wings. In the case of escape, the opposite is true; pigeons learn faster if the response is wing flapping rather than pecking (Bolles, 1970).

Again, the results are not consistent with the assumption that the same laws of learning apply to all situations, but they make sense from an ethological perspective. The reward case with the pigeons involved eating, and pecking (but not wing flapping) is part of the bird's natural eating activities. Hence, a genetically determined connection between pecking and eating is reasonable. Similarly, the escape case involved a danger situation, and the pigeon's natural reactions to danger include flapping its wings (but not pecking). Birds are known to have a small repertoire of defensive reactions, and they will quickly learn to escape only if the relevant response is one of these natural defensive reactions. In sum, rather than being a means for learning arbitrary associations, operant conditioning also honors the behavioral blueprint.

DIFFERENT KINDS OF LEARNING   Constraints on associations are not the only problem that ethologists have raised for behaviorists. Ethologists have also studied some important forms of animal learning that differ from associative learning. Two striking instances of such learning are imprinting and song learning in birds.

Imprinting refers to the type of learning that forms the basis for a young bird's attachment to its parents. A newly hatched duckling reared without its mother will follow a human being, a wooden decoy, or almost any other moving object that it first sees after birth (see the Critical Discussion, "Instincts and Maternal Behavior," in Chapter 10). Imprinting is different from standard associative learning because it occurs *only* during a *critical period*, which begins right after birth and typically ends when a suitable parent model is learned. No form of associative learning seems to have the feature that it occurs *only* very early in life.

Bird songs offer another challenge to associative learning. In part, birds learn their songs from other birds. For example, if a male white-crowned sparrow is raised in isolation, as an adult it will not vocalize normally; instead, it will sing a crude version of its species song. Imitation, therefore, seems to be involved. But imitation is not the whole story, for if the white-crowned sparrow is exposed only to the songs of other species, the songs will have no effect on the sparrow's learning. These results suggest that the sparrow has a kind of inborn *template* or model of what its adult song is like, and its learning is influenced only by songs that fit the template (Marler, 1970). The idea of "fitting an inborn template" is far removed from associative learning.

Cognitive Challenge

In a sense, the cognitive challenge is the opposite of the ethological one. Whereas the ethologist tells us that animals are not as flexible as the behaviorists thought, the cognitivist argues that animals, particularly higher species, are more intelligent than the behaviorists thought. According to the cognitivist, the crux of intelligence lies in an organism's ability to represent mentally aspects of the world and then to *operate* on these *mental representations* rather than on the world itself. In some cases, the costly trial and error of actual behavior can be replaced by a "mental trial and error," in which the organism tries out different possibilities in its mind. In other cases, the operations on mental representations are less like trial and error and more like a multistep strategy; that is, the organism takes some mental steps only because they enable subsequent ones. Such notions contradict the behaviorist assumption that an organism's behavior can be explained without considering its internal processes. Furthermore, the idea of a strategy seems at odds with the behaviorist assumption that complex learning is built out of simple associations.

The cognitive view of learning has gained support rapidly. No doubt, this is partly due to the advent of computers. Computers are capable of complex learning (for example, learning to play chess), yet no one thinks that the way to understand a computer is by considering just its external behavior—its inputs and outputs. Rather, the standard way to understand the behavior of a computer is in terms of its internal representations (its data, for example) and its procedures for operating on them. Animal and human learning may require the same kind of explanation. The analogy of a computer, however, is not the only reason for adopting a cognitive view of learning. There are numerous phenomena in learning that directly point to the need to consider mental representations. This is clearly the case with humans—as the next two chapters will testify—but it also holds for lower species. Some of these cognitive phenomena in lower species have long been known; other cognitive phenomena in animals have been discovered only recently.

EARLY COGNITIVE CHALLENGES TO BEHAVIORISM An early advocate of the cognitive approach to learning was Edward C. Tolman, whose research dealt with the problem of rats learning their way through complex mazes (Tolman, 1932). In his view, a rat running through a complex maze was not learning a sequence of right- and left-turning responses but rather was developing a *cognitive map*—a mental representation of the layout of the maze. Thus, if a familiar path was blocked, the animal adopted another route based on the spatial relations represented in its cognitive map.

To bolster the position that rats are learning representations of layouts, Tolman and his students performed experiments like the following. Rats were first passively transported in air by a "tram" from a starting place (distinguished by vertical stripes) to a destination (distinguished by horizontal stripes). (Think of the trams at ski resorts.) The rats experienced shocks throughout their journey until they arrived at the destination. Though they made no relevant responses, the rats had clearly learned something about the signposts of their journey. For when the starting place and destination of their journey became the two end points of a simple T-maze, most rats chose to run to the end that had been the destination which is where the shock had ended. Their aversion to the starting place had to be due to something they had learned in the absence of responding. Thus, overt behavior is not necessary for learning to occur (Gleitman, 1963).

While Tolman and his students tried to make the case for the cognitive view with lower species, other researchers assumed that the best evidence for a cognitive approach would come from higher species, especially primates. Among these researchers, Wolfgang Köhler's work with chimpanzees, carried out in the 1920s, remains particularly important. The problems that Köhler set for his chimpanzees left some room for insight, because no parts of the problem were hidden from view (in contrast, the workings of a food dispenser in a Skinner box are hidden from the animal's view). Typically, Köhler placed a chimpanzee in an enclosed area with a desirable piece of fruit, often a banana, out of reach. To obtain the fruit, the animal had to use a nearby object as a tool. Usually the chimpanzee solved the problem, and in a way that suggested it had some insight. The following description from Köhler is typical:

> Sultan [Köhler's most intelligent chimpanzee] is squatting at the bars but cannot reach the fruit which lies outside by means of his only available short stick. A longer stick is deposited outside the bars, about two meters on one side of the object and parallel with the grating. It cannot be grasped with the hand, but it can be pulled within reach by means of the small stick. [See Figure 7-18 for an illustration of a similar multiple-stick problem.] Sultan tries to reach the fruit with the smaller of the two sticks. Not succeeding, he tears at a piece of wire that

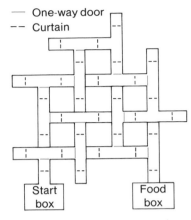

Diagram of One of Tolman's Mazes
A diagram of a maze used by Tolman in his learning experiments with rats. The complexity of the maze (with right and left turns, one-way doors, and curtains limiting the view of the route) tested the rat's ability to form a cognitive map.

FIGURE 7-18
A Chimpanzee Solving a Multiple-stick Problem *Using the shorter sticks, the chimpanzee pulls in a stick long enough to reach the piece of fruit. It has learned to solve this problem by understanding the relationship between the sticks and the piece of fruit—an example of insight.*

projects from the netting of his cage, but that too is in vain. Then he gazes about him (there are always in the course of these tests some long pauses, during which the animals scrutinize the whole visible area). He suddenly picks up the little stick once more, goes up to the bars directly opposite to the long stick, scratches it towards him with the "auxiliary," seizes it, and goes with it to the point opposite the objective (the fruit), which he secures. From the moment that his eyes fall upon the long stick, his procedure forms one consecutive whole, without hiatus, and although the angling of the bigger stick by means of the smaller is an action that could be complete and distinct in itself, yet observation shows that it follows, quite suddenly, on an interval of hesitation and doubt — staring about — which undoubtedly has a relation to the final objective, and is immediately merged in the final action of the attainment of the end goal. (Köhler, 1925, pp. 174–75)

Several aspects of the performance of these chimpanzees are unlike those of Thorndyke's cats or Skinner's rats and pigeons. For one thing, the solution was sudden, rather than being the result of a gradual trial-and-error process. Another point is that once a chimpanzee solved a problem, thereafter it would solve the problem with few irrelevant moves. This is most unlike a rat, which continues to make irrelevant responses in the Skinner box for many trials. Also, Köhler's chimpanzees could readily transfer what they had learned to a novel situation. For example, in one problem, Sultan was not encaged, but some bananas were placed too high for him to reach, as shown in Figure 7-19. To solve the problem, Sultan stacked some boxes strewn around him, climbed the "platform," and grabbed the bananas. In subsequent problems, if the fruit was again too high to reach, Sultan found other objects to construct a platform; in some cases, Sultan used a table and a small ladder, and in one case Sultan pulled Köhler himself over and used the experimenter as a platform.

There are, therefore, three critical aspects of the chimpanzee's solution: its suddenness, its availability once discovered, and its transferability. These aspects are at odds with the behaviorist notion of trial-and-error behaviors of the type observed by Thorndyke, Skinner, and their students. Instead, the chimpanzee's solutions may reflect a mental trial and error. That is, the animal forms a mental representation of the problem, manipulates components of the representation until it hits upon a solution, and then enacts the solution in the real world. The solution, therefore, appears sudden because the researchers do not have access to

FIGURE 7-19
A Chimpanzee Constructing a Platform *To reach the bananas hanging from the ceiling, the chimpanzee stacks boxes to form a platform.*

the chimpanzee's mental process. The solution is available thereafter because a mental representation persists over time, and the solution is transferable because the representation is either abstract enough to cover more than the original situation or malleable enough to be extended to a novel situation.

CURRENT COGNITIVE CHALLENGES TO BEHAVIORISM We have already described some phenomena in classical and operant conditioning that require a cognitive interpretation, particularly the importance of predictability and control in conditioning. Recall that in classical conditioning a rat will learn an association between a tone and a shock to the extent the tone predicts the shock; in operant conditioning, dogs will not learn to jump a hurdle to avoid shock if they have previously learned that shocks are not under their control. The notions of *predictability* and *control* are cognitive; *predictability*, for example, refers to a belief that something will happen, and *beliefs* are part of the mental world, not the physical one.

Moreover, *predictability* can be tied to other cognitive facets, such as those involving memory, to provide a more detailed account of classical conditioning. According to Wagner (1981), just as humans have a short-term memory in which they can rehearse information (see Chapter 8, p. 250), so do lower animals. Furthermore, an animal's short-term memory plays a critical role in conditioning. Early in the course of conditioning, a UCS is novel and unpredictable. Consequently, the organism actively rehearses the CS-UCS connection in short-term memory; this rehearsal process is presumably what mediates the acquisition of a classically conditioned response. Once the UCS is no longer surprising, rehearsal decreases and no further learning occurs.

Other research has revived Tolman's pioneering studies of cognitive maps in rats. To illustrate, consider the maze diagrammed in Figure 7-20. The maze consists of a center platform with eight identical arms radiating out. On each trial, the researcher places food at the end of each arm; the rat needs to learn to visit each arm (and obtain the food there) without returning to those it has already visited. Rats learn this remarkably well; after 20 trials, they will virtually never return to an arm they have already visited. (Rats will do this even when the maze has been doused with after-shave lotion to eliminate odor cues about which arms still have food.) Most important, a rat rarely employs the strategy that would occur to humans—such as always to go through the arms in an obvious order, say

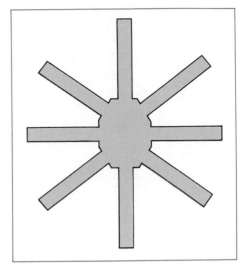

FIGURE 7-20
Maze for Studying Cognitive Maps *In experiments using this maze, rats must learn to visit each of the eight arms, without returning to one they have already visited. (After Olton & Samuelson, 1976)*

"Psst — want a map?"

clockwise. Instead, the rat visits the arms randomly, indicating that it has not learned a rigid sequence of responses. What, then, has it learned? Probably, the rat has developed a representation of the maze, which specifies the spatial relations between arms, and on each trial it makes a "mental note" of each arm that it has visited (Olton, 1978, 1979).

As was true in the past, the strongest evidence for cognition in animal learning comes from studies with primates. Particularly striking are studies showing that chimpanzees can acquire abstract concepts that were once believed to be the sole province of humans. In the typical study, chimpanzees learn to use plastic tokens of different shapes, sizes, and colors as words. For example, they might learn that one token refers to *apples* and another to *paper*, where there is no physical resemblance between the token and the object. The fact that chimpanzees can learn these references means they understand concrete concepts like *apple* and *paper*. More impressively, they also have abstract concepts like *same*, *different*, and *cause*. Thus, chimpanzees can learn to use their *same* token when presented either two *apple* tokens or two *orange* ones and their *different* token when presented one *apple* and one *orange* token. Likewise, chimpanzees seem to understand causal relations: they will apply the token for *cause* when shown some cut paper and scissors, but not when shown some intact paper and scissors (Premack, 1985a; Premack & Premack, 1983).

Though the experiments just described are important, the strongest evidence for a cognitive view comes from studies with people. Such studies demonstrate the need for a cognitive approach in understanding learning, memory, thinking, and language, and they are the concern of the next two chapters.

SUMMARY

1. Two forms of *associative learning* are *classical conditioning* and *operant conditioning*. In classical conditioning, an organism learns that one event follows another. In operant conditioning, an organism learns that a response leads to a particular consequence.

2. The behavioristic approach to conditioning assumes that: (a) simple associations are the building blocks of all learning, (b) the laws of association are the same for all species and situations, and (c) learning is better understood in terms of external causes than internal ones.

3. Pavlov's experiments showed that if a *conditioned stimulus* (CS) consistently precedes an *unconditioned stimulus* (UCS), the CS will come to serve as a signal for the UCS and will elicit a *conditioned response* (CR) that often resembles the *unconditioned response* (UCR). Stimuli that are similar to the CS will also elicit the CR to some extent, though such *generalization* can be curbed by *discrimination training*. These phenomena occur in organisms as diverse as flatworms and humans.

4. For classical conditioning to occur, the CS must be a reliable predictor of the UCS; that is, there must be a higher probability that the UCS will occur when the CS has been presented than when it has not.

5. Operant conditioning deals with situations where the response operates on the environment rather than being elicited by an unconditioned stimulus. The earliest systematic studies were performed by Thorndyke, who showed that animals engage in *trial-and-error* behavior, and that any behavior followed by reinforcement is strengthened (the *law of effect*).

6. In Skinner's experiments, typically a rat or pigeon learns to make a simple response, such as pressing a lever, to obtain reinforcement. The rate of response is a useful measure of *operant strength*. Even responses mediated by the autonomic nervous system, like blood pressure, can be modified through operant conditioning.

7. In *shaping*, which is used when the desired response is novel, the organism is reinforced for any behavior that brings it closer to the desired response. In *partial reinforcement*, the organism is reinforced for making the desired response only some fraction of the time. Responses learned under partial reinforcement are more difficult to extinguish (the *partial-reinforcement effect*). For operant conditioning to occur at all, the organism must interpret the reinforcement as being under the *control* of its response.

8. *Conditioned reinforcement*, the fact that a stimulus associated with a reinforcer acquires its own reinforcing properties, increases the range of conditioning. According to *Premack's principle*, activities that are engaged in more frequently reinforce activities that are engaged in less frequently.

9. *Punishments* are events that suppress or eliminate responses. Punishment is beneficial to learning to the extent that it is informative. An organism can learn to avoid punishment by responding to a signal that precedes the punishing event. In such *avoidance learning*, the reinforcement may be a reduction of fear.

10. The *ethological challenge* to behaviorism disputes that the laws of learning are the same for all species or for all situations within a species. According to ethologists, what an animal learns is constrained by its genetically determined "behavioral blueprint." Evidence for such constraints on learning comes from studies of *taste aversion*. While rats readily learn to associate the feeling of being sick with the taste of a solution, they cannot learn to associate sickness with a light. Conversely, birds can learn to associate light and sickness, but not taste and sickness. These distinctions are the result of innate differences between rats and birds in their food-gathering activities.

11. The *cognitive challenge* to behaviorism disputes that behavior can be understood by considering only external or environmental factors. According to cognitivists, intelligence is an organism's ability to represent aspects of the world mentally and then to operate on those *mental representations* rather than on the world itself. In some cases, the operations are like mental trial and error.

12. Some early cognitive studies demonstrated that rats learned about locations even when they made no overt responses to them. Other early studies suggested that chimpanzees could solve problems by mental trial and error. Some current studies provide strong evidence that rats develop a mental representation, or *cognitive map*, of a maze; other studies demonstrate that chimpanzees can acquire abstract concepts such as *same*, *different*, and *cause*.

FURTHER READING

Pavlov's *Conditioned Reflexes* (1927) is the classic work on classical conditioning. Skinner's *The Behavior of Organisms* (1938) is the corresponding statement on operant conditioning. The major points of view about conditioning and learning, presented in their historical settings, are summarized in Bower and Hilgard, *Theories of Learning* (5th ed., 1981).

For a general introduction to learning, a number of textbooks are recommended. Schwartz's *Psychology of Learning and Behavior* (2nd ed., 1984) is a particularly well-balanced review of conditioning, including discussion of ethology and cognition. Another useful textbook is Domjan and Burkhard's *The Principles of Learning and Behavior* (1985). Staddon's *Adaptive Behavior and Learning* (1983) tries to synthesize traditional work on conditioning with the ethological findings, while Mackintosh's *Conditioning and Associative Learning* (1983) takes a cognitive approach to classical conditioning. At the advanced level, the six-volume Estes (ed.), *Handbook of Learning and Cognitive Processes* (1975–1979), covers most aspects of learning and conditioning; and Honig and Staddon (eds.), *Handbook of Operant Behavior* (1977), provides a comprehensive treatment of operant conditioning.

The early cognitive approach is well described in two classics: Tolman's *Purposive Behavior in Animals and Men* (1932; reprint ed. 1967) and Köhler's *The Mentality of Apes* (1925; reprint ed. 1976). A recent statement of the cognitive approach to animal learning is presented in Premack's unusually titled *Gavagai: The Future of the Animal Language Controversy* (1985b).

Memory

ALL LEARNING IMPLIES MEMORY. IF WE remembered nothing from our experiences, we could learn nothing. Life would consist of momentary experiences that had little relation to one another. We could not even carry on a simple conversation. To communicate, we have to remember the thoughts we want to express as well as what has just been said to us. Without memory we could not even reflect upon ourselves, for the very notion of a self depends on a sense of continuity that only memory can bring. In short, when we think of what it means to be human, we must acknowledge the centrality of memory.

DISTINCTIONS ABOUT MEMORY

Psychologists find it useful to make a few basic distinctions about memory. One distinction concerns three stages of memory: *encoding, storage,* and *retrieval.* Other distinctions deal with different types of memory. Different memories may be used to store information for short and long periods and to store different kinds of information (for example, one memory for facts and another for skills).

Three Stages of Memory

Suppose one morning you are introduced to a student and told her name is Barbara Cohn. That afternoon you see her again and say something like, "You're Barbara Cohn. We met this morning." Clearly, you have remembered her name. But how exactly did you remember it?

Your minor memory feat can be broken into three stages (see Figure 8-1). First, when you were introduced, you somehow deposited Barbara Cohn's name into memory; this is the *encoding stage.* You transformed a physical input (sound waves) that corresponds to her spoken name into the kind of code or representation that memory accepts, and you placed that representation in memory. Second, you retained—or stored—the name during the time between the two meetings; this is the *storage stage.* And, third, you recovered the name from storage at the time of your second meeting; this is the *retrieval stage.*

Memory can fail at any of these three stages. Had you been unable to recall Barbara's name at the second meeting, this could have reflected a failure in encoding, storage, or retrieval. Much of current research on memory attempts to specify the mental operations that occur at each stage in different situations and to explain how these operations can go awry and result in memory failure.

245

FIGURE 8-1
Three Stages of Memory *Modern theories of memory attribute forgetting to a failure at one or more of these stages.*

FIGURE 8-1
Three Stages of Memory *Modern theories of memory attribute forgetting to a failure at one or more of these stages.*

Different Types of Memory

SHORT-TERM VERSUS LONG-TERM MEMORY The three stages of memory do not operate the same way in all situations. Memory seems to differ between those situations that require us to store material for a matter of seconds and those that require us to store material for longer intervals — from minutes to years. The former situations are said to tap *short-term memory,* whereas the latter reflect *long-term memory.*

We can illustrate this distinction by amending our story about meeting Barbara Cohn. Suppose that during the first meeting, as soon as you had heard her name, a friend came up and you said, "Doug, have you met Barbara Cohn?" In this case, remembering Barbara's name would be an example of short-term memory: you retrieved the name after only a second or two. Remembering her name at the time of your second meeting would be an example of long-term memory, because then retrieval would take place hours after the name was encoded.

When we recall a name immediately after encountering it, retrieval seems effortless, as if the name were still active, still in our consciousness. But when we try to recall the same name hours later, retrieval is often difficult because the name is no longer in our consciousness. This contrast between short- and long-term memory is similar to the contrast between conscious knowledge and preconscious knowledge — the knowledge we have but are not currently thinking about. We can think of memory as a vast body of knowledge, only a small part of which can ever be active at any moment. The rest is passive. Short-term memory corresponds to the active part, long-term memory to the passive part.

The need to distinguish between short- and long-term memory is further supported by studies of people with *amnesia,* or severe memory loss. In virtually every form of amnesia, people have profound difficulty remembering material for long time intervals but rarely have any trouble remembering material for a few seconds. Thus, a patient with severe amnesia may be unable to recognize his doctor when he enters the room — even though the patient has seen this doctor every day for years — yet will have no trouble repeating back the physician's full name when he is reintroduced (Milner, Corkin, & Teuber, 1968).

DIFFERENT MEMORIES FOR DIFFERENT KINDS OF INFORMATION Until recently, psychologists assumed that the same memory system was used for all contents that had to be stored. For example, the same long-term memory was presumably used to store both one's recollection of a grandmother's funeral and the skill one needs to ride a bike. Recent evidence suggests that this assumption is wrong. In particular, we seem to use a different long-term memory for storing *facts* (such as who the current president is) than we do for retaining *skills* (such as how to ride a bicycle). We may also use different long-term memories for storing *general facts* about the world (for example, "12 squared is 144") versus *personal facts* about our experiences ("I couldn't stand the teacher who taught me squares").

Ideally, we should first specify the different memory systems corresponding to different contents and for each one describe the nature of encoding, storage, and retrieval stages in its short-term and long-term memory. This goal is too ambitious given present knowledge. Most of what we know concerns memory for facts, particularly personal ones, and unless otherwise noted such memory will be the focus of this chapter. The next two sections consider the nature of encoding, storage, and retrieval in short-term and long-term fact memory. Then we will examine how long-term memory can be improved. In the last section, we will focus on memory for more complex factual material, with an emphasis on how we embellish what we put into memory.

SHORT-TERM MEMORY

Even in situations where we must remember information for only a few seconds, memory involves the three stages of encoding, storage, and retrieval.

Encoding

To encode information into short-term memory, we must attend to it. Since we are selective about what we attend to (see Chapter 6), our short-term memory will contain only what has been selected. This means that much of what we are exposed to never even enters short-term memory and, of course, will not be available for later retrieval. Indeed, many difficulties labeled "memory problems" are really lapses in attention. For example, if you bought some groceries and someone asked you later for the color of the checkout clerk's eyes, you might well be unable to answer because you had not paid attention to them in the first place.

ACOUSTIC CODING   When information is encoded into memory, it is deposited in a certain code or representation. For example, when you look up a phone number and retain it until you have dialed it, in what form do you represent the digits? Is the representation visual — a mental picture of the digits? Is it acoustic — the sounds of the names of the digits? Or is it semantic (based on meaning) — some meaningful association that the digits have? Research indicates that we can use any of these possibilities to encode information into short-term memory, although we seem to favor an acoustic code when we are trying to keep the information active by *rehearsing* it — that is, by repeating it over and over in our minds. Rehearsal is a particularly popular strategy when the information consists of verbal items such as digits, letters, or words. So in trying to remember a phone number, we are most likely to encode the number as the sounds of the digit names and to rehearse these sounds to ourselves until we have dialed the number.

In one experiment that provided evidence for an acoustic code, researchers briefly showed subjects a list of six consonants (for example, RLBKSJ); when the letters were removed, the subject had to write all six letters in order. Although the entire procedure took only a second or two, subjects occasionally made errors. When they did, the incorrect letter tended to be similar in sound to the correct one. For the list mentioned, a subject might have written RLTKSJ, replacing the B with the similar-sounding T (Conrad, 1964). This finding supports the idea that the subjects encoded each letter acoustically (for example, "bee" for B), sometimes lost part of this code (only the "ee" part of the sound remained), and then responded with a letter ("tee") that was consistent with the remaining part of the code.

Experiments such as this one have produced another result that points to an acoustic code: it is more difficult to recall the items in order when they are acoustically similar (for example, TBCGVE) than when they are acoustically

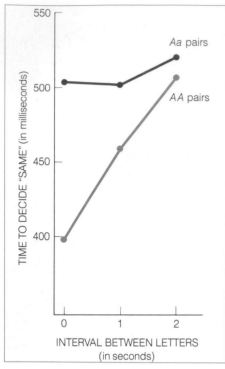

FIGURE 8-2

Fading of Visual Code   On each trial, subjects were shown two letters in succession; the interval between the letters varied from 0 to 2 seconds. Subjects had to determine whether the second letter had the same name as the first. In the two sample trials shown below, the pair of letters have the same name.

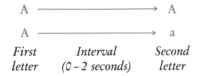

First letter   Interval (0 – 2 seconds)   Second letter

When the interval between the letters was roughly a second, the visual code for the first letter should not yet have faded. Consequently, subjects could make a direct visual comparison between letters. This kind of comparison will work for pairs like **AA.** *But pairs like* **Aa** *can only be determined to have the same name by comparing their names acoustically. So we might expect* **AA** *decisions to be made faster than* **Aa** *decisions. When the interval between the letters is about 2 seconds, however, the visual code has faded and only the sounds of the letters remain in short-term memory. Now decisions about* **AA** *and* **Aa** *should take the same amount of time because both must be based on acoustic codes. (After Posner & Keele, 1967)*

distinct (RLTKSJ). A striking example of this occurs with Chinese readers. Written Chinese consists of syllable-like units called "characters." Usually, there are two characters per word, and each character typically shares its name with several others. When Chinese subjects are briefly shown a sequence of characters that they then have to write down in order, they get about six correct if all the characters have different names but only three correct if all have the same name (and hence cannot be coded acoustically). Eliminating the use of an acoustic code thus cuts recall in half (Zhang & Simon, 1985).

VISUAL CODING   The fact that the Chinese readers in the previous study were able to remember the correct order of three characters with the same name suggests that they also maintained these items in a visual representation. Other experiments indicate that while we can use a visual code for verbal material, the code often fades quickly. To illustrate, after looking at the address 7915 THIRD AVENUE, you may have a visual code of it for a second or two. This representation would preserve visual details, such as the fact that the address is written in all capital letters. After a couple of seconds, however, all that would remain would be the sound of the address (the acoustic code), and this code would not preserve information about the form of the letters. The experiment in Figure 8-2 demonstrates the fading of the visual code.

This dominance of the acoustic code may apply mainly to verbal materials. When a person must store nonverbal items (such as pictures that are difficult to describe and therefore difficult to rehearse acoustically), the visual code may become more important. A few people, most of them children, are able to hold in their short-term memory images of visual material that are almost photographic in clarity. They can look briefly at a picture and, when it is removed, still "see" its image before their eyes. They can maintain the image for as long as several minutes, scan it, and when questioned, provide a wealth of detail, such as the number of stripes on a cat's tail (see Figure 8-3). Such children seem to be reading the details directly from an "eidetic" image (Haber, 1969). Eidetic imagery is quite rare, though. Studies with children indicate that only about 5 percent report visual images that are long-lasting and possess sharp detail. The existing evidence suggests that even fewer individuals have eidetic images after adolescence.

Storage

LIMITED CAPACITY   Perhaps the most striking fact about short-term memory is that it has a very limited capacity. On the average, the limit is seven items, give or take two (7 ± 2). Some people store as few as five items; others can retain as many as nine. It may seem strange to give such an exact number to cover all people when it is clear that individuals differ greatly in their memory abilities. These differences, however, are primarily due to long-term memory. For short-term memory, most normal adults have a capacity of 7 ± 2. This constancy has been known since the earliest days of experimental psychology. Hermann Ebbinghaus, who began the experimental study of memory in 1885, reported results showing that his own limit was seven items. Some 70 years later, George Miller (1956) was so struck by the constancy that he referred to it as the "magic number seven." And the limit has been shown to hold in non-Western cultures (Yu et al., 1985).

Psychologists determined this number by showing subjects various sequences of unrelated items (digits, letters, or words) and asking them to recall the items in order. The items are presented rapidly, and the subject does not have time to relate them to information stored in long-term memory; hence, the number of items recalled reflects only the storage capacity for short-term memory. On the initial trials, subjects have to recall just a few items, say, three or four digits, which they can easily do. Then the number of digits increases over trials until the experimenter determines the maximum number a subject can recall in perfect order. The maximum (almost always between five and nine) is the subject's *memory span*. This task is so simple that you can easily try it yourself. The next time you come across a list of names (a directory in a business or university building, for example), read through the list once and then look away and see how many names you can recall in order. It will probably be between five and nine.

FORGETTING   We may be able to hold on to seven items briefly, but in most cases they will soon be forgotten. Forgetting occurs either because the items are *displaced* by newer ones or because the items *decay* with time.

The notion of displacement fits with short-term memory having a fixed capacity. The fixed capacity suggests that we might think of short-term memory as a sort of mental box with roughly seven slots. Each item entering short-term memory goes into its own slot. As long as the number of items does not exceed the number of slots, we can recall the items perfectly, but when all the slots are filled and a new item enters, one of the old ones must go. The new item displaces an old one. To illustrate, suppose your short-term memory is empty (see Figure 8-4). An item enters. Let us say you have been introduced to Barbara Cohn (remember her?), and the name Cohn enters your short-term memory. Others are introduced soon after, and the list of names in short-term memory grows. Finally, the limit of your memory span is reached. Then each new item that enters short-term memory has a chance to displace Cohn. After one new item, there has been only one chance to displace Cohn; after two new items, there have been two chances; and so on. The likelihood that Cohn will be lost from short-term memory increases steadily with the number of items that have followed it. Eventually, Cohn will go.

Displacement has been demonstrated experimentally many times. In one study, subjects were given a list of 13 digits, presented one at a time. After the last digit in the list was presented, a *probe* digit was given (it is called a probe because subjects must use it to probe their memory). The probe was always the same as one of the digits in the list, and the subject was required to recall the item that came after the probe. For example, given the list 3 9 1 6 9 7 5 3 8 2 5 6 4 and the probe 2, subjects should report 5. (The probe always occurred just once in

FIGURE 8-3
Testing for Eidetic Images   *This test picture was shown for 30 seconds to elementary school children. After removal of the picture, one boy saw in his eidetic image "about 14" stripes in the cat's tail. The painting, by Marjorie Torrey, appears in Lewis Carroll's* Alice in Wonderland, *abridged by Josette Frank.*

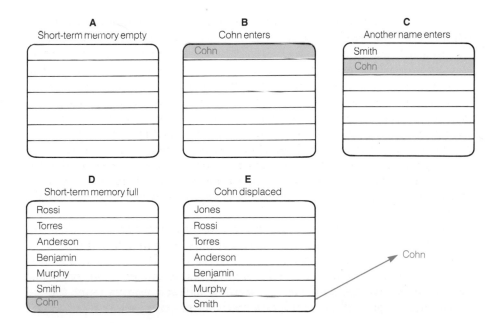

A	**B**	**C**
Short-term memory empty	Cohn enters	Another name enters

D
Short-term memory full

Rossi
Torres
Anderson
Benjamin
Murphy
Smith
Cohn

E
Cohn displaced

Jones
Rossi
Torres
Anderson
Benjamin
Murphy
Smith

→ Cohn

FIGURE 8-4
Forgetting Due to Displacement   *Due to the limited capacity of short-term memory, 7 ± 2 "slots," the addition of a new item can result in the displacement or loss of an old one.*

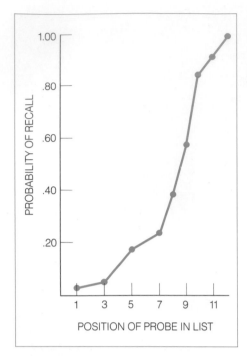

FIGURE 8-5
Recall as a Function of Probe Position
When probes are drawn from the end of the list, few items have followed the one to be recalled, and the probability of recall is high. When probes are drawn from the beginning of the list, many items have followed the one to be recalled, and the probability of recall is low. (After Waugh & Norman, 1965)

the list.) When the probe is drawn from the end of the list, the item following it should still be in short-term memory (because it has just been presented) and hence should be very likely to be recalled. When the probe is from the beginning of the list, however, many items have followed the one to be recalled. Most likely it has been displaced and will not be recalled. For probes drawn from the middle of the list, the chance of displacement is moderate, as is the chance of recall. Figure 8-5 shows that the data from this experiment support the principle of displacement. The more items that intervene between the occurrence of a particular digit and the attempt to recall it, the less the chance of recall.

The other major cause of forgetting in short-term memory is that information simply decays in time. We may think of the representation of an item as a trace that fades within a matter of seconds. One piece of evidence for this view is that an item may be lost from memory within seconds even if no new information follows it (Reitman, 1974). Another source of evidence for decay is that our short-term memory span holds fewer words when the words take longer to say; for example, the span is less for long words such as "harpoon" and "cyclone" than for shorter words such as "bishop" and "pewter" (try saying the words to yourself to see the difference in duration). Presumably this effect arises because as the words are presented we say them to ourselves, and the longer it takes to do so, the more likely it is that some of the words' traces will have faded before they can be recalled (Baddeley, Thompson, & Buchanan, 1975).

It appears, then, that information at the forefront of our memory must soon give way. The one major exception to this involves rehearsal: items that we rehearse are not readily subject to displacement or decay. (In experiments that demonstrate displacement or decay, subjects are typically discouraged from rehearsing.) Rehearsing information may protect it from displacement because we cannot encode new items at the same time we are rehearsing old ones. In other words, rehearsal may prevent displacement by preventing the encoding of new items. Rehearsal may offset decay more directly: rehearsing an item that has partly faded may bring it to full strength again.

Retrieval

Let us think of the contents of short-term memory as being active in consciousness. Intuition suggests that access to this information is immediate. You do not have to "dig for it"; it is right there. Retrieval, then, should not depend on the number of items in consciousness. But in this case intuition is wrong.

Evidence shows that the more items there are in short-term memory, the slower retrieval becomes, suggesting that retrieval requires a search of short-term memory in which the items are examined one at a time (just as you might examine a set of dishes one at a time to find the one with a chip). This *serial* search of short-term memory takes place at a very fast rate — so fast, in fact, that we are not aware of it. Most of the evidence for such a search comes from a type of experiment introduced by Sternberg (1966). On each trial of the experiment, a subject is shown a set of digits, called the *memory list,* that he or she must temporarily hold in short-term memory. It is easy for the subject to maintain the information in short-term memory because each memory list contains between one and six digits. The memory list is then removed from view, and a probe digit is presented. The subject must decide whether the probe was on the memory list. For example, if the memory list is 3 6 1 and the probe is 6, the subject should respond "yes"; given the same memory list and a probe of 2, the subject should respond "no." Subjects rarely make an error on this task; what is of interest, however, is the speed at which the subject makes the decision. The *decision time* is the elapsed time between the onset of the probe and the subject's press of a "yes" or a "no" button to indicate whether the probe was or was not on the memory list. The decision times are extremely fast and must be measured with equipment that permits accuracy in milliseconds (thousandths of a second).

Figure 8-6 presents data from such an experiment, indicating that decision time increases directly with the length of the memory list. What is remarkable about these decision times is that they fall along a straight line. This means that each additional item in short-term memory adds a fixed amount of time to the search process—approximately 40 milliseconds. The subject, of course, is not aware of such brief time intervals, but the data indicate that decision time increases with the amount of information that must be searched through in short-term memory. The same results are found when the items are letters, words, auditory tones, or pictures of people's faces: the addition of an extra item usually adds about 40 milliseconds to retrieval time (Sternberg, 1969). Psychologists have obtained similar results with groups as varied as schizophrenic patients, college students under the influence of marijuana, and people from preliterate societies.*

Short-term Memory and Thought

Short-term memory plays an important role in conscious thought. When consciously trying to solve a problem, we often use short-term memory as a mental work space: we use it to store parts of the problem as well as information accessed from long-term memory that is relevant to the problem. To illustrate, consider what it takes to multiply 35 by 8 in your head. You need short-term memory to store the given numbers (35 and 8), the nature of the operation required (multiplication), and arithmetic facts such as $8 \times 5 = 40$ and $3 \times 8 = 24$. Not surprisingly, performance on mental arithmetic declines substantially if you have to remember simultaneously some words or digits; try doing the above mental multiplication while remembering the phone number 745-1739 (Baddeley & Hitch, 1974). Other research indicates that short-term memory is used not only in numerical problems but also in the whole gamut of complex problems that we routinely confront (Ericsson & Simon, 1984).

The role that short-term memory plays in understanding language is less straightforward. The short-term memory system we have described appears not to be involved in such relatively "low-level" processes as understanding a single sentence (see Crowder, 1982). One piece of evidence for this is that people who have below-normal memory spans because of brain damage have no difficulty understanding simple sentences. Apparently, a normal memory span is not needed for normal comprehension of a sentence. Furthermore, even with normal subjects, the ability to understand sentences and later recognize them is not affected by blocking the use of auditory short-term memory (blocking is accomplished by having subjects say irrelevant words while first reading the sentences).

On the other hand, short-term memory appears to play a substantial role in higher-level language processes, such as following a conversation or reading a text. When reading for understanding, we often must consciously relate new sentences to some prior material in the text. This relating of new to old seems to occur in short-term memory because people who have more short-term capacity

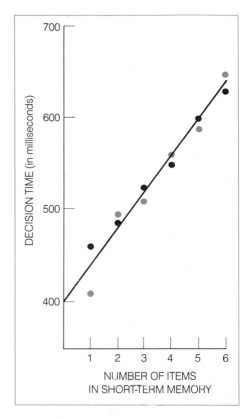

FIGURE 8-6
Retrieval as a Search Process *Decision times increase in direct proportion to the number of items in short-term memory. Colored circles represent "yes" responses; black circles, "no" responses. The times for both types of decision fall along a straight line. (After Sternberg, 1966)*

---

* While the data in Figure 8-6 are consistent with a serial (one at a time) search of short-term memory, other interpretations are possible. Some researchers have argued that the probe is compared to all memory items *simultaneously*, but the time required for each comparison increases with the number of items in short-term memory (Townsend, 1971). Others have argued that retrieval is based on an *activation process;* one decides a probe is in short-term memory if its representation is above a critical level of activation, and the more items in short-term memory, the less the activation for any one of them (Monsell, 1979).

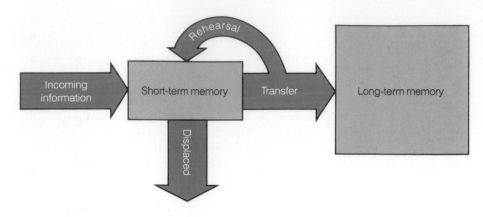

FIGURE 8-7

Dual-memory Theory *Incoming items enter the memory system through short-term memory. Once in short-term memory, an item can be maintained there by rehearsal. As an item is rehearsed, information about it is transferred to long-term memory. Once rehearsal of an item is terminated, the item soon will be displaced by a new incoming item and thus be lost from short-term memory. (After Atkinson & Shiffrin, 1971; © 1971 by Scientific American, Inc. All rights reserved.)*

score higher than others on reading comprehension tests (Daneman & Carpenter, 1981). Other work shows that the readability of text depends partly on the likelihood that relevant connecting material is still in short-term memory (Miller & Kintsch, 1980; Malt, 1985).

Short-term memory also seems to be involved in the everyday thinking we do about other people. In research on personality, for example, when subjects are asked to form an impression of someone on the basis of one meeting, they tend to describe the person in terms of roughly 7 ± 2 traits (Mischel, 1968). It is as if the capacity of short-term memory, 7 ± 2, places a limit on the number of ideas or impressions we can entertain at one time.

Chunking

In the preceding discussion, we considered only short-term memory, but in real life, both short-term and long-term memory often play a role in the same situation. One particularly important interaction between short-term and long-term memory is the phenomenon of *chunking,* which can occur in memory-span tasks.

Recall that in a memory-span task, subjects can repeat a sequence of verbal items in perfect order as long as the number of items is 7 ± 2. As a result, you would probably be unable to repeat the letter sequence SRUOYYLERECNIS since it contains 14 letters. Should you notice, however, that these letters spell the familiar phrase SINCERELY YOURS in reverse order, your task would become easier. By using this knowledge, you have decreased the number of items that must be held in short-term memory from 14 to 2. But where did this spelling knowledge come from? From long-term memory, of course, where knowledge about words is stored. Thus, you can use long-term memory to recode new material into larger meaningful units and then store those units in short-term memory. Such units are called *chunks,* and the capacity of short-term memory is best expressed as 7 ± 2 chunks (Miller, 1956).

Sometimes we can chunk letters without forming words when the letters stand for some meaningful (but nonword) unit. The letter string IB-MFB-ITVU-SA is hard to recall. But suppose the spacing is changed so that the string reads IBM-FBI-TV-USA. Each component is now a familiar unit. The result is four chunks and a string that is easy to remember (Bower & Springston, 1970). Chunking can occur with numbers as well. The string 149-2177-619-87 is beyond our capacity, but 1492-1776-1987 is well within it. The general principle is that we can boost our short-term memory by regrouping sequences of letters and digits into units that can be found in long-term memory.

Transfer From Short-term to Long-term Memory

DUAL-MEMORY THEORY If information is to persist, it must be transferred from short-term to long-term memory. A number of theories about this transfer have been advanced. One such proposal, called *dual-memory theory*, illustrates the ideas involved (Atkinson & Shiffrin, 1971, 1977).

This theory assumes that information we have attended to enters short-term memory, wherein it can be either maintained by rehearsal or lost by displacement or decay (see Figure 8-7). In addition, in order for information to be encoded into long-term memory, it must be transferred there from short-term memory. This assumption implies that we can learn something (encode it in long-term memory) only by first processing it in short-term memory. What about the transfer processes themselves? While there are a number of different ways to implement the transfer, one of the most commonly investigated is rehearsal. As the diagram in Figure 8-7 suggests, rehearsing an item not only maintains it in short-term memory but also causes it to be transferred to long-term memory.

Some of the best support for the dual-memory theory comes from experiments on *free recall*. In a free-recall experiment, subjects first see a list of, say, 20 or 40 unrelated words, which are presented one at a time. After all the words have been presented, subjects must immediately recall them in any order (hence the designation "free"). The results from such an experiment are shown in Figure 8-8A. The chance of correctly recalling a word is graphed as a function of the word's position in the list. The part of the curve to the left in the graph is for the first few words presented, whereas the part to the right is for the last few words presented.

The dual-memory theory assumes that at the time of recall the last few words presented are still likely to be in short-term memory, whereas the remaining words are in long-term memory. Hence, we would expect recall of the last few words to be high, because items in short-term memory can easily be retrieved. Figure 8-8A shows this is the case. But recall for the first words presented is also quite good. Why is this? Dual-memory theory has an answer. When the first words were presented, they were entered into short-term memory and rehearsed. Since there was little else in short-term memory, they were rehearsed often and were therefore likely to be transferred to long-term memory. As more items were presented, short-term memory quickly filled up, and the opportunity to rehearse and transfer any given item to long-term memory decreased to a low level. So, only the first few items presented enjoyed the extra opportunity of transfer, which is why they were later recalled so well from long-term memory.

Varying the procedure of the free-recall experiment produces results that support the preceding analysis. Suppose that after the list is presented but before subjects try to recall it they do arithmetic problems for 30 seconds. Doing arithmetic requires short-term memory capacity and should therefore displace many of the list words that are in short-term memory (the last words presented). Figure 8-8B shows that, as expected, the last few words were displaced.

The rate at which the words are presented should also affect recall. A slower rate of presentation—for instance, a word every two seconds instead of every second—will allow more time for rehearsal and, hence, for transfer to long-term memory. The slower rate should therefore boost recall for the words that have to be retrieved from long-term memory—that is, all words but the last few. The results of this variation, shown in Figure 8-8C, again conform to predictions. The slower rate improved recall for all but the last few words.

PROBLEMS FOR THE THEORY Although the dual-memory theory has successfully accounted for a wide range of phenomena, it does not answer some

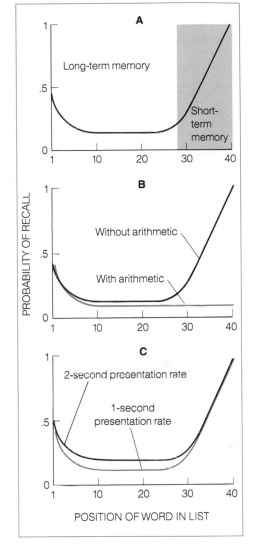

FIGURE 8-8
Curves of Free-recall Experiments
Probability of recall varies with an item's position in a list, with the probability being highest for the last five or so positions, next highest for the first few positions, and lowest for the intermediate positions. Recall of the last few items is based on short-term memory, whereas recall of the remaining items is based on long-term memory (A). If an arithmetic task occurs between the list presentation and free recall, only recall from short-term memory is reduced (B). Slower presentation of items results in better recall from long-term memory (C). (After Murdock, 1962; and Glanzer, 1972)

"Can we hurry up and get to the test? My short-term memory is better than my long-term memory."

© 1985, reprinted courtesy of Bill Hoest and *Parade* Magazine.

questions (Craik & Lockhart, 1972). One major dispute concerns rehearsal. The dual-memory theory assumes that rehearsal can transfer information to permanent memory. That is, simply repeating words to yourself, with no attempt to organize them or relate them to other memories, should increase your long-term recall. While some experiments support this prediction (Nelson, 1977), others do not (Craik & Watkins, 1973). Indeed, some psychologists have suspected for a long time that simple rehearsal is not an effective means for transferring information to long-term memory. Three-quarters of a century ago, the psychologist E. C. Sanford noted that his reading a group of five morning prayers aloud almost every day for 25 years (at least 5,000 repetitions) did not succeed in implanting the prayers in permanent memory. When Sanford tested his memory by cueing himself with a word from a prayer to see how much of the litany he could recall, he found that for some of the prayers he could not even recall three words per cue. That is not much memory for two and a half decades of rehearsal (Sanford, 1917; cited in Neisser, 1982).

Another challenge for dual-memory theory involves the free-recall evidence for the theory. When presenting this evidence, we noted that recall was particularly good for the most recently presented items and assumed that this *recency effect* was due to the words still being in short-term memory. However, a recency effect does not necessarily implicate short-term memory, because such an effect can arise even when recall is from long-term memory. For example, when soccer players were asked at the end of a season to free-recall all their rivals, recall was best for the last few competitors. This recency effect cannot possibly reflect short-term memory because the recall occurred weeks after the games. Rather, this effect probably results from searching long-term memory chronologically (Baddeley & Hitch, 1977). Perhaps the same is true of the recency effect in the free-recall studies described earlier. Thus, the existence of a long-term memory recency effect dilutes the evidence for the dual-memory model.

LONG-TERM MEMORY

Long-term memory involves information that has been retained for intervals as brief as a few minutes (such as a point made earlier in a conversation) or as long as a lifetime (such as an adult's childhood memories). In experiments on long-term memory, psychologists generally have studied forgetting over intervals of minutes, hours, or weeks, but a few studies have involved years or even decades.

Our discussion of long-term memory will again distinguish between the three stages of memory — encoding, storage, and retrieval — but this time there are two complications. First, unlike the situation in short-term memory, important interactions between encoding and retrieval occur in long-term memory. In view of these interactions, we will consider some aspects of retrieval in our discussion of encoding and will present a separate discussion of encoding-retrieval interactions. The other complication is that it is often difficult to know whether forgetting from long-term memory is due to a loss from storage or a failure in retrieval. To deal with this problem, we will delay our discussion of storage until after we have considered retrieval, so that we will have a clearer idea of what constitutes good evidence for a storage loss.

Encoding

ENCODING MEANING   For verbal materials, the dominant long-term memory representation is neither acoustic nor visual; instead, it is based on the meanings of the items. If you memorize a long list of unrelated words and try to recall them an hour later, you will undoubtedly make errors. Many of the erroneous words, however, will be similar in meaning to the correct ones. For example, if "quick" is on the original list, you may mistakenly recall "fast" instead (Kintsch & Buschke, 1969). Encoding items according to their meanings is more striking when the items are sentences. Several minutes after hearing a sentence, most of what is left in memory is its meaning. Suppose you heard the sentence, "The author sent the committee a long letter." Two minutes later you could not tell whether you had heard that sentence or one that has the same meaning: "A long letter was sent to the committee by the author" (Sachs, 1967).

Encoding meaning is pervasive in real life. When people report on complex social or political situations, they may misremember many of the specifics (who said what to whom, when something was said, who else was there) yet can accurately describe the basic situation that took place. Thus, in the famous Watergate scandal of the early 1970s, the chief government witness (John Dean) was subsequently shown to have made many mistakes about what was said and done in particular situations, yet his overall testimony accurately described the events that had taken place (Neisser, 1981).

ADDING MEANINGFUL CONNECTIONS   Often the items we have to remember are meaningful but the connections between them are not. In such cases, memory can be improved by creating real or artificial links between the items. For example, people learning to read music must remember that the five lines in printed music are referred to as EGBDF; although the symbols themselves are meaningful (they refer to notes on a keyboard), their order seems arbitrary. What many learners do is convert the symbols into the sentence "Every Good Boy Does Fine"; the first letter of each word names each symbol, and the relations between the words in the sentence supply meaningful connections between the symbols. These connections aid memory because they provide retrieval paths between the words: once the word "Good" has been retrieved, for example, there is a path or connection to "Boy," the next word that has to be recalled.

Numerous experiments have shown that adding meaningful connections is a powerful memory aid. In one study, subjects were asked to memorize a long list of unrelated word pairs. Later, when given the first item of a pair (the *stimulus*), the subjects were required to supply the second term (the *response*). If "horse-table" was one pair on the list to be memorized, subjects had to respond "table" when later tested with the stimulus term "horse." The relationship between the terms in each pair was arbitrary. One group of subjects was instructed to memorize each pair by thinking of a sentence that used both terms. For example, for the "horse-table" pair, they might think of the sentence "The horse kicked the table." Each sentence thus related the items in a meaningful way, which presumably set up a retrieval path between them. A second group, the control group, was left to its own devices to learn the list. The group instructed to think of sentences recalled about 75 percent of the word pairs, whereas the control group recalled only 35 percent (Bower, 1972).

Making sentences out of unrelated letters or words is not the only means of adding meaningful connections to verbal materials. Another way is to use imagery. In a variation of the experiment just described, the first group was instructed to memorize each pair by forming a visual image that related the two words — for example, an image of a horse jumping over a table. In this experiment, too, the first group recalled roughly twice as much as the control group. Thus, using either images or sentences to add meaningful connections increases the number of retrieval paths between the words; this in turn improves memory.

Although meaning may be the dominant way of representing verbal material in long-term memory, we sometimes code other aspects as well. We can, for example, memorize poems and recite them word for word. In such cases, we have coded not only the meaning of the poem but the words themselves. We can also use an acoustic code in long-term memory. When you get a phone call and the other party says "hello," you often recognize the voice. To do this, you must have coded the sound of that person's voice in long-term memory. Visual impressions, tastes, and smells are also coded in long-term memory. Thus, like short-term memory, long-term memory has a preferred code for verbal material (namely, meaning for long-term memory and acoustic for short-term memory), but other codes can be used as well.

ELABORATIONS Not only does coding by meaning result in the best recall, the more deeply or elaborately one encodes the meaning, the better memory will be. If you have to remember a point made in a textbook, you will recall it better if you concentrate on its meaning rather than on the exact words. And the more deeply and thoroughly you expand on its meaning, the better you will recall it.

An experiment by Bradshaw and Anderson (1982) illustrates some of these points. Subjects read facts about famous people that they would later have to recall, such as "At a critical point in his life, Mozart made a journey from Munich to Paris." Some facts were elaborated by either their causes or consequences, as in "Mozart wanted to leave Munich to avoid a romantic entanglement." Other facts were presented alone. When subjects were later tested for memory, they recalled more facts that were given elaborations than those presented alone. Presumably, in adding the cause (or consequence) to their memory representation, subjects set up a retrieval path from the cause to the target fact in the following manner:

Mozart journeyed from Munich to Paris

Mozart wanted to avoid romantic entanglement in Munich

At the time of recall, subjects could retrieve the target fact directly, or indirectly by following the path from its cause. Even if they forgot the target fact entirely, they could infer it if they retrieved the cause.

Material as complex as a textbook chapter also benefits from elaboration. This has been demonstrated in an experiment where subjects had to read part of a text and later answer questions about the material. Prior to reading the text, one group of subjects was given a set of advance questions (which were different from the test questions they would later be asked). These subjects were to find answers to the advance questions while reading the text. Trying to find these answers should have led the subjects to elaborate on parts of the text as it was being read. A control group of subjects studied the text without any advance questions. When both groups were later given the test questions, the first group answered more correctly than the control group. Again, an experimental technique that fostered elaboration enhanced memory (Frase, 1975; Anderson, 1985).

Retrieval

Many cases of forgetting from long-term memory result from a loss of access to the information rather than from a loss of the information itself. That is, poor memory often reflects a retrieval failure rather than a storage failure. (Note that this is unlike short-term memory, where forgetting is a result of exceeding the storage capacity, while retrieval is thought to be error free.) Trying to retrieve an item from long-term memory is analogous to trying to find a book in a large library. Failure to find the book does not necessarily mean it is not there; you may be looking in the wrong place, or it may simply be misfiled and therefore inaccessible.

EVIDENCE FOR RETRIEVAL FAILURES   Common experience provides much evidence for retrieval failures. Everyone at some point has been unable to recall a fact or an experience, only to have it come to mind later. How many times have you taken an exam and not been able to recall a specific name or date, only to remember it after the exam? Another example is the "tip-of-the-tongue" experience in which a particular word or name lies tantalizingly outside our ability to recall it (Brown & McNeill, 1966). We may feel quite tormented until a search of memory (dredging up and then discarding words that are close but not quite right) finally retrieves the correct word.

A more striking example of retrieval failure is the occasional recovery by a person under hypnosis of a childhood memory that had previously been forgotten. Similar experiences may occur in psychotherapy. Although we lack firm evidence for some of these observations, they at least suggest that some seemingly forgotten memories are not lost. They are just difficult to get at and require the right kind of *retrieval cue* (anything that can help us retrieve a memory).

For stronger evidence that retrieval failures can cause forgetting, consider the following experiment. Subjects were asked to memorize a long list of words. Some of the words were names of animals, such as dog, cat, horse; some named specific fruits, such as apple, pear, orange; some named items of furniture, and so on (see Table 8-1). At the time of recall, the subjects were divided into two groups. One group was supplied with retrieval cues such as "animal," "fruit," and so on; the other group, the control group, was not. The group given the retrieval cues recalled more words than the control group. In a subsequent test, when both groups were given the retrieval cues, they recalled the same number of words. Hence, the initial difference in recall between the two groups must have been due to retrieval failures.

Thus, the better the retrieval cues, the better our memory. This principle explains why we usually do better on a recognition test of memory than on a recall test. In a recognition test, we are asked if we have seen a particular item before (for example, "Was Harry Smith one of the people you met at the party?"). The test item itself is an excellent retrieval cue for our memory of that item. In contrast, in a recall test we have to produce the memorized items with minimal retrieval cues (for example, "Recall the names of everyone you met at the party."). Since the retrieval cues in a recognition test are generally more useful than those in a recall test, recognition tests usually show better memory performance than recall tests (Tulving, 1974).

INTERFERENCE   Among the factors that can impair retrieval, the most important is *interference*. If we associate different items with the same cue, when we try to use that cue to retrieve one of the items (the target item), the other items may come to mind and interfere with our recovery of the target. For example, if your friend, Dan, moves and you finally learn his new phone number, you will find it difficult to retrieve the old number. Why? You are using the cue "Dan's phone number" to retrieve the old number, but instead this cue activates the new number, which interferes with recovery of the old one. Or suppose that your reserved space in a parking garage, which you have used for a year, is changed. You may initially find it difficult to retrieve from memory your new parking location. Why? You are trying to learn to associate your new location with the cue "my parking place," but this cue retrieves the old location, which interferes with

William James Writing in 1890
"Suppose we try to recall a forgotten name. The state of our consciousness is peculiar. There is a gap therein; but no mere gap. It is a gap that is intensely active. A sort of wraith of the name is in it, beckoning us in a given direction, making us at moments tingle with the sense of our closeness and then letting us sink back without the longed-for term. If wrong names are proposed to us, this singularly definite gap acts immediately so as to negate them. They do not fit into its mold. And the gap of one word does not feel like the gap of another, all empty of content as both might seem necessarily to be when described as gaps." (James, 1890)

TABLE 8-1

Examples From a Study of Retrieval Failures   *Subjects not given the retrieval cues recall fewer words from the memorized list than other subjects who did have the cues. This finding shows that problems at the retrieval stage of long-term memory are responsible for some memory failures. (After Tulving & Pearlstone, 1966)*

LIST TO BE MEMORIZED		
dog	cotton	oil
cat	wool	gas
horse	silk	coal
cow	rayon	wood
apple	blue	doctor
orange	red	lawyer
pear	green	teacher
banana	yellow	dentist
chair	knife	football
table	spoon	baseball
bed	fork	basketball
sofa	pan	tennis
knife	hammer	shirt
gun	saw	socks
rifle	nails	pants
bomb	screwdriver	shoes

RETRIEVAL CUES		
animals	cloth	fuels
fruit	color	professions
furniture	utensils	sports
weapons	tools	clothing

the learning of the new one. In both examples, the power of retrieval cues ("Dan's phone number" or "my parking place") to activate particular target items decreases with the number of other items associated with those cues. The more items associated with a cue, the more overloaded it becomes and the less effectively it can retrieve.

Interference can operate at various levels, including that of facts. In one experiment, subjects first learned to associate various facts with the names of professions. For example, they learned that:

1. The banker was asked to address the crowd.
2. The banker broke the bottle.
3. The banker did not delay the trip.
4. The lawyer realized the seam was split.
5. The lawyer painted an old barn.

The occupational names "banker" and "lawyer" were the retrieval cues here. Since "banker" was associated with three facts, whereas "lawyer" was associated with just two, "banker" should have been less useful in retrieving any one of its associated facts than "lawyer" was ("banker" was the more overloaded retrieval cue). When subjects were later given a recognition test, they did take longer to recognize the facts learned about the banker than those learned about the lawyer. In this study, then, interference slowed the speed of retrieval. Many other experiments show that interference can lead to a complete retrieval failure if the target items are very weak or the interference is very strong (Anderson, 1983).

These interference effects suggest that retrieval from long-term memory involves a search process. To illustrate, consider how a sentence from the preceding study, "The banker broke the bottle," might be recognized. The term

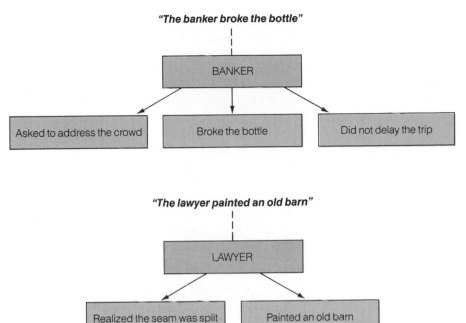

"The banker broke the bottle"

BANKER

Asked to address the crowd | Broke the bottle | Did not delay the trip

"The lawyer painted an old barn"

LAWYER

Realized the seam was split | Painted an old barn

FIGURE 8-9
Illustration of Retrieval as a Search Process *When presented the sentence, "The banker broke the bottle," the term "banker" accesses the banker representation in long-term memory; once at this representation, there are three paths to be searched. When presented "The lawyer painted an old barn," "lawyer" accesses the lawyer representation, from which there are two paths to be searched. Alternatively, the term "banker" may activate the banker representation, where this activation then spreads simultaneously along the three paths (and similarly for the "lawyer" example).*

"banker" accesses its representation in memory, which localizes the search to the relevant "part" of long-term memory (see Figure 8-9). Once there, three paths need to be searched to find the fact "broke the bottle." In contrast, if the test sentence was "The lawyer painted an old barn," there are only two paths to be searched (see Figure 8-9). Since the duration of a search increases with the number of paths to be considered, retrieval will be slower for the "banker" sentence than the "lawyer" one. Retrieval generally is more difficult when more facts are associated with a retrieval cue, because each fact adds a path to be searched.

An alternative way to think about the search process is in terms of activation. When trying to recognize "The banker broke the bottle," for example, the subject activates the representation for "banker," which then spreads simultaneously along the three paths emanating from "banker" (see Figure 8-9). When sufficient activation reaches "broke the bottle," the sentence can be recognized. Interference arises because the activation from the banker representation must be subdivided among the paths emanating from it. Hence, the more facts associated with "banker," the thinner the activation on each path, and the longer it will take for sufficient activation to reach any particular fact. So, thinking of retrieval in terms of spreading activation can also account for why interference slows retrieval (Anderson, 1983).

Storage

Retrieval failures are unlikely to be the only cause of forgetting. The fact that *some* forgetting is due to retrieval failures does not imply that *all* forgetting is. It seems most unlikely that everything we ever learned is still there in memory waiting for the right retrieval cue. Some information is almost certainly lost from storage (Loftus & Loftus, 1980).

Direct evidence of storage loss comes from people who receive *electroconvulsive shock* to alleviate severe depression (a mild electric current applied to the brain produces a brief epileptic-like seizure and momentary unconsciousness; see Chapter 16, p. 555). In such cases, the patient loses some memory for events that occurred in the months prior to the shock, but not for earlier events (Squire &

Fox, 1980). Memory loss due to electroconvulsive shock has been demonstrated with animal subjects in the laboratory (though with rats, the memory loss covers a period of minutes rather than months [McGaugh & Herz, 1972]). These memory losses are unlikely to be due to retrieval failures, because if the shock disrupted retrieval, then all memories should be affected, not just the more recent ones. More likely, the shock disrupts storage processes that *consolidate* new memories over a period of months or longer, and information that is not consolidated is lost from storage.

Psychologists have made some progress in determining the physiological basis of consolidation. The *hippocampus,* a brain structure located below the cerebral cortex, is clearly involved. Its role in consolidation seems to be that of a cross-referencing system, linking together aspects of a particular memory that are stored in separate parts of the brain (Squire, Cohen, & Nadel, 1984). The hippocampus, however, is not the place where memories are ultimately stored, for when it is removed, old memories are left intact. Rather, the locus of long-term storage is almost certainly the cortex.

Encoding-Retrieval Interactions

In describing the encoding stage, we noted that operations carried out during encoding (for instance, elaboration) later make retrieval easier. Two other encoding factors also increase the chances of successful retrieval: (1) organizing the information at the time of encoding and (2) ensuring that the context in which information is encoded is similar to that in which it will be retrieved.

ORGANIZATION   The more we organize the material we encode, the easier it is to retrieve. Suppose you were at a conference where you met various professionals — doctors, lawyers, and journalists. When you later try to recall their names, you will do better if you initially organize the information by profession. Then you can ask yourself, Who were the doctors I met? Who were the lawyers? And so forth. A list of names or words is far easier to recall when we encode the information into categories and then retrieve it on a category-by-category basis.

The following experiment illustrates the use of categories in organizing encoding. The subjects were asked to memorize lists of words. For some subjects, the words in a list were arranged in the form of a hierarchical tree, much like the example shown in Figure 8-10. For the other subjects, the words were arranged

FIGURE 8-10
Hierarchical Organization to Improve Retrieval   *Trees like this are constructed according to the following rule: all items below a node are included in the class labeled by that node. For example, the items "bronze," "steel," and "brass" are included in the class labeled "alloys." (After Bower, Clark, Winzenz, & Lesgold, 1969)*

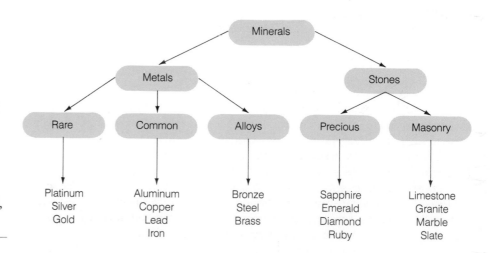

randomly. When tested later, the subjects presented with the hierarchical organization recalled 65 percent of the words, whereas the subjects presented with random arrangements recalled only 19 percent of the same words. Studies like this leave little doubt that memory is best when the material is highly organized.

Why does hierarchical organization improve memory? Probably because it makes the search process underlying retrieval more efficient. To illustrate, suppose that subjects in the preceding experiment used a serial search. Subjects who had seen the words hierarchically organized, as in Figure 8-10, might have proceeded as follows: first they found a high-level cluster, such as "metals"; from that high-level cluster, they then searched for a low-level cluster, such as "common metals"; and then they searched that low-level cluster for specific words ("aluminum," "copper," "lead," "iron,"); and so on. By operating in this way, at no point would subjects have to search a large set. There are only two high-level clusters, never more than three low-level clusters connected to a high-level one, and never more than four specific words in a low-level cluster. Hierarchical organization thus allows us to divide a big search into a sequence of little ones. And with a little search, there is less chance we will bog down by turning up the same words again and again, which is exactly what seems to happen when we search material that is not organized (Raaijmakers & Shiffrin, 1981; Gillund & Shiffrin, 1984).

Organization can also offset the detrimental effects of interference. In the experiment where subjects memorized such facts as "The banker was asked to address the crowd," "The banker broke the bottle," and "The banker did not delay the trip," subjects took longer to recognize one of these three facts than they did to recognize one of two facts learned about some other occupation term. This interference effect can be eliminated by organizing the facts. Thus, if the first sentence is replaced by "The banker was asked to christen the ship," the "banker" facts will be integrated around the theme of christening a ship. Now, subjects take no longer to recognize one of the three facts about the banker than one of the two learned about some other occupation; organization has offset interference (Smith, Adams, & Schorr, 1978).

CONTEXT It is easier to retrieve a particular episode if you are in the same context in which you encoded it (Estes, 1972). For example, it is a good bet that your ability to retrieve the names of your classmates in the first and second grades would improve were you to walk through the corridors of your elementary school. Similarly, your ability to retrieve, say, an emotional moment with your parents would be greater if you were back in the place where the incident occurred. This may explain why we are sometimes overcome with a torrent of memories about our earlier life when we visit a place we once lived. The context in which an event was encoded is itself one of the most powerful retrieval cues possible, and a mass of experimental evidence supports this (see Figure 8-11 for a representative study).

Context is not always external to the memorizer, such as a physical location or a specific face. What is happening inside of us when we encode information — our internal state — is also part of context. To take an extreme example, if we experience an event while under the influence of a particular drug (for instance, alcohol or marijuana), perhaps we can best retrieve it when we are again in that drug-induced state. In such cases, memory would be partly dependent on the internal state during learning; we call this *state-dependent learning*. While the evidence on state-dependent learning is controversial, it suggests that memory does indeed improve when our internal state during retrieval matches that during encoding (Eich, Weingartner, Stillman, & Gillian, 1975).

FIGURE 8-11

Effects of Context on Retrieval *In an experiment to demonstrate how context affects retrieval, subjects first studied pairs of faces like the one at the top. (Since only the right-hand face was ever tested, it was the* **test** *face, whereas the left-hand one was the* **context** *face.) Later, in a memory test, subjects were again shown pairs of faces and asked whether the test face (the one on the right) was one they had previously studied. In some cases, the context face was the same one that had appeared in the original pair; in other cases, it was not. Subjects made more accurate decisions when the context face was the same. (After Watkins, Ho, & Tulving, 1976)*

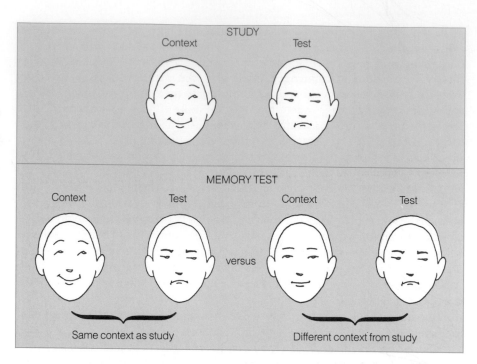

Emotional Factors in Forgetting

So far, we have treated memory as if it were divorced from the emotional part of our lives. But don't we sometimes fail to remember material because of its emotional content? There has been a great deal of research on this question. The results suggest that emotion can influence long-term memory in at least four distinct ways.

The simplest idea is that we tend to think about emotionally charged situations, negative as well as positive, more than we think about neutral ones. We rehearse and organize exciting memories more than we do their blander counterparts. For example, you may forget where you saw this or that movie, but if a fire breaks out while you are in a theater, you will describe the setting over and over to friends, thereby rehearsing and organizing it. Since we know that rehearsal and organization can improve retrieval from long-term memory, it is not surprising that many researchers have found better memory for emotional than for unemotional situations (Rapaport, 1942).

In some cases, however, negative emotions hinder retrieval. An experience that many students have at one time or another illustrates this:

> You are taking an exam about which you are not very confident. You can barely understand the initial question, let alone answer it. Signs of panic appear. Although the second question really isn't hard, the anxiety triggered by the previous question spreads to this one. By the time you look at the third question, it wouldn't matter if it just asked for your name. There's no way you can answer it. You're in a complete panic.

What is happening to memory here? Failure to deal with the first question produced anxiety. Anxiety is often accompanied by extraneous thoughts, such as "I'm going to flunk out" or "Everybody will know how stupid I am." These thoughts then interfere with any attempt to retrieve the information relevant to the question, and that may be why memory utterly fails. According to this view, anxiety does not directly cause memory failure; rather, it causes, or is associated with, extraneous thoughts, and these thoughts cause memory failure by interfering with retrieval (Holmes, 1974).

Emotion may also affect memory by *context effects*. As we have noted, memory is best when the context at retrieval matches that at encoding. Since our emotional state during learning is part of the context, if we feel sad when we learn some material, then we can best retrieve that material when we feel sad again. Experimenters have demonstrated such an emotional-context effect in the laboratory. Subjects agreed to keep diaries for a week, recording daily every emotional incident that occurred and noting whether it was pleasant or unpleasant. One week after they handed in their diaries, the subjects returned to the laboratory and were hypnotized (they had been preselected to be highly hypnotizable). Half the subjects were put in a pleasant mood, and the other half were put in an unpleasant mood. All were asked to recall the incidents recorded in their diaries. For subjects in a pleasant mood, most of the incidents they recalled had been rated as pleasant when experienced; for subjects in an unpleasant mood at retrieval, most of the incidents recalled had been rated as unpleasant when experienced. As expected, recall was best when the dominant emotion during retrieval matched that during encoding (Bower, 1981).

We have considered three means by which emotion can influence memory, each relying on principles already discussed—namely, rehearsal, interference, and context effects. The fourth view of emotion and memory, Freud's theory of the unconscious, brings up new principles. Freud proposed that some emotional experiences in childhood are so traumatic that allowing them to enter consciousness many years later would cause the individual to be totally overwhelmed by anxiety. (This is different from the example of the exam, where the anxiety was tolerable to consciousness.) Such traumatic experiences, as well as later ones associated with them, are said to be stored in the unconscious, or *repressed;* and they can be retrieved only when some of the emotion associated with them is defused, usually by therapeutic means. Repression, therefore, represents the ultimate retrieval failure: access to the target memories is actively blocked. This notion of active blocking makes the *repression hypothesis* qualitatively different from the views we considered earlier. (For a fuller discussion of Freud's theory, see Chapter 14.)

Repression is such a striking phenomenon that we would of course like to study it in the laboratory, but this has proved difficult to do. To induce true repression in the laboratory, the experimenter must have the subject experience something extremely traumatic; ethical considerations prohibit this. The studies that have been done have exposed subjects to only mildly upsetting experiences. The bulk of the evidence from these studies lends some support to the repression hypothesis (Erdelyi, 1985).

"And then I say to myself, 'If I really wanted to talk to her, why do I keep forgetting to dial 1 first?'"

Drawing by Modell; © 1981 *The New Yorker Magazine,* Inc.

Amnesia: Breakdown of Memory

We have learned a great deal about memory from people who have suffered *amnesia*. Amnesia refers to a partial or total loss of memory. It may result from very different causes, including accidental injuries to the brain, strokes, encephalitis, alcoholism, electroconvulsive shock, and surgical procedures (for example, removal of the hippocampus to reduce epilepsy). Whatever its cause, the primary symptom of amnesia is a profound inability to acquire *new* information or to remember day-to-day events; this is referred to as *anterograde amnesia,* and it can be very extensive. There are cases of amnesiacs who have spent years in the same hospital but have never learned their way to the bathroom. There is an intensively studied patient, identified as NA, who is unable to participate in a normal conversation because he loses his train of thought with the least distraction.

CRITICAL DISCUSSION

Childhood Amnesia

One of the most striking aspects of human memory is that everyone suffers from a particular kind of amnesia: virtually no person can recall events from the first years of life, though this is the time when experience is at its richest. This curious phenomenon was first discussed by Freud (1948), who called it *childhood amnesia.*

Freud discovered the phenomenon by observing that his patients were generally unable to recall events from their first three to five years of life. At first you might think there is nothing unusual about this, because memory for events declines with time, and for adults there has been a lot of intervening time since early childhood. But childhood amnesia cannot be reduced to a case of normal forgetting. Most 30-year-olds can recall a good deal about their high school years, but it is a rare 18-year-old that can tell you anything about his third year of life; yet the time interval is roughly the same in the two cases (about 15 years). More rigorous evidence along these lines comes from a study where 18-year-old subjects tried to recall personal memories from all periods of their lives. Memory for an event, of course, declined with the number of years that had passed since that event, but the *rate* of decline was much steeper for events in the first six years of life than for events thereafter (Wetzler & Sweeney, cited in Rubin, 1986).

In other studies, people have been asked to recall and date their childhood memories. For most subjects, their first memory is of something that occurred when they were age 3 or older; a few subjects, however, will report memories prior to the age of 1. A problem with these reports, however, is that we can never be sure that the "remembered" event actually occurred (the person may have reconstructed what he or she thought happened). This problem was overcome in an experiment in which subjects were asked a total of 20 questions about a childhood event that was known to have occurred—the birth of a younger sibling—the details of which could be verified by another person. The questions asked of each subject dealt with events that transpired during the mother's leaving for the hospital (for example, "What time of day did she leave?"), when the mother was in the hospital ("Did you visit her?"), and when the mother and infant returned home ("What time of day did she come back?"). The subjects were college students, and their ages at the birth of their siblings varied from 1 to 17 years. The results are shown in Figure 8-12: the number of questions answered is plotted as a function of the subject's age when the sibling was born. If the sibling was born before the subject was 3 years old, the person could not recall a thing about it! If the birth occurred after that, recall increased with age at the time of the event. These results suggest an almost total amnesia for the first three years of life.

What causes childhood amnesia? Freud (1948) thought that it was due to the

Another patient identified as HM—the most intensively studied of all amnesiacs—reads the same magazines over and over and continually needs to be reintroduced to doctors who have been treating him for more than two decades.

A secondary symptom of amnesia is an inability to remember events that occurred *prior* to the injury or disease. The extent of such *retrograde amnesia* varies from patient to patient. Aside from retrograde and anterograde memory losses, the typical amnesiac appears normal: he or she has a normal vocabulary, the usual knowledge about the world, and in general shows no loss of intelligence.

EFFECTS ON DIFFERENT STAGES Do the memory losses in amnesia reflect a breakdown in a particular stage of memory or in all of them? The evidence indicates that each stage can be affected. Some patients show an encoding deficit. If they are allowed more time than normal subjects to encode the material in a recall task, their subsequent recall can equal that of normals. Other patients may exhibit retrieval and storage deficits. For some amnesiacs, memory loss for events prior to the injury or disease (retrograde amnesia) extends over the majority of

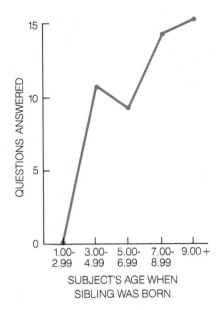

FIGURE 8-12
Recall of an Early Memory *In an experiment on childhood amnesia, college-age subjects were asked 20 questions about the events surrounding the birth of a younger sibling. The average number of questions answered is plotted as a function of the subject's age when the sibling was born. If the birth occurred before the fourth year of life, no subject could recall a thing about it; if the birth occurred after that, recall increased with age at the time of the event. (After Sheingold & Tenney, 1982)*

repression of sexual and aggressive feelings that a young child experiences toward his or her parents. But this account predicts amnesia for only events related to sexual and aggressive thoughts, when in fact childhood amnesia extends to all kinds of events. A more accepted explanation is that childhood amnesia is due to a massive difference between how young children encode experience and how adults organize their memories. Adults structure their memories in terms of categories and schemata ("She's that kind of person," "It's that kind of situation"), while young children encode their experiences without embellishing them or connecting them to related events. Once a child begins to form associations between events and to categorize those events, early experiences become lost (Schactel, 1947).

What causes the shift from early-childhood to adult forms of memory? One factor is biological development. The hippocampus, a brain structure involved in consolidating memories, is not mature until roughly a year or two after birth. Therefore, events that take place in the first two years of life cannot be sufficiently consolidated and consequently cannot be recalled later. Other causes of the shift to adult memory involve more cognitive factors, particularly the development of language and the beginning of schooling. Both language and the kind of thinking emphasized in school provide new ways of organizing experiences, ways that may be in-

compatible with how the young child encodes experiences. Interestingly, language development reaches an early peak at age 3, while schooling generally begins at age 5; and the age span from 3 to 5 is when childhood amnesia seems to end.

Organizational changes may not be the whole story of childhood amnesia. The difference between memory for skills and memory for facts may also play a role. Much of what we learn in infancy are skills, and they will not be represented in fact memory, which develops later. There is evidence for this hypothesis in studies with monkeys. Three-month-old monkeys can learn a "skill" task (really, a conditioning task) as readily as adult monkeys, but they cannot master a fact task that adults find easy (Mishkin, Malamut, & Bachevalier, 1984).

their lives. This loss must be due to retrieval failure, because events that occurred many years prior to the injury must have been normally encoded and consolidated. In contrast, in other patients, retrograde amnesia extends only over a period of months. Such a restricted memory loss suggests a disruption of the storage stage, because consolidation processes presumably require only a period of months (Hirst, 1982; Squire & Cohen, 1984).

It is possible that there are two distinct kinds of amnesia, each corresponding to a distinct site of brain damage and affecting different stages of memory. Thus, patients who have damage in their hippocampal regions may suffer primarily from a storage deficit; these are the patients whose retrograde amnesia is limited to relatively recent events. In contrast, a person with an intact hippocampus but a damaged thalamus may suffer from encoding and retrieval deficits; these are the patients whose retrograde amnesia is unlimited in time and whose recall of new information is relatively normal only if given extra encoding time. While the hypothesis that different kinds of amnesia are related to damage in different regions of the brain makes sense of the varied findings, it is quite controversial (Squire & Cohen, 1984; Corkin et al., 1985).

FACT VERSUS SKILL MEMORY   A striking aspect of amnesia is that not all kinds of memory are disrupted. Thus, while amnesiacs are generally unable to remember old facts about their lives or to learn new ones, they have no difficulty remembering and learning perceptual and motor skills. This suggests that there are different memories for facts and skills.

The skills preserved in amnesia include *motor skills,* such as tieing our shoelaces or riding a bike; *perceptual skills,* such as normal reading or reading words that are projected into a mirror (and hence reversed); and *cognitive skills,* such as defining a word or generating a word given only a fragment of its letters. Consider the ability of reading mirror-reversed words. To do this well takes a bit of practice (try holding this book in front of a mirror). Amnesiacs improve with practice at the very same rate as normal subjects, though they have no memory of having participated in prior practice sessions (Cohen & Squire, 1980). They show normal memory for the skill but virtually no memory for the learning episodes that developed it (the latter being *facts*).

A similar story emerges for cognitive skills, like that involved in word completion (for example, what word is *mot__?*). In one experiment, both amnesiac and normal subjects were first presented a list of words to study. Then fragments of words on the list and fragments of words not on the list were presented, and subjects tried to complete them. The normal subjects performed as expected, completing more words when the fragmented words were drawn from the list than when they were not, but interestingly, amnesiacs were also able to complete more words for fragments drawn from the list. In fact, the extent to which amnesiacs did better with fragments from the list than with fragments not on the list was the same as normal subjects. Hence, when memory is manifested in skill, amnesiacs perform normally. However, in another condition of the experiment, the original words were presented again along with some novel words, and subjects had to recognize which words had appeared on the list. Now, amnesiacs remembered far fewer than normals. Thus, when memory is manifested in "facts" ("This was one of the words that I saw on this list"), amnesiacs perform far below normals (Warrington & Weiskrantz, 1978).

The notion of different memories for skills and facts is not surprising once we reflect on how different these two kinds of knowledge are. Skill knowledge is "knowing how"; fact knowledge is "knowing that" (Ryle, 1949), and often the twain never meet. We know how to tie our shoelaces, for example, but we would have trouble describing it as a set of facts. The knowledge in a skill seems to be represented by the procedures needed to perform the skill, and such knowledge can be retrieved only by executing the procedures (Anderson, 1982).

PERSONAL-FACT VERSUS GENERAL-FACT MEMORY   Even within the domain of facts, there is an important distinction to be drawn. Some facts refer to personal episodes, while others are general truths. To illustrate, your memory of high school graduation is a *personal fact,* and so is your memory for what you had for dinner last night. Even your memory for a memory experiment you read about in which amnesiacs had to read mirror-reversed words is a personal fact. In each of these cases, the episode is encoded with respect to you the individual (your graduation, your dinner, and so on), and often the episode is coded with respect to a specific time and place as well. All of this is in contrast to *general facts,* examples of which include your memory, or knowledge, that the word "bachelor" means an unmarried man, that September has 30 days, and that Abraham Lincoln was president of the United States. In these cases, the knowledge is encoded in relation to other knowledge rather than in relation to yourself, and there is no coding of time and place. For example, you probably cannot remember much about the context in which you learned that February has 29 days every fourth year (Tulving, 1985).

Are personal facts and general facts stored in different memories? The very existence of amnesia suggests that they are. Aside from their severe memory loss, most amnesiacs seem to have normal intelligence. This implies they have a normal vocabulary and normal knowledge about the world, which in turn imply they are relatively normal with respect to general facts. In most forms of amnesia, then, memory for general facts is spared while memory for personal episodes is disrupted, suggesting that the two types of facts are indeed stored in different memories. In addition, specific experiments have shown that amnesiacs perform normally on tasks requiring the retrieval of general facts (Weingarten et al., 1983).

IMPROVING MEMORY

Having considered the basics of short-term and long-term memory, we are ready to tackle the question of improving memory. First, we will consider how to increase the short-term memory span. Then we will turn to a variety of methods for improving long-term memory; these methods work by increasing the efficiency of encoding and retrieval.

Chunking and Memory Span

For most of us, the capacity of short-term memory cannot be increased beyond 7 ± 2 chunks. However, we can enlarge the size of a chunk and thereby increase the number of items in our memory span. We demonstrated this point earlier: given the string 149-2177-619-87, we can recall all 12 digits if we recode the string into 1492-1776-1987 and then store just these three chunks in short-term memory. Although recoding digits into familiar dates works nicely in this example, it will not work with most digit strings because we have not memorized enough significant dates. But if a recoding system could be developed that worked with virtually *any* string, then short-term memory span could be dramatically improved.

There is a study of a particular subject who discovered such a general-purpose recoding system and used it to increase his memory span from 7 to almost 80 random digits (see Figure 8-13). The subject, referred to as SF, had average memory abilities and average intelligence for a college student. For a year and a half, he engaged in a memory-span task for about three to five hours per week. During this extensive practice, SF, a good long-distance runner, devised the strategy of recoding sets of four digits into running times. For example, SF would recode 3492 as "3:49.2—world class time for the mile," which for him was a single chunk. Since SF was familiar with many running times (that is, had them stored in long-term memory), he could readily chunk most sets of four digits. In those cases where he could not (1771 cannot be a running time because the second digit is too large), SF tried to recode the four digits into a familiar date.

Use of the above recoding systems enabled SF to increase his memory span from 7 to 28 digits (because each of SF's seven chunks contains 4 digits). But how did SF build to nearly 80 digits? By hierarchically organizing the running times. Thus, one chunk in SF's short-term memory might have pointed to three running times; at the time of recall, SF would go from this chunk to the first running time and produce its 4 digits, then move to the second running time in the chunk and produce its digits, and so on. One chunk was therefore worth 12 digits. Now we can see how SF could achieve his remarkable span of nearly 80 digits, the largest ever documented in the psychological literature. It was due to increasing the *size*

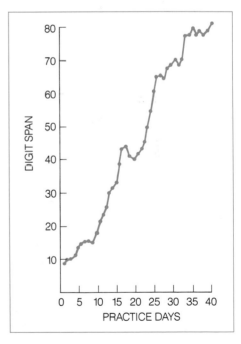

FIGURE 8-13
Number of Digits Recalled by SF *This subject greatly increased his memory span for digits by devising a recoding system using chunking and hierarchical organization. Total practice time was about 215 hours. (After Ericsson, Chase, & Faloon, 1980)*

FIGURE 8-14
A Mnemonic System *The method of loci aids memory by associating items (here, entries on a shopping list) with an ordered sequence of places.*

Caballo → eye → Horse

Pato → pot → Duck

FIGURE 8-15
Foreign Language Learning *Mental images can be used to associate spoken Spanish words with corresponding English words.*

of a chunk (by relating the items to information in long-term memory), not to increasing the *number* of chunks that short-term memory can hold. For when SF switched from digits to letters, his memory span went back to seven — that is, seven letters (Ericsson, Chase, & Faloon, 1980).

This research was among the first major projects to deal with improvement in a short-term memory task. In contrast, there has long been interest in how to improve long-term memory, which is the focus of the rest of this section. We will look first at how material can be encoded to make it easier to retrieve and then consider how the act of retrieval itself can be improved.

Imagery and Encoding

We mentioned earlier that recall for a word pair improved greatly when the two words were connected by an image. When we link the terms "horse" and "table" by an image, we establish a meaningful connection between them, which then serves as a retrieval path. Imagery, then, connects pieces of information in memory, and connections facilitate retrieval. This is the main principle behind many *mnemonic* (memory-aiding) systems.

One famous mnemonic system is called the *method of loci* (*loci* is Latin for "places"). The method works especially well with an ordered sequence of arbitrary items, like unrelated words. The first step is to commit to memory an ordered sequence of places, say the locations you would come upon in a slow walk through your house. You enter through the front door into a hallway, move next to the bookcase in the living room, then to the television in the living room, then to the curtains at the window, and so on. Once you can easily take this mental walk, you are ready to memorize as many unrelated words as there are locations on your walk. You form an image that relates the first word to the first location, another image that relates the second word to the second location, and so on. If the words are items on a shopping list — for example, "bread," "eggs," "beer," "milk," and "bacon" — you might imagine a slice of bread nailed to your front door, an egg hanging from the light cord in the hallway, a can of beer in the bookcase, a milk commercial playing on your television, and curtains made from giant strips of bacon (see Figure 8-14). Once you have memorized the items this way, you can easily recall them in order by simply taking your mental walk again. Each location will retrieve an image, and each image will retrieve a word. The method clearly works and is a favorite among those who perform memory feats professionally.

Imagery is also used in the *key-word method* of learning a foreign vocabulary. Suppose you had to learn that the Spanish word *caballo* means "horse." The key-word method has two steps. The first is to find a part of the foreign word that sounds like an English word. Since *caballo* is pronounced "cob-eye-yo," "eye" could serve as the key word. The next step is to form an image that connects the key word and the English equivalent — for example, a horse kicking a giant eye (see Figure 8-15). This should establish a meaningful connection between the Spanish and English words. To recall the meaning of *caballo,* you would first retrieve the key word "eye" and then the stored image that links it to "horse." Note that the key-word method can also be used to get from English words to Spanish words. If you want to recall the Spanish word for "horse," you would first retrieve the image involving a horse, thereby obtaining the key word "eye" that serves as a retrieval cue for *caballo.* The key-word method may sound complicated, but studies have shown that it greatly facilitates learning the vocabulary of a foreign language (Atkinson, 1975; Pressley, Levin, & Delaney, 1982).

Elaboration and Encoding

We have seen that the more we elaborate items, the more we remember. This phenomenon arises because the more connections we establish between items, the larger the number of retrieval possibilities. The practical implications of these findings are straightforward: if you want to remember something, expand on its meaning. To illustrate, suppose you read a newspaper article about an epidemic in Boston that health officials are trying to contain. To expand on this, you could ask yourself questions about the causes and consequences of the epidemic: Was the disease carried by a person or an animal? Was the disease transmitted through the water supply? To contain the epidemic, will officials go so far as to stop outsiders from visiting the city? How long is the epidemic likely to last? Questions about the causes and consequences of an event are particularly effective elaborations because each question sets up a meaningful connection, or retrieval path, to the event.

Context and Retrieval

Since context is a powerful retrieval cue, we can improve our memory by restoring the context in which the learning took place. If your psychology lecture always meets in one room, your memory for the lecture material will be best when you are in that room, because the context of the room is a retrieval cue for the lecture material. This has direct educational implications. Students will do better on exams when they are tested in their habitual classroom and when the proctor is their instructor than they will when these factors are changed (Abernathy, 1940).

Most often, though, when we have to remember something, we cannot physically return to the context in which we learned it. If you are having difficulty remembering the name of a particular high school classmate, you are not about to go back to your high school just to recall it. In these situations, however, you can try to re-create the context mentally. To retrieve the long-forgotten name, you might think of different classes, clubs, and other activities that you were in during high school to see if any of these bring to mind the name you are seeking. When subjects used these techniques in an actual experiment, they were often able to recall the names of high school classmates that they were sure had been forgotten (Williams & Hollan, 1981).

Another illustration of mentally re-creating context is as follows (adapted from Norman, 1976). Suppose someone asks you, "What were you doing at 1:00 P.M. on the third Monday of October two years ago?" "Ridiculous," you might say. "No one can remember things like that." But re-creating the context can lead to surprising results:

> Well, two years ago, I was a senior in high school; let me see, October—that's fall semester. Now what courses did I take that semester? Oh yes, chemistry. That's it—I had a chemistry lab every afternoon; that's where I was at 1:00 P.M. on the third Monday of October two years ago.

In this example, restoring the context seems to have done the trick. However, we cannot be sure that you actually remembered being in chemistry lab. Perhaps you inferred that you must have been there. Either way, though, you may come up with the right answer.

SPANISH	KEY WORD	ENGLISH
caballo	[eye]	horse
charco	[charcoal]	puddle
muleta	[mule]	crutch
clavo	[claw]	nail
lagartija	[log]	lizard
cebolla	[boy]	onion
payaso	[pie]	clown
hiio	[eel]	thread
tenaza	[tennis]	pliers
jabon	[bone]	soap
carpa	[carp]	tent
pato	[pot]	duck

Key-word Method *Examples of key words used to link Spanish words to their English translation. For example, when the Spanish word* **muleta** *is pronounced, part of it sounds like the English word "mule." Thus, "mule" could be used as the key word and linked to the English translation by forming an image of a mule standing erect on a crutch.*

Organization

We know that organization during encoding improves subsequent retrieval, presumably by making memory search more efficient. This principle can be put to great practical use: we are capable of storing and retrieving a massive amount of information if only we organize it.

Some experiments have investigated organizational devices that can be used to learn many unrelated items. In one study, subjects memorized lists of unrelated words by organizing the words in each list into a story, as illustrated in Figure 8-16. Later, when tested for 12 such lists (a total of 120 words), subjects recalled more than 90 percent of the words. This appears to be a truly remarkable memory feat, but anyone can easily do it.

At this point, you might concede that psychologists have devised some ingenious techniques for organizing lists of unrelated items. But, you argue, what you have to remember are not lists of unrelated items but stories you were told, lectures you have heard, and readings like the present chapter. Isn't this kind of material already organized, and doesn't this mean that the previously mentioned techniques are of limited value? Yes and no. Yes, this chapter is more than a list of unrelated words, but—and this is the critical point—there is always a problem of organization with any lengthy material, including this chapter. Later you may be able to recall that imagery aids learning, but this may not bring to mind anything about, say, acoustic coding in short-term memory. The two topics do not seem to be intimately related, but there is a relation between them: both deal with encoding phenomena. The best way to see that relationship is to note the headings and subheadings in the chapter, because these show how the material in the chapter is organized. A most effective way to study is to keep this organization in mind. You might, for example, try to capture part of this chapter's organization by sketching a hierarchical tree like the one shown below. Then you can use such a hierarchy to guide your memory search whenever you have to retrieve information about this chapter. It may be even more helpful, though, to make your own hierarchical outline of the chapter. Memory seems to benefit most when the organization is done by the rememberers themselves.

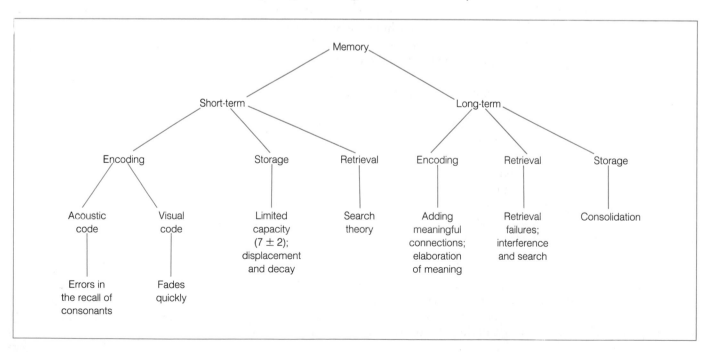

A LUMBERJACK DARTed out of a forest, SKATEd around a HEDGE past a COLONY of DUCKs. He tripped on some FURNITURE, tearing his STOCKING while hastening toward the PILLOW where his MISTRESS lay.

A VEGETABLE can be a useful INSTRUMENT for a COLLEGE student. A carrot can be a NAIL for your FENCE or BASIN. But a MERCHANT of the QUEEN would SCALE that fence and feed the carrot to a GOAT.

One night at DINNER I had the NERVE to bring my TEACHER. There had been a FLOOD that day, and the rain BARREL was sure to RATTLE. There was, however, a VESSEL in the HARBOR carrying this ARTIST to my CASTLE.

FIGURE 8-16
Organizing Words Into a Story *Three examples of turning a list of 10 unrelated words into a story. The capitalized items are the words on the list. (After Bower & Clark, 1969)*

Practicing Retrieval

Another way to improve retrieval is to practice it—that is, to ask yourself questions about what you are trying to learn. Suppose you have two hours in which to study an assignment that can be read in approximately 30 minutes. Reading and rereading the assignment four times is generally much less effective than reading it once and asking yourself questions about it. You can then reread selected parts to clear up points that were difficult to retrieve the first time around, perhaps elaborating these points so they become particularly well connected to each other and to the rest of the assignment. Attempting retrieval is an efficient use of study time. This was demonstrated long ago by experiments using unrelated items, as well as material like that actually learned in courses (see Figure 8-17).

PQRST Method

Thus far in this section, we have considered particular principles of memory (for example, the principle that organization aids memory search) and then shown their implications for improving memory. In establishing the practical application of memory principles, we can also go in the opposite direction. We can start with a well-known technique for improving memory and show how it is based on principles of memory.

One of the best-known techniques for improving memory, called the *PQRST method*, is intended to improve a student's ability to study and remember material presented in a textbook (Thomas & Robinson, 1982). The method takes its name from the first letters of its five stages: *Preview, Question, Read, Self-recitation*, and *Test*. We can illustrate the method by showing how it would apply to studying a chapter in this textbook. In the first stage, students preview the material in a chapter to get an idea of its major topics and sections. Previewing involves reading the table of contents at the beginning of the chapter, skimming the chapter while paying special attention to the headings of main sections and subsections, and carefully reading the summary at the end of the chapter. This kind of preview induces students to organize the chapter, perhaps even leading to the rudiments of a hierarchical organization like that just shown. As we have repeatedly noted, organizing material aids one's ability to retrieve it.

The second, third, and fourth stages (Question, Read, and Self-recitation) apply to each major section of the chapter as it is encountered. In this book, for example, a chapter typically has five to eight major sections, and students would

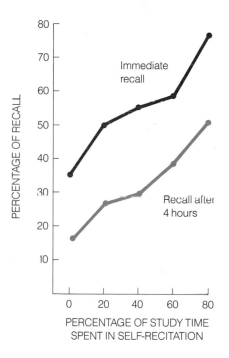

FIGURE 8-17
Practicing Retrieval *Recall can be improved by spending a large proportion of study time attempting retrieval rather than silently studying. Results are shown for tests given immediately and 4 hours after completing study. (After Gates, 1917)*

apply the Question, Read, and Self-recitation stages to each section before going on to the next one. In the Question stage, students carefully read the section and subsection headings and turn these into questions. In the Read stage, students read the section with an eye toward answering these questions. And in the Self-recitation stage, the reader tries to recall the main ideas in the section and recites the information (either subvocally or, preferably, aloud if alone). For example, if you were applying these stages to the present section of this chapter, you might look at the headings and make up such questions as "How much can the short-term memory span be increased?" or "What exactly is the PQRST method?" Next you would read this section and try to determine answers to your questions (for example, "One person was able to increase his short-term memory span to nearly 80 digits"). Then you would try to recall the main ideas (for example, "You can increase the size of a chunk but not the number of chunks"). The Question and Read stages almost certainly induce students to elaborate the material while encoding it; the Self-recitation stage induces the student to practice retrieval.

The fifth, or Test, stage occurs after finishing an entire chapter. Students try to recall the main facts from what they have read and to understand how the various facts relate to one another. This stage prompts elaboration and offers further practice at retrieval. In summary, the PQRST method relies on three basic principles for improving memory: organizing the material, elaborating the material, and practicing retrieval. (For a fuller description of the method, see Appendix I.)

CONSTRUCTIVE MEMORY

Throughout this chapter, we have considered research using simple verbal materials (lists of unrelated words, for instance) and more complex materials (sentences, textbook chapters). We did this because many principles apply to both simple and complex materials. However, some principles seem to apply only to memory for complex, meaningful materials; the most important of these principles is that memory can be *constructive*.

When we hear a sentence or story, we often take it as an incomplete description of a real event, and we use our general knowledge about how the world works to *construct* a more complete description of the event. How do we do this? By adding to the sentences and stories statements that are likely to follow from them. For example, on hearing "Mike broke the bottle in a barroom brawl," we are likely to infer that it was a beer or whiskey bottle, not a milk or soda bottle. We add this inference to our memory of the sentence itself. Our total memory therefore goes beyond the original information given. We fill in the original information by using our general knowledge about what goes with what (for example, that beer bottles go with bars). We do this because we are trying to explain to ourselves the events we are hearing about. Constructive memory, then, is a by-product of our need to understand the world.

Simple Inferences

Often when we read a sentence we draw inferences from it and store the inferences along with the sentence. In one study, subjects studied such sentences as

1. *Three turtles sat on a log and a fish swam beneath it.*

Now if the fish swam beneath the log, it must have swum beneath the turtles. If subjects made this inference, it would become part of their memory for that sentence. Later, subjects thought that they had seen Sentence No. 2:

2. *Three turtles sat on a log and a fish swam beneath them.*

Sentence No. 2 is such a natural inference from Sentence No. 1 that subjects had difficulty telling which of the two they had actually seen (Bransford, Barclay, & Franks, 1972).

The inference in the above study was necessarily true. If turtles are on a log and something goes beneath the log, the basic spatial facts of the world dictate that something went beneath the turtles, as well. But other studies show that people tend to draw inferences and make them part of their memory even when the inference is not necessarily true. This tendency is particularly strong when reading real text, because inferences are often needed to connect different lines. To illustrate, consider the following story, which was presented to subjects in an experiment.

1. Provo is a picturesque kingdom in France.
2. Corman was heir to the throne of Provo.
3. He was so tired of waiting.
4. He thought arsenic would work well.

When reading this story, subjects draw inferences at certain points. At line 3, they infer that Corman wanted to be king, which permits them to connect line 3 to the preceding line. But this is not a necessary inference (Corman could have been waiting for the king to receive him). At line 4, subjects infer that Corman had decided to poison the king, so they can connect this line to what preceded it. Again, the inference is not a necessary one (there are people other than the king to poison, and there are other uses of arsenic). When subjects' memories were later tested for exactly which lines had been presented, they had trouble distinguishing the story lines from the inferences we just described. Again, it is hard to keep separate what was actually presented from what we added to it (Seifert, Robertson, & Black, 1985).

Inferences can also affect memory for visual scenes, as illustrated by the following study. Subjects were shown a film of a traffic accident and then were asked questions about their memory of the accident. One question about the speed of the vehicles was asked in two different ways. Some subjects were asked, "How fast were the cars going when they smashed into each other?" whereas others were asked, "How fast were the cars going when they hit each other?" Subjects asked the "smashed" question might infer that the accident was a very destructive one, perhaps more destructive than they had actually remembered. These subjects were likely to use this inference somehow to alter their memory of the accident to make it more destructive (see Figure 8-18). Subjects asked the "hit" question, however, should be less likely to do this, since "hit" implies a less severe accident than does "smashed."

This line of reasoning was supported by the results of a memory test given one week later. In this test, subjects were asked, "Did you see any broken glass?" There was no broken glass in the film of the accident, but subjects who had been asked the "smashed" question were more likely to say mistakenly that there had been glass than were subjects who had been asked the "hit" question. The "smashed" question may have led to reconstruction of the memory for the accident, and the reconstructed memory contained details, such as broken glass,

FIGURE 8-18
Reconstructing a Memory of an Accident *The picture at the top represents the subject's original memory for the accident. Then comes the "smashed" question, which leads the subject to draw inferences about the destructiveness of the accident. These inferences may be used to reconstruct the original memory so that it looks more like the picture on the bottom. (After Loftus & Loftus, 1975)*

that were never actually part of the accident (Loftus, Schooler, & Wagenaar, 1985). Alternatively, subjects may not have integrated inferences about "smashed" with their memory of the accident; rather, they may have consulted such inferences at the time of the memory test (McCloskey & Zaragoza, 1985). Either interpretation of the results has important implications for eyewitness identification in our legal system. A question phrased in a particular way ("smashed" rather than "hit") can alter a witness's memory structures that an attorney is trying to probe.

Stereotypes

Another means by which we fill in, or construct, memories is through the use of social *stereotypes*. A stereotype is a packet of inferences about the personality traits or physical attributes of a whole class of people. We may, for example, have a stereotype of the typical German (intelligent, meticulous, serious) or of the typical Italian (artistic, carefree, fun loving). These descriptions rarely apply to many people in the class and can often be misleading guides for social interaction. Our concern here, however, is not with the effects of stereotypes on social interaction (see Chapter 17 for a discussion of this) but with the effects of stereotypes on memory.

When presented with information about a person, we sometimes stereotype that person (for example, "He's your typical Italian") and then combine the information presented with that in our stereotype. Our memory of the person is thus partly constructed from the stereotype. To the extent that our stereotype does not fit the person, our recall can be terribly distorted. Hunter, a British psychologist, provides a firsthand account of such a distortion:

> In the week beginning 23 October, I encountered in the university, a male student of very conspicuously Scandinavian appearance. I recall being very forcibly impressed by the man's nordic, Viking-like appearance — his fair hair, his blue eyes, and long bones. On several occasions, I recalled his appearance in connection with a Scandinavian correspondence I was then conducting and thought of him as the "perfect Viking," visualizing him at the helm of a long-ship crossing the North Sea in quest of adventure. When I again saw the man on 23 November, I did not recognize him, and he had to introduce himself. It was not that I had forgotten what he looked like but that his appearance, as I recalled it, had become grossly distorted. He was very different from my recollection of him. His hair was darker, his eyes less blue, his build less muscular, and he was wearing spectacles (as he always does). (Hunter, 1974, pp. 265 – 66)

Clearly, Hunter's memory of the student was severely distorted. His stereotype of Scandinavians seems to have so overwhelmed any information he actually encoded about the student's appearance that the result was a highly constructed memory. It bore so little resemblance to the student that it could not even serve as a basis for recognition.

Stereotypes may also work retroactively on memory. We may first hear a relatively neutral description of a person, later find out this person belongs to a particular category, and then use our stereotype of that category to augment our memory of the original description. In a study demonstrating this phenomenon, subjects first read a narrative about events in the life of a woman named Betty K. The narrative followed Betty K's life from birth to early adulthood and contained facts about her social life, such as, "Although she never had a steady boyfriend in high school, she did go out on dates." After reading the story, subjects were given additional facts about Betty K that would lead to stereotyping her. One group of subjects was told that Betty later adopted a lesbian life-style. A second group was told that she later married. Apparently, the first group fit Betty to their stereotype of lesbians, whereas the second group fit her to their stereotype of married women. Such stereotyping affected subsequent recognition of the original narrative. Subjects told about Betty's later lesbian activities were more likely to remember that "she never had a steady boyfriend" than that "she did go out on dates." Subjects told about Betty's later marriage did the reverse. Both groups may have reconstructed their memory of the original narrative to make it fit their stereotypes, or they may have used their stereotypes to answer questions when they could not remember the original narrative (Snyder & Uranowitz, 1978; Bellezza & Bower, 1981). Thus, memory for people seems to be particularly susceptible to construction; our memory is a compromise between what is and what we think should be.

Schemata

Psychologists use the term *schema* (*schemata* for plural) to refer to a mental representation of a class of people, objects, events, or situations. Stereotypes, as described above, are thus a kind of schema because they represent classes of people (for example, Italians, women, homosexuals). Similarly, common categories such as *dog* and *table* are another kind of schema because they represent classes of objects. Schemata can be used to describe not only our knowledge about particular objects and events but also our knowledge about how to act in certain situations. For example, most adults have a schema for how to drive a car (sit behind the wheel, insert the key into the ignition, turn the key while pressing the gas pedal, and so on) and a schema for how to eat in a restaurant (enter the restaurant, find a table, get a menu from the waiter, order food, and so on). Everyone but very young children would have schemata for how to find his or her way home from various locations.

Perceiving and thinking in terms of schemata permits us to filter, organize, and process large amounts of information swiftly and economically. Instead of having to perceive and remember all the details of each new person, object, or event we encounter, we can simply note that it is like a schema already in memory and encode and remember only its most distinctive features. The price we pay for such "cognitive economy," however, is that an object or event can be distorted if the schema used to encode it does not quite fit.

Bartlett (1932) was perhaps the first psychologist to study systematically the effect of schemata on memory. He suggested that memory distortions, much like those that occur when we fit people into stereotypes, can occur when we attempt to fit stories into schemata. Research has confirmed Bartlett's suggestion. For example, after reading a brief story about a character going to a restaurant, subjects are likely to recall statements about the character eating and paying for a meal, even when those actions were never mentioned in the story (Bower, Black, & Turner, 1979).

On the other hand, schemata are often a great aid to memory. For example, some stories we read may be difficult to comprehend and remember unless we can fit them into their appropriate schemata. To illustrate this, read the following paragraph and try to recall it.

The procedure is actually quite simple. First you arrange things into different groups. Of course, one pile may be sufficient, depending on how much there is to do. If you have to go somewhere else due to lack of facilities, that is the next step; otherwise you are pretty well set. It is important not to overdo things. That is, it is better to do too few things at once than too many. In the short run this may not seem important but complications can easily arise. A mistake can be expensive as well. At first the whole procedure will seem complicated. Soon, however, it will become just another facet of life. It is difficult to foresee any end to the necessity for this task in the immediate future, but then one never can tell. After the procedure is completed, one arranges the materials into different groups again. Then they can be put into their appropriate places. Eventually, they will be used once more and the whole cycle will then have to be repeated. However, that is part of life. (After Bransford & Johnson, 1973)

In reading the paragraph, you no doubt had some difficulty in trying to understand exactly what it was about. Consequently, your recall of it is probably relatively poor. But given the hint that the paragraph describes ''washing clothes,'' you can now use your schema for washing clothes to interpret all the cryptic parts of the passage. The *procedure* referred to in the first sentence is that of *washing clothes*, the *things* referred to in the second sentence are *clothes*, the *different groups* are *groups of clothing of different colors*, and so on. Your memory for the paragraph, if you reread it, should now be quite good. Schemata, then, can help or hurt memory.

Schemata seem to affect both the encoding and retrieval stages of long-term memory. If a particular schema is active when we read a story, we tend to encode mainly the facts that are related to the schema. We can illustrate with the following simple story:

1. Steven and Edgar went to a movie.
2. Steven and Edgar talked about business while waiting in line.
3. Steven liked the film, but Edgar thought it was too sentimental.

Assuming that Sentence No. 1 activates our movie schema, we are more likely to encode Sentence No. 3 than No. 2 because Sentence No. 3 is more related to the schema. In later recalling this story, if we could remember that it had to do with going to a movie, we could use our movie schema to search our memory: for example, was there anything in the story about a reaction to the film? Thus, schemata can affect retrieval by guiding search processes (Brewer & Nakamura, 1984).

In the case of a difficult memory task, retrieval may be almost totally guided by schemata. If asked to remember where you met a particular person, for example, you might check one schema after another to see if any of them have been used as the encoding context for the target person (''Was it a party, a class, a restaurant, a movie?''). The relevant schemata—parties, classes, and so on—have become the critical retrieval cues, and memory is almost entirely constructive (Kolodner, 1983).

Situations where memory is heavily constructive seem a far cry from the simpler situations we covered earlier. Consider, for example, memory for a list of unrelated words: here, memory processes appear more to *preserve* the input than to *construct* something new. However, there is a constructive aspect even to this simple situation, for techniques such as using imagery give meaning to the input. Similarly, when we read a paragraph such as the one about washing clothes, we must still preserve some of its specifics if we are to recall it correctly in detail. Thus, the two aspects of memory—to preserve and to construct—may always be present, although their relative emphasis may depend on the exact situation.

1. There are three stages of memory: *encoding, storage,* and *retrieval*. Encoding refers to the transformation of information into the kind of code or representation that memory can accept; storage is the retention of the encoded information; and retrieval refers to the process by which information is recovered from memory. The three stages may operate differently in situations that require us to store material for a matter of seconds *(short-term memory)* and in situations that require us to store material for longer intervals *(long-term memory)*.

2. Information in short-term memory tends to be encoded *acoustically,* although we can also use a *visual code*. The dominance of the acoustic code may apply mainly to verbal materials.

3. The most striking fact about short-term memory is that its storage capacity is limited to 7 ± 2 items, or *chunks*. When this limit is reached, a form of forgetting occurs: a new item can enter short-term memory only by *displacing* an old one. The other major cause of forgetting in short-term memory is that information *decays* with time. Both displacement and decay can be offset by *rehearsal*.

4. Retrieval slows down as the number of items in short-term memory increases, suggesting that retrieval may involve a *search process*. Short-term memory seems to serve as a mental "work space" in solving certain kinds of problems, such as mental arithmetic and answering questions about text.

5. There are interactions between short-term and long-term memory. In *chunking*, information in long-term memory is used to recode incoming material into large, meaningful units (chunks), which are then stored in short-term memory. Information may also be transferred from short-term to long-term memory, sometimes by the process of *rehearsal*. A theory of this transfer process *(dual-memory theory)* accounts for the results of experiments on *free recall*: items at the end of a list are remembered well because they are still in short-term memory, whereas items at the beginning of a list are remembered well because they are rehearsed more often.

6. Information in long-term memory is usually encoded according to its *meaning*. If the items to be remembered are meaningful but the connections between them are not, memory can be improved by adding meaningful connections that provide retrieval paths. The more one *elaborates* the meaning, the better memory will be.

7. Many cases of forgetting in long-term memory are due to *retrieval failures* (the information is there, but cannot be found). Retrieval failures are more likely to occur when there is *interference* from items associated with the same retrieval cue. Such interference effects indicate that retrieval from long-term memory is accomplished by a search process. The search may be either a process of checking paths one at a time or a *spreading activation* process.

8. Some forgetting from long-term memory is due to a loss from storage, particularly when there is a disruption of the processes that *consolidate* new memories. The biological locus of consolidation includes the *hippocampus*, a brain structure below the cerebral cortex.

9. Retrieval failures in long-term memory are less likely to happen when the items are *organized* during encoding and when the *context* at retrieval is similar to that at encoding. Retrieval processes can also be disrupted by *emotional factors*. In some cases, anxious thoughts interfere with retrieval of the target memory; in others, the target memory *(repression hypothesis)* may be actively blocked.

10. The symptoms common to all forms of amnesia are an inability to acquire new information *(anterograde amnesia)* and an inability to remember events that occurred prior to the injury or disease *(retrograde amnesia)*. In some cases of amnesia, the breakdown of memory seems to happen at the storage stage, while in other cases the breakdown seems to occur at the encoding and retrieval stages. In most forms of amnesia, the lost memories are for personal episodes or facts. Memory for skills and for general facts are usually spared, suggesting that there may be separate memories for *personal facts, general facts,* and *skills*.

11. Although we cannot increase the capacity of short-term memory, we can use *recoding* schemes to enlarge the size of a chunk and thereby increase the memory span. Long-term memory can be improved at the encoding and retrieval stages. One way to improve encoding and retrieval is to use imagery, which is the basic principle underlying mnemonic systems such as the *method of loci* and the *key-word method*.

12. Other ways to improve encoding (and subsequent retrieval) are to elaborate the meaning of the items and to organize the material during encoding (hierarchical organization seems best). The best ways to improve retrieval are to attempt to restore the encoding context at the time of retrieval and to practice retrieving information while learning it. Most of these principles for improving encoding and retrieval are incorporated into the *PQRST method* of studying a textbook, whose five stages are *Preview, Question, Read, Self-recitation,* and *Test*.

13. Memory for complex materials, such as stories, is often *constructive*. We tend to use our general knowledge of the world to construct a more complete memory of a story or an event. Construction can involve adding simple *inferences* to the material presented; it can also involve fitting the material into *stereotypes* and other kinds of *schemata* (mental representations of classes of people, objects, events, or situations).

There are several introductory books on memory that are readable and up-to-date: Anderson, *Cognitive Psychology and Its Implications* (2nd ed., 1985); Glass and Holyoak, *Cognition* (2nd ed., 1986); Klatzky, *Human Memory: Structures and Processes* (2nd ed., 1980); Norman, *Learning and Memory* (1982); and Reed, *Cognition: Theory and Applications* (1981). In addition to these textbooks, Neisser (ed.), *Memory Observed* (1982), provides a survey of remembering in natural contexts.

For an advanced treatment of theoretical issues in memory, see Anderson, *The Architecture of Cognition* (1983); Tulving, *Elements of Episodic Memory* (1983); the six-volume *Handbook of Learning and Cognitive Processes*, edited by Estes (1975–1979); Baddeley, *The Psychology of Memory* (1976); and Crowder, *Principles of Learning and Memory* (1976).

For a review of research on the biological bases of memory and learning, see Squire and Butters (eds.), *The Neuropsychology of Memory* (1984); and Bower and Hilgard, *Theories of Learning* (5th ed., 1981).

FURTHER READING

Thought and Language

THE GREATEST ACCOMPLISHMENTS OF our species stem from our ability to entertain complex thoughts and to communicate them. Thinking includes a wide range of mental activities. We think when we try to solve a problem that has been presented to us in class; we think when we daydream while waiting for that class to begin. We think when we decide what groceries to buy, plan a vacation, write a letter, or worry about a troubled relationship.

In all cases, thought can be conceived of as a "language of the brain." Introspection suggests that there is more than one language. One *mode of thought* corresponds to the stream of sentences that we seem to "hear in our mind"; this is referred to as *propositional thought*. Another mode corresponds to images, particularly visual ones, that we can "see" in our mind; this is *imaginal thought*. Finally, there may be a third mode, *motoric thought,* which corresponds to sequences of "mental movements" (Bruner, Olver, Greenfield, et al., 1966). While studies of cognitive development have paid some attention to motoric thought in children, research on thinking in adults has emphasized the other two modes, particularly the propositional one; this emphasis is reflected in the current chapter.

The next four sections discuss major topics in propositional thinking, including: the components of a proposition, or the study of *concepts;* the organization of propositional thought, or the study of *reasoning;* the communication of propositional thought, or the study of *language;* and the development of such communication, or the study of *language acquisition*. We then turn to the visual mode of thought. In the final section, we will discuss thought in action — the study of *problem solving* — and consider the uses of both propositional and imaginal thought.

CONCEPTS

We can think of a proposition as a statement that makes a factual claim. *Irene is a mother* is one proposition, and *Cats are animals* is another. It is easy to see that a proposition consists of concepts — such as *Irene* and *mother* or *cat* and *animal* — combined by a particular relation. To understand propositional thought, we first need to understand the concepts that compose it.

Concepts are our means of dividing the world into manageable units. The world is full of so many different objects that if we treated each one as distinct, we would soon be overwhelmed. For example, if we had to refer to every single object we encountered by a different name, our vocabulary would have to be gigantic — so immense that communication might be impossible. Fortunately, we do not treat each object as unique; rather, we see it as an instance of a concept or class. Thus, many different objects are seen as instances of the concept *apple,* many others as instances of the concept *chair,* and so on. By treating different objects as if they were roughly the same with respect to certain properties, we reduce the complexity of the world that we have to represent mentally.

To have a concept is to know the properties common to all or most instances of the concept. Thus, our concept of *apple* comprises properties shared by all or most apples: an apple has seeds, grows on a tree, is edible, is round, has distinctive colors, and so on. Knowledge of these common properties has an enormous impact on how we deal with the objects around us. Having perceived some visible properties of an object (something round and red on a tree), we assign it to the concept of *apple.* This allows us to infer properties that are not visible — for instance, that it has seeds inside of it and is edible. Concepts, then, enable us to go beyond the information immediately available.

We also have concepts of activities, such as *eating;* of states, such as *being old;* and of abstractions, such as *truth, justice,* or even the number *two.* In each case, we know something about the properties common to members of the concept. Widely used concepts like these generally are associated with a one-word name: "apple," "doctor," "eating," "old," "truth," and so forth. This allows us to communicate quickly about experiences that occur frequently.

Components of a Concept

Every concept includes a *prototype* and a *core.* The prototype contains the properties that describe the best examples of the concept, whereas the core comprises the properties that are more important for being a member of the concept. In the concept *bachelor,* for example, your prototype might include such properties as a man who is in his 30s, lives alone, and has an active social life. These properties may be true of the typical examples of a bachelor, but they are clearly not true of all instances (think of an uncle in his 60s who boards with his sister and rarely goes out). In contrast, your core of the concept *bachelor* would probably include the properties of being adult, male, and unmarried; these properties are essential for being a member of the concept (Armstrong, Gleitman, & Gleitman, 1983).

As another example, consider the concept *bird.* Your prototype likely includes the properties of flying and chirping — which works for the best examples of *bird,* such as robins and blue jays, but not for other examples, such as ostriches and penguins. Your core would likely specify something about the biological basis of birdhood — the fact that it involves having certain genes or, at least having parents that are birds. Note that in this example and the previous one, the prototype properties are salient but not perfect indicators of concept membership, whereas the core properties are diagnostic of concept membership.

The prototype and core play different roles in concepts like *bachelor* than they do in concepts like *bird.* In *bachelor,* because the core properties (being adult, for example) are as salient as the prototype properties (being in one's 30s), we primarily use the core to determine whether or not something is an instance of the concept. In *bird,* the core properties (genes) are hidden from view, and consequently we primarily use the prototype in determining membership in the concept. Thus, happening upon a small animal, we can hardly inspect its genes or inquire about its parentage. All we can do is check whether it does certain things such as fly and chirp, and use this information to decide whether it is a bird. Concepts like *bachelor* are called *classical* concepts, while concepts like *bird* are called *fuzzy* — because we cannot always be sure about our decisions (Smith & Medin, 1981).

Some instances of fuzzy concepts will have more prototype properties than other instances. Among birds, for example, a robin will have the property of flying, whereas an ostrich will not. And the more prototype properties an instance has, the more typical people will consider that instance to be of the concept. Thus, of *bird*, most people rate a robin as more typical than an ostrich; of *apple*, they rate red apples as more typical than green ones (since red seems to be a property of the concept *apple*); and so on.

Further, the *typicality* of an instance affects many mental processes (Rosch, 1978). One is *categorization*. When people are asked whether or not a pictured animal is a *bird*, a robin produces an immediate "yes," whereas a chicken requires a longer decision time. Another process affected by typicality is *memory*. When asked to retrieve the names of all the pieces of clothing they can think of, people produce such typical items as *suit* before the less typical ones such as *vest*. Typicality also affects our everyday inferences. Suppose you are away from home, feel ill, and think about seeing a doctor. The object of your thought will likely be the American prototype of *doctor*, and it will fit middle-aged, male doctors better than others. Why? Because most doctors you have seen, either directly or through the media, have been middle-aged males, and these properties have become part of your prototype. If you choose to see a Dr. Jones and the person turns out to be young and female, you will probably be surprised.

Hierarchies of Concepts

In addition to knowing the properties of concepts, we also know how they relate to one another. For example, *apples* are members (or a subset) of a larger concept, *fruit; robins* are a subset of *birds*, which in turn are a subset of *animals*. These two types of knowledge (properties of a concept and relationships between concepts) are represented in Figure 9-1 as a hierarchy. Such a hierarchy allows us to infer that a concept has a particular property even when it is not associated directly with that concept. Suppose you do not have the property of being alive associated directly with *bird*. If you were asked, "Is a bird a living creature?" presumably you would enter your mental hierarchy at *bird* (see Figure 9-1), trace a path from *bird* to *animal*, find the property of living stored at *animal*, and respond "yes." This idea implies that the time needed to establish a relation between a concept and a property should increase with the distance between them in the hierarchy. This prediction was confirmed in an experiment where subjects were asked questions such as, *Is a bird a living creature?* and *Is a blue jay a living creature?* Subjects took longer to answer the *blue jay* question than the *bird* one, because the distance in the hierarchy between *blue jay* and living is greater than that between *bird* and living (Collins & Quillian, 1969).

FIGURE 9-1
Hierarchy of Concepts *Words in capital letters represent concepts; lowercase words depict properties of these concepts. The black lines show relationships between concepts, and the colored lines connect properties and concepts.*

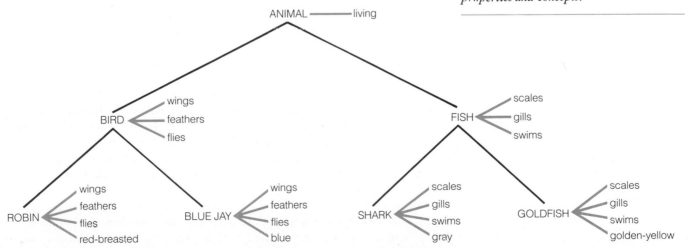

As the hierarchy in Figure 9-1 makes clear, an object can be classified at different levels. The same object is at once a *robin*, a *bird*, and an *animal*. However, for any particular culture or subculture, one level is the *basic* or preferred one for classification. For many city dwellers, the concept *bird* would be the basic level; these people would be faster at classifying something as a *bird* than as a *robin*, and would be more likely to call it a "bird" than a "robin." For people from rural areas, the basic level would move down to *robin*. What determines which level is basic? The answer seems to be that the basic level is the one that has the most *distinctive* properties. In Figure 9-1, *bird* has several properties that are distinctive — they are not shared by other kinds of animals (for example, wings and feathers are not properties of fish). *Robin*, as shown in this hierarchy, has fewer distinctive properties; most of a robin's properties are shared by a blue jay. However, *robin* also has properties distinguishing it from *blue jay* that are not shown in the figure, such as migrates and sings. These properties would be familiar to people living in rural areas. As we learn more about a conceptual domain, then, we shift (downward) the level at which we prefer to operate (Mervis & Rosch, 1981).

Acquiring Concepts

We can learn about a concept in two different ways: either we are explicitly taught something about the concept, or we learn it through experience. Which way we learn depends on *what* we are learning. Explicit teaching is likely to be the means by which we learn cores of concepts, while experience seems to be the standard means by which we acquire prototypes. Thus, someone explicitly tells a child a *robber* is someone who takes another person's possessions with no intention of returning them (the core), while the child's experiences lead him or her to expect robbers to be shiftless, disheveled, and dangerous (the prototype).

Children must also learn that the core is a better indicator of concept membership than the prototype is. It takes a while for them to learn this. In one study, children aged 5 to 10 were presented with descriptions of items and had to decide whether or not they belonged to particular concepts. We can illustrate the study with the concept of *robber*. One description given for *robber* depicted a person who matched its prototype but not its core:

> A smelly, mean old man with a gun in his pocket who came to your house and takes your TV set because your parents didn't want it anymore and told him he could have it.

Another description used for *robber* was of a person who matched its core but not its prototype:

> A very friendly and cheerful woman who gave you a hug, but then disconnected your toilet bowl and took it away without permission and no intention to return it. (Keil & Batterman, 1984, p. 226)

The younger children often thought the prototypical description was more likely than the core description to be an instance of the concept. Not until age 10 did children show a clear shift from the prototype to the core as the final arbitrator of concept decisions (Keil & Batterman, 1984).

Perhaps the reason why young children put so much stock in the prototype of a concept is that they learn it before they do the core. Even an 18-month-old child seems to have acquired the prototypes of *person, baby, dog, cup, food,* and so on. Children can learn prototypes very early because they can use a simple strategy that requires them only to note similarities, not to make abstractions. In this *exemplar strategy*, when children encounter a known instance (or *exemplar*) of a concept, they store a representation of it. Later, when they have to decide whether or not a new item is an instance of that concept, they determine its similarity to stored exemplars of the concept. If the similarity is great enough, they decide that the new item is an instance of the concept (Kemler Nelson, 1984).

The exemplar strategy works better with typical instances than atypical ones. Because the first exemplars a child learns tend to be typical ones, new instances are more likely to be correctly classified to the extent they are similar to typical instances. Thus, a young child's concept of *furniture* might consist of just the most typical instances (say, table and chair). The child could use the exemplar strategy to classify many other instances of the concept, such as desk and sofa, because they are so similar to the learned exemplars. But the child may not correctly classify instances of the concept that look different from the learned exemplars, such as lamp and bookshelf. When learning is based on exemplars, typical instances will fare well, but atypical ones may not even be included in the concept (Mervis & Pani, 1981).

Although the exemplar strategy remains part of our repertory for acquiring concepts, as we grow older we start to use another strategy, *hypothesis testing*. We hypothesize what properties are critical for determining whether an item belongs to a concept, analyze any potential instance for these critical properties, and then maintain our hypothesis if it leads to correct decisions. This strategy is clearly appropriate for classical concepts like *bachelor*, because the core properties may be taken as the critical ones.

Combining Concepts

We need to understand not only the nature of individual concepts but also how we combine them to form propositional thoughts. One general rule of combination is that we join concepts to produce a proposition that contains a descriptor and a person or object: the descriptor is called a *predicate*, and the person or object is called a *subject*. In the proposition *Lorri has beautiful eyes, Lorri* is the subject, and *has beautiful eyes* is the predicate. In the proposition *The tailor is asleep, the tailor* is the subject, and *is asleep* is the predicate. And in *Teachers work too hard, teachers* is the subject, and *work too hard* is the predicate. Note that in some cases the predicate is an attribute *(has beautiful eyes);* in other cases, it is a state *(is asleep);* and in still other cases, it is an activity *(works too hard).*

Combining concepts into propositions is the first step toward complex thoughts. The rest of the way is accomplished by combining the propositions themselves. Again, there appear to be only certain ways we can do this. The easiest way to combine propositions into thoughts is by simply joining them — for example, *Anne likes vegetables, but Ed prefers pizza.* A more complex way of combining propositions is to attach one proposition to part of another. In *Ben likes the blue blanket,* we have two propositions: *Ben likes the blanket,* and *the blanket is blue.* The second proposition is attached to part of the predicate of the first. Perhaps the most complex way to combine propositions or thoughts is to insert one into another. For example, *Anne's liking the restaurant was a surprise to everyone* contains two propositions. The first is *Anne liked the restaurant.* This proposition then serves as the subject of the second proposition, in which *was a surprise to everyone* is the predicate. Thus, the first proposition has been *embedded* into the second, and such embedding enables us to form very complex thoughts (Clark & Clark, 1977).

CRITICAL DISCUSSION

Linguistic Relativity Hypothesis

In our discussion of concepts, we assume that words reflect existing concepts. We assume that language is designed to express propositional thought and, therefore, that the structure of language reflects the structure of thought. However, some have suggested that the relationship between language and thought is the other way around. Rather than thought determining language, it may be that language determines thought. This is the *linguistic relativity hypothesis* proposed by Benjamin Whorf (1956). Whorf argued that the kinds of concepts and perceptions we can have are affected by the particular language we speak. Therefore, people who speak different languages perceive the world in different ways. This provocative idea has caused much debate.

Much of the evidence cited in favor of the hypothesis is based on vocabulary differences. For example, English has only one word for snow, whereas Eskimo has four. Consequently, speakers of Eskimo may perceive differences in snow that speakers of English cannot. Do such obser-

vations constitute strong evidence for the linguistic relativity hypothesis? Critics of the hypothesis argue that they do not (for example, Clark & Clark, 1977; Slobin, 1979). According to the critics, language may embody distinctions that are important to a culture, but it does not create those distinctions, nor does it limit its speakers' perceptions to them. English speakers may have the same capacity for perceiving variations in snow as Eskimo speakers, but since such variations are more important in Eskimo cultures than in Anglo cultures, one language assigns different words to the variations whereas the other does not. The best evidence for this view is the development of jargons. For example, American skiers talk of "powder" and "corn," not just "snow." This growth in vocabulary may be accompanied by changes in perception: Eskimos and skiers are more likely to notice variations in snow than are Hawaiians. But the critical point is that such changes do not depend on the language spoken. If anything, the language seems to depend on the changes.

REASONING

When we think propositionally, our sequence of thoughts is organized. Sometimes our thoughts are organized by the structure of long-term memory. A thought about calling your father, for example, leads to one about a recent conversation you had with him in your house, which in turn leads to a thought about fixing the house's attic. This sequence arises because different incidents about your father are interconnected in your memory, as are different facts about your house, and these connections supply the links between your thoughts. But memory associations are not the only means we have of organizing propositional thought. The kind of organization of interest to us here manifests itself when we try to *reason*. In such cases, our sequence of thoughts often takes the form of an argument, in which one proposition corresponds to a claim, or *conclusion*, that we are trying to draw. The remaining propositions are reasons for the claim, or *premises* for the conclusion.

Deductive Reasoning

ROLE OF LOGIC   According to logicians, certain arguments are *deductively valid*, which means that it is impossible for the conclusion of the argument to be false if its premises are true (Skyrms, 1986). An example of such an argument is the following:

1. If it's raining, I'll take an umbrella.
2. It's raining.
3. Therefore, I'll take an umbrella.

The linguistic relativity hypothesis has fared no better when it comes to explaining cultural variations in terms describing colors. At one time, many linguists believed that languages differed widely in how they divided the color spectrum and that this led to differences in the perception of colors. Subsequent research showed just the opposite. Berlin and Kay (1969), two anthropologists, studied the *basic color terms* of many languages. Basic color terms are simple, nonmetaphoric words that are used to describe the colors of many different objects. They found striking commonalities in such terms across languages. For instance, every language takes its basic color terms from a restricted set of 11 names. In English these are "black," "white," "red," "yellow," "green," "blue," "brown," "purple," "pink," "gray," and "orange." No matter what color terms a particular language has, they inevitably correspond to some subset of the colors listed here. In addition, if a language uses fewer than 11 terms, the basic terms chosen are not arbitrary. If a language has only two terms (none has fewer), they correspond to "black" and "white"; if it has three, they correspond to "black," "white," and "red"; if it has six, they correspond to these three plus "yellow," "green," and "blue." Thus, the ordering of basic color terms seems to be universal, rather than varying from language to language as the linguistic relativity hypothesis might suggest.

In addition, people whose languages use corresponding basic color terms agree on what particular color is most typical of a color term. Suppose two different languages have terms corresponding to "red." When speakers of these languages are asked to pick the best example of red from an array of hues, they make the same choice. Even though the range of hues for what they would call red may differ, their idea of a typical red is the same. Their perceptions are identical, even though their vocabularies are different. Further work by Rosch (1974) suggests that the Dani (a New Guinea people), whose language has only 2 basic color terms, perceive color variations in exactly the same way as people whose language has all 11. The perception of color gives little support to the linguistic relativity hypothesis.

We should not dismiss the hypothesis too quickly, however. Few language domains have been investigated in the same detail as color terms, and perhaps support for the hypothesis will be found in other domains (for example, whether a language codes a particular thing or event by a noun or a verb). Also, the linguistic relativity hypothesis calls attention to an important point. In learning to make fine discriminations in a particular field, it is helpful to have a vocabulary that expresses these discriminations. As we gain expertise in a field (whether skiing, psychology, or something else), we enlarge our vocabulary for distinctions in that field. Jargons help us to think about and communicate these distinctions. Although a distinction must exist in someone's mind before a term can be created to embody it, the importance of that embodiment should not be underestimated.

When asked to decide whether or not an argument is deductively valid, people are reasonably accurate in their assessments of simple arguments. The question is, How do we make such judgments? Most theories of deductive reasoning assume that we use logical rules in trying to prove that the conclusion of an argument follows from the premises. To illustrate, consider the following rule:

If you have a proposition of the form *If p then q*, and another proposition *p*, then you can infer the proposition *q*.

Presumably, adults know this rule (perhaps unconsciously) and use it to decide that the previous argument is valid. Specifically, they associate the first premise (*If it's raining, I'll take an umbrella*) with the *If p then q* part of the rule. They associate the second premise (*It's raining*) with the *p* part of the rule, and then they infer the *q* part (*I'll take an umbrella*).

Rule following becomes more conscious if we complicate the argument. Presumably, we apply our sample rule twice when evaluating the following argument:

1. If it's raining, I'll take an umbrella.
2. If I take an umbrella, I'll lose it.
3. It's raining.
4. Therefore, I'll lose my umbrella.

Applying our rule to Propositions No. 1 and No. 3 allows us to infer *I'll take an umbrella;* and applying our rule again to Proposition No. 2 and the inferred proposition allows us to infer *I'll lose my umbrella*, which is the conclusion. The

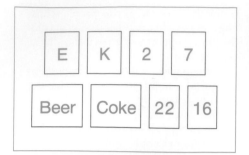

FIGURE 9-2
Content Effects in Deductive
Reasoning *The top half illustrates a
version of the problem where subjects had
to decide which two cards should be turned
over to test the hypothesis, "If a card has a
vowel on one side, it has an even number on
the other side" (After Wason &
Johnson-Laird, 1972). The bottom half
illustrates a version of the problem where
subjects had to decide which cards to turn
over to test the hypothesis, "If a person is
drinking beer, he or she must be over 19."
(After Griggs & Cox, 1982)*

best evidence that people are using rules like this is that the number of rules an
argument requires is a good predictor of the argument's difficulty. The more rules
that are needed, the more likely it is that people will make an error, and the longer
it will take them when they do make a correct decision (Osherson, 1976; Rips,
1983).

BIASES AND HEURISTICS Logical rules do not capture all aspects of deductive reasoning. Such rules are triggered only by the logical *form* of propositions,
yet our ability to evaluate a deductive argument often depends on the *content* of
the propositions, as well. We can illustrate this point by the following experimental problems. Subjects are presented four cards. In one version of the problem,
each card has a letter on one side and a digit on the other (see the top half of Figure
9-2). The subject must decide which two cards to turn over to determine whether
the following claim is correct: "If a card has a vowel on one side, then it has an
even number on the other side." While most subjects correctly choose the "E"
card, fewer than 10 percent of them also choose the "7" card, which is the other
correct choice. (To see that the "7" card is critical, note that if it has a vowel on its
other side, the claim is disconfirmed.)

Performance improves drastically, however, in another version of the above
problem (see the bottom half of Figure 9-2). Now the cards are labeled "Beer,"
"Coke," "22," and "16." The drink cards have either "22" or "16" on the reverse
side, and the number cards have either "Beer" or "Coke" on their reverse sides.
The claim that subjects must evaluate is "If a person is drinking beer, he or she
must be over 19." This version of the problem is logically equivalent to the
preceding version (in particular, "Beer" corresponds to "E," and "16," to "7");
but now most subjects make the correct choices (they turn over the "Beer" and
"16" cards). Thus, the content of the propositions biases our reasoning.

Results such as the above imply that we do not always use logical rules when
faced with deduction problems. Rather, we sometimes use *heuristics* — shortcut
procedures that are relatively easy to apply and that often yield the correct
answers, but not inevitably so. Subjects may solve the drinking version of the
aforementioned problem by retrieving from long-term memory a relevant fact
about drinking (that only young drinkers must be checked to see if the law is
being violated) and then applying this fact to the present problem (Rips, 1986).
Alternatively, subjects may solve the drinking problem by setting up a concrete
representation of the situation. They may, for example, imagine two people, each
with a number on his back and a drink in his hand. They may then inspect this
representation and see what happens, for example, if the drinker with "16" on his
back has a beer in his hand. According to this idea, we reason in terms of concrete
examples suggested by the content of the problem (Johnson-Laird, 1983).

Inductive Reasoning

ROLE OF LOGIC An argument can be good even if it is not deductively valid.
Such arguments are *inductively strong*, which means that it is *improbable* that the
conclusion is false if the premises are true (Skyrms, 1986). An example of an
inductively strong argument is as follows:

1. Mitch majored in accounting in college.
2. Mitch now works for an accounting firm.
3. Therefore, Mitch is an accountant.

This argument is not deductively valid (Mitch may have tired of accounting
courses and taken a night-watchman's job in the only place he had contacts).

Inductive strength, then, is a matter of probabilities, not certainties, and inductive logic is based on the theory of probability.

We make and evaluate inductive arguments all the time. In doing this, do we rely on the rules of probability theory? One probability rule that is relevant is the *base-rate rule,* which states that the probability of something being a member of a class (such as Mitch being a member of the class of accountants) is greater the more class members there are (that is, the higher the base rate of the class). Thus, our sample argument about Mitch being an accountant can be strengthened by adding the premise that Mitch joined a club where 90 percent of the members are accountants. Another relevant probability rule is the *conjunction rule:* the probability of a proposition cannot be less than the probability of that proposition conjoined with another proposition. For example, the probability that *Mitch is an accountant* cannot be less than the probability that *Mitch is an accountant and makes more than $30,000 a year.* The base-rate and conjunction rules are sensible guides to inductive reasoning, and most people will defer to them when the rules are made explicit. However, in the rough-and-tumble of everyday reasoning, people frequently violate these rules, as we are about to see.

BIASES AND HEURISTICS   In a series of ingenious experiments, Tversky and Kahneman have shown that people violate basic principles of probability theory when making inductive judgments. Violations of the base-rate rule are particularly common. In one experiment, one group of subjects was told that a panel of psychologists had interviewed 100 people — 30 engineers and 70 lawyers — and had written personality descriptions of them. These subjects were then given five descriptions and were asked to indicate the probability that the person described was an engineer. Some descriptions were prototypical of an engineer (for example, "Jack shows no interest in political issues and spends his free time on home carpentry"); other descriptions were neutral (for example, "Dick is a man of high ability and promises to be quite successful"). Not surprisingly, these subjects rated the prototypical description as more likely to be an engineer than the neutral description. Another group of subjects was given the identical instructions and five descriptions, except they were told that the 100 descriptions were of *70* engineers and *30* lawyers (the reverse of the first group). The base rate of engineers therefore differed greatly between the two groups. This difference had no effect: subjects in the second group gave essentially the same ratings as those in the first group. Subjects in both groups rated the neutral description as having a 50–50 chance of being an engineer. Subjects completely ignored the information about base rates (Tversky & Kahneman, 1973).

People pay no more heed to the conjunction rule. In one study, subjects were presented the following description:

Linda is 31 years old, single, outspoken, and very bright. In college, she majored in philosophy . . . and was deeply concerned with issues of discrimination.

Subjects then estimated the probabilities of the following statements:

1. Linda is a bank teller.
2. Linda is a bank teller and is active in the feminist movement.

Statement No. 2 is the conjunction of Statement No. 1 and the proposition *Linda is active in the feminist movement.* In flagrant violation of the conjunction rule, most subjects rated No. 2 more probable than No. 1. Note that this is a fallacy because every feminist bank teller is a bank teller, but some female bank tellers are not feminists, and Linda could be one of them (Tversky & Kahneman, 1983).

Subjects in this study based their judgments on the fact that Linda seems more similar to a feminist bank teller than to a bank teller. Though they were asked to estimate *probability,* subjects instead estimated the *similarity* of Linda to the prototype of the concepts *bank teller* and *feminist bank teller.* Thus, estimating similarity is used as a heuristic for estimating probability, because similarity often relates to probability yet is easier to calculate. Use of the *similarity heuristic* also explains why people ignore base rates. In the engineer-lawyer study described earlier, subjects may have considered only the similarity of the description to their prototypes of *engineer* and *lawyer.* Hence, given a description that matched the prototypes of *engineer* and *lawyer* equally well, subjects judged that that engineer and lawyer were equally probable.

Another heuristic that we employ to estimate probabilities is the *causality heuristic:* people estimate the probability of a situation by the strength of the causal connections between the events in the situation. For example, people judge Statement No. 4 to be more probable than Statement No. 3:

3. Sometime during 1990, there will be a massive flood in North America, in which more than 1,000 people will drown.
4. Sometime during 1990, there will be an earthquake in California, causing a massive flood, in which more than 1,000 people will drown.

Judging No. 4 to be more probable than No. 3 is another violation of the conjunction rule. This time, the violation arises because in Statement No. 4 the flood has a strong causal connection to another event, the earthquake; whereas in Statement No. 3, the flood alone is mentioned and hence has no causal connections. In sum, although inductive reasoning is supposed to be a matter of probabilities, often it involves judgments of causality and similarity.

LANGUAGE AND COMMUNICATION

Language is the means for communicating propositional thought. Moreover, it is the universal means: every human society has a language, and every human being of normal intelligence acquires his or her native language and uses it effortlessly. The naturalness of language sometimes lulls us into thinking that language use requires no special explanation. Nothing could be further from the truth. Some people can read, and others cannot; some can do arithmetic, and others cannot; some can play chess, and others cannot. But virtually everyone can master and use an enormously complex linguistic system. This is among the fundamental puzzles of human psychology.

Levels of Language

Language use has two aspects: *production* and *comprehension.* In producing language, we start with a propositional thought, somehow translate it into a sentence, and end up with sounds that express the sentence. In comprehending language, we start with sounds, attach meanings to the sounds in the form of words, combine the words to create a sentence, and then somehow extract a proposition from it. Language use thus seems to involve moving through various levels, and Figure 9-3 makes these levels explicit. At the highest level are sentence units, including sentences and phrases. The next level is that of basic meaning units, including words and parts of words that carry meaning (the prefix "non," for example). The lowest level contains speech sounds. The adjacent levels are closely related to one another: the phrases of a sentence are built from words and

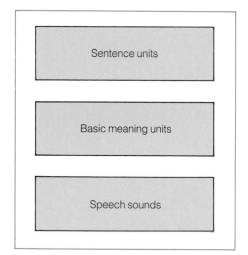

FIGURE 9-3
Levels of Language *At the highest level are sentence units, including phrases and sentences. The next level is that of basic meaning units, including words and parts of words that carry meaning. The lowest level contains speech sounds.*

other basic meaning units, which in turn are constructed from speech sounds. Language is therefore a multilevel system for relating thoughts to speech by basic meaning and sentence units (Chomsky, 1965).

There are striking differences in the number of units at each level. All languages have only a limited number of speech sounds; English has about 40 of them. But rules for combining these speech sounds make it possible to produce and understand thousands of words (a vocabulary of 20,000 to 30,000 words is not unusual for an adult). Similarly, rules for combining words make it possible to produce and understand millions of sentences (if not an infinite number of them). Thus, two of the basic properties of language are that it is *structured* at multiple levels and that it is *productive:* rules allow us to combine units at one level into a vastly greater number of units at the next level. Every human language has these two properties.

Language Units and Processes

With the above as background, let us now consider the units and processes involved at each level of language.

SPEECH SOUNDS In speaking, we use the lips, tongue, mouth, and vocal cords to produce a variety of physical sounds. Not all of these sounds are perceived as distinct, however. In English, we discriminate about 40 *phonemes*, or categories of speech sounds. The sound corresponding to the first letter in "boy" is a phoneme symbolized as /b/. We are good at discriminating different sounds that correspond to different phonemes. But we are poor at discriminating different sounds that correspond to the same phoneme — for example, the sound of the first letter in "pin" and the sound of the second letter in "spin" (Liberman, Cooper, Shankweiler, & Studdert-Kennedy, 1967). They are the same phoneme, /p/, and they sound the same to us even though they have different physical characteristics. The /p/ in "pin" is accompanied by a small puff of air, but the /p/ in "spin" is not (try holding your hand a short distance from your mouth as you say the two words). Thus, we are "equipped" with phonemic categories that act as filters; they convert a continuous stream of speech into the phonemes of our language.

Every language has a different set of phonemes, which is one reason why we often have difficulty learning to pronounce foreign words. Another language may use speech sounds that never appear in ours. It may take us a while even to hear the new phonemes, let alone produce them. Or another language may not make a distinction between two sounds that our language treats as two phonemes. For example, in Japanese the English sounds corresponding to *r* and *l* (/r/ and /l/) are treated as the same phoneme.

When phonemes are combined in the right way, they form words. Each language has its own rules about which phonemes can follow others. In English, for example, /b/ cannot follow /p/ at the beginning of a word (try pronouncing "pbet"). Such rules show their influence when we speak and listen. For example, we have no difficulty pronouncing the plurals of nonsense words we have never heard before. Consider "zuk" and "zug." In accordance with a simple rule, the plural of "zuk" is formed by adding the phoneme /s/, as in "hiss." In English, however, /s/ cannot follow *g* at the end of a word, so to form the plural of "zug" we must use another rule — one that adds the phoneme /z/, as in "fuzz." We may not be aware of these differences in forming plurals, but we have no difficulty producing them. It is as if we "know" the rules for combining phonemes even though we are not consciously aware of the rules: we conform to rules we cannot verbalize.

BASIC MEANING UNITS A *morpheme* is the smallest linguistic unit that carries meaning. Most morphemes are themselves words, such as "time." Others are suffixes, such as "ly," or prefixes, such as "un," which are added onto words to form more complex ones, such as "timely" or "untimely." Most words denote some specific content, such as "house" or "run." A few words, however, primarily serve to make sentences grammatical; such grammatical words or morphemes include what are commonly labeled articles and prepositions, such as "a," "the," "in," "of," "on," and "at." Some prefixes and suffixes also play primarily a grammatical role. These grammatical morphemes include the suffixes "ing" (added to verbs to form the progressive — "kicking"), "ed" (added to verbs to form the past—"kicked"), and "s" (added to nouns to form the plural—"boys"—and added to verbs in the present tense for the third person singular—"The boy kicks"). As we shall see later, grammatical morphemes are acquired in a different manner than are content words.

Many complex words are really just simple words with a host of prefixes and suffixes attached to them. An extreme case is "antidisestablishmentarianism," which breaks into "anti" + "dis" + "establish" + "ment" + "ary" + "an" + "ism" (a total of seven morphemes). Every language has rules about how prefixes or suffixes are combined with words. In English, for example, the suffix "er" is regularly added to many verbs to form nouns that refer to people who habitually perform the action described by the verb, as in "speak – speaker" and "paint – painter." Do we actually use these rules, or something like them, in production and comprehension? Our slips of the tongue suggest we do. For example, a speaker who intended to say "McGovern favors busting pushers" uttered instead "McGovern favors pushing busters" (Garrett, 1975). The morphemes "bust" and "push" were interchanged, whereas the morphemes "ing" and "er + s" stayed in their correct positions. This implies that the morphemes were treated as separate units.

The most important aspect of a word is, of course, its meaning. A word can be viewed as the name of a concept; hence, its meaning is the concept it names. Some words are *ambiguous* because they name more than one concept. "Club," for example, names both a social organization and an object used for striking. Sometimes we may be aware of a word's ambiguity, as when hearing the sentence "He was interested in the club." In most cases, however, the sentence context makes the meaning of the word sufficiently clear so we do not consciously experience any ambiguity—for example, "He wanted to join the club." Even in the latter cases, though, there is evidence that we *unconsciously* consider both meanings of the ambiguous word for a brief moment. Specifically, if a word is presented immediately after the end of the sentence "He wanted to join the club," subjects will respond to that word faster than they would normally if it is related to *either* meaning of "club" (for example, they will respond to either "group" or "stick" faster). This suggests that both meanings of "club" are activated during comprehension of the sentence, and that either meaning can prime related words (Swinney, 1979).

SENTENCE UNITS Sentence units include sentences and phrases. An important property of these units is that they can correspond to parts of a proposition. Such correspondences allow speakers to "put" propositions into sentences and listeners to "extract" propositions from sentences.

Recall that any proposition can be broken into a subject and predicate. A sentence can be broken into phrases in such a way that each phrase corresponds either to the subject or the predicate of a proposition or to an entire proposition. For example, intuitively we can divide the simple sentence "Irene sells insurance" into two phrases, "Irene" and "sells insurance." The first phrase, which is called

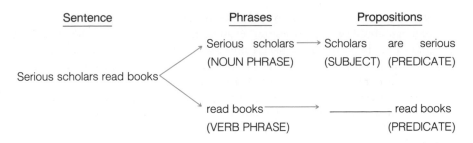

Sentence	Phrases	Propositions
	Serious scholars → (NOUN PHRASE)	Scholars are serious (SUBJECT) (PREDICATE)
Serious scholars read books		
	read books → (VERB PHRASE)	_____ read books (PREDICATE)

FIGURE 9-4

Phrases and Propositions *The first step in extracting the propositions from a complex sentence is to break the sentence into phrases.*

a *noun phrase* because it centers on a noun, specifies the subject of an underlying proposition. The second phrase, a *verb phrase*, gives the predicate of the proposition. For a more complex example, consider the sentence "Serious scholars read books." This sentence divides into two phrases, the noun phrase "serious scholars" and the verb phrase "read books." The noun phrase expresses an entire proposition, *scholars are serious;* the verb phrase expresses part (the predicate) of another proposition, *scholars read books* (see Figure 9-4). Again, there are marked correspondences between sentence units and propositional units.

Analyzing a sentence into subject and verb phrases and then dividing these phrases into smaller units (nouns, adjectives, verbs, and so on) is called a *syntactic analysis.* Such an analysis suggests the units that people use in understanding sentences. These suggested units have generally been confirmed in experiments. For example, in one study, subjects listened to sentences such as "The poor girl stole a warm coat." Immediately after each sentence was presented, they were given a probe word from the sentence and asked to say the word that came after it. People responded faster when the probe and the response words came from the same phrase ("poor" and "girl") than when they came from different phrases ("girl" and "stole"). Thus, people break the sentence into phrases, and each phrase becomes a unit in memory. When the probe and response are from the same phrase, only one unit needs to be retrieved (Wilkes & Kennedy, 1969).

Differences Between Comprehension and Production

Analyzing the levels of language provides a useful map of the areas of language study. However, the levels approach has some implications for the relation between language comprehension and production that need to be critically examined.

Figure 9-5 presents an amended version of our levels description of language. The figure suggests that understanding a sentence is the inverse of producing a sentence. To produce a sentence, we start with a propositional thought, translate it into the phrases and words of a sentence, and finally translate these words into phonemes. We work from the top level down to the bottom level ("top-down processing"). To understand a sentence, however, we move in the opposite direction—from the bottom level to the top. We hear phonemes, use them to construct the words and phrases of a sentence, and finally extract the proposition from the sentence unit ("bottom-up processing").

Although this analysis describes some of what occurs in sentence production and understanding, it is oversimplified. Understanding a sentence must be more than the simple inverse of producing it. There are many sentences we can understand but not produce (for example, sentences spoken in a foreign language that we have some familiarity with). Also, sometimes after comprehending just a few words, we jump to what we think the entire sentence means (the propositions behind it) and then use our guess about the propositions to help us understand the rest of the sentence. In such cases, understanding proceeds from the top level

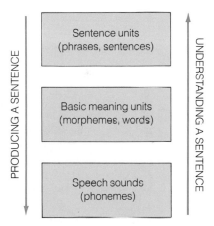

FIGURE 9-5

Levels of Language and Understanding and Producing Sentences *In producing a sentence, we translate a propositional thought into the phrases and words of a sentence and translate these words into speech sounds. In understanding a sentence, we go in the opposite direction — we use speech sounds to construct the words and phrases of a sentence and from these units extract the underlying propositions.*

down as well as from the bottom level up. To illustrate, suppose that in a conversation about eating in a restaurant, your friend says, "The food was so bad that I complained to the manager." Immediately after hearing the word "bad," you might hypothesize that the rest of the sentence will express a thought about complaining to someone on the staff. In this case, you could use your stored knowledge about eating in restaurants (what we called the restaurant schema in Chapter 8) to guide sentence understanding. Such schema guidance is very common in understanding conversations and stories (Adams & Collins, 1979; Schank, 1982).

Another limitation of our levels analysis is that it does not consider the *speaker's intentions* when he or she utters a particular sentence. One can say "This room is too cold" with the intention of answering the landlord's question "What's the problem?" or with the intention of getting one's host to close a window. The proposition involved is the same in both contexts (we are predicating coldness of a particular room), but the two goals for communicating that proposition are very different (Grice, 1975). Evidence shows that people "extract" the speaker's intention as part of the process of comprehension (Clark, 1984).

DEVELOPMENT OF LANGUAGE

Our discussion of language should indicate the enormity of the task confronting children. They must master all levels of language — not only the proper speech sounds but also how these sounds are combined into thousands of words and how these words can be combined into sentences to express thoughts. It is a wonder that virtually all children in all cultures accomplish so much of this in a mere four to five years. What is perhaps even more amazing is that all children, regardless of their culture, seem to go through the same sequence of development. At age 1, the child speaks a few isolated words; at about age 2, the child speaks two- and three-word sentences; at age 3, sentences become more grammatical; and at age 4, the child sounds much like an adult (Gleitman, 1984).

We will first discuss what is acquired at each level of language and then consider how it is acquired and what roles learning and innate factors play. Our discussion of innate factors will consider a number of critical issues, including the possibility of another species learning human language and the localization of language abilities in the human brain.

What Is Acquired?

Development occurs at all three levels of language. It starts at the level of phonemes, develops to the level of words and other morphemes, and then proceeds to the level of sentence units, or syntax.

PHONEMES AND THEIR COMBINATION Infants are preset to learn and discriminate between sounds corresponding to different phonemes (see Chapter 3), and they quickly learn which phonemes are relevant to their language (Eimas, Siqueland, Jusczyk, & Vigorito, 1971). However, it takes several years for children to learn how phonemes can be combined to form words. When children first begin to talk, they occasionally produce "impossible" words, like "dlumber" for "lumber." They do not yet know that in English /l/ cannot follow /d/ at the beginning of a word. By age 4, children have learned most of what they need to know about phoneme combinations. In one study, children of about 4 years of age were asked to say which of two made-up sequences of speech sounds would

"Darling! Justin verbalized!"

make a better name for a toy. One sequence was consistent with rules for combining phonemes (for example, "klek"), whereas the other was not (for example, "lkel"). Most of the children chose the name that conformed to the rules (Messer, 1967).

WORDS AND CONCEPTS   At about 1 year of age, children begin to speak. One-year-olds already have concepts for many things (including family members, household pets, food, toys, and body parts), and when they begin to speak, they are mapping these concepts onto words that adults use. To learn which word goes with which concept, children look at what is happening around them when a word is used and take the important aspects of the situation as the meaning of the word. For example, a child might think, "Mommy said 'Fang' when she pointed to my pet, so 'Fang' means my pet."

The beginning vocabulary is roughly the same for all children. Children 1 to 2 years old talk mainly about people ("Dada," "Mama," "baby"), animals ("dog," "cat," "duck"), vehicles ("car," "truck," "boat"), toys ("ball," "block," "book"), food ("juice," "milk," "cookie"), body parts ("eye," "nose," "mouth"), and household implements ("hat," "sock," "spoon"). While these words name some of the young child's concepts, by no means do they name all. Consequently, young children often have a gap between the concepts they want to communicate and the words they have at their disposal. To bridge this gap, children aged 1 to 2½ years old *overextend* their words to neighboring concepts. For example, a 2-year-old child might use the word "doggie" for cats and cows, as well as dogs (the child is not unsure of the word's meaning—if presented pictures of various animals and asked to pick the "doggie," the child makes the correct choice). At about the age of 2½ years, overextensions begin to disappear, presumably because the child's vocabulary begins to increase markedly, thereby eliminating many of the gaps (Rescorla, 1980; Clark, 1983).

Thereafter, vocabulary development virtually explodes. At 1½ years, a child might have a vocabulary of 25 words; at 6 years, the child's vocabulary is around 14,000 words. To achieve this incredible growth, children have to learn new words at the rate of 9 per day (Templin, 1957). Children seem to be tuned to learning new words. When they hear a word they do not know, they may assume it maps onto one of their concepts that is as yet unlabeled, and they use the context in which the word was spoken to find that concept (Clark, 1983; Markman, 1987).

FROM PRIMITIVE TO COMPLEX SENTENCES   At about 1½ to 2½ years, the acquisition of sentence units, or syntax, begins. Children start to combine single words into two-word utterances, such as "There cow" (where the underlying proposition is *There's the cow*), "Jimmy bike" (the proposition is *That's Jimmy's bike*), or "Towel bed" (the proposition is *The towel's on the bed*). There is a *telegraphic* quality about two-word speech. The child leaves out the grammatical words (such as "a," "an," "the," and "is"), as well as other grammatical morphemes (such as the suffixes "ing," "ed," and "s") and puts in only the words that carry the most important content. Despite their brevity, these utterances express most of the basic intentions of speakers, such as locating objects and describing events and actions (see Table 9-1).

Children progress rapidly from two-word utterances to more complex sentences that express propositions more precisely. Thus, "Daddy hat" may become "Daddy wear hat" and finally "Daddy is wearing a hat." Such expansions of the verb phrase appear to be the first complex, syntactic constructions that occur in children's speech. The next step is the use of conjunctions like "and" and "so" to form compound sentences ("You play with the doll *and* I play with the block")

INTENTION OF UTTERANCE	LANGUAGE			
	ENGLISH	GERMAN	RUSSIAN	SAMOAN
Locate, name	there book that car see doggie	buch da [book there] gukuk wauwau [see doggie]	Tosya tam [Tosya there]	Keith lea [Keith there]
Demand, desire	more milk give candy want gum	mehr milch [more milk] bitte apfel [please apple]	yeschĕ moloko [more milk] day chasy [give watch]	mai pepe [give doll] fia moe [want sleep]
Negate	no wet no wash no hungry allgone milk	nicht blasen [not blow] kaffee nein [coffee no]	vody net [water no] gus' tyu-tyu [goose gone]	le 'ai [not eat] uma mea [allgone thing]
Describe event, action, or situation	Bambi go mail come hit ball block fall baby highchair	puppe kommt [doll comes] tiktak hängt [clock hangs] sofa sitzen [sofa sit]	mama prua [mama walk] papa bay-bay [papa sleep] korka upala [crust fell]	pa'u pepe [fall doll] tapale 'oe [hit you] tu'u lalo [put down]
Indicate possession	my shoe mama dress	mein ball [my ball] mama hat [mama's hat]	mami chashka [mama's cup] pup moya [navel my]	lole a'u [candy my] polo 'oe [ball your]
Modify, qualify	pretty dress big boat	milch heiss [milk hot] armer wauwau [poor dog]	mama khoroshaya [mama good] papa bol'shoy [papa big]	fa'ali'i pepe [headstrong baby]
Question	where ball	wo ball [where ball]	gde papa [where papa]	fea Punafu [where Punafu]

TABLE 9-1
Intentions of Two-word Sentences in Children's Speech *Children's earliest sentences in many languages serve the same basic intentions. (After Slobin, 1971)*

and the use of grammatical morphemes like the past tense "ed." The sequence of development is remarkably similar for all children.

Learning Processes

Now that we have an idea about what children acquire in the language process, we ask how they acquire it. Learning undoubtedly plays a role; that is why children who are brought up in an English-speaking household learn English and why children raised in a French-speaking household learn French. And innate factors undoubtedly play a role; that is why all children in a household learn language but none of the pets do (Gleitman, 1984). We discuss learning in this section and consider innate factors in the next section. In both discussions, we emphasize sentence units and syntax, for it is at this level of language that the important issues about language acquisition are most clearly illustrated.

IMITATION AND CONDITIONING One possibility is that children learn language by *imitating* adults. While imitation may play some role in learning words (a parent points to a telephone, says "phone," and the child tries to repeat it), it cannot be the principal means by which children learn to produce and understand sentences. Young children constantly utter sentences they have never heard an adult say, such as "All gone milk." Even when children at the two-word stage try to imitate longer adult sentences (for example, "Mr. Miller will try"), they produce their usual telegraphic utterances ("Miller try"). In addition, the mistakes children make (for instance, "Daddy taked me") show that they are trying to apply something like rules, not simply trying to copy adults (Ervin-Tripp, 1964).

Some linguists and psychologists have argued that it is *impossible in principle* for a child to learn a language by imitation. Thus, the number of 20-word sentences that we can understand has been estimated to be 10^{20}. To learn sentences by imitation, a person first must listen to them; but if 10^{20} sentences were spoken at a normal rate, the amount of time needed to listen to them would exceed the estimated age of the earth (Miller, 1965)!

A second possibility is that children acquire language through *conditioning*. Adults may reward (positively reinforce) children when they produce a grammatical sentence and reprimand (punish) them when they make mistakes. For this to work, parents would have to respond to every detail in a child's speech. However, Brown, Cazden, and Bellugi (1969) found that parents do not pay attention to how the child says something as long as the statement is comprehensible. Rare attempts to correct a child (and hence to apply conditioning) are often futile.

CHILD: Nobody don't like me.
MOTHER: No, say, "nobody likes me."
CHILD: Nobody don't like me.
MOTHER: No, now listen carefully; say "nobody likes me."
CHILD: Oh! Nobody don't LIKES me.   (McNeill, 1966, p. 49)

HYPOTHESIS TESTING   The problem with imitation and conditioning is that they focus on specific utterances (one can only imitate or reinforce something specific). However, children often learn something general, such as a rule; they seem to form a hypothesis about a rule of language, test it, and retain it if it works.

Consider the morpheme "ed." As a general rule in English, "ed" is added to the present tense of verbs to form the past tense (as in "cook–cooked"). Many common verbs, however, are irregular and do not follow this rule (like "go–went" and "take–took"). Many of these irregular verbs express concepts that children use from the beginning. So at an early point, children use the past tense of some irregular verbs correctly (presumably because they learned them by imitation). They learn the past tense for some regular verbs and discover the hypothesis "add 'ed' to the present tense to form the past tense." This hypothesis leads them to add the "ed" ending to all verbs, including the irregular ones. They say things such as "Annie goed home" and "Jackie taked the book," which they have never heard before. Eventually, they learn that some verbs are irregular and stop overgeneralizing their use of "ed."

How do children generate these hypotheses? There are a few *operating principles* that all children use as a guide to forming hypotheses. One is to pay attention to the ends of words. Another is to look for prefixes and suffixes that indicate a change in meaning. A child armed with these two principles is likely to hit the hypothesis that "ed" at the end of verbs signals the past tense, since "ed" is a word ending associated with a change in meaning. A third operating principle is to avoid exceptions, which explains why children initially generalize their "ed"-equals-past-tense hypothesis to irregular verbs. Some of these principles appear in Table 9-2 and they seem to hold for the 40 languages studied by Slobin (1971, 1984).

TABLE 9-2
Operating Principles Used by Young Children in Generating Hypotheses   *Children from many countries seem to follow these principles in learning to talk and to understand speech. (After Slobin, 1971)*

1. Look for systematic changes in the form of words.
2. Look for grammatical markers that clearly indicate changes in meaning.
3. Avoid exceptions.
4. Pay attention to the ends of words.
5. Pay attention to the order of words, prefixes, and suffixes.
6. Avoid interruption or rearrangement of constituents (that is, sentence units).

Children also learn syntactic rules for ordering the words in a sentence, such as *The sentence subject precedes the verb* in English. How does a child become familiar with syntactic units like *sentence subject* and *verb*? Not by direct experience, for a child listening to a sentence has access only to a string of words and the concepts they name. The most likely possibility is that the child assumes that syntactic units correspond to familiar conceptual units. Suppose a little girl assumes that verbs correspond to actions (a conceptual unit) and sentence subjects, to actors (another conceptual unit). If the child hears the sentence "Daddy hit the ball," she can observe that the actor precedes the action and therefore hypothesize that *the sentence subject precedes the verb*. The problem with this approach, however, is that the assumed correspondences are not always true. What does the child do when confronted with the sentence "Daddy resembles grandpa," in which there is no action or actor? Because the child cannot rely on her correspondences, presumably she relies on her hypothesized rule; "Daddy" must be the sentence subject and "resembles" the verb because "Daddy" precedes "resembles." Thus, the child has bootstrapped her way to syntactic units and rules (Pinker, 1984).

Innate Factors

As noted earlier, some of our knowledge about language is inborn, or innate. There are, however, controversial questions about the extent and nature of this innate knowledge. One question concerns its *richness*. If our innate knowledge is very rich, or specific, then all human languages should bear strong similarities to one another (because they are all based on the same innate knowledge), and the process of language acquisition should be similar for different languages. A second question about innate factors involves *critical periods*. As noted in Chapter 7, a common feature of innate behavior is that it will be acquired only if the organism is exposed to the right cues during a critical time period. Are there such critical periods in language acquisition? A third question about the innate contribution to language concerns its possible *uniqueness:* Is the ability to learn a language system unique to the human species? We will consider these three questions in turn.

SIMILARITIES IN LANGUAGE AND LANGUAGE ACQUISITION   The study of different languages has revealed a number of specific features that may be common to *all* languages. We will illustrate with an example from Chomsky (1980a). In English, simple declarative sentences can be transformed into yes-no questions, as in:

The man is here. Is the man here?
The man will leave. Will the man leave?

What rule describes how to transform the declarative into the question form? One possibility is that the rule involves only word units, not syntactic units.

WORD RULE: Go through the declarative form from left to right until reaching the first occurrence of "is," "will," and so on; transpose this occurrence to the beginning of the sentence to get the question form.

Another possibility is that the rule involves a syntactic unit, namely that of a noun phrase:

SYNTACTIC RULE: Go through the declarative form from left to right until reaching the first occurrence of "is," "will," and so on, *following the first noun phrase;* transpose this occurrence to the beginning of the sentence to get the question form.

The syntactic rule is clearly the correct one for English. In the declarative "The man who is here is tall," we wait until the second occurrence of "is" — the one after the noun phrase ("the man who is here") — before transposing. The same principle — that the rule for transforming declaratives into questions depends on syntactic units, not just words — holds for every human language that has ever been studied. This universality is remarkable, given that there are thousands of natural languages. One might have thought that one or two languages would have evolved so that a simpler word rule could handle the transformation. The fact that there are *no* exceptions suggests that all languages must conform to specific innate constraints.

The sequence of language acquisition offers another source of evidence that our innate knowledge about language is very rich. The sequence (from single words to two-word telegraphs to complex sentences) is remarkably similar for all children, despite large variations in the language of the adults around them. Indeed, children go through the normal course of language acquisition even when there are no language users around them to serve as models. A group of researchers studied six deaf children of parents who could hear and who had decided not to have the children learn sign language. Before the children received any instruction in lip reading and vocalization — indeed, before they had acquired any knowledge of English — they began to use a system of gestures called *home sign*. Initially, their home sign was a kind of simple pantomime, but eventually it took on the properties of a language. For example, it was organized at both morphemic and syntactic levels, including individual signs and combinations of signs. In addition, these deaf children (who essentially created their own language) went through the same stages of development as normal hearing children. Thus, the deaf children initially gestured one sign at a time, then later put their pantomimes together into two- and three-concept "sentences." These striking results support the idea that our innate knowledge about language is indeed very specific (Feldman, Goldin-Meadow, & Gleitman, 1978).

CRITICAL PERIODS Like other innate behaviors, language learning has some critical periods. This is particularly evident when a person acquires the sound system of a new language — that is, learns new phonemes and their rules of combination. Young children readily learn to speak a second language without an accent, but if they learn the language after the age of 13, they inevitably will speak it with an accent. This difference between children and adults cannot be attributed to the children being more immersed in the new language. For even when children and adults have had comparable exposure to a language, as well as comparable practice in using it, only the children speak it without accent (Lenneberg, 1967).

The case is not as strong for a critical period in learning syntax. The evidence that exists concerns a few children whose dire circumstances prohibited them from learning any language until they were in their teens. The best-documented case is that of "Genie," who suffered as horrible a childhood as one can imagine. She was 14 when she was discovered. Apparently, Genie had lived tied to a chair without ever being spoken to since the age of 20 months. She had had virtually no social contact. Her blind mother would feed her hurriedly, and she was punished if she uttered a sound. Not surprisingly, Genie had developed no language. After her discovery, she was taught language by psychologists and linguists (Fromkin et al., 1974), but four years later she still had not become proficient, particularly at syntax. Although Genie had learned to use many words and to combine them into simple phrases, she could not combine phrases to form elaborate sentences. In this case, the crucial factor behind the lack of language development seems to be the relatively late age at which she learned language, which is consistent with the idea of a critical period for learning syntax.

Can Another Species Learn Human Language?

Some experts believe that our innate capacity to learn language is unique to our species (Chomsky, 1972). They acknowledge that other species have communication systems but argue that these are qualitatively different from ours. Consider the communication system of the chimpanzee. This species' vocalizations and gestures are limited in number, and the *productivity* of its communication system is very low in comparison to human language, which permits the combination of a relatively small number of phonemes into thousands of words and the combination of these words into an unlimited number of sentences. Another difference is that human language is structured at several levels whereas chimpanzee communications are not. In particular, in human language, a clear distinction exists between the level of morphemes — where the elements have meaning — and the level of sounds — where the elements do not. There is no hint of such a *duality of structure* in chimpanzee communication, because every symbol carries meaning. Still another difference is that chimpanzees do not vary the *order* of their symbols to vary the meaning of their messages, while we do. For instance, "Jonah ate the whale" means something quite different from "The whale ate Jonah."

The fact that chimpanzee communication is impoverished compared to our own does not mean that chimpanzees lack the capacity for a more productive system. Their system may be adequate for their needs. To determine if chimpanzees have the same innate capacity we do, we must see if they can learn our language.

Until about 1970, attempts to teach chimpanzees to *speak* had failed. The failures, however, may have been due to limitations in the chimpanzee's vocal abilities, not their linguistic abilities. More recent studies have attempted to teach chimpanzees to communicate with their hands. In one of the best-known studies, Gardner and Gardner (1972) taught a female chimpanzee, named Washoe, signs adapted from American Sign Language. Training began when Washoe was about a year old and continued until she was 5. During this time, Washoe's caretakers communicated with her only by means of sign language. They first taught her signs by shaping procedures, waiting for her to make a gesture that resembled a sign and then reinforcing her. Later they found that Washoe could learn signs if they put her hands into the proper position and guided her through the desired movement. Ultimately, Washoe learned signs simply by observing and imitating (see Figure 9-6).

By age 4, Washoe could produce 130 different signs and understand even more. She could also generalize a sign from one situation to another. For example, she first learned the sign for *more* in connection with *more tickling* and then generalized it to indicate *more milk*. Washoe is not unique. Other chimpanzees have acquired comparable vocabularies. Some of these studies have used methods of manual communication other than sign language. Premack (1971) taught a chimpanzee named Sarah to use plastic symbols as words and to communicate by manipulating these symbols. And Lana, a chimpanzee studied by Rumbaugh (1977), communicates by means of a keyboard console. The console has about a hundred keys, each representing a different word, and Lana types her messages

"Remember, don't talk sex, politics, or religion."

FIGURE 9-6
Two of Washoe's Signs *Washoe signs
"sweet" for lollipop (left) and "hat" for
woolen cap (right).*

on the keyboard. In a series of similar studies, Patterson (1978) taught sign
language to a gorilla named Koko, starting when Koko was 1 year old. By age 10,
Koko had a vocabulary of more than 600 signs (Patterson & Linden, 1981).

Do these studies prove that another species — the apes — can learn human
language? There seems to be little doubt that the apes' signs are equivalent to our
words and that the concepts behind these signs are equivalent to ours. But there
are grave doubts that apes can learn to combine these signs in the manner that
humans combine words into a sentence. Thus, not only can people combine the
words "snake," "Eve," "killed," and "the" into the sentence "The snake killed
Eve," but we can also combine the same words in a different order to produce a
sentence with a different meaning, "Eve killed the snake." Although we have
some evidence that apes can combine signs into a sequence resembling a sentence,
little evidence exists to show that they can alter the order of the signs to produce a
different sentence (Slobin, 1979).

Even the evidence that apes can combine signs into a sentence has come
under attack. In early work, researchers reported cases where an ape produced
what seemed to be a meaningful sequence of signs, such as *Gimme flower* and
Washoe sorry (Gardner & Gardner, 1972). As data have accumulated, it has
become apparent that, unlike human sentences, the utterances of an ape are often
highly repetitive. Thus, *you me banana me banana you* is typical of the signing
chimps but would be odd for a human child. These utterances are so repetitious
that some researchers have claimed they are qualitatively different from human
sentences (Seidenberg & Petitto, 1979). In the cases in which an ape utterance is
more like a sentence, the ape may simply be imitating the sequence of signs made
by its human teacher. Thus, some of Washoe's most sentencelike utterances
occurred when she was answering a question; for example, the teacher signed
Washoe eat?, and then Washoe signed *Washoe eat time*. Here, Washoe's combination of signs may have been a partial imitation of her teacher's combination,
which is not how human children learn to combine words (Terrace et al., 1979;
but see VanCantfort & Rimpau, 1982, for counterarguments).

No doubt, research and debate will continue on whether apes can learn our
language. Perhaps novel training methods will enable apes to learn to string signs
into sentences as we do. Alternatively, future research may support the conclusion that, although apes can develop a humanlike vocabulary, they cannot learn
to combine their signs in the systematic way we do. If this turns out to be the case,
we will at last have evidence to support the age-old belief that language separates
us from other species.

CRITICAL DISCUSSION

Brain Localization

Given that innate factors play a large role in language acquisition, it is not surprising that regions of the human brain are specialized for language. In a Critical Discussion in Chapter 2 ("Language and the Brain"), we discussed how damage to certain regions of the left hemisphere results in *aphasia,* or language deficits. There we emphasized the relationship between the site of the brain damage and whether the resulting deficit was primarily one of production or comprehension. In the current discussion, we focus on the relation between the site of the damage and whether the deficit involves syntactic or conceptual knowledge.

Recall from Chapter 2 that there are two regions of the left hemisphere of the cortex that are critical for language: *Broca's area,* which lies in the frontal lobes, and *Wernicke's area,* which lies in the temporal-occipital region (see Figure 2-9 and p. 51). Damage to either of these areas leads to specific kinds of aphasia.

The disrupted language of a patient with *Broca's aphasia* is illustrated by the following interview where "E" designates the interviewer and "P," the patient:

E: Were you in the Coast Guard?
P: No, er, yes, yes . . . ship . . . Massachu . . . chusetts . . . Coast Guard . . . years. [Raises hands twice indicating "19"]
E: Oh, you were in the Coast Guard for nineteen years.

P: Oh . . . boy . . . right . . . right.
E: Why are you in the hospital?
P: [Points to paralyzed arm] Arm no good. [Points to mouth] Speech . . . can't say . . . talk, you see.
E: What happened to make you lose your speech?
P: Head, fall, Jesus Christ, me no good, str, str . . . oh Jesus . . . stroke.
E: Could you tell me what you've been doing in the hospital?
P: Yes sure. Me go, er, uh, P. T. nine o'cot, speech . . . two times . . . read . . . wr . . . ripe, er, rike, er, write . . . practice . . . get-ting better.
(Gardner, 1975, p. 61)

The speech is very disfluent. Even in simple sentences, pauses and hesitations are plentiful. This is in contrast to the fluent speech of a patient with *Wernicke's aphasia:*

Boy, I'm sweating, I'm awful nervous, you know, once in a while I get caught up. I can't mention the tarripoi, a month ago, quite a little, I've done a lot well, I impose a lot, while, on the other hand, you know what I mean, I have to run around, look it over, trebbin and all that sort of stuff. (Gardner, 1975, p. 68)

In addition to fluency, there are other

IMAGINAL THOUGHT

We mentioned at the beginning of the chapter that, in addition to propositional thought, we can also think in an imaginal mode, particularly in terms of visual images. Such visual thinking is the concern of the present section.

Imagery and Perception

Many of us feel that we do some of our thinking visually. Often it seems that we retrieve past perceptions, or parts of them, and then operate on them in the way we would a real percept. For example, when asked, "What shape are a German shepherd's ears?" most people report that they form a visual image of a German shepherd's head and "look" at the ears to determine their shape. If asked, "What new letter is formed when an upper case *N* is rotated 90 degrees?" people report first forming an image of a capital *N,* then mentally "rotating" it 90 degrees and "looking" at it to determine its identity. And if asked, "How many windows are there in your parents' living room?" people report imagining the

marked differences between Broca's and Wernicke's aphasias. The speech of a Broca's aphasic consists mainly of content words. It contains few grammatical morphemes and complex sentences and, in general, has a telegraphic quality that is reminiscent of the two-word stage of language acquisition. In contrast, the language of a Wernicke's aphasic preserves syntax but is remarkably devoid of content. There are clear problems in finding the right noun, and occasionally words are invented for the occasion (as in the use of "tarripoi" and "trebbin"). These observations suggest that Broca's aphasia involves a disruption at the syntactic stage, while Wernicke's aphasia involves a disruption at the level of words and concepts.

These characterizations of the two aphasias are supported by experiments. In a study that tested for a syntactic deficit, subjects had to listen to a sentence on each trial and show that they understood it by selecting a picture (from a set) that the sentence described. Some sentences could be understood without using much syntactic knowledge. For example, given "The bicycle the boy is holding is broken," one can figure out that it is the bicycle that is broken and not the boy, solely from one's knowledge of the concepts involved. Understanding other sentences required extensive syntactic analysis. In "The lion that the tiger is chasing is fat," one must rely on word order to determine that it is the lion

who is fat and not the tiger. On those sentences that did not require much syntactic analysis, Broca's aphasics did almost as well as normals, scoring close to 90 percent correct. But with sentences that required extensive analysis, Broca's aphasics fell to the level of guessing (for example, given the sentence about the lion and tiger, they were as likely to select the picture with a fat tiger as the one with the fat lion). In contrast, the performance of Wernicke's aphasics did not depend on the syntactic demands of the sentence. Thus, Broca's aphasia, but not Wernicke's, seems to be partly a disruption of syntax (Caramazza & Zurif, 1976).

Other experiments have tested for a conceptual deficit. In one study, subjects were presented three words at a time and were asked to select the two that were most similar in meaning. The words included animal terms, such as "dog" and "crocodile," as well as human terms, such as "mother" and "knight." Normal subjects used the distinction between humans and animals as the major basis for their selections; given "dog," "crocodile," and "knight," for example, they selected the first two. Wernicke's patients, however, ignored this basic distinction. Although Broca's aphasics showed some differences from normals, their selections at least respected the human-animal distinction. A conceptual deficit is thus more pronounced in Wernicke's aphasics than in Broca's aphasics (Zurif,

Caramazza, Myerson, & Galvin, 1974).

While Broca's and Wernicke's are the most common forms of aphasia, other kinds exist as well, each associated with a specific area of brain damage. A particularly interesting case is *conduction aphasia*. A patient with this problem manifests relatively good syntax and conceptual knowledge but cannot repeat a sentence, or sometimes even a word, that he or she has just heard. Thus, one patient, after being prompted again and again to repeat just the word "no," exclaimed, "No, no, I told you I can't say no," and still could not repeat the word in isolation (Gardner, 1975). This peculiar symptom makes sense, given that the part of the brain damaged in conduction aphasia is the region connecting Broca's and Wernicke's areas. In order to repeat a spoken sentence, the sentence must first be registered by Wernicke's area and then passed to Broca's area, where it is given the syntactic frame needed for production. Since the passageway is damaged in conduction aphasia, repetition is disrupted, though comprehension and production remain intact. This line of reasoning indicates that the exact nature of a patient's language deficit can be used to diagnose the specific brain region that has been damaged (Geschwind, 1972).

room and then "scanning" the image while counting the windows (Shepard & Cooper, 1982; Kosslyn, 1983).

Although the above examples rest on subjective impressions, they suggest that imagery involves the same representations and processes that are used in perception. Our images of objects and places have visual detail: we see the German shepherd, the *N*, or our parents' living room in our "mind's eye." Moreover, the mental operations that we perform on these images seem to be analogous to the operations that we carry out on real visual objects: we scan the image of our parents' room in much the same way we would scan a real room, and we rotate our image of the *N* the way we would rotate the real object.

Imagery may be like perception because it is mediated by the same parts of the brain. Support for this idea comes from studies of people who have suffered brain damage in a certain region of the right hemisphere. Such patients may develop *visual neglect* of the left side; though not blind, they ignore everything on the left side of their visual field. A male patient, for example, may forget to shave the left side of his face. This visual neglect extends to imagery. When patients are asked to construct a mental image of a familiar location (say, a shopping area) and

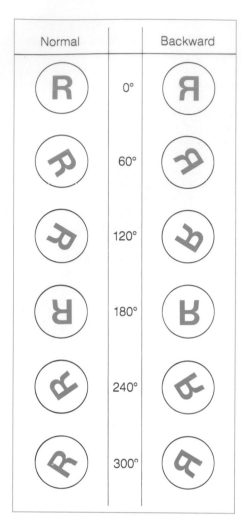

Normal		Backward
R	0°	Я
R	60°	Я
R	120°	Я
R	180°	Я
R	240°	Я
R	300°	Я

FIGURE 9-7

Study of Mental Rotation *Shown are examples of the letters presented to subjects in studies of mental rotation. On each presentation, subjects had to decide whether the letter was normal or backward. Numbers indicate deviation from the vertical in degrees. (After Cooper & Shepard, 1973)*

to report all of its contents, they may report only those things on the right side of their image (Bisiach & Luzzatti, 1978). The brain damage has led to the identical problem in perception and imagery.

Imaginal Operations

We have noted that the mental operations performed on images seem to be analogous to those we carry out on real visual objects. Numerous experiments provide objective evidence for these subjective impressions.

One operation that has been studied intensively is mental rotation. In one experiment, subjects saw the capital letter *R* on each trial. The letter was presented either normally *(R)* or backward (Я) and in its usual vertical orientation or rotated various degrees (see Figure 9-7). The subjects had to decide if the letter was normal or backward. The more the letter had been rotated from its vertical orientation, the longer it took the subjects to make the decision (see Figure 9-8). This finding suggests that subjects made their decisions by mentally rotating the image of the letter until it was vertical and then checking whether it was normal or backward.

Another operation that is similar in imagery and perception is that of scanning an object or array. In an experiment on scanning an image, subjects first studied the map of a fictional island, which contained seven critical locations. The map was removed, and subjects were asked to form an image of it and fixate on a particular location (see Figure 9-9). Then the experimenter named another location. Starting at the fixated location, the subjects were to scan their images until they found the named location and were to push a button on "arrival" there. The greater the distance between the fixated location and the named one, the longer the subjects took to respond. For example, responses were longer when the fixated and named locations were on different sides of the island than when they were on the same side. This suggests subjects were scanning their images in much the same way they scan real objects.

Another commonality between imaginal and perceptual processing is that both are limited by *grain size.* On a television screen, for instance, the grain of the picture tube determines how small the details of a picture can be and still remain perceptible. While there is no actual screen in the brain, we can think of our images as occurring in a mental medium, the grain in which limits the amount of detail we can detect in an image. If this grain size is fixed, then smaller images should be more difficult to inspect than larger ones. There is a good deal of support for this claim. In one experiment, subjects first formed an image of a familiar animal — say, a cat. Then they were asked to decide whether or not the imaged object had a particular property. Subjects made decisions faster for larger properties, such as the head, than for smaller ones, such as the claws. In another study, subjects were asked to image an animal at different relative sizes — small, medium, or large. Subjects were then asked to decide whether their images had a particular property. Their decisions were faster for larger images than smaller ones. Thus, in imagery as in perception, the larger the grain, the more readily we can see the details of an object (Kosslyn, 1980).

Visual Creativity

There are innumerable stories about scientists and artists producing their most creative work through visual thinking (Shepard, 1978). Although not hard evidence, these stories are among the best indicators that we have of the power of visual thinking. It is surprising that visual thinking appears to be quite effective in highly abstract areas like mathematics and physics. Albert Einstein, for example, said he rarely thought in words; rather, he worked out his ideas in terms of "more or less clear images which can be 'voluntarily' reproduced and combined." Perhaps the most celebrated example is in chemistry. Friedrich Kekule von Stradonitz was trying to determine the molecular structure of benzene. One night he dreamed that a writhing, snakelike figure suddenly twisted into a closed loop, biting its own tail. The structure of the snake proved to be the structure of benzene. A dream image had provided the solution to a major scientific problem. Visual images can also be a creative force for writers. Samuel Coleridge's famous poem "Kubla Khan" supposedly came to him in its entirety as a prolonged visual image.

THOUGHT IN ACTION: PROBLEM SOLVING

For many people, solving a problem epitomizes thinking itself. In problem solving, we are striving for a goal but have no ready means of obtaining it. We must break the goal into subgoals and perhaps divide these subgoals further into smaller subgoals, until we reach a level that we have the means to obtain (Anderson, 1985).

We can illustrate these points with a simple problem. Suppose you need to figure out the combination of an unfamiliar lock. You know only that the combination has four digits and that whenever you come across a correct digit, you will hear a click. Your overall goal is to find the combination. Most people decompose the overall goal into four subgoals, each corresponding to finding one of the four digits in the combination. Your first subgoal is to find the first digit, and you have a procedure for accomplishing this — namely, turning the lock slowly while listening for a click. Your second subgoal is to find the second digit, and you can use the same procedure, and so on for the remaining subgoals.

The strategies that people use to decompose goals into subgoals is thus a major issue in the study of problem solving. Another issue is how people mentally represent a problem, because this also affects how readily we can solve the problem. The following discussion considers both of these issues.

Problem-solving Strategies

Much of what we know about strategies for decomposing goals derives from the research of Newell and Simon (see, for example, Newell & Simon, 1972). Typically, the researchers have subjects think aloud while trying to solve a difficult problem, and they analyze the subjects' verbal responses for clues to the underlying strategy. A number of general-purpose strategies have been identified.

One strategy is to reduce the difference between our *current state* in a problem situation and our *goal state*, wherein a solution is obtained. Consider again the combination lock problem. Initially, our current state includes no knowledge of any of the digits, while our goal state includes knowledge of all four digits. We therefore set up the subgoal of reducing the difference between these two states; determining the first digit accomplishes this subgoal. Our current state now includes knowledge of the first digit. There is still a difference between our current state and our goal state, and we can reduce it by determining the second digit, and so on. Thus, the critical idea behind *difference reduction* is that we set up subgoals which, when obtained, put us in a state that is closer to our goal.

A similar but more sophisticated strategy is *means-ends analysis*. Here, we compare our current state to the goal state in order to find the most important difference between them; eliminating this difference becomes our main subgoal.

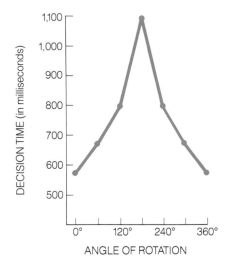

FIGURE 9-8
Decision Times in Mental Rotation Study *The time taken to decide whether a letter had normal or reversed orientation was greatest when the rotation was 180° so that the letter was upside down. Rotation was clockwise from upright (0°). (After Cooper & Shepard, 1973)*

FIGURE 9-9
Scanning Mental Images *The subject scans the image of the island from south to north, looking for the named location. It appears as though the subject's mental image is like a real map and that it takes longer to scan across the mental image if the distance to be scanned is greater. (After Kosslyn, Ball, & Reiser, 1978)*

We then search for a means or a procedure to achieve this subgoal. If we find such a procedure but discover that something in our current state prevents us from applying it, we introduce a new subgoal of eliminating this obstacle. Many commonsense problem-solving situations involve this strategy. Here is an example:

> I want to take my son to nursery school. What's the most important difference between what I have and what I want? One of distance. What [procedure] changes distance. My car. My car won't work. What is needed to make it work? A new battery. What has new batteries? My auto repair shop. (After Newell & Simon, 1972, as cited in Anderson, 1985, p. 211)

Means-ends analysis is more sophisticated than difference reduction because it allows us to take action even if it results in a temporary decrease in similarity between our current state and the goal state. In the example, the auto repair shop may be in the opposite direction from the nursery school. Going to the shop thus temporarily increases the distance from the goal, yet this step is essential for solving the problem.

Another strategy is to work backward from the goal. This is particularly useful in solving mathematical problems, such as that illustrated in Figure 9-10. The problem is this: given that ABDC is a rectangle, prove that AD and BC are the same length. In *working backward*, one might proceed as follows:

> What could prove that AD and BC are the same length? I could prove this if I could prove that the triangles ACD and BDC are congruent. I can prove that ACD and BDC are congruent if I could prove that two sides and an included angle are equal. (After Anderson, 1985, p. 216)

Thus, we reason from the goal to a subgoal (proving the triangles congruent), from that subgoal to another subgoal (proving the sides and angle equal), and so on, until we reach a subgoal that we have a ready means of obtaining.

Representing the Problem

Being able to solve a problem depends not only on our strategy for decomposing it but also on how we represent it. Sometimes a propositional mode, or representation, works best; at other times, a visual image is more effective. To illustrate, consider the following problem:

> One morning, exactly at sunrise, a monk began to climb a mountain. A narrow path, a foot or two wide, spiraled around the mountain to a temple at the summit. The monk ascended at varying rates, stopping many times along the way to rest. He reached the temple shortly before sunset. After several days at the temple, he began his journey back along the same path, starting at sunrise and again walking at variable speeds with many pauses along the way. His average speed descending was, of course, greater than his average climbing speed. Prove that there exists a particular spot along the path that the monk will occupy on both trips at precisely the same time of day. (Adams, 1974, p. 4)

In trying to solve this problem, many people start with a propositional representation. They may even try to write out a set of equations and soon confuse themselves. The problem is far easier to solve when it is represented visually. All you need do is visualize the upward journey of the monk superimposed on the downward journey. Imagine one monk starting at the bottom and the other, at the top. No matter what their speed, at some time and at some point

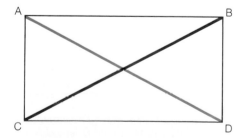

FIGURE 9-10
An Illustrative Geometry Problem
Given that ABDC is a rectangle, prove that the line segments AD and BC are the same length.

along the path the two monks will meet. Thus, there must be a spot along the path the monk occupied on both trips at precisely the same time of day. (Note that the problem did not ask you where the spot was.)

Some problems can be readily solved by manipulating either propositions or images. We can illustrate with the following problem: "Ed runs faster than David but slower than Dan; who's the slowest of the three men?" To solve this problem in terms of propositions, note that we can represent the first part of the problem as a proposition that has *David* as subject and *is slower than Ed* as predicate. We can represent the second part as a proposition with *Ed* as subject and *is slower than Dan* as predicate. We can then deduce that David is slower than Dan, which makes David the slowest. To solve the problem by imagery, we might, for example, imagine the three men's speeds as points on a line, like this:

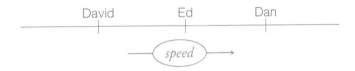

Then we can simply "read" the answer to the question directly from the image. Apparently, some people prefer to represent such problems as propositions, while others tend to represent them visually (Johnson-Laird, 1985).

In addition to the issue of propositions versus images, there are questions about *what* gets represented. Often, we have difficulty with a problem because we fail to include something critical in our representation or because we include something in our representation that is *not* an important part of the problem. We can illustrate with an experiment. One group of subjects was posed the problem of supporting a candle on a door, given only the materials depicted in Figure 9-11. The solution was to tack the box to the door and use the box as a platform for the candle. Most subjects had difficulty with the problem, presumably because they represented the box as a container, not as a platform. Another group of subjects was given the identical problem, except that the tacks were removed from the box. These subjects had more success in solving the problem, presumably because they were less likely to include the box's container property in their representation and more likely to include its supporter property.

Experts Versus Novices

In a given content area (physics, geography, or chess, for instance), experts solve problems qualitatively differently than novices. These differences are due to the

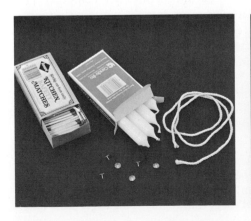

FIGURE 9-11
Materials Given in Candle Problem
Given the materials depicted (left), how can you support a candle on a door? The solution is shown in the right-hand photo.

representations and strategies that experts use and those that novices use. Experts have many more specific representations stored in memory that they can bring to bear on a problem. A master chess player, for example, can look for five seconds at a complex board configuration of over 20 pieces and reproduce it perfectly; a novice in this situation can reproduce only the usual 7 ± 2 items (see Chapter 8). Experts can accomplish this memory feat because, through years of practice, they have developed representations of many possible board configurations; these representations permit them to encode a complex configuration in just a chunk or two. Further, these representations are presumably what underlies their superior chess game. A master may have stored as many as 50,000 configurations and has learned what to do when each arises. Thus, master chess players can essentially "see" possible moves; they do not have to think them out the way novices do (Chase & Simon, 1973; Simon & Gilmartin, 1973).

Even when confronted with a novel problem, experts represent it differently than novices. This point is nicely illustrated in studies of problem solving in physics. An expert (say, a physics professor) represents a problem in terms of the physical principle that is needed for solution: for example, "this is one of those every-action-has-an-equal-and-opposite-reaction problems." In contrast, a novice (say, a student taking a first course in physics) tends to represent the same problem in terms of its surface features: for example, "this is one of those inclined-plane problems" (Chi, Glaser, & Rees, 1982).

Experts and novices also differ in the strategies they employ. In studies of physics problem solving, experts tend to reason from the givens of the problem toward a solution. Novices tend to work in the reverse direction (the working-backward strategy). Also, for difficult problems, experts generally try to formulate a plan for attacking the problem before generating equations, whereas novices typically start writing equations with no general plan in mind (Larkin, McDermott, Simon, & Simon, 1980).

Computer Simulation

To study how people solve problems, researchers often use the method of *computer simulation*. After having people think aloud while solving a complex problem, researchers use their verbal reports as a guide in programming a computer to solve the problem. Then the output of the computer can be compared to aspects of people's performance on the problem — say, the sequence of moves — to see if they match. If they match, the computer program offers a theory of some aspects of problem solving.

Why use computers to learn about people? Perhaps the most interesting answer is Simon's claim: "The reason human beings can think is because they are able to carry out with neurons the simple kinds of processes that computers do with tubes or chips" (1985, p. 3). These simple processes include reading, outputting, storing, and comparing symbols; we do one thing if the symbols match and another if they differ. To the extent that we can closely simulate human problem solving on a digital computer, which uses just these simple processes, we have support for Simon's claim.

Consider what is involved in trying to write a computer program that simulates the way many of us solve simple algebraic equations. When confronted with the equation $3X + 4 = X + 10$, you might have learned to reason as follows:

The solution of the equation looks like an X followed by an = sign followed by a number — not any number, it has to be one that will fit the equation if I substitute it back in. If I start out with something that has a number on the left side where I don't want it, then I better get rid of it since I'm trying to get something with an X and an = and a number. So given 3X + 4 = X + 10, I subtract the 4 (I know I have to subtract it from both sides). Then I have a new equation 3X = X + 6. But I don't want an X on the right side of the equation. So I subtract it and now have 2X = 6. Now I don't want a 2X, but instead just a plain X on the left side of the equation, so I divide by 2. Then I have X = 3. (After Simon, 1985, p. 6)

The above reasoning can be captured by four rules:

1. If there is a number on the left side of the equation, then subtract it from both sides.
2. If there is an X on the right side of the equation, then subtract it from both sides.
3. If there is a number in front of the X on the left side of the equation, then divide both sides of the equation by it.
4. If you arrive at an equation that looks like *X = Number,* quit and check your answer.

Though probably you do not articulate these rules, presumably they underlie your ability to solve algebraic equations. These rules can readily be translated into a computer program. A program is simply a detailed set of instructions (written in a language designed for a computer) that specifies every step the machine must take. Our rules can be treated as such instructions. Thus, simulation requires that we first be precise about the knowledge involved and then translate it into the language of a computer.

Computer simulation is not without its critics. Some argue that we do not yet know enough about human mental processes to evaluate the computer programs. How, for example, can we be sure that the computer memory resembles human memory? Other critics have challenged the basic analogy between computers and people: computers, they say, can only do what they have been programmed to do. However, it is quite possible that humans can also do only what heredity and experience have "programmed" them to do. Another criticism is that the physical basis of human thought, the brain, is very different from the electrical circuitry of computers. Clearly, a brain and a computer differ physically, but they may be similar in how they are organized and how they function. How far one can trust the computer as a guide to human mental life remains an open question.

At points in this chapter on human thought and language, we have raised questions about these abilities in nonhumans. We have discussed apes that talk or almost talk, and computers that appear to think. These discussions and comparisons suggest that we can improve our understanding of human intelligence by comparing it to nonhuman intelligence, be it natural or of our own making.

SUMMARY

1. Thought occurs in different modes, including *propositional, imaginal,* and *motoric.* The basic component of a proposition is a *concept,* the set of properties that we associate with a class. A concept includes both a *prototype* (properties that describe the best examples) and a *core* (properties that are most essential for being a member of the concept). Core properties play a major role in *classical* concepts, such as *bachelor;* prototype properties dominate in *fuzzy* concepts, such as *bird.*
2. Children often learn the prototype of a concept by an *exemplar strategy.* With this technique, a novel item is classified as an instance of a concept if it is sufficiently similar to a known exemplar of the concept. As children grow older, they use *hypothesis testing* as another strategy for learning concepts. Concepts can be combined to form *propositions,* with each proposition containing a *subject* (for example, *the tailor*) and a *predicate* (for example, *is asleep*).

3. In reasoning, we organize our propositions into an argument. Some arguments are *deductively valid:* it is impossible that the conclusion of the argument is false if its premises are true. When evaluating a deductive argument, we often try to prove that the conclusion follows from the premises by using logical rules. Other times, however, we use *heuristics* — rules of thumb — which operate on the content of propositions rather than on their logical form.

4. Some arguments are *inductively strong:* it is improbable that the conclusion is false if the premises are true. In generating and evaluating such arguments, we often ignore the principles of probability theory and rely instead on heuristics that focus on similarity or causality. For example, we may estimate the probability that a person belongs to a category by determining the person's similarity to the category's prototype.

5. Language, the means for communicating propositions, is structured at three levels. At the highest level are sentence units, including phrases that can be related to units of propositions. The next level is that of basic-meaning units, including words and parts of words that carry meaning. The lowest level contains speech sounds. The phrases of a sentence are built from words and other basic-meaning units, whereas the basic-meaning units are themselves constructed from speech sounds.

6. A *phoneme* is a category of speech sounds. Every language has its own set of phonemes and rules for combining them into words. A *morpheme* is the smallest unit that carries meaning. Most morphemes are words; others are prefixes and suffixes that are added onto words. A language also has *syntactic* rules for combining words into phrases and phrases into sentences.

7. Language development occurs at all three levels. Infants come into the world preset to learn phonemes, but they need several years to learn the rules for combining them. When children begin to speak, they learn words that name familiar concepts. If they want to communicate a concept that is as yet unnamed, they may *overextend* the name of a neighboring concept (for example, they use "doggie" to name cats and cows). In learning to produce sentences, children begin with one-word utterances, progress to two-word *telegraphic speech,* and then elaborate their noun and verb phrases.

8. Children acquire language mainly by testing hypotheses. Children's hypotheses appear to be guided by a small set of *operating principles,* which call the children's attention to critical characteristics of utterances, such as word endings. Innate factors also play a role in language acquisition. Our innate knowledge of language seems to be very rich, as suggested by the facts that all languages share some specific features and that all children seem to go through the same stages in acquiring a language. Like other innate behaviors, some language abilities are learned only during a *critical period* (we speak a language without an accent only if we learn it before puberty).

9. It is a matter of controversy whether or not our innate capacity to learn language is unique to our species. Recent studies suggest that chimpanzees and gorillas can learn signs that are equivalent to our words, but they have difficulty learning to combine these signs in the systematic manner that humans do. That innate factors play a large role in language acquisition fits with the fact that regions of the human brain are specialized for language. These regions include *Broca's area,* which may mediate syntax, and *Wernicke's area,* which seems to be concerned with concepts and meaning.

10. Not all thoughts are expressed in propositions; some are manifested as visual images. Such images contain the kind of visual detail found in perceptions. Moreover, brain damage that results in certain perceptual problems, *visual neglect,* also results in the comparable problem in imagery. In addition, the mental operations performed on images (such as scanning and rotation) are like the operations carried out on perceptions.

11. Problem solving requires decomposing a goal into subgoals that are easier to obtain. Strategies for such decomposition include *reducing differences* between

the *current state* and the *goal state; means-ends analysis* (eliminating the most important differences between the current and goal states); and *working backward*. Some problems are easier to solve by using a propositional representation; for other problems, a visual representation works best.

12. Expert problem solvers differ from novices in three basic ways: they have more representations to bring to bear on the problem; they represent novel problems in terms of solution principles rather than surface features; and they tend to reason forward rather than working backward. A useful method for studying problem solving is *computer simulation*, in which one tries to write a computer program that solves problems the same way people do.

FURTHER READING

The study of concepts is surveyed in Smith and Medin, *Categories and Concepts* (1981), and research on reasoning is reviewed by Kahneman, Slovic, and Tversky (eds.), *Judgement Under Uncertainty: Heuristics and Biases* (1982). For an introduction to the study of imagery, see Kosslyn, *Ghosts in the Mind's Machine* (1983). For more advanced treatments on imagery, see Kosslyn, *Image and Mind* (1980); and Shepard and Cooper, *Mental Images and Their Transformations* (1982). Problem-solving and computer simulation models are discussed in Newell and Simon, *Human Problem Solving* (1972); and Barr and Feigenbaum (eds.), *The Handbook of Artificial Intelligence* (1982).

Numerous books deal with the psychology of language. Standard introductions include Clark and Clark, *Psychology and Language: An Introduction to Psycholinguistics* (1977); Foss and Hakes, *Psycholinguistics: An Introduction to the Psychology of Language* (1978); Slobin, *Psycholinguistics* (2nd ed., 1979); Tartter, *Language Processes* (1986); and Carroll, *Psychology of Language* (1985). For a more advanced treatment, particularly of issues related to Chomsky's theory of language and thought, see Chomsky, *Rules and Representations* (1980b); and Fodor, Bever, and Garrett, *The Psychology of Language* (1974). For an account of early language development, see Brown, *A First Language: The Early Stages* (1973); and Pinker, *Language Learnability and Language Development* (1984).

Part Five

RALPH GIBSON
The Enchanted Hand, 1969

Gelatin-silver print, 12½ × 8⅜″.
Collection, The Museum of Modern Art,
New York. Gift of the photographer.

MOTIVATION AND EMOTION

Basic Motives

10

HAVING DISCUSSED WHAT PEOPLE CAN *do* — for instance, learn, remember, think — we will now consider what they *want*. The study of wants and needs goes under the heading of *motivation* and is concerned with factors that give behavior *direction* and *energize* it. A hungry organism will direct its behavior toward food and a thirsty organism toward drink. Both will engage in activity more vigorously than an unmotivated organism.

But hunger and thirst are just two among many motives. In this chapter, we deal with *basic* motives — unlearned motives that humans share with other animals. Such basic motives appear to be of several types: one corresponds to *survival* needs of the individual, such as hunger and thirst; a second deals with biologically based *social* needs, such as sex and maternal behavior; and a third involves *curiosity* motives, which are not directly related to the welfare of the organism. A fundamental question concerns what the motives within a type have in common. Do the motives corresponding to, say, survival needs all operate by the same principles? If so, do any of these principles apply to the other types of basic motives? We will consider these questions throughout our discussion.

SURVIVAL MOTIVES AND HOMEOSTASIS

Nature of Homeostasis

Many survival motives operate according to the principle of *homeostasis,* which is the body's tendency to maintain a constant internal environment in the face of a changing external environment. The healthy individual maintains a body temperature that varies only a degree or two, even though the temperature of the environment can vary by more than 100 degrees. Similarly, the healthy person maintains a relatively constant amount of water in his or her body, though the availability of water in the environment may vary drastically. Such internal constancies are essential for survival, since a body temperature that remains substantially above or below normal for hours can result in death, as can a lack of water for four to five days.

A thermostat is an example of a mechanical homeostatic system. Its purpose is to keep the temperature in your house (the internal environment) relatively constant while the temperature outside your house (the external environment) varies. The operation of a thermostat can tell us a good deal about the principles of homeostasis, as illustrated in the top half of Figure 10-1. The temperature of the room acts as input to the thermostat. The thermostat contains a *sensor* to measure the room temperature, an *ideal value* to represent the desired temperature, and a *comparator* to compare the sensed temperature to the ideal value. If the sensed temperature is less than the ideal value, the mechanism turns the furnace on; this

FIGURE 10-1
Homeostatic Systems *The top half of the figure illustrates the workings of a thermostat. The temperature of the room is input to the thermostat; there, a sensor detects the input temperature and compares it to an ideal value. If the sensed temperature is less than the ideal value, the furnace is turned on. The bottom half of the figure illustrates a homeostatic system in general. The system consists of a regulated variable, sensors that detect the variable, and a comparator that gauges the sensed variable against an ideal value. If the sensed variable is less than the ideal value, adjustments are made.*

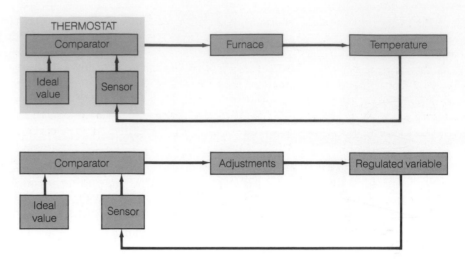

action raises the room temperature until it matches the ideal value, at which point the thermostat turns the furnace off.

We can generalize this description to all homeostatic systems, as shown in the bottom half of Figure 10-1. The core of the system is a particular variable that is being regulated (such as room temperature in the thermostat example). To regulate the variable, the system contains an ideal value of the variable, sensors that measure the variable, a comparator (or central control), and programmed adjustments that the system makes when the variable is at a value above or below the ideal (such as turning the furnace on or off). This framework enables us to understand a number of human motives. In the case of body temperature control, the variable regulated is body temperature; for thirst, the amounts of water in the cells and in the blood are the variables that are being regulated; and for hunger, several regulated variables correspond to various products of digestion (blood sugar, fat, and so on). In each case, sensors in the body detect changes from ideal values and activate adjustments that correct the imbalance. In studying these homeostatic systems, researchers seek to determine where the sensors are located, what adjustments are possible, and what region of the brain plays the role of a comparator.

We can use the homeostatic framework to distinguish between the concepts of *need* and *drive*. A need is any physiological departure from the ideal value; its psychological counterpart is a drive, an aroused state or urge that results from the need. Using hunger as an example, a need arises when the level of blood sugar drops below an ideal value. This physiological imbalance may be corrected automatically by the pancreas signaling the liver to release sugar into the bloodstream. But when these automatic mechanisms cannot maintain a balanced state, a drive is activated and the aroused organism takes action to restore the balance (it seeks foods with a high sugar content).

Temperature Regulation as a Homeostatic System

Of all human motives, the ability to keep ourselves at a comfortable temperature offers the most straightforward case of a homeostatic system. While temperature regulation may not be our prototype of a motive, it is critical for survival. Our cells cannot function outside certain limits of temperature: above 45 degrees Centigrade (113 degrees Fahrenheit), most proteins in cells become inactive and cannot carry out their functions; below 0 degrees Centigrade (32 degrees Fahrenheit), the water inside the cells begins to form ice crystals that destroy the cells.

The regulated variable is blood temperature, which is usually an accurate reflection of body temperature. There are sensors of blood temperature in the mouth (we can taste hot and cold foods), the skin (we can feel hot or cold), the spinal cord, and the brain. The chief region of the brain involved is the *hypothalamus*, a small collection of cell nuclei at the base of the brain that is directly linked with the pituitary gland and with other parts of the brain (see Figure 2-7, p. 39). In addition to sensors, the anterior (front) region of the hypothalamus appears to contain the comparator and the ideal temperature value (really, an ideal temperature *zone*). The anterior hypothalamus therefore functions like a thermostat. If this region is destroyed in a rat, the animal can no longer regulate its temperature. And if the anterior hypothalamus is heated directly (through a wire implanted there), the rat's body temperature drops, even though the body itself is not hot (Barbour, 1912); by heating the hypothalamus, the rest of the body had been "fooled" about its temperature. (This is analogous to applying a hot burst of air directly to a thermostat: even though room temperature is cool, the thermostat is fooled into dropping the temperature.)

Once the hypothalamic thermostat has determined that the body's temperature is outside of an ideal zone, it can make a variety of adjustments. Some adjustments are automatic, physiological responses. If body temperature is too high, the skin's capillaries may dilate, which increases the amount of warm blood just under the surface of the skin. The additional heat then radiates off the skin, which subsequently lowers the temperature of the blood. Sweating is another physiological means of heat loss for species that have sweat glands all over their bodies (such as humans, horses, and cattle). Species that have sweat glands in their tongues (dogs, cats, and rats) will pant to release heat. If body temperature dips too low, the first physiological adjustment is a constriction of the skin's capillaries; this pulls blood away from the cold periphery, which conserves the remaining heat for the vital organs. The body will also generate heat by shivering.

In addition to physiological reactions, we also make behavioral adjustments. When we feel cool or chilly, we put on extra clothing or seek a warmer place; when we feel too warm, we take off clothing or seek a cooler spot. These behavioral adjustments differ from the physiological ones in several respects. The behavioral adjustments are voluntary acts that we attribute to our "self," while the physiological adjustments are involuntary reactions that we attribute more to our body parts (for example, our sweat glands). Our bodies make a physiological adjustment in response to a physical need (a biological imbalance), and we make a behavioral adjustment in response to a drive. Physiological adjustments directly affect the internal environment, whereas behavioral adjustments affect the external environment (putting on a sweater protects us from the cool air), which in turn influences the internal environment. These two types of adjustments appear to be localized in different regions of the hypothalamus: the preoptic area regulates our physiological changes, whereas the lateral area regulates our behavior (Satinoff & Rutstein, 1970; Satinoff & Shan, 1971).

Thirst as a Homeostatic System

The regulation of water intake is another critical ingredient of our survival. Water is a major element of our bodies. It makes up more than half our weight; it is the main component of most tissues and blood; and it is used to carry nutrients and oxygen to our tissues, as well as to carry away wastes. But we are constantly losing water — either by evaporation from the surface of the lungs, or by sweating and urination. We therefore have to replace our water losses, and with the right amount.

The homeostatic system for thirst is more complex than that for temperature because our bodies must regulate two variables: the amount of water inside the body's cells *(intracellular fluid)*; and the amount outside the cells, including the blood *(extracellular fluid)*. We will examine these two regulated variables in turn.

The typical cause of intracellular fluid loss is a greater concentration of sodium in the water outside the cells than in the water inside the cells. Since sodium cannot permeate the cells' membranes, water leaves the cells by osmosis (a pressure to balance the concentrations of sodium on both sides of the membrane). While all cells may dehydrate, only certain ones play the role of sensors. These are *osmoreceptors* (so named because of their connection to osmosis), which are located in the hypothalamus and which respond to dehydration by becoming slightly deformed or shriveled. Thus, though the variable being regulated is water, the sensors are detecting changes in cell shape and size. In addition to the sensors, the anterior region of the hypothalamus may also contain the comparator and ideal values relevant to intracellular fluid loss.

Once the hypothalamus detects these changes, it sets homeostatic adjustments in motion. The physiological adjustment involves recovering water from the kidneys before it is excreted as urine. Specifically, neural activity from the osmoreceptors stimulates the pituitary gland (which is located just below the hypothalamus) to release the antidiuretic hormone (ADH). ADH regulates the kidneys so they release water back into the bloodstream and form only very concentrated urine. (After a night's sleep, you may notice that your urine is a darker color and has a stronger odor than it does at other times of the day; your body has recovered water from your kidneys to compensate for your not having consumed fluids while asleep.) This physiological mechanism can maintain the body's water balance only to a certain point, however. When the water deficit is too great, behavioral adjustments are required; you feel thirsty and seek water. All of this makes it clear why a hamburger and "fries" makes us thirsty. Eating the salty foods increases the concentration of salt outside the cells and causes water to leave the cells; the shrunken cells then activate sensors that mediate the drive of thirst.

There is more to thirst, though, than a deficit of intracellular fluid. Loss of blood volume, which is part of extracellular fluid, produces thirst even when the cells are not dehydrated. An injured person who has lost a considerable amount of blood feels extremely thirsty, even though the chemical concentration of the remaining blood is unchanged. Likewise, people engaged in vigorous exercise lose salt through perspiration but still have the urge to drink a lot of water, which will only further dilute the salt concentration of their blood. These observations indicate that there is another variable being regulated, namely the total volume of fluid in blood, regardless of its concentration.

The sensors for this variable are located in the kidneys, and what they actually detect is a change in blood pressure. The kidneys then secrete a substance called *renin* into the bloodstream. Renin plays a role in two different kinds of homeostatic adjustments to decreased blood volume. It causes the blood vessels to constrict, thereby preventing further blood loss; this reaction is a physiological adjustment. Through a complicated process that ultimately activates receptors in the hypothalamus, it also induces the feeling of thirst.

A homeostatic analysis suggests that a thirsty organism should drink until its intracellular and extracellular elements become rehydrated. But this is not the case. Subjects deprived of water and then allowed to drink will stop before their intracellular and extracellular levels are replenished. Thus, there must be a special mechanism to stop drinking—namely, satiety sensors which determine when there is sufficient water in the system to replenish the parched cells and the blood.

These sensors (osmoreceptors again) are located in the intestines. In experiments with monkeys, infusion of a small amount of water into the small intestine stops drinking, even if the animal has not had anywhere near enough water to make up its deficit. Thus, our system for regulating water intake is quite complex; it involves a satiety mechanism as well as the regulation of intracellular and extracellular fluid.

HUNGER

Hunger is a powerful motivator. When food becomes sparse, all of our energies and thoughts are directed to obtaining it. What exactly triggers eating? To say that people eat because it is mealtime is not sufficient. The number of meals people eat each day differs widely among cultures (as many as five in some European cultures and as few as one in some African cultures). Yet as long as food is available, people in different cultures weigh about the same. Similarly, it is not enough to say that we eat when we feel "hunger pangs" in our stomach, because people who have had their stomachs removed (due to cancer or large ulcers) still regulate their food intake. Nor do we eat simply because food tastes good, or smells good, or looks good, because when all these food cues are eliminated, people continue to regulate their food intake.

What, then, triggers eating? Current research suggests that we automatically monitor the quantities of various nutrients stored in our body (for example, glucose and fats) and are motivated to eat whenever these stores fall below critical levels. Again, the system is basically homeostatic; indeed, it is a common observation among researchers that most animals have stable body weights and that if they are given all they want to eat, they somehow eat just enough to maintain their weight. But hunger is too complex for us to give a simple homeostatic analysis. For one thing, several variables have to be regulated. For another, eating is terminated not by the food stores returning to their ideal values but, instead, by satiety sensors detecting that sufficient food has entered the system. Also, clearly

Social customs influence eating. Scene is the Great Hall of the People, Beijing, on May Day eve.

not every person is able to maintain homeostasis: just walking down a street, we can see examples of extreme overeating *(obesity)* and extreme undereating *(anorexia)*. In trying to understand hunger, we will first consider the variables that are regulated (along with the sensors that gauge them and trigger eating), then we will discuss the satiety detectors that tell us when we have eaten enough, the brain mechanisms that integrate the feeding and satiety cues, and finally the breakdown of homeostasis found in obesity.

Variables of Hunger

The study of hunger is closely tied to the study of metabolism and digestion. In order for our body cells to function, they require certain nutrients. These needed nutrients are the end products of digestion and include glucose (blood sugar), fats, and amino acids. All three appear to be regulated variables in hunger.

Glucose's role is the best documented. The brain can use only glucose for its energy supply (the rest of the body is more flexible), and it contains sensors for the nutrient. The sensors, located in the hypothalamus, measure the extent to which glucose has been absorbed by the cells. More precisely, they measure the difference in the amount of glucose in the arteries versus that in the veins. Researchers have implanted microelectrodes in the hypothalami of dogs and cats to record neural activity before and after injections of insulin (which lowers glucose level) and glucose. They found that after glucose injections cells in the lateral region of the hypothalamus decrease in activity (signaling that glucose levels are sufficient) and after insulin injections they increase their activity (signaling that glucose levels are insufficient). When the sensors indicate too low a glucose level, physiological and behavioral adjustments ensue: either the liver releases stored glucose into the bloodstream or the hungry organism searches for food. There are also glucose sensors outside the brain, specifically in the liver. These detectors are particularly well situated since the liver is among the first organs to receive the products of digestion (Stricker, Rowland, Saller, & Friedman, 1977).

We also regulate the amount of amino acids and of fat stored in special fat cells. We would expect amino acids to be regulated, for they are essential in building protein, but it is surprising that a decline in stored fat can trigger feeding. This makes sense, however, when one realizes that between meals stored fat is converted into free fatty acids, which are a major source of energy for the body. A lack of fat deposits can therefore lead to a lack of energy. The hypothalamus appears to be able to detect decreases in the size of fat cells. The substance *glycerol*, which is produced during the conversion of fat into free fatty acids, also seems to be a regulated variable. Hunger, then, involves multiple homeostatic systems.

Satiety Detectors

If we did not stop eating until our stores of nutrients reached their ideal levels, we would routinely eat for the roughly four hours that it takes to digest a meal. Nature has spared us this indignity by providing us with *satiety sensors*, which are detectors located in the early parts of the digestive system that signal the brain that the needed nutrients are on their way and that feeding can stop. The termination of feeding is thus handled by a different system — one located earlier in the digestive system — than that responsible for the initiation of feeding.

Where are the satiety sensors located? One obvious place to look is the mouth and throat. To establish definitively whether the mouth and throat contain satiety sensors, researchers have severed the esophagus of an animal and brought the cut ends out externally through incisions in the skin. When such an

External influences can arouse hunger.

animal eats, the food it swallows cannot make its way to the stomach (hence satiety sensors in the stomach and beyond can have no effect). Such an animal will swallow a somewhat larger than normal meal, then stop eating, which implies that satiety sensors must exist in the mouth and throat. However, the animal soon begins to eat again, which implies that these satiety sensors have only a short-term effect (Janowitz & Grossman, 1949). There must be other satiety sensors farther down the digestive tract.

The next places to look are the stomach and *duodenum* (the part of the small intestine connected directly to the stomach). Both organs also contain satiety sensors. If nutrients are injected directly into the stomach of a hungry animal before it is given access to food, it will eat less than usual. Thus, although the stomach may play little role in "feeling hungry," it has a substantial role in "feeling full." Nutrients injected directly into the duodenum also lead to a decrease in eating. Here, the satiety sensor may be the hormone *cholecystokinin* (CCK). When food enters the duodenum, the upper intestinal mucosa produces CCK, which limits the rate at which food passes from the stomach to the duodenum. Blood levels of CCK may be monitored by the brain as a satiety signal. Consistent with this hypothesis, many studies have found that injections of CCK inhibit eating (N. Carlson, 1985).

Another major depository of satiety sensors is the liver. It is the first organ to receive water-soluble nutrients from the digestive system, and hence its receptors have an accurate gauge of the nutrients being digested. If glucose is injected directly into the liver of a hungry animal, the animal will feed less. Sensors in the liver appear to monitor the level of nutrients that are in the intestines and then to pass this information on to the brain (Russek, 1971). In short, we can think of satiety sensors throughout the body as constituting a homeostatic system in which the variable being regulated is the total amount of nutrients in the system.

Brain Mechanisms

The system for satiety must be integrated with that for feeding. The likely locus of this is the brain, specifically the hypothalamus, which has already been shown to figure centrally in temperature control and fluid regulation and in aspects of feeding. The hypothalamus is particularly well suited for housing a control center for hunger, since it contains more blood vessels than any other area of the brain and consequently is readily influenced by the chemical state of the blood. Two regions of the hypothalamus are particularly important: the *lateral hypothalamus* and *ventromedial hypothalamus.*

One way to study the function of a brain area is to destroy cells and nerve fibers in the region and observe the animal's behavior when the area no longer exerts control. This technique has led to the discovery of two important syndromes. The first, *LH syndrome,* occurs when tissue in the lateral hypothalamus is destroyed. Initially, the animal — typically a rat — refuses to eat or drink and will die unless it is fed intravenously. After several weeks of being intravenously nourished, most of the rats begin to recover: first they eat only palatable wet food but will not drink; eventually they will eat dry food and begin to drink. The second syndrome, *VMH syndrome,* occurs when tissue in the ventromedial hypothalamus is destroyed. It has two distinct phases. In the initial or *dynamic phase,* which lasts between 4 and 12 weeks, the animal overeats voraciously, sometimes tripling its body weight within a matter of weeks (see Figure 10-2). In the second or *static phase,* the animal no longer overeats. Rather, it reduces its food intake to slightly more than normal level and maintains its new obese weight. The VMH syndrome has been observed in all animal species studied — from rat to chicken and monkey. For humans, researchers have noted that people with tumors or

FIGURE 10-2
Hypothalamic Overeating *Lesions in the ventromedial hypothalamus caused this rat to overeat and gain more than three times its normal weight. Its weight is 1,080 grams, not 80 grams.*

injuries in the ventromedial hypothalamus may overeat and become extremely obese.

Initially, psychologists interpreted the VMH and LH syndromes as implying the existence of dual hunger centers — a *feeding center* in the lateral hypothalamus and a *satiety center* in the ventromedial hypothalamus. They believed that destruction of the lateral tissue disrupts the feeding center, thereby making it difficult for the animal to eat, while destruction of ventromedial tissue disrupts the satiety center and makes it difficult for the animal not to eat. But why, then, do rats nursed through the first few weeks after their lateral-hypothalamic lesions eventually come to regulate their food intake with precision, albeit at a lower weight? Similarly, if destruction of the ventromedial hypothalamus impairs a satiety center, why do the animals actually reduce their food intake during the static phase? Recent findings have largely overthrown the dual-center interpretation.

One new account holds that the lateral and ventromedial areas are concerned with the regulation of overall body weight. Consider again a fat rat with a ventromedial lesion. We have already noted that eventually it will reach a static phase where it maintains its new obese weight. But if the animal's diet is restricted, body weight will decrease until it reaches the original, normal weight; if the rat is allowed to eat freely again, it will overeat until it returns to its obese state. Damage to the ventromedial area apparently disturbs the animal's long-term weight control system, so it regulates its weight at a higher level. Further, if these obese rats are force-fed until they become extremely obese, they will reduce their food intake until their weight returns to its "normal obese" level (see Figure 10-3).

Similarly, damage to the lateral hypothalamus apparently disturbs weight control so that the animal regulates its weight at a lower level. Recall that after initially refusing all food and water, rats with the LH syndrome resume eating and drinking on their own. But they stabilize at a lower weight level, just as rats with the VMH syndrome stabilize at an obese level (Mitchel & Keesey, 1974). Again, this behavior indicates impairment of a long-term weight control system. Rats that are starved prior to lesioning of the lateral hypothalamus do not refuse to eat after the operation. In fact, many of them overeat, but only until their weight reaches a new level that is lower than their normal weight but higher than their starved, preoperational weight (see Figure 10-4).

These findings indicate that the lateral and ventromedial hypothalamus have reciprocal effects on the *set point* for body weight, or the weight at which an individual body functions best. Damage to the ventromedial areas raises the set point; damage to the lateral area lowers it. If *both* areas in a rat are lesioned carefully so that an equivalent amount of tissue is destroyed in each area, the

FIGURE 10-3
Effects of Forced Feeding and Starvation on Body Weight of Rat with VMH Lesions *Following lesioning of the ventromedial hypothalamus, the rat overeats and gains weight until it stabilizes at a new, obese level. Forced feeding or starvation alters the weight level only temporarily; the rat returns to its stabilized level. (After Hoebel & Teitelbaum, 1966)*

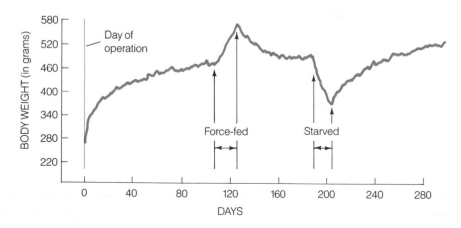

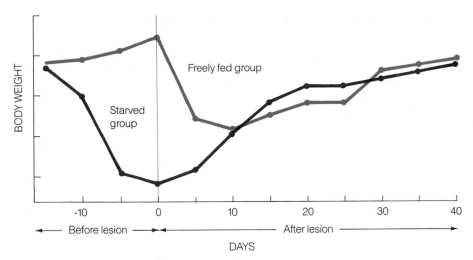

FIGURE 10-4
Body Weight and the Lateral Hypothalamus *Prior to lesioning the lateral hypothalamus, one group of rats was starved while another group was allowed to feed freely. Following surgery, the starved animals increased their food intake and gained weight while the freely fed group lost weight. Both groups stabilized at the same weight level. (After Powley & Keesey, 1970)*

animal does not overeat or undereat; rather, it maintains its presurgery weight level (Keesey & Powley, 1975).

Another explanation of the VMH and LH syndromes proposes that the effects are not due to the destruction of hypothalamic nuclei but to interference with some of the 50 different nerve tracts that pass through these hypothalamic locations. Consider again a fat rat with a lesion in its ventromedial hypothalamus. While the researchers may have been interested in the effects of the lesion on just the hypothalamus per se, such a lesion also affects certain branches of the parasympathetic nervous system that pass through this region. These latter effects alter metabolism so that too many nutrients are converted into fat (for storage) and too few are left as fuel for metabolic processes. As a result, the animal is constantly in need of nutrients, so it constantly overeats. Thus the VMH-lesioned rat may overeat because, in a sense, it is starving.

A lesion in the lateral hypothalamus also may interrupt an important set of nerve fibers called the *nigrostriatal bundle.* These fibers are involved in activating the organism to engage in all kinds of behaviors, not just feeding, and their destruction leads to activation problems and other general deficits (the same fibers are impaired in *Parkinson's disease,* which involves motor inactivation). These deficits in activation may be the reason why a rat with LH syndrome initially will not eat or drink at all. Indeed, when the nigrostriatal bundle is lesioned outside the hypothalamus (the tracts extend beyond the hypothalamus), animals show the same breakdowns in feeding that occur in the early stages of the LH syndrome (Friedman & Stricker, 1976).

Clearly, interpretations of the VMH and LH syndromes are controversial. Since the early 1960s, psychologists trying to explain hunger motivation have gone from hunger centers to set points to extraneous nerve tracts. Perhaps these interpretations are not incompatible: a lesion in the lateral hypothalamus may both lower the set point for body weight and interrupt nerve tracts that activate the organism. The brain is an enormously complex organ, and we cannot expect simple correspondences between its regions and psychological functions.

OBESITY

We have emphasized homeostatic processes in hunger, but our eating behavior shows several departures from homeostasis. Some people's body weights are not as constant as the homeostatic viewpoint suggests. And while the sight, taste, and smell of food may not be *the* basic factors in regulating feeding, they do have some influence. For example, after a full meal you may still want to eat dessert; here, your cue for hunger is not internal, because there is no physiological need.

The largest deviation from homeostatic regulation of eating—at least for humans—is obesity, which is very common in our culture. Roughly 34 million Americans are 20 percent or more above the appropriate weight for their body structure and height. Obesity is also dangerous: a 1985 National Institute of Health panel concluded that obesity is a major health hazard, contributing to a higher incidence of diabetes, high blood pressure, and heart disease. It is not surprising that each year millions of people spend millions of dollars on special diets and drugs to lose weight. Unfortunately, most of these people are not successful, and those who succeed in shedding pounds often regain them. Part of the difficulty in losing weight is that being fat is self-perpetuating: both gaining additional weight and dieting can change your metabolism and energy expenditure in such a way as to keep you fat. These problems have stimulated much research on the origin and control of obesity.

Most researchers agree that obesity is a complex problem and can involve genetic, metabolic, nutritional, psychological, sociological, and environmental factors. Obesity probably is not a single disorder but a host of disorders that all have fatness as their major symptom (Rodin, 1981). The question of how one becomes obese is like that of how one gets to Pittsburgh—there are many ways to do it, and which one you "choose" depends on where you are coming from (Offir, 1982).

We will be concerned with three major causes of weight gain: *calorie intake, calorie expenditure,* and *genetics.* Roughly speaking, people become obese because they (1) eat too much, (2) expend too little effort, or (3) are genetically predisposed to be fat. We reserve our consideration of genetic factors for the Critical Discussion. Keep in mind that no single factor needs to apply to all people (there are many ways to get to Pittsburgh).

Factors Increasing Calorie Intake

BREAKDOWN OF CONSCIOUS RESTRAINTS   Some people stay obese by binge eating after they diet. An obese man may break his two-day diet and then overeat so much that he eventually consumes more calories than he would have had he not dieted at all. Since the diet was a conscious restraint, the breakdown of control is a factor in increased calorie intake.

To have a more complete understanding of the role of conscious restraints, researchers have developed a questionnaire that asks about diet and weight history (for example, How often do you diet? and What is the maximum amount of weight that you have ever lost in a month?), as well as about the individual's concern with food and eating (for instance, Do you eat sensibly in front of others, yet overeat when alone? and Do you feel guilty after overeating?). The results show that almost everyone—whether thin, plump, or fat—can be classified into one of two categories: people who consciously restrain their eating and people who do not. In addition, regardless of their actual weight, the eating behavior of restrained eaters is closer to that of obese individuals than is that of unrestrained eaters (Herman & Polivy, 1980; Ruderman, 1986).

A laboratory study shows what happens when restraints are dropped. Restrained and unrestrained eaters (both of normal weight) were required to drink either two milk shakes, one milk shake, or none; they then sampled several flavors of ice cream and were encouraged to eat as much as they wanted. The more milk shakes the unrestrained eaters were required to drink, the less ice cream they consumed later. In contrast, the restrained eaters who had been preloaded with two milk shakes ate more ice cream than did those who drank one milk shake or none. A similar experiment with thin, normal, and obese subjects revealed that dieting was a more critical factor in predicting eating behavior than weight was. The three weight groups did not differ in the amount of ice cream they ate after being preloaded with two milk shakes or none. But when the data were analyzed for restrained versus unrestrained eaters, regardless of weight, nondieters (unrestrained subjects) were shown to eat much less after two milk shakes than after none, whereas dieters (restrained subjects) ate more (see Figure 10-5).

In these experiments, the forced loading of milk shakes makes the subjects lose control of their eating behavior. Once restrained eaters lose control, they eat much more than unrestrained eaters do. But loss of control may not be the only operative factor here. Deprivation per se can lead to binge eating, independent of the organism's feelings of control. In some experiments, rats were first deprived of food for four days, then allowed to feed back to their normal weights, and finally allowed to eat as much food as they wanted. These once-deprived rats ate more than did control rats that had no history of deprivation. Thus, prior deprivation leads to subsequent overeating, even after the weight lost from the deprivation has been regained (Coscina & Dixon, 1983). This may explain why many cases of anorexia nervosa — where the key symptom is extreme weight loss — paradoxically show binge eating: the deprivation required to stay very thin eventually leads to overeating. (The reason why anorexics do not gain weight from their binges is that they purge themselves by vomiting or taking laxatives.)

Why should prior deprivation lead to future overeating? Evolutionary theory suggests an answer. Until very recently in historical time — and, indeed, still in underdeveloped countries — whenever human beings experienced deprivation, it was because of scarcity in the environment. An adaptive response to such scarcity is to overeat and store in our bodies as much food as possible whenever it is available. Hence, evolution may have selected for an ability to overeat following deprivation. In times of famine, this tendency has served our species well, but once famine is not a concern, the tendency keeps obese dieters overweight (Polivy & Herman, 1985).

EMOTIONAL AROUSAL Overweight individuals often report that they tend to eat more when they are tense or anxious, and experiments support this. Obese subjects eat more in a high-anxiety situation than they do in a low-anxiety situation, while normal-weight subjects eat more in situations of low anxiety (McKenna, 1972). Other research indicates that any kind of emotional arousal seems to increase food intake in some obese people. In one study, overweight and normal-weight subjects saw a different film in each of four sessions. Three of the films aroused various emotions: one was distressing; one, amusing; and one, sexually arousing. The fourth film was a boring travelogue. After viewing each of the films, the subjects were asked to taste and evaluate different kinds of crackers. The obese subjects ate significantly more crackers after viewing any of the arousing films than they did after seeing the travelogue. Normal-weight individuals ate the same amount of crackers regardless of which film they had seen (White, 1977).

Two hypotheses may explain why obese people eat more when anxious. One possibility is that when they were babies, their caregivers interpreted all of their distress signals as requests for food; consequently, as adults, these people have difficulty distinguishing hunger from other feelings, including anxiety. A different possibility is that some obese persons may respond to an anxiety-producing situation by doing the one thing that has brought them comfort all their lives — namely, eating. The two hypotheses may apply to different kinds of obese people.

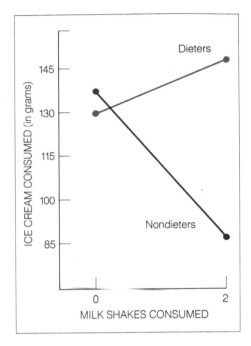

FIGURE 10-5
Restrained and Unrestrained Eaters
Subjects concerned with dieting consumed more ice cream after previously overindulging in milk shakes than did subjects who were unconcerned about controlling their food intake, regardless of body weight. (After Hibscher & Herman, 1977)

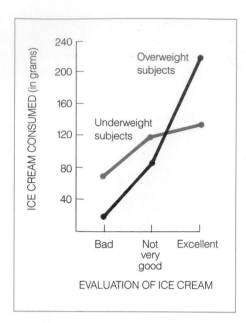

FIGURE 10-6
Taste and Obesity *The effects of food quality on the amount eaten by overweight and underweight subjects. The subjects rated the quality of ice cream and could eat as much as they desired. (After Nisbett, 1968)*

RESPONSIVENESS TO EXTERNAL CUES Compared to normal-weight people, obese individuals may be more sensitive to external hunger cues (the sight, aroma, and taste of food) and less sensitive to internal hunger cues (such as satiety signals from the intestines). One study examined the effects of taste on the eating behavior of underweight and overweight subjects. The subjects were allowed to eat as much vanilla ice cream as they wanted and then were asked to rate its quality. Some subjects were given a creamy, expensive brand; the others, a cheap brand with quinine added. Figure 10-6 plots the subjects' ratings against the amount of ice cream they ate. Overweight subjects ate much more ice cream when they rated it "excellent" than when they rated it "bad," while the ice-cream consumption by underweight subjects was less affected by taste.

Other experiments indicate that while people do indeed differ in their *externality* (sensitivity to external cues), by no means are all obese people "externals," nor are all externals obese. Rather, there are externals and internals in every weight category, and only a moderate correlation exists between degree of externality and degree of obesity. Perhaps externality contributes to obesity more in short-term situations than in long-term control of body weight. Hyper-responsive girls gained more weight in summer camp (where food was plentiful) than their less responsive cohorts did, but the difference between the two groups was greatest well before the end of camp and had started to fade by the last week of camp (Rodin, 1981).

Factors Decreasing Energy Expenditure

METABOLIC RATE Two-thirds of a normal person's energy expenditure is devoted to metabolic processes (basic bodily functions). Hence, our metabolic rate is a major determinant of weight control: low rates of metabolism expend fewer calories and result in more body weight. Metabolic rate is lower in fat tissue than it is in lean tissue. Thus, the individual's basal metabolic rate decreases as lean tissue is replaced by fat, which explains why obese people may stay fat even when their calorie intake is normal.

Metabolic rate also decreases during periods of deprivation, such as when dieting. Consequently, the calorie reduction during dieting is partly offset by the lowered metabolic rate, making it difficult for dieters to meet their goal. While it may seem that nature, in the guise of metabolism, is conspiring against the obese, an evolutionary account again provides some perspective. Since deprivation has usually indicated a scarcity of food in the environment, it is adaptive for organisms to respond to deprivation by decreasing the rate at which they expend their limited amount of calories.

ACTIVITY AND EXERCISE General activity and exercise account for the remaining third of a person's energy expenditure. Exercise, of course, burns off calories: the more that people exercise, the more calories they expend. But exercise also indirectly affects basal metabolism. If a person is sedentary, the metabolic mechanism fails to operate properly and so produces a lower metabolic rate (Garrow, 1978). Lack of exercise for an overweight person sets up a vicious cycle: obesity makes physical exercise more difficult and less enjoyable, and inactivity results in fewer calories being burned — directly through exercise and indirectly through a reduced basal metabolic rate. Thus, exercise is critical in weight loss, not only because it burns calories but also because it helps to regulate normal metabolic functioning (Thompson, Jarvie, Lakey, & Cureton, 1982).

Weight Control

Our discussion of obesity has uncovered a number of factors that tend to maintain fatness: eating to assuage emotions; the tendency of dieting to lead to binge

Exercise is critical in weight loss, not only because it burns calories but also because it helps regulate metabolic functioning.

eating; and the slowed metabolic rate caused by fat tissue, dieting, and lack of exercise. Each of these factors can perpetuate a vicious cycle. But in many cases the cycle can be broken, as witnessed by the success of certain weight-reduction programs. To lose weight and keep it off, overweight individuals must recognize that anxiety and emotional situations tend to cause them to overeat, that dieting can seduce them into binges, and — perhaps most important — that exercise is a vital part of success.

To control weight, the individual must establish a new set of eating and exercise habits. A study comparing methods for treating obesity illustrates this conclusion. For six months, obese individuals followed one of three treatment regimens: (1) behavior modification of eating and exercise habits, (2) drug therapy using an appetite suppressant (fenfluramine), and (3) a combination of behavior modification and drug therapy. Subjects in all three treatment groups were given information on exercise and extensive nutritional counseling, including a diet of no more than 1,200 calories per day. Subjects in the behavior modification groups were taught to keep a daily record of their eating habits, to become aware of situations that prompted them to overeat, to change the conditions associated with their overeating, to reward themselves for appropriate eating behavior, and to develop a suitable exercise regimen. In addition to the three treatment groups, there were two control groups: one consisted of subjects waiting to take part in the study, who received no treatment of any kind; and the other comprised subjects who saw a physician for traditional office treatment of weight problems.

Table 10-1 presents the results of the study. As might be expected, the subjects in all three treatment groups lost more weight than the subjects in the two control groups. At the end of treatment, the group combining behavior modification with drug therapy lost the most weight (an average of 33.7 pounds per person). The drug-therapy-only group did almost as well (averaging 31.9 pounds), but the behavior-modification-only group lost significantly less (an average of 24 pounds). However, during the year after treatment, a striking reversal developed. The behavior-modification-only group regained far less weight than the other two treatment groups; these subjects maintained an average

CRITICAL DISCUSSION

Are Some People Programmed to Be Fat?

Obesity runs in families: fat parents tend to have fat children. This observation does not necessarily imply a biological explanation (perhaps the child is simply imitating the parents), but there is evidence that some aspects of obesity are biologically based. For instance, twin studies indicate that genetics does play a role; identical twins share the same level of obesity twice as often as fraternal twins (Stunkard, Foch, & Hrubec, 1986).

Research on the biological basis of obesity has focused on *fat cells*, where all body fat is stored. Organisms — people and animals — vary in how many fat cells they have; the variation, due partly to genetics, has consequences for obesity. In one sample, obese subjects were found to have three times as many fat cells as normal subjects (Knittle & Hirsch, 1968). In other studies, researchers have shown that rats that have double the usual number of fat cells tend to be twice as fat as the control rats. And when researchers cut some of the fat cells out of young rats, so they had only half as many fat cells as their littermates, the operated rats grew up to be only half as fat as their littermates (Hirsch & Batchelor, 1976; Faust, 1984).

The number of fat cells is not entirely fixed by genes. Overeating during the early months of life can increase the number of fat cells. Recent work suggests that even in adulthood overeating can increase an organism's fat-cell count, though to a lesser extent. Still, genetics sets important limits on the total number of fat cells. It determines the minimum number of fat cells, since — barring surgery for obesity — an organism can never lose fat cells. In addition, the extent to which overeating produces new fat cells may itself be determined genetically.

The number of fat cells is not the only critical factor; the size of fat cells also matters. Overeating increases the size of fat cells, while deprivation decreases their size. In most organisms, however, fat cells stay relatively constant in size.

We therefore have two biologically based factors — the number and the size of fat cells — that vary from person to person

weight loss of 19.8 pounds by the end of year, whereas the weight losses for the drug-therapy-only group and the combined-treatment group averaged only 13.8 and 10.1 pounds each.

What caused this reversal? An increased sense of self-efficacy may have been a factor. Subjects who received the behavior-modification-only treatment could attribute their weight loss to their own efforts, thereby strengthening their resolve to continue controlling their weight after the treatment ended. Subjects who received an appetite suppressant, on the other hand, probably attributed their weight loss to the medication and so did not develop a sense of self-control; when the drug was withdrawn (releasing biological pressures to regain weight), their sense of self-efficacy was not strong enough to prevent them from returning to their old eating habits. The drug had also decreased the subjects' feelings of hunger; and so the subjects in the drug-therapy-only group and the combined-

TABLE 10-1
Weight Loss Following Different Treatments *Weight loss in pounds at the end of six months of treatment and on a follow-up one year later. Subjects in the two control groups were not available for the one-year follow-up. (After Craighead, Stunkard, & O'Brien, 1981)*

	WEIGHT LOSS AFTER TREATMENT	WEIGHT LOSS AFTER ONE YEAR
Treatment groups		
Behavior modification only	24.0	19.8
Drug therapy only	31.9	13.8
Combined treatment	33.7	10.1
Control groups		
Waiting list	2.9 (gain)	—
Physician office visits	13.2	—

and are critically related to obesity. Researchers believe that the combination of these two factors may determine an individual's set point (or ideal value), which the hypothalamus tries to maintain. Thus, the set point for obese and nonobese individuals who have the same height and bone structure may be different if the two people differ in the number and size of their fat cells. If this is true, obesity for some individuals is their "normal" weight. Attempts at weight reduction by such individuals would hold them below their biologically determined set point, in a state of chronic deprivation; they would feel hungry all the time — just as a thin person would feel on a starvation diet (Nisbett, 1972).

In pursuing the *set-point hypothesis,* Stunkard (1982) has argued that appetite-suppressant drugs such as fenfluramine act primarily to lower the set point and only secondarily to suppress appetite. His account explains the findings on drug therapy for obesity discussed in the text — namely, the rapid regaining of body weight following the withdrawal of fenfluramine in contrast to the relative stability of weight loss achieved by behavior modification. The drug lowered the set point of patients, thereby facilitating weight loss; but discontinuation of the drug caused the set point to return to its pretreatment level. The resulting biological pressure for the individuals to gain weight until they reached their original set points produced a greater weight gain in the drug-therapy subjects than in those who lost weight without the aid of drugs. These interpretations cast doubt on the effectiveness of appetite-suppressant medication in the treatment of obesity.

The set-point hypothesis is intriguing but controversial. For example, according to the hypothesis, increased responsiveness to food cues is a consequence rather than a cause of obesity. Many obese individuals remain below their set point by dieting, and this deprivation increases their receptivity to cues associated with food. Thus, proponents of the hypothesis argue that the longer obese individuals diet (that is, the more weight they lose), the more sensitive they become to food cues. But experiments do not seem to confirm this prediction. Sensitivity to cues associated with food appears to remain relatively constant, regardless of the amount of weight a person loses (Rodin, 1981).

The set-point hypothesis has generated considerable research, but there are too many contrary findings for it to serve as a general theory of obesity. However, as noted earlier, no such general theory may be possible. The set-point hypothesis may account for certain types of problems, particularly the individual who was moderately overweight as a child and remains moderately overweight throughout life. A higher than normal set point may be one reason for overconsumption, but undoubtedly others exist. Most overweight people do not suddenly become obese. Their fat accumulates over a period of months or years — a kind of "creeping obesity" that results from gradually consuming more calories than the body expends in energy.

treatment group may not have been sufficiently prepared to cope with the increase in hunger that they felt when the medication was stopped.

ADULT SEXUALITY

Sexual and maternal drives are other powerful motivators. Sexual desire sometimes can be so strong that it becomes almost an obsession, and a mother's (or father's) desire to protect its young can be so intense as to make her insensitive to pain. Like the survival motives we have considered, sex (and to some extent maternal behavior) is an unlearned motive that human beings share with other species, and whose biological basis psychologists are beginning to understand. There are, however, important differences between sex and maternal behavior, on the one hand, and temperature, thirst, and hunger on the other. Sex and maternal behavior are *social* motives — their satisfaction typically involves another organism — whereas the survival motives concern only the biological self. In addition, motives such as hunger and thirst stem from tissue needs, while sex and maternal behavior do not involve an internal deficit that needs to be regulated and remedied for the organism to survive. Consequently, social motives do not lend themselves to a homeostatic analysis.

With regard to sex, two critical distinctions should be kept in mind. The first stems from the fact that, although we begin to mature sexually at puberty, the basis for our sexual identity is established in the womb. We therefore distinguish between adult sexuality (that is, beginning with changes at puberty) and early sexual development. The second distinction is between the biological and environmental determinants of sexual behaviors and feelings. For many aspects of sexual development and adult sexuality, a fundamental question is the extent to which the behavior or feeling in question is a product of biology (particularly hormones), of environment (early experiences and cultural norms), or of an interaction between the two.

Hormonal Control

At puberty—roughly ages 11 to 14—changes in hormones occur, which lead to bodily changes that serve to distinguish males from females. The hormonal system involved is illustrated in Figure 10-7. Endocrine glands manufacture hormones (chemical messengers), which travel through the bloodstream to target organs. The process begins in the hypothalamus when it secretes *gonadotropin-releasing factors;* these chemical messengers direct the pituitary gland to produce *gonadotropins,* which are hormones whose targets are the *gonads*—the ovaries and testes. There are two kinds of gonadotropins. One is called *follicle-stimulating hormone* (FSH). In women, FSH stimulates the growth of *follicles,* clusters of cells in the ovaries that support developing eggs and secrete the female hormone *estrogen.* In men, FSH stimulates sperm production in the testes. The other gonadotropin produced by the pituitary is called *luteinizing hormone* (LH) in women and *interstitial-cell stimulating hormone* (ICSH) in men. The secretion of LH brings on ovulation—the release of a mature egg from the follicle—and then causes the ruptured follicle to secrete *progesterone,* another female hormone. ICSH, the male equivalent, stimulates the production of the male hormone *androgen.* Although a number of technical terms have been mentioned here, the basic scheme is simple: by way of hormones, the hypothalamus directs the pituitary, which in turn directs the gonads.

The hormones produced by the gonads—estrogen, progesterone, and androgen—are called the *sex hormones* (a bit of a misnomer because all three hormones are produced by males and females, albeit in different amounts). These hormones are responsible for the body changes at puberty. In girls, estrogen causes the development of breasts, the changes in the distribution of body fat that

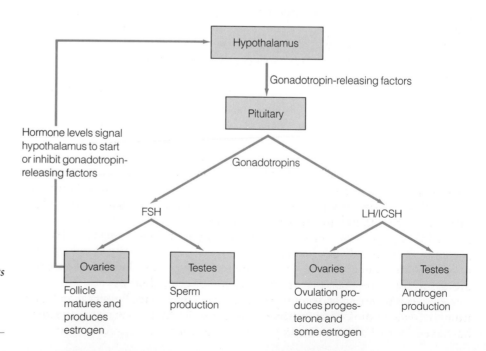

FIGURE 10-7
Hormonal System Involved in Sex *By way of hormones, the hypothalamus directs the pituitary, which in turn directs the gonads, to secrete the sex hormones. (After Offir, 1982)*

result in a more feminine form, and the maturation of the female genitals. In boys, *testosterone* (a kind of androgen) is responsible for the sudden growth of facial, underarm, and pubic hair; it also causes a deepening of the voice, the development of muscles that lead to a more masculine form, and the growth of the external genitals.

What role do these hormones play in adult sexual attraction and arousal? In other species, sexual attraction is closely tied to variations in hormonal levels; in humans, however, hormones play less of a role in sexual attraction. One way to assess the contribution of hormones to sexual arousal is to study the effects of castration. In males, castration usually involves removal of the testes, which essentially eliminates production of the sex hormones. In experiments with lower species (such as rats and guinea pigs), castration results in the rapid decline and eventual disappearance of sexual activity. For humans, of course, there are no controlled experiments; psychologists rely instead on observations of males with serious illnesses (for example, cancer of the testes) who have undergone *chemical castration* (synthetic hormones administered to suppress or block the use of androgen). These studies typically show that some men lose their interest in sex, while others continue to lead a normal sex life (Money, Wiedeking, Walker, & Gain, 1976; Walker, 1978). Apparently, androgen contributes to sexual desire only in some cases.

Another way to measure the contribution of hormones to sexual desire in men is to look for a relation between hormonal fluctuation and sexual arousal. Is a man more likely to feel aroused when his testosterone level is high? Thus far, researchers have found no conclusive evidence for such a relation, suggesting that once testosterone reaches a normal level, further increases may have little effect on sexual arousal.

The lack of hormonal effects on arousal in women is even more striking, particularly in contrast to other species. In all animals, from reptiles to monkeys, castration in a female (removal of the ovaries) results in cessation of sexual activity. The castrated female ceases to be receptive to the male and usually resists sexual advances. The major exception is the human female; following menopause (when the ovaries have ceased to function), sexual motivation in most women does not diminish. In fact, some women show an increased interest in sex after menopause, possibly because they are no longer concerned about becoming pregnant.

Studies looking at the relation between hormonal fluctuation and sexual arousal in premenopausal females present a similar conclusion: hormones have substantial control of arousal in lower species but not in humans. In female mammals, hormones fluctuate cyclically with accompanying changes in fertility. During the first part of the mammalian cycle (while the egg is being prepared for fertilization), the ovaries secrete estrogen, which prepares the uterus for implantation and also tends to arouse sexual interest. After ovulation occurs, both progesterone and estrogen are secreted. This *fertility* or *estrous cycle* is accompanied by a consequent variation in sexual motivation in most mammalian species. Most female animals are receptive to sexual advances by a male only during the period of ovulation, when the estrogen level is at its highest in the cycle (when they are "in heat"). Among primates, however, sexual activity is less influenced by the fertility cycle; monkey, ape, and chimpanzee females copulate during all phases of the cycle, although ovulation is still the period of most intense sexual activity. In the human female, sexual activity is barely influenced by the fertility cycle, being affected much more by social and emotional factors.

In sum, the degree of hormonal control over adult sexual behavior decreases from the lower to the higher vertebrates. Still, even for humans there may be some hormonal control, as witnessed by the effects of chemical castration on men.

Neural Control

The nervous system also is responsible for aspects of sexual arousal and behavior, the mechanisms of which are complex and vary from one species to the next. In humans, some of the neural mechanisms involved are at the level of the spinal cord. In males, an erection following direct stimulation of the penis is controlled by a spinal reflex, as are pelvic movements and ejaculations. All of these actions are still possible in men whose spinal cords have been severed by injury. Similarly, clinical studies of women with spinal cord injuries suggest that lubrication of the vagina may be controlled by a spinal reflex (Offir, 1982).

But the organ most responsible for the regulation of sexual arousal and behavior is the brain (sex therapists call it "the most erogenous zone"). The spinal reflexes are regulated by the brain, and erections can be directly controlled by the brain through thoughts and images. Some of our more precise knowledge about the role of the brain in sex comes from experiments with animals. In male rats, electrical stimulation of the posterior hypothalamus produces not only copulation but the entire repertoire of sexual behavior. A male rat stimulated in that area does not mount indiscriminately; instead, he courts the female by nibbling her ears and nipping the back of her neck until she responds. Intromission and ejaculation follow unless the electrical stimulation is terminated. Even a sexually satiated male rat will respond to electrical stimulation by pressing a bar to open a door leading to the female and will court and mate with her (Caggiula & Hoebel, 1966).

Early Experiences

The environment also has great influence on adult sexuality, one class of determinants being early experience. Experience has little influence on the mating behavior of lower mammals — inexperienced rats will copulate as efficiently as experienced ones — but it is a major determinant of the sexual behavior of higher mammals.

Experience can affect specific sexual responses. For instance, young monkeys exhibit in their play many of the postures required later for copulation. In wrestling with their peers, infant male monkeys display hindquarter grasping and thrusting responses that are components of adult sexual behavior. Infant female monkeys retreat when threatened by an aggressive male infant and stand steadfastly in a posture similar to the stance required to support the weight of the male during copulation. These presexual responses appear as early as 60 days of age and become more frequent and refined as the monkey matures (see Figure 10-8). Their early appearance suggests that they are innate responses to specific stimuli, and the modification and refinement of these responses through experience indicates that learning plays a role in the development of the adult sexual pattern.

Experience also affects the interpersonal aspect of sex. Monkeys raised in partial isolation (in separate wire cages, where they can see other monkeys but cannot have contact with them) are usually unable to copulate at maturity. The male monkeys are able to perform the mechanics of sex: they masturbate to ejaculation at about the same frequency as normal monkeys. But when confronted with a sexually receptive female, they do not seem to know how to assume the correct posture for copulation. They are aroused but aimlessly grope the female or their own bodies. Their problem is not just a deficiency of specific responses. These once-isolated monkeys have social or affectional problems:

A

B

C

D

FIGURE 10-8
Infant Play and Adult Sexual Behavior
A. The first presexual step.
B. Inappropriate sexual response: female correct, male incorrect. C. Basic sexual posture. D. Inappropriate sexual response: male correct, female incorrect.

even in nonsexual situations, they are unable to relate to other monkeys, exhibiting either fear and flight or extreme aggression. Apparently, normal heterosexual behavior in primates depends not only on hormones and the development of specific sexual responses but also on an affectional bond between two members of the opposite sex. This bond is an outgrowth of earlier interactions with the mother and peers, through which the young monkey learns to trust, to expose its delicate parts without fear of harm, to accept and enjoy physical contact with others, and to be motivated to seek the company of others (Harlow, 1971).

Although we must be cautious about generalizing these findings with monkeys to human sexual development, clinical observations of human infants suggest certain parallels. Human infants develop their first feelings of trust and affection through a warm and loving relationship with the mother or primary caretaker (see Chapter 3). This basic trust is a prerequisite for satisfactory interactions with peers. And affectionate relationships with other youngsters of both sexes lay the groundwork for the intimacy required for heterosexual relationships among adults.

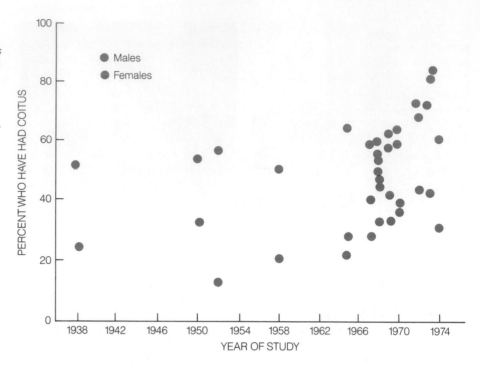

FIGURE 10-9
Reported Incidence of Premarital Coitus *Each data point represents findings from a study of the incidence of premarital sex among college men and women. Note the marked upward trend starting in the 1960s. (After Hopkins, 1977)*

Cultural Influences

Cultural influences constitute another class of environmental determinants. Unlike that of other primates, human sexual behavior is strongly determined by culture. Every society places some restrictions on sexual behavior. Incest (sexual relations within the family), for example, is prohibited by almost all cultures. Other aspects of sexual behavior—sexual activity among children, homosexuality, masturbation, and premarital sex—are permitted in varying degrees by different societies. Among preliterate cultures studied by anthropologists, acceptable sexual activity varies widely. Some very permissive societies encourage autoerotic activities and sex play among children of both sexes and allow them to observe adult sexual activity. The Chewa of Africa, for example, believe that if children are not allowed to exercise themselves sexually, they will be unable to produce offspring later.

In contrast, very restrictive societies try to control preadolescent sexual behavior and to keep children from learning about sex. The Cuna of South America believe that children should be totally ignorant about sex until they are married; they do not even permit their children to watch animals give birth. And among the Ashanti of Africa, intercourse with a girl who has not undergone the puberty rites is punishable by death for both participants. Similar extreme attitudes are found toward other aspects of sexual behavior: homosexuality, for example, is viewed by some nonliterate societies as an essential part of growing up and by others as an offense punishable by death.

In the 1940s and 1950s, the United States and most other Western countries would have been classified as sexually restrictive. Traditionally, the existence of prepubertal sexuality had been ignored or denied. Marital sex was considered the only legitimate sexual outlet, and other forms of sexual expression (homosexual activities, premarital and extramarital sex) were generally condemned and often prohibited by law. Of course, many members of these societies engaged in such activities, but often with feelings of shame.

Today, sexual activities are far less restricted. Premarital intercourse, for example, is now more acceptable and occurs more frequently. Among college-educated individuals interviewed in the 1940s, 27 percent of the women and 49 percent of the men had engaged in premarital sex by the age of 21 (Kinsey, Pomeroy, & Martin, 1948; Kinsey, Pomeroy, Martin, & Gebhard, 1953). In contrast, several surveys of college students in the 1970s report percentages ranging from 40 to over 80 for both males and females (Hunt, 1974; Tavris & Sadd, 1977). Figure 10-9 gives the reported incidence of premarital intercourse in studies conducted over a 35-year span. Note that the change in sexual behavior has been greater among women than men and that the biggest changes occurred in the late 1960s. These changes have led many observers of the social scene to conclude that there has been a sexual revolution.

The revolution, however, may pertain more to behavior than to feelings. In interviews with college-student couples, only 20 percent thought that sex between casual acquaintances was completely acceptable (Peplau, Rubin, & Hill, 1977). And in a study of first sexual experiences, although many respondents were proud of losing their virginity, few reported any sensual pleasures (Hunt, 1974). While heralding a revolution in sexual behavior, these and other results reveal traditional values and feelings.

In a similar vein, while women are becoming more like men with regard to sexual behavior, they continue to differ from men in certain critical attitudes toward sex before marriage. The majority of women who engage in premarital sex do so with only one or two partners with whom they are emotionally involved. Men, in contrast, are more likely to seek casual sex without involvement; in one survey, the median number of premarital partners reported by males was six (Hunt, 1974). Further, when college students were asked to list their problems with "any respect of sexual functioning," the concerns of males and females were quite different. Women most often expressed fears and insecurities:

- Fear of pregnancy
- Fear of rape
- Fear of being conquered and then regarded as of no further use
- Fear of being rejected if they said no
- Masturbation —accepting it
- Fear that their partners would be physically repulsed by them
- Fear of losing self-respect
- Fear of becoming too attached when the feeling was not mutual
- Guilt feelings about premarital sex
- Pressure to have sex even when they did not want to
- Fear of not satisfying their partners
- Embarrassment or concern over not being orgasmic

Men were more apt to list complaints about women rather than to express their own conflicts or worries:

- Finding partners who were open to varying sexual experiences
- Always having to be on the hunt
- Not being able to have sexual relations when they wanted to
- Women who tease, without wanting to engage in sexual activity
- Women's refusal to take responsibility for their own sexuality
- Women who used their sexual attractiveness in a manipulatory fashion

- The excessive modesty of women (they wanted the lights off)
- Passive women
- Aggressive women
- Necessity to say you loved the woman even if it was not true
- Being expected to know all about sex
- Inability to communicate feelings or needs during sex

(Tavris & Offir, 1977, p. 68)

These response differences reflect different attitudes — at least among males and females who are young and unmarried — about the relation between sex and love.

Homosexuality

The term "homosexual" can be applied to either a man or a woman, but female homosexuals are usually called "lesbians." Most experts agree with Kinsey's view that homosexuality is not an either-or matter; sexual behavior falls on a continuum, with exclusively heterosexual and exclusively homosexual individuals at either end and various mixtures of sexual behavior in between. Most young boys engage in erotic play with other boys at some time during their childhood, and many men have one or more homosexual encounters. According to some estimates, only about 4 percent of men become exclusively homosexual. Women are less apt than men to have sexual interactions with each other during childhood or a homosexual episode in later life; and only 1–2 percent of women are exclusively homosexual. Some individuals are *bisexual,* enjoying sexual relations with members of both sexes. And some married individuals may have homosexual encounters on the side.

Until the advent of the sexual revolution in the late 1960s, homosexuality was considered a mental illness or an abnormal perversion. Although many people still view homosexuality as unnatural, most psychologists and psychiatrists consider it to be a variant rather than a perversion of sexual expression and not, in itself, an indication or cause of mental illness. Indeed, in studies of mental health, homosexuals seem as well adjusted as comparable heterosexuals (see, for example, Hooker, 1957; Sahgir & Robins, 1973).

BIOLOGICAL AND ENVIRONMENTAL DETERMINANTS Despite considerable research, relatively little is known about the causes of homosexuality. With regard to possible biological determinants, there are no reliable differences in body characteristics between homosexuals and heterosexuals. Although some male homosexuals may look quite feminine — and some female homosexuals, quite masculine — this is often not the case. A more plausible locus of biological differences is hormones, and here the evidence is quite inconsistent. Some studies have found that male homosexuals have lower levels of testosterone than do heterosexual males, while other studies show no difference in overall levels of hormones. Moreover, when male homosexuals are given additional male hormones, their sex drive may increase but their sexual preferences do not change. Male homosexuals, however, may show a pattern of secreting the hormone LH in response to estrogen that is intermediate between that of heterosexual men and women (recall that LH is secreted by the pituitary and sent to the gonads). Four days after an injection of estrogen, heterosexual women's LH levels were 200 percent above their baseline, heterosexual men's LH levels averaged 88 percent above their baseline, and homosexual men had levels 138 percent above their baseline (Gladue, Green, & Hellman, 1984). No evidence, however, relates this pattern to the cause of homosexuality.

Some proposals about environmental causes of homosexuality seem equally tenuous. It is often proposed that parents are somehow responsible for their children's homosexuality, but a large study with homosexuals suggests that parental influence is, at best, only a minor determinant of sexual preference. The major results of this study, summarized in Table 10-2, suggest that sexual preference depends on a complex pattern of feelings and reactions within the child that cannot be traced to a single psychological or social factor.

A more promising approach is to consider the interaction between biology and environment. Storms (1981) has proposed that sexual preference results in part from an interaction between sex-drive development and social development during early adolescence. Specifically, the onset of the sex drive during adolescence (due to the surge of hormones) initiates the development of a sexual orientation, and the various people in an individual's social environment at that time determine the direction of the sexual orientation. An unusually early onset of the sex drive contributes to homosexuality, because the individual's social environment at that time is composed primarily of youngsters of the same sex (boys and girls tend to form separate, same-sexed groups from early childhood through preadolescence). Thus, sexual preference in adulthood depends on the social environment that is present when the individual's sex drive comes into full force during adolescence. If the environment is primarily of the same sex, the adult's sexual preference will tend to be homosexual; if heterosocial, the adult's sexual preference will tend to be heterosexual. This theory appears to explain a number of the observations regarding homosexuality reported in Table 10-2.

GENDER DIFFERENCES In our earlier discussion of heterosexuality, we noted that young men and women differ in their attitudes about sex, with women being more likely to view sex as part of a loving relationship. This same kind of

---

1. By the time both the boys and the girls reached adolescence, their sexual preference was likely to be determined, even though they might not yet have become very active sexually.

2. Among the respondents, homosexuality was indicated or reinforced by sexual feelings that typically occurred three years or so before their first "advanced" homosexual activity. These feelings, more than homosexual activities, appeared to play a crucial role in the development of adult homosexuality.

3. The homosexual men and women in the study were not particularly lacking in heterosexual experiences during their childhood and adolescent years. They were distinguishable from their heterosexual counterparts, however, in that they found such experiences ungratifying.

4. Among both the men and the women in the study, there was a powerful link between gender nonconformity as a child and the development of homosexuality.

5. The respondents' identification with their opposite-sex parents while growing up appeared to have had no significant impact on whether they turned out to be homosexual or heterosexual.

6. For both the men and the women in the study, poor relationships with fathers seemed to play a more important role in predisposing them to homosexuality than the quality of their relationships with their mothers.

7. Insofar as differences can be identified between male and female psychosexual development, gender nonconformity appeared to be somewhat more important for males and family relationships appeared to be more important for females in the development of sexual preference.

TABLE 10-2
Variables Influencing Sexual Preference *Results are based on interviews conducted in 1969–70 with approximately 1,500 homosexual men and women living in the San Francisco Bay area. The investigators analyzed the respondents' relationships with their parents and siblings while growing up, the degree to which the respondents conformed during childhood to the stereotypical concepts of what it means to be male or female, the respondents' relationships with peers and others outside the home, and the nature of their childhood and sexual experiences. Statistical analyses traced the relationship between such variables and adult sexual preference. (After Bell, Weinberg, & Hammersmith, 1981)*

difference appears between male and female homosexuals. Lesbians are more likely than male homosexuals to have long-term relations with their lovers. Lesbians also have many fewer sexual partners. In the study by Bell and Weinberg (1978), the majority of gay females reported having a total of fewer than ten sexual partners, while the average gay male reported hundreds of sexual partners. Also, lesbians place more emphasis on the romantic aspects of their relations than do gay men. The way that people conduct their sexual-romantic lives, therefore, may have less to do with being homosexual or heterosexual than with being male or female.

EARLY SEXUAL DEVELOPMENT

For social and sexual experiences to be gratifying in adult life, one needs to develop an appropriate *gender identity* — that is, males need to think of themselves as males, and females as females. This development is quite complex and begins early, in the womb.

Prenatal Hormones

For the first couple of months after conception, only the chromosomes of a human embryo indicate whether it will develop into a boy or girl. Up to this stage, both sexes are identical in appearance and have tissues that will eventually develop into testes or ovaries, as well as a genital tubercle that will become either a penis or a clitoris. But between 2 and 3 months, a primitive sex gland, or gonad, develops into testes if the embryo is genetically male (that is, has XY chromosomes — see Chapter 2) or into ovaries if the embryo is genetically female (XX chromosomes). Once testes or ovaries develop, they produce the sex hormones, which then control the development of the internal reproduction structures and the external genitals. The sex hormones are more important for prenatal development than they are for adult sexuality.

The critical hormone in genital development is androgen. If the embryonic sex glands produce enough androgen, the newborn will have male genitals; if there is insufficient androgen, the newborn will have female genitals, *even* if it is genetically male (XY). The anatomical development of the female embryo does not require female hormones, only the absence of male hormones. In short, nature will produce a female unless androgen intervenes.

The influence of androgen, called *androgenization*, extends beyond anatomy. Early androgenization may be responsible for masculine traits and behaviors that appear later. In a series of experiments, pregnant monkeys were injected with testosterone (a kind of androgen), and their female offspring were observed in detail. These female offspring showed some anatomical changes (penises instead of clitorises) and also acted differently than normal females. They were more aggressive in play, more masculine in sexual play, and less intimidated by approaching peers (Goy, 1968; Phoenix, Goy, & Resko, 1968). This indicates that some gender-appropriate behaviors (such as greater aggression for males) may be hormonally determined in monkeys. If the same is true in humans, then some typical aspects of our gender identity are controlled by hormones rather than social environment. Some researchers have even suggested that such unusual traits as musical genius and *dyslexia* (a reading disability), which are more common in men than women, are partly the products of excessive androgenization (Geschwind, 1984). The question of hormonal control in humans remains controversial.

Hormones Versus Environment

In humans, much of what is known about the effects of prenatal hormones and early environment has been uncovered by studies of *hermaphrodites*. Hermaphrodites are individuals who are born with both male and female tissue; they may have genitals that appear to be ambiguous (an external organ that could be described as a very large clitoris or a very small penis) or external genitals that conflict with internal sex organs (a penis and ovaries) (see Figure 10-10). These conditions arise because of prenatal hormonal imbalances, in which a genetically female fetus has too much androgen or a genetically male fetus has too little of it. What, then, will be the eventual gender identity of a hermaphroditic infant who is assigned the wrong sex label at birth — say, an infant with ambiguous external genitalia who is called a boy at birth but is later determined to be genetically female (XX) and to have ovaries?

In most cases such as this, the assigned label and the sex role in which the individual is raised have a much greater influence on gender identity than do the individual's genes and hormones. For example, two genetically female infants had ambiguous external genitals because their fetal sex glands had produced too much androgen (their internal organs were clearly female, though). Both infants had surgery to correct their enlarged clitorises. One infant's genitals were "feminized," and she was raised as a girl; the other infant's genitals were modified to resemble a penis, and he was raised as a boy. Reports indicate that both children grew up secure in their respective sex roles. The girl was somewhat "tomboyish," but feminine in appearance. The boy was accepted as a male by his peers and expressed a romantic interest in girls. Cases such as this suggest that an individual's gender identification is influenced more by the way a person is labeled and raised than by his or her hormones (Money, 1980).

But there are also cases that point to the opposite conclusion. The most famous occurred several years ago in remote villages of the Dominican Republic. It involved 18 genetic males who, owing to the fact that their cells were insensitive to the androgen their bodies generated prenatally, were born with internal organs that were clearly male but external genitals that were closer to females, including a clitoris-like sex organ. All 18 were raised as girls, which was at odds with both their genes and their prenatal hormonal environment. When they reached puberty, the surge of male hormones produced the usual bodily changes and turned their clitoris-like sex organs into penis-like organs. The vast majority of these males-reared-as-females rapidly turned into males. They seemed to have little difficulty adjusting to a male gender identity; they went off to work as miners and woodsmen and soon found female sexual partners. In this case, biology triumphed over environment (Imperato-McGinley, Peterson, Gautier, & Sturla, 1979). There is controversy, however, about these Dominican hermaphrodites; it is not clear how consistent their female upbringing was, particularly since they had ambiguous genitals.

Proponents of environmental determination can point to their own incredible case. Identical twin boys had a completely normal prenatal environment. But at the age of 7 months, in a tragic mistake, one of the boys had his penis completely severed in what was supposed to be a routine circumcision. Ten months later, the agonized parents authorized surgery to turn their child into a little girl — the testes were removed and a vagina was given preliminary shape. The child was then given female sex hormones and raised as a girl. Within a few years, the child seemed to have assumed a female gender identity: she preferred more feminine clothes, toys, and activities than her twin brother. What is striking about this case is (1) that environment won out over both genes and a *normal* prenatal environment (in all other cases considered, the prenatal environment has not

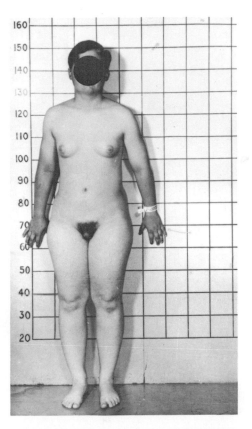

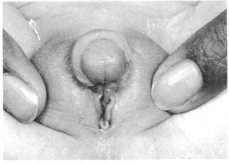

FIGURE 10-10

Hermaphroditism *Too much androgen in female fetuses and too little androgen in male fetuses may result in external genitals that are ambiguous in appearance. The full-body picture shows a late-treated boy who had a mastectomy after the picture was taken. The close-up shows clitoral enlargement in an infant female.*

been entirely normal), and (2) that a comparison can be made between individuals who have identical genes and prenatal hormones but different upbringings. Still, advocates of biological determination are skeptical about basing too much on a single case.

What can we conclude about gender identity? Clearly, prenatal hormones and environment are both major determinants of gender identity that typically work in harmony. When they clash, as they do in certain hermaphrodites, most experts believe that environment will dominate. But this is a controversial area, and expert opinion may change as additional data are gathered.

Transsexualism

Some people feel that their body is compatible with one sex—say, their internal and external organs are all male—but their gender identity is that of the other sex—they think of themselves as females. Such *transsexuals* (usually males) feel that they were born into the wrong body. They are not homosexuals in the usual sense. Most homosexuals are satisfied with their anatomy and identify themselves as appropriately male or female; they simply prefer members of their own sex. Transsexuals, in contrast, think of themselves as members of the *opposite* sex (often from early childhood) and may be so desperately unhappy with their physical appearance that they request hormonal and surgical treatment to change their genitals and secondary sex characteristics.

Doctors have performed several thousand sex-change operations in the United States. For males, hormone treatments can enlarge their breasts, reduce beard growth, and make their figures more rounded; surgical procedures involve removing the testes and part of the penis and shaping the remaining tissue into a vagina and labia. For women, hormone treatments can increase beard growth, firm their muscles, and deepen their voices; surgical procedures involve removing the ovaries and the uterus, reducing breast tissue, and in some instances constructing a penislike organ. Although a sex-change operation does not make reproduction possible, it can produce a remarkable change in physical appearance. Because the surgery is so drastic, though, it is undertaken only after careful consideration. The individual is usually given counseling and hormone treatments and is required to live as a member of the opposite sex for a year or more prior to the operation. Expert opinion remains divided on whether sex-change surgery genuinely helps transsexual individuals to feel better adjusted (Hunt & Hampson, 1980).

What explains transsexualism? An interesting hypothesis is that some cases of transsexualism may result from a prenatal hormonal error, which is similar to the one producing hermaphrodites but which occurs at a later stage of fetal development. If such an error were to occur after the formation of the external genitals but before the complete development of the brain mechanisms that influence sexual behavior, the individual's sense of sexual identity could contradict his or her physical sex. This is only speculation, however; we can reasonably assume that environmental and biological factors play a role in transsexualism (Money, 1980).

MATERNAL BEHAVIOR

In many species, care of the offspring is a more powerful determinant of behavior than is sex, or even hunger and thirst. A mother rat, for example, will more frequently overcome barriers and suffer pain to reach its young than it will to obtain food when hungry or water when thirsty. While humans are not always as dutiful parents as rats are, caring for the young is one of the basic motives in our species, too.

Biological Determinants

As is the case with sex, hormones play a major role in the maternal behavior of lower species, but not primates. Virgin rats presented with rat pups for several days will begin to build a nest, lick the pups, retrieve them, and finally hover in a nursing posture. If blood plasma from a mother rat that has just given birth is injected into a virgin rat, it will begin to exhibit maternal behavior in less than a day (Terkel & Rosenblatt, 1972). Maternal behavior patterns appear to be innately programmed in the rat's brain, and hormones serve to increase the excitability of these neural mechanisms. The hormonal effects depend on the balance between the female hormones (estrogen and progesterone) and prolactin from the anterior pituitary gland, which stimulates the production of milk.

For humans, hormones have much less influence. If human maternal behavior were chiefly guided by hormones, one would not expect parents to abuse their children as often as they do. Some women abandon their newborn infants or even kill them, and battered children are more commonplace than people realize. In the United States, according to a conservative estimate, approximately 350,000 children each year are physically, sexually, or emotionally abused by their caretakers; a less conservative estimate holds that between 1.4 and 1.9 million children each year are at risk of a serious injury from a family member (Wolfe, 1985). The parents involved in these cases generally received little or no love as children and frequently were beaten by their own parents, indicating the importance of early experience on parental behavior. In primates and humans, experience far overrides whatever influence "maternal hormones" may have.

But we cannot dismiss biology entirely. A number of possible biological determinants of human parental behavior have been suggested by *ethologists* (scientists who study animal behavior in the natural environment). One such possibility is that the distinctive, "cute" features of a baby (large head and eyes, upturned nose, chubby cheeks, and so forth) serve as *innate releasers* of parental feelings and behavior. That is, our species — and most others — may have evolved so that the characteristic "cute" features of babies elicit feelings of parenting in adults. In a similar vein, a baby's smile, which appears to be innately determined, seems to be a preprogrammed elicitor of parental behavior. (See the Critical Discussion, "Instincts and Maternal Behavior," for greater detail.)

Environmental Determinants

Among primates, maternal behavior is largely influenced by experience and learning. If female monkeys are raised in isolation, they exhibit none of the normal maternal behaviors when they later become mothers (see Chapter 3, p. 78). They appear to develop little love for their offspring and generally ignore them. When they do pay attention to their young, they sometimes abuse them savagely. A mother might try to crush her infant's head or, in extreme cases, even bite the infant to death (Suomi, Harlow, & McKinney, 1972). There is a parallel here between the dreadful parenting of these monkey mothers originally reared in isolation and the child abuse by people who were raised by inadequate parents. Those who are themselves subjected to poor parenting seem destined to pass it on to their offspring.

Cuteness acts as an innate releaser of parental feelings.

CRITICAL DISCUSSION

Instincts and Maternal Behavior

The concept of an *instinct* has a long history in the study of behavior. Around the turn of the century, psychologists relied heavily on the concept, attempting to explain all human behavior in terms of instincts (McDougall, 1908). During the 1920s, the concept fell into disrepute, partly because many acts were being cavalierly labeled "instinctive" and partly because the concept did not fit with the emerging theory of behaviorism (Stellar & Stellar, 1985). But later, starting in the 1950s, a group of European ethologists brought the study of instinct under scientific scrutiny and revived interest in the concept. For a behavior to be labeled instinctive, it has to be innately determined and it must be specific to a certain species and appear in the same form in all members of the species. Thus, *innateness, species specificity,* and *fixed-action patterns* are the hallmarks of the ethological approach to instinctive behavior.

One area where the ethological approach has succeeded is the maternal behavior of animals. The response patterns that animals display in the care of their young provide a clear example of instinctive behavior. Building nests, removing the amniotic sac so the newborn can breathe, feeding the young, and retrieving them when they stray from the nest are all complex behavior patterns that animals exhibit without having had the opportunity to have learned them; hence, they must be innate. A squirrel performs maternal duties in the same manner as all other mothers of its species; therefore, the behavior is species-specific and fixed in its action pattern.

Among the more startling discoveries of ethologists is the phenomenon of *imprinting.* As you may recall from Chapter 7, imprinting refers to a type of early learning that forms the basis for the young animal's attachment to its parents. A newly hatched duckling that has been incubated artificially will follow a human being, a wooden decoy, or almost any other moving object that it first sees after birth. Following a wooden decoy for as little as 10 minutes is enough to imprint the duckling on the decoy; the duckling will then remain attached to this object, follow it even under adverse circumstances, and prefer it to a live duck. Imprinting occurs most readily 14 hours after hatching, but can happen any time during the first two days of life. After this interval, imprinting is difficult, probably because the duckling has acquired a fear of strange objects.

Ethologists have found imprinting in a number of species—including dogs, sheep, and guinea pigs—but it is most clearly developed in birds that are able to walk or swim immediately after birth. An innate mechanism ensures that the young will follow and will remain close to their mothers (normally the first moving object they see), rather than wander off into a perilous world.

Studies of mallard ducks have identified the stimuli that are important for imprinting in birds and indicate that the phenomenon begins even before birth. Ducklings begin to make sounds in their eggs a week before they break through the shells. Mallard mothers respond to these sounds with clucking signals, which increase in frequency about the time the

CURIOSITY MOTIVES

Thus far, all of the motives discussed have been related to the survival of either the individual or the species. An earlier generation of psychologists believed that once an organism has satisfied its motives, it prefers a quiescent state, but this belief has turned out to be wrong. Both people and animals are motivated to *seek* stimulation—to explore actively their environment, even when the activity satisfies no bodily need. Thus, there appears to be a third general class of motives, *curiosity,* which we will briefly survey.

Exploration and Manipulation

We seem to have inborn drives to manipulate and investigate objects. We give babies rattles, crib gymnasiums, and other toys because we know they like to

ducklings hatch. Auditory stimuli before and after hatching, together with tactile stimulation in the nest after birth, thoroughly imprint the ducklings on the female mallard in the nest. An unhatched duckling that hears a recording of a human voice

Imprinting in Ducklings *The newly hatched duckling follows the model duck around a circular track. The duckling soon becomes imprinted on the model and will follow it in preference to a live duck of its own species. The more effort the duckling has to exert to follow the model (such as climbing a hurdle), the stronger the imprinting. (After Hess, 1958; © 1958 by Scientific American, Inc. All rights reserved.)*

saying "Come, come, come" instead of its mother's clucking will imprint on a decoy that utters "Come, come, come" as easily as it will imprint on a decoy that utters normal mallard clucks. Ducklings that have been exposed to a mallard female's call prior to hatching are more likely to imprint on decoys that utter mallard clucks (Hess, 1972).

In addition to the concepts of species specificity and fixed-action patterns, ethologists have developed the concept of a *releaser*, a particular environmental stimulus that sets off a species-specific behavior. In some young sea gulls, a red or yellow spot on the mother's beak "releases" a pecking response by the hatchling, which causes the mother to regurgitate the food that the infant will eat. By varying the color and shape of the spot on cardboard models and by observing whether the young gull pecks at the "beak," researchers can determine the characteristics of the releaser to which the bird responds.

Releasers also play a major role in the sexual behavior of lower animals. The swollen abdomen of the female stickleback fish initiates courtship behavior by the male. The bowing and cooing behavior of the male ringdove releases an entire sequence of reproductive behavior in the female (nest building and laying and incubating the eggs) and is responsible for the hormonal changes that accompany these activities (Lehrman, 1964).

The higher an animal is on the evolutionary scale, the fewer instinctive behaviors it exhibits and the more that learning determines its actions. But even humans

have some instinctual behavior patterns, including the *rooting reflex* of the human infant. Touching a nipple (or a finger) to the cheek of a newborn elicits head turning and simultaneous mouth opening. If the mouth contacts the nipple, it closes on the nipple and begins to suck. This behavior pattern is automatic and can occur even when the infant is sleeping. At about 6 months, the rooting reflex is superseded by voluntary behavior; the typical 6-month-old sees the nipple, reaches for it, and tries to bring it to his or her mouth.

Austrian ethologist Konrad Lorenz demonstrates how young ducklings follow him instead of their mother because he was the first moving object they saw after they were hatched.

hold, shake, and pull them. Monkeys enjoy the same sort of activities; in fact, the word "monkey," used as a verb, describes casual manipulation for whatever satisfaction it brings. A number of experiments have shown that monkeys do indeed like to "monkey." If various mechanical devices are placed in a monkey's cage, it will begin to take them apart, becoming more skilled with practice, without receiving any evident reward other than the satisfaction of manipulating them. If the monkey is fed each time it takes a puzzle apart, its behavior changes; it loses interest in manipulation and views the puzzle as a means of acquiring food (Harlow, Harlow, & Meyer, 1950).

While manipulation sometimes is done for its own sake, other times it is for purposes of *investigation*. The monkey — or person — picks up the object, looks at it, tears it apart, and examines the parts, apparently attempting to discover more about it. Piaget made a number of observations bearing on such responses in the early life of the human infant. Within the first few months of life, infants learn

Some young monkeys "monkeying"

to pull a string to activate a hanging rattle — a form of manipulation that might be considered merely entertaining. Between 5 and 7 months, they will remove a cloth from their faces in anticipation of the peekaboo game. At 8 to 10 months, infants look for objects behind or beneath other objects; by 11 months, they begin to experiment with objects, varying the toys' placement or positions (Piaget, 1952). This kind of inquisitive or investigative behavior is typical of the growing child, and it seems to develop as a motive apart from any physiological need of the organism.

Sensory Stimulation

SENSORY DEPRIVATION STUDIES   Both exploration and manipulation provide the organism with new and changing sensory input. This change in input may be one reason why humans and animals manipulate and investigate objects: perhaps we have a need for sensory stimulation. Studies in which sensory stimulation is markedly reduced support this hypothesis. In the first study of this type, college students were paid to lie on a cot in a lighted, partially sound-deadened room. They wore translucent goggles so that they could see diffuse light but no shapes or patterns. Gloves and cardboard cuffs reduced tactile stimulation (see Figure 10-11). The hum of an exhaust fan and an air conditioner provided a constant masking noise. Brief "time-outs" were allowed for meals and bathroom needs, but otherwise the subjects remained in a condition of very restricted stimulation. After two or three days, most of the subjects refused to continue the experiment; the situation was sufficiently intolerable to them to offset even a large financial payment. Some of the subjects began to experience visual hallucinations that varied from light flashes and geometric patterns to dreamlike scenes. They became disoriented in time and space, were unable to think clearly or concentrate for any length of time, and did poorly when given problems to solve. In short, the condition of *sensory deprivation* had a detrimental effect on normal functioning and produced symptoms not unlike those experienced by some mental patients (Heron, Doane, & Scott, 1956).

A number of similar studies have subsequently been conducted. In some studies, subjects lay immersed to the neck in a tub of warm water for several days in an attempt to reduce sensory stimulation further. Results have differed somewhat, depending on the procedure, but in most instances the subjects eventually

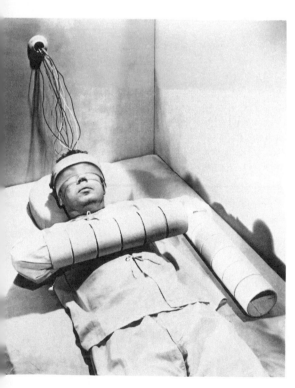

FIGURE 10-11
Sensory Deprivation Experiment
Cardboard cuffs and a translucent blindfold reduce stimulation.

became bored, restless, irritable, and emotionally upset. People apparently require sensory stimulation and react adversely to its absence (Zubek, 1969).

INDIVIDUAL DIFFERENCES IN STIMULATION SEEKING   While persons differ in the extent to which they manifest some of the other motives discussed in this chapter, individual differences in curiosity motives seem particularly salient. To try to measure these differences, Zuckerman (1979) has developed a test called the *Sensation Seeking Scale,* abbreviated SSS. The scale includes a range of items designed to assess an individual's desire to engage in adventurous activities, to seek new kinds of sensory experiences, to enjoy the excitement of social stimulation, and to avoid boredom. Table 10-3 presents a sample of the items on the scale; you may want to answer them before reading further.

---

1. A. I have no patience with dull or boring persons.
    B. I find something interesting in almost every person I talk to.
2. A. A good painting should shock or jolt the senses.
    B. A good painting should provide a feeling of peace and security.
3. A. People who ride motorcycles must have some kind of unconscious need to hurt themselves.
    B. I would like to drive or ride a motorcycle.
4. A. I would prefer living in an ideal society in which everyone is safe, secure, and happy.
    B. I would have preferred living in the unsettled days of history.
5. A. I sometimes like to do things that are a little frightening.
    B. A sensible person avoids dangerous activities.
6. A. I would not like to be hypnotized.
    B. I would like to be hypnotized.
7. A. The most important goal of life is to live to the fullest and experience as much as possible.
    B. The most important goal of life is to find peace and happiness.
8. A. I would like to try parachute jumping.
    B. I would never want to try jumping from a plane, with or without a parachute.
9. A. I enter cold water gradually, giving myself time to get used to it.
    B. I like to dive or jump right into the ocean or a cold pool.
10. A. When I go on a vacation, I prefer the comfort of a good room and bed.
    B. When I go on a vacation, I prefer the change of camping out.
11. A. I prefer people who are emotionally expressive even if they are a bit unstable.
    B. I prefer people who are calm and even-tempered.
12. A. I would prefer a job in one location.
    B. I would like a job that requires traveling.
13. A. I can't wait to get indoors on a cold day.
    B. I am invigorated by a brisk, cold day.
14. A. I get bored seeing the same faces.
    B. I like the comfortable familiarity of everyday friends.

Scoring:

Count one point for each of the following items that you have circled: 1A, 2A, 3B, 4B, 5A, 6B, 7A, 8A, 9B, 10B, 11A, 12B, 13B, 14A. Add your total for sensation seeking and compare it with the norms below:

0–3	Very low	6–9	Average	12–14	Very high
4–5	Low	10–11	High		

TABLE 10-3
Sensation Seeking Scale   *A sample of items from the SSS and a scoring procedure. Each item contains two choices. Choose the one that best describes your likes or feelings. If you do not like either choice, mark the choice you dislike the least. Do not leave any items blank. (Test items courtesy of Marvin Zuckerman)*

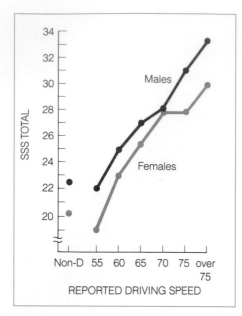

FIGURE 10-12

SSS Scores and Driving Speed *Subjects were asked at what speed they would usually drive on a highway if conditions were good and the posted speed limit was 55 MPH. Results revealed a significant relationship between reported driving speed and SSS score. Nondrivers (Non-D) and those who drove at or below the speed limit had the lowest SSS scores; scores increased with each increment in driving speed. The sex difference observed in this study is generally the case; males typically score higher on SSS than females. (After Zuckerman & Neeb, 1980)*

Research using the SSS has revealed large individual differences in stimulation seeking (Carrol, Zuckerman, & Vogel, 1982). Moreover, sensation seeking appears to be a trait that is consistent across a variety of situations; individuals who report enjoying new experiences in one area of life tend to describe themselves as adventurous in other areas. Psychologists have related high scores on the SSS to a number of behavioral characteristics: engaging in risky sports, occupations, or hobbies (parachuting, motorcycle riding, fire fighting, scuba diving); seeking variety in sexual and drug experiences; behaving fearlessly in common phobic situations (heights, darkness, snakes); taking risks when gambling; and preferring exotic foods. Even when asked to describe their normal driving habits, high-sensation seekers report driving at faster speeds than low-sensation seekers (see Figure 10-12).

Variations in sensation seeking can influence the way in which individuals react to each other. High-sensation seekers may feel that low-sensation seekers are boring and lead restricted lives; conversely, low-sensation seekers may feel that high-sensation seekers are engaged in unproductive and foolhardy activities. These attitudes can be important in the choice of marital partners. There is a significant correlation between the SSS scores of husbands and wives: high-sensation seekers tend to marry highs, and low-sensation seekers tend to marry lows. Compatibility on this trait seems to be a predictor of marital adjustment (Fisher, Zuckerman, & Neeb, 1981; Farley, 1986). If one partner has a very high SSS score and the other has a very low SSS score, the likelihood of marital disharmony increases.

COMMON PRINCIPLES FOR DIFFERENT MOTIVES

Motives generally can be categorized according to survival needs, social needs, and the need to satisfy curiosity. While the differences between these types are real, we have not addressed some similarities among them. In this closing section, we explore two principles that psychologists believe are common to all basic motives.

Drive Reduction

In the 1940s and 1950s, many psychologists believed that all basic motives operated according to the principle of *drive reduction:* motives are directed at the reduction of a psychological state which a person experiences as tension, and the person experiences pleasure from this reduction in tension or drive. Drive reduction seems applicable to the survival motives. When deprived of food, we do indeed feel a tension that is reduced by eating, and we experience that reduction as pleasurable. But for such motives as sex, drive reduction sounds less plausible; to make it more plausible, drive-reduction theorists have argued that what is rewarding about sexual activity is the drop in tension that occurs during orgasm (Hull, 1943).

The theory of drive reduction has lost favor over the years, in part because its account of sex proved unsatisfactory. Experiments with rats showed that a male would choose to spend time with a sexually receptive female even though every time he mounted her, the experimenter removed him before ejaculation could occur. In this case, tension should have kept increasing, and there should have been no drive reduction and no reward; but apparently sexual stimulation is rewarding in its own right (Friedman, Sheffield, Wulff, & Backer, 1951). Similarly, drive-reduction theory has never been able to come to grips with the curiosity motive. According to the theory, low levels of sensory stimulation should produce little drive and hence be attractive. But studies of sensory deprivation have shown that low levels of stimulation are very unpleasant and, if anything, they induce drive. On the opposite side of the coin, drive-reduction theory suggests that everyone would avoid extreme tension-producing situations; but some people (perhaps mainly those who are high on the SSS) seek out such situations, like riding roller coasters and sky diving (Geen, Beatty, & Arkin, 1984).

Arousal Level

Psychologists today generally reject drive reduction in favor of the principle of *arousal level*, according to which people seek an optimal level of drive or arousal. The optimal level varies from person to person — as demonstrated by individual differences in stimulation seeking. Physiological deprivation, as in hunger and thirst, increases arousal level above the optimum and leads to behavior that brings the level down. In contrast, too little stimulation, as in sensory deprivation situations, can motivate an organism to increase its arousal level. We seek stimulation (including sexual stimulation), novelty, and complexity in our environments, but only up to a point. Though the notion of arousal level is not without its critics, it seems more likely than drive reduction to emerge as a unifying principle of the basic drives.

SUMMARY

1. Motives, which give behavior *direction* and *energize* it, are of different types, including *survival*, *social*, and *curiosity*. Survival motives, such as hunger and thirst, operate according to *homeostasis:* they maintain a constant internal environment. Homeostasis involves a *regulated variable, sensors* that measure the variable, an *ideal value* of the variable, a *comparator,* and *adjustments* that the system makes when the variable is at a value above or below the ideal value.

2. Our regulation of temperature is an example of homeostasis. The regulated variable is the temperature of the blood, and sensors for this are located in various regions of the body, including the *hypothalamus*. The ideal value and comparator are also located in the hypothalamus. Adjustments are either automatic physiological responses (for example, shivering) or voluntary behavioral ones (such as putting on a sweater).

3. Thirst is another homeostatic motive. There are two regulated variables, *intracellular fluid* and *extracellular fluid*. The loss of intracellular fluid is detected by *osmoreceptors,* cells in the hypothalamus that respond to dehydration; this in turn leads to the release of the *antidiuretic hormone* (ADH), which regulates the kidneys, allowing water to be reabsorbed into the bloodstream. Extracellular fluid is detected by *blood-pressure sensors* in the kidneys.

4. Hunger is a complex, homeostatic motive with numerous regulated variables, including *glucose, fats,* and *amino acids.* Glucose sensors have been found in the hypothalamus and liver. In addition to sensors that trigger feeding, there are also *satiety detectors,* which are found in the digestive system (particularly the stomach, duodenum, and liver) and signal the brain that the needed nutrients are on their way.

5. Two regions of the brain are critical for hunger: the *lateral hypothalamus* and the *ventromedial hypothalamus*. Destruction of the lateral hypothalamus leads to undereating; destruction of the ventromedial hypothalamus to overeating. One interpretation of these effects is that the ventromedial and lateral regions have

reciprocal effects on the *set point* for body weight: damage to the ventromedial region raises the set point, whereas damage to the lateral region lowers it. Another interpretation proposes that the effects are due to interference with nerve tracts that pass through the hypothalamic locations.

6. People become obese when they (1) take in too many calories, (2) expend too few calories, or (3) are genetically predisposed to be fat. With regard to why they take in too many calories, obese people tend to overeat when they break a diet, they eat more when emotionally aroused, and they are more responsive than normal-weight individuals to external hunger cues. With regard to why they expend too few calories, obese people often have a relatively low metabolic rate (due to dieting or to a high proportion of fat tissue) and usually do not exercise enough. In treating obesity, it appears that keeping weight off permanently depends on establishing self-control over eating habits, which can be done by behavior modification, and exercising regularly.

7. The female hormones *(estrogen* and *progesterone)* and male hormones *(androgens)* are responsible for the body changes at puberty but play only a limited role in human sexual arousal. In contrast, there is substantial hormonal control over sex in lower species.

8. Early social experiences with parents and peers have a large influence on adult sexuality. Monkeys raised in isolation have sexual problems as adults. For humans, other environmental determinants of adult sexuality are cultural norms and attitudes. Although Western society is becoming increasingly permissive about premarital sex, men and women still differ in their attitudes toward it. Sexual interactions with members of the same sex are not uncommon during childhood, but only a small percentage of people become exclusively *homosexual* as adults. Homosexuality is probably a result of a number of psychological and social factors.

9. Prenatal hormones are important for sexual development. If the embryonic sex glands produce enough androgen, the newborn will have male genitals; if there is insufficient androgen, the newborn will have female genitals, even if it is genetically male. In cases where hormonal imbalances result in *hermaphrodites* (individuals born with both male and female tissue), the assigned label and the sex role in which the individual is raised have greater influence on gender identity than do the individual's genes and hormones.

10. In lower animals, maternal behavior appears to be innately programmed and triggered by hormones. In primates and humans, however, maternal behavior is largely influenced by experience. Monkeys reared in isolation exhibit none of the usual maternal behaviors when they later become mothers.

11. People and animals appear to have inborn curiosity motives to explore and manipulate objects. Manipulation of objects provides the organism with changing sensory input, and studies of *sensory deprivation* show that the absence of changing input disrupts normal functioning.

12. Psychologists used to believe that all basic motives operated by *drive reduction,* the principle that all motives are directed at the reduction of tension. But drive reduction does not offer a satisfactory account of sex or the curiosity motives. A more promising principle is that people seek an *optimal level of arousal.*

The biological approach to temperature regulation, thirst, hunger, and sex is well surveyed in Carlson, *Physiology of Behavior* (3rd ed., 1985); and Rosenzweig and Leiman, *Physiological Psychology* (1982). An introduction to human sexuality is provided by Offir, *Human Sexuality* (1982). An explanation of normal and abnormal patterns of eating and drinking is given in Logue, *The Psychology of Eating and Drinking* (1986); also see Stunkard (ed.), *Obesity* (1980).

For reviews of motivation in general, see Geen, Beatty, and Arkin, *Human Motivation: Physiological, Behavioral, and Social Approaches* (1984); Atkinson and Birch, *An Introduction to Motivation* (1978); and Stellar and Stellar, *The Neurobiology of Motivation and Reward* (1985). A review of ethology is presented in Lorenz, *The Foundations of Ethology* (1981); and in McFarland, *Animal Behaviour: Psychobiology, Ethology and Evolution* (1985).

FURTHER READING

Emotion

THE MOST BASIC FEELINGS THAT WE experience include not only motives such as hunger and sex but also emotions such as joy and anger. Emotions and motives are closely related. Emotions can activate and direct behavior in the same way that basic motives do. Emotions may also accompany motivated behavior: sex, for example, is not only a powerful motive but a potential source of joy, as well.

Despite their similarities, motives and emotions need to be distinguished. The most common basis for distinguishing between them assumes that emotions are triggered from the outside, while motives are activated from within. That is, emotions are usually aroused by external events, and emotional reactions are directed toward these events; motives, in contrast, are often aroused by internal events (a homeostatic imbalance, for example) and are naturally directed toward certain objects in the environment (such as food, water, or a mate). Another distinction between emotions and motives is that emotions invariably activate the autonomic nervous system, whereas motives may not. These distinctions are not absolute. An external source can sometimes trigger a motive, as when the sight of food triggers hunger. And the discomfort caused by a homeostatic imbalance — severe hunger, for example — can arouse emotions. Nevertheless, emotions and motives are sufficiently different in their sources of activation, subjective experience, and effects on behavior that they merit separate treatment.

COMPONENTS OF AN EMOTION

In a paper written a century ago, the Harvard psychologist William James raised the question, "What is an emotion?" (James, 1884). Psychologists and physiologists have been struggling with a response ever since. Proposed answers have focused on the following five components of an emotion:

1. Subjective experience
2. Internal bodily responses, particularly those involving the autonomic nervous system
3. Belief or cognitive appraisal that a particular positive or negative state of affairs is occurring
4. Facial expression
5. Reaction to the perceived source of the emotion

The critical questions in the study of emotion concern the relationships between these components. One question is, How do the other components contribute to the subjective experience of an emotion? That is, must one have autonomic arousal to experience an emotion? Must one have a particular kind of belief — or a particular kind of facial expression? A second critical question is, Which components are responsible for making the different emotions feel different? Or to put it another way, Which components *differentiate* the emotions? To appreciate the difference between the two questions, note that it is possible that a person *must* have autonomic arousal to experience an emotion but that the pattern of autonomic arousal is roughly the same for all emotions and, hence, cannot differentiate them.

These two questions will guide our discussion for most of this chapter, as we consider in turn autonomic arousal, cognitive appraisal, and facial expressions. In the remainder of the chapter, we will turn our attention to the last component, emotional reactions, and focus on aggression. Throughout the chapter, we will be concerned primarily with the more intense affective states, though the ideas and principles that will emerge in our discussion are relevant to a variety of feelings.

AUTONOMIC AROUSAL

Physiological Basis

When we experience an intense emotion, such as fear or anger, usually we are aware of a number of bodily changes — including rapid heartbeat and breathing, dryness of the throat and mouth, increased muscle tension, perspiration, trembling of the extremities, and a "sinking feeling" in the stomach (see Table 11-1).

TABLE 11-1
Symptoms of Fear in Combat Flying   *Based on reports of combat pilots during World War II. (After Shaffer, 1947)*

DURING COMBAT MISSIONS DID YOU FEEL	OFTEN	SOMETIMES	TOTAL
A pounding heart and rapid pulse	30%	56%	86%
That your muscles were very tense	30	53	83
Easily irritated, angry, or "sore"	22	58	80
Dryness of the throat or mouth	30	50	80
"Nervous perspiration" or "cold sweat"	26	53	79
"Butterflies" in the stomach	23	53	76
A sense of unreality — that this could not be happening to you	20	49	69
A need to urinate very frequently	25	40	65
Trembling	11	53	64
Confused or rattled	3	50	53
Weak or faint	4	37	41
That right after a mission you were unable to remember the details of what had happened	5	34	39
Sick to the stomach	5	33	38
Unable to concentrate	3	32	35
That you had wet or soiled your pants	1	4	5

Most of the physiological changes that take place during emotional arousal result from activation of the *sympathetic division* of the autonomic nervous system as it prepares the body for emergency action (see Chapter 2, p. 51). The sympathetic system is responsible for the following changes:

1. Blood pressure and heart rate increase.
2. Respiration becomes more rapid.
3. The pupils dilate.
4. Perspiration increases while secretion of saliva and mucous decreases.
5. Blood-sugar level increases to provide more energy.
6. The blood clots more quickly in case of wounds.
7. Motility of the gastrointestinal tract decreases; blood is diverted from the stomach and intestines to the brain and skeletal muscles.
8. The hairs on the skin become erect, causing "goose pimples."

The sympathetic system gears the organism for energy output. As the emotion subsides, the *parasympathetic system* — the energy-conserving system — takes over and returns the organism to its normal state.

These activities of the autonomic nervous system are themselves triggered by activity in certain critical regions of the brain, including the *hypothalamus* (which, as we saw in the last chapter, plays a major role in many biological motives) and parts of the limbic system. Impulses from these areas are transmitted to nuclei in the brain stem that control the functioning of the autonomic nervous system. The autonomic nervous system then acts directly on the muscles and internal organs to initiate some of the bodily changes previously described and acts indirectly by stimulating the adrenal hormones to produce other bodily changes. Additional hormones that play a crucial role in an individual's reaction to stress are secreted by the pituitary gland on direct signal from the hypothalamus.

Note that the kind of heightened physiological arousal we have described is characteristic of emotional states such as anger and fear, during which the organism must prepare for action — for example, to fight or flee. (The role of this "fight-or-flight response" in threatening or stressful situations is elaborated in Chapter 14, p. 462.) Some of the same responses may also occur during joyful excitement or sexual arousal. During emotions such as sorrow or grief, however, some bodily processes may be depressed, or slowed down.

Intensity of Emotions

To determine the relation between heightened physiological arousal and the subjective experience of an emotion, researchers have studied the emotional life of individuals with spinal cord injuries. When the spinal cord is severed, sensations below the point of injury cannot reach the brain. Since some of these sensations arise from the sympathetic nervous system, the injuries reduce the contributions of autonomic arousal to felt emotion. In one study, army veterans with spinal cord injuries were divided into five groups, according to the level on the spinal cord at which the lesion occurred. In one group, the lesions were near the neck (at the cervical level), with only one branch of the parasympathetic nervous system intact and no innervation of the sympathetic system. In another group, the lesions were near the base of the spine (at the sacral level), with at least partial innervation of both sympathetic and parasympathetic nerves. The other three groups fell between these two extremes. The five groups represented a continuum of bodily sensation: the higher the lesion on the spinal cord, the less the feedback of the autonomic nervous system to the brain.

CRITICAL
DISCUSSION

Using

Arousal

to Detect

Lies

If autonomic arousal is an inevitable part of an emotion and if experiencing an emotion is a likely consequence of lying, then we can use the presence of arousal to infer that a person is lying. This is the theory behind the *lie-detector* test, in which a machine called a *polygraph* (meaning "many writings") simultaneously measures several physiological responses known to be part of autonomic arousal. The measures most frequently recorded are changes in heart rate, blood pressure, respiration, and the galvanic skin response or GSR (a rapid change in the electrical conductivity of the skin that occurs with emotional arousal).

In operating a polygraph, the standard procedure is to make the first recording while the subject is relaxed; this recording serves as a *baseline* for evaluating subsequent responses. The examiner then asks a series of carefully worded questions that the subject has been instructed to answer with a "yes" or "no" response. Some of the questions are "critical," which means that the guilty are likely to lie in response to them (for example, "Did you rob Bert's Cleaners on December 11?"). Other questions are "controls"; even innocent people are somewhat likely to lie in response to these questions (for example, "Have you ever taken something that didn't belong to you?"). Yet other questions are "neutral" (for example, "Do you live in San Diego?"). Critical questions are interspersed among control and neutral ones; sufficient time is allowed between questions for the polygraph measures to return to normal. Presumably, only the guilty should show greater physiological responses to the critical questions than to the others.

However, the use of the polygraph in detecting lies is far from foolproof. A response to a question may show that a subject is aroused but not *why* he or she is aroused. An innocent subject may be very tense or may react emotionally to certain words in the questions and therefore appear to be lying when telling the truth. On the other hand, a practiced liar may show little arousal when lying. And a knowledgeable subject may be able to "beat" the machine by thinking about something exciting or by tensing muscles during neutral questions, thereby creating a baseline comparable to reactions to the critical questions. The recording in Figure 11-1 shows

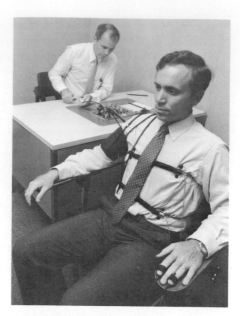

FIGURE 11-1

Polygraph   *The arm cuff measures blood pressure and heart rate, the pneumograph around the rib cage measures rate of breathing, and the finger electrodes measure GSR. The recording on the right shows the physiological responses of a subject as he lies and as he simulates lying. The respiratory trace (top line) shows that he held his breath as he prepared for the first simulation. He was able to produce sizable changes in heart rate and GSR at the second simulation. (After Kubis, 1962)*

the responses to an actual lie and a simulated lie. In this experiment, the subject picked a number and then tried to conceal its identity from the examiner. The number was 27, and a marked change in heart rate and GSR can be seen when the subject denies number 27. The subject simulates lying to number 22 by tensing his toes, producing noticeable reactions in heart rate and GSR.

Because of these and other problems, most state and federal courts will not admit polygraph tests; those that do generally require that both sides agree to its introduction. Such tests are frequently used, however, in preliminary criminal investigations and by employers interviewing prospective personnel for trusted positions.

Representatives of the American Polygraph Association have claimed an ac-

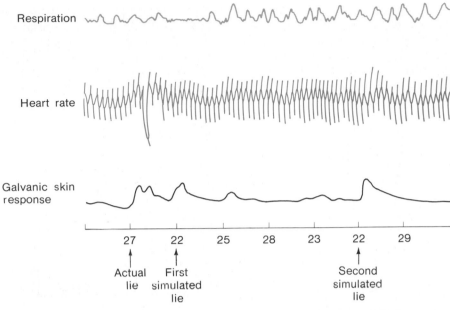

Respiration

Heart rate

Galvanic skin response

27   22   25   28   23   22   29

↑   ↑   ↑
Actual First   Second
lie   simulated   simulated
      lie   lie

curacy rate of 90 percent or better for polygraph tests conducted by a skilled operator. Critics, however, consider the accuracy rate to be much lower. For example, Lykken (1984) claims that in studies involving real-life situations, the lie-detector test is correct only about 65 percent of the time, and an innocent person has a 50-50 chance of failing the test. He argues that the polygraph detects not only the arousal that accompanies lying but also the stress that an honest person experiences when strapped to the equipment. Nevertheless, many businesses believe that the benefits of these tests outweigh the risks, and the use of polygraph tests is increasing in private industry. Their use in law enforcement is also increasing. The FBI, for example, administers several thousand polygraph tests per year, mostly to follow up leads and to verify

specific facts—areas in which, experts agree, the polygraph is more useful. Tests given by the FBI to several government officials led to evidence of the Watergate cover-up in the early 1970s. In criminal and private cases, anyone has the legal right to refuse a polygraph test. However, this is hardly a safeguard for someone whose refusal, for whatever reason, may endanger a career or job opportunity.

Another type of lie detector measures certain changes in a person's voice that are undetectable to the human ear. All muscles, including those controlling the vocal cords, vibrate slightly when in use. This tremor, which is transmitted to the vocal cords, is suppressed by activity of the autonomic nervous system when a speaker is under stress. When a tape recording of a person's voice is played through a device called a

voice-stress analyzer (at a speed four times slower than that at which it is recorded), a visual representation of the voice can be produced on a strip of graph paper. The tremors of the vocal cords in the voice of a relaxed speaker resemble a series of waves (see the left-hand graph in Figure 11-2). When a speaker is under stress, the tremors are suppressed (see the right-hand graph in Figure 11-2).

The voice-stress analyzer is used in lie detection in essentially the same way as a polygraph; neutral questions are interspersed with critical questions, and recordings of the subject's responses to both are compared. If answers to the critical questions produce the relaxed wave form, the person is probably telling the truth (as far as we know, vocal cord tremors cannot be controlled voluntarily). A stressed wave form, on the other hand, indicates only that the individual is tense or anxious, not necessarily that he or she is lying.

The advantage of using the voice-stress analyzer rather than the polygraph is that the subject does not have to be hooked up to a lot of equipment. In fact, the subject does not even have to be present; the analyzer can work over the telephone, from radio or TV messages, or from tape recordings. Since people's voices can be analyzed without their knowledge, there is considerable concern about the potential for the unethical use of this instrument. Another concern is the accuracy of the voice-stress analyzer. Some investigators claim that it is as accurate as the polygraph in distinguishing between the guilty and the innocent; others claim that it is no more accurate than chance. Much more research is required to determine the relationship between voice changes and other physiological measures of emotion (Rice, 1978; Lykken, 1980).

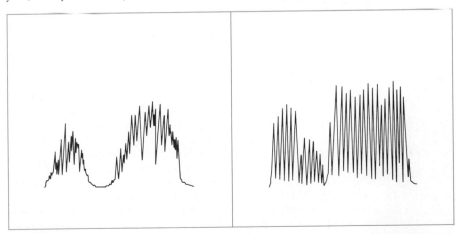

FIGURE 11-2
Effects of Stress on Voice Patterns *A voice-stress analyzer produces graphic records of speech. The voice printout for a relaxed speaker resembles a series of waves, such as those shown on the left. The waves are produced by tiny tremors of the vocal cords. Under stress, the tremors are suppressed, producing a printout similar to that shown on the right. (After Holden, 1975)*

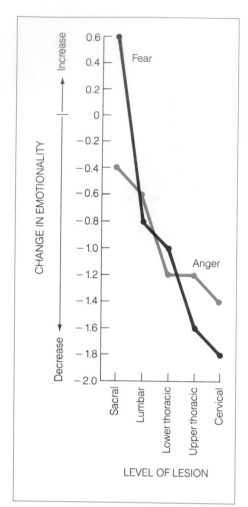

The subjects were interviewed to determine their feelings in situations of fear, anger, grief, and sexual excitement. Each person was asked to recall an emotion-arousing incident prior to the injury and a comparable incident following the injury and to compare the intensity of emotional experience in each case. The data for states of fear and anger are shown in Figure 11-3. It is apparent that the higher the person's lesion was on the spinal cord (that is, the less the feedback from the autonomic nervous system), the more his emotionality decreased following injury. The same relation was true for states of sexual excitement and grief. Deprivation of autonomic arousal resulted in a marked decrease in subjectively experienced emotion.

Comments by patients with the highest spinal cord lesions suggested that they could *react* emotionally to arousing situations, but that they did not really *feel* emotional. For example, "It's sort of a cold anger. Sometimes I act angry when I see some injustice. I yell and cuss and raise hell, because if you don't do it sometimes, I've learned people will take advantage of you; but it doesn't have the heat to it that it used to. It's a mental kind of anger." Or, "I say I am afraid, like when I'm going into a real stiff exam at school, but I don't really feel afraid, not all tense and shaky with the hollow feeling in my stomach, like I used to."

The preceding experiment is important, but it is not entirely objective — the emotional situations varied from person to person, and subjects rated their own experiences. A follow-up study provides a more objective situation: all subjects were exposed to the same situations, and their emotional experiences were rated by independent judges. Male subjects with spinal cord injuries were presented with pictures of clothed and nude females and were told to imagine that they were alone with each woman. Subjects reported their "thoughts and feelings," which then were rated by judges for expressed emotion. Patients who had higher lesions reported less sexual excitement than those whose lesions were lower on their spines (Jasmos & Hakmiller, 1975).

FIGURE 11-3
Relationship Between Spinal Cord Lesions and Emotionality   *Subjects with spinal cord lesions compared the intensity of their emotional experiences before and after injury. Their reports were coded according to the degree of change: 0 indicates no change; a mild change ("I feel it less, I guess") is scored −1 for a decrease or +1 for an increase; and a strong change ("I feel it a helluva lot less") is scored −2 or +2. Note that the higher the lesion, the greater the decrease in emotionality following injury. (After Schachter, 1971; and Hohmann, 1962)*

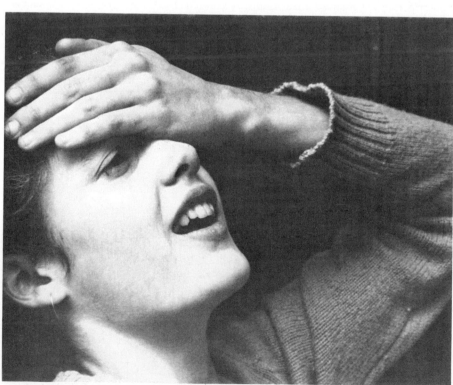

Differentiation of Emotions

Clearly, autonomic arousal contributes to the intensity of emotional experience. But does it differentiate the emotions? Is there one pattern of physiological activity for joy, another for anger, still another for fear, and so on? This question dates back to William James's seminal paper on emotion (James, 1884), in which he proposed that the perception of bodily changes *is* the subjective experience of an emotion: "We are afraid because we run"; "we are angry because we strike." The Danish physiologist Carl Lange arrived at a similar position at about the same time, but for him the bodily changes included autonomic arousal. Their combined position is referred to as the *James-Lange theory,* and it argues as follows: because the perception of autonomic arousal (and perhaps of other bodily changes) constitutes the experience of an emotion, and because different emotions feel different, there must be a distinct pattern of autonomic activity for each emotion. The James-Lange theory therefore holds that autonomic arousal differentiates the emotions.

The theory came under severe attack in the 1920s by the physiologist Walter Cannon (1927), who offered three major criticisms:

1. Since the internal organs are relatively insensitive structures and not well supplied with nerves, internal changes occur too slowly to be a source of emotional feeling.
2. Artificially inducing the bodily changes associated with an emotion—for example, injecting a drug such as epinephrine—does not produce the experience of a true emotion.
3. The pattern of autonomic arousal does not seem to differ much from one emotional state to another; for example, while anger makes our heart beat faster, so does the sight of a loved one.

The third argument, then, explicitly denies that autonomic arousal can differentiate the emotions.

Psychologists have pursued Cannon's third point while developing increasingly more accurate measures of the components of autonomic arousal. While many of the earlier experiments failed to find distinct physiological patterns for different emotions, recent studies have been more successful. In particular, a study by Ekman and his collaborators (1983) shows that there are autonomic patterns distinct to different emotions. Subjects produced emotional expressions for each of six emotions—surprise, disgust, sadness, anger, fear, and happiness—by following instructions about which particular facial muscles to contract (most of the subjects were actors, and they were aided in their task by a mirror and coaching). While they held an emotional expression for ten seconds, the researchers measured their heart rate, skin temperature, and other indicators of autonomic arousal. A number of these measures revealed differences between the emotions (see Figure 11-4). Heart rate was faster for the negative emotions of anger, fear, and sadness than it was for happiness, surprise, and disgust; and the former three emotions themselves could be partially distinguished by the fact that skin temperature was higher in anger than in fear or sadness. Thus, even though both anger and the sight of a loved one make our heart beat faster, only anger makes it beat *much* faster; and though anger and fear have much in common, anger is "hot" and fear "cold" (no wonder people describe their anger as their "blood boiling").

These results are important, but by no means do they provide unequivocal evidence for the James-Lange theory or the claim that autonomic arousal is the *only* component that differentiates the emotions. All the Ekman study demonstrated was that there are some physiological differences between emotions, not

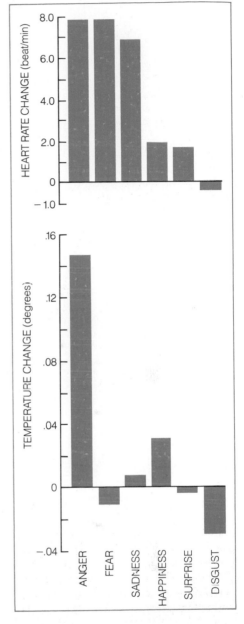

FIGURE 11-4
Arousal Differences for Different Emotions *Changes in heart rate (A) and right finger temperature (B). For heart rate, the changes associated with anger, fear, and sadness were all significantly greater than those for happiness, surprise, and disgust. For finger temperature, the change associated with anger was significantly different from that for all other emotions. (After Ekman, Levenson, & Frieson, 1983)*

that these differences are perceived and experienced as *the* qualitative differences between the emotions. Even if autonomic arousal does help differentiate some emotions, it is unlikely that it differentiates *all* emotions; the difference between contentment and pride, for example, is unlikely to be found in visceral reactions. Also, the first two points that Cannon raised against the James-Lange theory still stand: autonomic arousal is too slow to differentiate emotional experiences, and artificial induction of arousal does not yield a true emotion. For these reasons, many psychologists still believe that something other than autonomic arousal must be involved in differentiating the emotions. That something else is usually thought to be one's cognitive appraisal of the eliciting situation.

COGNITIVE APPRAISAL

When we experience an event or action, we interpret the situation with respect to our personal goals and well-being; the outcome of the appraisal is a cognition, or belief, that is either positive or negative ("I won the match and feel happy" or "I failed the test and feel depressed"). This interpretation is known as a *cognitive appraisal*, which has two distinct parts: the appraisal process and the resulting belief.

Intensity and Differentiation of Emotions

Clearly, our appraisal of a situation contributes to our emotional experience. If we are in a car that starts to roll down a steep incline, we experience fear, if not terror; but if we know the "car" is part of a roller coaster, the fear is usually much less. If we are told by someone that he or she cannot stand the sight of us, we may feel very angry or hurt if that person is a friend, but feel barely perturbed if the person is a mental patient whom we have never met before. If we watch a film of African tribesmen making an incision in a young boy's body, we may feel outrage if we believe the men are torturing the boy but feel relatively detached if we believe the men are performing a rites-of-passage ritual. In these cases, and countless others, our cognitive appraisal of the situation determines the intensity of our emotional experience (Lazarus, Kanner, & Folkman, 1980).

Cognitive appraisal is also heavily responsible for differentiating the emotions. Unlike autonomic arousal, the beliefs resulting from appraisal are rich enough to distinguish among many different kinds of feelings, and the appraisal process itself may be fast enough to account for the speed with which some emotions arise. Also, we almost always emphasize emotional beliefs when we describe the quality of an emotion. We say, "I felt angry because she was unfair" or "I felt frightened because I was abandoned"; unfairness and abandonment are clearly beliefs that result from a cognitive process.

Observations suggest that cognitive appraisals are often sufficient to determine the quality of experience. That is, if people could be induced to be in a neutral state of autonomic arousal, the quality of their emotion would be determined solely by their appraisal of the situation. Schacter and Singer (1962) first tested this claim in an important experiment.

Subjects were given an injection of epinephrine, which typically causes autonomic arousal, such as an increase in heart and respiration rates, muscle tremors, and a "jittery" feeling. The experimenter then manipulated the information that the subjects were given regarding the effects of epinephrine. Some subjects were told that the drug would produce a state of euphoria; others were

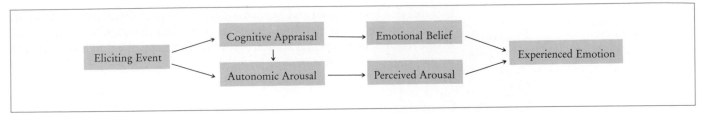

FIGURE 11-5
Components of an Emotional
Experience: 1 *The beliefs resulting from
a cognitive appraisal and the perception of
autonomic arousal both contribute to the
experience of an emotion. (After Reisenzein,
1983)*

told that the drug would make them feel angry. After each subject was informed of the "effects" of the injection, he or she was left in a waiting room with a person who was ostensibly another subject but who was actually a confederate of the experimenter. If the real subject had been told the drug produced euphoria, the confederate acted euphoric (made paper airplanes, played "basketball" by throwing wads of paper into the wastebasket, and so on). If the real subject had been told the drug produced anger, the confederate acted angry (complained about the experiment, showed his resentment of the questionnaire that the subjects had to complete, then tore up the questionnaire, and stomped out of the room).

These manipulations in information were intended to influence the subjects' appraisal of the situation, which is exactly what happened: the subjects molded their emotional experience to conform to the available information. If the information suggested that the injection would produce a feeling of euphoria, subjects were more likely to rate their feelings as happy; conversely, if they were told that the injection would make them feel angry, they were more likely to rate their feelings as angry. Although the autonomic arousal was the same in the two situations, the experienced emotion was not; the emotion was determined by the subjects' appraisals of the situations.

However, while the autonomic arousal may have been the same in the happy and angry situations, apparently it was not neutral (Marshall, 1976; Maslach, 1979). Subjects rated their experiences more negatively (less happy, or more angry) than the actions of the confederate warranted, suggesting that the physiological arousal produced by epinephrine is experienced as somewhat unpleasant. Hence, we still need a demonstration that completely neutral arousal may be misattributed. A subsequent study supplied this demonstration. Subjects first engaged in strenuous physical exercise and then participated in a task where they were provoked by a confederate of the experimenter. The exercise induced physiological arousal that was neutral and that persisted until the subject was provoked; this arousal should have combined with any that was elicited by the provocation, thereby resulting in a more intense experience of anger. In fact, subjects who exercised responded more aggressively to the provocation than subjects who did not (Zillman & Bryant, 1974).

The conclusions that emerge from this line of research are depicted in Figure 11-5. In an emotional situation, an eliciting event typically results in both autonomic arousal and cognitive appraisal; the arousal and appraisal lead, respectively, to *perceived* arousal and an emotional belief, which then determine the experienced emotion. (The perceived arousal and emotional belief are not experienced as independent; rather, the arousal is *attributed* to the belief—"My heart is racing *because* I'm so angry.") Usually, the same eliciting event is responsible for both the arousal and the appraisal. In the studies just reviewed, however, the experimenters arranged the situation so that arousal and appraisal had different sources (for example, injection versus confederate's behavior), thereby allowing the experimenter to analyze separately the role of each component. These studies

TABLE 11-2
Primary Emotions and Their
Causes   *Eight primary emotions and their
associated situations. (After Plutchik, 1980)*

EMOTION	SITUATION
Grief (Sorrow)	Loss of loved one
Fear	Threat
Anger	Obstacle
Joy	Potential mate
Trust	Group member
Disgust	Gruesome object
Anticipation	New territory
Surprise	Sudden novel object

indicate that both arousal and appraisal contribute to the intensity of experience —and that sometimes appraisal alone can determine the quality of experience. While research indicates that arousal may aid in differentiating emotions, it seems to play less of a role than does appraisal.*

Contents of Appraisal

Of course, not every situation elicits an emotion, so there must be a special aspect that leads to an emotive response. Mandler (1984) has argued that this special aspect is an *interruption of ongoing behavior or thought.* In anger or fear, the interruption is often a block to an intended activity; in joy or surprise, the interruption may be an unexpected positive event. In all cases, the interruption serves as a trigger for appraisal processes to determine the exact nature of the interruption. Although interruption also triggers autonomic arousal, it is the nature of the interrupted situation that mainly determines the quality of the experience.

We therefore need to specify which aspects of an interrupted situation lead to an appraisal of fear, which lead to joy, and so on for various emotions. In essence, we are asking for the causes of the different emotions. Psychologists have taken two different approaches to this problem. One approach assumes that there is a relatively small set of "primary" emotions and associates each emotion with a fundamental life situation. Table 11-2 lists several emotions (such as fear) and their respective triggering situations (threat). These primary emotions can be found in every human culture and throughout the animal kingdom. Their universality provides a reason for singling out these emotions as primary and for specifying the fundamental interrupted situations in terms that are appropriate even for lower species.

The other approach to specifying the situational aspects of emotion emphasizes cognitive processes and, consequently, may be more appropriate for humans than for lower species. Instead of starting with a primary set of emotions, this approach begins with a primary set of situational aspects that a person attends to. The theory then associates various combinations of these aspects with specific emotions. An example is given in Table 11-3. One aspect of a situation is the desirability of an anticipated event, and another is whether or not the event occurs. When we combine these two aspects (the left-hand side of Table 11-3), we get four possible situations, each of which seems to produce a distinct emotion. (We are using only four emotions in our example just to keep the explanation simple.) When a desired event occurs, we experience *joy;* when a desired event does not occur, we experience *sorrow;* when an undesired event occurs, we experience *distress;* and when an undesired event does not occur, we experience *relief.* To illustrate, if a young woman marries an attractive young man who is known to have a drinking problem, she may feel mainly joy, her rival sorrow, her parents distress, and his parents relief. The virtue of this approach is that it specifies the appraisal process in detail and accounts for a wide range of affective experiences.

TABLE 11-3
Primary Situation Aspects and Their
Consequences   *Combinations of two
situational aspects and their associated
emotions. (After Roseman, 1979)*

SITUATION	EMOTION
Desirable and occurs	Joy
Desirable and doesn't occur	Sorrow
Undesirable and occurs	Distress
Undesirable and doesn't occur	Relief

* There are cases of emotion, however, where no cognitive appraisal is involved (Zajonc, 1984). In particular, some fear experiences may be the result of classical conditioning in childhood (see Chapter 7). For example, if painful sessions with a doctor were reliably preceded by being in a waiting room, the person may experience substantial fear when in a waiting room even as an adult. In this case, the adult experience is not the result of an interpretation of a situation with respect to present goals.

Some Clinical Implications

The fact that cognitive appraisals can differentiate emotions helps make sense of a puzzling clinical observation. Clinicians report that sometimes a patient appears to be experiencing an emotion but is not conscious of it. That is, the patient has no subjective experience of the emotion, yet reacts in a manner consistent with the emotion — for example, though the patient may not feel angry, he acts in a hostile manner. Also, at a later point he may experience the emotion and agree that in some sense he must have been having it earlier. Freud (1976) thought that this phenomenon involved the repression of "painful" ideas, and modern work on appraisal and emotion is compatible with his hypothesis. Because the belief about a situation usually gives the emotion its quality, preventing that belief from entering consciousness (repression) prevents one from experiencing the quality of the emotion.

Another point of contact between clinical analysis and experimental research concerns emotional development. Clinical work suggests that a person's sensations of pleasure and distress change very little as he or she develops from child to adult; what does develop, however, are the ideas associated with the sensations (Brenner, 1980). Thus, the sensation of joy may be the same when we are 3 or 30, but what makes us joyous is very different. This developmental pattern fits perfectly with the facts that we have reviewed about emotion. Sensations of pleasure and distress are probably due to feedback from autonomic arousal, and the nature of this arousal may not change over the life span. In contrast, ideas associated with the sensations are simply emotional beliefs, and they should show the same kind of development as other aspects of cognition.

Finally, the work on appraisal fits with a phenomenon that is familiar not just to clinicians but to all of us: the extent to which a situation elicits an emotion depends on our past experience. When confronted with an overly critical employer, some people will be annoyed while others will be enraged. Why the difference? Presumably because of differences in past experience: perhaps those who are enraged suffered a hypercritical authority figure in the past, while those who are only annoyed had no such experience. A likely link between past experience and current emotion is the appraisal process; that is, our past experience affects our beliefs about the current situation, and these beliefs then influence the emotion we experience. (Another possible link between past experience and current emotion is classical conditioning, particularly when the emotion is fear.)

EMOTIONAL EXPRESSION

The facial expression that accompanies an emotion clearly serves to communicate that emotion. Since the publication of Charles Darwin's 1872 classic, *The Expression of Emotion in Man and Animals*, psychologists have regarded the communication of emotion as an important function, one with survival value for the species. Thus, looking frightened may warn others that danger is present, and perceiving that someone is angry tells us that he or she may be about to act aggressively. More recent work goes beyond the Darwinian tradition, suggesting that, in addition to their communicative function, emotional expressions contribute to the subjective experience of emotion, just as arousal and appraisal do.

Communication of Emotional Expressions

Certain facial expressions seem to have a universal meaning, regardless of the culture in which an individual is raised. When people from five different countries (the United States, Brazil, Chile, Argentina, and Japan) viewed photographs showing facial expressions of happiness, anger, sadness, disgust, fear, and surprise, they had little difficulty in identifying the emotion that each expression conveyed. Even members of remote, preliterate tribes that had had virtually no contact with Western cultures (the Fore and Dani tribes in New Guinea) were able to identify the facial expressions correctly. Likewise, American college students who viewed videotapes of emotions expressed by Fore natives identified the emotions accurately, although they sometimes confused fear and surprise (Ekman, 1982).

The universality of certain emotional expressions supports Darwin's claim that they are innate responses with an evolutionary history. According to Darwin, many of the ways in which we express emotion are inherited patterns that originally had some survival value. For example, the expression of disgust or rejection is based on the organism's attempt to rid itself of something unpleasant that it has ingested. To quote Darwin (1872),

Facial expressions are universal in the emotions they convey. Photographs of people from New Guinea and from the United States demonstrate that emotions are conveyed by the same facial expressions. From left to right are happiness, sadness, and disgust for each culture.

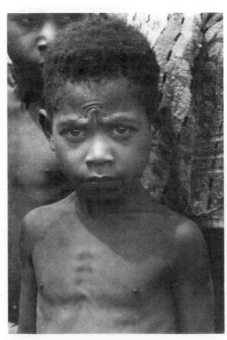

The term "disgust," in its simplest sense, means something offensive to the taste. But as disgust also causes annoyance, it is generally accompanied by a frown, and often by gestures as if to push away or to guard oneself against the offensive object. Extreme disgust is expressed by movements around the mouth identical with those preparatory to the act of vomiting. The mouth is opened widely, with the upper lip strongly retracted. The partial closure of the eyelids, or the turning away of the eyes or of the whole body, are likewise highly expressive of disdain. These actions seem to declare that the despised person is not worth looking at, or is disagreeable to behold. Spitting seems an almost universal sign of contempt or disgust; and spitting obviously represents the rejection of anything offensive from the mouth.

While some facial expressions and gestures seem to be innately associated with particular emotions, others are learned from culture. One psychologist reviewed Chinese novels to determine how Chinese writers portray various human emotions. Many of the bodily changes in emotion (flushing, paling, cold perspiration, trembling, goose pimples) represent the same symptoms of emotion in Chinese fiction as they do in Western writing. However, the Chinese have other, quite different ways of expressing emotion. The following quotations from Chinese novels would surely be misinterpreted by an American reader unfamiliar with the culture (Klineberg, 1938).

"They stretched out their tongues."
(They showed signs of surprise.)

"He clapped his hands."
(He was worried or disappointed.)

"He scratched his ears and cheeks."
(He was happy.)

"Her eyes grew round and opened wide."
(She became angry.)

Thus, superimposed on the basic expressions of emotion, which appear to be

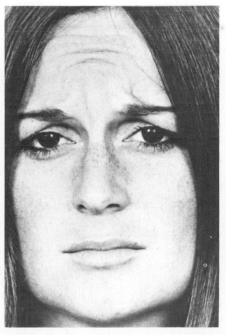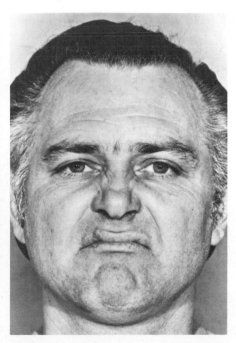

universal, are conventional or stereotyped forms of expressions — a kind of "language of emotion" recognized by others within a culture. Skilled actors are able to convey to their audiences an intended emotion by using facial expressions, tones of voice, and gestures in patterns that the audience will recognize. In simulating emotion, those of us who are less skilled actors can convey our intent by exaggerating the conventional expressions: gritting our teeth and clenching our fists to indicate anger, raising our eyebrows to express doubt or disapproval, and so on.

Brain Localization

The emotional expressions that are universal (for example, those associated with joy, anger, and disgust) are also highly specific: particular muscles are used to express particular emotions. This combination of universality and specificity suggests that a specialized neurological system may have evolved in humans to interpret the primitive emotional expressions, and recent evidence indicates that this system is localized in the right cerebral hemisphere.

One source of evidence comes from studies where pictures of emotional expressions are presented to either the left side or the right side of the subject's visual field. (Recall from Chapter 2 [p. 44] that input presented to the left visual field projects to the right hemisphere, and input presented to the right visual field projects to the left hemisphere.) When subjects have to decide which of two emotions the picture manifests, they are faster and more accurate when the picture is presented to their left visual field — that is, when it is projected to their right hemisphere. In addition, when the two halves of the face convey different emotions (one half may be smiling while the other half is frowning), the expression presented to the left visual field has the most impact on the subject's decision. Another source of evidence about the localization of emotional expressions comes from studies of patients who have suffered brain damage from strokes or accidents. Patients who have only right-hemisphere damage have more difficulty recognizing facial expressions of emotion than do patients who have only left-hemisphere damage (Etcoff, 1985).

Our system for recognizing emotional expressions seems to be highly specialized. In particular, it is distinct from our ability to recognize faces. Consider a *prosopagnosic*, a person who has such extreme difficulty recognizing familiar faces that he (or she) sometimes fails to recognize his own face! He can, however, recognize emotional expressions: he can tell you that a particular person is happy even when he does not know that the person is his spouse (Bruyer et al., 1983). The abilities to recognize faces and to recognize emotions also are differentially affected by electrical stimulation of various regions of the right hemisphere: face recognition is disrupted by stimulation in the parieto-occipital region, while emotion recognition is disrupted by stimulation of the middle temporal gyrus (Fried et al., 1982).

Emotions, in addition to being communicated by facial expressions, are also expressed by variations in voice patterns (particularly variations in pitch, timing, and stress). Some of these variations appear to be universal and specific: a sharp increase in pitch indicates fear, for example. The specialized neurological system for perceiving these emotional clues is located in the right cerebral hemisphere, and the evidence for this is similar to that for facial expressions. If an emotional voice is presented to either the left or right ear (which project to the right and left hemispheres, respectively), subjects are more accurate in identifying the emotion when the sound is presented to the left ear. And patients who have solely right-hemisphere damage have more trouble identifying emotions from voice

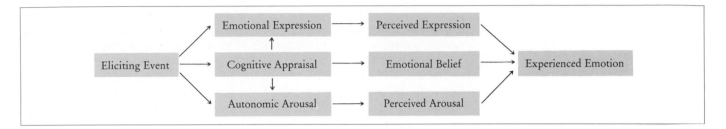

FIGURE 11-6
Components of an Emotional Experience: 2 *Emotional expression, emotional belief, and perceived arousal all contribute to the experience of an emotion. (After Reisenzein, 1983)*

clues than do patients who have solely left-hemisphere damage (Ley & Bryden, 1982).

Intensity and Differentiation of Emotions

The idea that facial expressions, in addition to their communicative function, also contribute to our experience of emotions is sometimes called the *facial feedback hypothesis*. According to the hypothesis, just as we receive feedback about (or "perceive") our autonomic arousal, so we receive feedback about (or "perceive") our facial expression, and this feedback combines with the other components of an emotion to produce a more intense experience. This implies that if you make yourself smile and hold the smile for several seconds, you will begin to feel happier; if you scowl, you will feel tense and angry. (Try it.) In support of the hypothesis, subjects who exaggerate their facial reactions to emotion-producing situations report more emotional response than subjects who do not (Laird, 1974). Other studies indicate that facial expressions may have an indirect effect on emotion by increasing autonomic arousal. Such an indirect influence was demonstrated in an experiment we discussed earlier, where producing particular emotional expressions led to changes in heartbeat and skin temperature. We therefore need to add emotional expression to our list of contributors to emotional experience (see Figure 11-6).

But exactly *how* do facial expressions influence either autonomic arousal or the subjective experience of emotion? An interesting answer was formulated in 1906 by Israel Waynbaum, a French physician, and rediscovered recently by Zajonc (1985). According to Waynbaum and Zajonc, the contraction of certain facial muscles affects blood flow in neighboring blood vessels. This, in turn, affects cerebral blood flow, which can determine brain temperature and neurotransmitter activity — and the latter may well be part of the cortical activity that underlies emotion. Thus, during laughter, contracting the facial muscles results in an increase in blood flow to the brain, which may contribute to the feeling of euphoria. The critical point is the link between facial muscles and blood, because once the expression "enters" the bloodstream, it can be communicated anywhere.

There are also many contemporary researchers who believe that facial expressions can determine the *quality* of emotions. Since the expressions for the primary emotions are distinct and occur rapidly, they are at least plausible candidates for contributing to the differentiation of emotions. Tompkins (1980) has suggested that the feedback from a facial expression is inherently acceptable or unacceptable, thereby providing a means by which facial expressions can distinguish the positive from the negative emotions. Should future research support the idea that facial expression can differentiate emotions, we are back (in part) to William James, who proposed that emotion *is* the perception of certain bodily changes; facial expressions are bodily changes — we are happy *because* we laugh.

Are we happy because *we laugh?*

CRITICAL DISCUSSION

Opponent Processes in Emotion

Given the evidence that intense emotions can be disruptive, why do some people repeatedly engage in highly arousing activities such as skydiving? According to an old joke, they do it because "it feels good when they stop." Surprisingly, there appears to be some truth to this punch line, which is captured by the *opponent-process theory* of emotion (Solomon & Corbit, 1974; Solomon, 1980).

The theory assumes that the brain is organized to oppose or suppress emotional states, whether the states are positive or negative. Each emotional state has an opposite that can cancel it; when one member of a pair is elicited (call it A), it soon triggers its opposite (call it B), which in time returns the system to its baseline:

Baseline → State A → State B → Baseline

This type of process is illustrated by reports on the emotional reactions typically experienced by parachutists in training (Epstein, 1967). During their first free-fall (before the parachute opens), the response is one of fear (this is State A). After landing, a trainee usually walks about with a stunned expression for a few minutes and then begins to smile and become very sociable. A feeling of euphoria follows (this is State B), which eventually fades to a baseline of normal behavior. (See Figure 11-7A.)

The temporal course of this emotional process can be understood by looking at the left-hand panel of Figure 11-7B. When the emotional event occurs, it elicits an *a*-process; this gives rise to State A. Sometime after the *a*-process is activated, the *b*-process is aroused and functions to oppose and suppress the affective state generated by the *a*-process. At any moment, the difference between the magnitude of the *a*-process and the magnitude of the *b*-process specifies the manifest emotional state or response; this difference is plotted in the top left-hand curve of Figure 11-7B.

The top left-hand curve also gives us the time course of an emotional experience. When an emotion-producing stimulus is first presented, an emotion occurs that rises to a peak in a few seconds. Then, as the event continues, the emotion recedes slightly from its peak and remains steady. This sequence occurs because initially the *a*-process is unopposed, giving rise to a

peak level for State A; but as the *b*-process gradually becomes activated, it subtracts from the *a*-process, thereby reducing the peak level for State A. Once the emotion-producing stimulus is removed, the opposite emotion is experienced. This happens because the *a*-process disappears almost immediately but the *b*-process recedes more slowly; thus, State B is experienced until the *b*-process has run its course.

Let us return to skydiving and interpret it in terms of these underlying processes. The free-fall is clearly an emotion-producing event. At its onset, the *a*-process will be activated immediately, leading to an emotional peak for State A—namely, intense fear. Shortly afterward (still during free-fall), the *b*-process will be aroused gradually and will reduce the intensity of State A, but the jumper will still feel considerable fear. When the parachute opens, fear will be lessened further. When the jumper lands, removing the fear-producing event, the *a*-process will disappear quickly

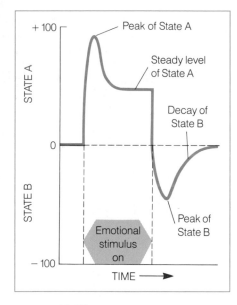

FIGURE 11-7A
Temporal Dynamics of an Affective Response *The standard pattern of an affective response produced by an emotion-arousing stimulus on its initial presentation. This curve is the same as the one at the top of the left-hand panel in Figure 11-7B.*

but the b-process will persist, giving rise to State B — a feeling of relief. This pattern of emotional response can be observed in our everyday experiences, but it is often complicated by cultural factors and our efforts to suppress or control our emotions. In well-controlled laboratory situations, the temporal course of an emotional state presented in Figure 11-7B can be demonstrated.

Thus far, we have considered only the first time an emotion-producing event is encountered. But skydivers repeat the activity of parachuting many times, and opponent-process theory considers this repetition of the event. According to the theory, the first time an arousing stimulus is experienced, the b-process is fairly weak and slow to occur. Repeated exposures to the stimulus strengthen the b-process until it becomes activated much more quickly and with much greater intensity; this is indicated in the right-hand panel of Figure 11-7B. As a result, the manifest level for State A is reduced, and when the stimulus is removed, the intensity of state B is greatly amplified. The time course for an emotional response to a stimulus encountered many times is illustrated by the curve in the top right-hand panel of Figure 11-7B. This pattern of reactions also has been verified by experimentation. Thus, the initial encounter with an arousing event will lead to a strong State A experience followed by a mild State B experience; but after repeated experiences, the intensity of State A will be diminished, whereas the intensity of State B will be greatly amplified. Hence, we can see why some people continue to engage in highly arousing activities such as skydiving and roller-coaster riding: the negative A state is more than compensated for by the positive B state.

This analysis of the effects of repeated exposures to arousing events can also illuminate drug addictions. The first few doses of an opiate produce a potent experience of pleasure, called a "rush," which has been described as an intense type of sexual pleasure felt throughout the body. The rush is followed by a less intense state of euphoria. After the drug has worn off, the user lapses into an aversive state of craving called "withdrawal," which fades in time. This pattern conforms to the curve in the top left-hand panel of Figure 11-7B. The opiate

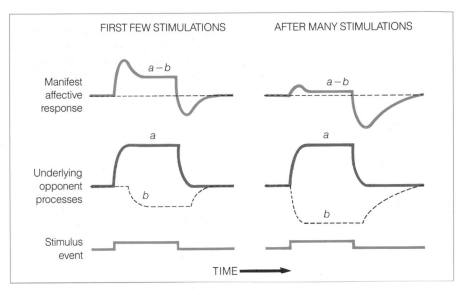

FIGURE 11-7B

Opponent Processes in Emotion   *The left-hand panel illustrates the affective response to the first few presentations of a stimulus; the right-hand panel shows the response after repeated presentations of the stimulus. The top curve in each panel is the manifest response produced by the interplay of the opponent processes; it is obtained by taking the difference between the underlying opponent processes a and b shown in the middle row of the figure (that is, subtracting the b-curve from the a-curve). The bottom row in the figure indicates the onset and offset of the emotion-arousing stimulus. Note that the b-process has a shorter latency, an increased intensity, and a slower decay as the stimulus is presented repeatedly and becomes familiar. These changes in the b-process explain why there is a change in the manifest emotional response as a stimulus is repeatedly experienced. (After Solomon, 1980)*

produces a peak level for State A (the rush), followed by a slight decline in intensity (euphoria); when the drug dose loses its effect, State B (withdrawal) emerges and then gradually disappears. If the user repeats the drug doses frequently, the course of the emotional experience changes as predicted by the opponent-process theory (see the right-hand panel of Figure 11-7B). The rush is no longer experienced, and the feeling of euphoria is minimal or absent. The withdrawal syndrome becomes much more intense, and its duration lengthens dramatically. Experienced drug users have mild "highs" followed by intense and extended "lows."

Initially, addictive drugs are taken because they produce pleasant effects. After repeated use, however, they are taken to counteract the unpleasant opponent process that persists from prior drug use. A vicious circle is formed: the more often a drug is used, the more intense and longer-lasting the opponent process becomes. To get rid of this unpleasant aftereffect, the drug user takes the drug again, further strengthening the opponent process. An experienced drug user continues to take a drug to reduce the low that occurs after the previous dose rather than to produce the high originally associated with the drug. This cycle is not easily broken, as the high failure rates of most drug-treatment programs indicate. The opponent-process theory does not offer a prescription for the treatment of drug addiction, but it provides a useful framework within which to evaluate such programs (Solomon, 1980).

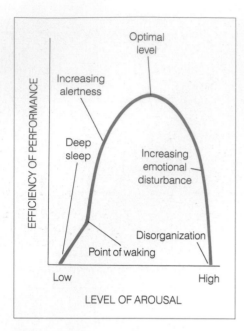

FIGURE 11-8
Emotional Arousal and Performance
The curve shows the hypothetical relationship between level of emotional arousal and efficiency of performance. The precise shape of the curve differs for various tasks or behaviors. (After Hebb, 1972)

HOW ADAPTIVE ARE EMOTIONS?

To what extent are emotional experiences beneficial? To what extent are they harmful? Do they mainly help us to survive, or are they chiefly sources of disturbance? The answers to these questions depend, in part, on the intensity and the duration of the emotion experienced.

With regard to intensity, a mild level of emotional arousal tends to produce alertness and interest in the current situation. When emotions become intense, however, whether pleasant or unpleasant, they usually result in some disruption of thought or behavior. The curve in Figure 11-8 represents the relation between a person's level of emotional arousal and his or her effectiveness on a task. At very low levels of emotional arousal (for example, at the point of waking up), sensory information may not be well attended to, and performance will be relatively poor. Performance is optimal at moderate levels of arousal. At high levels of emotional arousal, performance begins to decline, probably because the person cannot devote enough cognitive resources to the task.

The optimum level of arousal and the shape of the curve differ for different tasks. A simple, well-learned routine would be much less susceptible to disruption by emotional arousal than a more complex activity that depends on the integration of several thought processes. During a moment of intense fear, you would probably still be able to spell your name but not play good chess. Exactly what constitutes an excessive level of emotional arousal depends on the individual, as shown by studies of behavior during crises such as fires or sudden floods. About 15 percent of people show organized, effective behavior, suggesting that their optimum level of emotional arousal has not been exceeded. The majority of people, about 70 percent, show various degrees of disorganization but are still able to function with some effectiveness. The remaining 15 percent are so disorganized that they are unable to function at all; they may panic or exhibit aimless and completely inappropriate behavior, suggesting they are far above their optimal level of emotional arousal (Tyhurst, 1951).

Sometimes intense emotions are not quickly discharged but continue to remain unresolved. Perhaps the situation that makes a person angry (for example, prolonged conflict with an employer) or fearful (such as worry over the illness of a loved one) continues for a long time period. While the physiological changes that accompany anger and fear can have adaptive value (they mobilize us to fight or flee), when maintained too long they can exhaust our resources and even cause tissue damage. A chronic state of heightened arousal can thus take its toll on the individual's health. We will have more to say about the relationship between stress and illness in Chapter 14. At this point, however, it should be noted that long-term emotional stress can impair a person's physical health, as well as his or her mental efficiency.

AGGRESSION AS AN EMOTIONAL REACTION

We may respond in different ways when we experience an emotion. Sometimes we inhibit any expression of the emotion, or we express it only verbally ("I'm very angry even though I'm not showing it"). Other times we may display a typical emotional reaction—smiling and laughing when happy, withdrawing when frightened, being aggressive when angry, and so forth. Among these typical emotional reactions, psychologists have singled out one in particular for extensive study: aggression.

This special treatment is partly due to the social significance of aggression. At the societal level, a single aggressive act can spell disaster in an age when nuclear weapons are widely available. At the individual level, many people experience aggressive thoughts and impulses frequently, and how they handle these thoughts will have major effects on their health and interpersonal relations. Another reason why aggression is so important is that it is a primary object of study by different theories of social interactions. Thus, Freud's *psychoanalytic theory* views aggression as a drive, and *social-learning theory* views it as a learned response. These two views have dominated much of the research on aggression.

In the following discussion, we first describe these different views along with related research, and then consider how the views differ with respect to the effects of viewing aggression in the mass media. Keep in mind that what we mean by "aggression" is behavior that is *intended* to injure another person (physically or verbally) or to destroy property. The key concept in this definition is intent. If a person accidentally steps on your foot in a crowded elevator and immediately apologizes, you would not interpret the behavior as aggressive; but if someone walks up to you as you sit at your desk and stomps on your foot, you would not hesitate to label the act as aggressive.

Is aggression a drive or a learned response?

Aggression as a Drive

We will present only those aspects of psychoanalytic theory and social-learning theory that are relevant to aggression. Both theories will be presented in more detail in Chapter 13, where we focus on personality, and Chapters 15 and 16, where we discuss abnormal behavior and its treatment.

According to Freud's early psychoanalytic theory, many of our actions are determined by instincts, particularly the sexual instinct. When expression of these instincts is frustrated, an aggressive drive is induced. Later theorists in the psychoanalytic tradition broadened this *frustration-aggression hypothesis* to the following claim: whenever a person's effort to reach *any* goal is blocked, an aggressive drive is induced that motivates behavior to injure the obstacle (person or object) causing the frustration (Dollard et al., 1939). There are two critical aspects of this proposal: one is that the usual cause of aggression is frustration; the other is that aggression has the properties of a basic drive — being a form of *energy* that *persists* until its goal is satisfied, as well as an *inborn* reaction (hunger, sex, and other basic drives have these properties). As we will see, it is the drive aspect of the frustration-aggression hypothesis that has proved to be particularly controversial.

SUDDEN VIOLENCE   The idea of an aggressive drive fits with the popular notion of violence as a sudden, explosive, irrational type of behavior: it is as if aggressive energy builds up until it has to find an outlet. Newspaper and television accounts of crimes tend to encourage this view. Usually, however, the offender's background is not as innocent as media accounts would have us believe. In the 1960s, for example, a University of Texas student positioned himself in the campus bell tower and shot as many people as he could until he was finally gunned down. Newspaper reports described him as a model American youth, a former altar boy and Eagle Scout. Subsequent investigation revealed, however, that his life had been replete with aggressive acts, including assaults on his wife and others and a court-martial as a marine recruit for insubordination and fighting. He also had a passion for collecting firearms.

The above case is typical; most people who commit aggressive acts have a history of aggressive behavior (with the exception of some psychotic individuals who may be driven to violent acts by delusional beliefs). Today's most aggressive

FIGURE 11-9
Brain Stimulation and Aggression *A mild electrical current is delivered to electrodes implanted in the monkey's hypothalamus via remote radio control. The animal's response (attack or flight) depends on its position in the dominance hierarchy of the colony. (Courtesy Dr. José Delgado)*

30-year-olds were yesterday's most aggressive 10-year-olds. Aggressiveness seems to be established during childhood and remains relatively stable thereafter (Huesmann, Eron, Lefkowitz, & Walder, 1984).

BIOLOGICAL BASIS OF AGGRESSION Findings on the biological basis of aggression in animals provide better evidence for an aggressive drive. Some studies show that mild electrical stimulation of a specific region of the hypothalamus produces aggressive, even deadly, behavior in animals. When a cat's hypothalamus is stimulated via implanted electrodes, the animal hisses, its hair bristles, its pupils dilate, and it will strike at a rat or other objects placed in its cage. Stimulation of a different area of the hypothalamus produces quite different behavior: instead of exhibiting any of these "rage" responses, the cat coldly stalks and kills a rat.

Similar techniques have produced aggressive behavior in rats. A laboratory-bred rat that has never killed a mouse, nor seen a wild rat kill one, may live quite peacefully in the same cage with a mouse. But if the rat's hypothalamus is stimulated, the animal will pounce on its mouse cage mate and kill it with exactly the same response exhibited by a wild rat (a hard bite to the neck that severs the spinal cord). The stimulation seems to trigger an innate killing response that had previously been dormant. Conversely, if a neurochemical blocker is injected into the same brain site in rats that spontaneously kill mice on sight, the rats become temporarily peaceful (Smith, King, & Hoebel, 1970).

In higher mammals, such instinctive patterns of aggression are controlled by the cortex and therefore are influenced more by experience. Monkeys living in groups establish a dominance hierarchy: one or two males become leaders, and the others assume various levels of subordination. When the hypothalamus of a dominant monkey is electrically stimulated, the monkey attacks subordinate males but not females. When a low-ranking monkey is stimulated in the same way, it cowers and behaves submissively (see Figure 11-9). Thus, aggressive behavior in a monkey is not automatically elicited by stimulation of the hypothalamus; rather, in making its response a monkey "considers" the environment and its memory of past experiences. Humans are similar. Although we are equipped with neurological mechanisms that are tied to aggression, the activation of these mechanisms is usually under cortical control (except in some cases of brain damage). Indeed, in most individuals, the frequency with which aggressive behavior is expressed, the forms it takes, and the situations in which it is displayed are determined largely by experience and social influences. (For more comparisons between aggression in humans and that in other animals, see the Critical Discussion, "On Aggressive Instincts and Their Inhibition," p. 374.)

Aggression as a Learned Response

Social-learning theory is concerned with human interaction, but it has its origins in behavioristic studies of animal learning (such as those discussed in Chapter 7). It focuses on the behavior patterns that people develop in response to environmental contingencies. Some behaviors may be rewarded while others may produce unfavorable results; through the process of differential reinforcement, people eventually select the more successful behavior patterns. Social-learning theory, however, differs from strict behaviorism in that it stresses the importance of cognitive processes. Because people can represent situations symbolically, they are able to foresee the probable consequences of their actions and to alter their behavior accordingly.

Social-learning theory further differs from strict behaviorism in that it stresses the importance of *vicarious learning,* or learning by observation. Many behavior patterns are learned by watching the behavior of others and observing what consequences it produces for them. A child who observes the pained expressions of an older sibling in the dentist's chair will probably be fearful when the time comes for his or her first dental appointment. Social-learning theory emphasizes the role of *models* in transmitting both specific behaviors and emotional responses, and it focuses on such questions as what types of models are most effective and what factors determine whether the modeled behavior that is learned will actually be performed (Bandura, 1973).

With this emphasis on learning, it is no surprise that social-learning theory rejects the concept of aggression as an instinct or as a frustration-produced drive; the theory proposes instead that aggression is similar to any other learned response. Aggression can be learned through observation or imitation, and the more often it is reinforced, the more likely it is to occur. A person who is frustrated by a blocked goal or disturbed by some stressful event experiences unpleasant emotional arousal. The response that this arousal elicits will differ, depending on the kinds of responses the individual has learned to use in coping with stressful situations. The frustrated individual may seek help from others, aggress, withdraw, try even harder to surmount the obstacle, or anesthetize himself or herself with drugs or alcohol. The chosen response will be the one that has relieved frustration most successfully in the past. According to this view, frustration provokes aggression mainly in people who have learned to respond to adverse situations with aggressive behavior (Bandura, 1977).

Figure 11-10 shows how social-learning theory differs from psychoanalytic theory (the frustration-aggression hypothesis) in conceptualizing aggression. Social-learning theory assumes that (1) frustration is just one of several causes of aggression, and (2) aggression is a response with no drivelike properties.

IMITATION OF AGGRESSION   One source of evidence for social-learning theory is studies showing that aggression, like any other response, can be learned through imitation. Nursery school children who observed an adult expressing various forms of aggression toward a large, inflated doll subsequently imitated many of the adult's actions, including unconventional and unusual ones (see Figure 11-11). The experiment was expanded to include two filmed versions of aggressive modeling (one showing an adult behaving aggressively toward the doll; the other showing a cartoon character displaying the same aggressive behavior). The results were equally striking. Children who watched either of the two

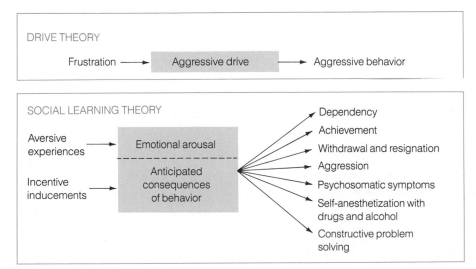

DRIVE THEORY

Frustration ⟶ Aggressive drive ⟶ Aggressive behavior

SOCIAL LEARNING THEORY

Aversive experiences ⟶ Emotional arousal
Incentive inducements ⟶ Anticipated consequences of behavior

⟶ Dependency
⟶ Achievement
⟶ Withdrawal and resignation
⟶ Aggression
⟶ Psychosomatic symptoms
⟶ Self-anesthetization with drugs and alcohol
⟶ Constructive problem solving

FIGURE 11-10
Two Views of Aggression   *The diagram schematically represents the determinants of aggression according to psychoanalytic theory (the frustration-aggression hypothesis) and social-learning theory. From the viewpoint of social-learning theory, the emotional arousal caused by unpleasant experiences can lead to any number of different behaviors, depending on the behavior that has been reinforced in the past.*

FIGURE 11-11
Children's Imitation of Adult Aggression *Nursery school children observed an adult express various forms of aggressive behavior toward an inflated doll. After watching the adult, both boys and girls behaved aggressively toward the doll, performing many of the detailed acts of aggression the adult had displayed, including lifting and throwing the doll, striking it with a hammer, and kicking it.*

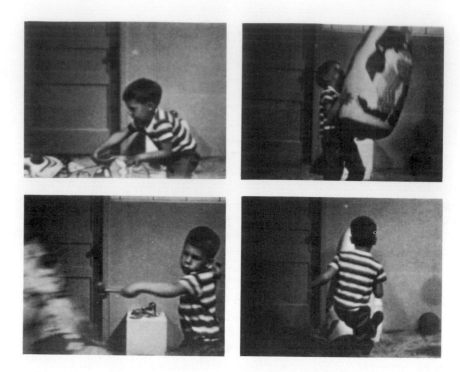

films behaved as aggressively toward the doll as children who had observed a live model displaying aggression. Figure 11-12 measures aggressive behavior for each of the groups and for two control groups who observed either no model or a nonaggressive model. The conclusion of such studies is that observation of either live or filmed models of aggression increases the likelihood of aggression in the viewer.

REINFORCEMENT OF AGGRESSION   Another source of evidence for social-learning theory is demonstrations that aggression is sensitive to reinforcement contingencies in the same manner that other responses are. A number of studies show that children are more likely to express the aggressive responses they learned by watching aggressive models when they are reinforced for such actions or when they observe aggressive models being reinforced. In one study, investigators observed children for ten weeks, recording instances of interpersonal aggression and the events that immediately followed aggression, such as positive reinforcers (victim winced or cried), punishment (victim counterattacked), or neutral reactions (victim ignored the aggressor). For the children who showed the highest overall level of aggression, positive reinforcement was the most common reaction to their aggressive act. Children who initially were unaggressive, but occasionally succeeded in stopping attacks by counteraggression, gradually began to initiate attacks of their own (their aggression was being reinforced). Children who showed the least aggression were those whose counteraggression was unsuccessful (nonreinforced). Clearly, the consequences of aggression play an important role in shaping behavior (Patterson, Littman, & Bricker, 1967).

Aggressive Expression and Catharsis

Studies that try to distinguish between aggression as a drive and aggression as a learned response often focus on *catharsis* (purging an emotion by experiencing it intensely). If aggression is persistent energy, then the expression of aggression should be cathartic, resulting in a reduction in the intensity of aggressive feelings and actions. On the other hand, if aggression is a learned response, the expression of aggression could result in an increase in such actions (if the aggression is reinforced). Currently, the evidence favors the learned-response view.

ACTING AGGRESSIVELY Psychologists have conducted numerous laboratory studies to determine whether or not aggression decreases once it has been partially expressed. Studies of children indicate that participation in aggressive activities either increases aggressive behavior or maintains it at the same level. Experiments with adults produce similar results. When given repeated opportunities to shock another person (who cannot retaliate), college students become more and more punitive. And subjects who are angry become even more punitive on successive attacks than subjects who are not angry. If aggression were cathartic, the angry subjects should reduce their aggressive drive by acting aggressively and become less punitive the more they aggress (Berkowitz, 1965; Geen & Quanty, 1977).

Some evidence about catharsis is also taken from real-life situations. In one case, California aerospace workers who had been laid off were first interviewed about how they felt about their companies and supervisors and subsequently were asked to describe their feelings in writing. If aggression were cathartic, men who expressed a lot of anger in the interviews should have expressed relatively little in the written reports. The results, however, showed otherwise: the men who let out anger in conversation expressed even more in their reports. Fuming in conversation may have "kindled" the aggression. Another study looked at the relation between the hostility of a culture (vis-à-vis its neighbors) and the kinds of games it plays. More belligerent cultures were found to play more combative games. Again, aggression seems to breed aggression rather than dissipate it (Ebbesen, Duncan, & Konečni, 1975).

These results argue against aggression being cathartic. However, there are circumstances in which the expression of aggression decreases its incidence. For example, behaving aggressively may arouse feelings of anxiety in the aggressors that inhibit further aggression, particularly if they observe the injurious consequences of their actions. But in these instances, the effect on aggressive behavior can be explained without concluding that an aggressive drive is being reduced. Also, although expressing hostile feelings in action does not usually reduce the aggression, it may make the person feel better. But this may happen because the person feels more powerful and more in control, rather than because the person has reduced an aggressive drive.

VIEWING VIOLENCE Most of the studies we have discussed deal with the consequences of directly expressing aggression. What about the effects of indirectly or vicariously expressing aggression through watching violence on television or in the movies? Is viewing violence cathartic, providing fantasy outlets for an aggressive drive? Or does it elicit aggression by modeling violent behavior? We have already seen that children will imitate live or filmed aggressive behavior in an experimental setting, but how will they react in more natural settings? The amount of violence to which we are exposed through the media makes this an important question.

Several experimental studies have controlled children's viewing of television: one group watched violent cartoons for a specified amount of time each day; another group watched nonviolent cartoons for the same amount of time. The amount of aggression the children showed in their daily activities was carefully recorded. The children who watched violent cartoons became more aggressive in their interactions with their peers, whereas the children who viewed nonviolent cartoons showed no change in interpersonal aggression (Steuer, Applefield, & Smith, 1971).

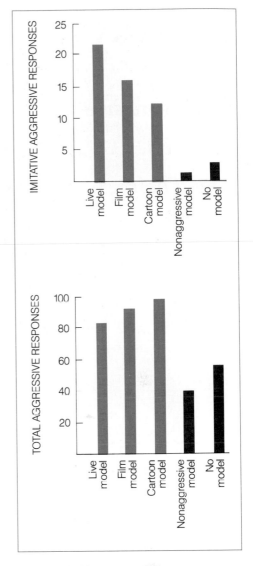

FIGURE 11-12

Imitation of Aggression *Observing aggressive models (either live or on film) greatly increases the amount of aggressive behavior that children display, compared to observing a nonaggressive model or no model at all. Note that observation of the live model results in the imitation of more specific aggressive acts, whereas observation of filmed (either real-life or cartoon) models instigates more aggressive responses of all kinds. (After Bandura, 1973)*

CRITICAL DISCUSSION

On Aggressive Instincts and Their Inhibition

In the early phase of his work, Freud proposed that aggression is a frustration-induced drive. In later years, he adopted the more extreme position that aggression is based on instinct. Freud postulated a *death instinct* that can be directed either inward in the form of self-destructive behavior or outward in the form of aggression. The claim that aggression is an instinct means that people aggress to express an inborn desire: the ultimate goal of aggression is not removal of a frustrating agent but aggression itself.

Freud came to this pessimistic stance in an attempt to account for the senseless carnage of World War I. He expressed his views in a letter written to Albert Einstein in 1932. Einstein, concerned with the efforts of the League of Nations to promote world peace, asked Freud for his opinions on why people engage in war. Is it possible, Einstein inquired, that human beings have a "lust for hatred and destruction"? Freud replied:

You express astonishment at the fact that it is so easy to make men enthusiastic about a war and add your suspicion that there is something at work in them — an instinct for hatred and destruction — which goes halfway to meet the efforts of warmongers. I can only express my entire agreement. We believe in an instinct of that kind and have been occupied during the last few years in studying its manifestations. The death instinct turns into the destructive instinct. It is directed outwards, onto objects. The living creature preserves its own life, so to say, by destroying an extraneous one. (1963, p. 41)

FIGURE 11-13

Ritualistic Patterns of Fighting Behavior   *The wildebeest bull defends its territory against a rival in a stylized challenge duel. These skirmishes, which may occur many times a day, seldom result in bloodshed. A. The two antagonists stand grazing head to head, taking each other's measure. B. Suddenly, they drop to their knees in the eye-to-eye combat attitude. C. Pretending to sense danger, they raise their heads in mock alarm, apparently a means of easing tension. D. At this point, the challenge may be called off or may progress to a brief, horn-locked battle.*

Though Freud's instinct view of aggression is not widely accepted by clinicians, it is in agreement with theories of aggression proposed by ethologists. The view of many ethologists is that both animals and humans have an aggressive instinct that must find some outlet (for example, Eibl-Eibesfeldt, 1970; Lorenz, 1981). Earlier work in ethology assumed that a major difference exists between humans and lower species—namely, that animals have evolved mechanisms to control their aggressive instincts, whereas humans have not (for example, Ardrey, 1966; Lorenz, 1966). More recent work, however, suggests that animals are no better at controlling their instincts than we are.

In the 1960s, Lorenz and other ethologists made a number of observations about animal aggression and its limits. They noted that, among their own species, animals usually fight to protect their young and to compete for food, mates, and nesting sites. Such aggression ensures that the strongest males will procreate—since they will be the winners in the competition for females—and also makes it likely that animals will be spaced over the inhabited area so that each group establishes a specific "territory." According to Lorenz, animals can safely enjoy these benefits of aggression because, through the process of evolution, they have developed inhibitions that prevent them from destroying their own species. Many species exhibit ritualistic fighting behavior that appears to be largely innate (see Figure 11-13). They ward off combat by threatening displays. They fight according to a stylized pattern that seldom results in serious injury, because the loser can display signals of submission that inhibit further aggression on the part of the victor (for example, a wolf lies down and exposes its throat). All of this, according to Lorenz, is in contrast to humans, who have developed powerful weapons that can cause instant death at great distances and who have no inhibitions to offset these destructive instincts.

More recent observations by ethologists challenge the earlier belief that animals "know how" to inhibit their aggression. It is now known that many animals do not employ innate signals to stop attacks, and that the stereotyped signals that

Mutual grooming is a social response that inhibits aggression.

they do employ have varying effects on the responses of their foes. The incidence of murder, rape, and infanticide among animals is much greater than was thought in the 1960s. One kind of murder involves border wars between chimpanzees (Goodall, 1978). In one well-documented case in the Gombe Stream National Park in Tanzania, a "gang" of five male chimpanzees defended their territory against any strange male that wandered into it. If the gang encountered a group of two or more strangers, their response would be raucous, but not deadly; but if there was only one intruder, then one member of the gang might hold his arm, another a leg, while a third member pounded the intruder to death. Or a couple of members of the gang would drag the intruder over the rocks until he died. In another chimpanzee border war observed during the 1970s, a tribe of about 15 chimpanzees destroyed a smaller neighboring group by killing the members off one male at a time. Observations such as this have led to a drastic revision in beliefs about the extent of animal aggression. Indeed, the well-known sociobiologist E. O. Wilson has gone so far as to claim that: "If you calculate the number of murders per individual animal per hour of observation, you realize that the murder rate is higher than for human beings, even taking into account our wars" (1983, p. 79).

Some experts believe that, in addition to comparable incidences of aggression, animals and humans have comparable inhibitions on aggression. Animal behaviors that appear to inhibit aggression include maintaining distance from a potential foe (strong odors and loud vocalizations that permit animals to detect and withdraw from one another at a distance serve this purpose) and evoking a social response that is incompatible with aggression. One such response is mutual grooming—touching or fingering the fur or feathers of another animal. Perhaps the most important factor in reducing aggression is familiarity. Many of the social rituals in which animals engage (such as sniffing and inspecting body parts and stereotyped greeting behaviors) familiarize them with each other's smell and appearance, which helps them to distinguish group members from strangers.

Maintaining distance, engaging in social responses incompatible with aggression, and gaining familiarity are also activities that people use to ward off aggression. These parallels (and others mentioned in this discussion) between humans and other animals are of considerable interest, but they are only weak evidence for an aggressive instinct or drive in humans. At this point, there is more evidence that aggression is a learned behavior (see the section "Aggression as a Learned Response").

The above study involves an experimental group and a control group. However, most studies that deal with children's viewing habits are correlational; they determine the relation between the amount of exposure to televised violence and the degree to which children use aggressive behavior to solve interpersonal conflicts. This correlation is clearly positive (Singer & Singer, 1981), even for children in Finland, which has a limited number of violent programs (Lagerspetz, Viemero, & Akademi, 1986). Correlations, however, do not imply causal relationships. It may be that children who are more aggressive prefer to watch violent TV programs — that is, aggression causes one to view violence, rather than vice versa.

To evaluate this alternative hypothesis, a longitudinal study traced TV viewing habits over a ten-year period. More than 800 children were studied between the ages of 8 and 9 years. Investigators collected information about each child's viewing preferences and aggressiveness (as rated by schoolmates). Boys who preferred programs that contained a considerable amount of violence were found to be much more aggressive in their interpersonal relationships than boys who preferred programs that contained little violence. So far, the evidence is of the same nature as that in previous studies. But ten years later, more than half of the original subjects were interviewed concerning their TV preferences, given a test that measured delinquency tendencies, and rated by their peers for aggressiveness. Figure 11-14 shows that high exposure to violence on television at age 9 is positively related to aggressiveness in boys at age 19. Most important, the correlation remains significant even when statistical methods are used to control for the degree of childhood aggressiveness, thereby reducing the possibility that the initial level of aggression determines both childhood viewing preferences and adult aggressiveness.

It is interesting that the results showed no consistent relation between the TV viewing habits of girls and their aggressive behavior at either age. This agrees with the results of other studies indicating that girls tend to imitate aggressive behavior much less than boys do unless specifically reinforced for doing so. In our society, girls are less likely to be reinforced for behaving aggressively. And since most of the aggressive roles on television are male, females are less likely to find aggressive models to imitate.

In summary, the majority of studies point to the conclusion that viewing violence does increase interpersonal aggression, particularly in young children. This argues against aggression catharsis and the view that aggression is a drive.

WHY VIEWING VIOLENCE AFFECTS SOCIAL BEHAVIOR   Exactly *why* should viewing violence lead to aggressive behavior? One reason, mentioned earlier, is that filmed violence provides aggressive models. While this is likely part of the story, there are other reasons for the link between viewing violence and behaving aggressively, some of which go beyond social-learning theory. A survey of plausible reasons follows:

Children often imitate what they see on television.

1. *Modeling aggressive styles of conduct.* We have already seen that children imitate the behavior of aggressive models. A number of cases have been reported of young children or teenagers duplicating a violent act previously seen on television. In one instance, the parents of a victim took legal action against a TV network, claiming that a program shown during the hours when children were watching was responsible for a brutal attack on their 9-year-old daughter. The three youngsters responsible admitted that they had copied the method of assault shown on the program. Police departments report that a number of violent crimes are the result of people trying to copy the plot of a TV show (Mankiewicz & Swerdlow, 1977).

2. *Increasing arousal.* When children watch violent TV programs, they become more emotionally aroused than when they watch nonviolent programs, as measured by a significant increase in their galvanic skin response, or GSR (Osborn & Endsley, 1971). This arousal may combine with other anger-induced arousal if the viewer is already frustrated or annoyed.

3. *Desensitizing people to violence.* Young children are emotionally aroused by viewing violence, but with repeated exposures their physiological reactions to displays of violence decrease. Indeed, exposure to TV violence decreases emotional responsiveness to real-life aggression in news films in both children and adults (Thomas, Horton, Lippincott, & Drabman, 1977). The emotional blunting produced by continual exposure to filmed violence may affect our ability to empathize with a victim's suffering in real life and may decrease our readiness to help.

4. *Reducing restraints on aggressive behavior.* Although we may be angry and feel like injuring someone who has provoked us, numerous restraints usually prevent us from doing so. Experiments indicate, however, that observing another person behaving aggressively weakens these restraints (Doob & Wood, 1972; Diener, 1976).

5. *Distorting views about conflict resolution.* On television or in the movies, interpersonal conflicts are solved by physical aggression much more often than by any other means. Watching the "good guys" triumph over the "bad guys" by violent means makes such behavior seem not only acceptable but perhaps even morally justified, particularly to young children who may have difficulty keeping fiction and reality separate.

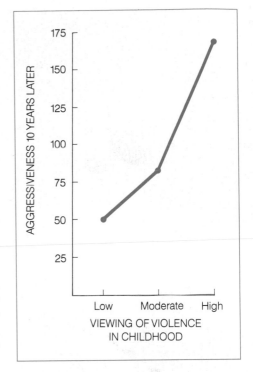

FIGURE 11-14
Relationship Between Childhood Viewing of Violent Television and Adult Aggression *Preference for viewing violent TV programs by boys at age 9 is positively correlated with aggressive behavior at age 19. (After Eron, Huesmann, Lefkowitz, & Walder, 1972)*

The different reasons may apply to different kinds of children. For example, perhaps only aggressive children learn to reduce their restraints on aggressive behavior by viewing violence. Other kinds of differences among children also influence the relation between TV violence and aggression. Children who are having school or social problems, or who identify more with violent characters, are more likely to be affected by TV violence (Huesmann, Lagerspetz, & Eron, 1984).

Our survey has by no means considered all plausible causes of aggression. Common causes of anger and aggression include a loss of self-esteem or a perception that another person has acted unfairly (Averill, 1983); neither of these factors has figured centrally in our discussion of aggression as a drive versus aggression as a learned response. Also, many societal factors are involved in the instigation of aggression; conditions of poverty, overcrowding, the actions of authorities such as the police, and the values of one's cultural group are only a few. Some of these social influences will be considered in Chapter 18.

The study of aggression makes it clear that an emotional reaction is a complex event. Similarly, each component of an emotion that we considered—autonomic arousal, cognitive appraisal, and emotional expression—is itself a complex phenomenon involving multiple factors. It is no wonder that we still know so little about this side of our lives.

SUMMARY

1. The components of an emotion include *subjective experience, autonomic arousal, cognitive appraisal,* and *emotional expression.* One critical question is, How do arousal, appraisal, and expression contribute to the subjective experience of an emotion? Another question is, Which components *differentiate* the emotions?

2. Intense emotions involve physiological arousal caused by activation of the *sympathetic division* of the *autonomic nervous system*. People who have spinal cord injuries, which limit feedback from the autonomic nervous system, report experiencing less intense emotions. Autonomic arousal may also help differentiate the emotions, since the pattern of arousal (for example, heartbeat, skin temperature) differs for different emotions.

3. A *cognitive appraisal* is an analysis of a situation that results in an emotional belief. Such appraisals affect both the intensity and quality of an emotion. When people are induced into a state of undifferentiated arousal (say, by injection of epinephrine), the quality of their emotional experience is determined almost entirely by their appraisal of the situation. That appraisals can differentiate emotions helps explain why past experience influences emotion and why people can have an emotion without being aware of it.

4. The facial expressions that accompany primary emotions have a universal meaning: people from different cultures agree on what emotion a person in a particular photograph is expressing. The ability to recognize emotional expression is localized in the right cerebral hemisphere and is neurologically distinct from the ability to recognize faces. In addition to their communicative functions, emotional expressions may also contribute to the subjective experience of an emotion.

5. The adaptive value of an emotional experience depends on its intensity and duration. A mild emotion produces alertness; an intense one can be disruptive. Intense emotions that persist too long can even cause tissue damage.

6. *Aggression* is a typical reaction to anger (though it can occur for other reasons as well). According to early *psychoanalytic theory*, aggression is a *frustration-produced drive;* according to *social-learning theory*, aggression is a *learned response.*

7. In lower animals, aggression is controlled by neurological mechanisms in the *hypothalamus*. Stimulation of the hypothalamus of a rat or cat can lead to a "rage" or "killing" response. In humans and other higher mammals, aggressive behavior is under cortical control.

8. In keeping with the social-learning theory of aggression, aggressive responses can be learned through *imitation* and increased in frequency when positively reinforced.

9. Evidence indicates that aggression either increases subsequent aggressive behavior or maintains it at the same level. The indirect or vicarious expression of aggression has similar effects: there is a positive relation between the amount of exposure children have to TV violence and the extent to which they act aggressively.

10. Viewing violence may lead to aggressive behavior because it teaches aggressive styles of conduct, increases arousal, desensitizes people to violence, reduces restraints on aggression, and distorts views about conflict resolution.

For an introduction to contemporary views on emotion, see Strongman, *The Psychology of Emotion* (2nd ed., 1978). For a more technical treatment, see Mandler, *Mind and Emotion* (1982); and Plutchik and Kellerman (eds.), *Emotion: Theory, Research, and Experience* (1980). Interesting books on facial expressions and emotion include Ekman's *Emotion in the Human Face* (2nd ed., 1982) and his *Telling Lies: Clues to Deceit in the Marketplace, Politics and Marriage* (1985). For a review and critical analysis of lie detection procedures, see Lykken, *A Tremor in the Blood: Uses and Abuses of the Lie Detector* (1980).

The psychoanalytic theory of emotion is presented in two books by Freud: *Beyond the Pleasure Principle* (1975) and *New Introductory Lectures on Psychoanalysis* (1965). For the social-learning approach, see Bandura, *Social Learning Theory* (1977).

Books on aggression include Johnson, *Aggression in Man and Animals* (1972); Bandura, *Aggression: A Social Learning Analysis* (1973); Montagu (ed.), *Learning Non-aggression: The Experience of Non-literate Societies* (1978); Tavris, *Anger: The Misunderstood Emotion* (1984); and Hamburg and Trudeau (eds.), *Biobehavioral Aspects of Aggression* (1981).

FURTHER READING

Part Six

NATHAN LYONS

Untitled, New York, 1967
From "Notations in Passing," M.I.T., 1974

PERSONALITY AND INDIVIDUALITY

Mental Abilities and Their Measurement

12

PEOPLE VARY WIDELY IN PERSONALITY characteristics and mental abilities. In this chapter, we will look at individual differences in ability and at tests designed to measure these differences. Methods of assessing personality differences will be discussed in Chapter 13. The features that make a test useful, however, are the same regardless of the test's purpose; the requirements for a good test apply equally to ability and personality tests.

The use of ability tests to assign schoolchildren to special classes, to admit students to college and professional schools, and to select individuals for jobs is a topic of public debate and controversy. When ability tests were first developed around the turn of the century, they were hailed as an objective and impartial method of identifying talent and ensuring individual opportunity. Testing permitted people to be selected for jobs or advanced schooling on the basis of merit rather than family background, wealth, social class, or political influence. America—a democratic society with a large, heterogeneous population—was particularly enthusiastic about the use of tests to classify students and select employees. To cite one example, the Civil Service Examinations that thousands of people now take annually when applying for government jobs were initiated during the 1880s in an attempt to ensure that such jobs would be given to qualified people instead of to those who had gained favor by supporting the newly elected politicians.

Many people still view ability tests as the best available means of determining what people can do and for advising them on jobs and professions. Others claim that such tests are narrow and restrictive: they do not measure the characteristics that are most important in determining how well a person will do in college or on the job — specifically, motivation, social skills, and qualities of leadership — and they discriminate against minorities. We will look at the evidence on both sides of this controversy.

TYPES OF ABILITY TESTS

By the time we finish high school, most of us have had some experience with ability tests. Driver's license examinations, grade school tests of reading and math skills, the competency examinations required for graduation from many high schools, and tests that assess mastery of a particular course (typing, American history, chemistry, and so on) are all ability tests.

A test is essentially a sample of behavior taken at a given point in time. A distinction is often made between *achievement tests* (which are designed to measure accomplished skills and indicate what the person can do at present) and *aptitude tests* (which are designed to predict what a person can accomplish with training). But the distinction between these two types of tests is not clear-cut. All tests assess the individual's current status, whether the purpose of the test is to assess what has been learned or to predict future performance. Both kinds of tests often include similar types of questions and yield results that are highly correlated. Rather than considering aptitude and achievement tests as two distinct categories, it is more useful to think of them as falling along a continuum.

Aptitude Versus Achievement

Tests at either end of the aptitude-achievement continuum are distinguished from each other primarily in terms of purpose. For example, a test of knowledge of mechanical principles might be given on completion of a course in mechanics to measure the student's mastery of the course material—to provide a measure of *achievement*. Similar questions might be included in a battery of tests administered to select applicants for pilot training, since knowledge of mechanical principles has been found to be a good predictor of success in flying. The latter test would be considered a measure of *aptitude*, since its results are used to predict a candidate's performance as a student pilot. Thus, whether the test is labeled an aptitude or an achievement test depends more on its purpose than on its content.

Tests at the two ends of the aptitude-achievement continuum can also be distinguished in terms of the *specificity of relevant prior experience*. At one end of the continuum are achievement tests designed to measure mastery of a fairly specific subject matter, such as music theory, European history, or the safe and legal operation of a motor vehicle. At the other extreme are aptitude tests that assume little more in terms of prior experience than the general experience of growing up in the United States. A musical aptitude test, for example, is intended to predict the degree to which a student will benefit from music lessons prior to any instruction. Thus, the Musical Aptitude Profile (Gordon, 1967) does not require any knowledge of musical techniques. It tests a person's ability to identify tones and rhythms that sound similar and to discriminate musical selections that are tastefully performed. However, although no specific experience is required, a person's ability to understand instructions given in English and his or her prior experience listening to music (Western versus Eastern music, for example) would undoubtedly influence the test results.

Two Dimensions That Describe Ability Tests *Any given test falls somewhere along an aptitude-achievement continuum and also along a general-specific continuum. For example, a Spanish vocabulary test or a typing test that measures how many words a minute the subject can type accurately would fall toward the achievement end of the aptitude-achievement continuum and toward the specific end of the general-specific continuum. The Musical Aptitude Profile, which requires no prior musical knowledge and is designed to predict an individual's capacity to profit from music lessons, also taps a fairly specific area of ability but falls toward the aptitude end of the aptitude-achievement dimension. Most intelligence tests (such as the Stanford-Binet and Wechsler Intelligence Scales) are fairly general in that they sample a range of abilities and are designed to measure aptitude more than achievement of skills. Scholastic achievement tests, such as the SAT and ACT (American College Testing Program), are fairly general; they measure achievement in verbal and mathematical reasoning and comprehension but do not presume the mastery of certain courses.*

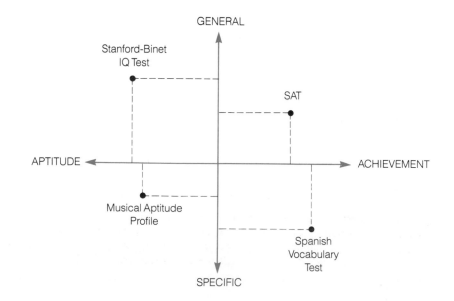

We will see later that performance on "intelligence" tests (aptitude tests designed to measure a person's general capacity for learning) does depend to some extent on prior experience, even though every attempt is made to devise questions that do not reflect the results of special training.

Somewhere between aptitude tests (which assume little in terms of relevant prior experience) and achievement tests (which measure the mastery of specific subject matter) are tests that measure both aptitude and achievement. An example is the Scholastic Aptitude Test (SAT), which is required for admission to many colleges. The SAT consists of a verbal section (see Table 12-1A), which measures vocabulary skills and the ability to understand what is read, and a mathematical section (see Table 12-1B), which tests the ability to solve problems requiring arithmetic reasoning, algebra, and geometry. Thus, although the test taps learned material (the verbal and quantitative skills that a person has acquired during 12 years of education), it attempts to avoid questions that depend on knowledge of particular topics and focuses instead on the ability to use acquired skills to solve newly posed problems.

TABLE 12-1A
Scholastic Aptitude Test *A sample of items from the verbal section of the SAT. These items are of middle difficulty and are answered correctly by 50–60 percent of the test takers. The answers are as follows: 1 — B, 2 — A, 3 — D.*

VERBAL ITEMS

Antonyms (tests extent of vocabulary)

1. Choose the word or phrase that is most nearly the *opposite* in meaning to the word in capital letters.

   PARTISAN: A commoner   D ascetic
                B neutral   E pacifist
                C unifier

Analogies (tests ability to see a relationship in a pair of words, to understand the ideas expressed in the relationship, and to recognize a similar or parallel relationship)

2. Select the lettered pair that *best* expresses a relationship similar to that expressed in the original pair.

   FLURRY: BLIZZARD: A trickle: deluge   D spray: foam
                       B rapids: rock   E mountain:
                       C lightning: cloudburst   summit

Sentence completion (tests ability to recognize the relationships among parts of a sentence)

3. Choose the word or set of words that *best* fits the meaning of the sentence as a whole.

   Prominent psychologists believe that people act violently because they have been _____ to do so, not because they were born _____:

   A forced – gregarious   D taught – aggressive
   B forbidden – complacent E inclined – belligerent
   C expected – innocent

Reading passages (tests ability to comprehend a written passage)

Blocks of questions are presented following passages of roughly 400 to 500 words. Some questions ask about information that is directly stated in the passage; others require applications of the author's principles or opinions; still others ask for judgments (e.g., how well the author supports claims).

TABLE 12-1B
Scholastic Aptitude Test   *A sample of items from the mathematical section of the SAT, also of middle difficulty. The answers are as follows: 1 — C, 2 — C, 3 — B, 4 — C.*

MATHEMATICAL ITEMS

Regular items

Algebra:

1. If $x^3 = (2x)^2$ and $x \neq 0$, then $x =$
   A 1   D 6
   B 2   E 8
   C 4

Geometry:

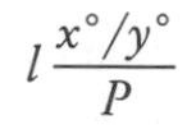

$$l\frac{x°/y°}{P}$$

Note: Figure is not drawn to scale.

2. If P is a point on line l in the figure above and $x - y = 0$, then $y =$

   A 0   D 135
   B 45   E 180
   C 90

Quantitative comparison

Each question consists of two quantities, one in Column A and one in Column B. You are to compare the two quantities and on the answer sheet blacken space:

   A   if the quantity in Column A is greater;
   B   if the quantity in Column B is greater;
   C   if the two quantities are equal;
   D   if the relationship cannot be determined from the information given.

   Note: In certain questions, information concerning one or both of the quantities to be compared is centered above the two columns.

	Column A	**Column B**
Arithmetic:		
3.	Number of minutes in 1 week	Number of seconds in 7 hours
Algebra:	$$\frac{5}{x} = \frac{1}{3}$$	
4.	$\dfrac{3}{x}$	$\dfrac{1}{5}$

Generality Versus Specificity

Ability tests can also be distinguished along a general-specific continuum, because they vary in the broadness of their content. The Musical Aptitude Profile would be at the specific end of the continuum, as would a typing test, a driver's license examination, a test of mathematical ability, or a reading comprehension test. All of these tests measure fairly specific abilities. At the general end of the continuum would be high school competency exams and scholastic aptitude tests (like the SAT), which attempt to measure educational development in a number of areas, as well as most tests that are called "intelligence tests." An *intelligence test* is an aptitude test designed to predict performance over a range of abilities. Such tests usually do not contain items that can be answered by simple recall or the application of practiced skills. Instead, they focus on items that require a mixture of the abilities to analyze, to understand abstract concepts, and to apply prior knowledge to the solution of new problems. Intelligence tests usually include verbal, figurative, and quantitative tasks. Although the attempt to measure general intellectual ability in order to predict what an individual can accomplish with education or training is certainly worthwhile, the label "intelligence test" is unfortunate. The wording implies that people possess an innate capacity, called intelligence, that is fixed in amount and is not influenced by education or experience. Later, we will see that many variables can influence a person's score on an intelligence test. In addition, although some individuals may be more able than others to accomplish a variety of tasks, abilities are not so consistent that a person who is above average at one task is above average at all tasks.

High school student taking the Scholastic Aptitude Test (SAT).

REQUIREMENTS FOR A GOOD TEST

In our society, much depends on test scores. In the elementary school grades, children are often placed in instructional groups on the basis of their performances on tests of math and reading skills. Some high schools require students to pass minimum competency tests in order to graduate. Tests are part of the admissions procedure in many colleges and most professional and graduate schools. Most high school students who are college-bound must take either the SAT or a similar admission test, the American College Testing Program (ACT). Scores on these tests, as well as high school grades and other criteria, determine who is admitted to college. Applicants to law schools and medical schools must take special admission tests — the Law School Admissions Test (LSAT) and the Medical College Admissions Test (MCAT); many graduate school departments require students to take the Graduate Record Exam (GRE). People applying to programs to be trained in most professions (dentistry, nursing, pharmacology, accounting, and business administration, to name a few) must also take special admission tests. And once the training program is completed, more tests must be passed to obtain a license to practice or a certificate of competency. Becoming certified or licensed in almost every trade or profession — as a plumber, beautician, physical therapist, doctor, clinical psychologist, or lawyer — requires the passage of a written examination. In addition, many industries and government agencies select job applicants and place or promote employees on the basis of test scores.

Since tests play such an important role in our lives, it is essential that they measure what they are intended to measure and that the scores accurately reflect the test taker's knowledge and skills. If a test is to be useful, its scores must be both *reliable* and *valid*.

Reliability

Test scores are *reliable* when they are reproducible and consistent. Tests may be unreliable for a number of reasons. Confusing or ambiguous test items may mean different things to a test taker at different times. Tests may be too short to sample the abilities being tested adequately, or scoring may be too subjective. If a test yields different results when it is administered on different occasions or scored by different people, it is unreliable. A simple analogy is a rubber yardstick. If we did not know how much it stretched each time we took a measurement, the results would be unreliable no matter how carefully we marked the measurement. Tests must be reliable if the results are to be used with confidence.

To evaluate reliability, two measures must be obtained for the same individual on the same test. This can be done by repeating the test, by giving the test in two different but equivalent forms, or by treating each half of the test separately. If each individual tested achieves roughly the same score on both measures, then the test is reliable. Of course, even for a reliable test, some differences are to be expected between the pair of scores due to chance and errors of measurement. Consequently, a statistical measure of the degree of relationship between the set of paired scores is needed. This degree of relationship is provided by the coefficient of correlation, r (discussed in Chapter 1, p. 23). The coefficient of correlation between paired scores for a group of individuals on a given test is called a *reliability coefficient*. Well-constructed tests usually have a reliability coefficient of $r = .90$ or greater.

Validity

Tests are *valid* when they measure what they are intended to measure. A college examination in economics that is full of questions containing complex or tricky wording might be a test of a student's verbal ability rather than of the economics learned in the course. Such an examination might be *reliable* (a student would achieve about the same score on a retest), but it would not be a *valid* test of achievement for the course. Or a test of sense of humor might be made up of jokes that are hard to understand unless the test taker is very bright and well read. This test might be a reliable measure of something (perhaps intelligence or educational achievement), but it would not be a valid test of humor.

To measure validity, we must also obtain two scores for each person: the test score and some other measure of the ability in question. This measure is called a *criterion*. Suppose that a test is designed to predict success in learning to type. To determine whether the test is valid, it is given to a group of individuals before they study typing. After completing the course, the students are tested on the number of words per minute that they can type accurately. This is a measure of their success and serves as a criterion. A coefficient of correlation between the early test scores and the scores on the criterion can now be obtained. This correlation coefficient, known as a *validity coefficient*, tells something about the value of a given test for a given purpose. The higher the validity coefficient, the more accurate the prediction that can be made from the test results.

Many tests, however, are intended to predict abilities that are more wide-ranging and difficult to measure than typing skills. Scores on the Medical College Admissions Test (MCAT), for example, are used (along with other information) to select medical students. If the purpose of the test is to predict success in medical school, a person's grade point average could be used as a criterion; correlating his or her MCAT score with the grade point average would be one way of validating the test. But if the MCAT is intended to predict success as a physician, the problem of validation becomes much more difficult. What criterion should be chosen: annual income, research achievements, contributions to community welfare, evaluation by patients or colleagues, number of malpractice suits? Even if the test administrators could agree on one of these criteria, that criterion would probably be difficult to measure.

The validity of ability tests — how well they predict performance — will be discussed later. The important point to remember here is that the evaluation of a test's validity must take into account the intended uses of the test and the inferences to be made from its scores.

Uniform Procedures

To a large extent, the reliability and validity of a test depend on the uniformity of the procedures followed in administering and scoring the test. In measuring ability, as in obtaining any scientific measurement, we attempt to control conditions in order to minimize the influence of extraneous variables. Thus, well-accepted ability tests contain clearly specified instructions, time limits (or, in some cases, no time restrictions), and scoring methods. The explanations given by the examiner and the manner in which the examiner presents the test materials must be standard from one test administration to the next.

Of course, not all extraneous variables can be anticipated or controlled. The sex and race of the examiner, for example, will vary. These characteristics could influence a test taker's performance, as could the examiner's general demeanor (facial expression, tone of voice, and so on). Although such variables cannot be controlled, their influence should be taken into consideration in evaluating test results. Thus, if a black male child does poorly when tested by a white female examiner, the possibility that the child's motivation and anxiety levels would have been different with a black male examiner should be considered.

TESTS OF INTELLECTUAL ABILITY

Reliability, validity, and uniform testing procedures are essential requirements for any test—whether the test is designed to measure personality characteristics (to be discussed in Chapter 13), mastery of a specific subject matter, job skills, or the probability of succeeding in college or professional school. This chapter focuses primarily on tests that measure general intellectual ability. Such tests are often called "intelligence tests," but as we noted earlier, many psychologists consider that term inappropriate. There is no general agreement as to what constitutes intelligence, and intelligence cannot be considered apart from an individual's culture and experiences. During this discussion of intelligence tests, these qualifications should be kept in mind.

Historical Background

The first person to attempt to develop tests of intellectual ability was Sir Francis Galton a century ago. A naturalist and mathematician, Galton developed an interest in individual differences from the evolutionary theory of his cousin, Charles Darwin. Galton believed that certain families are biologically superior—stronger and smarter—than others. Intelligence, he reasoned, is a question of exceptional sensory and perceptual skills, which are passed from one generation to the next. Since all information is acquired through the senses, the more sensitive and accurate an individual's perceptual apparatus, the more intelligent the person. In 1884, Galton administered a battery of tests (measuring such variables as head size, reaction time, visual acuity, auditory thresholds, and memory for visual forms) to over 9,000 visitors at the London Exhibition. To his disappointment, he discovered that eminent British scientists could not be distinguished from ordinary citizens on the basis of their head size and that measurements such as speed of reaction were not particularly related to other measures of intelligence. Although his tests did not prove very useful, Galton did invent the correlation coefficient, which plays an important role in psychology.

The first tests that approximated contemporary intelligence tests were devised by the French psychologist Alfred Binet. In 1881, the French government

Alfred Binet with his daughters.

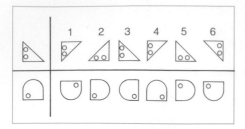

FIGURE 12-1
Novel Items Used in Intelligence Tests
The following instructions accompany the test: **Mark every card to the right that matches the sample card on the left. You can rotate the sample card but not flip it over.** *(Cards 2, 3, and 6 are correct in the first line; cards 1, 3, and 5 are correct in the second line.)*

passed a law making school attendance compulsory for all children. Previously, slow learners had usually been kept at home; now teachers had to cope with a wide range of individual differences. The government asked Binet to create a test that would detect children who were too slow intellectually to benefit from a regular school curriculum.

Binet assumed that intelligence should be measured by tasks that required reasoning and problem-solving abilities rather than perceptual-motor skills. In collaboration with another French psychologist, Théophile Simon, Binet published a scale in 1905, which he revised in 1908 and again in 1911.

Binet's Method: A Mental-age Scale

Binet reasoned that a slow or "dull" child was like a normal child retarded in mental growth. On tests, the slow child would perform like a normal child of younger age, whereas the mental abilities of a "bright" child were characteristic of older children. Binet devised a scale of *mental age* to measure intelligence in terms of the kinds of changes that are ordinarily associated with growing older. *Average mental-age* (MA) scores correspond to *chronological age* (CA), which is the age determined from the child's date of birth. A bright child's MA is above his or her CA; a slow child's MA is below his or her CA. The mental-age scale is easily interpreted by teachers and others who deal with children of differing mental abilities.

ITEM SELECTION   Since intelligence tests are designed to measure brightness rather than the results of special training (that is, aptitude more than achievement), they should consist of items that do not assume any special training. There are two chief ways to select such items. One way is to choose *novel items,* which provide an uneducated child with just as much chance to succeed as a child who has been taught at home or in school. Figure 12-1 illustrates a novel item; in this particular test, the child is asked to choose figures that are alike, on the assumption that the designs are unfamiliar to all children. The other way is to choose *familiar items,* on the assumption that all those for whom the test is designed have had the requisite prior experience to deal with the items. The following problem provides an example of a supposedly familiar item:

Mark F *if the sentence is foolish; mark* S *if it is sensible.*

S   F   Mrs. Smith has had no children, and I understand that the same was true of her mother.

Of course, this item is "fair" only for children who know the English language, who can read, and who understand all the words in the sentence. For such children, detection of the fallacy in the statement becomes a valid test of intellectual ability.

Many of the items on intelligence tests assume general knowledge and familiarity with the language of the test. But such assumptions can never be strictly met. The language spoken in one home is never exactly the same as that spoken in another; the available reading material and the stress on cognitive abilities also vary. Even the novel items test perceptual discriminations that may be acquired in one culture and not in another. Despite these difficulties, items can be chosen that work reasonably well. The items included in contemporary intelligence tests have survived in practice after many others have been tried and found defective. It should be remembered, however, that intelligence tests have been validated according to their success in predicting school performance within a particular culture.

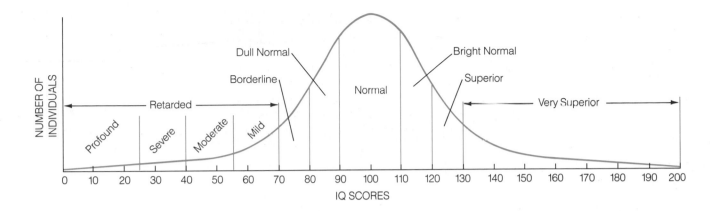

FIGURE 12-2
IQ Distribution *The distribution of IQ
scores expected for a large sample of
individuals and the adjectives used to
describe various levels of IQ. An IQ
between 90 and 110 is judged to be normal;
above 130, very superior; and below 70,
retarded.*

STANFORD-BINET INTELLIGENCE SCALE The test items originally developed by Binet were adapted for American schoolchildren by Lewis Terman at Stanford University. He standardized the administration of the test and developed age-level norms by giving the test to thousands of children. In 1916, he published the Stanford revision of the Binet tests, now referred to as the Stanford-Binet Intelligence Scale. This test has become one of the best known and widely used intelligence tests; it was revised in 1937, 1960, 1972, and most recently in 1986.

Terman retained Binet's concept of mental age. Each test item was age-graded at the level at which a substantial majority of the children passed it. A child's mental age could be obtained by summing the number of items passed at each age level. In addition, Terman adopted a convenient index of intelligence suggested by the German psychologist William Stern. This index is the *intelligence quotient,* commonly known as the IQ. It expresses intelligence as a ratio of mental age (MA) to chronological age (CA):

$$IQ = \frac{MA}{CA} \times 100$$

The 100 is used as a multiplier so that the IQ will have a value of 100 when MA is equal to CA. If MA is lower than CA, then the IQ will be less than 100; if MA is higher than CA, then the IQ will be more than 100.

How is the IQ to be interpreted? The distribution of IQs approximates the form of curve found for many differences among individuals, such as differences in height; this bell-shaped *normal distribution curve* is shown in Figure 12-2. Most cases cluster around a midvalue on the normal curve; from there, the number gradually decreases to just a few cases at both extremes. The adjectives commonly used to describe various IQ levels are also shown in the figure.*

Testing Specific Mental Abilities

The Stanford-Binet uses an assortment of different items to test intelligence. Until the 1986 revision, all items had contributed equally to the total IQ score. A child might perform very well on a test of vocabulary but poorly on a test

---

* The most recent revision of the Stanford-Binet (Thorndike, Hagen, & Sattler, 1986) uses Standard Age Scores, instead of IQ scores. These can be interpreted in terms of percentiles which show the percent of subjects in the standardization group falling above or below a given score.

TABLE 12-2
Examples of Items From the 1986
Stanford-Binet Intelligence
Scale   *Although the test is not age-graded,
these are typical items for a 6- to 8-year-old.*

VERBAL REASONING

Vocabulary   Defines words, such as "dollar" and "envelope."
Comprehension   Answers questions, such as "Where do people buy food?" and "Why do people comb their hair?"
Absurdities   Identifies the "funny" aspect of a picture, such as a girl riding a bicycle in a lake or a bald man combing his head.
Verbal Relations   Tells how the first three items in a sequence are alike and how they differ from the fourth: scarf, tie, muffler, shirt.

QUANTITATIVE REASONING

Quantitative   Performs simple arithmetic tasks, such as selecting a die with six spots because the number of spots equals the combination of a two-spot and a four-spot die.
Number Series   Gives the next two numbers in a series, such as
$$20 \quad 16 \quad 12 \quad 8 \quad \_\_ \quad \_\_ .$$
Equation Building   Builds an equation from the following array: $2 \quad 3 \quad 5 \quad + \quad =$. One of several correct responses would be $2 + 3 = 5$.

ABSTRACT/VISUAL REASONING

Pattern Analysis   Copies a simple design with blocks.
Copying   Copies a geometrical drawing demonstrated by the examiner, such as a rectangle intersected by two diagonals.

SHORT-TERM MEMORY

Bead Memory   Shown a picture of different-shaped beads stacked on a stick. Reproduces the sequence from memory by placing real beads on a stick.
Memory for Sentences   Repeats after the examiner sentences such as "It is time to go to sleep" and "Ken painted a picture for his mother's birthday."
Memory for Digits   Repeats after the examiner a series of digits, such as 5-7-8-3, forward and backward.
Memory for Objects   Shown pictures of individual objects, such as a clock and an elephant, one at a time. Identifies the objects in the correct order of their appearance in a picture that also includes extraneous objects; for example, a bus, a clown, an *elephant*, eggs, and a *clock*.

Bead Memory Test materials for the 1986 Stanford-Binet.

requiring drawing geometric forms. These strengths and weaknesses might be noted by the examiner but would not be reflected in the IQ score. In line with the current view of intelligence as a composite of different abilities, the 1986 revision groups its tests into four broad areas of intellectual abilities: *verbal reasoning, abstract/visual reasoning, quantitative reasoning*, and *short-term memory*. A separate score is obtained for each area; Table 12-2 gives some examples of items, grouped by area.

WECHSLER INTELLIGENCE SCALES   The 1986 revision of the Stanford-Binet has not been in use long enough for researchers and clinicians to assess the diagnostic value of identifying these particular intellectual abilities. In contrast, one of the first intelligence tests to measure separate abilities, developed by David

TEST	DESCRIPTION
Verbal scale	
Information	Questions tap a general range of information; for example, "How many nickels make a dime?"
Comprehension	Tests practical information and ability to evaluate past experience; for example, "What is the advantage of keeping money in a bank?"
Arithmetic	Verbal problems testing arithmetic reasoning.
Similarities	Asks in what way certain objects or concepts (for example, *egg* and *seed*) are similar; measures abstract thinking.
Digit span	A series of digits presented auditorily (for example, 7-5-6-3-8) is repeated in a forward or backward direction; tests attention and rote memory.
Vocabulary	Tests word knowledge.
Performance scale	
Digit symbol	A timed coding task in which numbers must be associated with marks of various shapes; tests speed of learning and writing.
Picture completion	The missing part of an incompletely drawn picture must be discovered and named; tests visual alertness and visual memory.
Block design	Pictured designs must be copied with blocks; tests ability to perceive and analyze patterns.
Picture arrangement	A series of comic-strip pictures must be arranged in the right sequence to tell a story; tests understanding of social situations.
Object assembly	Puzzle pieces must be assembled to form a complete object; tests ability to deal with part–whole relationships.

TABLE 12-3
Tests Composing the Wechsler Adult Intelligence Scale *The tests of the Wechsler Intelligence Scale for Children are similar with some modifications.*

The block design test for the Wechsler Scale.

Wechsler in 1939, has been extensively used. Wechsler originally developed his test because he felt the Stanford-Binet was not appropriate for adults, and also he felt it depended too heavily on language ability. The Wechsler Adult Intelligence Scale, or WAIS (1939, 1955, 1981), is divided into two parts —a *verbal* scale and a *performance* scale —which yield separate scores as well as a full-scale IQ. The test items are described in Table 12-3. A similar test for children, the Wechsler Intelligence Scale for Children (WISC), was developed later (1958, 1974).

Items on the performance scale require the manipulation or arrangement of blocks, pictures, or other materials. Both the stimulus displays and the responses are nonverbal. The Wechsler scales also provide scores for each of the subtests, so the examiner has a clearer picture of the individual's intellectual strengths and weaknesses. For example, separate scores can indicate how well the person performs under pressure (some subtests are timed; others are not) or how verbal skills compare with the ability to manipulate nonverbal material. Figure 12-3 shows a test profile and how scores are summed to yield IQs. The subject who obtained these particular scores tends to do better on performance (nonverbal) tasks. Looking at the profile of scores, this 16-year-old does not appear to be

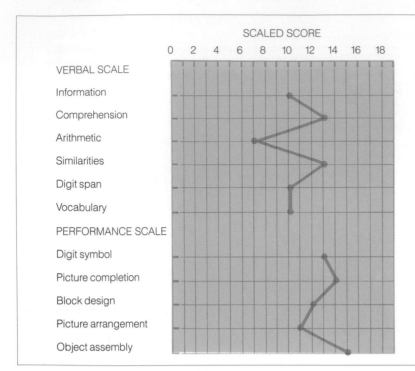

SCALED SCORE										
0	2	4	6	8	10	12	14	16	18	

TEST		Scaled score	
Information		10	
Comprehension		13	
Arithmetic		7	
Similarities		13	
Digit span		10	
Vocabulary		10	
Verbal score		63	
Digit symbol		13	
Picture completion		14	
Block design		12	
Picture arrangement		11	
Object assembly		15	
Performance score		65	
Total score		128	
VERBAL SCORE 63	IQ 108		
PERFORMANCE SCORE 65	IQ 121		
FULL SCALE SCORE 128	IQ 115		

FIGURE 12-3

Profile for Wechsler Adult Intelligence Scale *The table on the right shows the test scores for a 16-year-old male combined to yield verbal, performance, and full-scale scores. The manual that accompanies the test provides tables (adjusted for age) for use in converting these scores into IQs. Note that the test taker's performance IQ is 13 points above his verbal IQ.*

doing as well scholastically as he could be; he scores lowest on subtests that are more closely related to "school learning" (information, arithmetic, and vocabulary). A discrepancy between verbal and performance scores prompts the examiner to look for specific learning problems, such as reading disabilities or language handicaps.

Both the Stanford-Binet and the Wechsler scales meet the requirements for a good test; that is, they show good reliability and validity. The Stanford-Binet scale has a reliability coefficient of about .90 on retest; the WAIS has a retest reliability of .91. Both tests are fairly valid predictors of achievement in school; the correlation between IQ scores on these tests and school grades is approximately .40 to .60.

Group Tests

The Stanford-Binet and the Wechsler scales are *individual ability tests;* that is, they are administered to a single individual by a specially trained tester. *Group ability tests,* in contrast, can be administered to a large number of people by a single examiner and are usually in pencil-and-paper form (see Figure 12-4). The advantages of an individual test over a group test are many. The tester can be certain the subject understands the questions, can evaluate the person's motivation (is the subject really trying?), and can gain additional clues to intellectual strengths and weaknesses by carefully observing the subject's approaches to different tasks. Group ability tests are useful, however, when large numbers of people have to be evaluated. The armed services, for example, use a number of group tests which measure general intellectual ability and special skills and help in selecting men and women for special jobs, including pilots, navigators, electronic technicians, and computer programmers.

Other examples of group tests used to measure general ability are the SAT and the Professional and Administrative Career Examination (PACE), which

Space Perception

Which of the four patterns would result when the box is unfolded?

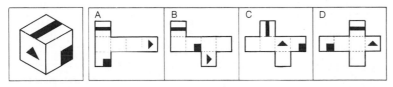

Mechanical Comprehension

Which bridge is the strongest?

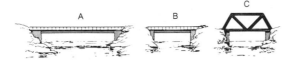

Word Knowledge

Stench most nearly means

A. Puddle of slimy water.
B. Pile of debris.
C. Foul odor.
D. Dead animal.

Camaraderie most nearly means

A. Interest in photography.
B. Close friendship.
C. Petty jealousies.
D. Arts and crafts projects.

General Information

For which of the following taxes was it necessary to amend the U.S. Constitution?

A. Income.
B. Sales.
C. Liquor.
D. Tobacco.

Picasso was a famous

A. poet.
B. painter.
C. philosopher.
D. soldier.

Arithmetic Reasoning

It cost $0.50 per square yard to waterproof canvas. What will it cost to waterproof a canvas truck cover that is 15′ x 24′?

A. $6.67
B. $18.00
C. $20.00
D. $180.00

The parcel post rate in the local zone is 18 cents for the first pound and 1½ cents for each additional pound. How many pounds can be sent in the local zone for $1.50?

A. 88
B. 89
C. 100
D. 225

FIGURE 12-4

Group Test *These are sample items from the Armed Services Vocational Aptitude Battery (ASVAB), the basic recruit selection and placement test used by all military services.*

was developed by the U.S. Civil Service Commission for use in selecting employees for government jobs.

PREDICTIVE VALIDITY OF TESTS

Tests of general ability, such as the Stanford-Binet and Wechsler Intelligence Scales, do predict achievement in school and do provide a measure of what most people think of as "brightness." When elementary school teachers are asked to rank children in their classrooms in terms of "brightness," correlations between the teachers' rankings and scores on intelligence tests range from .60 to .80. These correlations would probably be higher except for some interesting biases in judgment. For example, teachers tend to overrate the youngest children in their classrooms and underrate the oldest; apparently, they base their judgments on mental age rather than on IQ, which expresses the relationship between mental age and chronological age. Teachers also tend to overrate girls and underrate boys. In general, children who are sociable, eager, and self-confident—who volunteer for activities and raise their hands to recite—are viewed by their teachers and peers as brighter than children who are withdrawn and quiet, even though their test scores may be the same. In such instances, ability test scores provide a more accurate estimate of ability than the teacher's judgments.

CRITICAL DISCUSSION

Culture-fair Tests

A person's performance on an ability test clearly is dependent on the culture in which he or she is raised. Obviously, this is true of verbal tests that require familiarity with a particular language. We would not expect a child from a home in which English is spoken as a second language to score as well on verbal items as a child whose parents speak only English. But even among children from English-speaking families, the vocabulary in a middle-class home may differ significantly from the vocabulary in a lower-class home. In one study, for example, children were asked to consider the following item:

Pick ONE WORD that does not belong with the others.

cello   harp   drum
violin   guitar

Most children from upper- or middle-class homes chose "drum," the intended correct answer. Children from lower-class homes commonly answered "cello," an unfamiliar word that they thought did not belong (Eells et al., 1951). Children from upper-class homes are more likely to be acquainted with cellos, or at least to have heard the word, than are children from poorer homes.

Several tests have been developed that are based on black culture and language (see Williams, 1972; Boone & Adesso, 1974). The vocabulary and idioms used in these tests are more or less characteristic of Black English and include items similar to the following:

"Running a game" means:
A   writing a bad check
B   looking at something
C   directing a contest
D   getting what one wants

Those familiar with Black English will recognize that D is the correct answer.

These tests emphasize the extent to which cultural factors can influence test scores; blacks may score 20 IQ points higher than whites on such tests. But the test scores apparently bear little relationship to other measures of intelligence or achievement for members of either race (Matarazzo & Wiens, 1977).

Cultural experiences can also affect performance on nonverbal items. Numerical operations and mathematical concepts are taught primarily in school. And even items that presumably are unrelated to schooling (such as recognizing the missing element in a drawing of a common object or manipulating blocks to form a pattern) are not wholly independent of culture. For

EDUCATIONAL LEVEL	TYPICAL CORRELATIONS
Elementary School	.60 – .70
High School	.50 – .60
College	.40 – .50
Graduate School	.30 – .40

TABLE 12-4
Correlation Between IQ Scores and Academic Achievement   *Table entries give the correlations typically observed between intelligence test scores and other measures of academic achievement (for example, grades or achievement test scores) at different levels of schooling. (Data from various sources.)*

Test Scores and Academic Performance

Intelligence test scores correlate quite highly with measures of academic performance (for example, grades, continuation in school, likelihood of graduating), at least during the elementary and high school years. Youngsters who achieve higher scores on tests like the Stanford-Binet and Wechsler Intelligence Scales get better grades, enjoy school more, and stay in school longer. But as students move up the educational ladder—from elementary school to high school to college to graduate school—the correlations between intelligence test scores and measures of academic performance become progressively lower (see Table 12-4). A number of factors contribute to the progressive decrease in the size of validity coefficients as schooling increases. We will see shortly that one of the most important factors is *selection*.

Thus far, we have talked about the relationship between academic performance and tests designed to measure general aptitude for learning (so-called intelligence tests that yield an IQ score). What about scholastic aptitude tests, like the SAT, that measure developed abilities and are designed to predict performance in college? The SAT has been given to millions of college applicants over many years, and numerous studies have correlated SAT scores with freshman grade point averages. The correlations vary from study to study, with a median

example, if children from poor families are shown a drawing of a comb with several teeth missing and asked to name the missing part (an item on the WISC), they may be puzzled; to them, a broken comb may be more common than a whole one (Hewitt & Massey, 1969).

In some nonliterate societies, drawings and pictures are rare. When Nigerian children were asked to manipulate colored blocks to form a design (a task included in several intelligence tests), they did quite well when the design to be copied was also made of blocks. But it was difficult for them to copy a design from a picture until the examiner demonstrated with the blocks (D'Andrade, 1967).

Psychologists have made a number of attempts to develop tests that are culture-fair (see Figure 12-5), but the results have not been promising. For one thing, the culture-fair tests do not predict scholastic performance (or, in some instances, performance on the job) as well as do more conventional ability tests. This finding is not surprising, since what is considered a good performance in school or on the job is also culture-dependent. For another thing, group differences on culture-fair tests are often as large as the differences on the tests they have been designed to replace.

In principle, it is probably impossible

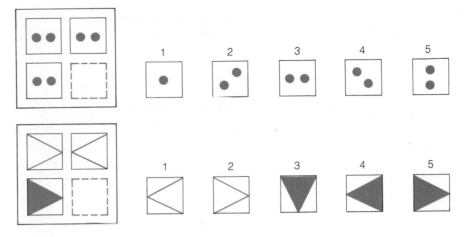

FIGURE 12-5

Culture-fair Test *Sample items from a test designed to be relatively independent of the culture in which one is raised. The test taker is to select one of the five items on the right that best completes the pattern on the left.*

to design a completely culture-fair test; an individual's performance will always be affected by his or her cultural background. The abilities that a society considers important are the ones it will take the trouble to test. If writing and quantitative skills are valued in a society, these skills will be viewed as predictive of success. If social skills and the use of complex riddles in storytelling are valued (as they are among the Kpelle people of Liberia), these skills will be considered the important ones to test (Cole, 1981).

In the absence of satisfactory culture-fair tests, the best we can do at present is to recognize the cultural basis of our standard intelligence tests and interpret the scores with caution, always keeping in mind the individual's background—the language spoken in the home and the kinds of learning experiences provided.

correlation of about .38 for the verbal section of the SAT and .34 for the mathematics section (Linn, 1982).

These correlations underestimate to some extent the relationship between test scores and college grades, because the criterion data (grade point averages) are collected only for those individuals who actually attend college. If everyone who took the SAT attended college, and the test scores were correlated with his or her freshman grades, the correlations would be much higher. The size of a correlation coefficient is affected by the amount of variability in the measures being correlated; in general, the more select the group, the narrower the range of scores and the lower the correlation. College students are more capable than the population at large. If the entire college-age population were tested and attended college, the correlation between test scores and freshman grades would be higher still.

An example may help to explain why correlations are lower in a selected group. Before there were weight classifications in the sport of boxing, weight was a fairly good predictor of the outcome of a match. A 250-pound boxer could usually defeat a 150-pounder, regardless of differences in training; the correlation between weight and winning was quite high. However, once weight classifications were introduced and boxers fought only boxers of similar weight (heavyweights against heavyweights, lightweights against lightweights, and so on), weight became a poor predictor of outcome (Fricke, 1975).

Although the effects of selection on correlations between SAT scores and grades are less extreme than in the above example, they still can be substantial. For instance, for colleges with freshman classes that show a wide range of scores on the verbal section of the SAT, the correlation between SAT-Verbal scores and freshman grade point averages is .44. For colleges with less variability, the correlation is .31 (Schrader, 1971). The more select or homogeneous the group is, the lower the correlation.

If correlations between SAT scores and freshman grades are "corrected" statistically to take into account the selective nature of the population, the resulting correlations are around .50. What does a correlation of this size mean in terms of predictability? A correlation of .50 indicates that the chances are 44 out of 100 that a student in the top fifth of the distribution of SAT scores will also be in the top fifth of the distribution of freshman grade point averages, whereas the chances that a student in the bottom fifth of the SAT scores will earn such grades are only 4 out of 100 (Schrader, 1965). With no knowledge of the test scores, the chances would, of course, be 20 out of 100. Thus, SAT scores improve prediction considerably, but it is also clear that the freshman grades of students with the same SAT scores will vary widely.

Group Differences in Test Performance

Differences in average performance on ability tests are often found when certain subgroups of the population are studied. For example, children from middle- or upper-income families score higher, on the average, than children from poor families. Mean differences are found in performance on tests of general ability as well as on achievement tests, whether the group of children is defined in terms of parental occupation, education, or income (Speath, 1976). Members of some minority groups — blacks, Hispanic Americans, American Indians — also tend to score lower on ability tests than members of the white majority (Coleman et al., 1966; Bock & Moore, 1982; Jones, 1984).

Males and females also score differently on some tests, depending on how the test was developed. Most intelligence tests (such as the Stanford-Binet and the

Wechsler Intelligence Scales) have been constructed to minimize sex differences, either by deleting items showing large sex differences or by balancing items advantageous to females with those advantageous to males. One test of general ability that was not designed to eliminate sex differences (Differential Aptitude Test) shows that high school girls perform much better than boys of the same age group on tests of clerical speed and accuracy and language usage, whereas boys perform much better than girls on tests of mechanical reasoning and spatial relationships (Linn, 1982). On the SAT, males and females score equally well on the verbal section, but males score higher on the mathematical section (Benbow & Stanley, 1980).

Two points should be emphasized whenever group differences in performance are discussed. First, these are only *average* differences; the size of the differences between subgroups is usually small compared to the variability within groups. Thus, some children from poor families will score higher than most children from upper-income families, and conversely, some wealthier children will score lower than most poor children. Second, as we will see later, group differences in average test scores cannot be viewed as evidence of innate differences in ability. They may reflect differences in factors related to home environment and opportunities to learn. However, to the extent that group differences in average test scores reflect differences in the probability of success in school or on the job, the distinctions need to be understood.

We will discuss later some possible reasons for differences in test performance among racial, ethnic, and socioeconomic groups. But the existence of group differences does not mean that tests are not useful for predicting performance. Ability tests predict scholastic performance for minority students as well as they do for white students. For example, if black grade school children are ranked according to scores on an intelligence test, the rankings predict school performance in mathematics and reading as well as they do for white children. And SAT scores predict college freshman grades for blacks and Mexican-Americans as well as they do for whites (Linn, 1982).

Saying that ability tests are not biased does not deny that society discriminates against minority groups. There is undoubtedly a bias in opportunity against minority groups that results in their lower scores on ability tests and on the criterion measure (grades, class standing, and so forth).

Using Tests to Predict Performance

Although ability tests are useful in predicting academic performance, they are only one measure and should always be used in combination with other information. For example, senior-year high school grades correlate about as highly with freshman grade point averages as SAT scores do. This fact raises some questions about the usefulness of admissions tests. However, it can be argued that college admission test scores provide an adjustment for the variability in the quality of education among different high schools (grades from one high school may not be equivalent to grades from another). Indeed, a combination of SAT scores and high school grades does predict college grades better than either of these variables alone.

Ability tests can provide a reasonably good indication of whether a person can read and comprehend certain material or solve quantitative problems. But tests cannot assess an individual's social concerns, willingness to work, or interpersonal skills. Tests provide some basis for predicting academic success, but they do not indicate which students will become creative scientists or writers, talented teachers or lawyers, and outstanding medical researchers or physicians.

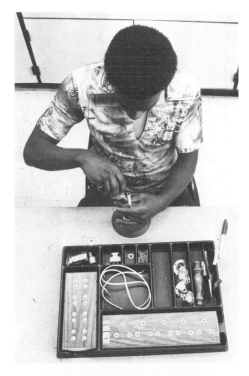

A mechanical aptitude test: assembling a lamp against time.

Coaching and Test Sophistication

Courses that claim to improve an applicant's score on such admissions tests as the Scholastic Aptitude Test (SAT), the Law School Admissions Test (LSAT), the Medical College Admissions Test (MCAT), the Graduate Record Examination (GRE), and the Graduate Management Aptitude Test (GMAT) are offered daily in the newspapers. Coaching for such tests has become a profitable business. The degree to which coaching can improve test scores, however, is a controversial issue: if coaching does result in higher scores, applicants who can afford to pay for such courses have an advantage over those who cannot.

Being familiar with testing procedures is clearly helpful. An individual who has had prior experience in taking tests and who knows what to expect will be more confident than a person who has had limited test-taking experience. *Test sophistication* includes being familiar with separate answer sheets, considering *all* the answers in a multiple-choice item rather than picking the first one that seems right, knowing not to spend too much time on puzzling items, and spotting flaws in items that provide additional clues. It also helps to know when to guess. If there is no penalty for incorrect answers, it makes sense to guess when you do not know the correct answer. On tests such as the SAT, where a wrong answer on a four-choice item is scored $-\frac{1}{4}$ (compared to 1 point for a correct answer and 0 for no response), it pays to guess if the answer can be narrowed to two or three possible alternatives.

Instruction in test-taking strategies and practice with sample test questions are included in most courses that prepare applicants for admissions tests. Commercially published practice booklets, available for the major admissions tests, can be used for a similar kind of self-coaching. Familiarity with the test format, knowledge of test-taking strategies, and practice on sample test items do result in higher test scores, but the gain is substantial only for naive test takers (for example, recent immigrants or students from schools that require little testing). Students who have graduated from American high schools, which provide substantial exposure to objective tests, probably would not benefit from spending more than a day on practice test items.

What about instruction in specific subjects? Admissions tests are designed to measure an individual's aptitude for a par-

Scores on admissions tests provide one piece of information. They should be evaluated along with other measures (high school grades, recommendations, special achievements) to predict an applicant's academic performance.

NATURE OF INTELLIGENCE

Some psychologists view intelligence as a general capacity for comprehension and reasoning that manifests itself in various ways. This was Binet's assumption. Although his test contained many different kinds of items (testing such abilities as memory span, arithmetic skills, and vocabulary knowledge), Binet noted that bright children tended to score higher than dull children on all of them. He assumed, therefore, that the different tasks sampled a basic ability or faculty.

> It seems to us that in intelligence there is a fundamental faculty, the alteration or the lack of which is of the utmost importance for practical life. This faculty is judgment, otherwise called good sense, practical sense, initiative, the faculty of adapting one's self to circumstances. To judge well, to comprehend well, to reason well, these are the essential activities of intelligence. (Binet & Simon, 1905)

Despite the diverse subscales that compose his tests, David Wechsler also believed that "intelligence is the aggregate or global capacity of the individual to act

ticular program of study, and test constructors try to avoid items on which performance can be raised by short-term drill or instruction in specialized topics. However, the verbal section of the SAT (and of the LSAT, MCAT, and GRE) relies heavily on vocabulary, and many of the problems in the quantitative section presume knowledge of high school algebra and geometry. For individuals who feel deficient in these subjects, a review would be worthwhile. Several studies have shown that coaching in mathematics raises scores on the quantitative section of the SAT for high school students who are not currently studying math, but it is of little benefit for those enrolled in mathematics courses. Vocabulary flashcards and reading with the aid of a dictionary would be helpful in preparing for the verbal section.

Over the past 30 years, numerous studies have been conducted to determine the effects of coaching on SAT scores. The studies covered a variety of coaching methods and included commercial programs as well as programs offered to students in public and private high schools. The results vary markedly, depending on the length and type of program and the presence or absence of a control group. (Control groups are important because students who enroll in coaching courses are apt to differ from those who do not in a number of ways — especially in level of motivation — and it is difficult to evaluate their test-score gains without referring to a comparable group of students.)

Messick and Jungeblut (1981) have published an analysis of research studies on SAT coaching that include control groups. They conclude that 30 hours of instruction in verbal skills, for instance, can result in average score gains of about 14 points on the verbal section of the SAT. An additional 30 hours of instruction in mathematics skills can result in average score gains of about 26 points on the mathematics section. These gains from 60 hours of instruction represent 40 points on the combined SAT scale. Since SAT scores range from a minimum of 400 to a maximum of 1600, gains of this size are not likely to affect college admission decisions. A subsequent study by Der Simonian and Laird (1983) comes to similar conclusions.

Several studies (without control groups) report much larger gains of 50–80 points on both sections of the SAT (Pallone, 1961; Marron, 1965). However, the subjects in these studies were enrolled in fairly intensive, long-term coaching programs of up to six months. The issue here is the difference between *education* and *coaching*. The SAT is designed to assess *developed* abilities. One year of high school courses in English and algebra does increase SAT scores; it is not surprising that a six-month coaching course produces a similar effect (Jones, 1984).

What recommendations should be made regarding coaching for admissions tests? For purposes of equity, a brief course in test strategies plus practice on sample test items under examination conditions would help to equalize test sophistication among individuals who have different amounts of experience in taking objective tests. Reviews of vocabulary and of algebra and geometry skills would probably benefit individuals whose background in these areas is deficient. It is probably not worthwhile for people with a normal high school education to spend much time or money on coaching courses.

purposefully, to think rationally, and to deal effectively with his environment" (Wechsler, 1958).

Factorial Approach

Other psychologists question whether there is such a thing as "general intelligence." They believe that intelligence tests sample a number of mental abilities that are relatively *independent of one another*. One method of obtaining more precise information about the kinds of abilities that determine performance on intelligence tests is *factor analysis*. This mathematical technique is used to determine the minimum number of *factors*, or abilities, that are required to explain the observed pattern of correlations for an array of different tests. The basic idea is that two tests that correlate very highly with each other are probably measuring the same underlying ability. Factor analyzing data from an array of tests indicate how many distinguishable factors enter the set of correlations and the weight (or influence) of each factor. Factor analysis is too complicated to describe in detail, but Table 12-5 provides a brief account of the method.

The originator of factor analysis, Charles Spearman (1904), proposed that all individuals possess a general intelligence factor (called *g*) in varying amounts. A person could be described as generally bright or generally dull, depending on the amount of *g* he or she possessed. According to Spearman, the *g* factor is the major determinant of performance on intelligence test items. In addition, special factors, each called *s*, are specific to particular abilities or tests. For example, tests of arithmetic or spatial relationships would each tap a separate *s*. An individual's

TABLE 12-5
Method of Factor Analysis

What are the data that enter into factor analysis, and what are the major steps in the analysis? The data are simply scores on a variety of tests designed to measure various psychological contents or processes. Each of a large number of individuals obtains a score for each of a number of tests. All these scores can then be intercorrelated; that is, we know how the scores of many individuals on Test 1 relate to their scores on Test 2, and so on. These intercorrelationships yield a table of correlations known as a *correlation matrix.* An example of such a correlation matrix, based on only nine tests, is given below.

TESTS	2	3	4	5	6	7	8	9
1	.38	.55	.06	−.04	.05	.07	.05	.09
2		.36	.40	.28	.40	.11	.15	.13
3			.10	.01	.18	.13	.12	.10
4				.32	.60	.04	.06	.13
5					.35	.08	.13	.11
6						.01	.06	.07
7							.45	.32
8								.32

The three outlined clusters of correlations indicate that these are groups of tests with something in common not shared by other tests (that is, they show high correlations). The inadequacy of making such a judgment from a table of correlations of this kind is shown by noting the additional high correlations of Test 2 with Tests 4, 5, and 6, not included in the outlined clusters. We can use factor analysis to tell us more precisely what underlies these correlations. If the correlation matrix contains a number of statistically significant correlations and a number of near-zero correlations, it is apparent that some tests measure similar abilities of one kind and that others measure abilities of other kinds. The purpose of factor analysis is to be more precise about these underlying abilities.

tested intelligence would reflect the amount of *g* plus the magnitude of the various *s* factors. Performance in mathematics would be a function of a person's general intelligence and mathematical aptitude.

A later investigator, Louis Thurstone (1938), objected to Spearman's emphasis on general intelligence. Thurstone felt that intelligence could be broken down into a number of primary abilities. To determine these abilities, he applied factor analysis to results from a large number of different tests. One set of test items was designed to measure verbal comprehension; another, to measure arithmetical computation; and so on. Thurstone hoped to find a more definitive way of grouping intelligence test items than the rather crude method of item sorting used in the Wechsler verbal and performance scales.

After intercorrelating the scores of all the tests (that is, correlating each test with every other test), Thurstone applied factor analysis to arrive at a set of basic factors. Test items that best represented each of the discovered factors were used to form new tests; these tests were then given to another group of subjects and the intercorrelations were reanalyzed. After several studies of this kind, Thurstone identified seven factors as the *primary mental abilities* revealed by intelligence tests: verbal comprehension, word fluency, number, space, memory, perceptual speed, and reasoning (see Table 12-6).

Thurstone devised a battery of tests, known as the *Test of Primary Mental Abilities,* to measure each of these abilities. Revised versions of this test are still

Factor analysis then uses mathematical methods (assisted by high-speed computers) to compute the correlation of each of the tests with each of several possible underlying factors. Such correlations between test scores and factors are known as *factor loadings;* if a test correlates .05 on factor I, .10 on factor II, and .70 on factor III, it is most heavily "loaded" on factor III. For example, the nine tests with the above correlation matrix yield the *factor matrix* below.

TESTS	FACTORS		
	I	II	III
1	.75	−.01	.08
2	.44	.48	.16
3	.72	.07	.15
4	.08	.76	.08
5	−.01	.49	−.01
6	.16	.73	.02
7	−.03	.04	.64
8	.02	.05	.66
9	−.01	.10	.47

The outlined loadings in the factor matrix show which tests are most highly correlated with each of the underlying factors. The clusters are the same as the clusters in the correlation matrix but are now assigned greater precision. The problem of Test 2 remains because it is loaded almost equally on factor I and factor II; it is obviously not a "factor-pure" test. Having found the three factors that account for the intercorrelations of the nine tests, the factors can be interpreted by studying the content of the tests most highly weighted on each factor. The factor analysis itself is strictly a mathematical process, but the naming and interpretation of the factors depends on a psychological analysis.

widely used, but its predictive power is no greater than the predictability of general intelligence tests, such as the Wechsler scales. Thurstone's hope of discovering the basic elements of intelligence through factor analysis was not fully realized for several reasons. His primary abilities are not completely independent; the significant intercorrelations among them provide some support for Spearman's concept of a general intelligence factor. In addition, the number of basic abilities identified by factor analysis depends on the nature of the test items. Other investigators, using different test items and alternative methods of factor analysis, have identified from 20 to 150 factors to represent the range of intellectual abilities (Ekstrom, French, Harman, & Derman, 1976; Ekstrom, French, & Harman, 1979; Guilford, 1982). This lack of consistency in the number and kinds of factors raises doubts about the validity of the *factorial approach*. Nevertheless, factor analysis continues to be a principal technique for studying intellectual performance (Cronbach, 1984).

Information-processing Approach

Until the 1960s, research on intelligence was dominated by the factorial approach. However, with the development of cognitive psychology and its emphasis on *information-processing models* (p. 9), a new approach has emerged. This approach is defined somewhat differently by different investigators, but the basic

ABILITY	DESCRIPTION
Verbal comprehension	The ability to understand the meaning of words; vocabulary tests represent this factor.
Word fluency	The ability to think of words rapidly, as in solving anagrams or thinking of words that rhyme.
Number	The ability to work with numbers and perform computations.
Space	The ability to visualize space-form relationships, as in recognizing the same figure presented in different orientations.
Memory	The ability to recall verbal stimuli, such as word pairs or sentences.
Perceptual speed	The ability to grasp visual details quickly and to see similarities and differences between pictured objects.
Reasoning	The ability to find a general rule on the basis of presented instances, as in determining how a number series is constructed after being presented with only a portion of that series.

idea is to try to understand intelligence in terms of the cognitive processes that operate when we engage in intellectual activities (Hunt, 1985). More specifically, the information-processing approach asks:

1. What mental processes are involved in the various tests of intelligence?
2. How rapidly and accurately are these processes carried out?
3. What types of mental representations of information do these processes act upon?

Rather than trying to explain intelligence in terms of factors, this approach attempts to identify the mental processes that underlie intelligent behavior. The information-processing approach assumes that individual differences on a given task depend on the specific processes that different individuals bring into play and the speed and accuracy of these processes. The goal is to use an information-processing model of a particular task to identify appropriate measures of the component processes. These measures may be as simple as the response to a multiple-choice item, or they may include the subject's speed of response, perhaps even eye movements and cortical evoked potentials associated with the response. The idea is to use whatever information is needed to estimate the efficiency of each component process.

   The information-processing approach can be illustrated by the work of Sternberg (1985) and his *componential model* of intelligence. He assumes that the test taker possesses a set of mental processes, which he calls *components,* that operate in an organized way to produce the responses observed on an intelligence test. There are many components that fall into the five classes given in Table 12-7. Sternberg selects a specific task from an intelligence test and uses it in a series of experiments to try to identify the components involved in the task. For example, consider analogy tests of the following sort:

lawyer : client :: doctor : (medicine, patient)

COMPONENTS	PROCESSES
Metacomponents	Higher-order control processes used for executive planning and decision making in problem solving.
Performance components	Processes that execute the plans and implement the decisions selected by metacomponents.
Acquisition components	Processes involved in learning new information.
Retention components	Processes involved in retrieving information previously stored in memory.
Transfer components	Processes involved in carrying over retained information from one situation to another.

TABLE 12-7
Components of Intelligence   *Sternberg's scheme for classifying the many component processes operative in solving problems. (After Sternberg, 1985)*

A series of experiments with analogy problems led Sternberg to conclude that the critical components were the *encoding process* and the *comparison process.* The subject encodes each of the words in the analogy by forming a mental representation of the word — in this case, a list of attributes of the word that are retrieved from the subject's long-term memory. For example, a mental representation of the word "lawyer" might include the following attributes: college-educated, versed in legal procedures, represents clients in court, and so on. Once the subject has formed a mental representation for each word in the analogy, the comparison process scans the representations looking for matching attributes that solve the analogy.

Other processes are involved in analogy problems, but Sternberg has shown that individual differences on this task are principally determined by the efficiency of the encoding and comparison processes. The experimental evidence shows that individuals who score high on analogy problems (skilled performers) spend more time encoding and form more accurate mental representations than do individuals who score low on such problems (less skilled performers). In contrast, during the comparison stage, the skilled performers are *faster* than the less skilled performers in matching attributes, but both are *equally accurate* on matching attributes. Thus the better test scores for skilled performers are based on the increased efficiency of their encoding process, but the time they require to solve the problem is a complicated mix of slow encoding speeds and fast comparisons (Pellegrino, 1985).

A factorial approach and an information-processing approach provide complementary interpretations of performance on intelligence tests. Factors such as Thurstone's primary mental abilities are useful in identifying broad areas of strengths and weaknesses. They may indicate that a person is strong in word fluency and verbal comprehension but weak in reasoning. If additional testing is conducted, an information-processing analysis could provide a diagnostic profile of the processes responsible for the observed deficiency. A process analysis may indicate a deficiency at the level of metacomponents (such as the choice of strategies used to attack the problem), or retention components (such as slow or inaccurate recall of relevant information), or transfer components (such as poor ability to transfer what has been learned in one situation to another).

Aspects of Intelligence

Sternberg (1985), in an attempt to generalize his approach, argues that a comprehensive theory of intelligence would involve a much larger set of component

CRITICAL
DISCUSSION

Theory
of Multiple
Intelligences

Howard Gardner (1983) has proposed an approach to intelligence that is similar in many ways to the factorial and information-processing approaches. Nevertheless, his approach has so many unique features that it deserves special consideration.

According to Gardner, there is no such thing as a singular intelligence; rather, there are at least six distinct kinds of intelligence. These six intelligences are independent of one another, each operating as a separate system (or module) in the brain according to its own rules. The six intelligences are:

1. Linguistic
2. Logical-mathematical
3. Spatial
4. Musical
5. Bodily-kinesthetic
6. Personal

The first three are familiar components of intelligence, and Gardner's description of them is similar to what other theorists have proposed; they are what standard intelligence tests measure. The last three are surprising and may even seem frivolous in a discussion of intelligence, but Gardner believes that they deserve comparable status to the first three. He argues that

musical intelligence, for example, has been more important than logical-mathematical intelligence throughout most of human history. The development of logical scientific thought occurred late in the evolution of the human species (as an invention of Western culture in the aftermath of the Renaissance); in contrast, musical and artistic skills have been with us from the dawn of civilization.

Musical intelligence involves the ability to perceive pitch and rhythm and is the basis for the development of musical competence. Bodily-kinesthetic intelligence involves the control of one's own body motions and the ability to manipulate and handle objects skillfully: examples are dancers and gymnasts, who develop precise control over movements of their body; or artisans, tennis players, and neurosurgeons, who are able to manipulate objects with finesse.

Personal intelligence has two components that can be regarded as separate — namely, intrapersonal and interpersonal intelligence. Intrapersonal intelligence is the ability to monitor one's own feelings and emotions, to discriminate among them and use the information to guide one's actions. Interpersonal intelligence, on the other hand, is the ability to notice and understand the needs and intentions of other

processes than have been identified to date by psychologists working in the restricted environment of a laboratory or a typical testing situation. He suggests that this larger set of components would relate not only to "academic intelligence" but also to "practical intelligence"; they would be organized and operate in clusters that might be labeled roughly as follows:

1. Ability to learn and profit from experience
2. Ability to think or reason abstractly
3. Ability to adapt to the vagaries of a changing and uncertain world
4. Ability to motivate oneself to accomplish expeditiously the tasks one needs to accomplish.

Other psychologists — whether working from the perspective of the factorial approach or the information-processing approach — would generally agree with this list. Most intelligence tests in use today are fairly effective in assessing the first two abilities, but they are of minimal value in assessing the last two. Undoubtedly, this is why conventional intelligence tests are very effective in predicting academic achievement but are far less predictive of personal achievement outside the academic world. Our ability to measure intelligence with the type of tests in

individuals and to monitor their moods and temperament as a way of predicting how they will behave in new situations.

Gardner analyzes each kind of intelligence from several viewpoints: the cognitive operations involved, the appearance of prodigies and other exceptional individuals, evidence from cases of brain damage, manifestations in different cultures, and the possible course of evolutionary development.

Because of heredity or training, some individuals will develop certain intelligences more than others, but every normal person should develop each to some extent. The intelligences interact with, and build upon, one another but still operate as semi-autonomous systems. Each intelligence is an "encapsulated module" within the brain, operating according to its own rules and procedures; certain kinds of brain damage can impair one type of intelligence and have no effect on the others. Gardner is not the first to argue for the modularity of different mental functions, but most theorists of this persuasion still assume that a central control process (or executive routine) coordinates the activities of the various modules. Gardner, however, believes that one can explain behavior without postulating an executive control process.

In Western society, the first three types of intelligence are highly regarded; they are what standard intelligence tests measure. But historical and anthropological evidence suggests that other intelligences have been more highly valued at earlier periods in human history and even today in some non-Western cultures. Further, the activities a culture emphasizes will influence how a specific intelligence develops: for example, a boy endowed with unusual bodily-kinesthetic intelligence may become a baseball player in the United States or a ballet dancer in the Soviet Union.

Gardner's ideas about personal, musical, and bodily-kinesthetic intelligences are provocative and will undoubtedly lead to new efforts to measure these abilities and to use them as predictors of other variables. As noted earlier, conventional IQ tests are good predictors of college grades, but are not particularly useful in predicting performance in later life on such indices as job success or career advancement. Measures of other abilities, such as personal intelligence, may help explain why some people with brilliant college records fail miserably in later life, while lesser students become charismatic leaders. No matter how one judges Gardner's work, he makes a forceful case for the idea that intelligence encompasses more than verbal and quantitative skills, and that society would be better served by a broader conception of what we call intelligence.

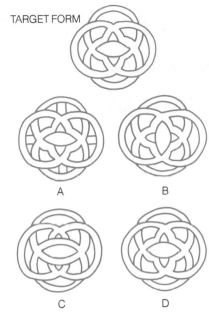

TARGET FORM

A   B

C   D

Spatial Ability *How quickly patterns can be matched is an indicator of spatial intelligence. From the array of four, choose the pattern that is identical to the target form. (After Gardner, 1983)*

use today probably has reached a ceiling. New methods will have to be developed that more accurately assess motivation and practical problem-solving ability in order to improve the predictive power of intelligence tests. These new methods will probably require a more interactive testing situation than that provided by paper-and-pencil tests. Computer-controlled testing may provide the flexibility and richness of interaction required; research along these lines is underway.

GENETIC AND ENVIRONMENTAL INFLUENCES

People differ in intellectual ability. How much of this difference is due to the particular genes we inherit, and how much is due to the environment in which we are raised? The heredity-environment issue, which has been debated in regard to many aspects of human behavior, has focused primarily on the area of intelligence. Most experts agree that at least some aspects of intelligence are inherited, but opinions differ as to the relative contributions made by heredity and environment.

RELATIONSHIP	CORRELATION
Identical twins	
Reared together	.86
Reared apart	.72
Fraternal twins	
Reared together	.60
Siblings	
Reared together	.47
Reared apart	.24
Parent/child	.40
Foster parent/ child	.31
Cousins	.15

TABLE 12-8

Familial Studies of Intelligence *A summary of 111 studies identified in a survey of the world literature on familial resemblances in measured intelligence. The data represent average correlation coefficients for IQ test scores between persons of various relationships. In general, the pattern of correlations indicates that the higher the proportion of genes two family members have in common, the higher the average correlation between their IQs. (After Bouchard & McGue, 1981)*

Genetic Relationships and Intelligence

Most of the evidence bearing on the inheritance of intelligence is derived from studies correlating IQs between persons of various degrees of genetic relationship. Table 12-8 summarizes the results of over 100 studies of this type. In general, the closer the genetic relationship, the more similar the tested intelligence. The average correlation between the IQs of parents and their natural children is .40; between parents and their adopted children, the correlation is about .31. Identical twins, because they develop from a single egg, share precisely the same heredity; the correlation between their IQs is very high — about .86. The IQs of fraternal twins (who develop from separate eggs and are no more alike genetically than ordinary siblings) have a correlation coefficient of about .60.

Although genetic determinants of intelligence are strong, the results shown in Table 12-8 indicate that environment is also important. Note that when siblings are reared together — in the same home environment — IQ similarity increases. Other studies have shown that the intellectual ability of adopted children is higher than would be predicted on the basis of their natural parents' ability (see Scarr & Weinberg, 1976). Environment does make a difference in intelligence.

It is possible to estimate what portion of the variability in test scores is due to environment and what portion is due to heredity from data similar to those given in Table 12-8. Several methods are used to make these estimates; the most common is to compare the variability of fraternal and identical twins on a given trait. To do this, two quantities are estimated: (1) the total variability due to both environment and heredity (V_T) is estimated from the observed differences between pairs of fraternal twins, and (2) the environmental variability alone (V_E) is estimated from the observed differences between pairs of identical twins. The difference between the two quantities (V_G) is the variability due to genetic factors (that is, $V_T = V_E + V_G$). The heritability ratio, or simply *heritability* (H), is the ratio between genetic variability and total variability:

$$H = \frac{V_G}{V_T}$$

In other words, heritability is the proportion of a trait's variation within a specified population that can be attributed to genetic differences. Heritability ranges between 0 and 1. When identical twins resemble each other much more than fraternal twins on a given trait, H approaches 1. When the resemblance between identical twins is about the same as the resemblance between fraternal twins on a given trait, H approaches 0.

There are a number of ways to estimate H other than comparing identical and fraternal twins. The theory that permits us to make such estimates is too lengthy to present here, but it is discussed in most genetics textbooks. For our purposes, it is sufficient to say that H measures the fraction of the observed variance in a population that is caused by differences in heredity. It is important to note that H refers to a *population* of individuals, not to a single individual. For example, height has an H of .90, which means that 90 percent of the variance in height observed in a population is due to genetic differences and 10 percent is due to environmental differences. (It does not mean that an individual who is 5 feet 10 inches tall grew to a height of 63 inches due to genetic factors and grew another 7 inches due to environmental factors.) In discussing intelligence, H is often misused to designate the fraction of an individual's intelligence that is due to heredity; the use of the term in this way is incorrect.

Heritability estimates for intelligence have ranged widely from one study to another. Some researchers have reported values as high as .87; others, values as low as .10. For the data presented in Table 12-8, the estimate of H is .74. The fact that heritability estimates vary so widely suggests that the research is plagued by a number of uncontrolled variables that influence the results in ways that cannot be specified. It must be kept in mind that heritability research is based on field studies and not on well-controlled laboratory experiments; individual cases are observed where they can be found. Field studies are always subject to the influence of uncontrolled variables and are particularly suspect when different investigators report quite different conclusions (Teasdale & Owen, 1984).

Complicating the situation further is the fact that assumptions made in assessing heritability may not always be correct. In research on twins, for example, it is assumed that twins who are reared together experience roughly the same environment, whether they are fraternal or identical twins. But this may not be true. Identical twins look more alike than fraternal twins, and this fact alone may cause parents and others to treat them more alike than fraternal twins (for example, identical twins are more likely to be dressed in identical outfits than fraternal twins).

In the absence of better-controlled studies, a reliable estimate of heritability is not possible. Heredity clearly has an effect on intelligence, but the degree of this effect is uncertain. It is probably less influential than some researchers have claimed (see Jensen, 1980) but not completely nonexistent, as some critics of the research have claimed (Kamin, 1976). Most probably, intellectual ability is determined by a number of genes whose individual effects are small but cumulative. If as few as 5 to 10 pairs of genes are involved, the possible combinations would produce a normal distribution of IQ scores and would allow for a wide range of intellectual ability, even within a single family; it would not be uncommon for offspring of high IQ parents to have low IQs and vice versa (Bouchard, 1976).

Environmental Influences

We can think of a person's genes as imposing a top and a bottom limit on intelligence or establishing a range of intellectual ability. Environmental influences — what happens to the individual during the course of development — will determine where the person's IQ will fall within that range. In other words, genes do not specify behavior; rather, they establish a range of probable responses to the environment, which is called the *reaction range*. Figure 12-6

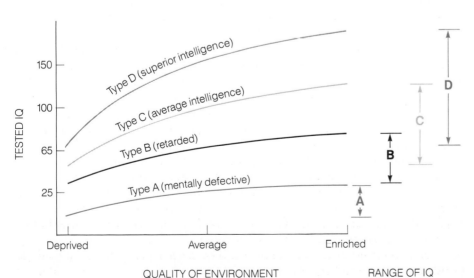

QUALITY OF ENVIRONMENT   RANGE OF IQ

FIGURE 12-6
Effects of Different Environments on IQ *The curves represent hypothetical reaction ranges for four individuals who vary in inherited intellectual potential. For example, the individual labeled Type D has an IQ of about 65 when raised in a deprived environment but an IQ of over 180 when raised in a maximally enriched environment. The vertical arrows to the right indicate the range of possible IQ scores for each type. (After Gottesman, 1963)*

CRITICAL DISCUSSION

Race and Intelligence

The debate over genetic contributions to intelligence has focused on the possibility of inherited racial differences in intelligence — specifically, on the question of whether blacks are innately less intelligent than whites. In view of the heated controversy about this issue and its significance for social policy, it is important that we examine the available evidence.

On standard intelligence tests, black Americans as a group score 10–15 points lower than white Americans as a group. This fact is not debated; the controversy revolves around the interpretation of this difference. Some behavioral scientists and geneticists believe that the two groups differ in inherited ability (see Jensen, 1980). Others argue that black-white differences in average IQ can be attributed entirely to environmental differences between the two groups (see Kamin, 1976). Many believe that genetic and environmental differences are so confounded that the question is unanswerable at present (Loehlin, Lindzey, & Spuhler, 1975). The issues involved are exceedingly complex; the best we can do here is to summarize a few of the main points.

1. Although blacks and whites may differ in physical appearance, they do not represent two distinct biological groups. In fact, differences in gene structures (where known) in most cases are greater *within* the races than between them.

2. Heritability is a population statistic (like infant mortality or birthrate); it depends on the environmental and genetic variation among a given group of people at a given time. Thus, although heritability ratios estimated for white populations indicate that variations in IQ are partly a function of heredity, such estimates do not permit us to make inferences about heritability ratios among black populations. More importantly, heritability estimates do not tell us anything about differences *between* populations. The heritability of a characteristic could be the same for two groups, even though the differences between them are caused entirely by environmental factors. For example, suppose the heritability of height is the same for two populations, A and B. If individuals in Population A are raised on a starvation diet, they will be shorter, on the average, than individuals in Population B. Variations in

illustrates this concept, showing hypothetical IQ reaction ranges for individuals of different genetic potential raised in deprived, average, and enriched environments. In each case, an enriched environment raises the individual's IQ and a deprived one lowers it. But each type of individual has a specific reaction range; a person with the genetic potential for average or superior intelligence under normal environmental conditions (Types C and D) has a much larger reaction range than an individual who is retarded (Type B) or mentally defective (Type A). Presumably, the person with the superior potential (Type D) has the greatest capacity to utilize an enriched environment and would show the greatest decrease in IQ under deprived conditions. Several studies suggest that an adverse environment does have the greatest effect on children of above-average ability (Weisman, 1966; Scarr-Salapatek, 1971; Scarr, 1981).

The environmental conditions that determine how an individual's intellectual potential will develop include nutrition, health, quality of stimulation, emotional climate of the home, and type of feedback elicited by behavior. Given two children with the same genes, the child with the better prenatal and postnatal nutrition, the more intellectually stimulating and emotionally secure home, and the more appropriate rewards for academic accomplishments will attain the higher IQ score when tested in first grade. Studies have shown that IQ differences between children of low and high socioeconomic status become progressively greater between birth and entrance into school, suggesting that environmental conditions accentuate whatever differences in intelligence are present at birth (Bayley, 1970).

adult height within each group are still influenced by heredity (that is, undernourished individuals with tall parents will be taller than undernourished individuals with short parents), but the difference in average height between the two groups is clearly the result of environment. To summarize, heritability estimates do not permit us to draw conclusions about differences between populations (Mackenzie, 1984).

3. Among black populations, there is some tendency for lightness of skin color (presumably an indication of the degrees of intermixture with whites) to correlate positively with IQ. But such correlations are very low (typically .15) and can be explained on the basis of environmental differences — a lighter skin color is associated with less discrimination and greater opportunity.

4. A study of illegitimate children fathered by U.S. servicemen during the occupation of Germany after World War II found no overall difference in average IQ between children whose fathers were black and those whose fathers were white. Since these children were all raised by German mothers of similar social status and were matched with children of the same age in the classroom, the results provide strong support for viewing environment as the major determinant of racial IQ differences (Eyferth, Brandt, & Wolfgang, 1960).

5. When black or interracial children (those with one black parent) are adopted before they are 1 year old and raised by white families with above-average incomes and educations, they score more than 15 IQ points higher than underprivileged black children reared by their biological families. The performance of the adopted children on school achievement tests is slightly above the national norms (Scarr & Weinberg, 1976).

6. Findings from the National Assessment of Educational Progress and from the College Entrance Examination Board demonstrate a consistent reduction over the last 20 years in the achievement differences between black and white students. These reductions occur for reading and mathematics achievement tests in grades 1 through 12 and for the SAT. The consistency of the trend suggests that further reductions in white-black differences will be seen in future years (Jones, 1984). The social changes affecting blacks have been enormous in the last 20 years; such profound changes might be expected to elevate aspirations of black youth and give them evidence that school achievement will enhance their prospects for career success. The improvement of black achievement levels in recent years is consistent with this supposition.

The authors of this text believe that it is not possible to draw valid conclusions about innate racial differences in intelligence from the available evidence. Cultural and environmental differences between blacks and whites influence the development of cognitive abilities in complex ways, and no study has succeeded in estimating or eliminating these effects. As long as systematic differences remain in the conditions under which blacks and whites are raised (and as long as the effects of these differences cannot be reliably estimated), no valid conclusions can be drawn concerning innate differences in intelligence.

HEAD START PROGRAMS   Because children from underprivileged families tend to fall behind in cognitive development even before they enter school, efforts have been made to provide more intellectual stimulation for these children during their early years. In 1965, as part of President Johnson's War on Poverty, Congress authorized funds for a number of programs designed to provide learning experiences for 2- to 5-year-olds from poor homes. These programs, funded by Project Head Start, varied in approach. In some, special teachers visited the children at home several times a week to play with them. They engaged the children in such activities as building with blocks, looking at pictures, and naming colors and taught them such concepts as big–little and rough–smooth. In brief, the teachers provided the kind of intellectual stimulation that children in upper-class homes usually receive from their parents. The visiting teachers also taught the parents how to provide the same kinds of activities for their children. In other programs, the children attended special classes, where they interacted with teachers in similar play-learning activities. Some of these programs involved the parents; others did not.

In general, the results of these early education programs have been promising. Children who have participated in such programs score higher on the Stanford-Binet or WISC on entering school and tend to be more self-confident and socially competent than children who have not received special attention.

Follow-up studies indicate that early education programs produce some lasting benefits. For example, several studies have followed progress through high school of disadvantaged children who participated in special preschool

Head Start programs give preschoolers an opportunity to prepare for grade school by providing them with increased intellectual stimulation.

programs when they were 3 years old. By the age of 15, these students were more than a full grade ahead of a matched control group of students who had received no preschool experience. In addition, compared with the control group, the students with preschool experience (1) scored higher on tests of reading, arithmetic, and language usage; (2) were less apt to need special remedial classes; (3) exhibited less antisocial behavior; and (4) were more likely to hold after-school jobs (Hohmann, Banet, & Weikart, 1979; Palmer & Anderson, 1979; Lazar & Darlington, 1982; Zigler & Berman, 1983).

Head Start programs have shown that early intellectual stimulation can have a significant impact on later school performance. But the specific method used appears to be less important than parental involvement. Programs that actively involve the parents, that interest them in their children's development and show them how to provide a more stimulating home environment, tend to produce the greatest gains.

Environmental effects on intellectual performance even more dramatic than Head Start are evidenced by studies of children living in Israeli kibbutzim. For some time, Israel has been faced with the problem of large differences in intellectual and educational background among Jews of different cultural ancestry. The average intellectual ability of Jews of European ancestry generally is considerably higher than that of Jews from Arabic countries. The average difference in IQ between the two groups is at least as large as the average difference in IQ between blacks and whites in the United States. The exceptions to this observation are Israeli children who are raised on certain types of kibbutzim, where they do not reside with their parents but live in a children's house under the care of women specially trained in child rearing. Under these special conditions, the children's IQ scores tend to be unrelated to the country of parental origin. Children whose parents came from Arabic countries score as well as children whose parents came from Europe. Although individual differences in IQ scores still exist, the differences are not related to ancestry (Smilansky, 1974). Thus, we have some indication of the contribution an enriched environment can make toward helping children reach their intellectual potential.

ABILITY TESTS IN PERSPECTIVE

Despite their limitations, ability tests are one of the most widely used tools that psychology has developed. If these tests are to continue to be useful, however, they must be viewed realistically. They should not be overvalued as providing a fixed, unchangeable measure of what a person can do. Nor should they be discarded because of their obvious shortcomings and replaced by other methods of evaluation that may be less valid.

One area of concern has been the use of ability tests to determine class placement for schoolchildren. Children who achieve low scores may be assigned to a slower "track" or placed in a special class for "slow learners"; children who earn high scores may be placed in accelerated or "enriched" programs. Unless schools provide periodic reassessment and unless slow-learner classes emphasize academic skills, a child's initial placement may well determine his or her academic future. Some youngsters who have the potential to succeed in college may be discouraged on the basis of early test scores from taking college preparatory courses. Both parents and teachers must realize that test scores — whether the test is called an intelligence test or an achievement test — can only measure current performance. Questions on an intelligence test are less dependent on schooling, but they do not measure innate capacity; thus, test scores can change with changes in the environment.

The use of tests to classify schoolchildren is a controversial social issue, because a disproportionately large number of minority and underprivileged children have been assigned to special classes for slow learners on the basis of their scores on group intelligence and achievement tests. Legal suits by parents have prompted some states to prohibit the use of group intelligence tests for purposes of classification (see Wigdor & Garner, 1982, pp. 110 – 16).

The issue is complicated. Ability tests (both intelligence and achievement) probably have been overused and misused in the schools. Teachers often do not know how to interpret test results and may draw sweeping conclusions about a child's ability on the basis of a single test score. More importantly, decisions about placement in special classes should be based on many factors — never on test scores alone. A child's medical and developmental history, social competency, and home environment are some of the variables that should be considered before the child is classified as a slow learner.

Ability tests can serve an important function when properly used. They help the teacher separate a large class of pupils of varying skills into homogeneous learning groups. (Children who are roughly at the same level in mastering reading or mathematical concepts can be taught together.) Ability tests can also be used diagnostically to improve the educational opportunities for disadvantaged and minority children. A child who scores low on a group intelligence test (and such tests should be used only as initial screening devices) should be given a more intensive evaluation. Individual testing can help to reveal (1) whether the group test scores represent an accurate assessment of the child's current abilities, (2) the child's particular intellectual strengths and weaknesses, and (3) the best instructional program for improving his or her skills. Tests should be used to match instruction with individual needs, not to label a child.

A comparison of intelligence and achievement test scores often yields valuable information. For example, some children whose achievement test scores in math or reading are low may score quite high on an intelligence test. This discrepancy should alert the teacher to the possibility that the child's math and reading skills are not well developed and require special attention. This child may do quite well scholastically once his or her specific learning problems are

"I'm sorry, but these records are somewhat mixed up. It turns out that 184 is your weight, not your IQ."

remedied. Without the information from the intelligence test, such a child might be inappropriately placed in a slow-learner group.

Another point of concern is the type of talent measured by ability tests. As noted earlier, the SAT and other admissions tests have proved successful in predicting college grades. But when college admission officials place too much emphasis on test scores, they are apt to overlook students who may have an extraordinary talent in art, drama, or music. They may also overlook students who have aimed all of their energy and enthusiasm toward creative efforts in a specific area (for example, an award-winning science project or an innovative community program). In any selection procedure, scores on intelligence and scholastic aptitude tests should be considered in conjunction with other information.

We must always question the validity of a test score for a particular individual or for a particular purpose, and we must continue to improve methods of assessment. But despite their limitations, ability tests are still the most effective aids we have for judging what job or class or type of training is most appropriate for a given individual. The alternatives are few. To rely entirely on subjective judgment would introduce the kinds of biases that such tests were designed to eliminate. To assign people at random to jobs or educational programs would benefit neither society nor the individual.

SUMMARY

1. Ability tests include *aptitude tests* (which are designed to predict what a person can accomplish with training) and *achievement tests* (which measure accomplished skills and indicate what the individual can do at present). Both tests may contain similar types of items, but they differ in their purposes and in the amount of *prior experience* they assume. Some ability tests measure very specific abilities; others cover a range of skills.

2. To be useful, tests must meet certain specifications. Studies of *reliability* tell us whether test scores are consistent over time. Studies of *validity* tell us how well a test measures what it is intended to measure — how well it predicts according to an acceptable criterion. *Uniform testing procedures* are necessary for a test to be reliable and valid.

3. The first successful intelligence tests were developed by the French psychologist Alfred Binet, who proposed the concept of *mental age.* A bright child's mental age is above his or her chronological age; a slow child's mental age is below his or her chronological age. The revision of the Binet scales (the Stanford-Binet) adopts the *intelligence quotient* (IQ) as an index of mental development. The IQ expresses intelligence as a ratio of mental age (MA) to chronological age (CA).

4. Two widely used ability tests, the Wechsler Adult Intelligence Scale (WAIS) and the Wechsler Intelligence Scale for Children (WISC), have both verbal and performance scales so that separate information can be obtained about each type of ability. The Stanford-Binet and the Wechsler scales are *individual tests* that are administered to a single individual by a specially trained tester. *Group ability tests* can be administered to a large number of people at one time.

5. Scores on ability tests correlate quite highly with what we think of as "brightness" and with measures of academic performance. But they do not measure motivation, leadership, and other characteristics that are important for success.

6. Both Binet and Wechsler assumed that intelligence is a *general capacity* for reasoning. Spearman proposed a general factor *(g)* plus specific abilities (each called *s*), which could be identified by the method of *factor analysis.* Thurstone used factor analysis to arrive at seven *primary mental abilities* he considered to be the basic elements of intelligence; variants of his test are still widely used, but their predictive power is no greater than that of tests of general intelligence, such

as the Wechsler scales. Factor analysis continues to be an important method for the analysis of test data; this perspective on intelligence is called the *factorial approach*.

7. An alternative perspective on intelligence is the *information-processing approach*. The basic idea of this approach is to try to understand intellectual behavior in terms of the underlying cognitive processes that are brought into play when we are confronted with a problem-solving task. The information-processing approach has yielded some detailed analyses of the mental processes involved in many tasks used to assess intelligence. A factorial approach and an information-processing approach provide complementary interpretations of performance on intelligence tests. Both approaches have enhanced our understanding of academic intelligence, but their common shortcoming is that they have not proved particularly effective in assessing practical intelligence.

8. Studies correlating IQs between persons with varying degrees of genetic relationship show that heredity plays a role in intelligence. Estimates of *heritability* vary, however; such environmental factors as nutrition, intellectual stimulation, and the emotional climate of the home will influence where a person's IQ will fall within the *reaction range* determined by heredity.

9. Despite their limitations, ability tests are still the most objective method available for assessing individual capabilities. But test scores must be considered in conjunction with other information.

FURTHER READING

For a general introduction to individual differences and psychological testing, see Cronbach, *Essentials of Psychological Testing* (4th ed., 1984); Kail and Pellegrino, *Human Intelligence: Perspectives and Prospects* (1985); Sternberg (ed.), *Human Abilities: An Information-processing Approach* (1984); and Anastasi, *Psychological Testing* (5th ed., 1982). More advanced treatments of these topics are Sternberg (ed.), *Handbook of Human Intelligence* (1982); and Wigdor and Garner (eds.), *Ability Testing: Uses, Consequences, and Controversies* (1982).

For a more general overview of intellectual abilities, see Sternberg, *Intelligence Applied: Understanding and Increasing Your Intellectual Skills* (1986). For a historical perspective on intelligence tests and the controversies associated with them, see Fancher, *The Intelligence Men: Makers of the IQ Controversy* (1985).

The genetics of intelligence is discussed in Plomin, Defries, and McClearn, *Behavioral Genetics: A Primer* (1980). For a discussion of racial and social class differences in intelligence, see Scarr, *Race, Social Class, and Individual Differences in IQ* (1981); and Lewontin, Rose, and Kamin, *Not in Our Genes: Biology, Ideology and Human Nature* (1984).

For a discussion of Head Start programs and day care for children, see Bond and Joffe (eds.), *Facilitating Infant and Early Childhood Development* (1982); and Zigler and Gordon (eds.), *Day Care: Scientific and Social Policy Issues* (1981).

Personality and Its Assessment

13

As POPULARLY USED, THE WORD *PERsonality* has a number of meanings. When we say that someone has "a lot of personality," we are usually referring to that individual's social effectiveness and appeal. Courses advertised to "improve your personality" attempt to teach social skills and to enhance your appearance or manner of speaking in order to elicit favorable reactions from others. Sometimes we use the word "personality" to describe an individual's most striking characteristic. We may refer to someone as having an "aggressive personality" or a "shy personality."

When psychologists talk about personality, however, they are concerned primarily with *individual differences*—the characteristics that distinguish one individual from another. Psychologists do not agree on an exact definition of the term. But for our purposes, we will define personality as the *characteristic patterns of behavior, thought, and emotion that determine a person's adjustment to the environment*.

The term *characteristic* in the definition implies some consistency in behavior—a tendency to act or think in certain ways in many different situations. For example, you can probably think of an acquaintance who seldom expresses anger, no matter what the provocation, and another who flies off the handle at the slightest irritation. Behavior is the result of interaction between personality characteristics and the social and physical conditions of the environment. But, as we will see later, personality theorists differ in the extent to which they believe behavior is *internally controlled* (determined by the personal characteristics of the individual and therefore fairly consistent) or *externally controlled* (determined by the particular situation in which the behavior occurs).

When we discuss behavior, we refer to the *public personality*—the "you" that others observe and listen to, the view of yourself that you present to the world. Your public personality includes expressive features and mannerisms (your speech patterns, the way you carry yourself), your general disposition (whether you are usually cheerful or grumpy), the way you react to threatening situations, the attitudes you express, and much more. You may behave differently at a large social gathering than you do in a small group of close friends, but the public side of your personality still can be observed by others and can be measured in various ways.

There is also a private, hidden part of your personality. Your *private personality* includes the fantasies, thoughts, and experiences that you do not share with others. You may have had some special experiences you have never told anyone about, wishes that seem too childish or embarrassing to reveal, dreams and memories that remain yours alone. The thoughts and memories that cycle through your mind as you wait for class to begin or as you stroll through the woods are part of your private personality. You may reveal some of these in a close, intimate relationship with another person, but generally they are yours alone.

SHAPING OF PERSONALITY

An infant is born with certain potentials. Physical characteristics — such as eye and hair color, body build, and the shape of one's nose — are essentially determined at the moment of conception. Intelligence and certain special abilities, such as musical and artistic talent, also depend to some extent on heredity. In addition, there is increasing evidence that differences in emotional reactivity may be innate. A study of newborns found that reliable differences can be observed shortly after birth in such characteristics as activity level, attention span, adaptability to changes in the environment, and general mood. One infant might tend to be active, easily distracted, and willing to accept new objects and people; another might be predominantly quiet, persistent in concentrating on an activity, and apprehensive of anything new. For many of the children in this study, these early characteristics of temperament persisted into adulthood (Thomas & Chess, 1977).

Parents respond differently to babies who have different characteristics. In this way, a reciprocal process starts that may exaggerate some of the personality characteristics present at birth. For example, an infant who stops crying when picked up and snuggles closely is more pleasant to hold than one who stiffens, turns his or her head away, and continues to cry. Consequently, the "snuggler" is apt to be held more often than the "nonsnuggler"; the initial behavioral predispositions are reinforced by the responses of the parent.

The biological predispositions with which an individual is born are shaped by experiences encountered in the course of growing up. Some of these experiences are *common*, shared by most people in a given culture; others are *unique* to the individual.

Biological Influences

The fact that differences in mood and activity level can be observed so soon after birth suggests the influence of genetic factors. Research on the inheritance of personality characteristics has focused on the study of twins. As illustrated in the discussion of intelligence in Chapter 12, comparison of identical twins (who share the same heredity because they develop from a single egg) with fraternal twins (who are no more alike genetically than ordinary siblings) provides a basis for estimating heritability.

In one study, same-sex twins (average age, 4½ years) were rated by their mothers on a number of personality characteristics. Identical twins were judged to be much more alike in emotional reactivity, activity level, and sociability than fraternal twins (see Table 13-1). When personality tests are administered to adult twins, identical twins generally give more similar answers than fraternal twins (Loehlin & Nichols, 1976).

TABLE 13-1
Personality Similarities in Twins   *In this study, 139 same-sex twins (average age, 4½ years) were rated by their mothers on three personality characteristics. Although identical twins may be treated more alike than fraternal twins (and therefore may have more similar environments), the size of these correlations suggests that genetic inheritance is an important determinant of personality. (After Buss & Plomin, 1975)*

| | CORRELATIONS FOR BOYS | | CORRELATIONS FOR GIRLS | |
	IDENTICAL	FRATERNAL	IDENTICAL	FRATERNAL
Emotionality	.68	.00	.60	.05
Activity	.73	.18	.50	.00
Sociability	.65	.20	.58	.06

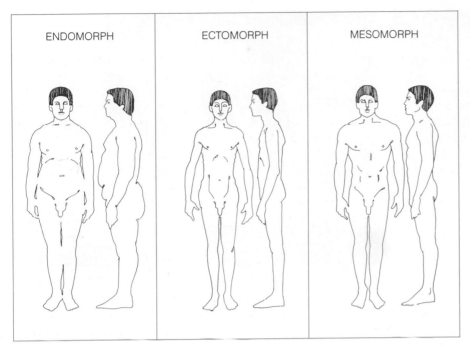

| ENDOMORPH | ECTOMORPH | MESOMORPH |

FIGURE 13-1
Body Types and Per *drawings illustrate Kretschmer (1925) individuals into personau. basis of body build. Research has little support for these ideas, and most psychologists now doubt the usefulness of such classifications.*

However, as we noted earlier, identical twins are often treated more alike than fraternal twins, and the similarities in their personalities may result from a greater similarity in treatment. One way to circumvent this problem is to study identical twins who have been reared apart. Interestingly, a survey of studies that compared twins who were separated for part of their lives with twins who were reared together found no indication that being separated decreased personality similarity (Willerman, 1979). On the contrary, there is some indication that identical twins reared apart may be *more* alike than identical twins reared together. Presumably, twins reared together feel the need to develop separate or complementary identities. If one twin plays soccer, the other may decide to join the debate team; or if one excels at the piano, the other may turn to painting. Twins reared apart have no need to complement or to compete with each other and thus may be more apt to follow their natural inclinations. (See the Critical Discussion "Genetic Influences on Personality: Identical Twins Reared Apart" for a further consideration of this topic.)

Although twin studies suggest that some personality characteristics are inherited, there is no evidence that these characteristics are determined by specific genes. The similarities in body build and physiology shared by identical twins may account in part for their personality similarities.

BODY BUILD The idea that body build and personality characteristics are related is reflected in such popular stereotypes as "fat people are jolly" or "tall, skinny people who wear glasses are intellectuals." This idea is far from new. Even Shakespeare had Julius Caesar say, "Let me have men about me that are fat; sleek-headed men, and such as sleep o' nights. Yond Cassius has a lean and hungry look; he thinks too much: such men are dangerous. . . . Would he were fatter" (*Julius Caesar,* act 1, scene 2).

One early personality theory classified individuals into three categories on the basis of body build and related these body types to personality characteristics (see Figure 13-1). A short, plump person *(endomorph)* was said to be sociable, relaxed, and even-tempered; a tall, thin person *(ectomorph)* was characterized as restrained, self-conscious, and fond of solitude; a heavy-set, muscular individual

Examples of high and low sensation seekers.

(mesomorph) was described as noisy, aggressive, and physically active (Kretschmer, 1925; Sheldon, 1954).

Attempts to relate body build to specific personality characteristics, however, usually produce very low correlations, and most psychologists do not consider this classification useful. People's body weight and muscular strength change with age, diet, and exercise. You may know some short, plump individuals who are sociable and relaxed, but you probably also know some who are shy and withdrawn.

Yet there is little doubt that a person's physique has some influence on personality, primarily through the limits it imposes on abilities and the reactions it evokes from other people. For example, a girl with a short, stocky build cannot realistically aspire to be a ballet dancer, a fashion model, or an all-star basketball player; one who is over six feet tall probably will not become an Olympic gymnast. Boys who are strong and muscular may be willing to risk physical danger and to assert themselves, whereas their weaker classmates may learn early in life to avoid fights and to depend on intellectual abilities to get what they want. Our physiques do not determine specific personality characteristics, but they may shape our personalities by affecting the way that others treat us, the nature of our interactions with others, and the kinds of situations we seek or avoid.

BODY PHYSIOLOGY In addition to differences in body build, people differ in a number of physiological measures (for example, the size of the endocrine glands, the reactivity of the autonomic nervous system, and the balance among various neurotransmitters). Ultimately, we may find that some personality differences are related to physiological and biochemical differences. Research has investigated some intriguing possibilities. One example is a series of studies examining the physiological basis of a personality characteristic called "sensation seeking," or "thrill seeking." A person's desire for new experiences and his or her willingness to take risks to achieve them can be measured by a personality test (see p. 345). Those who score high on the test (the sensation seekers) tend to have lower blood levels of an enzyme that affects neural transmission in the brain than do those who score low (Zuckerman, 1979). The enzyme (monoamine oxidase, or MAO) regulates the concentration of two neurotransmitters that are believed to play an important role in emotional and motivated behavior.

The relationship is tentative for a number of reasons. MAO levels are affected by a person's age and balance of sex hormones, and the level of MAO in the blood may not accurately reflect the level in the brain. Nevertheless, the implications are intriguing: the stunt pilot and the chess player may differ in their body chemistry. And since MAO levels are heritable, sensation seeking may be a family trait.

There is no doubt that energy level and mood are influenced by complex physiological and biochemical processes (Chapter 15 examines some biochemical theories of anxiety and depression). At this point, however, it is difficult to separate cause and effect — to determine the extent to which such differences are part of our biological inheritance and the extent to which they stem from experiences encountered over the course of a lifetime.

Common Experiences

All families in a given culture share certain common beliefs, customs, and values. While growing up, the child learns to behave in ways expected by the culture. One of these expectations has to do with *sex roles* (see Chapter 3). Most cultures expect different behaviors from males than from females. Sex roles may vary from culture to culture, but it is considered "natural" in any culture for boys and girls to have predictable differences in personality merely because they belong to one sex or the other.

A culture as complex as that of the United States contains numerous subcultures, each with its own views about such issues as moral values, standards of cleanliness, style of dress, and definitions of success. The cultural subgroup exerts its influence on the developing person. All boys are expected to exhibit certain personality characteristics, but a boy raised in an urban slum is expected to behave differently in some respects than a boy raised in a middle-class suburb.

Some roles, such as occupations, are of our own choosing. But these roles are also patterned by cultural dictates. We have formed stereotypes about doctors, truck drivers, rock stars, and opera singers. Within an occupation, however, stereotypes have become much less rigid. The greatest change has been in sex roles: we are no longer surprised by female taxicab drivers, telephone repairers, or construction workers, or by male secretaries, nurses, or telephone operators. And styles of dress and appearance are more flexible: football players can wear hair that curls below their helmets, female office workers can wear slacks, male doctors and lawyers can sport beards and jewelry, and opera stars can appear in blue jeans. Nevertheless, people tend to feel comfortable in an occupation if they behave — and appear — as others in that occupation do.

CRITICAL DISCUSSION

Genetic Influences on Personality: Identical Twins Reared Apart

Identical twins, as we have already noted, tend to be more alike in personality characteristics than fraternal twins. Although this fact suggests the influence of heredity, it is difficult to separate the effects of environment and heredity. Because identical twins look alike, they may be treated more alike by their parents and by other people and therefore may experience a more similar environment than fraternal twins.

An ideal situation for studying the effects of heredity on personality and behavior would be to separate identical twins at birth and raise them in radically different environments. Although humanitarian considerations prohibit a controlled experiment of this sort, a research project at the University of Minnesota, called the Minnesota Study of Twins Reared Apart, comes close to fulfilling these conditions (Bouchard et al., 1981; Lykken, 1982; McGue & Bouchard, 1984). Experimenters located

and brought to the laboratory for study 30 pairs of identical twins who were separated, on the average, at 6 weeks of age and reared by different families. The twins had not lived together since infancy, nor had they met each other before they were in their teens. (In fact, some of the twins had never met until the study brought them together.)

The twins participated in lengthy interviews, during which they were asked questions about such topics as childhood experiences, fears, hobbies, musical tastes, social attitudes, and sexual interests. A variety of medical and psychological tests were also administered. Analysis of the enormous amount of data collected will continue for several years, and at least 20 more sets of twins will be studied before conclusions are drawn. But the preliminary findings point to some startling similarities.

The twins with the most dramatically

Adult behavior is predictable to the extent that it conforms to social and occupational roles. Basically, we know how people will behave at a formal reception, a political demonstration, a football game, or a funeral.

Although cultural and subcultural pressures impose some personality similarities, individual personalities can never be completely predicted from a knowledge of the group in which a person is raised. There are two reasons for this: (1) the cultural influences on the individual are not uniform because they are transmitted by parents and by other people who may not all share the same values and practices, and (2) the individual has some experiences that are unique.

Unique Experiences

Each person reacts in his or her own way to social pressures. As we noted earlier, personal differences in behavior may result from biological differences. They may also develop from the rewards and punishments the parents impose on the child's behavior and from the type of role models the parents provide. Even though they may not resemble their parents, children are influenced by them. The contrasting possibilities of these influences are described by two brothers in Sinclair Lewis' novel *Work of Art*. Each brother ascribes his personality to his home surroundings.

> My father [said Ora] was a sloppy, lazy, booze-hoisting old bum, and my mother didn't know much besides cooking, and she was too busy to give me much attention, and the kids I knew were a bunch of foul-mouthed loafers that used to hang around the hoboes up near the water tank, and I never had a chance to get any formal schooling, and I got thrown on my own as just a brat. So naturally I've become a sort of vagabond that can't be bored by thinking about his "debts" to a lot of little shopkeeping lice, and I suppose I'm inclined to be

different backgrounds are Oskar Stohr and Jack Yufe. Born in Trinidad of a Jewish father and a German mother, they were separated shortly after birth. The mother took Oskar to Germany, where he was raised by his grandmother as a Catholic and a Nazi. Jack remained with his father, was raised as a Jew, and spent part of his youth on an Israeli kibbutz. Although the families never corresponded, and the two brothers now lead quite different lives, remarkable similarities were evident when the pair met for the first time to participate in the study. Both men have mustaches and wear wire-rimmed glasses. Their mannerisms and temperaments are similar, and they share certain idiosyncrasies: both like spicy foods and sweet liqueurs, are absentminded, flush the toilet before using it, and like to dip buttered toast in their coffee. Oskar tends to yell at his wife; Jack did also before he and his wife separated.

Another pair of twins with fairly different backgrounds are now British housewives who were separated during World War II and were raised by families of different socioeconomic status. Both twins, who had never met before, startled the experimenters by arriving for their interviews wearing seven rings on their fingers! Before we conclude that a fondness for rings is inherited, however, we should consider the more likely possibility that the twins inherited their pretty hands, thereby prompting their interest in rings. Despite the differences in their socioeconomic backgrounds, the twins showed striking similarities on many of the tests. Both performed about the same on ability tests, although the twin raised in the lower-class environment achieved a slightly higher score.

In the absence of carefully analyzed data, it is easy to be impressed by the personality similarities between twins and to ignore the differences. Nevertheless, the preliminary findings have surprised investigators, who note that the scores of the twins on many of the ability and personality tests were closer than would be expected if the same person took the test twice. Looking at the data obtained from all of the twin pairs, the greatest concordance has been in ability test scores, brain-wave patterns, sociability, and what might be called "tempo" or "energy level."

Even when the results are tabulated, they will not be definitive, because the sample will still be small. The discovery of personality *differences* between members of a twin pair may turn out to be more significant than the discovery of similarities. If identical twins are found to differ on some variable, we know that the variable is not genetically determined.

---

lazy, and not too scrupulous about the dames and the liquor. But my early rearing did have one swell result. Brought up so unconventionally, I'll always be an Anti-Puritan. I'll never deny the joys of the flesh and the sanctity of beauty.

My father [said Myron] was pretty easy-going and always did like drinking and swapping stories with the boys, and my mother was hard-driven taking care of us, and I heard a lot of filth from the hoboes up near the water tank. Maybe just sort of as a reaction I've become almost too much of a crank about paying debts, and fussing over my work, and being scared of liquor and women. But my rearing did have one swell result. Just by way of contrast, it made me a good, sound, old-fashioned New English Puritan. (Lewis, 1934, p. 278)

Although such divergent reactions to the same early environment are unlikely to occur in real life, individuals do respond differently to similar circumstances.

Beyond a unique biological inheritance and the specific ways in which the culture is transmitted, the individual is shaped by particular experiences. An illness accompanied by a long period of convalescence may create a fondness for being cared for and waited on that profoundly affects the personality. The death of a parent may disrupt the usual sex-role identifications. A traumatic accident, an opportunity to display heroism, leaving friends to move to another part of the country — countless personal experiences such as these influence development.

The individual's common and unique experiences interact with inherited potential to shape personality. How this occurs and how the resulting personality can best be described have been the subject of many theories. Most personality theories can be grouped into one of four classes: trait, social learning, psychoanalytic, or phenomenological. In the remainder of this chapter, we will briefly describe these theoretical approaches and provide examples of some of the methods used to assess personality. Personality cannot be studied scientifically unless there are satisfactory ways of measuring personality variables.

TRAIT APPROACH

The *trait approach* to personality attempts to isolate and to describe the basic properties of the individual that direct behavior. This approach focuses on the public personality and is concerned more with personality description and prediction of behavior than with personality development. Trait theories assume that people vary on a number of personality *dimensions*, or *scales*, each representing a *trait*. Thus, we could rate an individual on scales of intelligence, emotional stability, aggressiveness, and so on. To arrive at a global description of personality, we would need to know how the individual rated on a number of dimensions.

A trait refers to any characteristic that differs from person to person in a relatively permanent and consistent way. When we informally describe ourselves and others with such adjectives as "aggressive," "cautious," "excitable," "intelligent," or "anxious," we are using trait terms. Psychologists working in the area of trait theory are concerned with determining the basic traits that provide a meaningful description of personality and finding ways to measure these traits.

Determining Basic Traits

The English language contains thousands of words that refer to characteristics of behavior. How do we reduce these to a manageable number of traits that are meaningful in describing personality? One approach uses *factor analysis* (see p. 401). As we noted in Chapter 12, factor analysis is a complex statistical technique for reducing a large number of measures to a smaller number of independent dimensions.

For example, suppose you select a large number of words that describe personality characteristics and arrange them in pairs representing opposites (tidy–careless, calm–anxious, responsive–insensitive, cooperative–negativistic, and so on). You ask a group of people to rate their friends on each of these word pairs. Subjecting these ratings to factor analysis would yield a fairly small number of dimensions, or *factors*, that would account for most of the intercorrelations among the ratings. The five trait dimensions listed in Table 13-2 were

TABLE 13-2

Traits and Their Components   *The table presents five traits identified in a study using factor analysis. The adjective pairs describe the two ends of the scales for each dimension. (After Norman, 1963)*

TRAIT DIMENSION	DESCRIPTIVE ADJECTIVE PAIRS
Extraversion	Talkative – Silent Open – Secretive Adventurous – Cautious
Agreeableness	Good-natured – Irritable Gentle – Headstrong Cooperative – Negativistic
Conscientiousness	Tidy – Careless Responsible – Undependable Persevering – Quitting
Emotional stability	Calm – Anxious Poised – Nervous Not hypochondriacal – Hypochondriacal
Culture	Artistically sensitive – Artistically insensitive Refined – Boorish Intellectual – Unreflective

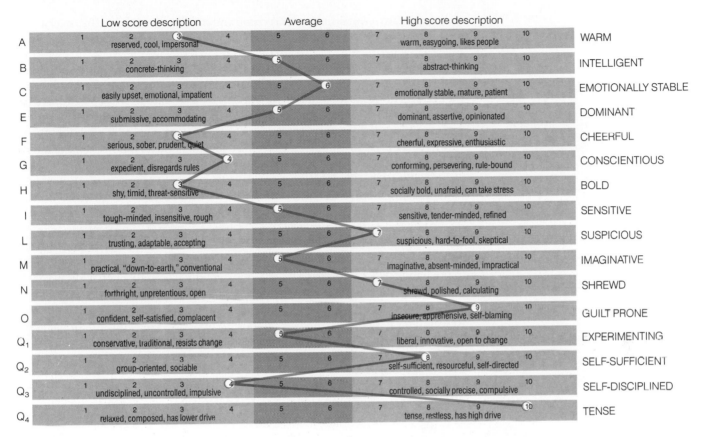

	Low score description	Average	High score description	
A	reserved, cool, impersonal		warm, easygoing, likes people	WARM
B	concrete-thinking		abstract-thinking	INTELLIGENT
C	easily upset, emotional, impatient		emotionally stable, mature, patient	EMOTIONALLY STABLE
E	submissive, accommodating		dominant, assertive, opinionated	DOMINANT
F	serious, sober, prudent, quiet		cheerful, expressive, enthusiastic	CHEERFUL
G	expedient, disregards rules		conforming, persevering, rule-bound	CONSCIENTIOUS
H	shy, timid, threat-sensitive		socially bold, unafraid, can take stress	BOLD
I	tough-minded, insensitive, rough		sensitive, tender-minded, refined	SENSITIVE
L	trusting, adaptable, accepting		suspicious, hard-to-fool, skeptical	SUSPICIOUS
M	practical, "down-to-earth," conventional		imaginative, absent-minded, impractical	IMAGINATIVE
N	forthright, unpretentious, open		shrewd, polished, calculating	SHREWD
O	confident, self-satisfied, complacent		insecure, apprehensive, self-blaming	GUILT PRONE
Q_1	conservative, traditional, resists change		liberal, innovative, open to change	EXPERIMENTING
Q_2	group-oriented, sociable		self-sufficient, resourceful, self-directed	SELF-SUFFICIENT
Q_3	undisciplined, uncontrolled, impulsive		controlled, socially precise, compulsive	SELF-DISCIPLINED
Q_4	relaxed, composed, has lower drive		tense, restless, has high drive	TENSE

FIGURE 13-2

Personality Profiles *The trait names represent the 16 personality factors obtained by factor analysis of a large number of ratings. Factors A – O were obtained from factor analyses of ratings of one person by another; the 4 Q factors were found only in data from self-ratings. A personality test based on the 16 factors measures the level of each factor, and the scores can be graphed as a profile. (After Cattell, 1986)*

found in several studies that used this type of procedure (Norman, 1963; Digman & Inouye, 1986).

The most extensive study of personality traits has been conducted by Raymond Cattell, who has collected data over three decades from questionnaires, personality tests, and observations of behavior in real-life situations. Cattell has identified 16 factors that he believes are the basic traits underlying personality. These factors and the adjectives describing them are shown in Figure 13-2.

Cattell has devised a questionnaire to measure his 16 traits: the Sixteen Personality Factor Questionnaire (16 PF, for short). The yes or no answers that a subject gives to more than 100 questions are compiled to yield a score for each factor. For example, answering no to the question "Do you tend to keep in the background on social occasions?" will earn a point toward the "dominant" side of the scale. By plotting an individual's test score for each factor, we arrive at a *personality profile* — a kind of shorthand description of the individual's personality. A typical profile is shown in Figure 13-2.

Evaluation of Trait Approach

Although the trait approach appears to be an objective, scientific way to study personality, some problems arise when this method is used. The personality factors found in a given study often depend on the type of data being analyzed (for example, self-ratings versus ratings of one person by another) and the specific factor-analytic technique used. Some investigators have identified as few as 5 factors as the basic dimensions of personality; others, more than 20.

Despite the lack of agreement on the number of basic personality traits, some overlap does occur. Two dimensions found in most factor-analytic studies of personality are *introversion – extraversion* and *stability – instability*. Introversion – extraversion refers to the degree to which a person's basic orientation is turned inward toward the self or outward toward the external world. At the introversion end of the scale are individuals who are shy and prefer to work alone; they tend to withdraw into themselves, particularly in times of emotional stress or conflict. At the extraversion end are individuals who are sociable and prefer occupations that permit them to work directly with other people; in times of stress, they seek company. Stability – instability is a dimension of emotionality, with calm, well-adjusted, reliable individuals at the stable end and moody, anxious, temperamental, and unreliable individuals at the other.

Another criticism of the trait approach is that behavior may vary widely from one situation to another. A young boy who obtains a high score on the "dominant" factor of the 16 PF may assume a dominant role with his schoolmates but not with his parents and teachers; even with his peers, he may be aggressive on some occasions and docile on others. As we will see later, tests designed to measure traits have not been as successful as psychologists would like in predicting behavior across a variety of situations. To predict behavior, we need to know how personal characteristics — tendencies to be sociable, aggressive, anxious, and so on — are influenced by particular environmental conditions. Research results indicate that the *interaction* between traits and situational variables is the most important factor.

SOCIAL-LEARNING APPROACH

Trait theorists focus on *personal* determinants of behavior. They assume that traits predispose the individual to respond consistently in different situations. Situations have some impact: Tom does not respond as aggressively when an attractive waitress accidently spills a cup of coffee on him as he does when a truck driver cuts in front of him in congested traffic. But trait theorists assume that Tom will behave more aggressively in both situations than will Mike, who scores lower on the aggression scale of the 16 PF Questionnaire.

Social-learning theory, in contrast, emphasizes the importance of *environmental,* or *situational,* determinants of behavior. For social-learning theorists, behavior is the result of a continuous interaction between personal and environmental variables. Environmental conditions shape behavior through learning; a person's behavior, in turn, shapes the environment. Persons and situations influence each other reciprocally. To predict behavior, we need to know how the characteristics of the individual interact with the characteristics of the situation.

Reinforcement and Social Learning

The effect of other people — the rewards and punishments they provide — is an important influence on an individual's behavior. According to social-learning theory, individual differences in behavior result in large part from differences in the kinds of learning experiences a person encounters in the course of growing up. Some behavior patterns are learned through direct experience: the individual is rewarded or punished for behaving in a certain manner. But a person acquires many responses without direct reinforcement, through *observational,* or *vicarious, learning* (see Chapter 11, p. 370). People can learn by observing the actions of others and by noting the consequences of those actions. It would be a slow and inefficient process indeed if all of our behavior had to be learned through the

Social learning

direct reinforcement of our responses. According to social-learning theorists, reinforcement is not *necessary* for learning, although it may *facilitate* learning by focusing the individual's attention in the appropriate direction.

Although reinforcement is not necessary for learning, it is crucial to the *performance* of learned behavior. A main assumption of social-learning theory is that people behave in ways that are likely to produce reinforcement. A person's repertoire of learned behaviors is extensive; the particular action chosen in a specific situation depends on the expected outcome. Most adolescent girls know how to fight, having watched male classmates or TV characters aggress by hitting with the fist, kicking, and so on. But since this kind of behavior is seldom reinforced in girls, it is unlikely to occur except under unusual circumstances.

The reinforcement that controls the expression of learned behavior may be *direct* (tangible rewards, social approval or disapproval, or alleviation of aversive conditions), *vicarious* (observation of someone receiving reward or punishment for behavior similar to one's own), or *self-administered* (evaluation of one's own performance with self-praise or self-reproach).

Person-Situation Interaction

According to social-learning theorists, a person's actions in a given situation depend on the specific characteristics of the situation, the individual's appraisal of the situation, and past reinforcement for behavior in similar situations (or observations of others in similar situations). People behave consistently insofar as the situations they encounter and the roles they are expected to play remain relatively stable.

Most social behaviors, however, are not uniformly rewarded in all settings. The individual learns to discriminate the contexts in which certain behavior is appropriate and those in which it is not. To the extent that a person is rewarded for the same response in many different situations, *generalization* takes place, ensuring that the same behavior will occur in a variety of settings. Thus, a boy whose father reinforces him for physical aggression at home, as well as at school and at play, will probably develop a personality that is pervasively aggressive. But, more often, aggressive responses are differentially rewarded, and learned *discriminations* determine the situations in which the individual will display aggression (for example, aggression is acceptable on the football field but not in the classroom).

PERSON VARIABLES   In predicting how a person will behave in a specific situation, social-learning theorists emphasize the importance of individual differences in cognitive development and in social-learning experiences over motivational traits (such as aggression or dependency). Some of the individual differences, or *person variables,* that interact with situational conditions to influence behavior are listed here.

1. *Competencies: What can you do?* Competencies include intellectual abilities, social and physical skills, and other special abilities.
2. *Encoding strategies: How do you see it?* People differ in the way they selectively attend to information, encode (represent) events, and group the information into meaningful categories. An event perceived by one person as threatening may be seen as challenging by another.
3. *Expectancies: What will happen?* Expectations about the consequences of different behaviors will guide the individual's choice of behavior. If you cheat on an examination and are caught, what do you expect the consequences to be? If you tell your friend what you really think of him or her, what will happen to your

Environments can be self-generated.

relationship? Expectations about our own abilities will also influence behavior: we may anticipate the consequences of a certain behavior but fail to act because we are uncertain of our ability to execute the behavior.

4. *Subjective values: What is it worth?* Individuals who have similar expectancies may choose to behave differently because they assign different values to the outcomes. Two students may expect a certain behavior to please their professor; however, this outcome is important to one student but is not important to the other.

5. *Self-regulatory systems and plans: How can you achieve it?* People differ in the standards and rules they adopt for regulating their behavior (including self-imposed rewards for success or punishments for failure), as well as in their ability to make realistic plans for reaching a goal. (After Mischel, 1986, pp. 305–13)

All of these person variables (sometimes referred to as cognitive social-learning person variables) interact with the conditions of a particular situation to determine what an individual will do in that situation.

SELF-GENERATED ENVIRONMENTS We are not simply passive reactors to situational conditions. The relationship between our behavior and the situations we encounter in life is reciprocal. Through our own actions, we produce the environmental conditions that affect our behavior. To use a simple experimental example, consider a rat in a Skinner box with an electrically charged grid for a floor. A brief shock is scheduled to occur each minute, but the animal can avoid the shocks by pressing a bar. The animals that learn the controlling behavior can create a punishment-free environment; the slow learners experience an unpleasant situation. Thus, the *potential environment* is the same for all animals, but the *actual environment* depends on their behavior (Bandura, 1977).

In a similar way, we choose and influence our own life situations. First, we prefer to enter and spend time in situations that make us feel comfortable. These are usually situations that encourage the expression of our characteristic attitudes and dispositions or that sustain our conceptions of ourselves. Thus, extraverts are much more likely than introverts to seek out stimulating social situations that involve assertiveness, competitiveness, and intimacy (Furnham, 1981); sensation seekers choose activities that provide thrills (Zuckerman, 1979); and people concerned with maintaining their images of self-competence choose settings where success will enhance their image as competent and where failure can be attributed to external circumstances, thereby not threatening their image (Jones & Berglas, 1978).

Second, once we enter a situation—whether or not it is of our choosing—much of what happens is determined by our own actions. A highly competitive individual can manage to turn even a noncompetitive situation into a challenging one. A person who acts abrasively will elicit hostility from others, whereas one who behaves in a warm and friendly manner will be responded to in kind. Situations are partly of our own devising.

Evaluation of Social-learning Approach

Social-learning theory, through its emphasis on specifying the environmental variables that elicit specific behaviors, has made a major contribution to both clinical psychology and personality theory. It has led us to see human actions as reactions to specific environments, and it has helped us to focus on the way in which environments control our behavior and how they can be changed to modify behavior. As we will see in Chapter 16, the careful application of learning principles has proved successful in changing maladaptive behavior.

Social-learning theorists have been criticized for overemphasizing the importance of situational influences on behavior and thus "losing the person" in personality psychology (Carlson, 1971). As we will see later, many personality theorists are unwilling to concede that personality has as little stability as social-learning theory implies.

PSYCHOANALYTIC APPROACH

Psychoanalytic theory approaches personality from a viewpoint that is quite different from either of the two theories discussed so far. Both trait and social-learning theories focus on the public personality; they are concerned primarily with behavior. Psychoanalytic theories, in contrast, explore the private personality — the *unconscious* motives that direct behavior. Psychoanalytic theory is also concerned with the way in which personality develops.

Freud's theories, formulated during 50 years of treating emotionally disturbed persons, fill 24 volumes. His final treatise, *Outline of Psychoanalysis*, was published in 1940, a year after his death. We can present only the barest outline of Freud's theory of personality here.

Freud compared the human mind to an iceberg. The small part that shows above the surface of the water represents *conscious experience;* the much larger mass below water level represents the *unconscious*, a storehouse of impulses, passions, and inaccessible memories that affect our thoughts and behavior. It was this unconscious portion of the mind that Freud sought to explore by the technique of *free association*, which requires the person to talk about everything that comes into his or her consciousness, no matter how ridiculous or trivial it might seem. By analyzing free associations, including the recall of dreams and early childhood memories, Freud sought to help his patients become aware of much that had been unconscious and thereby to discover the basic determinants of personality.

Personality Structure

Freud believed that personality is composed of three major systems: the *id*, the *ego*, and the *superego*. Each system has its own functions, but the three interact to govern behavior.

THE ID The *id* is the most primitive part of the personality, from which the ego and the superego later develop. It is present in the newborn infant and consists of the basic biological impulses (or drives): the need to eat, to drink, to eliminate wastes, to avoid pain, and to gain sexual pleasure. Freud believed that aggression is also a basic biological drive (see Chapter 11). The id seeks immediate gratification of these impulses. Like a young child, the id operates on the *pleasure principle:* it endeavors to avoid pain and to obtain pleasure, regardless of the external circumstances.

THE EGO Children soon learn that their impulses cannot always be gratified immediately. Hunger must wait until someone provides food. The satisfaction of relieving bladder or bowel pressure must be delayed until the bathroom is reached. Certain impulses — hitting someone or playing with the genitals — may elicit punishment from a parent. A new part of the personality, the *ego*, develops as the young child learns to consider the demands of reality. The ego obeys the

"Very well, I'll introduce you. Ego, meet Id. Now get back to work."

reality principle: the gratification of impulses must be delayed until the appropriate environmental conditions are found. For example, taking the real world into consideration, the ego delays satisfaction of sexual impulses until conditions are appropriate. It is essentially the "executive" of the personality: it decides what actions are appropriate and which id impulses will be satisfied and in what manner. The ego mediates among the demands of the id, the realities of the world, and the demands of the superego.

THE SUPEREGO   The third part of the personality, the *superego,* is the internalized representation of the values and morals of society as taught to the child by the parents and others. It is essentially the individual's conscience. The superego judges whether an action is right or wrong. The id seeks pleasure, the ego tests reality, and the superego strives for perfection. The superego develops in response to parental rewards and punishments. It incorporates all the actions for which the child is punished or reprimanded, as well as all the actions for which the child is rewarded.

Initially, parents control children's behavior directly by reward and punishment. Through the incorporation of parental standards into the superego, a child brings behavior under control. Children no longer need anyone to tell them it is wrong to steal; their superego tells them. Violation of the superego's standards, or even the impulse to do so, produces anxiety over the loss of parental love. According to Freud, this anxiety is largely unconscious; the *conscious* emotion is guilt. If parental standards are overly rigid, the individual may be guilt-ridden and inhibit all aggressive or sexual impulses. In contrast, an individual who fails to incorporate any standards for acceptable social behavior will have few behavioral constraints and may engage in excessively self-indulgent or criminal behavior. Such a person is considered to have a weak superego.

Sometimes the three components of personality are in opposition: the ego postpones the gratification that the id wants immediately, and the superego battles with both the id and the ego because behavior often falls short of the moral code it represents. But more often in the normal person, the three work together to produce integrated behavior.

ANXIETY AND DEFENSES AGAINST IT   Freud believed that the conflict between the id impulses (primarily sexual and aggressive instincts) and the restraining influences of the ego and the superego constitutes the motivating source of much behavior. Because society condemns free expression of aggression and sexual behavior, such impulses cannot be expressed immediately and directly. Children learn early that they should not handle their genitals in public or hit their siblings. They eventually internalize parental restrictions on impulse satisfaction, thereby forming the superego. The more restraints a society (or its representatives, the parents) places on impulse expression, the greater the potential for conflict among the three parts of the personality.

The desires of the id are powerful forces that must be expressed in some way; prohibiting their expression does not abolish them. Individuals with an urge to do something for which they will be punished become anxious. One way of reducing anxiety is to express the impulse in disguised form, thereby avoiding punishment by society and condemnation by the superego. Aggressive impulses, for example, may be displaced to racing sports cars or to championing political causes.

Another method of reducing anxiety, called *repression,* is to push the impulse out of awareness into the unconscious. These methods of anxiety reduction, called *defense mechanisms,* are means of defending oneself against painful anxiety. They are never totally successful in relieving tension, and the residue may spill over in the form of nervousness or restlessness — which, as Freud pointed out, is the price we must pay for being civilized. Presumably, a society that placed no restrictions on free expression of the id's instincts would produce people who were completely free of anxiety or tension. But such a society would probably not survive; all societies must place some restrictions on behavior for the well-being of the group.

Defense mechanisms form the basis of Freud's theory of maladaptive behavior and will be examined more fully in Chapter 14. At this point, we will note only that people differ in the balance among their id, ego, and superego systems and in the defenses they use to deal with anxiety. The individual's approach to a problem situation reflects his or her manner of coping with the conflicting demands of the id, the ego, and the superego.

Personality Development

Freud believed that during the first five years of life, the individual progresses through several developmental stages that affect personality. Applying a broad definition of sexuality, he called these periods *psychosexual stages*. During each stage, the pleasure-seeking impulses of the id (the libido) focus on a particular area of the body and on activities connected with that area.

Freud called the first year of life the *oral stage* of psychosexual development. During this period, infants derive pleasure from nursing and sucking. Indeed, they will put their thumb or anything else they can reach into their mouths. During the second year of life, the *anal stage*, children have their first experience with imposed control in the form of toilet training. Gratification presumably is derived from withholding or expelling feces. In the *phallic stage*, from about age 3 to age 6, children begin to derive pleasure from fondling their genitals. They observe the differences between males and females and may direct their awakening sexual impulses toward the parent of the opposite sex.

A *latency period* follows the end of the phallic stage, and during this time children become less concerned with their bodies and turn their attention to the skills needed for coping with the environment. The final period, the *genital stage*, occurs during adolescence. Youngsters begin to turn their sexual interests toward others and become capable of loving in a mature way.

Freud felt that special problems at any stage could arrest (or fixate) development and have a lasting effect on the individual's personality. The libido would remain attached to the activities appropriate for that stage. Thus, a person who was weaned very early and who did not have enough sucking pleasure might become *fixated* at the oral stage. As an adult, this person may be excessively dependent on others and overly fond of such oral pleasures as eating, drinking, and smoking. Such a person is called an oral personality. The person fixated at the anal stage of psychosexual development may be abnormally concerned with cleanliness, orderliness, and saving and may tend to resist external pressure.

Modifications of Freud's Theories

Later psychoanalysts felt that Freud placed too much emphasis on the instinctive and biological aspects of personality and failed to recognize that people are products of the society in which they live. The neo-Freudians — including Alfred Adler, Karen Horney, Erich Fromm, and Harry Stack Sullivan — considered personality to be shaped more by the people, society, and culture surrounding the individual than by the individual's biological needs. They placed less emphasis on the controlling power of the unconscious, believing that people are more rational in their planning and decisions than Freud had thought.

More recent psychoanalytic theorists have stressed the role of the ego. *Ego analysts* — such as Heinz Hartman and David Rapaport — believe that the ego is

Toilet training is one of the child's first experiences with imposed control.

present at birth, develops independently of the id, and performs functions in addition to finding realistic ways of satisfying id impulses. These ego functions are learning how to cope with the environment and making sense of experience. Ego satisfactions include exploration, manipulation, and competency in performance. This approach ties the concept of the ego more closely to cognitive processes. Contemporary psychoanalysts have not rejected the concept of the id or the importance of biological drives in motivating behavior. But they have an equal interest in such questions as the degree of psychological separateness from parents, the degree of attachment to and involvement with other people versus self-preoccupation, and the strength of the individual's feelings of self-esteem and competency.

Evaluation of Psychoanalytic Approach

Psychoanalytic theory has had an enormous impact on psychological and philosophical conceptions of human nature. Freud's major contributions are his recognition that unconscious needs and conflicts motivate much of our behavior and his emphasis on the importance of early childhood experiences in personality development. His emphasis on sexual factors led to an awareness of their role in adjustment problems and paved the way for the scientific study of sexuality. But Freud made his observations during the Victorian period, when sexual standards were very strict. So it is understandable that many of his patients' conflicts centered on their sexual desires. Today, feelings of guilt about sex are less frequent, but the incidence of mental illness remains about the same. Sexual conflicts are not the only cause of personality disturbances — and may not even be a major cause.

Some critics also point out that Freud's theory of personality is based almost entirely on his observations of emotionally disturbed individuals and may not be an appropriate description of the normal, healthy personality. In addition, many of Freud's ideas were decidedly sexist. For example, his theory that female psychosexual development is shaped by "penis envy" — and by the accompanying feelings of unworthiness due to the lack of such equipment — is certainly inadequate in view of our current awareness of the role that social factors play in gender identification (Chodorow, 1978). It was probably not her brother's penis that a little girl during the Victorian era envied but his greater independence, power, and social status.

Although psychoanalysis has exerted a powerful influence on our thinking about human nature, it has been seriously questioned as a scientific theory. Freud's constructs are ambiguous and difficult to define. He does not specify, for example, what behaviors indicate that a child is fixated at the anal stage of psychosexual development and what behaviors indicate that he or she is not fixated. Research efforts to identify oral and anal personality types suggest that the parents' characteristic ways of handling the child (for example, continual demands for neatness and precision or attempts to make the child excessively dependent) have more influence on later personality than do specific events that occur during particular psychosexual stages.

Psychoanalytic theory assumes that very different behaviors may be signs of the same underlying impulse or conflict. For example, a mother who feels resentful of her child may be punitive and abusive, or she may deny her hostile impulses by becoming overly concerned and protective toward the child — what Freud would call a *reaction formation* (see Chapter 14). When opposing behaviors are said to result from the same underlying motive, it is difficult to confirm the presence or absence of the motive. And, in turn, it is difficult to make theoretical predictions that can be empirically verified.

Most of the psychoanalysts who modified and expanded Freud's theories were interested in concepts that would help them understand their patients; they had little or no training in theory construction or research methods. Recently, there has been a renewed interest in reformulating psychoanalytic theory in testable terms and subjecting the theory to experimental evaluation (Silverman & Weinberger, 1985).

PHENOMENOLOGICAL APPROACH

The phenomenological approach to the study of personality focuses on the individual's *subjective experience* — his or her personal view of the world. Phenomenological theories differ from the theories we have discussed so far in that they generally are not concerned with the person's motivational history or with predicting behavior. They focus instead on how the individual perceives and interprets events — on the individual's *phenomenology*.

In a sense, the phenomenological approach is a reaction against both the psychoanalytic view that human beings are motivated by unconscious impulses and the behaviorists' emphasis on overt behavior. Rather than looking at objective measures of a situation or delving into childhood motives, phenomenologists focus on the individual's subjective view of what is taking place now. While most personality theories look at the individual from the outside, phenomenological theories attempt to enter into the person's own psychological experience — to understand how that particular person interprets and experiences the world.

The phenomenological approach to personality includes concepts that have been labeled "humanistic" (because they focus on the qualities that differentiate humans from animals — namely, self-direction and freedom of choice) and "self" theories (because they deal with the subjective, internal experiences that constitute a person's sense of being). Most phenomenological theories also emphasize the positive nature of human beings and their push toward personal growth and *self-actualization*. Some of the features of the phenomenological approach to personality will become clearer as we discuss the views of one of its leading spokesmen, the late Carl Rogers.

Rogers' Self Theory

Like Freud, Rogers developed his theory from his work with emotionally troubled people (Rogers, 1951, 1977). Rogers was impressed with what he saw as the individual's innate tendency to move in the direction of growth, maturity, and positive change. He came to believe that the basic force motivating the human organism is self-actualization — a tendency toward fulfillment or actualization of all the capacities of the organism. A growing organism seeks to fulfill its potential within the limits of its heredity. A person may not always clearly perceive which actions lead to growth and which actions are regressive. But once the course is clear, the individual chooses to grow rather than to regress. Rogers does not deny that there are other needs, some of them biological, but he sees them as subservient to the organism's motivation to enhance itself.

Rogers' belief in the primacy of self-actualization forms the basis of his "nondirective" or *person-centered therapy*. This method of psychotherapy assumes that every individual (given the proper circumstances) has the motivation and ability to change and that the individual himself is the best qualified to decide on the direction that such change should take. The therapist's role is to act as a sounding board while the individual explores and analyzes his or her problems.

Carl Rogers writing on the phenomenological approach *"The best vantage point for understanding behavior is from the internal frame of reference of the individual himself."*
"The organism has one basic tendency and striving — to actualize, maintain, and enhance the experiencing organism."
"When the individual perceives and accepts into one consistent and integrated system all his sensory and visceral experiences, then he is necessarily more understanding of others and is more accepting of others as separate individuals." (Rogers, 1951)

This approach differs from psychoanalytic therapy, during which the therapist analyzes the patient's history to determine the problem and devise a course of remedial action. (See Chapter 16 for a discussion of various approaches to psychotherapy.)

The central concept in Rogers' theory of personality is the *self*. Rogers admits that at first he was reluctant to use the concept of self because he felt it was not scientific:

> Speaking personally, I began my work with the settled notion that "self" was a vague, ambiguous, scientifically meaningless term which had gone out of the psychologist's vocabulary with the departure of the introspectionists. Consequently I was slow in recognizing that when clients were given the opportunity to express their problems and their attitudes in their own terms, without any guidance or interpretation, they tended to talk in terms of the self. Characteristic expressions were attitudes such as these: "I feel I'm not being my real self." "I wonder who I am, really." "I wouldn't want anyone to know the real me." "I never had a chance to be myself." "It feels good to let myself go and just *be* myself here." "I think if I chip off the plaster façade I've got a pretty solid self—a good substantial brick building, underneath." It seemed clear from such expressions that the self was an important element in the experience of the client, and that in some odd sense his goal was to become his "real self." (Rogers, 1959, pp. 200–201)

The self, or self-concept, (Rogers uses the terms interchangeably) became the cornerstone of Rogers' theory. The self consists of all the ideas, perceptions, and values that characterize "I" or "me"; it includes the awareness of "what I am" and "what I can do." This perceived self, in turn, influences both the person's perception of the world and his or her behavior. For example, a woman who perceives herself as strong and competent views the world quite differently and acts differently than does a woman who considers herself weak and ineffectual. The self-concept does not necessarily reflect reality: a person may be highly successful and respected but still view himself or herself as a failure.

According to Rogers, the individual evaluates every experience in relation to this self-concept. People want to behave in ways that are consistent with their self-image; experiences and feelings that are not consistent are threatening and may be denied admittance to consciousness. This is essentially Freud's concept of repression, although Rogers feels that such repression is neither necessary nor permanent. (Freud would say that repression is inevitable and that some aspects of the individual's experiences always remain unconscious.)

The more areas of experience that a person denies, because they are inconsistent with his or her self-concept, the wider the gulf between the self and reality and the greater the potential for maladjustment. An individual whose self-concept is incongruent with personal feelings and experiences must defend himself or herself against the truth because the truth will result in anxiety. If the incongruence becomes too great, the defenses may break down, resulting in severe anxiety or other forms of emotional disturbance. The well-adjusted person, in contrast, has a self-concept that is consistent with thought, experience, and behavior; the self is not rigid, but flexible, and can change as it assimilates new experiences and ideas.

The other self in Rogers' theory is the *ideal self*. We all have a conception of the kind of person we would like to be. The closer the ideal self is to the real self, the more fulfilled and happy the individual becomes. A large discrepancy between the ideal self and the real self results in an unhappy, dissatisfied person.

Thus, two kinds of incongruence can develop: one, between the self and the experiences of reality; the other, between the self and the ideal self. Rogers has some hypotheses about how these incongruences may develop.

Development of the Self

Because the child's behavior is continually being evaluated by parents and others (sometimes positively and sometimes negatively), the child soon learns to discriminate between thoughts and actions that are considered worthy and those that are not. In order to retain the *positive regard* of others (a need that Rogers assumes is universal), unworthy experiences are excluded from the self-concept, even though they may be quite valid. For example, relieving physiological tension in the bowel or bladder is a pleasurable experience for the child. However, unless the child urinates or defecates privately and in the proper place, parents usually condemn such activities as "bad" or "naughty." To retain the parents' positive regard, the child must deny his or her own experience — that defecating or urinating provides satisfaction.

Feelings of competition and hostility toward a younger sibling who has usurped the center of attention are natural. But parents disapprove of hitting a baby brother or sister and usually punish such actions. Children must somehow integrate this experience into their self-concept. They may decide that they are bad and so may feel ashamed. They may decide that their parents do not like them and so may feel rejected. Or they may deny their feelings and decide they do not want to hit the baby. Each of these attitudes contains a distortion of the truth. The third alternative is the easiest for children to accept; but in so doing, they deny their real feelings, which then become unconscious. The more people are forced to deny their own feelings and to accept the values of others, the more uncomfortable they will feel about themselves.

Obviously, there must be certain restrictions on behavior. Sanitary considerations require some restraints on defecating and urinating, and children cannot be permitted to beat their siblings. Rogers suggests that the best approach is for the parents to recognize the child's feelings as valid while explaining their own feelings and the reasons for restraint.

Other Perspectives on the Self

In recent years, there has been a renewed interest in the importance of the self-concept in understanding personality. The research has studied two main areas. Cognitive psychologists have focused on the self-concept as a memory structure that guides the processing of information. Social psychologists are interested in the way a person's self-concept shapes and is shaped by social interactions. Let us look at a few examples of research in both areas.

SELF-CONCEPTS AND COGNITION In Chapter 1, we distinguished between the cognitive and phenomenological approaches to the study of psychology. In many instances, however, the different approaches we described there overlap; it is difficult to classify a particular theory or theorist into a single category. In a broad sense, Rogers' theory of personality is cognitive because it is concerned with how we perceive and understand the world and ourselves. It is also phenomenological, because it is based on the individual's report of his or her subjective experiences rather than measures of overt behavior or observations by others. For example, in studies of the outcome of person-centered psychotherapy, personal growth is often assessed by comparing the congruence between the individual's description of his "real self" and his "ideal self" at different points in time — say, at the beginning of psychotherapy and after six months of treatment. A greater congruence between the two selves, as reported by the individual, is a measure of the personal growth achieved through psychotherapy. Thus, self-reports, rather than observations of behavior, form the basis of Rogers' theories.

Other psychologists, taking a cognitive approach, view the self as a system of self-concepts, or *self-schemata*, that organize and guide the processing of information relevant to the self. As noted in earlier chapters, schemata are cognitive structures stored in memory that are abstract representations of events, objects, and relationships in the real world. Self-schemata are generalizations, or theories, about the self derived from past experience. Over the course of a lifetime, we become increasingly aware of the distinctive characteristics of our appearance, temperament, abilities, and preferences. We become experts about ourselves. We may come to understand that we are shy, creative, stubborn, intimidated by large groups, a loving parent, and so forth. At the same time, we come to know a good deal about what it means to be "shy," "stubborn," or "a loving parent." These generalizations about the self, or self-schemata, organize and guide the way we process information relevant to ourselves. We search for information that is congruent with our self-schemata, and we direct our behavior so that it is consistent with the schemata (Markus & Sentis, 1982).

Suppose, for example, that you privately disagree with an opinion expressed by your roommate, but publicly you indicate agreement with the opinion. If "tactful" and "independent" are prominent self-schemata for you, you are likely to interpret your behavior in this situation (publicly agreeing while privately disagreeing) as demonstrating tact rather than conformity. If, on the other hand, "compliant" and "nonassertive" are prominent self-schemata for you, you are apt to view your behavior as another disgusting example of your inability to assert yourself.

Cognitive psychologists, in contrast to phenomenologists, usually test their ideas about the self in laboratory experiments. These experiments have shown that our self-schemata do influence the way we process personally relevant information. Individuals who have a well-articulated self-schema for a particular domain — such as independence – dependence — can make judgments about themselves more readily than can individuals who have no firm view of themselves as either dependent or independent. That is, they can decide more quickly whether trait adjectives related to this domain (such as "conforming," "obliging," "self-sufficient") apply to them than can individuals for whom the independent – dependent dimension is not an important part of their self-concept. Similar results have been found for other personality dimensions, such as masculinity – femininity or extraversion – introversion (Markus & Smith, 1981).

Our self-schemata also influence the way we attend to and recall information. We spend more time scrutinizing feedback that confirms our self-concepts than we do attending to information that is discrepant with them (Swann & Read, 1981). And we remember confirmatory information better than information that contradicts our self-schemata. In fact, we may find reasons to dismiss feedback that does not fit our self-schemata (Markus, 1977), or we may twist the facts in ways that allow us to remain confident in our self-concepts (Simon & Feather, 1973). These findings suggest that self-concepts help us integrate our experiences and thereby create a more stable world. Since self-schemata are resistant to discrepant feedback, it is not surprising that people's self-concepts are sometimes at odds with the way others appraise them (Felson, 1981).

PRIVATE AND PUBLIC SELF   As noted earlier, the self has both private and public aspects. The private self consists of our personal thoughts, emotions, and

PRIVATE SELF-CONSCIOUSNESS
I reflect about myself a lot.
I'm generally attentive to my inner feelings.
I'm always trying to figure myself out.
I'm constantly examining my motives.
I'm alert to changes in my mood.
I tend to scrutinize myself.
Generally, I'm aware of myself.
I'm aware of the way my mind works when I work through a problem.
I'm often the subject of my own fantasies.
I sometimes have the feeling that I'm off somewhere watching myself.
PUBLIC SELF-CONSCIOUSNESS
I'm concerned about what other people think of me.
I usually worry about making a good impression.
I'm concerned about the way I present myself.
I'm self-conscious about the way I look.
I'm usually aware of my appearance.
One of the last things I do before leaving my house is look in the mirror.
I'm concerned about my style of doing things.

TABLE 13-3
Questionnaire Assessing Private and Public Self-consciousness (*After Fenigstein, Scheier, & Buss, 1975*)

beliefs. The public self is what we present to others — the behavior, mannerisms, and ways of expressing ourselves that create people's impressions of us. Both aspects of the self influence behavior: our actions are guided by our personal feelings and beliefs as well as by the social context in which we find ourselves — that is, by considering how others will react to what we do.

Some circumstances may heighten our awareness of the private self, while other circumstances focus attention on the public self. Placing a mirror in front of a person while he or she is engaged in an experimental task appears to heighten private self-awareness — as indicated, for example, by an increased tendency to behave in accordance with personal beliefs or by an increased awareness of one's emotions. The presence of a TV camera or an audience, on the other hand, heightens awareness of the public self — as indicated by an increased tendency to change one's attitudes to conform to the opinions of others (Scheier & Carver, 1983). Thus, momentary circumstances may make us selectively aware of either the private or public aspect of the self and may affect our experiences and actions accordingly.

Superimposed on these transitory situations that affect all of us are individual differences in self-attentiveness. People differ in the degree to which they habitually attend to themselves as well as in the focus of their self-preoccupations. For example, some people are prone to introspect, to examine frequently their feelings and motives. Some are habitually concerned with how they appear to others.

The disposition to be self-attentive has been called *self-consciousness*. Some items from a questionnaire designed to measure self-consciousness are shown in Table 13-3. An analysis of responses indicates that the private and public self-consciousness dimensions are relatively independent; they are not simply two ends of the same continuum but distinct dispositional tendencies. Thus, being low in one aspect of self-consciousness does *not* automatically imply that the person is high on the other aspect. In fact, the scale makes it possible to distinguish four different groups of people. One group is quite aware of its private self, but relatively oblivious to its public self. Another set of individuals is quite attentive to the public self, but not very conscious of the private self. A third group is very aware of both aspects of the self. And a fourth group is not particularly attentive to either aspect of the self.

Most of the research has focused on the first two groups. Persons who score high in private self-consciousness (that is, the disposition to introspect) tend to be more responsive to transient affective states than do persons who score low in that category. They show more behavioral signs of anger when provoked and are more affected by viewing pleasant and unpleasant slides (Scheier, 1976; Scheier & Carver, 1977). They are also less suggestible, more resistant to political propaganda, and more accurate in describing their own behavior (Scheier, Buss, & Buss, 1978; Scheier, Carver, & Gibbons, 1979; Carver & Scheier, 1981). In essence, they seem to know themselves better than do those low in private self-consciousness. They are also more likely to disclose private aspects of themselves to their spouses or intimate partners (Franzoi, Davis, & Young, 1985).

What about persons who score high on the scale of public self-consciousness? Studies indicate that they are more sensitive to group rejection than are those who score low on this dimension. Individuals high in public self-awareness also are better at predicting the kind of impression they make on others and place more importance on their "social" identity in describing themselves — for example, their physical characteristics, gestures and mannerisms, and group memberships (Fenigstein, 1979; Tobey & Tunnell, 1981; Cheek & Briggs, 1982). If they are female, they are apt to wear more makeup than are those who score low on public self-consciousness (Miller & Cox, 1981).

The dimensions of private and public self-consciousness have implications for the question of personality consistency discussed at the end of this chapter. Individuals who score high on private and low on public self-consciousness show greater consistency in behavior over different situations than do individuals who score low on private and high on public self-consciousness. Persons high in private self-consciousness tend to behave in accordance with their own attitudes and beliefs rather than to tailor their actions to fit the social demands of changing situations (Scheier & Carver, 1983).

Evaluation of Phenomenological Approach

By focusing on the individual's unique perception and interpretation of events, the phenomenological approach brings back the role of private experience to the study of personality. More than any other theory we have discussed, Rogers' theory concentrates on the whole, healthy person and emphasizes a positive, optimistic view of human nature. However, a phenomenological theory of personality is incomplete; it does not provide a sufficient analysis of the causes of behavior. A person's self-concept may be an important determinant of behavior, but what determines the particular self-concept he or she holds? A complete explanation should include the conditions and variables that influence the person's self-concept.

In addition, though a person's self-concept certainly influences behavior, the nature of this relationship is not clear. An individual may believe himself or herself to be honest and trustworthy but behave with varying degrees of honesty in different situations. And changes in personal beliefs and attitudes do not always result in changes in behavior. Often the reverse is true: people modify their beliefs to make them consistent with their behavior.

The construct of the self has a long history in psychology. Early efforts to define the self proved difficult and led to theories that could not be tested against observable phenomena. The self also was sometimes identified with psychic agents, such as the soul and the will; thus, the concept lacked credibility and was dismissed as unscientific. In recent years, a combination of cognitive and phenomenological approaches has led to the re-emergence of the self as a key concept in theories of personality, but it is now formulated in ways that permit it to be rigorously evaluated.

PERSONALITY ASSESSMENT

In order to study personality—according to whatever theory—methods of assessing personality variables are necessary. We make informal appraisals of personality all the time. In selecting friends, sizing up potential co-workers, choosing candidates for political office, or deciding on a marriage partner, we make predictions about future behavior. Sometimes our predictions are erroneous. First impressions may be distorted because we focus on one particular characteristic that we especially like or dislike and let it bias our perception of other aspects of the individual. This tendency to bias our judgment on the basis of one particular feature is known as the *halo effect*. Sometimes our first impression of a person is based on a *stereotype* of the characteristics believed to be typical of the group to which he or she belongs. And sometimes the person being appraised may be putting his or her "best foot forward." For these and other reasons, informal evaluations of others may be in error.

On many occasions, a more objective assessment of personality is desirable. In selecting individuals for high-level positions, employers need to know something about their honesty, their ability to handle stress, and so on. In helping students to make career choices, counselors can offer wiser advice if they know something about a student's personality, in addition to his or her school performance. Decisions about the kind of treatment that will be most beneficial to a mentally ill person or that will help to rehabilitate a convicted felon require an objective assessment of the individual's personality. The many methods that have been used to assess personality can generally be classified under three headings: *observational methods*, *personality inventories*, and *projective techniques*.

Observational Methods

A trained observer can study an individual in a natural setting (watching a child interact with classmates), in an experimental situation (observing a student try to complete a test deliberately designed to be too difficult to finish in the allotted time), or in the context of an interview. The interview differs from casual conversation because it has a purpose—for example, to evaluate a job applicant, to determine whether a patient is suicidal, to estimate the extent of an individual's emotional problems, or to predict whether a prisoner is apt to violate parole. The interview may be *unstructured*, in which case the person being interviewed largely determines what is discussed, although the interviewer usually elicits additional information through the skilled use of supplementary questions. Or the interview may be *structured*, following a standard pattern—much like a questionnaire— that ensures all relevant topics are covered. The unstructured interview is used more frequently in a clinical or counseling situation; the structured interview is used more often with job applicants or research subjects when comparable data are required of all respondents.

The accuracy of the information obtained in an interview depends on factors too detailed to discuss here. But research on the interview process has made it clear that even slight changes in the behavior of the interviewer have a marked effect on what the person being interviewed says and does. For example, a simple nod of the interviewer's head at the right moment may encourage the person being interviewed to talk much more. If the interviewer increases the length of time that he or she speaks, the person being interviewed tends to do the same (Matarazzo & Wiens, 1972). As a means of measuring personality, the interview is subject to many sources of error and bias; the success of the technique depends on the skill and awareness of the interviewer.

Impressions gained from an interview or from observing behavior can be recorded in a standardized form by means of *rating scales*. A rating scale is a device for recording judgments about a personality trait. Some examples of rating scales appear in Table 13-4. Such scales give the observer a frame of reference within which to record impressions.

For the rating to be meaningful, the rater must (1) understand the scale, (2) be sufficiently acquainted with the person being rated to make meaningful judgments, and (3) avoid the halo effect. Unless the rater knows the person fairly well or unless the behavior being rated is very specific, ratings may be influenced by social stereotypes; that is, the rater may base a judgment on how he or she believes a "suburban housewife," a "college professor," or a "high school athlete" acts and thinks rather than on the actual behavior of the subject being rated. Despite such problems, descriptions of the same person provided by different raters in different situations often yield good agreement.

TABLE 13-4
Some Examples of Rating Scales

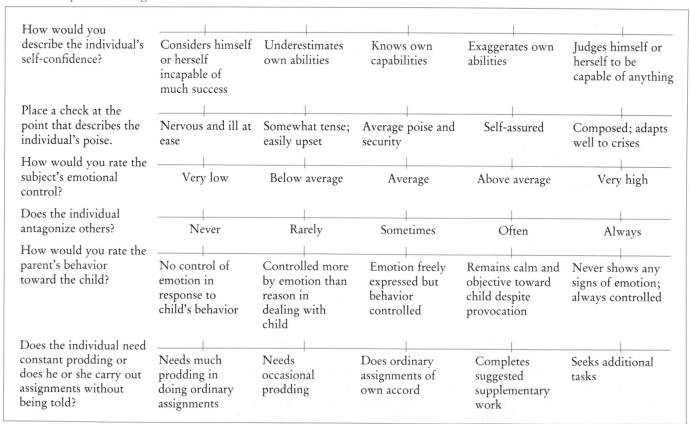

How would you describe the individual's self-confidence?	Considers himself or herself incapable of much success	Underestimates own abilities	Knows own capabilities	Exaggerates own abilities	Judges himself or herself to be capable of anything
Place a check at the point that describes the individual's poise.	Nervous and ill at ease	Somewhat tense; easily upset	Average poise and security	Self-assured	Composed; adapts well to crises
How would you rate the subject's emotional control?	Very low	Below average	Average	Above average	Very high
Does the individual antagonize others?	Never	Rarely	Sometimes	Often	Always
How would you rate the parent's behavior toward the child?	No control of emotion in response to child's behavior	Controlled more by emotion than by reason in dealing with child	Emotion freely expressed but behavior controlled	Remains calm and objective toward child despite provocation	Never shows any signs of emotion; always controlled
Does the individual need constant prodding or does he or she carry out assignments without being told?	Needs much prodding in doing ordinary assignments	Needs occasional prodding	Does ordinary assignments of own accord	Completes suggested supplementary work	Seeks additional tasks

Personality Inventories

Another method of personality assessment relies on the individual's self-observations. A *personality inventory* is essentially a questionnaire in which the person reports his or her reactions or feelings in certain situations. The personality inventory resembles a structured interview in that it asks the same questions of each person, and the answers are usually given in a form that can be easily scored, often by a computer. A personality inventory may be designed to measure a single dimension of personality (such as anxiety level) or several personality traits simultaneously. The Sixteen Personality Factor Questionnaire (16 PF) discussed earlier in this chapter, for example, produces a personality profile showing the individual's scores on 16 different traits.

Recall that the 16 PF is based on the statistical technique of *factor analysis*. Cattell used factor analysis to identify the 16 basic personality traits, then selected questions that best represented each trait and assembled them into a test that yielded scores on such personality characteristics as dominance, emotional stability, and self-discipline. A different method of test construction was used in the development of the Minnesota Multiphasic Personality Inventory (MMPI).

MINNESOTA MULTIPHASIC PERSONALITY INVENTORY The MMPI is composed of approximately 550 statements about attitudes, emotional reactions, physical and psychological symptoms, and past experiences. The subject responds to each statement by answering "true," "false," or "cannot say." Some sample test items follow:

- I have never done anything dangerous for the thrill of it.
- I daydream very little.
- My mother or father often made me obey, even when I thought it was unreasonable.
- At times my thoughts have raced ahead faster than I could speak them.

The responses are scored according to their correspondence to answers given by people with different kinds of psychological problems (see Table 13-5).

The MMPI was developed to aid clinicians in diagnosing personality disturbances. But instead of assuming specific personality traits and formulating questions to measure them, the test designers gave hundreds of test questions to groups of individuals. Each group was known to differ from the norm on a particular criterion. Only the questions that discriminated between groups were retained to form the inventory. This technique is known as *empirical construction*, because the test items bear an actual (empirical) relationship to the personality characteristic being measured. For example, to develop a scale of items that distinguish between paranoid and normal individuals, the same questions were given to two groups. The *criterion group* consisted of individuals who were hospitalized with the diagnosis of paranoia; the *control group* comprised people who had never been diagnosed as having psychiatric problems but who were similar to the criterion group in age, sex, socioeconomic status, and other important variables. Questions that at face value might seem to distinguish normal from paranoid individuals (for instance, "I think that most people would lie to get ahead") may or may not do so when put to an empirical test. In fact, patients diagnosed as paranoid were significantly *less* apt to respond "true" to this statement than were normal individuals.

Since the MMPI is derived from differences between criterion and control groups, it does not really matter whether what the person says is true. What is important is the fact that he or she says it. If schizophrenics answer "true" and normal subjects answer "false" to the statement "My mother never loved me,"

TABLE 13-5

MMPI Scales *The first three scales are "validity" scales, which help to determine whether the person has answered the test items carefully and honestly. For example, the F (Frequency) scale measures the degree to which infrequent or atypical answers are given. A high score on this scale usually indicates that the individual was careless or confused in responding. (However, high F scores often accompany high scores on the Schizophrenia scale, which measures bizarre thinking.) The remaining "clinical" scales were originally named for categories of psychiatric disorders, but interpretation now emphasizes personality attributes rather than diagnostic categories.*

SCALE NAME	SCALE ABBREVIATION	INTERPRETATION OF HIGH SCORES
Lie	L	Denial of common frailties
Frequency	F	Invalidity of profile
Correction	K	Defensive, evasive
Hypochondriasis	Hs	Emphasis on physical complaints
Depression	D	Unhappy, depressed
Hysteria	Hy	Reacts to stress by denying problems
Psychopathic deviancy	Pd	Lack of social conformity; often in trouble with the law
Masculinity–femininity	Mf	Feminine orientation (males); masculine orientation (females)
Paranoia	Pa	Suspicious
Psychasthenia	Pt	Worried, anxious
Schizophrenia	Sc	Withdrawn, bizarre thinking
Hypomania	Ma	Impulsive, excitable
Social introversion–extraversion	Si	Introverted, shy

their answers distinguish the two groups regardless of how their mothers actually behaved. This is an advantage of a test based on the method of empirical construction over one based on a test constructor's assumption that certain answers indicate specific personality traits.

Although the MMPI scales were originally designed to identify people with serious personality disorders, they have been widely used in studying normal populations. Sufficient data have been collected to provide personality descriptions of people with different patterns of high and low scores on the various scales. A recent development is the use of a computer to score and interpret the test results (see Figure 13-3). Because the MMPI does not adequately sample some of the traits useful in describing the normal personality (such as conscientiousness or cooperativeness), psychologists recommend that it be supplemented with tests that measure a broader range of normal personality characteristics (Costa, Zonderman, McCrae, & Williams, 1985).

CALIFORNIA PSYCHOLOGICAL INVENTORY Another personality test based on the method of empirical construction is the *California Psychological Inventory* (CPI). The CPI uses some of the same questions as the MMPI but is designed to measure more "normal" personality traits. The CPI scales measure such traits as dominance, sociability, self-acceptance, responsibility, and socialization. The comparison groups for some of the scales were obtained by asking high school and college students to nominate the classmates they would rate high or low on the trait in question. Thus, for the dominance scale, the criterion group consisted of students who were described by their peers as high in dominance (aggressive, confident, self-reliant) and the control group consisted of students who were described by their peers as low in dominance (retiring, lacking in

ROCHE PSYCHIATRIC SERVICE INSTITUTE

MMPI REPORT

CASE NO: 718365
AGE 39 MALE

RPSI. NO: 10000

THE PATIENT'S RESPONSES TO THE TEST SUGGEST THAT HE UNDERSTOOD ITEMS AND FOLLOWED THE INSTRUCTIONS ADEQUATELY. IT APPEARS HOWEVER, THAT HE MAY HAVE BEEN OVERLY SELF-CRITICAL. THE VALIDITY OF THE TEST MAY HAVE BEEN AFFECTED BY HIS TENDENCY TO ADMIT TO SYMPTOMS EVEN WHEN THEY ARE MINIMAL. THIS MAY REPRESENT AN EFFORT TO CALL ATTENTION TO HIS DIFFICULTIES TO ASSURE OBTAINING HELP. IT FURTHER SUGGESTS THAT HE CURRENTLY FEELS VULNERABLE AND DEFENSELESS, WHICH MAY REFLECT A READINESS TO ACCEPT PROFESSIONAL ASSISTANCE.

THIS PATIENT MAY EXHIBIT CONCERN OVER PHYSICAL SYMPTOMS WHICH, ON EXAMINATION, REVEAL NO ORGANIC PATHOLOGY. HE MAY BE IRRITABLE, DEPRESSED, SHY AND SECLUSIVE, WITH A RIGIDITY OF OUTLOOK AND AN INABILITY TO FEEL COMFORTABLE WITH PEOPLE. HE SHOWS LITTLE INSIGHT INTO HIS PERSONAL ADJUSTMENT. PSYCHIATRIC PATIENTS WITH THIS PATTERN ARE LIKELY TO BE DIAGNOSED NEUROTIC, CHIEFLY WITH SOMATIC FEATURES. MEDICAL PATIENTS WITH THIS PATTERN ARE DIFFICULT TO TREAT BECAUSE THEY APPEAR TO HAVE LEARNED TO LIVE WITH AND TO USE THEIR COMPLAINTS. ALTHOUGH THE PATIENT MAY SHOW A GOOD RESPONSE TO SHORT-TERM TREATMENT, THE SYMPTOMS ARE LIKELY TO RETURN.

IN TIMES OF PROLONGED EMOTIONAL STRESS HE MAY DEVELOP PSYCHOPHYSIOLOGICAL SYMPTOMS SUCH AS HEADACHES AND GASTROINTESTINAL DISORDERS. HE APPEARS TO BE A PERSON WHO REPRESSES AND DENIES EMOTIONAL DISTRESS. WHILE HE MAY RESPOND READILY TO ADVICE AND REASSURANCE, HE MAY BE UNWILLING TO ACCEPT A PSYCHOLOGICAL INTERPRETATION OF HIS DIFFICULTIES.

THERE ARE SOME UNUSUAL QUALITIES IN THIS PATIENT'S THINKING WHICH MAY REPRESENT AN ORIGINAL OR INVENTIVE ORIENTATION OR PERHAPS SOME SCHIZOID TENDENCIES. FURTHER INFORMATION WOULD BE REQUIRED TO MAKE THIS DETERMINATION.

THIS PERSON MAY BE HESITANT TO BECOME INVOLVED IN SOCIAL RELATIONSHIPS. HE IS SENSITIVE, RESERVED AND SOMEWHAT UNCOMFORTABLE, ESPECIALLY IN NEW AND UNFAMILIAR SITUATIONS.

THIS PERSON IS LIKELY TO BE AN INDECISIVE INDIVIDUAL WHO LACKS SELF-CONFIDENCE AND POISE AND IS LIKELY TO BE INHIBITED AND SLOW IN RESPONSE. HE HAS DIFFICULTY CONCENTRATING, AND MAY BECOME DISORGANIZED UNDER STRESS. ALTHOUGH SUPERFICIALLY CONFORMING AND COMPLIANT, HE MAY EXHIBIT CONSIDERABLE PASSIVE RESISTANCE.

THIS PATIENT HAS A TEST PATTERN WHICH SUGGESTS THE POSSIBILITY OF SEVERE EMOTIONAL PROBLEMS. PROFESSIONAL CARE IS INDICATED.

THIS PATIENT'S CONDITION APPEARS TO FALL WITHIN THE NEUROTIC RANGE. HE IS USING NEUROTIC DEFENSES IN AN EFFORT TO CONTROL HIS ANXIETY.

NOTE: ALTHOUGH NOT A SUBSTITUTE FOR THE CLINICIAN'S PROFESSIONAL JUDGMENT AND SKILL, THE MMPI CAN BE A USEFUL ADJUNCT IN THE EVALUATION AND MANAGEMENT OF EMOTIONAL DISORDERS. THE REPORT IS FOR PROFESSIONAL USE ONLY AND SHOULD NOT BE SHOWN OR RELEASED TO THE PATIENT.

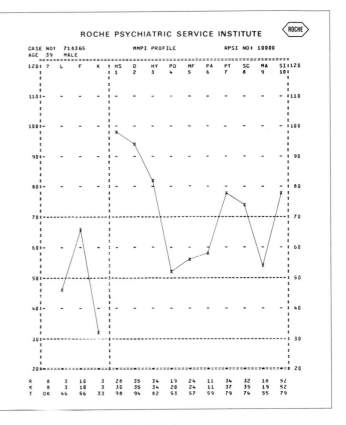

FIGURE 13-3
Computer Printout of an MMPI Profile With Interpretation

self-confidence, inhibited). Items that revealed a statistically significant difference between the criterion group and the control group formed the dominance scale.

Several CPI scales measure traits that are related to academic achievement, and studies have correlated scores on these scales with college grades. One study, for example, found that students who scored high on the scale measuring "achievement via conformance" tended to do well in courses that rewarded conformity — courses in which fixed core material had to be learned and then regurgitated on objective tests. Students who scored high on the scale measuring "achievement via independence" tended to do well in courses that emphasized independent study and self-direction. The highest grade point averages were obtained by students who scored high on both scales (Domino, 1971).

Most personality inventories rely on the individual's ability to understand the questions and his or her willingness to answer them honestly. However, the best answer to many personality test items is fairly apparent, and individuals may try to bias their answers. If the test is given by a prospective employer, job applicants will clearly want to present themselves in the best light. If admission to a psychotherapy program depends on the test results, applicants may bias their answers so that they appear to need help. Even if a person is trying to be accurate and objective, he or she may tend to give answers that are considered socially desirable. It is difficult to answer yes to the MMPI statement "I am certainly lacking in self-confidence," even though you may feel that way. Self-confidence is a desirable trait in our society; to be lacking in self-confidence is socially undesirable.

Another personality variable that influences test responses is the tendency of some people to acquiesce — to agree with the questions. For example, a person might answer yes to "I am a happy and carefree person" and later to "I frequently

"Rorschach! What's to become of you?"

have periods when I am extremely depressed." The test results would reflect something about the person's behavior—a tendency to agree with questions—but would tell us little about the individual's general mood. To counteract agreement tendencies, test constructors try (whenever possible) to reverse the wording of questions to provide yes and no versions of each item. Various other methods have been used to counteract deliberate falsifying, tendencies toward social desirability, and acquiescence on personality inventories, but they have been only partially successful.

Projective Techniques

Personality inventories strive for objectivity. They are easy to score and can be evaluated for reliability and validity. But their fixed structure—specific questions to which the individual must respond by selecting one of the answers presented—severely limits freedom of expression. *Projective tests,* in contrast, attempt to explore the private personality and to allow the individual to become much more involved in the responses. A projective test presents an ambiguous stimulus to which the person may respond as he or she wishes. Theoretically, because the stimulus is ambiguous and does not demand a specific response, the individual *projects* his or her personality onto the stimulus. Projective tests tap the individual's imagination and are based on the assumption that the person reveals something about himself or herself through imaginative productions. Two of the most widely used projective techniques are the Rorschach Test and the Thematic Apperception Test.

RORSCHACH TEST   The Rorschach Test, developed by the Swiss psychiatrist Hermann Rorschach in the 1920s, consists of a series of ten cards, each displaying a rather complex inkblot like the one shown in Figure 13-4. Some of the blots are color; some are black and white. The subject is instructed to look at one card at a time and report everything the inkblot resembles. After the subject has finished the ten cards, the examiner usually goes over each response, asking the subject to clarify some responses and to tell what features of the blot gave a particular impression.

The subject's responses may be scored in various ways. Three main categories are *location* (whether the response involves the entire inkblot or a part of it), *determinants* (whether the subject responds to the shape of the blot, its color, or differences in texture and shading), and *content* (what the response represents). Most testers also score responses according to frequency of occurrence; for example, a response is "popular" if many people assign it to the same inkblot.

Several elaborate scoring systems have been devised based on these categories. But because these systems have proved to have a limited predictive value, many psychologists base their interpretations on an impressionistic evaluation of the response record, as well as on the subject's general reaction to the test situation (for example, whether the individual is defensive, open, competitive, cooperative, and so on). Interpretation of the Rorschach requires more training and experience than interpretation of any of the other personality tests.

THEMATIC APPERCEPTION TEST   Another popular projective test, the Thematic Apperception Test (TAT), was developed at Harvard University by Henry Murray in the 1930s. The subject is shown as many as 20 ambiguous pictures of persons and scenes, similar to the one in Figure 13-5, and is asked to make up a story about each. The subject is encouraged to give free rein to his or her imagination and to tell whatever story comes to mind. The test is intended to reveal basic themes that recur in a person's imaginative productions. *Apperception*

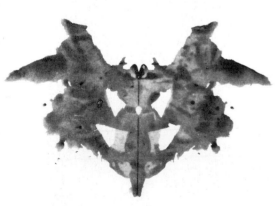

FIGURE 13-4
Rorschach Inkblot   *This inkblot is one of the standardized blots used in the Rorschach Test. The subject is asked to tell what is seen in the blot; it may be viewed from any angle.*

is a readiness to perceive in certain ways based on prior experiences. People interpret ambiguous pictures according to their apperceptions and elaborate stories in terms of preferred plots or themes that reflect personal fantasies. If particular problems are bothering the subject, they may become evident in a number of the stories or in striking deviations from the usual theme in one or two stories. When shown a picture similar to the one in Figure 13-5, a 21-year-old male told the following story:

> She has prepared this room for someone's arrival and is opening the door for a last general look over the room. She is probably expecting her son home. She tries to place everything as it was when he left. She seems like a very tyrannical character. She led her son's life for him and is going to take over again as soon as he gets back. This is merely the beginning of her rule, and the son is definitely cowed by this overbearing attitude of hers and will slip back into her well-ordered way of life. He will go through life plodding down the tracks she has laid down for him. All this represents her complete domination of his life until she dies. (Arnold, 1949, p. 100)

FIGURE 13-5
Thematic Apperception Test *This picture is similar to the pictures used on the Thematic Apperception Test. The pictures usually have elements of ambiguity so that the subject can "read into" them something from personal experience or fantasy.*

Although the original picture shows only a woman standing in an open doorway looking into a room, the subject's readiness to talk about his relationship with his mother led to this story of a woman's domination of her son. Facts obtained later confirmed the clinician's interpretation that the story reflected the subject's own problems.

In analyzing responses to the TAT cards, the psychologist looks for recurrent themes that may reveal the individual's needs, motives, or characteristic way of handling interpersonal relationships.

PROBLEMS WITH PROJECTIVE TESTS   Many other projective tests have been devised. Some ask the subject to draw pictures of people, houses, trees, and so on. Others involve completing sentences that start with "I often wish . . . ," "My mother . . . ," or "I feel like quitting when they. . . ." In fact, any stimulus to which a person can respond in an individualistic way could be considered the basis for a projective test. But most projective tests have not been subjected to enough research to establish their usefulness in assessing personality.

The Rorschach Test and the TAT, in contrast, have been intensively researched. The results, however, have not always been encouraging. Reliability of the Rorschach Test has been generally poor because the interpretation of responses is too dependent on the clinician's judgment; the same test protocol may be evaluated quite differently by two trained examiners. And attempts to demonstrate the Rorschach's ability to predict behavior or discriminate between groups have met with limited success.

The TAT has fared somewhat better. When specific scoring systems are used (for example, to measure achievement motives or aggressive themes), the interscorer reliability is fairly good. But the relationship of TAT scores to overt behavior is complex. Preoccupations are not necessarily acted on. A person who produces a number of stories with aggressive themes may not actually behave aggressively. The individual may be compensating for a need to inhibit aggressive tendencies by expressing such impulses in fantasy. When inhibitions about expressing aggression *and* strength of aggressive tendencies are estimated from the TAT stories, the relationship to behavior becomes more predictable. Among boys whose tests indicated that they were not very inhibited, the correlation between amount of aggression in the TAT stories and overt aggression was .55. Among boys showing a high degree of inhibition, the correlation between the number of aggressive themes and overt aggression was −.50 (Olweus, 1969).

Thematic Apperception Test

CRITICAL DISCUSSION

The Barnum Effect

There is no scientific evidence that the position of the stars and planets at the moment of a person's birth has any influence on personality (Carlson, 1985). Yet astrology, the study of "how heavenly bodies influence the destinies of individuals," is extremely popular. People buy books on astrology and avidly read their daily horoscopes in the newspapers, accepting the personality characterizations and predictions as at least probabilities, if not facts. What reinforces their belief? The answer seems to be that the astrological descriptions are general enough to be true of almost anyone.

Studies have shown that people tend to view generalized descriptions as accurate summaries of their own personality. In one experiment, college students were given a personality inventory. A few days later, each student was handed a typed report in a sealed envelope and asked to rate the accuracy of the evaluation. Unknown to the subjects, all the personality descriptions were *identical*. Most students said they felt that the description fit them fairly well (Forer, 1949). A glance at some of the evaluative statements will show why:

- You have a tendency to be critical of yourself. At times, you are extraverted, affable, sociable, while at other times you are introverted, wary, reserved.

Defenders of the Rorschach Test and the TAT point out that it is not fair to expect accurate predictions based on test responses alone; story themes or responses to inkblots are meaningful only when considered in light of additional information, such as the person's life history, other test data, and observations of behavior. The skilled clinician uses the results of projective tests to make tentative interpretations about the individual's personality and then verifies or discards them, depending on further information. The tests are helpful in suggesting possible areas of conflict to be explored.

CONSISTENCY OF PERSONALITY

Our everyday experience tells us that people have fairly stable personalities. We all know friendly people, overbearing people, competitive people, and easygoing people. We perceive consistency in the personalities of individuals we know well, and we believe that we can predict how they will behave in a variety of situations.

Most personality theories also postulate a stable core of personality. Trait theories assume that certain basic personality traits characterize an individual over a variety of day-to-day situations and, to some extent, over the course of a lifetime. Thus, if an individual appears to behave honestly or conscientiously in several situations, we assume that we can predict how that person will act in other situations and even how the person will behave several years from now. Psychoanalytic theory also assumes consistency; unresolved childhood conflicts (for example, centering on toilet training) lead to a cluster of personality characteristics (obstinacy, excessive cleanliness, and concern with details) that characterize a person throughout life.

Self theories assume that the self-concept plays a central role in integrating our behavior and, thus, providing consistency. Even though we may change in important ways, we still think of ourselves as the same, stable person. Indeed, the feeling of consistency within our thoughts and behavior is essential to our well-being. The loss of a sense of consistency is characteristic of personality disorganization.

However, in many instances, research has failed to show as much personality

- Under stressful circumstances, you occasionally experience some feelings of self-doubt.
- Although you have considerable affections for your parents, there have been times when you disagreed with them.
- Your sexual adjustment has presented problems for you.

These statements resemble the kinds of statements found in astrological characterizations of personality based on the signs of the zodiac. Because such descriptions are true of many people, they create the illusion of accuracy when applied to the individual case. This phenomenon has been dubbed the *Barnum effect,* in reference to the frequently quoted statement by the circus entrepreneur P. T. Barnum, "There's a sucker born every minute."

Several studies indicate that people are more likely to accept a personality description of themselves as accurate when they are told that the report is based on a projective test than when they are told that it is based on an interview or a personality inventory (Snyder, 1974). Apparently, a certain mystique is associated with projective tests: people believe they are revealing themselves in ways they do not quite understand. Interviews and personality inventories are more familiar techniques, and people assume that responses to them can be controlled consciously.

The popularity and acceptance of personality evaluations by astrologers, palmists, and readers of tea leaves or tarot cards appear to stem from the mystical quality associated with the procedure and from the universality of the personality descriptions. In addition, some fortune-tellers are quite skilled in picking up cues from the individual's appearance and reactions. The surprising accuracy of a small part of the personality description may predispose the subject to accept the total evaluation.

consistency as either theories or our intuitions lead us to expect. The consistency of personality is an issue much debated among psychologists.

Consistency Over Time

Longitudinal studies of individuals indicate considerable consistency of personality characteristics. In one large-scale study, more than 100 subjects were followed over a 35-year period. They were first evaluated in junior high school by psychologists who rated each individual on a number of personality traits, using a standardized rating procedure. The same subjects were rated again in senior high school, in their mid-30s, and in their mid-40s; each rating was conducted by a different group of judges. Over the three-year period from junior high school to senior high school, 58 percent of personality variables showed a significant positive correlation. Over the 30-year period from junior high school to the subjects' mid-40s, 31 percent of the items showed a significant correlation. Table 13-6 lists some of the personality characteristics that displayed the greatest consistency over time (Block, 1971, 1981).

Other studies of individuals across the adult life span (from age 20 to about age 68) have found three broad traits — called social extraversion, impulse control, and emotional stability — that remain relatively stable as measured by self-ratings, spouse ratings, and ratings by five acquaintances (Conley, 1985).

STABILITY AND CHANGE Although some individuals exhibit fairly stable characteristics over a lifetime, others show dramatic changes in personality. In today's world of rapid social and technological change, many people are confronted with a conflict between maintaining their self-concept (remaining consistent) and realizing their full potential (exploring new roles and behaviors). Personality development involves both constancy and change.

Although personality changes can occur at any time in life, they are most apt to take place during adolescence and early adulthood. The longitudinal study of junior high students found marked individual differences in the degree of personality consistency over the age periods studied. Some individuals appeared to stabilize their personality quite early in life; others changed considerably over the years from high school to middle adulthood. In general, the changers were those

TABLE 13-6
Consistency of Personality   *The table lists some of the personality traits that showed the greatest consistency in ratings over the years from junior high school to adulthood. With correlations of this size, adult characteristics can be predicted fairly well from earlier ratings. (After Block, 1971)*

CORRELATION JUNIOR HIGH TO SENIOR HIGH SCHOOL	CORRELATION SENIOR HIGH SCHOOL TO ADULTHOOD	ITEM RATED
Males		
.58	.53	Is a genuinely dependable and responsible person
.57	.59	Tends toward undercontrol of needs and impulses; unable to delay gratification
.50	.42	Is self-defeating
.35	.58	Enjoys aesthetic impressions; is aesthetically reactive
Females		
.50	.46	Basically submissive
.39	.43	Emphasizes being with others; gregarious
.48	.49	Tends to be rebellious and nonconforming
.45	.42	Is concerned with philosophical problems (for example, religion, values, the meaning of life)

whose adolescence was marked by conflict and tension, both within themselves and in relation to society and adult values. For example, male changers were described during their high school years as insecure, vulnerable, lacking in direction, immature, and oriented toward the peer culture. Female changers were described as insecure and rebellious; they placed a high value on independence and viewed their parents as old-fashioned.

Nonchangers, in contrast, were relaxed, effective individuals who comfortably pursued culturally valued goals. They appeared to accept themselves and to assimilate traditional roles and the values of their culture. Male nonchangers were described as self-confident, mature, adaptable, and productive. Female nonchangers tended to have positive relationships with their parents and other adults; they were described as submissive, productive, and accepting of traditional sex roles. Thus, although there are undoubtedly many individual reasons for seeking change, we can draw a general conclusion that changers of both sexes found life a struggle and were impelled to change; for the nonchangers, life was a smoother process.

Consistency Across Situations

As we have seen, the broad dispositional traits of most people remain fairly stable over time. There is less evidence, however, for personality consistency when we look at measures of behavior across different situations — for example, aggressive behavior at home and aggressive behavior at school. This area of research has caused the greatest controversy among psychologists interested in personality. The debate centers around whether behavior is consistent enough across different situations to make the trait approach useful in predicting behavior.

A classic study of the consistency of behavior was conducted by Hartshorne and May in the late 1920s. They gave some 11,000 elementary and high school students a large number of behavioral tests designed to measure the traits of altruism, self-control, and honesty in a number of different situations — at home, in the classroom, during athletic competition, and in church. To test honesty, for instance, the children were placed in situations where they had a chance to be dishonest while believing they would not be detected — to keep some of the money they were given to play with, to cheat on a test, to report falsely about the number of push-ups they could do, or the amount of work done at home. The correlations among behaviors in the different situations turned out to be quite low. For example, correlating scores on any two tests used to measure honesty yielded an average correlation of .23. These low correlations led Hartshorne and May to conclude that neither honesty nor dishonesty is a unified character trait; behavior is specific to the situation (Hartshorne & May, 1929).

The debate over the usefulness of the trait approach was reactivated some 40 years later by Walter Mischel (1968). Mischel, like Hartshorne and May, concluded that the situation is more important than the person in determining behavior. He came to this conclusion after repeated efforts to predict the effectiveness of Peace Corps teachers, once they were overseas, on the basis of personality tests administered while they were still in training in the United States. He was discouraged to discover that, despite his best efforts, he could not predict teacher performance very well (Mischel, 1965). He subsequently reviewed the literature to examine the relationship between scores on personality tests designed to measure a specific trait and other independent measures of the same trait as it might be elicited in a particular experimental task or observed in a natural setting. He found that the correlations between personality tests and situational measures of a trait were quite low for most studies — typically less than .30. Correlations between measures of the same trait in two different situations were equally low (Mischel, 1968).

Mischel's review initiated a vigorous debate about whether the characteristics of the person or the characteristics of the situation are more important in determining behavior. It led personality psychologists to reexamine their data-collection procedures and to offer various explanations for the *consistency paradox*. The consistency paradox refers to the fact that our intuition tells us that people are characterized by broad traits that produce consistent behavior across situations, and yet research often fails to support this intuition.

Some social-learning theorists who believe that behavior is largely situationally determined (more dependent on the nature of the specific situation than on enduring dispositions or traits of the individual) say that our tendency to see consistency in people is largely an illusion. They maintain that traits are more often in "the eye of the beholder" than in the person being observed. We tend to attribute more consistency to a person's behavior than actually exists. There are numerous reasons why we may do this. We will mention four:

1. Many features of an individual remain fairly constant — physical appearance, manner of speaking, expressive gestures, and so on. These constancies help to create an impression of personality consistency.

2. Our preconceived notions of how people behave may lead us to generalize beyond our actual observations. We may fill in the missing data according to our implicit personality theories of which traits and behaviors go together. Stereotypes of how a "homosexual," a "career woman," or an "athlete" behaves may cause us to attribute greater consistency to a person's actions than actual observations warrant.

3. Our presence can cause people to behave in certain ways. Thus, our acquaintances may appear to behave consistently because we are present as a stimulus during every observation we make. They may behave quite differently when we are not there.

4. Because the actions of another person are such a salient feature of any scene, we tend to overestimate the extent to which behavior is caused by personality characteristics and underestimate the importance of situational forces that may cause the person to act as he or she does. If we observe someone behaving aggressively, we assume that the person has an aggressive disposition and will behave similarly in other settings, even though the situational factors may be quite different. This tendency to underestimate situational influences on behavior has been called the *fundamental attribution error* (see Chapter 17).

Personality theorists who believe that behavior is determined by enduring dispositions (for example, trait theorists and psychoanalytic theorists) maintain that personality is much more consistent than the cross-situational research indicates. They point to problems with the methodology of many personality studies and emphasize the need for aggregating measures of behavior over a variety of situations and taking into account individual differences in consistency.

AGGREGATED MEASURES   Most of the studies that find little cross-situational consistency are based on a small sample of behaviors. For example, such studies may correlate an individual's score on a scale measuring aggression with aggressive behavior in a laboratory experiment. Or they may try to relate helpfulness in one situation (giving money to charity) with helpfulness in another (coming to the aid of a person in distress). The correlation between any two behavioral measures of this sort may not be representative. A more accurate picture can be obtained by combining several behavioral measures of the same trait to arrive at an *aggregated score*. In the Hartshorne and May study, for example, much higher correlations are found using aggregated scores. When the children's aggregated scores on half of the honesty tests are correlated with those on the other half of the tests, the correlation is .72. This is much higher than the average correlation of a .23 between any two tests for honesty and indicates considerable consistency (Rushton, Jackson, & Paunonen, 1981).

The method of aggregation can also be used to demonstrate the stability of traits over time. In one study, college students kept a daily log for several weeks, noting their most pleasant and unpleasant experiences each day and detailing the emotions associated with each experience, their impulses to act (what they felt like doing in response to the situation), and their actual behavior. When a subject's responses on any two days were compared, the correlations were quite low (usually below .30). However, when the subject's responses were averaged over a 14-day or 28-day period, the correlations were much higher (often over .80). As the number of days in the sample increased, the reliability coefficients of the measures increased steadily (Epstein, 1979; Epstein & O'Brien, 1985).

Other studies have shown similar results when behavior is observed over a period of time. For example, in a study by Leon (1977), observers followed people for four weeks and rated them on variables related to their sociability or their tendency to be impulsive. Although the correlations for any two days were quite low, the ratings averaged over the first 14 days correlated .81 with the ratings averaged over the second 14 days. Thus, it appears that we can find considerable consistency in traits, given a large enough sample of behavior. The practical implication is that if we wish to be accurate in our judgments about other people — in deciding whether they would be trustworthy business associates, reliable friends, or appropriate marriage partners — we need to observe them on a number of occasions. Too small a sample of behavior (a first impression) may prove inadequate. As one psychologist has noted,

> There is a considerable payoff, whether one is gambling for money or taking one's chances in interpersonal relationships, in being right most of the time. I considered the woman I was to marry to be a warm, considerate person. This does not mean I believed she would never get angry at me or would never misunderstand me. If her behavior were that invariant across situations, she would be rigid, a robot. It does mean that according to my assessment, her behavior, in general, would place her high on these attributes, high enough to make me willing to gamble my future happiness on my estimates, which fortunately were accurate. Note that in essence what was involved was being exposed to a sample of events from which a prediction was made of the average behavior in another sample of events. (Epstein, 1977, p. 84)

INDIVIDUAL DIFFERENCES IN CONSISTENCY Most of the research on personality traits assumes that every person can be described by every trait — that people differ from one another only in how much of the trait they possess. But although some people might be consistent on some traits, few people would be consistent on all traits. When we are asked to describe a friend, we pick a few traits that strike us as pertinent. When we are asked to describe another friend, we select a different set of traits. It may be that for any given individual, we should expect to find consistency only on the traits that are central to his or her personality.

In one study, college students were asked to rate their own cross-situational variability on a set of traits (Bem & Allen, 1974). Students who identified themselves as consistent on a particular trait tended to show much more consistency across different situations than students who identified themselves as variable on that trait. For example, students who said they were consistently friendly tended to show a fairly consistent level of friendliness in ratings by their parents and peers and by direct observation in several settings (a cross-situational correlation of .57). Students who described themselves as variable in friendliness tended to be less consistent (a cross-situational correlation of .27).

If, as this study indicates, people do vary in their consistency on different traits, a random selection of subjects will contain some individuals who show consistency and some who show variability on a particular trait. An attempt to demonstrate cross-situational consistency with such a mixed group of subjects is bound to yield poor results.

Subsequent studies indicate that people who show behavioral consistency fall into two groups: those who are consistent across many dimensions of behavior (indeed, for them, consistency may be a trait) and those who are consistent on only one or two traits (for example, aggression or sociability). An individual difference related to behavioral consistency is awareness of inner feelings. People who score high on the Private Self-consciousness Scale (indicating that they are attentive to their inner feelings) show more consistent behavior across situations than do people who achieve a low score on the scale (Underwood & Moore, 1981). They tend to respond on the basis of their feelings rather than according to the social demands of the situation.

Interactionism

The person-versus-situation debate is gradually being resolved. Most psychologists agree that we need to know the characteristics of the individual *and* of the particular situation if we want to predict behavior. People have consistent personality dispositions that predispose them to act in certain ways, but they also make discriminations among environmental conditions. Thus, even the most aggressive individual will behave relatively peacefully in church, whereas the least aggressive person will behave somewhat forcefully on the football field. Consistency and flexibility are both necessary attributes of human personality.

In addition to tailoring their behavior to meet the demands of a situation, people also seek or avoid certain situations as a result of their personality characteristics. Thus, a person who feels the need to dominate others might seek confrontation, whereas a more submissive individual would try to avoid such situations. And once people enter a situation, their behavior influences what happens. A person who acts in an abrasive manner is apt to create a more hostile social environment than one who is tactful and sensitive to the feelings of others.

This complex interplay between the person and the environment is called *interactionism* (Bandura, 1978; Endler, 1981). It suggests that human behavior results from the ongoing interaction between consistent personality dispositions and the situations in which people find themselves. Personal dispositions, overt behavior, and situational variables form an interlocking chain, with each component reciprocally influencing the others. Thus, behavior shapes the situation, but it can influence our dispositions as well. For example, successfully confronting a challenging situation may change one's tendency to be submissive.

TOWARD AN INTEGRATED VIEW OF PERSONALITY

We have looked at different ways of conceptualizing personality. Each approach has dealt in some way with how individual characteristics develop and how they interact with environmental conditions to determine behavior. But what is the best perspective from which to view personality, to form a cohesive view of the individual person? Psychologists are attempting to answer this question. The field of personality psychology is in a state of flux and transition. Clearly, no simplified theory will suffice to explain personality, and the current trend is toward a synthesis of several influences.

In trying to weigh the relative importance of individual differences and environmental conditions in determining behavior, it is helpful to think of the situation as *providing information* that the person interprets and acts on according to his or her past experiences and abilities. Some situations are powerful. A red traffic light causes most drivers to stop; they know what it means, are motivated to obey it, and have the ability to stop when they see it. We would be fairly successful in predicting the number of individuals who would respond in the same manner to a red traffic light. Other situations are weak. If an art teacher shows students a slide of an abstract painting and asks them to comment on its meaning, we would expect a variety of responses. The picture does not convey the same meaning to all the viewers, and there are no universal expectancies regarding the desired response. In weak situations, individual differences, rather than the stimulus, are the most important determinant of behavior. Some researchers are attempting to categorize social situations according to the variability of behavior associated with them and to specify the attributes that make a situation weak or strong (see, for example, Schutte, Kenrick, & Sadalla, 1985).

Current research on personality places more emphasis on cognitive processes and attempts to balance them with other aspects of personality. People differ in intellectual abilities, in the way they perceive events and represent them in memory, and in the strategies they employ in solving problems. Traditionally, intellectual abilities have been considered separately from personality, and although these topics are treated in different chapters of this book, they are actually closely interrelated. For example, studies indicate that the way in which people categorize objects and events is related to their personality characteristics. People whose categories are broad tend to be more open to experience than individuals who restrict their categories to a narrower group of stimuli (Block, Buss, Block, & Gjerde, 1981). Future research will probably expand the definition of personality to include intellectual factors, particularly the variety of cognitive processes that an individual employs in solving problems and dealing with new situations.

Another area that is beginning to form an important part of personality theory has to do with social interactions. Other people are a central part of most situations, and behavior in social situations is a process of continuous reciprocal interaction. Your behavior determines how another person reacts, and his or her response in turn influences your behavior, ad infinitum. Prescribed social roles, the impressions we form of other people, and the qualities we attribute to them are all important influences on behavior. These social-psychological processes will be discussed in Chapters 17 and 18.

SUMMARY

1. *Personality* refers to the characteristic patterns of behavior, thought, and emotion that determine a person's adjustment to the environment. It includes a *public personality* that can be observed by others as well as a *private personality* that consists of thoughts and experiences seldom revealed.

2. Some personality characteristics (such as general mood and energy level) are influenced by inherited *biological factors*. Experiences that are common to the *culture* and the *subcultural group* (such as sex roles) and experiences that are unique to the individual interact with inborn predispositions to shape personality. The major theoretical approaches to an understanding of personality include *trait*, *social-learning*, *psychoanalytic*, and *phenomenological* theories.

3. *Trait theories* assume that a personality can be described by its position on a number of *continuous dimensions*, or *scales*, each of which represents a trait. The method of *factor analysis* has been used to determine the basic traits. Two dimensions found fairly consistently in factor-analytic studies of personality are *introversion – extraversion* and *stability – instability*.

4. *Social-learning theory* assumes that personality differences result from variations in learning experiences. Responses may be learned through *observation*, without reinforcement, but reinforcement is important in determining whether the learned responses will be *performed*. A person's behavior depends on the specific characteristics of the situation in interaction with the individual's appraisal of the situation and reinforcement history. People behave consistently insofar as the situations they encounter and the roles they are expected to play remain relatively stable.

5. *Psychoanalytic theory* assumes that much of human motivation is *unconscious* and must be inferred indirectly from behavior. Freud viewed personality as composed of three systems — the *id*, the *ego*, and the *superego* — which interact and sometimes conflict. The id operates on the *pleasure principle*, seeking immediate

gratification of biological impulses. The ego obeys the *reality principle,* postponing gratification until it can be achieved in socially acceptable ways. The super-ego (conscience) imposes *moral standards* on the individual.

6. The dynamic aspects of psychoanalytic theory assume that repressed id impulses cause anxiety, which can be reduced by *defense mechanisms.* The developmental aspects propose that some kinds of personality types (such as oral or anal) result from *fixation* (arrested development) at one of the *psychosexual stages.*

7. *Phenomenological theories* are concerned with the individual's subjective experience. They emphasize a person's *self-concept* and push toward growth, or *self-actualization.* For Rogers, the most important aspect of personality is the *congruence* between the *self* and *reality* and between the *self* and the *ideal self.* Two more recent approaches focus on (a) the self as a system of *self-schemata* (generalizations about the self) that organize and guide the processing of information relevant to the self and (b) individual differences in *private self-consciousness* and *public self-consciousness.*

8. Personality can be assessed by *observing* an individual in a natural setting or during an interview. The observers may record their impressions on a *rating scale,* taking care to avoid the *halo effect* and *stereotypes.* Self-observations can be reported by means of *personality inventories,* such as the Minnesota Multiphasic Personality Inventory (MMPI) and the California Psychological Inventory (CPI).

9. Less structured approaches to personality assessment are *projective tests,* such as the Rorschach Test and the Thematic Apperception Test (TAT). Because the test stimuli are ambiguous, it is assumed that the individual projects his or her personality onto the stimulus.

10. Longitudinal studies indicate that personality characteristics are fairly stable over time, although some people stabilize their personality early in life and others change markedly from high school to middle adulthood.

11. Studies finding low correlations between measures of the same trait in two different situations and personality test scores and situational measures of a trait initiated a debate about the relative importance of personal versus situational determinants of behavior. Social-learning theorists argued that behavior is more dependent on the situation than on enduring traits. Trait and psychoanalytic theorists pointed out that personal consistency can be shown by *aggregating measures* across situations or over time and allowing for *individual differences in consistency.*

12. *Interactionism* resolves the debate by recognizing that behavior results from an ongoing reciprocal interaction between personal dispositions and situational variables. The situation provides information that the person interprets and acts on according to his or her past experiences and abilities.

General books on personality include Hall, Lindzey, Loehlin, and Manosevitz, *Introduction to Theories of Personality* (1985); Mischel, *Introduction to Personality* (4th ed., 1986); Feshback and Weiner, *Personality* (2nd ed., 1986); Singer, *The Human Personality: An Introductory Textbook* (1984); and Phares, *Introduction to Personality* (1984).

For a social-learning approach to personality, see Bandura, *Social Learning Theory* (1977); and Mischel's *Introduction to Personality*.

Freud's theories are presented in their most readable form in his *New Introductory Lectures on Psychoanalysis* (1933; reprint ed., 1965). Other references for psychoanalytical theories of personality include Holzman, *Psychoanalysis and Psychopathology* (1970); and Eagle, *Recent Developments in Psychoanalysis: A Critical Evaluation* (1984).

The phenomenological viewpoint is represented in Maddi and Costa, *Humanism in Personology: Allport, Maslow, and Murray* (1972); and Keen, *A Primer in Phenomenological Psychology* (1982). For Carl Rogers' views, see Rogers and Stevens, *Person to Person: The Problem of Being Human* (1967); and Rogers, *Carl Rogers on Personal Power* (1977). For research on the self, see Suls (ed.), *Psychological Perspectives on the Self* (Vol. 1, 1982); and Suls and Greenwald (eds.), *Psychological Perspectives on the Self* (Vol. 2, 1983). *Personality and Personal Growth* (2nd ed., 1984) by Frager and Fadiman focuses on the personality theories that are most concerned with understanding human nature and includes a section on such Eastern theories of personality as Yoga, Zen Buddhism, and Sufism.

Cronbach, *Essentials of Psychological Testing* (4th ed., 1984), has a number of chapters on personality appraisal.

FURTHER READING

Part Seven

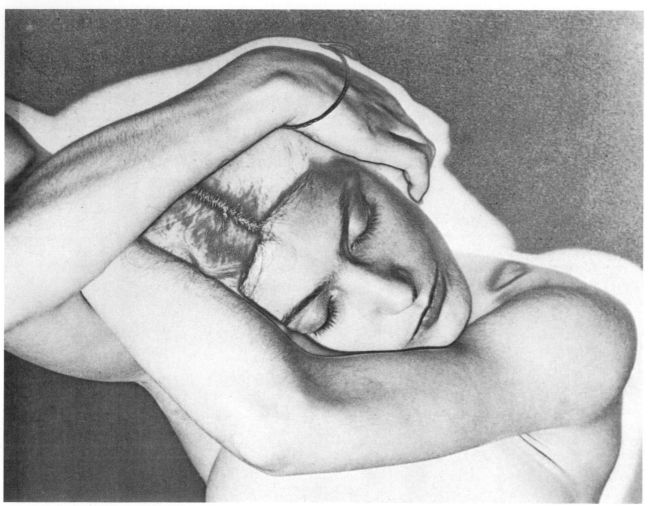

Solarization, 1929

STRESS, PSYCHOPATHOLOGY, AND THERAPY

Stress
and Coping

REGARDLESS OF HOW RESOURCEFUL WE may be in coping with problems, the circumstances of life inevitably involve stress. Our motives are not always easily satisfied: obstacles must be overcome, choices need to be made, and delays have to be tolerated. Today's rapidly paced society creates many pressures for each of us. We are constantly faced with a sense of urgency, the pressure to accomplish more and more in less and less time. Environmental and job stressors—air and noise pollution, traffic congestion, job deadlines, and work overload—are increasingly present in our everyday lives. Each of us develops characteristic ways of responding to such pressures. To a large extent, our responses to stressful situations determine how adequately we adjust to life. In the next three chapters, we will look at the ways in which people respond to stress and what happens when inadequate coping techniques pose a threat to adjustment. We will also discuss a variety of abnormal behaviors and the methods used to treat them.

CONCEPT OF STRESS

Stress has become a popular topic. We are flooded with messages about its harmful effects and how it can be managed or prevented. But what is stress? There is little agreement on how the term should be defined. Different researchers define it differently depending on their orientations.

Definitions of Stress

Approaches to studying stress fall into three broad categories. One approach defines stress as a *response;* researchers are interested in identifying the patterns of psychological and physiological responses that occur in difficult situations. When the response is emphasized, we speak of a state of stress or an organism being under stress. One of the pioneers in stress research, Hans Selye, defined stress as the "nonspecific response of the body to any demand made upon it" (Selye, 1979). By "nonspecific," he meant that the same pattern of responses could be produced by any number of different stressful stimuli, or *stressors.* We will look at this stress-response pattern in a moment.

Another approach focuses on the *stimulus,* conceptualizing stress in environmental terms as an event or a set of circumstances that requires an unusual response. Within this framework, researchers have studied catastrophic events such as tornadoes, earthquakes, or fires, as well as more chronic stressful circumstances such as imprisonment or crowding. As we will see later, they have also studied the relationship between the accumulation of stressful life events (such as job loss, divorce, or the death of a spouse) and the risk of subsequent physical illness. And they have tried to identify the characteristics of a situation that make it stressful.

A third approach views stress as neither a stimulus nor a response, but as a *transaction* — or relationship — between the person and the environment that taxes or exceeds the person's resources. The transactional approach argues that focusing on stimuli and responses is not sufficient. While some situations are stressful for everyone (natural disaster, life-threatening illness, or the loss of a loved one), many less dramatic experiences (taking an examination, arguing with a spouse, getting stuck in traffic) are stressful for some people but not for others. Responses to stressful situations, even physiological responses to painful stimuli, can be powerfully influenced by psychological factors. To understand stress, we need to know how the individual appraises a situation in terms of his or her particular (1) motives and needs and (2) resources for coping. From a transactional perspective, stress reflects a relationship between a person and the environment that is appraised by the person as taxing his or her resources and endangering his or her well-being (Lazarus & Folkman, 1984). Two critical processes that determine the stressfulness of the person-environment relationship are *cognitive appraisal* and *coping*. Cognitive appraisal is an evaluative process that determines why and to what extent a person views a situation as threatening. And coping refers to the behavioral and cognitive strategies used to manage the demands of the situation that are appraised as stressful and the emotions generated by it.

Cognitive Appraisal

In Chapter 11 we discussed how the cognitive appraisal of a situation influences the quality and intensity of the emotion experienced. When we talk specifically about stress, cognitive appraisal is the process of evaluating an event with respect to its significance for a person's well-being. This appraisal is twofold. The *primary appraisal* asks, What does this mean to me? Am I okay or in trouble? The *secondary appraisal* asks, What can I do about it? The primary appraisal may judge the situation as (1) irrelevant to the person's well-being, (2) benign-positive, or (3) stressful. A situation appraised as stressful involves three types of judgments. The

person may judge that he or she has already sustained some damage (for example, the loss of a loved one, an incapacitating injury, or damage to esteem). Or the judgment may involve the *threat* of such damage or loss. A third judgment is that the situation is a *challenge:* there are potential benefits to the individual, but these also contain risks (Lazarus & Folkman, 1984).

A job promotion may be viewed as both a threat and a challenge. Either way, the situation is stressful because an individual must mobilize coping efforts to meet new demands. The main difference is that challenge appraisals are characterized by pleasurable emotions such as eagerness and excitement, whereas threat is characterized by negative emotions such as fear and anxiety. In a study of stress about taking examinations, most students reported feelings of both threat and challenge two days before a midterm exam (Folkman & Lazarus, 1985).

If the primary appraisal evaluates the situation as stressful (I'm in trouble), then the secondary appraisal answers the question, What, if anything, can I do about it? The answer to a given stressful event depends on the person's past experiences in similar situations and his or her resources—problem-solving skills, morale, social supports, and material resources.

PHYSIOLOGICAL REACTIONS TO STRESS

The body reacts by initiating a complex sequence of innate responses to a perceived threat. If the threat is dealt with quickly, these emergency responses subside, and our physiological state returns to normal. If the stressful situation continues, a different set of internal responses occurs as we attempt to adapt to a chronic stressor.

Emergency Response

Whether you fall into an icy stream, encounter a knife-wielding assailant, or are terrified by your first parachute jump, your body responds in similar ways.

Regardless of the stressor, your body automatically prepares to handle the emergency. Quick energy is needed, so the liver releases extra sugar (glucose) to fuel the muscles; and hormones are released that stimulate the conversion of fats and proteins to sugar. The body's metabolism increases in preparation for expending energy on physical action. Heart rate, blood pressure, and breathing rate increase, and the muscles tense. At the same time, certain unessential activities, such as digestion, are curtailed. Saliva and mucus dry up, increasing the size of the air passages to the lungs. Thus, an early sign of stress is a dry mouth. Endorphins, the body's natural painkillers, are secreted, and the surface blood vessels constrict to reduce bleeding in case of injury. The spleen releases more red blood cells to help carry oxygen, and the bone marrow produces more white corpuscles to fight infection.

Most of these physiological responses are regulated by the autonomic nervous system (see Chapter 2, p. 50) under the control of the hypothalamus. The hypothalamus has been called the "stress center" because of its dual function in emergencies: controlling the autonomic nervous system and activating the pituitary gland.

The autonomic nervous system and the endocrine system orchestrate the stress response in complex ways. For example, the autonomic nervous system stimulates the inner core of the adrenal glands (the adrenal medulla), which floods the bloodstream with the hormone *epinephrine* (adrenaline). Epinephrine interacts with the receptors on cells in various organs of the body to increase heart rate and blood pressure and to prompt the liver to release extra sugar.

The hypothalamus also signals the pituitary to secrete two important hormones. One of these stimulates the thyroid gland, which in turn makes more energy available to the body. The other, adrenocorticotrophic hormone (ACTH), stimulates the outer layer of the adrenal glands (the adrenal cortex) resulting in the release of a group of hormones called corticosteroids, which are important in metabolic processes and in the release of glucose from the liver. ACTH also signals other organs of the body to release about 30 hormones, each of which plays a role in the body's adjustment to emergency situations.

This complex and innate pattern of responses has been called both the "fight-or-flight" response, because it prepares the organism to attack or flee (Cannon, 1929), and the "alarm reaction" (Selye, 1979). The response is triggered by a wide variety of physical and psychological stressors. While the physiological components of the fight-or-flight response are valuable in helping the person — or animal — deal with a physical threat, they are not very adaptive for dealing with many modern-day sources of stress. In fact, chronic arousal that is not discharged through appropriate physical activity may contribute to illness, as we shall see later.

General Adaptation Syndrome

What happens if the stressor is not terminated but continues over time? How does the body adapt? Selye studied this question experimentally for many years. He subjected rats to a variety of stressors — cold, heat, nonlethal doses of poison, trauma — and found that they all produced a similar pattern of physiological changes. He called these physiological reactions the *general adaptation syndrome* (GAS), which comprises three stages: *alarm reaction*, *resistance*, and *exhaustion* (see Figure 14-1).

The alarm reaction, the body's initial response to a stressor, has two phases. In the *shock phase*, temperature and blood pressure drop, heart rate quickens, and the muscles go slack. These reactions are instantly followed by a *countershock*

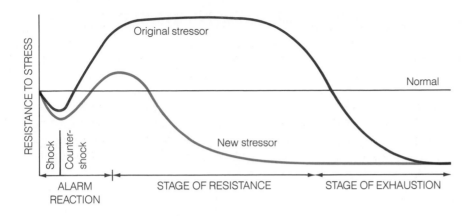

FIGURE 14-1
General Adaptation Syndrome *The upper curve shows resistance to a stressor over time. During the alarm reaction stage, resistance drops briefly (shock phase) and thereafter increases strongly (countershock phase). Resistance continues to increase in the resistance stage and stays high throughout that stage. If the stressor remains for an extended period of time, the body reaches a stage of exhaustion and its ability to resist ultimately collapses. If a new stressor is introduced while the body is still exposed to the original stressor, the ability to resist it is greatly reduced, as indicated by the lower curve. (After Selye, 1956)*

phase, in which the body rebounds and mobilizes its defenses. The countershock phase of the alarm reaction is essentially the emergency response described earlier. However, the body cannot maintain such a heightened degree of arousal for long. If the stressor is not severe enough to cause death, the organism enters a stage of resistance.

In the resistance stage, the pituitary continues to secrete ACTH, which stimulates the adrenal cortex to continue releasing corticosteroids. These hormones help increase the body's resistance. The adrenal glands actually expand in size in the resistance stage, reflecting their heightened activity. As resistance to the specific stressor increases, most of the physiological processes that were disrupted during the alarm reaction return to normal. After a few days of exposure to a stressor, experimental animals appear to adapt. The adrenal glands return to normal size and begin to renew their steroids. However, although things appear normal, they are not. If a second stressor is introduced at this point, the animal is unable to resist it and may die. Thus, while specific resistance to the original stressor has increased, general resistance is low.

If exposure to the harmful stressor continues for an extended period of time, the organism's ability to resist it or other stressors collapses and the exhaustion stage sets in. The pituitary and the adrenal cortex are unable to continue secreting their hormones, some of the alarm reaction symptoms reappear, and death may occur. When experimental animals died following prolonged exposure to stressors, their adrenal glands were found to be damaged. Their lymph nodes and thymuses, which play an important role in immunity, were shrunken, and their stomachs had bleeding ulcers.

The general adaptation syndrome describes the physiological changes observed in laboratory animals, but Selye suggests that any prolonged stressful experience may follow the same course—for humans as well as animals. For example, if we are engaging in an unaccustomed strenuous task, at first it is very difficult and requires much psychological and physical energy. We then go through a period of adaptation as we manage the task and resist the stress. Finally, we lose our ability to tolerate the burden and become exhausted by its continued demands (Selye, 1979).

The GAS concept has been valuable in explaining some of the stress-related illnesses we will discuss later. However, since the experimental work was conducted with animals, the conclusions of the studies do not recognize the importance of cognitive appraisal in human reactions to stress, where the perceived meaning of the situation determines which physiological reactions occur (Mason, 1971). In addition, evidence indicates that physiological responses differ depending on the nature of the stressor (Terman et al., 1984).

Test anxiety can interfere with a student's performance on an exam.

PSYCHOLOGICAL REACTIONS TO STRESS

Accompanying the physiological responses that occur with stress are some negative emotions, as well as an impairment of cognitive functioning.

Cognitive Impairment

Performance on a task, particularly a complex task, tends to deteriorate at high levels of emotional arousal (see Figure 11-8, p. 368). Stress impairs our ability to concentrate and to organize our thoughts logically. Instead of concentrating on the task at hand, our thinking tends to be dominated by worries about the consequences of our actions and by self-deprecatory thoughts. For instance, students who are especially prone to worry about examinations—a condition called *test anxiety*—tend to worry about possible failures and about their inadequacies. They can become so distracted by these negative thoughts that they fail to follow instructions and neglect or misinterpret obvious informational cues provided by the questions. As anxiety mounts, they have difficulty retrieving facts they had learned well.

In times of stress, people tend to resort to behavior patterns that have worked in the past. The cautious person may become even more cautious and withdraw entirely, whereas the aggressive person may lose control and strike out heedlessly in all directions. If the initial attempts at coping are unsuccessful, anxiety often intensifies and the individual becomes more rigid in his or her efforts, unable to perceive alternative solutions to the problem. People have been trapped in flaming buildings because they persisted in pushing against exit doors that opened inward; in their panic, they failed to consider the possibility of an alternative action.

Emotional Responses

Stressful situations produce emotional reactions ranging from exhilaration (when the event is appraised as a demanding but manageable challenge) to the more common emotions of anxiety, anger, discouragement, and depression. If the stressful situation continues, our emotions may switch back and forth among any of these, depending on the success of our coping efforts.

ANXIETY   The primary response to a situation appraised as threatening is anxiety. By anxiety, we mean the unpleasant emotion characterized by such terms as "worry," "apprehension," "tension," and "fear" that we all experience at times in varying degrees. Different theorists conceptualize anxiety differently, depending on what they view as threatening for people. Consequently, we will not attempt to provide a more precise definition.

Anxiety is generally characterized as "normal" or "neurotic," depending on whether an individual's reaction seems appropriate to the situation that caused it. Normal anxiety, or *objective anxiety*, is adaptive; it motivates the person to deal with the harmful situation. *Neurotic anxiety*, which is out of proportion to the actual danger posed (such as stage fright), often reduces the person's ability to cope. We will discuss some neurotic anxiety reactions in Chapter 15 when we consider phobias and other anxiety disorders.

Freud viewed objective anxiety as a realistic response to external danger, synonymous with fear. He believed that neurotic anxiety stems from unacceptable internal impulses that the individual is trying to control. Since these impulses are largely unconscious, the person is not aware of the reason for his or her anxiety. Many psychologists still find it meaningful to distinguish between fear and anxiety. However, since it is not clear that the two emotions can be differentiated — either on the basis of physiological responses or on the basis of the individual's descriptions of feelings — we will use the terms "anxiety" and "fear" interchangeably. Just as there are varying degrees of anxiety, ranging from mild apprehension to panic, there are probably varying degrees of awareness of the cause of an individual's discomfort. People who suffer from internal conflicts often have some idea of why they are anxious, even though they cannot specify all the factors involved clearly.

Freud believed that neurotic anxiety is the result of an unconscious conflict between *id impulses* (mainly sexual and aggressive) and the constraints imposed by the *ego* and *superego* (see Chapter 13). Many id impulses pose a threat to the individual because they are contradictory to personal or social values. A young girl may not consciously acknowledge that she has strong hostile feelings toward her mother because these feelings conflict with her belief that a child should love her parents. If she acknowledged her true feelings, she would destroy her self-concept as a loving daughter and would risk the loss of her mother's love and support. When she begins to feel angry toward her mother, the aroused anxiety serves as a *signal* of potential danger. The girl then engages in defensive maneuvers to exclude anxiety-producing impulses from her conscious awareness. These maneuvers, or *defense mechanisms,* form an important part of Freud's theory of maladaptive behavior and will be discussed in the section on coping with stress.

When a person reacts with intense anxiety to a situation that others view as only mildly stressful, then we assume that the source of danger is associated more with internal feelings than with the external stressor. While Freud saw unconscious conflicts as the internal source of anxiety, behaviorists have focused on ways in which anxiety becomes associated with certain situations via learning. For instance, a little girl who is punished by her parents whenever she rebels against their wishes and attempts to assert herself eventually learns to associate the pain of punishment with assertive behavior. When she thinks about asserting her own wishes and defying her parents, she becomes anxious.

Sometimes fears learned in childhood are difficult to extinguish. If a child's first reaction is to avoid or escape the anxiety-producing situation, he or she may not be able to determine when the situation is no longer dangerous. The little girl who has been punished for assertive behavior may never learn that it is appropriate and rewarding for her to express her wishes in certain situations.

A third approach suggests that people experience anxiety whenever they encounter a situation that seems beyond their control. It might be a new situation that we somehow must organize and integrate into our view of the world and of ourselves. It might be an ambiguous situation — as many of our experiences are — that we must fit into our concept of how the world operates. A feeling of being helpless and not in control of what is happening seems central to the experience of anxiety. As we will see later, the degree of anxiety we feel in stressful situations is largely dependent on how much control we believe we have over the situation.

ANGER AND AGGRESSION   Another common reaction to a stressful situation is anger, which may lead to aggression. Laboratory studies have shown that some animals behave aggressively in response to a variety of stressors, including overcrowding, electric shock, and the failure to receive an expected food reward. If a pair of animals is shocked in a cage from which they cannot escape, they begin fighting when the shock starts and stop fighting when it ends.

Children often become angry and exhibit aggressive behavior when they experience *frustration.* As we noted in Chapter 11, the *frustration-aggression hypothesis* assumes that whenever a person's effort to reach a goal is blocked, an aggressive drive is induced that motivates behavior to injure the object — or

*CRITICAL
DISCUSSION*

*Coping

With

Captivity*

Imagine yourself locked in a small, windowless cell with no one to talk to, no books or newspapers to read, and no paper or pencil with which to write. Months go by with no chance for you to breathe fresh air or to see the sun, moon, grass, or trees. The sparse food your captors provide is of little nutritional value; you are constantly hungry. Injuries and illnesses go untreated, as do abscessed teeth; there is no medical or dental care. Your hands are often bound, or you may be chained to your bed for days on end.

It is difficult to conceive of many situations that would engender greater feelings of frustration, helplessness, and hopelessness. Yet many U.S. servicemen captured during the Korean and Vietnam wars endured this type of solitary confinement for months or, in some cases, for years. One factor that helped the Vietnam prisoners cope with captivity was their previous training in prison-survival techniques.

Studies of people who are confined as hostages, as prisoners of war, or as inmates of concentration camps indicate that apathy and depression are common reac-

tions to frustrating and traumatic conditions from which there is no hope of escape. Faced with continual deprivation, torture, and threats of death, many prisoners become detached, emotionless, and indifferent to events taking place around them. Some may abandon any attempt to cope with the situation or to continue living. Interviews with American servicemen released from prison camps after the Korean War showed that almost all experienced feelings of withdrawal and apathy at some time during their imprisonment. Some men gave up altogether; they curled up on their bunks and waited to die, making no effort to eat or to take care of themselves. Two remedies seemed helpful in saving a man close to death: getting him on his feet and doing something, no matter how trivial, and getting him interested in some current or future project. In a sense, both remedies provided the individual with a goal toward which he could direct his efforts (Strassman, Thaler, & Schein, 1956).

Concern about the reactions of American prisoners during the Korean War led military officials to develop programs that

person — causing the frustration. While research has shown that aggression is not an inevitable response to frustration, it is certainly one of them. When one child takes a toy from another, the second is likely to attack the first in an attempt to regain the toy. Adults usually express their aggression verbally rather than physically; they are more apt to exchange insults than they are blows.

Direct aggression toward the source of frustration is not always possible or wise. Sometimes the source is vague and intangible. The person does not know what to attack but feels angry and seeks an object on which to vent these feelings. Sometimes the individual responsible for the frustration is so powerful that an attack would be dangerous. When circumstances block direct attack on the cause of frustration, aggression may be *displaced:* the aggressive action may be directed toward an innocent person or object rather than toward the actual cause of the frustration. A woman who is reprimanded at work may take out unexpressed resentment on her family. A student, angry at his professor for an unfair grade, may blow up at his roommate. A child frustrated by experiences at school may resort to vandalism of school property.

Prejudice against minority groups often contains an element of displaced aggression, or *scapegoating*. During periods of economic depression, when money and jobs are scarce, people are tempted to blame their troubles on relatively powerless minority groups. In the past, Nazis blamed Jews, farmers in the southern United States blamed blacks, Protestant laborers in Boston blamed Irish Catholics, California farm workers blamed Mexican illegal aliens, and so forth. Many factors contribute to prejudice, and displaced aggression in response to frustration is one of them.

would prepare servicemen to cope with the frustrations of imprisonment. Reports from men imprisoned during the Vietnam War indicate that their survival training had been helpful. Knowing how to keep physically and mentally active, to provide support for each other, and to focus on ways to solve daily problems did much to combat depression and feelings of helplessness. Returned POWs reported that the most helpful behaviors included *communication, thinking about the future,* and *physical exercise.* The least useful behaviors were *thinking about suicide, talking to oneself,* and *worrying about the family* (Richlin, 1977).

In many Vietcong prison camps, the prisoners were placed in solitary cells, and rules forbidding communication were strictly enforced by the guards. To be caught talking to a fellow prisoner meant severe torture. However, some POWs developed ingenious methods of communication, which they taught to each other. The sounds of finger tapping, coughing, spitting, and clearing the throat were used to convey messages. A prisoner could also

communicate by dragging his sandals according to a code as he walked past another prisoner's cell. And a POW sweeping the prison compound could send a message to every prisoner in the area by the way he moved his broom (Stockdale, 1984).

Having strategies for coping with the stress of imprisonment appears to have aided survival. Although American POWs were held captive in Vietnam more than twice as long (eight years in some cases) as American POWs in Korea, the servicemen who had been imprisoned in Vietnam returned in better physical and emotional condition than did the Korean War POWs. The Vietnam prisoner mortality rate during captivity also was much lower: roughly 38 percent of all American servicemen imprisoned during the Korean War did not survive captivity, whereas only about 15 percent of the American POWs in Vietnam died while imprisoned.

However, before concluding that survival training produced the differences in mortality rates, we should realize that the Korean and Vietnam POWs differed in other respects. Most of the men captured

during the Korean War were in the infantry. Some were officers, but the majority were enlisted men. Most of the men imprisoned in North Vietnam were pilots. On the average, they were more mature at the time of capture (average age 31 years) and more highly educated than the Korean POWs. Due to the nature of pilot selection procedures, the Vietnam POWs also were probably more emotionally stable and more highly motivated than the average serviceman. Their maturity, emotional stability, and intellectual resources undoubtedly played vital roles in their ability to survive. Another factor that contributed to the lower survival rate in Korea was the extreme cold to which POWs were subjected, which depleted their physical strength.

Thus, survival training was not the only variable affecting the ability of Vietnam POWs to endure imprisonment. However, such preparation does appear to help people cope with the stress of captivity. As a result, the U.S. government now provides survival training for military and diplomatic personnel who have a high risk of capture.

APATHY AND DEPRESSION   Complicating the study of human behavior is the tendency of different individuals to respond to similar situations in different ways. Although a common response to frustration is active aggression, the opposite response of withdrawal and apathy is not uncommon. If the stressful conditions continue and the individual is not successful in coping with them, apathy may deepen into depression.

We do not know why one person reacts with aggression and another reacts with apathy to the same situation, but it seems likely that learning is an important factor. Reactions to frustration can be learned in much the same manner as other behaviors. Children who strike out angrily when frustrated and find that their needs are then satisfied (either through their own efforts or because a parent rushes to placate them) will probably resort to the same behavior the next time their motives are thwarted. Children whose aggressive outbursts are never successful (who find they have no power to satisfy their needs by means of their own actions) may give up and withdraw when confronted with subsequent frustrating situations.

Studies have shown that animals and people can learn to be helpless when faced with stressful situations. The theory of *learned helplessness* originated with a laboratory experiment similar to those discussed in Chapter 7. A dog placed in a shuttle box (an apparatus with two compartments separated by a barrier) quickly learns to jump to the opposite compartment to escape a mild electric shock delivered to its feet through a grid on the floor. If a light is turned on a few seconds before the grid is electrified, the dog can learn to avoid the shock entirely by jumping to the safe compartment when signaled by the light. However, if the dog

World War II prisoners in a Nazi concentration camp at the moment of liberation (Buchenwald, Germany; 1945).

has had a previous history of being in another enclosure in which shocks are unavoidable and inescapable — where nothing the animal does terminates the shock — then it is very difficult for the dog to learn the avoidance response in a new situation when it is appropriate. The animal simply sits and endures the shock in the shuttle box, even though an easy jump to the opposite compartment would eliminate discomfort. Some dogs never learn, even if the experimenter demonstrates the proper procedure by carrying them over the barrier.

The experimenters concluded that the animals had learned through prior conditioning that they were helpless to avoid the shock and so gave up trying to do so, even in a new situation. This learned helplessness was difficult to overcome (Overmeier & Seligman, 1967).

Numerous experiments have attempted to demonstrate learned helplessness with human subjects, but the results have been difficult to interpret. Uncontrollable conditions do not always produce helplessness and passivity; sometimes they generate anxiety and invigorated effort (Wortman & Brehm, 1975). Clearly, the animal model of learned helplessness is too simple to account for human behavior. As we will see when we discuss depression in the next chapter (p. 508), the theory of learned helplessness has been elaborated to take into account the attributions a person makes about negative events. It is not uncontrollable events per se but how the individual interprets them that creates feelings of helplessness and depression. Nevertheless, the feeling that we have control over our lives and over what happens to us is an extremely important factor in our ability to cope with stress.

SOURCES OF STRESS

Countless events create stress. Some are major changes affecting large numbers of people — events such as war, industrial accidents that release radioactivity or toxic chemicals, and natural disasters such as earthquakes and floods, to name a few. Others are major changes in the life of an individual — for instance, moving to a new area, changing jobs, getting married, losing a friend, suffering a serious illness. In addition to the big changes that require major adjustments are life's "little hassles," such as losing your wallet, getting stuck in traffic, arguing with your boss, and so on.

Although it has become popular to focus on environmental stressors, the source of stress is often within the individual in the form of a *conflict* between opposing motives.

Conflict

When two motives conflict, the satisfaction of one leads to the frustration of the other. For example, a student may not be able to gain recognition as an outstanding athlete and still earn the grades required to enter law school. Even when only one motive is involved, conflict may arise if the goal can be approached in several different ways. For example, you can get a good education at many colleges, but choosing which college to attend presents a conflict situation. Although you will eventually reach the goal, progress toward it is disrupted by the necessity of making a choice.

In our society, the conflicts that are most pervasive and difficult to resolve generally occur between the following motives:

1. *Independence versus dependence* In times of stress, we may want to resort to the dependence characteristic of childhood, to have someone take care of us and solve our problems. But we are taught that the ability to stand on our own and to assume responsibilities is a mark of maturity.

2. *Intimacy versus isolation* The desire to be close to another person and to share our innermost thoughts and emotions may conflict with the fear of being hurt or rejected if we expose too much of ourselves.

3. *Cooperation versus competition* In our society much emphasis is placed on competition and success. Competition begins in early childhood among siblings, continues through school, and culminates in business and professional rivalry. At the same time, we are urged to cooperate and to help others.

4. *Impulse expression versus moral standards* Impulses must be regulated to some degree in all societies. We noted in Chapter 3 that much of childhood learning involves internalizing the cultural restrictions placed on innate impulses. Sex and aggression are two areas in which our impulses most frequently conflict with moral standards, and violation of these standards can generate strong feelings of guilt.

These four areas present the greatest potential for serious conflict. Trying to find a workable compromise between opposing motives can create considerable stress.

Life Changes

Any change in an individual's life—whether it is pleasant or unpleasant—requires some readjustment. Studies of personal histories suggest that physical and emotional disorders tend to cluster around periods of major change. In an attempt to measure life changes, researchers have developed the *Life Events Scale,* shown in Table 14-1. The life events are ranked in order from the most stressful (death of a spouse) to the least stressful (minor violations of the law).

To arrive at this scale, the investigators examined thousands of interviews and medical histories to identify the kinds of events that people found stressful. Because marriage (a positive event, but one that requires a considerable amount of adjustment) appeared to be a critical event for most people, it was placed in the middle of the scale and was assigned an arbitrary value of 50. The investigators then asked approximately 400 men and women (of varying ages, backgrounds, and marital status) to compare marriage with a number of other life events. They were asked such questions as, "Does the event call for more or less readjustment than marriage?" and "Would the readjustment take shorter or longer to accomplish?" The interviewees were then asked to assign a point value to each event on the basis of their evaluation of its severity and the time required for adjustment. These ratings were used to construct the scale in Table 14-1.

To arrive at a measure of the amount of stress an individual has experienced, the person is asked to check off the items that apply over a given time period. The life-change values are then summed to give a total stress score. Studies using the Life Events Scale have found a consistent relationship between the number of stressful events in a person's life and that person's emotional and physical health. More than half of the people whose life-change values summed to between 200 and 300 in a single year exhibited health problems the following year; 79 percent of the people whose total scores were over 300 became ill the following year.

To account for the findings relating life changes to illness, the compilers of the Life Events Scale hypothesized that the more major changes an individual experiences, the greater effort the individual must expend to adapt. This effort presumably lowers the body's natural resistance to disease. However, other researchers have questioned these conclusions for the following reasons.

LIFE EVENT	VALUE
Death of spouse	100
Divorce	73
Marital separation	65
Jail term	63
Death of close family member	63
Personal injury or illness	53
Marriage	50
Fired from job	47
Marital reconciliation	45
Retirement	45
Change in health of family member	44
Pregnancy	40
Sex difficulties	39
Gain of new family member	39
Business readjustment	39
Change in financial state	38
Death of close friend	37
Change to different line of work	36
Foreclosure of mortgage	30
Change in responsibilities at work	29
Son or daughter leaving home	29
Trouble with in-laws	29
Outstanding personal achievement	28
Wife begins or stops work	26
Begin or end school	26
Change in living conditions	25
Revision of personal habits	24
Trouble with boss	23
Change in residence	20
Change in school	20
Change in recreation	19
Change in church activities	19
Change in social activities	18
Change in sleeping habits	16
Change in eating habits	15
Vacation	13
Christmas	12
Minor legal violations	11

TABLE 14-1
Life Events Scale *This scale, also known as the Holmes and Rahe Social Readjustment Rating Scale, measures stress in terms of life changes. (After Holmes & Rahe, 1967)*

1. It is difficult to separate the effects of stress from such factors as diet, smoking, drinking, and other general health habits. Individuals who are trying to cope with major life changes (a new job, the loss of a spouse) may increase their alcohol intake, may eat more snack foods, may get less sleep, and may fail to exercise. An increased susceptibility to illness in such cases is more likely to stem from changes in health habits than from the direct action of stress on resistance to disease.

2. People differ in their tendencies to focus on physical symptoms and to seek medical help. A respiratory infection or stomachache that one person ignores may send another person to a doctor. Individuals who are unhappy and discontented with their lives are more apt to focus on symptoms and to go to a doctor than are people who are involved in activities they enjoy. Since the data for many life-change studies are derived from medical reports, the selective factor in help seeking may be significant. Stress may be more important in triggering help-seeking behavior than in triggering actual illness.

3. Some of the items on the Life Events Scale may be the *result* of illness rather than the cause. An individual's poor emotional or physical health may contribute to marital, job, and financial difficulties or to changes in social activities and sleeping habits.

4. The scale assumes that change, per se, is stressful. However, subsequent research has not found *positive* life changes to be related to poor health, and sometimes the absence of change (boredom) is stressful. Whether or not change (or its absence) is stressful depends on the individual's personal history and present life circumstances.

A more recently developed scale deals with this last objection by asking individuals to indicate the desirability and impact of each event—to judge it as good or bad and to estimate its effect on their lives. Thus, whether a new job or change of residence is good or bad is left up to the person answering the survey. Studies using this scale have found that people with a large number of events they regard as bad are more likely to report physical and emotional problems six months later (Sarason, Johnson, & Siegel, 1978).

Daily Hassles

Perhaps it is not the major life events but the minor frustrations and annoyances in our daily lives that produce the greatest stress. To investigate this possibility, a group of investigators conducted a year-long study of the effects of life's daily hassles on middle-aged men and women. They gave their subjects life-events questionnaires and checklists on which to record the "hassles," or irritating things that happened every day, as well as the "uplifts," or pleasant things. Examples of hassles include misplacing items, concerns about owing money, too many interruptions, too many responsibilities, not enough time for family, and arguments. The researchers found that the accumulation of daily hassles was an even better predictor of emotional and physical health than were the major events in people's lives (DeLongis et al., 1982).

It appears, too, that the stressfulness of major life changes is partly a function of the daily hassles they create. For example, a widow's grief over the loss of her husband may be compounded when she has to cope with such unfamiliar responsibilities as auto repairs, handling the changed finances, and preparing tax returns. To the extent that life changes (job loss, divorce, death of a loved one) disrupt an individual's patterns of daily living, they are apt to create hassles.

Before concluding that life changes and daily hassles per se *cause* poor physical and mental health, we must consider how the individual appraises an event and what his or her coping skills are. A job change that may be distressing to

one person may be considered an exciting challenge by another. One person may react to a traffic jam philosophically, with only minimal irritation, while another person may be infuriated. What a person considers a hassle depends on his or her life situation and coping skills. Some hassles may reflect coping ineptitudes. A person who finds it difficult to handle criticism is likely to have more authority-centered hassles at work than is the individual who lacks such vulnerability. Hassles generated by coping ineptitudes and vulnerabilities turn out to affect health and morale more than hassles that stem from chance circumstances in the environment.

Situational Factors That Influence Stress

Cognitive appraisal and coping skills are personal variables that influence the severity of stress. People respond differently to the same stressful situation, depending on its meaning for them and the amount of confidence they have in their ability to cope with it. But certain characteristics of the stressor have been found to influence the severity of stress — namely, its predictability and controllability.

PREDICTABILITY   Being able to predict the occurrence of a stressful event — even if the individual cannot control it — usually reduces the severity of the stress. Laboratory experiments show that both human beings and animals prefer predictable aversive events to unpredictable ones. In one study, rats were given a choice between a signaled shock and an unsignaled shock. If the rat pressed a bar at the start of a series of shock trials, each shock was preceded by a warning tone. If the rat failed to press the bar, no warning tones sounded during that series of trials. All of the rats quickly learned to press the bar, showing a marked preference for predictable shock (Abbott, Schoen, & Badia, 1984).

Human subjects generally choose predictable over unpredictable shocks, too. They also show less emotional arousal and report less distress while waiting for predictable shocks to occur, and they perceive predictable shocks as less aversive than unpredictable ones of the same intensity (Katz & Wykes, 1985). How do we explain these results? With unpredictable shock, there is no "safe" period; with predictable shock, the subject (human or animal) can relax to some extent until the signal warns that shock is about to occur. Another possibility is that a warning signal before an aversive event allows the subject to initiate some sort of preparatory process that acts to lessen the effects of a noxious stimulus on the nervous system.

In real-life situations, lack of predictability—or *uncertainty*—can make it very difficult for an individual to deal with stressful events. For example, one of the major problems faced by cancer patients who receive treatment is that they cannot be sure whether or not they have been cured until many years have passed. They must confront, every day, the uncertainty of a potentially disastrous future.

A similar gnawing uncertainty has created chronic stress for people who lived near Three Mile Island (Middletown, Pennsylvania) when an accident at the nuclear power plant released radioactive gases. Many of the residents believe that they were exposed to radiation and are apprehensive about the future effects of that exposure. Compared to a control group, these residents reported more emotional and physical problems and showed poorer task performance two years after the accident (Baum, Gatchel, Fleming, & Lake, 1981).

Another example is women whose husbands were reported missing in action in Vietnam. Not knowing whether their husbands were alive or dead made it difficult for them to resolve their grief and proceed with their lives. Compared with wives of men who were killed in action and with wives of men who were prisoners, these women showed the poorest physical and emotional health (Hunter, 1979).

CONTROLLABILITY   Having some control over a stressful event also reduces the severity of the stress. In one study, subjects were shown color photographs of victims of violent deaths. The experimental group could terminate the viewing by pressing a button. The control subjects saw the same photographs for the time duration determined by the experimental group, but they could not terminate exposure. The experimental group showed much less anxiety (measured by the galvanic skin response, GSR) in response to the photographs than did the group that had no control over the duration of viewing (Geer & Maisel, 1972).

In another study, two groups of subjects were exposed to a loud, extremely unpleasant noise. Subjects in one group were told that they could terminate the noise by pressing a button, but they were urged not to do so unless it was absolutely necessary. Subjects in the other group had no control over the noise. None of the subjects who had a control button actually pressed it, so the noise exposure was the same for both groups. Nevertheless, performance on subsequent problem-solving tasks was significantly worse for the group that had no control, indicating that they were more disturbed by the noise than was the group that had the potential for control. The belief that we can control the duration of an aversive event appears to lessen anxiety, even if the control is never exercised or if the belief is erroneous (Glass & Singer, 1972).

SOCIAL SUPPORTS   The emotional support and concern of other people can make stress more bearable. Divorce, the death of a loved one, or a serious illness is usually more devastating if an individual must face it alone. Numerous studies indicate that people who have many social ties (spouse, friends, relatives, and group memberships) live longer and are less apt to succumb to stress-related illnesses than are people who have few supportive social contacts (Cohen & Wills, 1985). Friends and family can provide support in many ways. They can bolster self-esteem by loving us despite our problems. They can provide information and advice, companionship to distract us from our worries, and financial or material aid. All of these tend to reduce feelings of helplessness and to increase our confidence in our ability to cope.

Sometimes, however, family and friends can increase the stress. Minimizing the seriousness of the problem or giving blind assurance that everything will be all right may produce more anxiety than failing to offer support at all. A study of graduate students facing crucial examinations suggests that spouses who are realistically supportive ("I'm worried, but I know you'll do the best you can") are more helpful than spouses who deny any possibility of failure ("I'm not worried; I'm sure you'll pass"). In the latter case, the student has to worry not only about failing the exam but also about losing respect in the eyes of the spouse (Mechanic, 1962).

Stress is easier to tolerate when the cause of the stress is shared by others. Community disasters (floods, earthquakes, tornadoes, wars) often seem to bring out the best in people (Nilson et al., 1981). Individual anxieties and conflicts tend to be forgotten when people are working together against a common enemy or toward a common goal. During the intensive bombing of London in World War II, for instance, there was a marked decline in the number of people seeking help for emotional problems.

COPING WITH STRESS

Because the anxiety and physiological arousal created by stressful situations are highly uncomfortable, the individual is motivated to do something to alleviate the discomfort. The process by which a person attempts to manage stressful demands is called *coping,* and it takes two major forms. One focuses on the problem: the individual evaluates the stressful situation and does something to change or avoid it. The other focuses on the emotional response to the problem: the individual tries to reduce anxiety without dealing directly with the anxiety-producing situation. The former is referred to as *problem-focused coping* and the latter, as *emotion-focused coping* (Lazarus & Folkman, 1984).

Suppose that you receive a warning that you are about to fail a course required for graduation. You might confer with the professor, devise a work schedule to fulfill the requirements, and then follow it; or you might decide that you cannot fulfill the requirements in the time remaining and so sign up to retake the course in summer school. Both of these actions are problem-focused methods of coping. On the other hand, you might try to reduce your anxiety about the failure warning by refusing to acknowledge the possibility of failing or by convincing yourself that a college degree is worthless — or you might deaden your anxiety with alcohol. These are emotion-focused coping strategies.

Each individual deals with stressful situations in his or her unique way, often using a combination of problem-focused and emotion-focused strategies. In most instances, problem solving is the healthier approach. But not all problems can be solved. In such instances as an incapacitating illness or the loss of a loved one, individuals may need to reduce emotional distress until they can face the situation in its entirety. We often use emotion-focused coping to maintain hope, to keep up our morale so that we can continue to function. In general, emotion-focused forms of coping are more likely to occur when a person is experiencing a high level of stress and has decided that nothing can be done to modify the threatening conditions. Problem-focused forms of coping, on the other hand, are more probable at moderate levels of stress, where the situation is appraised as changeable (Lazarus & Folkman, 1984).

Some emotion-focused strategies are behavioral — for example, engaging in physical exercise to get one's mind off a problem, taking a drink, venting anger, seeking emotional support from friends. Others are cognitive: examples are

Disasters, such as the earthquake that devastated Mexico City in 1985, tend to rally individuals to work toward a common goal. Stress is easier to tolerate when it is shared by others.

temporarily setting aside thoughts about the problem—"I decided it wasn't worth worrying about"—and reducing the threat by changing the meaning of the situation—"I decided her friendship wasn't that important to me." These two statements indicate that the person is reappraising a stressful situation to make it less of a threat.

Our reappraisal of a problem may be realistic: perhaps, on second thought, the problem is not worth serious concern. Sometimes, however, in seeking to reduce anxiety we deceive ourselves and distort the reality of the situation.

Defense Mechanisms as Emotion-focused Coping

Freud used the term *defense mechanisms* to refer to unconscious processes that defend a person against anxiety by distorting reality in some way. These emotion-focused strategies do not alter the stressful situation; they simply change the way the person perceives or thinks about it. Thus, all defense mechanisms involve an element of *self-deception.*

The word "mechanism" is not the most appropriate term, because it implies that a form of mechanical device is involved. Freud was influenced by the nineteenth-century tendency to think of the human being as a complicated machine. Actually, we will be talking about some emotion-focused strategies that people employ to minimize anxiety in situations they cannot handle effectively. But since "defense mechanism" is still the most commonly applied term, we will continue to use it.

We all use defense mechanisms at times. They help us over the rough spots until we can deal more directly with the stressful situation. Defense mechanisms indicate personality maladjustment only when they become the dominant mode of responding to problems.

REPRESSION   Freud considered *repression* to be the basic, and most important, defense mechanism. In repression, impulses or memories that are too frightening or painful are excluded from conscious awareness. Memories that evoke shame, guilt, or self-deprecation are often repressed. Freud believed that repression of certain childhood impulses is universal. He maintained that all young boys have feelings of sexual attraction toward the mother and feelings of rivalry and hostility toward the father (the *Oedipus complex*); these impulses are repressed to avoid the painful consequences of acting on them. In later life, an individual may repress feelings and memories that could cause anxiety because they are inconsistent with his or her self-concept. Feelings of hostility toward a loved one and experiences of failure may be banished from conscious memory.

Repression must be distinguished from *suppression*. Suppression is the process of deliberate self-control, keeping impulses and desires in check (perhaps holding them privately while denying them publicly) or temporarily pushing aside painful memories in order to concentrate on a task. Individuals are aware of suppressed thoughts but are largely *unaware* of impulses or memories that are repressed.

Freud believed that repression is seldom completely successful. The repressed impulses threaten to break through into consciousness; the individual becomes anxious (although unaware of the reason) and employs one of the following defense mechanisms to keep the partially repressed impulses from awareness. Thus, these other defense mechanisms are said to aid repression.

RATIONALIZATION   When the fox in Aesop's fable rejected the grapes he could not reach "because they were sour," he illustrated a defense mechanism known as *rationalization*. Rationalization does not mean "to act rationally"; it is the assignment of logical or socially desirable motives to what we do so that we seem to have acted rationally. Rationalization serves two purposes: it eases our disappointment when we fail to reach a goal ("I didn't want it anyway"), and it provides us with acceptable motives for our behavior. If we act impulsively or on the basis of motives we do not wish to acknowledge even to ourselves, we rationalize what we have done to place our behavior in a more favorable light.

In the search for the "good" reason rather than the "true" reason, individuals make a number of excuses. These excuses are usually plausible; they simply do not tell the whole story. For example, "My roommate failed to wake me" or "I had too many other things to do." Both statements may be true, but they are not the real reasons for the individual's failure to perform the behavior in question. Individuals who are really concerned set an alarm clock or find the time.

An experiment involving posthypnotic suggestion (see Chapter 4, p. 138) demonstrates the process of rationalization. A subject under hypnosis is told that when he wakes from the trance he will watch the hypnotist. When the hypnotist takes off his glasses, the subject will raise the window, but he will not remember that the hypnotist told him to do this. Aroused from the trance, the subject feels a little drowsy but presently circulates among the people in the room and carries on a normal conversation, furtively watching the hypnotist. When the hypnotist casually removes his glasses, the subject feels an impulse to open the window. He takes a step in that direction but hesitates. Unconsciously, he mobilizes his wishes to be a reasonable person; seeking a reason for his impulse to open the window, he says "Isn't it a little stuffy in here?" Having found the needed excuse, he opens the window and feels more comfortable (Hilgard, 1965).

REACTION FORMATION   Sometimes individuals can conceal a motive from themselves by giving strong expression to the opposite motive. Such a tendency is called *reaction formation*. A mother who feels guilty about not wanting her child may become overindulgent and overprotective to assure the child of her love and to assure herself that she is a good mother. In one case, a mother who wished to do everything for her daughter could not understand why the child was so unappreciative. At great sacrifice, she had the daughter take expensive piano lessons and assisted her in the daily practice sessions. Although the mother thought she was being extremely kind, she was actually being very demanding—in fact, hostile. She was unaware of her own hostility, but when confronted with it, the mother admitted that she had hated piano lessons as a child. Under the conscious guise of being kind, she was unconsciously being cruel to her daughter. The daughter vaguely sensed what was going on and developed symptoms that required psychological treatment.

Some people who crusade with fanatical zeal against loose morals, alcohol, and gambling may be manifesting reaction formation. Often such individuals have a background of earlier difficulties with these problems, and their zealous crusading may be a means of defending themselves against the possibility of backsliding.

PROJECTION   All of us have undesirable traits that we do not acknowledge, even to ourselves. One unconscious mechanism, *projection*, protects us from recognizing our own undesirable qualities by assigning them in exaggerated amounts to other people. Suppose you have a tendency to be critical of or unkind to other people, but you would dislike yourself if you admitted this tendency. If you are convinced that the people around you are cruel or unkind, your harsh treatment of them is not based on *your* bad qualities—you are simply "giving them what they deserve." If you can assure yourself that everybody else cheats on college examinations, your unacknowledged tendency to take some academic shortcuts is not so bad. Projection is really a form of rationalization, but it is so pervasive in our culture that it merits discussion in its own right.

© 1975 United Features Syndicate

INTELLECTUALIZATION   *Intellectualization* is an attempt to gain detachment from a stressful situation by dealing with it in abstract, intellectual terms. This kind of defense is frequently a necessity for people who must deal with life-and-death matters in their daily job. The doctor who is continually confronted with human suffering cannot afford to become emotionally involved with each patient. In fact, a certain amount of detachment may be essential for the doctor to function competently. This kind of intellectualization is a problem only when it becomes such a pervasive life-style that individuals cut themselves off from all emotional experiences.

DENIAL   When an external reality is too unpleasant to face, an individual may deny that it exists. The parents of a fatally ill child may refuse to admit that anything is seriously wrong, even though they are fully informed of the diagnosis and the expected outcome. Because they cannot tolerate the pain that acknowledging reality would produce, they resort to the defense mechanism of *denial*. Less extreme forms of denial may be seen in individuals who consistently ignore criticism, fail to perceive that others are angry with them, or disregard all kinds of clues suggesting that a marriage partner is having an affair.

Sometimes, denying facts may be better than facing them. In a severe crisis, denial may give the person time to face the grim facts at a more gradual pace. For example, victims of a stroke or a spinal cord injury might give up altogether if they were fully aware of the seriousness of their conditions. Hope gives the individual the incentive to keep trying. Servicemen who have faced combat or imprisonment report that denying the possibility of death helped them to function. In these situations, denial clearly has an adaptive value. On the other hand, the negative aspects of denial are evident when people postpone seeking medical help: for example, a woman may deny that a lump in the breast may be cancerous and so delay going to a physician.

DISPLACEMENT   The last defense mechanism we consider fulfills its function (reduces anxiety) while partially gratifying the unacceptable motive. Through the mechanism of *displacement*, a motive that cannot be gratified in one form is directed into a new channel. An example of displacement was provided in our discussion of anger that could not be expressed toward the source of frustration and was redirected toward a less threatening object.

Freud felt that displacement was the most satisfactory way of handling aggressive and sexual impulses. The basic drives cannot be changed, but the object toward which a drive is directed can be changed. For example, sexual impulses toward the parents cannot be safely gratified, but such impulses can be displaced toward a more suitable love object. Erotic impulses that cannot be expressed directly may be expressed indirectly in creative activities such as art, poetry, and music. Hostile impulses may find socially acceptable expression through participation in physical-contact sports.

It seems unlikely that displacement actually eliminates the frustrated impulses, but substitute activities do help to reduce tension when a basic drive is thwarted. For example, the activities of mothering, being mothered, or seeking companionship may help to reduce the tension associated with unsatisfied sexual needs.

Problem-focused Coping

In coping with the stressful situation itself, rather than with the emotions it generates, we can flee from the problem or we can try to find some way of altering or solving it. Strategies for solving problems include defining the problem, generating alternative solutions, weighing the alternatives in terms of costs and bene-

fits, choosing among them, and implementing the selected alternative. How skillfully the individual employs these strategies depends on his or her range of experiences, intellectual ability, and capacity for self-control.

Problem-focused strategies can also be directed inward: the person changes something about himself or herself instead of changing the environment. Changing one's level of aspiration, finding alternative sources of gratification, and learning new skills are examples. When a person's job is a chronic source of stress, for instance, such strategies might be the best solution.

It should be emphasized that most people use *both* emotion-focused and problem-focused coping in dealing with the stresses of daily life. Several studies asked people to record the stressful events they experienced over the course of a year. The subjects reported on a checklist the thoughts and behaviors they used to handle the demands of each event. The results indicate that almost everyone used both emotion-focused and problem-focused strategies to deal with virtually every stressful encounter (Folkman & Lazarus, 1980; Folkman et al., 1986).

Sometimes the two forms of coping can facilitate each other. For example, a student feels extremely anxious at the beginning of a major exam. But as she turns her attention to taking the exam, her anxiety diminishes. In this instance, problem-focused coping (turning to the task) reduces emotional distress. Sometimes emotion-focused and problem-focused coping can impede each other. A person suffering over having to make a difficult decision finds the distress unbearable and, in order to reduce distress, makes a premature decision. Here, the strategy used to reduce distress interferes with effective problem solving.

STRESS AND ILLNESS

In discussing the resistance stage of the general adaptation syndrome, we noted that the body's attempts to adapt to the continued presence of a stressor deplete the body's resources and make it vulnerable to illness. Chronic stress can lead to such physical disorders as ulcers, high blood pressure, and heart disease. It can also impair the immune system, decreasing the body's ability to fight invading bacteria and viruses. Indeed, doctors estimate that emotional stress plays an important role in more than half of all medical problems.

Psychosomatic disorders are physical disorders in which emotions are believed to play a central role. The term "psychosomatic" is derived from the Greek words *psyche* ("mind") and *soma* ("body"). A common misconception is that people with psychosomatic disorders are not really sick and do not need medical attention. On the contrary, the symptoms of psychosomatic illness reflect physiological disturbances associated with tissue damage and pain; a peptic ulcer caused by stress is indistinguishable from an ulcer that results from long-term heavy usage of aspirin.

Traditionally, research in psychosomatic medicine focused on such illnesses as asthma, hypertension (high blood pressure), ulcers, colitis, and rheumatoid arthritis. Researchers looked for relationships between specific illnesses and

Air traffic controllers, who work under intense pressure and must make instant decisions that affect the safety of hundreds of people, have a high incidence of peptic ulcers.

characteristic attitudes toward, or ways of coping with, stressful life events. For example, individuals with hypertension were said to feel that life was threatening and, consequently, they must be on guard at all times. Those suffering from colitis were believed to be angry but unable to express their anger. However, most studies that reported characteristic attitudes to be related to specific illnesses have not been replicated. Thus, the hypothesis that people who share the same ways of reacting to stress will be vulnerable to the same illnesses has generally not been confirmed. An important exception is the research on coronary heart disease and *Type A* behavior patterns, as we will see shortly.

Today the focus of psychosomatic research is much broader, and the term "psychosomatic medicine" is being replaced by *behavioral medicine*. Behavioral medicine is an interdisciplinary field that attracts specialists from psychology and medicine. It seeks to learn how social, psychological, and biological variables combine to cause illness, and how behavior and environments can be changed to promote health.

Ulcers

A peptic ulcer is a lesion (a hole) in the lining of the stomach or duodenum that is produced by the excessive secretion of hydrochloric acid. In the process of digestion, hydrochloric acid interacts with enzymes to break down food into components that can be utilized by the body. When the acid is secreted in excessive amounts, it gradually erodes the mucous layer protecting the stomach wall, producing small lesions. A number of factors can cause an increased secretion of hydrochloric acid, and psychological stress appears to be one of them.

Animal studies have shown that stress can cause ulcers. In a series of experiments with rats, stress was produced by administering a mild electric shock to the

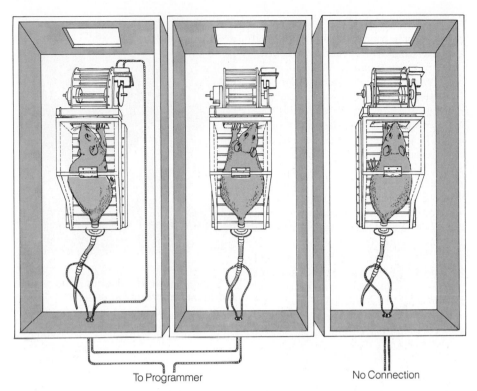

To Programmer   No Connection

tail. The rats, tested in sets of three, were placed in the apparatus shown in Figure 14-2. The rat in the left-hand chamber can terminate the programmed shocks by turning a wheel. Moreover, each shock is preceded by a warning signal; if the animal turns the wheel at the appropriate time, it can postpone the next shock. The rat in the middle compartment is "yoked" to the rat on the left so that it receives shocks of the same intensity and duration as the left-hand rat but can do nothing to control the shocks. The rat in the right-hand chamber is hooked up like the other two, but the electrodes are not connected so that it receives no shocks.

After the animals had participated in this procedure for some time, they were examined for ulcers. The rats who could do something to control the shocks showed much less ulceration than their helpless, yoked companions. The control animals, who received no shocks, showed no ulceration (Weiss, 1972).

This and similar experiments suggest that prolonged exposure to uncontrollable stress does contribute to the development of ulcers. Although we cannot generalize from animal subjects to human subjects without further research, it seems likely that stress is one factor that leads to ulcers — particularly in individuals who are biologically predisposed to secrete a high level of hydrochloric acid.

Heart Disease

Stress also plays a role in heart disease. One area of research has identified a behavior pattern, called "Type A," that appears to characterize people who have heart attacks (Friedman & Rosenman, 1974). Type A individuals are described as extremely competitive and achievement oriented; they have a sense of time urgency, find it difficult to relax, and become impatient and angry when confronted with delays or with people they view as incompetent. The assumption is that such individuals, although outwardly self-confident, are prey to constant feelings of

CRITICAL DISCUSSION

Controlling Physiological Responses to Stress

Among the techniques that have been used to help people control their physiological responses to stressful situations are *biofeedback*, *relaxation training*, and *cognitive behavior therapy*. In biofeedback training, individuals receive information (feedback) about an aspect of their physiological state and then attempt to alter that state. For example, in a procedure for learning to control tension headaches, electrodes are attached to the forehead so that any movement in the forehead muscle can be electronically detected, amplified, and fed back to the person as an auditory signal. The signal, or tone, increases in pitch when the muscle contracts and decreases when it relaxes. By learning to control the pitch of the tone, the individual learns to keep the muscle relaxed. (Relaxation of the forehead muscle usually ensures relaxation of scalp and neck muscles also.) After four to eight weeks of biofeedback training, the subject learns to recognize the onset of tension and to reduce it without feedback from the machine (Tarler-Benlolo, 1978).

Physiological processes that are controlled by the autonomic nervous system, such as heart rate and blood pressure, have traditionally been assumed to be automatic and not under voluntary control. However, experiments in the 1960s showed that rats could be operantly conditioned (see Chapter 7, p. 225) to raise or lower their heart rates (see DiCara & Miller, 1968). Subsequent laboratory studies have demonstrated that human subjects can also learn to modify heart rate and blood pressure (see Figure 14-3). The results of these studies have led to new procedures for treating patients with high blood pressure (hypertension). One procedure is to show patients a graph of their blood pressure while it is being monitored and to teach them techniques for relaxing different muscle groups. The patients are instructed to tense their muscles (for example, to clench a fist or to tighten the abdomen), release the tension, and notice the difference in sensation. By starting with the feet and ankle muscles and progressing through the body to the muscles that control the neck and face, the patients learn to modify muscular tension. This combination of biofeedback with relaxation training has proved effective in lowering blood pressure for some individuals (Tarler-Benlolo, 1978).

Biofeedback for Headaches *The sensors measure forehead muscle contractions and finger temperature. Cold fingers are often a sign of tension.*

Reviews of numerous studies using biofeedback and relaxation training to control headaches and hypertension conclude that the most important variable is *learning how to relax* (Runck, 1980). Some people may learn to relax faster when they receive biofeedback. Others may learn to relax equally well when they receive training in muscle relaxation without any specific biofeedback. The usefulness of relaxation training seems to depend on the individual. Some people who are not conscientious about taking drugs to relieve high blood pressure are more responsive to relaxation training, whereas others who have learned to control their blood pressure through relaxation may eventually drop the procedure because they find it too time-consuming.

People who are able to control their physiological responses by biofeedback and relaxation training in the laboratory will have more difficulty doing so in actual stressful situations, particularly if they continue to interact in ways that make them tense. Consequently, an additional approach to stress management focuses on changing the individual's cognitive and behavioral responses to stressful situations. *Cognitive behavior therapy* attempts to help people to identify the kinds of stressful situations that produce their physiological symptoms and to alter the way they cope with these situations. For example, a man who suffers from tension headaches would be asked to begin by keeping a record of their occurrence and rating the severity of each headache and the circumstances in which it occurred. Next he is taught how to monitor his responses to these stressful events and is asked to record his feelings, thoughts, and behavior prior to, during, and following the event. After a period of self-monitoring, certain relationships often become evident among situational variables (for example, criticism by a supervisor or coworker); thoughts ("I can't do anything right"); and emotional, behavioral, and physiological responses (depression, withdrawal, and headache).

The next step is trying to identify the expectations or beliefs that might explain the headache reactions (for example, "I expect to do everything perfectly, so the slightest criticism upsets me" or "I judge myself harshly, become depressed, and end up with a headache"). The final and most difficult step is trying to change something about the stressful situation, his way of thinking about it, or his behavior. The options might include finding a less stressful job, recognizing that his need to perform perfectly leads to unnecessary anguish over errors, or learning to behave more assertively in interactions instead of withdrawing.

This capsule summary of cognitive behavior therapy for coping with stressful situations does not do justice to the procedures involved. A more detailed description is found in Chapter 16 (p. 538). Biofeedback, relaxation training, and cognitive behavior therapy have all proved useful in helping people control their physiological responses to stress. Some research suggests that the improvement gained with cognitive behavior therapy is more likely to be maintained over time (Holroyd, Appel, & Andrasik, 1983). This is not surprising, since the complex demands of everyday life often require flexible coping skills; being able to relax may not be an effective method of coping with some of life's stresses. Programs for stress management frequently employ a combination of biofeedback, relaxation training, and cognitive behavior modification techniques.

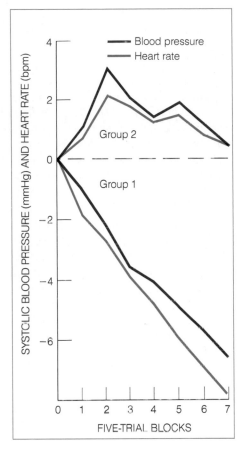

FIGURE 14-3
Operant Conditioning of Blood Pressure and Heart Rate *One group of male subjects received biofeedback (a light and a tone) whenever their blood pressure and heart rate decreased simultaneously (Group 1); the other group received the same feedback whenever their blood pressure and heart rate increased simultaneously (Group 2). Whenever a subject in either group produced 12 consecutive correct heart-rate/blood-pressure responses, he was reinforced with slides (landscapes and nude females) and a cash bonus. The subjects achieved significant simultaneous control of blood pressure and heart rate during a single conditioning session. The group reinforced for lowering both functions achieved increasingly more control over trials; the group reinforced for raising both functions was less consistent. (After Schwartz, 1975)*

self-doubt; they push themselves to accomplish more and more in less and less time. Some common Type A behaviors are listed in Table 14-2. Type B individuals are defined as those who do not exhibit the characteristics listed for Type A. Type B individuals are able to relax without feeling guilty and to work without becoming agitated; they lack a sense of urgency with its accompanying impatience and are not easily roused to anger.

Several long-range studies indicate that people who exhibit Type A behavior are more likely to suffer a heart attack than are Type B individuals (Rosenman et al., 1975; Haynes, Feinleib, & Kannel, 1980). How Type A behavior affects the cardiovascular system is still not clearly understood. The physiological effects of the kind of stress that Type A individuals experience may involve increased blood cholesterol levels, an enhanced tendency to form blood clots, elevated blood pressure, or increased secretion of the hormone norepinephrine, which can trigger abnormalities in heart rhythm. Studies indicate that Type A individuals, compared with Type B individuals, show greater changes on all of these measures when confronted with stressful tasks (Wright, Contrada, & Glass, 1985).

In 1981 the American Heart Association, after reviewing the evidence on Type A individuals, decided that Type A behavior should be classified as a risk factor for heart disease. However, two more recent studies failed to find any relationship between A and B personality types and subsequent heart attacks (Case, Heller, Case, & Moss, 1985; Shekelle et al., 1983). Some researchers believe that this is because the current definition of Type A behavior is too diffuse. They suggest that time urgency and competitiveness are not the most important com-

TABLE 14-2
Type A Behavior Characteristics *Some behaviors that characterize people prone to heart disease. (After Friedman & Rosenman, 1974)*

Thinking of or doing two things at once

Scheduling more and more activities into less and less time

Failing to notice or be interested in the environment or things of beauty

Hurrying the speech of others

Becoming unduly irritated when forced to wait in line or when driving behind a car you think is moving too slowly

Believing that if you want something done well, you have to do it yourself

Gesticulating when you talk

Frequent knee jiggling or rapid tapping of your fingers

Explosive speech patterns or frequent use of obscenities

Making a fetish of always being on time

Having difficulty sitting and doing nothing

Playing nearly every game to win, even when playing with children

Measuring your own and others' success in terms of numbers (number of patients seen, articles written, etc.)

Lip clicking, head nodding, fist clenching, table pounding, or sucking in of air when speaking

Becoming impatient while watching others do things you think you can do better or faster

Rapid eye blinking or ticlike eyebrow lifting

ponents; the crucial variable appears to be anger. Several studies have found that a person's level of hostility is a better predictor of heart disease than is his overall level of Type A behavior (Thoresen, Telch, & Eagleston, 1981; Dembroski, Mac-Dougall, Williams, & Haney, 1985). Thus, impatience and ambition seem less damaging than being constantly annoyed.

A project aimed at modifying Type A behavior and involving more than 1,000 individuals who have experienced at least one heart attack reports considerable success. The subjects in the experimental group were helped to change their Type A behavior. For example, to reduce their sense of time urgency, individuals were asked to practice standing in line (a situation Type A individuals find extremely irritating) and to use the opportunity to reflect on things that they do not normally have time to think about, or to watch people, or to strike up a conversation with a stranger. Treatment also included learning to alter certain specific behaviors (such as interrupting the speech of others or talking or eating hurriedly), reevaluating basic beliefs (such as the notion that success depends on the quantity of work produced), and finding ways to make the home and work environment less stressful (such as encouraging spouses to reduce the number of unnecessary social engagements).

The critical dependent variable in this study is the occurrence of another heart attack. By the end of the study, four and a half years later, the experimental group had a cardiac recurrence rate almost half that of control subjects who were not taught how to alter their life-style pattern. Clearly, learning to modify Type A behavior is beneficial to one's health (Friedman et al., 1985).

This study also found hostility to be the most significant predictor of heart disease. Individuals who suffered a subsequent heart attack, many of whom died, did not differ from individuals who remained healthy in terms of total Type A scores, family background, and overall measures of chronic stress. But they scored two or three times higher on measures of hostile behavior.

Another study reports considerable success in reducing hostility among Type A individuals. The subjects were officer-students at the U.S. Army War College who showed no signs of heart disease but who, by virtue of their high Type A scores, were likely candidates for future cardiac problems. An eight-month counseling program designed to modify Type A behavior produced a number of desired changes, the most dramatic being a reduction in hostility and time urgency. The subjects who experienced the greatest reduction in Type A characteristics had significantly lower levels of blood cholesterol at the end of the study (Gill et al., 1985). It remains to be seen, however, how long the effects of Type A counseling will last and whether or not the experimental subjects will have fewer heart attacks than the control subjects who received no counseling.

The Immune System

One relatively new area of research in behavioral medicine is *psychoimmunology*, the study of how the body's immune system is affected by psychological variables. The immune system is a surveillance mechanism that protects the body from disease-causing microorganisms. It regulates our susceptibility to cancers, infectious diseases, allergies, and autoimmune disorders (that is, diseases such as rheumatoid arthritis, in which the immune cells attack the normal tissue of the body). Evidence is mounting that stress affects the ability of the immune system to defend the body.

Many animal studies have demonstrated that experimentally induced stress increases susceptibility to a variety of infectious agents (Borysenko & Borysenko, 1982) and the incidence and rate of tumor growth (Riley, 1981). Data for human subjects are, of course, more difficult to obtain and to interpret. As noted earlier, the effect of stressful events on health-related behaviors (diet, sleep, cigarette and drug use) cannot be ignored when considering the relationship between stress and illness. Nevertheless, a review of the literature indicates that stress can influence the functioning of the immune system and our vulnerability to infectious diseases (Jemmott & Locke, 1984).

Two studies illustrate the kinds of psychological stressors that have been associated with lowered immune responses. One study found that during exams or periods of academic pressure, students show lower levels of an antibody that defends against respiratory infections (Jemmott et al., 1985). Another study, involving men whose wives had died from breast cancer, demonstrated that the responsiveness of the men's lymphocytes (a class of white blood cells that is an essential part of the immune system) declined significantly within the month following their wives' deaths, and in some cases remained low for a year thereafter (Schleifer, Keller, McKegney, & Stein, 1979).

While the link between stressors and impaired immune functioning is quite strong, only some stressed individuals become ill. Why? Two researchers devised an experiment to determine whether the ability to control a stressor would alter the functioning of the immune system. Controllability, as we noted earlier, is one of the factors that reduces the severity of stress. Using an apparatus similar to that shown in Figure 14-2, rats were exposed to either controllable or uncontrollable electric shock. Both groups received the same amount of shock, but only one group could terminate the shock by turning the wheel.

As a measure of immune-system response, the investigators studied how readily the rat's T-cells (a type of lymphocyte that kills invading viruses) multiplied when "challenged" by an invader. They found that the T-cells from rats that could control the shock multiplied as readily as did those from rats who were not stressed at all. T-cells from rats exposed to uncontrollable shock, on the other hand, multiplied only weakly. Thus shocks (stress) interfered with the immune response only in rats that could not control them (Laudenslager et al., 1983).

Using a similar experimental arrangement, the same investigators studied the effect of uncontrollable shock on another immune-system measure: the tumor-killing ability of a type of T-cell called "natural killer cells." Natural killer (NK) cells play a key role in tumor surveillance and help to prevent the development of cancerous tumors. The NK cells from unstressed rats or from rats that could control the stressor killed tumor cells normally, whereas NK cells from rats exposed to an uncontrollable stressor were less able to kill tumor cells (Maier & Laudenslager, 1985).

Perhaps when stressful life events (such as the loss of a spouse) result in suppressed immune responses, they do so because the individuals feel they have no control over the negative events. There is some support for this view. One study found that people who experienced many negative life events but did not react to these events with anxiety or depression had very high NK-cell activity, even higher than people who experienced few life stresses. Those who had high levels of anxiety and depression in response to life stresses had the lowest NK-cell activity. Coping well with stress seems to be accompanied by high levels of NK-cell activity (Locke et al., 1984).

The immune system is incredibly complicated, employing a number of different weapons that interact in complex ways to defend the body. Much remains unknown about how it does the job, and even less is known about its relationship to the nervous system. Scientists once believed that the immune system operated quite independently, isolated from other physiological systems. But current studies are making it increasingly evident that the immune system and the nervous system have numerous anatomical and physiological connections. To mention one example, researchers are discovering that lymphocytes have receptors for a number of different neurotransmitters. Thus, these immune-system cells are equipped to receive messages from the brain that may alter the way they behave.

As research in psychoimmunology yields additional information about the links between the nervous and immune systems, we will gain a clearer understanding of how mental attitudes affect health.

Stress-resistant Individuals

Some people experience one stressful event after another and do not break down. Others are seriously upset by even low-level stressors. As noted throughout the chapter, two important variables that mediate the effects of stressors are the individual's cognitive appraisal of the situation and his or her resources for coping with it. Several investigators have attempted to determine more precisely the personality characteristics that make people resistant to stress. In one study, more than 600 men who were executives or managers in the same company were given checklists and were asked to describe all of the stressful events and illnesses they had experienced over the previous three years. Two groups were selected for comparison: the first group scored above average on both stressful events and illness; the second group scored equally high on stress but *below average* on illness. Members of both groups then filled out detailed personality questionnaires. Analysis of the results indicated that the high-stress/low-illness men differed from the men who became ill under stress on three major dimensions: they were more actively involved in their work and social lives, they were more oriented toward challenge and change, and they felt more in control of events in their lives (Kobasa, 1979).

Of course, it could be argued that these personality differences were the *result* rather than the *cause* of illness. For example, it is hard for people to be involved in work or social activity when they are ill. The investigators therefore conducted a longitudinal study that considered the personality characteristics of business executives before they became ill, then monitored their life stress scores and the extent of their illnesses for a period of two years. The results showed that the executives whose attitudes toward life could be rated high on involvement, feelings of control, and positive responses to change remained healthier than the men who scored low on these dimensions (Kobasa, Maddi, & Kahn, 1982). The most important factor appears to be attitude toward change. People who view change as a challenge — for example, regarding the loss of a job as an opportunity to find a new career rather than as a serious setback — are apt to experience less stress and to turn the situation to their advantage.

The personality characteristics of stress-resistant or *hardy* individuals have been summarized by the terms *commitment, control,* and *challenge.* These characteristics are interrelated with the factors we have discussed as influencing the severity of stress. For example, commitment to relationships with other people provides social support in times of stress. The sense of being in control of life events reflects feelings of competency and also influences the way in which stressful events are appraised. People who feel they are able to exert control over stressful situations (instead of feeling helpless) are more likely to take action to remedy the situation. Challenge also involves cognitive evaluation, the belief that change is normal in life and should be viewed as an opportunity for growth rather than as a threat to security.

SUMMARY

1. Stress has been defined as a *response*, a *stimulus*, and a *transaction* between the demands of the environment and the person's ability to deal with them. According to the transactional approach, stress occurs when an individual appraises an event as taxing his or her resources and endangering his or her well-being.

2. The person's *cognitive appraisal* determines the degree of stress. The *primary appraisal* evaluates a situation as either irrelevant, benign-positive, or stressful (that is, constituting loss, threat of loss, or challenge). The *secondary appraisal* evaluates the individual's resources for coping with the threat.

3. The physiological responses that prepare the organism to deal with a perceived threat (the emergency, *fight-or-flight reaction*) are regulated by the *autonomic nervous system* under the control of the *hypothalamus*. The hypothalamus also signals the *pituitary gland* to secrete *adrenocorticotrophic hormone* (ACTH), which activates the release of numerous other hormones that play a role in the body's adjustment to emergencies.

4. The *general adaptation syndrome* (GAS) describes the body's adaptation to continued stress. Its stages include *alarm reaction* (shock and countershock phases), *resistance*, and *exhaustion*.

5. Psychological reactions to stress include *cognitive impairment* (difficulty in concentrating and rigidity of behavior) and such diverse emotional responses as *anxiety* (both objective and neurotic), *anger* and *aggression* (both direct and displaced), and *apathy* and *depression* (which may reflect *learned helplessness*).

6. Sources of stress include *conflict* between opposing motives, major *life changes*, and *daily hassles*. The ability to *predict* the occurrence of a stressful event and to exert some *control* over its duration reduces the severity of stress, as does the *social support* provided by other people.

7. In coping with stressful situations, people use a combination of *problem-focused strategies*, aimed at changing the situation in some way, and *emotion-focused strategies*, aimed at reducing anxiety without dealing directly with the problem. Some emotion-focused strategies that distort reality are called *defense mechanisms*. They include *repression*, *rationalization*, *reaction formation*, *projection*, *intellectualization*, *denial*, and *displacement*.

8. *Psychosomatic disorders* are physical disorders in which emotions are believed to play a central role. *Behavioral medicine*, an interdisciplinary field, seeks to discover how social, psychological, and biological variables combine to cause illness, and how behavior and environments can be changed to promote health.

9. Chronic stress can contribute to physical disorders, such as ulcers and heart disease, and can increase our vulnerability to infectious diseases by impairing the functioning of the body's immune system. *Type A personality* characteristics (hostile, impatient, time-pressured, and ambitious) predispose a person to heart disease. An inability to control stressful events appears to play a role in the development of ulcers and decreased immune functioning.

10. The personality characteristics of stress-resistant individuals (those who remain healthy despite many stressful life events) can be summarized by the terms *commitment*, *control*, and *challenge*.

Stress and Stress Management: Research and Applications (1984) by Hamberger and Lohr discusses the different models of stress, some relevant research findings, and various methods for controlling stress. The transactional model of stress is presented in *Stress, Appraisal, and Coping* (1984) by Lazarus and Folkman. For a cognitive behavior approach to stress prevention and management, see Meichenbaum and Jaremko (eds.), *Stress Reduction and Prevention* (1983); and a paperback, *Stress Inoculation Training* (1985), by Meichenbaum.

The *Handbook of Clinical Health Psychology* (1982), edited by Millon, Green, and Meagher, includes articles on most of the topics discussed in this chapter and also covers issues in the developing field of health psychology—for example, coping with the problems of life-threatening illness, chronic illness and disability, aging, and patient compliance with medical procedures. See also *Behavioral Medicine: The Biopsychological Approach* (1985), edited by Schneiderman and Tapp.

A classic account of defense mechanisms is given by Anna Freud in *The Ego and the Mechanisms of Defense* (rev. ed., 1967). An introductory treatment may be found in Coleman, Butcher, and Carson, *Abnormal Psychology and Modern Life* (7th ed., 1984).

FURTHER READING

Abnormal Psychology

MOST OF US HAVE PERIODS WHEN WE feel anxious, depressed, unreasonably angry, or inadequate in dealing with life's complexities. Trying to lead a satisfying and meaningful life is not easy in an era of rapid social and technological change. Many of our traditional assumptions about work, religion, sex, marriage, and family are being questioned, and the social and religious values that gave our grandparents a sense of security no longer provide clear guidelines for behavior. It is an unusual person who manages to get through life without periods of loneliness, self-doubt, and despair. In fact, about a third of Americans will experience a severe enough mental or emotional problem at least once during their lifetime that, if diagnosed, would be classified as a mental disorder (Robins et al., 1984).

In this chapter, we will look at some individuals who have serious mental disorders and some who have developed self-destructive life-styles. We will also consider a variety of ineffective ways of dealing with stress and with the problems of living. The behaviors we discuss are classified as "abnormal," but as we will see, the dividing line between "normal" and "abnormal" behavior is far from clear.

ABNORMAL BEHAVIOR

Defining Abnormality

What do we mean by "abnormal" behavior? By what criteria do we distinguish it from "normal" behavior? There is no general agreement, but most attempts to describe abnormality are based on one or more of the following definitions.

DEVIATION FROM STATISTICAL NORMS The word *abnormal* means "away from the norm." Many characteristics, such as height, weight, and intelligence, cover a range of values when measured over a population. Most people fall within the middle range of height, while a few individuals are abnormally tall or abnormally short. One definition of abnormality is based on *statistical frequency:* "abnormal behavior" is statistically infrequent or deviant from the norm. But according to this definition, the person who is extremely intelligent or extremely happy would be classified as abnormal. Thus, in defining abnormal behavior, we must consider more than statistical frequency.

DEVIATION FROM SOCIAL NORMS Every society has certain standards, or norms, for acceptable behavior; behavior that deviates markedly from these norms is considered abnormal. Usually, but not always, such behavior is also statistically infrequent in that society. However, several problems arise when deviation from social norms is used as a criterion for defining abnormality.

Behavior that is considered normal by one society may be considered abnormal by another. For example, members of some African tribes do not consider it unusual to hear voices when no one is actually talking or to see visions when nothing is actually there, but such behaviors are considered abnormal in most societies. Another problem is that the concept of abnormality changes over time within the same society. Most Americans would have considered smoking marijuana or appearing nude at the beach abnormal behaviors 30 years ago. Today, such behaviors tend to be viewed as differences in life-style rather than as signs of abnormality.

Thus, ideas of normality and abnormality differ from one society to another and over time within the same society. Any definition of abnormality must include more than social compliance.

MALADAPTIVENESS OF BEHAVIOR   Rather than defining abnormal behavior in terms of deviance from either statistical or societal norms, many social scientists believe that the most important criterion is how the behavior affects the well-being of the individual or of the social group. According to this criterion, behavior is abnormal if it is *maladaptive,* if it has adverse effects on the individual or society. Some kinds of deviant behavior interfere with the welfare of the individual (a man who is so fearful of crowds that he cannot ride the bus to work; an alcoholic who drinks so heavily that he or she cannot keep a job; a woman who attempts suicide). Other forms of deviant behavior are harmful to society (an adolescent who has violent aggressive outbursts; a paranoid individual who plots to assassinate national leaders). If we use the criterion of maladaptiveness, all of these behaviors would be considered abnormal.

PERSONAL DISTRESS   A fourth criterion considers abnormality in terms of the individual's subjective feelings of distress rather than the individual's behavior. Most people diagnosed as mentally ill feel acutely miserable. They are anxious, depressed, or agitated and may suffer from insomnia, loss of appetite, or numerous aches and pains. Sometimes personal distress may be the only symptom of abnormality; the individual's behavior may appear normal to the casual observer.

None of these definitions provides a completely satisfactory description of abnormal behavior. In most instances, all four criteria — statistical frequency, social deviation, maladaptive behavior, and personal distress — are considered in diagnosing abnormality. The *legal* definition of abnormality (which declares a person *insane* largely on the basis of the individual's inability to judge between right and wrong or to exert control over behavior) is less satisfactory for diagnostic purposes than are any of these four criteria. It should be emphasized that *insanity* is a legal term and is not used by psychologists in discussing abnormality.

What Is Normality?

Normality is even more difficult to define than abnormality, but most psychologists would agree that the following qualities indicate emotional well-being. These characteristics do not make sharp distinctions between the mentally healthy and the mentally ill; rather, they represent traits that the normal person possesses to a *greater degree* than the individual who is diagnosed as abnormal.

1. *Efficient perception of reality*   Normal individuals are fairly realistic in appraising their reactions and capabilities and in interpreting what is going on in the world around them. They do not consistently misperceive what others say and do, and they do not consistently overevaluate their abilities and tackle more than they

The Scream *by Edvard Munch (1893).*

can accomplish, nor do they underestimate their abilities and shy away from difficult tasks.

2. *Self-knowledge*   Well-adjusted people have some awareness of their own motives and feelings. Although none of us can fully understand our feelings or behavior, normal people do not hide important feelings and motives from themselves. They have more self-awareness than individuals who are diagnosed as mentally ill.

3. *An ability to exercise voluntary control over behavior*   Normal individuals feel fairly confident about their ability to control their behavior. Occasionally, they may act impulsively, but they are able to restrain sexual and aggressive urges when necessary. They may fail to conform to social norms, but their decision to act as such is voluntary rather than the result of uncontrollable impulses.

4. *Self-esteem and acceptance*   Well-adjusted people have some appreciation of their own self-worth and feel accepted by those around them. They are comfortable with other people and are able to react spontaneously in social situations. At the same time, they do not feel obligated to subjugate their opinions to those of the group. Feelings of worthlessness, alienation, and lack of acceptance are prevalent among individuals who are diagnosed as abnormal.

5. *An ability to form affectionate relationships*   Normal individuals are able to form close and satisfying relationships with other people. They are sensitive to the feelings of others and do not make excessive demands on others to gratify their own needs. Often, mentally disturbed people are so concerned with protecting their own security that they become extremely self-centered. Preoccupied with their own feelings and strivings, they seek affection but are unable to reciprocate. Sometimes they fear intimacy because their past relationships have been destructive.

6. *Productivity*   Well-adjusted people are able to channel their abilities into productive activity. They are enthusiastic about life and do not need to drive themselves to meet the demands of the day. A chronic lack of energy and excessive susceptibility to fatigue are often symptoms of psychological tension resulting from unresolved problems.

Some people turn to creative work as an outlet for their unresolved conflicts. The artists van Gogh and Munch were probably seriously disturbed (judging from descriptions of their behavior), and one wonders if their creative powers would have been as great if they had been better adjusted emotionally. The question is debatable, but it is clear from accounts of the lives of these artists that their works were produced at great expense in the form of pain to themselves and to those close to them. Although a few disturbed people manage to turn their troubles to their advantage, most mentally ill individuals are unable to use their full creative abilities because their emotional problems inhibit productivity.

Classifying Abnormal Behavior

A broad range of behaviors has been classified as abnormal. Some abnormal behaviors are acute and transitory, resulting from particularly stressful events, whereas others are chronic and lifelong. Some abnormal behaviors result from disease or damage to the nervous system. Others are the products of undesirable social environments or faulty learning experiences. Often these factors overlap and interact. Each person's behavior and emotional problems are unique; no two individuals behave in exactly the same manner or share the same life experiences. However, enough similarities exist for mental health professionals to classify cases into categories.

A classification system has advantages and disadvantages. If the various types of abnormal behavior have different causes, we can hope to uncover them

Vincent van Gogh's **Self Portrait** *(1887).*

TABLE 15-1
Categories of Mental Disorders   *Listed are the main diagnostic categories of DSM-III. Each category includes numerous subclassifications. A few leftover categories ("not elsewhere classified") have been omitted from this table. (After American Psychiatric Association, 1980)*

1. **Disorders first evident in infancy, childhood, or adolescence**

   Includes mental retardation, hyperactivity, childhood anxieties, eating disorders (for example, anorexia), and other deviations from normal development.

2. **Organic mental disorders**

   Covers disorders in which the psychological symptoms are directly related to injury to the brain or abnormality of its biochemical environment; may be the result of aging, degenerative diseases of the nervous system (for example, syphilis or Alzheimer's disease), or the ingestion of toxic substances (for example, lead poisoning or extreme alcoholism).

3. **Substance use disorders**

   Includes excessive use of alcohol, barbiturates, amphetamines, cocaine, and other drugs that alter behavior. Marijuana and tobacco are also included in this category, which is causing considerable controversy.

4. **Schizophrenic disorders**

   A group of disorders characterized by loss of contact with reality, marked disturbances of thought and perception, and bizarre behavior.

5. **Paranoid disorders**

   Disorders characterized by excessive suspicions and hostility accompanied by feelings of being persecuted; reality contact in other areas is satisfactory.

6. **Affective disorders**

   Disturbances of normal mood; the person may be extremely depressed, abnormally elated, or may alternate between periods of elation and depression.

7. **Anxiety disorders**

   Includes disorders in which anxiety is the main symptom (generalized anxiety or panic disorders) or anxiety is experienced unless the individual avoids certain

by grouping individuals according to similarities in behavior and then looking for other ways in which the persons may be similar. A diagnostic label also enables those who work with disturbed individuals to communicate information more quickly and concisely. The diagnosis of a *schizophrenic disorder* indicates quite a bit about a person's behavior. Knowing that an individual's symptoms are similar to those of other patients (whose progress followed a particular course or who benefited from a certain kind of treatment) is also helpful in deciding how to treat the patient.

Disadvantages arise, however, if we allow a diagnostic label to carry too much weight. Labeling induces us to overlook the unique features of each case and to expect the person to conform to the classification. We may also forget that a label for maladaptive behavior is not an explanation of that behavior; the classification does not tell us how the behavior originated or what maintains the behavior. It is also important to remember that we are labeling the individual's behaviors — *not* the individual — abnormal. Thus, we speak of someone as having a schizophrenic disorder (which may or may not change over time) rather than saying that person is a schizophrenic. Labels should be attached to the condition, not to the individual.

The classification of mental disorders used by most mental health professionals in this country is the *Diagnostic and Statistical Manual of Mental Disorders*, 3rd edition (DSM-III, for short), which corresponds closely to the international

feared situations (phobic disorders) or tries to resist performing certain rituals or thinking persistent thoughts (obsessive-compulsive disorders).

8. **Somatoform disorders**

The symptoms are physical, but no organic basis can be found and psychological factors appear to play the major role. Included are conversion disorders (for example, a woman who resents having to care for her invalid mother suddenly develops a paralyzed arm) and hypochondriasis (excessive preoccupation with health and fear of disease when there is no basis for concern).

9. **Dissociative disorders**

Temporary alterations in the functions of consciousness, memory, or identity due to emotional problems. Included are amnesia (the individual cannot recall anything about his or her history following a traumatic experience) and multiple personality (two or more independent personality systems existing within the same individual).

10. **Psychosexual disorders**

Includes problems of sexual identity (for example, transsexualism), sexual performance (for example, impotence, premature ejaculation, and frigidity), and sexual aim (for example, sexual interest in children). Homosexuality is considered a disorder only when the individual is unhappy with his or her sexual orientation and wishes to change it.

11. **Conditions not attributable to a mental disorder**

This category includes many of the problems for which people seek help, such as marital problems, parent-child difficulties, child abuse.

12. **Personality disorders**

Long-standing patterns of maladaptive behavior that constitute immature and inappropriate ways of coping with stress or solving problems. Antisocial personality disorder and narcissistic personality disorder are two examples.

system formulated by the World Health Organization. The major categories of mental disorders classified by DSM-III are listed in Table 15-1. Some of these disorders will be discussed in more detail later in the chapter.

DSM-III provides an extensive list of subcategories under each of these headings, as well as a description of the symptoms that must be present for the diagnosis to be applicable. The complete diagnosis for an individual is fairly comprehensive. In addition to the major diagnostic category, it includes

1. A description of the individual's prominent personality characteristics and ways of coping with stress
2. A list of any current physical disorders that may be relevant to understanding and treating the person
3. Documentation of stressful events that may have precipitated the disorder (such as divorce, death of a loved one)
4. An evaluation of how well the individual has functioned socially and occupationally during the previous year.

All of these variables are helpful in determining treatment and prognosis.

You have probably heard the terms "neurosis" and "psychosis" and may be wondering where they fit into the categories of mental disorders listed in Table 15-1. Traditionally, these terms denoted major diagnostic categories. *Neuroses*

I am often bothered by the thumping of my heart.

Little annoyances get on my nerves and irritate me.

I often become suddenly scared for no good reason.

I worry continuously and that gets me down.

I frequently get spells of complete exhaustion and fatigue.

It is always hard for me to make up my mind.

I always seem to be dreading something.

I feel nervous and high-strung all the time.

I often feel I cannot overcome my difficulties.

I feel constantly under strain.

(plural of *neurosis*) included a group of disorders characterized by anxiety, personal unhappiness, and maladaptive behavior that were seldom serious enough to require hospitalization. The individual could usually function in society, although not at full capacity. *Psychoses* (plural of *psychosis*) included more serious mental disorders. The individual's behavior and thought processes were so disturbed that he or she was out of touch with reality, could not cope with the demands of daily life, and usually had to be hospitalized.

Neither neuroses nor psychoses appear as major categories in DSM-III. There are several reasons for this departure from earlier classification systems, but the main one concerns precision of diagnosis. Both categories were fairly broad and included a number of mental disorders with quite dissimilar symptoms. Consequently, mental health professionals did not always agree on the diagnosis for a particular case. DSM-III attempts to achieve greater consensus by grouping disorders according to very specific behavioral symptoms, without implying anything about their origins or treatment. The intention is to describe what clinical workers *observe* about individuals who have psychological problems in a way that ensures accurate communication among mental health professionals. Consequently, DSM-III includes many more categories than previous editions of the manual. Disorders that were formerly categorized as neuroses (because they were assumed to be ways of coping with internal conflicts) are listed in DSM-III under three separate categories: anxiety disorders, somatoform disorders, and dissociative disorders.

Although psychosis is no longer a major category, DSM-III recognizes that people diagnosed as having schizophrenic and paranoid disorders, some affective disorders, and certain organic mental disorders exhibit *psychotic behavior* at some point during their illness. The individual inaccurately evaluates his or her perceptions and thoughts and makes incorrect inferences about what is happening. The person may have *hallucinations* (false sensory experiences, such as hearing voices or seeing strange visions) and/or *delusions* (false beliefs, such as the conviction that all thoughts are controlled by a powerful being from another planet).

These issues will become clearer as we look more closely at some of the mental disorders listed in Table 15-1. In the remainder of this chapter, we will examine anxiety disorders, affective disorders, schizophrenia, and one type of personality disorder. Alcoholism and drug dependence (both classified as substance use disorders) are covered in Chapter 4. Multiple personality, a dissociative disorder, is also discussed in Chapter 4.

ANXIETY DISORDERS

Most of us feel anxious and tense in the face of threatening or stressful situations. Such feelings are normal reactions to stress. Anxiety is considered abnormal only when it occurs in situations that most people can handle with little difficulty. *Anxiety disorders* include a group of disorders in which anxiety either is the main symptom (*generalized anxiety* and *panic disorders*) or is experienced when the individual attempts to control certain maladaptive behaviors (*phobic* and *obsessive-compulsive disorders*).

Generalized Anxiety and Panic Disorders

A person who suffers from a *generalized anxiety disorder* lives each day in a state of high tension. She or he feels vaguely uneasy or apprehensive much of the time and tends to overreact even to mild stresses. An inability to relax, disturbed sleep, fatigue, headaches, dizziness, and rapid heart rate are the most common physical complaints. In addition, the individual continually worries about potential problems and has difficulty concentrating or making decisions. When the individual finally makes a decision, it becomes the source of further worry ("Did I foresee all possible consequences?" or "Will disaster result?"). Some self-descriptions provided by people with chronically high levels of anxiety appear in Table 15-2.

People who suffer generalized anxiety may also experience panic attacks — episodes of acute and overwhelming apprehension or terror. During panic attacks, the individual feels certain that something dreadful is about to happen. This feeling is usually accompanied by such symptoms as heart palpitations, shortness of breath, perspiration, muscle tremors, faintness, and nausea. The symptoms result from excitation of the sympathetic division of the autonomic nervous system (see p. 51) and are the same reactions an individual experiences when extremely frightened. During severe panic attacks, the person fears that he or she will die. The following personal account describes how terrifying such experiences can be:

> I remember walking up the street, the moon was shining and suddenly everything around me seemed unfamiliar, as it would be in a dream. I felt panic rising inside me, but managed to push it away and carry on. I walked a quarter of a mile or so, with the panic getting worse every minute. . . . By now, I was sweating, yet trembling; my heart was pounding and my legs felt like jelly. . . . Terrified, I stood, not knowing what to do. The only bit of sanity left in me told me to get home. Somehow this I did very slowly, holding onto the fence in the road. I cannot remember the actual journey back, until I was going into the house, then I broke down and cried helplessly. . . . I did not go out again for a few days. When I did, it was with my mother and baby to my grandmother's a few miles away. I felt panicky there and couldn't cope with the baby. My cousin suggested we go to my Aunt's house, but I had another attack there. I was sure I was going to die. Following this, I was totally unable to go out alone, and even with someone else I had great difficulty. Not only did I get the panicky fainting spells, but I lived in constant fear of getting them. (Melville, 1977, pp. 1, 14)

People who experience generalized anxiety and panic disorders usually have no clear idea of why they are frightened. This kind of anxiety is sometimes called "free-floating" because it is not triggered by a particular event; rather, it occurs in a variety of situations.

Phobias

In contrast to the vague apprehension of generalized anxiety disorders, the fears in phobic disorders are more specific. Someone who responds with intense fear to a stimulus or situation that most people do not consider particularly dangerous is said to have a *phobia*. The individual usually realizes that his or her fear is irrational but still feels anxiety (ranging from strong uneasiness to panic) that can be alleviated only by avoiding the feared object or situation.

Most of us are afraid of something. Snakes, high places, storms, doctors, sickness, injury, and death are the seven fears most commonly reported by adults (Agras, 1975). As you can see from Figure 15-1, the prevalence of specific fears changes with age. There appears to be a continuum between these common fears and phobias, making their distinctions somewhat arbitrary. However, a fear is usually not diagnosed as a phobic disorder unless it interferes considerably with the person's daily life. Examples of phobic disorders would be a woman whose fear of enclosed places prevents her from entering elevators or a man whose fear

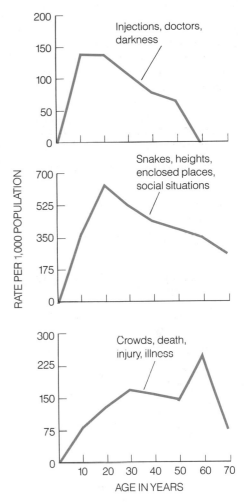

FIGURE 15-1
Fears Change With Age *The graphs show the prevalence of specific fears reported by people of different ages. Fears that follow the same general age pattern are represented together. For example, fears of injections, doctors, and darkness peak at about age 10 and decline thereafter. Fears of snakes, heights, enclosed places, and social situations reach a peak at age 20. Fears of crowds, death, injury, or illness become more prevalent later in life. (After Agras, Sylvester, & Oliveau, 1969)*

FIGURE 15-2
Phobias

An 18-year-old college freshman came for help at the student health center because each time he left his dormitory room and headed toward class, he experienced a feeling of panic. "It would get so bad at times that I thought I would collapse on the way to class. It was a frightening feeling, and I began to be afraid to leave the dorm." He could not understand these feelings because he was reasonably well pleased with his classes and professors. Even after he returned to the dormitory, he would be unable to face anyone for hours or to concentrate on his homework. But if he remained in or near his room, he felt reasonably comfortable.

During interviews with his therapist, the youth reported other fears, including becoming contaminated by syphilis and growing prematurely bald. Occasionally, these fears were sufficiently intense and persistent to cause him to scrub his hands, genitals, and head compulsively until these parts became red and sometimes even bled. In addition, he touched doorknobs only reluctantly, never drank water from a public fountain, and only used the toilet in his home or dormitory. He realized that his fears were unfounded and exaggerated but also felt that many of his precautions and constant worrying were necessary to avoid even greater "mental anguish."

The student's past history revealed that he had serious concerns about his sexual identity and his adequacy as a male. When he was young, he had avoided playing with the other boys because he could not run as fast or hit a ball as far. His mother had strongly rewarded his tendency not to join others because she was convinced that he would get hurt if he participated in their "rough-housing." He was a late maturer and had spent a traumatic summer at camp about the time that most of his peers were reaching puberty. Discovering that he was sexually underdeveloped in comparison to the other boys, he worried about his deficiency; he wondered whether he was destined to become a girl, and he feared that the other boys might attack him sexually.

Although his puberty made a belated appearance, he continued to worry about his masculine identity and even fantasized on occasion that he was a girl. At these times, he became extremely anxious and seriously considered suicide as a solution.

The therapist's immediate goal in treatment was to remove the student's irrational fear of leaving the dormitory, which was accomplished with the method of systematic desensitization [see p. 534]. However, the phobias in this case were clearly part of a deep-rooted problem of sexual identity that would require extensive psychotherapy (Kleinmuntz, 1974, pp. 168–69).

---

of crowds prevents him from attending the theater or walking along congested sidewalks.

DSM-III divides phobic disorders into three broad categories: simple phobias, social phobias, and agoraphobia. A *simple phobia* is a fear of a specific object, animal, or situation. Irrational fears of snakes, heights, enclosed places, and darkness are examples. Some people may develop a simple phobia but be normal in other respects. In more serious cases, the individual has a number of phobias that interfere with many aspects of life and may be intertwined with obsessive or compulsive behavior (see Figure 15-2).

People with *social phobias* feel extremely insecure in social situations and have an exaggerated fear of embarrassing themselves. Often they are fearful that they will betray their anxiety by such signs as hand tremors, blushing, or a quavering voice. These fears are usually unrealistic: individuals who fear they might shake do not do so; those who fear they will stutter or quaver actually speak quite normally. Fear of public speaking or of eating in public are the most common complaints of socially phobic individuals.

Agoraphobia is the most common phobia among people seeking professional help. It is also the most disabling. The word is Greek for "fear of the marketplace." Individuals suffering from agoraphobia are afraid of entering unfamiliar settings. They avoid open spaces, crowds, and traveling. In extreme cases, the individual may be afraid to leave the familiar setting of home. The following incident in the life of a woman suffering from agoraphobia shows how distressing such fears can be.

The woman who lives next door is a very nice person and I like her. One day she asked me if I would drive over to a big shopping center that had recently opened about five miles from where we live. I didn't know how to tell her that there isn't a chance in the world that I'd go to that shopping center or any other place outside our neighborhood. She must have seen how upset I got, but I was shaking like a leaf even more inside. I imagined myself in the crowd, getting lost, or passing out. I was terrified by the openness of the shopping center and the crowds. I made an excuse this time, but I don't know what I'll say next time. Maybe I'll just have to let her in on my little bit of craziness. (Sarason & Sarason, 1984, p. 140)

Agoraphobics usually have a history of panic attacks. They become fearful of being incapacitated by an attack away from the security of home and where no one may be available to help them. Crowded enclosed places where escape to safety would be difficult (such as a bus or a theater) are especially terrifying. But agoraphobics also fear open spaces (large bodies of water, bare landscapes, an empty street) and feel more comfortable when the space is circumscribed by trees, or when an enclosed space (perhaps symbolic of home) is easily reached. Agoraphobics are usually very dependent. A large percentage of them exhibited separation anxiety (fear of being away from mother) in childhood, long before developing agoraphobia (Gittelman & Klein, 1985). While simple phobias and social phobias are fairly easy to treat, agoraphobia is much more difficult.

Obsessive-Compulsive Disorders

Individuals with an *obsessive-compulsive disorder* feel compelled to think about things they would rather not think about or perform acts they do not wish to carry out. *Obsessions* are persistent intrusions of unwelcome thoughts or images. *Compulsions* are irresistible urges to carry out certain acts or rituals. Obsessive thoughts may be linked with compulsive acts (for example, thoughts of lurking germs combined with the compulsion to wash eating utensils many times before using them).

At times, all of us have persistently recurring thoughts ("Did I leave the door locked?") and urges to perform ritualistic behavior (knocking on wood after boasting of good fortune). But when a person has an obsessive-compulsive disorder, such thoughts occupy so much time that they seriously interfere with daily life. The individual recognizes that these thoughts are irrational but is unable to control them. Obsessive thoughts cover a variety of topics, but most often they are concerned with committing aggressive or sexual acts. A mother may have persistent thoughts of drowning her infant in the bathtub. A young man may have recurrent thoughts of exposing his genitals in public or shouting obscenities in church. The likelihood that these thoughts will be transformed into actions is slim. Nevertheless, individuals who experience such obsessive thoughts are horrified by them, cannot understand why they persist, and live in fear that they will perform these "dreadful" acts. Figure 15-3 reports the history of a young mother who was distressed by recurrent thoughts of murdering her two small children. The kind of prohibition her parents placed on any expression of negative feelings is fairly characteristic of the background of persons who develop obsessive-compulsive disorders. When normal feelings of anger are suppressed or denied, they become an "alien" part of the personality and find expression only in indirect ways.

Compulsive acts range from mild kinds of superstitious behavior (such as not stepping on the cracks in sidewalks or arranging the material on a desk in a precise

FIGURE 15-3
Obsessive Thoughts

A 32-year-old mother of two small children sought help because she was distressed over obsessively intrusive and repugnant thoughts related to injuring or murdering her children. On infrequent occasions, her husband was also a "victim." These thoughts were so repugnant, made so little sense, and were so foreign to her conscious feelings that she had been afraid and embarrassed to seek help. She had kept this problem to herself for nearly two years, despite considerable psychological pain, tension, and turmoil. Finally, the steadily increasing difficulty had reached an intolerable level.

The thoughts that were so terribly disturbing to this patient really did not differ greatly in quality from what every normal young woman may occasionally feel toward her children. Many less inhibited and more spontaneous young parents than this one might occasionally say, "Oh,

I feel just like throwing Johnny out of the window today! He makes me so mad!" Most mothers would not feel threatened by such a thought or guilty about having had it and would probably forget it rather quickly. But this patient greatly feared and condemned such thoughts. To her, the thought was nearly as threatening and as guilt-provoking as the act.

Early in life, this woman had developed a defensive need to deny the presence of all negative feelings. To defend herself against the guilt occasioned by having such "terrible" thoughts, she endeavored to dissociate herself from them—to deny that they were her thoughts. "It's just awful words that pop into my head. . . . They have nothing at all to do with the way I feel. They couldn't be my thoughts at all. . . ."

The patient had been raised by an anxious and insecure mother who was un-

able to permit herself or her children the slightest expression of negative feelings. The daughter soon realized that any feelings other than loving ones must be repressed or denied. The patient was the eldest of three siblings and had been assigned undue responsibility for their care. She felt deprived of her share of her parents' affection, was greatly resentful of her younger sister and brother, and fantasized about what it would be like if they were not around. Her occasional murderous fantasies about them were accompanied by tremendous guilt and anxiety. As a result, the fantasies and associated emotional feelings had been completely repressed from conscious awareness. These early conflicts were reactivated during her marriage when the needs of her husband and children seemed to take precedence over her own needs (Laughlin, 1967, pp. 324–25).

order before starting an assignment) to elaborate rituals like those described in Figure 15-4.

Most of us find comfort in certain familiar routines or rituals, particularly in times of stress. But people with obsessive-compulsive disorders become intensely anxious when they try to resist their compulsions, and they feel a release of tension once their acts are carried out.

We sometimes label a person who is exceedingly neat, meticulous, and exasperatingly attentive to details a compulsive personality—or sometimes an obsessive-compulsive personality. Such people also tend to be rigid in their thinking and behavior and highly moralistic. It is tempting to suppose that when an obsessive-compulsive personality is under stress, he or she reacts by developing an obsessive-compulsive disorder. However, this hypothesis is not supported by evidence. The results of personality tests indicate that people with *obsessive-compulsive disorders* do not have the characteristics of an *obsessive-compulsive personality* (Rachman & Hodgson, 1980). We should note, in addition, that people with obsessive-compulsive personalities tend to be proud of their meticulousness and attention to detail. Individuals with obsessive-compulsive disorders, in contrast, abhor their symptoms and wish to be rid of them.

Understanding Anxiety Disorders

We do not know why some people become chronically anxious, but their reactions seem to reflect feelings of inadequacy in situations that they perceive as threatening. Theories of anxiety disorders have focused on internal conflicts, learned responses to external events, maladaptive cognitions, and biological factors.

PSYCHOANALYTIC PERSPECTIVE Psychoanalytic theory assumes that the sources of anxiety are internal and unconscious. The person has repressed certain unacceptable or "dangerous" impulses that would endanger self-esteem or relationships with other people if they were expressed. In situations where these impulses (usually sexual or aggressive in nature) are likely to be aroused, the individual experiences intense anxiety. Because the source of anxiety is unconscious, the person does not know why he or she feels apprehensive.

From a psychoanalytic viewpoint, phobias are ways of coping with anxiety by displacing it onto an object or situation that can be avoided. For example, the student whose case is reported in Figure 15-2 could avoid the arousal of homosexual impulses by staying in his room away from other men and by not using public restrooms. Obsessions and compulsions also serve to protect the individual from recognizing the true source of his or her anxiety. Obsessive thoughts are unacceptable impulses (hostility, destructiveness, inappropriate sexual urges) that have been repressed and somehow reappear in a disguised form. The individual feels that they are not a part of herself or himself and may commit compulsive acts to undo or atone for forbidden impulses. A mother who is obsessed with thoughts of murdering her infant may feel compelled to check many times during the night to assure herself that the child is well. Compulsive rituals also serve to keep threatening impulses out of the individual's conscious awareness: a person who is continually busy has little opportunity to think improper thoughts or commit improper actions.

BEHAVIORAL PERSPECTIVE Psychologists who work within the framework of learning theory view anxiety as triggered more by specific external events than by internal conflicts. Generalized anxiety occurs when a person feels unable to cope with many everyday situations and consequently feels apprehensive much of the time. Phobias are viewed as avoidance responses that may be learned either directly from frightening experiences (developing a fear of dogs after being attacked by one) or vicariously by observing fearful responses in others.

"Ronald is *extremely* compulsive."

FIGURE 15-4

Compulsive Rituals

A 30-year-old woman had developed such an elaborate sequence of ritual acts that their consummation occupied most of her waking hours. She could not go to bed at night before she had checked each door and window three times to ensure that it was locked. The gas range and the pilot lights to the furnace and hot water heater also had to be checked to make certain that no gas was escaping. Bathing and dressing took up much of her time; she often took three or four showers in succession — scrubbing her body thoroughly with a special antibacterial cleanser each time — before she was convinced that she was clean enough to put on her clothes. She wore only clothing that could be washed at home, because she did not trust the dry cleaner to remove all possible germs. And each article had to be washed and rinsed three times before she would wear it. Similar hygienic procedures were involved whenever she prepared food: she scalded each dish and utensil with boiling water before and after using it and would not eat a meal unless she had prepared it herself.

This woman had always been unusually neat and clean, but her "security operations" had intensified over the years until they reached pathological proportions. At times, she realized the foolishness of her precautions, but she experienced intense anxiety whenever she attempted to cut short any of her procedures or omit a step in one of her rituals (R. L. Atkinson, unpublished case report).

The classical conditioning paradigm (see p. 216) provides an explanation of how innocuous objects or situations can become the focus of a phobia: a neutral object (the conditioned stimulus) paired with a traumatic event (the unconditioned stimulus) produces fear of the neutral object (the conditioned response). For example, a child who is stung by a bee while picking a yellow flower develops a phobia for yellow flowers. The precipitating trauma, when it can be identified in phobic cases, is well described by classical conditioning. There is considerable evidence from laboratory experiments with animals and humans that pairing a neutral object with a frightening situation produces strong fear of the neutral object. However, there are problems with this explanation of phobias. Simple phobias almost always are restricted to a certain set of objects, rather than to any object that happens to be present at the same time as the traumatic event. Why, for example, are phobias of the dark common, but phobias of pajamas nonexistent, although both are paired with nighttime trauma? Why do we have phobias of snakes and insects but not phobias of kittens or lambs? And why are phobias of knives and guns rare, even though both objects are often paired with injury?

The notion of *prepared conditioning* has been proposed as an explanation. Humans are biologically predisposed, or "prepared," to react with fear only to certain classes of dangerous objects or situations. When these objects or situations are paired with trauma, fear conditioning occurs rapidly and is very resistant to extinction (Seligman, 1971; Seligman & Rosenhan, 1984). The majority of common phobias were once actually dangerous to our early ancestors. Natural selection may have favored those ancestors who learned quickly (with only minimal exposure to trauma) that strangers, heights, snakes, large animals, and the dark were dangerous. Evolution may have selected certain objects, all dangerous in an earlier time, that are readily conditionable to trauma. We are less likely to become conditioned to fear other objects (such as lambs, guns, and electric outlets) either because they were never dangerous or because their origin is too recent to have been subject to natural selection. Thus, phobias are instances not of ordinary classical conditioning but of prepared classical conditioning.

A series of laboratory experiments lends support to the idea that people are more prepared to learn to be afraid of certain objects than they are of others. Fear was conditioned in student volunteers using a variety of prepared conditioned stimuli (pictures of snakes or spiders) and unprepared stimuli (pictures of houses, faces, or flowers). The pictures were followed by a brief, painful electric shock. Fear conditioning, as measured by galvanic skin response (see p. 219), occurred much more rapidly to prepared stimuli than to unprepared ones. In fact, conditioning occurred in one pairing of electric shock with pictures of snakes and spiders, but it took four or five pairings for subjects' fear to be conditioned to faces, houses, or flowers. A subsequent experiment, found the conditioning properties of guns to be similar to those for flowers, not snakes and spiders (Ohman, Fredrikson, Hugdahl, & Rimmo, 1976).

Viewing phobias as a form of prepared learning helps explain their irrationality and their resistance to extinction. With normal fear conditioning, once the unconditioned stimulus (for instance, the electric shock) is no longer paired with the conditioned stimulus, fear extinguishes rapidly. This does not appear to be the case for prepared fear conditioning. In one study, students were conditioned to fear either snakes and spiders or houses and faces by pairing each with shock. At the end of the conditioning (when the electrodes were removed), fear extinguished immediately to houses and faces but remained intense to snakes and spiders (Hugdahl & Ohman, 1977).

While some phobias appear to result from actual frightening experiences, others may be learned vicariously, through observation. Fearful parents tend to produce children who share their fears. A child who observes his or her parents react with fear to a variety of situations may accept such reactions as normal. Indeed, studies find a high correlation between the fears of a mother and those of her child.

As we will see in the next chapter, the treatment of phobias within the framework of learning theory uses various techniques to extinguish fear responses to the phobic object or situation.

COGNITIVE PERSPECTIVE A cognitive analysis of anxiety disorders focuses on the way that anxious people think about situations and potential dangers. Individuals who suffer from generalized anxiety tend to make unrealistic appraisals of certain situations, primarily those where the possibility of danger is remote. They consistently overestimate both the *degree* of harm and the *likelihood* of harm. This kind of mental set makes a person hypervigilant, always on the lookout for signs of danger. For example, a sudden noise in the house is interpreted as burglars; the screech of brakes in the street means one's child is in danger. This hypervigilance and expectation of harm result in continual bodily mobilization for danger. Thus, the physiological responses characteristic of the fight-or-flight reaction (tremors, rapid heart rate, clammy hands, muscle tension) are present much of the time.

The cognitive theory of obsessions assumes that we all have unwanted and repetitive thoughts on occasion. For example, song lyrics or advertising jingles often intrude unbidden into consciousness. But we are able to dismiss them, as well as the more abhorrent thoughts that occasionally run through our heads. The more anxiety-provoking the content of the obsession, the more difficult it is for anyone — obsessive or nonobsessive — to dismiss the thought. And the more stressed we are, the more frequent and intense are these thoughts. If a person is anxious to begin with, obsessive thoughts will be more disturbing and more difficult to dismiss.

If an event triggers a disturbing thought in a nonobsessive person, he or she may find the thought unacceptable but will not become anxious and will easily dismiss it. In contrast, the obsessive person will be made anxious by the thought, and the anxiety will reduce his or her ability to dismiss it. The thought will persist, and the obsessive's inability to disregard it will lead to further anxiety, which will increase his or her susceptibility to the intrusive thought.

Compulsive rituals, according to the cognitive view, are attempts to neutralize the bad thought by an action that ensures safety. Thus, the person obsessed with thoughts of disease and germs washes his hands and food dozens of times. The one obsessed with thoughts that the doors are unlocked checks them many times a night. These rituals are reinforced by the relief from anxiety. But the relief is temporary. The obsessive thoughts return with increased frequency and intensity, and the ritual must be performed each time the thought recurs.

As we will see in the next chapter, the cognitive approach to treating obsessive disorders uses the technique of thought stopping to help the individual terminate obsessive thoughts. The treatment for generalized anxiety and phobias focuses on helping individuals develop more realistic and rational appraisals of themselves and the situations they encounter.

BIOLOGICAL PERSPECTIVE Anxiety disorders tend to run in families. About 15 percent of parents and siblings of people who have anxiety disorders are similarly affected (Carey & Gottesman, 1981). This finding does not, of course, prove a hereditary basis for such disorders, since these individuals usually live together and thus experience similar environments. However, the results of twin studies provide firmer evidence for an inherited predisposition for two types of anxiety disorders: panic disorders and agoraphobia with panic attacks. Identical twins, as you recall, develop from the same egg and share the same heredity;

fraternal twins develop from different eggs and are no more alike genetically than ordinary siblings. Both identical twins are three times more likely to suffer from panic attacks, if one does, than are fraternal twins (Torgersen, 1983).

We do not know yet what is inherited, but researchers are investigating the possibility that it may be an imbalance in a chemical system in the brain that regulates anxiety. In 1960, a group of drugs called *benzodiazepines* were developed and marketed under such trade names as Valium and Librium. These drugs proved effective in reducing anxiety (see p. 553 for a discussion of their merits and disadvantages). Researchers subsequently discovered that the drugs were effective because they bind to specific receptor molecules in certain neurons of the brain, thereby influencing neural transmission (see Chapter 2, p. 36). The discovery of receptor sites for antianxiety drugs set off a search for a natural body substance that might act in the same way to keep anxiety in proper balance. So far, a "natural Valium" has not been found, but investigators have learned a great deal about the benzodiazepine receptors and how certain chemicals operate to increase or decrease anxiety (Costa, 1985).

There appear to be three specific "docking" areas on the benzodiazepine receptor site: one for the benzodiazepine molecule with its antianxiety effects, another for compounds that cause anxiety (the effects of which are blocked by administration of the benzodiazepines), and the third for a group of substances that block the effects of both the benzodiazepines and the anxiety-provoking compounds. The identification of these three receptor sites suggests that some substances secreted in the brain produce the subjective experience of fear and anxiety and other substances block this effect. The ratio of these substances may lead either to an emotionally stable or to an anxious individual (Agras, 1985).

Among the anxiety disorders, biological factors are most evident for panic attacks. Certain chemicals can produce an attack in individuals who suffer from spontaneous panic attacks, although the same chemicals usually have no effect on normal individuals or on phobics who experience anxiety in response to an external stimulus. Other drugs are capable of blocking spontaneous panic attacks (Lader, 1985). However, even if panic disorders have a biochemical basis, environmental experiences undoubtedly play an important role. Such disorders may develop through an interaction between biological predispositions and childhood experiences. Some children may be born with a lowered threshold for the arousal of anxiety. These children would be more prone than others to develop separation anxiety if deprived of the mother's care. And, as noted earlier, separation anxiety is often the forerunner of panic disorder in adulthood.

AFFECTIVE DISORDERS

Affective disorders are disturbances of *affect* or mood. The person may be severely depressed or manic (widely elated) or may alternate between periods of depression and elation. These mood changes may be so extreme that the individual requires hospitalization.

Depression

Almost everyone gets depressed at times. Most of us have periods when we feel sad, lethargic, and not interested in any activities — even pleasurable ones. Depression is a normal response to many of life's stresses. Among the situations that most often precipitate depression are failure at school or at work, the loss of a loved one, and the realization that illness or aging is depleting one's resources.

Depression is considered abnormal only when it is out of proportion to the event and continues past the point at which most people begin to recover.

Although depression is characterized as a disorder of mood, there are actually four sets of symptoms. In addition to emotional — or mood — symptoms, there are cognitive, motivational, and physical symptoms. An individual need not have all of these to be diagnosed as depressed, but the more symptoms he or she has, and the more intense they are, the more certain we can be that the individual is suffering from depression.

Sadness and dejection are the most salient emotional symptoms in depression. The individual feels hopeless and unhappy, often has crying spells, and may contemplate suicide. Equally pervasive in depression is the loss of gratification or pleasure in life. Activities that used to bring satisfaction seem dull and joyless. The depressed person gradually loses interest in hobbies, recreation, and family activities. Most depressed patients report that they no longer derive gratification from what had been major interests in life, and many report losing interest in and affection for other people.

The cognitive symptoms consist primarily of negative thoughts. Depressed individuals tend to have low self-esteem, feel inadequate, and blame themselves for their failures. They feel hopeless about the future and are pessimistic that they can do anything to improve their life.

Motivation is at a low ebb in depression. The depressed person tends to be passive and has difficulty initiating activities. The following conversation between a patient and his therapist illustrates this passivity. The man, who had been hospitalized after a suicide attempt, spent his days sitting motionless in the lounge. His therapist decided to try to engage him in some activities:

THERAPIST: I understand that you spend most of your day in the lounge. Is that true?
PATIENT: Yes, being quiet gives me the peace of mind I need.
THERAPIST: When you sit here, how's your mood?
PATIENT: I feel awful all the time. I just wish I could fall in a hole somewhere and die.
THERAPIST: Do you feel better after sitting for two or three hours?
PATIENT: No, the same.
THERAPIST: So you're sitting in the hope that you'll find peace of mind, but it doesn't sound like your depression improves.
PATIENT: I get so bored.
THERAPIST: Would you consider being more active? There are a number of reasons why I think increasing your activity level might help.
PATIENT: There's nothing to do around here.
THERAPIST: Would you consider trying some activities if I could come up with a list?
PATIENT: If you think it will help, but I think you're wasting your time. I don't have any interests.

(Beck, Rush, Shaw, & Emery, 1979, p. 200)

The physical symptoms of depression include loss of appetite, sleep disturbances, fatigue, and loss of energy. Since a depressed person's thoughts are focused inward, rather than toward external events, he or she may magnify aches and pains and worry about health.

As we see from this description of its many symptoms, depression can be a debilitating disorder. Fortunately, most depressive episodes are of relatively short duration. Depressed people gradually recover, with or without treatment. About one-quarter of depressive episodes last less than a month, half last less than three months, and one-quarter last a year or longer. Only about 10 percent of the latter group do not recover and remain chronically depressed (Lewinsohn, Fenn, & Franklin, 1982). Unfortunately, depressive episodes tend to recur. About half the

CRITICAL DISCUSSION

Suicide and Depression

The most disastrous consequence of depression is suicide. Of the reported 25,000 people who end their lives by suicide in the United States every year, the vast majority (at least 80 percent) are suffering from depression. However, suicide deaths are underreported for a variety of reasons. Because of the stigma attached to suicide, physicians and coroners may be persuaded by the family to list a death as accidental when the circumstances are questionable. In addition, many single-car accidents are probably suicides. And some people who engage in dangerous sports and occupations, who adopt lethal habits (such as heavy use of drugs), or who are physically ill and terminate their medication may be seeking death. Consequently, the number of actual suicides per year may well be closer to 50,000. The number of people who attempt suicide but fail has been estimated at anywhere from two to eight times the number of suicides (Shneidman, 1985).

Women attempt to commit suicide about three times more often than men do, but men succeed in killing themselves three times more often than women. The greater number of suicide attempts by women is probably related to the greater incidence of depression among women. The fact that men are more successful in their attempts is related to the choice of method: women tend to use less lethal means, such as cutting their wrists or overdosing on sleeping pills; men are more apt to use firearms or carbon monoxide fumes or to hang themselves.

Among the reasons most frequently cited by those who have attempted suicide are depression, loneliness, ill health, marital problems, and (for men) financial or job difficulties (Farberow & Shneidman, 1965; Shneidman, 1985).

The greatest number of suicides occurs among people in their 40s, and the rate continues to be high through age 60 and over. Recently, however, suicide has increased among adolescents and young adults. In fact, the incidence of suicide among 15- to 24-year-olds in the United States has tripled over the last two decades. Every year some 250,000 young people in this age group attempt suicide, and more than 5,000 of them succeed (Davis, 1983). College students are twice as likely to kill themselves as are nonstudents of the same age (Murphy & Wetzel, 1980).

The increased suicide rate among college students is found not only in the United States but in European countries, India, and Japan, as well. There are a number of possible reasons for the greater despair among college students: living away from home for the first time and having to cope with new problems; trying to stay at the top academically when the competition is much fiercer than it had been in high school; indecision about a career choice; loneliness caused by the absence of long-time friends and anxiety about new ones.

A study of the lives and academic records of college students who committed suicide found that they were moodier, drove themselves harder, and were depressed more frequently than their nonsuicidal classmates. They had also given recur-

individuals who have a depressive episode will experience another one. Generally, the more stable a person is before the first episode, the less likely that depression will recur.

Manic-Depression

The majority of depressions occur without mania. But between 5 percent and 10 percent of depressions occur as part of *manic-depression*. Manic-depression is also called a *bipolar disorder;* the individual goes from one pole of the affect continuum to the other.

People experiencing manic episodes behave in a way that appears, on the surface, to be the opposite of depression. During mild manic episodes, the individual is energetic, enthusiastic, and full of self-confidence. He or she talks

rent warnings of their suicidal intent to others. The major precipitating events appear to have been worry about academic work and physical health and difficulties in their relationships with others (Seiden, 1966). However, we cannot be sure whether these factors caused the suicides or whether academic difficulties and interpersonal problems were secondary to a severe depression. Worry about health is frequently a symptom of depression.

Suicidal college students, on the average, have higher records of academic achievement than their nonsuicidal classmates, whereas most adolescents who commit suicide have exceptionally poor high school records. The adolescents tend to be dropouts or to have behavior problems in school. The outstanding characteristic of adolescents who attempt suicide is social isolation: they describe themselves as loners, most have parents who were divorced or separated, a large number have alcoholic parents, and one-fourth were not living at home at the time of their suicide attempt (Rohn et al., 1977).

Another factor that contributes to suicide among younger people is drug use. One study found that half of the people under age 30 who committed suicide showed evidence of heavy drug use. It is not clear if the drug abuse *caused* these people to become depressed and kill themselves or if they turned to drugs as a way of coping with depression and killed themselves when the drugs did not help. But in many of the cases, drug abuse appears to have preceded the psychological

problems (Rich, Young, & Fowler, 1985).

Some individuals commit suicide because they find their emotional distress intolerable and see no solution to their problems other than death. Their sole motivation is to end their life. In other cases, the person does not really wish to die but seeks to impress others with the seriousness of his or her dilemma. The suicide attempt is motivated by a desire to communicate feelings of despair and to change the behavior of other people. Examples would be a woman who takes an overdose of sleeping pills when her lover threatens to leave or a student who does the same when pressured by his parents to achieve beyond his abilities. The suicide attempt is a cry for help.

Some experts use the term *parasuicide* for nonfatal acts in which a person deliberately causes self-injury or ingests a substance in excess of any prescribed or generally recognized therapeutic dosage (Kreitman, 1977). The term "parasuicide" is preferred to "suicide attempt" because it does not necessarily imply a wish to die. As noted earlier, there are many more parasuicides than suicides. However, most people who commit suicidal acts are experiencing such turmoil and stress that their thinking is far from clear. They are not sure whether they want to live or die; they want to do both at the same time, usually one more than the other. Since the best predictor of a future suicide is a prior attempt, all parasuicides should be taken seriously. Few people commit suicide without signaling their intentions to someone. Thus, a person

who talks about suicide may actually do it. Many communities have established suicide-prevention centers where troubled individuals can seek help, either through telephone contact or in person (see p. 557).

Dramatic instances of suicide, such as jumping from a bridge, are usually given sensational coverage by newspapers and television. There is some evidence that such publicity encourages suicidal individuals to act on their impulses. A seven-year California study showed that in the week following a suicide that was highly publicized by the press, the suicide rate rose about 9 percent above the normal rate. Fatal automobile accidents and fatal crashes of private planes (which could be a disguised form of suicide) also increased (Phillips, 1978).

Publicity may also make famous landmarks attractive for would-be suicides. The Golden Gate Bridge in San Francisco is currently the world's favorite suicide spot, with close to 700 officially reported suicide deaths and perhaps an additional 200 deaths that have escaped notice. The Bay Bridge, which is six miles away and the same height, is the scene of very few suicides, and those that occur receive little publicity. One researcher found that half the people from the East Bay Area who had committed bridge suicides had traveled across the Bay Bridge in order to leap from the Golden Gate Bridge. Apparently, no one had reversed this process (Seiden, 1981, as cited in Markham, 1981). Thus, media publicity does appear to play a role, perhaps by providing a model for suicide-prone individuals to copy.

continually, rushes from one activity to another with little need of sleep, and makes grandiose plans, paying little attention to their practicality. Unlike the kind of joyful exuberance that characterizes normal elation, manic behavior has a driven quality and often expresses hostility more than it does elation.

People experiencing severe manic episodes behave somewhat like the popular concept of a "raving maniac." They are extremely excited and constantly active. They may pace about, sing, shout, or pound the walls for hours. They are angered by attempts to interfere with their activities and may become abusive. Impulses (including sexual ones) are immediately expressed in actions or words. These individuals are confused and disoriented and may experience delusions of great wealth, accomplishment, or power.

Manic episodes can occur without depression, but this is very rare. Usually a depressive episode will occur eventually, once a person has experienced a manic episode. The depression is similar to what we have already described.

Manic-depression is relatively rare. Whereas about 20 percent of adult females and 10 percent of adult males in the United States have experienced a major depression at some time, only about 1 percent of the adult population has had a manic-depressive disorder, which appears to be equally common in men and women. Manic-depression differs from other affective disorders in that it tends to occur at an earlier age, is more likely to run in families, responds to different therapeutic medications, and is apt to recur unless treated. These facts suggest that biological variables play a more important role than psychological variables in manic-depression.

Understanding Affective Disorders

Depression is one of the most prevalent emotional disorders. Because depression is so common and can be so debilitating, much effort has been devoted to determining its causes. We will look briefly at several approaches to understanding affective disorders.

PSYCHOANALYTIC PERSPECTIVE Psychoanalytic theories interpret depression as a *reaction to loss*. Whatever the nature of the loss (loss of a loved one, loss of status, loss of moral support provided by a group of friends), the depressed person reacts to it intensely because the current situation brings back all the fears of an earlier loss that occurred in childhood—that being the loss of parental affection. For some reason, the individual's needs for affection and care were not satisfied in childhood. A loss in later life causes the individual to regress to his or her helpless, dependent state when the original loss occurred. Part of the depressed person's behavior, therefore, represents a cry for love—a display of helplessness and an appeal for affection and security (White & Watt, 1981).

Reaction to loss is complicated by angry feelings toward the deserting person. An underlying assumption of psychoanalytic theories is that people who are prone to depression have learned to repress their hostile feelings because they are afraid of alienating those on whom they depend for support. When things go wrong, they turn their anger inward and blame themselves. For example, a woman may feel extremely hostile toward the employer who fired her. But because her anger arouses anxiety, she uses the defense mechanism of projection to internalize her feelings: she is not angry; rather, others are angry at her. She assumes the employer had a good reason for rejecting her: she is incompetent and worthless.

Psychoanalytic theories suggest that the depressed person's low self-esteem and feelings of worthlessness stem from a childlike need for parental approval. A small child's self-esteem depends on the approval and affection of the parents. But as a person matures, feelings of worth also should be derived from the individual's sense of his or her own accomplishments and effectiveness. The self-esteem of a person prone to depression depends primarily on external sources: the approval and support of others. When these supports fail, the individual may be thrown into a state of depression.

Psychoanalytic theories of depression, therefore, focus on loss, overdependence on external approval, and internalization of anger. They seem to provide a reasonable explanation for some of the behaviors exhibited by depressed individuals, but they are difficult to prove or to refute. Some studies indicate that people who are prone to depression are more likely than the average person to have lost a parent in early life (Roy, 1981; Barnes & Prosen, 1985). But parental loss (through death or separation) is also found in the case histories of people who suffer from other types of mental disorders, and most people who suffer such a loss do not

develop emotional problems in adulthood (Tennant, Smith, Bebbington, & Hurry, 1981).

BEHAVIORAL PERSPECTIVE Learning theorists assume that lack of reinforcement plays a major role in depression. The inactivity of the depressed person and the feelings of sadness are due to a low rate of positive reinforcement and/or a high rate of unpleasant experiences (Lewinsohn, Mischel, Chaplin, & Barton, 1980; Lewinsohn, Hoberman, Teri, & Hautziner, 1985). Many of the events that precipitate depression (such as the death of a loved one, loss of a job, or impaired health) reduce accustomed reinforcement. In addition, people prone to depression may lack the social skills either to attract positive reinforcement or to cope effectively with aversive events.

Once people become depressed and inactive, their main source of reinforcement is the sympathy and attention they receive from relatives and friends. This attention may initially reinforce the very behaviors that are maladaptive (weeping, complaining, criticizing themselves, talking about suicide). But because it is tiresome to be around someone who refuses to cheer up, the depressed person's behavior eventually alienates even close associates, producing a further reduction in reinforcement and increasing the individual's social isolation and unhappiness. A low rate of positive reinforcement further reduces the individual's activities and the expression of behavior that might be rewarded. Both activities and rewards decrease in a vicious cycle.

COGNITIVE PERSPECTIVE Cognitive theories of depression focus not on what people *do* but on how they view themselves and the world. One of the more influential cognitive theories, developed by Aaron Beck, is derived from extensive therapeutic experience with depressed patients (Beck, 1976; Beck, Rush, Shaw, & Emery, 1979). Beck's theory suggests that individuals prone to depression have developed a general attitude of appraising events from a negative and self-critical viewpoint. They expect to fail rather than to succeed, and they tend to magnify failures and minimize successes in evaluating their performance. (For example, a student who receives a poor grade on only one examination out of many considers himself an academic misfit; a lawyer views herself as inadequate, despite a succession of praiseworthy achievements.) They also tend to blame themselves rather than the circumstances when things go wrong. (When rain dampens spirits at an outdoor buffet, the host blames himself rather than the

Helpless to control the situation.

weather.) According to this view, encouraging depressed people to become more socially active so they can receive more positive reinforcement will not, in itself, be helpful. They will simply find new opportunities to criticize themselves. Instead, cognitive therapy for depression attempts to identify and correct the distorted thinking underlying depression (see Chapter 16, p. 538). In addition, depressed individuals are taught to master situations they thought were insurmountable.

Another cognitive approach to depression, developed by Martin Seligman, derives from experiments on *learned helplessness* discussed in Chapter 14 (see p. 467). According to this theory, people become depressed when they *believe* that their actions make no difference in bringing about either pleasure or pain. Depression is caused by the expectation of future helplessness. A depressed person expects bad events to occur and believes that there is nothing he or she can do to prevent them from happening.

According to Seligman, three dimensions contribute to this feeling of helplessness. The first has to do with whether the person sees the problem as *internal* or *external*. The helplessness theory assumes that a person is more likely to become depressed if he or she believes the problem is internal, the result of his or her personal inability to control the outcome. Thus, a student who fails a course required for graduation and who attributes this failure to inadequate effort (she did not study enough) is more likely to feel depressed than one who attributes his failure to external factors (the teacher did an inferior job of presenting the material, and the final exam was unfair).

The second dimension has to do with whether the person views the situation as *stable* or *unstable*. For example, another student may attribute his course failure to a lack of ability — he worked hard, and his past performance in similar courses also has been poor. According to the theory, this student should be more severely depressed than the two students mentioned above, because he attributes his failure to something internal that is stable (not likely to change in the future).

The third dimension of helplessness has to do with the *global-specific* continuum. A person who interprets what happens as proof that he is totally helpless is more likely to be depressed than someone who sees himself as helpless only in a specific situation. Thus, a student who fails a variety of courses and decides he is "stupid" is more likely to become depressed than one who fails only language courses and decides he lacks this specific ability.

To summarize, Seligman's theory predicts that individuals who explain negative events in terms of internal, stable, and global causes — "It's me, it's going to last forever, and it's going to affect everything I do" — tend to become depressed when bad events occur (Peterson & Seligman, 1984).

The theories of Beck and Seligman have stimulated a great deal of research on the cognitive processes of depressed individuals, and the results have demonstrated that self-critical attitudes and attributions of helplessness are important components of depression. However, the extent to which such thoughts *precede* rather than *accompany* a depressed episode is far from clear. Both Beck's and Seligman's theories assume that individuals who become depressed possess a stable, traitlike depressive cognitive style that predisposes them to periods of depression. A number of studies using mildly depressed individuals as subjects (mostly college students) have found a relationship between a self-critical and helpless cognitive style and the degree of depression experienced when faced with bad events (Peterson & Seligman, 1984). However, most studies of severely depressed, hospitalized patients find that patterns of depressive cognitions accompany depression but are *not* apparent after a depressive episode. Once the patients' depression had lifted, they did not differ from control subjects (who had never been depressed) in the way they interpreted bad events (Hamilton & Abramson, 1983; Fennell & Campbell, 1984). Thus a depressive explanatory style may be a *symptom* rather than a *cause* of depression. It is an important symptom, however, because the intensity of a patient's negative beliefs does predict the speed of recovery from a period of depression (Brewin, 1985).

The way a person interprets bad events may be less important for the development of depression than is the belief that one has control over one's life. We noted in Chapter 14 that stressful situations are less disturbing if the individual believes that he or she can exert some control over them. Confidence in one's ability to cope with bad events may increase resistance to depression.

BIOLOGICAL PERSPECTIVE   A tendency to develop affective disorders, particularly manic-depressive disorders, appears to be inherited. Evidence from twin studies shows that if one identical twin is diagnosed as manic-depressive, there is a 72 percent chance that the other twin will suffer from the same disorder. The corresponding figure for fraternal twins is only 14 percent. These figures, called *concordance rates,* represent the likelihood that both twins will have a specific characteristic, given that one of the twins has the characteristic. The concordance rate for identical twins suffering from depression (40 percent) also exceeds the rate for fraternal twins (11 percent), but the difference between these two rates is much less than is the difference between the rates for manic-depressive twins (Allen, 1976). This comparison indicates that manic-depressive disorders are more closely related to genetic factors than are depressive disorders.

The specific role that genetic factors play in affective disorders is far from clear. However, it seems likely that a biochemical abnormality is involved. Mounting evidence indicates that our moods are regulated by the *neurotransmitters* that transmit nerve impulses from one neuron to another (see pp. 34–35). A number of chemicals serve as neurotransmitters in different parts of the nervous system, and normal behavior requires a careful balance among them. Two neurotransmitters believed to play an important role in affective disorders are *norepinephrine* and *serotonin*. Both of these neurotransmitters, which belong to a class of compounds called *biogenic amines,* are localized in areas of the brain that regulate emotional behavior (the limbic system and the hypothalamus). A widely accepted hypothesis is that depression is associated with a deficiency of one or both of these neurotransmitters and that mania is associated with an excess of one or both of them. However, the evidence is indirect, based largely on the effects that certain drugs have on behavior and on neurotransmitter activity. For example, the drug reserpine, which is used to treat high blood pressure, sometimes produces severe depression as a side effect. Animal research has shown that the drug causes a decrease in the brain levels of serotonin and norepinephrine. In contrast, amphetamines (or "speed"), which produce an emotional high, facilitate the release of both of these neurotransmitters.

Drugs that are effective in relieving depression increase the availability of both norepinephrine and serotonin in the nervous system. Two major classes of antidepressant drugs act in different ways to increase neurotransmitter levels. The *monoamine oxidase* (MAO) *inhibitors* block the activity of an enzyme that can destroy both norepinephrine and serotonin, thereby increasing the concentration of these two neurotransmitters in the brain. The *tricyclic antidepressants* prevent *reuptake* (the process by which neurotransmitters are taken back by the nerve terminals from which they were released) of serotonin and norepinephrine, thereby prolonging the duration of their activity. Since these drugs affect both serotonin and norepinephrine, it is difficult to distinguish between the roles of these two neurotransmitters in depressive disorders. Some studies indicate that serotonin plays the major role; others imply that norepinephrine does. It is possible that each neurotransmitter may be involved but in different subtypes of depression.

Research using new techniques is studying the long-term effects of antidepressants on the neuron's postsynaptic receptors. Antidepressant drugs require time to be effective: both tricyclics and MAO inhibitors take from one to three weeks before they begin to relieve the symptoms of depression. These observations do not fit with the discovery that the drugs, when they are first taken, increase norepinephrine and serotonin levels only temporarily; after several days, the neurotransmitters return to their previous levels. Thus, an increase in norepinephrine or serotonin per se cannot be the mechanism that relieves depression. Preliminary evidence indicates that these antidepressants increase the sensitivity of both norepinephrine and serotonin postsynaptic receptors. The time frame within which this occurs corresponds well with the course of drug action on symptoms (Charney & Heninger, 1983; Charney, Heninger, & Sternberg, 1984). Thus, even though the patient's levels of norepinephrine or serotonin are low once again, they may be able to use these neurotransmitters more effectively because the receptors receiving them have become more sensitive.

The neurotransmitter systems that regulate mood and emotion are incredibly complex, and we are only beginning to understand them. The fact that some of the newest drugs that have proved successful in relieving depression do not appear to influence serotonin and norepinephrine levels suggests that other neurotransmitter systems are also involved. Several neurotransmitter systems, acting alone or in combination, may be responsible for depressive symptoms (McNeal & Cimbolic, 1986).

There is no doubt that affective disorders involve biochemical changes in the nervous system. The unresolved question is whether the physiological changes are the cause or the result of the psychological changes. For example, people who deliberately behave as if they were experiencing a manic episode exhibit changes in neurotransmitter levels similar to those found among actual manic patients (Post, Kotin, Goodwin, & Gordon, 1973). The depletion of norepinephrine may cause certain kinds of depression, but an earlier link in the causal chain leading to depression may be feelings of helplessness or loss of emotional support.

VULNERABILITY AND STRESS   All of the theories we have discussed make important points about the nature of depression. Inherited physiological characteristics may predispose an individual to extreme mood changes. Early experiences (the loss of parental affection or the inability to gain gratification through one's own efforts) may also make a person *vulnerable* to depression in later life. The kinds of stressful events that depressed patients report precipitated their disorder are usually within the range of normal life experiences; they are experiences most people can handle without becoming abnormally depressed. Thus, the concept of vulnerability is helpful in understanding why some people develop depression but others do not when confronted with a particular stressful experience.

Some additional factors that have been found to increase vulnerability to depression include having few social skills, being poor, being very dependent on others, having children below the age of 7, and *not* having a close and intimate confidant. The last of these appears to be the most important, at least for women, since it has been the most consistently identified over various studies (Brown & Harris, 1978; Campbell, Cope, & Teasdale, 1983; Bebbington, Sturt, Tennant, & Hurry, 1984). Having an intimate, confiding relationship with a husband or friend decreased the risk of a woman's becoming depressed when confronted with a stressful life situation. This is consistent with the research (discussed in

Chapter 14) indicating that social supports reduce the severity of stressful events.

Depression has many causes, which may range from being determined almost entirely by an inherited biochemical abnormality to being exclusively the result of psychological or environmental factors. Most cases fall in between the two extremes and involve a mixture of genetic, early developmental, and environmental factors.

SCHIZOPHRENIA

Schizophrenia is the label applied to a group of disorders characterized by severe personality disorganization, distortion of reality, and an inability to function in daily life. *Schizophrenic disorders*, the category listed in DSM-III (see Table 15-1), is a more accurate term because most experts believe that schizophrenia encompasses several disorders, each of which may have a different cause. However, "schizophrenia" is the historical term and the one still most commonly used.

Schizophrenia occurs in all cultures, even those that are remote from the stresses of industrialized civilization, and appears to have plagued humanity throughout history. In the United States, about 6 out of every 1,000 people are treated for schizophrenia in any given year. The disorder usually appears in young adulthood, the peak of incidence being between ages 25 and 35. Sometimes schizophrenia develops slowly as a gradual process of increasing seclusiveness and inappropriate behavior. Sometimes the onset of schizophrenia is sudden, marked by intense confusion and emotional turmoil; such cases are usually precipitated by a period of stress in individuals whose lives have tended toward isolation, self-preoccupation, and feelings of insecurity. The case described in Figure 15-5 seems to fall into the latter category, although it lacks the intensity of onset that sometimes occurs.

Characteristics of Schizophrenia

Whether a schizophrenic disorder develops slowly or suddenly, the symptoms are many and varied. The primary characteristics of schizophrenia can be summarized under the following headings, although not every person diagnosed as schizophrenic will exhibit all of these symptoms.

DISTURBANCES OF THOUGHT AND ATTENTION Whereas affective disorders are characterized by disturbances of mood, schizophrenia is characterized by disturbances of *thought*. The following excerpt from a patient's writings illustrates how difficult it is to understand schizophrenic thinking.

> If things turn by rotation of agriculture or levels in regards and timed to everything; I am referring to a previous document when I made some remarks that were facts also tested and there is another that concerns my daughter she has a lobed bottom right ear, her name being Mary Lou. Much of abstraction has been left unsaid and undone in these productmilk syrup, and others, due to economics, differentials, subsidies, bankruptcy, tools, buildings, bonds, national stocks, foundation craps, weather, trades, government in levels of breakages and fuses in electronics too all formerly states not necessarily factuated. (Maher, 1966, p. 395)

By themselves, the words and phrases make sense, but they are meaningless in relation to each other. The juxtaposition of unrelated words and phrases and the

FIGURE 15-5
Schizophrenic Disorder

WG, a handsome, athletic-looking youth of 19, was admitted to the psychiatric service on the referral of his family physician. The boy's parents said, on his admission, that their son's behavior during the previous several months had changed drastically. He had been an adequate student in high school, but he had had to leave college recently because he was failing all his subjects. He had excelled in a variety of non-team sports—swimming, weightlifting, track—winning several letters, but now he did not exercise at all. Although he had always been careful about his health and had hardly ever mentioned any physical problems, within the past several weeks he had repeatedly expressed vague complaints about his head and chest, which, he said, indicated that he was "in very bad shape." During the past several days, the patient had spent most of his time sitting in his room, staring vacantly out of his window. He had become (quite uncharacteristically) careless about his personal appearance and habits.

Although there was no doubt that the patient had exhibited serious recent changes in behavior, further conversation with the parents indicated that the patient's childhood and adolescent adjustment had not been healthy. He had always been painfully shy, except in highly structured situations, and had spent much of his free time alone (often working out with weights). Despite his athletic achievements, he had no really close friends. . . .

The personnel of the psychiatric service found it difficult to converse with the patient; an ordinary diagnostic interview was impossible. For the most part, the boy volunteered no information. He would usually answer direct questions, but often in a flat, toneless way devoid of emotional coloring. Frequently, his answers were not logically connected to the questions. Observers often found it taxing to record their conversations with the patient. After speaking to him for a while, they would find themselves wondering just what the conversation had been about.

At times, the disharmony between the content of the patient's words and his emotional expression was striking. For example, while speaking sympathetically of an acute illness that had rendered his mother bedridden during a portion of the previous fall, the boy giggled constantly.

At times, WG became agitated and spoke with a curious intensity. On one occasion, he spoke of "electrical sensations" and "an electrical current" in his brain. On another, he revealed that when lying awake at night, he often heard a voice repeating the command, "You'll have to do it." The patient felt that he was somehow being influenced by a force outside himself to commit an act of violence—as yet undefined—toward his parents (Hofling, 1975, pp. 372–73).

idiosyncratic word associations (sometimes called a "word salad") are characteristic of schizophrenic writing and speech.

The thought disorder in schizophrenia appears to be a general difficulty in filtering out irrelevant stimuli. Most of us are able to focus our attention selectively. From a mass of incoming sensory information, we are able to select the stimuli that are relevant to the task at hand and to ignore the rest. A person who suffers from schizophrenia appears to be unable to screen out irrelevant stimuli. The individual is perceptually receptive to many stimuli at the same time and has trouble making sense of the profusion of inputs, as the following statement by a schizophrenic patient illustrates.

> I can't concentrate. It's diversions of attention that trouble me. I am picking up different conversations. It's like being a transmitter. The sounds are coming through to me, but I feel my mind cannot cope with everything. It's difficult to concentrate on any one sound. (McGhie & Chapman, 1961, p. 104)

The inability to filter out irrelevant stimuli is evident in many aspects of the schizophrenic person's thinking. The disjointed nature of schizophrenic speech reflects the intrusion of irrelevant associations. Often one word will set off a string of associations, as illustrated by the following sentence written by a schizophrenic patient.

> I may be a "Blue Baby" but "Social Baby" not, but yet a blue heart baby could be in the Blue Book published before the war.

This patient had suffered from heart trouble and may have started out to say "I was a blue baby." The association of "blue baby" with "blue blood" in the sense of social status prompted the interruption of "'Social Baby' not." The last phrase shows the interplay between the two meanings: the intention was to say "yet a blue baby could have been in the Society Blue Book" (Maher, 1966, p. 413).

DISTURBANCES OF PERCEPTION   During acute schizophrenic episodes, people often report that the world appears *different* to them (noises seem louder; colors, more intense). Their own bodies may no longer appear the same (their hands may seem to be too large or too small; their legs, overly extended; their eyes, dislocated in the face). Some patients fail to recognize themselves in a mirror or see their reflection as a triple image. During the acute stage of schizophrenia, many patients go through periods when they are unable to perceive wholes. For instance, they cannot see nurses or physicians as persons but can perceive them only in parts (a nose, the left eye, an arm, and so on). The drawing in Figure 15-6 shows a schizophrenic patient's fragmentation of the whole.

DISTURBANCES OF AFFECT   Schizophrenic individuals usually fail to exhibit "normal" or appropriate emotional responses. They often are withdrawn and unresponsive in situations that should make them sad or happy. For example, a man may show no emotional response when informed that his daughter has cancer. However, this blunting or flattening of emotional expression can conceal inner turmoil, and the person may erupt with angry outbursts.

Sometimes the schizophrenic individual expresses emotions that are inappropriately linked to the situation or to the thought being expressed. For instance, a patient may smile while speaking of tragic events. Since our emotions are influenced by cognitive processes, it is not surprising that disorganized thoughts and perceptions are accompanied by changes in emotional responses.

> Half the time I am talking about one thing and thinking about half a dozen other things at the same time. It must look queer to people when I laugh about something that has got nothing to do with what I am talking about, but they don't know what's going on inside and how much of it is running around in my head. You see I might be talking about something quite serious to you and other things come into my head at the same time that are funny and this makes me laugh. If I could only concentrate on one thing at the one time I wouldn't look half so silly. (McGhie & Chapman, 1961, p. 104)

WITHDRAWAL FROM REALITY   During schizophrenic episodes, the individual tends to withdraw from interaction with others and to become absorbed in his or her inner thoughts and fantasies. This state of self-absorption is known as *autism* (from the Greek word *autos,* meaning "self"). As the preceding quotation suggests, a person displaying inappropriate emotional behavior may be reacting to what is going on in his or her private world rather than to external events. Self-absorption can be so intense that the person may not know the day or month or where he or she is.

In acute cases of schizophrenia, withdrawal from reality is temporary. In chronic cases, withdrawal may become more enduring and can progress to the point where the individual is completely unresponsive to external events, remains silent and immobile for days, and must be cared for like an infant.

DELUSIONS AND HALLUCINATIONS   During the acute stage of schizophrenia, distorted thought processes and perceptions are accompanied by delusions. The most common delusions are beliefs that external forces are trying to control the individual's thoughts and actions. These *delusions of influence* include the

FIGURE 15-6
Perceptual Fragmentation   *This drawing by a schizophrenic woman shows the difficulty she has perceiving the face as a whole. (After Arieti, 1974)*

A rigidly held position is characteristic of some schizophrenic patients.

belief that one's thoughts are being broadcast to the world so that others can hear them, that strange thoughts (not one's own) are being inserted into the individual's mind, or that feelings and actions are being imposed on the person by some external force. Also frequent are beliefs that certain people or certain groups are threatening or plotting against the individual (*delusions of persecution*). Less common are beliefs that the person is powerful and important (*delusions of grandeur*).

A person who has persecutory delusions is called *paranoid*. He or she may become suspicious of friends and relatives, may fear being poisoned, or may complain of being watched, followed, and talked about. So-called motiveless crimes, when an individual attacks or kills someone for no apparent cause, are sometimes committed by people who are later diagnosed as suffering from paranoid schizophrenia.

Hallucinations may occur independently or as part of a delusional belief. Auditory hallucinations — usually voices telling the person what to do or commenting on his or her actions — are the most common. Visual hallucinations — such as seeing strange creatures or heavenly beings — are somewhat less frequent. Other sensory hallucinations (a bad odor emanating from the individual's body, the taste of poison in food, the feeling of being touched or pricked by needles) occur infrequently. Mark Vonnegut, in writing about his own schizophrenic experience, describes his first visual hallucination.

And then one night, as I was trying to get to sleep, I started listening to and feeling my heart beat. Suddenly I became terribly frightened that it would stop. And from out of nowhere came an incredibly wrinkled, iridescent face. Starting as a small point infinitely distant, it rushed forward, becoming infinitely huge. I could see nothing else. My heart had stopped. The moment stretched forever. I tried to make the face go away, but it mocked me. I had somehow gained control over my heartbeat, but I didn't know how to use it. I was holding my life in my hands and was powerless to stop it from dripping through my fingers. I tried to look the face in the eyes and realized I had left all familiar ground.

He, she, or whatever seemed not to like me much. But the worst of it was it didn't stop coming. It had no respect for my personal space, no inclination to maintain a conversational distance. When I could easily make out all its features, when it and I were more or less on the same scale, when I thought there was maybe a foot or two between us, it had actually been hundreds of miles away, and it kept coming and coming till I was lost somewhere in some pore in its nose and it still kept coming.

There was nothing at all unreal about that face. Its concreteness made the Rock of Gibraltar look like so much cotton candy. I hoped I could get enough rest simply by lying motionless. In any event, the prospect of not sleeping frightened me far less than the possibility of losing contact with the world. (Vonnegut, 1975, pp. 96-98)

The signs of schizophrenia are many and varied. Trying to make sense of the variety of symptoms is complicated by the fact that some may result directly from the disorder, while others may result from a reaction to the restrictive and often boring life in a mental hospital or from the effects of medication.

Understanding Schizophrenia

More research has been devoted to trying to understand the nature of schizophrenia than to any other mental disorder. In an attempt to explain the disturbances in communication and perception that often characterize the schizophrenic state, some investigators have studied the cognitive functioning of people diagnosed as schizophrenic — the way they selectively attend to stimuli, store information in memory, and use language. Others have looked at the ways in which schizo-phrenic individuals differ biologically from other people in terms of genetic inheritance, the functioning of the nervous system, and brain biochemistry. Still others have examined the effects on schizophrenia of such environmental factors as social class, family interaction, and stressful life events.

Despite a voluminous body of research, the causes of schizophrenia are still not well understood. Nevertheless, some areas of research are promising, and we will consider three of them here.

BIOLOGICAL PERSPECTIVE   It has become increasingly evident that there is a hereditary predisposition toward developing schizophrenia. Family studies show that relatives of schizophrenics are more likely to develop the disorder than are people from families free of schizophrenia. Figure 15-7 gives the lifetime risk of developing schizophrenia as a function of how closely an individual is geneti-cally related to a person diagnosed as schizophrenic. Note that an identical twin of a schizophrenic is more than 3 times as likely as a fraternal twin to develop schizophrenia and 46 times as likely as an unrelated person from the general population to develop the disorder. However, fewer than half of the identical twins of schizophrenics have schizophrenia themselves, even though they share the same genes. This fact demonstrates the importance of environmental vari-ables.

The means of genetic transmission is not known, nor is it possible at present to predict which individuals known to be at risk will develop schizophrenia. The pattern of inheritance suggests that several genes are involved, rather than a single dominant or recessive gene (Nicol & Gottesman, 1983).

Assuming that the genetic predisposition to schizophrenia involves a defect or imbalance in body chemistry, researchers over the years have sought to find biochemical differences between schizophrenic and normal individuals. A num-ber of differences between the chemistry of blood or urine samples from normals and that of hospitalized schizophrenics have been reported, often heralded as

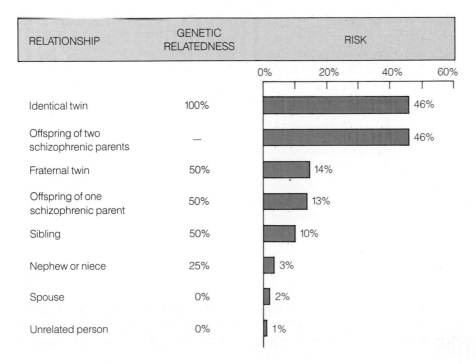

RELATIONSHIP	GENETIC RELATEDNESS	RISK
Identical twin	100%	46%
Offspring of two schizophrenic parents	—	46%
Fraternal twin	50%	14%
Offspring of one schizophrenic parent	50%	13%
Sibling	50%	10%
Nephew or niece	25%	3%
Spouse	0%	2%
Unrelated person	0%	1%

FIGURE 15-7
Genetic Relationships and Schizophrenia   *The lifetime risk of developing schizophrenia is largely a function of how closely an individual is genetically related to a schizophrenic and not a function of how much their environment is shared. In the case of an individual with two schizophrenic parents, genetic relatedness cannot be expressed in terms of percentage, but the regression of the individual's "genetic value" on that of the parents is 1, the same as it is for identical twins. (After Gottesman & Shields, 1982)*

"There are several reasons for your problem: environmental stress, early childhood experience, chemical imbalance, and, primarily, the fact that both of your parents are as cuckoo as a Bavarian clock."

breakthroughs in understanding the cause of schizophrenia. Unfortunately, most of these discoveries either have not been replicable or have been found to be related to a condition of the individual other than his or her schizophrenic disorder. The latter constitutes one of the major problems in the search for a causal explanation of schizophrenia: an abnormality found in schizophrenic patients but not in control subjects may be the *cause* of the disorder or the *result* of the disorder, or it may stem from some aspect of *treatment*. For example, a schizophrenic's first admission to a hospital is often preceded by weeks of intense panic and agitation that undoubtedly produce bodily changes. These changes — related to lack of sleep, inadequate diet, and general stress — cannot be considered the cause of the disorder. Other biochemical abnormalities may be related to treatment. Most schizophrenic patients receive medication, traces of which may remain in the blood for some time. Some of the conditions of prolonged hospitalization, such as a change in diet, may also produce biochemical changes.

All of these factors compound the problem of finding differences between schizophrenic and control subjects that tell us something about the origin of schizophrenia. Despite such obstacles, current research, based on increased knowledge of neurotransmitters and the use of new techniques for measuring brain activity, provides promising leads.

Biochemical theories of affective disorders have focused on norepinephrine and serotonin, but research on schizophrenia has centered on *dopamine*, a neurotransmitter active in an area of the brain believed to be involved in the regulation of emotion (the limbic system). The *dopamine hypothesis* proposes that schizophrenia is caused by too much dopamine at certain synapses in the brain. This excess may be due to overproduction of the neurotransmitter or to faulty regulation of the reuptake mechanism by which dopamine returns to and is stored by vesicles in the presynaptic neurons. It might also be due to oversensitive dopamine receptors or to too many dopamine receptors. Evidence for the importance of dopamine comes from two sources. First, drugs that are effective in relieving the symptoms of schizophrenia, called *antipsychotic drugs*, reduce the amount of usable dopamine in the brain. Researchers believe that they do so by blocking the dopamine receptors. These drugs do not completely cure schizophrenia, but they do reduce hallucinations and delusions, improve concentration, and make schizophrenic symptoms less bizarre. Moreover, the therapeutic effectiveness of a particular drug has been found to parallel its potency in blocking dopamine receptors (Creese, Burt, & Snyder, 1978).

Further evidence that an abnormality in dopamine metabolism may be the underlying cause of schizophrenia comes from observations of the effects of amphetamines, which increase the release of dopamine. Drug users who overdose on amphetamines exhibit psychotic behavior that closely resembles schizophrenia, and their symptoms can be relieved by the same antipsychotic drugs used to treat schizophrenia. When low doses of amphetamines are given to schizophrenic patients, their symptoms become much worse. In these cases, the drug does not produce a psychosis of its own; rather, it exacerbates whatever symptoms the patient may be experiencing (Snyder, 1980).

Thus, enhancing the action of dopamine aggravates schizophrenic symptoms, and blocking dopamine receptors alleviates them. The exact way in which the dopamine metabolisms of schizophrenic and normal individuals differ is not known.

While the dopamine hypothesis seems promising, it still has problems. For example, some schizophrenics do *not* improve when given antipsychotic drugs. Undoubtedly, schizophrenia is not a single disease but a group of disorders; some cases may be due to an excess of dopamine, while others may result from causes as yet unidentified. Investigators are currently using new techniques — positron emission tomography (PET) and computerized axial tomography (CT), discussed on pp. 40 and 41 — to study the brain activity of schizophrenic patients and to look for functional and structural abnormalities.

SOCIAL AND PSYCHOLOGICAL PERSPECTIVE Numerous studies in the United States and other countries have revealed that the incidence of schizophrenia is significantly higher among the lower classes than among the middle and upper classes (Dohrenwend, 1973; Strauss, 1982). No one knows why social class is related to schizophrenia, but several explanations have been suggested.

1. *Differential diagnosis* Therapists are reluctant to apply the label "schizophrenia" to higher-income patients because it could have a damaging effect on their clients' careers.
2. *Downward drift* Because their coping skills are poor, individuals who suffer from schizophrenia have difficulty completing their education and getting a decent job. They gradually drift downward in society and become part of the lower classes.
3. *Increased stress* Living under conditions of poverty in areas with high crime rates, run-down housing, and inadequate schools creates enough additional stress to precipitate schizophrenic disorders, particularly in individuals who are genetically predisposed to schizophrenia.

Evidence shows that all of these explanations, especially the last two, may be true (Kosa & Zola, 1975; Brenner, 1982; Fried, 1982).

Research on the role of psychological factors in the origins of schizophrenia has focused on parent-child relationships and patterns of communication within the family. Studies of the families of schizophrenic patients have identified two types of family relationships that seem to contribute to the disorder. In one type, the parents are sharply divided and are unwilling to cooperate in the pursuit of mutual goals; each devalues and tries to dominate the other and competes for the children's loyalty. In the second type, there is no open strife; the dominant parent shows serious psychopathology that the other parent passively accepts as normal (Lidz, 1973). Both family types include parents who are peculiar, immature, and who use their children to fulfill their own needs, and both are apt to produce children who feel confused, rejected, and uncertain about people's true feelings. In a sense, the children grow up learning to accept their parents' distortions of reality as normal.

Observations of interactions in schizophrenic families suggest that problems in communication constitute an important part of the parents' deviance. They often seem unable to focus their attention and to communicate a coherent message to their listener. Their conversation is therefore disjointed and confused, as the following example illustrates.

DAUGHTER: (the patient, *complainingly*) Nobody will listen to me. Everybody is trying to still me.
MOTHER: Nobody wants to kill you.
FATHER: If you're going to associate with intellectual people, you're going to have to remember that *still* is a noun and not a verb.

(Singer & Wynne, 1963, p. 195)

The members of this family are clearly not talking to each other in a meaningful way. Each is following his or her own idiosyncratic train of thought. After several conversations like this, a normal person might end up with a thought disorder!

In addition to communicating in ways that create confusion and uncertainty, the parents of children who later develop schizophrenia tend to deal with their offspring in a hostile and critical manner: when the child misbehaves, they criticize him rather than his actions ("You're no good"), and they *tell* him what he thinks and feels rather than *listen* to what he says ("You know you don't like that kid you go around with"). The combination of confused communication and negative parental attitudes appears to be more predictive of future schizophrenia than either variable alone (Goldstein, 1985). However, the causal relationship is not clear. It is possible that communication problems and negative parental attitudes result from the parents' attempts to cope with a child whose behavior is disturbed or unusual even before he or she is diagnosed as schizophrenic. In other words, is the parents' deviance a cause of the child's maladaptive behavior, or are the child's atypical characteristics (distractibility, difficulty focusing attention, and so forth) a cause of the parents' behavior? This question is as yet unanswered. But whatever their role in causing the initial schizophrenic behavior, family disorganization and parental rejection are important in determining the severity of the illness and the prognosis for recovery (Roff & Knight, 1981).

In addition to disturbed family relationships, other traumatic events (such as the early death of one or both parents) are found with greater than average frequency in the backgrounds of people who develop schizophrenia. Stressful childhoods of various kinds may contribute to the disorder. In general, the more stressful the childhood, the more severe the schizophrenic disorder.

VULNERABILITY AND STRESS   Most individuals who live in poverty or who experience a disturbing and stressful childhood do *not* develop schizophrenia. Some individuals who are eventually labeled schizophrenic may begin life with a hereditary predisposition to the disorder. But it seems unlikely that heredity alone can account for schizophrenia. Undoubtedly, genetic predisposition and environmental stress interact to produce the disorder. The situation may be similar to the development of allergies: there is an inherited predisposition to allergic sensitivities, but certain environmental events are necessary to trigger the reaction.

Currently, some 50 longitudinal studies are being conducted with children who have been identified as having a high risk of developing schizophrenia. The studies follow the children from their early years to adulthood in an attempt to pinpoint some of the factors that determine whether or not the disorder will develop. In most of these studies, the children are considered to have a high risk because they have at least one schizophrenic parent (Mednick, 1973; John, Mednick, & Schulsinger, 1982; Steffy et al., 1984). Other investigators have selected their high-risk group on the basis of psychophysiological measures or behavioral characteristics that they believe to be precursors of schizophrenia (Garmezy, 1974; Mednick et al., 1984).

The high-risk subjects are usually matched with a control group of children who have no family background of mental illness and who show no early signs of psychopathology. The development of both groups is carefully monitored through periodic testing and interviews with parents, teachers, and peers. Once a high-risk subject has a schizophrenic breakdown, he or she is matched both with a subject from the high-risk group who has remained well and with a well member of the control group. Thus, the background of the individual who develops schizophrenia can be compared with that of a high-risk subject and a normal, low-risk subject.

Most of these studies, started in the 1960s and 1970s, are still in progress, and the subjects are now young adults. Some have already become schizophrenic, and many more are expected to do so within the next decade. Consequently, the data available at present consist mainly of comparisons between high-risk and low-risk groups. These data indicate that the high-risk child is similar to an adult schizophrenic in many ways. For example, high-risk children are rated low in social competence and tend to perform poorly on tasks that require sustained attention or abstract thinking.

Preliminary data on high-risk subjects who later developed schizophrenia indicate that they differ from the high-risk subjects who have remained well in the following ways. The subjects who developed the disorder

1. Were more apt to have experienced birth complications that may have affected the functioning of their nervous system.
2. Were more likely to have been separated from their mothers at an early age.
3. Had fathers who were more likely to have been hospitalized, with diagnoses ranging from alcoholism to schizophrenia.
4. Were more likely to show inappropriate behavior in school. The boys were described by their teachers as anxious, lonely, and causing disciplinary problems; the girls, as withdrawn, isolated, and poorly controlled.

When more data from these ongoing high-risk studies become available, we should have a better understanding of how innate and environmental factors interact to produce schizophrenia.

PERSONALITY DISORDERS

Personality disorders are long-standing patterns of maladaptive behavior. In Chapter 13, we described *personality traits* as enduring ways of perceiving or relating to the environment and thinking about oneself. When personality traits become so inflexible and maladaptive that they significantly impair the individual's ability to function, they are called personality disorders. Personality disorders constitute immature and inappropriate ways of coping with stress or solving problems. They are usually evident by early adolescence and may continue throughout adult life.

Unlike people with affective or anxiety disorders, which also involve maladaptive behavior, people who have personality disorders usually do not feel upset or anxious and are not motivated to change their behavior. They do not lose contact with reality or display marked disorganization of behavior, unlike individuals who have schizophrenic disorders.

DSM-III lists 12 personality disorders. For example, someone who has a *narcissistic personality disorder* is described as having an inflated sense of self-importance, being preoccupied with fantasies of success, constantly seeking admiration and attention, and being insensitive to the needs of others and often exploiting them. *Dependent personality disorders* are characterized by a passive orientation to life, an inability to make decisions or accept responsibility, a tendency to be self-deprecating, and a need for continual support from others.

Most of the personality disorders listed in DSM-III have not been the subject of much research. Moreover, the characteristics of the various personality disorders overlap, so that agreement in classifying individuals is poor. The personality disorder that has been studied the most and is the most reliably diagnosed is the antisocial personality.

Antisocial Personality

People who have *antisocial personalities* (also called *psychopathic personalities*) seem to have little sense of responsibility, morality, or concern for others. Their behavior is determined almost entirely by their own needs. In other words, they lack a *conscience*. Whereas the average person realizes at an early age that some restrictions are placed on behavior and that pleasures must sometimes be postponed in consideration of the needs of others, individuals who have antisocial personalities seldom consider any desires except their own. They behave impulsively, seek immediate gratification of their needs, and cannot tolerate frustration.

The term "antisocial personality" is somewhat misleading, because these characteristics do not describe most people who commit antisocial acts. Antisocial *behavior* results from a number of causes, including membership in a delinquent gang or a criminal subculture, the need for attention and status, loss of contact with reality, and an inability to control impulses. Most juvenile delinquents and adult criminals do have some concern for others (for family or gang members) and some code of moral conduct ("You don't squeal on a friend"). In contrast, antisocial *personalities* have little feeling for anyone except themselves and seem to experience little guilt or remorse, regardless of how much suffering their behavior may cause others. Other characteristics of the antisocial personality include a great facility for lying, a need for thrills and excitement with little concern for possible injury, and an inability to alter behavior as a consequence of punishment. Such individuals are often attractive, intelligent, charming people who are quite facile in manipulating others — in other words, good "con artists." Their façade of competence and sincerity wins them promising jobs, but they have little staying power. Their restlessness and impulsiveness soon lead them into an escapade that reveals their true nature; they accumulate debts, desert their families, squander company money, or commit crimes. When caught, their declarations of repentance are so convincing that they often escape punishment and are given another chance. But they seldom live up to expectations; what they say has little relation to what they feel or do (see Figure 15-8).

The two most diagnostic characteristics of an antisocial personality disorder are considered to be lovelessness (the inability to feel any empathy for, or loyalty to, another person) and guiltlessness (the inability to feel any remorse for one's action, regardless of how reprehensible it is).

Understanding Antisocial Personalities

What factors contribute to the development of the antisocial personality? We might expect individuals with such personalities to have been raised by parents who provided no discipline or moral training, but the answer is not that simple. Although some individuals come from environments in which antisocial behavior is reinforced and adult criminals serve as models for personality development, many more come from "good" homes and were raised by parents who are prominent and respected members of the community.

As yet, there is no well-supported theory to explain why antisocial personalities develop. Many factors are probably involved and vary from case to case. Current research focuses on biological determinants and on the quality of the parent-child relationship.

BIOLOGICAL FACTORS   The clinical impression that the antisocial individual experiences little anxiety about future discomforts or punishments has been supported by experimental studies. One study compared two groups of adolescent male delinquents selected from the detention unit of a juvenile court. One group had been diagnosed as having antisocial personality disorders; the other, adjustment reactions of adolescence. The experimenters tested galvanic skin response (GSR, see p. 219) under stress. Dummy electrodes were attached to each

FIGURE 15-8

Antisocial Personality

A 40-year-old man was convicted of check forgery and embezzlement. He was arrested with a young woman, age 18, whom he had married bigamously some months before. She was unaware of the existence of any previous marriage. The subject in this case had already been convicted for two previous bigamous marriages and for 40 other cases of passing fraudulent checks.

The circumstances of his arrest illustrate the impulsivity and lack of insight characteristic of many antisocial personalities. He had gotten a job managing a small restaurant; the absentee owner, who lived in a neighboring town, had arranged to stop by at the end of each week to check on progress and to collect the income. The subject was provided with living quarters over the restaurant, a small salary, and a percentage of the cash register receipts. At the end of the first week, the subject took all the money (he had failed to bank it nightly as he had been instructed) and departed shortly before the employer arrived; he left a series of vulgar messages scribbled on the walls saying he had taken the money because the salary was "too low." He found lodgings with "his wife" a few blocks from the restaurant and made no effort to escape detection. He was arrested a few days later.

During the inquiry, it emerged that the subject had spent the past few months cashing checks in department stores in various cities. He would make out the check and send his wife in to cash it; he commented that her genuine innocence of the fact that he had no bank account made her very effective in not arousing suspicion. He had not bothered to use a false name when he signed the checks or the bigamous marriage contract, but he seemed surprised that the police discovered him so quickly.

Inquiry into the subject's past history revealed that he had been educated mostly in private schools and that his parents were financially well-to-do. They had planned for him to go to college, but his academic record was not good enough (although on examination he proved to have superior intelligence). Failing to get into college, he started work as an insurance salesman trainee and did very well. He was a distinguished-looking young man and an exceptionally fluent speaker.

Just as it appeared that he could anticipate a successful career in the insurance business, he ran into trouble because he failed to turn in the checks that customers had given him to pay their initial premiums. He admitted to having cashed these checks and to spending the money (mostly on clothes and liquor). It apparently did not occur to him that the company's accounting system would quickly discern this type of embezzlement. In fact, he expressed amused indignation at the company's failure to realize that he intended to pay back the money from his salary. No legal action was taken, but he was requested to resign. His parents reimbursed the company for the missing money.

At this point, the subject enlisted in the army and was sent to Officer Candidate School, from which he graduated as a second lieutenant. He was assigned to an infantry unit, where he soon got into trouble that progressed from minor infractions (drunk on duty, smuggling women into his quarters) to cashing fraudulent checks. He was court-martialed and given a dishonorable discharge. From then on, his life followed a pattern of finding a woman to support him (with or without marriage) and then running off with her money to the next woman when life became too tedious.

At his trial, where he was sentenced to five years in prison, he gave a long and articulate speech, pleading clemency for the young woman who was being tried with him, expressing repentance for having ruined her life, and stating that he was glad to have the opportunity to repay society for his crimes (Maher, 1966, pp. 214–15).

subject's leg, and he was told that in 10 minutes he would be given a very strong but not harmful shock. (A large clock was visible so that the subject knew precisely when the shock was supposed to occur—no shock was actually administered.) The two groups showed no difference in GSR measures during periods of rest or in response to auditory or visual stimulation. However, during the 10 minutes of shock anticipation, the maladjusted group showed significantly more tension than the antisocial group. At the moment when the clock indicated the shock was due, most of the maladjusted subjects exhibited an abrupt drop in skin resistance (indicating a sharp increase in anxiety). *None* of the antisocial subjects showed this reaction (Lippert & Senter, 1966).

Studies in prisons have shown that, compared to other prisoners, antisocial personalities do not learn to avoid shocks as quickly and do not exhibit as much autonomic nervous system activity under a variety of conditions (Lykken, 1957; Hare, 1970). These findings have led to the hypothesis that antisocial individuals may have been born with an *underreactive autonomic nervous system,* which would explain why they seem to require so much excitement and why they fail to respond normally to threats of danger that deter most people from antisocial acts.

CRITICAL DISCUSSION

Insanity as a Legal Defense

How should the law treat a mentally disturbed person who commits a criminal offense? Should individuals whose mental faculties are impaired be held responsible for their actions? These questions are of concern to behavioral and social scientists, to members of the legal profession, and to individuals who work with criminal offenders.

Over the centuries, an important part of Western law has been the concept that a civilized society should not punish a person who is mentally incapable of controlling his or her conduct. In 1724, an English court maintained that a man was not responsible for an act if "he doth not know what he is doing, no more than . . . a wild beast." Modern standards of legal responsibility, however, have been based on the M'Naghten decision of 1843. M'Naghten, a Scotsman, suffered the paranoid delusion that he was being persecuted by the English prime minister, Sir Robert Peel. In an attempt to kill Peel, he mistakenly shot Peel's secretary. Everyone involved in the trial was convinced by M'Naghten's senseless ramblings that he was insane. He was judged not responsible by reason of insanity and sent to a mental hospital, where he remained until his death. But Queen Victoria was not pleased with the verdict—apparently she felt that political assassinations should not be taken lightly—and called on the House of Lords to review the decision. The decision was upheld, and rules for the legal definition of insanity were put into writing. The M'Naghten Rule states that a defendant may be found not guilty by reason of insanity only if he were so severely disturbed at the time of his act that he did not know what he was doing, or if he did know what he was doing, did not know that it was wrong.

The M'Naghten Rule was adopted in the United States, and the distinction of knowing right from wrong remained the basis of most decisions of legal insanity for over a century. Some states added to their statutes the doctrine of "irresistible impulse," which recognizes that some mentally ill individuals may respond correctly when asked if a particular act is morally right or wrong but may be unable to control their behavior.

During the 1970s, a number of state and federal courts adopted a broader legal definition of insanity proposed by the American Law Institute, which states: "A person is not responsible for criminal conduct if at the time of such conduct, as a result of mental disease or defect, he lacks substantial capacity either to appreciate the wrongfulness of his conduct or to conform his conduct to the requirements of the law." The word *substantial* suggests that any incapacity is not enough to avoid criminal responsibility but that total incapacity is not required either. The use of the word *appreciate* rather than *know* implies that intellectual awareness of right or wrong is not enough; individuals must have some understanding of the moral or legal consequences of their behavior before they can be held criminally responsible.

The problem of legal responsibility in the case of mentally disordered individuals

Interpretations must be made with caution, however. It is possible that antisocial personalities may view an experimental situation as a game and may try to play it "extra cool" by attempting to control their responses.

PARENTAL INFLUENCES   According to psychoanalytic theory, the development of a conscience, or superego, depends on an affectionate relationship with an adult during early childhood. Normal children internalize their parents' values (which generally reflect the values of society) because they want to be like their parents and fear the loss of their parents' love if they do not behave in accordance with these values. A child who receives no love from either parent does not fear its loss; he or she does not identify with the rejecting parents and does not internalize their rules. Reasonable as this theory seems, it does not conform to all of the data. Many rejected children do not develop antisocial personalities, and some people who do were indulged in childhood.

has become a topic of increased debate in the wake of John Hinckley, Jr.'s, acquittal, by reason of insanity, for the attempted assassination of President Reagan in 1981. Many Americans seem to feel that the insanity defense is a legal loophole that allows too many guilty people to go free. Some legal and mental health professionals argue that the current courtroom procedures—in which psychiatrists and psychologists for the prosecution and the defense present contradictory evidence as to the defendant's mental state—is confusing to the jury and does little to help the cause of justice. One suggestion is to restrict expert testimony to evidence of abnormality that bears on the defendant's conscious awareness and perception at the time of the crime—that is, the defendant's intent to commit the crime. Other testimony concerning more subtle impairments of judgment and ability to control behavior would no longer be relevant when deciding on a verdict but could be introduced at the time of sentencing. Another proposal calls for a pool of expert witnesses to be selected by the court. These experts would not testify for the prosecution or the defense but would attempt to arrive at an impartial conclusion regarding the defendant's mental state at the time the crime was committed.

At present, in the United States the laws concerning the insanity defense are in a state of flux. In 1984, Congress passed a bill limiting the insanity test to a determination of whether the defendant knew that he was committing a crime. Federal courts are expected to follow this law, and a number of states have passed similar laws. Three states (Idaho, Montana, and Utah) have abolished the insanity plea altogether, and several other states have replaced the verdict of not guilty by reason of insanity with a new verdict of guilty but mentally ill. The person subject to this verdict would be given psychotherapeutic treatment in jail or would be treated in a mental hospital and returned to jail when he or she was deemed mentally fit to complete the sentence. The problem remains as to whether treatment in either place would be sufficient to rehabilitate the individual.

Despite the current controversy, actual cases of acquittal by reason of insanity are quite rare. Jurors seem reluctant to believe that people are not morally responsible for their acts, and lawyers, knowing that an insanity plea is apt to fail, tend to use it only as a last resort. Fewer than 1 percent of defendants charged with serious crimes are found not guilty by reason of insanity.

The question of mental disorder exerts its greatest impact earlier in the legal process. Many accused people who are mentally ill never come to trial. In the United States, the law requires that the defendant be *competent to stand trial*. An individual is judged competent to stand trial if he or she is able (1) to understand the charges and (2) to cooperate with a lawyer in preparing a defense. The competency issue is basic to the American ideal of a fair trial and is quite separate from the question of whether the person was "insane" at the time the crime was committed. In a preliminary hearing, the judge receives evidence about the accused's mental competency. The judge may drop the charges and commit the individual to a psychiatric facility (if the crime is not serious) or commit the accused and file the charges until he or she is deemed competent to stand trial. Because court calendars are congested and trials are expensive, judges often prefer to deal with mentally disturbed defendants in this way, particularly if they believe that the psychiatric hospital will provide adequate treatment and secure confinement.

Many more persons are confined to mental institutions because they are found incompetent to stand trial than because they are found not guilty by reason of insanity. These people, many of whom are not dangerous, often are confined longer than they would have been if they had been convicted of the crime in question. Indeed, before the widespread use of antipsychotic drugs, individuals deemed incompetent to stand trial were often committed to mental institutions for life. However, in 1972, the Supreme Court ruled that defendants found incompetent to stand trial due to mental illness could not be held indefinitely. Judges now attempt to bring such individuals to trial or to release them within 18 months. In deciding on release, the seriousness of the crime and the potential for future dangerous behavior are important considerations. Unfortunately, at present our data for predicting whether an individual is likely to commit a dangerous act are not very reliable.

According to learning theory, antisocial behavior is influenced by the kind of models the parents provide and the kind of behavior they reward. A child may develop an antisocial personality if he or she learns that punishment can be avoided by being charming, lovable, and repentant. A child who is consistently able to avoid punishment by claiming to be sorry and promising never to do it again may learn that it is not the deed that counts but charm and ability to act repentant. If the same child is indulged in other respects and never has to wait or to work for a reward, he or she does not learn to tolerate frustration. Two characteristics of the antisocial personality are a lack of frustration tolerance and the conviction that being charming and appearing contrite excuses wrongdoing. In addition, a child who is always protected from frustration or distress may have no ability to empathize with the distress of others (Maher, 1966). Undoubtedly, a number of family interaction patterns foster the development of an antisocial personality.

SUMMARY

1. The diagnosis of abnormal behavior is based on *statistical frequency, social norms, adaptiveness of behavior,* and *personal distress.* Characteristics indicative of good mental health include an *efficient perception of reality, self-knowledge, control of behavior, self-esteem,* an *ability to form affectionate relationships,* and *productivity.*

2. DSM-III classifies mental disorders according to specific behavioral symptoms. Such a classification system helps to communicate information and provides a basis for research. However, each case is unique, and diagnostic labels should not be used to pigeonhole individuals.

3. Anxiety disorders include *generalized anxiety* (constant worry and tension), *panic disorders* (sudden attacks of overwhelming apprehension), *phobias* (irrational fears of specific objects or situations), and *obsessive-compulsive disorders* (persistent unwanted thoughts, or *obsessions,* combined with urges, or *compulsions,* to perform certain acts).

4. Psychoanalytic theories attribute anxiety disorders to unresolved, unconscious conflicts. Learning theories focus on anxiety as a learned response to external events and invoke the concept of *prepared conditioning* to explain phobias. Cognitive theories emphasize the way anxious people think about potential dangers: their overestimation of the likelihood and degree of harm makes them tense and physiologically prepared for danger; they are unable to dismiss obsessive thoughts and so attempt to neutralize bad thoughts by compulsive acts. Biological theories suggest that some cases of anxiety disorder (particularly panic attacks) result from an imbalance in the brain's neurotransmitters that regulate anxiety.

5. *Affective disorders* are disturbances of mood: *depression; mania;* or an alternation between the two moods, referred to as *manic-depression.* Sadness, loss of gratification in life, negative thoughts, and lack of motivation are the main symptoms of depression. Psychoanalytic theories view depression as a *reactivation of the loss of parental affection* in a person who is *dependent on external approval* and tends *to turn anger inward.* Learning theories focus on *reduced positive reinforcement.*

6. Beck's cognitive theory of depression proposes that individuals prone to depression consistently appraise events from a negative and self-critical viewpoint. Seligman's *learned helplessness* theory attributes depression to an explanatory style that invokes *internal, stable,* and *global causes for bad events.* Depressive cognitions accompany depression but may not be a primary cause.

7. Some affective disorders may be influenced by inherited abnormalities in the metabolism of certain *neurotransmitters* (such as *norepinephrine* and *serotonin*). Inherited predispositions and early experiences may make people *vulnerable* to depression when under stress.

8. *Schizophrenia* is primarily a thought disorder characterized by difficulty in filtering out irrelevant stimuli, disturbances in perception, inappropriate affect, delusions and hallucinations, and withdrawal. Research on the causes of schizophrenia has focused on evidence for a hereditary disposition to the disorder, possible defects in the metabolism of neurotransmitters (the *dopamine hypothesis*), social factors, and deviant family relationships. Studies of high-risk children point to some predictors of schizophrenia.

9. *Personality disorders* are long-standing patterns of maladaptive behavior that constitute immature and inappropriate ways of coping with stress or solving problems. Individuals classified as having *antisocial personalities* are impulsive, show little guilt, are concerned only with their own needs, and are frequently in trouble with the law. An underreactive nervous system and inconsistent parental rewards and punishments are two possible explanations for the disorder.

General textbooks on abnormal psychology include Davison and Neale, *Abnormal Psychology: An Experimental Clinical Approach* (4th ed., 1986); Sarason and Sarason, *Abnormal Psychology: The Problem of Maladaptive Behavior* (4th ed., 1984); Seligman and Rosenhan, *Abnormal Psychology* (1984); Coleman, Butcher, and Carson, *Abnormal Psychology and Modern Life* (7th ed., 1984); Goldstein, Baker, and Jamison, *Abnormal Psychology: Experiences, Origins, and Interventions* (2nd ed., 1986).

The hereditary aspects of mental illness are reviewed in Plomin, DeFries, and McClearn, *Behavioral Genetics: A Primer* (1980); and in Gottesman and Shields, *Schizophrenia: The Epigenetic Puzzle* (1982).

Panic: Facing Fears, Phobias, and Anxiety (1985) by Agras provides an interesting discussion of the way fears develop into phobias. The world of psychosis from the patient's viewpoint is graphically described in Green, *I Never Promised You a Rose Garden* (1971); and Vonnegut, *The Eden Express* (1975). In *Holiday of Darkness* (1982) by Endler, a well-known psychologist provides an account of his personal battle with depression and discusses the effects of various treatments.

FURTHER READING

Methods of Therapy

16

IN THIS CHAPTER, WE WILL LOOK AT methods for treating abnormal behavior. Some of these methods focus on helping individuals gain an understanding of the causes of their problems, some attempt to modify thoughts and behavior directly, some involve biological interventions, and some specify ways in which the community can help. The treatment of mental disorders is closely linked to theories about the causes of such disorders. A brief history of the treatment of the mentally ill will illustrate how methods change as theories about human nature and the causes of its disorders change.

HISTORICAL BACKGROUND

According to one of the earliest beliefs (espoused by the ancient Chinese, Egyptians, and Hebrews), a person with a mental disorder was possessed by evil spirits. These demons were exorcised by such techniques as prayer, incantation, magic, and the use of purgatives concocted from herbs. If these treatments were unsuccessful, more extreme measures were taken to ensure that the body would be an unpleasant dwelling place for the evil spirit. Flogging, starving, burning, and even stoning to death were not infrequent forms of "treatment."

The first progress in understanding mental disorders was made by the Greek physician Hippocrates (circa 460–377 B.C.), who rejected demonology and maintained that mental disorders were the result of a disturbance in the balance of body fluids. Hippocrates, and the Greek and Roman physicians who followed him, argued for a more humane treatment of the mentally ill. They stressed the importance of pleasant surroundings, exercise, proper diet, massage, and soothing baths, as well as some less desirable treatments, such as bleeding, purging, and mechanical restraints. Although there were no institutions for the mentally ill during this period, many individuals were cared for with great kindness by physicians in temples dedicated to the Greek and Roman gods.

This progressive view of mental illness did not continue, however. Primitive superstitions and a belief in demonology were revived during the Middle Ages. The mentally ill were considered to be in league with Satan and to possess supernatural powers with which they could cause floods, pestilence, and injuries to others. Seriously disturbed individuals were treated cruelly: people believed that by beating, starving, and torturing the mentally ill, they were punishing the devil. This type of cruelty culminated in the witchcraft trials that sentenced to death thousands of people (many of them mentally ill) during the fifteenth, sixteenth, and seventeenth centuries.

Early Asylums

In the latter part of the Middle Ages, cities created asylums to cope with the mentally ill. These asylums were simply prisons; the inmates were chained in dark, filthy cells and were treated more as animals than as human beings. It was not until 1792, when Philippe Pinel was placed in charge of an asylum in Paris, that some improvements were made. As an experiment, Pinel was allowed to remove the chains that restrained the inmates. Much to the amazement of skeptics who thought Pinel was mad to unchain such "animals," the experiment was a success. When released from their restraints, placed in clean, sunny rooms, and treated kindly, many people who for years had been considered hopelessly mad improved enough to leave the asylum.

By the beginning of the twentieth century, the fields of medicine and psychology were making great advances. In 1905, a mental disorder known as *general paresis* was shown to have a physical cause: a syphilis infection acquired many years before the symptoms of the disorder appeared. General paresis is characterized by a gradual decline in mental and physical functions, marked personality changes, and delusions and hallucinations. Without treatment, death occurs within a few years. The syphilis spirochete remains in the body after the initial genital infection disappears, and it gradually destroys the nervous system. At one time, general paresis accounted for more than 10 percent of all admissions to mental hospitals, but today few cases are reported, due to the effectiveness of penicillin in treating syphilis (Dale, 1975).

The discovery that general paresis was the result of a disease encouraged those who believed that mental illness was biological in origin. At about the same time, Sigmund Freud and his followers laid the groundwork for understanding mental illness in terms of psychological factors, and Pavlov's laboratory experiments demonstrated that animals could become emotionally disturbed if forced to make decisions beyond their capacities.

Despite these scientific advances, the public in the early 1900s still did not understand mental illness and viewed mental hospitals and their inmates with fear and horror. Clifford Beers undertook the task of educating the public about mental health. As a young man, Beers developed a manic-depressive disorder and was confined for three years in several private and state hospitals. Although chains and other methods of torture had been abandoned long before, the straitjacket was still widely used to restrain excited patients. Lack of funds made the average state mental hospital—with its overcrowded wards, poor food, and unsympathetic attendants—a far from pleasant place to live. After his recovery, Beers wrote about his experiences in the now-famous book *A Mind That Found Itself* (1908), which aroused considerable public interest. Beers worked ceaselessly to educate the public about mental illness and helped to organize the

As late as the early nineteenth century, English asylums used rotating devices (top), in which patients were whirled around at high speeds.
A "tranquilizing chair" (above) used to restrain patients in a Pennsylvania hospital, circa 1800.
The "crib" (right) — a restraining device used in a New York mental institution in 1882.

National Committee for Mental Hygiene. In 1950, this organization joined with two related groups to form the National Association for Mental Health. The mental hygiene movement played an invaluable role in stimulating the organization of child-guidance clinics and community mental health centers to aid in the prevention and treatment of mental disorders.

Modern Treatment Facilities

Mental hospitals have been upgraded markedly since the time of Beers, but there is still much room for improvement. Most people who require hospitalization for mental disorders are first admitted to the psychiatric ward of a general hospital, where their condition is evaluated. If more than a brief period of hospitalization is indicated, they may be transferred to a public or private mental hospital. The best of these hospitals are comfortable and well-kept places that provide a number of therapeutic activities: individual and group psychotherapy, recreation, occupational therapy (designed to teach skills, as well as to provide relaxation), and educational courses to help patients prepare for a job upon release from the hospital. The worst are primarily custodial institutions where inmates lead a boring existence in run-down, overcrowded wards and receive little treatment except for medication. Most mental hospitals fall somewhere in between these two extremes.

Since the early 1960s, emphasis has shifted from treating mentally disturbed patients in hospitals to treating them within their home community. Regardless of how good the facilities are, hospitalization has inherent disadvantages. It cuts the patient off from family and friends, tends to make the individual feel "sick" and unable to cope with the outside world, encourages dependency, and may discourage active problem solving.

When antipsychotic and antidepressant drugs (see pp. 554–55) became widely available in the early 1960s, large numbers of patients were able to leave mental hospitals and to return home, receiving treatment as outpatients. The Community Mental Health Centers Act of 1963 made federal funds available for the establishment of community treatment centers. These centers provide outpatient treatment and a number of other services, including short-term hospitalization and partial hospitalization. Partial hospitalization is more flexible than traditional hospitalization: individuals may receive treatment at the center during the day and return home in the evening or may work during the day and spend nights at the center.

Treating mentally ill people in their home communities is a worthwhile goal. However, the move toward shorter hospital stays and the closing of many state and county mental hospitals have produced some unfortunate consequences, largely because the facilities in most communities are far from adequate. Some discharged patients are too incapacitated to support themselves or to function without custodial care; they may live in dirty, overcrowded housing or roam the streets. The disheveled man standing on the corner talking to himself and occasionally shouting gibberish to passersby may be one victim of "deinstitutionalization." The woman who has all of her worldly possessions piled in a shopping bag, and who spends one night in the doorway of an office building and the next in a subway station, may be another.

Many individuals who improve with hospitalization and could manage on their own with assistance do not receive adequate follow-up care in terms of outpatient therapy or help in finding friends, housing, and a job. As a consequence, countless numbers of the mentally ill lead a "revolving door" existence, going in and out of institutions between unsuccessful attempts to cope on their

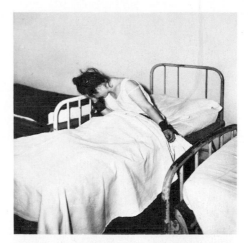

Conditions in a mental hospital in the 1950s.

Deinstitutionalization has resulted in many patients essentially living on the street.

own. About half of all patients discharged from state hospitals are readmitted within a year.

While there is no easy solution to this problem, it seems clear that funds need to be directed toward two areas. One is the improvement of outpatient services to help those who can make it on their own with adequate assistance. The other is the development of alternative residential facilities (such as small-group homes) for patients who are unable to function outside of a sheltered environment, as well as for those who need help in the transition from hospital to independent living. Evidence indicates that residential treatment centers cost less to operate and are more effective for many patients than are traditional hospitals (Kiesler, 1982). Nevertheless, 70 percent of all U.S. funds spent on mental health go to hospital care.

Professions Involved in Psychotherapy

Whether a person receives therapy in a hospital, a community mental health center, a private clinic, or an office, several different types of professionals may be involved. A psychiatrist, a clinical psychologist, and a psychiatric social worker may work together or independently on a given case.

A *psychiatrist* has an M.D. degree and has taken postgraduate training, called a residency, during which he or she received supervision in the diagnosis of abnormal behavior and in psychotherapy. Subsequently, many but not all psychiatrists take an examination in psychiatry and become board-certified. As a physician, the psychiatrist is the only mental health professional who can prescribe medication.

The term *psychoanalyst* is reserved for individuals who have received specialized training at a psychoanalytic institute learning the methods and theories derived from Freud. The program usually takes several years, during which the trainees must undergo their own personal psychoanalysis as well as treat several clients psychoanalytically while under supervision. Until recently, most psychoanalytic institutes required their graduates to have an M.D. degree. Thus, most psychoanalysts are psychiatrists. However, most psychiatrists are not psychoanalysts.

A *clinical psychologist* has a Ph.D. in psychology, which entails four to five years of graduate study, and has served special internships in the fields of testing and diagnosis, psychotherapy, and research. The clinical psychologist administers and interprets psychological tests, conducts psychotherapy, and is also active in research. A *counseling psychologist* has earned an M.A. or a Ph.D. and has had graduate training similar to that of the clinical psychologist, but usually with less emphasis on research. The training is concerned more with problems of adjustment than with mental disorders and often concentrates on specific areas such as student, marriage, or family counseling.

A *psychiatric social worker* usually has an M.A. or an M.S. from a graduate school of social work, as well as special training in interviewing and in extending treatment procedures to the home and community. The social worker is often called on to collect information about the patient's home and to interview relatives, in addition to participating in therapeutic procedures with the patient.

In mental hospitals, a fourth professional is involved: the *psychiatric nurse*. Psychiatric nursing is a field within the nursing profession that requires special training in the understanding and treatment of mental disorders. In our discussion of psychotherapeutic techniques, we will not specify the profession of the psychotherapists; we will assume that they are trained and competent members of any one of these professions.

TECHNIQUES OF PSYCHOTHERAPY

Psychotherapy refers to the treatment of mental disorders by *psychological* (rather than physical or biological) means. The term embraces a variety of techniques, all of which are intended to help emotionally disturbed individuals modify their behavior, thoughts, and emotions so that they can develop more useful ways of dealing with stress and with other people. Some psychotherapists believe that modification of behavior is dependent on the individual's understanding of his or her unconscious motives and conflicts. Others feel that people can learn to cope with their problems without necessarily exploring the factors that have led to their development. Despite differences in techniques, most methods of psychotherapy have certain basic features in common. They involve communication between two individuals: the *client* (patient) and the *therapist*. The client is encouraged to express intimate fears, emotions, and experiences freely without fear of being judged or condemned by the therapist. The therapist, in turn, offers sympathy and understanding and tries to help the client develop more effective ways of handling his or her problems.

Psychoanalysis

Freud and his colleagues developed *psychoanalysis,* the first formalized method of psychotherapy. Freud believed that most mental disorders are the result of unconscious conflicts between the aggressive and sexual impulses of the id and the constraints imposed by the ego and superego. These conflicts, repressed since early childhood, prevent the individual from coping with the environment in a mature fashion. The purpose of psychoanalysis is to bring repressed fears and motives into awareness so they can be dealt with in a more rational and realistic way. When people understand what is motivating them, they can deal more effectively with their problems.

FREE ASSOCIATION   One of the main techniques psychoanalysts use to facilitate the recovery of unconscious conflicts is *free association*. The client is

Freud's office in Vienna offered the comfort of his famous couch as well as a collection of Egyptian, Greek, and Roman antiquities.

encouraged to give free rein to thoughts and feelings and to verbalize whatever comes to mind without editing or censoring. This is not easy to do, however. In conversation, we usually try to keep a connecting thread running through our remarks and to exclude irrelevant ideas so that we do not wander too far from the point. In addition, most of us have spent a lifetime learning to be cautious and to think before speaking; passing thoughts that strike us as inappropriate, stupid, or shameful usually remain unspoken.

With practice, however, and with encouragement from the analyst, free association becomes easier. But even individuals who conscientiously try to give free rein to their thoughts will occasionally find themselves blocked. When a client remains silent, abruptly changes the subject, or is unable to recall the details of an event, the analyst assumes that the person is resisting the recall of certain thoughts or feelings. Freud believed that blocking, or *resistance,* results from the individual's unconscious control over sensitive areas and that these are precisely the areas the analyst should explore.

INTERPRETATION   The psychoanalyst attempts to overcome the client's resistance and to encourage fuller self-understanding through *interpretation.* The interpretation usually assumes one of two forms. In the first, the analyst calls attention to the individual's resistances. People often learn something about themselves simply by discovering when a train of associations is suddenly blocked, when they forget an appointment, when they want to change the subject, and so on. In the second form of interpretation, the analyst may privately deduce the nature of what lies behind the client's statements and may attempt to facilitate further associations. For example, a client may say something that he or she thinks is trivial and half apologize for its unimportance. At this point, the analyst may point out that what seems trivial may allude to something important. If the interpretation is appropriately timed, this hint may lead to significant new associations. The analyst is careful not to suggest *just what it is* that is important; the goal is to have the client discover this on his or her own.

TRANSFERENCE   In psychoanalysis, the client's attitudes toward the analyst are considered to be an important part of treatment. Sooner or later, the client develops strong emotional responses to the psychoanalyst. Sometimes the responses are positive and friendly; sometimes, negative and hostile. Often these reactions are inappropriate responses to what is taking place in the therapy sessions. The tendency for the client to make the therapist the object of emotional responses is known as *transference:* the client expresses attitudes toward the analyst that the client actually feels toward other people who are, or were, important in his or her life. Freud assumed that transference represents relics of childhood reactions to parents, and he utilized this transference of attitudes as a means of explaining to clients the childhood origin of many of their concerns and fears. By studying how their clients feel toward them, analysts help their patients achieve a better understanding of emotional reactions to others. For example, a man who has always professed admiration for an older brother detects something in the analyst's attitude that reminds him of the brother. An angry attack on the analyst may lead the client to uncover hostile feelings toward his brother that were never acknowledged before.

ABREACTION, INSIGHT, AND WORKING THROUGH   The course of improvement during psychoanalytic therapy is commonly attributed to three main experiences: *abreaction,* gradual *insight* into one's difficulties, and a repeated *working through* of conflicts and one's reactions to them.

Abreaction is the release of suppressed emotion. Expressing intense emotions or reliving earlier emotional experiences in the safety of the therapy session often brings relief to the client. (The process is also called *catharsis,* as though it were a kind of emotional cleansing.) Abreaction does not eliminate the causes of conflict, but it may open the way for further exploration of repressed feelings and experiences.

A person achieves *insight* when he or she understands the roots of the conflict. Sometimes insight comes when the patient recovers the memory of a repressed experience, but the popular notion that psychoanalytic cures result from the sudden recall of a single dramatic episode is untrue. The individual's troubles seldom stem from a single source, and the client gains insight through a gradual increase in self-knowledge. Insight and abreaction must work together: patients must understand their feelings and feel what they understand. The reorientation is never simply an intellectual process.

As analysis progresses, the patient goes through a lengthy process of re-education known as *working through*. By examining the same conflicts over and over as they have appeared in a variety of situations, the person learns to face rather than to deny reality and to react in more mature and effective ways. By working through these conflicts during therapy, the person becomes strong enough to face the threat of the original conflict situation and to react to it without undue anxiety. The goal of psychoanalysis is a deep-seated modification of the individual's personality that allows him or her to cope with problems on a realistic basis.

Psychoanalysis is a lengthy, intensive, and expensive process. Client and analyst usually meet for 50-minute sessions several times a week for at least a year, and often several years. Psychoanalysis is most successful with individuals who are highly motivated to solve their problems, who can verbalize their feelings with some ease, and who can afford it.

Psychoanalytic Psychotherapy

Since Freud's time, numerous forms of psychotherapy based on Freudian concepts have developed. They share in common the premise that mental disorders stem from unconscious conflicts and fears, but they differ from classical psychoanalysis in several ways and are usually called *psychoanalytic psychotherapies*. As noted in Chapter 13, the psychoanalysts who came after Freud gave greater recognition to the importance of social and cultural factors, as opposed to biological drives, in shaping human behavior. They also placed increased emphasis on the role of the ego in directing behavior and solving problems and correspondingly less emphasis on the role of unconscious sexual and aggressive drives.

The classical methods of psychoanalysis have been modified, too. Contemporary psychoanalytic psychotherapy tends to be briefer and less intense. The therapist often limits the length of therapy, giving both client and therapist a fixed time within which to work on problems and to achieve certain goals. Sessions are scheduled less frequently, usually once or twice a week, so that the client has time between meetings to think about what was discussed and to examine his or her daily interactions in light of the analysis. There is less emphasis on a complete reconstruction of childhood experiences and more attention to problems arising from the way the individual is currently interacting with others. Free association is often replaced with a direct discussion of critical issues, and the psychoanalytic psychotherapist may be more direct, raising pertinent topics when it seems appropriate rather than waiting for the client to bring them up. While transference is still considered an important part of the therapeutic process, the therapist may try to limit the intensity of the transference feelings.

Still central, however, is the psychoanalytic therapist's conviction that unconscious motives and fears are at the core of most emotional problems and that insight and the working-through process are essential to a cure. As we will see in the next section, behavior therapists do not agree with these views.

"Leave us alone! I am a behavior therapist! I am helping my patient overcome a fear of heights!"

Behavior Therapies

The term *behavior therapy* includes a number of different therapeutic methods based on learning theory. Behavior therapists assume that maladaptive behaviors are learned ways of coping with stress and that some of the techniques developed in experimental work on learning can be used to substitute more appropriate responses for maladaptive ones. Whereas psychoanalysis is concerned with understanding how the individual's past conflicts influence behavior, behavior therapy focuses more directly on the behavior itself.

Behavior therapists point out that, although the achievement of insight is a worthwhile goal, it does not ensure behavior change. Often we understand why we behave the way we do in a certain situation but are not able to change our behavior. If you are unusually timid about speaking in class, you may be able to trace this fear to past events (your father criticized your opinions whenever you expressed them, your mother made a point of correcting your grammar, you had little experience in public speaking during high school because you were afraid to compete with your older brother who was captain of the debate team). Understanding the reasons behind your fear probably will not make it easier for you to contribute to class discussions.

In contrast to psychoanalysis, which attempts to change the individual's personality, behavior therapies tend to focus on fairly circumscribed goals: the modification of maladaptive behaviors in specific situations. Behavior therapists are also more concerned than psychoanalysts with obtaining scientific validation of their techniques.

SYSTEMATIC DESENSITIZATION   *Systematic desensitization* can be viewed as a "deconditioning" or "counterconditioning" process. This procedure is highly effective in eliminating fears or phobias. The principle of the treatment is to weaken a maladaptive response by strengthening an incompatible or antagonistic response. For example, relaxation is antagonistic to anxiety—it is difficult to be both relaxed and anxious at the same time. One method of systematically desensitizing a person to a feared situation involves first training the individual to relax and then gradually exposing him or her to the feared situation, either in imagination or in reality. Through relaxation training, the individual learns to contract and relax various muscles, starting, for example, with the feet and ankles and proceeding up the body to facial and neck muscles. The person learns what muscles feel like when they are truly relaxed and how to discriminate among various degrees of tension. Sometimes the therapist uses drugs and hypnosis to help people who cannot relax otherwise.

While learning to relax, the individual works with the behavior therapist to construct an *anxiety hierarchy*, a list of situations or stimuli that make the person feel anxious. The situations are ranked in order from the one that produces the least anxiety to the one that is most fearful. For example, a woman who suffers from agoraphobia (p. 496) and experiences intense anxiety whenever she leaves the security of her home might construct a hierarchy that begins with a walk to the corner mailbox. Somewhere around the middle of the list might be a drive to the supermarket, and at the top, a plane trip alone to a distant city. After the woman has learned to relax and has constructed the hierarchy, desensitization begins. She sits with her eyes closed in a comfortable chair while the therapist describes the least anxiety-producing situation to her. If she can imagine herself in the situation without any increase in muscle tension, the therapist proceeds to the next item on the list. If the woman reports any anxiety while visualizing a scene, she concentrates on relaxing; the same scene is visualized until all anxiety is neutralized. This process continues through a series of sessions until the situation that originally provoked the most anxiety now elicits only relaxation. At this point, the woman has been systematically desensitized to anxiety-provoking situations through the strengthening of an antagonistic or incompatible response —relaxation.

Although desensitization through visually imagined scenes has been effective in reducing fears or phobias, it is less effective than desensitization through actual encounters with the feared stimuli. The woman in our hypothetical case would probably lose her fears more readily if she actually exposed herself to the anxiety-producing situations in a sequence of graduated steps and managed to tolerate each situation until her anxiety subsided (Sherman, 1972). Whenever possible, a behavior therapist tries to combine real-life and symbolic desensitization.

ASSERTIVENESS TRAINING   Another kind of response that is antagonistic to anxiety is an *assertive response*. Some people feel anxious in social situations because they do not know how to speak up for what they feel is right or to say no when others take advantage of them. By practicing *assertive responses* (first in role playing with the therapist and then in real-life situations), the individual not only reduces anxiety but also develops more effective coping techniques. The therapist determines the kinds of situations in which the person is passive and then helps him or her to think of and to practice some assertive responses that might be effective. The following situations might be worked through during a sequence of therapy sessions:

A class meeting at LaGuardia Airport in New York City to overcome a fear of flying. The first stage — learning to relax in an airplane — is accomplished on the ground!

- Someone steps in front of you in line.
- A friend asks you to do something you do not want to do.
- Your boss criticizes you unjustly.
- You return defective merchandise to a store.
- You are annoyed by the conversation of people behind you in the movies.
- The mechanic did an unsatisfactory job of repairing your car.

Most people do not enjoy dealing with such situations, but some individuals are so fearful of asserting themselves that they say nothing and instead build up feelings of resentment and inadequacy. In assertiveness training, the client rehearses with the therapist effective responses that could be made in such situations and gradually tries them in real life.

POSITIVE REINFORCEMENT AND EXTINCTION   When a timid person learns and practices assertive responses, he or she is likely to receive considerable *positive reinforcement* from the therapist who praises such new skills, from other people who are impressed by the change in behavior, and from the worthwhile results of the actions themselves. *Systematic reinforcement*, based on the principles of operant conditioning (see Chapter 7), has proved to be an effective method of modifying behavior, especially with children.

The procedure can be illustrated by the case of a third-grade student who was inattentive in school, refused to complete assignments or to participate in class, and spent most of her time daydreaming. In addition, her social skills were poor and she had few friends. The behavior to be reinforced was defined as "on task" behavior, which included paying attention to schoolwork or instructions from the teacher, completing reading assignments, and taking part in class discussions. The reinforcement consisted of beans that were used as tokens to be exchanged for special privileges that the girl valued, such as standing first in line (three beans) or being allowed to stay after school to help the teacher with special projects (nine beans). Anytime the teacher observed the student performing on-task behaviors, she placed one bean in a jar.

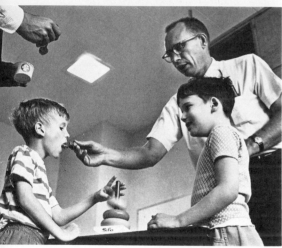

FIGURE 16-1

Behavior Reinforcement *These two autistic children were enrolled in an intensive behavior therapy program at the UCLA Neuropsychiatric Institute. Here they are shown receiving immediate reinforcement in the form of food for interacting with each other. Other techniques included modeling of the appropriate behavior and punishment (electric shock) for self-destructive behavior. The boy on the right, mute and self-destructive when he entered the program, was able to return home in less than a year, and two years later he was doing first grade work in a special school.*

During the first three months of treatment, the girl completed 12 units of work, compared to 0 units during the three months before the reinforcement regime started. In the final three months, she completed 36 units and was performing at the same level as the rest of the class. A follow-up the next year showed that the girl was maintaining her academic performance. She also showed a marked improvement in social skills and was accepted more by the other children (Walker, Hedberg, Clement, & Wright, 1981). This is a common finding: improving behavior in one area of life often produces added benefits (Kazdin, 1982).

Reinforcement of desirable responses can be accompanied by extinction of undesirable ones. For example, a young boy who habitually shouts to get his mother's attention could be ignored whenever he does so and reinforced by her attention only when he comes to where she is and speaks in a conversational tone.

Sometimes the behavior that the therapist wants to reinforce occurs infrequently or is totally absent, such as talking in a mute child. In this case, a technique similar to Skinner's *shaping* of behavior (p. 226) is used: responses that approximate the desired behavior are reinforced, and the therapist gradually requires closer and closer approximations until the desired behavior occurs. A procedure of this sort was used to develop language in a seriously disturbed 6-year-old boy whose speech consisted almost entirely of two-word phrases. The boy was trained to respond to pictures showing people in various activities. At first, he was reinforced (with food and praise) for any verbal response to the pictures. Next he was taught to use simple sentences to describe the pictures and was reinforced only when he responded with a sentence. Finally, he learned to use the connective "and" between two sentences and was rewarded only when he produced two correct sentences relevant to a picture (for example, "The boy is reading and the teacher is putting away the book"). Once the boy reached the point where he consistently produced correct compound sentences to the training pictures, trials with new pictures were interspersed among trials with the training stimuli. The boy had to produce complete, grammatically correct, and relevant sentences to the new pictures in order to be rewarded. After 30 half-hour training sessions, the child responded correctly to the novel stimuli on 70 perent of the trials. Moreover, he began describing objects and events in classroom and playground conversations (Stevens-Long, Schwarz, & Bliss, 1976).

Similar procedures have been effective in teaching seriously disturbed children to interact with other children, to sit quietly at a desk, and to respond appropriately to questions (see Figure 16-1). Instead of receiving regular breakfasts or lunches, these children were provided with bits of food when their responses approximated the desired behaviors. Although such procedures may seem cruel, they are an effective means of establishing more normal behavior when all other attempts have failed. Once the child begins to respond to primary forms of reward (such as food), social rewards (praise, attention, and special privileges) become effective reinforcers.

A number of mental hospitals have instituted "token economies" on wards with very regressed, chronic patients to induce socially appropriate behavior. Tokens (which can later be exchanged for food and privileges such as watching television) are given for dressing properly, interacting with other patients, eliminating "psychotic talk," helping on the wards, and so on. Such programs have proved successful in improving both the patients' behavior and the general functioning of the ward.

MODELING   Another effective means of changing behavior is *modeling* (see p. 371). Observing the behavior of a model (either live or videotaped) has proved successful in reducing fears and in teaching new skills. A classic study illustrates the use of modeling in the treatment of snake phobias (Bandura, Blanchard, &

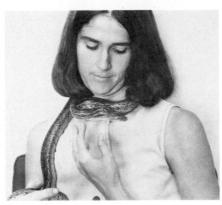

Ritter, 1969). The subjects were young adults whose fear of snakes was severe enough to restrict their activities in various ways (for example, some could not participate in gardening or hiking for fear of encountering snakes). After an initial test to determine how closely they would approach a live but harmless king snake in a glass tank, the subjects were rated according to their degree of fearfulness and were divided into four matched groups. One group underwent the systematic desensitization procedure described earlier: they learned to relax while imagining increasingly anxiety-provoked situations involving snakes. A second group, after learning muscle relaxation procedures, watched a film in which child and adult models enjoyed progressively more intimate interactions with a large king snake. The subjects were instructed to stop the film if a particular scene provoked anxiety, reverse the film to the beginning of that sequence, and reinduce relaxation. (This procedure is called "symbolic modeling.") A third group imitated the behavior of a live model as the model performed progressively more fearful activities with the snake (see Figure 16-2). Gradually, the subjects were guided in such activities as touching the snake with a gloved hand, touching the snake with their bare hands, holding the snake, letting it coil around their arms, and finally letting the snake loose in the room, retrieving it, and letting it crawl over their bodies. (This procedure is termed "live modeling with participation.") The fourth group served as a control group and received no training.

Figure 16-3 indicates the number of snake-approach responses by the subjects before and after the different treatments. All three treatment groups showed improvement in comparison with the control group, but the group that combined live modeling with guided participation achieved the best results. Almost all the subjects in this group completely overcame their fear of snakes.

Subsequent studies have shown that the most effective method of eliminating snake phobias is to start with participant modeling, during which the individual is guided in handling the snake, and then to let the person proceed through various degrees of snake intimacy on his or her own (Bandura, Adams, & Beyer, 1976). In this way, the individual gains a sense of mastery over the situation—a feeling that effective performance is the result of his or her own actions (Bandura, Adams, Hardy, & Howells, 1980).

Modeling is often combined with role playing, during which the therapist helps the individual rehearse or practice more adaptive behaviors. In the following excerpt, a therapist helps a young man overcome his anxieties about asking girls for dates. The young man has been pretending to talk to a girl over the phone and finishes by asking for a date.

CLIENT: By the way (pause), I don't suppose you want to go out Saturday night?
THERAPIST: Up to actually asking for the date, you were very good. However, if I were the girl, I think I might have been a bit offended when you said,

FIGURE 16-2
Modeling as a Treatment for Snake Phobia *The photos show an individual modeling interactions with a live king snake.*

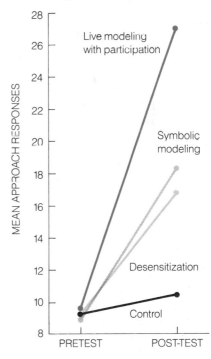

FIGURE 16-3
Treatment of Snake Phobia *The mean number of snake-approach responses by subjects before and after they received different behavior therapy treatments. (After Bandura, Blanchard, & Ritter, 1969)*

"By the way." It's like your asking her out is pretty casual. Also, the way you phrased the question, you are kind of suggesting to her that she doesn't want to go out with you. Pretend for the moment I'm you. Now, how does this sound: "There is a movie at the Varsity Theater this Saturday that I want to see. If you don't have other plans, I'd like very much to take you."

CLIENT: That sounded good. Like you were sure of yourself and liked the girl, too.

THERAPIST: Why don't you try it.

CLIENT: You know that movie at the Varsity? Well, I'd like to go, and I'd like to take you Saturday, if you don't have anything better to do.

THERAPIST: Well, that certainly was better. Your tone of voice was especially good. But the last line "if you don't have anything better to do" sounds like you don't think you have too much to offer. Why not run through it one more time.

CLIENT: I'd like to see the show at the Varsity Saturday, and if you haven't made other plans, I'd like to take you.

THERAPIST: Much better. Excellent, in fact. You were confident, forceful, and sincere.

(Rimm & Masters, 1979, p. 74)

SELF-REGULATION   Because client and therapist seldom meet more than once per week, the client must learn to control or regulate his or her own behavior so that progress can be made outside the therapy hour. Moreover, if people feel they are responsible for their own improvement, they are more likely to maintain such gains. Self-regulation involves monitoring, or observing, one's own behavior and using various techniques — *self-reinforcement, self-punishment, control of stimulus conditions, development of incompatible responses* — to change the maladaptive behavior. An individual monitors his or her behavior by keeping a careful record of the kinds of situations that elicit the maladaptive behavior and the kinds of responses that are incompatible with it. A person concerned with alcohol dependency would note the kinds of situations in which he or she is most tempted to drink and would try to control such situations or to devise a response that is incompatible with drinking. A man who finds it hard not to join his coworkers in a noontime cocktail might plan to eat lunch at his desk, thereby avoiding the situation. If he is tempted to relax with a drink on arriving home from work, he might substitute a game of tennis or a jog around the block as a means of relieving tension. Both of these activities would be incompatible with drinking.

Self-reinforcement is rewarding yourself immediately for achieving a specific goal; the reward could be praising yourself, watching a favorite TV program, telephoning a friend, eating a favorite food. Self-punishment is arranging some aversive consequence for failing to achieve a goal, such as depriving yourself of something you enjoy (*not* watching a favorite TV program, for instance) or making yourself do an unpleasant task (such as cleaning your room). Depending on the kind of behavior the individual wants to change, various combinations of self-reinforcement, self-punishment, or control of stimuli and response may be used. Table 16-1 outlines a program for self-regulation of eating.

Cognitive Behavior Therapies

The behavior therapy procedures we have discussed thus far have focused on modifying behavior directly with little attention paid to the individual's thinking and reasoning processes. Initially, behavior therapists discounted the importance of cognition, preferring a strict stimulus-response approach. They regarded any consideration of beliefs and attitudes as a return to the kind of unscientific

TABLE 16-1
Self-regulation of Eating *The program illustrates the use of learning principles to help control food intake. (After Stuart & Davis, 1972; O'Leary & Wilson, 1975)*

SELF-MONITORING

Daily Log   Keep a detailed record of everything you eat. Note amount eaten, type of food and caloric value, time of day, and the circumstances of eating. This record will establish the caloric intake that is maintaining your present weight. It will also help to identify the stimuli that elicit and reinforce your eating behavior.

Weight Chart   Decide how much you want to lose and set a weekly goal for weight loss. Your weekly goal should be realistic (between 1 and 2 pounds). Record your weight each day on graph paper. In addition to showing how your weight varies with food intake, this visual record will reinforce your dieting efforts as you observe progress toward your goal.

CONTROLLING STIMULUS CONDITIONS

Use these procedures to narrow the range of stimuli associated with eating:
1. Eat only at predetermined times, at a specific table, using a special place mat, napkin, dishes, and so forth. Do *not* eat at other times or in other places (for example, while standing in the kitchen).
2. Do *not* combine eating with other activities, such as reading or watching television.
3. Keep in the house only those foods that are permitted on your diet.
4. Shop for food only after having had a full meal; buy only those items that are on a previously prepared list.

MODIFYING ACTUAL EATING BEHAVIOR

Use these procedures to break the chain of responses that make eating automatic:
1. Eat very slowly, paying close attention to the food.
2. Finish chewing and swallowing before putting more food on the fork.
3. Put your utensils down for periodic short breaks before continuing to eat.

DEVELOPING INCOMPATIBLE RESPONSES

When tempted to eat at times other than those specified, find a substitute activity that is incompatible with eating. For example, exercise to music, go for a walk, talk with a friend (preferably one who knows you are dieting), study your diet plan and weight graph, noting how much weight you have lost.

SELF-REINFORCEMENT

Arrange to reward yourself with an activity you enjoy (watching television, reading, planning a new wardrobe, visiting a friend) when you have maintained appropriate eating behavior for a day. Plan larger rewards (for example, buying something you want) for a specified amount of weight loss. Self-punishment (other than forgoing a reward) is probably less effective because dieting is a fairly depressing business anyway. But you might decrease the frequency of binge eating by immediately reciting to yourself the aversive consequences or by looking at an unattractive picture of yourself in a bathing suit.

introspection that Watson objected to at the beginning of this century (see p. 7). However, in recent years behavior therapists have paid increased attention to the role of cognitive factors — the individual's thoughts, expectations, and interpretation of events — in determining behavior and in mediating behavior change.

Cognitive behavior therapy is a general term for treatment methods that use behavior modification techniques but also incorporate procedures designed to change maladaptive beliefs. The therapist attempts to help people control

Cognitive behavior therapy attempts to change a client's maladaptive beliefs.

disturbing emotional reactions, such as anxiety and depression, by teaching them more effective ways of interpreting and thinking about their experiences. For example, as we noted in discussing Beck's cognitive theory of depression (see p. 507), depressed individuals tend to appraise events from a negative and self-critical viewpoint. They expect to fail rather than to succeed, and they tend to magnify failures and to minimize successes in evaluating their performance. In treating depression, cognitive behavior therapists try to help their clients recognize the distortions in their thinking and make changes that are more in line with reality. The following dialogue illustrates how a therapist, by carefully directed questioning, makes a client aware of the unrealistic nature of her beliefs.

THERAPIST: Why do you want to end your life?

CLIENT: Without Raymond, I am nothing. . . . I can't be happy without Raymond. . . . But I can't save our marriage.

THERAPIST: What has your marriage been like?

CLIENT: It has been miserable from the very beginning. . . . Raymond has always been unfaithful. . . . I have hardly seen him in the past five years.

THERAPIST: You say that you can't be happy without Raymond. . . . Have you found yourself happy when you are with Raymond?

CLIENT: No, we fight all the time and I feel worse.

THERAPIST: You say you are nothing without Raymond. Before you met Raymond, did you feel you were nothing?

CLIENT: No, I felt I was somebody.

THERAPIST: If you were somebody before you knew Raymond, why do you need him [in order] to be somebody now?

CLIENT: (puzzled) Hmmm. . . .

THERAPIST: If you were free of the marriage, do you think that men might be interested in you—knowing that you were available?

CLIENT: I guess that maybe they would be.

THERAPIST: Is it possible that you might find a man who would be more constant than Raymond?

CLIENT: I don't know. . . . I guess it's possible. . . .

THERAPIST: Then what have you actually lost if you break up the marriage?

CLIENT: I don't know.

THERAPIST: Is it possible that you'll get along better if you end the marriage?

CLIENT: There is no guarantee of that.

THERAPIST: Do you have a *real marriage?*

CLIENT: I guess not.

THERAPIST: If you don't have a real marriage, what do you actually lose if you decide to end the marriage?

CLIENT: (long pause) Nothing, I guess.

(Beck, 1976, pp. 280–91)

The behavioral component of the treatment comes into play when the therapist encourages the client to formulate alternative ways of viewing her situation and then test the implications. For example, the woman in this dialogue might be asked to record her moods at regular intervals and then to note how her depression and feelings of self-esteem fluctuate as a function of what she is doing. If she finds she feels worse after interacting with her husband than when she is alone or is interacting with someone else, this information could serve to challenge her belief that she "can't be happy without Raymond."

Cognitive behavior therapists often combine behavior modification techniques with specific instructions for handling negative thoughts. A program to help someone overcome agoraphobia might include systematic desensitization (at first with imagery and later with actual excursions going progressively farther from home), along with training in positive thinking. The therapist teaches the

INSTRUCTION IN SELF-CHANGE SKILLS

Pinpointing the target behavior and recording its baseline rate of occurrence; discovering the events or situations that precede the target behavior and the consequences (either positive or negative) that follow it; setting goals for change and choosing reinforcers

RELAXATION TRAINING

Learning progressive muscle relaxation to handle the anxiety that often accompanies depression; monitoring tension in daily situations and applying relaxation techniques

INCREASING PLEASANT EVENTS

Monitoring the frequency of enjoyable activities and planning weekly schedules so that each day contains a balance between negative/neutral activities and pleasant ones

COGNITIVE STRATEGIES

Learning methods for increasing positive thoughts and decreasing negative thoughts; for identifying "irrational" thoughts and challenging them; and for using self-instructions (self-talk) to help handle problem situations

ASSERTIVENESS TRAINING

Identifying situations where being nonassertive adds to feelings of depression; learning to handle social interactions more assertively via modeling and role playing

INCREASING SOCIAL INTERACTION

Identifying the factors that are contributing to low social interaction (such as getting in the habit of doing things alone, feeling uncomfortable due to few social skills); deciding on activities that need to be increased (such as calling friends to suggest getting together) or decreased (such as watching television) in order to improve the level of pleasant social interaction

TABLE 16-2
Coping With Depression   *A program for the treatment of depression that combines behavioral and cognitive techniques. This is a condensed description of a 12-session course used successfully to treat depressed individuals in small groups. (After Lewinsohn, Antonuccio, Steinmetz, & Teri, 1984)*

client to replace self-defeating internal dialogues ("I'm so nervous, I know I'll faint as soon as I leave the house") with positive self-instructions ("Be calm; I'm not alone; even if I have a panic attack there is someone to help me"). Table 16-2 describes a program for the treatment of depression that includes techniques for modifying behavior and for changing attitudes.

Cognitive behavior therapists agree that it is important to alter a person's beliefs in order to bring about an enduring change in behavior. Nevertheless, most maintain that behavioral procedures are more powerful than strictly verbal ones in affecting cognitive processes. For example, to overcome anxiety about giving a speech in class, it is helpful to think positively: "I know the material well, and I'm sure I can present my ideas effectively"; "The topic is interesting, and the other students will enjoy what I have to say." But successfully presenting the speech to a roommate and again before a group of friends will probably do more to reduce anxiety. Successful performance increases our feeling of mastery. In fact, Bandura suggests that all therapeutic procedures that are effective give the person a sense of mastery or *self-efficacy*. Observing others cope and succeed, being verbally persuaded that we can handle a difficult situation, and judging from internal cues that we are relaxed and in control contribute to our feeling of self-efficacy. But the greatest sense of efficacy comes from actual performance, from personal mastery experiences. In essence, nothing succeeds like success (Bandura, 1984).

Carl Rogers (top, center) facilitating discussion in a therapy group.

Humanistic Therapies

Practitioners of *humanistic therapy* are concerned with the uniqueness of the individual and focus on the person's natural tendency toward growth and self-actualization (see p. 433). The humanistic therapist does not interpret the person's behavior, as a psychoanalyst would, or try to modify it, as a behavior therapist would. The goal of the humanistic therapist is to facilitate exploration of the individual's own thoughts and feelings and to assist the individual in arriving at his or her own solutions. This approach will become clearer as we look at *person-centered therapy* (formerly called *client-centered therapy*), one of the first humanistic therapies.

Person-centered therapy, developed by Carl Rogers, is based on the assumption that the client is the best expert on himself or herself and that people are capable of working out the solutions to their own problems. The task of the therapist is to facilitate this progress — not to ask probing questions, to make interpretations, or to suggest courses of action. In fact, Rogers prefers the term "facilitator" to "therapist."

Person-centered therapy can be described rather simply, but in practice, it requires great skill and is much more subtle than it first appears. The therapist begins by explaining the nature of the interviews. The responsibility for working out problems is the client's. He or she is free to leave at any time and to choose whether to return. The relationship is private and confidential; the person is free to speak of intimate matters without fear of reproof or of the information being revealed to others. Once the situation is structured, the client does most of the talking. Usually, the client has much to say. The therapist is a patient but alert listener. When the client stops, as though expecting the therapist to say something, the therapist usually acknowledges and accepts the feelings the person has expressed. For example, if a man has been talking about his nagging mother, the therapist may say, "You feel that your mother tries to control you." The object is to *clarify* the feelings that the person has been expressing, not to judge them or to elaborate on them.

Generally, individuals begin therapy with rather low evaluations of themselves, but in the course of facing their problems and of trying to arrive at solutions, they begin to view themselves more positively. For instance, one client began the initial session with the following statements:

> Everything is wrong with me. I feel abnormal. I don't do even the ordinary things of life. I'm sure I will fail on anything I undertake. I'm inferior. When I try to imitate successful people, I'm only acting. I can't go on like this.

By the final interview, the client expressed attitudes that contrasted strikingly with the statements in the first interview:

> I am taking a new course of my own choosing. I am really changing. I have always tried to live up to others' standards that were beyond my abilities. I've come to realize that I'm not so bright, but I can get along anyway. I no longer think so much about myself. I'm much more comfortable with people. I'm getting a feeling of success out of my job. I don't feel quite steady yet and would like to feel that I can come for more help if I need it. (Snyder et al., 1947)

To determine whether this kind of progress is typical, researchers have analyzed recorded interviews. When clients' statements are classified and plotted, the course of therapy turns out to be fairly predictable. In the early interviews, people spend a good deal of time talking about their problems and describing symptoms. During the course of therapy, they make more and more statements that indicate they are achieving an *understanding* of their particular problems. By classifying all clients' remarks as either "problem restatements" or "statements of understanding and insight," the progressive increase in insight as therapy proceeds becomes evident (see Figure 16-4).

What do person-centered therapists do to bring about these changes? Rogers believes that the most important qualities for a therapist are empathy, warmth, and genuineness. *Empathy* refers to the ability to understand the feelings the client is trying to express *and* the ability to communicate this understanding to the client. The therapist must adopt the client's frame of reference and must strive to see the problems as the client sees them. By *warmth*, Rogers means a deep acceptance of the individual as he or she is, including the conviction that this person has the capacity to deal constructively with his or her problems. A therapist who is *genuine* is open and honest and does not play a role or operate behind a professional façade. People are reluctant to reveal themselves to those they perceive as phony. Rogers believes that a therapist who possesses these attributes will facilitate the client's growth and self-exploration (Rogers, 1970; Truax & Mitchell, 1971).

Rogers and his colleagues, by their insistence on an empirical analysis of the therapy process, have contributed much to the field of psychotherapy research. For example, they initiated the practice of tape-recording therapy sessions for subsequent analysis by researchers. Person-centered therapy has some limitations, however. Like psychoanalysis, it appears to be successful only with individuals who are fairly verbal and who are motivated to discuss their problems. For people who do not voluntarily seek help or who are seriously disturbed and are unable to discuss their feelings, more directive methods are usually necessary. In addition, by using the client's self-reports as the only measure of psychotherapeutic effectiveness, the person-centered therapist ignores behavior outside of the therapy session. Individuals who feel insecure and ineffective in their interpersonal relationships often need help in modifying their behavior.

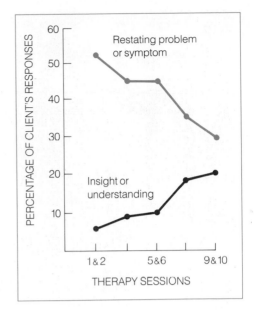

FIGURE 16-4

Changes During Person-centered Therapy *Description and restatement of the problem on the part of the client gradually gives way during the course of therapy to increased frequency of statements, indicating understanding. (After Seeman, 1949)*

Group Therapy

Many emotional problems involve an individual's difficulties in relating to others, including feelings of isolation, rejection, and loneliness and the inability to form meaningful relationships. Although the therapist can help the individual to work out some of these problems, the final test lies in how well the person can apply the attitudes and responses learned in therapy to relationships in everyday life. *Group therapy* permits clients to work out their problems in the presence of others, to observe how other people react to their behavior, and to try out new methods of responding when old ones prove unsatisfactory.

Therapists of various orientations (psychoanalytic, humanistic, and cognitive behaviorist) have modified their techniques to be applicable to therapy groups. Group therapy has been used in a variety of settings: in hospital wards and outpatient psychiatric clinics, with parents of disturbed children, and with teenagers in correctional institutions, to name a few. Typically, the groups consist of a small number of individuals (6 to 12 is considered optimal) who have similar problems. The therapist generally remains in the background, allowing the members to exchange experiences, to comment on one another's behavior, and to discuss their own problems as well as those of the other members. Initially, the members tend to be defensive and uncomfortable when exposing their weaknesses, but they gradually become more objective about their own behavior and more aware of the effect their attitudes and behavior have on others. They gain an increased ability to identify and empathize with others in the group and a feeling

Group therapy gives individuals an opportunity to work through their problems in interaction with others.

of self-esteem when they are able to help another member by offering an understanding remark or a meaningful interpretation.

Group therapy has several advantages over individual therapy. It saves time because one therapist can help several people at once. An individual can derive comfort and support from observing that others have similar, perhaps more severe problems. A person can learn vicariously by watching how others behave and can explore attitudes and reactions by interacting with a variety of people, not just with the therapist. Groups are particularly effective when they provide the participants with opportunities to acquire new social skills through modeling and to practice these skills in the group.

ENCOUNTER GROUPS An offshoot of group therapy that became popular during the 1960s and 1970s is the *encounter group,* also known as the *sensitivity-training group (T-group,* for short). Encounter groups offer people the opportunity to become more aware of how they relate to others and of how others see them and to become more open in their interactions. The groups usually consist of 12 to 20 individuals who may meet for only one intensive weekend session or for sessions over a period of several months. Members are urged to express attitudes and feelings not usually displayed in public. The group leader (or *facilitator,* as he or she is sometimes called, because the job is not really to lead) encourages participants to explore their feelings and motives, as well as those of other group members. The objective is to stimulate an exchange that is not inhibited by defensiveness and that achieves openness and honesty.

Carl Rogers, who has studied various types of encounter groups, describes a fairly consistent pattern of change as the sessions progress (Rogers, 1970). Initially, there tends to be confusion and some frustration when the facilitator makes it clear that he or she will not take the responsibility for directing the group. Members also resist expressing their feelings; if one member describes a personal feeling, other members may try to stop the person, questioning whether it is appropriate to express such feelings in the group. At the next stage, the participants gradually begin to talk about feelings and problems they have encountered outside the group. They then begin to discuss relationships within the group; often, the first feeling expressed is a negative attitude toward oneself or toward another group member. When the individual finds that these feelings are accepted, a climate of trust begins to develop. By the final sessions, the group members have become impatient with defensiveness; they attempt to undercut façades, insisting that individuals be themselves. The tact and polite cover-up that are acceptable outside the group are not tolerated within it.

In theory, the feedback the individual receives about how his or her behavior affects others and the feelings of acceptance by group members lead to increased self-awareness and to behavior change both within and outside the group. Studies of the effects of encounter-group participation, however, raise doubts about the extent of behavior change that actually occurs. One study of more than 200 college students who participated in encounter groups with well-trained leaders revealed that only one-third of the students showed positive changes following their experience (based on self-reports and ratings by close friends). Another third of the students showed no change, and the remainder displayed negative changes — either dropping out of the group because it was disturbing or feeling afterward that the experience aggravated personal problems without resolving them (Lieberman, Yalom, & Miles, 1973).

Although encounter groups provide an opportunity for psychologically healthy people to learn something about themselves from the honest reactions of others, they generally do not help individuals who have emotional problems.

Encounter groups have proved to be less effective in producing behavior change than individual therapy or more traditional therapy groups, and the gains produced by encounter-group participation appear to be temporary (Bednar & Kaul, 1978). In more traditional groups, participants are carefully selected, and meetings extend over a longer period so that interpersonal problems can be worked out. In addition, the emphasis on the free expression of emotion in encounter groups may prove harmful to individuals whose self-esteem is too tenuous to withstand group criticism and pressure (Kirsch & Glass, 1977).

Encounter groups appear to be waning in popularity. In their stead are an increasing number of self-help groups, voluntary organizations of people who meet regularly to exchange information and to support each other's efforts to overcome a common problem. Alcoholics Anonymous is the best known of the self-help groups (see p. 133). Another is Recovery, Inc., an organization open to former mental patients. Other groups help people cope with specific stressful situations such as bereavement, divorce, and single parenthood.

MARITAL AND FAMILY THERAPY Problems in communicating feelings, satisfying one's needs, and responding appropriately to the needs and demands of others become intensified in the intimate context of marriage and family life. To the extent that they involve more than one client and focus on interpersonal relationships, *marital therapy* and *family therapy* can be considered specialized forms of group therapy.

The high divorce rate and the number of couples seeking help for difficulties centering around their relationship have made marital, or couple, therapy a growing field. Studies show that joint therapy for both partners is more effective in solving marital problems than is individual therapy for only one partner (Gurman & Kniskern, 1981).

There are many approaches to marital therapy, but most focus on helping the partners communicate their feelings, develop greater understanding and sensitivity to each other's needs, and work on more effective ways of handling their conflicts. Some couples enter marriage with very different, and often unrealistic, expectations about the roles of husband and wife, which can wreak havoc with their relationship. The therapist can help them clarify their expectations and work out a mutually agreeable compromise. Sometimes the couple negotiates *behavioral contracts,* agreeing on the behavior changes each person is willing to make in order to create a more satisfying relationship and specifying the rewards and penalties they can use with each other to ensure the changes.

Family therapy overlaps with marital therapy but has a somewhat different origin. It developed in response to the discovery that many people who improved in individual therapy while away from their family — often in institutional settings — relapsed when they returned home. It became apparent that many of these people came from a disturbed family setting that required modification itself if the individual's gains were to be maintained. The basic premise of family therapy is that the problem shown by the "identified patient" is a sign that something is wrong with the entire family; the *family system* is not operating properly. The difficulty may lie in poor communication among family members or in an alliance between some family members that excludes others. For example, a mother whose relationship with her husband is unsatisfactory may focus all her attention on her son. As a result, the husband and daughter feel neglected and the son, upset by his mother's smothering and the resentment directed toward him by his father and sister, develops problems in school. While the boy's school difficulties may be the reason for seeking treatment, it is clear that they are only a symptom of a more basic family problem.

Family therapy analyzes interpersonal relationships between family members.

NAME	FOCUS	METHODS
Gestalt therapy	To become aware of the "whole" personality by working through unresolved conflicts and discovering those aspects of the individual's being that are blocked from awareness. Emphasis is on becoming intensely aware of how one is feeling and behaving at the moment.	Therapy in a group setting, but therapist works with one individual at a time. Acting out fantasies, dreams, or the two sides to a conflict are methods used to increase awareness. Combines psychoanalytic emphasis on resolving internal conflicts with behaviorist emphasis on awareness of one's behavior and humanistic concern for self-actualization.
Reality therapy	To clarify the individual's values and to evaluate current behavior and future plans in relation to these values. To force the individual to accept responsibility.	Therapist helps the individual perceive the consequences of possible courses of action and decide on a realistic solution or goal. Once a plan of action is chosen, a "contract" may be signed in which the client agrees to follow through.
Rational-emotive therapy	To replace certain "irrational" ideas (It is essential to be loved and admired by everyone all the time; I should be competent in all respects; People have little control over their sorrow and unhappiness) with more realistic ones. Assumes that cognitive change will produce emotional changes.	Therapist attacks and contradicts the individual's ideas (sometimes subtly, sometimes directly) in an attempt to persuade her or him to take a more "rational" view of the situation. Similar to Beck's cognitive therapy, but therapist is more direct and confrontive.
Transactional analysis	To become aware of the intent behind the individual's communications; to eliminate subterfuge and deceit so that the individual can interpret his or her behavior accurately.	Therapy in a group setting. Communications between married couples or group members are analyzed in terms of the part of the personality that is speaking— "parent," "child," or "adult" (similar to Freud's superego, id, and ego) — and the intent of the message. Destructive social interactions or "games" are exposed for what they are.
Hypnotherapy	To relieve symptoms and strengthen ego processes by helping the individual set reality aside and make constructive use of imagery.	Therapist uses various hypnotic procedures in an attempt to reduce conflict and doubt by focusing the individual's attention, modify symptoms through direct suggestion or displacement, and strengthen the individual's ability to cope.

TABLE 16-3
Some Approaches to Psychotherapy

In family therapy, the entire family meets regularly with one or two therapists (usually a male and a female). The therapist, after observing the interactions among family members, tries to help each member become aware of the way he or she relates to the others and how his or her actions may be contributing to the family's problems. Sometimes videotape recordings are played back to make the family members aware of how they interact with each other. Other times, the therapist may visit the family in the home to observe conflicts and verbal exchanges as they occur in their natural setting. It often becomes apparent that problem behaviors are being reinforced by the responses of family members. For example, a young child's temper tantrums or a teenager's eating problems may be inadvertently reinforced by the attention they elicit from the parents. The therapist can teach the parents to monitor their own and their children's behavior, to determine how their reactions may be reinforcing the problem behavior, and then to alter the reinforcement contingencies.

An Eclectic Approach

There are many variations of psychotherapy in addition to the ones we have discussed here. Several other approaches to psychotherapy are listed in Table 16-3. Most psychotherapists do not adhere strictly to any *single* method. Instead, they take an *eclectic approach,* selecting from the different techniques the ones they feel are most appropriate for the individual client. Although their theoretical orientation may be toward a particular method or school (for example, more psychoanalytic than behaviorist), eclectic psychotherapists feel free to discard the concepts they view as not especially helpful and to select techniques from other schools. In short, they are flexible in their approach to therapy. In dealing with a highly anxious individual, for instance, an eclectic psychotherapist might first prescribe tranquilizers and relaxation training to help reduce the person's level of anxiety. (Most psychoanalysts would not take this approach, however, because they believe that anxiety is necessary to motivate the client to explore his or her conflicts.) To help the client understand the origins of his or her problems, the eclectic therapist might discuss certain aspects of the patient's history but might feel it unnecessary to explore childhood experiences to the extent that a psychoanalyst would. (An exception to this would be the person-centered therapist, who does not delve into the past.) The therapist might use educational techniques, such as providing information about sex and reproduction to help relieve the anxieties of an adolescent boy who feels guilty about his sexual impulses or explaining the functioning of the autonomic nervous system to reassure an anxious woman that some of her symptoms, such as heart palpitations and hand tremors, are not indications of a disease.

Another psychotherapeutic technique is to change the patient's environment. The therapist might feel, for example, that a young man who has serious conflicts in his relationship with his parents can make little progress in overcoming his difficulties while remaining at home. In this instance, the therapist might recommend that the youth attend school away from home or seek employment in another community. Occasionally, with a younger child, the home environment may be so seriously detrimental to the child's mental health that the therapist, with the help of a walfare agency and the courts, may have the child placed in a foster home.

EFFECTIVENESS OF PSYCHOTHERAPY

How effective is psychotherapy? Which methods work best? These questions are not easy to answer. Research into the effectiveness of psychotherapy is hampered by several major difficulties. How do we decide whether an individual has improved? What measures of improvement are valid? How do we know what caused the change?

Evaluating Psychotherapy

Evaluating the effectiveness of psychotherapy is a very difficult task because so many variables must be considered. For instance, a large percentage of people with psychological problems get better without any professional treatment. This phenomenon is called *spontaneous remission,* a term borrowed from medicine.

"Today we'll try aversion therapy. Every time you say something stupid, I'll spill a bucket of water on your head."

Many physical illnesses run a certain course, and barring complications, the individual will recover without specific treatment. However, the word "spontaneous" is not really appropriate in describing recovery from psychological disorders without professional help. Some mental disorders do improve by themselves, simply with the passage of time — much like the common cold. This is particularly true of depression (see p. 503). But more often, improvement that occurs in the absence of treatment is not spontaneous; rather, it is the result of external events — usually changes in the individual's life situation or the help of another person.

Many emotionally disturbed people who do not seek professional assistance are able to improve with the help of a nonprofessional, such as a friend, teacher, or religious adviser. We cannot consider these recoveries to be spontaneous; but since they are not due to psychotherapy, they are included in the rate of spontaneous remission, which ranges from about 30 to 60 percent, depending on the particular disorder being studied (Bergin & Lambert, 1978). To allow for those who would have improved without treatment, any evaluation of psychotherapy must compare a treated group with an untreated control group. Psychotherapy is judged to be effective if the client's improvement after therapy is greater than any improvement that occurs without therapy over the same period. The ethical problem of allowing someone to go without treatment is usually resolved by composing the control group of individuals on a waiting list. Members of the waiting list control group are interviewed at the start of the study to gather baseline information but receive no treatment until the study has ended. Unfortunately, the longer the study (and time is needed to measure improvement, especially with insight therapies), the harder it is to maintain people on a waiting list.

A second major problem in evaluating psychotherapy is measuring the outcome. How do we decide whether a person has been helped by therapy? We cannot always rely on the individual's own assessment. Some people report that they are feeling better simply to please the therapist or to convince themselves that their money was well spent. The *hello – goodbye effect* has long been recognized by therapists. At the beginning of therapy (the "hello"), people tend to exaggerate their unhappiness and their problems to convince the therapist that they really need help. At the end of therapy (the "goodbye"), they tend to exaggerate their well-being to express appreciation to the therapist for his or her efforts or to convince themselves that their time and money were not wasted. These phenomena must be considered when evaluating the client's view of his or her progress.

The therapist's evaluation of the treatment as "successful" cannot always be considered an objective criterion, either. The therapist has a vested interest in proclaiming that the client is better. But sometimes the changes that the therapist observes during the therapy session do not carry over into real-life situations. Assessment of improvement, therefore, should include at least three independent measures: the client's evaluation of progress; the therapist's evaluation; and the judgment of a third party, such as family members and friends or a clinician not involved in the treatment.

Other outcome measures that may be used in evaluating the effectiveness of psychotherapy include scores on tests (such as the Minnesota Multiphasic Personality Inventory or the Beck Depression Inventory) and, in the case of behavior therapy, changes in the target behavior (such as a decrease in compulsive acts). Measures of improvement in a person's life outside of the therapy situation — performing more effectively at work or school, drinking less, a decrease in antisocial activities — are more meaningful but are often difficult to obtain in long-term studies of psychotherapeutic effectiveness.

Despite these problems, researchers have been able to conduct many psychotherapy evaluation studies. Rather than discuss individual studies, we will look at a major evaluation that attempted to answer the question of whether psychotherapy works. The investigators located 475 published studies that compared at least one therapy group with an untreated control group. Using a complicated statistical procedure, they determined the magnitude of effect for each study by comparing the average change produced in treatment (on measures such as self-esteem, anxiety, and achievement in work and school) with that of the control group. They concluded that individuals receiving therapy were better off than those who had received no treatment. The average psychotherapy patient showed greater improvement than 80 percent of the untreated control-group patients (Smith, Glass, & Miller, 1980).

Comparing Psychotherapies

Psychotherapy produces greater improvement than no treatment, but are the different therapeutic approaches equally effective? The evaluation study attempted to answer this question by analyzing the results from 50 studies in which a behavioral therapy (including systematic desensitization and behavior modification) was compared with a nonbehavioral therapy (including person-centered, psychoanalytic, and eclectic therapies); and both types of therapy were compared, in turn, with an untreated control group. They found that both behavioral and nonbehavioral therapies were superior to no treatment. Also, on the average, there was little difference in effectiveness between the two classes of therapy. This result has been confirmed by other researchers (Sloane et al., 1975; Luborsky, Singer, & Luborsky, 1975; Berman, Miller, & Massman, 1985). How can therapies that espouse such different methods produce such similar results? Numerous possible explanations have been suggested (see Stiles, Shapiro, & Elliott, 1986). We will mention only two.

Perhaps certain therapies are effective for certain problems or disorders but are relatively ineffective for others. When specific therapies are used to treat a wide range of disorders, they may help some cases but not others. Thus, averaging results over cases may conceal the special strengths of a particular therapy. We need to know which treatment is effective for which problem.

There are some clues. We know, for example, that systematic desensitization and modeling are effective for eliminating specific fears or phobias, whereas psychoanalytic and person-centered therapies are not. When we want to change specific behaviors, cognitive behavior therapies generally work better than insight therapies. But if the goal is self-understanding, then more global therapies such as psychoanalytic and person-centered therapy are appropriate.

We know, too, that none of the psychotherapies are very successful in treating schizophrenia or manic-depression. However, psychotherapy can be beneficial (when used in combination with some of the biological therapies described in the next section) in helping the patient deal with the problems of daily living.

The task for future evaluators is to determine the disorder for which each therapy is particularly effective. Matching the right therapy and therapist with the right patient will improve the overall effectiveness of treatment. A large-scale study of treatment for depression sponsored by the National Institute of Mental Health is aimed toward this goal. The study, which involved 28 therapists and 240 patients, compares the effectiveness of two forms of brief psychotherapy (cognitive behavior therapy and interpersonal therapy) and treatment with an antidepressant drug. The cognitive behavior therapy focused on correcting the patients' distorted thinking and negative views of themselves; the interpersonal therapy attempted to help the patients to develop better ways of relating to family members, coworkers, and others. In both cases, weekly one-hour sessions were conducted for 12 to 16 weeks. The antidepressant drug was dispensed weekly by experienced clinicians who also provided support and encouragement.

Preliminary results indicate that, *on the average,* the three treatments did equally well in alleviating the symptoms of depression; more than half of the patients in each group recovered. But indications are that certain types of patients responded best to specific treatments. This aspect of the data is being analyzed, as is the degree of improvement the subjects maintained during the 18-month follow-up (Elkin et al., 1986).

Another reason why different psychotherapies may be equally effective in helping clients is because they all share certain factors. It may be these common factors, rather than the specific therapeutic techniques employed, that promote positive change.

Common Factors in Psychotherapies

One school of therapy emphasizes insight; another, modeling and reinforcement; and yet another, empathy and warmth. But perhaps these variables are not the crucial ones. Other factors that are common to most psychotherapies, but which receive little emphasis when therapists write about what they do, may be more important (Garfield, 1980).

AN INTERPERSONAL RELATIONSHIP OF WARMTH AND TRUST Regardless of the type of therapy provided, in a good therapeutic relationship, client and therapist have mutual respect and regard for one another. The client must believe that the therapist understands and is concerned with his or her problems. Although behavior therapy may sound like a rather impersonal procedure when it is described in a textbook, studies indicate that experienced behavior therapists show as much empathy and depth of interpersonal involvement as experienced psychoanalytically oriented therapists (Sloane et al., 1975). A therapist who understands our problems and believes we can solve them earns our trust, which increases our sense of competence and our confidence that we can succeed.

REASSURANCE AND SUPPORT Our problems often seem insurmountable and unique to us. Discussing them with an "expert" who accepts our difficulties as not unusual and indicates that they can be resolved is reassuring. Having someone help us with problems we have not been able to solve alone also provides a sense of support and a feeling of hope. In fact, the most successful therapists, regardless of their method of psychotherapy, are those who form a helpful, supportive relationship with their clients (Luborsky et al., 1985).

DESENSITIZATION We have already talked about systematic desensitization, the specific techniques of behavior therapy aimed at helping individuals to lose their fear of certain objects or situations. But many types of psychotherapy can encourage a broader kind of desensitization. When we discuss events and emotions that have been troubling us in the accepting atmosphere of a therapy session, they gradually lose their threatening quality. Problems that we brood about alone can become magnified beyond proportion; sharing problems with someone else often makes them seem less serious. Several other hypotheses can also explain how desensitization occurs in psychotherapy. For example, putting events that are disturbing into words may help us reappraise the situation in a more realistic manner. From the viewpoint of learning theory, repeatedly discussing distressing experiences in the security of a therapeutic setting (where

For treatment to be effective, the therapist must give the client reassurance and support and must maintain a relationship of warmth and trust.

punishment is not forthcoming) may gradually extinguish the anxiety associated with them. Whatever the process, desensitization does appear to be a factor common to many kinds of psychotherapy.

REINFORCEMENT OF ADAPTIVE RESPONSES   Behavior therapists use reinforcement as a technique to increase positive attitudes and actions. But any therapist in whom a client places trust and confidence functions as a reinforcing agent; that is, the therapist tends to express approval of the behaviors or attitudes deemed conducive to better adjustment and to ignore or express disapproval of maladaptive attitudes or responses. Which responses are reinforced depends on the therapist's orientation and therapeutic goals. The use of reinforcement may be intentional or unintentional; in some instances, the therapist may be unaware that he or she is reinforcing or failing to reinforce a particular client behavior. For example, person-centered therapists believe in letting the client determine what is discussed during the therapy sessions and do not wish to influence the trend of the client's conversation. However, reinforcement can be subtle; a smile, a nod of the head, or a simple "um hmm" following certain client statements may increase the likelihood of their recurrence.

Since the goal of all psychotherapies is to bring about a change in the client's attitudes and behaviors, some type of learning must take place in therapy. The therapist needs to be aware of his or her role in influencing the client by means of reinforcement and should use this knowledge consciously to facilitate desired changes.

UNDERSTANDING OR INSIGHT   All of the psychotherapies we have been discussing provide the client with an *explanation* of his or her difficulties — how they arose, why they persist, and how they can be changed. For the individual in psychoanalysis, this explanation may take the form of a gradual understanding of repressed childhood fears and the ways in which these unconscious feelings have contributed to current problems. A behavior therapist might inform the client that current fears are the result of previous conditioning and can be conquered by learning responses that are antagonistic to the current ones. A client seeing a cognitive behavior therapist might be told that his or her difficulties stem from the irrational belief that one must be perfect or must be loved by everyone.

How can such different explanations all produce positive results? Perhaps the precise nature of the insights and understanding provided by the therapist is relatively unimportant. It may be more important to provide the client with an explanation for the behavior or feelings that he or she finds so distressing and to present a set of activities (such as free association or relaxation training) that both therapist and client believe will alleviate the distress. When a person is experiencing disturbing symptoms and is unsure of their cause or how serious they might be, he or she will feel reassured contacting a professional who seems to know what the problem is and offers ways of relieving it. The knowledge that change is possible gives the individual hope, and hope is an important variable in facilitating change. (See the Critical Discussion, "The Placebo Response.")

Our discussion of common factors among psychotherapies is not intended to deny the value of some specific treatment methods. Perhaps the most effective therapist is one who recognizes the importance of the common factors and utilizes them in a planned manner for all patients, but who also selects the specific procedures most appropriate for each individual case. This suggests that the training of future therapists should be more eclectic, less committed to a particular school of psychotherapy, and more open to a variety of procedures. It should encourage a systematic search for the procedures that are most effective and efficient for specific problems.

CRITICAL DISCUSSION

The Placebo Response

Placebos are commonly used in research on the effectiveness of drugs. A placebo is an inert substance (known to have no pharmacological effect) that is made to look like an active drug—in essence, a sugar pill. Placebos are used in drug research as controls (1) for the patients' expectations that the medicine will make them feel better, (2) for the researcher's belief that the medicine is effective, and (3) for the beneficial effects of extra attention from nurses and other personnel that stem from being a research subject. A *double-blind* procedure is usually employed: one group of patients is given the drug and a comparable group is given the placebo, but neither the patients nor the researchers (or whoever judges the results) knows until the end of the study which pills contain the active medication and which are the placebos. Since both the patients and the researchers are "blind" to the nature of the pills, the method is termed "double-blind." If the rate of improvement is greater in those who received the drug, then the drug is considered to be therapeutically effective. If both groups of patients show similar improvement, then whatever positive response occurs with the drug is considered to be a placebo effect and the drug is judged to be ineffective.

All responses that cannot be explained on the basis of actual drug effects are considered to be placebo responses — that is, due to unknown and nonpharmacological causes. Such unknown causes are generally assumed to be psychological in nature.

Placebo responses can be very powerful. For example, 40 percent of patients who were suffering from a painful heart disease (angina pectoris) reported marked relief from their symptoms after undergoing a diagnostic procedure that they believed was an operation to cure the problem (Beecher, 1961). In treating psychological disorders, placebos are often as effective as medication. A review of studies in which patients were given either an antianxiety drug or a placebo found that improvement rates for patients receiving placebos were usually as good as, and often better than, the rates for those receiving drugs (Lowinger & Dobie, 1969).

Until the beginning of modern scientific medicine, almost all medications were placebos. Patients were given every conceivable substance — crocodile dung, lozenges of dried vipers, spermatic fluid of frogs, spiders, worms, and human excrement — prepared in every possible manner to treat their symptoms. Throughout medical history, patients have been purged, poisoned, leached, bled, heated, frozen, sweated, and shocked (Shapiro & Morris, 1978). Since physicians and healers traditionally have held positions of honor and respect, their "treatments" must have helped at least some of their patients. We assume their effectiveness was due to the placebo response. Scientists also attribute

BIOLOGICAL THERAPIES

The biological approach to abnormal behavior assumes that mental disorders, like physical illnesses, are caused by biochemical or physiological dysfunctions of the brain. Several biological theories were mentioned in discussing the etiology of schizophrenia and the affective disorders in Chapter 15. Biological therapies include the use of drugs, electroconvulsive shock, and surgical procedures.

Psychotherapeutic Drugs

By far the most successful biological therapy is the use of drugs to modify mood and behavior. The discovery in the early 1950s of drugs that relieved some of the symptoms of schizophrenia represented a major breakthrough in the treatment of severely disturbed individuals. Intensely agitated patients no longer had to be physically restrained by straitjackets, and patients who had been spending most of their time hallucinating and exhibiting bizarre behavior became more responsive and functional. As a result, psychiatric wards became more manageable, and

documented cases of faith healing and various forms of miraculous cures to placebo effects.

Some clinicians have suggested that the placebo response may be one of the reasons why psychotherapy works (Lieberman & Dunlap, 1979; Wilkins, 1984). According to this view, almost any method of psychotherapy should show positive results if the client believes it will be effective. If this is true, it becomes important for the therapist to convey to the client his or her conviction that the method of treatment will be successful.

The idea that placebo responses play a central role in psychotherapy is disturbing to some clinicians. They feel that it links psychotherapy with quackery or charlatanism and implies that the process is one of self-deception. This is not the case. Physicians and psychotherapists have known for a long time that a patient's attitudes and beliefs are very important in determining the effectiveness of treatment. Any treatment will be more effective if the patient believes in it and is motivated to use it in the proper manner. Rather than deny the importance of the placebo effect, it would be better to continue investigating the variables that contribute to it.

In addition, researchers who wish to demonstrate the effectiveness of a specific therapeutic technique should control for the placebo response. Sophisticated studies do this by including a placebo control group, as well as an untreated control group. For example, an experiment designed to test the efficacy of systematic desensitization in reducing anxiety about public speaking included the following groups: systematic desensitization, insight therapy, attention-placebo, and untreated control. The subjects in the attention-placebo group met with a sympathetic therapist who led them to believe that a pill would reduce their overall sensitivity to stress. To convince them, the therapist had them listen to a "stress tape" (presumably one used in training astronauts to function under stress) for several sessions after ingesting the "tranquilizer." In reality, the pill was a placebo and the tape contained nonverbal sounds that had been found in other research to be boring rather than stressful. In this way, the researcher raised the subjects' expectations that their speech anxiety would be lessened by taking a pill. The results of this study revealed that the systematic desensitization group improved much more than the no-treatment group and more than the attention-placebo and insight therapy groups, who reacted about the same to their forms of therapy. The latter two groups, however, did show significant improvement (Paul, 1967). By including the attention-placebo group, the experimenter was able to conclude that the success of the systematic desensitization procedure was not due solely to the placebo effect.

The mechanism that causes placebo responses is unknown. Numerous hypotheses have been proposed, but so far there is little empirical verification for any of them. One group of explanations focuses on social influence (see Chapter 18). Because patients tend to view physicians and therapists as socially powerful individuals, they may be very suggestible to the influence of such "authorities" and may be easily persuaded that beneficial results will occur. In addition, the role of patient entails certain prescribed behaviors. A "good patient" is one who gets better; getting better justifies the therapists' initial concern and subsequent interest.

Other explanations focus on the individual's expectations. The person who administers the treatment may communicate, by intended or unintended means, expectations about the effects of the treatment. The patients also arrive with certain expectations, based on their previous experiences. Expectations that one will get better and a strong desire that it happen are the essential ingredients of hope. And hope can have a powerful influence on our emotions and bodily processes. Some researchers speculate that this influence may be mediated by the endorphin group of neurotransmitters. We noted earlier (p. 36) how endorphins, the "brain's natural opiates," affect mood and the subjective experience of pain. Endorphins may turn out to play an important role in the placebo response.

patients could be discharged more quickly. A few years later, the discovery of drugs that could relieve severe depression had a similar beneficial effect on hospital management and population. Figure 16-5 shows the reduction in the number of mental-hospital residents that occurred following the introduction of antipsychotic and antidepressant drugs. About the same time, a group of drugs were being developed to relieve anxiety.

ANTIANXIETY DRUGS Drugs that reduce anxiety belong to the family called *benzodiazepines*. They are commonly known as *tranquilizers* and are marketed under such trade names as Valium (diazepam), Librium (chlordiazepoxide), and Xanax (alprazolam). These drugs reduce tension and cause drowsiness. Like alcohol and the barbiturates, they depress the action of the central nervous system. Family physicians often prescribe tranquilizers to help people cope during difficult periods in their lives. The drugs are also used to treat anxiety disorders, withdrawal from alcohol, and physical disorders related to stress. For example, antianxiety drugs may be combined with systematic desensitization in the treatment of a phobia to help the individual relax when confronting the feared situation.

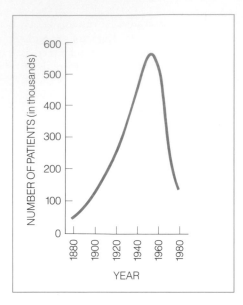

FIGURE 16-5
Patients in Public Mental Hospitals
The graph presents the number of residents in state and county mental hospitals from 1880 to 1980. In the mid-1950s, the number of hospitalized patients began to decline dramatically. The most important factor contributing to this decline has been the widespread use of antipsychotic and antidepressant drugs. Other factors include more adequate outpatient clinics, day hospitals, and related community health facilities. (Data from the National Institute of Mental Health)

Although tranquilizers may be useful on a short-term basis, the overall benefits are debatable, and such drugs clearly are overprescribed and misused. Until quite recently (before some of the dangers became apparent), Valium and Librium were the two most widely prescribed drugs in this country (Julien, 1985). The dangers of tranquilizer overuse are several. Depending on a pill to relieve anxiety may prevent a person from exploring the *cause* of the anxiety and from learning more effective ways of coping with tension. More importantly, long-term use of tranquilizers can lead to physical dependency, or addiction (see p. 122). Although tranquilizers are not as addictive as barbiturates, tolerance does develop with repeated use and the individual experiences severe withdrawal symptoms if the drug is discontinued. In addition, tranquilizers impair concentration, including driving performance, and can cause death if combined with alcohol.

ANTIPSYCHOTIC DRUGS   Most of the *antipsychotic drugs* that relieve the symptoms of schizophrenia belong to the family called *phenothiazines*. Examples are Thorazine (chlorpromazine) and Prolixin (fluphenazine). These drugs have been called "major tranquilizers," but the term is not really appropriate, because they do not act on the nervous system in the same way as barbiturates or antianxiety drugs. They may cause some drowsiness and lethargy, but they do not induce deep sleep even in massive doses (the person can be easily aroused). They also seldom create the pleasant, slightly euphoric feeling associated with low doses of antianxiety drugs. In fact, the psychological effects of the antipsychotic drugs when administered to normal individuals are usually unpleasant. Hence, these drugs are seldom abused.

In Chapter 15, we discussed the theory that schizophrenia is caused by excessive activity of the neurotransmitter dopamine. Antipsychotic drugs block dopamine receptors. Because their molecules are structurally similar to dopamine molecules, they bind to the postsynaptic receptors of dopamine neurons, thereby blocking the access of dopamine to its receptors. (The drug cannot activate the receptors.) A single synapse has many receptor molecules. If all of them are blocked, transmission across the synapse will fail. If only some of them are blocked, transmission will be weakened. The clinical potency of an antipsychotic drug is directly related to its ability to compete for dopamine receptors.

Neurons that have receptors for dopamine are concentrated in the reticular system, the limbic system, and the hypothalamus. The reticular system selectively filters the flow of messages from the sense organs to the cerebral cortex and controls the individual's state of arousal. The limbic system and the hypothalamus are important in the regulation of emotion. Alteration of neural activity in these areas may account for the calming effects of antipsychotic drugs, although we have no idea as yet of the processes involved.

Whatever their method of action, antipsychotic drugs are effective in alleviating the hallucinations and confusion of an acute schizophrenic episode and in restoring rational thought processes. These drugs do not "cure" schizophrenia; most patients must continue to receive a maintenance dosage in order to function outside of a hospital. Many of the characteristic symptoms of schizophrenia — emotional blunting, seclusiveness, difficulties in sustaining attention — remain. Nevertheless, antipsychotic drugs shorten the length of time patients must be hospitalized, and they prevent relapse. Studies of schizophrenics living in the community find that the relapse rate for those taking one of the phenothiazines is typically half the relapse rate of those receiving a placebo (Hogarty et al., 1979).

Unfortunately, antipsychotic drugs do not help all schizophrenic patients. In addition, the drugs have unpleasant side effects — dryness of the mouth, blurred vision, difficulty concentrating — which prompt many patients to discontinue their medication. With long-term usage, more serious side effects may also occur (for example, low blood pressure and a muscular disorder in which there are involuntary movements of the mouth and chin). Researchers continue to search for drugs that will relieve the symptoms of schizophrenia with fewer side effects.

ANTIDEPRESSANT DRUGS *Antidepressant drugs* help to elevate the mood of depressed individuals. These drugs energize rather than tranquilize, apparently by increasing the availability of two neurotransmitters (norepinephrine and serotonin) that are deficient in some cases of depression (see p. 509). The two major classes of antidepressant drugs act in different ways to increase neurotransmitter levels. The *monoamine oxidase* (MAO) *inhibitors* (examples are Nardil and Parnate) block the activity of an enzyme that can destroy both norepinephrine and serotonin, thereby increasing the concentration of these two neurotransmitters in the brain. The *tricyclic antidepressants* (examples are Tofranil and Elavil) prevent the *reuptake* of serotonin and norepinephrine, thereby prolonging the duration of the neurotransmitters' actions. (Recall that *reuptake* is the process by which neurotransmitters are drawn back into the nerve terminals that released them.) Both classes of drugs have proved effective in relieving certain types of depression, presumably those caused more by biological factors than environmental ones. However, like the antipsychotic drugs, the antidepressants can produce some undesirable side effects.

Antidepressants are not stimulants, as amphetamines are (see p. 127); they do not produce feelings of euphoria and increased energy. In fact, a patient may undergo several weeks of medication before a change in mood is observed. This is one reason why electroconvulsive therapy, which acts more quickly, is sometimes the preferred treatment for severely depressed, suicidal individuals. We will discuss electroconvulsive therapy in the next section.

Antidepressants are not effective in treating the depression that occurs with manic-depressive disorders. However, another drug, lithium, has proved very successful. Lithium reduces extreme mood swings and returns the individual to a more normal state of emotional equilibrium.

Drug therapy has successfully reduced the severity of some types of mental disorders. Many individuals who otherwise would require hospitalization can function within the community with the help of these drugs. On the other hand, there are limitations to the application of drug therapy. All therapeutic drugs can produce undesirable side effects. In addition, many psychologists feel that these drugs alleviate symptoms without requiring the individual to face the personal problems that are contributing to the disorder. Biochemical abnormalities undoubtedly play a role in schizophrenia and in the more severe affective disorders, but psychological factors are equally important. Attitudes and methods of coping with problems that have developed gradually over a lifetime cannot be changed suddenly by the administration of a drug. When therapeutic drugs are prescribed, psychotherapeutic help is usually also required.

Electroconvulsive Therapy and Psychosurgery

In *electroconvulsive therapy* (ECT), also known as *electroshock therapy,* a mild electric current is applied to the brain to produce a seizure similar to an epileptic convulsion. ECT was a popular treatment from about 1940 to 1960, before antipsychotic and antidepressant drugs became readily available. Today, ECT is used only in cases of severe depression when patients fail to respond to drug therapy.

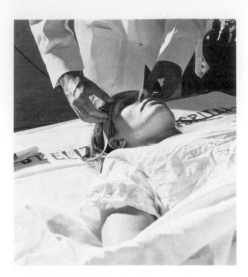

Electroshock therapy being administered to a patient.

ECT has been the subject of much controversy and public apprehension for several reasons. At one time, it was used indiscriminately in mental hospitals to treat such disorders as alcoholism and schizophrenia, for which it produced no beneficial results. Before more refined procedures were developed, ECT was a frightening experience for the patient, who was often awake until the electric current triggered the seizure and produced momentary unconsciousness. The patient frequently suffered confusion and memory loss afterward. Occasionally, the intensity of the muscle spasms accompanying the brain seizure resulted in physical injuries.

Today, ECT involves little discomfort. The patient is given a short-acting anesthesia and then is injected with a muscle relaxant. A brief, very weak electric current is delivered to the brain either across both temples or to the temple on the side of the nondominant cerebral hemisphere. The minimum current required to produce a brain seizure is administered, since the seizure itself—*not* the electricity—is therapeutic. The muscle relaxant prevents the convulsive spasm of body muscles and possible injury. The individual awakens within a few minutes and remembers nothing about the treatment. Four to six treatments are usually administered over a period of several weeks.

The most troublesome side effect of ECT is memory loss. Some patients report a gap in memory for events that occurred up to six months before ECT, as well as an impaired ability to retain new information for a month or two following treatment. However, if very low dosages of electricity are used (the amount is carefully calibrated for each patient to be just sufficient to produce a seizure), memory problems are minimal (Sackeim & Malitz, 1985).

No one knows how the electrically induced seizures relieve depression. Brain seizures do cause the massive release of a number of neurotransmitters, including norepinephrine and serotonin; deficiencies of these two neurotransmitters may be an important factor in some cases of depression (see p. 509). Whichever way it works, ECT is effective in bringing people out of severe, immobilizing depression and does so faster than drug therapy (Janicak et al., 1985).

In *psychosurgery,* selected areas of the brain are destroyed by cutting nerve fibers or by ultrasonic irradiation. Most often, the fibers that connect the frontal lobes with the limbic system or with certain regions of the hypothalamus are destroyed. (Both the limbic system and the hypothalamus are believed to play important roles in emotion.) Psychosurgery is a highly controversial procedure, and congressional committees have investigated the issue of whether it should be legally banned. Some early surgical methods produced individuals who were relaxed and cheerful (no longer violent or suicidal) but whose brains were so impaired that they could not function efficiently. Newer techniques appear to cause minimal intellectual impairment, and the procedure may help severely depressed and suicidal patients, or those who suffer from intractable pain, when all other forms of treatment have failed (Valenstein, 1980).

ENHANCING MENTAL HEALTH

The prevention and treatment of mental disorders is a problem of tremendous concern for both the community and the nation. Considerable progress has been made in this area since the 1950s. Early in this chapter, we noted that the Community Mental Health Centers Act, passed by Congress in 1963, provided funds for the establishment of community mental health centers where people could be treated close to family and friends rather than in large state psychiatric hospitals. These community centers provide short-term hospitalization, outpatient treatment, and a 24-hour emergency service. They are also concerned with preventing emotional problems and so consult with schools, juvenile courts, and other community agencies.

Community Resources and Paraprofessionals

A variety of community resources have been developed in response to the psychological needs of different groups. One such resource is the *halfway house,* where patients who have been hospitalized can live while making the transition back to an independent life in the community. Residential centers are also available to people recovering from alcohol and drug problems, to delinquent or runaway youths, and to battered wives. *Rap centers,* where troubled teenagers can discuss their problems with each other and with sympathetic counselors, play an important role in many communities; *youth centers* provide job counseling, remedial education, and help with family and personal problems.

CRISIS INTERVENTION   *Crisis intervention,* a fairly recent development, provides immediate help for individuals and families undergoing intense stress. During periods of acute emotional turmoil, people often feel overwhelmed and incapable of dealing with the situation. They may not be able to wait for a therapy appointment, or they may not know where to turn. One form of crisis intervention is provided by 24-hour, walk-in services, often in a community mental health center, where the individual receives immediate attention. There, a therapist helps to clarify the problem, provides reassurance, suggests a plan of action, and mobilizes the support of other agencies or family members. This kind of therapy is usually short-term (five or six sessions) and provides the support the person requires to handle the crisis at hand. Such short-term intervention often prevents the need for hospitalization.

Another form of crisis intervention is the *telephone hot line.* Telephone crisis centers are usually staffed by volunteers under the direction of mental health professionals. Some focus specifically on suicide prevention; others are more general and help distressed callers find the particular kind of assistance they need. The volunteers usually receive training that emphasizes listening with care, evaluating the potential for suicide, conveying empathy and understanding, providing information about community resources, giving hope and reassurance, and recording the caller's name and phone number before he or she hangs up so that a professional can follow up on the problem. Most major cities in the United States have developed some form of telephone hot line to help people who are undergoing periods of severe stress, as well as specialized hot lines to deal with child abuse, rape victims, battered wives, and runaways. The phone numbers are widely publicized in the hope of reaching those who need help.

PARAPROFESSIONALS AS THERAPISTS   Most of the community programs we have discussed could not function without the help of paraprofessionals. Because the need for psychological services outstrips the supply of available therapists, concerned citizens can play a valuable role. People of all ages and backgrounds have been trained to work in the area of community mental health. College students have served as companions for hospitalized patients. Older women who have successfully raised families have been trained as mental health counselors to work with adolescents in community clinics, to counsel mothers of youngsters who have behavior problems, and to work with schizophrenic children. Former mental patients, recovered drug addicts, and exconvicts have been trained to help those faced with problems similar to the ones they have experienced.

Nonprofessionals as Therapists
College students and other volunteers can do much to augment therapeutic programs in hospitals and mental health centers, whether they are trained in special therapeutic techniques or they simply provide conversation and companionship. This young woman is working with a disturbed child.

FIGURE 16-6
Residential Program for Delinquent
Youths   *A family conference at
Achievement Place — a group home for
youngsters with behavior problems who are
referred by the courts. The youngsters and
their professional teacher-parents meet
daily to discuss rules of conduct, decide on
consequences for violations of the rules,
criticize aspects of the program, and
evaluate a peer manager who oversees many
of the activities.*

Many residential mental health programs are run by nonprofessionals in consultation with trained therapists. An outstanding example is Achievement Place, which is a home-style facility in Kansas where couples act as surrogate parents for a group of youngsters referred by the courts because of their delinquent behavior (see Figure 16-6). Behavior therapy methods are used to extinguish aggressive behavior and to reward social skills. Follow-up data show that youths who graduate from Achievement Place have fewer contacts with courts and police and achieve slightly higher grades than do individuals who are placed on probation or in a traditional institution for delinquents (Fixsen, Phillips, Phillips, & Wolf, 1976). At present, there are 80 Achievement Places throughout the United States modeled after the original Kansas facility.

Promoting Your Own Emotional Well-being

The problems that people face vary greatly, and there are no universal guidelines for staying psychologically healthy. However, a few general suggestions have emerged from the experiences of therapists.

ACCEPT YOUR FEELINGS   Strong emotions can produce anxiety. Anger, sorrow, fear, and a feeling of having fallen short of ideals or goals are all unpleasant emotions, and we may try to escape anxiety by denying these feelings. Sometimes we try to avoid anxiety by facing situations unemotionally, which leads to a false kind of detachment or "cool" that may be destructive. We may try to suppress all emotions, thereby losing the ability to accept as normal the joys and sorrows that are a part of our involvement with other people.

Unpleasant emotions are a normal reaction to many situations. There is no reason to be ashamed of feeling homesick, of being afraid when learning to ski, or of becoming angry at someone who has disappointed us. These emotions are natural, and it is better to recognize them than to deny them. When emotions cannot be expressed directly (for example, it may not be wise to tell off your boss), it helps to find another outlet for releasing tension. Taking a long walk, pounding a tennis ball, or discussing the situation with a friend can help to dissipate anger. As long as you accept your right to feel emotion, you can express it in indirect or substitute ways when direct channels of expression are blocked.

KNOW YOUR VULNERABILITIES Discovering the kinds of situations that upset you or cause you to overreact may help to guard against stress. Perhaps certain people annoy you. You could avoid them, or you could try to understand just what it is about them that disturbs you. Maybe they seem so poised and confident that they make you feel insecure. Trying to pinpoint the cause of your discomfort may help you to see the situation in a new light. Perhaps you become very anxious when you have to speak in class or present a paper. Again, you could try to avoid such situations, or you could gain confidence by taking a course in public speaking. (Many colleges offer courses specifically aimed at learning to control speech anxiety.) You could also reinterpret the situation. Instead of thinking "Everyone is waiting to criticize me as soon as I open my mouth," you could tell yourself "The class will be interested in what I have to say, and I'm not going to let it worry me if I make a few mistakes."

Many people feel especially anxious when they are under pressure. Careful planning and spacing of work can help you avoid feeling overwhelmed at the last minute. The strategy of purposely allowing more time than you think you need to get to classes or to appointments can eliminate one source of stress.

DEVELOP YOUR TALENTS AND INTERESTS People who are bored and unhappy seldom have many interests. Today's college and community programs offer almost unlimited opportunities for people of all ages to explore their talents in many areas, including sports, academic interests, music, art, drama, and crafts. Often, the more you know about a subject, the more interesting it (and life) becomes. In addition, the feeling of competency gained from developing skills can do a great deal to bolster self-esteem.

BECOME INVOLVED WITH OTHER PEOPLE Feelings of isolation and loneliness form the core of most emotional disorders. We are social beings, and we need the support, comfort, and reassurance provided by other people. Focusing all of your attention on your own problems can lead to an unhealthy preoccupation with yourself. Sharing your concerns with others often helps you to view your troubles in a clearer perspective. Also, being concerned for the welfare of other people can reinforce your feelings of self-worth.

KNOW WHEN TO SEEK HELP Although these suggestions can help to promote emotional well-being, there are limits to self-understanding and self-help. Some problems are difficult to solve alone. Our tendency toward self-deception makes it hard to view problems objectively, and we may not know all of the possible solutions. When you feel that you are making little headway in gaining control over a problem, it is time to seek professional help from a counseling or clinical psychologist, a psychiatrist, or some other trained therapist. The willingness to seek help is a sign of emotional maturity, not a sign of weakness; do not wait until you feel overwhelmed. Obtaining psychological help when it is needed should be as accepted a practice as going to a physician for medical problems.

SUMMARY

1. Treatment of the mentally ill has progressed from the ancient notion that abnormal behavior resulted from the possession of evil spirits that needed to be punished, to custodial care in ill-kept and isolated asylums, to our modern mental hospitals and community mental health centers, which offer a variety of activities designed to help people understand and modify their behavior.

2. *Psychotherapy* is the treatment of mental disorders by psychological means. One type of psychotherapy is *psychoanalysis,* which was developed by Freud. Through the method of *free association,* repressed thoughts and feelings are

brought to the client's conscious awareness. By *interpreting* these associations, the analyst helps the individual to understand the roots of his or her problems. *Transference,* the tendency to express feelings toward the analyst that the client has for important people in his or her life, provides another source of interpretation. Through the processes of *abreaction, insight,* and *working through,* the individual becomes able to cope with problems more realistically.

3. *Psychoanalytic psychotherapy,* based on Freudian concepts, is briefer than psychoanalysis and places more emphasis on the problem-solving functions of the ego (as opposed to the id's sexual and aggressive impulses) and the individual's current interpersonal problems (as opposed to a complete reconstruction of childhood experiences).

4. *Behavior therapy* applies methods based on learning principles to *modify* the individual's behavior. These methods include *systematic desensitization* (the individual learns to relax in situations that previously produced anxiety), *assertiveness training, reinforcement* of adaptive behaviors and *extinction* of maladaptive ones, *modeling* of appropriate behavior, and techniques for *self-regulation* of behavior.

5. *Cognitive behavior therapy* uses behavior modification techniques but also incorporates procedures for changing maladaptive beliefs. The therapist helps the individual to replace irrational interpretations of events with more realistic ones.

6. *Humanistic therapies* help the individual to explore his or her problems and to solve them with a minimum of therapist intervention. Carl Rogers, who developed *person-centered psychotherapy,* believes that the *therapist's characteristics* necessary for the client's growth and self-exploration are *empathy, warmth,* and *genuineness.*

7. *Group therapy* provides an opportunity for the individual to explore his or her attitudes and behavior in interaction with others who have similar problems. *Encounter groups,* an offshoot of group therapy, may help psychologically healthy individuals to learn about themselves, but they do not appear to help individuals who have emotional problems. *Marital therapy* and *family therapy* are specialized forms of group therapy that help couples, or parents and children, to learn more effective ways of relating to one another and of handlng their problems.

8. The effectiveness of psychotherapy is difficult to evaluate because of the difficulty of defining a *successful outcome* and of controlling for *spontaneous remission.* Research indicates that psychotherapy does help but that different approaches do not differ greatly in effectiveness. Factors common to the various psychotherapies — a *warm and trustful interpersonal relationship, reassurance and support, desensitization, insight,* and *reinforcement of adaptive responses* — may be more important in producing positive change than are specific therapeutic methods.

9. *Biological therapies* include *electroconvulsive therapy* (ECT), *psychosurgery,* and the use of *psychotherapeutic drugs.* Of these three treatments, drug therapy has proved by far to be the most successful. *Antianxiety drugs* are used to reduce severe anxiety and to help individuals cope with life crises. *Antipsychotic drugs* have proved effective in the treatment of schizophrenia, *antidepressants* help to elevate the mood of depressed patients, and *lithium* has been successful in treating manic-depressive disorders.

10. The *prevention* and *treatment* of mental disorders is of great concern in our society. Community resources that offer help include *halfway houses, residential centers* for people who have special problems, and various forms of *crisis intervention.* We can promote our own emotional health by accepting our feelings as natural, discovering our vulnerabilities, developing talents and interests, becoming involved with others, and recognizing when to seek professional help.

Interesting material on the historical treatment of the mentally ill can be found in Veith, *Hysteria: The History of a Disease* (1970); and Bell, *Treating the Mentally Ill: From Colonial Times to the Present* (1980).

A review of the various methods of psychotherapy is provided by Martin, *Introduction to Psychotherapy* (1971); and Corsini, *Current Psychotherapies* (1984). *Psychotherapy: An Eclectic Approach* (1980) by Garfield describes the process of psychotherapy, the features common to most psychotherapies, and psychotherapy research. *The Handbook of Research Methods in Clinical Psychology* (1982), edited by Kendall and Butcher, includes a section on methods for evaluating the outcome of psychotherapy.

For an introduction to psychoanalytic methods, see Menninger and Holzman, *Theory of Psychoanalytic Technique* (2nd ed., 1973). For person-centered therapy, see *On Becoming a Person: A Therapist's View of Psychotherapy* (1970) and *Carl Rogers on Personal Power* (1977), both by Rogers. The principles of behavior therapy are presented in Craighead, Kazdin, and Mahoney, *Behavior Modification: Principles, Issues, and Applications* (2nd ed., 1981); and Turner, Calhoun, and Adams (eds.), *The Handbook of Clinical Behavior Therapy* (1981). *Panic: Facing Fears, Phobias, and Anxiety* (1985) by Agras describes behavior therapy methods for overcoming fears.

An overview of group therapy is presented in Yalom, *The Theory and Practice of Group Psychotherapy* (2nd ed., 1975). On encounter groups, see Lieberman, Yalom, and Miles, *Encounter Groups: First Facts* (1973).

Drugs for Mental Illness: A Revolution in Psychiatry (1983), a paperback by Lickey and Gordon, presents a very readable summary of biological research on the major mental disorders. It includes case histories and describes diagnostic procedures, evidence of drug effectiveness, and how psychotherapeutic drugs affect the brain.

For ways to modify your own behavior, see Bower and Bower, *Asserting Yourself: A Practical Guide for Positive Change* (1976); and Watson and Tharp, *Self-directed Behavior: Self-modification for Personal Adjustment* (4th ed., 1985).

FURTHER READING

Part Eight

VILHO SETÄLÄ
Photographic Museum of Finland, Helsinki

Little Men, Long Shadows, 1929

SOCIAL
BEHAVIOR

Social Information Processing

17

SOCIAL PSYCHOLOGY IS THE STUDY OF social interaction, of how we think, feel, and act in the presence of other people, and of how, in turn, our thoughts, feelings, and actions are influenced by others. How do we perceive and interpret the behaviors and motives of others? How consistent are our social beliefs, attitudes, and behaviors? What determines whom we like and dislike? What are the processes of social influence?

Social psychologists base their approach to such topics on two fundamental observations. Both of these have been mentioned earlier (see Chapters 13 and 14), but they are especially relevant to the study of social interaction. The first observation is that human behavior is a function of both the person and the situation. Each person brings a unique set of personal attributes to a situation, leading different persons to act in different ways in the same situation. But each situation also brings a unique set of forces to bear on the person, leading him or her to act in different ways in different situations.

The second observation is that if persons define situations as real, those situations are real in their consequences (Thomas & Thomas, 1928). That is, people do not react simply to the objective features of a situation but to their own subjective interpretations, or cognitive appraisals, of it. This is one reason why different persons behave in different ways in the same objective situation. The person who interprets a hurtful act as the product of hostility reacts differently from the person who interprets that same act as the product of insensitivity. Thus, an understanding of social interaction requires a particularly detailed understanding of social information processing — the ways in which we perceive and interpret the behaviors and motives of others. Accordingly, this chapter deals entirely with social information processing. Chapter 18 will discuss social influence.

INTUITIVE SCIENCE OF SOCIAL JUDGMENTS

We are all psychologists. In attempting to understand other people and ourselves, we are informal scientists who construct our own intuitive theories of human behavior. In doing so, we face the same basic tasks as the formal scientist (Nisbett & Ross, 1985). First, we *observe* or *collect data* ("My friend Chris asserts that women should have the right to obtain abortions"; "Lee Yamuri achieved the highest score on the math test"; "My heart is pounding"). Second, we try to *detect covariation*, to discern what goes with what ("Most people who support the right to abortion also seem to oppose the death penalty"; "On the average, Asians seem to do better in math and science than non-Asians"; "My heart seems to pound when Robin is around"). And third, we attempt to *infer cause and effect*, to evaluate what causes what ("Does Chris support the right to abortion out of genuine conviction or because of peer pressure to express liberal attitudes?" "Do Asian students excel in math and science because they are inherently smarter or because their families stress the value of education?" "Am I in love with Robin or is it just sexual passion?").

Our intuitive attempts to apply scientific reasoning to everyday life work surprisingly well. Social interaction would be chaos if our informal theories of human behavior did not possess substantial validity. But we also make a number of systematic errors in arriving at social judgments, and ironically, our theories themselves often interfere with accurate information processing. As we shall see, our theories can actually shape our perceptions of the data, distort our estimates of what goes with what, and bias our evaluations of cause and effect.

Collecting Data

The first difficulty we face as informal scientists is to collect our data in a systematic and unbiased way. When a survey researcher wants to estimate how many Americans support a woman's right to abortion, he or she takes great care to ensure that a random or representative sample of people are contacted so that the numbers of Catholics, Protestants, men, women, and so forth are interviewed in proportion to their percentage of the total population. But when we, as informal survey researchers, try to make this estimate intuitively, our major source of data is likely to be the people we see daily. Obviously, this is not a representative sample of the population.

Another major source of data for us is the mass media, which also provide a nonrandom and nonrepresentative sample of data. For example, the media necessarily give more attention to a small number of antiabortion protesters publicly demonstrating at a medical clinic than they do to a larger number of people who silently support the clinic's abortion service. The media are not being biased here in the usual sense, they are simply reporting the news. But the data they give us are still not a reliable sample from which to estimate public opinion.

A survey researcher also keeps accurate records of the data. But in everyday life, we constantly accumulate information in our heads, and then later, when we are called upon to make a judgment, we must attempt to recall the pertinent data from memory. Thus, not only are the data we collect a biased sample in the first place, but the data we actually bring to bear on our social judgments are further biased by problems of selective recall.

VIVIDNESS   One of the factors that influences both the information we attend to and the information we recall is its *vividness*. Research has shown that our estimates and judgments are often more influenced by vivid information than they are by pallid information of equal or greater reliability (Nisbett & Ross, 1985).

In one study, introductory psychology students who planned to major in psychology were given information about upper-level psychology courses and then were asked to indicate which courses they planned to take. The subjects either saw a statistical summary of course evaluations made by students who had already taken the courses (made on five-point scales from Poor to Excellent) or heard two or three students make some informal remarks about each course in a face-to-face session. The subjects were less influenced in their choices by the statistical summary than they were by the face-to-face remarks — even if the summary was accompanied by written quotations of those same remarks. The

Protesters on the abortion issue illustrate the vividness effect.

pallid written information was less influential than the vivid face-to-face information even though the written information was based on more complete and representative data (Borgida & Nisbett, 1977).

In a study showing the effects of vividness on judgments based on recalled information, subjects read testimony allegedly from a trial in which a person of otherwise good character was accused of drunk driving. Half the subjects read pallid prosecution testimony and vivid defense testimony, while the other half read vivid prosecution testimony and pallid defense testimony. For example, in describing the man's behavior at a party before he left to drive home, the pallid prosecution testimony stated that he had staggered against a table, knocking a bowl to the floor. The vivid version stated that he had knocked a bowl of guacamole dip to the floor, splattering the dip all over the white shag carpet. Pallid defense testimony argued that the man was not drunk because he was alert enough to avoid an oncoming car, whereas the vivid version had him avoiding a bright orange Volkswagen. Note that the vivid descriptions should not logically affect the nature of the evidence, and in fact, the vividness of testimony did not affect subjects' judgments of the defendants guilt immediately after they had read the testimony. But when subjects were asked to judge the defendant's guilt again the next day, the subjects who had read the vivid prosecution testimony shifted toward guilty verdicts and those who had read the vivid defense testimony shifted toward nonguilty verdicts (Thompson, Reyes, & Bower, 1979).

The vividness effect is a particular problem with information from the mass media. Even if reporters scrupulously gave equal coverage to both the vivid and nonvivid sides of an issue — which they usually do not — our own information-processing tendencies would supply the bias. The studies described here suggest, for example, that even if a television newscast reports survey results showing that a national majority supports abortion rights, we are still more likely to store and later to recall the vivid pictures of the antiabortion protest as the relevant "data" about public opinion.

SCHEMATA   Even if we could collect data in a systematic and unbiased way, our perceptions of the data can still be biased by our existing expectations and preconceptions — our theories — of what the data *should* look like. Whenever we perceive any object or event, we compare the incoming information with our memories of previous encounters with similar objects and events. In earlier chapters, we saw that our memories of objects and events often are not photograph-like reproductions of the original stimuli, but simplified reconstructions of our original perceptions. As noted in Chapter 8, such representations or memory structures are called *schemata* and are the result of perceiving and thinking in terms of mental representations of classes of people, objects, events, or situations. The process of searching for the schema in memory that is most consistent with the incoming data is called *schematic processing*. Schemata and schematic processing permit us to organize and to process an enormous amount of information with great efficiency. Instead of having to perceive and to remember all the details of each new object or event, we can simply note that it is like one of our preexisting schemata and encode or remember only its most prominent features. Schematic processing typically occurs rapidly and automatically; usually we are not even aware that any information processing is taking place at all.

For example, we have schemata for different kinds of people. When someone tells you that you are about to meet an extravert, you immediately retrieve your extravert schema in anticipation of the coming encounter. The extravert schema consists of a set of interrelated traits such as sociability, warmth, and possibly loudness and impulsiveness. General person-schemata such as these are sometimes called *stereotypes*. We also have schemata of particular persons such as the president of the United States, our best friend, even ourselves (see Chapter 13). When you see a job advertisement for a peer counselor, you can quickly and automatically evaluate the match between your schema for a counselor and your self-schema to decide if you should apply.

Research confirms that schemata help us to process information. If people are explicitly instructed to remember as much information as they can about a stimulus person, they actually remember *less* than if they are simply told to try to form an impression of the person (Hamilton, 1979). The instruction to form an impression induces the subjects to search for various person-relevant schemata that help them organize and recall material better. Similarly, people can recall a list of traits better if they are told to think about each trait as it applies to them than if they just try to learn them in the abstract (Rogers, Kuiper, & Kirker, 1977). The self-schema provides a way of organizing items to be memorized. Without schemata and schematic processing, we would simply be overwhelmed by the information that floods us. We would be very poor information processors.

But the price we pay for such efficiency is a bias in our perception of the data. Consider, for example, the impression you form of Jim from the following observations of his behavior.

> Jim left the house to get some stationery. He walked out into the sun-filled street with two of his friends, basking in the sun as he walked. Jim entered the stationery store, which was full of people. Jim talked with an acquaintance while he waited to catch the clerk's eye. On his way out, he stopped to chat with a school friend who was just coming into the store. Leaving the store, he walked toward the school. On his way he met the girl to whom he had been introduced the night before. They talked for a short while, and then Jim left for school. After school Jim left the classroom alone. Leaving the school, he started on his long walk home. The street was brilliantly filled with sunshine. Jim walked down the street on the shady side. Coming down the street toward him, he saw the pretty girl whom he had met on the previous evening. Jim crossed the street and entered a candy store. The store was crowded with students, and he noticed a few familiar faces. Jim waited quietly until he caught the counterman's eye and then gave his order. Taking his drink, he sat down at a side table. When he had finished his drink he went home. (Luchins, 1957, pp. 34–35)

What impression do you have of Jim? Do you think of him as friendly and outgoing or shy and introverted? If you think Jim is better described as friendly, you agree with 78 percent of people who read this description. But examine the description closely; it is actually composed of two very different portraits. Up to the sentence that begins "After school, Jim left . . . ," Jim is portrayed in several situations as fairly friendly. After that point, however, a nearly identical set of situations shows him to be much more of a loner. In fact, 95 percent of the people who are shown only the first half of the description rate Jim as friendly, whereas only 3 percent of the people who are shown only the second half do so. Thus, in the combined description that you read, Jim's "friendliness" seems to win out over his unfriendliness. But when individuals read the same description with the unfriendly half of the paragraph appearing first, only 18 percent rate Jim as friendly; Jim's unfriendly behavior leaves the major impression (see Table 17-1). In general, the first information we receive has the greatest impact on our overall impressions. This is known as the *primacy effect*.

The primacy effect has been found repeatedly in several different kinds of impression formation studies, including studies using real rather than hypothetical persons. For example, subjects who watched a male student attempt to solve a series of difficult multiple-choice problems were asked to assess his general

CONDITIONS	PERCENTAGE RATING JIM FRIENDLY
Friendly description only	95
Friendly first— unfriendly last	78
Unfriendly first— friendly last	18
Unfriendly description only	3

TABLE 17-1
Schematic Processing and the Primacy Effect   *Once a schema of Jim has been established, later information is assimilated to it. (After Luchins, 1957)*

ability (Jones et al., 1968). Although the student always solved exactly 15 of the 30 problems correctly, he was judged more capable if the successes came mostly at the beginning of the series than if they came near the end. Moreover, when asked to recall how many problems the student had solved, subjects who had seen the 15 successes bunched at the beginning estimated an average of 20.6, whereas subjects who had seen the successes at the end estimated an average of 12.5.

Although several factors contribute to the primacy effect, it appears to be primarily a consequence of schematic processing. When we are first attempting to form our impressions of a person, we actively search in memory for the person schema or schemata that best matches the incoming data. At some point we make a preliminary decision: This person is "friendly" (or whatever). We then assimilate any further information to that schema and dismiss any discrepant information as not representative of the "real" person we have come to know. For instance, when explicitly asked to reconcile the apparent contradictions in Jim's behavior, subjects sometimes say that Jim is "really" friendly but was probably tired by the end of the day (Luchins, 1957). Thus, our perceptions become "schema-driven" and hence relatively impervious to new data. Our "theory" of Jim shapes our perception of all subsequent data.

Such theories can also affect the retrieval of data from memory. For example, in Chapter 8 we described a study in which subjects read statements about a woman's early life (for instance, "Although she never had a steady boyfriend in high school, she did go out on dates"). At a subsequent session, subjects were further told either that she had adopted a lesbian life-style as an adult or that she had gotten married. When asked to recall what they remembered about her earlier history, subjects selectively recalled facts and events that were consistent with their new schema about her. Subjects given the lesbian outcome were more likely to remember that she never had a steady boyfriend, whereas subjects given the marriage outcome were more likely to remember that she went out on dates (Snyder & Uranowitz, 1978). This study illustrates how a new schema can affect the recall of old data. The primacy effect demonstrates how a preexisting schema can affect the interpretation of new data.

SCRIPTS   In addition to schemata of people, we also have schemata for events and social interactions. Such schemata are sometimes called *scripts* (Abelson, 1976). One of the most familiar is the greeting script. When we greet an acquaintance with the phrase "How are you," the script calls for the response "Fine, how are you." A person who responds instead with a long list of woes fails to understand this common social script. Some scripts are more complex and abstract. When we are invited to a birthday party, we invoke a general birthday party script, an abstract picture or cognitive structure in our minds that informs us what would be appropriate to wear, reminds us to take a gift, and generally helps us to anticipate what will take place. Like other schemata, scripts permit us to process information quickly and automatically — even mindlessly — by permitting us to gloss over the particular details of each new interaction.

This aspect of scripts was amusingly demonstrated in an experiment in which a person about to use a photocopy machine was approached by an experimental confederate who asked for permission to use the machine first (Langer, Blank, & Chanowitz, 1978). The confederate stated that she had either a small or a large number of copies to make and made the request in one of three ways.

1. Request only: "Excuse me. I have 5 [20] pages. May I use the Xerox machine?"
2. Request plus genuine reason: "Excuse me, I have 5 [20] pages. May I use the Xerox machine because I'm in a rush?"

The greeting script

3. Request plus nonreason: "Excuse me, I have 5 [20] pages. May I use the Xerox machine because I have to make copies?"

How much compliance should we expect with each of these requests? It is reasonable, of course, to expect more compliance with the smaller, 5-page requests than with the larger, 20-page requests. Moreover, we all know that the polite — and most effective — way to phrase a request is to accompany it with a reason. This is the "request script" we have all learned. Thus, it is reasonable to expect more compliance with Request No. 2 than with Request No. 1. The interesting condition is Request No. 3, which appears to follow the polite script, but the reason given — "I have to make copies" — conveys no information. Why else would someone want to use a copying machine if not to make copies? Thus, despite its appearance, Request No. 3 conveys no more information than does Request No. 1.

Table 17-2 shows the percentage of subjects who complied with the request in each condition. When the request is small, a nonreason embedded in the proper script obtains the same result as a genuine reason. Apparently the person responds to the form of the request "mindlessly" — that is, without thinking about its meaning. The larger request appears to give the person enough pause to think consciously about its meaning, and hence a nonreason becomes no more effective than no reason at all.

THEORIES   Schemata and scripts are actually minitheories of everyday objects and events. But more elaborate theories also affect our perception of data. In one particularly elegant demonstration of this, students who held strongly divergent beliefs about whether or not capital punishment (the death penalty) acts as a deterrent for potential murderers read a summary of two purportedly authentic studies. One of the studies appeared to show that capital punishment was a deterrent, and the other appeared to show that it was not (Lord, Ross, & Lepper, 1979). The students also read a critique of each study that criticized its methodology. The investigators report that students on both sides of the issue found the study supporting their own position to be significantly more convincing and better conducted than the other study. Moreover, they were more convinced about the correctness of their initial position than they were before reading about *any* evidence! One disturbing implication of these results is that evidence introduced into public debate in the hope of resolving an issue — or at least of moderating extreme views — will tend instead to polarize public opinion even further. Proponents of each side will pick and choose from the evidence so as to bolster their initial opinions (Nisbett & Ross, 1985).

In 1982, a tragic series of events in the Middle East permitted researchers to examine how strongly held beliefs affect the perception of information in a real-life situation. Israeli-supported elements in Lebanon massacred a number of civilians in Lebanese refugee camps. Television coverage of the event was extensive, and Israel's role was quite controversial. The researchers questioned both pro-Israeli and pro-Arab individuals about the television news coverage and found that each group believed that media coverage had been biased against its side. For example, pro-Israeli subjects estimated that only 17 percent of the references to Israel in the news programs were favorable, whereas 57 percent were unfavorable. Pro-Arab subjects estimated that 42 percent of the references to Israel were favorable and that only 26 percent were unfavorable. Both groups predicted that neutral viewers had been swayed in the direction hostile to their own beliefs (Vallone, Ross, & Lepper, 1985). Our theories shape our perceptions of data!

CONDITION	PERCENTAGE OF SUBJECTS COMPLYING WITH REQUEST TO USE THE COPIER	
	SMALL REQUEST	LARGE REQUEST
Request only	60	24
Request plus genuine reason	94	42
Request plus nonreason	93	24

TABLE 17-2
Automatic Processing of the Request Script *When the request was small, a nonreason couched in the appropriate script format was as effective as a genuine reason. When the request was large, a nonreason was no more effective than no reason at all. (After Langer, Blank, & Chanowitz, 1978)*

Detecting Covariation

When two things vary in relation to each other (for instance, height and weight or education and income), they are said to *covary* or *correlate*. The detection of such covariation or correlation is a fundamental task in every science, and as intuitive scientists of human behavior, we perceive — or think we perceive — such correlations all the time ("People who hold a pro-choice position on abortion seem more likely to be against capital punishment"; "Asians seem to do better in math and science than do non-Asians"; "My heart seems to pound when Robin is around").

Research shows, however, that we are not very good at this task. Once again, it is our theories that mislead us. In particular, when our schemata or theories lead us to expect two things to covary, we overestimate the correlation between them, even seeing "illusory correlations" that do not exist. But when we do not have a theory, we underestimate the correlation; we may even fail to spot a correlation that is strongly present in the data.

This was nicely demonstrated in a series of studies initiated by two researchers who were puzzled by the fact that clinical psychologists routinely report associations between patients' responses to projective tests and their personality characteristics or symptoms, even though research studies repeatedly fail to find such correlations. First, the researchers obtained reports from 32 clinicians who, in the course of their practices, had analyzed the Rorschach inkblot responses (see p. 444) of many homosexual men. These clinicians reported that homosexual men are more likely than heterosexual men to see anal images and feminine clothing in the inkblots — despite the fact that carefully controlled research studies have failed to confirm the validity of these images as indicators of male homosexuality. Moreover, only 2 of the 32 clinicians listed either of two Rorschach images (a monster in one of the inkblots and an animal in another) that research studies *have* shown to be valid indicators of male homosexuality (Chapman & Chapman, 1969).

The researchers suggest that the invalid images are erroneously seen to correlate with homosexuality because they are part of a popular stereotype — a schema — of male homosexuality, whereas the two valid images are not detected because they are not part of the stereotype. Several experiments have now confirmed this hypothesis.

Student subjects in one of these experiments were asked to study a set of Rorschach cards. Each card contained the inkblot, a description of the image that the patient reported seeing in it, and a statement of two "symptoms" that the patient displayed. The reported images included five stereotyped but invalid

CRITICAL DISCUSSION

The Gender Schema

Most of the schemata discussed in the previous section apply to limited domains of objects or events (such as particular persons, the birthday party), helping us to organize and interpret small and specific areas of everyday life. But some schemata have a much wider scope, organizing broad areas of experience and becoming, in effect, a set of lenses through which we view vast aspects of our world. Gender is often such a schema, because in most cultures the distinction between male and female tends to organize many features of daily life. Not only are young boys and girls expected to acquire sex-specific skills and behaviors, they are also expected to have or to acquire sex-specific self-concepts and personality attributes; to be masculine or feminine as defined by that particular culture. As we saw in Chapter 3, the process by which a society teaches children to conform to such expectations is called *sex typing*.

Psychologist Sandra Bem (1981) has suggested that in addition to learning the specific concepts and behaviors that the culture associates with sex, the child learns to perceive and organize diverse kinds of information in terms of a *gender schema*.

According to her theory, sex-typed individuals within any given culture should use the gender schema more than non-sex-typed individuals.

In her research, Bem identifies sex-typed persons by asking individuals to rate themselves on a list of sex-typed personality traits. Individuals who rate themselves high on stereotypically masculine traits (such as *assertive, independent*) but low on stereotypically feminine traits (such as *compassionate, tender*) are defined as masculine; individuals with the reverse pattern are defined as feminine; and individuals who describe themselves as having both masculine and feminine traits are defined as *androgynous* (*andro* means male; *gyn* means female).

In a series of studies validating this classification procedure, androgynous individuals displayed both "masculine" independence and "feminine" nurturance, whereas sex-typed individuals (masculine men and feminine women) tended to display only the behavior stereotypically considered appropriate for their sex (Bem, 1975; Bem, Martyna, & Watson, 1976).

In one study designed to test whether or not sex-typed individuals use the gender

signs of homosexuality, the two unstereotyped but valid signs, and unrelated control signs (for example, food images). The "symptoms" were either homosexuality ("has sexual feelings toward other men") or unrelated problems ("feels sad and depressed much of the time"). The cards were carefully constructed so that *no* sign was systematically associated with homosexuality.

After studying all of the cards, subjects were presented with four symptoms and were asked to report if they had noticed "any general kind of thing that was seen most often by men with this problem." Like the practicing clinical psychologists, subjects erroneously reported the invalid signs — but not the valid signs or the control signs — to be associated with homosexuality. Even when the cards were reconstructed so that the valid signs were associated with homosexuality 100 percent of the time, subjects still reported seeing the nonexistent correlation with the invalid signs more than twice as often as the perfect correlation with the valid signs.

As intuitive scientists, we are theory-driven. We see covariations our theories have prepared us to see and fail to see covariations our theories have not prepared us to see.

SELF-FULFILLING STEREOTYPES   As the studies just described indicate, our schemata of classes of persons — stereotypes — are actually miniature theories of covariation. The stereotypes of an extravert or of a homosexual is a theory of what particular traits or behaviors go with certain other traits or behaviors. For this reason, stereotypes have also been called *implicit personality theories* (Schneider, 1973).

schema to organize information, subjects were shown a list of words and were later asked to recall as many of the words as they could in any order. The list included proper names, animal names, verbs, and articles of clothing. Half of the proper names were male and half were female, and one-third of the words within each of the other categories had been rated by judges as masculine (for instance, *gorilla, hurling, trousers*), one-third as feminine (for instance, *butterfly, blushing, bikini*), and one-third as neutral (for instance, *ant, stepping, sweater*). Research in memory has shown that if an individual has encoded a number of words in terms of an underlying schema or network of associations, then thinking of one schema-related word enhances the probability of thinking of another. Accordingly, an individual's sequence of recall should reveal runs or clusters of words that are linked in memory by the schema. If a subject thinks of an animal word, he or she is likely to think next of another animal word. Note that subjects in this experiment could cluster words either according to semantic category (proper names, animals, verbs, clothing) or according to gender.

The sex-typed individuals showed significantly more gender clustering than did non-sex-typed individuals. For example, if a sex-typed person happened to recall the "feminine" animal *butterfly*, he or she was more likely to follow that with another "feminine" word such as *bikini*, whereas a non-sex-typed individual was more likely to follow *butterfly* with another animal name. Thus, sex-typed subjects were more likely to link words together in memory on the basis of gender; as the theory predicts, they were more likely to use the gender schema to organize information.

Sex-typed individuals also organize information about themselves in terms of the gender schema. In one study, they were much faster at rating themselves on sex-typed traits than they were on other traits. For example, masculine males rated themselves more quickly on the masculine trait *assertive* than on a sex-neutral trait such as *honest*. According to the theory, they had encoded in memory both their self-concepts and the terms for sex-typed personality traits according to the gender schema; instead of reviewing their person-

ality in detail, they just had to "look up" the trait in the schema to see if it was there. In contrast, non-sex-typed individuals—who organize neither their self-concepts nor personality trait terms according to the gender schema—were no faster on sex-typed traits than they were on sex-neutral traits (Girvin, 1978, as cited in Bem, 1981). Later studies have yielded similar results (Markus, Crane, Bernstein, & Siladi, 1982).

Bem believes that the lesson to be learned from gender schema theory is *not* that every individual ought to be androgynous, to be both masculine and feminine. This prescription would constrain the person from being a unique individual just as much as the traditional prescription would that men must be masculine and women must be feminine. Rather, she argues that human behaviors and personality attributes should cease to have gender and that society should stop projecting gender into situations that are irrelevant to genitalia. The individual, in short, should not have to be androgynous, but the society should be less gender schematic.

Stereotypes have a bad reputation because they are associated with prejudice and discrimination. But it is important to recognize that the thinking process behind stereotypes—schematic processing—is not itself evil or pathological. Because it is simply not possible for us to deal with every new person as a unique individual, our use of schemata or working stereotypes is inevitable until further experiences either refine or discredit the schemata. For example, some students from rural areas of the country who attend college in New York City spend their first few weeks of college thinking that all New Yorkers are Jews and all Jews are New Yorkers. There is not necessarily any malice or ill will behind such a stereotype; the new student has simply not yet seen enough Catholic New Yorkers or Texas Jews to sort the social environment into more accurate and finely differentiated categories or schemata. Many of our stereotypes are of this benign variety and are discarded as our experiences multiply.

As we have seen, however, schemata are resistant to change, because they lead us to misperceive the very data that could potentially disconfirm them. For this reason alone, stereotypes are not easily discarded, even as experiences multiply. But there is an even more insidious process at work: our schemata influence not only our perceptions but also our behaviors and social interactions. Our stereotypes can lead us to interact with those we stereotype in ways that cause them to fulfill our expectations. Thus, our stereotypes can become both self-perpetuating and self-fulfilling.

This was illustrated in a study in which white college students played the role of job interviewers. They were assigned to interview both black and white job applicants, who were actually confederates of the experimenters. The

The attractiveness stereotype attributes many desirable characteristics to good-looking individuals.

experimenters found that the subjects (the interviewers) were less friendly when interviewing black applicants than they were when interviewing white applicants. The subjects also maintained greater interpersonal distance, made more speech errors, and terminated the interview sooner when speaking to the black applicants.

But that was only the first part of the study. The experimenters then trained white interviewers to reproduce both the friendly and the less friendly interviewing styles shown by the original subjects. New subjects — all white — were then recruited, this time to play the role of the job applicants. Some received the friendly interview treatment; others, the less friendly treatment. Viewing videotapes of the interviews, judges later rated the subjects' performance and composure. The results showed that subjects who received the less friendly pattern of behavior from the interviewer (as had the black applicants in the first experiment) were rated significantly lower on both performance and demeanor than were those who had received the more friendly pattern (Word, Zanna, & Cooper, 1974). This study indicates that prejudiced individuals may interact in ways that actually evoke the stereotyped behaviors and thus sustain the prejudice.

Stereotypes may be self-fulfilling in more profound ways, actually shaping the long-term personalities of those stereotyped. Evidence for this comes from research on physical attractiveness. First, a commonly held stereotype is that physically attractive persons have many other desirable characteristics. In one study, male and female subjects were shown photographs of men and women from a college yearbook and were asked to rate the pictured individuals on a number of traits. The photographs had been previously rated as very attractive, average, or unattractive. Compared to the unattractive individuals, the more attractive individuals were rated as being more sensitive, kind, interesting, strong, poised, sociable, outgoing, exciting, and sexually responsive. They were also rated as having higher status, more likely to get married, likely to have a more successful marriage, and likely to be happier (Dion, Berscheid, & Walster, 1972).

Second, evidence shows that such a stereotype can be self-fulfilling, even in a brief interaction. In one study, male students engaged in a ten-minute telephone conversation with a female student they had never seen but who they believed to be either physically attractive or unattractive. The experimenters established this belief by showing the man a photograph allegedly taken of his phone partner — a photograph whose attractiveness was, in fact, unrelated to the actual attractiveness of the woman on the phone. Analyses of the conversations showed that men who believed they were talking to an attractive woman were friendlier, more outgoing, and more sociable than were men who believed they were talking to a less attractive woman. This is interesting in itself, but there is more. The phone conversations were recorded on two-track tapes, and judges listened to the woman's half of each conversation without hearing the male partner and without knowing the partner's belief about the woman's attractiveness. These judges rated women whose partners believed they were attractive as more sociable, poised, and humorous than women whose partners believed they were unattractive. The men's stereotype of physically attractive women became self-fulfilling in a ten-minute phone conversation (Snyder, Tanke, & Berscheid, 1977).

Finally, indirect evidence suggests that this self-fulfilling process has long-term effects in the real world; the common stereotype of the physically attractive person appears to have a grain of truth. In one study, male students spoke on the phone for about five minutes with female students they had never seen and then rated the women's social skills. Independent observers rated the physical attractiveness of the women. The researchers found that the more attractive women, in fact, were rated higher in social skills by their phone partners than were the less attractive women (Goldman & Lewis, 1977). Other studies have shown that physical attractiveness correlates with a positive self-concept (Lerner & Karabenick, 1974), good mental health (Adams, 1981), assertiveness and self-confidence (Jackson & Huston, 1975; Goldman & Lewis, 1977; Dion & Stein, 1978), and a variety of other positive characteristics.

The suggestion, then, is that more attractive individuals have higher self-esteem, better mental health, and greater social skills than do unattractive individuals because the former are treated better in everyday life. They develop these desirable traits because they are hired first, paid more, promoted faster, and so forth. And, as we shall see later in this chapter, they also have the edge in dating and mating.

Inferring Causality

The heart of most sciences is the discovery of causes and effects. Similarly, as intuitive scientists, we feel we truly understand some instance of human behavior when we know why it occurred or what caused it. Suppose, for example, that a famous athlete endorses a breakfast cereal on television. Why does she do it? Does she really like the cereal, or is she doing it for the money? A man kisses his female companion at the end of an evening out. Is this just a social norm, or is he really fond of her? Perhaps this particular man kisses everyone. Or perhaps everyone would kiss this particular woman. You give a five-dollar donation to Planned Parenthood. Why? You are altruistic? You were being pressured? You need a tax write-off? You believe in the work of the organization?

Each of these cases creates an attribution problem. We see a behavior— perhaps our own—and must decide to which of many possible causes the action should be attributed. In social psychology, the task of attempting to infer the causes of behavior is known as the *attribution problem*, and the study of the attribution process has become a central concern in social psychology (Heider, 1958; Kelley, 1967).

Inferring cause and effect is a special case of detecting covariations. Suppose that you wake up one morning with a runny nose. You see that the azaleas in your yard have just bloomed and hypothesize that they are causing your sniffles. Note how you test this hypothesis. You look to see if your symptoms come and go as you enter and leave areas containing azaleas. That is, you run an experiment to see if your symptoms and azaleas covary. Does the effect come and go with the suspected cause? If it does, azaleas are convicted. But if your sniffles remain constant—there is no covariation—then there is nothing distinctive about azaleas, and you conclude that they are not the cause. Thus, you use the *distinctiveness* of your reactions to the suspected stimulus as a criterion for deciding if it caused the problem.

Another criterion is *consistency*. If you had the same symptoms the last three years when the azaleas bloomed, you are fairly certain that they are the culprit. But if this is the first time the symptoms have occurred—this is not a consistent event—you might not be as certain.

Finally, you call your doctor, who says that yours is the 16th such complaint of the day and that "this always happens when the azaleas bloom." In other words, you are not unique. Others share the same reaction to the same stimulus. This is the criterion of *consensus*.

Thus, you attempt to detect a covariation that satisfies three criteria: the effect must vary only with the suspected cause (distinctiveness); it must do so every time the experiment is conducted (consistency); and other people must get the same result (consensus).

"Folks, I endorse Scrunchies because I *eat* Scrunchies. As God is my witness, I don't just *say* I eat them, I really and truly *do* eat them. In fact, folks, I never eat anything but. And if you don't believe me, I can supply documentation from my personal physician."

Drawing by Ross; © 1976 *The New Yorker Magazine*, Inc.

We use these same criteria when we attempt to understand the behavior of our friends and acquaintances (Kelley, 1973). Suppose that Julia raves about a recent meal at a local Chinese restaurant. In very general terms, there are three potential causes of her praise. The first is the stimulus itself: maybe the food really was terrific. The second possible source of the praise is something about the person: Julia is a Chinese-food nut. The third possibility is the particular situation: it was her birthday and anything would have seemed great to her. To choose among these three classes of causes, we again invoke the three criteria of distinctiveness, consistency, and consensus. If she praises no restaurants but this one (distinctiveness), does so every time she eats there (consistency), and so does everyone else (consensus), then the restaurant must be terrific. But if Julia praises all Chinese restaurants all of the time — but nobody else does — we are probably learning more about Julia than about the restaurant. Finally, if she has never praised any restaurant before — including this one — and nobody else in Julia's party liked it much, then we can probably conclude that something about this particular situation (such as her birthday) is coloring her perceptions of the meal.

Research confirms that people do, in fact, utilize these criteria in this way (McArthur, 1972), but research also reveals that we frequently fail to apply the criteria correctly or sufficiently (Nisbett & Ross, 1985). For example, we may fail to utilize the consensus criterion as fully as we should. But the main problem — as you must be able to guess by now — is that we have theories of causality that bias our inferences.

FUNDAMENTAL ATTRIBUTION ERROR   As several of the above examples illustrate, one of the major attribution tasks we face daily is deciding whether an observed behavior reflects something unique about the person (his or her attitudes, personality characteristics, and so forth) or something about the situation in which we observe the person. If we infer that something about the person is primarily responsible for the behavior (for instance, the athlete really loves the cereal), then our inference is called an *internal* or *dispositional attribution* ("disposition" here refers to a person's beliefs, attitudes, and personality characteristics). If, however, we conclude that an external cause is primarily responsible for the behavior (for instance, money, strong social norms, threats), it is called an *external* or *situational attribution*.

The founder of modern attribution theory, Fritz Heider, noted that an individual's behavior is so compelling to observers that they take it at face value and give insufficient weight to the circumstances surrounding it (1958). Recent research has confirmed Heider's speculation. We underestimate the situational causes of behavior, jumping too easily to conclusions about the dispositions of the person. Another way of stating it is that we (in Western society, at any rate) have a schema of cause and effect in human behavior that gives too much weight to the person and too little to the situation. One psychologist has termed this bias toward dispositional rather than situational attributions the *fundamental attribution error* (Ross, 1977).

In one of the first studies to reveal this bias, subjects were asked to listen to an individual giving a speech either favoring or opposing racial segregation. The subjects were explicitly informed that the individual was participating in an experiment and had been told which side of the issue to argue; the speaker had no choice. Despite this knowledge, when asked to estimate the individual's actual attitude toward racial segregation, subjects inferred that the individual held a position close to the one argued in the speech. In other words, the subjects made a dispositional attribution even though situational forces were fully sufficient to account for the behavior (Jones & Harris, 1967). This effect is quite powerful. Even if the presentations are deliberately designed to be drab and unenthusiastic, and even if the speaker simply reads a transcribed version of the talk, speaking in a monotone and using no gestures, observers are still willing to attribute to the speaker the attitudes expressed (Schneider & Miller, 1975).

SELF-PERCEPTION   Understanding ourselves is one of our major tasks as informal scientists of human behavior, and one *theory of self-perception* proposes that we make judgments about ourselves using the same inferential processes — and making the same kinds of errors — that we use for making judgments about others (Bem, 1972). Just as we try to evaluate the surrounding situational forces to decide if the athlete on television really loves the cereal she endorses, we also sometimes look at our own behavior and its surrounding circumstances to decide what we ourselves feel or believe. This may sound odd, because we generally assume that we have direct knowledge of our own feelings and beliefs. But we don't always. Consider the common remark: "This is my second sandwich; I guess I was hungrier than I thought." Clearly, this person originally misjudged an internal state and has now decided on the basis of observing his or her own behavior that he or she was wrong. This suggests that, whenever internal feelings are not very strong, an individual is actually forced into the role of an outside observer to make the correct attributions. Thus, the self-observation "I've been biting my nails all day; something must be bugging me" is based on the same kind of evidence as a friend's observation, "You've been biting your nails all day; something must be bugging you": the nail biter's overt behavior.

Consider the following experiment. College students were taken one at a time to a small room to work for an hour on dull, repetitive tasks (stacking spools and turning pegs). After completing the tasks, some were offered $1 to tell the next subject that the tasks had been fun and interesting. Others were offered $20 to say the same. All subjects complied with this request. Later, they were asked how much they had enjoyed the tasks. As shown in Figure 17-1, subjects who had been paid only $1 stated that they had, in fact, enjoyed the tasks. But subjects who had been paid $20 did not find them significantly more enjoyable than did control subjects who were not asked to speak to another subject (Festinger & Carlsmith, 1959).

This study is an example of what is called an *induced-compliance experiment* and was actually conducted in order to test Festinger's theory of *cognitive dissonance* (Festinger, 1957), which is discussed later in the chapter. For now, let us look at these results from the perspective of self-perception theory. Why might the small sum of money, but not the large sum, lead individuals to believe what they had heard themselves say?

Self-perception theory assumes that the subjects looked at their behavior (saying that the tasks were fun and interesting) and had to solve the attribution problem, "Why did I say this?" It further assumes that they solved the problem the same way an outside observer would. Such a hypothetical observer hears the individual say the tasks were enjoyable and must decide whether to make a dispositional attribution (the individual did it because he or she believes it) or a situational attribution (the individual did it for the money). When the individual is paid $20, the observer is most likely to make a situational attribution: "Anyone would have done it for that sum." But if the individual is paid only $1, the observer is more likely to make a dispositional attribution: "This person wouldn't be willing to say it for only $1 and so must believe it." If we assume that the individual follows the same inferential process as the outside observer, then subjects paid $20 attribute their behavior to situational factors and decide they

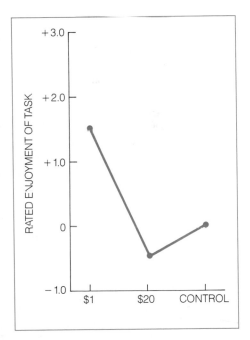

FIGURE 17-1

Induced-compliance Experiment   *The smaller the incentive for complying with the experimenter's request, the greater the attitude change. (After Festinger & Carlsmith, 1959)*

CRITICAL DISCUSSION

Information-processing Biases: Cognitive or Motivational?

So far, this chapter has suggested that *information-processing biases* are rooted in cognitive or perceptual factors, especially schematic processing. But when dealing with an individual's interpretation of his or her own behavior, we must also consider the possibility that some of the biases of judgment are motivational, that they are self-serving distortions that enhance the person's self-esteem or defend the self-image. The Freudian defense mechanisms, discussed in Chapter 14, are examples of such motivational processes. A question currently under debate within social psychology is whether the biases of the kind we have been discussing in this chapter can all be explained by cognitive factors or whether some of them require motivational explanations.

A commonplace example comes from a study of college students' explanations for the grades they received in three examinations. Students attributed A and B grades to personal internal factors, such as ability and effort, but they attributed C, D, and F grades to external factors, such as test difficulty and bad luck (Bernstein, Stephan, & Davis, 1979). In another study, subjects played a competitive game that was rigged so that winners and losers were randomly determined. The results showed that winners attributed their wins to skill and effort, whereas losers blamed their losses on luck (Snyder, Stephan, & Rosenfeld, 1976). These attributions would certainly seem to be self-serving.

It is important, however, to be cautious before concluding that the causes are necessarily motivational. Because we usually try to succeed and rarely try to fail, it makes some sense to attribute our successes to internal factors and failures to external factors. We fail *despite* our abilities and efforts, not because of them. And if we have a history of success, then it is certainly rational to attribute an unexpected failure to external rather than to enduring internal causes. Thus, these apparently self-serving attributions may not only derive from purely cognitive factors, but may well be correct! On the other hand, one well-designed study controlled for the subjects' expectancies of success and failure and still found self-serving bias (Ross & Sicoly, 1979).

Similar debates are waging over other biases. For example, the $1-$20 experiment (in which the smaller incentive led subjects to say that they enjoyed the tasks) was interpreted earlier as a purely cognitive phenomenon of self-perception, a set of self-attributions biased by the fundamental attribution error. But as we shall see in the section on attitudes, these same results have been interpreted motivationally in at least two different ways. Other apparent biases of information processing are being similarly debated, and several ingenious experiments have been devised to support one or the other sides of the argument. A resolution, though, does not seem to be at hand. In fact, some authors have argued that the cognitive and motivational positions are formulated in ways that do not even permit the debate to be resolved on empirical grounds (Tetlock & Levi, 1982).

did not really find the tasks enjoyable. But subjects paid $1 make a dispositional attribution: "I must think the tasks are enjoyable; otherwise, I would not have said so."

FUNDAMENTAL ATTRIBUTION ERROR IN SELF-PERCEPTION   There is a subtle point about the findings in the experiment just described. We know that all the subjects were willing to comply with the experimenter's request to tell the next subject that the tasks were enjoyable — even subjects who were offered only $1 to do so. But the subjects themselves do not know this. Thus, when subjects paid $1 implicitly conclude that they must think the tasks are enjoyable because otherwise they would not have complied with the request, they are wrong. They should be concluding that they complied with the request because they were paid $1. In other words, the subjects are making a dispositional attribution about their own behavior when they should be making a situational attribution. They are committing the fundamental attribution error.

An important demonstration of the fundamental attribution error was illustrated in a study in which pairs of male or female subjects were recruited to participate in a question-and-answer game of general knowledge. One member of the pair was randomly assigned to be the questioner and to make up ten difficult questions to which he or she knew the answers (for example, "What is the world's longest glacier?"). The other subject served as the contestant and attempted to answer the questions. When the contestant failed a question, the questioner would give the answer. In a reenactment of the study, observers also watched the contest. After the game was completed, both participants and observers were asked to rate the level of general knowledge possessed by the questioner and the contestant, relative to the "average student." It is important to note that participants and observers all knew that the roles of questioner and contestant had been assigned randomly.

As Figure 17-2 shows, questioners judged both themselves and the contestant to be about average in level of general knowledge. But contestants rated the questioner as superior and themselves as inferior to the average student. They attributed the outcome of the game to their (and the questioner's) level of knowledge rather than taking into account the overwhelming situational advantage enjoyed by the questioner—who gets to omit any questions to which he or she does not know the answer. Observers, aware that the questioner could ask questions which neither they nor the contestant could answer, rated the questioner's level of knowledge even higher. In other words, both contestants and observers gave too much weight to dispositional causes and too little weight to situational causes: the fundamental attribution error (Ross, Amabile, & Steinmetz, 1977).

One implication of this study is that people who select the topics discussed in a conversation will be seen as more knowledgeable than those who passively let others set the agenda—even if everyone is aware of the differential roles being played. This, in turn, has implications for contemporary sex roles. Research has shown that men talk more than women in mixed-sex interactions (Henley, Hamilton, & Thorne, 1985); they interrupt more (West & Zimmerman, 1983); and they are more likely to raise the topics discussed (Fishman, 1983). The questioner-contestant study implies that one consequence of these sex role patterns is that women depart most mixed-sex interactions thinking themselves less knowledgeable than the men, with bystanders of both sexes sharing this illusion. The moral is clear: the fundamental attribution error can work for or against you. If you want to appear knowledgeable both to yourself and to others, learn how to structure the situation so that you control the choice of topics discussed. Be the questioner, not the contestant.

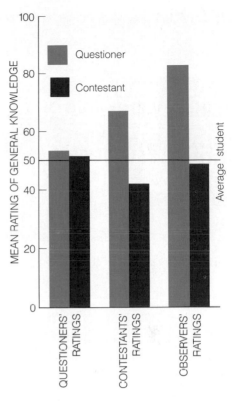

FIGURE 17-2
Fundamental Attribution Error
Ratings of questioners and contestants after they had participated in a quiz game. The questioner is rated as superior by both the contestant and observers even though the questioner had an overwhelming situational advantage. Both contestants and observers gave too much weight to dispositional causes and too little to situational causes. (After Ross, Amabile, & Steinmetz, 1977)

INTUITIVE LOGIC OF SOCIAL ATTITUDES

Except for the brief consideration of possible motivational biases in self-attributions, our discussion of social information processing has focused exclusively on cognitive functioning, the processes of perceiving and thinking. With the concept of *attitude*, social psychology's most central concept, we can begin to incorporate affective functioning—emotions and feelings—into our portrait of the person as a processor of social information.

Attitudes are likes and dislikes—affinities for and aversions to objects, persons, groups, situations, or any other identifiable aspects of the environment, including abstract ideas and social policies. We often express our attitudes in

Certain opinions seem to go together.

opinion statements: "I love oranges"; "I can't abide Republicans." But even though they express feelings, attitudes are often linked to cognitions, specifically to beliefs about the attitude objects ("Oranges contain lots of vitamins"; "Republicans have no compassion for the poor"). Moreover, attitudes are sometimes linked to actions that we take with respect to the attitude objects ("I eat an orange every morning"; "I never vote for Republicans"). Accordingly, social psychologists have typically studied attitudes as one component of a three-part system. The beliefs constitute the *cognitive* component, the attitude is the *affective* component, and the actions constitute the *behavioral* component.

Prior sections of this chapter have focused on how well we do as intuitive empirical scientists in making social judgments. It was appropriate to ask whether our judgments were true or false, correct or incorrect, accurate or inaccurate. But attitudes cannot be objectively judged to be right or wrong, hence the more appropriate question to ask is whether or not they are logically consistent with one another, with their associated beliefs, and with their associated actions. In this section, then, we assess not our adequacy as intuitive empirical scientists but our adequacy as intuitive logicians.

Cognitive Consistency

Certain opinions seem to go together. For example, people who support affirmative action often seem to be the same people who advocate stronger gun control, oppose book censorship, and are most concerned about nuclear disarmament. On the surface, these diverse attitudes do not seem to follow one another logically. Yet knowing that a person holds one of the attitudes often permits us to guess the others with fair accuracy, and there does seem to be a kind of logic involved. The attitudes all appear to follow more or less a common set of underlying values that we might label as "liberal."

The same kind of logic can be discerned among "conservative" attitudes. Many people who oppose affirmative action and gun control laws cite their belief in the value of individual freedom as the basis for their opinions. Even those who disagree with such opinions can appreciate the logic involved. But many such freedom-loving individuals also feel that women belong in the home, that marijuana use should be more heavily penalized, and that homosexual behavior should be illegal. Here the logic is less than clear, yet these opinions, too, seem strangely predictable.

In short, people's attitudes often appear to have a kind of internal logic to them, but it is not usually a strict kind of formal logic. Instead, it is a kind of psycho-logic, and it is this psycho-logic that social psychologists have studied under the label of *cognitive consistency*. The basic premise of cognitive consistency theories is that we all strive to be consistent in our beliefs, attitudes, and behaviors, and that inconsistency acts as an irritant or a stimulus that motivates us to modify or change one or more of these three components until they form a coherent, if not logical, package.

CONSISTENCY AMONG BELIEFS One of the earliest studies of cognitive consistency assessed the degree to which sets of beliefs did, in fact, follow the rules of formal logic. Subjects in the study were given a questionnaire containing 48 propositions that had been taken from 16 logical syllogisms. A *logical syllogism* contains three propositions — two premises and a conclusion drawn from those premises. For example, three of the propositions were drawn from the following syllogism:

Any form of recreation that constitutes a serious health menace will be outlawed by the City Health Authority.

The increasing water pollution in this area will make swimming a serious health menace.

Swimming at the local beaches will be outlawed by the City Health Authority.

The propositions did not appear in syllogistic form on the questionnaire; rather, they were dispersed among propositions from other syllogisms and filler items.

High school students filled out the questionnaire by indicating their belief in the truth of each proposition on a numerical scale. About a week later, these students received persuasive messages that argued for the truth of the first premise in each syllogism but did not mention the second premises or the conclusions. After receiving the messages, the students again indicated how much they believed each of the 48 propositions.

After the persuasion, the results showed a significant change toward stronger belief in the propositions explicitly mentioned in the persuasive messages, as might be expected. Of greater interest, however, was a significant though smaller change toward a stronger belief in the unmentioned conclusions —as a cognitive consistency hypothesis would predict (McGuire, 1960).

CONSISTENCY AMONG ATTITUDES   We implied earlier that a person's attitudes might cohere because they all derive from a core set of underlying values. A *value* can be defined as a basic attitude toward certain broad modes of conduct (for example, courage, honesty, friendship) or certain end states of existence (for example, equality, salvation, freedom, self-fulfillment) (Rokeach, 1968, 1973). Values are thus a kind of attitude, but they refer to ends, not means. A woman who has a positive attitude toward money, for instance, might explain it by saying that money would allow her to retire, retirement would permit her to take music lessons, and music lessons would help her to attain self-fulfillment. Money, retirement, and music lessons do not qualify as values because they are all seen as means, not ends — means toward the value of self-fulfillment. Such labels as "liberal" and "conservative" enable us to predict many of an individual's attitudes because these two terms refer to broad underlying values that are shared by large segments of the population. In fact, Americans — liberals and conservatives alike — share many values, and our differences of opinion stem from the relative importance we assign to them.

This was nicely illustrated in a study in which individuals were asked to rank 12 values in the order of the values' importance to them. The investigator was particularly interested in the values *freedom* and *equality,* and he tallied the rankings of these two values separately for individuals who had participated in civil rights demonstrations during the 1960s, for individuals who had not participated but who were sympathetic to them, and for individuals who were unsympathetic to them. Table 17-3 shows how each of these groups ranked freedom and

"And don't waste your time canvassing the whole building, young man. We all think alike."

Drawing by Stevenson; © 1980 *The New Yorker Magazine*, Inc.

TABLE 17-3
Freedom and Equality in Relation to Civil Rights Attitudes   *Three groups of individuals, with different attitudes toward civil rights, ranked* **freedom** *and* **equality** *among a list of 12 values. Although all subjects ranked the value of* **freedom** *high, only those who were favorable toward civil rights demonstrations also ranked* **equality** *high. (After Rokeach, 1968)*

	PARTICIPATED	SYMPATHETIC	UNSYMPATHETIC
Freedom	1	1	2
Equality	3	6	11

The degree of consistency between a person's values and attitudes is related to his or her involvement in social issues.

equality in the list of 12. As the table shows, freedom ranked high for all groups, but equality was considered relatively unimportant (next to last among the 12 values) for those unsympathetic to civil rights demonstrations.

The investigator then conducted a study similar to the one for syllogisms described earlier to see if inconsistency could induce attitude or value change. After obtaining students' value rankings and their attitudes toward civil rights demonstrations, he discussed with them the low ranking given to equality by those unsympathetic to civil rights demonstrations and speculated aloud that maybe such individuals cared a great deal about their own freedom but were indifferent to other people's freedom. Students were invited to ponder their own values and attitudes in this light. Three weeks later and then again three to five months later, they were asked to rank their values and to state their attitudes once more.

This study, like the syllogism study, found that inconsistency produced attitude change. In particular, students who had ranked equality high but who were initially against civil rights demonstrations became more pro–civil rights while retaining the importance of equality in their value rankings. Interestingly, the change in civil rights attitudes was greater after three to five months than it was only three weeks after the experiment — as if the changes needed time to filter through the belief system. Finally, students who had initially ranked equality low but were pro–civil rights raised the importance of equality in their value rankings and retained their pro–civil rights attitudes (Rokeach, 1968).

CONSISTENCY BETWEEN BELIEFS AND ATTITUDES Consistency between our beliefs and our attitudes is a common occurrence in daily life. If we come to believe that a certain automobile is highly reliable, gives a comfortable ride, and has good gas mileage, then we are likely to have a favorable attitude toward it. In such cases, our attitude seems to arise naturally and inevitably from the supporting beliefs. A number of researchers over the years have shown that it is even possible to make quantitative predictions of people's attitudes by using numerical scales and algebraic formulas to combine the relevant underlying beliefs and values (see Rosenberg, 1956; Fishbein, 1963). This kind of consistency closely follows the rules of formal logic demonstrated in the syllogism study.

But even the syllogism study revealed a kind of consistency between beliefs and attitudes that formal logic does not anticipate: there was a high correlation between the degree to which subjects believed the 48 propositions from the syllogisms to be true and their attitudes toward those propositions. The more they believed a proposition to be true, on the average, the more they thought it to be desirable. Furthermore, when subjects changed their degree of belief in a proposition, they also changed their attitude toward it. This kind of consistency is often called *rationalization*. If we come to believe that something is true, then we persuade ourselves that it is desirable, as well. The reverse sequence of reasoning may also take place: because we believe something to be desirable, we persuade ourselves that it is true. This is called *wishful thinking*. Both rationalization and wishful thinking could account for the correlation between the belief ratings and the attitude ratings. Both produce a consistency not of logic, but of psychologic, and they illustrate how beliefs and attitudes can affect one another.

CONSISTENCY BETWEEN ATTITUDES AND BEHAVIOR   A major reason for studying attitudes is the expectation that they enable us to predict behavior. A political candidate is interested in a survey of voter attitudes only if the attitudes expressed relate to voting behavior. The assumption that a person's attitudes determine his or her behavior is deeply ingrained in Western thinking, and in many instances the assumption holds. For example, a survey of presidential campaigns from 1952 to 1964 reveals that 85 percent of the voters surveyed showed a correspondence between their attitudes two months before the election and their actual vote in the election (Kelley & Mirer, 1974).

But in other cases, the assumption of attitude-behavior consistency appears to be violated. The classic study usually cited in this connection was conducted during the 1930s. A white professor traveled across the United States with a young Chinese couple. At that time, prejudice against Asians was quite strong, and no laws against racial discrimination in public accommodations existed. The three travelers stopped at over 200 hotels, motels, and restaurants and were served at all the restaurants and all but one of the hotels and motels without problem. Later, a letter was sent to all of the establishments visited asking them whether or not they would accept a Chinese couple as guests. Of the 128 replies received, 92 percent said they would not. In other words, these proprietors expressed attitudes that were much more prejudiced than their behavior (LaPiere, 1934).

This study illustrates that behavior is determined by many factors other than attitudes, and these other factors affect attitude-behavior consistency. One obvious factor is the degree of constraint in the situation: we must often act in ways that are not consonant with what we feel or believe. As children, we ate asparagus that we detested, and as adults we attend lectures and dinner parties that we would compare unfavorably to asparagus. In the racial discrimination study, the prejudiced proprietors may have found it difficult to act on their prejudices when actually faced with an Asian couple seeking service. Public accommodation laws against discrimination now make it even more difficult to display such prejudices than it was in 1934. Peer pressure can exert similar influences on behavior. For example, a teenager's attitude toward marijuana is moderately correlated with his or her actual use of marijuana, but the number of marijuana-using friends the teenager has is an even better predictor (Andrews & Kandel, 1979).

In general, attitudes tend to predict behavior best when they are (1) strong and consistent, (2) based upon the person's direct experience, and (3) specifically related to the behavior being predicted.

The importance of the strength and consistency of attitudes is illustrated by the surveys of presidential voting, mentioned earlier. Most of the attitude-vote

Attitudes and behaviors are not always consistent. Many health-minded individuals smoke nevertheless.

inconsistencies came from voters who had weak or ambivalent attitudes. Many such voters experience ambivalence because they are "cross-pressured" by friends and associates who do not agree with one another. For example, the Jewish businessperson belongs to an ethnic group that generally holds liberal political positions, but he or she also belongs to a business community that frequently holds conservative political positions, particularly on economic issues. When it comes time to vote, such a person experiences conflicting pressures. Ambivalence and conflict can arise from within the person as well. When the cognitive and affective components (the beliefs and the attitude, respectively) are not consistent with one another, then the attitude is usually not a reliable predictor of behavior (Norman, 1975).

Attitudes based on direct experience predict behavior better than do attitudes formed from just reading or hearing about an issue. For example, during a housing shortage at a university, many freshmen had to spend the first few weeks of the term in crowded temporary housing. Researchers measured attitudes of students toward the housing crisis and their willingness to sign and distribute petitions or to join committees to study it. For students who actually had to live in the temporary housing, there was a high correlation between their attitude toward the crisis and their willingness to take action to solve it. But for students who had not directly experienced the temporary housing, no such correlation existed (Regan & Fazio, 1977). There are many more examples of a strong relationship between behaviors and attitudes based on direct experiences (Fazio & Zanna, 1981).

Finally, specific attitudes tend to predict behavior better than attitudes only generally related to the behavior. For example, general environmental attitudes in one study were not related to a willingness to take action on behalf of the Sierra Club, but attitudes specifically toward the Sierra Club were strongly related (Weigel, Vernon, & Tognacci, 1974). Similarly, attitudes toward birth control correlated only .08 with a woman's use of oral contraceptives over a two-year span, but attitudes toward "the pill" in particular correlated .7 with that behavior (Davidson & Jaccard, 1979).

COGNITIVE DISSONANCE THEORY   Our discussion of attitude-behavior consistency has covered only half of the topic so far. We have examined how attitudes might lead to behavior, but it is also possible for behavior to lead to attitudes. The most influential theory of this sequence of events has been Leon Festinger's theory of cognitive dissonance. Like cognitive consistency theories in general, cognitive dissonance theory assumes that there is a drive toward cognitive consistency: two cognitions that are inconsistent with one another will produce discomfort that motivates the person to remove the inconsistency and to bring the cognitions into harmony. This inconsistency-produced discomfort is called *cognitive dissonance* (Festinger, 1957).

Although cognitive dissonance theory speaks generally about many kinds of inconsistency, it has been the most provocative in predicting that engaging in behavior that is counter to one's attitudes creates dissonance pressure to change the attitudes so they are consistent with the behavior. The theory further states that engaging in counterattitudinal behavior produces the most dissonance, and hence the most attitude change, when there are no other "consonant" reasons for engaging in the behavior. This was illustrated in an experiment that we have already discussed in the context of self-perception theory, the $1-$20 induced-compliance experiment by Festinger and Carlsmith (1959).

Recall that subjects in this study were induced to tell a waiting subject that a series of dull tasks had been fun and interesting. Subjects who had been paid $20 to do this did not change their attitudes, but subjects who had been paid only $1 came to believe that the tasks had, in fact, been enjoyable. According to cognitive dissonance theory, being paid $20 provides a consonant reason for complying with the experimenter's request to lie to the waiting subject, and hence the person experiences little or no dissonance. The inconsistency between the person's compliance and his or her attitude toward the tasks is swamped by the far greater consistency between the compliance and the incentive for complying. Accordingly, the subjects who were paid $20 did not change their attitudes. The subjects who were paid $1, however, had no consonant reason for complying. Accordingly, they experienced dissonance, which they reduced by coming to believe that they really did enjoy the tasks. The general conclusion is that dissonance-causing behavior will lead to attitude change when the behavior can be induced with a *minimum* amount of pressure, whether in the form of reward or punishment.

Experiments with children have confirmed the prediction about minimal punishment. If children obey a mild request not to play with an attractive toy, they come to believe that the toy is not as attractive as they first thought — a belief that is consistent with their observation that they are not playing with it. But if the children refrain from playing with the toy under a strong threat of punishment, they do not change their liking for the toy (Aronson & Carlsmith, 1963; Freedman, 1965).

Cognitive dissonance theory successfully predicts a number of other attitude change phenomena as well, and it has inspired extensive research and intensive debate.

Competing Theories of Induced Compliance

As we have now seen, both cognitive dissonance theory and self-perception theory claim to explain the results of induced-compliance studies. Dissonance theory is a motivational theory because it proposes that the inconsistency between the behavior and the person's initial attitude motivates him or her to change that attitude. In contrast, self-perception theory implies that the person's initial attitude is irrelevant and there is no discomfort produced by the behavior. People are seen not as *changing* their attitudes but as *inferring* what their own attitudes must be by observing their behavior. There is no drive or motivational process involved.

A third theory, *impression management theory*, proposes that subjects in such studies are motivated to make a good impression on the experimenter. In low incentive conditions (such as the $1 payment), their behavior appears to be an expression of their true attitudes, and hence expressing a contrary attitude at the end of the session would make them look inconsistent. Accordingly, they express an attitude consistent with their behavior. The attitude changes, then, are not seen as a result of internal cognitive dynamics but of a motivated attempt to avoid looking bad in a situation contrived by the experimenter (Tedeschi & Rosenfeld, 1981).

Each of these theories has been supported by several studies, and each of the theories has also generated data that the other theories cannot explain. Several investigators have now concluded that all the theories may be partially correct, and the focus of research should be on specifying when and where each theory applies (Fazio, Zanna, & Cooper, 1977; Paulhus, 1982; Baumeister & Tice, 1984).

This is a common outcome in the history of science. Scientists rarely adopt a new theory and discard another because a crucial experiment decides between them. Most often they switch theories because they are more interested in the problems that can be explored with the new theory and simply abandon for a time the problems dealt with by the older paradigm (Kuhn, 1970). For example, during the 1960s, when social psychologists were most interested in attitude change phenomena, cognitive dissonance theory was very popular. But when attention shifted to problems of attribution in the 1970s, self-perception theory seemed to provide a more congenial set of concepts. At the moment, the ways in which people present themselves to others is a topic of interest to many social psychologists, and thus impression management theories may become increasingly popular.

Beyond the Laboratory

Although the evidence for consistency among beliefs, attitudes, and behaviors seems impressive, psychologists and political scientists who have analyzed the public mind outside the social psychology laboratory are quite divided in their views about the ideological coherence of public opinion on important social and political issues (Kinder & Sears, 1985). One of those who believes the public to be ideologically innocent has said:

> As intellectuals and students of politics we are disposed by training and sensibility to take political ideas seriously. . . . We are therefore prone to forget that most people take them less seriously than we do, that they pay little attention to issues, rarely worry about the consistency of their opinions, and spend little or no time thinking about the values, presuppositions and implications that distinguish one political orientation from another. (McClosky, quoted by Abelson, 1968)

An example of such nonconsistency was revealed in a national survey taken by the *New York Times* and CBS News in the late 1970s. The survey showed that a majority of Americans said they disapprove of "most government-sponsored welfare programs." Yet 81 percent said they approve of the government's "program providing financial assistance for children raised in low-income homes where one parent is missing" (Aid to Families with Dependent Children, a major welfare program). Similarly, 81 percent endorsed the government's "helping poor people buy food for their families at cheaper prices" (the essence of the federal food-stamp program) and 82 percent approved of paying for health care for poor people (the Medicaid program). This pattern of support was similar among almost all types of people — rich and poor, liberal and conservative, Democrat and Republican.

An earlier national survey, designed specifically to probe this kind of inconsistency, found a similar contradiction between an *ideological* conservatism and an *operational* liberalism in attitudes toward welfare. One out of four Americans was classified as conservative on questions concerning the general concept of welfare but simultaneously classified as liberal on questions concerning specific welfare programs (Free & Cantril, 1967).

It is important to be cautious about accusing someone of being inconsistent, however, because his or her opinions may simply be inconsistent with the ideological framework of the investigator. Inconsistency may be in the eye of the beholder. Thus, opposition to capital punishment is usually characterized as a "liberal" position, whereas opposition to legalized abortion is usually thought of as a "conservative" position. And yet there is quite a logical coherence to the views of a person who, being against all taking of life, opposes both capital

Many Americans who are ideologically conservative — opposing government-sponsored welfare programs — are also operationally liberal, supporting, for example, housing and food assistance programs. Nonconsistency of beliefs and attitudes seems to be more prevalent than consistency.

punishment and legalized abortion. Another example is provided by "libertarians," who are opposed to any government interference in our lives. They are "conservative" on economic issues (the free market should govern the economic system) and in their opposition to government-enforced civil rights laws. But they are "liberal" on personal social issues, believing, for example, that the government should not criminalize the use of marijuana or concern itself with our private sexual behavior. To libertarians, both conservatives and liberals are inconsistent.

Nevertheless, the evidence suggests that most citizens do not organize their beliefs and attitudes according to any kind of overall ideology; nonconsistency, if not inconsistency, seems more prevalent than consistency. This has led one investigator to propose that many of our opinions exist as isolated *opinion molecules*. Each molecule is made up of (1) a belief, (2) an attitude, and (3) a perception of social support for the opinion. In other words, each opinion molecule contains a fact, a feeling, and a following (Abelson, 1968): "It's a fact that when my Uncle Charlie had back trouble, he was cured by a chiropractor *[fact]*"; "You know, I feel that chiropractors have been sneered at too much *[feeling]*, and I'm not ashamed to say so because I know a lot of people who feel the same way *[following]*." Or, "Americans don't really want the Equal Rights Amendment *[following]*, and neither do I *[feeling]*. It would lead to unisex bathrooms *[fact]*."

Opinion molecules serve important social functions. First, they act as conversational units, giving us something coherent to say when a particular topic comes up in conversation. They also give a rational appearance to our unexamined agreement with friends and neighbors on social issues. But most important, they serve as badges of identification with our important social groups. They stem from and reinforce our group identifications. Thus, the "fact" and the "feeling" are less important ingredients of an opinion molecule than the "following."

In general, this chapter has treated beliefs, attitudes, and values as cognitive artifacts. In Chapter 18, the chapter on social influence, we shall examine them as social artifacts.

SOCIAL PSYCHOLOGY OF INTERPERSONAL ATTRACTION

Of all our attitudes, the most important are undoubtedly our attitudes toward other people. The questions that often concern us most whenever we meet new people are whether or not they like us and we like them. Beyond the initial encounter, our concerns often center upon how to nurture and guide the relationship from an initial liking or attraction to a deeper friendship or possibly even to intimacy and love. It is probably not an exaggeration to say that fostering personal relationships is a top priority for most people much of the time. Accordingly, social psychologists have long been interested in the factors that promote liking or interpersonal attraction, and they have recently shown a willingness to enter the thickets of love and intimacy as well. Some of the findings have confirmed commonly held notions about liking and loving, but others have produced surprises. We begin with liking — namely, friendship and the early stages of more intimate love relationships.

Determinants of Liking

After years of speculation and gossip, Great Britain's Prince Charles finally married. To social psychologists, the least surprising aspect of his choice was that he married "the girl next door," a woman whom he had known for years and who shared many of his social background characteristics, attitudes, and interests. And as many proud British were quick to point out, she was as pretty as he was handsome. As we shall see, these are precisely the determinants of interpersonal attraction: proximity, familiarity, and similarity. It also helps, alas, to be beautiful.

PHYSICAL ATTRACTIVENESS To most of us, there is something mildly undemocratic about the possibility that a person's physical appearance is a determinant of how well others like him or her. Unlike character, niceness, and other personal attributes, physical appearance is a factor over which we have little control, and hence it seems unfair to use it as a criterion for liking someone. In fact, surveys taken over a span of several decades have shown that people do not rank physical attractiveness as very important in their liking of other people (Perrin, 1921; Tesser & Brodie, 1971).

But research on actual behavior shows otherwise. A group of psychologists set up a "computer dance" in which each person was randomly paired with a partner. At intermission, each person filled out an anonymous questionnaire evaluating his or her date. In addition, the experimenters obtained several personality test scores for each person, as well as an independent estimate of his or her physical attractiveness. The results showed that only physical attractiveness played a role in how much each person was liked by his or her partner. None of the measures of intelligence, social skills, or personality were related to the partners' liking for one another (Walster, Aronson, Abrahams, & Rottmann, 1966). Moreover, the importance of physical attractiveness continues to operate not only on first dates but on subsequent ones, as well (Mathes, 1975).

The importance of physical attractiveness is not confined just to dating and mating patterns. For example, physically attractive boys and girls (5 and 6 years of age) are more popular with their peers than are less attractive children (Dion & Berscheid, 1972). Even adults are affected by a child's physical attractiveness. One investigator had women read a description of an aggressive act committed by a 7-year-old child. The description was accompanied by a photograph of either an attractive or an unattractive child. The women believed that attractive children were less likely than unattractive children to commit a similar aggressive act in the future (Dion, 1972).

Why is physical attractiveness so important? As this last finding reminds us, part of the reason is the popular stereotype of physically attractive people that was discussed earlier. Beautiful people not only are thought to have more beautiful personalities, but there is some evidence that they actually do — in part because we treat them more beautifully.

Research also suggests that our own social standing and self-esteem are enhanced when we are seen with physically attractive companions. Both men and women are rated more favorably when they are with an attractive romantic partner or friend than when they are with an unattractive companion (Sigall & Landy, 1973; Sheposh, Deming, & Young, 1977). But there is an interesting twist on this: both men and women are rated *less* favorably when they are seen with a *stranger* who is physically more attractive than they (Kernis & Wheeler, 1981). This suffer-by-contrast effect has been found in other studies. For example, male college students who had just watched a TV show starring beautiful young women gave lower attractiveness ratings to a photograph of a more typical-looking woman — as did both men and women who were first shown a photograph of a highly attractive woman (Kenrick & Gutierres, 1980).

Fortunately, there is hope for the unbeautiful among us. First of all, physical attractiveness appears to decline in importance when we are choosing a marriage partner (Stroebe, Insko, Thompson, & Layton, 1971). And, as we shall now see, several more democratic factors can work in our favor.

PROXIMITY   An examination of 5,000 marriage license applications in Philadelphia in the 1930s found that one-third of the couples lived within five blocks of each other (Rubin, 1973). Research shows that the best single predictor of whether two people are friends is how far apart they live. In a study of friendship patterns in apartment houses, residents were asked to name the three people they saw socially most often. Residents mentioned 41 percent of neighbors who lived in the apartment next door, 22 percent of those who lived two doors away (about 30 feet), and only 10 percent of those who lived at the other end of the hall (Festinger, Schachter, & Back, 1950).

Studies of college dormitories show the same effect. After a full academic year, roommates were twice as likely as floormates to be friends, and floormates were more than twice as likely as dormitory residents in general to be friends (Priest & Sawyer, 1967). A study of male students at the Training Academy of the Maryland State Police is even more striking. The academy assigns trainees to dormitory rooms and classroom seats by name in alphabetical order. Thus the closer two trainees' last names are alphabetically, the more likely they are to spend time in close proximity to one another. The researchers asked trainees who had been at the academy for six months to name their three closest friends there. Despite an intensive training course in which all trainees get to know one another quite well, there was a strong "alphabetical" proximity effect. On the average, each person chosen as a best friend was only 4.5 letters away from the person who chose him, which was an alphabetical proximity significantly closer than chance (Segal, 1974).

There are cases, of course, in which neighbors and roommates hate one another, and the major exception to the friendship-promoting effect of proximity seems to occur when there are initial antagonisms. In a test of this, a subject waited in a laboratory with a female confederate who acted in either a pleasant or an unpleasant way toward the subject. When she acted pleasantly, the closer she

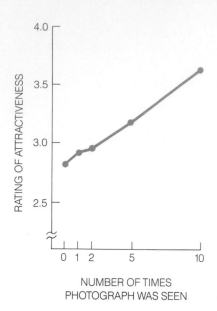

FIGURE 17-3
Familiarity Breeds Liking *Subjects were asked to rate photographs of unknown faces according to how much they thought they would like the person. The lowest ratings of attractiveness were made by subjects who had never seen the photograph before; the highest ratings of attractiveness were made by subjects who had seen the photograph most often. (After Zajonc, 1968)*

sat to the subject, the better she was liked; when she acted unpleasantly, the closer she sat to the subject, the less she was liked. Proximity simply increased the intensity of the initial reaction (Schiffenbauer & Schiavo, 1976). But since most initial encounters probably range from neutral to pleasant, the most frequent result of sustained proximity is friendship.

Those who believe in miracles when it comes to matters of the heart may believe that there is a perfect mate for each of us waiting to be discovered somewhere in the world. But if this is true, the far greater miracle is the frequency with which the Fates conspire to place this person within walking distance.

FAMILIARITY One of the major reasons that proximity creates liking is that it increases *familiarity,* and there is now abundant research that familiarity all by itself — sheer exposure — increases liking (Zajonc, 1968). This is a quite general phenomenon. For example, rats repeatedly exposed to either the music of Mozart or Schoenberg come to prefer the composer they have heard, and humans repeatedly exposed to selected nonsense syllables or Chinese characters come to prefer those they have seen most often. Perhaps more germane to the present discussion is a study in which subjects were exposed to pictures of faces and then were asked how much they thought they would like the person shown. The more frequently they had seen a particular face, the more they said they liked it and thought they would like the person (see Figure 17-3).

In one clever demonstration of the *familiarity breeds liking effect,* the investigators took photographs of college women and prepared prints of both the original face and its mirror image. These prints were then shown to the women themselves, their women friends, and their lovers. The women themselves preferred the mirror image prints by a margin of 68 percent to 32 percent, but the friends and lovers preferred the nonreversed prints by a margin of 61 percent to 39 percent (Mita, Dermer, & Knight, 1977). Can you guess why?

The familiarity breeds liking effect is quite robust. Investigators have found this in studies that use actual interaction, not just photographs, and also in studies in which the person remains unaware of the stimulus (Moreland & Zajonc, 1979; Wilson, 1979). The effect is observed even when the surrounding situation is unpleasant (Saegert, Swap, & Zajonc, 1973) and when the target stimuli themselves are neutral or moderately negative to begin with. Only when the stimuli are quite negative does the effect fail to occur (Perlman & Oskamp, 1971). There is a possibility, too, that extreme levels of repetition may induce boredom and limit the effect.

The moral is clear. If you are not beautiful or you find your admiration of someone unreciprocated, be persistent and hang around. Proximity and familiarity are your most powerful weapons.

SIMILARITY There is an old saying that opposites attract, and lovers are fond of recounting how different they are from each other: "I love boating, but she prefers mountain climbing"; "I'm in engineering, but he's a history major." What such lovers overlook is that they both like outdoor activities; they are both preprofessionals; they are both Democrats; they are both the same nationality, the same religion, the same social class, the same educational level, and they are probably within three years of each other in age and within two IQ points of each other in intelligence. In short, the old saying is mostly false.

Research all the way back to 1870 supports this conclusion. Over 99 percent of the married couples in the United States are of the same race, and 94 percent are of the same religion. Moreover, statistical surveys show that husbands and wives are significantly similar to each other not only on sociological characteristics — such as age, race, religion, education, and socioeconomic class — but also with respect to psychological characteristics, such as intelligence, and physical characteristics, such as height and eye color (Rubin, 1973). A study of dating couples finds the same patterns, in addition to finding that couples were also similar in their attitudes about sexual behavior and sex roles. Moreover, couples who were most similar in background at the beginning of the study were most likely to be together one year later (Hill, Rubin, & Peplau, 1976). Of particular pertinence to our earlier discussion of physical attractiveness is the finding that couples are closely matched on this dimension as well, a finding that has shown up in several studies (Berscheid & Walster, 1974).

For example, in one study, judges rated photographs of each partner of 99 couples for physical attractiveness without knowing who was paired with whom. The physical attractiveness ratings of the couples matched each other significantly more closely than did the ratings of photographs that were randomly paired into couples (Murstein, 1972). Similar results were obtained in a real-life field study in which separate observers rated the physical attractiveness of members of couples in bars and theater lobbies and at social events (Silverman, 1971).

This matching of couples on physical attractiveness is usually explained in terms of the *expectancy-value theory* of decision making. This theory states that we consider not only the reward value of the particular choice — the potential partner's attractiveness — but also the expectancy of success — the probability the person is willing to pair up with us. Put bluntly, less attractive people seek less attractive people because they expect to be rejected by someone more attractive than themselves. A study of a video dating service found that both men and women were most likely to pursue a relationship with someone who matched them on physical attractiveness. Only the most attractive people sought dates with the most attractive partners (Folkes, 1982). The overall result of this chilling marketplace process is attractiveness similarity: most of us end up with partners who are about as attractive as we are.

But similarities on dimensions other than physical attractiveness are probably even more important over the long-term course of a relationship. In one ambitious study of similarity and friendship, male students received free rent for the year in a large house at the University of Michigan in exchange for their participation. On the basis of information from tests and questionnaires, some men were assigned roommates who were quite similar to them and others were assigned roommates who were quite dissimilar. The investigator observed the friendship patterns that developed over the course of the year, obtaining more questionnaire and attitude data from the participants at regular intervals. In all other respects, the men lived as they would in any dormitory.

Roommates who were initially similar generally liked each other and ended up as better friends than those who were dissimilar. When the study was repeated with a new group of men the next year, however, the familiarity breeds liking effect turned out to be even more powerful than similarity. Regardless of whether low or high similarity had been the basis for room assignments, roommates came to like each other (Newcomb, 1961).

One reason that similarity produces liking is probably that people value their own opinions and preferences and enjoy being with others who validate their choices, possibly boosting their self-esteem in the process. But perhaps the major reason that similarity produces liking is just a repeat of factors we have seen before, proximity and familiarity. Both social norms and situational circumstances throw us together with people who are like us. Most religious groups prefer or insist that their members date and mate within the religion, and cultural norms regulate what is considered acceptable in terms of race and age

matches—a couple comprising an older woman and a younger man is still viewed as inappropriate. Situational circumstances also play an important role. Many couples meet in college or graduate school, thus assuring that they will be similar in educational level, general intelligence, professional aspirations, and probably in age and socioeconomic status. Moreover, tennis players will have met on the tennis courts, political liberals at the antiapartheid rally, and gay people at a meeting of the Gay People's Union.

Despite all this, the saying that opposites attract may still apply to certain complementary personality traits (Winch, Ktsanes, & Ktsanes, 1954). To take the most obvious example, one partner may be quite dominant and thus require someone who is relatively more submissive. A person with strong preferences may do best with someone who is very flexible or even wishy-washy. This has been called the *need-complementarity hypothesis.* But even in the case of complementary traits, an underlying similarity of attitudes can often be discerned. For example, the marital relationship in which the husband is dominant and the wife is submissive will be smooth only if both agree on the desirability of these traditional sex roles. Even successful complementarity requires a basic similarity of attitudes favoring the dissimilarity.

The major problem with the need-complementarity hypothesis, however, is that there is not much evidence for it (Levinger, Senn, & Jorgensen, 1970). In one study, marital adjustment among couples married for up to five years was found to depend more on similarity than on complementarity (Meyer & Pepper, 1977). And attempts to identify the pairs of personality traits that bring about complementarity have not been very successful. When all is said and done, it is similarity that wins the day.

Love

The process by which relationships move from liking toward greater closeness and intimacy has been called *social penetration* (Altman & Taylor, 1973). Social penetration has both breadth and depth. Breadth refers to the number of different areas of the partners' lives and personalities that are involved in the relationship, and depth refers to the degree to which the pair know and share things that are close to the cores of their personalities — hopes, desires, fears, anxieties, uncertainties, and so forth.

The key to social penetration is *reciprocal self-disclosure;* the partners must reveal themselves to each other, and this can be a very delicate process. At the beginning of a relationship, there is a strong *norm of reciprocity;* as one person begins to disclose things about himself or herself, the other person must also be willing to do so. In this way, trust builds and intimacy increases. Research shows that the pace of self-disclosure is very important. If one of the partners discloses too much too soon, it can cause the other person to pull back (Rubin, 1975).

In romantic relationships these days, self-disclosure takes place rather early. In one study, most of the couples who had been going together an average of eight months had engaged in full and equal disclosure about very personal and private areas of their lives (Rubin, Hill, Peplau, & Dunkel-Schetter, 1980). About three-fourths of the women and men said they had fully revealed their feelings about their sexual relationship, almost half had fully disclosed their thoughts about the future of the relationship, and over half had provided full information about their previous sexual experiences. One-third of each sex had revealed fully the things about themselves that they were most ashamed of.

Such rapid and full self-disclosure has not always been the norm. In one study, both college students and senior citizens were asked to describe relationships characteristic of 22-year-olds of their own generations. The results showed that today's young people expect pairs to disclose both positive and negative feelings more openly and freely than had previous generations (Rands & Levinger, 1979). Up through the 1950s, the middle-class norm emphasized much more self-restraint and self-protectiveness. The sexual revolution of the 1960s changed not only sexual behavior but also social norms concerning self-disclosure (Altman & Taylor, 1973). This was the era of the encounter group and instant intimacy. Although much of the popularity of encounter groups has declined, the new norms of self-disclosure have been sustained in romantic relationships.

The concept of romantic love is an old one, but the belief that it has much to do with marriage is more recent and far from universal. In some non-Western cultures, marriage is still considered to be a contractual or financial arrangement that has nothing whatever to do with love. In our own society, the link between love and marriage has actually become stronger in the past 20 years. In 1967, about two-thirds of college men but only about one-fourth of college women stated that they would not marry a person they did not love even if the person had all the other qualities they desired (Kephart, 1967). Perhaps the women at that time had to be more practical about their financial security. But in a 1976 replication of the study, a full 86 percent of the men and 80 percent of the women would now refuse to marry without being in love. In fact, these researchers report that many young men and women believe that if romantic love disappears from the relationship, that is sufficient reason to end it (Campbell & Berscheid, 1976).

A study of long-term marriages in the United States and Japan suggests that these romantic views may change with time. The American marriages started out with a higher level of love than did Japanese arranged marriages, as measured by expressions of affection, sexual interest, and marital satisfaction. The amount of love that couples shared decreased in both groups until there were no differences between the two groups after ten years (Blood, 1967). As the sixteenth-century writer Giraldi put it: "The history of a love affair is in some sense the drama of its fight against time."

This decline of romantic love does not spell marital failure, however. Many couples in this study reported quite gratifying marriages. These successful marriages were characterized by communication between the partners, an equitable division of labor, and equality of decision-making power. Romantic love is terrific for starters, but the sustaining forces of a good long-term relationship are less exciting, undoubtedly require more work, and have more to do with equality than with passion. A disappointment for romantics, perhaps, but heartening news and powerful propaganda for advocates of sexual equality.

SUMMARY

1. *Social psychology* is the study of social interaction, of how we think, feel, and act in the presence of other people, and of how, in turn, our thoughts, feelings, and actions are influenced by others. Social psychology emphasizes that human behavior is a function of both the person and the situation.
2. In attempting to understand others and ourselves, we construct intuitive theories of human behavior by performing the same tasks as a formal scientist: *collecting data, detecting covariation,* and *inferring causality.* Our theories themselves, however, can shape our perceptions of the data, distort our estimates of covariation, and bias our evaluations of cause and effect. For example, we tend to notice and recall information that is vivid rather than pallid, and this biases our social judgments.

3. *Schematic processing* is the perceiving and interpreting of incoming information in terms of simplified memory structures called *schemata*. Schemata of classes of persons are called *stereotypes*, and schemata of events and social interactions are called *scripts*. Schemata constitute miniature theories of everyday objects and events. They allow us to process social information efficiently by permitting us to encode and to remember only the unique or most prominent features of a new object or event.

4. Because schemata constitute simplifications of reality, schematic processing produces biases and errors in our processing of social information. In forming impressions of other people, for example, we are prone to the *primacy effect;* the first information we receive evokes an initial schema and, hence, becomes more powerful in determining our impression than does later information. In general, schematic processing produces perceptions that are resistant to change and relatively impervious to new data.

5. We are not very accurate at detecting covariations or correlations between variables. When our schemata or theories lead us to expect two things to covary, we overestimate their actual correlation; but when we do not have a theory, we underestimate their correlation.

6. Stereotypes, like other schemata, are resistant to change. Moreover, they can be self-perpetuating and self-fulfilling, because they influence those who hold them to behave in ways that actually evoke the stereotyped behavior in others.

7. *Attribution* is the process by which we attempt to interpret and to explain the behavior of other people — that is, to discern the causes of their actions. We tend to attribute an action or event to a potential cause with which it covaries — provided that it varies only with that potential cause *(distinctiveness)* and does so over several occasions *(consistency)* and for several observers *(consensus)*.

8. One major attribution task is to decide whether someone's action should be attributed to *dispositional causes* (the person's personality or attitudes) or to *situational* causes (social forces or other external circumstances). We tend to give too much weight to dispositional factors and too little to situational factors. This bias has been called the *fundamental attribution error*. Many principles of schematic processing and attribution apply to the process of *self-perception*. Individuals sometimes commit the fundamental attribution error about their own behavior.

9. *Attitudes* are likes and dislikes for identifiable aspects of the environment — objects, persons, events, or ideas. Attitudes are the *affective* component of a three-part system that also includes beliefs (the *cognitive* component) and actions (the *behavioral* component). A major question in attitude research is the degree of consistency among these components, particularly between attitudes and behavior. In general, attitudes predict behavior best when they are (1) strong and consistent, (2) based upon the person's direct experience, and (3) specifically related to the behavior being predicted.

10. *Cognitive dissonance theory* proposes that when a person's actions are inconsistent with his or her attitudes, the discomfort produced by this dissonance leads the person to bring the attitudes into line with the actions. *Self-perception theory* and *impression management theory* offer alternative explanations for the same phenomenon. All three theories may be partially correct but under different circumstances.

11. Social scientists are divided in their views about the degree to which citizens hold coherent opinions about social and political issues. Many opinions appear to serve social rather than intellectual functions for the person, such as reinforcing his or her group identifications.

12. Many factors influence whether we will be attracted to someone. The most important are *physical attractiveness, proximity, familiarity,* and *similarity*. The process by which relationships move from liking toward greater intimacy has been called *social penetration*. The key to social penetration is reciprocal self-

disclosure. Early and full self-disclosure among couples is much commoner now than it was in earlier years.

13. Cross-cultural observations suggest that the sustaining forces of a good long-term relationship have less to do with the intensity of romantic love than with communication between the partners, an equitable division of labor, and equality of decision making.

FURTHER READING

The major theme of this chapter—that persons act as informal scientists in arriving at social judgments—is treated in detail in Nisbett and Ross, *Human Inference: Strategies and Shortcomings of Social Judgment* (1985). A number of books deal in more depth with the other topics discussed. Recommended are Bem, *Beliefs, Attitudes, and Human Affairs* (1970); Berscheid and Walster, *Interpersonal Attraction* (2nd ed., 1978); and Aronson, *The Social Animal* (4th ed., 1984).

Two comprehensive textbooks in this area are Brown, *Social Psychology, the Second Edition* (1985); and Sears, Freedman, and Peplau, *Social Psychology* (5th ed., 1985). More technical, in-depth treatments are available in Lindzey and Aronson (eds), *The Handbook of Social Psychology* (3rd ed., 1985).

Social Influence

18

As we noted in Chapter 17, social psychology is, in part, the study of how an individual's thoughts, feelings, and behaviors are influenced by others. To most of us, the term *social influence* connotes a deliberate attempt by a person or a group to change our beliefs, attitudes, or behaviors. Examples include a parent's attempt to make a child eat spinach, a TV commercial's efforts to induce us to buy a particular product, and the more dramatic attempts of a religious cult to persuade a young person to abandon school and family and to devote full loyalty to a "higher" mission.

Social psychologists (Kelman, 1961) have identified three basic processes of social influence:

1. *Compliance* The person at whom the influence is directed (the "target") publicly conforms to the wishes of the influencing source but does not change his or her private beliefs or attitudes. (The child eats the spinach but continues to dislike it.)
2. *Internalization* The target changes his or her beliefs, attitudes, or behaviors because of a genuine belief in the validity of the position advocated by the influencing source. (A middle-aged man gives up smoking after reading—and believing—the surgeon general's warnings that smoking causes cancer.)
3. *Identification* The target changes his or her beliefs, attitudes, or behaviors in order to resemble an influencing source that is respected or admired. (A high school girl takes up smoking in order to be like a group of older girls she admires.)

We shall examine each of these processes in this chapter.

Many forms of social influence are both subtle and unintentional. For example, we shall see that the mere physical presence of others can influence us in a number of unexpected ways. In addition, we are strongly influenced by *social norms*—implicit rules and expectations that tell us what we ought to think and how we ought to behave. These range from the trivial to the profound. Social norms tell us to face forward when riding in an elevator and govern how long we can gaze at a stranger before being considered rude. Social norms can also create and maintain an entire ideology of racism or sexism in a society. Moreover, even the overt forms of influence often succeed because they rest on subtle social norms to which we give allegiance without being aware of it.

Because social norms can influence us even when other people are not actually present, the definition of social psychology usually includes how an individual's thoughts, feelings, and behaviors are influenced by the *actual, imagined, or implied* presence of others (G. Allport, 1985). And it is social influence in this broader sense that concerns us in this chapter.

Social influence is central to human interaction and to communal life. Cooperation, community, altruism, and love all involve social influence. But we tend to take these phenomena for granted and to focus our concern on influences that cause us grief. For sociohistorical reasons, psychologists have focused on the social influences that cause the society grief. Accordingly, just as the chapter on abnormal psychology focuses on the dark side of individual behavior, this chapter also dwells on the dark side of social behavior. Some of the findings are disturbing, even depressing. But just as the study of abnormal psychology has led to effective therapies, the study of problematic social influences has led us to more effective ways of dealing with them. As we shall see, the principles of social influence that can produce evil are the same principles that can produce the antidote to evil.

PRESENCE OF OTHERS

Social Facilitation

In 1897, the psychologist Norman Triplett was examining the speed records of bicycle racers and noticed that many cyclists achieved higher speeds when they raced against each other than when they raced alone against the clock. This led him to perform one of social psychology's earliest laboratory experiments. He instructed children to turn a fishing reel as fast as they could for a fixed period of time. Sometimes two children worked at the same time in the same room, each with his or her own reel. Other times they worked alone. Although his published data are difficult to interpret (Schmitt & Bem, 1986), Triplett reported that many children worked faster in *coaction* — that is, when another child doing the same task was present — than when they worked alone.

Since this experiment, many studies have demonstrated the facilitating effects of coaction with both human and animal subjects. For example, college students will complete more multiplication problems in coaction than when alone (F. Allport, 1920, 1924), worker ants in groups will dig more than three times as much sand per ant than when alone (Chen, 1937), and many animals will eat more food if other members of their species are present (for example, Platt, Yaksh, & Darby, 1967).

Soon after Triplett's experiment on coaction, psychologists discovered that the presence of a passive spectator — an audience rather than a coactor — also facilitates performance. For example, the presence of an audience had the same facilitating effect on students' multiplication performance as did that of the coactors in the earlier study (Dashiell, 1930). These coaction and audience effects collectively have been called *social facilitation*.

But even this simplest case of social influence turns out to be more complicated than social psychologists first thought. For example, researchers found that subjects made more errors on the multiplication problems when in coaction or in the presence of an audience than when they performed alone (Dashiell, 1930). In other words, the quality of performance declined even though quantity increased. In other studies, however, the quality of performance improved when coactors or audiences were present (for example, Dashiell, 1935; Cottrell, 1972). How can these contradictions be reconciled?

A close examination has revealed that behaviors showing improved performance in the presence of coactors or audiences usually involve either highly practiced responses or instinctive responses, such as eating. When performing such practiced or instinctive behaviors, the most likely or most dominant response is the correct one. Behaviors that show impaired performance are those in which the possibility is greater that the most likely or most dominant response

Social facilitation — the presence of an audience can facilitate performance.

could be wrong. On a multiplication problem, for example, there are many wrong answers but only one correct one. A well-known principle of motivation explains this pattern of findings: a high level of drive or arousal tends to energize the dominant responses of an organism. If the mere presence of another member of the species raises the general arousal or drive level of an organism, then simple or well-learned behaviors should show social facilitation, since these behaviors would be the dominant response. More complex behavior or behavior just being learned—in which the dominant or most likely response is more apt to be incorrect—would be impaired when the organism is in an aroused state (Zajonc, 1965, 1980).

A number of experiments with both human and animal subjects tested this theory of social facilitation. In one particularly clever study, cockroaches were permitted to run down a straight runway into a darkened goal box to escape a bright floodlight (see Figure 18-1). Researchers found that the roaches reached the goal box faster if they ran in pairs than if they ran alone. But when the escape response was made more complicated by requiring the roaches to make a right-angle turn to find the goal box, pairs of roaches took longer to reach the box than did single roaches. In other words, the presence of coactors facilitated performance in the simple runway but impaired performance in the complex runway (Zajonc, Heingartner, & Herman, 1969). This experiment was repeated by having all of the roaches run alone, but with an "audience" of four roaches which watched from small plexiglass boxes set alongside the runways. Again, the presence of other roaches— even if they were just spectators—facilitated performance when the dominant response (running down the straight runway) was correct and impaired performance when the dominant response was incorrect.

Studies with human subjects have also confirmed this theory of social facilitation. One such study was analogous to the cockroach experiment, showing that subjects learn a simple maze faster, but a complex maze more slowly, when an audience is present than when it is not (Hunt & Hillery, 1973). People also memorize easy word lists faster, but difficult word lists more slowly, in the presence of an audience than when alone (Cottrell, Rittle, & Wack, 1967).

Because social facilitation effects occur in lower organisms, they would not seem to be due to complex cognitive processes. But one theory suggests that social facilitation in humans is due not to the mere presence of others but to feelings of competition or to concerns about being evaluated, and it is these cognitive concerns that raise the drive level. Even the early studies of coaction found that, if all elements of rivalry and competition were removed, social facilitation effects would be reduced or eliminated (Dashiell, 1930). Other studies show that audience effects vary, depending on how much the person feels that he or she is being evaluated. For example, performance is enhanced if an "expert" is watching, but it is diminished if the audience consists only of "undergraduates who want to watch a psychology experiment" (Henchy & Glass, 1968; Paulus & Murdock, 1971). In one study, when the audience wore blindfolds and hence could not watch or evaluate the individual's performance, the subject's performance showed no social facilitation effects (Cottrell, Wack, Sekerak, & Rittle, 1968).

One problem with most of these studies, however, is that subjects may still feel concern about being evaluated, even in the alone and mere presence conditions, because they know that their performances are being recorded and evaluated by the experimenter. Thus, these studies still leave open the question of whether or not social facilitation effects in humans ever arise purely from the mere presence of others.

In a study designed to eliminate subjects' concerns about being evaluated in both the alone and mere presence conditions, each subject was shown to a waiting

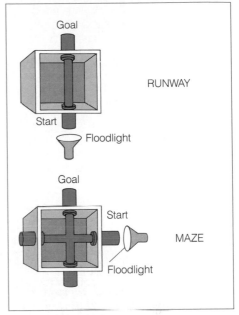

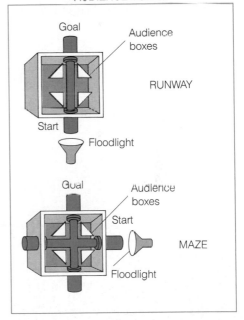

FIGURE 18-1
Social Facilitation Experiment
Diagrams of runways and mazes used in Zajonc's social facilitation experiment with cockroaches. (After Zajonc, 1965)

CONDITION	MEAN NUMBER OF SECONDS TO COMPLETE TYPING TASK	
	EASY TASK	DIFFICULT TASK
Alone (Baseline)	15	52
Evaluation	7	63
Mere Presence	10	73

TABLE 18-1
Social Facilitation in the Mere Presence of Another Individual   *The mere presence of another individual produces social facilitation effects. When subjects either are being evaluated or are merely in the presence of another individual, they perform an easy task more quickly but a difficult task more slowly than they would if alone. (After Schmitt, Gilovich, Goore, & Joseph, in press)*

room, seated in front of a computer, and asked to provide some "background information before the experiment begins." The computer first prompted the subject to enter his or her name (such as "Joan Smith") and then to construct a code name by typing his or her name backwards and alternating each letter with ascending digits (for example, "h1t2i3m4S5n6a7o8J"). In actuality, that was the entire experiment, and it was over before the subject realized that the experiment had even begun. The computer automatically recorded how long it took the subject to type his or her name (the easy task) and the code name (the difficult task). One group of subjects typed while alone in the room (alone condition). Another group of subjects typed while the experimenter looked over their shoulders (evaluation condition). A third group typed in the presence of a blindfolded person who wore headphones, faced away from the subject, and was said to be waiting to be in a sensory deprivation experiment (mere presence condition).

The results revealed that social facilitation effects *can* be produced by the mere presence of another individual (see Table 18-1). Compared to subjects in the alone condition, subjects in both the evaluation and mere presence conditions performed the easy task more quickly but the difficult task more slowly, which upheld the pattern of social facilitation (Schmitt, Gilovich, Goore, & Joseph, in press).

Two additional theories have been proposed to account for social facilitation effects. Distraction-conflict theory suggests that the presence of others distracts a person, causing a conflict over how to allocate attention between the others and the task to be performed. It is this attentional conflict — rather than a concern about another person's presence or ability to judge — that raises the drive level and causes social facilitation effects (Sanders & Baron, 1975; Baron, 1986). Self-presentation theory proposes that the presence of others enhances an individual's desire to present a favorable image. On easy tasks, this leads to greater effort and concentration and thus to improved performance. On difficult tasks, however, this desire magnifies the frustrations imposed by the task and leads to embarrassment, withdrawal, or excessive anxiety, all of which lead to poorer performance (Bond, 1982). There are research results that support each of these theories, and it seems likely that all of the proposed conditions — mere presence, concern over evaluation, distraction-conflict, and desire to present a favorable image — contribute to social facilitation effects (Sanders, 1984).

Deindividuation

At about the same time that Triplett was performing his laboratory experiment on social facilitation, another observer of human behavior, Gustave Le Bon, was taking a less dispassionate view of group coaction. In his book *The Crowd* (1895), he complained that "the crowd is always intellectually inferior to the isolated individual. . . . The mob man is fickle, credulous, and intolerant, showing the violence and ferocity of primitive beings . . . women, children, savages, and lower classes . . . operating under the influence of the spinal cord." Le Bon believed that the aggressive and immoral behaviors shown by lynch mobs (and, in his view, by the underclasses during the French Revolution) spread by "contagion" through a mob or crowd, breaking down the moral sense and self-control of men — if not of women, children, or savages. This caused crowds to commit destructive acts that no single individual would commit.

Despite his obvious prejudices, Le Bon's observations did seem to have some validity. The modern counterpart to his theory is built on the concept of *deindividuation*, an idea first proposed by Festinger, Pepitone, and Newcomb (1952) and extended by Zimbardo (1970) and Diener (1979, 1980). Their theories propose that certain conditions that are often present in groups can lead individuals

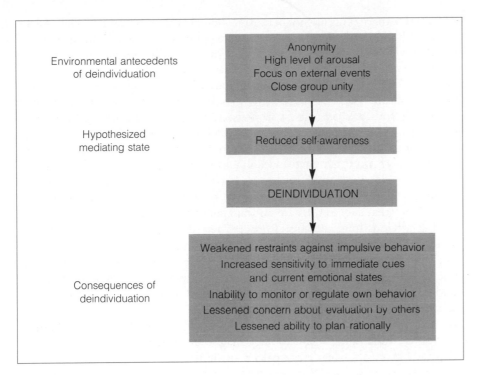

FIGURE 18-2
Antecedents and Consequences of Deindividuation *One explanation of crowd behavior traces it to a loss of personal identity in certain group situations. (After Diener, 1979)*

to experience a psychological state of *deindividuation*, a feeling that they have lost their personal identities and have merged anonymously into the group. This produces diminished restraints against impulsive behavior and other cognitive and emotional conditions associated with unruly mob behavior. The several antecedents and consequences of deindividuation proposed by Diener are illustrated in Figure 18-2. Note that antecedent conditions lead to deindividuation by producing a state of reduced self-awareness in the individual.

Most studies on deindividuation have explored the effects of the antecedent variable of anonymity. In one study, college women, participating in groups of four, were required to deliver electric shocks to another woman who was supposedly in a learning experiment. Half of the women were deindividuated by making them feel anonymous. They were dressed in bulky laboratory coats and hoods that hid their faces, and the experimenter only spoke to them as a group, never referring to any of them by name. The remaining women were individuated by having them remain in their own clothes and wear large identification tags. In addition, the women in the second group were introduced to each other by name. During the experiment, each woman had a button in front of her that she was to push when the learner made an error. Pushing the button would deliver a shock to the learner. The results showed that the deindividuated women delivered twice the intensity of shocks to the learner as did the women in the individuated groups (Zimbardo, 1970).

A clever demonstration of deindividuation took advantage of the Halloween custom of trick-or-treating in identity-hiding costumes. Children out trick-or-treating were greeted at the door by an adult who asked that each child take only one piece of candy. The adult then disappeared into the house briefly, giving the children the opportunity to take more candy. Some of the children had been asked their names, while others remained anonymous. The children who came in groups or who remained anonymous stole more candy than did children who came alone or who had given their names to the adult (Diener, Fraser, Beaman, & Kelem, 1976).

Deindividuation—merging into a group and becoming anonymous—makes it easier to violate social norms.

Mass Suicide at Jonestown, Guyana
More than 900 followers of religious-cult leader Jim Jones obeyed his orders and committed suicide by poison. Shared beliefs and identification with a charismatic leader can exert a powerful influence on people's actions.

These experiments are not definitive, however. For instance, the laboratory coats and hoods in the first study carried negative connotations (they resembled Ku Klux Klan outfits), and it may be that the roles suggested by the costumes, rather than the anonymity provided by the costumes, produced the behavior. To test this possibility, the shock experiment was repeated, but this time each subject wore one of three outfits: a Ku Klux Klan-type costume, a nurse's uniform, or his or her own clothes. The results of the revised experiment did not replicate those of the original study; wearing a Ku Klux Klan-type costume had only a small effect on the level of shock the subjects administered. More significantly, those wearing nurses' uniforms actually gave fewer shocks than did the control group subjects who wore their own clothes, suggesting that a uniform encourages the person to play the kind of role it connotes. Anonymity may increase aggression, but this study shows that such results are not inevitable (Johnson & Downing, 1979).

Deindividuation is a complex process, and the experiments have often confounded a number of different variables (for example, the effects of anonymity with the effects of being part of a group—anonymity seems to be the critical variable, not group membership). Nevertheless, several studies show that the factors hypothesized to produce deindividuation do reduce self-awareness and increase impulsive behavior as outlined in Figure 18-2 (Diener, 1979; Prentice-Dunn & Rogers, 1980). The theory of deindividuation appears to have some validity for explaining the phenomena that so discomforted Le Bon. However, other factors are also clearly at work. Some collective behaviors such as revolutions or the mass suicides that occurred within the religious cult at Jonestown, Guyana, in 1978 stem from shared and strongly held beliefs among group members or from the charisma of a group leader. It is also undoubtedly true that people in a mob may behave irresponsibly because they know they are less likely to be caught and punished than if they committed the same acts alone.

Bystander Intervention

In earlier chapters, we noted that people do not react simply to the objective features of a situation but to their own subjective interpretations of it. In this chapter, we have seen that even social facilitation, a primitive kind of social influence, depends in part on the individual's interpretation of what others are doing or thinking. But the process of defining or interpreting the situation is often the very mechanism through which individuals influence one another.

In 1964, a young woman, Kitty Genovese, was murdered outside her home in New York City late at night. Because she resisted, the murder took over half an hour. Forty neighbors heard her screams for help, but nobody came to her aid. No one even called the police (Rosenthal, 1964).

The American public was horrified by this incident, and social psychologists began to investigate the causes of what at first was termed "bystander apathy." Their work showed that "apathy," however, was not a very accurate term. It is not simple indifference that prevents bystanders from intervening in emergencies. First, there are realistic deterrents, such as physical danger. Second, "getting involved" may mean lengthy court appearances or other entanglements. Third, emergencies are unpredictable and require quick, unplanned action; few of us are prepared for them. Finally, one risks making a fool of oneself by misinterpreting a situation as an emergency when it is not. Researchers concluded that "the bystander to an emergency situation is in an unenviable position. It is perhaps surprising that anyone should intervene at all" (Latané & Darley, 1970, p. 247).

Although we might suppose that the presence of other bystanders would embolden an individual to act despite the risks, research demonstrates the reverse.

Often it is the presence of other people that prevents us from intervening. Specifically, the presence of others serves (1) to define the situation as a *non*emergency and (2) to diffuse the responsibility for acting.

DEFINING THE SITUATION   Most emergencies begin ambiguously. Is the man who is staggering about ill or simply drunk? Is the woman's life really being threatened, or is it just a family quarrel? Is that smoke or steam pouring out the window? One common way to deal with such dilemmas is to postpone action, to act as if nothing is wrong, and to look around to see how others are reacting. What are you likely to see? Other people who, for the same reasons, are also acting as if nothing is wrong. A state of *pluralistic ignorance* develops — that is, everybody in the group misleads everybody else by defining the situation as a nonemergency. We have all heard about crowds panicking because each person leads everybody else to overreact. The reverse, in which a crowd lulls its members to inaction, may be even more common. Several experiments demonstrate this effect.

In one, male college students were invited to an interview. As they sat in a small waiting room, a stream of smoke began to pour through a wall vent. Some subjects were alone in the waiting room when this occurred, whereas others were in groups of three. The experimenters observed them through a one-way window and waited six minutes. Of the subjects tested alone, 75 percent reported the smoke within about two minutes. In contrast, fewer than 13 percent of the people tested in groups reported the smoke within the entire six-minute period, even though the room was filled with smoke. Those who did not report the smoke had decided that it must have been steam, air conditioning vapors, smog, or practically anything but a real fire or emergency. This experiment thus showed that bystanders can define situations as nonemergencies for one another (Latané & Darley, 1968).

But perhaps these subjects were simply afraid to appear cowardly. In a similar study, the "emergency" did not involve personal danger. Subjects in the testing room heard a female experimenter in the next office climb up on a chair to reach a bookcase, fall to the floor, and yell, "Oh my god — my foot. . . . I . . . can't move it. Oh . . . my ankle. . . . I can't get this thing off me." She continued to moan for about a minute longer. The entire incident lasted about two minutes. Only a curtain separated the woman's office from the testing room where subjects waited, alone or in pairs. The results confirmed the findings of the smoke study. Of the subjects who were alone, 70 percent came to the woman's aid, whereas only 40 percent of those in two-person groups offered help. Again, those who had not intervened claimed later that they were unsure of what had happened but had decided that it was not serious (Latané & Rodin, 1969). The presence of others in these experiments produced pluralistic ignorance; each person, observing the calmness of the others, resolved the ambiguity of the situation by deciding that no emergency existed.

DIFFUSION OF RESPONSIBILITY   Pluralistic ignorance can lead individuals to define a situation as a nonemergency, but this process does not explain such incidents as the Genovese murder, in which the emergency is abundantly clear. Moreover, Genovese's neighbors could not observe one another behind their curtained windows and hence could not tell whether others were calm or panicked. The crucial process here was *diffusion of responsibility.* When each individual knows that many others are present, the burden of responsibility does not fall solely on him or her. Each can think, "certainly someone else must have done something by now; someone else will intervene."

To test this hypothesis, experimenters placed subjects individually in a booth and told them that they would participate in a group discussion about

Although each of these passers-by has undoubtedly noticed the man lying on the sidewalk, no one has stopped to help — to find out if he is asleep, sick, drunk, or dead. If others were not present, someone would be more likely to come to his aid.

CRITICAL DISCUSSION

Social Impact Theory

Each of the social influence phenomena discussed in this chapter has one or more theories that attempt to explain it. One of the investigators who initiated the research on bystander intervention has attempted to construct a more abstract theory that would summarize, if not exactly explain, all of these phenomena. He has called this a *theory of social impact* (Latané, 1981). The purpose of such a theory is not to replace the individual theories but to incorporate them into a more general framework as special cases.

Two propositions of the theory are of interest here. The first proposition is illustrated in Figure 18-3 and states that the social impact of any source of influence on a target individual increases with the number, immediacy, and strength or importance of the sources. For example, this proposition predicts that social facilitation effects will increase with the number of coactors or audience members present, with their immediacy or salience to the individual, and with their importance to the individual. Thus we have seen that social facilitation effects are weaker if an audience is blindfolded (less immediacy), and they are stronger if the audience consists of an "expert" rather than of undergraduates (greater importance).

A number of studies outside the arena of social facilitation are also consistent with this proposition. For example, when reciting a poem before an audience, individuals rate themselves as increasingly nervous as the number and the status of audience members increase (Latané & Harkins, 1976). Stutterers reading aloud in front of an audience stutter more as the audience increases in size (Porter, 1939). We will see additional illustrations of this proposition

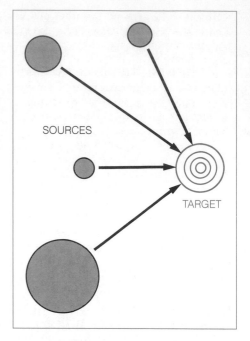

FIGURE 18-3
Multiplication of Social Impact *The social impact of a source of influence on a target individual increases with the number of sources (the number of circles), the immediacy of the sources (the nearness of the circles), and the strength or importance of the sources (the size of the circles). (After Latané, 1981)*

later when we discuss conformity and obedience.

The second proposition is illustrated in Figure 18-4 and states that the social impact of a source *decreases* as the number, immediacy, and importance of *targets* increase. Thus, the first proposition deals

personal problems faced by college students. To avoid embarrassment, the discussion would be held through an intercom. Each person would speak for two minutes. The microphone would be turned on only in the booth of the person speaking, and the experimenter would not be listening. Actually, the voices of all participants except the subject's were tape recordings. On the first round, one of the taped participants mentioned that he had problems with seizures. On the second round, this individual sounded as if he were actually starting to have a seizure and begged for help. The experimenters waited to see if the subject would leave the booth to report the emergency and how long it would take. Note that (1) the emergency was not at all ambiguous, (2) the subject could not tell how the

with the multiplication of impact due to numerous sources of influence; the second, with the diffusion of impact over multiple targets. For example, the second proposition describes the diffusion of responsibility in emergency situations: the more bystanders present in an emergency situation, the less pressure there is on any particular bystander to intervene.

A number of other studies also support this diffusion-of-impact proposition. For example, we illustrated the multiplication-of-impact proposition by noting that performers become increasingly nervous as the size of the audience increases—as the number of sources impinging on a single target increases. The diffusion-of-impact proposition is illustrated by a study of performers in a talent show. Solo performers were about six times more nervous than were those who performed in a ten-person act (Jackson & Latané, 1981). The impact of the source (the audience) was diffused over several targets (the performers).

In another study of impact diffusion, researchers kept records of how much diners in a restaurant tipped the waiter or waitress. The researchers reasoned that one motive for leaving a tip is a feeling of obligation and that this feeling of obligation should be diffused or divided when several diners share the check. In the restaurant they studied, the average tip was about 15 percent. An individual dining alone tipped an average of nearly 19 percent, whereas parties of five to six people tipped less than 13 percent (Freeman, Walker, Borden, & Latané, 1975). A study of Billy Graham's evangelical rallies varying in size from 2,000 to 143,000 persons revealed that the percentage of people present who were willing to come forth and "inquire for

Christ" declined as the size of the rally increased (Latané, 1981).

One of the major phenomena predicted by the diffusion-of-impact proposition is "social loafing." In the 1920s, a German researcher named Ringelmann conducted an unpublished study on how collective action influenced individual effort. Workers were asked to pull as hard as they could on a rope when they were working alone, in a group of three people, or in a group of six people. Even though total group effort increased with group size, the effort of each member decreased, with six-person groups performing at only 36 percent of potential capacity (calculated as the sum of individual-based efforts) (Moede, 1927, as reported by Latané, 1981). More recent studies have replicated this finding using different kinds of tasks (Petty, Harkins, Williams, & Latané, 1977; Latané, Williams, & Harkins, 1979).

Perhaps you have noticed an apparent contradiction here. The presence of coactors is supposed to produce social facilitation—increased drive and effort—not social loafing. According to social impact theory, the critical difference lies in the role played by the "others" in the situation. When each person performs a task independently, the others put competitive or evaluative pressure on each other. There are many sources acting on each individual target; thus, multiplication of impact occurs (Figure 18-3). When a group of individuals work on a shared task, the experimenter serves as a single source and his or her influence is diffused over many targets; hence, Figure 18-4 applies. Cognitive processes may also contribute to social loafing. Each person may believe that others in the group are not contributing their fair share and

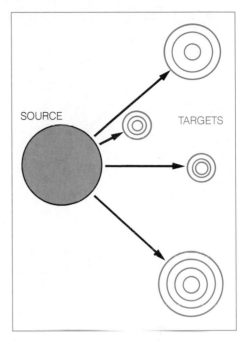

FIGURE 18-4
Diffusion of Social Impact *The impact of a source decreases as the number, immediacy, and importance of targets increase. (After Latané, 1981)*

thus may be less motivated to work to capacity. Or each individual may feel that his or her own contribution will be less recognizable when working in a group, leading to a diffusion of responsibility. A more recent study found that social loafing decreases when the task is made more challenging and when individuals believe they can make a unique contribution to the group effort (Harkins & Petty, 1982).

"bystanders" in the other booths were reacting, and (3) the subject knew the experimenter could not hear the emergency. Some subjects were led to believe that the discussion group consisted only of themselves and the seizure victim. Others were told it was a three-person group; and still others, a six-person group.

Of the subjects who thought that they alone knew of the victim's seizure, 85 percent reported it; of those who thought they were in a three-person group, 62 percent reported the seizure; and only 31 percent of those who thought they were in a six-person group reported the seizure (see Figure 18-5). Interviews showed that all the subjects perceived the situation to be a real emergency. Most were very emotional about the conflict between letting the victim suffer and

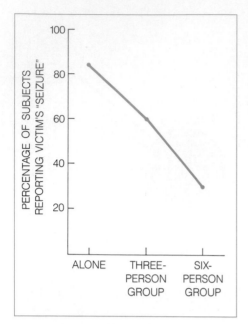

FIGURE 18-5
Diffusion of Responsibility *The percentage of subjects who reported a victim's apparent seizure declined as the number of other people the subject believed were in his or her discussion group increased. (After Darley & Latané, 1968)*

rushing, perhaps foolishly and unnecessarily, for help. In fact, subjects who did not report the seizure seemed far more upset than those who did. Clearly we cannot interpret their nonintervention as apathy or indifference. Instead, the presence of others diffused the responsibility for acting (Darley & Latané, 1968).

If pluralistic ignorance and diffusion of responsibility are minimized, will people help one another? Three psychologists used the New York City subway system as their laboratory (Piliavin, Rodin, & Piliavin, 1969). Two male experimenters and two female experimenters boarded a subway train separately. The female experimenters took seats and recorded the results, while the two men remained standing. As the train moved along, one of the men staggered forward and collapsed, remaining prone and staring at the ceiling until he received help. If no help came, the other man finally helped him to his feet. Several variations of the study were tried: the victim either carried a cane (so he would appear ill) or smelled of alcohol (so he would appear drunk). Sometimes the victim was white; other times, black. There was no ambiguity; clearly, the victim needed help. Diffusion of responsibility was minimized because each bystander could not continue to assume that someone else was intervening. Therefore, the people should help.

The results supported this optimistic expectation. The victim with the cane received spontaneous help on over 95 percent of the trials, within an average of 5 seconds. Even the "drunk" victim received help in half of the trials, on the average within 109 seconds. Both black and white "cane" victims were aided by black and white bystanders. There was no relationship between the number of bystanders and the speed of help, suggesting that diffusion of responsibility had indeed been minimized. And all of this occurred on the New York City subway system! This not only tends to support the proposed explanations of bystander nonintervention but should help us revise our stereotypes about New York City subway riders.

ROLE OF "HELPING" MODELS   In the subway study, as soon as one person moved to help, many others followed. This suggests that just as individuals use other people as models to define a situation as a nonemergency (pluralistic ignorance), they also use other people as models to indicate when to be helpful. This possibility was tested in a study by counting the number of drivers who stopped to help a woman whose car had a flat tire (the "test" car). During some test periods, another car with a flat tire (the "model" car) was parked alongside the highway one-quarter mile before the test car. The model car was raised on a jack and a woman was watching a man change the flat tire. Of 4,000 passing cars, 93 stopped to help the woman alone in the test car: 35 stopped when there was no model car and 58 when there was—a statistically significant difference. Others not only help us decide when *not* to act in an emergency but also show us how and when to be Good Samaritans (Bryan & Test, 1967).

ROLE OF INFORMATION   Would you be more likely to intervene in an emergency now that you have read this section? An experiment at the University of Montana suggests that you would. Undergraduates were either given a lecture or shown a film based on the material discussed in this section. Two weeks later, each undergraduate was confronted with a simulated emergency while walking with one other person (a confederate of the experimenters). A male "victim" was sprawled on the floor of a hallway. The confederate did not react as if the situation were an emergency. Of those who had heard the lecture or seen the film, 43 percent offered help, compared with only 25 percent of those who had not attended the session—a statistically significant difference (Beaman, Barnes, Klentz, & McQuirk, 1978). For society's sake, perhaps you should reread this section!

COMPLIANCE

As we noted at the beginning of the chapter, social influence produces *compliance* when a target individual publicly conforms to the wishes of an influencing source but does not change his or her private beliefs or attitudes. When a source obtains compliance by setting an example, we call that compliance *conformity*, and when a source obtains compliance by wielding authority, we call it *obedience*. In both cases, an individual complies because the source has the power to administer rewards and punishments. Most often these are social rewards and punishments, such as approval and disapproval or acceptance and rejection. In this section we examine both conformity to peer pressure and obedience to authority.

Conformity to a Majority

When we are in a group, we may find ourselves in the minority on some issue. This is a fact of life to which most of us have become accustomed. If we decide that the majority is a more valid source of information than our own experience, we may change our minds and conform to the majority opinion. But imagine yourself in a situation in which you are sure that your own opinion is correct and that the group is wrong. Would you yield to social pressure under those circumstances? This is the kind of conformity that social psychologist Solomon Asch decided to investigate in a series of classic studies (1952, 1955, 1958).

In Asch's standard procedure, a single subject was seated at a table with a group of seven to nine others (actually confederates of the experimenter). The group was shown a display of three vertical lines of different lengths, and members of the group were asked to judge which line was the same length as a standard in another display (see Figure 18-6). Each individual announced his or her decision in turn, and the subject sat in the next to last seat. The correct judgments were obvious, and on most trials everyone gave the same response. But on several predetermined "critical" trials, the confederates had been instructed to give the wrong answer. Asch then observed the amount of conformity this procedure would elicit from his subjects.

The results were striking. Even though the correct answer was always obvious, the average subject conformed to the group consensus on 32 percent of the critical trials, and 74 percent of the subjects conformed at least once. Moreover, the group did not have to be large to obtain such conformity. When Asch varied the size of the group from 2 to 16, he found that a group of 3 or 4 confederates was just as effective at producing conformity as were larger groups (Asch, 1958).

Why didn't the obviousness of the correct answer provide support for the individual's independence from the majority? Why isn't a person's confidence in his or her ability to make simple sensory judgments a strong force against conformity?

According to one line of argument, it is precisely the obviousness of the correct answer in the Asch experiment that produces the strong forces *toward* conformity (Ross, Bierbrauer, & Hoffman, 1976). Disagreements in real life typically involve difficult or subjective judgments, such as which economic policy will best reduce inflation or which of two paintings is more aesthetically pleasing. In these cases, we expect to disagree with others occasionally; we even know that being a minority of one in an otherwise unanimous group is a plausible, if uncomfortable, possibility.

The Asch situation is much more extreme. Here the individual is confronted with unanimous disagreement about a simple physical fact, a bizarre and unprecedented occurrence that appears to have no rational explanation. Subjects are

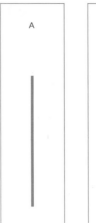
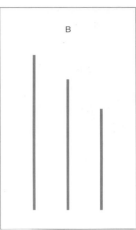

FIGURE 18-6
Representative Stimulus in Asch's Study *After viewing display A, the subjects were told to pick the matching line from display B. The displays shown here are typical in that the correct decision is obvious. (After Asch, 1958)*

"Wait a minute, you guys — I've decided to make it unanimous after all."

Drawing by Victor; © 1978 *The New Yorker Magazine,* Inc.

A

B

C

Resistance to Majority Opinion

A. All of the group members except the man sixth from the left are confederates previously instructed to give uniformly wrong answers on 12 of the 18 trials. No. 6, who has been told he is participating in an experiment in visual judgment, therefore finds himself a lone dissenter when he gives the correct answers.

B. The subject, showing the strain of repeated disagreement with the majority, leans forward anxiously to look at the pair of cards.

C. This particular subject persists in his opinion, saying that "he has to call them as he sees them."

"Well, heck! If all you smart cookies agree, who am I to dissent?"

Drawing by Handelsman; copyright © 1972 *The New Yorker Magazine*, Inc.

clearly puzzled and tense. They rub their eyes in disbelief and jump up to look more closely at the lines. They squirm, mumble, giggle in embarrassment, and look searchingly at others in the group for some clue to the mystery. After the experiment, they offer halfhearted hypotheses about optical illusions or suggest — quite aptly — that perhaps the first person occasionally made mistakes and each successive person followed suit because of conformity pressures (Asch, 1952).

Consider what it means to dissent from the majority under these circumstances. Just as the judgments of the group seem incomprehensible to the subject, so the subject believes that his or her dissent will be incomprehensible to the group. Group members will surely judge him or her to be incompetent, even out of touch with reality. Similarly, if the subject dissents repeatedly, this will seem to constitute a direct challenge to the group's competence, a challenge that requires enormous courage when one's own perceptual abilities are suddenly and inexplicably called into question. Such a challenge violates a strong social norm against insulting others. This fear of "What will they think of me?" and "What will they think I think of them?" inhibits dissent and generates the strong pressures to conform in the Asch situation.

Conformity pressures are far less strong when the group is not unanimous. If even one confederate breaks with the majority, the amount of subject conformity drops from 32 percent of the trials to about 6 percent. In fact, a group of eight containing only one dissenter produces less conformity than a unanimous majority of three (Asch, 1958). Surprisingly, the dissenter does not even have to give the correct answer. Even when the dissenter's answers are *more* incorrect than the majority's, the spell is broken and subjects are more inclined to give their own correct judgments (Asch, 1955; Allen & Levine, 1969). Nor does it matter who the dissenter is. A black dissenter reduces the conformity rate among racially prejudiced white subjects just as effectively as a white dissenter (Malof & Lott, 1962). In a variation that approaches the absurd, conformity was significantly reduced even though the subjects thought the dissenter was so visually handicapped that he could not see the stimuli (Allen & Levine, 1971). It seems clear that the presence of but one other deviant to share the potential disapproval or ridicule of the group permits the subject to dissent without feeling totally isolated. Social impact theory (see the previous Critical Discussion) would describe this as a result of diffusing the social forces over a larger number of targets.

If Asch's conformity situation is unlike most situations in real life, why did Asch use a task where the correct answer was obvious? The reason is that he wanted to study pure public conformity, uncontaminated by the possibility that subjects were actually changing their minds about the correct answers. In other words, he was investigating compliance, not internalization. Several variations of Asch's study have utilized more difficult or subjective judgments, and although they may reflect real life more faithfully, they do not permit us to assess the effects of pure pressure to conform to a majority when we are certain that our own minority judgment is correct. This critical difference between the original Asch situation and its later variations, which use more difficult, subjective, or ambiguous tasks, is almost never recognized (Ross, Bierbrauer, & Hoffman, 1976).

Obedience to Authority

In Nazi Germany from 1933 to 1945, millions of innocent people were systematically put to death in concentration camps. The mastermind of this horror, Adolf Hitler, may well have been a psychopathic monster. But he could not have done it alone. What about all those who ran the day-to-day operations, who built the ovens and gas chambers, filled them with human beings, counted bodies, and did the paperwork? Were they all monsters, too?

Not according to social philosopher Hannah Arendt (1963), who covered the trial of Adolf Eichmann, a Nazi war criminal who was found guilty and was executed for causing the murder of millions of Jews. She described him as a dull, ordinary, unaggressive bureaucrat who saw himself as a little cog in a big machine. The recent publication of a partial transcript of Eichmann's pretrial interrogation supports Arendt's view. Several psychiatrists found Eichmann to be quite sane, and his personal relationships were quite normal. He sincerely believed that the Jews should have been allowed to emigrate to a separate territory and had argued that position within Hitler's security service. Moreover, he had a secret Jewish mistress—a crime for an SS officer—and a Jewish half cousin whom he arranged to have protected during the war (Von Lang & Sibyll, 1983).

Arendt subtitled her book about Eichmann *A Report on the Banality of Evil* and concluded that most of the "evil men" of the Third Reich were just ordinary people following orders from superiors. This suggests that all of us might be capable of such evil and that Nazi Germany was an event less wildly alien from the normal human condition than we might like to think. As Arendt put it, "in certain circumstances the most ordinary decent person can become a criminal." This is not an easy conclusion to accept, because it is more comforting to believe that monstrous evil is done only by monstrous persons. In fact, our emotional attachment to this explanation of evil was vividly shown by the intensity of the attacks on Arendt and her conclusions.

The problem of obedience to authority arose again in 1969, when a group of American soldiers serving in Vietnam killed a number of civilians in the community of My Lai, claiming that they were simply following orders. Again the public was forced to ponder the possibility that ordinary citizens are willing to obey authority in violation of their own moral conscience.

This issue was explored empirically in a series of important and controversial studies conducted by Stanley Milgram (1963, 1974) at Yale University. Ordinary men and women were recruited through a newspaper ad that offered four dollars for one hour's participation in a "study of memory." On arriving at the laboratory, the subject was told that he or she would be playing the role of teacher in the study. The subject was to read a series of word pairs to another subject and then to test the "learner's" memory by reading the first word of each pair and asking him to select the correct second word from four alternatives. Each time the learner made an error, the subject was to press a lever that delivered an electric shock to him.

The subject watched while the learner was strapped into an electrically wired chair and an electrode was attached to his wrist. The subject was then seated in an adjoining room in front of a shock generator whose front panel contained 30 lever switches set in a horizontal line. Each switch was labeled with a voltage rating, ranging in sequence from 15 to 450 volts, and groups of adjacent switches were

FIGURE 18-7
Milgram Obedience Experiment *The subject was told to give the "learner" a more intense shock after each error. If he or she objected, the experimenter insisted it was necessary to go on. (After Milgram, 1974)*

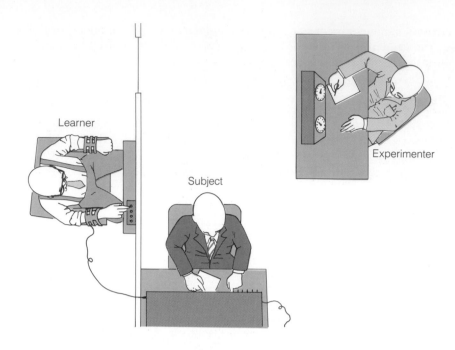

labeled descriptively, ranging from "Slight Shock" up to "Danger: Severe Shock." When a switch was depressed, an electric buzz sounded, lights flashed, and the needle on a voltage meter deflected to the right. To illustrate how it worked, the subject was given a sample shock of 45 volts from the generator. As the procedure began, the experimenter instructed the subject to move one level higher on the shock generator after each successive error (see Figure 18-7).

The learner did not, of course, actually receive any shocks. He was a 47-year-old, mild-mannered accountant who had been specially trained for his role. As he began to make errors and the shock levels escalated, he could be heard protesting through the adjoining wall. As the shocks became stronger, he began to shout and curse. At 300 volts he began to kick the wall, and at the next shock level (marked "Extreme Intensity Shock"), he no longer answered the questions or made any noise. As you might expect, many subjects began to object to this excruciating procedure, pleading with the experimenter to call a halt. But the experimenter responded with a sequence of "prods," using as many as necessary to get the subject to go on: "Please continue"; "The experiment requires that you continue"; "It is absolutely essential that you continue"; and "You have no other choice — you *must* go on." Obedience to authority was measured by the maximum amount of shock the subject would administer before refusing to continue.

Milgram found that 65 percent of the subjects continued to obey throughout, going all the way to the end of the shock series (450 volts). Not one subject stopped prior to administering 300 volts, the point at which the learner began to kick the wall (see Figure 18-8). What produces such obedience?

The potential for obedience to authority, Milgram suggests, is such a necessary requirement for communal life that it has probably been built into our species by evolution. The division of labor in a society requires that individuals have the capacity to subordinate and to coordinate their actions to serve the goals and purposes of the larger social organization. Parents, school systems, and businesses all nurture this capacity by reminding the individual about the importance of following the directives of others who "know the larger picture." To understand obedience in a particular situation, then, we need to understand the factors that persuade individuals to relinquish their autonomy and to become

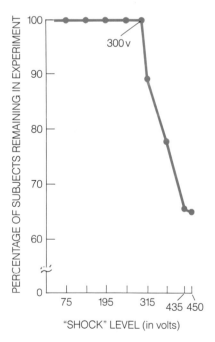

FIGURE 18-8
Obedience to Authority *The percentage of subjects willing to administer a punishing shock did not begin to decline until the intensity level of the shock reached 300 volts. (After Milgram, 1963)*

Milgram Experiment *(top left) The "shock generator" used in Milgram's experiment on obedience. (top right) The victim is strapped into the "electric chair." (bottom left) A subject receives the sample shock before starting the "teaching session." (bottom right) A subject refuses to go on with the experiment. Most subjects became deeply disturbed by the role they were asked to play, whether they continued in the experiment to the end or refused at some point to go on any longer. (From the film* Obedience, *distributed by New York University Film Library; copyright © 1965 by Stanley Milgram)*

voluntary agents of the system. Four such factors — social norms, surveillance, buffers, and ideological justification — are well illustrated in the Milgram experiments.

SOCIAL NORMS By replying to the advertisement and agreeing to be in the study, subjects in Milgram's experiments had voluntarily assented to an implicit contract to cooperate with the experimenter, to follow the directions of the person in charge, and to see the job through to completion. This is a very strong social norm, and we tend to underestimate how difficult it is to break such an agreement and to go back on our implied word to cooperate.

The experiment was also designed to reinforce this norm by making it particularly difficult for subjects to stop once they had begun. The procedure starts rather innocently as an experiment in memory and then gradually escalates. Once subjects begin to give shocks and to raise the shock levels, there is no longer a natural stopping point. By the time they want to quit, they are trapped. The experimenter makes no new demands, only that they continue to do what they are already doing. In order to break off, they must suffer the guilt and embarrassment of acknowledging that they were wrong to begin at all. And the longer they put off quitting, the harder it is to admit their misjudgment in going as far as they have. It is easier to continue. Imagine how much less obedience there would be if subjects had to begin by giving the strongest shock first.

Finally, the potential quitter faces the dilemma of violating a social norm of etiquette (being polite) similar to the one confronting a subject in the Asch situation. Dissenting in that case implied that the subject thought the group was incompetent. Dissenting in the Milgram situation is equivalent to accusing the experimenter of being evil and immoral — an even more compelling force pushing the subject to stay in line and not make waves.

If social norms such as these can produce so much obedience in Milgram's studies, then it is easy to imagine how much more powerful the penalties for quitting would be in Nazi Germany or in military service once one has already "signed on."

SURVEILLANCE An obvious factor in the Milgram experiment is the constant presence or surveillance of the experimenter. When the experimenter left the room and issued his orders by telephone, obedience dropped from 65 percent to 21 percent (Milgram, 1974). Moreover, several of the subjects who continued under these conditions "cheated" by administering shocks of lower intensity than they were supposed to without telling the experimenter. In general, continued compliance rests upon continuing surveillance, because the influencing agent is obtaining only public conformity from the target individual, not private acceptance. As we shall see in later sections, social influence based on processes of internalization or identification does not require surveillance for its maintenance.

BUFFERS Milgram's subjects believed that they were committing acts of violence, but several buffers obscured this fact or diluted the immediacy of the experience. For example, the learner was in the next room, out of sight and unable to communicate. Milgram has reported that obedience drops from 65 percent to 40 percent if the learner is in the same room as the subject. If the subject must personally ensure that the learner holds his hand on the shock plate, obedience declines to 30 percent. The more direct the person's experience with the victim — the fewer buffers between the person and the consequences of his or her act — the less the subject will obey.

The most common buffer found in warlike situations is the remoteness of the person from the final act of violence. Thus, Eichmann argued that he was not directly responsible for killing Jews; he merely arranged for their deaths indirectly. Milgram conducted an analogue to this "link-in-the-chain" situation by requiring a subject only to pull a switch that enabled another teacher (a confederate) to deliver the shocks to the learner. Under these conditions, obedience soared: a full 93 percent of the subjects continued to the end of the shock series. In this situation, the subject can shift the blame to the person who actually delivers the shock.

The shock generator itself served as a buffer — an impersonal mechanical "agent" that actually delivered the shock. Imagine how obedience would have declined if subjects were required to hit the learner with their fists. In real life, we have analogous technologies that permit us to destroy distant fellow humans by remote control, thereby removing us from the sight of their suffering. Although we probably all agree that it is worse to kill thousands of people by pushing a button that releases a guided missile than it is to beat one individual to death with a rock, it is still psychologically easier to push the button. Such are the effects of buffers.

IDEOLOGICAL JUSTIFICATION The fourth and most important factor producing voluntary obedience is the individual's acceptance of an ideology that legitimizes the authority of the person in charge and justifies following his or her directives. Nazi officers such as Eichmann believed in the primacy of the German state and hence in the legitimacy of orders issued in the name of its ideology. Similarly, the American soldiers who followed orders to shoot enemy civilians in Vietnam had already committed themselves to the premise that national security requires strict obedience to military commands.

In the Milgram experiments, "science" provides the ideology that legitimizes even quite extraordinary demands. Some critics of the Milgram experiments have argued that they were artificial, that the prestige of a scientific experiment led people to obey without questioning the dubious procedures in which they participated and that people in "real life" would never do such a thing. Indeed, when Milgram repeated his experiment in a run-down set of offices and removed any association with Yale University from the setting, obedience dropped from 65 percent to 48 percent (Milgram, 1974).

Remoteness from the final act of violence: (left) aerial view of the Pentagon; (right) War Room of the Pentagon.

But this criticism misses the major point. The prestige of science is not an irrelevant artificiality but an integral part of Milgram's demonstration. Science serves precisely the same legitimizing role in the experiment that the German state served in Nazi Germany and that national security serves in wartime killing. A belief in the primacy of "scientific research" *is* the ideology that prompts individuals to relinquish their personal moral autonomy and to voluntarily subordinate their own independence to goals and purposes of a larger social organization.

Obedience to Authority in Everyday Life

Because the Milgram experiments have been criticized for being artificial (see Orne & Holland, 1968), it is instructive to look at an example of obedience to authority under more ordinary conditions. Researchers investigated whether nurses in public and private hospitals would obey an order that violated hospital rules and professional practice (Hofling et al., 1966). While on regular duty, the subject (a nurse) received a phone call from a doctor she knew to be on the staff but had not met: "This is Dr. Smith from Psychiatry calling. I was asked to see Mr. Jones this morning, and I'm going to have to see him again tonight. I'd like him to have had some medication by the time I get to the ward. Will you please check your medicine cabinet and see if you have some Astroten? That's ASTRO-TEN." When the nurse checked the medicine cabinet, she saw a pillbox labeled

ASTROTEN
5 mg. capsules
Usual dose: 5 mg.
Maximum daily dose: 10 mg.

After she reported that she had found it, the doctor continued, "Now will you please give Mr. Jones a dose of 20 milligrams of Astroten. I'll be up within ten minutes; I'll sign the order then, but I'd like the drug to have started taking effect." A staff psychiatrist, posted unobtrusively nearby, terminated each trial by disclosing its true nature when the nurse either poured the medication

CRITICAL DISCUSSION

The Power of Situational Influences

In Chapter 17, we saw that people typically underestimate the degree to which external forces control behavior, thus making the *fundamental attribution error*. Studies on conformity and obedience illustrate this point—not through their results but through our surprise at their results. In his social psychology class every year, one psychologist describes the Milgram procedure to students and asks them to predict whether they would continue to administer the shocks after the "learner" begins to pound on the wall. About 99 percent of the students say they would not (Aronson, 1984). Milgram himself surveyed psychiatrists at a leading medical school; they predicted that most subjects would refuse to go on after reaching 150 volts, that only about 4 percent would administer more than 300 volts, and that fewer than 1 percent would go all the way to 450 volts. In another study, subjects were asked to "walk through" the entire Milgram procedure complete with shock apparatus and a tape recording of the protesting "learner." Whether they role-played the part of the subject or the part of an observer, all subjects continued to vastly underestimate the compliance rates actually obtained by Milgram, as shown in Figure 18-9 (Bierbrauer, 1973). The nursing study on administering medication yields comparable findings. When nurses who had not been subjects were given a complete description of the situation and asked how they themselves would respond, 83 percent reported that they would not have given the medication, and most of them thought a majority of nurses would also refuse. Of 21 nursing students asked the same question, all of them reported that they would not have given the medication as ordered.

The obedience experiments thus dramatically illustrate a major lesson of social

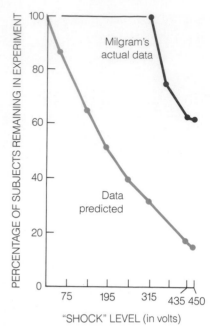

FIGURE 18-9

Predicted and Actual Compliance *The upper curve presents the Milgram data and shows the percentage of subjects who remained obedient in the situation, continuing to administer shocks as the voltage increased. The lower curve is from a study where observers witnessed a reenactment of the Milgram experiment and attempted to predict what percentage of the subjects would continue to be obedient as shock increased. The observers vastly underestimated the magnitude of the situational forces and the likelihood of obedience in the Milgram situation. (After Bierbrauer, 1973)*

psychology: we seriously underestimate the extent and power of social and situational forces on human behavior.

(actually a harmless placebo), refused to accept the order, or tried to contact another professional.

This order violated several rules. The dose was clearly excessive. Medication orders are not permitted to be given by telephone. The medication was unauthorized—that is, it was not on the ward stock list clearing it for use. Finally, the order was given by an unfamiliar person. Despite all this, 95 percent of the nurses started to give the medication. Moreover, the telephone calls were all brief, and the nurses put up no resistance. None of them insisted on a written order, although several sought reassurance that the doctor would arrive promptly. In interviews after the experiment, all the nurses stated that such orders had been received in the past and that doctors became annoyed if the nurses balked.

Rebellion

One reason compliance experiments generate so much conformity and obedience may be that the social pressures in these studies are directed toward a lone individual. According to social impact theory, social influence will be less powerful if it is diffused over many target individuals, suggesting that a group of individuals might be less susceptible to it—perhaps even showing a bit of rebellion. We have already seen some data to support this suggestion: a subject in the Asch conformity situation is less likely to go along with the group's incorrect judgments if there is at least one other dissenter.

A similar phenomenon occurs in the Milgram obedience situation. In one variation of the procedure, two additional confederates were employed. They were introduced as subjects who would also play teacher roles. Teacher No. 1 would read the list of word pairs; Teacher No. 2 would tell the learner if he was right or wrong; and Teacher No. 3 (the subject) would deliver the shocks. The confederates complied with the instructions through the 150 volt shock, at which point Teacher No. 1 informed the experimenter that he was quitting. Despite the experimenter's insistence that he continue, Teacher No. 1 got up from his chair and sat in another part of the room. After the 210-volt shock, Teacher No. 2 also quit. The experimenter then turned to the subject and ordered him to continue alone. Only 10 percent of the subjects were willing to complete the series in this situation. In a second variation, there were two experimenters rather than two additional teachers. After a few shocks, they began to argue — one of them saying that they should stop the experiment; the other saying that they should continue. Under these circumstances, not a single subject would continue despite the orders to do so by the second experimenter (Milgram, 1974).

In these variations, the instigation to nonconformity or disobedience came from planted confederates. A more recent experiment explored the possibility that groups of subjects with no confederates present would be moved to rebel against unjust authority. Citizens from a nonuniversity community were recruited by phone for ten dollars to spend two hours at a local Holiday Inn assisting in research on "group standards" sponsored by the "Manufacturer's Human Relations Consultants" or "MHRC" (Gamson, Fireman, & Rytina, 1982). Nine subjects, both male and female, were recruited for each group session. When they arrived, they were given a letter explaining that legal cases sometimes hinge on the notion of community standards and that MHRC collects evidence on such standards by bringing together concerned citizens for group discussions. The subjects were then seated in front of video cameras and microphones at a U-shaped table, where they filled out a background questionnaire and signed a "participation agreement" giving MHRC permission to videotape them as they engaged in group discussion. The man in charge, who introduced himself as the coordinator, then read the background of a pending court case. The basic facts were as follows:

> A service station manager was suing an oil company because it had canceled the franchise on his service station. The oil company had conducted an investigation of the man and discovered that he was living with a woman to whom he was not married. The company claimed that his life-style violated the moral standards of the local community and that he would therefore not be able to maintain good

relations with customers; accordingly they decided to revoke his franchise license. The man sued for breach of contract and invasion of privacy, arguing that the company was out to get him because he had publicly criticized the company's gas pricing policies in a local TV interview.

After presenting the case, the coordinator asked the group to discuss it while being videotaped. After a general discussion, the cameras were turned off and the group was given a short break. Before resuming the videotaping, the coordinator requested three of the group members to argue as if they were personally offended by the station manager's life-style. This second discussion was taped, there was another break, and three additional individuals were designated to argue in the same way in the next discussion. Finally, the coordinator asked each individual to go on camera alone and voice objections to the station manager's affair, stating an intention to boycott the station, and arguing that the manager should lose his franchise. Group members were also told that they would be asked to sign notarized affidavits giving MHRC the right to introduce the tapes as evidence in court after editing them as it saw fit.

As MHRC's motives began to dawn on them, all but one of the 33 groups in this experiment began to dissent: "Can you assure us that the court is going to know these aren't our real opinions?"; "Would you mind leaving the tape on while you give us these instructions, so that it doesn't appear . . . "; "Do these professional people know what you're doing in fact is suborning perjury?" (Gamson, Fireman, & Rytina, 1982, pp. 62, 65). One group even decided to take direct action by gathering up materials from the table and taking them to the local newspaper.

Overall, 16 of the 33 groups rebelled completely—all members refused to sign the final affidavit—and a majority refused to do so in 9 additional groups. Only a minority refused in the remaining 8 groups, although a number of dissenting comments were voiced. Compared to the Milgram situation, then, obedience to authority had clearly been undermined in this study. But why?

The two studies differ in several respects, so we cannot be certain that the important difference was having a group rather than a lone individual as the target. Nevertheless, this seems to be the most likely element. In fact, the circumstances producing rebellion in the MHRC study appear to be the same ones that we have seen operating in other group contexts: defining the situation, and conformity.

In the bystander intervention studies, we noted that individuals in a group define an ambiguous situation for one another. Subjects in the MHRC study were given ample opportunity during the breaks to discuss the situation with one another and to share their suspicions of MHRC's motives. Some of the comments were "How are people going to know that these aren't our opinions?" "We don't want to be faced with the situation where you read in the *New York Times* one day that thanks to a new method of litigation [group laughter] that this poor schnook [group laughter] lost his license" (Gamson, Fireman, & Rytina, 1982, pp. 101, 102).

The preliminary questionnaires also indicated that 80 to 90 percent of the subjects initially disagreed with the position they were asked to take: they were quite tolerant of an unmarried couple living together; they were critical of large oil companies; and they believed that an employee's private life was none of a company's business. The group members could also share these opinions with one another. The researchers compared the 23 groups in which a majority of subjects initially held the dissenting opinions with the 10 groups that initially held less dissenting opinions. They found that 65 percent of the former groups produced complete rebellion — nobody signed the affidavits — whereas only 10 percent of the latter groups did so. A majority of the groups also contained some individuals who had been active in past protests and strikes, and these groups were also more likely to rebel than were groups without such "role models." Lone subjects in the Milgram obedience studies obviously had none of these opportunities for sharing information, receiving social support for dissent, or seeing role models for disobedience.

But before we congratulate the human species for heroic independence and autonomy in the face of social pressure, we should consider the implication of these findings more closely. They suggest that many of the individuals in the groups were not choosing between obedience and autonomy but between obedience and conformity: obey the coordinator or conform to the developing group norm to disobey. As the researchers observed, "Many were uncertain at this point, waiting to see what others would do, delaying decision as long as possible. Ultimately, they were faced with an unavoidable choice — to sign or not to sign — and loyalty to the group became one major factor in their decision." They also report that some who had already signed the affidavit crossed out their names or tore up the form. As one subject told the coordinator, "I didn't personally say anything I didn't believe, but I'm not going to sign this either, if the rest of the group isn't signing" (Gamson, Fireman, & Rytina, 1982, p. 99).

Obeying or conforming may not strike you as a very heroic choice. But these are among the processes that provide the social glue for the human species. Several years before this study was conducted, a social historian noted that "disobedience when it is not criminally but morally, religiously or politically motivated is always a collective act and it is justified by the values of the collectivity and the mutual engagements of its members" (Walzer, 1970, p. 4).

INTERNALIZATION

Individuals are said to comply when they change their behavior in accordance with the wishes of a person who exercises power and maintains continued surveillance over the influence target. But in everyday life, most sources of influence strive to obtain change that the individual "believes in" and that will therefore sustain itself after the source has departed. Such long-term change is called *internalization*. Certainly the major goal of parents, educators, clergy, politicians, and advertisers is internalization, not just compliance. In general, internalization is obtained by an influence source who has *credibility*, whose message is itself persuasive and believable. In this section, we examine two sources of influence whose goal is to persuade rather than to coerce: minority influences on majority opinion, and the mass media.

Minority Influence

A number of European scholars have been critical of social psychological research in North America because of its preoccupation with conformity and the influence of the majority on the minority. As they correctly point out, intellectual innovation, social change, and political revolution inevitably occur because an informed and articulate minority — sometimes a minority of one — begins to convert others to its point of view (Moscovici, 1976). Therefore, why not study innovation and the influence that minorities can have on the majority?

Gay rights issue — action by the minority can change the attitude of the majority.

To make their point, these European investigators deliberately began their work by setting up a laboratory situation virtually identical to Asch's conformity situation. Subjects were asked to make a series of simple perceptual judgments in the face of confederates who consistently gave the incorrect answer. But instead of placing a single subject in the midst of several confederates, these investigators planted two confederates, who consistently gave incorrect responses, in the midst of four real subjects. The experimenters found that the minority was able to influence about 32 percent of the subjects to make at least one incorrect judgment. For this to occur, however, the minority had to remain consistent throughout the experiment. If they wavered or showed any inconsistency in their judgments, they were unable to influence the majority (Moscovici, Lage, & Naffrechoux, 1969).

Since this initial demonstration of minority influence, many additional studies have been conducted in both Europe and North America, including several that required groups to debate social and political issues rather than to make simple perceptual judgments. The general finding is that minorities can move majorities toward their point of view if they present a consistent position without appearing rigid, dogmatic, or arrogant. Such minorities are perceived to be more confident and, occasionally, more competent than the majority (Maass & Clark, 1984). Minorities are also more effective if they argue a position that is consistent with the developing social norms of the larger society. For example, in two experiments in which feminist issues were discussed, subjects were moved significantly more by a minority position that was in line with recent social norms (feminist) than by one opposed to the new norms (antifeminist) (Paicheler, 1976, 1977).

But the most interesting finding from this research is that the majority members in these studies show internalization — a change of private attitudes — not just compliance or public conformity. In fact, minorities sometimes obtain internalization from majority members even when they fail to obtain public conformity. In one study, groups of subjects read a purported summary of a discussion of gay rights held by five undergraduates like themselves. In all cases, four discussants had favored one position and a minority of one had consistently favored the opposite position. In some discussions, the majority had been for gay rights and the minority against; in other discussions, the majority and minority positions were reversed. After reading the summary, subjects voiced considerable public agreement with the majority view — regardless of whether it had been for or against gay rights — but written ratings revealed that opinions had shifted toward the minority position (Maass & Clark, 1983).

These findings serve to remind us that the majorities of the world typically have the social power to approve and disapprove, to accept or reject, and it is this power that can obtain compliance. In contrast, minorities rarely have such social power. But if they have credibility, then they have the power to produce internalization and, hence, innovation, social change, and revolution.

Mass Media Persuasion

The mass media have had an enormous effect on our society. Television, in particular, has become a potent social presence in our lives. By age 16, the average child has spent more time in front of the TV set than in the classroom (Waters & Malamud, 1975), and it is estimated that one-third of all American adults watch an average of four or more hours of television per day (Gerbner & Gross, 1976). Understandably, many people have been concerned about the influences of the mass media on our beliefs, attitudes, and behaviors. In Chapter 11 we discussed the effects of TV violence on behavior. Here we look at the success of media persuasion.

Given the amount of money that companies and candidates spend on TV advertising, one would conclude that persuasion via the mass media must be very effective. It is and it is not. In a highly competitive market or in a close political campaign, a competitive edge of a few percentage points makes an enormous difference. Media advertising can sometimes provide that extra edge. It can also create consumer knowledge of and demand for a new product or create "name recognition" for a political unknown. Finally, intense, long-term media promotion can help a small group of manufacturers dominate a particular market, even though they are in close competition among themselves. For example, despite repeated medical findings that all nonprescription pain relievers provide the same amount of relief, equally fast and with equal safety, the market is totally dominated by three or four heavily advertised national brands (Consumers Union, 1980). Such advertising costs money, of course, and these national brands cost the buyer up to seven times more than the less advertised brands available in virtually every drugstore and supermarket in the country. If you use one of these well-known brands, your headache dollar is spent primarily for the privilege of being persuaded to spend it, and you have first-hand knowledge that media persuasion is effective (Bem, 1970).

But when one considers how small a proportion of its intended audience that mass media persuasion affects or how little it affects a single individual's beliefs or attitudes, the effectiveness of media persuasion looks much less impressive. For example, after an intensive image-building campaign for the oil industry, 13 percent of the sample surveyed had become more favorable, but 9 percent had become less favorable (Watson, 1966). During the 1960 presidential campaign, 55 percent of the adult population watched the famous debates between John F. Kennedy and Richard M. Nixon; 80 percent watched at least one of the debates. Moreover, there was a clear perception among journalists that Kennedy won the debates. But research surveys showed that there were no substantial changes in votes as a result of the debates (Katz & Feldman, 1962). The 1980 debate between Jimmy Carter and Ronald Reagan was held one week before the presidential election and is often cited as a major influence in Reagan's last-minute victorious surge. But a CBS News poll taken immediately after the debate showed that only 7 percent of viewers changed their preference from Carter to Reagan and 1 percent of Reagan's supporters moved to Carter. Again, in a close race such tiny percentages can be important, but they do not reveal massive influence on the part of the mass media. Why aren't the mass media more influential?

NOBODY IS WATCHING Perhaps the most mundane, but most critical, reason is that only a small proportion of the target audience is watching or paying attention. For example, even though the Nielsen ratings showed that the average household in 1976 had a TV set on almost 7 hours per day, one study found that nobody was in the room 19 percent of the time while the television was on, and 21 percent of the time people were in the room but no one was watching. Even when people were watching, they were often doing other things, including ironing, playing games, talking on the telephone, wrestling, dancing, and undressing (Comstock et al., 1978).

Moreover, with the exception of events such as the presidential debates, most political news and advertising reach only a tiny proportion of the population. A majority of adult Americans do not see any national news broadcast in an average two-week period (Robinson, 1971). Even those who do watch fail to retain much of what they see. One telephone survey found that viewers could recall fewer than 2 of the 20 news stories covered on the national news earlier in the evening. Even when reminded of the stories, viewers still could not remember having heard half of them (Neuman, 1976).

SELECTIVE EXPOSURE   A second reason the media fail to change our beliefs and attitudes is that we are more likely to be exposed to opinions we already agree with. Democrats listen mainly to speeches by Democrats; Republicans, to speeches by Republicans. Liberals read *The New Republic* but are unlikely to read *The National Review.* Research shows that most selective exposure is unintentional; we simply tend to be around sources of information that support our views. The conservative businessperson probably reads the *Wall Street Journal* because he or she is interested in business news; the fact that it also supports his or her political views is incidental. Again, the major obstacle facing a would-be persuader is to get the message to us in the first place.

SELECTIVE ATTENTION   Even the persuader whose message does reach us cannot control very well how we attend to it. This was shown in two clever experiments in which subjects listened to persuasive communications that were difficult to hear because of static in the sound channel. In order to hear the message more clearly, the subject could push a button that removed the static (Brock & Balloun, 1967; Kleinhesselink & Edwards, 1975). The subjects were more likely to remove the static from messages that supported their views than to messages that did not. For example, students who were strongly in favor of legalizing marijuana removed the static from neutral messages, from messages supporting legalization, and even from messages opposing legalization with arguments that were easy to refute; but they let the static interfere when the messages opposed legalization with arguments that were difficult to refute (Kleinhesselink & Edwards, 1975).

SELECTIVE INTERPRETATION   Even when we listen carefully to a message, we are likely to interpret it in the context of our own beliefs and attitudes. Political figures learn to state their positions — or nonpositions — with enough ambiguity so that the maximum number of people can interpret the message as agreeing with their own position. Moreover, we will perceive messages from sources we already agree with as more supportive of our own positions than they might actually be. For instance, in presidential elections voters tend to see the positions taken by the candidates they prefer as being more consistent with their own views than they actually are (Granberg & Brent, 1974).

A SUCCESSFUL COUNTEREXAMPLE   It is clear that the mass media are not going to brainwash us. When we consider the many obstacles a would-be persuader faces in trying to reach us, it is a wonder that mass media persuasion works at all. But in some cases these obstacles have been overcome, as the following study demonstrates.

In 1972, the Stanford Heart Disease Prevention Program launched a three-community field study to see if people could be persuaded to alter their exercise, smoking, and dietary habits in the interest of reducing their risk of heart disease (Maccoby, Farquhar, Wood, & Alexander, 1977). This was a collaborative effort involving social psychologists, communications experts, media production people, and cardiovascular disease experts. Note that such an effort not only faces the usual obstacles of media persuasion already discussed, but it also requires people to change deeply embedded habits, such as smoking and overeating. Accordingly, the research team put everything they knew about persuasion, communication, and behavior modification into the program.

Two northern California communities (each with a population of about

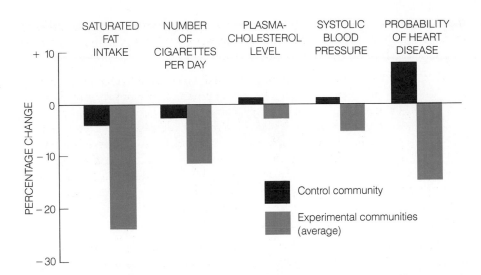

FIGURE 18-10

Mass Media Persuasion Campaign *An intensive two-year mass media campaign successfully persuaded citizens from the experimental communities to alter their daily habits in order to reduce their risk of developing heart disease. (After Farquhar et al., 1977)*

13,000) were selected to be the experimental communities; and a third community, similar to the others, served as the control. A randomly selected sample of about 400 people in each of the three communities was surveyed before, during, and after the two-year study in order to assess the effects of the campaign. Over the two years, the entire population of the experimental communities was exposed to about three hours of TV programs, over 50 TV spot announcements, 100 radio spots, several hours of radio programming, weekly newspaper columns, and newspaper advertisements and stories that dealt with the heart disease campaign. Posters were put up in buses, stores, and worksites, and printed material was sent via direct mail to the participants. The campaign was presented in both English and Spanish because of the sizable Spanish-speaking population in the communities.

The research team found that the level of knowledge about risk factors associated with heart disease increased dramatically in the two experimental communities, showing about a 30 percent increase, compared with about a 6 percent increase for the control community (Maccoby, Farquhar, Wood, & Alexander, 1977). Figure 18-10 shows that participants in the experimental communities demonstrated significantly greater decreases than the control community participants in saturated fat intake, cigarette smoking, plasma-cholesterol levels, systolic blood pressure, and overall probability of contracting heart disease (Farquhar et al., 1977).

These results are even more impressive when compared with results obtained from a specially selected group of participants who were enrolled in an intensive ten-week program involving weekly counseling and instruction on how to reduce the risk of heart disease. These were all people identified as being at high risk for contracting such disease. During the second year of the program, the individuals again received counseling and were encouraged to maintain any previous changes. The participants were also exposed to the overall media campaign. The results show that this group significantly reduced their risk-related behaviors during the first year of the program, doing better than media-only participants. But by the end of the second year, the media-only campaign had almost caught up, producing nearly as much change as the intensive counseling (Farquhar et al., 1977). This highly successful study has led to several others in both North America and other countries. The original Stanford group now conducts workshops for communities that wish to implement such programs on their own, and

This scene, from a 60-second TV spot sponsored by the Stanford Heart Disease Prevention Program, features a local man who reports that he can now run marathon races after having lost 60 pounds through exercise and jogging.

current research is testing to see if existing community organizations can obtain and maintain similar beneficial behavior changes in the community (Farquhar, Maccoby, & Solomon, 1984).

This study shows that persuasion via the mass media *can* be effective if it is carefully and intensively carried out. It is also important to note that the sources of influence in this study had very high credibility. They were experts on the topic of heart disease, and their motives in trying to obtain behavior change from the target audience could not be seen as self-serving—as a product advertisement or political speech would be. Credibility is the key to internalization.

IDENTIFICATION

Nearly every group to which we belong, from our family to the society as a whole, has an implicit or explicit set of beliefs, attitudes, and behaviors that it considers to be correct. Any member of the group who strays from these social norms risks isolation and social disapproval. Thus, through social rewards and punishments, the groups to which we belong obtain compliance from us. In addition, if we respect or admire other individuals or groups we may obey their norms and adopt their beliefs, attitudes, and behaviors in order to be like them, to identify with them. This is the process of *identification*.

Reference Groups

Groups with whom we identify are called our *reference groups*, because we refer to them in order to evaluate and to regulate our opinions and actions. A reference group can also serve as a frame of reference by providing us not only with specific beliefs and attitudes but also with a general perspective by which we view the world—an ideology or set of ready-made interpretations of social issues and events. If we eventually adopt these views as our own and integrate the group's ideology into our value system, then the reference group will have produced internalization. The process of identification can provide a bridge between compliance and internalization.

The influence of reference groups was illustrated by a study in which students at a progressive teachers' college listened to a recorded speech that called for a return to traditional classroom methods. The speech was interrupted several times by applause. Half the students had been told that the audience in the recording was composed of students from their own college; the other half, that it was composed of local townspeople. Members of the first group changed their opinions about progressive education more than did the students who believed the applause came from "outsiders" (Kelley & Woodruff, 1956).

An individual does not necessarily have to be a member of a reference group in order to be influenced by its values. For example, lower-middle-class individuals often use the middle-class as a reference group. A young, aspiring athlete may use professional athletes as a reference group, adopting their views and otherwise trying to model himself or herself after them.

Life would be simple if each of us identified with only one reference group. But most of us identify with several reference groups, which often leads to conflicting pressures on us. We noted in Chapter 17, for example, that the Jewish businessperson might experience cross-pressures because his or her ethnic reference group usually holds more liberal political positions than does his or her business reference group. But perhaps the most enduring example of competing reference groups is the conflict that many young people experience between their family reference group and their college or peer reference group, which is repeated every generation. The most extensive study of this conflict is Theodore Newcomb's classic Bennington study—an examination of the political attitudes of the entire population of Bennington College, a small, politically liberal college in Vermont. The dates of the study (1935–39) are a useful reminder to those who are just now discovering the generation gap for themselves; it is not a new phenomenon.

Today, Bennington College tends to attract liberal students, but in 1935 most students were from wealthy, conservative families. (It is coed today, but in 1935, it was a women's college.) Over two-thirds of the parents of Bennington students were affiliated with the Republican party. The Bennington College community was liberal during the 1930s, but this was not why most of the women selected the college.

Newcomb's main finding was that with each year at Bennington, students moved further away from their parents' attitudes and closer to the attitudes of the college community. For example, in the 1936 presidential campaign, about 66 percent of parents favored the Republican candidate, Landon, over the Democratic candidate, Roosevelt. Landon was supported by 62 percent of the Bennington freshmen and 43 percent of the sophomores, but only 15 percent of the juniors and seniors.

For most of the women, increasing liberalism reflected a deliberate choice between the two competing reference groups. Two women discuss how they made this choice:

> All my life I've resented the protection of governesses and parents. At college I got away from that, or rather, I guess I should say, I changed it to wanting the intellectual approval of teachers and more advanced students. Then I found that you can't be reactionary and be intellectually respectable.

> Becoming radical meant thinking for myself and, figuratively, thumbing my nose at my family. It also meant intellectual identification with the faculty and students that I most wanted to be like. (Newcomb, 1943, pp. 134, 131)

Individuals belong to a number of reference groups. This young woman's attitudes and behavior may be influenced by her fellow cheerleaders, but she probably also identifies with other reference groups which may emphasize similar or different values.

Reference groups provide their members with a ready-made viewpoint on social issues.

Note that the second woman uses the term "identification" in the sense that we have been using it. Note, too, how the women describe a mixture of change produced by social rewards and punishments (compliance) and change produced by an attraction to an admired group whom they strive to emulate (identification).

From Identification to Internalization

As mentioned earlier, reference groups also serve as frames of reference by providing their members with new perspectives on the world. The Bennington community, particularly the faculty, gave students a perspective on the depression of the 1930s and the threat of World War II that their wealthy and conservative home environments had not, and this began to move the women from identification to internalization:

> It didn't take me long to see that liberal attitudes had prestige value. . . . I became liberal at first because of its prestige value; I remain so because the problems around which my liberalism centers are important. What I want now is to be effective in solving problems.

> Prestige and recognition have always meant everything to me. . . . But I've sweat blood in trying to be honest with myself, and the result is that I really know what I want my attitudes to be, and I see what their consequences will be in my own life. (Newcomb, 1943, pp. 136–137)

Many of our most important beliefs and attitudes probably are initially based on identification. Whenever we start to identify with a new reference group, we engage in a process of "trying on" the new set of beliefs and attitudes they prescribe. What we "really believe" is in flux, capable of changing from day to day. The first year of college often has this effect on students; many of the views students bring from the family reference group are challenged by students and faculty from very different backgrounds, with different beliefs. Students often "try on" the new beliefs with great intensity and strong conviction, only to discard them for still newer beliefs when the first set does not quite fit. This is a natural process of growth. Although the process never really ends for people who remain open to new experiences, it is greatly accelerated during the college years, before the person has formed a nucleus of permanent beliefs on which to build more slowly and less radically. The real "work" of college is to evolve an ideological identity from the several beliefs and attitudes that are tested in order to move from identification to internalization.

It also appears that the college experience moves most students toward greater political liberalism—just as it did years ago at Bennington. Surveys from 1961 to 1963 and again from 1969 to 1970, conducted by a politically conservative magazine, showed this trend at a diverse array of colleges and universities (*National Review*, 1963, 1971). About 77 percent of the students in the 1970 survey said their political attitudes had moved toward the left since they had entered college, whereas only 9 percent had moved toward the right. And although fewer college students in the 1980s describe themselves as politically liberal or radical than did those in the 1970s, liberal political protest is still widely supported by students on college campuses. Surveys continue to show that younger people are more liberal than older people, particularly on social issues such as women's rights, abortion, acceptance of homosexuality, and so forth (Yankelovich, 1974, 1981).

As noted earlier, the advantage of internalization over compliance is that the changes are self-sustaining. The original source of influence does not have to monitor the individual to maintain the induced changes. The test of internalization, then, is the long-term stability of the induced beliefs, attitudes, and behaviors. Was the identification-induced liberalism of the Bennington women maintained when the students returned to the "real world"? The answer is yes. A follow-up study of the women 25 years later found that they had remained liberal. For example, in the 1960 presidential election, 60 percent of Bennington alumnae preferred the Democrat Kennedy over the Republican Nixon, compared with fewer than 30 percent of women from a similar socioeconomic class and geographical location and with a similar educational level. Moreover, about 60 percent of Bennington alumnae were politically active, most (66 percent) within the Democratic party (Newcomb, Koening, Flacks, & Warwick, 1967).

But we never outgrow our need for identification with supporting reference groups. The political attitudes of Bennington women remained stable, in part, because they selected new reference groups — friends and husbands — after college who supported the attitudes they had developed in college. Those who married more conservative men were more likely to be politically conservative in 1960. As Newcomb noted, we often select our reference groups because they share our attitudes, and then our reference groups, in turn, help to develop and to sustain our attitudes. The relationship is circular. The distinction between identification and internalization is a useful one for understanding social influence, but in practice it is not always possible to disentangle them.

SUMMARY

1. Social psychology is, in part, the study of how an individual's thoughts, feelings, and behaviors are influenced by others. Three processes of social influence have been identified: (a) *compliance*, in which the person publicly conforms outwardly to the wishes of the influencing source but does not change his or her private beliefs or attitudes; (b) *internalization*, in which the person changes his or her beliefs, attitudes, or behaviors because he or she genuinely believes in the validity of the position advocated by the influencing source; and (c) *identification*, in which the person changes his or her beliefs, attitudes, or behaviors in order to identify with, or be like, an influencing source that is respected or admired.

2. We are also influenced by *social norms*, implicit rules and expectations that tell us what we ought to think and how we ought to behave. Because norms influence us even when others are not actually present, the definition of social psychology broadens to include the study of how an individual's thoughts, feelings, and behaviors are influenced by the *actual, imagined,* or *implied presence* of others.

3. Both humans and animals respond more quickly in the presence of other members of their species. This effect, called *social facilitation,* occurs whether the others are performing the same task (coactors) or are simply watching (an audience). The presence of others appears to raise the organism's drive level. For humans, cognitive factors, such as a concern with evaluation, also play a role, and there are several competing theories about social facilitation effects.

4. The uninhibited aggressive behavior sometimes shown by mobs and crowds may be the result of a state of *deindividuation*, in which individuals feel that they have lost their personal identities and have merged into the group. Anonymity and close group unity seem to reduce self-awareness and to contribute to deindividuation. Some of the consequences of deindividuation are weakened restraints against impulsive behavior, increased sensitivity to immediate cues and current emotional states, and a lessened concern about the evaluation by others.

5. A bystander to an emergency is less likely to intervene or to help if in a group than if alone. Two major factors that deter intervention are *defining the situation* and *diffusion of responsibility.* Bystanders, by attempting to appear calm, may define the situation for each other as a nonemergency, thereby producing a state

of *pluralistic ignorance.* The presence of other people also diffuses responsibility so that no one person feels the necessity to act. Bystanders are more likely to intervene when these factors are minimized, particularly if at least one person displays helping behavior.

6. *Social impact theory* summarizes many phenomena of social influence by proposing that (1) the social impact or effectiveness of influence on a target individual *increases* with the number, immediacy, and importance of the sources of influence; and (2) the social impact of a source of influence *decreases* as the number, immediacy, and importance of targets increase.

7. When a source of influence obtains compliance by setting an example, it is called *conformity.* When the source obtains compliance by wielding authority, it is called *obedience.* Asch studied conformity to social pressure by using a simple perceptual task with an obvious correct answer. He found that incorrect responses by the group placed strong pressure on the individual to conform to the group's judgments. Pressures to conform appear to arise from the message that dissent would communicate to the group — namely, that the other members of the group are incompetent or that the individual is out of touch with reality. Much less conformity is observed if the group is not unanimous.

8. A dramatic and controversial set of studies by Milgram demonstrated that people will obey an experimenter's order to deliver strong electric shocks to an innocent victim. Factors conspiring to produce the high obedience rates include social norms (for example, the implied contract to continue the experiment until completed); the surveillance of the experimenter; features of the setting (buffers) that distance the person from the consequences of his or her acts; and the legitimizing role of science, which leads people to abandon their autonomy to the experimenter.

9. Obedience to illegitimate authority can be undermined — and rebellion provoked — if the individual is with a group whose members have the opportunity to share their opinions about the situation with one another, can give each other social support for dissenting, and can provide role models for disobedience. But the individual may then have to choose between obedience to the authority and conformity to the group that has decided to rebel.

10. Studies of conformity and obedience reveal that situational factors exert more influence over behavior than most of us realize. We tend to underestimate situational forces on behavior.

11. A source of influence with social power can produce compliance, but only an influence source with credibility (persuasiveness and believability) can produce internalization, actual belief and attitude change. Research has shown that a minority of persons within a larger group can move the majority toward its point of view if it presents and maintains a consistent dissenting position without appearing rigid, dogmatic, or arrogant. Such minorities are perceived to be more confident and, occasionally, more competent than the majority. Sometimes the minority obtains such internalization even without obtaining compliance; members of the majority modify their private opinions while publicly continuing to express the initial majority position.

12. Despite the amount of money spent on persuasion in the mass media, the effects are not great. The main problem lies in reaching the intended audience. People tend not to attend to the persuasive message, they expose themselves primarily to opinions they already agree with, they "tune out" messages they disagree with, and they tend to interpret the message as more similar to their original beliefs than it actually is. However, a large-scale, two-year campaign aimed at changing people's habits in order to reduce the risk of heart disease showed that the mass media can be very effective when skillfully used.

13. We display the process of *identification* when we obey the norms and adopt the beliefs, attitudes, and behaviors of groups that we respect and admire. We use such *reference groups* to evaluate and to regulate our opinions and actions. A

reference group can regulate our attitudes and behavior by administering social rewards and punishments or by providing us with a frame of reference, a ready-made interpretation of events and social issues.

14. Most of us identify with more than one reference group, and this can lead to conflicting pressures on our beliefs, attitudes, and behaviors. College students frequently move away from the views of their family reference group toward the college reference group. Typically, they move in a politically liberal direction, and this change sustains itself over subsequent years. The new views, usually adopted through the process of identification, thus become internalized. They are also sustained because we tend to select new reference groups after college — spouses and friends — that agree with us already.

FURTHER READING

Many of the topics in this chapter are covered in paperback books written for general audiences, often by the original investigators. Aronson, *The Social Animal* (4th ed., 1984), covers several topics in social influence. Milgram, *Obedience to Authority* (1974) is well worth reading, especially before forming an opinion about this controversial series of studies. Latané and Darley's *The Unresponsive Bystander: Why Doesn't He Help?* (1970) is a report by two of the original researchers in that area. Le Bon's classic book *The Crowd* (1895) is available in several editions.

The Bennington study and its follow-up of both the original women and Bennington College itself are reported in Newcomb, *Personality and Social Change* (1943); and in Newcomb, Koening, Flacks, and Warwick, *Persistence and Change: Bennington College and Its Students After Twenty-five Years* (1967).

Brown, *Social Psychology, the Second Edition* (1985); and Sears, Freedman, and Peplau, *Social Psychology* (5th ed., 1985), are general social psychology textbooks that cover the topics discussed in this chapter. More technical, in-depth treatments are available in Lindzey and Aronson (eds.), *The Handbook of Social Psychology* (3rd ed., 1985).

How to Read a Textbook: The PQRST Method

A CENTRAL TOPIC IN PSYCHOLOGY IS the study of learning and memory. Almost every chapter of this book refers to these phenomena, and Chapter 7 ("Learning and Conditioning") and Chapter 8 ("Memory") are devoted exclusively to them. In this appendix we review a method for reading and studying information presented in textbook form. The theoretical ideas underlying this method are discussed in Chapter 8 (p. 271); the method is described here for readers who wish to apply it in studying this textbook.

This approach for reading textbook chapters, called the PQRST method, has been shown to be very effective in improving the reader's understanding of and memory for key ideas and information.* The method takes its name from the first letter of the five steps one follows in reading a chapter. The steps or stages are diagramed in the margin of the next page. The first and last stages (Preview and Test) apply to the chapter as a whole; the middle three stages (Question, Read, Self-recitation) apply to each major section of the chapter as it is encountered.

STAGE P (PREVIEW) In the first step, you preview the entire chapter by skimming through it to get an idea of major topics. This is done by reading the table of contents at the start of the chapter and then skimming the chapter, paying special attention to the headings of main sections and subsections and glancing at pictures and illustrations. The most important aspect of the preview stage is to read carefully the summary section at the end of the chapter once you have skimmed through the chapter. Take time to consider each point in the summary;

---

* The PQRST method as described here is based on the work of Thomas and H. A. Robinson (1982) and Spache and Berg (1978); their work, in turn, is based on the earlier contributions of F. P. Robinson (1970).

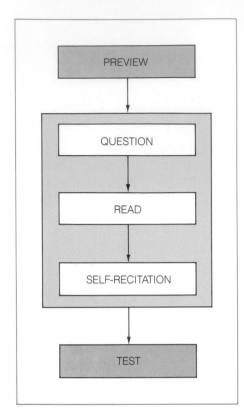

The PQRST Method

questions will come to mind that should be answered as you read the full text. The preview stage will give you an overall picture of the topics covered in the chapter and how they are organized.

STAGE Q (QUESTION) As noted earlier, you should apply Stages Q, R, and S to each major section of the chapter as it is encountered. The typical chapter in this textbook has about five to eight major sections. Work through the chapter one section at a time, applying Stages Q, R, and S to each section before going on to the next section. Before reading a section, read the heading of the section and the headings of the subsections. Then turn the topic headings into one or more questions that you should expect to answer while reading the section. This is the Question Stage.

STAGE R (READ) As you read the section, try to answer the questions you asked in Stage Q. Reflect on what you are reading, and try to make connections to other things you know. You may choose to mark or underline key words, phrases, or sentences in the text. It is probably best to delay taking notes until you have read the entire section and encountered all the key ideas, so you can judge their relative importance.

STAGE S (SELF-RECITATION) After you have finished reading the section, try to recall the main ideas and recite the information. Self-recitation is a powerful means of fixing the material in your memory. Put the ideas you have read into words and recite the information (preferably aloud or, if you are not alone, subvocally). Self-recitation will reveal blanks in your knowledge and at the same time will help you organize and consolidate the information in your mind. After you have completed one section of the chapter in this way, turn to the next section and again follow Stages Q, R, and S. Continue in this manner until you have finished all the sections of the chapter.

STAGE T (TEST) When you have finished reading the chapter, you should test and review all of the material. Look over your notes and test your recall for the main facts. Try to understand how the various facts relate to each other and how they were organized in the chapter. The test stage may require that you thumb back through the chapter to check key facts and ideas. You should also reread the chapter summary at this time; as you are doing so, you should be able to elaborate each sentence of the summary with several sentences of additional detail.

Research indicates that the PQRST method is very helpful and definitely preferable to simply reading straight through a chapter (Thomas & Robinson, 1982). Self-recitation is particularly important; it is better to spend as much as 80 percent of study time in an active attempt to recite than it is to devote the entire time to reading and rereading the material (Gates, 1917). Studies also show that a careful reading of the summary of the chapter *before* reading the chapter itself is especially productive (Reder & Anderson, 1980). Reading the summary first provides an overview of the chapter that helps organize the material as you read through the chapter. Even if you choose not to follow every step of the PQRST method, special attention should be directed to the value of self-recitation and reading the chapter summary as an introduction to the material.

Brief History of Psychology

ALTHOUGH PSYCHOLOGY IS A YOUNG science, people throughout history have been concerned with psychological issues. Books on the history of psychology discuss the views of early Greek philosophers, especially those of Plato and Aristotle. After the Greeks, Saint Augustine (A.D. 354–430) is considered the next great precursor of modern psychology because of his interest in introspection and his curiosity about psychological phenomena, including the behavior of young infants and of crowds at chariot races. Descartes (1596–1650) left his mark on psychology by theorizing that animals are machines that can be studied much as other machines are studied. He also introduced the concept of reflex action, which has occupied a significant place in psychology. Many prominent philosophers of the seventeenth and eighteenth centuries — Leibnitz, Hobbes, Locke, Kant, and Hume, to name five — grappled with psychological questions.

ROOTS OF CONTEMPORARY PSYCHOLOGY

Two Early Approaches

In the nineteenth century, two theories of the mind competed for support. One, known as *faculty psychology,* was a doctrine of inherited mental powers. According to this theory, the mind has a few distinct and independent "faculties" or mental agencies — such as thinking, feeling, and willing — that account for its activities. These faculties were further broken into subfaculties: we remember through the subfaculty of memory, imagine through the subfaculty of imagination, and so on. Faculty psychology encouraged early nineteenth-century *phrenologists,* such as Gall, to try to localize special faculties in different parts of the brain.

The *association psychologists* held an opposing view. They denied inborn faculties of the mind; instead, they limited the mind's content to ideas that enter by way of the senses and then become associated through such principles as similarity, contrast, and contiguity. They explained all mental activity through the *association of ideas* — a concept principally developed by British philosophers.

Wilhelm Wundt

Sir Francis Galton

Both faculty psychology and association psychology have present-day counterparts. The search for mental abilities as factors in psychological tests is related to faculty psychology. Current research on memory and learning is related to earlier association theory. Faculty psychology took note of the inherited aspects of behavior, whereas associationism emphasized the environment as the determiner of behavior. The environment versus heredity issue runs throughout the history of psychology.

Wundt's Laboratory

Wilhelm Wundt is given credit for founding psychology as an academic discipline. The founding date is usually cited as 1879, the year that Wundt established the first formal psychological laboratory at the University of Leipzig in Germany. Wundt's research was primarily concerned with the senses, especially vision; but he and his coworkers also studied attention, emotion, and memory.

Wundt's psychology relied on *introspection* as a method of studying mental processes. The introspective method was inherited from philosophy, but Wundt added a new dimension to the concept. Pure self-observation was not sufficient; it had to be supplemented by experiments. His experiments systematically varied some physical dimension of a stimulus, and the introspective method was used to determine how these physical changes modified consciousness.

Wundt's approach to research can be illustrated by one of his experiments on *reaction time*. In this experiment, the subject was required to press a key as quickly as possible after the onset of a light, and the subject's reaction time was carefully measured. Wundt found that the response time was longer when a subject paid careful attention to detecting the onset of light than it was when the subject's attention was directed to making a quick finger movement to press the key. The subject reacted very quickly in both cases, but there was a difference in reaction time of about .1 second. To explain this strange finding, Wundt distinguished between *perception* and *apperception*. When attention was focused on the finger movement, simple perception occurred and the light triggered the response promptly. But when attention was focused on the stimulus, an additional activity of apperception occurred, which involved a "richer" perception of the light. Wundt decided that this apperception required about .1 second. His interpretation is no longer accepted, for we now know that the processes intervening between stimulus and response are organized in more complex ways; but such studies helped to launch psychology as an experimental science.

Until his death in 1920, Wundt's personal influence on psychology was singularly important. Many pioneers in American psychology were trained in Wundt's laboratory. The first formal psychology laboratory in the United States was established in 1883 at Johns Hopkins University by G. Stanley Hall (who had studied with Wundt), although William James had set up a small demonstration laboratory at Harvard by 1875. The first person to be called "professor of psychology" in the United States was J. McKeen Cattell, another Wundt student, who acquired that title at the University of Pennsylvania in 1888. Before the end of the 1890s, Wundt's students were to be found in many American universities.

Other Roots of Contemporary Psychology

Although the impetus for establishing psychological laboratories came largely from Germany, there were other influences. In England, Sir Francis Galton was a pioneer in the study of individual differences and also exerted an important influence on the development of intelligence tests. Galton invented the statistical technique of correlation and developed the index that later became known as the *coefficient of correlation*.

The influence of the theory of evolution through natural selection, propounded by Charles Darwin, also came from England. Darwin's theory established the continuity between animals and human beings and thus led to comparative studies in psychology.

Another area of influence on psychology came from medicine, especially from the treatment of the mentally ill. Hypnotism, for example, has a long history as a form of therapy, dating from the work of Anton Mesmer in the late 1700s. Another Viennese physician, Sigmund Freud, founded psychoanalysis early in the present century.

SCHOOLS OF PSYCHOLOGY

Structuralism and Functionalism

When scientific psychology emerged in the latter part of the nineteenth century, researchers were making great advances in chemistry and physics by analyzing complex compounds (molecules) into their elements (atoms). These successes encouraged psychologists to look for the mental elements of which more complex experiences were composed. If the chemist made headway by analyzing water into hydrogen and oxygen, perhaps the psychologist could make progress by considering the taste of lemonade (perception) as a molecule of conscious experience to be analyzed into elements (sensations) — such as sweet, bitter, cold, and whatever — that could be identified by introspection. This was the approach taken by Wundt and his students; its major proponent in the United States was E. B. Titchener, a Wundt-trained psychologist at Cornell University. Since the goal was to specify mental structures, Titchener introduced the term *structuralism* to describe this brand of psychology.

But there was vigorous opposition to the purely analytical character of structuralism. William James — a distinguished psychologist at Harvard University — was impatient with the restrictions on psychology as it was developing under the structuralists. James felt that less emphasis should be placed on analyzing the elements of consciousness and more emphasis should be placed on understanding its fluid, streaming, personal character. His principal interest was in studying how the mind worked so that an organism could adapt to its environment. Because James asked how consciousness functions (particularly in the adaptive process), his approach to psychology was named *functionalism*. James' writing on *habits* as a mode of adaptation helped set the stage for a psychology that included the learning process as a central topic of study.

Interest in adaptation was influenced by Darwin's theory of natural selection. Consciousness evolved, so the argument ran, only because it served some purpose in guiding the activities of the individual. With this emphasis on the functional role of consciousness came a recognition that the introspective method of structuralism was too restrictive. To find out how the organism adapts to its environment, the functionalists argued that data derived from introspection had to be supplemented by observations of actual behavior, including the study of animal behavior and the development of behavior (developmental psychology). Thus, functionalism broadened the scope of psychology to include behavior as a dependent variable. But along with the structuralists, functionalists still regarded psychology as the science of conscious experience and the principal investigative method as introspection.

William James

Important Dates in the History of Psychology

B.C.	400	Hippocrates relates personality characteristics to body types and proposes a physiological (as opposed to demonological) theory of mental illness.
B.C.	350	Aristotle stresses the objective observation of man's behavior and proposes three principles to account for the association of ideas.
A.D.	400	Saint Augustine, influenced by Platonic ideas, makes careful introspections in his *Confessions*.
	1650	René Descartes characterizes the mind–body relationship as one of interaction.
	1651	Thomas Hobbes foreshadows associationism by declaring that all ideas come from sensory experience.
	1690	John Locke carries Hobbes' notion a step further by declaring that the mind at birth is a blank slate *(tabula rasa)*.
	1749	David Hartley formalizes a doctrine of associationism and suggests a neurological basis for memory.
	1781	Immanuel Kant's *Critique of Pure Reason* attacks associationism and the nativistic approach; it strongly influences later philosophers and psychologists.
	1809	Franz Gall and Johann Spurzheim give prominence through phrenology to the study of mental faculties and brain function.
	1821	Pierre Flourens performs the first significant experiments in localization of brain functions.
	1822	Friedrich Bessel measures individual differences in reaction time for astronomical observations.
	1838	Johannes Müller formulates the doctrine of specific nerve energies.
	1846	Ernst Weber derives the first quantitative law in psychology.
	1850	Hermann von Helmholtz measures the rates of conduction of nerve impulses.
	1859	Charles Darwin publishes *The Origin of Species*, propounding the theory of evolution through natural selection.
	1860	Gustav Fechner publishes *Elements of Psychophysics*, in which he presents various methods for measuring the relationship between physical stimuli and sensations.
	1869	Sir Francis Galton studies individual differences and applies Darwin's concept of selective adaptation to the evolution of races.
	1879	Wilhelm Wundt opens the first formal psychological laboratory at the University of Leipzig.
	1883	G. Stanley Hall establishes the first psychological laboratory in America at Johns Hopkins University.

1885   Hermann Ebbinghaus publishes the first experimental studies of memory.

1890   William James' *Principles of Psychology* is published in the United States.

1892   Edward Titchener at Cornell University establishes "structuralism" as a major influence in American psychology.

1898   Edward Thorndike performs some of the first controlled experiments on animal learning.

1900   Sigmund Freud publishes *The Interpretation of Dreams*, which presents many of his ideas on psychoanalysis.

1905   Alfred Binet and Theodore Simon devise the first intelligence test.

1906   Ivan Pavlov publishes the results of his studies on classical conditioning.

1908   William McDougall's publication of *An Introduction to Social Psychology* marks the formal inauguration of the field of social psychology.

1912   Max Wertheimer publishes the first formulation of Gestalt psychology.

1913   John B. Watson exerts a major impact on the course of psychology with his behaviorist manifesto.

1917   Wolfgang Köhler publishes the results of his studies on problem solving in primates.

1922   Edward Tolman presents his initial ideas on purposive behaviorism.

1929   Karl Lashley publishes *Brain Mechanisms and Intelligence*.

1935   Louis Thurstone develops factor analysis.

1938   B. F. Skinner publishes *The Behavior of Organisms*, which summarizes early research on operant conditioning.

1949   Donald Hebb, in *Organization of Behavior*, presents a theory that bridges the gap between neurophysiology and psychology.

1950   William Estes lays the foundation for a mathematical approach to theories of learning.

1954   The Swiss psychologist Jean Piaget publishes *The Construction of Reality in the Child*, which focuses attention on cognitive development.

1957   Noam Chomsky publishes *Syntactic Structures*, a book that presents a cognitive approach to language behavior.

1958   Herbert Simon and colleagues publish *Elements of a Theory of Human Problem Solving*, which reformulates classical psychological problems in terms of information-processing models.

Events since 1960 are not listed because not enough time has elapsed to judge their long-term impact on the field.

John B. Watson

Structuralism and functionalism played important roles in the early development of psychology. Because each viewpoint provided a systematic approach to the field, the two were considered competing *schools of psychology*. As psychology developed, other schools evolved and vied for leadership. By 1920, structuralism and functionalism were being displaced by three newer schools: behaviorism, Gestalt psychology, and psychoanalysis.

Behaviorism

Of the three new schools, behaviorism had the greatest influence on scientific psychology. Its founder, John B. Watson, reacted against the tradition of his time — that conscious experience was the province of psychology — and boldly proclaimed a psychology *without* introspection. Watson made no assertions about consciousness when he studied the behavior of animals and infants. He decided not only that the results of animal psychology and child psychology could stand on their own as a science, but also that they set a pattern that adult psychology might well follow.

In order to make psychology a science, Watson said, psychological data must be open to public inspection like the data of any other science. Behavior is public; consciousness is private. Science should deal with public facts. Because psychologists were growing impatient with introspection, the new behaviorism caught on rapidly, particularly in the 1920s; for a time, most of the younger psychologists in the United States called themselves "behaviorists." In Russia, the work of Ivan Pavlov on the conditioned response was regarded as an important area of research by the behaviorists. The conditioned response was being investigated in the United States in a limited way before the advent of behaviorism, but Watson was responsible for its subsequent widespread influence on psychology.

Watson argued that nearly all behavior is the result of conditioning, and that the environment shapes our behavior by reinforcing specific habits. The conditioned response was viewed as the smallest indivisible unit of behavior, an "atom of behavior" from which more complicated behaviors could be built. All types of complex behavioral repertoires arising from special training or education were regarded as nothing more than an interlinked fabric of conditioned responses.

Behaviorists found it congenial to discuss psychological phenomena as beginning with a stimulus and ending with a response — giving rise to the term *stimulus-response (S-R) psychology*. S-R psychology, as it evolved from behaviorism, went beyond the earlier behaviorists in its willingness to infer hypothetical processes between the stimulus input and the response output, processes that were called *intervening variables*.

If broad definitions are used, so that "stimulus" refers to a whole class of antecedent conditions and "response" refers to a whole class of outcomes (actual behavior and products of behavior), S-R psychology becomes merely a psychology of independent and dependent variables. Viewed in this way, S-R psychology is not a particular theory but a *language* that can be used to make psychological information explicit and communicable. As such, the S-R outlook is widely prevalent in psychology today.

Gestalt Psychology

At about the same time that Watson announced behaviorism in America, Gestalt psychology was appearing in Germany. The word *Gestalt* translates from the German as "form" or "configuration," and the psychology announced by Max Wertheimer in 1912 was a psychology concerned with the organization of mental processes. The position came to be identified most closely with Wertheimer and his colleagues Kurt Koffka and Wolfgang Köhler, all of whom migrated to the United States.

The earliest Gestalt experiments dealt with perceived motion, particularly the *phi phenomenon*. When two separated lights are flashed in succession (provided the timing and spatial locations are proper), the subject sees a single light moving from the position of the first light to that of the second. The phenomenon of apparent motion was familiar, but the Gestalt psychologists sensed the theoretical importance of the patterning of stimuli in producing the effect. Our experiences depend on the *patterns* formed by stimuli and on the *organization* of experience, they decided. What we see is relative to background, to other aspects of the whole. The whole is different from the sum of its parts; the whole consists of parts in relationship.

Although the Gestalt psychologists did not subscribe to the introspective psychology of their day any more than Watson did, they were vigorous opponents of behaviorism. They did not want to give up a kind of free introspection that goes by the name of *phenomenology*. They wanted to be able to ask a person what something looked like, what it meant. They were interested in the perception of motion, in how people judged sizes, and in the appearance of colors under changes in illumination.

The importance of perception in all psychological events has led those influenced by Gestalt psychology to a number of perception-centered interpretations of learning, memory, and problem solving. These interpretations, spoken of as forms of cognitive theory, were instrumental in laying the groundwork for current developments in cognitive psychology.

Wolfgang Köhler

Psychoanalysis

Sigmund Freud introduced psychoanalytic psychology to the United States in a series of lectures given at Clark University in 1909 on the invitation of psychologist G. Stanley Hall. Thus, the first scholarly recognition of Freud's work in the United States came from psychologists. Freud's influence became so pervasive that those who know nothing else about psychology have at least a nodding acquaintance with psychoanalysis.

If one of Freud's theories is to be singled out for consideration along with behaviorism and Gestalt psychology, it is his interpretation of the *unconscious*. Basic to Freud's theory of the unconscious is the conception that the unacceptable (forbidden, punished) wishes of childhood are driven out of awareness and become part of the unconscious, where (while out of awareness) they remain influential. The unconscious presses to find expression, which it does in numerous ways, including dreams, slips of speech, and unconscious mannerisms. The method of psychoanalysis — free association under the guidance of the analyst — is itself a way of helping unconscious wishes find verbal expression. In classical Freudian theory, these unconscious wishes were almost exclusively sexual. This emphasis on childhood sexuality was one of the barriers to the acceptance of Freud's theories when they were first announced.

RECENT DEVELOPMENTS

Despite the important contribution of Gestalt psychology and psychoanalysis, psychology was dominated by behaviorism until World War II, particularly in the United States. With the end of the war, interest in psychology increased and

Sigmund Freud

Herbert Simon

many people were attracted to careers in the field. Sophisticated instruments and electronic equipment became available, and a wider range of problems could be examined. This expanded program of research made it evident that earlier theoretical approaches were too restrictive.

This viewpoint was strengthened by the development of computers in the 1950s. Computers, properly programmed, were able to perform tasks — such as playing chess and proving mathematical theorems — that previously could only be done by human beings. It became apparent that the computer offered psychologists a powerful tool with which to theorize about psychological processes. A series of brilliant papers, published in the late 1950s by Herbert Simon (who was later awarded the Nobel prize) and his colleagues, indicated how psychological phenomena could be *simulated* using the computer. Many old psychological issues were recast in terms of *information-processing systems*. The human being could now be viewed as a processor of information. The senses provide an input channel for information; mental operations are applied to the input; the transformed input creates a mental structure that is stored in memory; that structure interacts with others in memory to generate a response. The power of the computer permitted psychologists to theorize about complex mental processes and then to investigate the implications of the theory by simulating it on a computer. If the response (output) stage of the computer simulation agreed with the observed behavior of actual people, the psychologist could have some confidence in the theory.

The information-processing approach provided a richer and more dynamic approach to psychology than S-R theory with its intervening variables. Similarly, the information-processing approach permitted some of the speculations of Gestalt psychology and psychoanalysis to be formulated in a precise fashion as programs in a computer; in this way, earlier ideas about the nature of the mind could be made concrete and checked against actual data.

Another factor that led to a changing viewpoint in psychology in the 1950s was the development of modern linguistics. Prior to that time, linguists were primarily concerned with a description of a language; now they began to theorize about the mental structures required to comprehend and to speak a language. Work in this area was pioneered by Noam Chomsky, whose book *Syntactic Structures*, published in 1957, provided the basis for an active collaboration between psychologists and linguists. A rapid development of the field of *psycholinguistics* followed, providing the first significant psychological analyses of language.

At the same time, important advances were occurring in neuropsychology. A number of discoveries about the brain and the nervous system established clear relationships between neurobiological events and mental processes. It became increasingly difficult to assert, as some of the early behaviorists had, that a science of psychology could be established without links to neurophysiology.

The development of information-processing models, psycholinguistics, and neuropsychology has produced a psychology that is highly cognitive in orientation. There is no agreed definition of *cognitive psychology,* but its principal concern is the scientific analysis of mental processes and mental structures. Cognitive psychology is not exclusively concerned with thought and knowledge. Its early concerns with the representation of knowledge and complex aspects of human thought led to the label "cognitive psychology," but the approach has been expanded to all areas of psychology, including clinical psychology.

Within a period of 50 years, the focus of psychology has come full circle. After rejecting conscious experience as ill-suited to scientific investigation and turning to the study of behavior, psychologists are once again theorizing about the mind, but this time with new and more powerful tools. The gain from behaviorism has been an emphasis in the objectivity and reproducibility of findings—an emphasis that has found a place in cognitive psychology.

From a historical perspective, it is too early to judge the long-term significance of recent developments in psychology. What is evident, however, is that there is great excitement in the field today, and many psychologists believe that it is in a period of revolutionary change and progress. Understanding how the mind works is a worthy challenge that deserves the best intellectual effort we can put forth.

FURTHER READING

For a general survey of the history of psychology, see Hilgard, *Psychology in America: A Historical Survey* (1987); Watson, *The Great Psychologists: From Aristotle to Freud* (4th ed., 1978); Wertheimer, *A Brief History of Psychology* (rev. ed., 1979); and Schultz, *A History of Modern Psychology* (4th ed., 1987). See also Boring, *A History of Experimental Psychology* (2nd ed., 1950); and Herrnstein and Boring, *A Source Book in the History of Psychology* (1965).

APPENDIX III ▰

Statistical Methods and Measurement

MUCH OF THE WORK OF PSYCHOLOGISTS calls for making measurements — either in the laboratory or under field conditions. This work may involve measuring the eye movements of infants when first exposed to a novel stimulus, recording the galvanic skin response of people under stress, counting the number of trials required to condition a monkey that has a prefrontal lobotomy, determining achievement test scores for students using computer-assisted learning, or counting the number of patients who show improvement following a particular type of psychotherapy. In all these examples, the *measurement operation* yields numbers; the psychologist's problem is to interpret them and to arrive at some general conclusions. Basic to this task is *statistics* — the discipline that deals with collecting numerical data and with making inferences from such data. The purpose of this appendix is to review certain statistical methods that play an important role in psychology.

The appendix is written on the assumption that the problems students have with statistics are essentially problems of clear thinking about data. An introductory acquaintance with statistics is *not* beyond the scope of anyone who understands enough algebra to use plus and minus signs and to substitute numbers for letters in equations.

84	75	91
61	75	67
72	87	79
75	79	83
77	51	69

TABLE 1
Raw Scores   *College entrance examination scores for 15 students, listed in the order in which they were tested.*

DESCRIPTIVE STATISTICS

Statistics serves, first of all, to provide a shorthand description of large amounts of data. Suppose that we want to study the college entrance examination scores of 5,000 students recorded on cards in the registrar's office. These scores are the raw data. Thumbing through the cards will give us some impressions of the students' scores, but it will be impossible for us to keep all of them in mind. So we make some kind of summary of the data, possibly averaging all the scores or finding the highest and lowest scores. These statistical summaries make it easier to remember and to think about the data. Such summarizing statements are called *descriptive statistics*.

Frequency Distributions

Items of raw data become comprehensible when they are grouped in a *frequency distribution*. To group data, we must first divide the scale along which they are measured into intervals and then count the number of items that fall into each interval. An interval in which scores are grouped is called a *class interval*. The decision of how many class intervals the data are to be grouped into is not fixed by any rules but is based on the judgment of the investigator.

Table 1 provides a sample of raw data representing college entrance examination scores for 15 students. The scores are listed in the order in which the students were tested (the first student tested had a score of 84; the second, 61; and so on). Table 2 shows these data arranged in a frequency distribution for which the class interval has been set at 10. One score falls in the interval from 50 to 59, three scores fall in the interval from 60 to 69, and so on. Note that most scores fall in the interval from 70 to 79 and that no scores fall below the 50 to 59 interval or above the 90 to 99 interval.

A frequency distribution is often easier to understand if it is presented graphically. The most widely used graph form is the *frequency histogram;* an example is shown in the top panel of Figure 1. Histograms are constructed by drawing bars, the bases of which are given by the class intervals and the heights of which are determined by the corresponding class frequencies. An alternative way of presenting frequency distributions in graph form is to use a *frequency polygon*, an example of which is shown in the bottom panel of Figure 1. Frequency polygons are constructed by plotting the class frequencies at the center of the class interval and connecting the points obtained by straight lines. To complete the picture, one extra class is added at each end of the distribution; since these classes have zero frequencies, both ends of the figure will touch the horizontal axis. The frequency polygon gives the same information as the frequency histogram but by means of lines rather than bars.

In practice, we would obtain a much greater number of items than those plotted in Figure 1, but a minimum amount of data is shown in all of the illustrations in this appendix so that you can easily check the steps in tabulating and plotting.

Measures of Central Tendency

A *measure of central tendency* is simply a representative point on our scale — a central point with scores scattered on either side. Three such measures are commonly used: the *mean*, the *median*, and the *mode*.

The *mean* is the familiar arithmetic average obtained by adding the scores and dividing by the number of scores. The sum of the raw scores in Table 1 is 1125. If we divide this by 15 (the number of students' scores), the mean turns out to be 75.

The *median* is the score of the middle item, which is obtained by arranging the scores in order and then counting into the middle from either end. When the 15 scores in Table 1 are placed in order from highest to lowest, the eighth score

CLASS INTERVAL	NUMBER OF PERSONS IN CLASS
50 – 59	1
60 – 69	3
70 – 79	7
80 – 89	3
90 – 99	1

TABLE 2

Frequency Distribution   *Scores from Table 1 accumulated with class intervals of 10.*

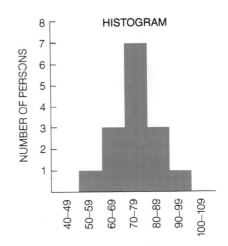

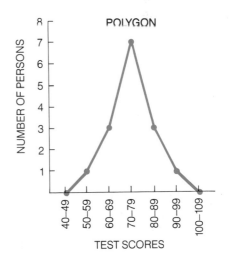

FIGURE 1

Frequency Diagrams   *The data from Table 2 are plotted here. A frequency histogram is on the top; a frequency polygon, on the bottom.*

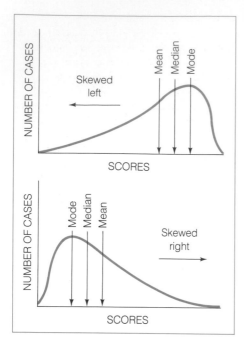

FIGURE 2

Skewed Distribution Curves *Note that skewed distributions are designated by the direction in which the tail falls. Also note that the mean, median, and mode are not identical for a skewed distribution; the median commonly falls between the mode and the mean.*

from either end turns out to be 75. If the number of cases is even, we simply average the two cases on either side of the middle. For instance, the median of 10 items is the arithmetic average of the fifth and sixth cases.

The *mode* is the most frequent score in a given distribution. In Table 1, the most frequent score is 75; hence, the mode of the distribution is 75.

In a *symmetrical distribution,* in which the scores are distributed evenly on either side of the middle (as in Figure 1), the mean, median, and mode all fall together. This is not true for distributions that are *skewed,* or unbalanced. Suppose we want to analyze the departure times of a morning train. The train usually leaves on time; occasionally it leaves late, but it never leaves early. For a train with a scheduled departure time of 8:00 A.M., one week's record might be as follows:

M	8:00	Mean = 8:07
Tu	8:04	Median = 8:02
W	8:02	Mode = 8:00
Th	8:19	
F	8:22	
Sat	8:00	
Sun	8:00	

The distribution of departure times in this example is skewed because of the two late departures; they raise the mean departure time but do not have much effect on the median or the mode.

Skewness is important because unless it is understood, the differences between the median and the mean may sometimes be misleading (see Figure 2). If, for example, two political parties are arguing about the prosperity of the country, it is possible for the mean and median incomes to move in opposite directions. Suppose that a round of wage increases has been combined with a reduction in extremely high incomes. The median income might have gone up while the mean went down. The party wanting to show that incomes were getting higher would choose the median; whereas the party wishing to show that incomes were getting lower would choose the mean.

The mean is the most widely used measure of central tendency, but there are times when the mode or the median is a more appropriate measure.

Measures of Variation

Usually more information is needed about a distribution than can be obtained from a measure of central tendency. For example, we need a measure to tell us whether scores cluster closely around their average or whether they scatter widely. A measure of the spread of scores around the average is called a *measure of variation.*

Measures of variation are useful in at least two ways. First, they tell us how representative the average is. If the variation is small, we know that individual scores are close to it. If the variation is large, we cannot use the mean as a representative value with as much assurance. Suppose that clothing is being designed for a group of people without the benefit of precise measurements. Knowing their average size would be helpful, but it also would be important to know the spread of sizes. The second measure provides a "yardstick" that we can use to measure the amount of variability among the sizes.

To illustrate, consider the data in Figure 3, which show frequency distributions of entrance examination scores for two classes of 30 students. Both classes have the same mean of 75, but they exhibit clearly different degrees of variation. The scores of all the students in Class I are clustered close to the mean, whereas

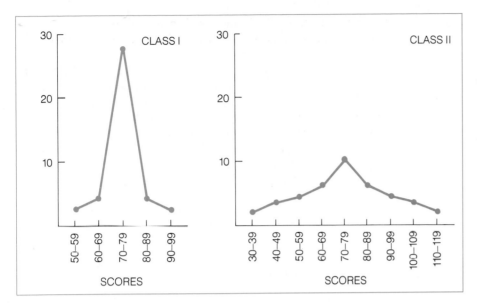

FIGURE 3

Distributions Differing in Variation *It is easy to see that the scores for Class I cluster closer to the mean than the scores for Class II, even though the means of the two classes are identical (75). For Class I, all the scores fall between 60 and 89, with most of the scores falling in the interval from 70 through 79. For Class II, the scores are distributed fairly uniformly over a wide range from 40 through 109. This difference in variability between the two distributions can be measured using the standard deviation, which is smaller for Class I than it is for Class II.*

the scores of the students in Class II are spread over a wide range. Some measure is required to specify more exactly how these two distributions differ. Two measures of variation frequently used by psychologists are the *range* and the *standard deviation*.

To simplify arithmetic computation, we will suppose that five students from each class seek entrance to college and that their entrance examination scores are as follows:

Student scores from Class I:
73, 74, 75, 76, 77 (mean = 75)

Student scores from Class II:
60, 65, 75, 85, 90 (mean = 75)

We will now compute the measures of variation for these two samples.

The *range* is the spread between the highest score and the lowest score. The range of scores for the five students from Class I is 4 (from 73 to 77); the range of scores from Class II is 30 (from 60 to 90).

The range is easy to compute, but the *standard deviation* is more frequently used because it has certain properties that make it the preferred measure. One such property is that it is an extremely sensitive measure of variation because it accounts for every score, not just extreme values as the range does. The standard deviation, denoted by the lowercase Greek letter *sigma* (σ), measures how far the scores making up a distribution depart from that distribution's mean. The deviation *d* of each score from the mean is computed and squared; then the average of these squared values is obtained. The standard deviation is the square root of this average.* Written as a formula,

---

* For this introductory treatment, we will use *sigma* (σ) throughout. However, in scientific literature, the lowercase letter *s* is used to denote the standard deviation of a *sample* and σ is used to denote the standard deviation of the *population*. Moreover, in computing the standard deviation of a sample *s*, the sum of d^2 is divided by $N - 1$ rather than by N. For reasonably large samples, however, the actual value of the standard deviation is only slightly affected whether we divide by $N - 1$ or N. To simplify this presentation, we will not distinguish between the standard deviation of a sample and that of a population; instead, we will use the same formula to compute both. For a discussion of this point, see Phillips (1982).

CLASS I SCORES (MEAN = 75)		
	d	d^2
$77 - 75 =$	2	4
$76 - 75 =$	1	1
$75 - 75 =$	0	0
$74 - 75 =$	−1	1
$73 - 75 =$	−2	4
		10

Sum of $d^2 = 10$
Mean of $d^2 = \frac{10}{5} = 2.0$
Standard deviation $(\sigma) = \sqrt{2.0} = 1.4$

CLASS II SCORES (MEAN = 75)		
	d	d^2
$90 - 75 =$	15	225
$85 - 75 =$	10	100
$75 - 75 =$	0	0
$65 - 75 =$	−10	100
$60 - 75 =$	−15	225
		650

Sum of $d^2 = 650$
Mean of $d^2 = \frac{650}{5} = 130$
Standard deviation $(\sigma) = \sqrt{130} = 11.4$

TABLE 3
Computation of the Standard Deviation

$$\sigma = \sqrt{\frac{\text{sum of } d^2}{N}}$$

Specimen computation of the standard deviation. The scores for the samples from the two classes are arranged in Table 3 for computation of the standard deviation. The first step involves subtracting the mean from each score (the mean is 75 for both classes). This operation yields positive d values for scores above the mean and negative d values for scores below the mean. The minus signs disappear when the d values are squared in the next column. The squared deviations are added and then divided by N, the number of cases in the sample; in our example, $N = 5$. Taking the square root yields the standard deviation. In this example, the two standard deviations give us much the same information as the ranges.

STATISTICAL INFERENCE

Now that we have become familiar with statistics as ways of describing data, we are ready to turn to the processes of interpretation — to the making of inferences from data.

Populations and Samples

First, it is necessary to distinguish between a *population* and a *sample* drawn from that population. The United States Census Bureau attempts to describe the whole population by obtaining descriptive material on age, marital status, and so on from everyone in the country. The word *population* is appropriate to the census because it represents *all* the people living in the United States.

In statistics, the word "population" is not limited to people or animals or things. The population may be all of the temperatures registered on a thermometer during the last decade, all of the words in the English language, or all of any other specified supply of data. Often we do not have access to the total population, and so we try to represent it by a sample drawn in a *random* (unbiased) fashion. We may ask some questions of a random fraction of the people, as the United States Census Bureau has done as part of recent censuses; we may derive average temperatures by reading the thermometer at specified times, without taking a continuous record; we may estimate the number of words in the encyclopedia by counting the words on a random number of pages. These illustrations all involve the selection of a *sample* from the population. If any of these processes are repeated, we will obtain slightly different results due to the fact that a sample does not fully represent the whole population and therefore contains *errors of sampling.* This is where statistical inference enters.

A sample of data is collected from a population in order to make inferences about that population. A sample of census data may be examined to see whether the population is getting older or whether there is a trend of migration to the suburbs. Similarly, experimental results are studied to determine what effects experimental manipulations have had on behavior — whether the threshold for pitch is affected by loudness, whether child-rearing practices have detectable effects later in life. To make *statistical inferences,* we have to evaluate the relationships revealed by the sample data. These inferences are always made under some degree of uncertainty due to sampling errors. If the statistical tests indicate that the magnitude of the effect found in the sample is fairly large (relative to the estimate of the sampling error), then we can be confident that the effect observed in the sample holds for the population at large.

Thus, statistical inference deals with the problem of making an inference or judgment about a feature of a population based solely on information obtained from a sample of that population. As an introduction to statistical inference, we will consider the normal distribution and its use in interpreting standard deviations.

Normal Distribution

When large amounts of data are collected, tabulated, and plotted as a histogram or polygon, they often fall into a roughly bell-shaped symmetrical distribution known as the *normal distribution*. Most items fall near the mean (the high point of the bell), and the bell tapers off sharply at very high and very low scores. This form of curve is of special interest because it also arises when the outcome of a process is based on a large number of *chance* events all occurring independently. The demonstration device displayed in Figure 4 illustrates how a sequence of chance events gives rise to a normal distribution. The chance factor of whether a steel ball will fall to the left or right each time it encounters a point where the channel branches results in a symmetrical distribution: more balls fall straight down the middle, but occasionally one reaches one of the end compartments. This is a useful way of visualizing what is meant by a chance distribution closely approximating the normal distribution.

The normal distribution (Figure 5) is the mathematical representation of the idealized distribution approximated by the device shown in Figure 4. The normal distribution represents the likelihood that items within a normally distributed population will depart from the mean by any stated amount. The percentages shown in Figure 5 represent the *percentage of the area* lying under the curve between the indicated scale values; the total area under the curve represents the whole population. Roughly two-thirds of the cases (68 percent) will fall between plus and minus one standard deviation from the mean ($\pm 1\sigma$); 95 percent of the cases within $\pm 2\sigma$; and virtually all cases (99.7 percent) within $\pm 3\sigma$. A more detailed listing of areas under portions of the normal curve is given in Table 4.

Using Table 4, let us trace how the 68 percent and 95 percent values in Figure 5 are derived. We find from Column 3 of Table 4 that between -1σ and the mean lies .341 of the total area and between $+1\sigma$ and the mean also lies .341 of the area. Adding these values gives us .682, which is expressed in Figure 5 as 68 percent. Similarly, the area between -2σ and $+2\sigma$ is $2 \times .477 = .954$, which is expressed as 95 percent.

These percentages have several uses. One is in connection with the interpretation of standard scores, to which we turn next. Another is in connection with tests of significance.

Scaling of Data

In order to interpret a score, we often need to know whether it is high or low in relation to other scores. If a person taking a driver's test requires .500 seconds to brake after a danger signal, how can we tell whether the performance is fast or slow? Does a student who scores 60 on a physics examination pass the course? To answer questions of this kind, we have to derive a *scale* against which the scores can be compared.

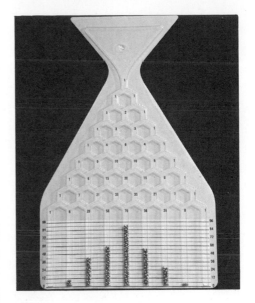

FIGURE 4

Device to Demonstrate a Chance Distribution *The board is held upside down until all the steel balls fall into the reservoir. Then the board is turned over and held vertically until the balls fall into the nine columns. The precise number of balls falling into each column will vary from one demonstration to the next. On the average, however, the heights of the columns of balls will approximate a normal distribution, with the greatest height in the center column and gradually decreasing heights in the outer columns.*

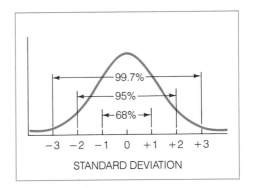

FIGURE 5

Normal Distribution *The normal distribution curve can be constructed using the mean and the standard deviation. The area under the curve below -3σ and above $+3\sigma$ is negligible.*

STANDARD DEVIATION	(1) AREA TO THE LEFT OF THIS VALUE	(2) AREA TO THE RIGHT OF THIS VALUE	(3) AREA BETWEEN THIS VALUE AND MEAN
-3.0σ	.001	.999	.499
-2.5σ	.006	.994	.494
-2.0σ	.023	.977	.477
-1.5σ	.067	.933	.433
-1.0σ	.159	.841	.341
-0.5σ	.309	.691	.191
0.0σ	.500	.500	.000
$+0.5\sigma$	.691	.309	.191
$+1.0\sigma$	.841	.159	.341
$+1.5\sigma$	.933	.067	.433
$+2.0\sigma$	.977	.023	.477
$+2.5\sigma$	.994	.006	.494
$+3.0\sigma$	.999	.001	.499

TABLE 4
Area of the Normal Distribution as
Proportion of Total Area

RANKED DATA By placing scores in rank order from high to low, we derive one kind of scale. An individual score is interpreted on the basis of where it ranks among the group of scores. For example, the graduates of West Point know where they stand in their class—perhaps 35th or 125th in a class of 400.

STANDARD SCORES The standard deviation is a convenient unit to use in scaling because we can interpret how far away 1σ or 2σ is from the mean (see Table 4). A score based on a multiple of the standard deviation is known as a *standard score*. Many scales used in psychological measurement are based on the principle of standard scores.

Specimen computations of standard scores. Table 1 presented college entrance scores for 15 students. Without more information, we do not know whether these scores are representative of the population of all college applicants. On this examination, however, we will assume that the population mean is 75 and the standard deviation is 10.

What, then, is the *standard score* for a student who had 90 on the examination? We must express how far this score lies above the mean in multiples of the standard deviation.

Standard score for grade of 90:

$$\frac{90 - 75}{10} = \frac{15}{10} = 1.5\sigma$$

As a second example, consider a student with a score of 53.

Standard score for grade of 53:

$$\frac{53 - 75}{10} = \frac{-22}{10} = -2.2\sigma$$

In this case, the minus sign tells us that the student's score is below the mean by 2.2 standard deviations. Thus, the sign of the standard score (+ or −) indicates whether the score is above or below the mean, and its value indicates how far from the mean the score lies in standard deviations.

How Representative Is a Mean?

How useful is the mean of a sample in estimating the population mean? If we measure the height of a random sample of 100 college students, how well does the sample mean predict the true population mean (that is, the mean height of *all* college students)? These questions raise the issue of making an *inference* about a population based on information from a sample.

The accuracy of such inferences depends on *errors of sampling*. Suppose we were to select two random samples from the same population, make the necessary measurements, and compute the mean for each sample. What differences between the first and the second mean could be expected to occur by chance?

Successive random samples drawn from the same population will have different means, forming a distribution of *sample means* around the *true mean* of the population. These sample means are themselves numbers for which the standard deviation can be computed. We call this standard deviation the *standard error of the mean*, or σ_M, and can estimate it on the basis of the following formula:

$$\sigma_M = \frac{\sigma}{\sqrt{N}}$$

where σ is the standard deviation of the sample and N is the number of cases from which each sample mean is computed.

According to the formula, the size of the standard error of the mean decreases as the sample size increases; thus, a mean based on a large sample is more trustworthy (more likely to be close to the actual population mean) than a mean based on a smaller sample. Common sense would lead us to expect this. Computations of the standard error of the mean permit us to make clear assertions about the degree of uncertainty in our computed mean. The more cases in the sample, the more uncertainty has been reduced.

Significance of a Difference

In many psychological experiments, data are collected on two groups of subjects; one group is exposed to certain specified experimental conditions, and the other serves as a control group. The question is whether there is a difference in the mean performance of the two groups, and if such a difference is observed, whether it holds for the population from which these groups of subjects have been sampled. Basically, we are asking whether a difference between two sample means reflects a true difference or whether this difference is simply the result of sampling error.

As an example, we will compare the scores on a reading test for a sample of first grade boys with the scores for a sample of first grade girls. The boys score lower than the girls as far as mean performances are concerned, but there is a great deal of overlap; some boys do extremely well, and some girls do very poorly. Thus, we cannot accept the obtained difference in means without making a test of its *statistical significance*. Only then can we decide whether the observed differences in sample means reflect true differences in the population or are due to sampling error. If some of the brighter girls and some of the duller boys are sampled by sheer luck, the difference could be due to sampling error.

As another example, suppose that we have set up an experiment to compare the grip strength of right-handed and left-handed men. The top panel of Table 5 presents hypothetical data from such an experiment. A sample of five right-handed men averaged 8 kilograms stronger than a sample of five left-handed men. In general, what can we infer from these data about left-handed and right-handed men? Can we argue that right-handed men are stronger than left-handed men? Obviously not, because the averages derived from most of the right-handed men would not differ from those from the left-handed men; the one markedly deviant score of 100 tells us we are dealing with an uncertain situation.

Now suppose that the results of the experiment were those shown in the bottom panel of Table 5. Again, we find the same mean difference of 8 kilograms, but we are now inclined to have greater confidence in the results, because the left-handed men scored consistently lower than the right-handed men. Statistics provides a precise way of taking into account the reliability of the mean differences so that we do not have to depend solely on intuition to determine that one difference is more reliable than another.

These examples suggest that the significance of a difference will depend on both the size of the obtained difference and the variability of the means being compared. From the standard error of the means, we can compute the *standard error of the difference between two means* σ_{D_M}. We can then evaluate the obtained difference by using a *critical ratio* — the ratio of the obtained difference between the means D_M to the standard error of the difference between the means:

$$\text{Critical ratio} = \frac{D_M}{\sigma_{D_M}}$$

STRENGTH OF GRIP IN KILOGRAMS, RIGHT-HANDED MEN	STRENGTH OF GRIP IN KILOGRAMS, LEFT-HANDED MEN
40	40
45	45
50	50
55	55
100	60
Sum 290	Sum 250
Mean 58	Mean 50

STRENGTH OF GRIP IN KILOGRAMS, RIGHT-HANDED MEN	STRENGTH OF GRIP IN KILOGRAMS, LEFT-HANDED MEN
56	48
57	49
58	50
59	51
60	52
Sum 290	Sum 250
Mean 58	Mean 50

TABLE 5
Significance of a Difference   *Two examples that compare the difference between means are shown above. The difference between means is the same (8 kilograms) in both the top and the bottom panel. However, the data in the bottom panel indicate a more reliable difference between means than do the data in the top panel.*

This ratio helps us to evaluate the significance of the difference between the two means. As a rule of thumb, a critical ratio should be 2.0 or larger for the difference between means to be accepted as significant. Throughout this book, statements that the difference between means is "statistically significant" indicate that the critical ratio is at least that large.

Why is a critical ratio of 2.0 selected as statistically significant? Simply because a value this large or larger can occur by chance only 5 out of 100 times. Where do we get the 5 out of 100? We can treat the critical ratio as a standard score because it is merely the difference between two means, expressed as a multiple of its standard error. Referring to Column 2 in Table 4, we note that the likelihood is .023 that a standard deviation as high as or higher than +2.0 will occur by chance. Because the chance of deviating in the opposite direction is also .023, the total probability is .046. This means than 46 times out of 1,000, or about 5 times out of 100, a critical ratio as large as 2.0 would be found by chance if the population means were identical.

The rule of thumb that says a critical ratio should be at least 2.0 is just that — an arbitrary but convenient rule that defines the "5 percent level of significance." Following this rule, we will make fewer than 5 errors in 100 decisions by concluding on the basis of sample data that a difference in means exists when in fact there is none. The 5 percent level need not always be used; a higher level of significance may be appropriate in certain experiments, depending on how willing we are to make an occasional error in inference.

Specimen computation of the critical ratio. The computation of the critical ratio calls for finding the *standard error of the difference between two means,* which is given by the following formula:

$$\sigma_{D_M} = \sqrt{(\sigma_{M_1})^2 + (\sigma_{M_2})^2}$$

In this formula, σ_{M_1} and σ_{M_2} are the standard errors of the two means being compared.

As an illustration, suppose we wanted to compare reading achievement test scores for first grade boys and girls in the United States. A random sample of boys and girls would be identified and given the test. We will assume that the mean score for the boys was 70 with a standard error of .40 and that the mean score for the girls was 72 with a standard error of .30. On the basis of these samples, we want to decide whether there is a real difference between the reading achievement of boys and girls in the population as a whole. The sample data suggest that girls do achieve better reading scores than boys, but can we infer that this would have been the case if we had tested all the girls and all the boys in the United States? The critical ratio helps us make this decision.

$$\sigma_{D_M} = \sqrt{(\sigma_{M_1})^2 + (\sigma_{M_2})^2}$$
$$= \sqrt{.16 + .09} = \sqrt{.25}$$
$$= .5$$

$$\text{Critical ratio} = \frac{D_M}{\sigma_{D_M}} = \frac{72 - 70}{.5} = \frac{2.0}{.5} = 4.0$$

Because the critical ratio is well above 2.0, we may assert that the observed mean difference is statistically significant at the 5 percent level. Thus, we can conclude that there is a reliable difference in performance on the reading test between boys and girls. Note that the sign of the critical ratio could be positive or negative, depending on which mean is subtracted from which; when the critical ratio is interpreted, only its magnitude (not its sign) is considered.

COEFFICIENT OF CORRELATION

Correlation refers to the concomitant variation of paired measures. Suppose that a test is designed to predict success in college. If it is a good test, high scores on it will be related to high performance in college and low scores will be related to poor performance. The *coefficient of correlation* gives us a way of stating the degree of relationship more precisely. (This topic was discussed on pp. 23–25. You may find it helpful to review that material.)

Product-Moment Correlation

The most frequently used method of determining the coefficient of correlation is the *product-moment method,* which yields the index conventionally designated r. The product-moment coefficient r varies between perfect positive correlation ($r = +1.00$) and perfect negative correlation ($r = -1.00$). Lack of any relationship yields $r = .00$.

The formula for computing the product-moment correlation is

$$r = \frac{\text{Sum } (dx)(dy)}{N\sigma_x\sigma_y}$$

Here, one of the paired measures has been labeled the x-score; the other, the y-score. The dx and dy refer to the deviations of each score from its mean, N is the number of paired measures, and σ_x and σ_y are the standard deviations of the x-scores and the y-scores.

The computation of the coefficient of correlation requires the determination of the sum of the $(dx)(dy)$ products. This sum, in addition to the computed standard deviations for the x-scores and y-scores, can then be entered into the formula.

Specimen computation of product-moment correlation. Suppose that we have collected the data shown in Table 6. For each subject, we have obtained two scores — the first being a score on a college entrance test (to be labeled arbitrarily the x-score) and the second being freshman grades (the y-score).

TABLE 6
Computation of a Product-Moment Correlation

STUDENT	ENTRANCE TEST (x-score)	FRESHMAN GRADES (y-score)	(dx)	(dy)	$(dx)(dy)$
Adam	71	39	6	9	+54
Bill	67	27	2	−3	−6
Charles	65	33	0	3	0
David	63	30	−2	0	0
Edward	59	21	−6	−9	+54
Sum	325	150	0	0	+102
Mean	65	30			

$$\sigma_x = 4 \qquad \sigma_y = 6 \qquad r = \frac{\text{Sum } (dx)(dy)}{N\sigma_x\sigma_y} = \frac{+102}{5 \times 4 \times 6} = +.85$$

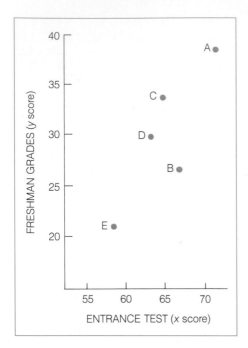

FIGURE 6

Scatter Diagram   *Each point represents the x- and y-scores for a particular student. The letters next to the points identify the students in the data table (A = Adam, B = Bill, and so on).*

Figure 6 is a *scatter diagram* of these data. Each point represents the x-score and y-score for a given subject; for example, the uppermost right-hand point is for Adam (labeled A). Looking at these data, we can easily detect that there is some positive correlation between the x-scores and the y-scores. Adam attained the highest score on the entrance test and also earned the highest freshman grades; Edward received the lowest scores on both. The other students' test scores and grades are a little irregular, so we know that the correlation is not perfect; hence, r is less than 1.00.

We will compute the correlation to illustrate the method, although no researcher would consent, in practice, to determining a correlation for so few cases. The details are given in Table 6. Following the procedure outlined in Table 3, we compute the standard deviation of the x-scores and then the standard deviation of the y-scores. Next, we compute the $(dx)(dy)$ products for each subject and total the five cases. Entering these results in our equation yields an r of +.85.

Interpreting a Correlation Coefficient

We can use correlations in making predictions. For example, if we know from past experience that a certain entrance test correlates with freshman grades, we can predict the freshman grades for beginning college students who have taken the test. If the correlation were perfect, we could predict their grades without error. But r is usually less than 1.00, and some errors in prediction will be made; the closer r is to 0, the greater the sizes of the errors in prediction.

Although we cannot go into the technical problems of predicting freshman grades from entrance examinations or of making other similar predictions, we can consider the meanings of correlation coefficients of different sizes. It is evident that with a correlation of 0 between x and y, knowledge of x will not help to predict y. If weight is unrelated to intelligence, it does us no good to know a subject's weight when we are trying to predict his or her intelligence. At the other extreme, a perfect correlation would mean 100 percent predictive efficiency—knowing x, we can predict y perfectly. What about intermediate values of r? Some appreciation of the meaning of correlations of intermediate sizes can be gained by examining the scatter diagrams in Figure 7.

In the preceding discussion, we did not emphasize the sign of the correlation coefficient, since this has no bearing on the strength of a relationship. The only distinction between a correlation of r = +.70 and r = −.70 is that increases in x are accompanied by increases in y for the former, and increases in x are accompanied by decreases in y for the latter.

Although the correlation coefficient is one of the most widely used statistics in psychology, it is also one of the most widely misused procedures. Those who use it sometimes overlook the fact that r does not imply a cause-and-effect relationship between x and y. When two sets of scores are correlated, we may suspect that they have some causal factors in common, but we cannot conclude that one of them causes the other (see pp. 23–25).

Correlations sometimes appear paradoxical. For example, the correlation between study time and college grades has been found to be slightly negative (about −.10). If a causal interpretation were assumed, we might conclude that the best way to raise grades would be to stop studying. The negative correlation arises because some students have advantages over others in grade making (possibly due to better college preparation), so that often those who study the hardest are those who have difficulty earning the best grades.

This example provides sufficient warning against assigning a causal interpretation to a coefficient of correlation. It is possible, however, that when two

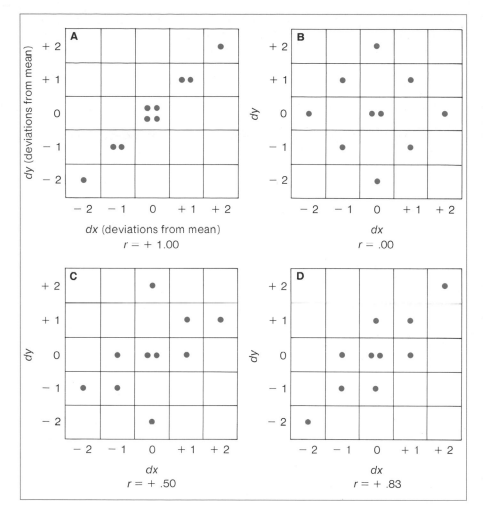

FIGURE 7

Scatter Diagrams Illustrating Correlations of Various Sizes *Each dot represents one individual's score on two tests, x and y. In A, all cases fall on the diagonal and the correlation is perfect (r = +1.00); if we know a subject's score on x, we know that it will be the same on y. In B, the correlation is 0; knowing a subject's score on x, we cannot predict whether it will be at, above, or below the mean on y. For example, of the four subjects who score at the mean of x (dx = 0), one makes a very high score on y (dy = +2), one a very low score (dy = −2), and two remain average. In both C and D, there is a diagonal trend to the scores, so that a high score on x is associated with a high score on y and a low score on x with a low score on y, but the relationship is imperfect. It is possible to check the value of the correlations by using the formulas given in the text for the coefficient of correlation. The computation has been greatly simplified by presenting the scores in the deviation form that permits entering them directly into the formulas. The fact that the axes do not have conventional scales does not change the interpretation. For example, if we assigned the values 1 through 5 to the x and y coordinates and then computed r for these new values, the correlation coefficients would be the same.*

variables are correlated, one may be the cause of the other. The search for causes is a logical one, and correlations can help us by providing leads to experiments that can verify cause-and-effect relationships.

FURTHER READING

There are a number of textbooks on statistics written from the viewpoint of psychological research. Excellent examples are McCall, *Fundamental Statistics for Behavioral Sciences* (4th ed., 1986); Welkowitz, Ewen, and Cohen, *Introductory Statistics for the Behavioral Sciences,* (3rd ed., 1982); Loftus and Loftus, *Essence of Statistics* (1982); Minium and Clark, *Elements of Statistical Reasoning* (1982); and Phillips, *Statistical Thinking* (2nd ed., 1982).

The role of statistics in the design of psychological experiments is discussed in Keppel and Saufley, *Introduction to Design and Analysis* (1980).

APPENDIX IV

Psychology Journals

LISTED ALPHABETICALLY ARE SOME OF the major American psychology journals and a description of the types of articles they publish. These journals are available in most college and university libraries; current issues of the journals usually can be found on racks in an open area of the library. An excellent introduction to psychology can be gained by spending some time perusing recent issues of these journals.

- *American Psychologist:* Official papers of the American Psychological Association; articles on psychology; comments, announcements, and lists of regional, national, and international conventions.
- *Animal Learning and Behavior:* Studies of animal learning, motivation, emotion, and comparative animal behavior.
- *Behavioral Neuroscience:* Original research papers concerned with the biological bases of psychological phenomena; studies cover the entire range of relevant biological and neural sciences.
- *Cognitive Psychology:* Theory and research in the area of cognitive processes and related fields of psychology.
- *Contemporary Psychology:* Critical reviews of recent books, films, and other media; brief notes on new texts; previews of textbooks in psychology.
- *Developmental Psychology:* Studies of the variables influencing growth, development, and aging.
- *Journal of Abnormal Psychology:* Basic research and theory in the field of abnormal behavior, its determinants, and its correlates.
- *Journal of Applied Psychology:* Theoretical and research contributions in applied fields such as business and industry; government, urban, and consumer affairs; legal, health, transportation, defense, and educational systems; and space and other new environments.
- *Journal of Comparative Psychology:* Research reports in comparative psychology; laboratory and field studies of the behavioral patterns of various species as they relate to such factors as evolution, development, ecology, and functional significance.

- *Journal of Consulting and Clinical Psychology:* Research and theory concerning clinical psychology, including psychological diagnoses, psychotherapy, personality, and psychopathology.
- *Journal of Counseling Psychology:* Theory, research, and practice concerning counseling and related activities of counselors and personnel workers.
- *Journal of Educational Psychology:* Studies of learning and teaching, including measurement of psychological development, methods of instruction, and school adjustment.
- *Journal of Experimental Psychology — Animal Behavior Processes:* Studies of the basic mechanisms of perception, learning, motivation, and performance, especially with infrahuman animals.
- *Journal of Experimental Psychology — General:* Long, integrative reports leading to an advance in knowledge of interest to all experimental psychologists.
- *Journal of Experimental Psychology — Human Learning and Memory:* Studies of human acquisition, retention, and transfer processes.
- *Journal of Experimental Psychology — Human Perception and Performance:* Studies of information-processing operations as they relate to experience and performance.
- *Journal of Mathematical Psychology:* Theoretical contributions in all fields of psychology, in which the work involves theories or models employing mathematical methods, formal logic, or computer simulation.
- *Journal of Personality and Social Psychology:* Research on personality dynamics, group processes, and the psychological aspects of social structure.
- *Journal of Phenomenological Psychology:* Theoretical and empirical contributions to psychology that emphasize a humanistic-phenomenological approach.
- *Memory and Cognition:* Studies of human memory and learning, conceptual processes, psycholinguistics, problem solving, thinking, decision making, and skilled performance.
- *Perception and Psychophysics:* Studies that deal with sensory processes, perception, and psychophysics.
- *Physiological Psychology:* Basic studies in structural, chemical, and electrical aspects of brain organization and functions that have implications for behavior.
- *Psychological Abstracts:* Noncritical abstracts of the world's literature in psychology and related subjects.
- *Psychological Bulletin:* Evaluative reviews of research literature and discussions of research methodology in psychology.
- *Psychological Review:* Theoretical contributions attempting to integrate and discuss a broad range of psychological phenomena.
- *Psychology and Aging:* Focuses on adult development and aging. The journal's two major aims are to disseminate new research findings and to highlight the importance of the physiological and behavioral aspects of aging.
- *Psychometrika:* Articles on the development of quantitative models for psychological phenomena, including new mathematical and statistical techniques for the evaluation of psychological data.

Glossary

The glossary defines the technical words that appear in the text and some common words that have special meanings when they are used in psychology. No attempt is made to give the range of meanings beyond those used in the text. For fuller definitions and other shades of meaning, consult any standard dictionary of psychology.

A

ability. Demonstrable knowledge or skill. Ability includes aptitude and achievement. See also **achievement, aptitude.**

abreaction. In psychoanalysis, the process of reducing emotional tension by reliving (in speech or action or both) the experience that caused the tension.

absolute threshold. The intensity or frequency at which a stimulus becomes effective or ceases to become effective, as measured under experimental conditions. See also **difference threshold, threshold.**

accommodation. The process by which the lens of the eye varies its focus.

acetylcholine. The most common of the neurotransmitters. It is found in many synapses in the brain and spinal cord, and is particularly prevalent in an area of the brain called the hippocampus, which plays a key role in the formation of new memories. See also **neurotransmitter.**

achievement. Acquired ability, such as school attainment in spelling. See also **aptitude.**

achromatic colors. Black, white, and gray. See also **chromatic colors.**

acquisition. The stage during which a new response is learned and gradually strengthened. See also **classical conditioning.**

ACTH. See **adrenocorticotrophic hormone.**

action potential. Synonymous with *nerve impulse.* The wave of electrical activity that is transmitted down the axon of the neuron when the cell membrane becomes depolarized. See also **depolarization, graded potentials, resting potential.**

addiction. See **physical dependence.**

additive mixture. The mixture of colored lights; two spotlights of different colors focused on the same spot yield an additive color mixture. See also **subtractive mixture.**

ADH. See **antidiuretic hormone.**

adipocytes. Special fat cells in the body. Obese individuals have many more of them and thus, perhaps, a higher body fat base line.

adolescence. In human beings, the period from puberty to maturity, roughly the early teens to the early twenties. See also **puberty.**

adolescent growth spurt. The period of rapid physical growth that precedes puberty and is accompanied by the gradual development of the reproductive organs and the secondary sex characteristics. See also **puberty, secondary sex characteristics.**

adrenal gland. One of a pair of endocrine glands located above the kidneys. The medulla of the gland secretes the hormones epinephrine and norepinephrine. The cortex of the gland secretes a number of hormones, collectively called the *adrenocortical hormones,* which include cortisone. See also **endocrine gland.**

adrenalin. See **epinephrine.**

adrenocorticotrophic hormone (ACTH). A hormone released by the pituitary gland in response to stress; known as the body's major "stress" hormone. It is carried by the bloodstream to the adrenal glands and various other organs of the body, causing the release of some 30 hormones, each of which plays a role in the body's adjustment to emergency situations. See also corticotropin-release factor.

affective disorder. A mental disorder characterized by disturbances of mood, or affect. Mania (exaggerated excitement), depression, and a cyclical manic-depression are examples. See also **bipolar disorder, depression, manic-depressive disorder.**

affective experience. An emotional experience, whether pleasant or unpleasant, mild or intense. See also **emotion.**

afferent neuron. See **sensory neuron.**

afterimage. The sensory experience that remains when a stimulus is withdrawn. Usually refers to visual experience — for example, the negative afterimage of a picture or the train of colored images that results after staring at the sun.

age regression. In hypnosis, the reliving through fantasy of experiences that are based on early memories or appropriate to a younger age. See also **hypnosis.**

aggregated score. A combination of several measures of the same behavior or characteristic.

aggression. Behavior intended to harm another person. See also **hostile aggression, instrumental aggression.**

agoraphobia. Fear of being alone or being in a public place where escape might be difficult or help unavailable should the individual be incapacitated by a panic attack. See also **panic disorder, phobia.**

AI. See **artificial intelligence.**

all-or-none principle. The rule that the nerve impulse in a single neuron is independent of the strength of stimulation; the neuron either responds completely (fires its action potential) or not at all.

alpha waves. See **electroencephalogram.**

ambivalence. Simultaneous liking and disliking of an object or person; the conflict caused by an incentive that is at once positive and negative. See also **conflict.**

amnesia. A partial or complete loss of memory. May be due to psychological factors (e.g., emotional trauma) or physiological factors (some form of brain damage) and may involve loss of memory for events occurring prior to or subsequent to the amnesia-causing trauma.

See also **anterograde amnesia, retrograde amnesia.**

amphetamines. Central nervous system stimulants that produce restlessness, irritability, anxiety, and rapid heart rate. Dexedrine sulfate ("speed") and methamphetamine ("meth") are two types of amphetamines. See also **depressants, stimulants.**

anal stage. The second stage according to the psychoanalytic theory of psychosexual development, following the oral stage. The sources of gratification and conflict have to do with the expulsion and retention of feces. See also **psychosexual development.**

androgens. The collective name for male sex hormones, of which testosterone, secreted by the testes, is best known. See also **gonads.**

androgyny. The condition in which some male and some female characteristics are present in the same individual. An **androgynous** individual has both so-called masculine and feminine personality traits.

anterograde amnesia. Loss of memory for events and experiences occurring subsequent to an amnesia-causing trauma; the patient is unable to acquire new information, although recall of information learned prior to the onset may be largely unaffected. See also **amnesia, retrograde amnesia.**

anthropology. The science that studies chiefly preliterate ("primitive") societies. Its main divisions are archaeology (the study of the physical monuments and remains from earlier civilizations), physical anthropology (concerned with the anatomical differences among men and their evolutionary origins), linguistic anthropology, and social anthropology (concerned with social institutions and behavior). See also **behavioral sciences.**

antianxiety drug. Central nervous system depressant that reduces tension. Causes some drowsiness but less than barbiturates. Examples are Valium and Librium (syn. *tranquilizer*).

antidepressant. Drug used to elevate the mood of depressed individuals, presumably by increasing the availability of the neurotransmitters norepinephrine and/or serotonin. Examples are imipramine (Tofranil), isocarboxazid (Marplan), and tranylcypromine (Parnate).

antidiuretic hormone (ADH). Hormone

secreted by the pituitary gland that signals the kidney to reabsorb water into the bloodstream instead of excreting it as urine.

antipsychotic drug. A drug that reduces psychotic symptoms, used most frequently in the treatment of schizophrenia. Chlorpromazine and reserpine are examples (syn. *neuroleptic drug*). See also **psychotic behavior.**

antisocial personality. A type of personality disorder marked by impulsivity, inability to abide by the customs and laws of society, and lack of anxiety or guilt regarding behavior (syn. *psychopathic personality*).

anxiety. A state of apprehension, tension, and worry. Synonymous with fear for some theorists, although others view the object of anxiety (such as a vague danger or foreboding) as less specific than the object of a fear (such as a vicious animal). See also **neurotic anxiety, objective anxiety.**

anxiety disorders. A group of mental disorders characterized by intense anxiety or by maladaptive behavior designed to relieve anxiety. Includes generalized anxiety and panic disorders, phobic and obsessive-compulsive disorders. Major category of DSM-III covering most of the disorders formerly called neuroses. See also **generalized anxiety disorder, neurosis, obsessive-compulsive disorder, panic disorder, phobic disorder.**

anxiety hierarchy. A list of situations or stimuli to which a person responds with anxiety ranked in order from the least anxiety-producing to the most fearful. Used by behavior therapists in systematically desensitizing patients to feared stimuli by associating deep relaxation with the situations rather than anxiety. See also **behavior therapy, systematic desensitization.**

apathy. Listlessness, indifference; one of the consequences of frustration. See also **frustration.**

aphagia. Inability to eat. See also **hyperphagia.**

aphasia. Impairment or loss of ability to articulate words or comprehend speech.

apnea. A sleep disturbance characterized by inhibited breathing during sleep.

apparent motion. See **phi phenomenon, stroboscopic motion.**

appetitive behavior. Seeking behavior. See also **aversive behavior.**

aptitude. The capacity to learn—for instance, a person's typing aptitude prior to practice on a typewriter. Aptitude tests are designed to predict the outcome of training, hence to predict future ability on the basis of present ability. See also **achievement.**

archetypes. In the psychology of Carl Jung, a basic idea, such as "God" or "mother," said to characterize a universal unconscious.

arousal level. The principle according to which people seek an optimal level of drive or arousal.

artificial intelligence (AI). A relatively new field of research combining computer science and cognitive psychology; it is concerned with (1) using computers to simulate human thought processes and (2) devising computer programs that act "intelligently" and can adapt to changing circumstances. In essence, it is the science of making machines (computers) do things that are normally done by the human mind. See also **computer simulation, cognitive psychology, cognitive science.**

assertive training. A form of counter-conditioning in which assertive or approach responses are reinforced in an attempt to extinguish passivity or anxiety in certain situations. See also **behavior therapy, counterconditioning.**

association areas. Areas of the cerebral cortex that are not directly concerned with sensory or motor processes; they integrate inputs from various sensory channels and presumably function in learning, memory, and thinking.

associative learning. Learning that certain contingencies (or relations) exist between events; learning that one event is associated with another.

attachment. The tendency of the young organism to seek closeness to particular individuals and to feel more secure in their presence.

attention. The focusing of perception leading to heightened awareness of a limited range of stimuli. It has both overt behavioral components and internal components. See also **orienting reflex.**

attitude. A like or dislike; an affinity for or aversion to objects, persons, groups, situations or other aspects of the environment including abstract ideas and social

policies. Treated by social psychologists as one component in a three-part system. Beliefs constitute the cognitive component; the attitude is the affective component; actions constitute the behavioral component.

attribution. The process by which we attempt to explain the behavior of other people. Attribution theory deals with the rules people use to infer the causes of observed behavior. See also **dispositional attribution, situational attribution.**

autism. Absorption in fantasy to the exclusion of interest in reality; a symptom of schizophrenia. See also **schizophrenia.**

autistic thinking. A form of associative thinking, controlled more by the thinker's needs or desires than by reality; wishful thinking. See also **daydreaming, rationalization.**

automatic writing. Writing that the writer is unaware of (does not know that he or she is producing); familiar in hypnosis. See also **hypnosis.**

autonomic nervous system. The division of the peripheral nervous system that regulates smooth muscle (organ and glandular activities). It is divided into the sympathetic and parasympathetic divisions. See also **parasympathetic division, peripheral nervous system, sympathetic division.**

autoshaping. A shaping procedure that involves aspects of both operant and classical conditioning and does not require the presence of an experimenter. See also **shaping of behavior.**

average. See **measure of central tendency.**

aversive behavior. Avoidance behavior. See also **appetitive behavior.**

aversive conditioning. A form of conditioning in which an undesirable response is extinguished through association with punishment; has been used in behavior therapy to treat alcoholism, smoking, and sexual problems. See also **behavior therapy, counterconditioning.**

avoidance learning. A form of conditioned behavior in which an organism learns to avoid a punishing event by responding to a warning signal. See also **conditioning.**

awareness. See **consciousness.**

axon. That portion of a neuron that trans-

mits impulses to other neurons. See also **dendrite, neuron.**

B

Barnum effect. Refers to the readiness of people to believe that general descriptions, as given in astrological characterizations, refer to them personally.

basal mental age. In individual tests of the Binet type, the highest age level at which, and below which, all tests are passed. See also **mental age.**

basilar membrane. A membrane of the ear within the coils of the cochlea supporting the organ of Corti. Movements of the basilar membrane stimulate the hair cells of the organ of Corti, producing the neural effects of auditory stimulation. See also **cochlea, organ of Corti.**

behavior. Those activities of an organism that can be observed by another organism or by an experimenter's instruments. Included within behavior are verbal reports made about subjective, conscious experiences. See also **conscious processes.**

behavior genetics. The study of the inheritance of behavioral characteristics.

behavior modification. See **behavior therapy.**

behavior therapy. A method of psychotherapy based on learning principles. It uses such techniques as counter-conditioning, reinforcement, and shaping to modify behavior (syn. *behavior modification*). See also **cognitive behavior therapy.**

behavioral medicine. An interdisciplinary field that focuses on how social, psychological, and biological variables contribute to illness and how behavior and environments can be changed to promote health. An outgrowth of earlier research on psychosomatic aspects of illness. See also **psychosomatic disorder.**

behavioral sciences. The sciences concerned in one way or another with the behavior of humans and lower organisms (especially social anthropology, psychology, and sociology but including some aspects of biology, economics, political science, history, philosophy, and other fields of study).

behaviorism. A school or system of psychology associated with the name of John B. Watson; it defined psychology as the study of behavior and limited the data of psychology to observable activities. In its classical form it was more restrictive than the contemporary behavioral viewpoint in psychology.

binocular cues. See distance cues.

binocular disparity. The fact that an object projects slightly different images on the two retinas due to the different positions of the right and left eyes.

biofeedback. A procedure that permits individuals to monitor their own physiological processes (such as heart rate, blood pressure), which they are normally unaware of, to learn to control them.

biological therapy. Treatment of personality maladjustment or mental illness by drugs, electric shock, or other methods directly affecting bodily processes. See also psychotherapy.

bipolar disorder. An affective disorder in which people experience episodes of both mania and depression or of mania alone. The term in DSM-III for manic-depressive disorder. See also affective disorder, manic-depressive disorder.

blind spot. An insensitive area of the retina where the nerve fibers from the ganglion cells join to form the optic nerve.

blood pressure. The pressure of the blood against the walls of the blood vessels. Changes in blood pressure following stimulation serve as one indicator of emotion.

brain stem. The structures lying near the core of the brain; essentially all of the brain with the exception of the cerebrum and the cerebellum and their dependent parts.

brightness. The dimension of color that describes its nearness in brilliance to white (as contrasted to black). A bright color reflects more light than a dark one. See also hue, saturation.

Broca's area. A portion of the left cerebral hemisphere involved in the control of speech. Individuals with damage in this area have difficulty enunciating words correctly and speak in a slow and labored way; their speech often makes sense, but it includes only key words.

C

Cannon-Bard theory. A classical theory of emotion proposed by Cannon and Bard. The theory states that an emotion-producing stimulus activates the cortex and bodily responses at the same time; bodily changes and the experience of emotion occur simultaneously. See also cognitive-appraisal theory, James–Lange theory.

cardiac muscle. A special kind of muscle found only in the heart. See also smooth muscle, striate muscle.

case history. A biography obtained for scientific purposes; the material is sometimes supplied by interview, sometimes collected over the years. See also longitudinal study.

castration. Surgical removal of the gonads; in the male, removal of testes; in the female, removal of the ovaries.

catharsis. Reduction of an impulse or emotion through direct or indirect expression, particularly verbal and fantasy expression.

central core. The most central and the evolutionarily oldest portion of the brain. It includes structures that regulate basic life processes, including most of the brain stem. See also brain stem, cerebellum, hypothalamus, reticular system.

central fissure. A fissure of each cerebral hemisphere that separates the frontal and parietal lobes (syn. *fissure of Rolando*).

central nervous system. In vertebrates, the brain and spinal cord, as distinct from the nerve trunks and their peripheral connections. See also autonomic nervous system, peripheral nervous system.

cerebellum. Lobed structure attached to the rear of the brain stem that regulates muscle tone and coordination of intricate movements.

cerebral cortex. The surface layer of the cerebral hemispheres in higher animals, including humans. It is commonly called gray matter because its many cell bodies give it a gray appearance in cross section, in contrast with the myelinated nerve fibers that make up the white matter in the center.

cerebral hemispheres. Two large masses of nerve cells and fibers constituting the bulk of the brain in humans and other higher animals. The hemispheres are separated by a deep fissure, but connected by a broad band of fibers, the corpus callosum (syn. *cerebrum*). See also cerebral cortex, left hemisphere, right hemisphere, split-brain subject.

cerebrum. See cerebral hemispheres.

childhood amnesia. The inability to recall events from the first years of one's life.

chlorpromazine. See antipsychotic drug.

chromatic colors. All colors other than black, white, and gray; for instance, red, yellow, blue. See also achromatic colors.

chromosome. Rodlike structures found in pairs in all the cells of the body, carrying the genetic determiners (genes) that are transmitted from parent to offspring. A human cell has 46 chromosomes, arranged in 23 pairs, one member of each pair deriving from the mother, one from the father. See also gene.

chronological age (CA). Age from birth; calendar age. See also mental age.

chunk. The largest meaningful unit of information that can be stored in short-term memory; short-term memory holds 7 ± 2 chunks. See also short-term memory.

circadian rhythm. A cycle or rhythm that is roughly 24 hours long. Sleep-wakefulness, body temperature, and water excretion follow a circadian rhythm, as do a number of behavioral and physiological variables.

clairvoyance. A form of extrasensory perception in which the perceiver is said to identify a stimulus that is influencing neither his or her own sense organs nor those of another person. See also extrasensory perception, precognition, psychokinesis, telepathy.

classical concept. A concept where every instance must have every property mentioned in the concept. An example is the concept of *bachelor;* every instance must have the properties of being adult, male, and unmarried. See also fuzzy concept.

classical conditioning. Conditioned-response experiments conforming to the pattern of Pavlov's experiment. The main feature is that the originally neutral conditioned stimulus, through repeated pairing with the unconditioned one, acquires the response originally given to the unconditioned stimulus. See also operant conditioning.

claustrophobia. Fear of closed places. See also phobia.

client-centered therapy. See person-centered therapy.

clinical psychologist. A psychologist, usually with a Ph.D. degree, trained in the diagnosis and treatment of emotional or behavioral problems and mental disorders. See also **counseling psychologist, psychiatrist.**

cocaine. A central nervous system stimulant derived from leaves of the coca plant. Increases energy, produces euphoria, and in large doses causes paranoia.

cochlea. The portion of the inner ear containing the receptors for hearing. See also **basilar membrane, organ of Corti.**

coding. See **encoding.**

coefficient of correlation. A numerical index used to indicate the degree of correspondence between two sets of paired measurements. The most common kind is the product-moment coefficient designated by *r*.

cognition. An individual's thoughts, knowledge, interpretations, understandings, or ideas. See also **cognitive processes.**

cognitive appraisal. The interpretation of an event or situation with respect to one's goals and well-being. The cognitive appraisal of an event influences both the quality and intensity of the emotion experienced and the degree of perceived threat.

cognitive-appraisal theory. A theory of emotion which proposes that the subjective emotional state is a function of the individual's appraisal, or analysis, of the emotion-arousing situation. A state of physiological arousal can produce different emotions (even antithetical ones) depending on how the person appraises the situation. See also **Cannon–Bard theory, James–Lange theory.**

cognitive behavior therapy. A psychotherapy approach that emphasizes the influence of a person's beliefs, thoughts, and self-statements on behavior. Combines behavior therapy methods with techniques designed to change the way the individual thinks about self and events. See also **behavior therapy.**

cognitive dissonance. The condition in which one has beliefs or attitudes that disagree with each other or with behavioral tendencies; when such cognitive dissonance arises, the subject is motivated to reduce the dissonance through changes in behavior or cognition.

cognitive map. A hypothetical structure in memory that preserves and organizes information about the various events that occur in a learning situation; a mental picture of the learning situation. See also **schema.**

cognitive processes. Mental processes of perception, memory, and information processing by which the individual acquires information, makes plans, and solves problems.

cognitive psychology. A general approach to psychology that stresses the role of mental processes in understanding behavior. The cognitive psychologist explains behavior at the level of mental representations and the mental processes that operate on these representations to produce products (including responses). The approach is not restricted to the study of thought and knowledge; its early concerns with these topics led to the label "cognitive psychology," but in recent years has been generalized to all areas of psychology. See also **artificial intelligence, cognitive science, information-processing model.**

cognitive science. A term introduced in the 1970s to focus attention on how humans acquire and organize knowledge; a "new" science dedicated to understanding cognition. In addition to psychology, the disciplines relevant to cognitive science are neuroscience, linguistics, philosophy, mathematics, and computer science (particularly that branch of computer science known as artificial intelliegnce). See also **artificial intelligence, cognitive psychology.**

color blindness. Defective discrimination of chromatic colors. See also **dichromatism, monochromatism, red-green color blindness, trichromatism.**

color circle. An arrangement of chromatic colors on the circumference of a circle in the order in which they appear in the spectrum but with the addition of nonspectral reds and purples. The colors are so arranged that those opposite each other are complementaries in additive mixture. See also **color solid.**

color constancy. The tendency to see a familiar object as of the same color, regardless of changes in illumination on it that alter its stimulus properties. See also **perceptual constancy.**

color solid. A three-dimensional representation of the psychological dimensions of color, with hue around the circumference, saturation along each radius, and brightness from top to bottom. See also **color circle.**

complementary colors. Two colors that in additive mixture yield either a gray or an unsaturated color of the hue of the stronger component.

complex cell. A cell in the visual cortex that responds to a bar of light or straight edge of a particular orientation located anywhere in the visual field. See also **simple cell.**

compliance. A response to social influence in which the person at whom the influence is directed publicly conforms to the wishes of the influencing source but does not change his or her private beliefs or attitudes. When a source obtains compliance by setting an example, it is called *conformity;* when a source obtains compliance by wielding authority, it is called *obedience.* See also **identification, internalization.**

compulsion. A repetitive action that a person feels driven to make and is unable to resist; ritualistic behavior. See also **obsession, obsessive-compulsive disorder.**

computer program. See **program.**

computer simulation. The use of a computer to simulate a phenomenon or system in order to study its properties. In psychology, the simulation usually involves an attempt to program a computer to mimic how the mind processes information and solves problems. In this sense, the computer program is literally a theory of how the mind functions. See also **artificial intelligence, cognitive psychology, information-processing model.**

concept. The properties or relationships common to a class of objects or ideas. Concepts may be of concrete things (such as the concept *poodle* referring to a given variety of dog) or of abstract ideas (such as *equality, justice, number*), implying relationships common to many different kinds of objects or ideas. See also **classical concept, fuzzy concept.**

concrete operational stage. Piaget's third stage of cognitive development (ages 7 to 12 years) during which a child becomes capable of logical thought and achieves conservation concepts. See also **conservation.**

conditioned emotion. An emotional response acquired by conditioning: one aroused by a stimulus that did not originally evoke it. See also **conditioning.**

conditioned reinforcer. A stimulus that has become reinforcing through prior association with a reinforcing stimulus (syn. *secondary reinforcer*). See also **reinforcing stimulus.**

conditioned response (CR). In classical conditioning, the learned or acquired response to a conditioned stimulus; i.e., to a stimulus that did not evoke the response originally. See also **conditioned stimulus, unconditioned response, unconditioned stimulus.**

conditioned stimulus (CS). In classical conditioning, a stimulus previously neutral that comes to elicit a conditioned response through association with an unconditioned stimulus. See also **conditioned response, unconditioned response, unconditioned stimulus.**

conditioning. The process by which conditioned responses are learned. See also **classical conditioning, operant conditioning.**

cone. In the eye, a specialized cell of the retina found predominantly in the fovea and more sparsely throughout the retina. The cones mediate both chromatic and achromatic sensations. See also **fovea, retina, rod.**

conflict. The simultaneous presence of opposing or mutually exclusive impulses, desires, or tendencies. See also **ambivalence.**

connotative meaning. The suggestive and emotional meanings of a word or symbol, beyond its denotative meaning. Thus, *naked* and *nude* both refer to an unclothed body (denotative meaning), but they have somewhat different connotations. See also **denotative meaning.**

conscience. An internal recognition of standards of right and wrong by which the individual judges his or her conduct. See also **superego.**

conscious processes. Events such as perceptions, afterimages, private thoughts, and dreams, of which only the person is aware. They are accessible to others through verbal report or by way of inference from other behavior (syn. *experience, awareness*).

consciousness. We are conscious when we are aware of external events, reflect on past experiences, engage in problem solving, are selective in attending to some stimuli rather than others, and deliberately choose an action in response to environmental conditions and personal goals. In short, consciousness has to do with (1) *monitoring* ourselves and our environment so that percepts, memories,

and thoughts are accurately represented in awareness; and (2)*controlling* ourselves and our environment so that we are able to initiate and terminate behavioral and cognitive activities. In some contexts, the term is used as a synonym for *awareness.*

conservation. Piaget's term for the ability of the child to recognize that certain properties of objects (such as mass, volume, number) do not change despite transformations in the appearance of the objects. See also **preoperational stage.**

constructive memory. Using general knowledge stored in memory to construct and elaborate a more complete and detailed account of some events.

control group. In an experimental design contrasting two groups, that group not given the treatment whose effect is under study. See also **experimental group.**

control processes. Regulatory processes that serve to establish equilibrium or monitor goal-directed activities. See also **homeostasis.**

conventional morality. Level II of Kohlberg's stages of moral reasoning in which actions are evaluated in terms of external sanctions, i.e., whether the actions gain approval from others and adhere to laws and social norms. See also **preconventional morality, postconventional morality.**

convergent thinking. In tests of intellect, producing a specified "correct" response in accordance with truth and fact. See also **divergent thinking.**

core. The part of a concept that contains the properties that are more essential for determining membership in the concept. See also **prototype.**

corpus callosum. A large band of nerve fibers connecting the two cerebral hemispheres.

correlation. See **coefficient of correlation.**

corticotropin-release factor (CRF). A substance secreted by neurons in the hypothalamus in response to stress. It, in turn, is carried through a channel-like structure to the pituitary gland, causing ACTH (the body's major "stress" hormone) to be released. See also **adrenocorticotrophic hormone.**

counseling psychologist. A trained psychologist usually with a Ph.D. or Ed.D. degree, who deals with personal problems not classified as illness, such as academic, social, or vocational problems of

students. He or she has skills similar to those of the clinical psychologist but usually works in a nonmedical setting. See also **clinical psychologist, psychiatrist.**

counterconditioning. In behavior therapy, the replacement of a particular response to a stimulus by the establishment of another (usually incompatible) response. See also **assertive training.**

CRF. See corticotropin-release factor.

criterion. (1) A set of scores or other records against which the success of a predictive test is verified. (2) A standard selected as the goal to be achieved in a learning task; for example, the number of runs through a maze to be made without error as an indication that the maze has been mastered.

critical period. A stage in development during which the organism is optimally ready to learn certain response patterns. There is some evidence for a critical period in language learning; a child not exposed to language prior to adolescence has great difficulty acquiring language thereafter.

cross-pressure. Conflicting social influences on an individual's beliefs, attitudes, or behaviors. Usually arises when a person identifies with more than one reference group.

cues to distance. See **distance cues.**

culture-fair test. A type of intelligence test that has been constructed to minimize bias due to the differing experiences of children raised in a rural rather than an urban culture or in a lower-class rather than in a middle-class or upper-class culture (syn. *culture-free test*).

cumulative curve. A graphic record of the responses emitted during an operant conditioning session. The slope of the cumulative curve indicates the rate of response.

D

dark adaptation. The increased sensitivity to light when the subject has been continuously in the dark or under conditions of reduced illumination. See also **light adaptation.**

daydreaming. Reverie; free play of thought or imagination. Because of self-reference, usually a form of autistic thinking. See also **autistic thinking.**

db. See **decibel.**

decibel (db). A unit for measuring sound intensity.

deductive reasoning. Reasoning about arguments in which the conclusion cannot be false if the premises are true. See also **inductive reasoning.**

defense mechanism. An adjustment made, often unconsciously, either through action or the avoidance of action to keep from recognizing personal qualities or motives that might lower self-esteem or heighten anxiety. Denial and projection are two examples.

deindividuation. A psychological state in which persons feel that they have lost their personal identities and have merged anonymously into a group. Hypothesized to be the basis for the impulsive, aggressive behaviors sometimes shown by mobs and crowds.

delayed conditioning. A classical conditioning procedure in which the CS begins several seconds or more before the onset of the UCS and continues with it until the response occurs. See also **simultaneous conditioning, trace conditioning.**

delta waves. See **electroencephalogram.**

delusion. False beliefs characteristic of some forms of psychotic disorder. They often take the form of delusions of grandeur or delusions of persecution. See also **hallucination, illusion, paranoid schizophrenia.**

dendrite. The specialized portion of the neuron that (together with the cell body) receives impulses from other neurons. See also **axon, neuron.**

denial. A defense mechanism by which unacceptable impulses or ideas are not perceived or allowed into full awareness. See also **defense mechanism.**

denotative meaning. The primary meaning of a symbol, something specific to which the symbol refers or points (for example, my street address is denotative; whether I live in a desirable neighborhood is a connotative meaning secondary to the address itself). See also **connotative meaning.**

deoxyribonucleic acid (DNA). The basic hereditary material of all organisms; a nucleic acid polymer incorporating the sugar deoxyribose. In higher organisms, the great bulk of DNA is located within the chromosomes.

dependent variable. The variable whose measured changes are attributed to (or correspond to) changes in the independent variable. In psychological experiments, the dependent variable is often a response to a measured stimulus. See also **independent variable.**

depolarization. Change in the resting potential of the nerve cell membrane in the direction of the action potential; the inside of the membrane becomes more positive. See also **action potential, resting potential.**

depressants. Psychoactive drugs that tend to reduce arousal. Alcohol, barbiturates, and opiates are examples.

depression. An affective, or mood, disorder characterized by sadness and dejection, decreased motivation and interest in life, negative thoughts (e.g., feelings of helplessness, inadequacy, and low self-esteem) and such physical symptoms as sleep disturbances, loss of appetite, and fatigue. See also **affective disorder.**

depth perception. The perception of the distance of an object from the observer or the distance from front to back of a solid object. See also **distance cues.**

developmental psychologist. A psychologist whose research interest lies in studying the changes that occur as a function of the growth and development of the organism, in particular the relationship between early and later behavior.

deviation IQ. An intelligence quotient (IQ) computed as a standard score with a mean of 100 and a standard deviation of 15 (Wechsler) or 16 (Stanford–Binet), to correspond approximately to traditional intelligence quotient. See also **intelligence quotient.**

dichromatism. Color blindness in which either the red-green or the blue-yellow system is lacking. The red-green form is relatively common; the blue-yellow form is the rarest of all forms of color blindness. See also **monochromatism, red-green color blindness, trichromatism.**

difference threshold. The minimum difference between a pair of stimuli that can be perceived under experimental conditions. See also **absolute threshold, just noticeable difference, threshold, Weber's law.**

diffusion of responsibility. The tendency for persons in a group situation to fail to take action (as in an emergency) because others are present, thus diffusing the re-

sponsibility for acting. A major factor in inhibiting bystanders from intervening in emergencies.

discrimination. (1) In perception, the detection of differences between two stimuli. (2) In conditioning, the differential response to the positive (reinforced) stimulus and to the negative (nonreinforced) stimulus. See also **generalization.** (3) In social psychology, prejudicial treatment, as in racial discrimination.

discriminative stimulus. A stimulus that becomes an occasion for an operant response; for example, a knock that leads one to open the door. The stimulus does not elicit the operant response in the same sense that a stimulus elicits respondent behavior. See also **operant behavior.**

displaced aggression. Aggression against a person or object other than that that was (or is) the source of frustration. See also **scapegoat.**

displacement. (1) A defense mechanism whereby a motive that may not be directly expressed (such as sex or aggression) appears in a more acceptable form. See also **defense mechanism.** (2) The principle of loss of items from short-term memory as too many new items are added. See also **chunk, short-term memory.**

dispositional attribution. Attributing a person's actions to internal dispositions (attitudes, traits, motives), as opposed to situational factors. See also **situational attribution.**

dissociation. The process whereby some ideas, feelings, or activities lose relationship to other aspects of consciousness and personality and operate automatically or independently.

dissonance. (1) In music, an inharmonious combination of sounds; contrasted with consonance. (2) In social psychology, Festinger's term for discomfort arising from a perceived inconsistency between one's attitudes and one's behavior. See also **cognitive dissonance.**

distance cues. (1) In vision, the monocular cues according to which the distance of objects is perceived — such as superposition of objects, perspective, light and shadow, and relative movement — and the binocular cues used in stereoscopic vision. See also **stereoscopic vision.** (2) In audition, the corresponding cues governing perception of distance and direction, such as intensity and time differences of sound reaching the two ears.

divergent thinking. In tests of intellect (or creativity), producing one or more "possible" answers rather than a single "correct" one. See also **convergent thinking.**

dizygotic (DZ) twins. Twins developed from separate eggs. They are no more alike genetically than ordinary brothers and sisters and can be of the same or different sexes (syn. *fraternal twins*). See also **monozygotic twins.**

DNA. See **deoxyribonucleic acid.**

dominance. The higher status position when social rank is organized according to a dominance-submission hierarchy; commonly found in human societies and in certain animal groups.

dominant gene. A member of a gene pair, which, if present, determines that the individual will show the trait controlled by the gene, regardless of whether the other member of the pair is the same or different (that is, recessive). See also **recessive gene.**

dopamine. A neurotransmitter of the central nervous system believed to play a role in schizophrenia. It is synthesized from an amino acid by the action of certain body enzymes and, in turn, is converted into norepinephrine. See also **neurotransmitter, norepinephrine.**

dopamine hypothesis. The hypothesis that schizophrenia is related to an excess of the neurotransmitter dopamine; either schizophrenics produce too much dopamine or are deficient in the enzyme that converts dopamine to norepinephrine. See also **dopamine, norepinephrine, schizophrenia.**

double blind. An experimental design, often used in drug research, in which neither the investigator nor the patients know which subjects are in the treatment and which in the nontreatment condition until the experiment has been completed.

Down's syndrome. A form of mental deficiency produced by a genetic abnormality (an extra chromosome on pair 21). Characteristics include a thick tongue, extra eyelid folds, and short, stubby fingers (also known as **mongolism**).

drive. (1) An aroused condition of the organism based on deprivation or noxious stimulation, including tissue needs, drug or hormonal conditions, and specified internal or external stimuli, as in pain. (2) Loosely, any motive. See also **motive, need.**

drive-reduction theory. The theory that a motivated sequence of behavior can be best explained as moving from an aversive state of heightened tension (or drive) to a goal state in which the drive is reduced. The goal of the sequence, in other words, is drive reduction. See also **drive, incentive theory, motive, need.**

DSM-III. The third edition of the *Diagnostic and Statistical Manual of the American Psychiatric Association*.

dual-memory theory. A theory that distinguishes between a short-term memory of limited capacity and a virtually unlimited long-term memory. Information can only be encoded into long-term memory via short-term memory. See also **long-term memory, short-term memory.**

DZ twins. See **dizygotic twins.**

E

eardrum. The membrane at the inner end of the auditory canal, leading to the middle ear. See also **middle ear.**

ectomorph. The third of the three types of physique in Sheldon's type theory. It comprises delicacy of skin, fine hair, and ultrasensitive nervous system. See also **endomorph, mesomorph, type theory.**

educational psychologist. A psychologist whose research interest lies in the application of psychological principles to the education of children and adults in schools. See also **school psychologist.**

EEG. See **electroencephalogram.**

efferent neuron. See **motor neuron.**

ego. In Freud's tripartite division of the personality, that part corresponding most nearly to the perceived self, the controlling self that holds back the impulsiveness of the id in the effort to delay gratification until it can be found in socially approved ways. See also **id, superego.**

ego analyst. A psychoanalyst who focuses on the integrative, positive functions of the ego (e.g., coping with the environment) rather than the functions of the id (e.g., gratifying sexual impulses). Heinz Hartman and David Rapaport are considered ego analysts. See also **ego, id, psychoanalyst.**

eidetic imagery. The ability to retain visual images of pictures that are almost photographic in clarity. Such images can be described in far greater detail than would be possible from memory alone. See also **mental imagery.**

elaboration. A memory process wherein one expands verbal material so as to increase the number of ways to retrieve the material.

electroconvulsive therapy (ECT). A treatment for severe depression in which a mild electric current is applied to the brain, producing a seizure similar to an epileptic convulsion. Also known as **electroshock therapy.**

electroencephalogram (EEG). A record obtained by attaching electrodes to the scalp (or occasionally to the exposed brain) and amplifying the spontaneous electrical activity of the brain. Familiar aspects of the EEG are alpha waves (8–13 Hz) and delta waves of slower frequency.

electroshock therapy. See **electroconvulsive therapy.**

emotion. The condition of the organism during affectively toned experience, whether mild or intense. See also **affective experience.**

emotion-focused coping. Ways of reducing anxiety or stress that do not deal directly with the anxiety-producing situation; defense mechanisms are a form of emotion-focused coping. See also **problem-focused coping.**

empiricism. The view that behavior is learned as a result of experience. See also **nativism.**

encoding. Transforming a sensory input into a form (code) that can be processed by the memory system.

encounter group. A general term for various types of groups in which people meet to learn more about themselves in relation to other people (syn. *sensitivity group, T-group*).

endocrine gland. A ductless gland, or gland of internal secretion, that discharges its products directly into the bloodstream. The hormones secreted by the endocrine glands are important chemical integrators of bodily activity. See also **hormones.**

endomorph. The first of three types of physique in Sheldon's type theory. It comprises prominence of intestines and other visceral organs, including a prominent abdomen, as in the obese individual.

See also **ectomorph, mesomorph, type theory.**

endorphins. A group of neurotransmitters in the brain released in response to stress that have the effect of blocking pain. Opiates, a class of drugs that includes heroin and morphine, are similar in molecular shape to endorphins and mimic this naturally occurring substance.

engineering psychologist. A psychologist who specializes in the relationship between people and machines, seeking, for example, to design machines that minimize human error.

epinephrine. The principal hormone secreted by the adrenal medulla in response to stressful situations. Its effects are similar to those brought about by stimulation of the sympathetic division of the autonomic nervous system (e.g., arousal, increased heart rate and blood pressure). It is also an excitatory neurotransmitter in the central nervous system (syn. *adrenalin*). See also **adrenal gland, norepinephrine.**

equilibratory senses. The senses that give discrimination of the position of the body in space and of the movement of the body as a whole. See also **kinesthesis, semicircular canals, vestibular sacs.**

ESP. See **extrasensory perception.**

estrogen. A female sex hormone manufactured and secreted by the ovaries; it is partially responsible for the growth of the female secondary sex characteristics and influences the sex drive. See also **androgens.**

estrous. The sexually receptive state in female mammals. It is a cyclical state, related to menstruation in the primates and humans (syn. *heat*). See also **menstruation.**

ethology. An interdisciplinary science combining zoology, biology, and psychology to study animal behavior, primarily in the natural environment of the species being observed. Most of the work has been on insects, birds, and fish, but in recent years the approach has been applied to human behavior. Naturalistic observation characterizes the approach, and the theoretical ideas tend to focus on the interplay of genetic and environmental factors in understanding behavior. See also **imprinting, instinct.**

evoked potential. An electrical discharge in some part of the nervous system produced by stimulation elsewhere. The measured potential is commonly based on response averaging by a computer.

excitatory synapse. A synapse at which the neurotransmitter changes the membrane permeability of the receiving cell in the direction of depolarization. See also **depolarization, inhibitory synapse, synapse.**

exemplar strategy. A categorization strategy in which (1) old instances of a concept are memorized and (2) a new item is declared a member of that concept if it is sufficiently similar to the memorized instances.

expectation. An anticipation or prediction of future events based on past experience and present stimuli.

experimental design. A plan for collecting and treating the data of a proposed experiment. The design is evolved after preliminary exploration, with the aims of economy, precision, and control, so that appropriate inferences and decisions can be made from the data.

experimental group. In an experimental design contrasting two groups, that group of subjects given the treatment whose effect is under investigation. See also **control group.**

experimental method. The method of investigation of natural events that seeks to control the variables involved so as to more precisely define cause-and-effect relationships. Most frequently done in a laboratory, but need not be. See also **observational method, variable.**

experimental psychologist. A psychologist whose research interest is in the laboratory study of general psychological principles as revealed in the behavior of lower organisms and human beings.

extinction. (1) The experimental procedure, following classical or operant conditioning, of presenting the conditioned stimulus without the usual reinforcement. (2) The reduction in response that results from this procedure. See also **reinforcement.**

extracellular fluid. Fluid, including the blood, outside the cells; one of the critical variables monitored in the control of thirst.

extrasensory perception (ESP). A controversial category of experience consisting of perception not mediated by sense-organ stimulation. See also **clairvoyance, parapsychology, precognition, psychokinesis, telepathy.**

extravert. One of the psychological types proposed by Jung. The extravert is more preoccupied with social life and the external world than with his or her inward experience. See also **introvert.**

F

fact memory. The kind of memory that presumably stores factual information. See also **skill memory.**

factor analysis. A statistical method used in test construction and in interpreting scores from batteries of tests. The method enables the investigator to compute the minimum number of determiners (factors) required to account for the intercorrelations among the scores on the tests making up the battery. See also **general factor, special factor.**

family therapy. Psychotherapy with the family members as a group rather than treatment of the patient alone. See also **group therapy.**

fantasy. Daydreaming, "woolgathering" imagination; sometimes a consequence of frustration. It is used as a personality indicator in projective tests. See also **projective test.**

feature detector. A general term for any perceptual mechanism that detects distinctive features in a complex display. An example is a line (or edge) detector in vision. Since anything we see can be approximated by a series of line segments at angles to each other, feature detectors have been postulated to be the building blocks for recognizing more complex forms.

Fechner's law. The assertion that the perceived magnitude of a stimulus increases in proportion to the logarithm of its physical intensity.

figure-ground perception. Perceiving a pattern as foreground against a background. Patterns are commonly perceived this way even when the stimuli are ambiguous and the foreground-background relationships are reversible.

filter. Any device that allows some things to pass through it and not others; for example, an electronic device that allows only particular sound frequencies to pass or an optical lens that transmits only certain wavelengths of light. Various types of filters are embedded in the sensory system (optical, mechanical, chemical, neural) that pass some signals and not others. A neuron in the sensory system that is preceded by a filter will respond only to signals that pass through the filter; such a neuron is said to be "tuned" to those signals. See also **specific neuron code hypothesis.**

fixation. In psychoanalysis, arrested development through failure to pass beyond one of the earlier stages of psychosexual development or to change the objects of attachment (such as fixated at the oral stage or fixated on the mother).

flow chart. A diagramatic representation of the sequence of choices and actions in an activity.

formal operational stage. Piaget's fourth stage of cognitive development (age 12 and up) in which the child becomes able to use abstract rules.

fovea. In the eye, a small area in the central part of the retina, packed with cones; in daylight, the most sensitive part of the retina for detail vision and color vision. See also **cone, retina.**

fraternal twins. See **dizygotic twins.**

free association. (1) The form of word-association experiment in which the subject gives any word he or she thinks of in response to the stimulus word. (2) In psychoanalysis, the effort to report without modification everything that comes into awareness.

free recall. A memory task in which a subject is given a list of items (usually one at a time) and is later asked to recall them in any order.

frontal lobe. A portion of each cerebral hemisphere, in front of the central fissure. See also **occipital lobe, parietal lobe, temporal lobe.**

frustration. (1) As an event, the thwarting circumstances that block or interfere with goal-directed activity. (2) As a state, the annoyance, confusion, or anger engendered by being thwarted, disappointed, defeated.

frustration-aggression hypothesis. The hypothesis that frustration (thwarting a person's goal-directed efforts) induces an aggressive drive, which, in turn, motivates aggressive behavior.

fundamental attribution error. The tendency to underestimate situational influences on behavior and assume that some personal characteristic of the individual is responsible; the bias toward dispositional rather than situational attributions. See also **attribution, dispositional attribution, situational attribution.**

fuzzy concept. A concept where one primarily relies on prototype properties in determining membership, and hence cannot always be sure of one's decisions. See also **prototype.**

G

galvanic skin response (GSR). Changes in electrical conductivity of, or activity in, the skin, detected by a sensitive galvanometer. The reactions are commonly used as an emotional indicator.

ganglia (sing. *ganglion*). A collection of nerve cell bodies and synapses, constituting a center lying outside the brain and spinal cord, as in the sympathetic ganglia. See also **nuclei.**

gastrointestinal motility. Movements of parts of the digestive tract caused by contraction of smooth muscle; one form of emotional indicator.

gate control theory of pain. According to this theory, the sensation of pain requires not only that pain receptors be activated, but also that a neural gate in the spinal cord allow these signals to continue to the brain. Pressure stimulation tends to close the gate; this is why rubbing a hurt area can relieve pain. Attitudes, suggestions, and drugs may act to close the gate.

gender identity. The degree to which one regards oneself as male or female. See also **sex role, sex typing.**

gender schema. An abstract cognitive structure that organizes a diverse array of information in terms of its male-female connotations. According to gender schema theory (S. Bem), sex-typed individuals are more likely to use a gender schema than non–sex-typed individuals. See also **schema, sex typing.**

gene. The basic unit of hereditary transmission, localized within the chromosomes. Each chromosome contains many genes. Genes are typically in pairs, one member of the pair being found in the chromosome from the father, the other in the corresponding chromosome from the mother. See also **chromosome, dominant gene, recessive gene.**

general adaptation syndrome (GAS). Selye's three-stage characterization of the biological reactions to a severe stressor. The first stage (the alarm reaction) has two phases: the shock phase in which temperature and blood pressure drop, muscle tone weakens, and heart rate increases; followed by the countershock phase in which the body mobilizes for action. In the second stage (resistance) bodily functions return to near normal, but resistance to a second stressor is low. If the stressful situation is severe or prolonged, the third stage (exhaustion) ensues; the pattern of the alarm reaction reappears and death may result.

general factor (g). (1) A general ability underlying test scores, especially in tests of intelligence, as distinct from special abilities unique to each test. (2) A general ability with which each of the primary factors correlates. See also **factor analysis, special factor.**

General Problem Solver (GPS). A computer program to simulate human problem solving by setting up subgoals and reducing the discrepancies to each subsequent subgoal. See also **simulation.**

generalization. (1) In concept formation, problem solving, and transfer of learning, the detection by the learner of a characteristic or principle common to a class of objects, events, or problems. (2) In conditioning, the principle that once a conditioned response has been established to a given stimulus, similar stimuli will also evoke that response. See also **discrimination.**

generalized anxiety disorder. An anxiety disorder characterized by persistent tension and apprehension. May be accompanied by such physical symptoms as rapid heart rate, fatigue, disturbed sleep, and dizziness. See also **anxiety disorders.**

genetics. That branch of biology concerned with heredity and the means by which hereditary characteristics are transmitted.

genital stage. In classical psychoanalysis, the final stage of psychosexual development, culminating in sexual union with a member of the opposite sex. See also **psychosexual development.**

genotype. In genetics, the characteristics that an individual has inherited and will transmit to his or her descendants, whether or not the individual manifests these characteristics. See also **phenotype.**

Gestalt psychology. A system of psychological theory concerned primarily with perception that emphasizes pattern, organization, wholes, and field properties.

glia cells. Supporting cells (not neurons) composing a substantial portion of brain tissue; recent speculation suggests that they may play a role in neural conduction.

gonads. Testes in the male, ovaries in the female. As duct glands, the sex glands are active in mating behavior, but as endocrine glands their hormones affect secondary sex characteristics as well as maintaining functional sexual activity. The male hormones are known as androgens, the female hormones as estrogen (syn. *sex glands*). See also **androgens, endocrine gland, estrogen.**

graded potentials. Potential changes of varying size induced in a neuron's dendrites or cell body by stimulation from synapses from other neurons. When the graded potentials reach a threshold of depolarization, an action potential occurs. See also **action potential, depolarization.**

gradient of texture. If a surface is perceived visually as having substantial texture (hard, soft, smooth, rough, etc.) and if the texture has a noticeable grain, it becomes fine as the surface recedes from the viewing person, producing a gradient of texture that is important in judgments of slant and of distance. See also **distance cues.**

group test. A test administered to several people at once by a single tester. A college exam is usually a group test.

group therapy. A group discussion or other group activity with a therapeutic purpose participated in by more than one client or patient at a time. See also **psychotherapy.**

GSR. See **galvanic skin response.**

H

habit. A learned stimulus-response sequence. See also **conditioned response.**

habituation. The reduction in the strength of a response to a repeated stimulus. In general, almost any stimulus will produce habituation; e.g., a pure tone sounded for a half-hour may decrease as much as 20 db in perceived loudness.

hallucination. A sense experience in the absence of appropriate external stimuli; a misinterpretation of imaginary experiences as actual perceptions. See also **delusion, illusion, schizophrenia.**

hallucinogens. Drugs whose main effect is to change perceptual experience and "expand consciousness." LSD and marijuana are examples (syn. *psychedelic drugs*).

halo effect. The tendency to bias our perception of another person in the direction of one particular characteristic that we like or dislike.

hedonism. The theory that human beings seek pleasure and avoid pain; an extreme form of the theory (in philosophy) is that pleasure or happiness is the highest good.

heritability. The proportion of the total variability of a trait in a given population that is attributable to genetic differences among individuals within that population.

hermaphrodite. An individual born with genitals that are ambiguous in appearance or that are in conflict with the internal sex glands. See also **transsexual.**

heroin. An extemely addictive central nervous system depressant derived from opium. See also **opiates.**

hertz (Hz). The wave frequency of a sound source, or other cyclical phenomena, measured in cycles per second.

heterosexuality. Interest in or attachment to a member of the opposite sex; the usual adult outcome of psychosexual development.

heuristic. In problem solving, a strategy that can be applied to a variety of problems and that usually, but not always, yields a correct solution.

hidden observer. A metaphor to describe the concealed consciousness in hypnosis, inferred to have experiences differing from, but parallel to, the hypnotic consciousness.

hierarchies of concepts. The relationships among individual concepts. See also **concept.**

hierarchy of motives. Maslow's way of classifying motives, ascending from basic biological motives to a peak of self-actualization, supposedly the highest human motive.

home sign. A system of gestures used by deaf children that initially functions as a kind of simple pantomime but eventually takes on the properties of a language.

homeostasis. An optimal level of organic function, mainatined by regulatory mechanisms known as homeostatic mechanisms; for example, the mechanisms maintaining a uniform body temperature.

homosexual. A person who prefers to have sexual relations with others of the same sex. Can be male or female, but female homosexuals are often termed *lesbians. Not* to be confused with transsexual. See also **transsexual.**

hormones. The internal secretions of the endocrine glands that are distributed via the bloodstream and affect behavior. See also **endocrine gland.**

hostile aggression. Aggression whose primary aim is to inflict injury. See also **instrumental aggression.**

hue. The dimension of color from which the major color names are derived (red, yellow, green, etc.), corresponding to wavelength of light. See also **brightness, saturation.**

humanistic psychology. A psychological approach that emphasizes the uniqueness of human beings; it is concerned with subjective experience and human values. Often referred to as a third force in psychology in contrast to behaviorism and psychoanalysis. See also **phenomenology.**

hunger drive. A drive based on food deprivation. See also **drive, specific hunger.**

hyperphagia. Pathological overeating. See also **aphagia.**

hypnosis. The responsive state achieved following a hypnotic induction or its equivalent. In this state, one person (the subject) responds to suggestions offered by another person (the hypnotist) and experiences alterations in perception, memory, and voluntary action.

hypnotic induction. The procedure used in establishing hypnosis in a responsive person. It usually involves relaxation and stimulated imagination. See also **hypnosis.**

hypnotic trance. The dreamlike state of heightened suggestibility induced in a subject by a hypnotist. See also **posthypnotic suggestion.**

hypothalamus. A small but very important structure located just above the brain stem and just below the thalamus. Considered a part of the central core of the brain, it includes centers that govern motivated behavior such as eating, drinking, sex, and emotions; it also regulates endocrine activity and maintains body homeostasis. See also **lateral hypothalamus, ventromedial hypothalamus.**

hypothesis testing. Gathering information and testing alternative explanations of some phenomenon.

hypothetical construct. One form of inferred intermediate mechanism. The construct is conceived of as having properties of its own, other than those specifically required for the explanation; for example, drive that is inferred from the behavior of a deprived organism and is used in the explanation of later behavior.

Hz. See **hertz.**

I

id. In Freud's tripartite division of the personality, that part reflecting unorganized, instinctual impulses. If unbridled, it seeks immediate gratification of primitive needs. See also **ego, superego.**

ideal self. In Carl Roger's theory, the conception of the kind of person one would like to be. A large discrepancy between the ideal self and the real self creates unhappiness and dissatisfaction. See also **self-concept.**

identical twins. See **monozygotic twins.**

identification. (1) The normal process of acquiring appropriate social roles in childhood through copying, in part unconsciously, the behavior of significant adults; for example, the child's identification with his or her like-sexed parent. See also **imitation.** (2) Close affiliation with others of like interest, such as identifying with a group. (3) A response to social influence in which the person changes his or her beliefs, attitudes, or behaviors in order to be like an influencing source that is respected or admired. See also **compliance, internalization, reference group.**

identification figures. Adult models (especially parents) copied, partly unconsciously, by the child. See also **identification.**

identity confusion. A stage of develop-

ment characteristic of some adolescents (and others) in which various identifications have not been harmonized and integrated into a sense of personal identity. See also **identification, identity formation.**

identity formation. The process of achieving adult personality integration, as an outgrowth of earlier identifications and other influences. See also **identification.**

illusion. In perception, a misinterpretation of the relationships among presented stimuli so that what is perceived does not correspond to physical reality, especially, but not exclusively, an optical or visual illusion. See also **delusion, hallucination.**

imitation. Beahvior that is modeled on or copies that of another. See also **identification.**

imprinting. A term used by ethologists for a species-specific type of learning that occurs within a limited period early in the life of the organism and is relatively unmodifiable thereafter, such as young ducklings learning to follow one adult female (usually the mother) within 11–18 hours after birth. But whatever object they are given to follow at this time, they will thereafter continue to follow. See also **ethology.**

incentive. (1) A tangible goal object that provides the stimuli that lead to goal activity. (2) Loosely, any goal. See also **negative incentive, positive incentive.**

incentive theory. A theory of motivation that emphasizes the importance of negative and positive incentives in determining behavior; internal drives are not the sole instigators of activity. See also **drive-reduction theory.**

independent variable. The variable under experimental control with which the changes studied in the experiment are correlated. In psychological experiments, the independent variable is often a stimulus, responses to which are the dependent variables under investigation. See also **dependent variable.**

individual differences. Relatively persistent dissimilarities in structure or behavior among persons or members of the same species.

inductive reasoning. Reasoning about arguments in which it is improbable that the conclusion is false if the premises are true. See also **deductive reasoning.**

infancy. The period of helplessness and dependency in humans and other organisms; in humans, roughly the first two years.

information-processing model. In general, a model based on assumptions regarding the flow of information through a system; usually best realized in the form of a computer program. In cognitive psychology, theories of how the mind functions are often represented in the form of an information-processing model. By simulating the model on a computer, one can study the properties and implications of the theory. See also **cognitive psychology, computer simulation, model.**

inhibitory synapse. A synapse at which the neurotransmitter changes the membrane permeability of the receiving cell in the direction of the resting potential; i.e., keeps it from firing. See also **excitatory synapse, synapse.**

inner ear. The internal portion of the ear containing, in addition to the cochlea, the vestibular sacs and the semicircular canals. See also **cochlea, semicircular canals, vestibular sacs.**

insight. (1) In problem-solving experiments, the perception of relationships leading to solution. Such a solution can be repeated promptly when the problem is again confronted. (2) In psychotherapy, the discovery by the individuals of dynamic connections between earlier and later events so that they come to recognize the roots of their conflicts.

instinct. The name given to unlearned, patterned, goal-directed behavior, which is species-specific, as illustrated by nest-building in birds or by the migration of salmon (syn. *species-specific behavior*). See also **ethology.**

instrumental aggression. Aggression aimed at obtaining rewards other than the victim's suffering. See also **hostile aggression.**

insulin. The hormone secreted by the pancreas. See also **hormones.**

intellectualization. A defense mechanism whereby a person tries to gain detachment from an emotionally threatening situation by dealing with it in abstract, intellectual terms. See also **defense mechanism.**

intelligence. (1) That which a properly standardized intelligence test measures. (2) The ability to learn from experience, think in abstract terms, and deal effectively with one's environment. See also **intelligence quotient, mental age.**

intelligence quotient (IQ). A scale unit used in reporting intelligence test scores, based on the ratio between mental age and chronological age. The decimal point is omitted so that the average IQ for children of any one chronological age is set at 100. See also **chronological age, deviation IQ, mental age.**

interactionism. In personality theory, a framework in which behavior is seen as resulting from the interaction between consistent personality dispositions, or traits, and the situations in which people find themselves. A limited form of the model uses the statistical method of analysis of variance to separate the proportion of variance in behavior that is attributable to personality traits, situational influences, and the interaction between the two. A broader concept of the interactionist position considers the reciprocal sequence of actions that takes place between person and situation, including the reactions that a person's behavior elicits from others and the influence this feedback has on the person's subsequent actions.

intermittent reinforcement. See **partial reinforcement.**

internalization. A response to social influence in which the person changes his or her beliefs, attitudes, or behaviors because he or she genuinely believes in the validity of the position advocated by the influencing source. The incorporation of someone else's opinions or behaviors into one's own value system. See also **compliance, identification.**

interneurons. Neurons in the central nervous system that receive messages from sensory neurons and send them to other interneurons or to motor neurons. See also **sensory neuron, motor neuron.**

interpretation. In psychoanalysis, the analyst's calling attention to the patient's resistances in order to facilitate the flow of associations; also the explanation of symbols, as in dream interpretation. See also **resistance.**

intervening variable. A process inferred to occur between stimulus and response, thus accounting for one response rather than another to the same stimulus. The intervening variable may be inferred without further specification, or it may be given concrete properties and become an object of investigation.

interview. A conversation between an investigator (the interviewer) and a subject (the respondent) used for gathering pertinent data for the subject's benefit (as in the psychotherapeutic interview) or for information-gathering (as in a sample survey).

intracellular fluid. Water contained within the body's cells; one of the critical variables monitored in the control of thirst.

introspection. (1) A form of trained self-observation, in which individuals describe the content of their consciousness without the intrusion of meanings or interpretations. (2) Any form of reporting on subjective (conscious) events or experiences. See also **phenomenology.**

introvert. One of the psychological types proposed by Jung, referring to the individual who, especially in time of emotional stress, tends to withdraw into himself or herself and to avoid other people. See also **extravert.**

J

James–Lange theory. A classical theory of emotion, named for the two men who independently proposed it. The theory states that the stimulus first leads to bodily responses, and then the awareness of these responses constitutes the experience of emotion. See also **Cannon-Bard theory, cognitive-appraisal theory.**

jnd. See **just noticeable difference.**

just noticeable difference (*jnd*). A barely perceptible physical change in a stimulus; a measure of the difference threshold. The term is used also as a unit for scaling the steps of sensation corresponding to increase in the magnitude of stimulation. See also **difference threshold, Weber's law.**

K

key-word method. A technique for learning vocabulary of a foreign language via an intermediate key word related to the sound of the foreign word and the meaning of the English equivalent. See also **mnemonics.**

kinesthesis. The muscle, tendon, and joint senses, yielding discrimination of position and movement of parts of the body. See also **equilibratory senses.**

Klinefelter's syndrome. An abnormal condition of the sex chromosomes (XXY instead of XX or XY); the individual is physically a male with penis and testicles but has marked feminine characteristics.

L

latency. (1) A temporal measure of response, referring to the time delay between the occurrence of the stimulus and the onset of the response. (2) In psychoanalysis, a period in middle childhood, roughly the years from 6–12, when both sexual and aggressive impulses are said to be in a somewhat subdued state, so that the child's attention is directed outward, and curiosity about the environment makes him or her ready to learn. See also **psychosexual development.**

latent content. The underlying significance of a dream (such as the motives or wishes being expressed by it) as interpreted from the manifest content. See also **interpretation, manifest content.**

latent learning. Learning that is not demonstrated by behavior at the time of learning but can be shown to have occurred by increasing the reinforcement for such behavior.

lateral fissure. A deep fissure at the side of each cerebral hemisphere, below which lies the temporal lobe (syn. *fissure of Sylvius*).

lateral hypothalamus (LH). An area of the hypothalamus important to the regulation of food intake. Electrical stimulation of this area will make an experimental animal start to eat; destruction of brain tissue here causes an animal to stop eating. See also **hypothalamus, ventromedial hypothalamus.**

law of effect. The phenomenon that any behavior that is followed by reinforcement is strengthened; from the infinite pool of possible responses, those that lead to reinforcement are repeated, whereas those that do not are extinguished. Some argue that the law of effect is comparable to the principle of natural selection: adaptive responses are selected from the pool of possible responses and their occurrence is made more likely by reinforcement, whereas nonadaptive responses are allowed to become extinct. See also **reinforcement.**

learned helplessness. A condition of apathy or helplessness created experimentally by subjecting an organism to unavoidable trauma (such as shock, heat, or cold). Being unable to avoid or escape an aversive situation produces a feeling of helplessness that generalizes to subsequent situations.

learning. A relatively permanent change in behavior that occurs as the result of practice. Behavior changes due to maturation or temporary conditions of the organism (such as fatigue, the influence of drugs, adaptation) are not included.

learning curve. A graph plotting the course of learning, in which the vertical axis (ordinate) plots a measure of proficiency (amount per unit time, time per unit amount, errors made, etc.), while the horizontal axis (abscissa) represents some measure of practice (trials, times, etc.)

left hemisphere. The left cerebral hemisphere. Controls the right side of the body and, for most people, speech and other logical, sequential activities (syn. *major hemisphere*). See also **cerebral hemisphere, corpus callosum, right hemisphere, split-brain subject.**

lesbian. See **homosexual.**

LH. See **lateral hypothalamus.**

libido. In psychoanalysis, the energy of the sexual instinct, which throughout life becomes attached to new objects and is expressed through various types of motivated behavior.

lie detector. See **polygraph, voice stress analyzer.**

light adaptation. The decreased sensitivity of the eye to light when the subject has been continuously exposed to high levels of illumination. See also **dark adaptation.**

lightness constancy. The tendency to see a familiar object as of the same brightness, regardless of light and shadow that change its stimulus properties. See also **perceptual constancy.**

limbic system. A set of structures in and around the midbrain, forming a functional unit regulating motivational-emotional types of behavior, such as waking and sleeping, excitement and quiescence, feeding, and mating.

linguistic relativity hypothesis. The proposition that one's thought processes, the way one perceives the world, are related to one's language.

lithium carbonate. A compound based on lithium, an element related to sodium. Has been successful in treating manic-depressive disorders.

localized functions. Behavior controlled by known areas of the brain; for example, vision is localized in the occipital lobes.

location constancy. The tendency to perceive the place at which a resting object is located as remaining the same even though the relationship to the observer has changed. See also **perceptual constancy.**

long-term memory (LTM). The relatively permanent component of the memory system, as opposed to short-term memory. See also **short-term memory.**

longitudinal study. A research method that studies an individual through time, taking measurements at periodic intervals. See also **case history.**

loudness. An intensity dimension of hearing correlated with the amplitude of the sound waves that constitute the stimulus. Greater amplitudes yield greater loudnesses. See also **pitch, timbre.**

LSD. See **lysergic acid diethylamide.**

lysergic acid diethylamide. A powerful psychoactive drug capable of producing extreme alterations in consciousness, hallucinations, distortions in perception, and unpredictable mood swings.

M

major hemisphere. See **left hemisphere.**

manic-depressive disorder. An affective disorder characterized by alternating moods of excitement and elation (manic phase) and despondency and sadness (depressive phase), often with periods of normal mood in between. Some individuals experience only the manic phase. Alternations between normal mood and periods of depression are *not* diagnosed manic-depressive disorder. See also **affective disorder, bipolar disorder.**

manifest content. The remembered content of a dream, the characters, and their actions, as distinguished from the inferred latent content. See also **latent content.**

mantra. See **transcendental meditation.**

MAO. See **monoamine oxidase.**

MAOI. See **monoamine oxidase inhibitor.**

marijuana. The dried leaves of the hemp plant; also known as hashish, "pot," or "grass." Hashish is actually an extract of the plant material and, hence, is usually stronger than marijuana. Intake may enhance sensory experiences and produce a state of euphoria.

marital therapy. Psychotherapy with both members of a couple aimed at resolving problems in their relationship (syn. *couples therapy*). See also **psychotherapy.**

masochism. A pathological desire to inflict pain on oneself or to suffer pain at the hands of others. See also **sadism.**

maternal drive. The drive, particularly in animals, induced in the female through bearing and nursing young, leading to nest-building, retrieving, and other forms of care. See also **drive.**

maturation. Growth processes in the individual that result in orderly changes in behavior, whose timing and patterning are relatively independent of exercise or experience though they may require a normal environment.

maze. A device used in the study of animal and human learning, consisting of a correct path and blind alleys.

mean. The arithmetical average; the sum of all scores divided by their number. See also **measure of central tendency.**

measure of central tendency. A value representative of a frequency distribution, around which other values are dispersed; for example, the mean, median, or mode of a distribution of scores. See also **mean, median, mode.**

measure of variation. A measure of the dispersion or spread of scores in a frequency distribution, such as the range or the standard deviation. See also **standard deviation.**

median. The score of the middle case when cases are arranged in order of size of score. See also **measure of central tendency.**

meditation. An altered state of consciousness in which the individual is extremely relaxed and feels divorced from the outside world; the individual loses self-awareness and gains a sense of being involved in a wider consciousness. This meditative state is achieved by performing certain rituals, including regulating breathing, sharply restricting one's field of attention, and assuming yogic body positions. A commercialized form of meditation has been widely promoted under the name of *transcendental meditation* or *TM*.

memory decay. A major cause of forgetting in short-term memory in which information simply fades with time.

memory span. The number of items (digits, letters, words) that can be reproduced in order after a single presentation; usually 7 ± 2. See also **chunk, short-term memory.**

memory trace. The inferred change in the nervous system that persists between the time something is learned and the time it is recalled.

menarche. The first menstrual period, indicative of sexual maturation in a girl. See also **menstruation.**

menstruation. The approximately monthly discharge from the uterus. See also **menarche.**

mental age (MA). A scale unit proposed by Binet for use in intelligence testing. If an intelligence test is properly standardized, a representative group of children of age 6 should earn an average mental age of 6, those of age 7, a mental age of 7, etc. A child whose MA is above his or her chronological age (CA) is advanced; one whose MA lags behind is retarded. See also **chronological age, intelligence quotient.**

mental imagery. Mental pictures used as an aid to memory. *Not* the same as eidetic imagery. See also **eidetic imagery.**

mental retardation. Subnormal intellectual functioning with impairment in social adjustment.

mental rotation. The notion that a mental image of an object can be rotated in the mind in a fashion analogous to rotating the real object.

mesomorph. The second of three types of physique in Sheldon's type theory. Refers to the prominence of bone and muscle, as in the typical athlete. See also **ectomorph, endomorph, type theory.**

method of loci. An aid to serial memory. Verbal material is transformed into mental images, which are then located at successive positions along a visualized route, such as an imaged walk through the house or down a familiar street.

middle ear. The portion of the ear containing the hammer, anvil, and stirrup bones,

which connect the eardrum to the oval window of the inner ear.

minor hemisphere. See **right hemisphere.**

mnemonics. A system for improving memory often involving a set of symbols that can substitute for the material to be remembered; for example, in attempting to remember a number sequence, one may translate the sequence into letters of the alphabet that in turn approximate words that are easily remembered.

mode. The most frequent score in a distribution, or the class interval in which the greatest number of cases fall. See also **measure of central tendency.**

model. (1) Miniature systems are often constructed according to a logical, mathematical, or physical model. That is, the principles according to which data are organized and made understandable parallel those of the model; for instance, the piano keyboard is a model for understanding the basilar membrane; the thermostat is a model for the feedback principle of homeostasis. (2) In behavior therapy, one who *models* or performs behaviors that the therapist wishes the patient to imitate.

modeling. In social learning theory, the process by which a child learns social and cognitive behaviors by observing and imitating others. See also **identification.**

mongolism. See **Down's syndrome.**

monoamine oxidase (MAO). One of the enzymes responsible for the breakdown of a group of neurotransmitters called biogenic amines (norepinephrine, dopamine, and serotonin are examples); believed to be important in the regulation of emotion. Drugs that inhibit the action of this enzyme (MAO inhibitors) are used in treating depression. See also **antidepressant, monamine oxidase inhibitor, neurotransmitter.**

monoamine oxidase inhibitor (MAOI). A class of drugs used to treat depression; it inhibits the action of an enzyme (monoamine oxidase) that breaks down certain neurotransmitters (such as dopamine, norepinephrine, and serotonin), thereby prolonging the action of these neurotransmitters. See also **antidepressant, monoamine oxidase, neurotransmitter.**

monochromatism. Total color blindness, the visual system being achromatic. A

rare disorder. See also **dichromatism, trichromatism.**

monocular cues. See **distance cues.**

monozygotic (MZ) twins. Twins developed from a single egg. They are always of the same sex and commonly much alike in appearance, although some characteristics may be in mirror image; for example one right-handed, the other left-handed (syn. *identical twins*). See also **dizygotic twins.**

morpheme. The smallest meaningful unit in the structure of a language, whether a word, base, or affix; such as *man, strange, ing, pro*. See also **phoneme.**

motivation. A general term referring to the regulation of need-satisfying and goal-seeking behavior. See also **motive.**

motive. Any condition of the organism that affects its readiness to start on or continue in a sequence of behavior.

motor area. A projection area in the brain lying in front of the central fissure. Electrical stimulation commonly results in movement, or motor, responses. See also **somatosensory area.**

motor neuron. A neuron, or nerve cell, that conveys messages from the brain or spinal cord to the muscles and glands (syn. *efferent neuron*). See also **sensory neuron.**

multiple personality. The existence of two or more integrated and well-developed personalities within the same individual. Each personality has its own set of memories and characteristic behaviors. Typically, the attitudes and behavior of the alternating personalities are markedly different.

myelin sheath. The fatty sheath surrounding certain nerve fibers known as myelinated fibers. Impulses travel faster and with less energy expenditure in myelinated fibers than in unmyelinated fibers.

MZ twins. See **monozygotic twins.**

N

nanometer (nm). A billionth of a meter. Wavelength of light is measured in nanometers.

narcissism. Self-love; in psychoanalytic theory, the normal expression of pregenital development.

narcolepsy. A sleep disturbance characterized by an uncontrollable tendency to fall asleep for brief periods at inopportune times.

narcotics. See **opiates**.

nativism. The view that behavior is innately determined. See also **empiricism**.

nature-nurture issue. The problem of determining the relative importance of heredity (nature) and the result of upbringing in the particular environment (nurture) on mature ability.

need. A physical state involving any lack or deficit within the organism. See also **drive, motive**.

negative incentive. An object or circumstance away from which behavior is directed when the object or circumstance is perceived or anticipated. See also **positive incentive**.

negative reinforcement. Reinforcing a response by the removal of an aversive stimulus. See also **negative reinforcer**.

negative reinforcer. Any stimulus that, when removed following a response, increases the probability of the response. Loud noise, electric shock, and extreme heat or cold classify as negative reinforcers. See also **punishment**.

nerve. A bundle of elongated axons belonging to hundreds or thousands of neurons, possibly both afferent and efferent neurons. Connects portions of the nervous system to other portions and to receptors and effectors. See also **axon, neuron**.

nerve cell. See **neuron**.

neuron. The nerve cell; the unit of a synaptic nervous system.

neurosis (pl. *neuroses*). A mental disorder in which the individual is unable to cope with anxieties and conflicts and develops symptoms that he or she finds distressing, such as obsessions, compulsions, phobias, or anxiety attacks. In psychoanalytic theory, neurosis results from the use of defense mechanisms to ward off anxiety caused by unconscious conflicts. No longer a diagnostic category of DSM-III. See also **anxiety disorders, obsessive-compulsive disorder, phobia**.

neurotic anxiety. Fear that is out of proportion to the actual danger posed (such as stage fright). See also **anxiety, objective anxiety**.

neurotransmitter. A chemical involved in the transmission of nerve impulses across the synapse from one neuron to another. Usually released from small vesicles in the terminal button of the axon in response to the action potential; diffuses across synapse to influence electrical activity in another neuron. See also **dopamine, epinephrine, norepinephrine, serotonin**.

noncontingent reinforcement. Reinforcement not contingent on a specific response.

noradrenalin. See **norepinephrine**.

norepinephrine. One of the hormones secreted by the adrenal medulla; its action in emotional excitement is similar in some, but not all, respects to that of epinephrine. It is also a neurotransmitter of the central nervous system. Norepinephrine synapses can be either excitatory or inhibitory. Believed to play a role in depression and manic-depression (syn. *noradrenaline*). See also **adrenal gland, epinephrine**.

norm. An average, common, or standard performance under specified conditions; for example, the average achievement test score of 9-year-old children or the average birth weight of male children. See also **social norms, test standardization**.

normal curve. The plotted form of the normal distribution.

normal distribution. The standard symmetrical bell-shaped frequency distribution, whose properties are commonly used in making statistical inferences from measures derived from samples. See also **normal curve**.

nuclei (sing. *nucleus*). A collection of nerve cell bodies grouped in the brain or spinal cord. See also **ganglia**.

null hypothesis. A statistical hypothesis that any difference observed among treatment conditions occurs by chance and does not reflect a true difference. Rejection of the null hypothesis means that we believe the treatment conditions are actually having an effect.

O

object constancy. See **perceptual constancy**.

object permanence. Piaget's term for the child's realization that an object continues to exist even though it is hidden from view. See also **sensorimotor stage**.

object size. The size of an object as determined from measurement at its surface. When size constancy holds, the observer perceives a distant object as being near its object size. See also **retinal size**.

objective anxiety. Fear that is proportionate to the danger posed.

observational method. Studying events as they occur in nature, without experimental control of variables; for instance, studying the nest-building of birds or observing children's behavior in a play situation. See also **experimental method**.

obsession. A persistent, unwelcome, intrusive thought, often suggesting an aggressive or sexual act. See also **compulsion, obsessive-compulsive disorder**.

obsessive-compulsive disorder. An anxiety disorder taking one of three forms: (1) recurrent thoughts, often disturbing and unwelcome (obsessions); (2) irresistible urges to repeat stereotyped or ritualistic acts (compulsions); (3) both of these in combination. See also **anxiety disorders**.

occipital lobe. A portion of the cerebral hemisphere, behind the parietal and temporal lobes. See also **frontal lobe, parietal lobe, temporal lobe**.

Oedipal stage. In psychoanalysis, an alternative designation of the phallic stage of psychosexual development, because it is at this stage that the Oedipus complex arises. See also **Oedipus complex, psychosexual development**.

Oedipus complex. In psychoanalytic theory, sexual attachment to the parent of the opposite sex, originating as the normal culmination of the infantile period of development.

olfactory epithelium. The specialized skin within the nasal cavity that contains the receptors for the sense of smell.

operant behavior. Behavior defined by the stimulus to which it leads rather than by the stimulus that elicits it; such as behavior leading to reward (syn. *instrumental behavior*). See also **respondent behavior**.

operant conditioning. The strengthening of an operant response by presenting a reinforcing stimulus if, and only if, the response occurs (syn. *instrumental conditioning, reward learning*). See also **classical conditioning**.

opiates. Opium or one of its chemical derivatives: codeine, morphine, or heroin. Central nervous system depressants that relieve pain and produce euphoria, all highly addictive (syn. *narcotics*). See also **heroin**.

opponent-color theory. A theory of color perception that postulates two types of color-sensitive units that respond in opposite ways to the two colors of an opponent pair. One type of unit responds to red or green, the other to blue or yellow. Since a unit cannot respond in two ways at once, reddish-greens and yellowish-blues cannot occur. See also **trichromatic theory, two-stage color theory.**

opponent-process theory. In emotion, the theory that assumes the brain is organized to oppose or suppress emotional responses, whether they are pleasurable or aversive.

oral behavior. Behavior deriving from the infant's need to suck or, more generally, to be fed through the mouth.

oral stage. In psychoanalysis, first stage of psychosexual development, in which pleasure derives from the lips and mouth, as in sucking at the mother's breast. See also **psychosexual development.**

organ of Corti. In the ear, the actual receptor for hearing, lying on the basilar membrane in the cochlea and containing the hair cells where the fibers of the auditory nerve originate (syn. *Tunnel of Corti*). See also **basilar membrane, cochlea.**

orienting reflex. (1) A nonspecific response to change in stimulation involving depression of cortical alpha rhythm, galvanic skin response, pupillary dilation, and complex vasomotor responses (a term introduced by Russian psychologists). (2) Head or body movements that orient the organism's receptors to those parts of the environment in which stimulus changes are occurring.

osmoreceptors. Hypothesized cells in the hypothalamus that respond to dehydration by stimulating the release of ADH by the pituitary gland, which, in turn, signals the kidneys to reabsorb water into the bloodstream. See also **antidiuretic hormone, volumetric receptors.**

otoliths. "Ear stones." See also **vestibular sacs.**

ovarian hormones. See **estrogen.**

overextension. The tendency of a child, in learning a language, to apply a new word too widely; for example, to call all animals "doggie."

overtone. A higher frequency tone, a multiple of the fundamental frequency, that occurs when a tone is sounded by a musical instrument. See also **timbre.**

P

paired-associate learning. The learning of stimulus-response pairs, as in the acquisition of a foreign language vocabulary. When the first member of a pair (the stimulus) is presented, the subject's task is to give the second member (the response).

pancreas. A bodily organ situated near the stomach. As a duct gland, it secretes pancreatic juice into the intestines, but some specialized cells function as an endocrine gland, secreting the hormone insulin into the bloodstream. See also **endocrine gland.**

pandemonium theory. An early effort in the field of artificial intelligence to build a computer-based machine that could simulate the process of pattern recognition. The system was designed for the recognition of hand-printed letters, and many psychologists argue that it has important resemblances to human recognition. See also **artificial intelligence, simulation.**

panic disorder. An anxiety disorder in which the individual has sudden and inexplicable episodes of terror and feelings of impending doom accompanied by physiological symptoms of fear (such as heart palpitations, shortness of breath, muscle tremors, faintness). See also **anxiety, anxiety disorders.**

parallel processing. A theoretical interpretation of information processing in which several sources of information are all processed simultaneously. See also **serial processing.**

paranoid schizophrenia. A schizophrenic reaction in which the patient has delusions of persecution. See also **schizophrenia.**

parapsychology. A subfield of psychology that studies such paranormal phenomena as extrasensory perception and psychokinesis. See also **clairvoyance, extrasensory perception, precognition, psychokinesis, telepathy.**

parasympathetic division. A division of the autonomic nervous system, the nerve fibers of which originate in the cranial and sacral portions of the spinal cord. Active in relaxed or quiescent states of the body and to some extent antagonistic to the sympathetic division. See also **sympathetic division.**

parathyroid glands. Endocrine glands adjacent to the thyroid gland in the neck, whose hormones regulate calcium metabolism, thus maintaining the normal excitability of the nervous system. Parathyroid inadequacy leads to tetany. See also **endocrine gland.**

parietal lobe. A portion of the cerebral hemisphere, behind the central fissure and between the frontal and occipital lobes. See also **frontal lobe, occipital lobe, temporal lobe.**

partial reinforcement. Reinforcing a given response only some proportion of the times it occurs (syn. *intermittent reinforcement*). See also **reinforcement, reinforcement schedule.**

percept. The result of the perceptual process; that which the individual perceives.

perception. A general term to describe the whole process of how we come to know what is going on around us; the entire sequence of events from the presentation of a physical stimulus to the phenomenological experiencing of it. Perception is viewed as a set of subprocesses that occur in a multilevel, interactive system. The lower levels of this system, the parts closely associated with the sense organs, are called sensory processes. See also **sensory processes.**

perceptual constancy. The tendency to see objects as relatively unchanged under widely altered conditions of illumination, distance, and position. See also **color constancy, lightness constancy, location constancy, shape constancy, size constancy.**

perceptual patterning. The tendency to perceive stimuli according to principles such as proximity, similarity, continuity, and closure. Emphasized by Gestalt psychologists. See also **figure-ground perception, Gestalt psychology.**

performance. Overt behavior, as distinguished from knowledge or information not translated into action. The distinction is important in theories of learning.

peripheral nervous system. That part of the nervous system outside the brain and spinal cord; it includes the autonomic nervous system and the somatic nervous system. See also **autonomic nervous system, somatic nervous system.**

personality. The characteristic patterns of behavior, thought, and emotion that determine a person's adjustment to his or her environment (syn. *individuality*).

personality assessment. (1) Generally, the appraisal of personality by any method. (2) More specifically, personality appraisal through complex observations and judgments, usually based in part on behavior in contrived social situations.

personality disorders. Ingrained, habitual, and rigid patterns of behavior or character that severely limit the individual's adaptive potential; often society sees the behavior as maladaptive whereas the individual does not.

personality dynamics. Theories of personality that stress personality dynamics are concerned with the interactive aspects of behavior (as in conflict resolution), with value hierarchies, with the permeability of boundaries between differentiated aspects of personality, etc. Contrasted with developmental theories, though not incompatible with them.

personality inventory. An inventory for self-appraisal, consisting of many statements or questions about personal characteristics and behavior that the person judges to apply or not to apply to him or her. See also **projective test.**

personality psychologist. A psychologist whose area of interest focuses on classifying individuals and studying the differences between them. This specialty overlaps both developmental and social psychologists to some extent. See also **developmental psychologist, social psychologist.**

person-centered therapy. A method of psychotherapy developed by Carl Rogers in which the therapist is nondirective and reflective and does not interpret or advise. The operating assumption is that the client is the best expert on his or her problems and can work them out in a nonjudgmental, accepting atmosphere. Formerly called client-centered therapy (syn. *nondirective counseling*).

phallic stage. In psychoanalysis, that stage of psychosexual development in which gratification is associated with stimulation of the sex organs and the sexual attachment is to the parent of the opposite sex. See also **Oedipal stage, psychosexual development.**

phenomenology. The study of an individual's subjective experience or unique perception of the world. Emphasis is on understanding events from the subject's point of view rather than focusing on behavior. See also **humanistic psychology, introspection.**

phenotype. In genetics, the characteristics that are displayed by the individual organism—such as eye color or intelligence—as distinct from those traits that one may carry genetically but not display. See also **genotype.**

pheromones. Special chemicals secreted by many animals that float through the air to attract other members of the same species. They represent a primitive form of communication.

phi phenomenon. Stroboscopic motion in its simpler form. Commonly produced by successively turning on and off two separated stationary light sources; as the first is turned off and the second turned on, the subject perceives a spot of light moving from the position of the first to that of the second. See also **stroboscopic motion.**

phobia. Excessive fear in the absence of real danger. See also **agoraphobia, claustrophobia.**

phobic disorder. An anxiety disorder in which phobias are severe or pervasive enough to interfere seriously with the individual's daily life. See also **anxiety disorders, phobia.**

phoneme. The smallest unit in the sound system of a language; it serves to distinguish utterances from one another. See also **morpheme.**

physical dependence. With repeated use of a drug, an individual can become dependent on that drug. Physical dependence is characterized by tolerance (with continued use, the individual must take more and more of the drug to achieve the same effect) and withdrawal (if use is discontinued, the person experiences unpleasant physical symptoms) (syn. *addiction*).

physiological motive. A motive based on an evident bodily need, such as the need for food or water.

physiological psychologist. A psychologist concerned with the relationship between physiological functions and behavior.

physiology. That branch of biology concerned primarily with the functioning of organ systems within the body.

pitch. A qualitative dimension of hearing correlated with the frequency of the sound waves that constitute the stimulus. Higher frequencies yield higher pitches. See also **loudness, timbre.**

pituitary gland. An endocrine gland joined to the brain just below the hypothalamus. It consists of two parts, the anterior pituitary and the posterior pituitary. The anterior pituitary is the more important part because of its regulation of growth and of other endocrine glands (syn. *hypophysis*). See also **endocrine gland.**

place theory of pitch. A theory of hearing that associates pitch with the place on the basilar membrane where activation occurs. See also **temporal theory of pitch.**

placebo. An inert substance used in place of an active drug; given to the control group in an experimental test.

pluralistic ignorance. The tendency for persons in a group to mislead each other about a situation; e.g., to define an emergency as a nonemergency because others are remaining calm and are not taking action.

polygenic traits. Characteristics—intelligence, height, emotional stability—determined by many sets of genes.

polygraph. A device that measures simultaneously several physiological responses that accompany emotion; for instance, heart and respiration rate, blood pressure, and GSR. Commonly known as a "lie detector" because of its use in determining the guilt of a subject through responses while he or she answers questions. See also **voice stress analyzer.**

population. The total universe of all possible cases from which a sample is selected. The usual statistical formulas for making inferences from samples apply when the population is appreciably larger than the sample—for instance, 5 to 10 times larger than the sample. See also **sample.**

positive incentive. An object or circumstance toward which behavior is directed when the object or circumstance is perceived or anticipated. See also **negative incentive.**

positive reinforcement. Reinforcing a response by the presentation of a positive stimulus. See also **positive reinforcer.**

positive reinforcer. Any stimulus that, when applied following a response, increases the probability of the response (syn. *reward*). See also **negative reinforcer.**

postconventional morality. Level III of Kohlberg's stages of moral reasoning in which actions are evaluated in terms of their adherence to principles essential to the community welfare and/or personal ethics. See also **conventional morality, preconventional morality.**

posthypnotic amnesia. A particular form of posthypnotic suggestion in which the hypnotized person forgets what has happened during the hypnosis until signaled to remember. See also **posthypnotic suggestion.**

posthypnotic suggestion. A suggestion made to a hypnotized person that he or she will perform in a prescribed way (commonly to a prearranged signal) when no longer hypnotized. The activity is usually carried out without the subject's awareness of its origin. See also **hypnosis.**

PQRST method. A technique for reading and studying information presented in textbook form. The method takes its name from the first letter of the five steps one follows in reading a textbook chapter: *Preview, Question, Read, Self-recitation, Test.*

precognition. A claimed form of extrasensory perception in which a future event is perceived. See also **clairvoyance, extrasensory perception, telepathy.**

preconscious memories. Memories and thoughts that are not part of your consciousness at this moment, but that can be brought to consciousness when needed. They include specific memories of personal events as well as information accumulated over a lifetime. See also **consciousness.**

preconventional morality. Level I of Kohlberg's stages of moral reasoning in which actions are evaluated in terms of outcome (whether the actions avoid punishment or lead to reward) without any concept of right or wrong. See also **conventional morality, postconventional morality.**

prejudice. A prejudgment that something or someone is good or bad on the basis of little or no evidence; an attitude that is firmly fixed, not open to free and rational discussion, and resistant to change.

preoperational stage. Piaget's second stage of cognitive development (ages 2–7 years). The child can think in terms of symbols but does not yet comprehend certain rules or operations, such as the principle of conservation. See also **conservation.**

prepared conditioning. The proposal that humans are biologically predisposed, or prepared, by evolutionary selection to associate fear with objects or situations that were dangerous in earlier times. Explains why people develop phobias (conditioned fears) of snakes and heights but not of lambs or guns. See also **classical conditioning.**

primacy effect. (1) In memory experiments, the tendency for initial words in a list to be recalled more readily than later words. (2) In studies of impression formation, the tendency for initial information to carry more weight than information received later.

primary abilities. The abilities, discovered by factor analysis, that underlie intelligence test performance. See also **factor analysis.**

primary sex characteristics. The structural or physiological characteristics that make possible sexual union and reproduction. See also **secondary sex characteristics.**

private self-consciousness. The disposition to introspect, to examine one's feelings and motives. See also **public self-consciousness, self-consciousness.**

proactive interference. The interference of earlier learning with the learning and recall of new material. See also **retroactive interference.**

probe. In studies of memory, a digit or other item from a list to be remembered that is presented as a cue to the subject; for example, the subject could be asked to give the next digit in the list.

problem-focused coping. Reducing anxiety or stress by dealing in some way with the anxiety-producing situation. Escaping the situation or finding a way to alter it are examples. See also **emotion-focused coping.**

problem-solving strategies. The various strategies that can be employed in solving a problem. Of special interest are a class of strategies that involve breaking the solution to a problem into a series of subgoals. The subgoals are to be accomplished as intermediate steps toward ultimately reaching the final goal.

product-moment correlation. See **coefficient of correlation.**

progesterone. A female sex hormone produced by the ovaries; it helps prepare the uterus for pregnancy and the breasts for lactation.

program. (1) A plan for the solution of a problem; often used interchangeably with "routine" to specify the precise sequence of instructions enabling a computer to solve a problem. (2) In teaching, a set of materials arranged so as to maximize the learning process.

projection. A defense mechanism by which people protect themselves from awareness of their own undesirable traits by attributing those traits excessively to others. See also **defense mechanism.**

projective test. A personality test in which subjects reveal ("project") themselves through imaginative productions. The projective test gives much freer possibilities of response than the fixed-alternative personality inventory. Examples of projective tests are the Rorschach Test (ink blots to be interpreted) and the Thematic Apperception Test (pictures that elicit stories). See also **personality inventory.**

prolactin. Pituitary hormone prompting the secretion of milk. See also **hormones.**

proposition. A sentence or component of a sentence that asserts something, the predicate, about somebody (or something), the subject. All sentences can be broken into propositions.

prosopagnosia. The inability to recognize familiar faces; in severe cases, the person may be unable to recognize his or her own face.

prototype. The part of a concept that contains the properties that describe the best examples of the concept. See also **core.**

psi. The special ability said to be possessed by the subject who performs successfully in experiments on extrasensory perception and psychokinesis. See also **extrasensory perception, psychokinesis.**

psychedelic drugs. See **hallucinogens.**

psychiatric nurse. A nurse specially trained to deal with patients suffering from mental disorders. See also **psychiatrist.**

psychiatric social worker. A social worker trained to work with patients and their families on problems of mental health and illness, usually in close relationship with psychiatrists and clinical psychologists. See also **clinical psychologist, psychiatrist.**

psychiatrist. A medical doctor specializing in the treatment and prevention of mental disorders both mild and severe. See also **clinical psychologist, psychoanalyst.**

psychiatry. A branch of medicine concerned with mental health and mental illness. See also **psychiatrist, psychoanalyst.**

psychoactive drugs. Drugs that affect

one's behavior and thought processes. See also **depressants, hallucinogens, stimulants.**

psychoanalysis. (1) The method developed by Freud and extended by his followers for treating neuroses. (2) The system of psychological theory growing out of experiences with the psychoanalytic method.

psychoanalyst. A psychotherapist, usually trained as a psychiatrist, who uses methods related to those originally proposed by Freud for treating neuroses and other mental disorders. See also **clinical psychologist, psychiatrist.**

psychoanalytic psychotherapy. A method of treating mental disorders based on the theories of Freud but briefer and less intense than psychoanalysis. Less emphasis on exploration of childhood experiences and more attention to the client's current interpersonal problems. See also **psychoanalysis.**

psychodrama. A form of spontaneous play acting used in psychotherapy.

psychogenic. Caused by psychological factors (such as emotional conflict or faulty habits) rather than by disease, injury, or other somatic cause; functional rather than organic.

psychograph. See **trait profile.**

psychoimmunology. An area of research in behavioral medicine that studies how the body's immune system is affected by psychological variables. See also **behavioral medicine.**

psychokinesis (PK). A claimed form of mental operation said to affect a material body or an energy system without any evidence of more usual contact or energy transfer; for example, affecting the number that comes up in the throw of dice by a machine through wishing for that number. See also **extrasensory perception.**

psycholinguistics. The study of the psychological aspects of language and its acquisition.

psychological motive. A motive that is primarily learned rather than based on biological needs.

psychology. The science that studies behavior and mental processes.

psychometric function. A curve plotting the percentage of times the subject reports detecting a stimulus against a measure of the physical energy of the stimulus.

psychopathic personality. See **antisocial personality.**

psychopharmacology. The study of the effects of drugs on behavior.

psychophysics. A name used by Fechner for the science of the relationship between mental processes and the physical world. Now usually restricted to the study of the sensory consequences of controlled physical stimulation.

psychosexual development. In psychoanalysis, the theory that development takes place through stages (oral, anal, phallic, latent, genital), each stage characterized by a zone of pleasurable stimulation and appropriate objects of sexual attachment, culminating in normal heterosexual mating. See also **anal stage, genital stage, latency stage, oral stage, phallic stage, psychosocial stages.**

psychosis (pl. *psychoses*). A severe mental disorder in which thinking and emotion are so impaired that the individual is seriously out of contact with reality. No longer a major diagnostic category in DSM-III. See also **psychotic behavior.**

psychosocial stages. A modification by Erikson of the psychoanalytic theory of psychosexual development, giving more attention to the social and environmental problems associated with the various stages of development and adding some adult stages beyond genital maturing. See also **psychosexual development.**

psychosomatic disorder. Physical illness that has psychological causes (syn. *psycho-physiological disorder*).

psychosurgery. A form of biological therapy for abnormal behavior. Involves destroying selected areas of the brain, most often the nerve fibers connecting the frontal lobes to the limbic system and/or the hypothalamus.

psychotherapy. Treatment of personality maladjustment or mental illness by psychological means, usually, but not exclusively, through personal consultation. See also **biological therapy.**

psychotic behavior. Behavior indicating gross impairment in reality contact as evidenced by delusions and/or hallucinations. May result from damage to the brain or from a mental disorder such as schizophrenia or a manic-depressive disorder. See also **psychosis.**

puberty. The age at which the sex organs become reproductively functional; marked by menstruation in girls and the appearance of live sperm cells in the semen of boys. Sometimes used to refer to period during which the reproductive organs are becoming functionally mature, in which case the development of the secondary sex characteristics (particularly the growth and pigmentation of underarm and pubic hair) marks the onset of puberty and the capacity for reproduction, the culmination. See also **adolescent growth spurt, secondary sex characteristics.**

public self-consciousness. The disposition to be concerned with how one appears to others. See **private self-consciousness, self-consciousness.**

punishment. A procedure used to decrease the strength of a response by presenting an aversive stimulus whenever the response occurs. Note that such a stimulus when applied would be a punisher; when removed, it would act as a nagative reinforcer, reinforcing whatever led to its removal. See also **negative reinforcer.**

R

rapid eye movements (REMs). Eye movements that usually occur during dreaming and that can be measured by attaching small electrodes laterally to and above the subject's eye. These register changes in electrical activity associated with movements of the eyeball in its socket.

rapport. (1) A comfortable relationship between the subject and the tester, ensuring cooperation in replying to test questions. (2) A similar relationship between therapist and patient. (3) A special relationship of hypnotic subject to hypnotist.

rating scale. A device by which raters can record their judgments of others (or of themselves) on the traits defined by the scale.

rationalization. A defense mechanism in which self-esteem is maintained by assigning plausible and acceptable reasons for conduct entered on impulsively or for less acceptable reasons. See also **defense mechanism.**

reaction formation. A defense mechanism in which a person denies a disapproved motive through giving strong expression to its opposite. See also **defense mechanism.**

reaction range. The range of potential intellectual ability specified by a person's genes. According to this concept, the effects of an enriched, average, or deprived environment will be to change the person's IQ but only within his or her genetically specified reaction range.

reaction time. The time between the presentation of a stimulus and the occurrence of a response. See also **latency.**

receiver-operating-characteristic curve (ROC curve). The function relating the probability of hits and false alarms for a fixed signal level in a detection task. Factors influencing response bias may cause hits and false alarms to vary, but their variation is constrained to the ROC curve. See also **signal detection task.**

recency effect. In memory experiments, the tendency for the last words in a list to be recalled more readily than other list words.

receptor. A specialized portion of the body sensitive to particular kinds of stimuli and connected to nerves composed of afferent neurons (such as the retina of the eye). Used more loosely, the organ containing these sensitive portions (such as the eye or the ear).

recessive gene. A member of a gene pair that determines the characteristic trait or appearance of the individual only if the other member of the pair is recessive. If the other member of the pair is dominant, the effect of the recessive gene is masked. See also **dominant gene.**

recoding. A process for improving short-term memory by grouping items into a familiar unit or chunk.

recognition. To recognize something is to associate it correctly with a category, such as "chair," or with a specific name, such as "John Jones." It is a high-level process that requires learning and remembering.

recurrent inhibition. A process whereby some receptors in the visual system when stimulated by nerve impulses inhibit the firing of other visual receptors, thus making the visual system responsive to changes in illumination.

red-green color blindness. The commonest form of color blindness, a variety of dichromatism. In the two subvarieties, red-blindness and green-blindness, both red and green vision are lacking, but achromatic bands are seen at different parts of the spectrum. See also **color blindness, dichromatism.**

reference group. Any group to which an individual refers for comparing, judging, and deciding on his or her opinions, and behaviors. We are said to "identify" with such groups. See also **identification.**

refractory phase. The period of temporary inactivity in a neuron after it has fired once.

registration. A term to describe receptive processing in which information is processed but not perceived. See also **perception.**

regression. A return to the more primitive or infantile modes of response.

rehearsal. The conscious repetition of information in short-term memory, usually involving speech. The process facilitates the short-term recall of information and its transfer to long-term memory. See also **dual-memory theory.**

reincarnation. The belief in rebirth; i.e., that a person has lived before.

reinforcement. (1) In classical conditioning, the experimental procedure of following the conditioned stimulus by the unconditioned stimulus. (2) In operant conditioning, the analogous procedure of following the occurrence of the operant response by the reinforcing stimulus. (3) The process that increases the strength of conditioning as a result of these arrangements. See also **negative reinforcement, partial reinforcement, positive reinforcement.**

reinforcement schedule. A well-defined procedure for reinforcing a given response only some proportion of the time it occurs. See also **partial reinforcement.**

reinforcing stimulus. (1) In classical conditioning, the unconditioned stimulus. (2) In operant conditioning, the stimulus that reinforces the operant (typically, a reward) (syn. *reinforcer*). See also **negative reinforcer, positive reinforcer.**

relaxation training. Training in various techniques for relaxing muscle tension. The procedure is based on Jacobson's progressive relaxation method, in which the person learns how to relax muscle groups one at a time, the assumption being that muscular relaxation is effective in bringing about emotional relaxation.

releaser. A term used by ethologists for a stimulus that sets off a cycle of instinctive behavior. See also **ethology, instinct.**

reliability. The self-consistency of a test as a measuring instrument. Reliability is measured by a coefficient of correlation between scores on two halves of a test, alternate forms of the test, or retests with the same test; a high correlation signifies high consistency of scores for the population tested. See also **validity.**

REMs. See **rapid eye movements.**

repression. (1) A defense mechanism in which an impulse or memory that is distressing or might provoke feelings of guilt is excluded from conscious awareness. See also **defense mechanism, suppression.** (2) A theory of forgetting.

reserpine. See **antipsychotic drugs.**

resistance. In psychoanalysis, a blocking of free association; a psychological barrier against bringing unconscious impulses to the level of awareness. Resistance is part of the process of maintaining repression. See also **interpretation, repression.**

respondent behavior. A type of behavior corresponding to reflex action, in that it is largely under the control of and predictable from the stimulus (syn. *elicited behavior*). See also **operant behavior.**

response. (1) The behavioral result of stimulation in the form of a movement or glandular secretion. (2) Sometimes, any activity of the organism, including central responses (such as an image or fantasy) regardless of whether the stimulus is identified and whether identifiable movements occur. (3) Products of the organism's activity, such as words typed per minute.

resting potential. The electrical potential across the nerve cell membrane when it is in its resting state (i.e., not responding to other neurons); the inside of the cell membrane is slightly more negative than the outside. See also **action potential.**

reticular system. A system of ill-defined nerve paths and connections within the brain stem, lying outside the well-defined nerve pathways, and important as an arousal mechanism.

retina. The portion of the eye sensitive to light, containing the rods and the cones. See also **cone, rod.**

retinal image. The image projected onto the retina by an object in the visual field.

retinal size. The size of the retinal image of

an object; retinal size decreases in direct proportion to the object's distance. See also **object size.**

retrieval. Locating information in memory.

retroactive interference. The interference in recall of something earlier learned by something subsequently learned. See also **proactive interference.**

retrograde amnesia. Loss of memory for events and experiences occurring in a period of time prior to the amnesia-causing trauma; usually considered to be a failure of the ability to retrieve the information rather than a true loss of that information. See also **amnesia, anterograde amnesia.**

reuptake. The process by which a neurotransmitter is "taken up" again (reabsorbed) by the synapse's terminal buttons from which it had been released. See also **neurotransmitter.**

reward. A synonym for *positive reinforcement.* See also **positive reinforcement.**

right hemisphere. The right cerebral hemisphere. Controls the left side of the body and, for most people, spatial and patterned activities (syn. **minor hemisphere**). See also **cerebral hemispheres, corpus callosum, left hemisphere, split-brain subject.**

ROC curve. See **receiver-operating-characteristic curve.**

rod. In the eye, an element of the retina mediating achromatic sensation only; particularly important in peripheral vision and night vision. See also **cone, retina.**

role playing. A method for teaching attitudes and behaviors important to interpersonal relations by having the subject assume a part in a spontaneous play, whether in psychotherapy or in leadership training. See also **psychodrama.**

S

saccade. The quick, almost instantaneous movement of the eyes between eye fixations.

sadism. A pathological motive that leads to inflicting pain on another person. See also **masochism.**

sample. A selection of scores from a total set of scores known as the "population." If selection is random, an unbiased sample results; if selection is nonrandom, the sample is biased and unrepresentative. See also **population.**

satiety sensors. Detectors located in different parts of the digestive or thirst systems that signal that the needed nutrients or fluids are on their way and that feeding or drinking can stop.

saturation. The dimension of color that describes its purity; if highly saturated, it appears to be pure hue and free of gray, but if of low saturation, it appears to have a great deal of gray mixed with it. See also **brightness, hue.**

scaling. Converting raw data into types of scores more readily interpreted, such as ranks, centiles, standard scores.

scapegoat. A form of displaced aggression in which an innocent but helpless victim is blamed or punished as the source of the scapegoater's frustration. See also **displaced aggression.**

schema (pl. *schemata*). Some psychologists use the term to designate specific theoretical ideas about mental events; others use it in a very broad and vaguely defined sense. However used, the term refers to cognitive structures stored in memory that are abstract representations of events, objects, and relationships in the real world. It is a key ingredient of cognitive theories of psychological phenomena. See also **cognitive map, schematic processing.**

schematic processing. The cognitive process of searching for the schema in memory that is most consistent with the incoming information. See also **schema.**

schizoid. Having some characteristics that resemble schizophrenia but are less severe. Occurs with higher frequency in families of schizophrenics and thus tends to support a genetic basis for schizophrenia. See also **schizophrenia.**

schizophrenia. A group of mental disorders characterized by major disturbances in thought, perception, emotion, and behavior. Thinking is illogical and usually includes delusional beliefs; distorted perceptions may take the form of hallucinations; emotions are flat or inappropriate; bizarre behavior includes unusual postures, sterotyped movements, and "crazy talk." The individual withdraws from other people and from reality. Inherited biochemical abnormalities are implicated.

school psychologist. A professional psy-

chologist employed by a school or school system, with responsibility for testing, guidance, research, etc. See also **educational psychologist.**

script. A schema or abstract cognitive representation of events and social interactions (e.g., a birthday party). See also **schema.**

secondary sex characteristics. The physical features distinguishing the mature male from the mature female, apart from the reproductive organs. In humans, the deeper voice of the male and the growth of the beard are illustrative. See also **primary sex characteristics.**

selective breeding. A method of studying genetic influences by mating animals that display certain traits and selecting for breeding from among their offspring those that express the trait. If the trait is primarily determined by heredity, continued selection for a number of generations will produce a strain that breeds true for that trait.

self-actualization. A person's fundamental tendency toward maximal realization of his or her potentials; a basic concept in humanistic theories of personality such as those developed by Maslow and Rogers.

self-concept. The composite of ideas, feelings, and attitudes people have about themselves. For some theorists, self-concept is synonymous with the *self.*

self-consciousness. A state of heightened self-awareness; the disposition to be self-attentive.

self-perception. The individual's awareness of himself or herself; differs from self-consciousness because it may take the form of objective self-appraisal. See also **self-consciousness.**

self-perception theory. The theory that attitudes and beliefs are influenced by observations of one's own behavior; sometimes we judge how we feel by observing how we act (Bem).

self-regulation. In behavior therapy, monitoring one's own behavior and using techniques such as self-reinforcement or controlling stimulus conditions to modify maladaptive behavior. See also **behavior therapy.**

self-schema (pl. *self-schemata*). A generalization or theory about oneself derived from past experience. Self-schemata are assumed to influence the way we selectively attend to, process, and recall personally relevant information (syn. *self-concept*). See also **schema**.

semantic conditioning. A form of classical conditioning in which semantic concepts are used as the conditioned stimuli and generalization occurs through semantic similarities.

semicircular canals. Three curved tubular canals, in three planes, which form part of the labyrinth of the inner ear and are concerned with equilibrium and motion. See also **equilibratory senses**.

sensation. The conscious experience associated with a very simple stimulus like the onset of a tone or light. At one time, the distinction between sensation and perception had great theoretical importance with perception viewed as a combination of sensations. Today, the dividing line between sensation and perception is much less clear, and it seems best to view such experiences as lying along a continuum.

sensorimotor stage. Piaget's first stage of cognitive development (birth–2 years) during which the infant discovers relationships between sensations and motor behavior. See also **object permanence**.

sensory adaptation. The reduction in sensitivity that occurs with prolonged stimulation and the increase in sensitivity that occurs with lack of stimulation; most noted in vision, smell, taste, and temperature sensitivity. See also **dark adaptation, light adaptation**.

sensory deprivation. A condition in which sensory stimulation is markedly reduced. The effects on functioning are usually detrimental.

sensory neuron. A neuron, or nerve cell, that conveys messages to the brain or spinal cord from the sense receptors informing the organism about events in the environment or within the body (syn. *afferent neuron*). See also **motor neuron, receptor**.

sensory processes. The subprocesses of the perceptual system that are closely associated with the sense organs. Sensory processes provide selectively filtered information about the stimuli that impinge on us; higher-level processes use this information to form a mental representation of the scene. See also **filter, perception**.

septal area. A portion of the brain deep in the central part, between the lateral ventricles, that appears to yeild a state akin

to pleasure when stimulated electrically (in a rat, at least).

serial memory search. Comparing a test stimulus in sequence to each item in short-term memory. See also **short-term memory**.

serial processing. A theoretical interpretation of information processing in which several sources of information are processed in a serial order; only one source being attended to at a time. See also **parallel processing**.

serotonin. A neurotransmitter in both the peripheral and central nervous systems. It is an inhibitory transmitter whose actions have been implicated in various processes including sleep, the perception of pain, and affective disorders (depression and manic-depression). See also **neurotransmitter**.

sex-linked trait. A trait determined by a gene transmitted on the same chromosomes that determine sex, such as red-green color blindness. See also **X, Y chromosome**.

sex role. The full complement of attitudes and behaviors that a society considers appropriate for the individual because of his or her sex. See also **sex typing**.

sex typing. The acquisition of attitudes and behaviors that a society considers appropriate for the individual because of his or her sex. Distinquished from *gender identity*, which is the degree to which one regards oneself as male or female. See also **sex role**.

shape constancy. The tendency to see a familiar object as of the same shape regardless of the viewing angle. See also **perceptual constancy**.

shaping of behavior. Modifying operant behavior by reinforcing only those variations in response that deviate in the direction desired by the experimenter.

shock therapy. See **electroconvulsive therapy**.

short-term memory (STM). The assumption that certain components of the memory system have limited capacity and will maintain information for only a brief time. The definition varies somewhat from theory to theory. See also **long-term memory**.

sibling. A brother or a sister.

sibling rivalry. Jealousy between siblings, often based on their competition for parental affection.

signal detectability theory. A theory of

the sensory and decision processes involved in psychophysical judgments, with special reference to the problem of detecting weak signals in noise. See also **signal detection task**.

signal detection task. A procedure whereby the subject must judge on each trial whether a weak signal was embedded in a noise background. Saying "yes" when the signal was presented is called a *hit* and saying "yes" when the signal was not presented is called a *false alarm*. See also **receiver-operating-characteristic curve**.

simple cell. A cell in the visual cortex that responds to a bar of light or straight edge of a particular orientation and location in the visual field. See also **complex cell**.

simple phobia. Excessive fear of a specific object, animal, or situation in the absence of real danger. See also **phobia, phobic disorder**.

simulation. See **computer simulation**.

simultaneous conditioning. A classical conditioning procedure in which the CS begins a fraction of a second before the onset of the UCS and continues with it until the response occurs. See also **delayed conditioning, trace conditioning**.

sine wave. A cyclical wave that when plotted corresponds to the plot of the trigonometric sine function. The sound waves of pure tones yield this function when plotted.

situational attribution. Attributing a person's actions to factors in the situation or environment, as opposed to internal attitudes and motives. See also **dispositional attribution**.

size constancy. The tendency to see a familiar object as of its actual size regardless of its distance. See also **perceptual constancy**.

skill memory. The kind of memory that presumably stores perceptual and motor skills, such as the ability to ride a bicycle. See also **fact memory**.

smooth muscle. The type of muscle found in the digestive organs, blood vessels, and other internal organs. Conrolled via the autonomic nervous system. See also **cardiac muscle, striate muscle**.

social facilitation. The phenomenon in which an organism performs responses more rapidly when other members of its species are present.

social impact theory. A general theory of

social influence which proposes that the impact of any source of influence on a target individual increases as the number, immediacy, and importance of sources increases, but decreases as the number, immediacy, and importance of targets increases (Latané).

social learning theory. The application of learning theory to the problems of personal and social behavior (syn. *social behavior theory*).

social loafing. The phenomenon in which individuals put in less effort when working in concert with others than when working alone.

social norms. A group or community's unwritten rules that govern its members' behavior, attitudes, and beliefs.

social phobia. Extreme insecurity in social situations accompanied by an exaggerated fear of embarrassing oneself. See also **phobia, phobic disorder.**

social psychologist. A psychologist who studies social interaction and the ways in which individuals influence one another.

socialization. The shaping of individual characteristics and behavior through the training that the social environment provides.

sociology. The science dealing with group life and social organization in literate societies. See also **behavioral sciences.**

somatic nervous system. A division of the peripheral nervous system consisting of nerves that connect the brain and spinal cord with the sense receptors, muscles, and body surface. See also **autonomic nervous system, peripheral nervous system.**

somatosensory area. Area in the parietal lobe of the brain that registers sensory experiences, such as heat, cold, touch, and pain. Also called *body-sense area*. See also **motor area.**

spatial resolution. The ability to see spatial patterns. Visual acuity and the contrast threshold are measures of spatial resolution.

special factor (s). A specialized ability underlying test scores, especially in tests of intelligence; for example, a special ability in mathematics, as distinct from general intelligence. See also **factor analysis, general factor.**

species-specific behavior. See **instinct.**

specific hunger. Hunger for a specific food incentive, such as a craving for sweets. See also **hunger drive.**

specific neuron code hypothesis. According to this hypothesis, the sensory system contains diffrent types of neurons, each tuned to (responsive to) specific features of a stimulus and each evoking a particular sensation. The fact that specific neurons are tuned to particular stimulus features occurs because filters are appropriately located at lower levels in the sensory system. From this theoretical perspective, a scene is represented in our mind not by a picture, but by a coded message composed of sensations that correspond to specific features of the stimulus. See also **feature detector, filter.**

spindle. An EEG characteristic of Stage 2 sleep, consisting of short bursts of rhythmical responses of 13–16 Hz; slightly higher than alpha. See also **electroencephalogram.**

split-brain subject. A person who has had an operation that severed the corpus callosum, thus separating the functions of the two cerebral hemispheres. See also **cerebral hemispheres, corpus callosum.**

spontaneous remission. Recovery from an illness or improvement without treatment.

sports psychology. The study of human behavior in sport. The goal of much of the work is to help athletes develop psychological skills that maximize performance and enhance the sport experience. For example, hypnosis and biofeedback have been used to control an athlete's anxiety level during competition and mental imagery has been employed to help perfect the synchrony and flow of certain body movements.

spreading activation. A proposed model of retrieval from long-term memory in which activation subdivides among paths emanating from an activated mental representation.

S-R psychology. See **stimulus-response psychology.**

stabilized retinal image. The image of an object on the retina when special techniques are used to counteract the minute movements of the eyeball that occur in normal vision. When an image is thus stabilized it quickly disappears, suggesting that the changes in stimulation of retinal cells provided by the eye movements are necessary for vision.

stages of development. Developmental periods, usually following a progressive sequence, that appear to represent qualitative changes in either the structure or the function of the organism (such as Freud's psychosexual stages, Piaget's cognitive stages).

standard deviation. The square root of the mean of the squares of the amount by which each case departs from the mean of all the cases (syn. *root mean square deviation*).

state-dependent learning. Learning that occurs during a particular biological state — such as when drugged — so that it can only be demonstrated or is most effective when the person is put in the same state again.

statistical significance. The trustworthiness of an obtained statisical measure as a statement about reality; for example, the probability that the population mean falls within the limits determined from a sample. The expression refers to the reliability of the statistical finding and not to its importance.

stereoscopic vision. (1) The binocular perception of depth and distance of an object owing to the overlapping fields of the two eyes. (2) The equivalent effect when slightly unlike pictures are presented individually to each eye in a stereoscope. See also **distance cues.**

stereotype. A schema, or abstract cognitive representation, of the personality traits or physical attributes of a class or group of people. The schema is usually an overgeneralization, leading us to assume that every member of the group possesses the particular characteristic; for instance the false stereotype that all male homosexuals are effeminate. See also **schema.**

steroids. Complex chemical substances, some of which are prominent in the secretions of the adrenal cortex and may be related to some forms of mental illness. See also **adrenal gland.**

stimulants. Psychoactive drugs that increase arousal. Amphetamines, cocaine, and caffeine are examples.

stimulus (pl. *stimuli*). (1) Some specific physical energy impinging on a receptor sensitive to that kind of energy. (2) Any objectively describable situation or event (whether outside or inside the organism) that is the occasion for an organism's response. See also **response.**

stimulus-response (S-R) psychology. A

psychological view that all behavior is in response to stimuli and that the appropriate tasks of psychological science are those identifying stimuli, the responses correlated with them, and the processes intervening between stimulus and response.

STM. See **short-term memory.**

stress. Defined variously as (1) a response, the pattern of psychological and physiological responses that occur in difficult situations; (2) a stimulus, an event or set of circumstances that requires an unusual response; (3) a transaction, a relationship between the person and the environment that is appraised by the person as taxing his or her resources and endangering his or her well-being.

striate muscle. Striped muscle; the characteristic muscles controlling the skeleton, as in the arms and legs. Activated by the somatic, as opposed to the autonomic, nervous system. See also **cardiac muscle, smooth muscle.**

stroboscopic motion. An illusion of motion resulting from the successive presentation of discrete stimulus patterns arranged in a progression corresponding to movement; such as motion pictures. See also **phi phenomenon.**

subconscious processes. A considerable body of research indicates that we register and evaluate stimuli that we are not consciously aware of. The stimuli are said to influence us subconsciously or to operate at a subconscious level of awareness. See also **consciousness.**

subtractive mixture. Color mixture in which absorption occurs so that results differ from additive mixture obtained by mixing projected lights. Subtractive mixture occurs when transparent collored filters are placed one in front of the other and when pigments are mixed. See also **additive mixture.**

superego. In Freud's tripartite division of the personality, that part corresponding most nearly to conscience, controlling through moral scruples rather than by way of social expediency. The superego is said to be an uncompromising and punishing conscience. See also **conscience, ego, id.**

suppression. A process of self-control in which impulses, tendencies to action, and wishes to perform disapproved acts are in awareness but not overtly revealed. See also **repression.**

survey method. A method of obtaining information by questioning a large sample of people.

symbol. Anything that stands for or refers to something other than itself.

sympathetic division. A division of the autonomic nervous system, characterized by a chain of ganglia on either side of the spinal cord, with nerve fibers originating in the thoracic and lumbar portions of the spinal cord. Active in emotional excitement and to some extent antagonistic to the parasympathetic division. See also **parasympathetic division.**

synapse. The close functional connection between the axon of one neuron and the dendrites or cell body of another neuron. See also **excitatory synapse, inhibitory synapse.**

systematic desensitization. A behavior therapy technique in which hierarchies of anxiety-producing situations are imagined (or sometimes confronted in reality) while the person is in a state of deep relaxation. Gradually the situations become dissociated from the anxiety response. See also **anxiety hierarchy, behavior therapy, counterconditioning.**

T

tabula rasa. Latin, meaning *blank slate.* The term refers to the view that human beings are born without any innate knowledge or ideas; all knowledge is acquired through learning and experience. Proposed by the 17th- and 18th-century British empiricists (Locke, Hume, Berkeley, Hartley).

tachistoscope. An instrument for the brief exposure of words, symbols, pictures, or other visually presented material; sometimes called a T-scope.

telegraphic speech. A stage in the development of speech where the child preserves only the most meaningful and perceptually salient elements of adult speech. The child tends to omit prepositions, articles, prefixes, suffixes, and auxiliary words.

telepathy. The claimed form of extrasensory perception in which what is perceived depends on thought transference from one person to another. See also

clairvoyance, extrasensory perception, precognition.

temperament. An individual's characteristic mood, sensitivity to stimulation, and energy level. Temperament is usually conceptualized as a genetic predisposition because striking differences in reactivity to stimulation, general mood, and activity level can be observed in newborns.

temperature regulation. The process by which an organism keeps its body temperature relatively constant.

temporal lobe. A portion of the cerebral hemisphere, at the side below the lateral fissure and in front of the occipital lobe. See also **frontal lobe, occipital lobe, parietal lobe.**

temporal theory of pitch. A theory of pitch perception which assumes that the neural impulses traveling up the auditory nerve correspond to a tone's vibrations. If the neural response follows the waveform of the sound, then the auditory system could pick out and respond to this overall frequency. See also **place theory of pitch.**

terminal button. A specialized knob at the end of the axon that releases a chemical into the synapse to continue transmission of the nerve impulse. See also **neurotransmitter.**

test battery. A collection of tests whose composite scores are used to appraise individual differences.

test method. A method of psychological investigation. Its advantages are that it allows the psychologist to collect large quantities of useful data from many people, with a minimum of disturbance of their routines of existence and with a minimum of laboratory equipment.

test profile. A chart plotting scores from a number of tests given to the same individual (or group of individuals) in parallel rows on a common scale, with the scores connected by lines, so that high and low scores can be readily perceived. See also **trait profile.**

test standardization. The establishment of norms for interpreting scores by giving a test to a representative population and by making appropriate studies of its reliability and validity. See also **norm, reliability, validity.**

testosterone. The primary male sex hormone produced by the testes; it is important for the growth of the male sex organs and the development of the secondary male sex characteristics. It influences the sex drive. See also **androgens, secondary sex characteristics.**

thalamus. Two groups of nerve cell nuclei located just above the brain stem and inside the cerebral hemispheres. Considered a part of the central core of the brain. One area acts as a sensory relay station, the other plays a role in sleep and waking; this portion is considered part of the limbic system. See also **hypothalamus.**

theory. A set of assumptions (axioms) advanced to explain existing data and predict new events; usually applicable to a wide array of phenomena.

thinking. The ability to imagine or represent objects or events in memory and to operate on these representations. Ideational problem solving as distinguished from solution through overt manipulation.

threshold. The transitional point at which an increasing stimulus or an increasing difference not previously perceived becomes perceptible (or at which a decreasing stimulus or previously perceived difference becomes imperceptible). The value obtained depends in part on the methods used in determining it. See also **absolute threshold, difference threshold.**

thyroid gland. An endocrine gland located in the neck, whose hormone thyroxin is important in determining metabolic rate. See also **endocrine gland.**

timbre. The quality distinguishing a tone of a given pitch sounded by one instrument from that sounded by another. The differences are due to overtones and other impurities. See also **overtone.**

tip-of-the-tongue phenomenon. The experience of failing to recall a word or name when we are quite certain we know it.

TM. See **meditation.**

T-maze. An apparatus in which an animal is presented with two alternative paths, one of which leads to a goal box. It is usually used with rats and lower organisms. See also **maze.**

tolerance. The need to take more and more of a drug to achieve the same effect. An important factor in physical dependency on drugs.

trace conditioning. A classical conditioning procedure in which the CS terminates before the onset of the UCS. See also **delayed conditioning, simultaneous conditioning.**

trait. A persisting characteristic or dimension of personality according to which individuals can be rated or measured. See also **trait profile.**

trait profile. A chart plotting the ratings of a number of traits of the same individual on a common scale in parallel rows so that the pattern of traits can be visually perceived (syn. *psychograph*). See also **test profile, trait.**

trait theory. The theory that human personality is most profitably characterized by the scores that an individual makes on a number of scales, each of which represents a trait or dimension of his or her personality.

tranquilizer. A drug that reduces anxiety and agitation, such as *Valium*.

transcendental meditation (TM). See **meditation.**

transducer. A device such as an electrode or gauge that, in psychophysiology, converts physiological indicators into other forms of energy that can be recorded and measured.

transference. In psychoanalysis, the patient's unconsciously making the therapist the object of emotional response, transferring to the therapist responses appropriate to other persons important in the patient's life history.

transsexual. An individual who is physically one sex but psychologically the other. Transsexuals sometimes resort to surgery and hormonal treatment to change their physical gender. They do not, however, consider themselves to be homosexual. See also **homosexual.**

trichromatic theory. A theory of color perception that postulates three basic color receptors (cones), a "red" receptor, a "green" receptor, and a "blue" receptor. The theory explains color blindness by the absence of one or more receptor types (syn. *Young–Helmholtz theory*). See also **opponent-color theory, two-stage color theory.**

trichromatism. Normal color vision, based on the classification of color vision according to three color systems: black-white, blue-yellow, and red-green. The normal eye sees all three; the colorblind eye is defective in one or two of the three systems. See also **dichromatism, monochromatism.**

tricyclic antidepressant. A class of antidepressants that relieves the symptoms of depression by preventing the reuptake of the neurotransmitters serotonin and norepinephrine, thereby prolonging their action. Imipramine (brand names, Tofranil and Elavil) is the drug most commonly prescribed. See also **antidepressant.**

Turner's syndrome. An abnormal condition of the sex chromosomes in which a female is born with one X chromosome instead of the usual XX. See also **X chromosome.**

two-stage color theory. A theory of color vision that postulates three types of cones (in agreement with trichromatic theory) followed by red-green and yellow-blue opponent processes (in agreement with opponent-color theory). This theory accounts for much of what is known about color vision, and serves as a prototype for the analysis of other sensory systems. See also **opponent-color theory, trichromatic theory.**

type A and type B. Two contrasting behavior patterns found in studies of coronary heart disease. Type A people are rushed, competitive, aggressive, and overcommitted to achieving; type Bs are more relaxed and feel less pressure. Type As are at risk for heart disease.

type theory. The theory that human subjects can profitably be classified into a small number of classes or types, each class or type having characteristics in common that set its members apart from other classes or types. See also **trait theory.**

U

unconditioned response (UCR). In classical conditioning, the response given originally to the unconditioned stimulus used as the basis for establishing a conditioned response to a previously neutral stimulus. See also **conditioned response, conditioned stimulus, unconditioned stimulus.**

unconditioned stimulus (UCS). In classical conditioning, a stimulus that automatically elicits a response, typically via a reflex, without prior conditioning. See also **conditioned response, condi-**

tioned stimulus, unconditioned response.

unconscious inference. A term used by the German scientist Hermann von Helmholtz to describe the process by which the perceiver progresses from experiencing sensations evoked by an object to recognizing the properties of the object. We make this inference automatically and unconsciously, and eventually we do not even notice the sensations on which it is based. Helmholtz argued that unconscious inference is the basis of many perceptual phenomena, including distance and object perception.

unconscious motive. A motive of which the subject is unaware or aware of in distorted form. Because there is no sharp dividing line between conscious and unconscious, many motives have both conscious and unconscious aspects.

unconscious processes. Memories, impulses, and desires that are not available to consciousness. According to the psychoanalytic theories of Sigmund Freud, painful memories and wishes are sometimes repressed — that is, diverted to the unconscious where they continue to influence our actions even though we are not aware of them. See also **consciousness.**

V

validity. The predictive significance of a test for its intended purposes. Validity can be measured by a coefficient of correlation between scores on the test and the scores that the test seeks to predict; i.e., scores on some criterion. See also **criterion, reliability.**

value. A basic attitude toward broad modes of conduct (e.g., courage, honesty) or end-states of existence (e.g., equality, salvation). See also **attitude.**

variable. One of the conditions measured or controlled in an experiment. See also **dependent variable, independent variable.**

variance. The square of a standard deviation.

ventromedial hypothalamus (VMH). Area of the hypothalamus important to the regulation of food intake. Electrical stimulation of this area will make an experimental animal stop eating; destruction of brain tissue here produces voracious eating, eventually leading to obesity. See also **hypothalamus, lateral hypothalamus.**

vestibular sacs. Two sacs in the labyrinth of the inner ear, called the *saccule* and *utricle,* which contain the otoliths ("ear stones"). Pressure of the otoliths on the hair cells in the gelatinous material of the utricle and saccule gives us the sense of upright position or departure from it. See also **equilibratory senses.**

vicarious learning. Learning by observing the behavior of others and noting the consequences of that behavior (syn. *observational learning*).

visual area. A projection area lying in the occipital lobe. In humans, damage to this area produces blindness in portions of the visual field corresponding to the amount and location of the damage.

visual cliff. An experimental apparatus with glass over a patterned surface, one half of which is just below the glass and the other half, several feet below. Used to test the depth perception of animals and human infants.

visual field. The total visual array acting on the eye when it is directed toward a fixation point.

VMH. See **ventromedial hypothalamus.**

voice stress analyzer. A device that graphically represents changes in a person's voice associated with emotion. Used in lie detection. See also **polygraph.**

volumetric receptors. Hypothesized receptors that regulate water intake by responding to the volume of blood and body fluids. Renin, a substance secreted by the kidneys into the bloodstream, may be one volumetric receptor; it constricts the blood vessels and stimulates the release of the hormone, angiotensin, which acts on cells in the hypothalamus to produce thirst. See also **osmoreceptors.**

voluntary processes. Activities selected by choice and controlled or monitored according to intention or plan. See also **control processes.**

W

Weber's law. A law stating that the difference threshold is proportional to the stimulus magnitude at which it is measured. The law is not accurate over the full stimulus range. See also **difference threshold.**

Wernicke's area. A portion of the left cerebral hemisphere involved in language understanding. Individuals with damage in this area are not able to comprehend words; they can hear words, but they do not know their meanings.

working through. In psychoanalytic therapy, the process of reeducation by having patients face the same conflicts over and over in the consultation room, until they can independently face and master the conflicts in ordinary life.

X

X chromosome. A chromosome that, if paired with another X chromosome, determines that the individual will be a female. If it is combined with a Y chromosome, the individual will be a male. The X chromosome transmits sex-linked traits. See also **chromosome, sex-linked trait, Y chromosome.**

XYY syndrome. An abnormal condition in which a male has an extra Y sex chromosome; reputedly associated with unusual aggressiveness, although the evidence is not conclusive. See also **Y chromosome.**

Y

Y chromosome. The chromosome that, combined with an X chromosome, determines maleness. See also **chromosome, sex-linked trait, X chromosome.**

Young–Helmholtz theory. See **trichromatic theory.**

Z

zygote. A fertilized ovum or egg. See also **dizygotic twins, monozygotic twins.**

Copyrights and Acknowledgments and Illustration Credits

TABLES

Chapter 1

1-2 Stapp, J., and Fulcher, R. (1981) "The employment of APA members," *American Psychologist,* 36:1263–1314. Copyright © 1981 by the American Psychological Association. Reprinted/adapted by permission of the authors.

Chapter 3

3-1 Adapted from *Review of Child Development Research,* Volume 1, edited by Martin L. Hoffman and Lois Wladis Hoffman. Copyright © 1964 by Russell Sage Foundation. Reprinted by permission of Basic Books, Inc., Publishers. **3-2** Adapted from Kohlberg, L. (1967) "Moral education, religious education, and the public schools: A developmental view," in T.R. Sizer (ed.), *Religion and Public Education.* Copyright © 1967 by Houghton Mifflin Co. Reprinted by permission of the publisher and the National Conference of Christians & Jews, Inc. **3-3** Kuhn, D., Nash, S.C., and Brucken, L. (1978) "Sex role concepts of two- and three-year-olds," *Child Development,* 49:445–51. Copyright © The Society for Research in Child Development, Inc. **3-5** Modified table of "The Eight Ages of psychosocial development," from Erikson, E.H. (1950) *Childhood and Society* (2nd ed.),

p. 274, is used with the permission of W.W. Norton & Company, Inc., and The Hogarth Press, Ltd. Copyright 1950, © 1963 by W.W. Norton & Company, Inc. Copyright renewed 1978 by Erik H. Erikson.

Chapter 4

4-1 Adapted from Brown, R., Galanter, E., Hess, E.H., and Mandler, G. (1962) *New Direction in Psychology:* Vol. 1. *Models of Attitude Change, Contemporary Psychophysics, Ethology: An Approach Toward the Complete Analysis of Behavior, Emotion.* Foreword by T.M. Newcomb. Copyright © 1962 by Holt, Rinehart & Winston, Publishers.

Chapter 6

6-1 Soal, S.G., and Bateman, F. (1954) *Modern Experiments in Telepathy.* New Haven: Yale University Press, p. 352.

Chapter 8

8-1 Tulving, E., and Pearlstone, Z. (1966) "Availability vs. accessibility of information in memory for words," *Journal of Verbal Learning and Verbal Behavior,* 5. Reprinted by permission of Academic Press, Inc., and the authors. **8-16** Bower, G.H., and Clark, M.C. (1969) "Narrative stories as mediators for serial learning," *Psychonomic Science,*

14:181–82. Reprinted by permission of Psychonomic Society, Inc.

Chapter 9

9-1 From "Functions of two-word sentences in child speech, with examples from several languages," in Slobin, D.I., *Psycholinguistics,* pp. 44–45. Copyright © 1971 by Scott, Foresman & Company. Reprinted by permission. **9-2** Revised version of Slobin, D.I. (1971) "Developmental psycholinguistics," in W.O. Dingwall (ed.), *A Survey of Linguistic Science.* Stamford, CT: Greylock Publishers, pp. 298–400. Reprinted by permission of Greylock Publishers.

Chapter 10

10-1 Craighead, L.W., Stunkard, A.J., and O'Brien, R.M. (1981) "Behavior therapy and pharmacotherapy for obesity," *Archives of General Psychiatry,* 38:763–68. **10-2** Bell, A.P., Weinberg, M.S., and Hammersmith, S.K. (1981) *Sexual Preference: Its Development in Men and Women.* Copyright © 1981 by Indiana University Press. Reprinted by permission of the publisher. **10-3** Zuckerman, M., and Neeb, M. (1980) "Demographic influences in sensation seeking and expressions of sensation seeking in religion, smoking, and driving habits," *Personality and Individual Differences,* 1(3):197–206. Copyright © 1980,

J.R. (1977) "Sexual behavior in adolescence," *Journal of Social Issues*, 33(2):67–85. **10-12** Zuckerman, M., and Neeb, M. (1980) "Demographic influences in sensation seeking and expressions of sensation seeking in religion, smoking, and driving habits," *Personality and Individual Differences*, 1:197–206. Reprinted with permission from Pergamon Press, Ltd.

Chapter 11

11-1 Kubis, J.F. (1962) cited in Smith, B.M., "The polygraph," in Atkinson, R.C. (ed.) *Contemporary Psychology*. San Francisco: Freeman, Cooper & Co. **11-3** After Schachter, S. (1961) and Hohmann, G.W. (1962). Schachter, S. (1964) "The interaction of cognitive and physiological determinants of emotional state," in P.H. Leiderman and D. Shapiro (eds.) *Psychobiological Approaches to Human Behavior*. Stanford: Stanford University Press, p. 166. **11-4** Ekman, P., Levenson, R.W., and Frieson, W.V. (1983) "Autonomic nervous system activity distinguishes among emotions," *Science*, 221:1208–10. Copyright © 1983 by the American Association for the Advancement of Science. **11-7** Solomon, R.L. (1980) "The opponent-process theory of acquired motivation," *American Psychologist*, 35:691–712. Copyright © 1980 by the American Psychological Association. Reprinted and adapted by permission of the publisher and author. **11-8** Hebb, D.O. (1972) "Emotional arousal and performance," *Textbook of Psychology* (3rd ed.). Copyright © 1972 by W.B. Saunders Co. Copyright © 1958 & 1966 by W.B. Saunders. Reprinted by permission of CBS College Publishers. **11-12** Bandura, A. (1973) *Aggression: A Social Learning Analysis*. Englewood Cliffs, NJ: Prentice-Hall. Figures 1-1 and 2-2 from data in Bandura, Ross, and Ross (1963) "Imitation of film-mediated aggressive models," *Journal of Abnormal Psychology*, 66:8. Copyright © 1963 by the American Psychological Association. Reprinted by permission. **11-14** Eron, L., Huesmann, L., Lefkowitz, M., and Walder, L. (1972) "Does television violence cause aggression?" *American Psychologist*, 27:253–63. Copyright © 1972 by the American Psychological Association. Reprinted by permission.

Chapter 12

12-1 Thurstone, L.L., and Thurstone, T.G. (1942) "Factorial studies of intelligence," *Psychometric Monographs*, No. 2. Copyright © 1942 by the University of Chicago. All rights reserved. **12-5** Cattell, R.B. (1977) Culture Fair Intelligence Test, Scale 2, Form A test booklet. Champaign, IL: Institute for Personality and Ability Testing, Inc. © 1949, 1960, 1977. Reproduced by permission of the copyright owner. **12-6** Gottesman, I.I. (1963) "Genetic aspects of intelligent behavior," in N. Ellis (ed.), *Handbook of Mental Deficiency: Psychological Theory and Research*. New York: McGraw-Hill Book Co. **Page 407** Gardner, H. (1983) *Frames of Mind*. New York: Basic Books, p. 170.

Chapter 13

13-2 From Cattell, R.B. (1986) *The Handbook for the 16 Personality Factor Questionnaire (16PF)*. Copyright © 1972, 1979, 1986 by the Institute for Personality and Ability Testing. Reproduced by permission.

Chapter 14

14-1 Selye, H. (1979) *The Stress of Life* (rev. ed.). New York: Van Nostrand Reinhold. **14-3** Schwarts, G.E. (1973) "Biofeedback, self-regulation, and the patterning of physiological processes," *American Scientist*, 63:316.

Chapter 15

15-1 Agras, S., Sylvester, D., and Oliveau, D. (1969) "The epidemiology of common fears and phobia," *Comprehensive Psychiatry*, 10:151–56. Reproduced by permission of Grune & Stratton, Inc. **15-2** Abridged and adapted from Case Report 11-4, "Phobic neurosis," in Kleinmuntz, B., *Essentials of Abnormal Psychology*. Copyright © 1980 by Benjamin Kleinmuntz. By permission of Benjamin Kleinmuntz. **15-3** Laughlin, H.P. (1967) *The Neuroses*. Woburn, MA: Butterworth Publishers, Inc., pp. 324–25. Reprinted by permission of the publisher. **15-5** Hofling, C.K. (1975) *Textbook of Psychiatry for Medical Practice* (3rd ed.). Philadelphia: Lippincott, p. 372. **15-7** Gottesman, I.I., and Shields, J. (1982) *Schizophrenia: The Epigenetic Puzzle*. © Cambridge University Press. Reprinted by permission. **15-8** From Maher, B.A. (1966) *Principles of Psychopathology*. Copyright © 1966 by McGraw-Hill, Inc. Used with permission of McGraw-Hill Book Co.

Chapter 16

16-3 Bandura, A.L., Blanchard, E.B., and Ritter, B. (1969) "The relative efficacy of desensitization of modeling approaches to inducing behavior, affective and attitudinal changes," *Journal of Personality and Social Psychology*, 3:173–79. Copyright © 1969 by the American Psychological Association. Reprinted by permission. **16-4** Based on data from Seeman, J. (1949) "A study of the process of non-directive therapy," *Journal of Consulting Psychology*, 13:157–68.

Chapter 17

17-1 Festinger, L., and Carlsmith, J.M. (1959) "Cognitive consequences of forced compliance," *Journal of Abnormal and Social Psychology*, 58:203–10. Copyright © 1959 by the American Psychological Association. Reprinted by permission. **17-2** Ross, L.D., Amabile, T.M., and Steinmetz, J.L. (1977) "Social roles, social control, and biases in social-perception processes," *Journal of Personality and Social Psychology*, 35:485–94. Copyright © 1977 by the American Psychological Association. Reprinted by permission. **17-3** Zajonc, R.B. (1968) "Attitudinal effects of mere exposure," *Journal of Personality and Social Psychology*, 8:18. Copyright © 1968 by the American Psychological Association. Reprinted by permission.

Chapter 18

18-2 Diener, E. (1979) "Deindividuation, self-awareness and disinhibition," *Journal of Personality and Social Psychology*. Copyright © 1979 by the American Psychological Association. Reprinted by permission. **18-3** and **18-4** Latané, B. (1981) "The Psychology of social impact," *American Psychologist*, 36:343–56. **18-5** Darley, J.M., and Latané, B. (1968) "Bystander intervention in emergencies: Diffusion of responsibility," *Journal of Personality and Social Psychology*, 8:377–83. Copyright © 1968 by the American Psychological Association. Reprinted by permission. **18-7** Fig. 13 (p. 91) from *Obedience to Authority: An Experimental View*. © 1974 by Stanley Milgram. Reprinted by permission of Harper & Row, Publishers, Inc. Milgram, S. (1963) "Behavioral study of obedience," *Journal of Abnormal and Social Psychology*, 67:371–78. Copyright © 1963 by the American Psychological Association. Reprinted by permission. **18-9** Beirbrauer, G. (1979) "Why did he do it? Attribution of obedience and the phenomenon of dispositional bias," *European Journal of Social Psychology*, 9:67–84. © 1979 by John Wiley & Sons Ltd. **18-10** Maccoby, N., Farquhar, J.W., Wood, P.D., and Alexander, J. (1977) "Reducing the risk of cardiovascular disease: Effects of a community-based campaign on knowledge and behavior," *Journal of Community Health*, 3:100–14.

PICTURES

References and
Index to Authors
of Works Cited

The numbers in boldface following each reference give the text pages on which the article or book is cited. Citations in the text are made by author and date of publication.

A

ABBOTT, B.B., SCHOEN, L.S., & BADIA, P. (1984) Predictable and unpredictable shock: Behavioral measures of aversion and physiological measures of stress. *Psychological Bulletin*, 96:45–71. **471**

ABELSON, R.P. (1968) Computers, polls, and public opinion—Some puzzles and paradoxes. *Transaction*, 5:20–27. **586, 587**

ABELSON, R.P. (1976) Script processing in attitude formation and decision waking. In Carroll, J.S., & Payne, J.W. (eds.), *Cognition and Social Behavior*. Hillsdale, N.J.: Erlbaum. **569**

ABERNATHY, E.M. (1940) The effect of changed environmental conditions upon the results of college examinations. *Journal of Psychology*, 10:293–301. **269**

ABRAHAMS, D., see WALSTER, ARONSON, ABRAHAMS, & ROTTMAN (1966).

ABRAMSON, L.Y., see HAMILTON & ABRAMSON (1983).

ACKERMAN, R.H., see CORKIN, COHEN, SULLIVAN, CLEG, ROSEN, & ACKERMAN (1985).

ADAMS, G.R. (1981) The effects of physical attractiveness on the socialization process. In Lucher, G.W., Ribbens, K.A., & McNamara, J.A., Jr. (eds.), *Psychological Aspects of Facial Form*. Craniofacial Growth Series. Ann Arbor: University of Michigan. **575**

ADAMS, H.E., see TURNER, CALHOUN, & ADAMS (1981).

ADAMS, J.L. (1974) *Conceptual Blockbusting*. Stanford, Calif.: Stanford Alumni Association. **306**

ADAMS, M., & COLLINS, A. (1979) A schema-theoretic view of reading. In Freedle, R.O. (ed.), *New Directions Discourse Processing*, Vol. 12. Norwood, N.J.: Ablex. **294**

ADAMS, N., see SMITH, ADAMS, & SCHORR (1978).

ADAMS, N.E., see BANDURA, ADAMS, & BEYER (1976).

ADAMS, N.E., see BANDURA, ADAMS, HARDY, & HOWELLS (1980).

ADELSON, E. (1982) Saturation and adaptation in the rod system. *Vision Research*, 22:1299–1312. **157**

ADESSO, V.J., see BOONE & ADESSO (1974).

AGRAS, W.S. (1975) Fears and phobias. *Stanford Magazine*, 3:59–62. **495**

AGRAS, W.S. (1985) *Panic: Facing Fears, Phobias, and Anxiety*. New York: Freeman. **502, 525, 561**

AGRAS, W.S., SYLVESTER, D., & OLIVEAU, D. (1969) The epidemiology of common fears and phobia. *Comprehensive Psychiatry*, 10:151–56. **495**

AINSWORTH, M.D.S. (1979) Infant-mother attachment. *American Psychologist*, 34:932–37. **79**

AINSWORTH, M.D.S., BLEHAR, M.C., WALTERS, E., & WALL, S. (1978) *Patterns of Attachment: A Psychological Study of the Strange Situation*. Hillsdale, N.J.: Erlbaum. **78**

AKADEMI, A., see LAGERSPETZ, VIEMERO, & AKADEMI (1986).

ALEXANDER, J., see MACCOBY, FARQUHAR, WOOD, & ALEXANDER (1977).

ALFORD, G.S. (1980) Alcoholics anonymous: An empirical outcome study. *Addictive Behaviors*, Vol. 5. Oxford: Pergamon Press. **133**

ALLEN, A., see BEM & ALLEN (1974).

ALLEN, M.G. (1976) Twin studies of affective illness. *Archives of General Psychiatry*, 35:1476–78. **509**

ALLEN, V.L., & LEVINE, J.M. (1969) Consensus and conformity. *Journal of Experimental and Social Psychology*, 5(No. 4):389. **608**

ALLEN, V.L., & LEVINE, J.M. (1971) Social support and conformity: The role of independent assessment of reality. *Journal of Experimental Social Psychology*, 7:48–58. **608**

ALLISON, J., see TIMBERLAKE & ALLISON (1974).

ALLPORT, F.H. (1920) The influence of the group upon association and thought. *Journal of Experimental Psychology*, 3:159–82. **598**

ALLPORT, F.H. (1924) *Social Psychology*. Boston: Houghton Mifflin. **598**

ALLPORT, G.H. (1985) The historical background of social psychology. In Lindzey, G., & Aronson, E. (eds.), *The Handbook of Social Psychology* (3rd ed.). New York: Random House. (Article originally published in 1954). **597**

ALTMAN, I., & TAYLOR, D.A. (1973) *Social Penetration: The Development of Interpersonal Relationships*. New York: Holt, Rinehart & Winston. **592, 593**

ALTUS, W.C. (1966) Birth order and its sequelae. *Science*, 151:44–49. **95**

AMABILE, T.M., see ROSS, AMABILE, & STEINMETZ (1977).

AMERICAN PSYCHIATRIC ASSOCIATION (1980) *Diagnostic and Statistical Manual of Mental Disorders* (3rd ed.). Washington, D.C.: American Psychiatric Association. **492**

AMOORE, J.E. (1970) *The Molecular Basis of Odor*. Springfield, Ill.: Thomas. **173**

ANASTASI, A. (1982) *Psychological Testing* (5th ed.). New York: Macmillan. **415**

ANDERSON, D.J., see ROSE, BRUGGE, ANDERSON, & HIND (1967).

ANDERSON, J.R. (1982) Acquisition of cognitive skill. *Psychological Review*, 89:369–406. **266**

ANDERSON, J.R. (1983) *The Architecture of Cognition*. Cambridge, Mass.: Harvard University Press. **258, 259, 279**

ANDERSON, J.R. (1985) *Cognitive Psychology and Its Implications* (2nd ed.). New York: Freeman. **27, 211, 256, 279, 305, 306**

ANDERSON, J.R., see BRADSHAW & ANDERSON (1982).

ANDERSON, J.R., see REDER & ANDERSON (1980).

ANDERSON, L.W., see PALMER & ANDERSON (1979).

ANDERSON, N.H., & BUTZIN, C.A. (1978) Integration theory applied to children's judgments of equity. *Developmental Psychology*, 14:593–606. **86**

ANDERTON, C.H., see WADDEN & ANDERTON (1982).

ANDRASIK, F., see HOLROYD, APPEL, & ANDRASIK (1983).

ANDRES, D., see GOLD, ANDRES, & GLORIEUX (1979).

ANDREWS, K.H., & KANDEL, D.B. (1979) Attitude and behavior. *American Sociological Review*, 44:298–310. **583**

ANDRYSIAK, T., see SCHAEFFER, ANDRYSIAK, & UNGERLEIDER (1981).

ANTONUCCIO, D.O., see LEWINSOHN, ANTONUCCIO, STEINMETZ, & TERI (1984).

ANTROBUS, J.S., see ARKIN, ANTROBUS, & ELLMAN (1978).

APPEL, M.A., see HOLROYD, APPEL, & ANDRASIK (1983).

APPLEFIELD, J.M., see STEUER, APPLEFIELD, & SMITH (1971).

ARAKAKI, K., see KOBASIGAWA, ARAKAKI, & AWIGUNI (1966).

ARDREY, R. (1966) *The Territorial Imperative*. New York: Dell. **375**

AREND, R.A., see MATAS, AREND, & SROUFE (1978).

ARENDT, H. (1963) *Eichmann in Jerusalem: A Report on the Banality of Evil*. New York: Viking Press. **609**

ARIETI, S. (1974) *Interpretation of Schizophrenia* (2nd ed.). New York: Basic Books. **513**

ARKIN, A.M., ANTROBUS, J.S., & ELLMAN, S.J. (eds.) (1978) *The Mind in Sleep*. Hillsdale, N.J.: Erlbaum. **145**

ARKIN, A.M., TOTH, M.F., BAKER, J., & HASTEY, J.M. (1970) The frequency of sleep talking in the laboratory among chronic sleep talkers and good dream recallers. *Journal of Nervous and Mental Disease*, 151:369–74. **120**

ARKIN, R.M., see GEEN, BEATTY, & ARKIN (1984).

ARMSTRONG, S.L., GLEITMAN, L.R., & GLEITMAN, H. (1983) What some concepts might not be. *Cognition*, 13:263–308. **282**

ARNOLD, M. (1949) A demonstrational analysis of the TAT in a clinical setting. *Journal of Abnormal and Social Psychology*, 44:97–111. **445**

ARONSON, E. (1984) *The Social Animal* (4th ed.). San Francisco: Freeman. **595, 614, 627**

ARONSON, E., & CARLSMITH, J.M. (1963) The effect of the severity of threat on the devaluation of forbidden behavior. *Journal of Abnormal and Social Psychology*, 66:584–88. **585**

ARONSON, E., see LINDZEY & ARONSON (1985).

ARONSON, E., see WALSTER, ARONSON, ABRAHAMS, & ROTTMAN (1966).

ASARNOW, J.R., see STEFFY, ASARNOW, ASARNOW, MACCRIMMON, & CLEGHORN (1984).

ASARNOW, R.F., see STEFFY, ASARNOW, ASARNOW, MACCRIMMON, & CLEGHORN (1984).

ASCH, S.E. (1952) *Social Psychology*. Englewood Cliffs, N.J.: Prentice-Hall. **607, 608**

ASCH, S.E. (1955) Opinions and social pressures. *Scientific American*, 193:31–35. **607, 608**

ASCH, S.E. (1958) Effects of group pressure upon modification and distortion of judgments. In Maccoby, E.E., Newcomb, T.M., & Hartley, E.L. (eds.), *Readings in Social Psychology* (3rd ed.). New York: Holt, Rinehart & Winston. **607, 608**

ASCHOFF, J. (1965) Circadian rhythm of a Russian vocabulary. *Journal of Experimental Psychology: Human Learning and Memory*, 104:126–33. **114**

ASLIN, R.N., & BANKS, M.S. (1978) Early visual experience in humans: Evidence for a critical period in the development of binocular vision. In Schneider, S., Liebowitz, H., Pick, H., & Stevenson, H. (eds.), *Psychology: From Basic Research to Practice*. New York: Plenum. **206**

ASLIN, R.N., see FOX, ASLIN, SHEA, & DUMAIS (1980).

ATKINSON, J.W., & BIRCH, D. (1978) *An Introduction to Motivation*. New York: Van Nostrand. **349**

ATKINSON, R.C. (1975) Mnemotechnics in second-language learning. *American Psychologist*, 30:821–28. **268**

ATKINSON, R.C. (1976) Teaching children to read using a computer. *American Psychologist*, 29:169–78. **22**

ATKINSON, R.C., & SHIFFRIN, R.M. (1971) The control of short-term memory. *Scientific American*, 224:82–90. **252**

ATKINSON, R.C., & SHIFFRIN, R.M. (1977) Human memory: A proposed system and its control processes. In Bower, G.H. (ed.), *Human Memory: Basic Processes*. New York: Academic Press. **253**

ATKINSON, R.C., see DARLEY, TINKLENBERG, ROTH, HOLLISTER, & ATKINSON (1973).

AUERBACH, A., see LUBORSKY, MCLELLAN, WOODY, O'BRIEN, & AUERBACH (1985).

AUTRUM, H., et al. (eds.) (1971–1973) *Handbook of Sensory Physiology*. New York: Springer-Verlag. **179**

AVERILL, J.R. (1983) Studies on anger and aggression: Implications for theories of emotion. *American Psychologist*, 38:1145–60. **377**

AWAYA, S., MIYAKE, Y., IMAYUMI, Y., SHIOSE, Y., KNADA, T., & KOMURO, K. (1973) Amblyopia. *Japanese Journal of Opthalmology*, 17:69–82. **206**

AWIGUNI, A., see KOBASIGAWA, ARAKAKI, & AWIGUNI (1966).

B

BACHEVALIER, J., see MISHKIN, MALAMUT, & BACHEVALIER (1984).

BACHMAN, J.G., see JOHNSTON, O'MALLEY, & BACHMAN (1986).

BACK, K., see FESTINGER, SCHACHTER, & BACK (1950).

BACKER, R., see FRIEDMAN, SHEFFIELD, WULFF, & BACKER (1951).

BADDELEY, A.D. (1976) *The Psychology of Memory*. New York: Basic Books. **279**

BADDELEY, A.D., & HITCH, G.J. (1974) Working memory. In Bower, G.H. (ed.), *The Psychology of Learning and Motivation*, Vol. 8. New York: Academic Press. **251**

BADDELEY, A.D., & HITCH, G.J. (1977) Recency re-examined. In Dornic, S. (ed.), *Attention and Performance*, Vol. 6. Hillsdale, N.J.: Erlbaum. **254**

BADDELEY, A.D., THOMPSON, N., & BUCHANAN, M. (1975) Word length and the structure of short-term memory. *Journal of Verbal Learning and Verbal Behavior*, 14:575–89. **250**

BADIA, P., see ABBOTT, SCHOEN, & BADIA (1984).

BAER, D.J., & CORRADO, J.J. (1974) Heroin addict relationships with parents during childhood and early adolescent years. *Journal of Genetic Psychology*, 124:99–103. **133**

BAER, P.E., & FUHRER, M.J. (1968) Cognitive processes during differential trace and delayed conditioning of the G.S.R. *Journal of Experimental Psychology*, 78:81–88. **222**

BAGCHI, B., see WENGER & BAGCHI (1961).

BAHRICK, L.E., & WATSON, J.S. (1985) Detection of intermodel proprioceptive-visual contingency as a potential basis of self-perception in infancy. *Developmental Psychology*, 21:693–973. **74**

BAKER, B.L., see GOLDSTEIN, BAKER, & JAMISON (1986).

BAKER, J., see ARKIN, TOTH, BAKER, & HASTEY (1970).

BALL, T.M., see KOSSLYN, BALL, & REISER (1978).

BALLOUN, J.L., see BROCK & BALLOUN (1967).

BANDUCCI, R. (1967) The effect of mother's employment on the achievement, aspirations, and expectations of the child. *Personnel and Guidance Journal*, 46:263–67. **80**

BANDURA, A. (1973) *Aggression: A Social Learning Analysis*. Englewood Cliffs, N.J.: Prentice-Hall. **371, 373, 379**

BANDURA, A. (1977) *Social Learning Theory*. Englewood Cliffs, N.J.: Prentice-Hall. **371, 379, 428, 455**

BANDURA, A. (1978) The self-system in reciprocal determinism. *American Psychologist*, 33:344–58. **452**

BANDURA, A. (1984) Recycling misconceptions of perceived self-efficacy. *Cognitive Therapy and Research*, 8:231–55. **541**

BANDURA, A., ADAMS, N.E., & BEYER, J. (1976) Cognitive processes mediating behavioral change. *Journal of Personality and Social Psychology*, 35:125–39. **537**

BANDURA, A., ADAMS, N.E., HARDY, A.B., & HOWELLS, G.N. (1980) Tests of the generality of self-efficacy theory. *Cognitive Therapy and Research*, 4:39–66. **537**

BANDURA, A., BLANCHARD, E.B., & RITTER, B. (1969) The relative efficacy of desensitization and modeling approaches for inducing behavioral, affective, and attitudinal changes. *Journal of Personality and Social Psychology*, 13:173–99. **536, 537**

BANDURA, A., & MCDONALD, F.J. (1963) Influence of social reinforcement and the behavior of models in shaping children's moral judgments. *Journal of Abnormal and Social Psychology*, 67:274–81. **86**

BANDURA, M.M., see NEWCOMBE & BANDURA (1983).

BANET, B., see HOHMANN, BANET, & WEIKART (1979).

BANKS, M.S. (1982) The development of spatial and temporal contrast sensitivity. *Current Eye Research*, 2:191–98. **204**

BANKS, M.S., see ASLIN & BANKS (1978).

BANYAI, E.I., & HILGARD, E.R. (1976) A comparison of active-alert hypnotic induction with traditional relaxation induction. *Journal of Abnormal Psychology*, 85:218–24. **137**

BARBOUR, H.G. (1912) Die Wirkung Unmittelbarer Erwarmung und Abkuhlung der Warmenzentrum auf die Korpertemperatur. *Achiv fur Experimentalle Pathalogie und Pharmakologie*, 70:1–26. **317**

BARCLAY, J.R., see BRANSFORD, BARCLAY, & FRANKS (1972).

BARLOW, H.B. (1972) Single units and sensation: A neuron doctrine for perceptual psychology. *Perception*, 1:371–94. **178**

BARLOW, H.B., BLAKEMORE, C., & PETTI-

GREW, J.D. (1967) The neural mechanism of binocular depth discrimination. *Journal of Physiology*, 193:327–42. **185**

BARLOW, H.B., & MOLLON, J.D. (1982) *The Senses*. Cambridge: Cambridge University Press. **179**

BARNES, G.E., & PROSEN, H. (1985) Parental death and depression. *Journal of Abnormal Psychology*, 94:64–69. **506**

BARNES, P.J., see BEAMAN, BARNES, KLENTZ, & MCQUIRK (1978).

BARON, R.S. (1986) Distraction-conflict theory: Progress and problems. In Berkowitz, L. (ed.), *Advances in Experimental Social Psychology*, Vol. 19. New York: Academic Press. **600**

BARON, R.S., see SANDERS & BARON (1975).

BARR, A., & FEIGENBAUM, E.A. (1982) *The Handbook of Artificial Intelligence*. Los Altos, Calif.: William Kaufman. **311**

BARTIS, S.P., see ZAMANSKY & BARTIS (1985).

BARTLETT, F.C. (1932) *Remembering: A Study in Experimental and Social Psychology*. Cambridge: Cambridge University Press. **275**

BARTON, R., see LEWINSOHN, MISCHEL, CHAPLIN, & BARTON (1980).

BATCHELOR, B.R., see HIRSCH & BATCHELOR (1976).

BATEMAN, F., see SOAL & BATEMAN (1954).

BATTERMAN, N.A., see KEIL & BATTERMAN (1984).

BATTERSBY, W., & WAGMAN, I. (1962) Neural limits of visual excitability: Pt. 4. Spatial determinants of retrochiasmal interaction. *American Journal of Physiology*, 203:359–65. **158**

BAUM, A., GATCHEL, R.J., FLEMING, R., & LAKE, C.R. (1981) Chronic and acute stress associated with the Three Mile Island accident and decontamination: Preliminary findings of a longitudinal study. Technical report submitted to the U.S. Nuclear Regulatory Commission. **472**

BAUMEISTER, R.F., & TICE, D.M. (1984) Role of self-presentation and choice in cognitive dissonance under forced compliance: Necessary or sufficient causes? *Journal of Personality and Social Psychology*, 43:838–52. **585**

BAUMRIND, D. (1967) Child care practices anteceding three patterns of preschool behavior. *Genetic Psychology Monographs*, 75:43–88. **88**

BAUMRIND, D. (1972) Socialization and instrumental competence in young children. In Hartup, W.W. (ed.), *The Young Child: Reviews of Research*, Vol. 2. Washington, D.C.: National Association for the Education of Young Children. **89**

BAYLEY, N. (1970) Development of mental abilities. In Mussen, P. (ed.), *Carmichael's*

Manual of Child Psychology, Vol. 1. New York: Wiley. **410**

BEAMAN, A.L., BARNES, P.J., KLENTZ, B., & MCQUIRK, B. (1978). Increasing helping rates through information dissemination: Teaching pays. *Personality and Social Psychology Bulletin,* 4:406–11. **606**

BEAMAN, A.L., see DIENER, FRASER, BEAMAN, & KELEM (1976).

BEATTY, W.W., see GEEN, BEATTY, & ARKIN (1984).

BEBBINGTON, P., STURT, E., TENNANT, C., & HURRY, J. (1984) Misfortune and resilience: A community study of women. *Psychological Medicine,* 14:347–63. **510**

BEBBINGTON, P., see TENNANT, SMITH, BEBBINGTON, & HURRY (1981).

BECK, A.T. (1976) *Cognitive Therapy and the Emotional Disorders.* New York: International Universities Press. **507, 540**

BECK, A.T., RUSH, A.J., SHAW, B.F., & EMERY, G. (1979) *Cognitive Therapy of Depression.* New York: Guilford Press. **503, 507**

BECKER, B.J. (1983) Item characteristics and sex differences on the SAT-M for mathematically able youths. Presented at Annual Meeting of American Educational Research Association, Montreal. **92**

BEDNAR, R.L., & KAUL, T.J. (1978) Experiential group research: Current perspectives. In Garfield, S.L., & Bergin, A.E. (eds.), *Handbook of Psychotherapy and Behavior Change* (2nd ed.). New York: Wiley. **545**

BEE, H. (1985) *The Developing Child* (4th ed.). New York: Harper & Row. **105**

BEECHER, H.K. (1961) Surgery as placebo. *Journal of American Medical Association,* 176:1102–107. **552**

BEERS, C.W. (1908) *A Mind That Found Itself.* New York: Doubleday. **528**

BEKESY, G. VON (1960) *Experiments in Hearing* (E.G. Weaver, trans.). New York: McGraw-Hill. **169**

BELL, A.P., & WEINBERG, M.S. (1978) *Homosexualities: A Study of Diversity Among Men and Women.* New York: Simon & Schuster. **338**

BELL, A.P., WEINBERG, M.S., & HAMMERSMITH, S.K. (1981) *Sexual Preference: Its Development in Men and Women.* Bloomington: Indiana University Press. **337**

BELL, L.V. (1980) *Treating the Mentally Ill: From Colonial Times to the Present.* New York: Praeger. **561**

BELLEZZA, F.S., & BOWER, G.H. (1981) Person stereotypes and memory for people. *Journal of Personality and Social Psychology,* 41(No. 5):856–65. **275**

BELLUGI, U., see BROWN, CAZDEN, & BELLUGI (1969).

BEM, D.J. (1970) *Beliefs, Attitudes and Human Affairs.* Belmont, Calif.: Brooks/Cole. **595, 619**

BEM, D.J. (1972) Self-perception theory. In Berkowitz, L. (ed.), *Advances in Experimental Social Psychology,* Vol. 6. New York: Academic Press. **577**

BEM, D.J., & ALLEN, A. (1974) On predicting some of the people some of the time: The search for cross-situational consistencies in behavior. *Psychological Review,* 81:506–20. **451**

BEM, D.J., see SCHMITT & BEM (1986).

BEM, S.L. (1975) Sex-role adaptability: One consequence of psychological androgyny. *Journal of Personality and Social Psychology,* 31:634–43. **572**

BEM, S.L. (1981) Gender schema theory: A cognitive account of sex typing. *Psychological Review,* 88:354–64. **572, 573**

BEM, S.L., MARTYNA, W., & WATSON, C. (1976) Sex typing and androgyny: Further explorations of the expressive domain. *Journal of Personality and Social Psychology,* 34:1016–23. **572**

BENBOW, C.P., & STANLEY, J.C. (1980) Sex differences in mathematical ability: Fact or artifact? *Science,* 210:1262–64. **399**

BENDFELDT, F., see LUDWIG, BRANDSMA, WILBUR, BENDFELDT, & JAMESON (1972).

BENSON, H. (1975) *The Relaxation Response.* New York: Morrow. **145**

BENSON, H., & FRIEDMAN, R. (1985) A rebuttal to the conclusions of David S. Holmes' article: "Meditation and somatic arousal reduction." *American Psychologist,* 40:725–28. **136**

BENSON, H., KOTCH, J.B., CRASSWELLER, K.D., & GREENWOOD, M.M. (1977) Historical and clinical considerations of the relaxation response. *American Scientist,* 65:441–43. **135**

BENSON, H., see JEMMOTT, BORYSENKO, MCCLELLAND, CHAPMAN, MEYER, & BENSON (1985).

BERG, P., see SPACHE & BERG (1978).

BERGIN, A.E., & LAMBERT, M.J. (1978) The evaluation of therapeutic outcomes. In Garfield, S.L., & Bergin, A.E. (eds.), *Handbook of Psychotherapy and Behavior Change,* (2nd ed.). New York: Wiley. **548**

BERGLAS, S., see JONES & BERGLAS (1978).

BERGMAN, T., see HAITH, BERGMAN, & MOORE (1977).

BERKELEY, G. (1709) Essay Towards a New Theory of Vision. Reprinted in A.A. Luce & T.E. Jessup (eds.), *The Works of George Berkeley,* Vol. 1. London: Nelson, 1948. **181, 190**

BERKOWITZ, L. (1965) The concept of aggressive drive. In Berkowitz, L. (ed.), *Ad-*

vances in Experimental Social Psychology, Vol. 2. New York: Academic Press. **373**

BERLIN, B., & KAY, P. (1969) *Basic Color Terms: Their Universality and Evolution.* Los Angeles: University of California Press. **287**

BERMAN, J.S., MILLER, R.C., & MASSMAN, P.J. (1985) Cognitive therapy versus systematic desensitization: Is one treatment superior? *Psychological Bulletin,* 97:451–61. **549**

BERMAN, L., see YUSSEN & BERMAN (1981).

BERMAN, W., see ZIGLER & BERMAN (1983).

BERNSTEIN, M. (1956) *The Search for Bridey Murphy.* New York: Doubleday. **143**

BERNSTEIN, S., see MARKUS, CRANE, BERNSTEIN, & SILADI (1982).

BERNSTEIN, W.M., STEPHAN, W.G., & DAVIS, M.H. (1979) Explaining attributions for achievement: A path analytic approach. *Journal of Personality and Social Psychology,* 37:1810–21. **578**

BERSCHEID, E., & WALSTER, E. (1974) Physical attractiveness. In Berkowitz, L. (ed.), *Advances in Experimental Social Psychology.* New York: Academic Press. **591**

BERSCHEID, E., & WALSTER, E. (1978) *Interpersonal Attraction* (2nd ed.). Menlo Park, Calif.: Addison-Wesley. **595**

BERSCHEID, E., see CAMPBELL & BERSCHEID (1976).

BERSCHEID, E., see DION & BERSCHEID (1972).

BERSCHEID, E., see DION, BERSCHEID, & WALSTER (1972).

BERSCHEID, E., see SNYDER, TANKE, & BERSCHEID (1977).

BERTERA, J.H., see RAYNER, INHOFF, MORRISON, SLOWIACZEK, & BERTERA (1981).

BERTRAND, L.D., see SPANOS, WEEKES, & BERTRAND (1985).

BEVER, T.G., see FODOR, BEVER, & GARRETT (1974).

BEVER, T.G., see TERRACE, PETITTO, SANDERS, & BEVER (1979).

BEVERLY, K.I., see REGAN, BEVERLEY, & CYNADER (1979).

BEYER, J., see BANDURA, ADAMS, & BEYER (1976).

BIEDERMAN, I. (1981) On the semantics of a glance at a scene. In Kubovy, M., & Pomerantz, J. (eds.), *Perceptual Organization.* Hillsdale, N.J.: Erlbaum. **196**

BIERBRAUER, G. (1973) Attribution and perspective: Effects of time, set, and role on interpersonal inference. Unpublished Ph.D. dissertation, Stanford University. **614**

BIERBRAUER, G., see ROSS, BIERBRAUER, & HOFFMAN (1976).

BINET, A., & SIMON, T. (1905) New methods for the diagnosis of the intellectual level of subnormals. *Annals of Psychology*, 11:191. **390, 400**

BIRCH, D., see ATKINSON & BIRCH (1978).

BIRNBAUM, J.A. (1975) Life patterns and self-esteem in gifted family oriented and career committed women. In Mednick, M.S., Tangri, S.S., & Hoffman, L.W. (eds.), *Women and Achievement*. Washington: Hemisphere Publisher. **80**

BISIACH, E., & LUZZATI, C. (1978) Unilateral neglect of representational space. *Cortex*, 14:129–33. **304**

BLACK, J.B., see BOWER, BLACK, & TURNER (1979).

BLACK, J.B., see SEIFERT, ROBERTSON, & BLACK (1985).

BLACKBURN, H., see SHEKELLE, NEATON, JACOBS, HULLEY, & BLACKBURN (1983).

BLAKE, R., see SEKULER, & BLAKE (1985).

BLAKEMORE, C., & COOPER, G.F. (1970) Development of the brain depends on the visual environment. *Nature*, 228:477–78. **206**

BLAKEMORE, C., see BARLOW, BLAKEMORE, & PETTIGREW (1967).

BLANCHARD, E.B., see BANDURA, BLANCHARD, & RITTER (1969).

BLANK, A., see LANGER, BLANK, & CHANOWITZ (1978).

BLEHAR, M.C., see AINSWORTH, BLEHAR, WALTERS, & WALL (1978).

BLISS, D., see STEVENS-LONG, SCHWARZ, & BLISS (1976).

BLISS, E.L. (1980) Multiple personalities: Report of fourteen cases with implications for schizophrenia and hysteria. *Archives of General Psychiatry*, 37:1388–97. **114**

BLOCK, J. (1971) *Lives Through Time*. Berkeley: Bancroft Books. **447, 448**

BLOCK, J. (1981) Some enduring and consequential structures of personality. In Rabin, A.I., Aronoff, J., Barclay, A.M., & Zucker, R.A. (eds.), *Further Explorations in Personality*. New York: Wiley-Interscience. **447**

BLOCK, J., BUSS, D.M., BLOCK, J.H., & GJERDE, P.F. (1981) The cognitive style of breadth of categorization: Longitudinal consistency of personality correlates. *Journal of Personality and Social Psychology*, 40:770–79. **453**

BLOCK, J.H. (1980) Another look at sex differentiation in the socialization behavior of mothers and fathers. In Denmark, F., & Sherman, J. (eds.), *Psychology of Women: Future Directions of Research*. New York: Psychological Dimensions. **91**

BLOCK, J.H., see BLOCK, BUSS, BLOCK, & GJERDE (1981).

BLOOD, R.O. (1967) *Love Match and Ar-ranged Marriage*. New York: Free Press. **593**

BLUM, R., & ASSOCIATES (1972) *Horatio Alger's Children*. San Francisco: Jossey-Bass. **133**

BOCK, R.D., & MOORE, E. (1982) *Advantage and Disadvantage: Vocational Prospects of American Young People*. Technical Report, National Opinion Research Center, University of Chicago. **398**

BODEN, M. (1981) *Artificial Intelligence and Natural Man* (reprint ed.). New York: Basic Books. **211**

BOFF, K.R., KAUFMAN, L., & THOMAS, J.P. (eds.) (1986) *Handbook of Perception and Human Performance: Vol. 1. Sensory Processes and Perception*. New York: Wiley. **179**

BOLLES, R.C. (1970) Species-specific defense reactions and avoidance learning. *Psychological Review*, 77:32–48. **238**

BOND, C.F. (1982) Social facilitation: A self-presentational view. *Journal of Personality and Social Psychology*, 42:1042–50. **600**

BOND, L.A., & JOFFE, J.M. (eds.) (1982) *Facilitating Infant and Early Childhood Development*. Hanover, N.H.: University Press of New England. **415**

BOONE, J.A., & ADESSO, V.J. (1974) Racial differences on a black intelligence test. *Journal of Negro Education*, 43:429–536. **396**

BORDEN, R., see FREEMAN, WALKER, BORDEN, & LATANE (1975).

BORGIDA, E., & NISBETT, R.E. (1977) The differential impact of abstract vs. concrete information on decisions. *Journal of Applied Social Psychology*, 7:258–71. **567**

BORING, E.G. (1930) A new ambiguous figure. *American Journal of Psychology*, 42:444–45. **195**

BORING, E.G. (1942) *Sensation and Perception in the History of Experimental Psychology*. New York: Appleton-Century-Crofts. **148**

BORING, E.G. (1950) *A History of Experimental Psychology* (2nd ed.). New York: Appleton-Century-Crofts. **639**

BORING, E.G., see HERRNSTEIN & BORING (1965).

BORTON, R., see TELLER, MORSE, BORTON, & REGAL (1974).

BORYSENKO, J., see BORYSENKO & BORYSENKO (1982).

BORYSENKO, M., & BORYSENKO, J. (1982) Stress, behavior, and immunity: Animal models and mediating mechanisms. *General Hospital Psychiatry*, 4:59–67. **483**

BORYSENKO, M., see JEMMOTT, BORYSENKO, MCCLELLAND, CHAPMAN, MEYER, & BENSON (1985).

BOUCHARD, T.J. (1976) Genetic factors in intelligence. In Kaplan, A.R. (ed.), *Human Behavior Genetics*. Springfield, Ill.: Charles Thomas. **409**

BOUCHARD, T.J., HESTON, L., ECKERT, E., KEYES, M., & RESNICK, S. (1981) The Minnesota study of twins reared apart: Project description and sample results in the developmental domain. *Twin Research:* Vol. 3. *Intelligence, Personality, and Development*. New York: Alan Liss. **422**

BOUCHARD, T.J., & MCGUE, M. (1981) Familial studies of intelligence: A review. *Science*, 212:1055–59. **408**

BOUCHARD, T.J., see MCGUE & BOUCHARD (1984).

BOUTELLE, W., see WEINGARTEN, GRAFMAN, BOUTELLE, KAYE, & MARTIN (1983).

BOWE-ANDERS, C., see ROFFWARG, HERMAN, BOWE-ANDERS, & TAUBER (1978).

BOWER, G.H. (1972) Mental imagery and associative learning. In Gregg L.W. (ed.), *Cognition in Learning and Memory*. New York: Wiley. **255**

BOWER, G.H. (1981) Mood and memory. *American Psychologist*, 36:129–48. **263**

BOWER, G.H., BLACK, J.B., & TURNER, T.R. (1979) Scripts in memory for text. *Cognitive Psychology*, 11:177–220. **275**

BOWER, G.H., & CLARK, M.C. (1969) Narrative stories as mediators for serial learning. *Psychonomic Science*, 14:181–82. **271**

BOWER, G.H., CLARK, M.C., WINZENZ, D., & LESGOLD, A. (1969) Hierarchical retrieval schemes in recall of categorized word lists. *Journal of Verbal Learning and Verbal Behavior*, 8:323–43. **260**

BOWER, G.H., & HILGARD, E.R. (1981) *Theories of Learning* (5th ed.). Englewood Cliffs, N.J.: Prentice-Hall. **243, 279**

BOWER, G.H., & SPRINGSTON, F. (1970) Pauses as recoding points in letter series. *Journal of Experimental Psychology*, 83:421–30. **252**

BOWER, G.H., see BELLEZZA & BOWER (1981).

BOWER, G.H., see BOWER & BOWER (1976).

BOWER, G.H., see THOMPSON, REYES, & BOWER (1979).

BOWER, S.A., & BOWER, G.H. (1976) *Asserting Yourself*. Reading, Mass.: Addison-Wesley. **561**

BOWER, T.G.R. (1982) *Development in Infancy* (2nd ed.). San Francisco: Freeman. **205, 211**

BOWERS, K.S. (1984) On being unconsciously influenced and informed. In Bowers, K.S., & Meichenbaum, D. (eds.), *The Unconscious Reconsidered*. New York: Wiley. **111**

BOWERS, K.S., & MEICHENBAUM, D.H. (eds.)

(1984) *The Unconscious Reconsidered.* New York: Wiley. **144**

BOWLBY, J. (1973) *Separation: Attachment and Loss,* Vol. 2. New York: Basic Books. **75, 78**

BOWMAKER, J.K., see DARTNALL, BOWMAKER, & MOLLON (1983).

BOYCOTT, B.B., see DOWLING & BOYCOTT (1966).

BOYNTON, R. (1979) *Human Color Vision.* New York: Holt, Rinehart & Winston. **151, 154, 179**

BRADSHAW, G.L., & ANDERSON, J.R. (1982) Elaborative encoding as an explanation of levels of processing. *Journal of Verbal Learning and Verbal Behavior,* 21:165–74. **256**

BRAND, R.J., see ROSENMAN, BRAND, JENKINS, FRIEDMAN, STRAUS, & WRUM (1975).

BRANDSMA, J.M., see LUDWIG, BRANDSMA, WILBUR, BENDFELDT, & JAMESON (1972).

BRANDT, U., see EYFERTH, BRANDT, & WOLFGANG (1960).

BRANSFORD, J.D., & JOHNSON, M.K. (1973) Considerations of some problems of comprehension. In Chase, W.G. (ed.), *Visual Information Processing.* New York: Academic Press. **276**

BRANSFORD, J.D., BARCLAY, J.R., & FRANKS, J.J. (1972) Sentence memory: A constructive versus interpretive approach. *Cognitive Psychology,* 3:193–209. **273**

BREHM, J.W., see WORTMAN & BREHM (1975).

BRELAND, K., & BRELAND, M. (1961) The misbehavior of organisms. *American Psychologist,* 16.681–84. **236**

BRELAND, K., & BRELAND, M. (1966) *Animal Behavior.* New York: Macmillan. **226**

BRELAND, M., see BRELAND & BRELAND (1961).

BRELAND, M., see BRELAND & BRELAND (1966).

BRENNER, C. (1980) A psychoanalytic theory of affects. In Plutchik, R., & Kellerman, H. (eds.), *Emotion: Theory, Research, and Experience,* Vol. 1. New York: Academic Press. **361**

BRENNER, M.H. (1982) Mental illness and the economy. In Parron, D.L., Solomon, F., & Jenkins, C.D. (eds.), *Behavior, Health Risks, and Social Disadvantage.* Washington, D.C.: National Academy Press. **517**

BRENT, E.E., see GRANBERG & BRENT (1974).

BREWER, W.F., & NAKAMURA, G.V. (1984) The nature and functions of schemas. In Wyer, R.S. & Srull, T.K. (eds.), *Handbook of Social Cognition,* Vol. 1. Hillsdale, N.J.: Erlbaum. **276**

BREWIN, C.R. (1985) Depression and causal attributions: What is their relation? *Psychological Bulletin,* 98:297–300. **509**

BRICKER, W.A., see PATTERSON, LITTMAN, & BRICKER (1967).

BRIDGER, W.H. (1961) Sensory habituation and discrimination in the human neonate. *American Journal of Psychiatry,* 117:991–96. **66**

BRIGGS, S.R., see CHEEK & BRIGGS (1982).

BROADBENT, D.E. (1958) *Perception and Communication.* London: Pergamon Press. **198**

BROCK, T.C., & BALLOUN, J.L. (1967) Behavior receptivity to dissonant information. *Journal of Personality and Social Psychology,* 6:413–28. **620**

BRODIE, M., see TESSER & BRODIE (1971).

BRONSON, G.W. (1972) Infants' reactions to unfamiliar persons and novel objects. *Monographs of the Society for Research in Child Development,* 37(3, Serial No. 148). **76**

BROOKS, B., see KENSHALO, NAFF, & BROOKS (1961).

BROTZMAN, E., see HOFLING, BROTZMAN, DALRYMPLE, GRAVES, & PIERCE (1966).

BROWN, A.E. (1936) Dreams in which the dreamer knows he is asleep. *Journal of Abnormal Psychology,* 31:59–66. **119**

BROWN, D.P. (1977) A model for the levels of concentrative meditation. *International Journal of Clinical and Experimental Hypnosis,* 25:236–73. **135**

BROWN, E.L., & DEFFENBACHER, K. (1979) *Perception and the Senses.* Oxford: Oxford University Press **174, 175, 179**

BROWN, G.W., & HARRIS, T. (1978) *Social Origins of Depression: A Study of Psychiatric Disorder in Women.* London: Tavistock. **510**

BROWN, P.L., & JENKINS, H.M. (1968) Autoshaping of the pigeon's keypeck. *Journal of the Experimental Analysis of Behavior,* 11:1–8. **227**

BROWN, R. (1973) *A First Language: The Early Stages.* Cambridge, Mass.: Harvard University Press. **311**

BROWN, R. (1985) *Social Psychology, the Second Edition.* New York: Free Press. **595, 627**

BROWN, R., CAZDEN, C.B., & BELLUGI, U. (1969) The child's grammar from 1 to 3. In Hill, J.P. (ed.), *Minnesota Symposium on Child Psychology,* Vol. 2. Minneapolis: University of Minnesota Press. **297**

BROWN, R.W., & MCNEILL, D. (1966) The "tip-of-the-tongue" phenomenon. *Journal of Verbal Learning and Verbal Behavior,* 5:325–37. **257**

BROWN, S.W. (1970) A comparative study of

maternal employment and nonemployment. Unpublished Ph.D. dissertation, Mississippi State University (University Microfilms, 70–8610). **80**

BROWN, T.S., & WALLACE, P.M. (1980) *Physiological Psychology.* New York: Academic Press. **59**

BROZAN, N. (1985) U.S. leads industrialized nations in teen-age births and abortions. *New York Times* (March 13), p. 1. **97, 99**

BRUCKEN, L., see KUHN, NASH, & BRUCKEN (1978).

BRUGGE, J.F., see ROSE, BRUGGE, ANDERSON, & HIND (1967).

BRUNER, J.S., OLVER, R.R., GREENFIELD, P.M., et al. (1966) *Studies in Cognitive Growth.* New York: Wiley. **281**

BRUYER, R., LATERRE, C., SERON, X., et al. (1983) A case of prosopagnosia with some preserved covert remembrance of familiar faces. *Brain and Cognition,* 2:257–84. **364**

BRYAN, J.H., & TEST, M.A. (1967) Models and helping: Naturalistic studies in aiding behavior. *Journal of Personality and Social Psychology,* 6:400–707. **606**

BRYANT, J., see ZILLMANN & BRYANT (1974).

BRYDEN, M.P., see LEY & BRYDEN (1982).

BUCHANAN, M., see BADDELEY, THOMPSON, & BUCHANAN (1975).

BURKHARD, B., see DOMJAN & BURKHARD (1985).

BURT, D.R., see CREESE, BURT, & SNYDER (1978).

BUSCHKE, H., see KINTSCH & BUSCHKE (1969).

BUSS, A.H., & PLOMIN, R. (1975) *A Temperament Theory of Personality Development.* New York: Wiley. **418**

BUSS, A.H., see FENIGSTEIN, SCHEIER, & BUSS (1975).

BUSS, A.H., see SCHEIER, BUSS, & BUSS (1978).

BUSS, D.M., see BLOCK, BUSS, BLOCK, & GJERDE (1981).

BUSS, D.M., see SCHEIER, BUSS, & BUSS (1978).

BUTCHER, J.N., see COLEMAN, BUTCHER, & CARSON (1984).

BUTCHER, J.N., see KENDALL & BUTCHER (1982).

BUTTERS, N., see SQUIRE & BUTTERS (1984).

BUTZIN, C.A., see ANDERSON & BUTZIN (1978).

C

CAGGIULA, A.R., & HOEBEL, B.G. (1966) A "copulation-reward site" in the posterior hypothalamus. *Science,* 153:1284–85. **332**

CAIN, W.S. (1978) The odoriferous environment and the application of olfactory research. In Carterette, E.C., & Friedman, M.P. (eds.), *Handbook of Perception*, Vol. 7. New York: Academic Press. **173**

CALDER, N. (1971) *The Mind of Man.* New York: Viking. **143**

CALHOUN, K.S., see TURNER, CALHOUN, & ADAMS (1981).

CAMPBELL, B., & BERSCHEID, E. (1976) The perceived importance of romantic love as a determinant of marital choice: Kephart revisited ten years later. Unpublished manuscript. **593**

CAMPBELL, E.A., COPE, S.J., & TEASDALE, J.D. (1983) Social factors and affective disorder: An investigation of Brown and Harris's model. *British Journal of Psychiatry*, 143:548–53. **510**

CAMPBELL, E.H., see FENNELL & CAMPBELL (1984).

CAMPBELL, E.Q., see COLEMAN, CAMPBELL, HOBSON, et al. (1966).

CAMPBELL, F.W., & ROBSON, J.G. (1968) Application of Fourier analysis to the visibility of gratings. *Journal of Physiology*, 197:551–66. **163**

CAMPBELL, H.J. (1973) *The Pleasure Areas.* London: Eyre Methuen. **231**

CAMPOS, J.J., see LAMB & CAMPOS (1982).

CANNON, J.T., see TERMAN, SHAVIT, LEWIS, CANNON, & LIEBESKIND (1984).

CANNON, W.B. (1927) The James-Lange theory of emotions: A critical examination and an alternative theory. *American Journal of Psychology*, 39:106–24. **357**

CANNON, W.B. (1929) *Bodily Changes in Pain, Hunger, Fear, and Rage.* New York: Appleton. **462**

CANTRIL, H., see FREE & CANTRIL (1967).

CARAMAZZA, A., & ZURIF, E.B. (1976) Dissociation of algorithmic and heuristic processes in language comprehension: Evidence from aphasia. *Brain and Language*, 3:572–82. **303**

CARAMAZZA, A., see ZURIF, CARAMAZZA, MYERSON, & GALVIN (1974).

CAREY, G., & GOTTESMAN, I.I. (1981) Twin and family studies of anxiety, phobic, and obsessive disorders. In Klein, D.F., & Rabkin, J. (eds.), *Anxiety: New Research and Changing Concepts.* New York: Haven Press. **501**

CARLSMITH, J.M., DORNBUSCH, S.M., & GROSS, R.T. (1983) Unpublished study, personal communication. **93**

CARLSMITH, J.M., see ARONSON & CARLSMITH (1963).

CARLSMITH, J.M., see FESTINGER & CARLSMITH (1959).

CARLSON, N.R. (1985) *Physiology of Behavior* (3rd ed.). Boston: Allyn & Bacon. **59, 321, 349**

CARLSON, R. (1971) Where is the person in personality research? *Psychological Bulletin*, 75:203–19. **429**

CARLSON, S. (1985) A double-blind test of astrology. *Nature*, 318:419–25. **446**

CARPENTER, P.A., see DANEMAN & CARPENTER (1981).

CARPENTER, P.A., see JUST & CARPENTER (1980).

CARPENTER, R.H.S. (1977) *Movements of the Eyes.* London: Pion. **158**

CARR, K.D., & COONS, E.E. (1982). Rats' self-administered nonrewarding brain stimulation to ameliorate aversion. *Science*, 215: 1516–17. **231**

CARROL, E.N., ZUCKERMAN, M., & VOGEL, W.H. (1982) A test of the optimal level of arousal theory of sensation seeking. *Journal of Personality and Social Psychology*, 42:572–75. **346**

CARROLL, D.W. (1985) *Psychology of Language.* Monterey, Calif.: Brooks/Cole. **311**

CARSKADON, M.A., MITLER, M.M., & DEMENT, W.C. (1974) A comparison of insomniacs and normals: Total sleep time and sleep latency. *Sleep Research*, 3:130. **117**

CARSON, R.C., see COLEMAN, BUTCHER, & CARSON (1984).

CARTERETTE, E.C., & FRIEDMAN, M.P. (eds.) (1974–1978) *Handbook of Perception*, Vols. 1–11. New York: Academic Press. **179**

CARTWRIGHT, R.D. (1974) The influence of a conscious wish on dreams: A methodological study of dream meaning and function. *Journal of Abnormal Psychology*, 83:387–93. **120**

CARTWRIGHT, R.D. (1978) *A Primer on Sleep and Dreaming.* Reading, Mass.: Addison-Wesley. **116, 145**

CARVER, C.S., & SCHEIER, M.F. (1981) Self-consciousness and reactance. *Journal of Research in Personality*, 15:16–29. **438**

CARVER, C.S., see SCHEIER & CARVER (1977).

CARVER, C.S., see SCHEIER & CARVER (1983).

CARVER, C.S., see SCHEIER, CARVER, & GIBBONS (1979).

CARVER, R.P. (1981) *Reading Comprehension and Reading Theory.* Springfield, Ill.: Thomas. **201**

CASE, N.B., see CASE, HELLER, CASE, & MOSS (1985).

CASE, R. (1985) *Intellectual Development: Birth to Adolescence.* New York: Academic Press. **75**

CASE, R.B., HELLER, S.S., CASE, N.B., & MOSS, A.J. (1985) Type A behavior and survival after acute myocardial infarction.

New England Journal of Medicine, 312:737. **482**

CASEY, K.L., see MELZAK & CASEY (1968).

CASTELLUCI, V., & KANDEL, E.R. (1976) Presynaptic facilitation as a mechanism for behavioral sensitization in Aplysia. *Science*, 194:1176–78. **221**

CATTELL, R.B. (1986) *The Handbook for the 16 Personality Factor Questionnaire.* Champaign, Ill.: Institute for Personality and Ability Testing. **425**

CAZDEN, C.B., see BROWN, CAZDEN, & BELLUGI (1969).

CHAFFEE, S., see COMSTOCK, CHAFFEE, KATZMAN, MCCOMBS, & ROBERTS (1978).

CHANOWITZ, B., see LANGER, BLANK, & CHANOWITZ (1978).

CHAPLIN, W., see LEWINSOHN, MISCHEL, CHAPLIN, & BARTON (1980).

CHAPMAN, J., see MCGHIE & CHAPMAN (1961).

CHAPMAN, J.P., see CHAPMAN & CHAPMAN (1969).

CHAPMAN, L.J., & CHAPMAN, J.P. (1969) Illusory correlation as an obstacle to the use of valid psychodiagnostic signs. *Journal of Abnormal Psychology*, 74:271–80. **571**

CHAPMAN, R., see JEMMOTT, BORYSENKO, MCCLELLAND, CHAPMAN, MEYER, & BENSON (1985).

CHARNEY, D.S., & HENINGER, G.R. (1983) Monoamine receptor sensitivity and depression: Clinical studies of antidepressant effects on serotonin and noradrenergic function. *Psychopharmacology Bulletin*, 20:213–23. **510**

CHARNEY, D.S., HENINGER, G.R., & STERNBERG, D.E. (1984) Serotonin function and mechanism of action of antidepressant treatment: Effects of amitriptyline and desipramine. *Archives of General Psychiatry*, 41:359–65. **510**

CHARNOV, E.L., see LAMB, THOMPSON, GARDNER, CHARNOV, & ESTES (1984).

CHASE, W.G., & SIMON, H.A. (1973) The mind's eye in chess. In Chase, W.G. (ed.), *Visual Information Processing.* New York: Academic Press. **308**

CHASE, W.G., see ERICSSON, CHASE, & FALOON (1980).

CHAUDURI, H. (1965) *Philosophy of Meditation.* New York: Philosophical Library. **134**

CHEEK, J.M., & BRIGGS, S.R. (1982) Self-consciousness and aspects of identity. *Journal of Research in Personality*, 16:401–408. **438**

CHEN, S.C. (1937) Social modification of the activity of ants in nest-building. *Physiological Zoology*, 10:420–36. **598**

CHESS, S., & THOMAS, A. (1982) Infant

bonding: Mystique and reality. *American Journal of Ortho-Psychiatry,* 52:213–22. **81**

CHESS, S., see THOMAS & CHESS (1977).

CHI, M., GLASER, R., & REES, E. (1982) Expertise in problem solving. In Sternberg, R. (ed.), *Advances in the Psychology of Human Intelligence,* Vol. 1. Hillsdale, N.J.: Erlbaum. **308**

CHODOROW, N. (1978) *The Reproduction of Mothering.* Los Angeles: University of California Press. **432**

CHOMSKY, N. (1957) *Syntactic Structures.* The Hague: Mouton. **638**

CHOMSKY, N. (1965) *Aspects of the Theory of Syntax.* Cambridge, Mass.: M.I.T. Press. **291**

CHOMSKY, N. (1972) *Language and Mind* (2nd ed.). New York: Harcourt Brace Jovanovich. **300**

CHOMSKY, N. (1980a) On cognitive structures and their development: A reply to Piaget. In Piatelli-Palmarini, M. (ed.), *Language and Learning: The Debate Between Jean Piaget and Noam Chomsky.* Cambridge, Mass.: Harvard University Press. **298**

CHOMSKY, N. (1980b) *Rules and Representations.* New York: Columbia University Press. **311**

CIMBOLIC, P., see MCNEAL & CIMBOLIC (1986).

CLARK, E.V. (1983) Meanings and concepts. In Mussen, P.H. (ed.), *Handbook of Child Psychology.* New York: Wiley. **295**

CLARK, E.V., see CLARK & CLARK (1977).

CLARK, H.H. (1984) Language use and language users. In Lindzey, G., & Aronson, E. (eds.), *The Handbook of Social Psychology,* Vol. 2 (3rd. ed.). New York: Harper & Row. **294**

CLARK, H.H., & CLARK, E.V. (1977) *Psychology and Language: An Introduction to Psycholinguistics.* New York: Harcourt Brace Jovanovich. **285, 286, 311**

CLARK, M.C., see BOWER & CLARK (1969).

CLARK, M.C., see BOWER, CLARK, WINZENZ, & LESGOLD (1969).

CLARK, R.D., III, see MAASS & CLARK (1983).

CLARK, R.D., III, see MAASS & CLARK (1984).

CLARK, R.W., see MINIUM & CLARK (1982).

CLARK, V., see TASHKIN, COULSON, CLARK, et al. (1985).

CLARKE-STEWART, K.A. (1973) Interactions between mothers and their young children: Characteristics and consequences. *Monographs of the Society for Research in Child Development,* 38. **79**

CLARKE-STEWART, K.A. (1982) *Daycare.* Cambridge, Mass.: Harvard University Press. **80, 81**

CLARKE-STEWART, K.A. (1978) Popular

primers for parents. *American Psychologist,* 35:359–69. **82**

CLARKE-STEWART, K.A., & FEIN, G.G. (1983) Early childhood programs. In Mussen, P.H. (ed.), *Handbook of Child Psychology,* Vol. 2 (4th ed.). New York: Wiley. **81**

CLARREN, S.K., see STREISSGUTH, CLARREN, & JONES (1985).

CLAYTON, R.R., see O'DONNELL & CLAYTON (1982).

CLECKLEY, H., see THIGPEN & CLECKLEY (1957).

CLEG, R.A., see CORKIN, COHEN, SULLIVAN, CLEG, ROSEN, & ACKERMAN (1985).

CLEGHORN, J.M., see STEFFY, ASARNOW, ASARNOW, MACCRIMMON, & CLEGHORN (1984).

CLEMENT, P.W., see WALKER, HEDBERG, CLEMENT, & WRIGHT (1981).

COATES, B., see HARTUP & COATES (1967).

COE, W.C., & SARBIN, T.R. (1977) Hypnosis from the standpoint of a contextualist. *Annals of the New York Academy of Sciences,* 296:2–13. **140**

COHEN, J., see WELKOWITZ, EWEN, & COHEN (1982).

COHEN, N.J., & SQUIRE, L.R. (1980) Preserved learning and retention of pattern analyzing skill in amnesia: Dissociation of knowing how and knowing that. *Science,* 210:207–09. **266**

COHEN, N.J., see CORKIN, COHEN, SULLIVAN, CLEGG, ROSEN, & ACKERMAN (1985).

COHEN, N.J., see SQUIRE & COHEN (1984).

COHEN, N.J., see SQUIRE, COHEN, & NADEL (1984).

COHEN, S., & WILLS, T.A. (1985) Stress, social support, and the buffering hypothesis. *Psychological Bulletin,* 98:310–57. **472**

COLBURN, H.S., see DURLACH & COLBURN (1978).

COLE, M. (1981) Mind as a cultural achievement: Implications for IQ testing. *Annual Report, 1979–1980.* Research and Clinical Center for Child Development. Faculty of Education, Hokkaido University, Sapporo, Japan. **397**

COLE, M., & COLE, S.R. (1987) *Human Development.* New York: Scientific American Books. **81**

COLEMAN, J.C., BUTCHER, J.N., & CARSON, R.C. (1984) *Abnormal Psychology and Modern Life* (7th ed.). Glenview, Ill.: Scott, Foresman. **487, 525**

COLEMAN, J.S., CAMPBELL, E.Q., HOBSON, C.J., et al. (1966) *Equality of Educational Opportunity, Supplemental Appendix 9.10.* Washington, D.C.: DHEW. **398**

COLLINS, A., see ADAMS & COLLINS (1979).

COLLINS, A.M., & QUILLIAN, M.R. (1969) Retrieval time from semantic memory.

Journal of Verbal Learning and Verbal Behavior, 8:240–48. **283**

COLLINS, J.K., see HARPER & COLLINS (1972).

COMSTOCK, G., CHAFFEE, S., KATZMAN, N., MCCOMBS, M., & ROBERTS, D. (1978) *Television and Human Behavior.* New York: Columbia University Press. **619**

CONDRY, J., & CONDRY, S. (1976) Sex differences: A study in the eye of the beholder. *Child Development,* 47:812–19. **90**

CONDRY, S., see CONDRY & CONDRY (1976).

CONGER, J.J., & PETERSON, A.C. (1983) *Adolescence and Youth: Psychological Development in a Changing World* (3rd ed.). New York: Harper & Row. **105**

CONGER, J.J., see MUSSEN, CONGER, KAGAN, & HUSTON (1984).

CONLEY, J.J. (1985) Longitudinal stability of personality traits: A multitrait-multimethod-multioccasion analysis. *Journal of Personality and Social Psychology,* 49:1266–82. **447**

CONNOLLY, C., see SYER & CONNOLLY (1984).

CONRAD, R. (1964) Acoustic confusions in immediate memory. *British Journal of Psychology,* 55:75–84. **247**

CONSUMERS UNION (1980) *The Medicine Show* (5th ed.). Mount Vernon, N.Y.: Consumers Union of U.S., Inc. **619**

CONTRADA, R.J., see WRIGHT, CONTRADA, & GLASS (1985).

COONS, E.E., see CARR & COONS (1982).

COOPER, F., see LIBERMAN, COOPER, SHANKWEILER, & STUDDERT-KENNEDY (1967).

COOPER, G.F., see BLAKEMORE & COOPER (1970).

COOPER, J., see FAZIO, ZANNA, & COOPER (1977).

COOPER, J., see WORD, ZANNA, & COOPER (1974).

COOPER, L.A., & SHEPARD, R.N. (1973) Chronometric studies of the rotation of mental images. In Chase, W.G. (ed.), *Visual Information Processing.* New York: Academic Press. **304, 305**

COOPER, L.A., see SHEPARD & COOPER (1981).

COOPER, L.M. (1979) Hypnotic amnesia. In Fromm, E., & Shor, R.E. (eds.), *Hypnosis: Developments in Research and New Perspectives* (rev. ed.). New York: Aldine. **139**

COPE, S.J., see CAMPBELL, COPE, & TEASDALE (1983).

CORBIT, J.D., see SOLOMON & CORBIT (1974).

CORDUA, G.D., MCGRAW, K.O., & DRABMAN, R.S. (1979) Doctor or nurse: Children's perception of sex-typed occupations. *Child Development,* 50:590–93. **94**

COREN, S., PORAC, C., & WARD, L.M. (1984) *Sensation and Perception* (2nd ed.). Orlando: Academic Press. **179**

CORKIN, S., COHEN, N.J., SULLIVAN, E.V., CLEGG, R.A., ROSEN, T.J., & ACKERMAN, R.H. (1985) Analyses of global memory impairments of different etiologies. In Olton, D.S., Gamzu, E., & Corkin, S. (eds.), *Memory Dysfunction*. New York: New York Academy of Sciences. **265**

CORKIN, S., see MILNER, CORKIN, & TEUBER (1968).

CORRADO, J.J., see BAER & CORRADO (1974).

CORSINI, R.J. (1984) *Current Psychotherapies* (3rd ed.). Itasca, Ill.: Peacock. **561**

COSCINA, D.V., & DIXON, L.M. (1983) Body weight regulation in anorexia nervosa: Insights from an animal model. In Darby, P.L., Garfinkel, P.E., Garner, D.M., & Coscina, D.V. (eds.), *Anorexia Nervosa: Recent Developments*. New York: Allan R. Liss. **325**

COSTA, P., see MADDI & COSTA (1972).

COSTA, E. (1985) Benzodiazepine/GABA interactions: A model to investigate the neurobiology of anxiety. In Tuma, A.H., and Maser, J.D. (eds.), *Anxiety and the Anxiety Disorders*. Hillsdale, N.J.: Erlbaum. **502**

COSTA, P.T., JR., ZONDERMAN, A.B., MCCRAE, R.R., WILLIAMS, R.B., JR. (1985) Content and comprehensiveness in the MMPI: An item factor analysis in a normal adult sample. *Journal of Personality and Social Psychology*, 48:925–33. **442**

COTMAN, C.W., & MCGAUGH, J.L. (1980) *Behavioral Neuroscience: An Introduction*. New York: Academic Press. **59**

COTTRELL, N.B. (1972) Social facilitation. In McClintock, C.G. (ed.), *Experimental Social Psychology*. New York: Holt, Rinehart & Winston. **598**

COTTRELL, N.B., RITTLE, R.H., & WACK, D.L. (1967) Presence of an audience and list type (competitional or noncompetitional) as joint determinants of performance in paired-associates learning. *Journal of Personality*, 35:425–34. **599**

COTTRELL, N.B., WACK, D.L., SEKERAK, G.J., & RITTLE, R.H. (1968) Social facilitation of dominant responses by the presence of an audience and the mere presence of others. *Journal of Personality and Social Psychology*, 9:245–50. **599**

COULSON, A., see TASHKIN, COULSON, CLARK, et al. (1985).

COX, C.L., see MILLER & COX (1981).

COX, J.R., see GRIGGS & COX (1982).

COYNE, J.C., see DELONGIS, COYNE, DAKOF, FOLKMAN, & LAZARUS (1982).

CRAIGHEAD, L.W., STUNKARD, A.J., & O'BRIEN, R.M. (1981) Behavior therapy and pharmacotherapy for obesity. *Archives of General Psychiatry*, 38:763–68. **328**

CRAIGHEAD, W.E., KAZDIN, A.E., & MAHONEY, M.J. (1981) *Behavior Modification: Principles, Issues, and Applications* (2nd ed.). Boston: Houghton Mifflin. **561**

CRAIK, F.I.M., & LOCKHART, R.S. (1972) Levels of processing: A framework for memory research. *Journal of Verbal Learning and Verbal Behavior*, 11:671–84. **254**

CRAIK, F.I.M., & WATKINS, M.J. (1973) The role of rehearsal in short-term memory. *Journal of Verbal Learning and Verbal Behavior*, 12:599–607. **254**

CRAIK, K. (1943) *The Nature of Explanation*. New York: Cambridge University Press. **9**

CRANE, M., see MARKUS, CRANE, BERNSTEIN, & SILADI (1982).

CRASSWELLER, K.D., see BENSON, KOTCH, CRASSWELLER, & GREENWOOD (1977).

CREESE, I., BURT, D.R., & SNYDER, S.H. (1978) Biochemical actions of neuroleptic drugs. In Iversen, L.L., Iversen, S.D., & Snyder, S.H. (eds.), *Handbook of Psychopharmacology*, Vol. 10. New York: Plenum. **516**

CRICK, F., & MITCHISON, G. (1983) The function of dream sleep. *Nature*, 304:111–14. **120**

CRISTOL, A.H., see SLOANE, STAPLES, CRISTOL, YORKSTON, & WHIPPLE (1975).

CRONBACH, L.J. (1984) *Essentials of Psychological Testing* (4th ed.). New York: Harper & Row. **403, 415, 455**

CROWDER, R.G. (1976) *Principles of Learning and Memory*. Hillsdale: N.J.: Erlbaum. **279**

CROWDER, R.G. (1982) The demise of short-term memory. *Acta Psychologica*, 50:291–323. **251**

CRUTCHFIELD, L., see KNOX, CRUTCHFIELD, & HILGARD (1975).

CUDECK, R., see MEDNICK, CUDECK, GRIFFITH, TALOVIC, & SCHULSINGER (1984).

CURETON, K.J., see THOMPSON, JARVIE, LAKEY, & CURETON (1982).

CURTISS, S., see FROMKIN, KRASHEN, CURTISS, RIGLER, & RIGLER (1974).

CYNADER, M., see REGAN, BEVERLEY, & CYNADER (1979).

D

D'ANDRADE, R.G. (1967) Report on some testing and training procedures at Bassawa Primary School, Zaria, Nigeria. Unpublished manuscript. **397**

D'AQUILA, J.M., see SANDERS, SOARES, & D'AQUILA (1982).

DAKOF, G., see DELONGIS, COYNE, DAKOF, FOLKMAN, & LAZARUS (1982).

DALE, A.J.D. (1975) Organic brain syndromes associated with infections. In Freedman, A.M., Kaplan, H.I., & Sadock, B.J. (eds.), *Comprehensive Textbook of Psychiatry*, Vol. 2. 1:1121–30. Baltimore, Md.: Williams & Wilkins. **528**

DALE, L.A., see WOLMAN, DALE, SCHMEIDLER, & ULLMAN (1985).

DALRYMPLE, S., see HOFLING, BROTZMAN, DALRYMPLE, GRAVES, & PIERCE (1966).

DAMON, W. (1977) *The Social World of the Child*. San Francisco: Jossey-Bass. **87**

DANEMAN, M., & CARPENTER, P.A. (1981) Individual differences in working memory and reading. *Journal of Verbal Learning and Verbal Behavior*, 19:450–66. **252**

DARBY, C.L., see PLATT, YAKSH, & DARBY (1967).

DARIAN-SMITH, I. (ed.) (1984) *Handbook of Physiology: The Nervous System:* Section 1, Vol. 3. *Sensory Processes*. Bethesda, Md.: American Physiological Society. **179**

DARLEY, C.F., TINKLENBERG, J.R., ROTH, W.T., HOLLISTER, L.E., & ATKINSON, R.C. (1973) Influence of marijuana on storage and retrieval processes in memory. *Memory and Cognition*, 1:196–200. **19**

DARLEY, I.M., see LATANE & DARLEY (1970).

DARLEY, J.M., & LATANE, B. (1968) Bystander intervention in emergencies: Diffusion of responsibility. *Journal of Personality and Social Psychology*, 8:377–83. **606**

DARLEY, J.M., see LATANE & DARLEY (1968).

DARLINGTON, R., see LAZAR & DARLINGTON (1982).

DARTNALL, H.J.A., BOWMAKER, J.K., & MOLLON, J.D. (1983) Microspectrometry of human photoreceptors. In Mollon, J.D. & Sharpe, L.T. (eds.), *Colour Vision*. New York: Academic Press. **161**

DARWIN, C. (1859) *On the Origin of the Species*. London: Murray. **62**

DARWIN, C. (1872) *The Expression of Emotion in Man and Animals*. New York: Philosophical Library. **362**

DASHIELL, J.F. (1930) An experimental analysis of some group effects. *Journal of Abnormal and Social Psychology*, 25:190–99. **598, 599**

DASHIELL, J.F. (1935) Experimental studies of the influence of social situations on the behavior of individual human adults. In Murchison, C. (ed.), *Handbook of Social Psychology*. Worcester, Mass.: Clark University. **598**

DAVIDSON, A.R., & JACCARD, J.J. (1979) Variables that moderate the attitude-behavior relations: Results of a longitudinal survey. *Journal of Personality and Social Psychology*, 37:1364–76. **584**

DAVIDSON, E.S., YASUNA, A., & TOWER, A. (1979) The effects of television cartoons on sex-role stereotyping in young girls. *Child Development*, 50:597–600. **92**

DAVIS, A., see EELLS, DAVIS, HAVIGHURST, HERRICK, & TYLER (1951).

DAVIS, B. see STUART & DAVIS (1972).

DAVIS, B.M., see MOHS, DAVIS, GREENWALD, et al. (1985).

DAVIS, J.M., see JANICAK, DAVIS, GIBBONS, ERICKSEN, CHANG, & GALLAGHER (1985).

DAVIS, M.H., see BERNSTEIN, STEPHAN, & DAVIS (1979).

DAVIS, M.H., see FRANZOI, DAVIS, & YOUNG (1985).

DAVISON, G.C., & NEALE, J.M. (1986) *Abnormal Psychology: An Experimental Clinical Approach* (4th ed.). New York: Wiley. **525**

DE BACA, P.C., see HOMME, DE BACA, DEVINE, STEINHORST, & RICKERT (1963).

DE CASPER, A.J., & FIFER, W.P. (1980) Of human bonding: Newborns prefer their mother's voices. *Science*, 208:1174–76. **66**

DEAUX, K. (1985) Sex and gender. *Annual Review of Psychology*, 36:49–81. **92**

DECINA, P., see SACKEIM, PORTNOY, NEELEY, STEIF, DECINA, & MALITZ (1985).

DEFFENBACHER, K., see BROWN & DEFFENBACHER (1979).

DEFRIES, J.C., see PLOMIN, DEFRIES, & MCCLEARN (1980).

DEIKMAN, A.J. (1963) Experimental meditation. *Journal of Nervous and Mental Disease*, 136:329–73. **135**

DELANEY, H.D., see PRESSLEY, LEVIN, & DELANEY (1982).

DELONGIS, A., COYNE, J.C., DAKOF, G., FOLKMAN, S., & LAZARUS, R.S. (1982) Relationship of daily hassles, uplifts, and major life events to health status. *Health Psychology* 1:119–36. **470**

DELONGIS, A., see FOLKMAN, LAZARUS, DUNKEL-SCHETTER, DELONGIS, & GRUEN (1986).

DEMBROSKI, T.M., MACDOUGALL, J.M., WILLIAMS, B., & HANEY, T.L. (1985) Components of Type A hostility and anger: Relationship to angiographic findings. *Psychosomatic Medicine*, 47:219–33. **483**

DEMENT, W.C. (1960) The effect of dream deprivation. *Science*, 131:1705–1707. **117**

DEMENT, W.C. (1976) *Some Must Watch While Some Must Sleep*. New York: Simon & Schuster. **117**

DEMENT, W.C., & KLEITMAN, N. (1957) The relation of eye movements during sleep to dream activity: An objective method for the study of dreaming. *Journal of Experimental Psychology*, 53:339–46. **115**

DEMENT, W.C., & WOLPERT, E. (1958) The relation of eye movements, bodily motility, and external stimuli to dream content. *Journal of Experimental Psychology*, 55:543–53. **119**

DEMENT, W.C., see CARSKADON, MITLER, & DEMENT (1974).

DEMENT, W.C., see GULEVICH, DEMENT, & JOHNSON (1966).

DEMING, M., see SHEPOSH, DEMING, & YOUNG (1977).

DENARI, M., see YESAVAGE, LEIER, DENARI, & HOLLISTER (1985).

DENNIS, W. (1960) Causes of retardation among institutional children: Iran. *Journal of Genetic Psychology*, 96:47–59. **69**

DENNIS, W. (1973) *Children of the Creche*. Englewood Cliffs, N.J.: Prentice-Hall. **70**

DER SIMONIAN, R., & LAIRD, N.M. (1983) Evaluating the effect of coaching on SAT scores: A meta-analysis, *Harvard Educational Review*, 53:1–15. **401**

DERMAN, D., see EKSTROM, FRENCH, HARMAN, & DERMAN (1976).

DERMER, M., see MITA, DERMER, & KNIGHT (1977).

DESILVA, R.A., see REICH, DESILVA, LOWN, & MURAWSKI (1981).

DEUTSCH, G., see SPRINGER & DEUTSCH (1985).

DEVALOIS, K.K., see DEVALOIS & DEVALOIS (1980).

DEVALOIS, R.L., & DEVALOIS, K.K. (1980) Spatial vision. *Annual Review of Psychology*, 31:309–41. **164**

DEVALOIS, R.L. & JACOBS, G.H. (1984) Neural mechanisms of color vision. In Darian-Smith, I. (ed.), *Handbook of Physiology*, Vol. 3. Bethesda, Md.: American Physiological Society. **161**

DEVINE, J.V., see HOMME, DE BACA, DEVINE, STEINHORST, & RICKERT (1963).

DICARA, L.V. (1970) Learning in the autonomous nervous system. *Scientific American*, 222:30–39. **225**

DICARA, L.V., & MILLER, W.E. (1968) Instrumental learning of systolic blood pressure responses by curarized rats. *Psychosomatic Medicine*, 30:489–94. **480**

DICK, L., see TART & DICK (1970).

DIENER, E. (1976) Effects of prior destructive behavior, anonymity, and group presence on deindividuation and aggression. *Journal of Personality and Social Psychology*, 33:497–507. **377**

DIENER, E. (1979) Deindividuation, self-awareness, and disinhibition. *Journal of Personality and Social Psychology*, 37:1160–71. **600, 601, 602**

DIENER, E. (1980) Deindividuation: The absence of self-awareness and self-regulation in group members. In Paulus, P.B. (ed.), *The Psychology of Group Influence*. Hillsdale, N.J.: Erlbaum. **600**

DIENER, E., FRASER, S.C., BEAMAN, A.L., & KELEM, R T. (1976) Effects of deindividuation variables on stealing among Halloween trick-or-treaters. *Journal of Personality and Social Psychology*, 33:178–83. **601**

DIGMAN, J.M., & INOUYE, J. (1986) Further specification of the five robust factors of personality. *Journal of Personality and Social Psychology*, 50:116–23. **425**

DION, K.K. (1972) Physical attractiveness and evaluations of children's transgressions. *Journal of Personality and Social Psychology*, 24:207–13. **589**

DION, K.K., & BERSCHEID, E. (1972) Physical attractiveness and social perception of peers in preschool children. Unpublished manuscript, University of Minnesota, Minneapolis. **588**

DION, K.K., BERSCHEID, E., & WALSTER, E. (1972) What is beautiful is good. *Journal of Personality and Social Psychology*, 24:285–90. **574**

DION, K.K., & STEIN, S. (1978) Physical attractiveness and interpersonal influence. *Journal of Experimental Social Psychology*, 14:97–108. **575**

DIPIETRO, J.A. (1981) Rough and tumble play: A function of gender. *Developmental Psychology*, 17:50–58. **93**

DIXON, L.M., see COSCINA & DIXON (1983).

DOANE, B.K., see HERON, DOANE, & SCOTT (1956).

DOBELLE, W.H., MEADEJOVSKY, M.G., & GIRVIN, J.P. (1974) Artificial vision for the blind: Electrical stimulation of visual cortex offers hope for a functional prosthesis. *Science*, 183:440–44. **171**

DOBIE, S., see LOWINGER & DOBIE (1969).

DODDS, J.B., see FRANKENBURG & DODDS (1967).

DOHRENWEND, B.S. (1973) Social status and stressful life events. *Journal of Personality and Social Psychology*, 28:225–35. **517**

DOLLARD, J., DOOB, L.W., MILLER, N.E., MOWRER, O.H., & SEARS, R.R. (1939) *Frustration and Aggression*. New Haven: Yale University Press. **369**

DOMINO, G. (1971) Interactive effects of achievement orientation and teaching style of academic achievement. *Journal of Educational Psychology*, 62:427–31. **443**

DOMJAN, M., & BURKHARD, B. (1985) *The Principles of Learning and Behavior*. Monterey, Calif.: Brooks/Cole. **243**

DOOB, A.N., & WOOD, L.E. (1972) Catharsis and aggression: Effects of annoyance and retaliation on aggressive behavior. *Journal of Personality and Social Psychology*, 22:156–62. **377**

ETCOFF, N.L. (1985) The neuropsychology of emotional expression. In Goldstein, G., & Tarter, R.E. (eds.), *Advances in Clinical Neuropsychology*, Vol. 3. New York: Plenum. **364**

EVANS, C. (1984) *Landscapes of the Night: How and Why We Dream*. New York: Viking. **120**

EWEN, R.B., see WELKOWITZ, EWEN, & COHEN (1982).

EYFERTH, K., BRANDT, U., & WOLFGANG, H. (1960) *Farbige Kinder in Deutschland*. Munich: Juventa. **411**

F

FADIMAN, J., see FRAGER & FADIMAN (1984).

FALOON, S., see ERICSSON, CHASE, & FALOON (1980).

FANCHER, R.E. (1985) *The Intelligence Men: Makers of the IQ Controversy*. New York: Norton. **415**

FANTINO, E., & LOGAN, C.A. (1979) *The Experimental Analysis of Behavior: A Biological Perspective*. San Francisco: Freeman. **222**

FANTZ, R.L. (1961) The origin of form perception. *Science*, 204:66–72. **66, 204**

FANTZ, R.L., ORDY, J.M., & UDELF, M.S. (1962) Maturation of pattern vision in infants during the first six months. *Journal of Comparative and Physiological Psychology*, 55:907–17. **204**

FARBEROW, N.L., & SHNEIDMAN, E.S. (1965) *The Cry for Help*. New York: McGraw Hill. **504**

FARLEY, F. (1986) The big T in personality. *Psychology Today*, 20:46–52. **346**

FARQUHAR, J.W., MACCOBY, N., & SOLOMON, D.S. (1984) Community applications of behavioral medicine. In Gentry, W.D. (ed.), *Handbook of Behavioral Medicine*. New York: Guilford Press. **622**

FARQUHAR, J.W., MACCOBY, N., WOOD, P.D., et al. (1977) Community education for cardiovascular health. *The Lancet*, 1(No. 8023):1192–95. **621**

FARQUHAR, J.W., see MACCOBY, FARQUHAR, WOOD, & ALEXANDER (1977).

FAUST, I.M. (1984) Role of the fat cell in energy balance physiology. In Stunkard, A.T., & Stellar, E. (eds.), *Eating and its Disorders*. New York: Raven Press. **328**

FAZIO, R., & ZANNA, M.P. (1981) Direct experience and attitude-behavior consistency. In Berkowitz, L. (ed.), *Advances in Experimental Social Psychology*, Vol. 14. New York: Academic Press. **584**

FAZIO, R., ZANNA, M.P., & COOPER, J. (1977) Dissonance and self-perception:

An integrative view of each theory's proper domain of application. *Journal of Experimental Social Psychology*, 13:464–79. **585**

FAZIO, R., see REGAN & FAZIO (1977).

FEATHER, N.T., see SIMON & FEATHER (1973).

FECHNER, G.T. (1860) *Elements of Psychophysics* (H.E. Adler, trans.). New York: Holt, Rinehart & Winston. (Reprint ed. 1966.) **157**

FEDIO, P., see FRIED, MATEER, OJEMANN, WOHNS, & FEDIO (1982).

FEDROV, C.N., see KUMAN, FEDROV, & NOVIKOVA (1983).

FEIGENBAUM, E.A., see BARR & FEIGENBAUM (1982).

FEIN, G.G., see CLARKE-STEWART & FEIN (1983).

FEINLEIB, M., see HAYNES, FEINLEIB, & KANNEL (1980).

FEJER, D., see SMART & FEJER (1972).

FELDMAN, H., GOLDIN-MEADOW, S., & GLEITMAN, L.R. (1978) Beyond Herodotus: The creation of language by linguistically deprived children. In Lock, A. (ed.), *Action, Gesture, and Symbol: The Emergence of Language*. London: Academic Press. **299**

FELDMAN, J.J., see KATZ & FELDMAN (1962).

FELSON, R.B. (1981) Self and reflected appraisal among football players. *Social Psychology Quarterly*, 44:116–26. **436**

FENIGSTEIN, A. (1979) Self-consciousness, self-attention, and social interaction. *Journal of Personality and Social Psychology*, 37:75–86. **438**

FENIGSTEIN, A., SCHEIER, M.F., & BUSS, A.H. (1975) Public and private self-consciousness: Assessment and theory. *Journal of Consulting and Clinical Psychology*, 43:522–24. **437**

FENN, D., see LEWINSOHN, FENN, & FRANKLIN (1982).

FENNELL, M.J.V., & CAMPBELL, E.H. (1984) The cognitions questionnaire: Specific thinking errors in depression. *British Journal of Clinical Psychology*, 23:81–92. **509**

FERRO, P., see HOGARTY, SCHOOLER, ULRICH, MUSSARE, FERRO, & HERRON (1979).

FESHBACH, N., see FESHBACH & FESHBACH (1973).

FESHBACH, S., & FESHBACH, N. (1973) The young aggressors. *Psychology Today*, 6:90–95. **93**

FESHBACH, S., & WEINER, B. (1986) *Personality* (2nd ed.). Lexington, Mass.: Heath. **455**

FESTINGER, L. (1957) *A Theory of Cognitive Dissonance*. Stanford: Stanford University Press. **577, 584**

FESTINGER, L., & CARLSMITH, J.M. (1959) Cognitive consequences of forced compliance. *Journal of Abnormal and Social Psychology*, 58:203–10. **577, 584**

FESTINGER, L., PEPITONE, A., & NEWCOMB, T.M. (1952) Some consequences of deindividuation in a group. *Journal of Abnormal and Social Psychology*, 47:383–89. **600**

FESTINGER, L., SCHACHTER, S., & BACK, K. (1950) *Social Pressures in Informal Groups: A Study of Human Factors in Housing*. New York: Harper & Row. **589**

FIFER, W.P., see DE CASPER & FIFER (1980).

FINKELSTEIN, M.A., see HOOD & FINKELSTEIN (1983).

FIORENTINI, A., see PIRCHIO, SPINELLI, FIORENTINI, & MAFFEI (1978).

FIREMAN, B., see GAMSON, FIREMAN, & RYTINA (1982).

FISCHER, K.W., & LAZERSON, A. (1984) *Human Development: From Conception Through Adolescence*. New York: Freeman. **105**

FISHBEIN, M. (1963) An investigation of the relationships between beliefs about an object and the attitude toward that object. *Human Relations*, 16:233–40. **582**

FISHER, G.H. (1967) Preparation of ambiguous stimulus materials. *Perception and Psychophysics*, 2:421–22. **195**

FISHER, I.V., ZUCKERMAN, M., & NEEB, M. (1981) Marital compatibility in sensation seeking trait as a factor in marital adjustment. *Journal of Sex and Marital Therapy*, 7:60–69. **346**

FISHMAN, P. (1983) Interaction: The work women do. In Thorne, B., Kramarae, C., & Henley, N. (eds.), *Language, Gender, and Society*. Rowley, Mass.: Newbury House. **579**

FIXSEN, D.L., PHILLIPS, E.L., PHILLIPS, E.A., & WOLF, M.M. (1976) The teaching-family model of group home treatment. In Craighead, W.E., Kazdin, A.E., & Mahoney, M.J. (eds.), *Behavior Modification: Principles, Issues, and Applications*. Boston: Houghton Mifflin. **558**

FLACKS, R., see NEWCOMB, KOENIG, FLACKS, & WARWICK (1967).

FLAVELL, J.H. (1985) *Cognitive Development* (2nd ed.). Englewood Cliffs, N.J.: Prentice-Hall. **105**

FLEMING, R., see BAUM, GATCHEL, FLEMING, & LAKE (1981).

FOCH, T.T., see STUNKARD, A.J., FOCH, T.T., & HRUBEC, Z. (1986).

FODOR, J.A., BEVER, T.G., & GARRETT, M.F. (1974) *The Psychology of Language: An Introduction to Psycholinguistics and Generative Grammar*. New York: McGraw-Hill. **311**

FOLEY, J.M. (1978) Primary distance perception. In Held, R., Leibowitz, H.W., & Teuber, H.L. (eds.), *Handbook of Sensory Physiology*, Vol. 8. Berlin: Springer-Verlag. **184**

FOLKES, V.S. (1982) Forming relationships and the matching hypothesis. *Personality and Social Psychology Bulletin*, 8:631–36. **591**

FOLKMAN, S., & LAZARUS, R.S. (1980) An analysis of coping in a middle-aged community sample. *Journal of Health and Social Behavior*, 21:219–39. **477**

FOLKMAN, S., & LAZARUS, R.S. (1985) If it changes it must be a process: A study of emotion and coping during three stages of a college examination. *Journal of Personality and Social Psychology*, 48:150–70. **461**

FOLKMAN, S., LAZARUS, R.S., DUNKEL-SCHETTER, C., DELONGIS, A., & GRUEN, R. (1986) The dynamics of a stressful encounter: Cognitive appraisal, coping, and encounter outcomes. *Journal of Personality and Social Psychology*, 50:992–1003. **477**

FOLKMAN, S., see DELONGIS, COYNE, DAKOF, FOLKMAN, & LAZARUS (1982).

FOLKMAN, S., see LAZARUS & FOLKMAN (1984).

FOLKMAN, S., see LAZARUS, KANNER, & FOLKMAN (1980).

FOREM, J. (1973) *Transcendental Meditation: Maharishi Mahesh Yogi and the Science of Creative Intelligence*. New York: Dutton. **135**

FORER, B.R. (1949) The fallacy of personality validation: A classroom demonstration of gullibility. *Journal of Abnormal and Social Psychology*, 44:118–23. **446**

FOSS, D.J., & HAKES, D.T. (1978) *Psycholinguistics: An Introduction to the Psychology of Language*. Englewood Cliffs, N.J.: Prentice-Hall. **311**

FOULKE, E., see SCHIFF & FOULKE (1982).

FOWLER, R.C., see RICH, YOUNG, & FOWLER (1985).

FOX, M.M., see SQUIRE & FOX (1980).

FOX, R., ASLIN, R.N., SHEA, S.L., & DUMAIS, S.T. (1980) Stereopsis in human infants. *Science*, 207:323–24. **205**

FRAGER, R., & FADIMAN, J. (1984) *Personality and Personal Growth* (2nd ed.). New York: Harper & Row. **455**

FRANKENBURG, W.K., & DODDS, J.B. (1967) The Denver developmental screening test. *Journal of Pediatrics*, 71:181–91. **64**

FRANKIE, G., see HETHERINGTON & FRANKIE (1967).

FRANKLIN, J., see LEWINSOHN, FENN, & FRANKLIN (1982).

FRANKS, J.J., see BRANSFORD, BARCLAY, & FRANKS (1972).

FRANZOI, S.L., DAVIS, M.H., & YOUNG, R.D.

(1985) The effects of private self-consciousness and perspective taking on satisfaction in close relationships. *Journal of Personality and Social Psychology*, 48: 1584–94. **438**

FRASE, L.T. (1975) Prose processing. In G.H. Bower (ed.), *The Psychology of Learning and Motivation*, Vol. 9. New York: Academic Press. **256**

FRASER, S.C., see DIENER, FRASER, BEAMAN, & KELEM (1976).

FRAZIER, K. (ed.) (1986) *Science Confronts the Paranormal*. Buffalo: Prometheus Books. **145, 209, 211**

FREDRIKSON, M., see OHMAN, FREDRIKSON, HUGDAHL, & RIMMO (1976).

FREE, L.A., & CANTRIL, H. (1967) *The Political Beliefs of Americans*. New Brunswick, N.J.: Rutgers University Press. **586**

FREEDMAN, J.L. (1965) Long-term behavioral effects of cognitive dissonance. *Journal of Experimental Social Psychology*, 1:145–55. **585**

FREEDMAN, J.L., see SEARS, FREEDMAN, & PEPLAU (1985).

FREEMAN, S., WALKER, M.R., BORDEN, R., & LATANE, B. (1975) Diffusion of responsibility and restaurant tipping: Cheaper by the bunch. *Personality and Social Psychology Bulletin*, 1:584–87. **605**

FRENCH, G.M., & HARLOW, H.F. (1962) Variability of delayed-reaction performance in normal and brain-damaged rhesus monkeys. *Journal of Neurophysiology*, 25:585–99. **45**

FRENCH, J.W., see EKSTROM, FRENCH, & HARMAN (1979).

FRENCH, J.W., see EKSTROM, FRENCH, HARMAN, & DERMAN (1976).

FREUD, A. (1967) *The Ego and the Mechanisms of Defense* (rev. ed.). London: Hogarth Press. **487**

FREUD, S. (1885) *Ueber Coca*. Vienna: Moritz Perles. (Translated in Freud, 1974.) **128**

FREUD, S. (1900) *The Interpretation of Dreams*, Vols. 4, 5. (Reprint ed., London: Hogarth Press, 1953.) **121**

FREUD, S. (1948) *Three Contributions to Theory of Sex* (4th ed.; A.A. Brill, trans.). New York: Nervous and Mental Disease Monograph. **374**

FREUD, S. (1965) Revision of the theory of dreams. In Strachey, J. (ed. and trans.), *New Introductory Lectures on Psychoanalysis*, Vol. 22, Lect. 29. New York: Norton. (Essay originally published in 1933.) **121, 379, 455**

FREUD, S. (1974) *Cocaine Papers* (edited and introduction by R. Byck; notes by A. Freud). New York: Stonehill. (Originally published in 1885.) **128**

FREUD, S. (1975) *Beyond the Pleasure Principle*. New York: Norton. (Originally published in 1920.) **379**

FREUD, S. (1976) Repression. In Strachey, J. (ed. and trans.), *The Complete Psychological Works: Standard Edition*, Vol. 14. (Essay originally published in 1915.) **361**

FRICKE, B.G. (1975) *Report to the Faculty*. Ann Arbor: Evaluation and Examinations Office, University of Michigan. **397**

FRIED, C., see JACOBSON, FRIED, & HOROWITZ (1967).

FRIED, I., MATEER, C., OJEMANN, G., WOHNS, R., & FEDIO, P. (1982) Organization of visuospatial functions in human cortex. *Brain*, 105:349–71. **364**

FRIED, M. (1982) Disadvantage, vulnerability, and mental illness. In Parron, D.L., Solomon, F., & Jenkins, C.D. (eds.), *Behavior, Health Risks, and Social Disadvantage*. Washington, D.C.: National Academy Press. **517**

FRIEDMAN, M., & ROSENMAN, R.H. (1974) *Type A behavior and your heart*. New York: Knopf. **479, 482**

FRIEDMAN, M., THORESEN, C.E., GILL, J.J., et al. (1985) Alteration of Type A behavior and its effect upon cardiac recurrences in post-myocardial infarction subjects: Summary results of the recurrent coronary prevention project. Paper presented at meetings of the Society of Behavioral Medicine, New Orleans, March 1985. **483**

FRIEDMAN, M., see GILL, PRICE, FRIEDMAN, et al. (1985).

FRIEDMAN, M., see ROSENMAN, BRAND JENKINS, FRIEDMAN, STRAUS, & WRUM (1975).

FRIEDMAN, M.I., SHEFFIELD, F.D., WULFF, J.J., & BACKER, R. (1951) Reward value of copulation without sex drive reduction. *Journal of Comparative and Physiological Psychology*, 44:3–8. **347**

FRIEDMAN, M.I., & STRICKER, E.M. (1976) The physiological psychology of hunger: A physiological perspective. *Psychological Review*, 83:401–31. **323**

FRIEDMAN, M.I., see STRICKER, ROWLAND, SALTER, & FRIEDMAN (1977).

FRIEDMAN, M.P., see CARTERETTE & FRIEDMAN (1974–1978).

FRIEDMAN, R., see BENSON & FRIEDMAN (1985).

FRIESON, W.V., see EKMAN, LEVENSON, & FRIESON (1983).

FRISCHHOLZ, E.J. (1985) The relationship among dissociation, hypnosis, and child abuse in the development of multiple personality disorder. In Kluft, R.P. (ed.), *Childhood Antecedents of Multiple Personality*. Washington, D.C.: American Psychiatric Press. **113**

FROMKIN, V., KRASHEN, S., CURTISS, S.

RIGLER, D., & RIGLER, M. (1974) The development of language in Genie a case of language acquisition beyond the "critical period." *Brain and Language,* 1:81–107. **300**

FROMM, E. (1970) Age regression with unexpected reappearance of a repressed childhood language. *International Journal of Clinical and Experimental Hypnosis,* 18:79–88. **139**

FROMM, E., & SHOR, R.E. (eds.) (1979) *Hypnosis: Developments in Research and New Perspectives* (2nd. ed.). Chicago: Aldine. **145**

FUHRER, M.J., see BAER & FUHRER (1968).

FULCHER, R., see STAPP & FULCHER (1981).

FURNHAM, A. (1981) Personality and activity preference. *British Journal of Social and Clinical Psychology,* 20:57–68. **428**

G

GAIN, D., see MONEY, WIEDEKING, WALKER, & GAIN (1976).

GALANTER, E. (1962) Contemporary psychophysics. In Brown, R., et al. (eds.), *New Directions in Psychology,* Vol. 1. New York: Holt, Rinehart & Winston. **149**

GALLAGHER, P., see JANICAK, DAVIS, GIBBONS, ERICKSEN, CHANG, & GALLAGHER (1985).

GALLISTEL, C.R. (1973) Self-stimulation: The neurophysiology of reward and motivation. In Deutsch, J.A. (ed.), *The Physiological Basis of Memory.* New York: Academic Press. **231**

GALLISTEL, C.R., see GELMAN & GALLISTEL (1978).

GALVIN, J., see ZURIF, CARAMAZZA, MYERSON, & GALVIN (1974).

GAMSON, W.B., FIREMAN, B., & RYTINA, S. (1982) *Encounters With Unjust Authority.* Homewood, Ill.: Dorsey Press. **615, 616, 617**

GAMZU, E., see SCHWARTZ & GAMZU (1977).

GANZ, L., see SEKULER & GANZ (1963).

GARCIA, J., & KOELLING, R.A. (1966) The relation of cue to consequence in avoidance learning. *Psychonomic Science,* 4:123–24. **237**

GARDNER, B.T., & GARDNER, R.A. (1972) Two-way communication with an infant chimpanzee. In A.M. Schrier, & F. Stollnitz (eds.), *Behavior of Nonhuman Primates,* Vol. 4. New York: Academic Press. **300, 301**

GARDNER, H. (1975) *The Shattered Mind.* New York: Knopf. **143, 302, 303**

GARDNER, H. (1983) *Frames of Mind: The Theory of Multiple Intelligences.* New York: Basic Books. **406, 407**

GARDNER, H. (1985) *The Mind's New Science: A History of the Cognitive Revolution.* New York: Basic Books. **18, 27**

GARDNER, M. (1981) *Science: Good, Bad, and Bogus.* New York: Prometheus. **145**

GARDNER, R.A., see GARDNER & GARDNER (1972).

GARDNER, W.P., see LAMB, THOMPSON, GARDNER, CHARNOV, & ESTES (1984).

GARFIELD, S.L. (1980) *Psychotherapy: An Eclectic Approach.* New York: Wiley-Interscience. **550, 561**

GARMEZY, N. (1974) Children at risk: The search for the antecedents of schizophrenia: Pt. 2. Ongoing research programs, issues and intervention. *Schizophrenia Bulletin,* 1(No. 9):55–125. **518**

GARNER, W.R., see WIGDOR & GARNER (1982).

GARRETT, M.F. (1975) The analysis of sentence production. In Bower, G.H. (ed.), *The Psychology of Learning and Motivation,* Vol. 9. New York: Academic Press. **292**

GARRETT, M.F., see FODOR, BEVER, & GARRETT (1974).

GARROW, J. (1978) The regulation of energy expenditure. In Bray, G.A. (ed.), *Recent Advances in Obesity Research,* Vol. 2. London: Newman. **326**

GATCHEL, R.J., see BAUM, GATCHEL, FLEMING, & LAKE (1981).

GATES, A.I. (1917) Recitation as a factor in memorizing. *Archives of Psychology,* No. 40. **271, 630**

GAUTIER, T., see IMPERATO-MCGINLEY, PETERSON, GAUTIER, & STURLA (1979).

GEBHARD, P.H., see KINSEY, POMEROY, MARTIN, & GEBHARD (1953).

GEEN, R.G., BEATTY, W.W., & ARKIN, R.M. (1984) *Human Motivation: Physiological, Behavioral, and Social Approaches.* Boston: Allyn & Bacon. **347, 349**

GEEN, R.G., & QUANTY, M.B. (1977) The catharsis of aggression. In Berkowitz, L. (ed.), *Advances in Experimental Social Psychology,* Vol. 10. New York: Academic Press. **373**

GEER, J., & MAISEL, E. (1972) Evaluating the effects of the prediction-control confound. *Journal of Personality and Social Psychology,* 23:314–19. **472**

GEISLER, W.S. (1978) Adaptation, afterimages and cone saturation. *Vision Research,* 18:279–89. **156**

GELMAN, R., & GALLISTEL, C.R. (1978) *The Young Child's Understanding of Number: A Window on Early Cognitive Development.* Cambridge, Mass.: Harvard University Press. **75**

GELMAN, R., see STARKEY, SPELKE, & GELMAN (1986).

GERBNER, G., & GROSS, L. (1976) The scary world of TV's heavy viewer. *Psychology Today,* 9:41–45. **618**

GESCHWIND, N. (1972) Language and the brain. *Scientific American,* 226:10, 76–83. **303**

GESCHWIND, N. (1979) Specializations of the human brain. *Scientific American,* 241:180–99. **51**

GESCHWIND, N. (1984) The biology of cerebral dominance: Implications for cognition. *Cognition,* 17:193–208. **338**

GESELL, A., & THOMPSON, H. (1929) Learning and growth in identical twins: An experimental study by the method of co-twin control. *Genetic Psychology Monographs,* 6:1–123. **69**

GIBBONS, F.X., see SCHEIER, CARVER, & GIBBONS (1979).

GIBBONS, R.D., see JANICAK, DAVIS, GIBBONS, ERICKSEN, CHANG, & GALLAGHER (1985).

GIBSON, E.J., & WALK, R.D. (1960) The "visual cliff." *Scientific American,* 202:64–71. **205**

GIBSON, J.J. (1979) *The Ecological Approach to Visual Perception.* Boston: Houghton-Mifflin. **187**

GILL, J.J., PRICE, V.A., FRIEDMAN, M., et al. (1985) Reduction in Type A behavior in healthy middle-aged American military officers. *American Heart Journal,* 110:503–14. **483**

GILL, J.J., see FRIEDMAN, THORESEN, GILL, et al (1985).

GILL, M.M. (1972) Hypnosis as an altered and regressed state. *International Journal of Clinical and Experimental Hypnosis,* 20:224–337. **140**

GILLAM, B. (1980) Geometrical illusions. *Scientific American,* 240(No. 1):102–11. **190**

GILLIAN, J.C., see EICH, WEINGARTNER, STILLMAN, & GILLIAN (1975).

GILLIN, J.C., see KRIPKE & GILLIN (1985).

GILLUND, G., & SHIFFRIN, R.M. (1984) A retrieval model for both recognition and recall. *Psychological Review,* 91(No. 1):1–61. **261**

GILMARTIN, K., see SIMON & GILMARTIN (1973).

GILOVICH, T., see SCHMITT, GILOVICH, GOORE, & JOSEPH (in press).

GIRVIN, B. (1978) The nature of being schematic: Sex-role, self-schemas and differential processing of masculine and feminine information. Unpublished Ph.D. dissertation, Stanford University. **573**

GIRVIN, J.P., see DOBELLE, MEADEJOVSKY, & GIRVIN (1974).

GITTELMAN, R., & KLEIN, D.F. (1985) Childhood separation anxiety and adult agoraphobia. In Tuma, A.H., & Maser, J.D. (eds.), *Anxiety and the Anxiety Disorders.* Hillsdale, N.J.: Erlbaum. **497**

GJERDE, P.F., see BLOCK, BUSS, BLOCK, & GJERDE (1981).

GLADUE, B.A., GREEN, R., & HELLMAN, R.E. (1984) Neuroendocrine response to estrogen and sexual orientation. *Science,* 225:1496–98. **336**

GLANZER, M. (1972) Storage mechanisms in recall. In Bower, G.H., & Spence, J.T. (eds.), *The Psychology of Learning and Motivation,* Vol. 5. New York: Academic Press. **253**

GLASER, R., see CHI, GLASER, & REES (1982).

GLASS, A.L., & HOLYOAK, K.J. (1986) *Cognition* (2nd ed.). New York: Random House. **279**

GLASS, D.C., & SINGER, J.E. (1972) *Urban Stress: Experiments on Noise and Social Stressors.* New York: Academic Press. **472**

GLASS, D.C., see HENCHY & GLASS (1968).

GLASS, D.C., see WRIGHT, CONTRADA, & GLASS (1985).

GLASS, G.V., see SMITH, GLASS, & MILLER (1980).

GLASS, L.L., see KIRSCH & GLASS (1977).

GLEITMAN, H. (1963) Place-learning. *Scientific American,* 209:116–22. **239**

GLEITMAN, H., see ARMSTRONG, GLEITMAN, & GLEITMAN (1983).

GLEITMAN, L.R. (1984) Biological predispositions to learn language. In Marler, P., & Terrace, H.S. (eds.), *The Biology of Learning.* New York: Springer-Verlag. **294, 296**

GLEITMAN, L.R., see ARMSTRONG, GLEITMAN, & GLEITMAN (1983).

GLEITMAN, L.R., see FELDMAN, GOLDIN-MEADOW, & GLEITMAN (1978).

GLORIEUX, J., see GOLD, ANDRES, & GLORIEUX (1979).

GLUCK, M.A., & THOMPSON, R.F. (1986) Modeling the neural substrates of associative learning and memory: A computational approach. *Psychological Review,* in press. **221**

GOETHALS, G.R., see JONES, ROCK, SHAVER, GOETHALS, & WARD (1968).

GOLD, D., ANDRES, D., & GLORIEUX, J. (1979) The development of Francophone nursery-school children with employed and nonemployed mothers. *Canadian Journal of Behavioral Science,* 11:169–73. **80**

GOLDBERG, R.J. (1978) Development in the family and school context: Who is responsible for the education of young children in America? Paper presented at the National Association for the Education of Young Children Annual Conference, New York City. **81**

GOLDIN-MEADOW, S. (1982) The resilience of recursion: A structure within a conventional model. In Wanner, E., & Gleitman, L.R. (eds.), *Language Acquisition: The State of the Art.* Cambridge: Cambridge University Press. **65**

GOLDIN-MEADOW, S., see FELDMAN, GOLDIN-MEADOW, & GLEITMAN (1978).

GOLDMAN, W., & LEWIS, P. (1977) Beautiful is good: Evidence that the physically attractive are more socially skillful. *Journal of Experimental Social Psychology,* 13:125–30. **575**

GOLDSTEIN, E.B. (1984) *Sensation and Perception* (2nd ed.). Belmont, Calif.: Wadsworth. **179**

GOLDSTEIN, J.L. (1973) An optimum processor theory for the central formation of the pitch of complex tones. *Journal of the Acoustical Society of America,* 54:1496–1516. **172**

GOLDSTEIN, M.J. (1985) The UCLA family project. Paper presented at the High Risk Consortium Conference, San Francisco, April 1985. **518**

GOLDSTEIN, M.J., BAKER, B.L., & JAMISON, K.R. (1986) *Abnormal Psychology: Experiences, Origins, and Interventions* (2nd ed.). Boston: Little, Brown. **525**

GOLEMAN, D.J. (1977) *The Varieties of Meditative Experience.* New York: Dutton. **145**

GOODALL, J. (1978) Chimp killings: Is it the man in them? *Science News,* 113:276. **375**

GOODELL, H., see HARDY, WOLFF, & GOODELL (1947).

GOODENOUGH, D.R., see KOULACK & GOODENOUGH (1976).

GOODWIN, D.W., see HALIKAS, GOODWIN, & GUZE (1971).

GOODWIN, F.K., see POST, KOTIN, GOODWIN, & GORDON (1973).

GOORE, N., see SCHMITT, GILOVICH, GOORE, & JOSEPH (in press).

GORDON, B., see LICKEY & GORDON (1983).

GORDON, E. (1967) *A Three-Year Longitudinal Predictive Validity Study of the Musical Aptitude Profile.* Studies in the Psychology of Music, Vol. 5. Iowa City: University of Iowa Press. **384**

GORDON, E., see POST, KOTIN, GOODWIN, & GORDON (1973).

GORDON, E.W., see ZIGLER & GORDON (1981).

GOTTESMAN, I.I. (1963) Genetic aspects of intelligent behavior. In Ellis, N. (ed.), *Handbook of Mental Deficiency: Psychological Theory and Research.* New York: McGraw-Hill. **409**

GOTTESMAN, I.I., & SHIELDS, J. (1982) *Schizophrenia: The Epigenetic Puzzle.* New York: Cambridge University Press. **515, 525**

GOTTESMAN, I.I., see CAREY & GOTTESMAN (1981).

GOTTESMAN, I.I., see NICOL & GOTTESMAN (1983).

GOULD, A. (1977) Discarnate survival. In Wolman, B.B. (ed.), *Handbook of Parapsychology.* New York: Van Nostrand Reinhold. **143**

GOY, R.H., see PHOENIX, GOY, & RESKO (1968).

GOY, R.W. (1968) Organizing effect of androgen on the behavior of rhesus monkeys. In Michael, R.P. (ed.), *Endocrinology of Human Behaviour.* London: Oxford University Press. **338**

GRAFMAN, J., see WEINGARTEN, GRAFMAN, BOUTELLE, KAYE, & MARTIN (1983).

GRAHAM, N., see YAGER, KRAMER, SHAW, & GRAHAM (1984).

GRANBERG, D., & BRENT, E.E. (1974) Dove-hawk placements in the 1968 election: Application of social judgment and balance theories. *Journal of Personality and Social Psychology,* 29:687–95. **620**

GRANRUD, C.E., see YONAS, PETTERSEN, & GRANRUD (1982).

GRAVES, N., see HOFLING, BROTZMAN, DALRYMPLE, GRAVES, & PIERCE (1966).

GREEN, C., see MILLON, GREEN, MEAGHER (1982).

GREEN, D.M., & SWETS, J.A. (1966) *Signal Detection Theory and Psychophysics.* New York: Wiley. **153**

GREEN, D.M., & WIER, C.C. (1984) Auditory perception. In Darian-Smith, I. (ed.), *Handbook of Physiology,* Vol. 3. Bethesda, Md.: American Physiological Society. **169**

GREEN, H. (1971) *I Never Promised You a Rose Garden.* New York: New American Library. **525**

GREEN, R., see GLADUE, GREEN, & HELLMAN (1984).

GREENFIELD, P.M., see BRUNER, OLVER, GREENFIELD, et al. (1966).

GREENWALD, A.G., see SULS & GREENWALD (1983).

GREENWALD, B.S., see MOHS, DAVIS, GREENWALD, et al. (1985).

GREENWOOD, M.M., see BENSON, KOTCH, CRASSWELLER, & GREENWOOD (1977).

GRICE, H.P. (1975) Logic and conversation. In Harman, G., & Davidson, D. (eds.), *The Logic of Grammar.* Encino, Calif.: Dickinson. **294**

GRIFFITH, J.J., see MEDNICK, CUDECK, GRIFFITH, TALOVIC, & SCHULSINGER (1984).

GRIGGS, R.A., & COX, J.R. (1982) The elusive thematic-materials effect in Wason's selection task. *British Journal of Psychology*, 73:407–20. **288**

GROSS, L., see GERBNER & GROSS (1976).

GROSS, R.T., see CARLSMITH, DORNBUSCH, & GROSS (1983).

GROSSMAN, M.I., see JANOWITZ & GROSSMAN (1949).

GROVES, P.M., & SCHLESINGER, K. (1982) *Introduction to Biological Psychology* (2nd ed.). Dubuque: Brown. **59**

GRUEN, R., see FOLKMAN, LAZARUS, DUNKEL-SCHETTER, DELONGIS, & GRUEN (1986).

GUILFORD, J.P. (1982) Cognitive psychology's ambiguities: Some suggested remedies. *Psychological Review*, 89:48–49. **403**

GULEVICH, G., DEMENT, W.C., & JOHNSON, L. (1966) Psychiatric and EEG observations on a case of prolonged wakefulness. *Archives of General Psychiatry*, 15:29–35. **117**

GURMAN, A.S., & KNISKERN, D.P. (1981) *Handbook of Family Therapy*. New York: Brunner/Mazel. **545**

GUTIERRES, S.E., see KENRICK & GUTIERRES (1980).

GUZE, S.B., see HALIKAS, GOODWIN, & GUZE (1971).

H

HABER, R.N. (1969) Eidetic images. *Scientific American*, 220:36–55. **248**

HAGEN, F.P., see THORNDIKE, HAGEN, & SATTLER (1986).

HAITH, M.M., BERGMAN, T., & MOORE, M.J. (1977) Eye contact and face scanning in early infancy. *Science*, 198:853–55. **66**

HAKES, D.T., see FOSS & HAKES (1978).

HAKMILLER, K.L., see JASMOS & HAKMILLER (1975).

HALIKAS, J.A., GOODWIN, D.W., & GUZE, S.B. (1971) Marijuana effects: A survey of regular users. *Journal of American Medical Association*, 217:692–94. **130**

HALL, C.S., & LINDZEY, G. (1978) *Theories of Personality* (3rd ed.). New York: Wiley. **27**

HALL, C.S., LINDZEY, G., LOEHLIN, J.C., & MANOSEVITZ, M. (1985) *Introduction to Theories of Personality*. New York: Wiley. **455**

HAMBERGER, L.K., & LOHR, J.M. (1984) *Stress and Stress Management: Research and Applications*. New York: Springer. **487**

HAMBURG, D., & TRUDEAU, M.B. (eds.) (1981) *Biobehavioral Aspects of Aggression*. New York: Alan Liss. **379**

HAMILTON, D.L. (1979) A cognitive-attributional analysis of stereotyping. In Berkowitz, L. (ed.), *Advances in Experimental Social Psychology*, Vol. 12. New York: Academic Press. **568**

HAMILTON, E.W., & ABRAMSON, L.Y. (1983) Cognitive patterns and major depressive disorder: A longitudinal study in a hospital setting. *Journal of Abnormal Psychology*, 92:173–84. **509**

HAMILTON, M., see HENLEY, HAMILTON, & THORNE (1985).

HAMMERSMITH, S.K., see BELL, WEINBERG, & HAMMERSMITH (1981).

HAMPSON, J.L., see HUNT & HAMPSON (1980).

HANEY, T.L., see DEMBROSKI, MACDOUGALL, WILLIAMS, & HANEY (1985).

HANSEL, C.E.M. (1980) *ESP and Parapsychology: A Critical Reevaluation*. Buffalo: Prometheus Books. **210**

HARDY, A.B., see BANDURA, ADAMS, HARDY, & HOWELLS (1980).

HARDY, J.D., WOLFF, H.G., & GOODELL, H. (1947) Studies in pain: Discrimination of differences in intensity of a pain stimulus as a basis for a scale of pain intensity. *Journal of Clinical Investigation*, 26:1152–58. **175**

HARE, R.D. (1970) *Psychopathy: Theory and Research*. New York: Wiley. **521**

HARKINS, S.G., & PETTY, R.E. (1982) Effects of task difficulty and task uniqueness on social loafing. *Journal of Personality and Social Psychology*, 43:1214–29. **605**

HARKINS, S.G., see LATANE & HARKINS (1976).

HARKINS, S.G., see LATANE, WILLIAMS, & HARKINS (1979).

HARKINS, S.G., see PETTY, HARKINS, WILLIAMS, & LATANE (1977).

HARLOW, H.F. (1971) *Learning to Love*. San Francisco: Albion. **333**

HARLOW, H.F., HARLOW, M.K., & MEYER, D.R. (1950) Learning motivated by a manipulation drive. *Journal of Experimental Psychology*, 40:228–34. **343**

HARLOW, H.F., & SUOMI, S.J. (1970) Nature of love-simplified. *American Psychologist*, 25:161–68. **77**

HARLOW, H.F., see FRENCH & HARLOW (1962).

HARLOW, H.F., see SUOMI, HARLOW, & MCKINNEY (1972).

HARLOW, M.K., see HARLOW, HARLOW, & MEYER (1950).

HARMAN, H.H., see EKSTROM, FRENCH, & HARMAN (1979).

HARMAN, H.H., see EKSTROM, FRENCH, HARMAN, & DERMAN (1976).

HARPER, J., & COLLINS, J.K. (1972) The ef-

fects of early or late maturation on the prestige of the adolescent girl. *Australian and New Zealand Journal of Sociology*, 8:83–88. **96**

HARRE, R., & LAMB, R. (eds.) (1983) *The Encyclopedic Dictionary of Psychology*. Cambridge, Mass.: M.I.T. Press. **136**

HARRIS, T., see BROWN & HARRIS (1978).

HARRIS, V.A., see JONES & HARRIS (1967).

HARTMANN, E. (1984) *The Nightmare*. New York: Basic Books. **116**

HARTSHORNE, H., & MAY, M.A. (1929) *Studies in the Nature of Character: Vol. 2. Studies in Service and Self Control*. New York: Macmillan. **449**

HARTUP, W.W., & COATES, B. (1967) Imitation of a peer as a function of reinforcement from the peer group and rewardingness of the model. *Child Development*, 38:1003–16. **83**

HARTUP, W.W., & MOORE, S.G. (1963) Avoidance of inappropriate sex-typing by young children. *Journal of Consulting Psychology*, 27:467–73. **91**

HARVEY, E.N., see LOOMIS, HARVEY, & HOBART (1937).

HASTEY, J.M., see ARKIN, TOTH, BAKER, & HASTEY (1970).

HATFIELD, E., see TRAUPMANN & HATFIELD (1981).

HAURI, P. (1982) *Sleep Disorders*. Kalamazoo, Mich.: Upjohn. **145**

HAUTZINER, M., see LEWINSOHN, HOBERMAN, TERI, & HAUTZINER (1985).

HAVIGHURST, R.J., see EELLS, DAVIS, HAVIGHURST, HERRICK, & TYLER (1951).

HAWKINS, R.D., & KANDEL, E.R. (1984) Is there a cell-biological alphabet for simple forms of learning? *Psychological Review*, 91:375–91. **221**

HAYNES, S.G., FEINLEIB, M., & KANNEL, W.B. (1980) The relationship of psychosocial factors to coronary heart disease in the Framingham Study: Pt. 3. Eight-year incidence of coronary heart disease. *American Journal of Epidemiology*, 111 (No. 1):37–58. **482**

HEALD, F.P., see ROHN, SARTES, KENNY, REYNOLDS, & HEALD (1977).

HEBB, D.O. (1972) *Textbook of Psychology* (3rd ed.). Philadelphia: Saunders. **368**

HEBB, D.O. (1982) Understanding psychological man: A state-of-the-science report. *Psychology Today*, 16:52–53. **140**

HECHT, S., & HSIA, Y. (1945) Dark adaptation following light adaptation to red and white lights. *Journal of the Optical Society of America*, 35:261–67. **156**

HEDBERG, A., see WALKER, HEDBERG, CLEMENT, & WRIGHT (1981).

HEIDER, F. (1958) *The Psychology of Inter-*

personal Relations. New York: Wiley. **575, 576**

HEIN, A., & HELD, R. (1967) Dissociation of the visual placing response into elicited and guided components. *Science,* 158: 390–92. **207**

HEINGARTNER, A., see ZAJONC, HEINGARTNER, & HERMAN (1969).

HEISEL, S., see LOCKE, KRAUS, LESERMAN, HURST, HEISEL, & WILLIAMS (1984).

HELD, R. (1965a) Object and effigy. In Kepes, G. (ed.), *Structure in Art and Science.* New York: Braziller. **147**

HELD, R. (1965b) Plasticity in sensory-motor systems. *Scientific American,* 21(No. 5):84–94. **207**

HELD, R., see HEIN & HELD (1967).

HELLER, S.S., see CASE, HELLER, CASE, & MOSS (1985).

HELLMAN, R.E., see GLADUE, GREEN, & HELLMAN (1984).

HELMHOLTZ, H. VON (1857) *Treatise on Physiological Optics* (J.P. Southhall, trans.). New York: Dover. **160, 181**

HELZER, J.E., see ROBINS, HELZER, WEISSMAN, et al. (1984).

HEMMI, T. (1969) How we have handled the problem of drug abuse in Japan. In Sjoqvist, F., & Tottie, M. (eds.), *Abuse of Central Stimulants.* New York: Raven Press. **128**

HENCHY, T., & GLASS, D.C. (1968) Evaluation apprehension and social facilitation of dominant and subordinate responses. *Journal of Personality and Social Psychology,* 10:446–54. **599**

HENINGER, G.R., see CHARNEY & HENINGER (1983).

HENINGER, G.R., see CHARNEY, HENINGER, & STERNBERG (1984).

HENLEY, N., HAMILTON, M., & THORNE, B. (1985) Womanspeak and manspeak: Sex differences and sexism in communication, verbal and nonverbal. In Sargent, A.G. (ed.), *Beyond Sex Roles.* St. Paul, Minn.: West. **579**

HENSEL, H. (1973) Cutaneous thermoreceptors. In Iggo, A. (ed.), *Handbook of Sensory Physiology,* Vol. 2. Berlin: Springer-Verlag. **175**

HERING, E. (1878) *Outlines of a Theory of the Light Sense* (L.M. Hurvich & D. Jameson, trans.). Cambridge, Mass.: Harvard University Press. **160**

HERMAN, C.P., & POLIVY, J. (1980) Restrained eating. In Stunkard, A.J. (ed.), *Obesity.* Philadelphia: Saunders. **324**

HERMAN, C.P., see HIBSCHER & HERMAN (1977).

HERMAN, C.P., see POLIVY & HERMAN (1985).

HERMAN, E.M., see ZAJONC, HEINGARTNER, & HERMAN (1969).

HERMAN, J.H., see ROFFWARG, HERMAN, BOWE-ANDERS, & TAUBER (1978).

HERON, W., DOANE, B.K., & SCOTT, T.H. (1956) Visual disturbances after prolonged perceptual isolation. *Canadian Journal of Psychology,* 10:13–16. **344**

HERRICK, V.E., see EELLS, DAVIS, HAVIGHURST, HERRICK, & TYLER (1951).

HERRNSTEIN, R.J., & BORING, E.G. (1965) *A Source Book in the History of Psychology.* Cambridge, Mass.: Harvard University Press. **639**

HERRON, E., see HOGARTY, SCHOOLER, ULRICH, MUSSARE, FERRO, & HERRON (1979).

HERZ, M.J., see MCGAUGH & HERZ (1972).

HESS, E.H. (1958) "Imprinting" in animals. *Scientific American,* 198:81–90. **343**

HESS, E.H. (1972) "Imprinting" in a natural laboratory. *Scientific American,* 227:24–31. **343**

HESTON, L., see BOUCHARD, HESTON, ECKERT, KEYES, & RESNICK (1981).

HETHERINGTON, E.M., & FRANKIE, G. (1967) Effects of parental dominance, warmth, and conflict on imitation in children. *Journal of Personality and Social Psychology,* 6:119–25. **94**

HEWITT, E.C., see SPANOS & HEWITT (1980).

HEWITT, P., & MASSEY, J.O. (1969) *Clinical Clues From the WISC.* Palo Alto, Calif.: Consulting Psychologists Press. **397**

HIBSCHER, J.A., & HERMAN, C.P. (1977) Obesity, dieting, and the expression of "obese" characteristics. *Journal of Comparative and Physiological Psychology,* 91:374–80. **325**

HILGARD, E.R. (1961) Hypnosis and experimental psychodynamics. In Brosin, H. (ed.), *Lectures on Experimental Psychiatry.* Pittsburgh: Pittsburgh University Press. **23**

HILGARD, E.R. (1965) *Hypnotic Susceptibility.* New York: Harcourt Brace Jovanovich. **138, 475**

HILGARD, E.R. (1968) *The Experience of Hypnosis.* New York: Harcourt Brace Jovanovich. **145**

HILGARD, E.R. (1977) *Divided Consciousness: Multiple Controls in Human Thought and Action.* New York: Wiley-Interscience. **140, 144**

HILGARD, E.R. (1987) *Psychology in America: A Historical Survey.* San Diego: Harcourt Brace Jovanovich. **27, 639**

HILGARD, E.R., & HILGARD, J.R. (1975) *Hypnosis in the Relief of Pain.* Los Altos, Calif.: Kaufmann. **139**

HILGARD, E.R., HILGARD, J.R., MACDON-ALD, H., MORGAN, A.H., & JOHNSON, L.S. (1978) Covert pain in hypnotic analgesia: Its reality as tested by the real-simulator design. *Journal of Abnormal Psychology,* 87:655–63. **141**

HILGARD, E.R., see BANYAI & HILGARD (1976).

HILGARD, E.R., see BOWER & HILGARD (1981).

HILGARD, E.R., see KNOX, CRUTCHFIELD, & HILGARD (1975).

HILGARD, E.R., see RUCH, MORGAN, & HILGARD (1973).

HILGARD, J.R. (1979) *Personality and Hypnosis: A Study of Imaginative Involvement* (2nd ed.). Chicago: University of Chicago Press. **94, 145**

HILGARD, J.R., see HILGARD & HILGARD (1975).

HILGARD, J.R., see HILGARD, HILGARD, MACDONALD, MORGAN, & JOHNSON (1978).

HILL, C.T., RUBIN, Z., & PEPLAU, L.A. (1976) Breakups before marriage: The end of 103 affairs. *Journal of Social Issues,* 32:147–68. **591**

HILL, C.T., see PEPLAU, RUBIN, & HILL (1977).

HILL, C.T., see RUBIN, HILL, PEPLAU, & DUNKEL-SCHETTER (1980).

HILLERY, J.M., see HUNT & HILLERY (1973).

HIND, J.E., see ROSE, BRUGGE, ANDERSON, & HIND (1967).

HIRSCH, H.V.B., & SPINELLI, D.N. (1970) Visual experience modifies distribution of horizontally and vertically oriented receptive fields in cats. *Science,* 168:869–71. **206**

HIRSCH, J., & BATCHELOR, B.R. (1976) Adipose tissue cellularity and human obesity. *Clinical Endocrinology and Metabolism,* 5:299–311. **328**

HIRSCH, J., see KNITTLE & HIRSCH (1968).

HIRSH, S.R., & NATELSON, B.J. (1981) Electrical brain stimulation and food reinforcement dissociated by demand elasticity. *Physiology and Behavior,* 18:141–50. **235**

HIRST, W. (1982) The amnesic syndrome: Descriptions and explanations. *Psychological Bulletin,* 91(No. 3):435–60. **265**

HITCH, G.J., see BADDELEY & HITCH (1974).

HITCH, G.J., see BADDELEY & HITCH (1977).

HO, E., see WATKINS, HO, & TULVING (1976).

HOBART, G.A., see LOOMIS, HARVEY, & HOBART (1937).

HOBERMAN, H., see LEWINSOHN, HOBERMAN, TERI, & HAUTZINER (1985).

HOBSON, C.J., see COLEMAN, CAMPBELL, HOBSON, et al. (1966).

HOBSON, J.A., & MCCARLEY, R.W. (1977) The brain as a dream state generator: An activation-synthesis hypothesis of the dream process. *American Journal of Psychiatry*, 134:1335–48. **116**

HOCHBERG, J. (1978) *Perception* (2nd ed.). Englewood Cliffs, N.J.: Prentice-Hall. **184, 192, 211**

HODGSON, R.J., see RACHMAN & HODGSON (1980).

HOEBEL, B.G., & TEITELBAUM, P. (1966) Effects of force-feeding and starvation on food intake and body weight on a rat with ventromedial hypothalamic lesions. *Journal of Comparative and Physiological Psychology*, 61:189–93. **322**

HOEBEL, B.G., see CAGGIULA & HOEBEL (1966).

HOEBEL, B.G., see SMITH, KING, & HOEBEL (1970).

HOFFMAN, L.W. (1980) The effects of maternal employment on the academic attitudes and performance of school-aged children. *School Psychology Review*, 9:319–35. **80**

HOFFMAN, S., see ROSS, BIERBRAUER, & HOFFMAN (1976).

HOFLING, C.K. (1975) *Textbook of Psychiatry for Medical Practice* (3rd ed.). Philadelphia: Lippincott. **512**

HOFLING, C.K., BROTZMAN, E., DALRYMPLE, S., GRAVES, N., & PIERCE, C.M. (1966) An experimental study in nurse-physician relationships. *Journal of Nervous and Mental Disease*, 143:171–80. **613**

HOGARTY, G.E., SCHOOLER, N.R., ULRICH, R., MUSSARE, F., FERRO, P., & HERRON, E. (1979) Fluphenazine and social therapy in the after care of schizophrenic patients. *Archives of General Psychiatry*, 36:1283–94. **554**

HOGNESS, D.S., see NATHANS, THOMAS, & HOGNESS (1986).

HOHMANN, G.W. (1962) Some effects of spinal cord lesions on experienced emotional feelings. *Psychophysiology*, 3:143–56. **356**

HOHMANN, M., BANET, B., & WEIKART, D. (1979) *Young Children in Action.* Ypsilanti, Mich.: High Scope Press. **412**

HOLDEN, C. (1975) Lie detectors: PSE gains audience despite critic's doubt. *Science*, 190:359–62. **355**

HOLLAN, J.D., see WILLIAMS & HOLLAN (1981).

HOLLAND, C.C., see ORNE & HOLLAND (1968).

HOLLISTER, L.E., see DARLEY, TINKLENBERG, ROTH, HOLLISTER, & ATKINSON (1973).

HOLLISTER, L.E., see YESAVAGE, LEIER, DENARI, & HOLLISTER (1985).

HOLMES, D.S. (1974) Investigations of repression: Differential recall of material experimentally or naturally associated with ego threat. *Psychological Bulletin*, 81:632–53. **263**

HOLMES, D.S. (1984) Meditation and somatic arousal reduction: A review of the evidence. *American Psychologist*, 39:1–10. **136**

HOLMES, D.S. (1985) To meditate or to simply rest, that is the question: A response to the comments of Shapiro. *American Psychologist*, 40:722–25. **136**

HOLMES, T.H., & RAHE, R.H. (1967) The social readjustment rating scale. *Journal of Psychosomatic Research*, 11:213–18. **469**

HOLROYD, K.A., APPEL, M.A., & ANDRASIK, F. (1983) A cognitive-behavioral approach to psychophysiological disorders. In Meichenbaum, D., & Jaremko, M.E. (eds.), *Stress Reduction and Prevention.* New York: Plenum. **481**

HOLYOAK, K.J., see GLASS & HOLYOAK (1986).

HOLZMAN, P.S. (1970) *Psychoanalysis and Psychopathology.* New York: McGraw-Hill. **455**

HOLZMAN, P.S., see MENNINGER & HOLZMAN (1973).

HOMME, L.E., DE BACA, P.C., DEVINE, J.V., STEINHORST, R., & RICKERT, E.J. (1963) Use of the Premack principle in controlling the behavior of nursery school children. *Journal of the Experimental Analysis of Behavior*, 6:544. **232**

HONIG, W.K., & STADDON, J.E.R. (eds.) (1977) *Handbook of Operant Behavior.* Englewood Cliffs, N.J.: Prentice-Hall. **243**

HOOD, D.C., & FINKELSTEIN, M.A. (1983) A case for the revision of textbook models of color vision: The detection and appearance of small, brief lights. In Mollon, J.D., & Sharpe, L.T. (eds.), *Colour Vision: Physiology and Psychophysics.* London: Academic Press. **162**

HOOK, E.B. (1973) Behavioral implications of the human XYY genotype. *Science*, 179:139–50. **57**

HOOKER, E. (1957) The adjustment of the male overt homosexual. *Journal of Projective Techniques*, 22:33–54. **336**

HOPKINS, J.R. (1977) Sexual behavior in adolescence. *Journal of Social Issues*, 33:67–85. **334**

HOROWITZ, S.D., see JACOBSON, FRIED, & HOROWITZ (1967).

HORTON, R.W., see THOMAS, HORTON, LIPPINCOTT, & DRABMAN (1977).

HOVLAND, C. (1937) The generalization of conditioned responses: Pt. 1. The sensory generalization of conditioned responses with varying frequencies of tone. *Journal of General Psychology*, 17:125–48. **219**

HOWELLS, G.N., see BANDURA, ADAMS, HARDY, & HOWELLS (1980).

HRUBEC, Z., see STUNKARD, FOCH, & HRUBEC (1986).

HSIA, Y., see HECHT & HSIA (1945).

HUBEL, D.H., & WIESEL, T.N. (1963) Receptive fields of cells in striate cortex of very young visually inexperienced kittens. *Journal of Neurophysiology*, 26:994–1002. **205**

HUBEL, D.H., & WIESEL, T.N. (1968) Receptive fields and functional architecture of monkey striate cortex. *Journal of Physiology*, 195:215–43. **164**

HUBEL, D.H., see WIESEL & HUBEL (1974).

HUESMANN, L.R., ERON, L.D., LEFKOWITZ, M.M., & WALDER, L.O. (1984) Stability of aggression over time and generations. *Developmental Psychology*, 20:1120–34. **510**

HUESMANN, L.R., LAGERSPETZ, K., & ERON, L.D. (1984) Intervening variable in the TV violence-aggression relation: Evidence from two countries. *Developmental Psychology*, 20:746–75. **377**

HUESMANN, L.R., see ERON, HUESMANN, LEFKOWITZ, & WALDER (1972).

HUGDAHL, K., & OHMAN, A. (1977) Effects of instruction on acquisition and extinction of electrodermal response to fear-relevant stimuli. *Journal of Experimental Psychology: Human Learning and Memory*, 3(No. 5):608–18. **500**

HUGDAHL, K., see OHMAN, FREDRIKSON, HUGDAHL, & RIMMO (1976).

HULL, C.L. (1943) *Principles of Behavior.* New York: Appleton-Century-Crofts. **346**

HULLEY, S. see SHEKELLE, NEATON, JACOBS, HULLEY, & BLACKBURN (1983).

HUNT, D.D., & HAMPSON, J.L. (1980) Follow up of 17 biologic male transsexuals after sex reassignment surgery. *American Journal of Psychiatry*, 137:432–38. **340**

HUNT, E. (1985) Verbal ability. In Sternberg, R.J. (ed.), *Human Abilities: An Information-Processing Approach.* New York: Freeman. **404**

HUNT, M. (1974) *Sexual Behavior in the 1970's.* Chicago: Playboy Press. **335**

HUNT, P.J., & HILLERY, J.M. (1973) Social facilitation at different stages in learning. Paper presented at the Midwestern Psychological Association Meetings, Cleveland. **599**

HUNTER, E.J. (1979) Combat casualties who remain at home. Paper presented at Western Regional Conference of the Interuniversity Seminar, "Technology in

Combat." Navy Postgraduate School, Monterey, Calif., May 1979. **472**

HUNTER, I.M.L. (1974) *Memory.* Baltimore: Penguin. **274**

HURRY, J., see BEBBINGTON, STURT, TENNANT & HURRY (1984).

HURRY, J., see TENNANT, SMITH, BEBBINGTON, & HURRY (1981).

HURST, M.W., see LOCKE, KRAUS, LESERMAN, HURST, HEISEL, & WILLIAMS (1984).

HURVICH, L.M. (1981) *Color Vision.* Sunderland, Mass.: Sinauer Associates. **161, 179**

HUSTON, A.C., see MUSSEN, CONGER, KAGAN, & HUSTON (1984).

HUSTON, A.C., SEE O'BRIEN & HUSTON (1985).

HUSTON, T.L., & KORTE, C. (1976) The responsive bystander. In Lickona, T. (ed.), *Moral Development and Behavior.* New York: Holt, Rinehart & Winston. **86**

HUSTON, T.L., see JACKSON & HUSTON (1975).

HYDE, J.S. (1981) How large are cognitive gender differences? *American Psychologist,* 36:892–901. **92**

HYSON, R.L., see LAUDENSLAGER, RYAN, DRUGAN, HYSON, & MAIER (1983).

I

IMAYUMI, Y., see AWAYA, MIYAKE, IMAYUMI, SHIOSE, KNADA, & KOMURO (1973).

IMBER, S., see ELKIN, SHEA, & IMBER (1986).

IMPERATO-MCGINLEY, J., PETERSON, R.E., GAUTIER, T., & STURLA, E. (1979) Androgens and the evolution of male gender identity among male pseudohermaphrodites with 5 alpha reductase deficiency. *New England Journal of Medicine,* 300:1233–37. **339**

INHOFF, A.W., see RAYNER, INHOFF, MORRISON, SLOWIACZEK, & BERTERA (1981).

INOUYE, J., see DIGMAN & INOUYE (1986).

INSKO, C.A., see STROEBE, INSKO, THOMPSON, & LAYTON (1971).

INSTITUTE OF MEDICINE (1982) *Marijuana and Health.* Washington, D.C.: National Academy Press. **131, 145**

J

JACCARD, J.J., see DAVIDSON & JACCARD (1979).

JACKLIN, C.N., see MACCOBY & JACKLIN (1974).

JACKSON, D.J., & HUSTON, T.L. (1975) Physical attractiveness and assertiveness. *Journal of Social Psychology,* 96:79–84. **575**

JACKSON, D.N., see RUSHTON, JACKSON, & PAUNONEN (1981).

JACKSON, J.M., & LATANE, B. (1981) All alone in front of all those people: Stage fright as a function of number and type of coperformers and audience. *Journal of Personality and Social Psychology,* 40:73–85. **605**

JACOBS, D., see SHEKELLE, NEATON, JACOBS, HULLEY, & BLACKBURN (1983).

JACOBS, G.H., see DEVALOIS & JACOBS (1984).

JACOBSON, A., & KALES, A. (1967) Somnambulism: All-night EEG and related studies. In Kety, S.S., Evarts, E.V., & Williams, H.L. (eds.), *Sleep and Altered States of Consciousness.* Baltimore: Williams & Wilkins. **120**

JACOBSON, A.L., FRIED, C., & HOROWITZ, S.D. (1967) Classical conditioning, pseudoconditioning, or sensitization in the planarian. *Journal of Comparative and Physiological Psychology,* 64:73–79. **218**

JAMES, W. (1884) What is an emotion? *Mind,* 9:188–205. **351, 357**

JAMES, W. (1890) *The Principles of Psychology.* New York: Holt, Rinehart & Winston. **13, 257**

JAMISON, K.R., see GOLSTEIN, BAKER, & JAMISON (1986).

JANET, P. (1889) *L'Automisme psychologique.* Paris: Felix Alcan. **112**

JANICAK, P.G., DAVIS, J.M., GIBBONS, R.D., ERICKSEN, S., CHANG, S., & GALLAGHER, P. (1985) Efficacy of ECT: A meta-analysis. *American Journal of Psychiatry,* 142(No. 3):297–302. **556**

JANOWITZ, H.D., & GROSSMAN, M.I. (1949) Some factors affecting the food intake of normal dogs and dogs esophagostomy and gastric fistula. *American Journal of Physiology,* 159:143–48. **321**

JAREMKO, M.E., see MEICHENBAUM & JAREMKO (1983).

JARVIE, G.J., see THOMPSON, JARVIE, LAKEY, & CURETON (1982).

JASMOS, T.M., & HAKMILLER, K.L. (1975) Some effects of lesion level, and emotional cues on affective expression in spinal cord patients. *Psychological Reports,* 37:859–70. **356**

JEMMOTT, J.B., III, BORYSENKO, M., MCCLELLAND, D.C., CHAPMAN, R., MEYER, D., & BENSON, H. (1985) Academic stress, power motivation, and decrease in salivary secretory immunoglubulin: A secretion rate. *Lancet,* 1:1400–402. **484**

JEMMOTT, J.B., III, & LOCKE, S.E. (1984) Psychosocial Factors, immunologic medi-

ation, and human susceptibility to infectious diseases: How much do we know? *Psychological Bulletin,* 95:78–108. **484**

JENKINS, C.D., see ROSENMAN, BRAND, JENKINS, FRIEDMAN, STRAUS, & WRUM (1975).

JENKINS, H.M., & MOORE, B.R. (1973) The form of the autoshaped response with food or water reinforcers. *Journal of the Experimental Analysis of Behavior,* 20:163–81. **228**

JENKINS, H.M., see BROWN & JENKINS (1968).

JENSEN, A.R. (1980) *Bias in Mental Testing.* New York: Free Press. **409, 410**

JENSEN, R.A., see MCGAUGH, JENSEN, & MARTINEZ (1979).

JING, Q., see YU, ZHANG, JING, PENG, ZHANG, & SIMON (1985).

JOFFE, J.M., see BOND & JOFFE (1982).

JOHN, R.S., MEDNICK, S.A., & SCHULSINGER, F. (1982) Teacher reports as a predictor of schizophrenia and borderline schizophrenia: A Bayesian decision analysis. *Journal of Abnormal Psychology,* 91:399–413. **518**

JOHNSON, H.H., & SOLSO, R.L. (1978) *An Introduction to Experimental Design in Psychology: A Case Approach* (2nd ed.). New York: Harper & Row. **27**

JOHNSON, L., see GULEVICH, DEMENT, & JOHNSON (1966).

JOHNSON, L.S., see HILGARD, HILGARD, MACDONALD, MORGAN, & JOHNSON (1978).

JOHNSON, M.K., see BRANSFORD & JOHNSON (1973).

JOHNSON, R.D., & DOWNING, L.L. (1979) Deindividuation and valence of cues: Effects on prosocial and antisocial behavior. *Journal of Personality and Social Psychology,* 37:1532–38. **602**

JOHNSON, R.N. (1972) *Aggression in Man and Animals.* Philadelphia: Saunders. **379**

JOHNSON, V.E., see MASTERS & JOHNSON (1966).

JOHNSON-LAIRD, P.N. (1983) *Mental Models: Toward a Cognitive Science of Language, Inference, and Consciousness.* Cambridge, Mass.: Harvard University Press. **288**

JOHNSON-LAIRD, P.N. (1985) The deductive reasoning ability. In Sternberg, R.J. (ed.), *Human Abilities: An Information-Processing Approach.* New York: Freeman. **307**

JOHNSON-LAIRD, P.N., see WASON & JOHNSON-LAIRD (1972).

JOHNSTON, L.D., O'MALLEY, P.M., & BACHMAN, J.G. (1986) *Drug Use Among American High School Students, College Students, and Other Young Adults.* Rockville, Md.: National Institute on Drug Abuse. DHHS

Publication No. (ADM) 86–1450. **123, 128**

JONES, E.E., & BERGLAS, S. (1978) Control of attributions about the self through self-handicapping strategies: The appeal of alcohol and the role of underachievement. *Personality and Social Psychology Bulletin,* 4:200–206. **428**

JONES, E.E., & HARRIS, V.A. (1967) The attribution of attitudes. *Journal of Experimental Social Psychology,* 3:1–24. **577**

JONES, E.E., ROCK, L., SHAVER, K.G., GOETHALS, G.R., & WARD, L.M. (1968) Pattern of performance and ability attribution: An unexpected primacy effect. *Journal of Personality and Social Psychology,* 9:317–40. **569**

JONES, H.C., & LOVINGER, P.W. (1985) *The Marijuana Question and Science's Search for an Answer.* New York: Dodd, Mead. **131**

JONES, K.L., see STREISSGUTH, CLARREN, & JONES (1985).

JONES, L.V. (1984) White-Black Achievement Differences: The Narrowing Gap. *American Psychologist,* 39:1207–13. **398, 401, 411**

JONES, M.C. (1965) Psychological correlates of somatic development. *Child Development,* 36:899–911. **96**

JORGENSON, B.W., see LEVINGER, SENN, & JORGENSEN (1970).

JOSEPH, L., see SCHMITT, GILOVICH, GOORE, & JOSEPH (in press).

JULESZ, B. (1971) *Foundations of Cyclopean Perception.* Chicago: University of Chicago Press. **185**

JULIEN, R.M. (1985) *A Primer of Drug Action* (4th ed.). New York: Freeman. **59, 145, 554**

JUNG, R. (1984) Sensory research in historical perspective: Some philosophical foundations of perception. In Darian-Smith, I. (ed.), *Handbook of Physiology,* Vol. 3. Bethesda, Md.: American Physiological Society. **147**

JUNGEBLUT, A., see MESSICK & JUNGEBLUT (1981).

JUSCZYK, P., see EIMAS, SIQUELAND, JUSCZYK, & VIGORITO (1971).

JUST, M.A., & CARPENTER, P.A. (1980) A theory of reading: From eye fixations to comprehension. *Psychological Review,* 87:329–54. **200**

K

KAGAN, J. (1979) Overview: Perspectives on human infancy. In Osofsky, J.D. (ed.), *Handbook of Infant Development.* New York: Wiley-Interscience. **63, 76**

KAGAN, J., KEARSLEY, R., & ZELAZO, P.R. (1978) *Infancy: Its Place in Human Development.* Cambridge, Mass.: Harvard University Press. **80, 81**

KAGAN, J., & KLEIN, R.E. (1973) Crosscultural perspectives on early development. *American Psychologist,* 28:947–61. **70**

KAGAN, J., see MUSSEN, CONGER, KAGAN, & HUSTON (1984).

KAHN, S., see KOBASA, MADDI, & KAHN (1982).

KAHNEMAN, D., SLOVIC, P., & TVERSKY, A. (eds.) (1982) *Judgment Under Uncertainty: Heuristics and Biases.* New York: Cambridge University Press. **311**

KAHNEMAN, D., & TREISMAN, A. (1984) Changing views of attention. In Parasuraman, R., Davies, D., & Beatty, J. (eds.), *Varieties of Attention.* New York: Academic Press. **199**

KAHNEMAN, D., see TVERSKY & KAHNEMAN (1973).

KAHNEMAN, D., see TVERSKY & KAHNEMAN (1983).

KAIL, R. (1984) *The Development of Memory in Children* (2nd ed.). New York: Freeman. **105**

KAIL, R., & PELLEGRINO, J.W. (1985) *Human Intelligence: Perspectives and Prospects.* New York: Freeman. **415**

KALES, A., see JACOBSON & KALES (1967).

KAMIN, L.J. (1969) Predictability, surprise, attention, and conditioning. In Campbell, B.A. & Church, R.M. (eds.), *Punishment and Aversive Behavior.* New York: Appleton-Century-Crofts. **222**

KAMIN, L.J. (1976) Heredity, intelligence, politics, and psychology. In Block, N.J., & Dworkin, G. (eds.), *The IQ Controversy.* New York: Pantheon. **409, 410**

KAMIN, L.J., see LEWONTIN, ROSE, & KAMIN (1984).

KAMMANN, R., see MARKS & KAMMANN (1977).

KAMMANN, R., see MARKS & KAMMANN (1980).

KANDEL, D.B. (1975) Stages in adolescent involvement in drug use. *Science,* 190:912–14. **132**

KANDEL, D.B., & LOGAN, J.A. (1984) Patterns of drug use from adolescence to young adulthood: Pt. 1. Periods of risk for initiation, continued use, and discontinuation. *American Journal of Public Health,* 74(No. 7). **132**

KANDEL, D.B., see ANDREWS AND KANDEL (1979).

KANDEL, E.R. (1979) Small systems of neurons. In Thompson, R. (ed.), *The Brain.* San Francisco: Freeman. **220, 221**

KANDEL, E.R., see CASTELLUCI & KANDEL (1976).

KANDEL, E.R., see HAWKINS & KANDEL (1984).

KANNEL, W.B., see HAYNES, FEINLEIB, & KANNEL (1980).

KANNER, A.D., see LAZARUS, KANNER, & FOLKMAN (1980).

KANTER, J.F., see ZELNIK & KANTER (1977).

KAPLAN, J. (1983) *The Hardest Drug: Heroin and Public Policy.* Chicago: University of Chicago Press. **145**

KARABENICK, S.A., see LERNER & KARABENICK (1974).

KATZ, E., & FELDMAN, J.J. (1962) The debates in the light of research: A survey of surveys. In Kraus, S. (ed.), *The Great Debates.* Bloomington: Indiana University Press. **619**

KATZ, R., & WYKES, T. (1985) The psychological difference between temporally predictable and unpredictable stressful events: Evidence for information control theories. *Journal of Personality and Social Psychology,* 48:781–90. **471**

KATZMAN, N., see COMSTOCK, CHAFFEE, KATZMAN, MCCOMBS, & ROBERTS (1978).

KAUFMAN, L., see BOFF, KAUFMAN, & THOMAS (1986).

KAUL, T.J., see BEDNAR & KAUL (1978).

KAY, P. see BERLIN & KAY (1969).

KAYE, W., see WEINGARTEN, GRAFMAN, BOUTELLE, KAYE, & MARTIN (1983).

KAZDIN, A.E. (1982) Symptom substitution, generalization, and response covariation: Implications for psychotherapy outcome. *Psychological Bulletin,* 91:349–65. **536**

KAZDIN, A.E., see CRAIGHEAD, KAZDIN, & MAHONEY (1981).

KEARSLEY, R., see KAGAN, KEARSLEY, & ZELAZO (1978).

KEELE, S.W., see POSNER & KEELE (1967).

KEEN, E. (1982) *A Primer in Phenomenological Psychology.* New York: Holt, Rinehart & Winston. **455**

KEESEY, R.E., & POWLEY, T.L. (1975) Hypothalamic regulation of body weight. *American Scientist,* 63:558–65. **323**

KEESEY, R.E., see MITCHEL & KEESEY (1974).

KEESEY, R.E., see POWLEY & KEESEY (1970).

KEIL, F.C., & BATTERMAN, N.A. (1984) Characteristic-to-defining shift in the development of word meaning. *Journal of Verbal Learning and Verbal Behavior,* 23:221–36. **284**

KELEM, R.T., see DIENER, FRASER, BEAMAN, & KELEM (1976).

KELLER, S.E., see SCHLEIFER, KELLER, MCKEGNEY, & STEIN (1979).

KELLERMAN, H., see PLUTCHIK & KELLERMAN (1980).

KELLEY, H.H. (1967) Attribution theory in social psychology. In Levine, D. (ed.), *Nebraska Symposium on Motivation,* Vol. 15.

Lincoln: University of Nebraska Press. **575**

KELLEY, H.H. (1973) The processes of causal attribution. *American Psychologist,* 28: 107–28. **576**

KELLEY, H.H., & WOODRUFF, C.L. (1956) Members' reactions to apparent group approval of a counternorm communication. *Journal of Abnormal and Social Psychology,* 52:67–74. **623**

KELLEY, S., JR., & MIRER, T.W. (1974) The simple act of voting. *American Political Science Review,* 68:572–91. **583**

KELMAN, H.C. (1961) Processes of opinion change. *Public Opinion Quarterly,* 25:57–78. **597**

KEMLER NELSON, D.G. (1984) The effect of intention on what concepts are acquired. *Journal of Verbal Learning and Verbal Behavior,* 23:734–59. **285**

KENDALL, P.C., & BUTCHER, J.N. (eds.) (1982) *The Handbook of Research Methods in Clinical Psychology.* New York: Wiley. **561**

KENNEDY, C.E. (1978) *Human Development: The Adult Years and Aging.* New York: Macmillan. **105**

KENNEDY, R.A., see WILKES & KENNEDY (1969).

KENNY, T.J., see ROHN, SARTES, KENNY, REYNOLDS, & HEALD (1977).

KENRICK, D.T., & GUTIERRES, S.E. (1980) Contrast effects and judgments of physical attractiveness: When beauty becomes a social problem. *Journal of Personality and Social Psychology,* 38, 131–40. **589**

KENRICK, D.T., see SCHUTTE, KENRICK & SADALLA (1985).

KENSHALO, D.R., NAFE, J.P., & BROOKS, B. (1961) Variations in thermal sensitivity. *Science,* 134, 104–105. **175**

KEPHART, W.M. (1967) Some correlates of romantic love. *Journal of Marriage and the Family,* 29:470–74. **593**

KEPPEL, G., & SAUFLEY, W.H., JR. (1980) *Introduction to Design and Analysis.* San Francisco: Freeman. **651**

KERNIS, M.H., & WHEELER, L. (1981) Beautiful friends and ugly strangers: Radiation and contrast effects in perception of same-sex pairs. *Journal of Personality and Social Psychology,* 7:617–20. **589**

KEYES, M., see BOUCHARD, HESTON, ECKERT, KEYES, & RESNICK (1981).

KIESLER, C.A. (1982) Mental hospitals and alternative care: Noninstitutionalization as potential policy for mental patients. *American Psychologist,* 34:349–60. **530**

KIHLSTROM, J.F. (1984) Conscious, subconscious, unconscious: A cognitive view. In Bowers, K.S., & Meichenbaum, D. (eds.),

The Unconscious: Reconsidered. New York: Wiley. **110, 111**

KIHLSTROM, J.F. (1985) Hypnosis. *Annual Review of Psychology,* 36:385–418. **137, 138, 139, 141**

KIMBLE, G.A., & PERLMUTER, L.C. (1970) The problem of volition. *Psychological Review,* 77:361–84. **225**

KIMMEL, D.C., & WEINER, I.B. (1985) *Adolescence: A Developmental Transition.* Hillsdale, N.J.: Erlbaum. **105**

KINDER, D.R., & SEARS, D.O. (1985) Public opinion and political action. In Lindzey, G., & Aronson, E. (eds.), *The Handbook of Social Psychology* (3rd ed.). New York: Random House. **586**

KING, M., see SMITH, KING, & HOEBEL (1970).

KINSEY, A.C., POMEROY, W.B., & MARTIN, C.E. (1948) *Sexual Behavior in the Human Male.* Philadelphia: Saunders. **20, 97, 335**

KINSEY, A.C., POMEROY, W.B., MARTIN, C.E., & GEBHARD, P.H. (1953) *Sexual Behavior in the Human Female.* Philadelphia: Saunders. **21, 97, 335**

KINTSCH, W., & BUSCHKE, H. (1969) Homophones and synonyms in short-term memory. *Journal of Experimental Psychology,* 80:403–407. **255**

KINTSCH, W., see MILLER & KINTSCH (1980).

KIRKER, W.S., see ROGERS, KUIPER, & KIRKER (1977).

KIRSCH, M.A., & GLASS L.L. (1977) Psychiatric disturbances associated with Erhard Seminars Training: Pt. 2. Additional cases and theoretical considerations. *American Journal of Psychiatry,* 134:1254–58. **545**

KLATZKY, R.L. (1980) *Human Memory: Structures and Processes* (2nd ed.). San Francisco: Freeman. **279**

KLATZKY, R.L., LEDERMAN, S.J., & METZGER, V.A. (1985) Identifying objects by touch: An expert system. *Perception and Psychophysics,* 37:299–302. **176**

KLEIN, D.F., see GITTELMAN & KLEIN (1985).

KLEIN, R.E., see KAGAN & KLEIN (1973).

KLEINHESSELINK, R.R., & EDWARDS, R.W. (1975) Seeking and avoiding belief-discrepant information as a function of its perceived refutability. *Journal of Personality and Social Psychology,* 31:787–90. **620**

KLEINMUNTZ, B. (1974) *Essentials of Abnormal Psychology.* New York: Harper & Row. **496**

KLEITMAN, N., see DEMENT & KLEITMAN (1957).

KLENTZ, B., see BEAMAN, BARNES, KLENTZ, & MCQUIRK (1978).

KLINEBERG, O. (1938) Emotional expression in Chinese literature. *Journal of Abnormal and Social Psychology,* 33:517–20. **363**

KLUFT, R.P. (ed.) (1985) *Childhood Antecedents of Multiple Personality.* Washington, D.C.: American Psychiatric Press. **144**

KNADA, T., see AWAYA, MIYAKE, IMAYUMI, SHIOSE, KNADA, & KOMURO (1973).

KNIGHT, J., see MITA, DERMER, & KNIGHT (1977).

KNIGHT, R., see ROFF & KNIGHT (1981).

KNISKERN, D.P., see GURMAN & KNISKERN (1981).

KNITTLE, J.L., & HIRSCH, J. (1968) Effect of early nutrition on the development of rat epididymal fat pads: Cellularity and metabolism. *Journal of Clinical Investigation,* 47:2091. **328**

KNOX, V.J., CRUTCHFIELD, L., & HILGARD, E.R. (1975) The nature of task interference in hypnotic dissociation: An investigation of hypnotic behavior. *International Journal of Clinical and Experimental Hypnosis,* 23:305–23. **141**

KOBASA, S.C. (1979) Stressful life events, personality, and health: An inquiry into hardiness. *Journal of Personality and Social Psychology,* 37:1–11. **485**

KOBASA, S.C., MADDI, S.R., & KAHN, S. (1982) Hardiness and health: A prospective study. *Journal of Personality and Social Psychology,* 42:168–77. **485**

KOBASIGAWA, A., ARAKAKI, K., & AWIGUNI, A. (1966) Avoidance of feminine toys by kindergarten boys: The effects of adult presence or absence, and an adult's attitudes toward sextyping. *Japanese Journal of Psychology,* 37:96–103. **91**

KOELLING, R.A., see GARCIA & KOELLING (1966).

KOENIG, K.E., see NEWCOMB, KOENIG, FLACKS, & WARWICK (1967).

KOHLBERG, L. (1969) Stage and sequence: The cognitive-developmental approach to socialization. In Goslin, D.A. (ed.), *Handbook of Socialization Theory and Research.* Chicago: Rand McNally. **84, 85, 86**

KOHLBERG, L. (1973) Implications of developmental psychology for education: Examples from moral development. *Educational Psychologist,* 10:2–14. **84, 85**

KOHLBERG, L. (1984) *The Psychology of Moral Development:* Vol. 1. *Moral Stages and the Life Cycle:* Vol. 2. *Essays on Moral Development.* New York: Harper & Row. **84, 85**

KÖHLER, W. (1925) *The Mentality of Apes.* New York: Harcourt Brace. (Reprint ed., 1976. New York: Liveright.) **240, 243**

KOLB, B., & WHISHAW, I.Q. (1985) *Fundamentals of Human Neuropsychology* (2nd ed.). San Francisco: Freeman. **59**

KOLB, S., see ZELAZO, ZELAZO, & KOLB (1972).

KOLODNER, J.L. (1983) Maintaining organization in a dynamic long-term memory. *Cognitive Science*, 7:243–80. **276**

KOMURO, K., see AWAYA, MIYAKE, IMAYUMI, SHIOSE, KNADA, & KOMURO (1973).

KORNER, A.F. (1973) Individual differences at birth: Implications for early experience and later development. In Westman, J.C. (ed.), *Individual Differences in Children*. New York: Wiley. **68**

KORTE, C., see HUSTON & KORTE (1976).

KOSA, J., & ZOLA, I.K. (eds.) (1975) *Poverty and Health: A Sociological Analysis*. Cambridge, Mass.: Harvard University Press. **517**

KOSSLYN, S.M. (1980) *Image and Mind*. Cambridge, Mass.: Harvard University Press. **304, 311**

KOSSLYN, S.M. (1983) *Ghosts in the Mind's Machine*. New York: Norton. **303, 311**

KOSSLYN, S.M., BALL, T.M., & REISER, B.J. (1978) Visual images preserve metric spatial information: Evidence from studies of image scanning. *Journal of Experimental Psychology: Human Perception and Performance*, 4:47–60. **305**

KOTCH, J.B., see BENSON, KOTCH, CRASSWELLER, & GREENWOOD (1977).

KOTELCHUCK, M. (1976) The infant's relationship to the father: Experimental evidence. In Lamb, M. (ed.), *The Role of the Father in Child Development*. New York: Wiley. **82**

KOTIN, J., see POST, KOTIN, GOODWIN, & GORDON (1973).

KOULACK, D., & GOODENOUGH, D.R. (1976) Dream recall and dream recall failure: An arousal-retrieval model. *Psychological Bulletin*, 83:975–84. **119**

KOVACH, J., see MURPHY & KOVACH (1972).

KOWET, D. (1983) *The Jet Lag Book*. New York: Crown. **115**

KRAMER, P., see YAGER, KRAMER, SHAW, & GRAHAM (1984).

KRASHEN, S., see FROMKIN, KRASHEN, CURTISS, RIGLER, & RIGLER (1974).

KRAUS, L., see LOCKE, KRAUS, LESERMAN, HURST, HEISEL, & WILLIAMS (1984).

KREITMAN, N. (1977) *Parasuicide*. London: Wiley. **505**

KRETSCHMER, E. (1925) *Physique and Character*. London: Kegan Paul. **419, 420**

KRIPKE, D.F., & GILLIN, J.C. (1985) Sleep disorders. In Klerman, G.L., Weissman, M.M., Applebaum, P.S., & Roth, L.N. (eds.), *Psychiatry*, Vol. 3. Philadelphia: Lippincott. **117**

KTSANES, T., see WINCH, KTSANES, & KTSANES (1954).

KTSANES, V., see WINCH, KTSANES, & KTSANES (1954).

KUBIS, J.F. (1962). Cited in B.M. Smith, "The polygraph." In Atkinson, R.C. (ed.), *Contemporary Psychology*. San Francisco: Freeman. **354**

KUHN, D., NASH, S.C., & BRUCKEN, L. (1978) Sex role concepts of two- and three-year-olds. *Child Development*, 49:445–51. **90**

KUHN, T.S. (1970) *The Structure of Scientific Revolutions* (2nd ed.). Chicago: University of Chicago Press. **586**

KUIPER, N.A., see ROGERS, KUIPER, & KIRKER (1977).

KUMAN, I.G., FEDROV, C.N., & NOVIKOVA, L.A. (1983) Investigation of the sensitive period in the development of the human visual system. *Zh. Vyshp. Nerv. Deyat (Journal of Higher Nervous Activity)*, 33:434–41. **65**

KURTZ, P. (ed.) (1985) *A Skeptic's Handbook of Parapsychology*. Buffalo: Prometheus Books. **145, 209, 211**

KWAN, M.W., see NEGRETE & KWAN (1972).

L

LADER, M. (1985) Benzodiasepines, anxiety and catecholamines: A commentary. In Tuma, A.H., & Maser, J.D. (eds.), *Anxiety and the Anxiety Disorders*. Hillsdale, N.J.: Erlbaum. **502**

LAGE, E., see MOSCOVICI, LAGE, & NAFFRECHOUX (1969).

LAGERSPETZ, K., VIEMERO, V., & AKADEMI, A. (1986) Television and aggressive behavior among Finnish children. In Huesmann, L.R., & Eron, L.D. (eds.), *Television and the Aggressive Child*. New York: Erlbaum. **376**

LAGERSPETZ, K., see HUESMANN, LAGERSPETZ, & ERON (1984).

LAIRD, J.D. (1974) Self-attribution of emotion: The effects of expressive behavior on the quality of emotional experience. *Journal of Personality and Social Psychology*, 29:475–86. **365**

LAIRD, N.M., see DER SIMONIAN & LAIRD (1983).

LAKE, C.R., see BAUM, GATCHEL, FLEMING, & LAKE (1981).

LAKEY, B.B., see THOMPSON, JARVIE, LAKEY, & CURETON (1982).

LAMB, M.E., & CAMPOS, J.J. (1982) *Development in Infancy: An Introduction*. New York: Random House. **105**

LAMB, M.E., THOMPSON, R.A., GARDNER, W.P., CHARNOV, E.L., & ESTES, D. (1984) Security of infantile attachment as assessed in the "Strange Situation": Its study and biological interpretation. *Behavioral and Brain Sciences*, 7:127–54. **81**

LAMB, R., see HARRE & LAMB (1983).

LAMBERT, M.J., see BERGIN & LAMBERT (1978).

LAND, E.H. (1977) The retinex theory of color vision. *Scientific American*, 237(No. 6):108–28. **188**

LANDY, D., see SIGALL & LANDY (1973).

LANGER, E.J., BLANK, A., & CHANOWITZ, B. (1978) The mindlessness of ostensibly thoughtful action. *Journal of Personality and Social Psychology*, 36:635–42. **569, 571**

LANGLOIS, J.H., & DOWNS, A.C. (1980) Mothers, fathers, and peers as socialization agents of sex-typed play behaviors in young children. *Child Development*, 51:1237–47. **91**

LAPIERE, R. (1934) Attitudes versus actions. *Social Forces*, 13:230–37. **583**

LARKIN, J.H., MCDERMOTT, J., SIMON, D.P., & SIMON, H.A. (1980) Expert and novice performance in solving physics problems. *Science*, 208:1335–42. **308**

LATANE, B. (1981) The psychology of social impact. *American Psychologist*, 36:343–56. **604, 605**

LATANE, B., & DARLEY, J.M. (1968) Group inhibition of bystander intervention in emergencies. *Journal of Personality and Social Psychology*, 10:215–21. **603**

LATANE, B., & DARLEY, J.M. (1970) *The Unresponsive Bystander: Why Doesn't He Help?* New York: Appleton-Century-Crofts. **602, 627**

LATANE, B., & HARKINS, S.G. (1976) Cross-modality matches suggest anticipated stage fright, a multiplicative power function of audience size and status. *Perception and Psychophysics*, 20:482–88. **604**

LATANE, B., & RODIN, J. (1969) A lady in distress: Inhibiting effects of friends and strangers on bystander intervention. *Journal of Experimental and Social Psychology*, 5:189–202. **603**

LATANE, B., WILLIAMS, K.D., & HARKINS, S.G. (1979) Many hands make light work: The causes and consequences of social loafing. *Journal of Personality and Social Psychology*, 37:822–32. **605**

LATANE, B., see DARLEY & LATANE (1968).

LATANE, B., see FREEMAN, WALKER, BORDEN, & LATANE (1975).

LATANE, B., see JACKSON & LATANE (1981).

LATANE, B., see PETTY, HARKINS, WILLIAMS, & LATANE (1977).

LATERRE, C., see BRUYER, LATERRE, SERON, et al. (1983).

LAUDENSLAGER, M., see MAIER & LAUDENSLAGER (1985).

LAUDENSLAGER, M.L., RYAN, S.M., DRUGAN, R.C., HYSON, R.L., & MAIER, S.F. (1983) Coping and immunosuppression:

710

Inescapable but not escapable shock suppresses lymphocyte proliferation. *Science,* 221:568–70. **484**

LAUER, J., & LAUER, R. (1985) Marriages made to last. *Psychology Today,* 19(No. 6):22–26. **102, 103**

LAUGHLIN, H.P. (1967) *The Neuroses.* Washington, D.C.: Butterworths. **498**

LAURENCE, J.R. (1980) Duality and dissociation in hypnosis. Unpublished M.A. thesis, Concordia University, Montreal. **141**

LAYTON, B.D., see STROEBE, INSKO, THOMPSON, & LAYTON (1971).

LAZAR, I., & DARLINGTON, R. (1982) Lasting effects of early education: A report from the Consortium for Longitudinal Studies. *Monographs of the Society for Research in Child Development,* 47:2–3. **412**

LAZARUS, R.S., & FOLKMAN, S. (1984) *Stress, Appraisal, and Coping.* New York: Springer. **460, 461, 473, 487**

LAZARUS, R.S., KANNER, A.D., & FOLKMAN, S. (1980) Emotions: A cognitive-phenomenological analysis. In Plutchik, R. & Kellerman, H. (eds.), *Emotion: Theory, Research, and Experience,* Vol. 1. New York: Academic Press. **358**

LAZARUS, R.S., see DELONGIS, COYNE, DAKOF, FOLKMAN, & LAZARUS (1982).

LAZARUS, R.S., see FOLKMAN & LAZARUS (1980).

LAZARUS, R.S., see FOLKMAN & LAZARUS (1985).

LAZARUS, R.S., see FOLKMAN, LAZARUS, DUNKEL-SCHETTER, DELONGIS, & GRUEN (1986).

LAZERSON, A., see FISCHER & LAZERSON (1984).

LE BON, G. (1895) *The Crowd.* London: Ernest Benn. **600, 627**

LEDERMAN, S.J., see KLATZKY, LEDERMAN, & METZGER (1985).

LEDERMAN, S.J., see LOOMIS & LEDERMAN (1986).

LEFKOWITZ, M.M., see ERON, HUESMANN, LEFKOWITZ, & WALDER (1972).

LEFKOWITZ, M.M., see HUESMANN, ERON, LEFKOWITZ, & WALDER (1984).

LEHMKUHLE, S.W., see SPOEHR & LEHMKUHLE (1982).

LEHRMAN, D.S. (1964) Control of behavior cycles in reproduction. In Etkin W. (ed.), *Social Behavior and Organization Among Vertebrates.* Chicago: University of Chicago Press. **343**

LEIBOWITZ, H., see ZEIGLER & LEIBOWITZ (1957).

LEIER, V.O., see YESAVAGE, LEIER, DENARI, & HOLLISTER (1985).

LEIKIND, B.J., & MCCARTHY, W.J. (1985) An investigation of firewalking. *The Skeptical Observer,* 10(No. 1):23–34. **142**

LEIMAN, A.L., see ROSENZWEIG & LEIMAN (1982).

LENNEBERG, E.H. (1967) *Biological Foundations of Language.* New York: Wiley. **299**

LENNIE, P., see SHAPLEY & LENNIE (1985).

LEON, M. (1977) *Coordination of Intent and Consequence Information in Children's Moral Judgments.* (Tech. Rep. CHIP 72.) La Jolla, Calif.: University of California, San Diego, Center for Human Information Processing. **450**

LEPPER, M.R., see LORD, ROSS, & LEPPER (1979).

LEPPER, M.R., see VALLONE, ROSS, & LEPPER (1985).

LERNER, R.M., & KARABENICK, S.A. (1974) Physical attractiveness, body attitudes, and self-concept in late adolescents. *Journal of Youth and Adolescence,* 3:307–16. **575**

LESERMAN, J., see LOCKE, KRAUS, LESERMAN, HURST, HEISEL, & WILLIAMS (1984).

LESGOLD, A., see BOWER, CLARK, WINZENZ, & LESGOLD (1969).

LEVENSON, R.W., see EKMAN, LEVENSON, & FRIESON (1983).

LEVI, A., see TETLOCK & LEVI (1982).

LEVIN, J.R., see PRESSLEY, LEVIN, & DELANEY (1982).

LEVINE, J.M., see ALLEN & LEVINE (1969).

LEVINE, J.M., see ALLEN & LEVINE (1971).

LEVINE, M.W., & SHEFNER, J.M. (1981) *Fundamentals of Sensation and Perception.* Reading, Mass.: Addison-Wesley. **179**

LEVINGER, G., SENN, D.J., & JORGENSEN, B.W. (1970) Progress toward permanence in courtship: A test of the Kerckhoff-Davis hypotheses. *Sociometry,* 33:427–43. **592**

LEVINGER, G., see RANDS & LEVINGER (1979).

LEVINTHAL, C.F. (1983) *Introduction to Physiological Psychology* (2nd ed.). Englewood Cliffs, N.J.: Prentice-Hall. **59**

LEVY, J. (1985) Right brain, left brain: Facts and fiction. *Psychology Today,* 19(No. 5):38–44. **49**

LEWINSOHN, P.M., ANTONUCCIO, D.O., STEINMETZ, J.L., & TERI, L. (1984) *The Coping With Depression Course: Psychoeducational Intervention for Unipolar Depression.* Eugene, Ore.: Castalia. **541**

LEWINSOHN, P.M., FENN, D., & FRANKLIN, J. (1982) The relationship of age of onset to duration of episode in unipolar depression. Unpublished manuscript, University of Oregon. **503**

LEWINSOHN, P.M., HOBERMAN, H., TERI, L., & HAUTZINER, M. (1985) An integrative theory of depression. In Reiss, S., & Boot-

sin, R. (eds.), *Theoretical Issues in Behavior Therapy.* New York: Academic Press. **507**

LEWINSOHN, P.M., MISCHEL, W., CHAPLIN, W., & BARTON, R. (1980) Social competence and depression: The role of illusory self-perceptions. *Journal of Abnormal Psychology,* 89:203–12. **507**

LEWIS, J.W., see TERMAN, SHAVIT, LEWIS, CANNON, & LIEBESKIND (1984).

LEWIS, P., see GOLDMAN & LEWIS (1977).

LEWIS, S. (1934) *Work of Art.* Garden City, N.Y.: Doubleday. **423**

LEWONTIN, R.C., ROSE, S., & KAMIN, L.J. (1984) *Not in Our Genes: Biology, Ideology, and Human Nature.* New York: Pantheon. **415**

LEY, R.G., & BRYDEN, M.P. (1982) A dissociation of right and left hemispheric effects for recognizing emotional tone and verbal content. *Brain and Cognition,* 1:3–9. **365**

LIBERMAN, A.M., COOPER, F., SHANKWEILER, D., & STUDDERT-KENNEDY, M. (1967) Perception of the speech code. *Psychological Review,* 74:431–59. **291**

LICKEY, M.E., & GORDON, B. (1983) *Drugs for Mental Illness.* New York: Freeman. **561**

LIDZ, T. (1973) *The Origin and Treatment of Schizophrenic Disorders.* New York: Basic Books. **517**

LIEBERMAN, L.R., & DUNLAP, J.T. (1979) O'Leary and Borkovec's conceptualization of placebo: The placebo paradox. *American Psychologist,* 34:553–54. **553**

LIEBERMAN, M.A., YALOM, I.D., & MILES, M.B. (1973) *Encounter Groups: First Facts.* New York: Basic Books. **544, 561**

LIEBESKIND, J.C., see TERMAN, SHAVIT, LEWIS, CANNON, & LIEBESKIND (1984).

LINDEN, E., see PATTERSON & LINDEN (1981).

LINDZEY, G., & ARONSON, E. (eds.) (1985) *The Handbook of Social Psychology* (3rd ed.). Hillsdale, N.J.: Erlbaum. **595, 627**

LINDZEY, G., see HALL & LINDZEY (1978).

LINDZEY, G., see HALL, LINDZEY, LOEHLIN, & MANOSEVITZ (1985).

LINDZEY, G., see LOEHLIN, LINDZEY, & SPUHLER (1975).

LINN, R.L. (1982) Ability Testing: Individual differences, prediction, and differential prediction. In Wigdor, A., & Gardner, W. (eds.), *Ability Testing: Uses, Consequences, and Controversies.* Washington, D.C.: National Academy Press. **397, 399**

LIPPERT, W.W., & SENTER, R.J. (1966) Electrodermal responses in the sociopath. *Psychonomic Science,* 4:25–26. **521**

LIPPINCOTT, E.C., see THOMAS, HORTON, LIPPINCOTT, & DRABMAN (1977).

LIPSITT, J.P., see SIQUELAND & LIPSITT (1966).

LITTMAN, R.A., see PATTERSON, LITTMAN, & BRICKER (1967).

LOCKE, S.E., KRAUS, L., LESERMAN, J., HURST, M.W., HEISEL, S., & WILLIAMS, R.M. (1984) Life change stress, psychiatric symptoms, and natural killer cell activity. *Psychosomatic Medicine,* 46:441–53. **484**

LOCKE, S.E., see JEMMOTT & LOCKE (1984).

LOCKHART, R.S., see CRAIK & LOCKHART (1972).

LOEB, G. (1985) The functional replacement of the ear. *Scientific American,* 252(No. 2):104–11. **171**

LOEHLIN, J.C., LINDZEY, G., & SPUHLER, J.N. (1975) *Race Differences in Intelligence.* San Francisco: Freeman. **410**

LOEHLIN, J.C., & NICHOLS, R.C. (1976) *Heredity, Environment, and Personality: A Study of 850 Twin Sets.* Austin: University of Texas Press. **418**

LOELHLIN, J.C., see HALL, LINDZEY, LOEHLIN, & MANOSEVITZ (1985).

LOFTUS, E.F., & LOFTUS, G.R. (1980) On the permanence of stored information in the human brain. *American Psychology,* 35:409–20. **259**

LOFTUS, E.F., see LOFTUS & LOFTUS (1975).

LOFTUS, E.F., see LOFTUS & LOFTUS (1982).

LOFTUS, E.F., SCHOOLER, J.W., & WAGENAAR, W.A. (1985) The fate of memory: Comment on McCloskey and Zaragoza. *Journal of Experimental Psychology: General,* 114(No. 3):375–80. **274**

LOFTUS, G.R., & LOFTUS, E.F. (1975) *Human Memos: The Processing of Information.* New York: Halsted Press. **273**

LOFTUS, G.R., & LOFTUS, E.F. (1982) *Essence of Statistics.* Monterey, Calif.: Brooks/Cole. **651**

LOFTUS, G.R., see LOFTUS & LOFTUS (1980).

LOGAN, C.A., see FANTINO & LOGAN (1979).

LOGAN, J.A., see KANDEL & LOGAN (1984).

LOGUE, A.W. (1986) *The Psychology of Eating and Drinking.* New York: Freeman. **349**

LOHR, J.M., see HAMBERGER & LOHR (1984).

LOOMIS, A.L., HARVEY, E.N., & HOBART, G.A. (1937) Cerebral states during sleep as studied by human potentials. *Journal of Experimental Psychology,* 21:127–44. **115**

LOOMIS, J.M., & LEDERMAN, S.J. (1986) Tactual perception. In Boff, K., Kaufman, L., & Thomas, J. (eds.), *Handbook of Perception and Human Performance,* Vol. 1. New York: Wiley. **175, 176**

LORD, C.G., ROSS, L., & LEPPER, M.R. (1979) Biased assimilation and attitude polarization: The effects of prior theories on subsequently considered evidence. *Journal of Personality and Social Psychology,* 37:2098–109. **570**

LORENZ, K. (1966) *On Aggression.* New York: Harcourt Brace Jovanovich. **375**

LORENZ, K. (1981) *The Foundations of Ethology.* New York: Springer-Verlag. **349, 375**

LOTT, A.J., see MALOF & LOTT (1962).

LOVINGER, P.W., see JONES & LOVINGER (1985).

LOWINGER, P., & DOBIE, S. (1969) What makes the placebo work? A study of placebo response rate. *Archives of General Psychiatry,* 20:84–88. **552**

LOWN, B., see REICH, DESILVA, LOWN, & MURAWSKI (1981).

LUBORSKY, L., SINGER, B., & LUBORSKY, L. (1975) Comparative studies of psychotherapies. *Archives of General Psychiatry,* 32:995–1008. **549**

LUBORSKY, L., see LUBORSKY, SINGER, & LUBORSKY (1975).

LUBORSKY, L.L., MCLELLAN, A.T., WOODY, G.E., O'BRIEN, E.P., & AUERBACH, A. (1985) Therapist success and its determinants. *Archives of General Psychiatry,* 42:602–11. **550**

LUCE, R.D., see KRANTZ, LUCE, SUPPES, & TVERSKY (1971).

LUCHINS, A. (1957) Primacy-recency in impression formation. In Hovland, C.I. (ed.), *The Order of Presentation in Persuasion.* New Haven: Yale University Press. **568, 569**

LUDWIG, A.M., BRANDSMA, J.M., WILBUR, C.B., BENDFELDT, F., & JAMESON, D.H. (1972) The objective study of a multiple personality. *Archives of General Psychiatry,* 26:298–310. **113**

LUNDIN, R.W. (1985) *Theories and Systems of Psychology,* (3rd ed.). Lexington, Mass.: Heath. **27**

LURIA, Z., & RUBIN, J.Z. (1974) The eye of the beholder: Parents' views on sex of newborns. *American Journal of Orthopsychiatry,* 44:512–19. **90**

LUZZATI, C., see BISIACH & LUZZATI (1978).

LYKKEN, D.T. (1957) A study of anxiety in the sociopathic personality. *Journal of Abnormal and Social Psychology,* 55:6–10. **521**

LYKKEN, D.T. (1980) *A Tremor in the Blood: Uses and Abuses of the Lie Detector.* New York: McGraw-Hill. **355, 379**

LYKKEN, D.T. (1982) Research with twins: The concept of emergencies. *The Society for Psychophysiological Research,* 19:361–73. **422**

LYKKEN, D.T. (1984) Polygraphic interrogation. *Nature,* 307:681–84. **355**

M

MAASS, A., & CLARK, R.D., III. (1983) Internalization versus compliance: Differential processes underlying minority influence and conformity. *European Journal of Social Psychology,* 13:45–55. **618**

MAASS, A., & CLARK, R.D., III. (1984) Hidden impact of minorities: Fifteen years of minority influence research. *Psychological Bulletin,* 95:428–50. **618**

MACCOBY, E.E., & JACKLIN, C.N. (1974) *The Psychology of Sex Differences.* Stanford: Stanford University Press. **92, 93**

MACCOBY, N., FARQUHAR, J.W., WOOD, P.D., & ALEXANDER, J. (1977) Reducing the risk of cardiovascular disease: Effects of a community-based campaign on knowledge and behavior. *Journal of Community Health,* 3:100–14. **620, 621**

MACCOBY, N., see FARQUHAR, MACCOBY, & SOLOMON (1984).

MACCOBY, N., see FARQUHAR, MACCOBY, WOOD, et al. (1977).

MACCRIMMON, D.J., see STEFFY, ASARNOW, ASARNOW, MACCRIMMON, & CLEGHORN (1984).

MACDONALD, H., see HILGARD, HILGARD, MACDONALD, MORGAN, & JOHNSON (1978).

MACDOUGALL, J.M., see DEMBROSKI, MACDOUGALL, WILLIAMS, & HANEY (1985).

MACKENZIE, B. (1984) Explaining race differences in IQ: The logic, the methodology, and the evidence. *American Psychologist,* 39:1214–33. **411**

MACKINTOSH, N.J. (1983) *Conditioning and Associative Learning.* New York: Oxford University Press. **243**

MADDI, S., & COSTA, P. (1972) *Humanism in Personology: Allport, Maslow, and Murray.* Chicago: Aldine. **455**

MADDI, S.R., see KOBASA, MADDI, & KAHN (1982).

MAFFEI, L., see PIRCHIO, SPINELLI, FIORENTINI, & MAFFEI (1978).

MAHER, B.A. (1966) *Principles of Psychotherapy: An Experimental Approach.* New York: McGraw-Hill. **511, 512, 521, 523**

MAHONEY, M.J., see CRAIGHEAD, KAZDIN, & MAHONEY (1981).

MAIER, S.F., & LAUDENSLAGER, M. (1985) Stress and health: Exploring the links. *Psychology Today,* 19(No. 8):44–49. **484**

MAIER, S.F., & SELIGMAN, M.E.P. (1976) Learned helplessness: Theory and evidence. *Journal of Experimental Psychology: General,* 105:3–46. **228**

MAIER, S.F., see LAUDENSLAGER, RYAN, DRUGAN, HYSON, & MAIER (1983).

MAISEL, E., see GEER & MAISEL (1972).

MALAMUT, B., see MISHKIN, MALAMUT, & BACHEVALIER (1984).

MALAUMD, P., see WATERS & MALAUMD (1975).

MALITZ, S., see SACKEIM, PORTNOY, NEELEY, STEIF, DECINA, & MALITZ (1985).

MALOF, M., & LOTT, A.J. (1962) Ethnocentrism and the acceptance of Negro support in a group pressure situation. *Journal of Abnormal and Social Psychology*, 65:254–58. **608**

MALT, B.C. (1985) The role of discourse structure in understanding anaphora. *Journal of Memory and Language*, 24:271–89. **252**

MANDLER, G. (1982) *Mind and Emotion*. New York: Norton. **379**

MANDLER, G. (1984) *Mind and Body*. New York: Norton. **360**

MANDLER, G. (1985) *Cognitive Psychology: An Essay in Cognitive Science*. Hillsdale, N.J.: Erlbaum. **9, 27**

MANKIEWICZ, F., & SWERDLOW, J. (1977) *Remote Control*. New York: Quadrangle. **376**

MANN, L., see KILHAM & MANN (1974).

MANN, M.B., see WABER, MANN, MEROLA, & MOYLAN (1985).

MANOSEVITZ, M., see HALL, LINDZEY, LOEHLIN, & MANOSEVITZ (1985).

MARCEL, A.J. (1983) Conscious and unconscious perception: An approach to the relations between phenomenal experience and perceptual processes. *Cognitive Psychology*, 15:238–300. **196**

MARGULIS, S., see YERKES & MARGOLIS (1909).

MARIN, O.S.M., see POSNER & MARIN (1985).

MARKHAM, M. (1981) Suicide without depression. *Psychiatric News*, 8:24–25. **505**

MARKMAN, E. (1987) How children constrain the possible meanings of words. In Neisser, U. (ed.), *Concepts and Conceptual Development: Ecological and Intellectual Factors in Categorization*. New York: Cambridge University Press. **295**

MARKS, D., & KAMMANN, R. (1977) The nonpsychic powers of Uri Geller. *The Zetetic*, 1:9–17. **143**

MARKS, D., & KAMMANN, R. (1980) *The Psychology of the Psychic*. Buffalo: Prometheus Books. **210, 211**

MARKUS, H. (1977) Self-schemata and processing information about the self. *Journal of Personality and Social Psychology*, 35:63–78. **436**

MARKUS, H., & SENTIS, K. (1982) The self in social information processing. In Suls, J. (ed.), *Psychological Perspectives on the Self*, Vol. 1. Hillsdale, N.J.: Erlbaum. **436**

MARKUS, H., & SMITH, J. (1981) The influence of self-schemas on the perception of others. In Cantor, N., & Kihlstrom, J. (eds.), *Personality, Cognition, and Social Interaction*. Hillsdale, N.J.: Erlbaum. **436**

MARKUS, H., CRANE, M., BERNSTEIN, S., & SILADI, M. (1982) Self-schemas and gender. *Journal of Personality and Social Psychology*, 42:38–50. **573**

MARLER, P. (1970) A comparative approach to vocal learning: Song development in white-crowned sparrows. *Journal of Comparative and Physiological Psychology*, 7: 1–25. **238**

MARR, D. (1982) *Vision*. San Francisco: Freeman. **194, 211**

MARRON, J.E. (1965) Special test preparation: Its effects on college board scores and the relationship of effected scores to subsequent college performance. Office of the Director of Admissions and Registrar. U.S. Military Academy, West Point, N.Y. **401**

MARSHALL, G. (1976) The affective consequences of "inadequately explained" physiological arousal. Unpublished Ph.D. dissertation, Stanford University. **359**

MARTIN, C.E., see KINSEY, POMEROY, & MARTIN (1948).

MARTIN, C.E., see KINSEY, POMEROY, MARTIN, & GEBHARD (1953).

MARTIN, D.G. (1971) *Introduction to Psychotherapy*. Monterey, Calif.: Brooks/Cole. **561**

MARTIN, P.R., see WEINGARTEN, GRAFMAN, BOUTELLE, KAYE, & MARTIN, (1983).

MARTINEZ, J.L., JR., see MCGAUGH, JENSEN, & MARTINEZ (1979).

MARTYNA, W., see BEM, MARTYNA, & WATSON (1976).

MASLACH, C. (1979) The emotional consequences of arousal without reason. In Izard, C.E. (ed.), *Emotion in Personality and Psychopathology*. New York: Plenum. **359**

MASON, J.W. (1971) A re-evaluation of the concept of "nonspecificity" in stress theory. *Journal of Psychiatric Research*, 8:323–33. **463**

MASSEY, J.O., see HEWITT & MASSEY (1969).

MASSMAN, P.J., see BERMAN, MILLER, & MASSMAN (1985).

MASTERS, J.C., see RIMM & MASTERS (1979).

MASTERS, W.H., & JOHNSON, V.E. (1966) *Human Sexual Response*. Boston: Little, Brown. **20**

MATARAZZO, J.D., & WIENS, A.W. (1972) *The Interview: Research on Its Anatomy and Structure*. Chicago: Aldine-Atherton. **440**

MATARAZZO, J.D., & WIENS, A.W. (1977) Black Intelligence Test of Cultural Homogeneity and Wechsler Adult Intelligence Scale scores of black and white police applicants. *Journal of Applied Psychology*, 62:57–63. **396**

MATAS, L., AREND, R.A., & SROUFE, L.A. (1978) Continuity of adaption in the second year: The relationship between quality of attachment and later competence. *Child Development* 49:547–56. **80**

MATEER, C., see FRIED, MATEER, OJEMANN, WOHNS, & FEDIO (1982).

MATHES, E.W. (1975) The effects of physical attractiveness and anxiety on heterosexual attraction over a series of five encounters. *Journal of Marriage and the Family*, 37:769–73. **588**

MAY, M.A., see HARTSHORNE & MAY (1929).

MAYER, R.E. (1981) *The Promise of Cognitive Psychology*. San Francisco: Freeman. **13**

MCALLISTER, B.H., see NILSON, NILSON, OLSON, & MCALLISTER (1981).

MCARTHUR, L.A. (1972) The how and what of why: Some determinants and consequences of causal attribution. *Journal of Personality and Social Psychology*, 22:171–93. **576**

MCBURNEY, D.H. (1978) Psychological dimensions and the perceptual analysis of taste. In Carterette, E.C., & Friedman, M.P. (eds.), *Handbook of Perception*, Vol. 6A. New York: Academic Press. **174**

MCCALL, R.B. (1986) *Fundamental Statistics for Behavioral Sciences* (4th ed.). San Diego: Harcourt Brace Jovanovich. **651**

MCCARLEY, R.W., see HOBSON & MCCARLEY (1977).

MCCARTHY, W.J., see LEIKIND & MCCARTHY (1985).

MCCLEARN, G.E., see PLOMIN, DEFRIES, & MCCLEARN (1980).

MCCLELLAND, D.C., see JEMMOTT, BORYSENKO, MCCLELLAND, CHAPMAN, MEYER, & BENSON (1985).

MCCLELLAND, J.L., & RUMELHART, D.E. (1981) An interactive model of context effects in letter perception: Pt. 1. An account of basic findings. *Psychological Review*, 88:375–407. **203**

MCCLOSKEY, M., & ZARAGOZA, M. (1985) Misleading post-event information and memory for events: Arguments and evidence against memory impairment hypotheses. *Journal of Experimental Psychology: General*, 114:1–16. **274**

MCCOMBS, M., see COMSTOCK, CHAFFEE, KATZMAN, MCCOMBS, & ROBERTS (1978).

MCCRAE, R.R., see COSTA, ZONDERMAN, MCCRAE, & WILLIAMS (1985).

MCDERMOTT, J., see LARKIN, MCDERMOTT, SIMON, & SIMON (1980).

MCDONALD, F.J., see BANDURA & MCDONALD (1963).

MCDOUGALL, W. (1908) *Social Psychology.* New York: G.P. Putnam's Sons. **342**

MCFARLAND, D. (1985) *Animal Behaviour: Psychobiology, Ethology and Evolution.* Menlo Park, Calif.: Benjamin-Cummings. **349**

MCGAUGH, J.L., & HERZ, M.J. (1972) *Memory Consolidation.* San Francisco: Albion. **260**

MCGAUGH, J.L., JENSEN, R.A., & MARTINEZ, J.L., JR. (1979) Sleep, brain state, and memory. In Drucker-Colin, R., Shkurovich, M., & Sterman, M.B. (eds.), *The Functions of Sleep.* New York: Academic Press. **118**

MCGAUGH, J.L., see COTMAN & MCGAUGH (1980).

MCGAUGH, J.L., see HUDSPETH, MCGAUGH, & THOMPSON (1964).

MCGHIE, A., & CHAPMAN, J. (1961) Disorders of attention and perception in early schizophrenia. *British Journal of Medical Psychology,* 34:103–16. **512, 513**

MCGINNES, E. (1949) Emotionality and perceptual defense. *Psychological Review,* 56:244–51. **196**

MCGRAW, K.O., see CORDUA, MCGRAW, & DRABMAN (1979).

MCGRAW, M.D. (1935) *Growth: A Study of Johnny and Jimmy.* Englewood Cliffs, N.J.: Prentice-Hall. **69**

MCGUE, M., & BOUCHARD, T.J., JR. (1984) Adjustment of twin data for the effects of age and sex. *Behavior Genetics* 14:325–43. **422**

MCGUE, M., see BOUCHARD & MCGUE (1981).

MCGUIRE, W.J. (1960) A syllogistic analysis of cognitive relationships. In Hovland, C.I., & Rosenberg, M.J. (eds.), *Attitude Organization and Change.* New Haven: Yale University Press. **581**

MCKEGNEY, F.P., see SCHLEIFER, KELLER, MCKEGNEY, & STEIN (1979).

MCKENNA, R.J. (1972) Some effects of anxiety level and food cues on the eating behavior of obese and normal subjects. *Journal of Personality and Social Psychology,* 22:311–19. **325**

MCKINNEY, W.T., see SUOMI, HARLOW, & MCKINNEY (1972).

MCLELLAN, A.T., see LUBORSKY, MCLELLAN, WOODY, O'BRIEN, & AUERBACH (1985).

MCNEAL, E.T., & CIMBOLIC, P. (1986) Antidepressants and biochemical theories of depression. *Psychological Bulletin,* 99:361–74. **510**

MCNEILL, D. (1966) Developmental psycholinguistics. In Smith, F., & Miller, G.A. (eds.), *The Genesis of Language: A Psycholinguistic Approach.* Cambridge, Mass.: M.I.T. Press. **297**

MCNEILL, D., see BROWN & MCNEILL (1966).

MCQUIRK, B., see BEAMAN, BARNES, KLENTZ, & MCQUIRK (1978).

MEADEJOVSKY, M.G., see DOBELLE, MEADEJOVSKY, & GIRVIN (1974).

MEAGHER, R., see MILLON, GREEN, MEAGHER (1982).

MECHANIC, D. (1962) *Students Under Stress.* New York: Free Press. **473**

MEDIN, D.L., see SMITH & MEDIN (1981).

MEDNICK, B.K. (1973) Breakdown in high-risk subjects: Familial and early environmental factors. *Journal of Abnormal Psychology,* 82:469–75. **518**

MEDNICK, S.A., CUDECK, R., GRIFFITH, J.J., TALOVIC, S.A., & SCHULSINGER, F. (1984) The Danish High-Risk Project: Recent methods and findings. In Watt, H.F., Anthony, E.J., Wynne, L.C., & Rolf, J.E. (eds.), *Children at Risk for Schizophrenia.* New York: Cambridge University Press. **518**

MEDNICK, S.A., see JOHN, MEDNICK, & SCHULSINGER (1982).

MEDNICK, S.A., see WITKIN, MEDNICK, SCHULSINGER, et al. (1976).

MEICHENBAUM, D.H. (1985) *Stress Inoculation Training.* New York: Pergamon. **487**

MEICHENBAUM, D.H., & JAREMKO, M.E. (eds.) (1983) *Stress Reduction and Prevention.* New York: Plenum. **487**

MEICHENBAUM, D.H., see BOWERS & MEICHENBAUM (1984).

MELVILLE, J. (1977) *Phobias and Obsessions.* New York: Coward, McCann, & Geoghegan. **495**

MELZAK, R., & CASEY, K.L. (1968) Sensory, motivational, and central control determinants of pain. In Kenshalo, D.R. (ed.), *The Skin Senses.* Springfield, Ill.: Thomas. **176**

MELZAK, R., & WALL, P.D. (1965) Pain mechanisms: A new theory. *Science,* 150:971–79. **176**

MENNINGER, K., & HOLZMAN, P.S. (1973) *Theory of Psychoanalytic Technique* (2nd ed.). New York: Basic Books. **561**

MENZIES, R. (1937) Conditioned vasomotor responses in human subjects. *Journal of Psychology,* 4:75–120. **218**

MEROLA, J., see WABER, MANN, MEROLA, & MOYLAN (1985).

MERVIS, C.B., & PANI, J.R. (1981) Acquisition of basic object categories. *Cognitive Psychology,* 12:496–522. **285**

MERVIS, C.B., & ROSCH, E. (1981) Categorization of natural objects. In Rosenzweig, M.R., & Porter, L.W. (eds.), *Annual Review of Psychology,* Vol. 21. Palo Alto, Calif.: Annual Reviews. **284**

MERVIS, C.B., see ROSCH & MERVIS (1975).

MESSER, S. (1967) Implicit phonology in children. *Journal of Verbal Learning and Verbal Behavior,* 6:609–13. **295**

MESSICK, S., & JUNGEBLUT, A. (1981) Time and method in coaching for the SAT. *Psychological Bulletin,* 89:191–216. **401**

METZGER, V.A., see KLATZKY, LEDERMAN, & METZGER (1985).

MEYER, D., see JEMMOTT, BORYSENKO, MCCLELLAND, CHAPMAN, MEYER, & BENSON (1985).

MEYER, D.E., see SCHVANEVELDT & MEYER (1973).

MEYER, D.R., see HARLOW, HARLOW, & MEYER (1950).

MEYER, J.P., & PEPPER, S. (1977) Need compatibility and marital adjustment in young married couples. *Journal of Personality and Social Psychology,* 35:331–42. **592**

MILES, L.E., RAYNAL, D.M., & WILSON, M.A. (1977) Blind man living in normal society has circadian rhythm of 24.9 hours. *Science,* 198:421–23. **115**

MILES, M.B., see LIEBERMAN, YALOM, & MILES (1973).

MILGRAM, S. (1963) Behavioral study of obedience. *Journal of Abnormal and Social Psychology,* 67:371–78. **609, 610**

MILGRAM, S. (1974) *Obedience to Authority: An Experimental View.* New York: Harper & Row. **609, 610, 612, 615, 627**

MILLER, G.A. (1956) The magical number seven plus or minus two: Some limits on our capacity for processing information. *Psychological Review,* 63:81–97. **252**

MILLER, G.A. (1965) Some preliminaries to psycholinguistics. *American Psychologist,* 20.15–20. **297**

MILLER, J.R., & KINTSCH, W. (1980) Readability and recall of short prose passages: A theoretical analysis. *Journal of Experimental Psychology: Human Learning and Memory,* 6:335–54. **252**

MILLER, L.C., & COX, C.L. (1981) Public self-consciousness and makeup use: Individual differences in preparational tactics. Paper presented at the annual meeting of the American Psychological Association, Los Angeles, August 1981. **438**

MILLER, N.E. (1969) Learning of visceral and glandular responses. *Science,* 169:434–45. **225**

MILLER, N.E. (1985) The value of behavioral research on animals. *American Psychologist,* 40:423–40. **226**

MILLER, N.E., see DOLLARD, DOOB, MILLER, MOWRER, & SEARS (1939).

MILLER, N.E., see DOLLARD & MILLER (1939).

MILLER, R.C., see BERMAN, MILLER, & MASSMAN (1985).

MILLER, R.S., see SCHNEIDER & MILLER (1975).

MILLER, T.I., see SMITH, GLASS, & MILLER (1980).

MILLER, W.E., see DICARA & MILLER (1968).

MILLER, W.E., see DICARA & MILLER (1970).

MILLON, T., GREEN, C., & MEAGHER, R. (eds.) (1982) *Handbook of Clinical Health Psychology.* New York: Plenum. **487**

MILNER, B. (1964) Some effects of frontal lobectomy in man. In Warren, J.M., & Akert, K. (eds.), *The Frontal Granular Cortex and Behavior.* New York: McGraw-Hill. **45**

MILNER, B., CORKIN, S., & TEUBER, H.L. (1968) Further analysis of the hippocampal amnesic syndrome: 14-year follow-up study of H.M. *Neuropsychologia,* 6:215–34. **246**

MINIUM, E.W., & CLARK, R.W. (1982) *Elements of Statistical Reasoning.* New York: Wiley. **651**

MIRER, T.W., see KELLEY & MIRER (1974).

MISCHEL, H., see MISCHEL & MISCHEL (1976).

MISCHEL, W. (1965) Predicting the success of Peace Corps volunteers in Nigeria. *Journal of Personality and Social Psychology,* 1:510–17. **449**

MISCHEL, W. (1968) *Personality and Assessment.* New York: Wiley. **252, 449**

MISCHEL, W. (1986) *Introduction to Personality* (4th ed.). New York: Holt, Rinehart & Winston. **428, 455**

MISCHEL, W., & MISCHEL, H. (1976) A cognitive social learning approach to morality and self regulation. In Lickona, T. (ed.), *Moral Development and Behavior.* New York: Holt, Rinehart & Winston. **86**

MISCHEL, W., see LEWINSOHN, MISCHEL, CHAPLIN, & BARTON (1980).

MISHKIN, M., MALAMUT, B., & BACHEVALIER, J. (1984) Memories and habits: Two neural systems. In Lynch, G.T., McGaugh, J.L., & Weinberger, N.M. (eds.), *Neurobiology of Learning and Memory.* New York: Guilford Press. **265**

MITA, T.H., DERMER, M., & KNIGHT, J. (1977) Reversed facial images and the mere-exposure hypothesis. *Journal of Personality and Social Psychology,* 35:597–601. **590**

MITCHEL, J.S., & KEESEY, R.E. (1974) The effects of lateral hypothalamic lesions and castration upon the body weight of male rats. *Behavioral Biology,* 11:69–82. **322**

MITCHELL, D.E., & WILKINSON, F. (1974) The effect of early astigmatism on the visual resolution of gratings. *Journal of Physiology,* 243:739–56. **206**

MITCHELL, K.M., see TRUAX & MITCHELL (1971).

MITCHISON, G., see CRICK & MITCHINSON (1983).

MITLER, M.M., see CARSKADON, MITLER, & DEMENT (1974).

MIYAKE, Y., see AWAYA, MIYAKE, IMAYUMI, SHIOSE, KNADA, & KOMURO (1973).

MOEDE, W. (1927) Die Richtlinien der Liestungs-Psychologie. *Industrielle Psychotechnik,* 4:193–207. **605**

MOHS, R.C, DAVIS, B.M., GREENWALD, B.S., et al. (1985) Clinical studies of the cholinergic deficit in Alzheimer's disease. *Journal of the American Geriatrics Society,* 33:749–57. **37**

MOLLON, J.D., see BARLOW & MOLLON (1982).

MOLLON, J.D., see DARTNALL, BOWMAKER, & MOLLON (1983).

MONEY, J. (1980) Endocrine influences and psychosexual status spanning the life cycle. In Van Praag, H.M. (ed.), *Handbook of Biological Psychiatry* (Part 3). New York: Marcel Dekker. **339, 340**

MONEY, J., WIEDEKING, C., WALKER, P.A., & GAIN, D. (1976) Combined antiandrogenic and counseling programs for treatment of 46 XY and 47 XXY sex offenders. In Sacher, E. (ed.), *Hormones, Behavior and Psychopathology.* New York: Raven Press. **331**

MONSELL, S. (1979) Recency, immediate recognition memory, and reaction time. *Cognitive Psychology,* 10:465–501. **251**

MONTAGU, A. (ed.) (1978) *Learning Non-aggression: The Experience of Non-literate Societies.* New York: Oxford University Press. **379**

MOORE, B.C.J. (1978) Psychophysical tuning curves measured in simultaneous and forward masking. *Journal of the Acoustical Society of America,* 63:524–32. **169**

MOORE, B.C.J. (1982) *An Introduction to the Psychology of Hearing* (2nd ed.). New York: Academic Press. **179**

MOORE, B.R., see JENKINS & MOORE (1973).

MOORE, B.S., see UNDERWOOD & MOORE (1981).

MOORE, E., see BOCK & MOORE (1982).

MOORE, M.J., see HAITH, BERGMAN, & MOORE (1977).

MOORE, S.G., see HARTUP & MOORE (1963).

MORAY, N. (1969) *Attention: Selective Processes in Vision and Hearing.* London: Hutchinson. **198**

MORELAND, R.L., & ZAJONC, R.B. (1979) Exposure effects may not depend on stimulus recognition. *Journal of Personality and Social Psychology,* 37:1085–89. **590**

MORGAN, A.H. (1973) The heritability of hypnotic susceptibility in twins. *Journal of Abnormal Psychology,* 82:55–61. **138**

MORGAN, A.H., see HILGARD, HILGARD, MACDONALD, MORGAN, & JOHNSON (1978).

MORGAN, A.H., see RUCH, MORGAN, & HILGARD (1973).

MORRIS, L.A., see SHAPIRO & MORRIS (1978).

MORRISON, D.M. (1985) Adolescent contraceptive behavior: A review. *Psychological Bulletin,* 98:538–68. **98, 99**

MORRISON, R.E., see RAYNER, INHOFF, MORRISON, SLOWIACZEK, & BERTERA (1981).

MORSE, R., see TELLER, MORSE, BORTON, & REGAL (1974).

MOS, L.P., see ROYCE & MOS (1981).

MOSCOVICI, S. (1976) *Social Influence and Social Change.* London: Academic Press. **617**

MOSCOVICI, S., LAGE, E., & NAFFRECHOUX, M. (1969) Influence of a consistent minority on the responses of a majority in a color perception task. *Sociometry,* 32:365–79. **618**

MOSS, A.J., see CASE, HELLER, CASE, & MOSS (1985).

MOVSHON, J.A., & VAN SLUYTERS, R.C. (1981) Visual neural development. *Annual Review of Psychology,* 32:477–522. **206**

MOWRER, O.H. (1947) On the dual nature of learning: A reinterpretation of "conditioning" and "problem solving." *Harvard Educational Review,* 17:102–48. **236**

MOWRER, O.H., see DOLLARD, DOOB, MILLER, MOWRER, & SEARS (1939).

MOYLAN, P.M., see WABER, MANN, MEROLA, & MOYLAN (1985).

MURAWSKI, B.J., see REICH, DESILVA, LOWN, & MURAWSKI (1981).

MURDOCK, B.B., JR. (1962) The serial position effect in free recall. *Journal of Experimental Psychology,* 64:482–88. **253**

MURDOCK, P., see PAULUS & MURDOCK (1971).

MURPHY, G., & KOVACH, J. (1972) *Historical Introduction to Modern Psychology* (3rd ed.). New York: Harcourt Brace Jovanovich. **27**

MURPHY, G.E., & WETZEL, R.D. (1980) Suicide risk by birth cohort in the United States, 1949 to 1974. *Archives of General Psychiatry,* 37:519–23. **504**

MURSTEIN, B.I. (1972) Physical attractiveness and marital choice. *Journal of Personality and Social Psychology,* 22:8–12. **591**

MUSSARE, F., see HOGARTY, SCHOOLER, URLICH, MUSSARE, FERRO, & HERRON (1979).

MUSSEN, P.H. (ed.) (1983) *Handbook of Child Psychology* (4th ed.). New York: Wiley. **105**

MUSSEN, P.H., CONGER, J.J., KAGAN, J., & HUSTON, A.C. (1984) *Child Development and Personality* (6th ed.). New York: Harper & Row. **105**

MUSSEN, P.H., & RUTHERFORD, E. (1963)

Parent-child relations and parental personality in relation to young children's sex-role preferences. *Child Development*, 34:589–607. **94**

MYERSON, R., see ZURIF, CARAMAZZA, MYERSON, & GALVIN (1974).

N

NADEL, L., see SQUIRE, COHEN, & NADEL (1984).

NAFE, J.P., see KENSHALO, NAFE, & BROOKS (1961).

NAFFRECHOUX, M., see MOSCOVICI, LAGE, & NAFFRECHOUX (1969).

NAKAMURA, G.V., see BREWER & NAKAMURA (1984).

NAKAYAMA, K. (1985) Biological image motion processing. *Vision Research*, 25:625–60. **186, 187**

NAKAYAMA, K., & TYLER, C.W. (1981) Psychophysical isolation of movement sensitivity by removal of familiar position cues. *Vision Research*, 21:427–33. **186**

NARANJO, C., & ORNSTEIN, R.E. (1977) *On the Psychology of Meditation*. New York: Penguin. **145**

NASH, S.C., see KUHN, NASH, & BRUCKEN (1978).

NATELSON, B.J., see HIRSH & NATELSON (1981).

NATHANS, J., THOMAS, D., & HOGNESS, D.S. (1986) Molecular genetics of human color vision: The genes encoding blue, green, and red pigments. *Science*, 232:193–202. **159**

NATIONAL REVIEW (1963) A survey of the political and religious attitudes of American college students. (October 8, 1963): 279–302. **624**

NATIONAL REVIEW (1971) Opinion on the campus. (June 15, 1971): 635–50. **624**

NEALE, J.M., see DAVISON & NEALE (1986).

NEATON, J.D., see SHEKELLE, NEATON, JACOBS, HULLEY, & BLACKBURN (1983).

NEBES, R.D., & SPERRY, R.W. (1971) Cerebral dominance in perception. *Neuropsychologia*, 9:247. **48**

NEEB, M., see FISHER, ZUCKERMAN, & NEEB (1981).

NEEB, M., see ZUCKERMAN & NEEB (1980).

NEELEY, P., see SACKEIM, PORTNOY, NEELEY, STEIF, DECINA, & MALITZ (1985).

NEELY, J.E., see THOMPSON & NEELY (1970).

NEGRETE, J.C., & KWAN, M.W. (1972) Relative value of various etiological factors in short lasting, adverse psychological reactions to cannabis smoking. *Internal Pharmacopsychiatry*, 7:249–59. **130**

NEISSER, U. (1981) John Dean's memory: A case study. *Cognition*, 9:1–22. **255**

NEISSER, U. (ed.) (1982) *Memory Observed: Remembering in Natural Contexts*. San Francisco: Freeman. **254, 255, 279**

NEISSER, U., see SELFRIDGE & NEISSER (1960).

NELSON, T.O. (1977) Repetition and depth of processing. *Journal of Verbal Learning and Verbal Behavior*, 16:152–71. **254**

NEUGARTEN, B. (1971) Grow old with me, the best is yet to be. *Psychology Today*, 5:45–49. **103**

NEUMAN, W.R. (1976) Patterns of recall among television news viewers. *Public Opinion Quarterly*, 40:115–23. **620**

NEWCOMB, T.M. (1943) *Personality and Social Change*. New York: Dryden Press. **623, 624, 627**

NEWCOMB, T.M. (1961) *The Acquaintance Process*. New York: Holt, Rinehart & Winston. **591**

NEWCOMB, T.M., KOENING, K.E., FLACKS, R., & WARWICK, D.P. (1967) *Persistence and Change: Bennington College and Its Students After Twenty-Five Years*. New York: Wiley. **625, 627**

NEWCOMB, T.M., see FESTINGER, PEPITONE, & NEWCOMB (1952).

NEWCOMBE, N., & BANDURA, M.M. (1983) The effect of age at puberty on spatial ability in girls: A question of mechanism. *Developmental Psychology*, 19:215–24. **93**

NEWELL, A., & SIMON, H.A. (1972) *Human Problem Solving*. Englewood Cliffs, N.J.: Prentice Hall. **305, 306, 311**

NEWMAN, E.B., see STEVENS & NEWMAN (1936).

NICHOLS, R.C. (1968) Nature and nurture in adolescence. In Adams, J.F. (ed.), *Understanding Adolescence*. Boston: Allyn & Bacon. **95**

NICHOLS, R.C., see LOEHLIN & NICHOLS (1976).

NICKLAUS, J. (1974) *Golf My Way*. New York: Simon & Schuster. **136**

NICOL, S.E., & GOTTESMAN, I.I. (1983) Clues to the genetics and neurobiology of schizophrenia. *American Scientist*, 71:398–404. **515**

NIELSON, D.W., see YOST & NIELSON (1985).

NILSON, D.C., NILSON, L.B., OLSON, R.S., & MCALLISTER, B.H. (1981) *The Planning Environment Report for the Southern California Earthquake Safety Advisory Board*. Redlands, Calif.: Social Research Advisory & Policy Research Center. **473**

NILSON, L.B., see NILSON, NILSON, OLSON, & MCALLISTER (1981).

NISBETT, R.E. (1968) Taste, deprivation, and weight determinants of eating behavior. *Journal of Personality and Social Psychology*, 10:107–16. **326**

NISBETT, R.E. (1972) Hunger, obesity, and the ventromedial hypothalamus. *Psychological Review*, 79:433–53. **329**

NISBETT, R.E., & ROSS, L. (1985) *Human Inference: Strategies and Shortcomings of Social Judgment* (reprint ed.). Englewood Cliffs, N.J.: Prentice-Hall. **565, 566, 570, 576, 595**

NISBETT, R.E., see BORGIDA & NISBETT (1977).

NORMAN, D.A. (1976) *Memory and Attention: An Introduction to Human Information Processing* (2nd ed.). New York: Wiley. **199, 269**

NORMAN, D.A. (1982) *Learning and Memory*. San Francisco: Freeman. **279**

NORMAN, D.A., see WAUGH & NORMAN (1965).

NORMAN, R. (1975) Affective-cognitive consistency, attitudes, conformity, and behavior. *Journal of Personality and Social Psychology*, 32:83–91. **584**

NORMAN, W.T. (1963) Toward an adequate taxonomy of personality attributes: Replicated factor structure in peer nomination personality ratings. *Journal of Abnormal and Social Psychology*, 66:574–83. **424, 425**

NOVIKOVA, L.A., see KUMAN, FEDROV, & NOVIKOVA (1983).

O

O'BRIEN, E.J., see EPSTEIN & O'BRIEN (1985).

O'BRIEN, E.P., see LUBORSKY, MCLELLAN, WOODY, O'BRIEN, & AUERBACH (1985).

O'BRIEN, M., & HUSTON, A.C. (1985) Development of sex-typed play behavior in toddlers. *Developmental Psychology* 21 (No. 5):866–71. **90**

O'BRIEN, R.M., see CRAIGHEAD, STUNKARD, & O'BRIEN (1981).

O'DONNELL, J.A., & CLAYTON, R.R. (1982) The stepping stone hypothesis: Marijuana, heroin, and causality. *Chemical Dependencies*, 4(No. 3). **132**

O'LEARY, K.D., & WILSON, G.T. (1975) *Behavior Therapy: Application and Outcome*. Englewood Cliffs, N.J.: Prentice-Hall. **539**

O'MALLEY, P.M., see JOHNSTON, O'MALLEY, & BACHMAN (1986).

OFFIR, C. (1982) *Human Sexuality*. San Diego: Harcourt Brace Jovanovich. **324, 330, 332, 349**

OFFIR, C., see TAVRIS & OFFIR (1977).

OHMAN, A., FREDRIKSON, M., HUGDAHL, K., & RIMMO, P. (1976) The premise of equipotentiality in human classical conditioning: Conditioned electrodermal responses to potentially phobic stimuli. *Journal of Experimental Psychology: General,* 105:313–37. **500**

OHMAN, A., see HUGDAHL & OHMAN (1977).

OJEMANN, G., see FRIED, MATEER, OJEMANN, WOHNS, & FEDIO (1982).

OLIVEAU, D., see AGRAS, SYLVESTER, & OLIVEAU (1969).

OLSON, R.S., see NILSON, NILSON, OLSON, & MCALLISTER (1981).

OLTON, D.S. (1978) Characteristics of spatial memory. In Hulse, S.H., Fowler, H.F., & Honig, W.K. (eds.), *Cognitive Processes in Animal Behavior.* Hillsdale, N.J.: Erlbaum. **242**

OLTON, D.S. (1979) Mazes, maps, and memory. *American Psychologist,* 34:583–96. **242**

OLTON, D.S., & SAMUELSON, R.J. (1976) Remembrance of places passed: Spatial memory in rats. *Journal of Experimental Psychology: Animal Behavior Process,* 2:96–116. **241**

OLVER, R.R., see BRUNER, OLVER, GREENFIELD, et al. (1966).

OLWEUS, D. (1969) *Prediction of Aggression.* Scandinavian Test Corporation. **445**

OLZAK, L.A., & THOMAS, J.P. (1986) Seeing spatial patterns. In Boff, K., Kaufman, L., & Thomas, J.P. (eds.), *Handbook of Perception and Human Performance,* Vol. 1. New York: Wiley. **163**

ORDY, J.M., see FANTZ, ORDY, & UDELF (1962).

ORNE, M.T., & HOLLAND, C.C. (1968) On the ecological validity of laboratory deceptions. *International Journal of Psychiatry,* 6:282–93. **613**

ORNSTEIN, R.E., see NARANJO & ORNSTEIN (1977).

ORR, W.C. (1982) Disorders of excessive somnolence. In Hauri, P. (ed.), *Sleep Disorders.* Kalamazoo, Mich.: Upjohn. **116**

OSBORN, D.K., & ENDSLEY, R.C. (1971) Emotional reactions of young children to TV violence. *Child Development,* 42:321–31. **377**

OSHERSON, D.N. (1976) *Logical Abilities in Children:* Vol. 4. *Reasoning and Concepts.* Hillsdale, N.J.: Erlbaum. **288**

OSKAMP, S., see PERLMAN & OSKAMP (1971).

OSOFSKY, J.D. (ed.) (1979) *Handbook of Infant Development.* New York: Wiley. **105**

OVERMEIER, J.B., & SELIGMAN, M.E.P. (1967) Effects of inescapable shock upon subsequent escape and avoidance responding. *Journal of Comparative and Physiological Psychology,* 63:28. **468**

OWEN, D.R. (1972) The 47 XYY male: A review. *Psychological Review,* 78:209–33. **57**

OWEN, D.R., see TEASDALE & OWEN (1984).

P

PAICHELER, G. (1976) Norms and attitude change: Pt. 1. Polarization and styles of behavior. *European Journal of Social Psychology,* 6:405–27. **618**

PAICHELER, G. (1977) Norms and attitude change: Pt. 2. The phenomenon of bipolarization. *European Journal of Social Psychology,* 7:5–14. **618**

PALLONE, N.J. (1961) Effects of short- and long-term developmental reading courses upon SAT verbal scores. *Personnel and Guidance Journal,* 39:654–57. **401**

PALMER, F.H., & ANDERSON, L.W. (1979) Long-term gains from early intervention: Findings from longitudinal studies. In Zigler, E., & Valentine, J. (eds.), *Project Head Start: A Legacy of the War on Poverty.* New York: Free Press. **412**

PALMER, S.E. (1975) The effects of contextual scenes on the identification of objects. *Memory and Cognition,* 3:519–26. **196**

PANATI, C. (ed.) (1976) *The Geller Papers: Scientific Observations on the Paranormal Powers of Uri Geller.* Boston: Houghton Mifflin. **142**

PANI, J.R., see MERVIS & PANI (1981).

PATTERSON, F.G. (1978) The gestures of a gorilla: Language acquisition in another pongid. *Brain and Language,* 5:72–97. **301**

PATTERSON, F.G., & LINDEN, E. (1981) *The Education of Koko.* New York: Holt, Rinehart & Winston. **301**

PATTERSON, G.R., LITTMAN, R.A., & BRICKER, W A. (1967) Assertive behavior in children: A step toward a theory of aggression. *Monographs of the Society for Research in Child Development,* 32(Serial No. 113):5. **372**

PAUL, G.L. (1967) Insight versus desensitization in psychotherapy two years after termination. *Journal of Consulting Psychology,* 31:333–48. **553**

PAULHUS, D. (1982) Individual differences, self-presentation, and cognitive dissonance: Their concurrent operation in forced compliance. *Journal of Personality and Social Psychology,* 43:838–52. **585**

PAULUS, P.B., & MURDOCK, P. (1971) Anticipated evaluation and audience presence in the enhancement of dominant responses. *Journal of Experimental Social Psychology,* 7:280–91. **599**

PAUNONEN, S.V., see RUSHTON, JACKSON, & PAUNONEN (1981).

PAVLOV, I.P. (1927) *Conditioned Reflexes.* New York: Oxford University Press. **217, 243**

PAXMAN, J.M., see SENDEROWITZ & PAXMAN (1985).

PEARLSTONE, Z., see TULVING & PEARLSTONE (1966).

PEEPLES, D.R., see TELLER, PEEPLES & SEKEL (1978).

PELLEGRINO, J.W. (1985) Inductive reasoning ability. In Sternberg, R.J. (ed.), *Human Abilities: An Information-Processing Approach.* New York: Freeman. **405**

PELLEGRINO, J.W., see KAIL & PELLEGRINO (1985).

PENG, R., see YU, ZHANG, JING, PENG, ZHANG, & SIMON (1985).

PEPITONE, A., see FESTINGER, PEPITONE, & NEWCOMB (1952).

PEPLAU, L.A., RUBIN, Z., & HILL, C.T. (1977) Sexual intimacy in dating relationships. *Journal of Social Issues,* 33:86–109. **335**

PEPLAU, L.A., see HILL, RUBIN, & PEPLAU (1976).

PEPLAU, L.A., see RUBIN, HILL, PEPLAU, & DUNKEL-SCHETTER (1980).

PEPLAU, L.A., see SEARS, FREEDMAN, & PEPLAU (1985).

PEPPER, S., see MEYER & PEPPER (1977).

PERLMAN, D., & OSKAMP, S. (1971) The effects of picture content and exposure frequency on evaluations of negroes and whites. *Journal of Experimental Social Psychology,* 7:503–14. **590**

PERLMUTER, L.C., see KIMBLE & PERLMUTER (1970).

PERRIN, F.A.C. (1921) Physical attractiveness and repulsiveness. *Journal of Experimental Psychology,* 4:203–17. **588**

PETERSEN, A.C. (1981) Sex differences in performance on spatial tasks: Biopsychological influences. In Ansara, H., Geschwind, N., Galaburda, A., Albert, M., & Gertrell, N. (eds.), *Sex Differences in Dyslexia.* Towson, Md.: Orton Society. **93**

PETERSON, A.C., see CONGER & PETERSON (1983).

PETERSON, C., & SELIGMAN, M.E.P. (1984) Causal explanations as a risk factor for depression: Theory and evidence. *Psychological Review,* 91:347–74. **508**

PETERSON, R.E., see IMPERATO-MCGINLEY, PETERSON, GAUTIER, & STURLA (1979).

PETITTO, L.A., see SEIDENBERG & PETITTO (1979).

PETITTO, L.A., see TERRACE, PETITTO, SANDERS, & BEVER (1979).

PETTERSEN, L., see YONAS, PETTERSEN, & GRANRUD (1982).

PETTIGREW, J.D., see BARLOW, BLAKEMORE, & PETTIGREW (1967).

PETTY, R.E., HARKINS, S.G., WILLIAMS, K.D., & LATANE, B. (1977) The effects of group size on cognitive effort and evaluation. *Personality and Social Psychology Bulletin* 3:575–78. **605**

PETTY, R.E., see HARKINS & PETTY (1982).

PHARES, E.J. (1984) *Introduction to Personality.* Columbus, Oh.: Merrill. **455**

PHILLIPS, D.P. (1978) Airplane accident fatalities increase just after newspaper stories about murder and suicide. *Science,* 201:748–49. **505**

PHILLIPS, E.A., see FIXSEN, PHILLIPS, PHILLIPS, & WOLF (1976).

PHILLIPS, E.L., see FIXSEN, PHILLIPS, PHILLIPS, & WOLF (1976).

PHILLIPS, J.L., JR. (1981) *Piaget's Theory: A Primer.* San Francisco: Freeman. **105**

PHILLIPS, J.L., JR. (1982) *Statistical Thinking: A Structural Approach* (2nd ed.). San Francisco: Freeman. **27, 643, 651**

PHOENIX, C.H., GOY, R.H., & RESKO, J.A. (1968) Psychosexual differentiation as a function of androgenic stimulation. In Diamond, M. (ed.), *Reproduction and Sexual Behavior.* Bloomington: Indiana University Press. **338**

PIAGET, J. (1932) *The Moral Judgment of the Child.* New York: Free Press. (Reprint ed., 1965.) **84, 86**

PIAGET, J. (1952) *The Origins of Intelligence in Children.* New York: International Universities Press. **344**

PIERCE, C.M., see HOFLING, BROTZMAN, DALRYMPLE, GRAVES, & PIERCE (1966).

PILIAVIN, I.M., RODIN, J., & PILIAVIN, J.A. (1969) Good Samaritanism: An underground phenomenon? *Journal of Personality and Social Psychology,* 13:289–99. **606**

PILIAVIN, J.A., see PILIAVIN, RODIN, & PILIAVIN (1969).

PINKER, S. (1984) *Language Learnability and Language Development.* Cambridge, Mass.: Harvard University Press. **298, 311**

PIRCHIO, M., SPINELLI, D., FIORENTINI, A., & MAFFEI, L. (1978) Infant contrast sensitivity evaluated by evoked potentials. *Brain Research,* 141:179–84. **204**

PITTILLO, E.S., see SIZEMORE & PITTILLO (1977).

PLATT, J.J., YAKSH, T., & DARBY, C.L. (1967) Social facilitation of eating behavior in armadillos. *Psychological Reports,* 20:1136. **598**

PLOMIN, R., DEFRIES, J.C., & MCCLEARN, G.E. (1980) *Behavioral Genetics: A Primer.* San Francisco: Freeman. **59, 415, 525**

PLOMIN, R., see BUSS & PLOMIN (1975).

PLUTCHIK, R. (1980) A general psychoevolutionary theory of emotion. In Plutchik, R., & Kellerman, H. (eds.), *Emotion: Theory, Research, and Experience,* Vol. 1. New York: Academic Press. **360**

PLUTCHIK, R., & KELLERMAN, H. (eds.) (1980) *Emotion: Theory, Research, and Experience,* Vol. 1. New York: Academic Press. **379**

POKORNY, J., see SMITH & POKORNY (1972).

POLIVY, J., & HERMAN, C.P. (1985) Dieting and binging: A causal analysis. *American Psychologist,* 40:193–201. **325**

POLIVY, J., see HERMAN & POLIVY (1980).

POLT, J.M., see HESS & POLT (1960).

POMEROY, A.C., see KINSEY, POMEROY, & MARTIN (1948).

POMEROY, W.B., see KINSEY, POMEROY, MARTIN, & GEBHARD (1953).

POON, L.W. (ed.) (1980) *Aging in the 1980s.* Washington, D.C.: American Psychological Association. **105**

POPE, K.S., & SINGER, J.L. (eds.) (1978) *The Stream of Consciousness.* New York: Plenum. **144**

PORAC, C., see COREN, PORAC, & WARD (1984).

PORTER, H. (1939) Studies in the psychology of stuttering: Pt. 14. Stuttering phenomena in relation to size and personnel of audience. *Journal of Speech Disorders,* 4:323–33. **604**

PORTNOY, S., see SACKEIM, PORTNOY, NEELEY, STEIF, DECINA, & MALITZ (1985).

POSNER, M.I. (1982) Cumulative development of attentional theory. *American Psychologist,* 37:168–79. **199**

POSNER, M.I., & KEELE, S.W. (1967) Decay of visual information from a single letter. *Science,* 158:137–39. **248**

POSNER, M.I., & MARIN, O.S.M. (eds.) (1985) *Mechanisms of Attention:* Vol. 11. *Attention and Performance.* Hillsdale, N.J.: Erlbaum. **211**

POST, R.M., KOTIN, J., GOODWIN, F.K., & GORDON, E. (1973) Psychomotor activity and cerebrospinal fluid amine metabolites in affective illness. *American Journal of Psychiatry,* 130:67–72. **510**

POWLEY, T.L., & KEESEY, R.E (1970) Relationship of body weight to the lateral hypothalamic feeding syndrome. *Journal of Comparative and Physiological Psychology,* 70:25–36. **323**

POWLEY, T.L., see KEESEY & POWLEY (1975).

PREMACK, A.J., see PREMACK & PREMACK (1983).

PREMACK, D. (1959) Toward empirical behavior laws: Pt. 1. Positive reinforcement. *Psychological Review,* 66:219–33. **231**

PREMACK, D. (1962) Reversibility of the reinforcement relation. *Science,* 136:255–57. **232**

PREMACK, D. (1971) Language in chimpanzees? *Science,* 172:808–22. **300**

PREMACK, D. (1985a) "Gavagai!" Or the future history of the animal language controversy. *Cognition,* 19:207–96. **242**

PREMACK, D. (1985b) *Gavagai! The Future of the Animal Language Controversy.* Cambridge, Mass.: M.I.T. Press. **243**

PREMACK, D., & PREMACK, A.J. (1983) *The Mind of an Ape.* New York: Norton. **242**

PRENTICE-DUNN, S., & ROGERS, R.W. (1980) Effects of deindividuating situational cues and aggressive models on subjective deindividuation and aggression. *Journal of Personality and Social Psychology,* 39:104–13. **602**

PRESSLEY, M., LEVIN, J.R., & DELANEY, H.D. (1982) The mnemonic keyword method. *Review of Educational Research,* 52:61–91. **268**

PRICE, V.A., see GILL, PRICE, FRIEDMAN, et al. (1985).

PRIEST, R.F., & SAWYER, J. (1967) Proximity and peership: Bases of balance in interpersonal attraction. *American Journal of Sociology,* 72:633–49. **589**

PROSEN, H., see BARNES & PROSEN (1985).

PUTNAM, F.W., JR. (1984) Cited in Restak, R.M., *The Brain.* New York: Bantam. **113**

Q

QUANTY, M.B., see GEEN & QUANTY (1977).

QUILLIAN, M.R., see COLLINS & QUILLIAN (1969).

R

RAAIJMAKERS, J.G., & SHIFFRIN, R.M. (1981) Search of associative memory. *Psychological Review,* 88:93–134. **261**

RACHLIN, H. (1980) Economics and behavioral psychology. In Staddon, J.E.R. (ed.), *Limits to Action.* New York: Academic Press. **234**

RACHMAN, S.J., & HODGSON, R.J. (1980) *Obsessions and Compulsions.* Englewood Cliffs, N.J.: Prentice-Hall. **498**

RAHE, R.H., see HOLMES & RAHE (1967).

RAMEY, C.T. (1981) Consequences of infant day care. In Weissbound, B., & Musick, J. (eds.), *Infants: Their Social Environments.* Washington, D.C.: National Association for the Education of Young Children. **81**

RANDI, J. (1982) *Flim-flam! Psychics, ESP, Unicorns and other delusions.* Buffalo: Prometheus Books. **142**

RANDS, M., & LEVINGER, G. (1979) Implicit theories of relationship: An intergenerational study. *Journal of Personality and Social Psychology*, 37:645–61. **593**

RAPAPORT, D. (1942) *Emotions and Memory.* Baltimore: Williams & Wilkins. **262**

RAVIZZA, R., see RAY & RAVIZZA (1984).

RAY, O.S. (1983) *Drugs, Society, and Human Behavior*, (3rd ed.). St. Louis: Mosby. **132, 145**

RAY, W.J., & RAVIZZA, R. (1984) *Methods Toward a Science of Behavior and Experience* (2nd ed.). Belmont, Calif.: Wadsworth. **27**

RAYNAL, D.M., see MILES, RAYNAL, & WILSON (1977).

RAYNER, K. (1978) Eye movements in reading and information processing. *Psychological Bulletin*, 85:618–60. **199**

RAYNER, K., INHOFF, A.W., MORRISON, R.E., SLOWIACZEK, M.L., & BERTERA, J.H. (1981) Masking of foveal and parafoveal vision during eye fixations in reading. *Journal of Experimental Psychology: Human Perception and Performance*, 7:167–79. **200**

READ, S.J., see SWANN & READ (1981).

REDER, L.M., & ANDERSON, J.R. (1980) A comparison of texts and their summaries: Memorial consequences. *Journal of Verbal Learning and Verbal Behavior*, 19:12–34. **630**

REES, E., see CHI, GLASER, & REES (1982).

REED, S.K. (1981) *Cognition: Theory and Applications*. Monterey, Calif.: Brooks/Cole. **279**

REGAL, D., see TELLER, MORSE, BORTON & REGAL (1974).

REGAN, D., BEVERLEY, K.I., & CYNADER, M. (1979) The visual perception of motion in depth. *Scientific American*, 241(No. 1):136–51. **86**

REGAN, D.T., & FAZIO, R. (1977) On the consistency between attitudes and behavior: Look to the method of attitude formation. *Journal of Experimental Social Psychology*, 13:28–45. **584**

REICHER, G.M. (1969) Perceptual recognition as a function of the meaningfulness of the material. *Journal of Experimental Psychology*, 81:275–80. **202**

REISENZEIN, R. (1983) The Schachter theory of emotion: Two decades later. *Psychological Bulletin*, 94:239–64. **359, 365**

REISER, B.J., see KOSSLYN, BALL, & REISER (1978).

REITMAN, J.S. (1974) Without surreptitious rehearsal, information in short-term memory decays. *Journal of Verbal Learning and Verbal Behavior*, 13:365–77. **250**

RESCORLA, R.A. (1967) Pavlovian conditioning and its proper control procedures. *Psychological Review*, 74:71–80. **220**

RESCORLA, R.A. (1972) Informational variables in Pavlovian conditioning. In Bower, G.H. (ed.), *Psychology of Learning and Motivation*, Vol. 6. New York: Academic Press. **222**

RESCORLA, R.A. (1980) Overextension in early language development. *Journal of Child Language*, 7:321–35. **295**

RESCORLA, R.A., & SOLOMON, R.L. (1967) Two-process learning theory: Relations between Pavlovian conditioning and instrumental learning. *Psychological Review*, 74:151–82. **236**

RESKO, J.A., see PHOENIX, GOY, & RESKO (1968).

RESNICK, S., see BOUCHARD, HESTON, ECKERT, KEYES, & RESNICK (1981).

REST, J.R. (1983) Morality. In Mussen, P.H. (ed.), *Handbook of Child Psychology* (4th ed.), Vol. 3. New York: Wiley. **86**

REYES, R.M., see THOMPSON, REYES, & BOWER (1979).

REYNOLDS, B.J., see ROHN, SARTES, KENNY, REYNOLDS, & HEALD (1977).

RHINE, J.B. (1942) Evidence of precognition in the covariation of salience ratios. *Journal of Parapsychology*, 6:111–43. **208**

RICE, B. (1978) The new truth machine. *Psychology Today*, 12:61–78. **355**

RICE, F.P. (1984) *The Adolescent: Development, Relationships, and Culture* (4th ed.). Boston: Allyn & Bacon. **105**

RICH, C.L., YOUNG, D., & FOWLER, R.C. (1985) The San Diego suicide study: Comparison of 133 cases under age 30 to 150 cases 30 and over. Paper presented to the American Association of Suicidology, April 1985. **505**

RICHLIN, M. (1977) Positive and negative residuals of prolonged stress. Paper presented at Military Family Research Conference, San Diego, September 3, 1977. **467**

RICKERT, E.J., see HOMME, DE BACA, DEVINE, STEINHORST, & RICKERT (1963).

RIESEN, A.H. (1947) The development of visual perception in man and chimpanzee. *Science*, 106:107–108. **205**

RIGLER, D., see FROMKIN, KRASHEN, CURTISS, RIGLER, & RIGLER (1974).

RIGLER, M., see FROMKIN, KRASHEN, CURTISS, RIGLER, & RIGLER (1974).

RILEY, V. (1981) Psychoneuroendocrine influence on immunocompetence and neoplasia. *Science*, 212:1100–109. **483**

RIMM, D.C., & MASTERS, J.C. (1979) *Behavior Therapy: Techniques and Empirical Findings* (2nd ed.). New York: Academic Press. **538**

RIMMO, P., see OHMAN, FREDRIKSON, HUGDAHL, & RIMMO (1976).

RIMPAU, J.B., see VAN CANTFORT & RIMPAU (1982).

RIPS, L.J. (1983) Cognitive processes in propositional reasoning. *Psychological Review*, 90:38–71. **288**

RIPS, L.J. (1986) Deduction. In Sternberg, R.J., & Smith, E.E. (eds.), *The Psychology of Human Thought*. New York: Cambridge University Press. **288**

RITTER, B., see BANDURA, BLANCHARD, & RITTER (1969).

RITTLE, R.H., see COTTRELL, WACK, SEKERAK, & RITTLE (1968).

ROBERTS, D., see COMSTOCK, CHAFFEE, KATZMAN, MCCOMBS, & ROBERTS (1978).

ROBERTSON, S.P., see SEIFERT, ROBERTSON, & BLACK (1985).

ROBINS, E., see SAHGIR & ROBINS (1973).

ROBINS, L. (1974) *The Viet Nam Drug Abuser Returns*. New York: McGraw-Hill. **126**

ROBINS, L.N., HELZER, J.E., WEISSMAN, M.M., et al. (1984) Lifetime prevalence of specific psychiatric disorders in three sites. *Archives of General Psychiatry*, 41:949–58. **489**

ROBINSON, D.L., & WURTZ, R. (1976) Use of an extra-retinal signal by monkey superior colliculus neurons to distinguish real from self-induced stimulus movement. *Journal of Neurophysiology*, 39:852–70. **189**

ROBINSON, F.P. (1970) *Effective Study*. New York: Harper & Row. **629**

ROBINSON, H.A., see THOMAS & ROBINSON (1982).

ROBINSON, J.P. (1971) The audience for national TV news programs. *Public Opinion Quarterly*, 35:403–405. **619**

ROBSON, J.G., see CAMPBELL & ROBSON (1968).

ROCK, I. (1983) *The Logic of Perception*. Cambridge, Mass.: M.I.T. Press. **211**

ROCK, L., see JONES, ROCK, SHAVER, GOETHALS, & WARD (1968).

RODIN, J. (1981) Current status of the internal-external hypothesis of obesity: What went wrong? *American Psychologist*, 36:361–72. **324, 326, 329**

RODIN, J., see LATANE & RODIN (1969).

RODIN, J., see PILIAVIN, RODIN, & PILIAVIN (1969).

ROFF, J.D., & KNIGHT, R. (1981) Family characteristics, childhood symptoms, and adult outcome in schizophrenia. *Journal of Abnormal Psychology*, 90:510–20. **518**

ROFFWARG, H.P., HERMAN, J.H., BOWEANDERS, C., & TAUBER, E.S. (1978) The effects of sustained alterations of waking visual input on dream content. In Arkin, A.M., Antrobus, J.S., & Ellman, S.J. (eds.), *The Mind in Sleep*. Hillsdale, N.J.: Erlbaum. **119**

ROGERS, C.R. (1951) *Client-Centered Therapy*. Boston: Houghton Mifflin. **433**

ROGERS, C.R. (1959) A theory of therapy, personality, and interpersonal relationships, as developed in the client-centered framework. In Koch, S. (ed.), *Formulations of the Person and the Social Context*, Vol. 3. New York: McGraw-Hill. **434**

ROGERS, C.R. (1970) *On Becoming a Person: A Therapist's View of Psychotherapy*. Boston: Houghton Mifflin. **543, 544, 561**

ROGERS, C.R. (1977) *Carl Rogers on Personal Power*. New York: Delacorte Press. **433, 455, 561**

ROGERS, C.R., & STEVENS, B. (1967) *Person to Person: The Problem of Being Human*. New York: Pocket Books. **455**

ROGERS, R.W., see PRENTICE-DUNN & ROGERS (1980).

ROGERS, T.B., KUIPER, N.A., & KIRKER, W.S. (1977) Self-reference and the encoding of personal information. *Journal of Personality and Social Psychology*, 35:677–88. **568**

ROHN, R.D., SARTES, R.M., KENNY, T.J., REYNOLDS, B.J., & HEALD, F.P. (1977) Adolescents who attempt suicide. *Journal of Pediatrics*, 90:636–38. **505**

ROKEACH, M. (1968) *Beliefs, Attitudes, and Values*. San Francisco: Jossey-Bass. **581, 582**

ROKEACH, M. (1973) *The Nature of Human Values*. New York: Free Press. **581**

ROSCH, E. (1974) Linguistic relativity. In Silverstein, A. (ed.), *Human Communication: Theoretical Perspectives*. New York: Halsted Press. **287**

ROSCH, E. (1978) Principles of categorization. In Rosch, E., & Lloyd, B.L. (eds.), *Cognition and Categorization*. Hillsdale, N.J.: Erlbaum. **283**

ROSCH, E., see MERVIS & ROSCH (1981).

ROSE, J.E., BRUGGE, J.F., ANDERSON, D.J., & HIND, J.E. (1967) Phase-locked response to lower frequency tones in single auditory nerve fibers of the squirrel monkey. *Journal of Neurophysiology*, 309:769–93. **170**

ROSE, S., see LEWONTIN, ROSE, & KAMIN (1984).

ROSEMAN, I. (1979) Cognitive aspects of emotion and emotional behavior. Paper read at the 87th Annual Convention of the American Psychological Association in New York City, September 1979. **360**

ROSEN, T.J., see CORKIN, COHEN, SULLIVAN, CLEGG, ROSEN, & ACKERMAN (1985).

ROSENBERG, M.J. (1956) Cognitive structure and attitudinal affect. *Journal of Abnormal and Social Psychology*, 53:367–72. **582**

ROSENBLATT, J.S., see TERKEL & ROSENBLATT (1972).

ROSENBLITH, J.F., & SIMS-KNIGHT, J. (1985) *In the Beginning: Development in the First Two Years*. Monterey, Calif.: Brooks/Cole. **105**

ROSENFELD, D., see SNYDER, STEPHAN, & ROSENFELD (1976).

ROSENFELD, P., see TEDESCHI & ROSENFELD (1981).

ROSENHAN, D.L., see SELIGMAN & ROSENHAN (1984).

ROSENMAN, R.H., BRAND, R.J., JENKINS, C.D., FRIEDMAN, M., STRAUS, R., & WRUM, M. (1975) Coronary heart disease in the Western Collaborative Group Study: Final follow-up experience of 8½ years. *JAMA*, 233:872–77. **482**

ROSENMAN, R.H., see FRIEDMAN & ROSENMAN (1974).

ROSENTHAL, R. (1964) Experimental outcome-orientation and the results of the psychological experiment. *Psychological Bulletin*, 61:405–12. **602**

ROSENZWEIG, M.R., & LEIMAN, A.L. (1982) *Physiological Psychology*. Lexington, Mass.: Heath. **59, 349**

ROSS, L. (1977) The intuitive psychologist and his shortcomings: Distortions in the attribution process. In Berkowitz, L. (ed.), *Advances in Experimental Social Psychology*, Vol. 10. New York: Academic Press. **576**

ROSS, L., AMABILE, T.M., & STEINMETZ, J.L. (1977) Social roles, social control, and biases in social-perception processes. *Journal of Personality and Social Psychology*, 35:485–94. **579**

ROSS, L., see LORD, ROSS, & LEPPER (1979).

ROSS, L., see NISBETT & ROSS (1985).

ROSS, L., see VALLONE, ROSS, & LEPPER (1985).

ROSS, M., & SICOLY, F. (1979) Egocentric biases in availability and attribution. *Journal of Personality and Social Psychology*, 37:322–36. **578**

ROSS, R., BIERBRAUER, G., & HOFFMAN, S. (1976) The role of attribution processes in conformity and dissent: Revisiting the Asch Situation. *American Psychologist*, 31:148–57. **607, 609**

ROTH, W.T., see DARLEY, TINKLENBERG, ROTH, HOLLISTER, & ATKINSON (1973).

ROTTMANN, L., see WALSTER, ARONSON, ABRAHAMS, & ROTTMANN (1966).

ROWLAND, N., see STICKER, ROWLAND, SALLER, & FRIEDMAN (1977).

ROY, A. (1981) Role of past loss in depression. *Archives of General Psychiatry*, 38(No. 3):301–302. **506**

ROYCE, J.R., & MOS, L.P. (eds.) (1981) *Humanistic Psychology: Concepts and Criticisms*. New York: Plenum. **27**

RUBIN, J.Z., see LURIA & RUBIN (1974).

RUBIN, Z. (1973) *Liking and Loving*. New York: Holt, Rinehart & Winston. **102, 589, 591**

RUBIN, Z. (1975) Disclosing oneself to a stranger: Reciprocity and its limits. *Journal of Experimental Social Psychology*, 11:233–60. **592**

RUBIN, Z., HILL, C.T., PEPLAU, L.A., & DUNKEL-SCHETTER, C. (1980) Self-disclosure in dating couples: Sex roles and ethic of openness. *Journal of Marriage and the Family*, 42:305–17. **592**

RUBIN, Z., see HILL, RUBIN, & PEPLAU (1976).

RUBIN, Z., see PEPLAU, RUBIN, & HILL (1977).

RUCH, J.C. (1975) Self-hypnosis: The result of heterohypnosis or vice versa? *International Journal of Clinical and Experimental Hypnosis*, 23:282–304. **137**

RUCH, J.C., MORGAN, A.H., & HILGARD, E.R. (1973) Behavioral predictions from hypnotic responsiveness scores when obtained with and without prior induction procedures. *Journal of Abnormal Psychology*, 82:543–46. **137**

RUDERMAN, A.J. (1986) Dietary restraint: A theoretical and empirical review. *Psychological Bulletin*, 99:247–62. **324**

RUMBAUGH, D.M. (ed.) (1977) *Language Learning by a Chimpanzee: The Lana Project*. New York: Academic Press. **300**

RUMELHART, D.E., see MCCLELLAND & RUMELHART (1981).

RUNCK, B. (1980) *Biofeedback: Issues in Treatment Assessment*. National Institute of Mental Health Science Reports. **480**

RUSH, A.J., see BECK, RUSH, SHAW, & EMERY (1979).

RUSHTON, J.P., JACKSON, D.N., & PAUNONEN, S.V. (1981) Personality: Nomothetic or idiographic? A response to Kenrick and Stringfield. *Psychological Review*, 88:582–89. **450**

RUSSEK, M. (1971) Hepatic receptors and the neurophysiological mechanisms controlling feeding behavior. In Ehreupreis, S. (ed.), *Neurosciences Research*, Vol. 4. New York: Academic Press. **321**

RUSSELL, M.J. (1976) Human olfactory communication. *Nature*, 260:520–22. **67**

RUTHERFORD, E., see MUSSEN & RUTHERFORD (1963).

RUTSTEIN, J., see SATINOFF & RUTSTEIN (1970).

RYAN, S.M., see LAUDENSLAGER, RYAN, DRUGAN, HYSON, & MAIER (1983).

RYLE, G. (1949) *The Concept of Mind.* San Francisco: Hutchinson. **266**

RYTINA, S., see GAMSON, FIREMAN, & RYTINA (1982).

S

SACHS, J.D.S. (1967) Recognition memory for syntactic and semantic aspects of connected discourse. *Perception and Psychophysics,* 2:437–42. **255**

SACKEIM, H.A., PORTNOY, S., NEELEY, P., STEIF, B.L., DECINA, P., & MALITZ, S. (1985) Cognitive consequences of low dosage ECT. In Malitz, S., & Sackeim, H.A., (eds.) *Electroconvulsive Therapy: Clinical and Basic Research Issues.* Annals of the New York Academy of Science. **556**

SADALLA, E.K., see SCHUTTE, KENRICK, & SADALLA (1985).

SADD, S., see TAVRIS & SADD (1977).

SAEGERT, S., SWAP, W., & ZAJONC, R.B. (1973) Exposure, context, and interpersonal attraction. *Journal of Personality and Social Psychology,* 25:234–42. **590**

SAHGIR, M.T., & ROBINS, E. (1973) *Male and Female Homosexuality.* Baltimore: Williams & Wilkins. **336**

SALAMY, J. (1970) Instrumental responding to internal cues associated with REM sleep. *Psychonomic Science,* 18:342–43. **119**

SALLER, C.F., see STRICKER, ROWLAND, SALLER, & FRIEDMAN (1977).

SANDERS, B., & SOARES, M.P. (1986) Sexual maturation and spatial ability in college students. *Developmental Psychology,* 22:199–203. **93**

SANDERS, B., SOARES, M.P., & D'AQUILA, J.M. (1982) The sex difference on one test of spatial visualization: A nontrivial difference. *Child Development,* 53:1106–10. **92**

SANDERS, D.J., see TERRACE, PETITTO, SANDERS, & BEVER (1979).

SANDERS, G.S. (1984) Self-presentation and drive in social facilitation. *Journal of Experimental Social Psychology,* 20:312–22. **600**

SANDERS, G.S., & BARON, R.S. (1975) The motivating effects of distraction on task performance. *Journal of Personality and Social Psychology,* 32:956–63. **600**

SARASON, B.R., see SARASON & SARASON (1984).

SARASON, I.G., JOHNSON, J.H., SIEGEL, J.M. (1978) Assessing the impact of life changes: Development of the life experi-

ences survey. *Journal of Consulting and Clinical Psychology,* 46:932–46. **470**

SARASON, I.G., & SARASON, B.R. (1984) *Abnormal Psychology: The Problem of Maladaptive Behavior.* Englewood Cliffs, N.J.: Prentice-Hall. **494, 497, 525**

SARBIN, T.R., see COE & SARBIN (1977).

SARTES, R.M., see ROHN, SARTES, KENNY, REYNOLDS, & HEALD (1977).

SATINOFF, E., & RUTSTEIN, J. (1970) Behavioral thermoregulations in rats with anterior hypothalamic lesions. *Journal of Comparative and Physiological Psychology,* 71:72–82. **317**

SATINOFF, E., & SHAN, S.Y. (1971) Loss of behavioral thermoregulation after lateral hypothalamic lesions in rats. *Journal of Comparative and Physiological Psychology,* 72:302–12. **317**

SAUFLEY, W.H., JR., see KEPPEL & SAUFLEY (1980).

SAWYER, J., see PRIEST & SAWYER (1967).

SCARR, S. (1981) *Race, Social Class, and Individual Differences in IQ.* Hillsdale, N.J.: Erlbaum. **410, 415**

SCARR, S. (1984) *Mother Care/Other Care.* New York: Basic Books. **81**

SCARR, S., & WEINBERG, R.A. (1976) IQ test performance of black children adopted by white families. *American Psychologist,* 31:726–39. **408, 411**

SCARR-SALAPATEK, S. (1971) Race, social class, and IQ. *Science,* 174:1285. **410**

SCHACTEL, E.G. (1947) On memory and child amnesia. *Psychiatry,* 10:1–26. **265**

SCHACHTER, S. (1971) *Emotion, Obesity, and Crime.* New York: Academic Press. **356**

SCHACHTER, S., & SINGER, J.E. (1962) Cognitive, social and physiological determinants of emotional state. *Psychological Review,* 69:379–99. **358**

SCHACHTER, S., see FESTINGER, SCHACHTER, & BACK (1950).

SCHAEFFER, J., ANDRYSIAK, T., & UNGERLEIDER, J.T. (1981) Cognition and long-term use of ganja (cannabis). *Science,* 213:456–66. **131**

SCHANK, R.C. (1982) *Dynamic Memory.* New York: Cambridge University Press. **294**

SCHEIER, M.F. (1976) Self-awareness, self-consciousness, and angry aggression. *Journal of Personality,* 44:627–44. **438**

SCHEIER, M.F., BUSS, A.H., & BUSS, D.M. (1978) Self-consciousness, self-report of aggressiveness, and aggression. *Journal of Research in Personality,* 12:133–40. **438**

SCHEIER, M.F., & CARVER, C.S. (1977) Self-focused attention and the experience of emotion: Attraction, repulsion, elation,

and depression. *Journal of Personality and Social Psychology,* 35:625–36. **438**

SCHEIER, M.F., & CARVER, C.S. (1983) Two sides of the self: One for you and one for me. In Suls, J., & Greenwald, A.G. (eds.), *Psychological Perspectives on the Self,* Vol. 2. Hillsdale, N.J.: Erlbaum. **437, 438**

SCHEIER, M.F., & CARVER, C.S., & GIBBONS, F.X. (1979) Self-directed attention, awareness of bodily states, and suggestibility. *Journal of Personality and Social Psychology,* 37:1576–88. **438**

SCHEIER, M.F., see CARVER & SCHEIER (1981).

SCHEIER, M.F., see FENIGSTEIN, SCHEIER, & BUSS (1975).

SCHEIN, E.H., see STRASSMAN, THALER, & SCHEIN (1956).

SCHIAVO, R.S., see SCHIFFENBAUER & SCHIAVO (1976).

SCHIFF, W., & FOULKE, E. (1982) *Tactual Perception: A Sourcebook.* Cambridge: Cambridge University Press. **179**

SCHIFFENBAUER, A., & SCHIAVO, R.S. (1976) Physical distance and attraction: An intensification effect. *Journal of Experimental Social Psychology,* 12:274–82. **590**

SCHIFFMAN, H.R. (1982) *Sensation and Perception: An Integrated Approach* (2nd ed.). New York: Wiley. **179**

SCHIFFMAN, S.S. (1974) Physiochemical correlates of olfactory quality. *Science,* 185:112–17. **173**

SCHIFFMAN, S.S., & ERICKSON, R.P. (1980) The issue of primary tastes versus a taste continuum. *Neuroscience and Biobehavioral Reviews,* 4:109–17. **174**

SCHLEIFER, S.J., KELLER, S.E., MCKEGNEY, F.P., & STEIN, M. (1979) The influence of stress and other psychosocial factors on human immunity. Paper presented at the 36th Annual Meeting of the Psychosomatic Society, Dallas, March 1979. **484**

SCHLESINGER, K., see GROVES & SCHLESINGER (1982).

SCHMEIDLER, G.R., see WOLMAN, DALE, SCHMEIDLER, & ULLMAN (1985).

SCHMITT, B.H., & BEM, D.J. (1986) Social facilitation: What did Triplett really find in 1898? Or was it 1897? Unpublished manuscript, Cornell University. **598**

SCHMITT, B.H., GILOVICH, T., GOORE, N., & JOSEPH, L. (in press) Mere presence and social facilitation: One more time. *Journal of Personality and Social Psychology.* **600**

SCHNEIDER, A.M., & TARSHIS, B. (1986) *An Introduction to Physiological Psychology* (3rd ed.). New York: Random House. **59**

SCHNEIDER, D.J. (1973) Implicit personality theory: A review. *Psychological Bulletin,* 79:294–309. **572**

SCHNEIDER, D.J., & MILLER, R.S. (1975) The

effects of enthusiasm and quality of arguments on attitude attribution. *Journal of Personality*, 43:693–708. **577**

SCHNEIDERMAN, N.S., & TAPP, J.T. (eds.) (1985) *Behavioral Medicine: The Biopsychosocial Approach*. New York: Erlbaum. **487**

SCHOEN, L.S., see ABBOTT, SCHOEN, & BADIA (1984).

SCHOOLER, J.W., see LOFTUS, SCHOOLER, & WAGENAAR (1985).

SCHOOLER, N.R., see HOGARTY, SCHOOLER, ULRICH, MUSSARE, FERRO, & HERRON (1979).

SCHORR, D., see SMITH, ADAMS, & SCHORR (1978).

SCHRADER, W.B. (1965) A taxonomy of expectancy tables. *Journal of Educational Measurement*, 2:29–35. **398**

SCHRADER, W.B. (1971) The predictive validity of College Board Admissions tests. In Angoff, W.H. (ed.), *The College Board Admissions Testing Program: A Technical Report on Research and Development Activities Relating to the Scholastic Aptitude Test and Achievement Tests*. New York: College Entrance Examination Board. **398**

SCHUCKIT, M.A. (1984) *Drug and Alcohol Abuse: A Clinical Guide to Diagnosis and Treatment* (2nd ed.). New York: Plenum. **125, 145**

SCHULSINGER, F., see JOHN, MEDNICK, & SCHULSINGER (1982).

SCHULSINGER, F., see MEDNICK, CUDECK, GRIFFITH, TALOVIC, & SCHULSINGER (1984)

SCHULSINGER, F., see WITKIN, MEDNICK, SCHULSINGER, et al. (1976).

SCHULTZ, D. (1987) *A History of Modern Psychology* (4th ed.). New York: Academic Press. **27, 639**

SCHUTTE, N.S., KENRICK, D.T., & SADALLA, E.K. (1985) The search for predictable settings: Situational prototypes, constraint, and behavioral variation. *Journal of Personality and Social Psychology*, 49:121–28. **453**

SCHVANEVELDT, R.W., & MEYER, D.E. (1973) Retrieval and comparison processes in semantic memory. In Kornblum, S. (ed.), *Attention and Performance*, Vol. 4. New York: Academic Press. **196**

SCHWARTZ, B. (1982) Failure to produce response variability with reinforcement. *Journal of the Experimental Analysis of Behavior*, 37:171–81. **235**

SCHWARTZ, B. (1984) *Psychology of Learning and Behavior*. (2nd ed.). New York: Norton. **223, 243**

SCHWARTZ, B., & GAMZU, E. (1977) Pavlovian control of operant behavior. In

Honig, W.K., & Staddon, J.E.R. (eds.), *Handbook of Operant Behavior*. Englewood Cliffs, N.J.: Prentice-Hall. **228**

SCHWARTZ, G.E. (1975) Biofeedback, self-regulation, and the patterning of physiological processes. *American Scientist*, 63:314–24. **481**

SCHWARZ, J.L., see STEVENS-LONG, SCHWARZ, & BLISS (1976).

SCOTT, T.H., see HERON, DOANE, & SCOTT (1956).

SEARS, D.O., FREEDMAN, J.L., & PEPLAU, L.A. (1985) *Social Psychology* (5th ed.). Englewood Cliffs, N.J.: Prentice-Hall. **595, 627**

SEARS, D.O., see KINDER & SEARS (1985).

SEARS, R.R., see DOLLARD, DOOB, MILLER, MOWRER, & SEARS (1939).

SEEMAN, J. (1949) A study of the process of nondirective therapy. *Journal of Consulting Psychology*, 13:157–68. **543**

SEGAL, M.W. (1974) Alphabet and attraction: An unobstrusive measure of the effect of propinquity in a field setting. *Journal of Personality and Social Psychology*, 30:654–57. **589**

SEIDEN, R.H. (1966) Campus tragedy: A study of student suicide. *Journal of Abnormal Psychology*, 71:388–99. **505**

SEIDENBERG, M.S., & PETITTO, L.A. (1979) Signing behavior in apes. *Cognition*, 7:177–215. **301**

SEIFERT, C.M., ROBERTSON, S.P., & BLACK, J.B. (1985) Types of inferences generated during reading. *Journal of Memory and Language*, 24:405–22. **273**

SEKEL, M., see TELLER, PEEPLES, & SEKEL (1978).

SEKERAK, G.J., see COTTRELL, WACK, SEKERAK, & RITTLE (1968).

SEKULER, R., & BLAKE, R. (1985) *Perception*. New York: Knopf. **179**

SEKULER, R., & GANZ, L. (1963) A new aftereffect of seen movement with a stabilized retinal image. *Science*, 139:1146–48. **186**

SELFRIDGE, O., & NEISSER, U. (1960) Pattern recognition by machine. *Scientific American*, 203:60–80. **192, 193**

SELIGMAN, M.E.P. (1971) Phobias and preparedness. *Behavior Therapy*, 2:307–20. **500**

SELIGMAN, M.E.P. (1975) *Helplessness*. San Francisco: Freeman. **222, 229**

SELIGMAN, M.E.P., & ROSENHAN, D.L. (1984) *Abnormal Psychology*. New York: Norton. **133, 500, 525**

SELIGMAN, M.E.P., see MAIER & SELIGMAN (1976).

SELIGMAN, M.E.P., see OVERMEIER & SELIGMAN (1967).

SELIGMAN, M.E.P., see PETERSON & SELIGMAN (1984).

SELYE, H. (1956) *The Stress of Life*. New York: McGraw-Hill. **463**

SELYE, H. (1979) *The Stress of Life* (rev. ed.). New York: Van Nostrand Reinhold. **459, 462, 463**

SENDEROWITZ, J., & PAXMAN, J.M. (1985) Adolescent fertility: World-wide concerns. *Population Bulletin*, 40(2). Washington, D.C.: Population Reference Bureau. **98**

SENN, D.J., see LEVINGER, SENN, & JORGENSEN (1970).

SENTER, R.J., see LIPPERT & SENTER (1966).

SENTIS, K., see MARKUS & SENTIS (1982).

SERBIN, L.A., see STERNGLANZ & SERBIN (1974).

SERON, X., see BRUYER, LATERRE, SERON, et al. (1983).

SHAFER, J. (1985) Designer drugs. *Science 85*, (March 1985):60–67. **132**

SHAFFER, L.F. (1947) Fear and courage in aerial combat. *Journal of Consulting Psychology*, 11:137–43. **352**

SHAN, S.Y., see SATINOFF & SHAN (1971).

SHANKWEILER, D., see LIBERMAN, COOPER, SHANKWEILER, & STUDDERT-KENNEDY (1967).

SHAPIRO, A.K., & MORRIS, L.A. (1978) The placebo effect in medical and psychological therapies. In Garfield, S.L., & Bergin, A.E. (eds.), *Handbook of Psychotherapy and Behavior Change*, (2nd ed.). New York: Wiley. **552**

SHAPIRO, D.A., see STILES, SHAPIRO, & ELLIOTT (1986).

SHAPIRO, D.H. (1985) Clinical use of meditation as a self-regulation strategy: Comments on Holme's (1984) conclusions and implications. *American Psychologist*, 40:719–22. **136**

SHAPLEY, R., & ENROTH-CUGELL, C. (1984) Visual adaptation and retinal gain controls. In Osborne, N., & Chaders, G. (eds.), *Progress in Retinal Research*, Vol. 3. Oxford: Pergamon Press. **158**

SHAPLEY, R., & LENNIE, P. (1985) Spatial frequency analysis in the visual system. *Annual Review of Neurosciences*, 8:547–83. **164**

SHAVER, K.G., see JONES, ROCK, SHAVER, GOETHALS, & WARD (1968).

SHAVIT, Y., see TERMAN, SHAVIT, LEWIS, CANNON, & LIEBESKIND (1984).

SHAW, B.J., see BECK, RUSH, SHAW, & EMERY (1979).

SHAW, M., see YAGER, KRAMER, SHAW, & GRAHAM (1984).

SHEA, S.L., see FOX, ASLIN, SHEA, & DUMAIS (1980).

SHEA, T., see ELKIN, SHEA, & IMBER (1986).

SHEFFIELD, F.D., see FRIEDMAN, SHEFFIELD, WULFF, & BACKER (1951).

SHEFNER, J.M., see LEVINE & SHEFNER (1981).

SHEINGOLD, K., & TENNEY, Y.J. (1982) Memory for a salient childhood event. In Neisser, U. (ed.), *Memory Observed: Remembering in Natural Contexts*. San Francisco: Freeman. **265**

SHEKELLE, R., NEATON, J.D., JACOBS, D., HULLEY, S., & BLACKBURN, H. (1983) Type A behavior pattern in MRFIT. A paper presented to the American Heart Association Council on Epidemiology Meetings, San Diego. **482**

SHELDON, W.H. (1954) *Atlas of Men: A Guide for Somatotyping the Adult Male at All Ages*. New York: Harper & Row. **420**

SHEPARD, R.N. (1978) The mental image. *American Psychologist*, 33:125–37. **304**

SHEPARD, R.N., & COOPER, L.A. (1982) *Mental Images and Their Transformations*. Cambridge, Mass.: M.I.T Press, Bradford Books. **303, 311**

SHEPARD R.N., see COOPER & SHEPARD (1973).

SHEPOSH, J.P., DEMING, M., & YOUNG, L.E. (1977) The radiating effects of status and attractiveness of a male upon evaluating his female partner. Paper presented at the annual meeting of the Western Psychological Association, Seattle, April 1977. **589**

SHERMAN, A.R. (1972) Real-life exposure as a primary therapeutic factor in the desensitization treatment of fear. *Journal of Abnormal Psychology*, 79:19–28. **535**

SHIELDS, J., see GOTTESMAN & SHIELDS (1982).

SHIFFRIN, R.M., see ATKINSON & SHIFFRIN (1971).

SHIFFRIN, R.M., see ATKINSON & SHIFFRIN (1977).

SHIFFRIN, R.M., see GILLUND & SHIFFRIN (1984).

SHIFFRIN, R.M., see RAAIJMAKERS & SHIFFRIN (1981).

SHIOSE, Y., see AWAYA, MIYAKE, IMAYUMI, SHIOSE, KNADA, & KOMURO (1973).

SHKUROVICH, M., see DRUCKER-COLIN, SHKUROVICH, & STERMAN (1979).

SHNEIDMAN, E.A. (1985) *Definition of Suicide*. New York: Wiley. **504**

SHNEIDMAN, E.S., see FARBEROW & SHNEIDMAN (1965).

SHOR, R.E., see FROMM & SHOR (1979).

SIBYLL, C., see VON LANG & SIBYLL (1983).

SICOLY, F., see ROSS & SICOLY (1979).

SIGALL, H., & LANDY, D. (1973) Radiating beauty: The effects of having a physically attractive partner on person perception. *Journal of Personality and Social Psychology*, 31:410–14. **589**

SILADI, M., see MARKUS, CRANE, BERNSTEIN, & SILADI (1982).

SILVERMAN, I. (1971) Physical attractiveness and courtship. *Sexual Behavior*, 1:22–25. **591**

SILVERMAN, L.H., & WEINBERGER, J. (1985) Mommy and I are one: Implications for psychotherapy. *American Psychologist*, 40:1296–308. **433**

SIMMONS, J.V. (1981) Project Sea Hunt: A report on prototype development and tests. Technical Report 746, Naval Ocean Systems Center, San Diego. **227**

SIMON, D.P., see LARKIN, MCDERMOTT, SIMON, & SIMON (1980).

SIMON, H.A. (1985) Using Cognitive Science to Solve Human Problems. Paper presented at Science and Public Policy Seminar, Federation of Behavioral, Psychological, and Cognitive Sciences, June 1985. **308, 309**

SIMON, H.A., & GILMARTIN, K. (1973) A simulation of memory for chess positions. *Cognitive Psychology*, 5:29–46. **308**

SIMON, H.A., see CHASE & SIMON (1973).

SIMON, H.A., see ERICSSON & SIMON (1984).

SIMON, H.A., see LARKIN, MCDERMOTT, SIMON, & SIMON (1980).

SIMON, H.A., see NEWELL & SIMON (1972).

SIMON, H.A., see YU, ZHANG, JING, PENG, ZHANG, & SIMON (1985).

SIMON, H.A., see ZHANG & SIMON (1985).

SIMON, J.G., & FEATHER, N.T. (1973) Causal attributions for success and failure at university examinations. *Journal of Educational Psychology*, 64:46–56. **436**

SIMON, T., see BINET & SIMON (1905).

SIMS-KNIGHT, J., see ROSENBLITH & SIMS-KNIGHT (1985).

SINGER, B., see LUBORSKY, SINGER, & LUBORSKY (1975).

SINGER, D.G., see SINGER & SINGER (1981).

SINGER, J.E., see GLASS & SINGER (1972).

SINGER, J.E., see SCHACHTER & SINGER (1962).

SINGER, J.L. (1984) *The Human Personality: An Introductory Textbook*. San Diego: Harcourt Brace Jovanovich. **455**

SINGER, J.L., & SINGER, D.G. (1981) *Television, Imagination and Aggression*. Hillsdale, N.J.: Erlbaum. **376**

SINGER, J.L., see POPE & SINGER (1978).

SINGER, M.T., & WYNNE, L.C. (1963) Thought disorder and family relations of schizophrenics: Pt. 1. A research strategy. *Archives of General Psychiatry*, 9:191–98. **517**

SIQUELAND, E.R., & LIPSITT, J.P. (1966) Conditioned head-turning in human newborns. *Journal of Experimental Child Psychology*, 3:356–76. **67**

SIQUELAND, E.R., see EIMAS, SIQUELAND, JUSCZYK, & VIGORITO (1971).

SIZEMORE, C.C., & PITTILLO, E.S. (1977) *I'm Eve*. Garden City, N.Y.: Doubleday. **112**

SKEELS, H.M. (1966) Adult status of children with contrasting early life experiences: A follow-up study. *Monographs of the Society for Research in Child Development*, 31(Serial No. 105). **70**

SKEELS, H.M., & DYE, H.B. (1939) A study of the effects of differential stimulation on mentally retarded children. *Proceedings of the American Association for Mental Deficiency*, 44:114–36. **70**

SKINNER, B.F. (1938) *The Behavior of Organisms*. New York: Appleton-Century-Crofts. **215, 224, 243**

SKINNER, B.F. (1948) "Superstition" in the pigeon. *Journal of Experimental Psychology*, 38:168–72. **228**

SKINNER, B.F. (1971) *Beyond Freedom and Dignity*. New York: Knopf. **215**

SKINNER, B.F. (1981) Selection by consequences. *Science*, 213:501–504. **8**

SKOLNICK, A.S. (1986) *The Psychology of Human Development*. San Diego: Harcourt Brace Jovanovich. **105**

SKYRMS, B. (1986) *Choice and Chance: An Introduction to Inductive Logic*. Belmont, Calif.: Dickenson. **286, 288**

SLOANE, R.B., STAPLES, F.R., CRISTOL, A.H., YORKSTON, N.J., & WHIPPLE, K. (1975) *Psychotherapy vs. Behavior Therapy*. Cambridge, Mass.: Harvard University Press. **549, 550**

SLOBIN, D.I. (1971) Cognitive prerequisites for the acquisition of grammar. In Ferguson, C.A., & Slobin, D.I. (eds.), *Studies of Child Language Development*. New York: Holt, Rinehart & Winston. **296, 297**

SLOBIN, D.I. (1979) *Psycholinguistics* (2nd. ed.). Glenville, Ill.: Scott, Foresman. **286, 301, 311**

SLOBIN, D.I. (ed.) (1984) *The Crosslinguistic Study of Language Acquisition*. Hillsdale, N.J.: Erlbaum. **297**

SLOVIC, P., see KAHNEMAN, SLOVIC, & TVERSKY (1982).

SLOWIACZEK, M.L., see RAYNER, INHOFF, MORRISON, SLOWIACZEK, & BERTERA (1981).

SMART, R.G., & FEJER, D. (1972) Drug use among adolescents and their parents: Closing the generation gap in mood modification. *Journal of Abnormal Psychology*, 79:153–60. **133**

SMILANSKY, B. (1974) Paper presented at the meeting of the American Educational Research Association, Chicago. **412**

SMITH, A., see TENNANT, SMITH, BEBBINGTON, & HURRY (1981).

SMITH, D., KING, M., & HOEBEL, B.G. (1970) Lateral hypothalamic control of killing: Evidence for a cholinoceptive mechanism. *Science,* 167:900–901. **370**

SMITH, E.E., ADAMS, N., & SCHORR, D. (1978) Fact retrieval and the paradox of interference. *Cognitive Psychology,* 10: 438–64. **261**

SMITH, E.E., & MEDIN, D.L. (1981) *Categories and Concepts.* Cambridge, Mass.: Harvard University Press. **282, 311**

SMITH, G.M. (1986) Adolescent personality traits that predict adult drug use. *Comprehensive Therapy,* 22:44–50. **134**

SMITH, J., see MARKUS & SMITH (1981).

SMITH, M.B. (1973) Is psychology relevant to new priorities? *American Psychologist,* 6:463–71. **11**

SMITH, M.L., GLASS, G.V., & MILLER, T.I. (1980) *The Benefits of Psychotherapy.* Baltimore: Johns Hopkins University Press. **549**

SMITH, R., see STEUER, APPLEFIELD, & SMITH (1971).

SMITH, V.C., & POKORNY, J. (1972) Spectral sensitivity of color-blind observers and the cone photopigments. *Vision Research,* 12:2059–71. **160**

SNYDER, C.R. (1974) Acceptance of personality interpretations as a function of assessment procedures. *Journal of Consulting Psychology,* 42:150. **447**

SNYDER, M., & URANOWITZ, S.W. (1978) Reconstructing the past: Some cognitive consequences of person perception. *Journal of Personality and Social Psychology,* 36:941–50. **275, 569**

SNYDER, M.L., STEPHAN, W.G., & ROSENFELD, D. (1976) Egotism and attribution. *Journal of Personality and Social Psychology,* 33:435–41. **578**

SNYDER, M.L., TANKE, E.D., & BERSCHEID, E. (1977) Social perception and interpersonal behavior: On the self-fulfilling nature of social stereotypes. *Journal of Personality and Social Psychology,* 35:656–66. **574**

SNYDER, S.H. (1980) *Biological Aspects of Mental Disorder.* New York: Oxford University Press. **516**

SNYDER, S.H., see CREESE, BURT, & SNYDER (1978).

SNYDER, W.U., et al. (1947) *Casebook of Nondirective Counseling.* Boston: Houghton Mifflin. **542**

SOAL, S.G., & BATEMAN, F. (1954) *Modern Experiments in Telepathy.* New Haven: Yale University Press. **209**

SOARES, M.P., see SANDERS & SOARES (1986).

SOARES, M.P., see SANDERS, SOARES, & D'AQUILA (1982).

SOLOMON, D.S., see FARQUHAR, MACCOBY, & SOLOMON (1984).

SOLOMON, R.L. (1980) The opponent-process theory of acquired motivation. *American Psychologist,* 35:691–712. **366, 367**

SOLOMON, R.L., & CORBIT, J.D. (1974) An opponent-process theory of motivation: Pt. 1. Temporal dynamics of affect. *Psychological Review,* 81:119–45. **366**

SOLOMON, R.L., see RESCORLA & SOLOMON (1967).

SOLSO, R.L., see JOHNSON & SOLSO (1978).

SORENSEN, R.C. (1973) *Adolescent Sexuality in Contemporary America.* New York: World. **97**

SPACHE, G., & BERG, P. (1978) *The Art of Efficient Reading* (3rd ed.). New York: Macmillan. **629**

SPANOS, N.P., & HEWITT, E.C. (1980) The hidden observer in hypnotic analgesia: Discovery or experimental creation? *Journal of Personality and Social Psychology,* 39:1201–14. **141**

SPANOS, N.P., WEEKES, J.R., & BERTRAND, L.D. (1985) Multiple personality: A social psychological perspective. *Journal of Abnormal Psychology,* 94:362–76. **114**

SPEARMAN, C. (1904) "General intelligence" objectively determined and measured. *American Journal of Psychology,* 15:201–93. **401**

SPEATH, J.L. (1976) Characteristics of the work setting and the job as determinants of income. In Sewell, W.H., Hauser, R.M., & Featherman, D.L. (eds.), *Schooling and Achievement in American Society.* New York: Academic Press. **398**

SPELKE, E.S., see STARKEY, SPELKE, & GELMAN (1986).

SPERLING, G. (1960) The information available in brief visual presentations. *Psychological Monographs,* 74(11, No. 498). **197**

SPERRY, R.W. (1970) Perception in the absence of neocortical commissures. In *Perception and Its Disorders* (Res. Publ. A.R.N.M.D., Vol. 48). New York: The Association for Research in Nervous & Mental Disease. **48**

SPERRY, R.W., see NEBES & SPERRY (1971).

SPINELLI, D., see PIRCHIO, SPINELLI, FIORENTINI, & MAFFEI (1978).

SPINELLI, D.N., see HIRSCH & SPINELLI (1970).

SPOEHR, K.T., & LEHMKUHLE, S.W. (1982) *Visual Information Processing.* San Francisco: Freeman. **211**

SPRINGER, S.P., & DEUTSCH, G. (1985) *Left Brain, Right Brain* (rev. ed.). San Francisco: Freeman. **49, 59**

SPRINGSTON, F., see BOWER & SPRINGSTON (1970).

SPUHLER, J.N., see LOEHLIN, LINDZEY, & SPUHLER (1975).

SQUIRE, L.R. (1986) Mechanisms of memory. *Science,* 232:1612–19. **41**

SQUIRE, L.R., & BUTTERS, N. (eds.) (1984) *The Neuropsychology of Memory.* New York: Guilford Press. **279**

SQUIRE, L.R., & COHEN, N.J. (1984) Human memory and amnesia. In McGaugh, J.L., Lynch, G.T., & Weinberger, N.M. (eds.). *The Neurobiology of Learning and Memory.* New York: Guilford Press. **265**

SQUIRE, L.R., COHEN, N.J., & NADEL, L. (1984) The medial temporal region and memory consolidations: A new hypothesis. In Weingartner, H., & Parker, E. (eds.), *Memory Consolidation.* Hillsdale, N.J.: Erlbaum. **260, 265**

SQUIRE, L.R., & FOX, M.M. (1980) Assessment of remote memory: Validation of the television test by repeated testing during a seven-day period. *Behavioral Research Methods and Instrumentation,* 12:583–86. **259, 260**

SQUIRE, L.R., see COHEN & SQUIRE (1980).

SROUFE, L.A., see MATAS, AREND, & SROUFE (1978).

SROUFE, L.A., see WATERS, WIPPMAN, & SROUFE (1979).

STAATS, A.W. (1968) *Language, Learning and Cognition.* New York: Holt, Rinehart & Winston. **215**

STADDON, J.E.R. (1983) *Adaptive Behavior and Learning.* New York: Cambridge University Press. **243**

STADDON, J.E.R., see HONIG & STADDON (1977).

STANLEY, J.C., see BENBOW AND STANLEY (1980).

STAPLES, F.R., see SLOANE, STAPLES, CRISTOL, YORKSTON, & WHIPPLE (1975).

STAPP, J., & FULCHER, R. (1981) The employment of APA members. *American Psychologist,* 36:1263–1314. **14**

STARKEY, P., SPELKE, E.S., & GELMAN, R. (1986) Numerical abstraction by human infants. *Cognition,* in press. **67**

STAYTON, D.J. (1973) Infant responses to brief everyday separations: Distress, following, and greeting. Paper presented at the meeting of the Society for Research in Child Development, March 1973. **79**

STEFFY, R.A., ASARNOW, R.F., ASARNOW, J.R., MACCRIMMON, D.J., & CLEGHORN, J.M. (1984) The McMaster-Waterloo High-Risk Project: Multifaceted strategy for high-risk research. In Watt, H.F., Anthony, E.J., Wynne, L.C., & Rolf, J.E. (eds.), *Children at Risk for Schizophrenia.* New York: Cambridge University Press. **518**

724

STEIF, B.L., see SACKEIM, PORTNOY, NEELEY, STEIF, DECINA, & MALITZ (1985).

STEIN, M., see SCHLEIFER, KELLER, MCKEGNEY, & STEIN (1979).

STEIN, S., see DION & STEIN (1978).

STEINHORST, R., see HOMME, DE BACA, DEVINE, STEINHORST, & RICKERT (1963).

STEINMETZ, J.L., see LEWINSOHN, ANTONUCCIO, STEINMETZ, & TERI (1984).

STEINMETZ, J.L., see ROSS, AMABILE, & STEINMETZ (1977).

STELLAR, E., see STELLAR & STELLAR (1985).

STELLAR, J.R., & STELLAR, E. (1985) The Neurobiology of Motivation and Reward. New York: Springer-Verlag. 231, 342, 349

STEPHAN, W.G., see BERNSTEIN, STEPHAN, & DAVIS (1979).

STEPHAN, W.G., see SNYDER, STEPHAN, & ROSENFELD (1976).

STERMAN, M.B., see DRUCKER-COLIN, SHKUROVICH, & STERMAN (1979).

STERNBACH, R.A. (1978) The Psychology of Pain. New York: Raven. 179

STERNBERG, D.E., see CHARNEY, HENINGER, & STERNBERG (1984).

STERNBERG, R.J. (1985) Beyond IQ: A Triarchic Theory of Human Intelligence. New York: Cambridge University Press. 404, 405

STERNBERG, R.J. (1986) Intelligence Applied: Understanding and Increasing Your Intellectual Skills. San Diego: Harcourt Brace Jovanovich. 415

STERNBERG, R.J. (ed.) (1982) Handbook of Human Intelligence. New York: Cambridge University Press. 415

STERNBERG, R.J. (ed.) (1984) Human Abilities: An Information-processing Approach. New York: Freeman. 415

STERNBERG, S. (1966) Highspeed scanning in human memory. Science, 153:652–54. 250, 251

STERNBERG, S. (1969) Memory-scanning: Mental processes revealed by reaction-time experiments. American Scientist, 57:421–57. 251

STERNGLANZ, S.H., & SERBIN, L.A. (1974) Sex-role stereotyping in children's television programs. Developmental Psychology, 10:710–15. 92

STEUER, F.B., APPLEFIELD, J.M., & SMITH, R. (1971) Televised aggression and the interpersonal aggression of preschool children. Journal of Experimental Child Psychology, 11:422–47. 373

STEVENS, B., see ROGERS & STEVENS (1967).

STEVENS, S.S. (1957) On the psychophysical law. Psychological Review, 64:153–81. 157

STEVENS, S.S. (1975) Psychophysics: Introduction to Its Perceptual, Neural and Social Prospects. New York: Wiley. 150

STEVENS, S.S., & NEWMAN, E.B. (1936) The localization of actual sources of sound. American Journal of Psychology, 48, 297–306. 172

STEVENS-LONG, J., SCHWARZ, J.L., & BLISS, D. (1976) The acquisition of compound sentence structure in an autistic child. Behavior Therapy, 7:397–404. 536

STEVENSON, I. (1977) Reincarnation: Field studies and theoretical issues. In Wolman, B.B. (ed.), Handbook of Parapsychology. New York: Van Nostrand Reinhold. 143

STILES, W.B., SHAPIRO, D.A., & ELLIOTT, R. (1986) Are all psychotherapies equivalent? American Psychologist, 41:165–80. 549

STILLMAN, R.C., see EICH, WEINGARTNER, STILLMAN, & GILLIAN (1975).

STOCKDALE, J.B. (1984) A Vietnam Experience. Stanford: Hoover Press. 467

STORMS, M.D. (1981) A theory of erotic orientation development. Psychological Review, 88:340–53. 337

STRASSMAN, H.D., THALER, M.B., & SCHEIN, E.H. (1956) A prisoner of war syndrome: Apathy as a reaction to severe stress. American Journal of Psychiatry, 112:998–1003. 466

STRAUS, R., see ROSENMAN, BRAND, JENKINS, FRIEDMAN, STRAUS, & WRUM (1975).

STRAUSS, J.S. (1982) Behavioral aspects of being disadvantaged and risk for schizophrenia. In Parron, D.L., Solomon, F., & Jenkins, C.D. (eds.), Behavior, Health Risks, and Social Disadvantage. Washington, D.C.: National Academy Press. 517

STREISSGUTH, A.P., CLARREN, S.K., & JONES, K.L. (1985) Natural history of the fetal alcohol syndrome: A 10-year follow-up of eleven patients. The Lancet, 2(No. 8446):85–91. 124

STRICKER, E.M., ROWLAND, N., SALLER, C.F., & FRIEDMAN, M.I. (1977) Homeostasis during hypoglycemia: Central control of adrenal secretion and peripheral control of feeding. Science, 196:79–81. 320

STRICKER, E.M., see FRIEDMAN & STRICKER (1976).

STROEBE, W., INSKO, C.A., THOMPSON, V.D., & LAYTON, B.D. (1971) Effects of physical attractiveness, attitude similarity and sex on various aspects of interpersonal attraction. Journal of Personality and Social Psychology, 18:79–91. 589

STRONGMAN, K.T. (1978) The Psychology of Emotion (2nd ed.). New York: Wiley. 379

STUART, R.B., & DAVIS, B. (1972) Slim Chance in a Fat World. Champaign, Ill.: Research Press. 539

STUDDERT-KENNEDY, M., see LIBERMAN, COOPER, SHANKWEILER, & STUDDERT-KENNEDY (1967).

STUNKARD, A.J. (1982) Obesity. In Hersen, M., Bellack, A., Kazdin, A. (eds.), International Handbook of Behavior Modification and Therapy. New York: Plenum. 329

STUNKARD, A.J. (ed.) (1980) Obesity. Philadelphia: Saunders. 349

STUNKARD, A.J., FOCH, T.T., & HRUBEC, Z. (1986) A twin study of human obesity. Journal of the American Medical Association, 256:51–54. 328

STUNKARD, A.J., see CRAIGHEAD, STUNKARD, & O'BRIEN (1981).

STURLA, E., see IMPERATO-MCGINLEY, PETERSON, GAUTIER, & STURLA (1979).

STURT, E., see BEBBINGTON, STURT, TENNANT, & HURRY (1984).

SULLIVAN, E.V., see CORKIN, COHEN, SULLIVAN, CLEGG, ROSEN, & ACKERMAN (1985).

SULS, J. (ed.) (1982) Psychological Perspectives on the Self, Vol. 1. Hillsdale, N.J.: Erlbaum. 455

SULS, J., & GREENWALD, A.G. (eds.) (1983) Psychological Perspectives on the Self, Vol. 2. Hillsdale, N.J.: Erlbaum. 455

SUOMI, S.J. (1977) Peers, play, and primary prevention in primates. In Proceedings of the Third Vermont Conference on the Primary Prevention of Psychopathology: Promoting Social Competence and Coping in Children. Hanover, N.H.: University Press of New England. 82

SUOMI, S.J., HARLOW, H.F., & MCKINNEY, W.T. (1972) Monkey psychiatrist. American Journal of Psychiatry, 28:41–46. 341

SUOMI, S.J., see HARLOW & SUOMI (1970).

SUPPES, P., see KRANTZ, LUCE, SUPPES, & TVERSKY (1971).

SURBER, C.F. (1977) Developmental processes in social inference: Averaging of intentions and consequences in moral judgment. Developmental Psychology, 13:654–65. 86

SUTTON-SMITH, B. (1982) Birth order and sibling status effects. In Lamb, M.E., & Sutton-Smith, B. (eds.), Sibling Relationships: Their Nature and Significance Across the Life-Span. Hillsdale, N.J.: Erlbaum. 95

SVAETICHIN, G. (1956) Spectral response curves from single cones. Acta Physiologica Scandinavica, 39(Suppl. 134):17–46. 161

SWANN, W.B., JR., & READ, S.J. (1981) Acquiring self-knowledge: The search for feedback that fits. Journal of Personality and Social Psychology, 41:1119–28. 436

SWAP, W., see SAEGERT, SWAP, & ZAJONC (1973).

SWEENEY, J.A., see WETZLER & SWEENEY (1986).

SWERDLOW, J., see MANKIEWICZ & SWERDLOW (1977).

SWETS, J.A., see GREEN & SWETS (1966).

SWINNEY, D.A. (1979) Lexical access during sentence comprehension: Consideration of context effects. *Journal of Verbal Learning and Verbal Behavior,* 18:645–59. **292**

SYER, J., & CONNOLLY, C. (1984) *Sporting Body Sporting Mind: An Athlete's Guide to Mental Training.* Cambridge: Cambridge University Press. **136, 145**

SYLVESTER, D., see AGRAS, SYLVESTER, & OLIVEAU (1969).

T

TAKAHASHI, K. (1986) Examining the strange-situation procedure with Japanese mothers and 12-month-old infants. *Development Psychology,* 22:265–70. **82**

TALOVIC, S.A., see MEDNICK, CUDECK, GRIFFITH, TALOVIC, & SCHULSINGER (1984).

TANNER, J.M. (1970) Physical growth. In Mussen, P.H. (ed.), *Carmichael's Manual of Child Psychology,* Vol. 1 (3rd ed.). New York: Wiley. **96**

TAPP, J.T., see SCHNEIDERMAN & TAPP (1985).

TARLER-BENLOLO, L. (1978) The role of relaxation in biofeedback training. *Psychological Bulletin,* 85:727–55. **480**

TARSHIS, B., see SCHNEIDER & TARSHIS (1986).

TART, C.T. (1979) Measuring the depth of an altered state of consciousness, with particular reference to self-report scales of hypnotic depth. In Fromm, E., & Shor, R.E. (eds.), *Hypnosis: Developments in Research and New Perspectives* (2nd ed.). New York: Aldine. **138**

TART, C.T. (ed.) (1975) *States of Consciousness.* New York: Dutton. **130, 144**

TART, C., & DICK, L. (1970) Conscious control of dreaming: Pt. 1. The post-hypnotic dream. *Journal of Abnormal Psychology,* 76:304–15. **120**

TARTTER, V.C. (1986) *Language Processes.* New York: Holt, Rinehart & Winston. **311**

TASHKIN, D.P., COULSON, A., CLARK, V., et al. (1985) Respiratory symptoms and lung function in heavy habitual smokers of marijuana alone and with tobacco, smokers of tobacco alone and nonsmokers. *American Review of Respiratory Disease,* 131: A198. **131**

TAUBER, E.S., see ROFFWARG, HERMAN, BOWE-ANDERS, & TAUBER (1978).

TAVRIS, C. (1984) *Anger: The Misunderstood Emotion.* New York: Simon & Schuster. **379**

TAVRIS, C., & OFFIR, C. (1977) *The Longest War: Sex Differences in Perspective.* New York: Harcourt Brace Jovanovich. **366**

TAVRIS, C., & SADD, S. (1977) *The Redbook Report on Female Sexuality.* New York: Dell. **335**

TAYLOR, D.A., see ALTMAN & TAYLOR (1973).

TEASDALE, J.D., see CAMPBELL, COPE, & TEASDALE (1983).

TEASDALE, T.W., & OWEN, D.R. (1984) Heredity and familial environment in intelligence and education level: A sibling study. *Nature,* 309:620–22. **409**

TEDESCHI, J.T., & ROSENFELD, P. (1981) Impression management and the forced compliance situation. In Tedeschi, J.T. (ed.) *Impression Management Theory and Social Psychological Research.* New York: Academic Press. **585**

TEITELBAUM, P., see HOEBEL & TEITELBAUM (1966).

TELCH, M.J., see THORESEN, TELCH, & EAGLESTON (1981).

TELLER, D.Y., MORSE, R., BORTON, R., & REGAL, D. (1974) Visual acuity for vertical and diagonal gratings in human infants. *Vision Research,* 14:1433–39. **204**

TELLER, D.Y., PEEPLES, D.R., & SEKEL, M. (1978) Discrimination of chromatic from white light by two-month old human infants. *Vision Research,* 18:41–48. **205**

TEMPLIN, M.C. (1957) *Certain Language Skills in Children: Their Development and Interrelationships.* Minneapolis: University of Minnesota Press. **295**

TENNANT, C., SMITH, A., BEBBINGTON, P. & HURRY, J. (1981) Parental loss in childhood: Relationship to adult psychiatric impairment and contact with psychiatric services. *Archives of General Psychiatry,* 38:309–14. **507**

TENNANT, C., see BEBBINGTON, STURT, TENNANT & HURRY (1984).

TENNEY, Y.J., see SHEINGOLD & TENNEY (1982).

TERI, L., see LEWINSOHN, ANTONUCCIO, STEINMETZ, & TERI (1984).

TERI, L., see LEWINSOHN, HOBERMAN, TERI, & HAUTZINER (1985).

TERKEL, J., & ROSENBLATT, J.S. (1972) Humoral factors underlying maternal behavior at parturition: Cross transfusion between freely moving rats. *Journal of Comparative and Physiological Psychology,* 80:365–71. **341**

TERMAN, G.W., SHAVIT, Y., LEWIS, J.W., CANNON, J.T., & LIEBESKIND, J.C. (1984) Intrinsic mechanisms of pain inhibition: Activation by stress. *Science,* 226:1270–77. **463**

TERRACE, H.S., PETITTO, L.A., SANDERS, D.J., & BEVER, T.G. (1979) Can an ape create a sentence? *Science,* 206:891–902. **301**

TESSER, A., & BRODIE, M. (1971) A note on the evaluation of a "computer date." *Psychonomic Science,* 23:300. **588**

TEST, M.A., see BRYAN & TEST (1967).

TETLOCK, P.E., & LEVI, A. (1982) Attribution bias: On the inconclusiveness of the cognition-motivation debate. *Journal of Experimental Social Psychology,* 18:68–88. **578**

TEUBER, H.L. see MILNER, CORKIN, & TEUBER (1968).

THALER, M.B., see STRASSMAN, THALER, & SCHEIN (1956).

THARP, R.G., see WATSON & THARP (1985).

THIGPEN, C.H., & CLECKLEY, H. (1957) *The Three Faces of Eve.* New York: McGraw-Hill. **112**

THOMAS, A., & CHESS, S. (1977) *Temperament and Development.* New York: Brunner/Mazel. **68, 418**

THOMAS, A., see CHESS & THOMAS (1982).

THOMAS, D., see NATHANS, THOMAS, & HOGNESS (1986).

THOMAS, D.S., see THOMAS & THOMAS (1928).

THOMAS, E.L., & ROBINSON, H.A. (1982) *Improving Reading in Every Class.* Boston: Allyn & Bacon. **271, 629, 630**

THOMAS, J.P., see BOFF, KAUFMAN, & THOMAS (1986).

THOMAS, J.P., see OLZAK & THOMAS (1986).

THOMAS, M.H., HORTON, R.W., LIPPINCOTT, E.C., & DRABMAN, R.S. (1977) Desensitization to portrayals of real-life aggression as a function of exposure to television violence. *Journal of Personality and Social Psychology,* 35:450–58. **377**

THOMAS, W.I., & THOMAS, D.S. (1928) *The Child in America.* New York: Knopf. **565**

THOMPSON, C.W., see HUDSPETH, MCGAUGH, & THOMPSON (1964).

THOMPSON, H., see GESELL & THOMPSON (1929).

THOMPSON, J.K., JARVIE, G.J., LAKEY, B.B. & CURETON, K.J. (1982) Exercise and obesity: Etiology, physiology, and intervention. *Psychological Bulletin,* 91:55–79. **326**

THOMPSON, N., see BADDELEY, THOMPSON, & BUCHANAN (1975).

THOMPSON, R.A., see LAMB, THOMPSON, GARDNER, CHARNOV, & ESTES (1984).

VIEMERO, V., see LAGERSPETZ, VIEMERO, & AKADEMI (1986).

VIGORITO, J., see EIMAS, SIQUELAND, JUSCZYK, & VIGORITO (1971).

VINEY, W., see TITLEY & VINEY (1969).

VOGEL, W.H., see CARROL, ZUCKERMAN, & VOGEL (1982).

VON LANG, J., & SIBYLL, C. (eds.) (1983) *Eichmann Interrogated* (R. Manheim, trans.). New York: Farrar, Straus & Giroux. **609**

VONNEGUT, M. (1975) *The Eden Express.* New York: Bantam. **514, 525**

W

WABER, D.P. (1977) Sex differences in mental abilities, hemispheric lateralization, and rate of physical growth at adolescence. *Developmental Psychology,* 13:29–38. **93**

WABER, D.P., MANN, M.B., MEROLA, J., & MOYLAN, P.M. (1985) Physical maturation rate and cognitive performance in early adolescence: A longitudinal examination. *Developmental Psychology,* 21:666–81. **93**

WACK, D.L., see COTTRELL, RITTLE, & WACK (1967).

WACK, D.L., see COTTRELL, WACK, SEKERAK, & RITTLE (1968).

WADDEN, T.A., & ANDERTON, C.H. (1982) The clinical use of hypnosis, *Psychological Bulletin,* 91:215–43. **139**

WAGENAAR, W.A., see LOFTUS, SCHOOLER, & WAGENAAR (1985).

WAGMAN, I., see BATTERSBY & WAGMAN (1962).

WAGNER, A.R. (1981) SOP: A model of automatic memory processing in animal behavior. In Spear, N.E., & Miller, R.R. (eds.), *Information Processing in Animals: Memory Mechanisms.* Hillsdale, N.J.: Erlbaum. **241**

WALDER, L.O., see ERON, HUESMANN, LEFKOWITZ, & WALDER (1972).

WALDER, L.O., see HUESMANN, ERON, LEFKOWITZ, & WALDER (1984).

WALK, R.D., see GIBSON & WALK (1960).

WALKER, C.E., HEDBERG, A., CLEMENT, P.W., & WRIGHT, L. (1981) *Clinical Procedures for Behavior Therapy.* Englewood Cliffs, N.J.: Prentice-Hall. **536**

WALKER, E. (1978) *Explorations in the Biology of Language.* Montgomery, Vt.: Bradford Books. **331**

WALKER, M.R., see FREEMAN, WALKER, BORDEN, & LATANE (1975).

WALKER, P.A., see MONEY, WIEDEKING, WALKER, & GAIN (1976).

WALL, P.D., see MELZAK & WALL (1965).

WALL, S., see AINSWORTH, BLEHAR, WALTERS, & WALL (1978).

WALLACE, P. (1977) Individual discrimination of humans by odor. *Physiology and Behavior,* 19:577–79. **173**

WALLACE, P.M., see BROWN & WALLACE (1980).

WALLEY, R.E., & WEIDEN, T.D. (1973) Lateral inhibition and cognitive masking: A neuropsychological theory of attention. *Psychological Review,* 80:284–302. **199**

WALSTER, E., ARONSON, E., ABRAHAMS, D., & ROTTMANN, L. (1966) Importance of physical attractiveness in dating behavior. *Journal of Personality and Social Psychology,* 4:508–16. **588**

WALSTER, E., see BERSCHEID & WALSTER (1974).

WALSTER, E., see BERSCHEID & WALSTER (1978).

WALSTER, E., see DION, BERSCHEID, & WALSTER (1972).

WALTERS, E., see AINSWORTH, BLEHAR, WALTERS, & WALL (1978).

WALZER, M. (1970) *Obligations.* Cambridge, Mass.: Harvard University Press. **617**

WARD, L.M., see COREN, PORAC, & WARD (1984).

WARD, L.M., see JONES, ROCK, SHAVER, GOETHALS, & WARD (1968).

WARNER, P., see MICHAEL, BONSALL, & WARNER (1974).

WARRINGTON, E.K., & WEISKRANTZ, L. (1978) Further analysis of the prior learning effect in amnesic patients. *Neuropsychologia,* 16:169–77. **266**

WARWICK, D.P., see NEWCOMB, KOENIG, FLACKS, & WARWICK (1967).

WASON, P.C., & JOHNSON-LAIRD, P.N. (1972) *Psychology of Reasoning: Structure and Content.* London: Batsford. **288**

WATERS, E., WIPPMAN, J., & SROUFE, L.A. (1979) Attachment, positive affect, and competence in the peer group: Two studies in construct validation. *Child Development,* 50:821–29. **80**

WATERS, H.F., & MALAUMD, P. (1975) Drop that gun, Captain Video. *Newsweek,* 85:81–82. **618**

WATKINS, M.J., HO, E., & TULVING, E. (1976) Context effects in recognition memory for faces. *Journal of Verbal Learning and Verbal Behavior,* 15:505–18. **262**

WATKINS, M.J., see CRAIK & WATKINS (1973).

WATSON, C., see BEM, MARTYNA, & WATSON (1976).

WATSON, D.L., & THARP, R.G. (1985) *Self-directed Behavior: Self-modification for Personal Adjustment* (4th ed.). Belmont, Calif.: Wadsworth. **561**

WATSON, G. (1966) *Social Psychology: Issues and Insights.* Philadelphia: Lippincott. **619**

WATSON, J.B. (1928) *Psychological Care of Infant and Child.* New York: Norton. **87**

WATSON, J.B. (1950) *Behaviorism.* New York: Norton. **62**

WATSON, J.S. (1983) Contingency perception in early social development. Unpublished paper, University of California, Berkeley. **74**

WATSON, J.S., see BAHRICK & WATSON (1985).

WATSON, R.I. (1978) *The Great Psychologists: From Aristotle to Freud* (4th ed.). Philadelphia: Lippincott. **639**

WATT, N.F., see WHITE & WATT (1981).

WAUGH, N.C., & NORMAN, D.A. (1965) Primary memory. *Psychological Review,* 72:89–104. **250**

WEATHERLY, D. (1964) Self-perceived rate of physical maturation and personality in late adolescence. *Child Development,* 35:1197–1210. **96**

WEBB, W.B. (1975) *Sleep the Gentle Tyrant.* Englewood Cliffs, N.J.: Prentice-Hall. **114, 117**

WEBER, E.H. (1834) *Concerning Touch.* (Reprint ed., 1978. H.E. Ross, trans.) New York: Academic Press. **155**

WECHSLER, D. (1958) *The Measurement and Appraisal of Adult Intelligence.* Baltimore: Williams. **393, 401**

WECHSLER, D. (1974) *Wechsler Intelligence Scale for Children, Revised.* New York: Psychological Corporation. **393**

WEEKES, J.R., see SPANOS, WEEKES, & BERTRAND (1985).

WEIDEN, T.D., see WALLEY & WEIDEN (1973).

WEIGEL, R.H., VERNON, D.T.A., & TOGNACCI, L.N. (1974) Specificity of the attitude as a determinant of attitude-behavior congruence. *Journal of Personality and Social Psychology,* 30:724–28. **584**

WEIKART, D., see HOHMANN, BANET, & WEIKART (1979).

WEINBERG, M.S., see BELL & WEINBERG (1978).

WEINBERG, M.S., see BELL, WEINBERG, & HAMMERSMITH (1981).

WEINBERG, R.A., see SCARR & WEINBERG (1976).

WEINBERGER, J., see SILVERMAN & WEINBERGER (1985).

WEINER, B., see FESHBACH & WEINER (1986).

WEINER, I.B., see KIMMEL & WEINER (1985).

WEINFELD, F.D., see COLEMAN, CAMPBELL, HOBSON, MCPARTLAND, MOODY, WEINFELD, & YORK (1966).

WEINGARTEN, H., GRAFMAN, J., BOUTELLE,

W., KAYE, W., & MARTIN, P.R. (1983) Forms of memory failure. *Science,* 221:380–82. **267**

WEINGARTNER, H., see EICH, WEINGARTNER, STILLMAN, & GILLIAN (1975).

WEINSTEIN, S. (1968) Intensive and extensive aspects of tactile sensitivity as a function of body part, sex, and laterality. In Kenshalo, D.R. (ed.), *The Skin Senses.* Springfield, Ill.: Thomas. **175**

WEISKRANTZ, L., see WARRINGTON & WEISKRANTZ (1978).

WEISMAN, S. (1966) Environmental and innate factors and educational attainment. In Meade, J.E., & Parkes, A.S. (eds.), *Genetic and Environmental Factors in Human Ability.* London: Oliver & Boyd. **410**

WEISS, J.M. (1972) Psychological factors in stress and disease. *Scientific American,* 226:106. **479**

WEISSMAN, M.M., see ROBINS, HELZER, WEISSMAN, et al. (1984).

WELKOWITZ, J., EWEN, R.B., & COHEN, J. (1982) *Introductory Statistics for the Behavioral Sciences* (3rd ed.). San Diego: Harcourt Brace Jovanovich. **651**

WENGER, M., & BAGCHI, B. (1961) Studies of autonomic function in practitioners of yoga in India. *Behavioral Science,* 6:312–23. **142**

WERTHEIMER, M. (1912) Experimentelle Studien uber das Sehen von Beuegung. *Zeitschrift fuer Psychologie,* 61:161–265. **185, 636**

WERTHEIMER, M. (1961) Psychomotor coordination of auditory and visual space at birth. *Science,* 134:1692–93. **205**

WERTHEIMER, M. (1979) *A Brief History of Psychology* (rev. ed.). New York: Holt, Rinehart & Winston. **27, 639**

WEST, C., & ZIMMERMAN, D.H. (1983) Small insults: A study of interruptions in cross-sex conversations between unacquainted persons. In Thorne, B., Kramarae, C., & Henley, N. (eds.), *Language, Gender, and Society.* Rowley, Mass.: Newbury House. **579**

WETZEL, R.D., see MURPHY & WETZEL (1980).

WETZLER, S.E., & SWEENEY, J.A. (1986) Childhood amnesia: An empirical demonstration. In Rubin, D.C. (ed.) *Autobiographical Memory.* New York: Cambridge University Press. **264**

WHEELER, L., see KERNIS & WHEELER (1981).

WHIPPLE, K., see SLOANE, STAPLES, CRISTOL, YORKSTON, & WHIPPLE (1975).

WHISHAW, I.Q., see KOLB & WHISHAW (1985).

WHITE, C. (1977) Unpublished Ph.D. dissertation, Catholic University, Washington, D.C. **325**

WHITE, R.W., & WATT, N.F. (1981) *The Abnormal Personality* (5th ed.). New York: Wiley. **506**

WHORF, B.L. (1956) Science and linguistics. In Carroll, J.B. (ed.), *Language, Thought and Reality: Selected Writings of Benjamin Lee Whorf.* Cambridge, Mass.: M.I.T. Press. **286**

WICKELGREN, W.A. (1979) *Cognitive Psychology.* Englewood Cliffs, N.J.: Prentice-Hall. **199, 211**

WIEDEKING, C., see MONEY, WIEDEKING, WALKER, & GAIN (1976).

WIENS, A.W., see MATARAZZO & WIENS (1972).

WIENS, A.W., see MATARAZZO & WIENS (1977).

WEIR, C.C., see GREEN & WEIR (1984).

WIESEL, T.N., & HUBEL, D.H. (1974) Ordered arrangement of orientation columns in monkeys lacking visual experience. *Journal of Comparative Neurology,* 158:307–18. **205**

WIESEL, T.N., see HUBEL & WIESEL (1963).

WIESEL, T.N., see HUBEL & WIESEL (1968).

WIGDOR, A.K., & GARNER, W.R. (eds.) (1982) *Ability Testing: Uses, Consequences, and Controversies.* Washington, D.C.: National Academy Press. **413, 415**

WILBUR, C.B., see LUDWIG, BRANDSMA, WILBUR, BENDFELDT, & JAMESON (1972).

WILKES, A.L., & KENNEDY, R.A. (1969) Relationship between pausing and retrieval latency in sentences of varying grammatical form. *Journal of Experimental Psychology,* 79:241–45. **293**

WILKINS, W. (1984) Psychotherapy: The powerful placebo. *Journal of Consulting and Clinical Psychology,* 52:570–73. **553**

WILKINSON, F., see MITCHELL & WILKINSON (1974).

WILLERMAN, L. (1979) *The Psychology of Individual Differences.* San Francisco: Freeman. **419**

WILLIAMS, B., see DEMBROSKI, MACDOUGALL, WILLIAMS, & HANEY (1985).

WILLIAMS, D.C. (1959) The elimination of tantrum behavior by extinction procedures. *Journal of Abnormal and Social Psychology,* 59:269. **225**

WILLIAMS, K.D., see LATANE, WILLIAMS, & HARKINS (1979).

WILLIAMS, K.D., see PETTY, HARKINS, WILLIAMS, & LATANE (1977).

WILLIAMS, M.D., & HOLLAN, J.D. (1981) The process of retrieval from very long-term memory. *Cognitive Science,* 5:87–119. **269**

WILLIAMS, R.B., JR., see COSTA, ZONDERMAN, MCCRAE, & WILLIAMS (1985).

WILLIAMS, R.L. (1972) *The BITCH Test (Black Intelligence Test of Cultural Homogeneity).* St. Louis: Black Studies Program, Washington University. **396**

WILLIAMS, R.M., see LOCKE, KRAUS, LESERMAN, HURST, HEISEL, & WILLIAMS (1984).

WILLS, T.A., see COHEN & WILLS (1985).

WILSON, E.O. (1983) Statement cited in "Mother nature's murderers," *Discovery* (October 1983), 79–82. **375**

WILSON, G.T., SEE O'LEARY & WILSON (1975).

WILSON, I. (1982) *All in the Mind: Reincarnation, Stigmata, Multiple Personality and Other Little-Understood Powers of the Mind.* Garden City, N.Y.: Doubleday. **143**

WILSON, M.A., see MILES, RAYNAL, & WILSON (1977).

WILSON, W.R. (1979) Feeling more than we can know: Exposure effects without learning. *Journal of Personality and Social Psychology,* 37:811–21. **590**

WINCH, R.F., KTSANES, T., & KTSANES, V. (1954) The theory of complementary needs in mate selection: An analytic and descriptive study. *American Sociological Review,* 29:241–49. **592**

WINZENZ, D., see BOWER, CLARK, WINZENZ, & LESGOLD (1969).

WIPPMAN, J., see WATERS, WIPPMAN, & SROUFE (1979).

WISE, R.A. (1984) Neuroleptic and operant behavior: The anhedonia hypothesis. *Behavior and Brain Sciences,* 5:39–87. **231**

WITKIN, H.A., MEDNICK, S.A., SCHULSINGER, F., et al. (1976) Criminality in XYY and XXY men, *Science,* 193:547–55. **57**

WOHNS, R., see FRIED, MATEER, OJEMANN, WOHNS, & FEDIO (1982).

WOLF, M.M., see PHILLIPS, PHILLIPS, FIXSEN, & WOLF, 1972.

WOLFE, D.A. (1985) Child-abusive parents: An empirical review and analysis. *Psychological Bulletin,* 97:462–82. **341**

WOLFF, H.G., see HARDY, WOLFF, & GOODELL (1947).

WOLFGANG, H., see EYFERTH, BRANDT, & WOLFGANG (1960).

WOLMAN, B.B., DALE, L.A., SCHMEIDLER, G.R., & ULLMAN, M. (eds.) (1985) *Handbook of Parapsychology.* New York: Van Nostrand Reinhold. **145, 211**

WOLPERT, E., see DEMENT & WOLPERT (1958).

WOOD, G. (1986) *Fundamentals of Psychological Research* (3rd ed.). Boston: Little, Brown. **27**

WOOD, L.E., see DOOB & WOOD (1972).

WOOD, P.D., see FARQUHAR, MACCOBY, WOOD, et al. (1977).

WOOD, P.D., see MACCOBY, FARQUHAR, WOOD, & ALEXANDER (1977).

WOODRUFF, C.L., see KELLEY & WOODRUFF (1956).

WOODY, G.E., see LUBORSKY, MCLELLAN, WOODY, O'BRIEN, & AUERBACH (1985).

WORD, C.O., ZANNA, M.P., & COOPER, J. (1974) The nonverbal mediation of self-fulfilling prophecies in interracial interaction. *Journal of Experimental Social Psychology*, 10:109–20. **574**

WORTMAN, C.B., BREHM, J.W. (1975) Responses to uncontrollable outcomes: An integration of reactance theory and the learned helplessness model. *Advances in Experimental and Social Psychology*, 8:277–36. **468**

WRIGHT, L., see WALKER, HEDBERG, CLEMENT, & WRIGHT (1981).

WRIGHT, R.A., CONTRADA, R.J., & GLASS, D.C. (1985) Psychophysiologic correlates of Type A behavior. In Katkin, E.S., & Manuck, S.B. (eds.), *Advances in Behavioral Medicine*. Greenwich, Conn.: JAI. **482**

WRIGHT, W.D. (1946) *Researches on Normal and Color Defective Vision*. London: Henry Kimpton. **159**

WRIGHTMAN, F.L. (1973) Pitch and stimulus fine structure. *Journal of the Acoustical Society of America*, 54:397–406. **172**

WRUM, M., see ROSENMAN, BRAND, JENKINS, FRIEDMAN, STRAUS, & WRUM (1975).

WULFF, J.J., see FRIEDMAN, SHEFFIELD, WULFF, & BACKER (1951).

WURTZ, R., see ROBINSON & WURTZ (1976).

WYKES, T., see KATZ & WYKES (1985).

WYNNE, L.C., see SINGER & WYNNE (1963).

Y

YAGER, D., KRAMER, P., SHAW, M., & GRAHAM, N. (1984) Detection and identification of spatial frequency: Models and data. *Vision Research*, 24:1021–25. **196**

YAKSH, T., see PLATT, YAKSH, & DARBY (1967).

YALOM, I.D. (1975) *The Theory and Practice of Group Psychotherapy* (2nd ed.). New York: Basic Books. **561**

YALOM, I.D., see LIEBERMAN, YALOM, & MILES (1973).

YANKELOVICH, D. (1974) *The New Morality: A Profile of American Youth in the Seventies*. New York: McGraw-Hill. **624**

YANKELOVICH, D. (1981) *New Rules: Searching for Self-Fulfillment in a World Turned Upside Down*. New York: Random House. **624**

YARBUS, D.L. (1967) *Eye Movements and Vision*. New York: Plenum. **198**

YASUNA, A., see DAVIDSON, YASUNA, & TOWER, (1979).

YERKES, R.M., & MARGULIS, S. (1909) The method of Pavlov in animal psychology. *Psychological Bulletin*, 6:257–73. **216**

YESAVAGE, J.A., LEIER, V.O., DENARI, M., & HOLLISTER, L.E. (1985) Carry-over effect of marijuana intoxication on aircraft pilot performance: A preliminary report. *American Journal of Psychiatry*, 142:1325–30. **131**

YONAS, A., PETTERSEN, L., & GRANRUD, C.E. (1982) Infants' sensitivity to familiar size as information for distance. *Child Development*, 53:1285–90. **205**

YORKSTON, N.J., see SLOANE, STAPLES, CRISTOL, YORKSTON, & WHIPPLE (1975).

YOST, W.A., & NIELSON, D.W. (1985) *Fundamentals of Hearing* (2nd ed.). New York: Holt, Rinehart & Winston. **167, 179**

YOUNG, D., see RICH, YOUNG, & FOWLER (1985).

YOUNG, L.E., see SHEPOSH, DEMING, & YOUNG (1977).

YOUNG, R.D., see FRANZOI, DAVIS, & YOUNG (1985).

YOUNG, T. (1807) *A Course of Lectures on Natural Philosophy*. London: William Savage. **160**

YU, B., ZHANG, W., JING, Q., PENG, R., ZHANG, G., & SIMON, H.A. (1985) STM capacity for Chinese and English language materials. *Memory and Cognition*, 13:202–207. **248**

YUSSEN, S.R., & BERMAN, L. (1981) Memory predictions for recall and recognition in first-, third-, and fifth-grade children. *Developmental Psychology*, 17:224–29. **75**

Z

ZAJONC, R.B. (1965) Social facilitation. *Science*, 149:269–74. **599**

ZAJONC, R.B. (1968) Attitudinal effects of mere exposure. *Journal of Personality and Social Psychology*, Monograph Supplement 9(No. 2):1–29. **590**

ZAJONC, R.B. (1980) Compresence. In Paulus, P.B. (ed.), *Psychology of Group Influence*. Hillsdale, N.J.: Erlbaum. **599**

ZAJONC, R.B. (1984) On the primacy of affect. *American Psychologist*, 39:117–23. **360**

ZAJONC, R.B. (1985) Emotion and facial efference: A theory reclaimed. *Science*, 228:15–21. **365**

ZAJONC, R.B., HEINGARTNER, A., & HERMAN, E.M. (1969) Social enhancement and impairment of performance in the cockroach. *Journal of Personality and Social Psychology*, 13:83–92. **599**

ZAJONC, R.B., see MORELAND & ZAJONC (1979).

ZAJONC, R.B., see SAEGERT, SWAP, & ZAJONC (1973).

ZAMANSKY, H.S., & BARTIS, S.P. (1985) The dissociation of an experience: The hidden observer observed. *Journal of Abnormal Psychology*, 94:243–48. **141**

ZANNA, M.P., see FAZIO & ZANNA (1981).

ZANNA, M.P., see FAZIO, ZANNA, & COOPER (1977).

ZANNA, M.P., see WORD, ZANNA, & COOPER (1974).

ZARAGOZA, M., see MCCLOSKEY & ZARAGOZA (1985).

ZEIGLER, H.P., & LEIBOWITZ, H. (1957) Apparent visual size as a function of distance for children and adults. *American Journal of Psychology*, 70:106–109. **205**

ZELAZO, N.A., see ZELAZO, ZELAZO, & KOLB (1972).

ZELAZO, P., see KAGAN, KEARSLEY, & ZELAZO (1978).

ZELAZO, P.R., ZELAZO, N.A., & KOLB, S. (1972) Walking: In the newborn. *Science*, 176:314–15. **70**

ZELAZO, P.R., see KAGAN, KEARSLEY, & ZELAZO (1978).

ZELNIK, M., & KANTER, J.F. (1977) Sexual and contraceptive experience of young unmarried women in the United States, 1976 and 1971. *Family Planning Perspectives*, 9:55–71. **97**

ZHANG, G. & SIMON, H.A. (1985) STM capacity for Chinese words and idioms: Chunking and acoustical loop hypothesis. *Memory and Cognition*, 13:193–201. **248**

ZHANG, G., see YU, ZHANG, JING, PENG, ZHANG, & SIMON (1985).

ZHANG, W., see YU, ZHANG, JING, PENG, ZHANG, & SIMON (1985).

ZIGLER, E., & BERMAN, W. (1983) Discerning the future of early childhood intervention. *American Psychologist*, 38:894–906. **412**

ZIGLER, E.F., & GORDON, E.W. (eds.) (1981) *Day Care: Scientific and Social Policy Issues*. Boston: Auburn House. **415**

ZILLMANN, D., & BRYANT, J. (1974) Effect of residual excitation on the emotional response to provocation and delayed aggressive behavior. *Journal of Personality and Social Psychology*, 30:782–91. **359**

ZIMBARDO, P.G. (1970) The human choice: Individuation, reason and order versus de-individuation, impulse and chaos. In Arnold, W.J., & Levine, D. (eds.), *Nebraska Symposium on Motivation, 1969*, Vol. 16. Lincoln: University of Nebraska Press. **600, 601**

ZIMMERMAN, D.H., see WEST & ZIMMERMAN (1983).

ZOLA, I.K., see KOSA & ZOLA (eds.) (1975).

ZONDERMAN, A.B., see COSTA, ZONDERMAN, MCCRAE, & WILLIAMS (1985).

ZUBEK, J.P. (1969) *Sensory Deprivation: Fifteen Years of Research.* New York: Appleton-Century-Crofts. **345**

ZUCKERMAN, M. (1979) *Sensation Seeking: Beyond the Optimal Level of Arousal.* Hillsdale, N.J.: Erlbaum. **345, 420, 428**

ZUCKERMAN, M., & NEEB, M. (1980) Demographic influences in sensation seeking and expressions of sensation seeking in religion, smoking and driving habits. *Personality and Individual Differences*, 1(No. 3):197–206. **346**

ZUCKERMAN, M., see CARROL, ZUCKERMAN, & VOGEL (1982).

ZUCKERMAN, M., see FISHER, ZUCKERMAN, & NEEB (1981).

ZURIF, E.B., CARAMAZZA, A., MYERSON, R., & GALVIN, J. (1974) Semantic feature representations for normal and aphasic language. *Brain and Language*, 1:167–87. **303**

ZURIF, E.B., see CARAMAZZA & ZURIF (1976).

Index

Page numbers in *italics* refer to figures and tables.

A

Ability tests, 383–414; generality vs. specificity, 386–87; group, 394–95, *395*; intellectual, 389–95, 400–407; predictive ability of, 395–400; reliability of, 387–88; requirements for, 387–99; types of, 383–87; use of, 413–14; validity of, 388–89

Abnormal behavior, 489–94; classifying, 491–94; treatment of, 527–59

Abnormal psychology, 489–523

Abnormality, 489–90; chromosomal, 56–57, defined, 489–90

Abreaction, 532–33

Absolute motion, 186

Absolute threshold, 148–49, *149*; for hearing, *168*; for light intensity, 155, *156*; for taste, 174

Absorption curves, 160, *161*

Abstract concepts, formation by infants, *67*

Abstract reasoning, testing for, 392

Abstractions, 285

Acetylcholine (ACh), 34

Achievement Place, *558*

Achievement tests, 383–85

Acoustic coding, 247–48; into short-term memory, 247–48

Acoustic nerve, 167

Acquired Immune Deficiency Syndrome (AIDS), 126

Acquisition stage, in conditioning, *217*

Action potential. *See* Nerve impulse

Activation process, 251*n*

Acuity, perceptual, 204

Acupuncture, 36–37

Adaptation: light, 157–58; motion, 186–87; odor, 173; pressure, 174; selective, 186–87; taste, 174; temperature, 175

Addiction, 122, 126–27

Additive mixture, 158–59

Adenine, 54

Adipocytes. *See* Fat cells

Adler, Alfred, 431

Adolescence, 95–100, *101*; maturation during, 63; role confusion during, 99; search for identity during, 98–100; sexuality during, 95–99

Adolescent growth spurt, 95–96, *96*

Adrenal cortex, 462, 463

Adrenal glands, *53*, 462

Adrenalin. *See* Epinephrine

Adrenocorticotrophic hormone (ACTH), 53, 462, 463

Adulthood: development during, 102–103; maturation during, 63; memory structure and, 265; sexuality during, 329–38; sleep schedules during, 114

Affect, schizophrenia and, 513. *See also* Affective disorders; Emotions

Affectionate relationships: normality and, 491; sexual development and, 333

Affective disorders, *492*, 502–11; depression, 502–506; manic-depression, 504–506; theories of, 506–11

Afferent neurons. *See* Sensory neurons

Afterimages, complementary, 160

Age, mental, 390–91

Age regression, 139

Aggregated scores, 450–51

Aggression, 368–77; biological basis of, 370; brain stimulation and, *370*; cathartic, 372–76; chromosomal abnormalities and, 56–57; as drive, 369–70; as emotional reaction, 368–77; instinct view of, 369, 370, 374–75; as learned response, 370–72; sex differences in, 93; stress as cause of, 465–66

Aging, 100–103; fears and, *495*, 495–96

Agoraphobia, 496–97

Alarm reaction, 462–63

Alcohol, 122–25, 131–32, 553

Alcoholics Anonymous (AA), 133, 545

Alcoholism, 124–25, *125*, 132–33

Alienation, 491

All-or-none principle of action, 33

Alpha waves, 115

Alprazolam, 553

Alzheimer's disease, 34

Amacrine cells, 152–53, *154*

Ambiguous stimulus, *195*, 195–96, *196*

American College Testing (ACT) Program, *384*, 387

Amino acids, 55

Amnesia, 246, 263–67; anterograde, 263–64; childhood, 264–65; posthypnotic, 138–39; retrograde, 264–65

Amphetamines, 34–35, 37, 127–28, 231, 509, 516, 555

Anal stage, 431

Analytic introspection, 148

Androgen, *330*, 331, 338, 339

Androgenization, 338